"A scholarly masterwork but also a highly r... tonishing. It is a book one would be proud to ... an entire bookcase by itself."
—*The Independent*

"Since it became a worldwide phenomenon, nobody has attempted to write an overall history of the game. Now David Goldblatt's stunning book will be the measure against which all other such volumes are judged. Weighing in at more than nine hundred pages, this might seem a mighty read. But Goldblatt has packed the book with detail, stories, match reports, and rumination. It can be read cover-to-cover or dipped into. It is both a magnificent work of synthesis of other people's research and a voyage into entirely new territory. I found myself zipping around the globe, and across time, from Saudi Arabia to Ireland, from Bolton to Calcutta. . . . It is difficult to do justice to the range of this work, which moves from a solid account of the origins of the game, on to tactics, globalization, administration, and corruption. . . . Elegant, witty, stylish, and crisp, the language of the book moves swiftly forward, taking the reader with it. . . . There is more food for thought in the few pages of the conclusion than in a hundred ghostwritten biographies of rich twentysomethings. Quite simply, *The Ball Is Round* takes football history to a new level."
—*The Guardian*

"A comprehensive history of world football, immense in scope and scholarship."
—*The Daily Telegraph* (London)

"An impeccably researched and impressively scholarly work that contains just about all you will ever need to know about how and why a game played in a handful of nineteenth-century English public schools rose to become the global industry it is today."
—*Belfast Telegraph*

"It is in its sheer span that Goldblatt's work takes one's breath away. No one has ever attempted something quite like this in the history of any sport, let alone football. When Goldblatt reveals that his goal is to trace, through a history of football, 'the Faustian bargain that all modern societies have made with the forces of money and power,' one is half-incredulous at the ambition. But he nets the goal all the same, with the flair of a Maradona taking on the English defense."
—*The Calcutta Telegraph*

"The ultimate book."
—SoccerBlog.com

DAVID GOLDBLATT

The Ball Is Round

A Global History of Soccer

RIVERHEAD BOOKS
New York

RIVERHEAD BOOKS
Published by the Penguin Group
Penguin Group (USA) Inc.
375 Hudson Street, New York, New York 10014, USA
Penguin Group (Canada), 90 Eglinton Avenue East, Suite 700, Toronto, Ontario M4P 2Y3, Canada
(a division of Pearson Penguin Canada Inc.)
Penguin Books Ltd., 80 Strand, London WC2R 0RL, England
Penguin Group Ireland, 25 St. Stephen's Green, Dublin 2, Ireland (a division of Penguin Books Ltd.)
Penguin Group (Australia), 250 Camberwell Road, Camberwell, Victoria 3124, Australia
(a division of Pearson Australia Group Pty. Ltd.)
Penguin Books India Pvt. Ltd., 11 Community Centre, Panchsheel Park, New Delhi—110 017, India
Penguin Group (NZ), 67 Apollo Drive, Rosedale, North Shore 0632, New Zealand
(a division of Pearson New Zealand Ltd.)
Penguin Books (South Africa) (Pty.) Ltd., 24 Sturdee Avenue, Rosebank, Johannesburg 2196,
South Africa

Penguin Books Ltd., Registered Offices: 80 Strand, London WC2R 0RL, England

THE BALL IS ROUND

The publisher has no control over and does not assume any responsibility for author or
third-party websites or their content.

Previously published in Great Britain by Viking Penguin: 2006
First Riverhead trade paperback edition: January 2008
Riverhead trade paperback ISBN: 978-1-59448-296-0

PRINTED IN THE UNITED STATES OF AMERICA

Contents

Contents

An astonishing void: official history ignores football. Contemporary history texts fail to mention it, even in passing, in countries where it has been and continues to be a primordial symbol of collective identity.

I play therefore I am: a style of play is a way of being that reveals the unique profile of each community and affirms its right to be different.

Tell me how you play and I will tell you who you are.

Eduardo Galeano

The only thing that has never changed in the history of the game is the shape of the ball.   **Denis Law**

Foreword to the American Edition

Everywhere else in the universe this book is selling, or not, as *The Ball Is Round: A Global History of Football*. In America it is *A Global History of Soccer*. As you can imagine, given the length and subject matter of this book, there would be an awful lot of alterations to make if we were to change every use of 'football' to 'soccer.' So, you're getting a foreword's worth of soccer and then it's football.

The global association of 'football' with soccer rather than gridiron reflects a central theme of *The Ball Is Round*, for it is the only history of the modern world that I know in which the United States is a transatlantic curiosity rather than a central attraction. The British historian Eric Hobsbawm encapsulated this oddity when he wrote 'The twentieth century was the American century in every way but one: sport.' This is not exactly news to anyone, but it remains an extraordinary and under-explored anomaly; an almost unique reversal of the dominant patterns of global influence and power.

The Ball Is Round attempted to answer Hobsbawm's question by looking at the reasons why soccer had fared so poorly in the United States. The main lines of the argument are well known. Basically, soccer's timing was bad. By the early 1870s when soccer, played according to the FA rules of 1863, was beginning in America, baseball had already claimed the emotional and cultural high ground of America's emerging sports culture.

Through the rest of the nineteenth century, soccer thrived in the United States amongst certain working-class communities, but was indelibly marked as European, foreign and in some quarters as un-American. The predominance of ethnic affiliations in team names—from Hakoah New York to Brooklyn Hispano—is testament to both soccer's deep local roots and its still unbroken connections to the old world. The cultural space and market share available to soccer was further narrowed over the twentieth century as, successively, ice hockey, American football, and basketball went professional.

Despite this, America did manage to sustain a small soccer culture and generate professional leagues, but none with the luck or the business model to survive. The current incarnation, Major League Soccer (MLS), may be able to overcome this history. Launched on the back of the 1994 World Cup, it has survived and even begun to prosper. The league has made uneven but increasingly serious attempts to draw upon America's vast reservoirs of participation in women's soccer, youth soccer, and in the soccer traditions of the new Latino communities. The recent arrival of new soccer-specific stadiums, new franchises, rich investors, reasonable crowds, and, finally, a TV deal that the league gets money for rather than paying out on are all considerable advances.

The arrival of David Beckham at L.A. Galaxy in summer 2007 signals a new departure in MLS's strategy and ambition. The highly restrictive but egalitarian wage policy of the last decade has been modified to allow in a small number of highly paid imports who will, it is hoped, significantly raise the quality and profile of the game. Becks himself seems to sense the immensity of the mission when he told *Good Morning America*: 'I'm going for the life, of course, for my kids to enjoy it and my wife to enjoy it, but the main thing for me is to improve the soccer and to improve the standard and to be part of history really.'

Seen from Europe, Beckham's departure for L.A. appears the perfect terminus for a career in which brand and image have always predominated over form and performance (which is not to ignore or diminish Beckham's considerable sporting talents or his heart and tenacity). Beckham's arrival suggests that MLS is now ready to try and add some glitz to the game in its bid to go mainstream. Minor masters of the dark arts of self-promotion and public relations, the Beckhams have constructed a global brand of considerable power. Whether that brand can make the shift from Europe to America and turn the power of celebrity into a world historical force, even with the help of Tom Cruise, remains to be seen. Becks is up against an awful lot of celebrity and an awful lot of history.

The Ball Is Round was finished a few hours before the opening ceremony of the 2006 World Cup began. It was proofread during the semifinals and signed off on the day after the final. After that I neither read nor wrote about soccer for six months. I did not listen to, watch, or play a game. Instead, I spent the summer with MLB, autumn with the NFL and the winter with the NBA and the NHL. It was, I think, a necessary corrective. While I remain broadly convinced of the structural, economic, and politico-cultural arguments for the limited progress of soccer in the United States, after spending a year with American sports they now appear to me an incomplete historical response to Hobsbawm's paradox.

The central pillars of American sports culture—American football, baseball, and basketball, along with hockey—have enjoyed only a limited global embrace, which has, I believe, entrenched their American rather than universal characteristics. This in turn has helped consolidate a wider American sports culture that finds soccer not merely foreign but alien, both incomprehensible and reprehensible. The private and mysterious timekeeping of the referee in soccer is contrasted with the open, public, and democratic clock in American football, basketball and hockey. The draw is considered nonsense at best, an outrage at worst. The rarity of not only goals, but clear scoring opportunities, is anathema not merely because it appears, at first sight, tedious, but more profoundly because it allocates such a large role to chance in determining the outcome of the game. The enormous number of scoring chances in basketball and the immense length of the baseball season are two devices that ensure, over both individual games and entire seasons, that luck evens out and other factors prevail. It is the same distaste for unaccountability and chance that finds the diving, faking, gamesmanship and chicanery of soccer unbearable.

Perhaps most fundamentally of all, soccer offers modes of storytelling and narrative structures that the American sporting public finds unsatisfactory. You have had, after all, a century of the most extraordinary and compelling sporting stories to savor and reflect upon. America possesses a literary culture that has, like no other, risen to the challenge of expressing them—a dual heritage I found condensed in Red Smith's homage to the "Shot Heard Round the World," Bobby Thomson's homerun that clinched the 1951 National League pennant race for the New York Giants after an epic chasing down of the Brooklyn Dodgers: 'Now it is done. Now the story ends. And there is no way to tell it. The art of fiction is dead. Reality has strangled invention. Only the utterly impossible, the inexpressibly fantastic, can ever be plausible again.' I now see that when this kind of performance is on offer, soccer, both domestic and international, appears to many, at best, a distraction.

Soccer can match the epic quality of the 1951 pennant race—European leagues have often featured season-long slugging matches between two or three top teams only resolved on the final day in the final minutes of multiple games. It can also offer the condensed moments of brilliance, beauty, and meaning that Thomson's homer exemplifies: Maradona's Hand of God, anyone? However, on a day-to-day basis, the level of narrative quality control is lower. Although soccer can do fantastical last-minute comebacks, collapses, turnovers, winners, and equalizers, there are less than in American sports. For all the really compelling o-o draws there are an awful lot of excruciating ones. For all the simple 5-o routs and hopelessly unjust 1-o victories for the poorer team, there are reams and reams of confusing, avant-garde, and just plain boring scripts. Ultimately, the entire logic of American sports culture chaffs at soccer's draws and low scores.

One could argue that American sports exceptionalism, its sense of glorious self-isolation, is in fact a perfect expression of the only superpower left standing and its willful unilateralism. However, American power has always rested on more than free agency. Its global hegemony has rested on the capacity to shape international institutions in its own image, determine the rules of the game to its own advantage, to force, cajole, and pressure others into accepting them and adapting to them. So it is, in reverse, in soccer. You will excuse me, I hope, if I express a preference for a multilateral world in which the United States is on occasion bound by collective agreements and meanings that are not entirely of its own making and that is an America that plays and understands soccer.

Soccer's mission in the United States is not, I think, to supplement or challenge American football, baseball, or basketball, but to offer a conduit to the rest of the world; a sporting antidote to the excesses of isolationism, a prism for understanding the world that the United States may currently shape but will increasingly be shaped by. A year with American sport has taught me more about America than I had ever learned before, opened my eyes and my heart to America's genius and to its tragedies. I have been enlightened and entertained. I offer *The Ball Is Round* as one route to the genius and the tragedies of the rest of us.

Introduction:
Life and Death,
Love and Money

The ball is round. The game lasts ninety minutes. This much is fact. Everything else is theory.   **Sepp Herberger**

Some people believe football is a matter of life and death: I am very disappointed with that attitude. I can assure you it is much, much more important than that.   **Bill Shankly**

Is there any cultural practice more global than football? Rites of birth, death and marriage are universal, but infinite in their diversity. Football is played by the same rules everywhere. No single world religion can match its geographical scope. Even Christianity, borne on the back of European expansion, is a relatively minor player across Asia, the Middle East and North Africa. The use of English and the vocabularies of science and mathematics must run football close for universality, but they remain the lingua francas of the world's elites, not of its masses. McDonald's, MTV? Only the most anodyne products of America's cultural industries can claim a reach as wide as football's, and then only for a fleeting moment in those parts of the world that can afford them. Around half the planet watched the 2006 World Cup Final – three billion humans have never done anything simultaneously before.

Football is available to anyone who can make a rag ball and find another pair of feet to pass to. Football has not merely been consumed by the world's societies, it has been embraced, embedded and then transformed by them. Football is a minority sport only in North America, Australasia and South Asia, where baseball, rugby and cricket are stronger, and even here it is a rising force. Whatever the course of its migration, whatever its geographical origins, whatever the hierarchies of the game, no single country or continent owns football.

Life and death? Can anything be that important? Football has claimed enough innocent victims in its hellish fires, tragic crushes and vicious little knife fights to ask the question. Important enough to be distrusted and banned by the last nervous Ottoman Sultanate, the neurotic demagogues of China's Cultural Revolution and Iran's revolutionary theocracy. Important enough that football has either outlasted its oppressors or forced them to relent. For football is driven by love and money, and if anything trumps life and death then they do.

Love of playing the game. Because before the great club colours were chosen and the monumental stadiums were raised and filled, people just played anywhere. They still do. No one knows how many people play football; how could you count them? But FIFA has tried – and their guess is that around a billion people play the game reasonably formally. That's 50 million referees, balls and pitches and 25 million kilometres of white lines, enough to circle the earth over a thousand times.

Love of watching the game. Because before the pitch was circled with fences and turnstiles, before the earth was circled with television satellites, before giant screens and action replays, people just came to watch. To capture singular moments of brilliance. Ninety minutes of grind and plod for a sly feint, an impish dribble, an unstoppable, rifled shot – and goals, always goals.

Love of following the game. Because the game is not just an art, it's drama, too. It has great metropolitan and minor provincial theatres, with free-spending and penny-pinching impresarios and their megalomaniac obsessive directors. It has legions of critics and a fantastical rotating cast of angels and devils, geniuses and journeymen, fallen giants and rising stars. It offers the spotlight for individual brilliance while relishing the defiance and heart of collective endeavour. It has staged tragedy and comedy, epic and pantomime, unsophisticated music hall and inaccessible experimental performances. It does imperious triumph, lucky escapes, impossible comebacks and stubborn stalemates. It captures the brilliance of unpredictability, the uncertainty of the human heart and human skill, of improvisation and chance. And those that follow it are not merely the crowd; they are the chorus. Consumers and commentators, spectators and participants, without whom every goal is just a ball in the back of the net, every victory just three points in the bag.

Love of us and hatred of them. Because, before clubs became global brands, before club crests competed with corporate logos, football had become entwined with every conceivable social identity and the social divisions that surely follow them: derby day in Glasgow, Belfast and Dundee pitches Catholic against Protestant; in Calcutta it aligns Hindu Mohun Bagan against Muslim Mohammedan Sporting. In Athens, AEK are the migrant refugees from the Graeco-Turkish war contesting the turf, eighty years later, with the locals of Olympiakos. In Manchester,

Turin and Munich, wealthy outsiders and parvenus play off against the authentic heart and soul of the city. In Rio, rich and poor, elite and mass, white and black take to the field alongside Fluminense and Flamengo. In Soviet Moscow, Dinamo play Spartak and the lumbering communist leviathan faces off against its surly public. Through the multiple acts of playing, organizing, watching and following, people have defined and expressed who they think they and their neighbours are.

And all for what? Because football matches do not change social structures. Because no victory, however comprehensive, can shift the real balance of power, or change the actual distribution of wealth and status. It is for the glory. For winning, and winning in style. For winning because you were the best, the quickest, the cleverest. Because, when it came to it on the pitch, when the whistle blew and money, power, status, reputation and history were all sent to the bench, you wanted it more.

But, in the never-ending arms race of competitive sport, glory – even the chance of glory – must be paid for, schemed for, planned for. From the first Lancashire industrialist coughing up for the works team's boots to Nike's virtual ownership of the Brazilian national squad, victory has been pursued through the relentless expenditure of hard cash. So relentless that football has not been and cannot be too choosy where it comes from. If money is not the currency of power then other more basic political means will do. Power, authority, threats and violence have acquired squads, built stadiums and ordained results. Football has served the greater glories and fed on the brute power of every imaginable political institution; all to borrow or steal their share of glory.

And yet the historians and the sporting press want to separate what is obviously connected: football and history, sport and politics, the game and money. The historians do so on grounds of causality; the press on grounds of morality. Perhaps the historians are right. Football has not altered the course of history. Football did not kick-start the industrial revolution or build the world's cities. Football does not start, end or replace wars; it does not make the peace or redraw the borders of the world. But is it not extraordinary that, in an epoch characterized by unprecedented global interconnectedness, the most universal cultural phenomenon in the world is football? Is it not worthy of note that, the moment male urban working classes have had a bit of time and money on their hands, they have chosen, almost everywhere, to play, watch, organize and follow football? Is it wise to recount the history of the modern world without some reference to this? Whether the historians like it or not, football cannot be taken out of the history of the modern world and the history of the modern world is unevenly, erratically but indisputably etched into the history of football.

Much of the sporting press would prefer us not to bring the big bad world into the game at all. Football has its history, its traditions, its turning points, but they are the work of great players, charismatic managers, unrepeatable performances, unquenchable team spirits and the serendipity of interlocking personal histories. History, yes, in the guise of heritage and urban myth, but economics, politics, never. And perhaps the reporters are right. The drama and its outcome cannot be decided by the forces of money and power. Victory should not be bought. Allegiances should not be imposed. Love is not tradable, nor can it be ruled. Yet so often it is. Referees have been bought, linesmen have been corralled and games been thrown. Players, clubs and fans have been exploited, liquidated, mistreated and thrown on the scrapheap. Across the world, football's bureaucracies have been run as personal fiefdoms and political campaign machines. Violence, racism and bigotry have constantly staked their place on and off the pitch. So what alternative explanations are there? Sepp Herberger expresses the virtually autistic refusal of the football world to see its own enmeshment with the social institutions and ideas of its day; its resistance to seeing the game explained by anything other than its own internal rules of chance; its meaning and significance restricted to its own protected times and spaces. Herberger lived the firestorm of the rise and fall of the Third Reich as Germany's national team coach. In his 361 notebooks compiled daily throughout the cataclysm there is not a single reference to anything other than football. But if you flee from theory, conjecture and engagement with power, what are you left with? Are these pathologies simply the work of evil men? Are they the random and unfortunate consequences of a few bad apples, secret coteries and plots?

No, and in this football expresses the Faustian bargain that all modern societies have made with the forces of money and power. For the modern world comes with strings attached. The logic of the market is to price, buy and sell everything. The logic of power is to control, monitor and regulate everything. Can your health be priced? The market will try. Can dignity or loyalty be bought? Money will ask the question.

Football, in its transition from a chaotic folk ritual to a sector of the global entertainment industry, has encountered the same dilemma. In the world of football, glory has the final say. The bottom line for those who follow football is not calculated in money or power, but in victories and pleasures. But spectaculars require backers, the circus must be paid for. Football attracts and must therefore deal with money and power and they will always be looking to buy or take their share of glory; and glory bought or stolen turns to dust.

So, what bargain can be struck with these forces? How will the line be policed? Who will seek to cross it? It is not just the bureaucrats and the moneymen, the cynical professionals and opportunist politicians who must make their deal, but everyone who plays, watches and follows football. We want to see the best professionals play at the highest level, but we cannot bear that their wages might diminish their heart and their hunger. We want to see grace and invention, but we will settle at half-time for a single grubby point. We want pantomime crooks and villains as club owners, but we also want them to obey the health and safety laws. We hate the way the media barons try to buy the game, but we pay our subscriptions anyway. Money and power, capitalism and the state: can't live with them, can't live without them. Football, the game the world plays, offers a metaphor for the dilemmas that sit at the very centre of any moral framework or political programme that takes the reformation rather than the abolition of modernity as its starting point.

No history of the modern world is complete without an account of football. No history of football can begin to disclose its meaning or describe its course without shadowing the economic, political and social histories of modern societies. *The Ball is Round* is my attempt to write the history of how humanity has played and watched and followed football; the stories of players and managers, fans and owners, clubs and national teams. It is a chronicle of who has won and lost, of how and why. Because if the currency is glory, it matters who scored, and when they scored and how they scored, who they beat and how they celebrated. But this book is also a history of states and markets, money and power. Above all, it is a history of how all these forces have interacted. A history which attempts to locate where the line between the realm of glory and the realm of power has been crossed, that celebrates the love of the game, but knows that it can be bought.

PART ONE

Ancients and Moderns:

Football and the Invention of Modern Sport, from the Beginning to 1914

1
Chasing Shadows: The Prehistory of Football

Football is as old as the world . . . People have always played some
form of football, from its very basic form of kicking a ball around
to the game it is today.   **Sepp Blatter, FIFA President**

I

Is it? Have we? Let us forgive the President of FIFA his hyperbole, let us not take him at his word. Football, at the very least, requires feet. The emergence of bipedal hominids, whose feet and hands are sufficiently differentiated that they can trap and kick or catch and throw rather than paw, pad or shove, can be dated to around 2 million years ago. The world is somewhat older. And the ball? Let us forgive Blatter his carelessness with the archaeological record, for there is no evidence of any human manufactured sphere that could be kicked before 2000 BCE. Perhaps those stitched ancient Egyptian balls were kicked, but the hiero-glyphic and mural evidence only shows throwing. No doubt, people have been kicking fruit and gourds for longer, rocks and pebbles at a pinch, skulls perhaps and any manner of the roughly spherical objects that the world throws up. Of course they have, it is an irresistible act; to spy the object, to imagine its future trajectory, to shape and balance one's body and then to take a mighty swing. Better still there comes the delicious moment of impact and the always extraordinary sensation of energy and motion passing from one's leg to the inanimate object. It soars into the air. It scuds across the ground. It finds its target or perhaps it bounces, tumbling, spinning on an unimagined course. This is not football. This is play. It has no rules and no obvious purpose. It is not a contest or a trial. It contains no strategy or tactics. Yes, it is pleasure and wonder and experiment, but if this is football, then peek-a-boo is drama. This is not to say that football is not a form of playing, or that even in its most modern, structured, commercialized forms that it does not draw upon the same spirit of play that animates a Neolithic rock-kicker. But football is the game modernity plays and the gulf between the modern world and prehistory, between sport and play, is so vast, so punctured by profound transformations in the organization of human life, that to declare an unbroken lineage between the two is to embrace an historical perspective only to render it utterly vacuous.

Undaunted, Mr Blatter has had another stab at constructing football's prehistory. He chose to make his intervention in the debate in a speech at the Beijing Football Expo 2004, an international bazaar devised to bring together the sporting-industrial complex of companies that create the game's elaborate infrastructure and the global and national bureaucrats and officials that run it. Blatter said, 'We honour the Chinese people for their country's role as the cradle of the earliest forms of football, having firmly planted the roots of our sport and helping set the course for it to grow into the beautiful game it is today.'[1] A statement which received a chorus of coordinated support from the Chinese Sports Ministry and the Asian Football Confederation. Blatter is at least on firmer ground here than on his excursion into the prehistory of play. Certainly, the China created and ruled by the Han dynasty (206 BCE–221 CE) widely played a game called *cuju*, simply translated as kick-ball. The technological and social precocity of ancient China is not in doubt; the Chinese invented a lot of things first. The emergence of settled societies, cities and social hierarchies provided the framework in which spontaneous play could be organized into rule-bound contests, and China came to all of these things early. In the initial attempts by nationalist historians of the 1920s and 1930s to write a Chinese history of sport these truths were applied to football.[2] Claims based on stories of the *cuju*-playing Yellow Emperor dated his political and sporting career as early as the third millennium BCE. The claims however were an attempt to give historical foundation to mythology, relying on legendary epics written just before the emergence of the great Han dynasty in the second century BCE. It seems most likely that *cuju*, although played in the era of the Warring States (in the third and fourth centuries BCE), was first formalized as an organized sport under the Han. The game was played with a stitched leather ball stuffed with fur or feathers, though some accounts suggest hemp. There were two teams on a marked pitch with goals at the two ends. It appears handling and rough tackling were allowed, but kicking was an important form of propulsion. In some accounts the goal was moon- or crescent-shaped, in others it was described as a hole in a silk sheet hung between bamboo posts. The game was clearly popular among the Royal Household – Emperor Wu Di has been described as both enthusiast and expert. But the game's home was most likely to have been in the army where it became an element of both training and recreation; some suggest that it warded off the leg numbness suffered by cavalry after a long ride.

Under the subsequent imperial dynasties – the Tang (618–907 CE) and the Song (960–1279 CE) – the game continued to be played but its form changed. The ball itself was transformed as players adopted the more technologically advanced but less physically robust hollow ball. It was easier to control, but less suited to combative mêlée. It may be that the new ball was only accessible to the rich, which would help explain the linguistic and formal separation of the common or popular game *Bai Da* and the courtly game *Zhu Qiu*. *Bai Da* was closer to the original Han version of *cuju*. Although details of the rules are not certain, in *Zhu Qiu* physical contest and direct confrontation appear to have been lost and a more stylized format adopted. Two goals merged into one. The ball was first passed among the players of one team until it was received by a designated player who alone could attempt to shoot at a target. Whether they scored or not, if the shooting side could keep the ball in the air afterwards they would retain possession and have another go at shooting. If the ball touched the ground the shooting initiative passed to the other side. The game was certainly ubiquitous enough for it to appear in *Tales of the Water Margin*, one of the four classics of Chinese literature. The tales feature a court official named Gao Qiu whose senior position in the imperial bureaucracy was won by his prodigious *cuju* skills. But *cuju* did not outlive its Tang and Song patrons. With their decline and the rise of the Ming dynasty (1368–1644 CE) that replaced them, *cuju* disappears.

Like many other Chinese innovations, the ball game appears to have spread along the tracks of imperial expansion and the networks of long-distance trade routes, land and marine, that radiated out from the Middle Kingdom. In the Malay Peninsula, for example, a cross between football and volleyball called *Sepak Raga* was played with a light rattan ball. It has recently been formalized and modernized as *Sepak Takraw* – a compromise between the Malay word for kick and the Thai word for ball – but its roots are at least four hundred years old and derive from its Chinese counterpart. Medieval Japan played *kemari*. Although Japanese nationalist historians have insisted on its indigenous origin as far back as the sixth century BCE, the earliest documented writing on the game dates from the twelfth century.[3] The form of the game is clearly related to the courtly version of *cuju* that the Song had been playing half a millennium before this. In the hands of the Japanese nobility the game became even more stylized than in China. *Kemari* was also known as 'standing among the trees'. The playing space was a six- or seven-metre dirt square demarcated by four trees placed at its corners. These could be cherry, willow or maple but pine trees were considered to have the highest status. Eight players would take the field, standing in pairs on either side of the trees. The ball was hollow, light and made of deerskin, often coated white with albumen or dyed yellow by smoke from a pine needle fire. The courtiers with the highest social status would kick-off and the players would simply try and keep the ball in the air as long as possible and used the trees to bounce it off, their branches pruned and trained to provide a path back on to the court for the ball. If a formal count of successful kicks and passes was being carried out, the official responsible could award extra kicks for particularly impressive or stylish plays. Individuals were admired for their ball skills, but also their attention to the etiquette and traditions of the game. A day's *kemari* was best ended by a single high kick from the most senior player gracefully caught in the folds of his kimono.

Kemari became an important pastime amongst the Japanese elite in the twelfth and thirteenth centuries. The first masters of the game appeared, wrote down the rules and displayed unheard-of levels of excellence. Retired and active emperors Goshirakawa and Gotoba became noted enthusiasts and participants. Distinct schools or houses of *kemari* emerged with their own take on training, technique and rules. Gotoba himself first set down the sartorial regulations covering the game, specifying the colour and pattern of playing socks according to social rank and *kemari* skill. The game continued to be represented in Japanese art and literature throughout the Tokagowa Shogunate and into the nineteenth century. But while *kemari* proved longer lived than *cuju* it was no more able to capture the imagination of a modernizing society. Within a few years of the Meiji Restoration (1868) and Japan's headlong drive for industrialization *kemari* had shrunk to a minority pastime of a minority social caste of aristocrats reduced to lobbying the emperor and government to preserve this fragment of the country's feudal past.

Although some imperial patronage was dispensed the game was virtually extinguished by the end of the Second World War.

So are *cuju* and its descendants the ancestors of football as Mr Blatter and the Chinese sports bureaucracies claim? What really marks these sports out in the ancient history of ball games was that they were primarily, though probably not exclusively, kicking games. Yet this preference for the foot over the hand or any other part of the body to propel the ball does not make *cuju* or *kemari* unique or even the most venerable. Among the Aboriginal Australians of what is now Victoria State, *Marn Gook* has been played for millennia. Accounts written by white Australians in the 1840s suggest that it was predominantly a kicking game. The Pacific Islands societies of Polynesia and Micronesia had their own indigenous kicking games with balls made from wrapped Pandanus leaves. Native Americans played many large-scale team ball games and showed a general disinclination to use their hands, preferring bats and feet. William Strachey, the first colonial governor of Virginia, described one game as:

a kynd of exercise that have often amongst them much like that which boyes call bandy in English and may be aunceynt game. They have the exercise of Footeball, in which yet they only forceibly encounter with the foote to carry the Balle the one from the other, and spurne it to the goale with a kind of dexterity and swift footmanshippe, which is the honour of it.[4]

Does that make these games and cultures the ancestors of football? *Marn Gook* is likely to be as old as and probably older than *cuju*. The Native Americans continued to play their games of football long after the Ming had abandoned theirs. They also continued to play the ball horizontally, passing it towards a goal. While early forms of *cuju* appear to take this form, its refined courtly versions as well as *kemari* play the ball upwards. The switch from the horizontal to the vertical as the main axis of movement was perfectly in tune with the shifting culture of the times. Late medieval China and Japan closed their doors to the world until Americans and Europeans forced them to open them again in the nineteenth century. Expansive territorial imperatives were abandoned for the delicate maintenance of vertical hierarchy. The price of over three hundred years of glorious internal order was social, military and technological inferiority; and that is why whatever the similarities of Han *cuju* or *Marn Gook* to football, neither can claim its origins.

What has ultimately determined which game modernity plays is not who played a kicking game earliest, nor even who kept the ball on the ground for longest, but who played the game at the moment of modernization. Perhaps, in an alternative history, in which China or Japan had industrialized before or alongside Europe, a sizeable portion of the world, at least in Asia and the Pacific, would be playing an alternative football code of their own. But they did not. The pallid remnants of *cuju* and *kemari* were, like the elites that still played them, swept aside by the whirlwind of East Asia's encounter with modernity.

The Chinese Tang imperial household may have dabbled in *cuju* but they revelled in *polo*. Roman senators might have warmed up in the gym with a game of catch but the slaughter at the Coliseum was the centre of their sporting world. Competitive ball games are present in nearly all the cultures of the ancient world, but only in Mesoamerica did the ball game take centre stage. In this respect the sporting universe of the modern world is closer to that of the cultures that lived in what is now Mexico, Guatemala, Belize and Honduras; the ball game was the only game. For 3,000 years, between the emergence of the Olmecs in Central Mexico and the fall of the Aztecs to the Spanish conquistadors in 1521, every society in Mesoamerica, every settlement from the great city of Teotihulucan to the scattered village compounds of the Gulf of Mexico played the game. The material archaeological record left behind cannot quite match the singular splendour of the Coliseum or Olympia but its breadth is unparalleled. Over 1,500 ball courts have been unearthed, from tiny plain rectangular troughs in small villages and ancient hilltop towns to the vast and elaborate stepped constructions of the great Mayan city of Chichen Itza. Many more must have been lost to the jungle or were destroyed by the Spanish occupation. In addition, the ruined ball courts and ransacked tombs have yielded an extraordinary trove of ceramic figurines, glyphs, carvings, reliefs and statues that depict the game and its rituals.[5]

The mythological record is even stronger. The *Popul Vuh* is the defining written document of the Qiche Mayan cultures that ruled over southern Mexico, Belize and Guatemala from around 800 to 1400 CE.

It consists of three parts. The first is the story of creation. The third is a dynastic history of the Mayan nobility. At the heart of the text, sandwiched between the two, is an account of the creation of the sun and the moon and with it all the dualities around which Mesoamerican life was organized: light and dark, day and night, good and evil, life and death. Its chief protagonists are the hero twins Hunahpu and Xbalanque. The twin's forefathers were the brothers Hun Hunahpu and Vucub Hunahpu. Both were ball players of considerable repute whose noisy game disturbed the gods of the underworld. The Dark Lords of Xibalba opened a portal on to the brothers' court and tricked them into entering their realm. There they challenged them to a game. The mortals lost and were immediately sacrificed, their bodies buried in the subterranean court and the head of Hun Hunahpu humiliatingly displayed on a calabash tree. When the goddess Xquic passed the tree Hun Hunahpu's dismembered head spat in her hand. The goddess was impregnated and when her pregnancy was discovered by the Xibalba lords she was banished to the upper world. Here she gave birth to the hero twins. The demi-god brothers proved to be divine ball players and once they reached adulthood were summoned to the underworld for the second leg of this intergenerational encounter. On and off the court the twins proved a match for their immortal foes and escaped back to earth with their father and uncle's bodies, exhumed from the diabolical ball court. The corpses were placed in the sky to become the sun and the moon.

It is worth pausing for a moment to reflect on this. These are not ancillary elements of Mesoamerican culture, a mere addendum to their central myths and narratives; they are at the core of their whole structure of belief. How can it be that a ball game provided the physical and symbolic fulcrum of an entire continental culture? We could ask a similar if secularized question of our own world. What appeared to strike the Spanish most of all on seeing the game for the first time was the ball and how it moved. Columbus brought examples back to the Spanish court for investigation. Royal chronicler Pedro Mártir de Anglería was flummoxed: 'I don't understand how when the balls hit the ground they are sent into the air with such incredible bounce.'[6]

Mesoamerica alone had balls that bounced, because it alone had rubber. Today rubber can be found all over the tropics but prior to the conquest it was indigenous to the forests of Mesoamerica. But rubber plants are not enough alone to make the ball. In the earliest settled communities of the second millennium somebody had to have the wit and the luck to mix the latex juice of the plant with the roots of the morning glory flower. What they got was a botanical form of vulcanization that created a solidified, elastic, jumping ball. When all you have known are pebbles and squashes, who wouldn't want to play with that? The playful energies of these ancient Mesoamericans must have been so intensely stimulated, so unreservedly released by the quicksilver bounce of the rubber ball that the game itself became sacred; a portal into the world of magical energies.

Archaeological fragments suggest that ball manufacture had begun as early as 1500 BCE, but it was around 1200 BCE that the expanding Olmec Empire, with its emergent cities, public architecture and hierarchical religious and political institutions, provided the context in which the rubber ball and the insatiable desire to play with it could be framed by settled rules to create a contested team game. The Olmec version of the ball game contained all of its lasting characteristics. The courts the game was played on were invariably part of a larger public space or temple complex. They were either rectangular or a capital I-shaped, flanked by high sloping whitewashed walls and often richly decorated with brightly coloured murals. The very biggest complexes would have further levels of stepped stone serving as seating for a considerable audience. The rubber ball, varying in size between a large softball and a small basketball, moved back and forth across a central line between two competitors or two teams. From the protective clothing worn by players in sculpture and pictures, it seems that the ball was struck with some combination of forearms, shins, shoulders, buttocks and hips. The heavy speeding ball would have been dangerous and difficult to control with the head or bare feet. The aim appears to have been akin to modern volleyball: to keep the ball aloft in one's own half or restrict it to a limited number of bounces before returning it to one's opponents.

The precise form and meanings of the ball game changed over the next 3,000 years. In the smaller cities of Pacific Mexican civilization, at their height around the second century BCE, the game was played at village level in modest courts. In the city-state of Teotihulucan three centuries later, the game was restricted to the elite who played with bats and sticks. Among the Maya the game's ritual and religious dimension peaked, while the greatest enthusiasts for just playing were probably the civilizations of Vera Cruz on the Caribbean coast whose urban ruins are studded with simple ball courts. The game even spread east to the island societies of what is now Hispaniola and Puerto Rico, and to the north it was taken up by the Hohokum Indian cultures of Arizona. The Aztecs, who knew the game as *Tchatali*, added decorated stone rings to the side of a court, and awarded the game to those who could send the ball through them.

The geographical spread of the ball game was matched by its social depth. From its inception the game was entwined with other features of Mesoamerican life. The sheer number of courts and ubiquity of objects indicated that the game was played informally by commoners as well as ritually by the elite. Aztec and Mayan records even point to the emergence of highly skilled players from the lower classes competing with nobles. The meaning of the game was tied to the complex systems of astronomy and calendrical time around which these societies were organized. The patron deity of the Aztec game was Xolotl who appeared in the night sky as Venus, and players appear in murals as representatives of other cosmic bodies. Statuettes and carvings show that the game was often accompanied or preceded by dramatic performances, and that gambling was rife. A number of Mesoamerican cultures record accounts of the nobility wagering their land and their tributary authority on the outcome of a game. Sometimes a substitute for war, the game could also provide its denouement as defeated opponents first played the game before being sacrificed – their heads cut off or their hearts torn out.

When the Spanish arrived they were amazed and appalled by the ball game. In 1528 Hernando Cortés was sufficiently intrigued to take ball players and equipment back to the court of King Charles V of Spain, where his captive athletes performed for the Castilian nobility. But the devil was in the ball, its capricious flight diabolical, its intrinsic rhythms pagan. The Spanish suppressed the game. They needn't have bothered: the introduction of Eurasian diseases into the continent, the enslavement of much of the population and the forced Christianization of those that survived were easily enough to destroy the societies and beliefs that sustained the ball game. All that is left are shadows; the odd, the quaint, the rural and the regional. For example, in the far north-western Mexican state of Sinaloa variants of the ball game – called *Ulama* – survive. Here the unpaved dirt streets provided the court for the rough rubber balls still hand-made by the players; broken Aztec words furnish its specialized language.

Modern football is now the game at the centre of the region's culture. The World Cup has been played out twice in a stadium called Azteca, on a site just a few miles south of the great Aztec capital Tenochtitlan. There, beneath the foundations of the Metropolitan Cathedral of Mexico City, lie the remains of its great ball courts. It is a cruel accident of global history that football's twentieth-century triumph in Mesoamerica was predicated on the epidemiological slaughter and cultural eradication performed by the Spanish conquest that preceded it.

III

The European civilization that eventually outpaced and dominated the societies of Asia, Africa and the Americas was an amalgam. It was forged from the remains of the Roman Empire and the Hellenistic culture that it had conquered and appropriated. Rome was in turn conquered from within by the new monotheism – Christianity – and from without by the invading nomads of the Eurasian steppes who arrived in the fifth century. Their fusion generated the fragmented, warring feudal Christendom of medieval Europe. None of these elements in the European mix can claim a significant ball-playing culture.

Classical Antiquity did not lack ball games, but they had little or no status.[7] In *The Odyssey*, Homer's description of Odysseus' encounter with the Phoenicians tells us that the Minoan cultures of the first millennium BCE knew the ball. The shipwrecked hero was woken by the excited shrieks of naked royal serving-girls playing catch ball while their clothes dried in the sun. In *The Iliad*, Homer's description of the funereal games held after the death of the Athenian warrior Patroclus includes athletics, archery, wrestling and chariot racing, but in this esteemed sporting and social company ball games do not merit a single mention. No laurel wreath was ever awarded at Olympia for any ball game of any kind, nor at the Greeks' other sacred sporting gatherings.

Rome's relationship with the ball was not dissimilar though if anything the Romans were more enthusiastic ball players than the Greeks. They had specially constructed indoor ball courts called *Sphaerista* for *Expulsum Ludere*, a competitive game not entirely unlike modern handball. Like the Greeks there were plenty of ball games based around circles, catching, throwing, feigning and dodging. Adults and children played Sky-ball, *Pila* and *Trigon*. Other games were played outdoors on playing fields or *Palaestra*, especially *Harpastum*. Like the Greek games it was based upon – *Episkyros* and *Phaininda* – the rules of *Harpastum* remain hazy but it appears to be something akin to rugby with kicking, catching and physical contact the order of the day. In one of the best accounts of the game to have survived, Athenaeus writes, 'He seized the ball and passed it on to a teammate while dodging another and laughing. He pushed it out of the way of another. Another fellow player he raised to his feet. All the while the crowd resounded with shouts of out of bounds. Too far. Right behind him. Over his head, on the ground, up in the air, too short, pass it back in the scrum.'[8] Like *cuju* in Han China, *Harpastum* seems to have been most popular in the army and may have formed an element of formal military training. But as a spectator sport or a game of social significance it was nowhere.

Harpastum could not be found at the Coliseum, where the Romans had built the single most important and impressive sporting architecture of the ancient world: a five-storey, 50,000-seat stadium that would aesthetically and practically remain superior to every other sports stadium until the twentieth century. Rome had mass, urban sporting spectacle that had no parallel, but in that spectacle there was no place for ball games. For the lumpenproletariat of the city and the senatorial class alike the preference was for real blood and guts. At the Circus Maximus, they crowded in to watch chariot racing, but this often proved as macabre and bloody as the staged fights down the road. The desperation of Rome's proletariat can be measured by the coarseness of its pleasures, the cynicism and manipulativeness of its ruling class by the baroque scale of the circus they created to sate them. In this important sense Rome's sporting culture is closer to the modern era than that of the ancient Far East or Mesoamerica. Rome had the crowd and the impresario. Of course, *cuju*, *kemari* and the Mesoamerican game had their audience, but it is a qualitative rather than just a quantitative shift to move from a few hundred cheering round the edge of a field or ball court to 50,000 encased in a cauldron. It is one thing to gather a refined selection of the local elite around a Zen Garden; it is quite another to sweep up every level of a deeply divided urban colossus and throw them together in an atmosphere of intimidation and contest. At the Circus Maximus, Rome even created the first secular sporting derby in which the blue and green chariot teams and their supporters faced off on the track, in the stands, and sometimes on the street or on the floor of the Senate. Rome's sporting legacy and tastes were lost. The intensity and scale of Rome's secular spectacle would only be recovered when societies evolved that could build and sustain cities of equal magnitude. It would be a long wait.

Of the barbarian invaders we know little. Whatever sporting practices the Visigoths and Vandals may have brought with them from the steppes were soon subsumed and lost, like the rest of their cultures, beneath the vast edifice of Christianity that their kings embraced. The dominant sporting cultures and practices of medieval Christendom that these invasions produced were not amicable to ball games. In short, knights don't play kickabouts, they fight wars. The feudal ruling classes of the era were more wholly militarized than the nobility of either Mesoamerica or the Far East. Europe's aristocracies were dependent on the use of organized violence for their social status, political power and economic wellbeing. The most powerful technology of war was the mounted, armoured knight and such force could not be conjured from a rural peasant levy or standing army; it had to be provided directly by the nobility itself. There was no time, no utility and no glamour in such trite pastimes as ball games; the joust, the hunt and the tournament were the only sports fit for a mounted warrior caste.

Yet despite this paucity of ball games in the European cultural mix, this is where modern football did emerge. Unlike the development of basketball or volleyball – which are games completely invented anew as exercises in modern sporting rationality – football in the far north-western corners of the continent did have traditional roots and practices to draw upon. These practices had survived despite their subservience to the games of aristocrats and their irrelevance to the tasks of warriors. They survived because the societies that incubated these games had themselves maintained a degree of independence and autonomy from medieval Europe's mainstream. They had eluded the control of Rome even at its height, absorbed Christianity without losing their pre-Christian festivities and retained networks of kinship and tribal authority that could challenge the feudal hierarchies of the medieval world. These were the Celtic cultures and societies of the Western Fringe.

IV

On the western edge of the European peninsula, Celtic-speaking cultures preserved a degree of autonomy and separateness throughout the medieval era. All appear to have played large-scale and often riotous ball games in large open spaces with innumerable participants divided into two teams trying to get the ball to a particular place with few formalities or restrictions. Often the games were played between two parishes or villages, the ball carried across the open fields between them. Alternatively a village could be divided by geography, or age, or between married men and bachelors in a game linked to courting rituals or Shrove Tuesday and saints' days. In Ireland the game was well known. In 1527 the Statutes of Galway referred to it by its English name stating that people should not play 'the hurlings of the littll ball with hockie sticks or staves nor use no hands ball to play without the walls but only the great footballe', while poets of the seventeenth and eighteenth century describe games in the Boyen Valley, Country Kildare and County Kerry.[9] A game called *La Soule* was played in Brittany but also further east in Normandy and Picardy and like its Irish counterpart was subject to repeated bans by ecclesiastical and secular authorities. In Cornwall the game was know as Hurling and on the Pembrokeshire peninsula in south Wales they played *Knappen*. In the Orkney Islands, Kirkwall hosted the *Ba* game between the uppies and downies of the town. The game was formalized and revived in 1850 but can claim a much older ancestry. Similar games were played in Perth, Jedburgh and Duns Castle in Berwickshire.

The only example of a team ball game of similar qualities played outside of the Celtic and Anglo-Saxon areas is *Calcio* – played in medieval and early modern Florence until its disappearance, possibly its banning, in the mid-eighteenth century. Today it survives as a tourist and civic spectacular, revived by the fascists in 1930 and played annually in the central squares of Florence in medieval pantaloons with accompanying gunfire. Legend claims that the game was played in 1530 while the city was under siege from the Medici, and that the aristocracy of the city liked to take the field on feast days, saints' days and Epiphany. The rules were first published in 1580 by Giovanni Bardi. Unlike the Celtic ball games there does not appear to be a rural or folk version that the urban aristocracy civilized – it was and is a purely urban phenomenon; and it was played, according to one English observer in the seventeenth century, with the same attention to rules of courtly procedure and etiquette.

As well as sharing linguistic and sporting ties, what all of these Celtic societies shared was an antipathy towards long conflict with their nearest expansive imperial neighbours – England and the English. Brittany would elude the English Plantagenet kings only to be subsumed by the expanding French monarchy. Wales, Ireland and Scotland were all subject to repeated incursions and colonial settlement. Political independence was eroded, as the English crown established its hegemony over the British Isles.

While the Angles, Saxons and Normans that made up much of the English mix may have had their own ball games, it seems as likely that they learned them in the course of their long struggles with their Celtic neighbours. By the early medieval era football was sufficiently commonplace as both a village occasion and an urban pastime that edicts were issued in the names of Edward II, Henry V, Edward IV, Henry VII and Henry VIII which sought to ban, control or restrict it. It was certainly violent enough for deaths and injuries to be recorded.

On some occasions the justification was one of public order. A law proclaimed in the name of Edward II in 1314 decried 'a great uproar in the city, through certain tumults arising from great footballs in the fields of the public, from which many evils may arise'.[10] An observer described its rural version as a game 'in which young men, in country sport, propel a huge ball not by throwing it into the air, but by striking and rolling it along the ground, and that not with their hands but with their feet. A game I say abominable enough, and in my judgment at least, more common, undignified, and worthless than any other kind of game, rarely ending but with some loss, accident or disadvantage to the players themselves.'[11] In other legal documents the need for the populace to focus on archery was the rationale for controlling the game. A statute of Edward IV from 1477 reads, 'No person shall practise any unlawful games such as dice, quoits, football and such games, but that every strong and able-bodied person shall practise with the bow for the reason that the national defence depends upon such bowmen.'[12] Court records show that individuals were fined and punished for playing the game. Provincial towns like Halifax, Leicester, Manchester and Liverpool banned the game at some point between 1450 and 1650. Yet for all the evident disapproval and repeated attempts to control it, football was an indelible feature of both rural and urban life for the lower orders. Even the determined efforts of the Puritan Commonwealth to purge Merrie England of its insufferable attraction to games and gaming failed. In the early years of the Restoration Charles II and his court dabbled in football.

By the eighteenth century all these quirky ball games were just a small element of the broader sporting culture that was emerging. Hunting and field sport still reigned supreme among the landed elites. Early forms of cricket, tennis and golf proved more attractive to their more pacific members. Horse racing and boxing were the preferred sports of the gambler from all social classes. All were played alongside the rise and remaking of a global imperial ruling class and in the furnace of the world's first industrial revolution. It was the chance encounter of those immense historical forces with the surviving rough Anglo-Celtic mêlées of the eighteenth century that created modern football. It would embrace the kicking spirit of the Far East and the Pacific, it would assume a secular cultural importance that parallels the Mesoamerican ball game, and it would revive the memory of Rome's urban furnace and the repertoire of bread and circuses. But it was only in the short-lived association of the game with aristocratic Corinthian amateurism that football would develop with conscious reference to or knowledge of Antiquity. The rest was confined to the shadows by the course of global history. The sphere is as old as the world. Kicking is as old as humanity. The Ancients knew the ball, but football is born of modernity.

2
The Simplest Game: Britain and the Invention of Modern Football

The game was formerly much in vogue among the common people, though of late years it seems to have fallen into disrepute and is but little practised. **Joseph Strutt, 1801**

Any lower boy in this house who does not play football once a day and twice on a half holiday will be fined half a crown and kicked.

Notice at Eton College, mid-nineteenth century

1

Joseph Strutt, author of the incomparable survey of England's sporting cultures in the late Georgian era, *Sports and Pastimes of the People of England*, would have been astonished to discover that a mere half century after he had noted the virtual disappearance of football it should have come to dominate the curriculum of the most prestigious and powerful public school in the land. It would surely have been beyond even the wildest reaches of Strutt's imagination to conceive that a century after he had casually written the obituary of traditional football it had in its modernized form become the national game of England and Scotland and was well on its way to becoming the single most popular global sport of the twentieth century. The very idea of a national game would have appeared odd to Strutt, for in 1801 almost no game or pastime could boast genuine national coverage or a single codified set of agreed rules. Rules, such as they were, were tied to context, unstably enshrined in unwritten traditions. Nor had any sense of emergent national identity been tied to something as seemingly marginal and trivial as the playing of games. But then many other aspects of the future were as yet unclear. It was by no means obvious to contemporary observers that by mid-century Britain would, without question, be the dominant global power or that it would possess an unrivalled empire and have assumed the leading edge of economic and technological development. In 1801 Britain was embroiled in the long Napoleonic wars and was uncertain of final victory. The empire, after the recent loss of the United States, did not look unassailable and the slow-burning fuse of industrialization, ignited by tiny pockets of mid-eighteenth-century development, had yet to explode into a juggernaut of sustained economic growth and urbanization.

Even if these social preconditions for football's growth in Britain and its eventual global spread had been apparent it was by no means certain that football would be the sport that Britain's elites would lionize. The organizational energies of the nation's aristocracy, which would reinvent and rationalize football as part of a wider and deeper commitment to games and sport, were otherwise engaged. Indeed a survey of the leading sports of the era suggests that the early processes of professionalization, agreed rules and a centralized organization – which were infrastructural preconditions of the emergence of modern football as the dominant national and global sport – were beginning in the worlds of boxing, rowing, horse racing and cricket.

In the early nineteenth century boxing was run by a network of pugilistic aristocrats and London publicans. This cross-class sporting alliance began life in the early eighteenth century in fights centred on Figg's Emporium in London where written rules were first agreed and nationally open competitions established. Jack Broughton, the leading prizefighter and then promoter of the age, devised these rules in 1743 in a format that was to last until the last official prize fight in Britain was held in 1860. The Duke of Cumberland was a big backer of Broughton, wagering £10,000 on his man in a bout fought in 1750. These patron–client relationships and the significant prize money to be won in the many fights held created a small but unmistakably professional caste of boxers from the mid-eighteenth century onwards. More than just giving money, the aristocracy occasionally took to the ring themselves and provided safe haven for the sport away from the prying eyes of the law. The estates of the Duke of York and the Prince of Wales served as venues in the 1780s with both supposed to have made boxing bets as large as £40,000 a time.

The aristocracy's love of gambling supplied the financial underpinning of both horse racing and rowing. Horse racing, in particular, had moved from informal, local and irregular contests between members of the gentry and aristocracy over open fields to a very highly organized sport. The arrival of thoroughbred Arabian bloodstock in the early eighteenth century provided both a different calibre of horse and a huge incentive for monitored, selective breeding and record keeping. Permanent race courses were built across the country, and the first classic races were run, establishing a hierarchy of competition and a truly national focus for the sport. A regular racing calendar followed and then the Jockey

Club was founded in 1752 to regulate the sport. Rowing races had an equally long pedigree. The many boatmen plying their trade on the country's major navigable rivers provided a ready-made pool of sporting talent. Annual challenge races, major regattas, and huge crowds hugging the banks of the Tyne and the Thames were regular features of urban sporting life in the late eighteenth and early nineteenth centuries. But the most formalized sport of all was undoubtedly cricket. The game had been played in something at least recognizable to the modern eye since the Restoration of the late seventeenth century. Once again rural land-owners' insatiable thirst for gambling was the catalyst for organized games and the nobility themselves were not above participating. The Duke of Richmond founded one of the first cricket clubs in 1727 and a thriving cricket-club culture was established in both the country and the city.

If football was being marginalized from above by a sporting aristocracy that preferred racing, fighting and cricket, it was also being squeezed from below by the persistent campaign against traditional sports and pastimes. In part, this movement drew on a gloomy Puritan heritage that equated play with impiety and used a fierce Sabbatarianism to articulate its disapproval for popular pleasure. However, traditional theology was then mixed with new arguments. The medieval church's interpretation of the relationship between humanity and the natural world, in which the former wielded unwavering sovereignty over the latter, was no longer tenable. And though humanity might remain the senior partners in creation, there was a tangible distaste among these new social forces for the brutish cruelty of older peasant and aristocratic pleasures. For the Methodists, other non-conformists and urban professionals who articulated these arguments, the abiding concern was with the cruel animal sports of cockfighting and bear-baiting. Together, they created the Society for the Prevention of Cruelty to Animals in 1825 and being among the first to benefit politically from the narrow expansion of the franchise in the 1832 Reform Act they used their new-found parliamentary power to push through the Prevention of Cruelty to Animals Act in 1835. From this milieu the emergence of a broader critique of the social disorder, personal danger and unregulated violence of traditional sports, like football, was inevitable. The new class of industrialists and business people were dismayed by the game's impact on both property and labour discipline. Shopkeepers on the council of

Kingston-upon-Thames lamented, 'It is not a trifling consideration that suspension of business for nearly two days should be created to the inhabitant for the mere gratification of a sport at once so useless and barbarous.'[1] Derbyshire Council cast the game in these terms: 'the assembly of a lawless rabble, suspending business to the loss of the industrious, creating terror and alarm to the peaceable, committing violence on the person and damage to the properties of the defenceless poor'.[2] The new business class found unlikely allies in the radical artisans of the era. This early aristocracy of labour attempted to put a considerable social distance between itself, the desperate rural proletariat and the new urban underclass that was emerging in late Georgian Britain. Thus the radical artisans of Derby could, with some contempt, describe the Ashbourne Shrovetide game as 'barbarous recklessness and supreme folly'.[3]

A reliance on the records of legal cases overemphasizes those games of football that were subject to ban or control rather than those that carried on as normal. Even so the trend appears clear: informal and traditional forms of football were on the decline. The 1835 Highways Act explicitly permitted the banning of street football in urban areas, and its provisions were used to that effect. Simultaneously the traditional Shrovetide games of football were being closed down across Middlesex and Surrey. In the 1840s and 1850s games were eradicated in Kingston-upon-Thames, Richmond and Hampton Wick. The rest of Europe might have been engulfed by the urban popular uprisings of 1848 but in England the rule of the ancient regime was not to be challenged by the mob. The notoriously large and violent Ashbourne Derby was, like the Chartist movement, controlled in the years 1846 to 1848 by the use of the army and the reading of the Riot Act. Where games of football had once helped reassert the people's control of common lands and by-ways, they were now being extinguished or tamed. That was certainly the fate of the famous football game in Alnwick, which was subdued and denuded of political content by the Duke of Northumberland who simply moved the game outside the town centre. This kind of direct action combined with the steady depopulation of nineteenth-century rural England saw traditional football games just peter out. The last game in Ashbourne was played in 1861 and the game of *Knappen*, once common in south Wales, was last recorded in the streets of Neath in 1884. By the end of the nineteenth century games of traditional football only survived in the most extreme peripheries and backwaters of the kingdom

– Workington, Chester-le-Street, Jedburgh, the Orkneys and Cornwall – and even here these games were already anachronisms; extinction loomed.

But football, as we know, survived. It did so because it was preserved and nurtured in institutions that were beyond the cultural reach of Methodists, industrialists and artisans. Britain's public schools were the ludic zoos of the age. They provided refuge for the wild and endangered games of rural Georgian Britain where they were bred and developed before being released into the new sporting and social ecology of industrial Victorian Britain.

The British public schools of the early nineteenth century existed to educate the sons of the country's old landed and new commercial families who stood at the apex of the social and economic hierarchy. Quite what they were being educated for was less clear. The curriculum was grim and fusty and dominated by Latin, Greek and Theology. Beyond the immediate disciplines of the classroom they were turbulent, brutal and occasionally anarchic institutions. The social superiority of most of the pupils over the staff, combined with the basic disposition of young male aristocrats, meant that life in the schools often constituted 'an irregular but continuous warfare against adult government', a government whose illegitimacy was greatly enhanced by its use of flogging and brutality to enforce its rule.[4] Mere indiscipline was often succeeded by openly seditious rebellions and occupations. The army was called to Rugby in 1797 to put down a pupils' revolt, while the militia were summoned to Winchester in 1818 with fixed bayonets. It was their sixth such visit to the school in fifty years.

Games were a central component of the boys' culture. All the usual playground amusements of tag, catch and hoop-la could be found, but public-school boys showed a distinct preference for cruelty and violence. Toozling was the slang at Harrow for killing small song birds. Duck hunting and beagling were favourites and stone throwing was greatly regarded. It was said that 'no dog could live on Harrow Hill' and 'ponies frequently lost their eyes if they had to pull their owners' carts near the school'.[5] When animals offered insufficient competition for the pugilists the locals would do instead. Fighting was endemic among the boys and with their geographical if not their social peers. Harrovians were known to enjoy a good punch-up with the railway navvies that cut the embankment nearby, while Etonians were often scrapping with the Windsor butcher boys. If the boys were not above mixing it with the locals, they were unlikely to disdain their pastimes, especially when they were as boisterous and anarchic as traditional street football. Thus all the leading public schools had developed some kind of footballing tradition among the pupils in the late eighteenth or early nineteenth centuries. Once established in these relatively closed institutions, informal rules and modes of playing were, like school slang and rites of initiation, developed and handed down from seniors to juniors.

The Eton Wall Game and the Eton Field Game had been played since the mid-eighteenth century. Harrow, whose pitches were poorly drained and heavy, developed a game using a large flat-bottomed ball that scudded pleasingly across the clay mud and puddles. Winchester football was played on a long narrow pitch with the emphasis on kicking and then chasing the ball. Westminster's enclosed spaces seemed to favour a short dribbling style of game, while Shrewsbury and Rugby appeared to put more emphasis on carrying the ball in the hands. Charterhouse, which was originally located in an old Carthusian monastery, also seemed to deploy dribbling, but they were not above a serious bundle: 'the ball very soon got into one of the buttresses, when a terrific squash would result, some fifty or sixty boys huddled together and vigorously "roughing", kicking and shoving to extricate the ball.'[6] Scrums, hots, rouges and squashes were synonymous with public-school football; indeed the Eton Wall Game was just one long scrum up and down a narrow strip of earth. The violence and danger engendered by so much teenage masculine energy in one space at one time saw the Eton Field Game actually banned between 1827 and 1836, while Samuel Butler, the headmaster of Shrewsbury, described football as 'more fit for farm boys and labourers than for young gentlemen'.[7]

While the disreputable and chaotic education of the elite, of which football was an element, failed to trouble many of Britain's aristocrats, there were some who became convinced that the changing nature of the world required something different from the public schools. The pivotal figure in the movement for reform was Thomas Arnold, who was headmaster at Rugby between 1828 and 1848. Arnold planned to civilize the education of the elite in the classroom and the chapel. The barbarous scions of the aristocracy and the philistine nouveau riche of the industrial bourgeoisie would both be transformed by a programme of discipline, prayer and rational learning into a more polished and mannered form of masculinity more suited to the tasks of imperial Christian gentlemen in an age of enlightenment.

Games and athleticism were not a central component of Arnold's programme of reform but in the hands of his contemporaries and sup-porters they came to acquire pride of place. The central dilemma faced by the teaching staff at Rugby and the other public schools was not initially how to create a different kind of student but simply how to take control. Engaging with team games, especially football, allowed staff to insert themselves into the pre-existing hierarchy of power with them-selves at the top, senior boys below and new arrivals at the bottom and then to delegate some of their power down to the seniors. Simul-taneously, games allowed staff to burn off some of the great flare of excess energy and hormonal transformation that large numbers of pubescent boys in confined spaces generate. *Sotto voce*, staff believed that regular physical exertion would provide an effective prophylactic to the unspoken evils of homosexuality and masturbation. Many of Arnold's key lieutenants at Rugby were games players and they and their protégés spread the gospel of games and athleticism from school to school during their itinerant teaching careers. G. E. L. Cotton was one of the key figures in Arnold's reform programme at Rugby and went on to be the headmaster of Marlborough. He formed the basis of the games master in Thomas Hughes's *Tom Brown's Schooldays*. A. G. Butler, the head at Haileybury, was so enthusiastic that he often joined the game himself, 'dashing into the fray, now emerging triumphant with the ball held aloft and at another moment bowled over in the mud like the humblest forward, eventually retiring from the field to the great detriment of his clothes, but none to his dignity'.[8] Charles Vaughan, headmaster at Harrow, was a very active proponent of the games ethic; and at the most extreme end of the scale we find characters like Edward Thring at Uppingham Grammar and the irrepressible Hely Hutchinson Almond of the Loretto School in Edinburgh who instituted the daily playing of games, created a school uniform that looked suspiciously like a football shirt, endorsed running in the winter snow and chose a school song called 'Go Like Blazes'.

Why was it that such a small group of admittedly dedicated even fanatical teachers should be able so to mould the ethos and practices of an entire ruling class? Their enthusiasm and energy were one thing, but these evangelists were fortunate enough to pursue their mission in a practical and cultural context that was closely supportive of their arguments. The Victorians were increasingly concerned with issues of physical health as evidenced by the transformation of medicine, biology and public health thinking at the time. Moreover, the Victorians were quite convinced of the relationship between physical, mental and moral health. Healthy nations require healthy elites and thus the psycho-sexual health of upper-class schoolboys went right to the heart of the concerns of Victorian bodily culture. Indeed it has been said that 'The Victorian Public School was the forcing house of a new kind of masculinity in which the distinguishing characteristics of the male sex were not intellectual or genital but physical and moral',[9] a combination that would become known as muscular Christianity and which chimed with many other elements of mid-Victorian thought.

This new ruling-class Christian masculinity would, it was proposed, best be nurtured and developed by playing team sports. Games provided a perfect instrument for welding together the old aristocracy and new bourgeoisie in a common pursuit through the schools, what Matthew Arnold called 'this beneficial salutary intermixture of classes'. Above all games shaped character. For Thring it was a matter of hardness or toughness. Others interpreted the role of sport in general and football in particular as an instrument of Darwinian selection, weeding out those incapable of taking on the mantle of imperial rule. Sport physically hardened up the Victorian ruling class for the task of imperial conquest and global hegemony in an era when office work would otherwise enfeeble them. Sport simultaneously taught the essential lessons of co-operation and competition that such an elite would require. As Richard Holt has put it, 'The idea of being a good loser was not just a matter of etiquette and upper-class style, it was a device for encouraging a healthy as opposed to a Hobbesian form of competition.'[10] Charles Kingsley, one of the leading proponents of a Christian athleticism, wrote:

Through sport boys acquire virtues which no books can give them: not merely daring and endurance, but better still, temper, self-restraint, fairness, honour, unenvious appropriation of another's success and all that 'give and take' of life which stand a man in good stead when he goes forth into the world and without which, indeed, his success is always maimed and partial.[11]

By mid-century the games ethic was central to the curriculum and ethos of the British public school. Indeed the headmaster of Fettes school went as far as to exclaim: 'Cleverness, what an aim! Cleverness neither makes nor keeps man nor nation.'[12] The internal hierarchies of school subcultures were now built around prowess in sport. The importance of games can also be measured by the size of playing fields. Harrow's grounds expanded from just 8 acres in 1845 to 146 in 1900. Charterhouse actually moved out of their original and rather cramped site for the open fields and plentiful land of Surrey in 1872. The public school's obsession with games was soon emulated by the leading aspirational urban grammar schools, like Ripon, Worcester and Bristol. These schools increasingly drew on public-school-educated teachers who brought the games ethic with them. A. B. Halsey, a former captain of football and head boy at Rugby, became headmaster of Ripon Grammar School and announced to parents during an open day that Wellington had indeed been right when he had claimed that the Battle of Waterloo had been won on the playing fields of Eton – though if Wellington had ever said such a thing he was probably referring to playground fisticuffs rather than team sport. While cricket remained immensely popular and the unchallenged summer game, and boxing, rowing, athletics and hockey all had their niches, it was football that most captivated the energies and imaginations of the staff and pupils.

Although the rules of each school's game were not yet fixed, they had begun to assume a reasonably settled form. The first written set of rules was produced by Rugby in 1845; the increasing involvement of masters in the organization of the game saw the other schools follow suit in the 1850s. The next stop for most of these public-school sportsmen was either Oxford and Cambridge Universities or the armed forces or both. All of these institutions proved fertile soil for the development of sport. Oxbridge colleges and army regiments replicated the system of houses, colours, regalia and sporting contests familiar at all the leading public schools. Academic study was not hugely demanding of most students' time and with the provision of magnificent sporting facilities at the universities in the late 1830s and 1840s the entire infrastructure for regular football was established. After the Crimean War the incidence of football within the army appeared to rise. Certainly it was widespread among convalescing soldiers on the Isle of Wight in this period. The only problem was what kind of football to play, for of course boys arrived with their own particular sets of school-specific rules. Two old boys from Shrewsbury School, Thring and De Winton, sought to establish the first set of compromise rules in Cambridge in 1846. As Thring later wrote, 'An attempt was made to get up some football in preference to hockey then in vogue. But the result was dire confusion, as every man played the rules he was accustomed to at his public school. I remember how the Eton man howled at the Rugby man for handling the ball. So it was agreed that two men should be chosen to represent each of the public schools and two who were not public-school men for the "varsity".'[13] The major conflict in these discussions arose from the division between those schools that had created a primarily kicking and dribbling game (Harrow, Eton, Charterhouse and Winchester), and those that involved more extensive handling of the ball (Rugby, Marlborough); though there were as yet no rules that completely prohibited handling and catching. These debates were based on more than mere sporting logic. Questions of status and hierarchy among the public schools were never far from the surface, while the character of the compromise rules was often denounced as a 'mongrel game'. The tone of the debate could become so bitter and the participants so unreasonably impassioned that in 1859 the editor of *Bell's London Life*, in whose pages the issue had been discussed, announced that he was curtailing correspondence on the subject.

While the public schools and the universities were clearly central to preserving and transforming old football traditions and disseminating the new football, they were not alone. In the provinces, among cricket clubs and in scratch sides centred on pubs, minor schools and military units, informal football games were being played from the late 1830s into the late 1850s. A survey of *Bell's London Life* – which despite its title was widely read across the country and across the socio-economic spectrum in these decades – reveals a wealth of letters, adverts and requests involving football teams. As far back as 1839 the Cumbrian town of Ulverston boasted two teams playing football, one seemingly open to all artisans and one concentrated in a single trade – the Ulverston Leathermen. In Scotland, Edinburgh yielded teams made up of domestic workers, waiters and members of various military regiments. Leicestershire, Derbyshire, Warwickshire and Lancashire all appeared to have football teams in these decades. Surrey Cricket Club created their own football-playing wing in the late 1840s and their own rule book. Christian Chartists in Birmingham who founded the Athenic Institution liked a game of football too. But the greatest concentration of footballing activity outside of the public schools was in Sheffield. Reports of games in the city's Hyde Park date back to 1831 and there was sufficient enthusiasm for the game for Sheffield Football Club to be formed in 1857. The club drew on former pupils of the Sheffield Collegiate schools from middle-class manufacturing and professional families. Only in London, it appears, were football clubs overwhelmingly the preserve of ex-public-school men. In south London the Blackheath club was formed in 1857 by advocates of the handling game, while Old Harrovians living in London and preferring their version of the sport formed Forest Club in 1858, renamed the Wanderers in 1860.

Any resolution to the resulting chaos and disorganization required at the very least that all the different rules be laid out against each other and systematically compared as a prelude to synthesis, and this was only achieved in 1861 when Lillywhites published nearly all of the competing rules together. That said, the editor of *The Field*, in whose pages much of the rule-making debate was being conducted, confessed that he still found the rules of Eton's Field Game unintelligible. In 1862 J. C. Thring, one of the convenors of the meeting to establish the first set of compromise Cambridge rules in 1846, was now headmaster at Uppingham Grammar School. He tried again to establish a shared set of regulations that could encourage widespread competition between different schools. Thring set out twelve rules which he described as 'the simplest game' but though this saw a massive increase in interest in the game at Uppingham and the rules were used in an eleven-a-side game between Old Harrovians and Old Etonians at Cambridge later that year, they failed to gain widespread acceptance. Once again in 1863 another attempt was made to generate a set of agreed rules in Cambridge but no definitive resolution seemed possible.

The problem must have been particularly acute in London where all of the public schools continued to be represented at different old boys' clubs. In November 1863 a meeting was held at the Freemasons' Tavern, Lincoln's Inn Fields, in central London. Representatives from eleven old boys' clubs in the London area were present: No Names of Kilburn, Barnes, the War Office, Crusaders, Forest, Perceval House, Crystal Palace, Blackheath, Kennington School, Surbiton, Blackheath School and an observer from Charterhouse. In a series of meetings over the next two months attempts were made to generate a single code from the many competing versions of football represented around the table. Although Thring's 1862 rules provided a useful starting point, it became increasingly clear that there were irreconcilable differences on two key issues. First, between those that favoured a catch-and-run game and those that preferred a dribbling-kicking game. Second, between those who favoured 'hacking' – where players deliberately targeted their opponents' shins as a way of stopping them in the tackle – and those who opposed the practice. Mr Campbell from the Blackheath Club remarked of the plan to dispense with hacking that, 'you will do away with the courage and pluck of the game, and I will be bound to bring over a lot of Frenchmen who would beat you with a week's practice.' But as Ebenezer Morley, the honorary secretary of the group – now referring to themselves as the Football Association – responded, 'If we have hacking, no one who has arrived at the age of discretion will play at football and it will be entirely left to schoolboys.'[14] The published rule book also banned tripping, holding, pushing and running with the ball, though one could still cleanly catch a ball and call a mark, giving rise to a free kick for the catcher.

History is written by the victors. The coterie of London-based old boys who created the Football Association and came to control the game in England have been seen as the sole inventors and codifiers of modern football. But as we have seen they were neither alone nor first in drawing up a set of agreed written rules for the game as played outside the public schools and universities. That honour lies with the Sheffield footballing fraternity who published their own rules book in October 1858 and whose revised version formed the basis for the play of the Sheffield Football Club. Teething problems with this code included a proliferation of 0–0 draws caused by having goals a mere four yards wide. Over the next five or six years the rules were adapted and defects improved upon as more and more clubs in South Yorkshire came to adopt them, culminating in the formation of a football association in 1867. Despite starting four years after the London-based FA, the Sheffield association had more players and more member clubs than its southern compatriots. The status of the London FA was barely any higher; the public schools snubbed its authority and its rule book, preferring to retreat into their own esoteric and idiosyncratic modes of play. Few other clubs adopted their rules, while many provincial clubs continued to play their own variants, often retaining the hacking and carrying practices that the FA had sought to abolish. Many teams chose to play more than one code, often during the same game. Some of the confusion was alleviated when the Sheffield- and London-based FAs resolved their differences and played by a shared set of rules, and the predominantly handling-based clubs finally decided to establish their own set of rules and created the Rugby Football Union in 1871. Association football, as it was now known, was a distinct entity at last. Whether it was popular, whether it would even survive, were as yet unanswered questions.

IV

In the early 1870s football remained a minor recreational pastime for a very narrow stratum of Victorian society. There were many for whom this state of affairs was quite satisfactory. Indeed the rugby-playing clubs would continue to do all they could to keep their game within the confines of the elite and discouraged and disapproved of organized competition and trophies; what they contemptuously referred to as 'pot hunting'. Football's ruling class, who despite their elevated social status retained a streak of populism, thought otherwise. C. W. Alcock, Old Harrovian and secretary of the FA, took Harrow's inter-house football competitions as his model and on 20 July 1871 announced: 'It is desirable that a challenge cup should be established in connection with the association, for which all clubs belonging to the association should be invited to compete.'[15] Fifty clubs were eligible to play in the first FA Challenge Cup but only fifteen entered. Many were deterred by the expense and complexity of nationwide travel, three never got further than registering their interest and only two came from north of Hertfordshire: Queen's Park, the first Scottish club, based in Glasgow, and Donnington Grammar School from Lincoln. The semi-finals saw the Old Harrovian side Wanderers get past Queen's Park when the Scots could not afford to come back down to London for a replay after the two sides had drawn, and the Royal Engineers beat the south London team Crystal Palace. Two thousand people came to the Oval cricket ground to see Morton Betts score a goal for Wanderers and win the first FA Cup. He played under an assumed name, A. H. Chequer, having played previously for Harrow Chequers. The social composition and range of the crowd meant that nearly all of them would have got the joke.

What would those spectators have seen? What kind of game had been created? The nature of the spectators can perhaps be gleaned from the social origins of the players who were exclusively drawn from the upper classes. The next few years would see among others in the FA Cup Finals the Lyttelton brothers, Alfred and Edward. Both were Old Etonians. Edward went on to be the headmaster of his old school, while Alfred, as well as playing cricket for England, served as an MP and member of the Cabinet. Edward described his brother's extraordinary performances in a classical cultural context, writing, 'When things grew to be exciting and his ardour rose to a formidable heat, he would come thundering down with the heavy knees far advanced and all the paraphernalia of a Homeric onset.'[16] William Kenyon Slaney, another fixture at FA Cup Finals, rose to be a colonel in the elite Household Cavalry before becoming an MP and Privy Counsellor. Quentin Hogg, who played in goal for the Old Etonians, went on to be one of the leading social philanthropists of Edwardian Britain while his fag, Lord Kinnaird, was the first true footballing star and later on in his life the Lord High Commissioner of the Church of Scotland. In 1873 the Cup Final was delayed so that the crowd and the players could attend the football and see their chums in the Varsity Boat Race scheduled for that day as well.

The precise dimensions of the playing field were not recorded but under the FA rules of the time it could have been anything up to 100 yards wide by 200 yards long (91–182 m), considerably bigger than modern-day football pitches (between 100 and 50 yards (91.4–45.7 m) wide and between 130 and 100 yards (118.8–91.4 m) long). There would have been no white lines on the turf, only flags marking the boundary. Two flimsy goalposts would have stood at each end of the pitch 24 feet (7.3 m) apart and with tape strung between them about 8 feet (2.5 m) above the ground. The tape was a recent innovation after committee members of the FA had seen a goal allowed at a game in Reigate where the ball had passed between the posts but around 100 feet (30 m) up in the air. Regular spectators at subsequent FA Cup Finals would have to wait until 1882 for a fixed crossbar to be added to the goal, and until 1892 for a goal net to be in place. The goal posts were square and remained so until early in the twentieth century, when they were replaced by round and oval variants. 1882 also saw the introduction of the compulsory marking of the pitch boundary and the addition of a halfway line which served to locate both the kick-off and the precise area in which each goalkeeper could handle the ball; it was not until 1912 that handling by the goalkeeper was restricted to his own penalty area. That said, in 1872 there was no penalty area and no penalties. The 12-yard penalty line arrived in 1887 when a penalty could finally be awarded for fouls in this vital attacking area. The centre circle arrived at the same time, forcing the opposition to keep their distance at the kick-off. In 1891 12- and 18-yard lines were introduced across the breadth of the pitch, the former marking the line over which any foul was a penalty. The latter metamorphosed into an 18-yard area in 1902 or the box as it colloquially became known. With this, pitch markings assumed their contemporary form (but for the D-shaped curve at the top of the box behind which all players must stand when a penalty is taken, added in 1937). The ball at least had taken on a familiar aspect by 1872. Till then the rules had only stipulated that it be round – now its circumference was to be limited to between 27 and 29 inches (68.5–73.6 cm).

The number of players on each side would have been familiar – eleven-a-side being pretty much fixed by this time. There were however only two officials. They were called umpires, with one drawn from each team, and they were confined to the sidelines of the game. They were first mentioned in the rules in 1874. A third official was added late in the 1870s so that a final decision could be made when the two umpires disagreed. The third official was soon known as the referee and made it into the FA rule book in 1881. It was not until 1891 that the referee was given overall control of the game and made a compulsory fixture. However, it was still down to the team captains to call for a foul or draw the referee's attention to a rule infringement rather than the referee initiating matters. This power finally passed to the referee in 1898 when neutral linesmen replaced club umpires.

Players had hitherto based their wardrobe on cricket kit: long trousers, flannel shirts, tassled caps and heavy boots. The drift from trousers to knickerbockers, often held up by belts, occurred during the 1870s when shirts also increasingly acquired distinct colours and patterns – though the earliest working men's teams simply wore their own clothes. Shirts were not numbered and goalkeepers as yet did not have to wear distinct colours. It was not until 1909 that goalkeepers were compelled to wear different coloured shirts from the rest of the team and not until 1912 that they were permitted to wear the ubiquitous green shirt. Shirt numbers did not arrive for another fifteen years. The first experiment was conducted in England in 1928–29 and they did not become compulsory in league games until 1938–39. Distinct cap designs were one way in which players could be distinguished by colleagues and crowds. Memorably in the 1875 FA Cup tie between Queen's Park and Wanderers, the Old Harrovian D. N. Kendrick sported a cerise and french grey design while his winger Heron had an orange, violet and black cap. Lord Kinnaird, for once a more restrained figure, wore white and blue, C. W. Alcock white and blue checks. Early shirt designs were on occasion equally flamboyant with Bolton Wanderers beginning life in white shirts with red spots which were said to make the players look larger than they really were. Everton, who later settled on royal blue, tried out black with a scarlet sash, and all manner of browns, pinks and purples were used until sides settled down into the dominant visual vocabulary of football shirts: predominantly single-colour shirts in red, white and blue with the occasional look-in for green, yellow, black; variety was provided by the use of hoops, stripes, halves and quarters. Boots were more prosaic, made of tough leather often with metal toecaps and of course with studs.

Catching the ball in any circumstances apart from by the goalkeeper had been ruled illegal in 1866, and in this respect the game was recognizably football. Other oddities remained: for example, teams would often change ends after every goal was scored. And beyond the goalkeeper both the formation and practice of teams was a long way from the style of the modern game. Most teams fielded two backs, one half-back and seven forwards. Although the backs would often hoof the ball far up the field, most of the time the ball moved at the feet of individuals dribbling the ball towards the opponent's goal. Passing was only considered as a last resort and indicated failure, even dishonour. During the 1877 England–Scotland game the Hon. Alfred Lyttelton, when challenged about his failure to pass the ball, remarked to his team-mate but social inferior Bill Mosforth, 'I am playing purely for my own pleasure, Sir!' High crosses and the heading of the ball were also absent from the players' repertoire. Thus most of the action was concentrated around the main dribbling player where a huge scrum of other players would gather, often bundling and charging into each other like a knot of schoolboys. Knocking one's opponents over, including the opposing goalkeeper, was not frowned upon, indeed it was integral to the game. As late as 1888 a goal by Aston Villa against the Corinthians could be described in these terms: 'The ball was soon transferred to Corinthian quarters, a fine tussle ending by Archie Hunter sending a grand one through the posts, while Allen grassed the goalkeeper in a most efficient unceremonious manner.'[17]

While barging and grassing remained features of the game for some time to come, the pre-eminence of dribbling was soon toppled by the advent of the passing game. This was certainly aided by the adoption of the offside rule, originally formulated by the Sheffield FA in the 1860s. Rugby had dealt with the problem of forward passing and 'goal hanging' by simply banning the manoeuvre, but in the process the game lost a degree of complexity, three-dimensionality and depth. Football was able to retain the swift shifts of pace and position that forward passing allowed, but by ruling that three opponents must stand between the recipient of the pass and the goal line for the play to be onside the rule prevented the game degenerating into an endless succession of long balls into the goal mouth.

Having saved the forward pass, it could only be a matter of time before the superiority of collective action over individual action in manoeuvring the ball towards goal became obvious, but quite who got there first is a matter of dispute. C. W. Alcock wrote that the 'passing-on' game was 'first introduced in any degree of perfection by the Northerners in the early matches between London and Sheffield' and that in the 1870s the short passing game was characteristic of the Scottish sides Queen's Park and Vale of Leven, while Blackburn Olympic and the other working-class teams of the Lancashire cotton belt were associated with the 'alternation of long passing and vigorous rushes'.[18] By contrast Frederick Wall, who later replaced Alcock as the secretary of the FA, wrote that 'the advantages of combination ... over the old style of individualism' were first formulated by the Royal Engineers who then took it to the provinces and the north in the early 1870s.[19] Whatever the origins of the passing game, it revolutionized the spectacle. Ten years after Wanderers lifted the FA Cup the Old Etonians' victory over Blackburn Rovers in the 1882 Cup Final would be the last in which a predominantly dribbling side beat a predominantly passing side. Moreover, the Old Etonians were perhaps the last to field a 2-1-7 formation. After this almost every club assumed the new 2-3-5 formation in which the defence was allocated two more team members. The ball now moved across the pitch as well as down it and came in the air as well as on the ground. Teams began to explore the wings more systematically rather than clogging up the centre; once the wings were brought into play, crossing and heading became the norm. Football as a game and a spectacle had been transformed and so, quietly, beneath the surface had its players, spectators and organizers.

A year after they had won their first FA Cup in 1872 the Wanderers were back in the final where they beat Oxford University 2–1. For the next seven years the final was contested by old boys, university students or military teams based in the south of England. Oxford University beat the Royal Engineers in 1874; the Old Etonians, after losing two finals, won the trophy in 1876 beating Clapham Rovers; the Old Carthusians won their only FA Cup in 1881. From these events it would appear that football remained a marginal phenomenon, an eccentric detail in the bigger picture of mid-Victorian culture. And certainly to most observers at the time it would have seemed so. But through the 1870s the popularity of the game was growing, reaching parts of the country and sectors of society hitherto untouched. Thus in 1882 the Old Etonians faced a rather different prospect in the final: Blackburn Rovers, a team from the north of England whose players were drawn from working-class backgrounds. The Etonians won 1–0, and Lord Kinnaird celebrated the winning goal by turning a handstand in front of the main pavilion at the Oval. Perhaps he knew that this was the final call for the amateur gentleman footballer.

The call had come because by 1882 football had spread from its southern English and upper-class strongholds into middle- and working-class neighbourhoods north of the Wash as well as to the Celtic nations.

There had already been a few warning shots, none more widely remarked upon at the time than Darwen's epic encounter with the Old Etonians in the quarter-finals of the 1879 FA Cup. Darwen, a team from a working-class cotton town in Lancashire, had taken the Etonians to a third replay after two bruising and unresolved encounters. In the first Darwen had recovered from 5–1 down with fifteen minutes to play to draw 5–5. The Old Etonians, perhaps sensing the drift of the game, refused to play extra time and settle the matter there and then. The second game ended 2–2 after extra time and only in the third did the Etonians settle it, winning 6–2 – though the accumulated costs and inconvenience of travelling for the Lancastrians must have been a factor in losing the tie. The new geography of lower-class football had four advanced zones: the South Yorkshire–Nottinghamshire borders, cotton-belt Lancashire, the central belt of Scotland and the West Midlands. South Yorkshire's importance was actually almost exclusively focused on Sheffield, for the rest of the county remained wedded to rugby, in part because so few of the local landed or commercial elite were educated in the main football-playing public schools of the south. With expansion blocked to the north, it seems that football turned south, hopping the short distance across the border with Nottinghamshire to the city of Nottingham where the late 1860s saw the founding of two serious football clubs: Notts County, founded in 1862, and Nottingham Forest in 1865. The pair quickly established a combative relationship and considerable local followings.

The dense network of small but growing industrial towns made Lancashire a hotbed of popular sport in the last quarter of the nineteenth century. Rugby was the leading game in the isolated north of the county around Barrow-in-Furness where football remained a marginal concern until the inter-war era. Further south rugby cut two swathes through the textile towns from Salford up to Rochdale in the east and from St Helens to Wigan and Warrington in the west. Football was concentrated between the two, centring on the triangle of Darwen, Blackburn and Bolton. The intensity of football's growth here can be gauged by the formation in 1878 of the Lancashire FA with all twenty-eight founding clubs coming from this micro-region. But it was not merely the number of clubs that marked out Lancashire; it was the sudden development of big clubs drawing big crowds that made the region so distinctive. Preston North End and Burnley both began life in the 1870s as rugby-playing clubs but made the transition to football; by 1884 they were getting 12,000 into Burnley's Turf Moor, and Preston was in the vanguard of professionalism.

The experience of Lancashire points to the role of educational institutions of all kinds in the diffusion of football. Ex-public-school and Oxbridge students returning to their family homes had carried the game north. The first club in the Lancashire cotton belt was probably Turton FC, founded in 1871 under the influence of two old Harrovians, John and Robert Kay, whose families owned land in the area. Among the earliest converts was J. J. Bentley, later president of the Football League, who wrote, 'Turton was the factory . . . of footballers for Lancashire and a good many other places beside.'[20] Darwen FC, just down the road, was also created by Old Harrovians returning to the family estate and teaching the locals. Grammar-school boys who had followed the lead of their social superiors did the same. Ex-pupils of Wygesston School in Leicester created Leicester Fosse; Chester City can be traced back to the King's School in the town, while Blackburn Grammar School was the source of Blackburn Rovers. By the 1880s the spread of football down the social scale was sufficiently entrenched that old boys of the most lowly state school could create sustainable football clubs. The boys of Droop Street Primary in west London founded Queens Park Rangers in 1885, while Sunderland AFC started life in 1879 in the local teacher-training college. Those colleges which supplied the massive influx of new teaching staff into the expanding state education system were amongst the most enthusiastic proponents of the game, not only playing amongst themselves, but even in the face of official opposition introducing the game to working-class boys. In so doing they created a pool of talent and enthusiasm that would be essential to the massive growth of professional football later in the century.

Scotland's two major cities, Edinburgh and Glasgow, had possessed football-playing clubs and schools since the 1850s. After 1863 there was a clear and sharp division between Edinburgh, which predominantly played the handling game, and Glasgow, which played the dribbling game. Queen's Park was the first Glasgow club, founded in 1867 from a group of gentlemen players who used the YMCA and which came to dominate Scottish football in the next two decades. A clutch of clubs soon followed suit. In Glasgow alone Dumbarton, Renton and Third Lanark were founded in 1872, Glasgow Rangers in 1873, Hamilton

Academicals and Cambuslang in 1875, Cowlairs, Partick Thistle and Vale of Leven in 1876. With the foundation of Heart of Midlothian and Hibernian in Edinburgh in 1874 and 1875, central-belt Scotland could boast a density of football clubs as great as anywhere in Britain. The Scottish Football Association was created in 1873 and an English-style FA Cup soon followed on. Glasgow's precocious reputation was enhanced by hosting the very first official international game in 1872 between England and Scotland at the West of Scotland cricket ground.

The development of football in the west midlands points to the role of the Church in the emergence of working-class football. In response to the decline of organized religion among the poor, evangelical sportsmen had spread the gospel of football through various forms of missionary and social work in working-class communities in the new industrial cities, though the initiative to create sports clubs came as much if not more from the congregation than from the clergy. In Birmingham over a quarter of all football and cricket clubs in the 1880s had their roots in the Church. Aston Villa were founded in 1874 as the Villa Cross Wesleyan Chapel cricket team. In the winter the club played half their games under the FA code and half under the rugby union code but quickly settled on football as its first love. The Church also provided the springboard for the formation in 1877 of Wolverhampton Wanderers. Hard on their heels came the cricketers of Holy Trinity Church who formed Small Heath FC, later Birmingham City. Similar routes created Everton in Liverpool from St Domingo's Church in 1878, and Bolton Wanderers sprang from Christ Church Sunday School in 1874.

Beyond these core areas, working- and middle-class clubs were beginning to form in the north-east and London, but they remained marginal. Considerable parts of Yorkshire, Lancashire and the far south-west were preoccupied with rugby while the south-east and East Anglia had yet to acquire much of an urban working class, let alone a battery of successful working-class sports clubs. Football arrived in north Wales from across the border with Cheshire. Wrexham cricket club set up a football-playing section as early as 1872, the Welsh FA was set up in 1876, the nation's first international (against Scotland at Wrexham) and a national cup competition were established the following year – but the game remained in the north. Transport connections from the north to the south of Wales were poor even by rural Victorian standards, but even had they been better it is unlikely that they would have effectively carried the north's enthusiasm for football. Wales possessed a new working class in the coalmining villages and valleys of the south who might have taken up the game, but they and the rest of urban south Wales were also populated by English immigrants from rugby-playing zones in the south-west. The new professional classes turned their considerable entrepreneurial sporting energies to developing a cross-class, semi-professional but hidden, rugby union culture. Football would develop in south Wales in the biggest cities – like Cardiff and Swansea – but not for another thirty years.

The diffusion of football and other British sports to Ireland met an even more implacable foe, for their arrival ran parallel to the most sustained and serious nationalist ferment of the century. Football quickly caught on among Catholics and Protestants in Belfast and in some of the smaller towns of the south, and later in parts of working-class Dublin. The Irish FA was based in Belfast and in the years before the First World War clubs from the north dominated both the Irish League and the Irish FA Cup. But aside from these predominantly Anglophile urban enclaves, football acquired an air bordering on collaborationism. In the increasingly bitter struggle over Irish sovereignty, home rule and independence, sport was being mobilized and football could not be the game of the Irish nation as conceived by the nationalist movement. The half-invented, half-revived games of rural Ireland – where much of the demographic strength of the nationalist movements lay – became emblematic of the struggle. Gaelic football and hurling expressed the oppressed but rising nation; football was the game of the colonist. This process culminated in the formation of the Gaelic Athletic Association (the GAA) in 1884, which explicitly set out to preserve and develop what were perceived to be indigenous Irish games and to oppose those games that appeared as just another instrument of cultural imperialism.

The Irish of course were not alone in welding together British imperialism and football. In the late nineteenth and early twentieth centuries it became clear that Scotland took on football as an opportunity to beat the English at their own game. Scotland, after all, was the nation that most clearly benefited from its association with the British Empire, staffing many of its key institutions including the army, civil service and imperial service. The Welsh, who felt their inferiority and minority status most acutely, and who had done less well out of their imperial connections, played rugby to distinguish themselves from the English without completely making a break from the anglophone cultural norm. New Zealanders and white South Africans would fit into the same category. The Irish, the Americans and Australians, all of whom were exposed to the new game of association football in the second half of the nineteenth century, would proclaim their fundamental opposition, separation and distance from the monopoly by playing their own distinct football codes.

If attitudes to the dominant metropolitan power and its game helps explain why, Scotland apart, the Celtic nations and the white dominions played football unenthusiastically, fitfully or chose to play other games entirely, what explains why people did play and watch the game? What was it about association football that captivated so many middle- and working-class town and city dwellers in England and Scotland in the 1870s and 1880s? Here let us just pause to consider the attractions of playing the game for the pioneering working-class players of the era. Remarkably little written material has been left behind by the first generation of lower-class footballers – they were, not surprisingly, not the most literate section of the population. So to some extent we are forced to try and re-create the choices and decisions made by this class. Certainly we can argue that there would have been a pent-up demand for recreation and exercise among the urban lower classes. Despite their often gruelling conditions of work they would have experienced physical activity as a regularized, soporific grind rather than as a sphere of exuberance and self-expression – football offered these pleasures. But if it were merely physical recreation and competition that was in demand, why not hockey or rugby? Football was and is cheaper and easier to organize, play and learn than either of these other team sports. More- over, football is played more easily and with less danger to the partici- pants on poor quality surfaces; for working men who could not afford to miss a day's pay this would not be an inconsiderable factor in choosing the kicking game over the handling game. Football's more flexible div- ision of playing labour would also have been attractive. But perhaps most important of all, football's upper-class participants proved mark- edly less insular and snobbish than rugby and hockey players – they alone among this cadre of upper-class sportsmen were evangelists for their game.

31 March 1883
Blackburn Olympic 2 Old Etonians 1
Kennington Oval, London

Say what you like about the British aristocracy but nothing became them more than their passing. They had the decency and good taste to depart without any of the fuss and rancour of the Europeans: no desperate pacts with authoritarians and ultra-nationalists, no nasty counter-revolutions. They seemed to know when they were beaten. After the collapse in land values, the decline of the House of Lords and the slaughter of the officer class in France, they dissolved into moneyed eccentricity and the higher reaches of high finance or sold their souls to the heritage industry; but they relinquished football first.

Blackburn Olympic: you couldn't ask for a better cross-section of the provincial industrial workforce. A certain S. Yeats Esq., owner of an iron foundry, provided the capital. Mr W. Braham Esq. was employed as a full-time trainer. In his team three weavers, a spinner, a cotton machine operative and an iron worker were his working-class spine; a plumber and a picture framer his skilled tradesmen; a clerk and a dental assistant from the lowest rungs of the white-collar middle class and up front, oiling the wheels, a publican. A whip-round from the shop floors of the mills and foundries sent them off to Blackpool for five days' training on the sand and a strict diet of kippers and porridge, beer and oysters. They even arrived in London two days early, resting up before the game. They meant business. Another couple of thousand from Blackburn arrive on the day, in their Sunday clogs with the brass rivets.

The Old Etonians are another matter. They just roll up at the last moment. They've been here before. Ten of the eleven have Cup Final experience and hard training is 'bad form'. Who needs training when you have the future Lord High Commissioner for the Church of Scotland, a dilettante gentleman farmer, a Professor of Latin, the leading commercial lawyer in British India and a baronet by the name of Percy de Paravicini?

The first half finishes 1–0 as the Etonians, riding the rough tackles, squeeze a goal past Olympic. While they leisurely sip their half-time pavilion tea, the Blackburn dressing room resounds with cursing and complaints. In the second half Olympic's organization begins to tell and they equalize. Arthur Dunn, the Etonians' best striking threat, departs the field injured. Down to ten men, they are forced to defend and are looking tired when the final whistle comes. Olympic ask to play on rather than return for a replay, with all the costs that involves. Lord Kinnaird agrees. When it's time to go it's time to go.

The Old Etonians go 2–1 down and Olympic's fans invade the pitch and exult in victory. On their return to Lancashire Blackburn Olympic parade through the town in a carriage drawn by six horses, preceded by six brass bands. Less than twenty years later they are broke, sell their ground and disappear. The silver cup, which never leaves the north and midlands, passes to Aston Villa in 1895 where it is stolen and melted down into half-crowns. Eton College is still with us.

VI

The shift in power announced by the 1883 Cup Final was confirmed in 1884 and 1885 when Blackburn Rovers twice beat the amateurs of Queen's Park, Glasgow. The Lancashire team won their third Cup in a row in 1886 against working-class, professional opposition in the shape of West Bromwich Albion. No amateur team would ever make the final again. In retrospect it might appear inevitable that the spread of the game to the working class and the emergence of large paying crowds would lead to the creation of an elite commercialized and professional game. But as the development of rugby shows, this was not automatically the case. When rugby was presented with a similar challenge from a similar cross-class alliance of northern working-class spectators and players and provincial middle-class club directors, its ruling elite could not bring themselves to compromise. Thus in 1895 the aristocratic majority in the Rugby Union effectively sanctioned an irrevocable split between northern professional working-class rugby league and southern amateur middle-class rugby union. In a generation they thereby consigned both codes to a marginal status in the sporting culture of Britain with Union the leading sport only in south Wales and among certain factions of the middle classes, while League was only dominant in the microzones of south Lancashire and the West Riding of Yorkshire. Football remained unified and universal; that it did so was primarily a consequence of the way in which the issue of professionalism was handled. In that regard the commercial politics of football mirrored the high politics of electoral reform – the middle and working classes were incorporated into the ruling order but on the managed terms of the old aristocratic elite. In so doing, revolutionary and radical politics was contained but at the cost of an incomplete modernization of politics and football alike.

Exactly which club paid which player first and how much is not clear. The illegality of the practice makes precision difficult. As with so many features of the game a reasonable claim for primacy can be made for Sheffield where the Heeley Club paid Peter Andrews while Wednesday employed the itinerant J. J. Lang. Both were Scots who came south with a Glasgow representative team to play against Sheffield and ended up staying. Lang, who it transpired was blind in one eye, was good enough to warrant a sinecure at a local knife works in return for his sporting services, while Andrews had a job as an insurance agent in Leeds. Although the clubs were prepared to pay for the services of these Scottish migrants, at the time the Sheffield FA remained implacably opposed to professionalism. The London FA was no different. But the fearsome rivalry that was developing between the leading clubs ensured that clubs' directors and supporters were prepared to pay out to acquire the skills of a key player.

The Blackburn–Bolton–Darwen Lancashire triangle was particularly important in forcing the pace of professionalism through the late 1870s. Turton were said to have hired the much touted Fergie Suter for £3 when he appeared for the club in the Turton Challenge Cup. Suter also played for Darwen and like many other players on their books he was a recently arrived Scot. Under-the-counter payments, jobs in local firms, mock testimonials and a variety of other devices hidden on the club's balance sheets were used to pay players. Bolton Wanderers and Blackburn Rovers seem to have gone down the same road in the early 1880s and Preston North End were not too far behind. Arrangements for paying players were not always so covert. Billy Mosforth was one of the leading players of the early 1880s in Sheffield and was notorious for his openly mercenary attitudes. 'He was once stripped to play for Hallam against Wednesday [but] when a supporter called "ten bob and free drinks all week, Billy if you'll change your shirt", he returned to the dressing room to re-emerge in Wednesday colours.'[21]

The Football Association, although slightly grudgingly, did actually allow 'broken-time' payments for players who were forced to miss work to fulfil their fixtures. Expenses and travel costs could also be covered for players. Even the high priests of amateurism, the Corinthians, liked their expenses set at around £150 a game. But direct payment or salaries were forbidden alongside the multitude of other sins that came with the arrival of money in the game, such as financial inducements for players a club wanted to sign, or the poaching of players by one club from another. The case against professionalism was multifaceted. There were certainly members of the liberal elite around the *Manchester Guardian* newspaper and among the radical artisan fraternity that were concerned by the negative moral and practical consequences of professionalism in sport, but the loudest voice and most fearsome opposition was an aristocratic and conservative one in which the moral argument failed to hide the extent to which this class felt itself displaced in the sporting firmament by its social inferiors. The sheer bitterness of the social and class prejudice that the growth of professionalism unleashed is captured by the claim that the 'Employment of the scum of Scottish villages has tended, in no small degree, to brutalise the game.'[22]

The Scottish presence was certainly overwhelming. Burnley were fielding nine Scots in their team in 1883, and the rising Scottish stars of Preston North End occupied ten of the first team's eleven places. Scots could be found at the Sheffield clubs, Darwen, Bolton, Blackburn and Aston Villa too. As the pioneer J. J. Lang had said of his career – and this could apply to all of these players – he 'hadn't crossed the border to play for nothing'.[23] Matters came to a head when an FA Cup tie in 1884 saw Preston North End beat Upton Park. The London club then complained to the FA, arguing that the professional status of the Preston players should make the result void. Preston counter-attacked in the shape of their powerful secretary Major William Sudell. His response was 'so what'. Preston, Burnley and Great Lever announced their departure from the Cup. This was followed by the very real threat from thirty-one clubs, mainly in Lancashire and the midlands, and all currently paying players in one form or another, that they would leave the FA altogether and form an independent British Football Association in which professionalism would be normalized and legalized. The landed and aristocratic interests at the pinnacle of the FA could see that alone they could not defeat the combined forces of provincial capital and the organized working class and that the principles of amateurism were not so precious that they should be retained whatever the cost. The FA retreated and in July 1885 offered this political compromise: 'It is now expedient in the interests of association football to legalise the employment of professional football players, but only under certain restrictions.'[24] Those restrictions included a pervasive sense of class superiority and apartheid: the first professional to play for England was made to wear a blue shirt while the rest of the team sported white. The FA attempted to maintain an annual Gentleman versus Players contest in emulation of cricket which kept its professionals very much in their place until after the Second World War. The FA also debarred former professionals from taking up places on any FA committees and issued rules that regulated wages, contracts and working conditions in favour of the clubs and their management.

Those players and clubs that were most threatened and most appalled by the legalization of professionalism pushed the FA to establish a separate Amateur Cup. The first was held in 1893 and won by the impeccably elite Old Carthusians. But there was to be no respite for the aristocratic footballer, no space for the gentleman player in a sport that demographically and culturally was becoming more and more working class. Middlesbrough beat the Old Carthusians to win the Amateur Cup in 1895 and the competition was subsequently dominated by amateur working-class clubs from the north of England. These kinds of clubs also sprung up in the midlands and the south and formed the backbone of the new amateur leagues like the Northern League and the Isthmian, Spartan and Athenian leagues in London and the south-east. There was persistent disquiet over ex-professionals finding their way into the amateur sides. In a desperate effort to preserve a realm in which the old order could not only be dominant ideologically but sportingly and competitively as well, the leading public-school sides established the Arthur Dunn Cup in 1903, named in honour of the Old Etonian and English international who had died tragically young. The secessionist impulse implicit in the creation of the Arthur Dunn Cup found its clearest expression in 1907. A row erupted over the FA's edict that the Middlesex and Surrey FAs, hitherto bastions of home counties' amateurism, must incorporate professional clubs. The issue in the end was peripheral but it provided a rallying point for the remnants of elite amateur football. A breakaway football association, the AFA, was formed and led by Old Etonian Lord Alverstone. It rapidly received the backing of the leading journals *Amateur Sport Illustrated* and *Amateur Football* and 500 clubs joined. However, the FA stood firm and banned contact between its own clubs and the breakaways. Amateur clubs in the midlands and the north refused to join, making the AFA appear the expression of an anachronistic social order that it undoubtedly was. It stumbled on until the outbreak of the First World War when the prevailing sentiment of patriotic unity and the hopelessness of its cause saw the AFA return to the FA's fold.

There was still a small space left open in the new professional game for the exceptionally gifted and dedicated amateur. The ludicrously talented C. B. Fry found space in his crowded timetable (England cricketer, world long-jump record holder, Olympian, Rugby Union three-quarter for Oxford and Surrey, classical scholar, journalist, schoolmaster and parliamentary candidate) to play as an amateur for Southampton, including their FA Cup Final defeat in 1902. Vivian Woodward, centre-forward for Spurs and England in the years before the First World War, was the last truly great amateur player able to compete at the highest level. Much was made at the time and in retrospect of the distinctive character of the amateur genius in the professional world. Woodward was said to be endowed with exceptional talent, intelligence and spontaneity compared to the dour drill and low-risk learned responses of the plodding workaday professional.

A more quixotic response to professionalization came from the illustrious N. L. Jackson, who in the early 1880s was the assistant secretary of the FA. He founded the Corinthians in 1882 as an elite standard bearer for the amateur game. He was able to draw on the cream of British aristocratic society, the universities and the public schools to assemble a considerable body of freewheeling talent. The club had no ground and for much of its existence refused to enter anything as vulgar as the FA Cup. Rather it issued and responded to challenges. The Corinthians played a self-consciously buccaneering, free-spirited attacking football that was emblematic of an older golden era of aristocratic sporting, political and ideological dominance. As Jackson himself put it, 'In the very early days of the game, when it was chiefly confined to old school boys, the laws were strictly observed, any infringement being purely accidental. This was doubtless due to that honourable understanding which it cultivated amongst boys at the better class schools and which prevents them taking unfair advantage of an opponent.'[25]

Despite the rapid progress of the professional game, the Corinthians were a force to be reckoned with. They beat Blackburn Rovers, the leading professional side and FA Cup holders, in 1884. Two years later the Corinthians provided nine of the eleven in the England team that played Scotland. In 1894 and 1895 they provided the whole of the England team that met Wales. Yet overt practising was considered bad form and the Corinthians cultivated an aura of Olympian indifference to their own brilliance: 'I remember how they walked onto the field, spotless in their white shirts and dark shorts. Their hands were in their pockets, sleeves hanging down. Yet there was about them an air of casual grandeur, a haughtiness that was not yet haughty, which seemed intangible. And how they played!'[26] The team never took up the opportunity to score a penalty and always left the goalmouth undefended when their opponents were awarded one – on the grounds that the foul must have been sufficiently serious in the first place to merit a goal. As late as 1904 the Corinthians were able to mix it with the best of the professionals – beating Bury, that year's FA Cup winners, 10–3 – and they continued to attract huge interest and crowds on their many foreign tours, including South Africa, Brazil, Australia and Continental Europe. But although the Corinthians and their class would survive the First World War, they would never take the field with the same élan. Passchendaele and the Somme ripped the heart out of the British aristocracy and in the inter-war years it was clear that their political, social and sporting superiority was over. The Corinthians' decline was such that they would be forced to merge with another club to survive, just as the class they sprung from would be forced to seek jobs in the City and merge with the industrial, professional and commercial middle classes that now ran football and the empire. The aristocracy joined the rat race, the Corinthians took part in the FA Cup, and the glorious, effortless superiority of the gentleman amateur was crushed by the relentless forces of modernity.

3

An Altogether More Splendid Life: Industrial Football and Working-class Britain, 1888–1914

The emancipation of their class appears to them as a foolish dream
. . . it is football, boxing, horse-racing which move them the deepest
and to which their entire leisure time, their individual powers, and
their material means are devoted.   **Karl Kautsky**

It turned you into a member of a new community, all brothers
together for an hour and half, for not only had you escaped from
the clanking machinery of this lesser life, from work, from wages,
rent, doles, sick pay, insurance cards, nagging wives, ailing children, bad bosses, idle workmen, but you had escaped with most of
your mates and your neighbours, with half the town, cheering
together, thumping one another on the shoulders, swapping judge-
ments like Lords of the Earth, having pushed your way through a
turnstile into another and altogether more splendid life.

                                                    J. B. Priestley

I

Between 1840 and the mid-1870s football had made the journey from
a dying folk ritual and the scorned pastime of urchins and urban undesir-
ables to the formalized if eccentric hobby of overgrown, aristocratic
schoolboys. In the last quarter of the nineteenth century it embarked on
a second transformation. Almost from the moment of its codification
football was colonized by the British working classes as both players
and spectators. While cricket remained immensely popular in England,
it had by the First World War ceded its place as the national game to
football. In Scotland *fitba*'s place as the cynosure of sporting and social

life was unchallenged. But if football's centrality to the social life of the majority of male, urban Britons in the late nineteenth and early twentieth centuries was without doubt, its function and consequences were disputed. To some observers, like the puritanical German Marxist Karl Kautsky, football functioned as an opiate, pure and simple – a diversion from the more pressing tasks of industrial organization and revolutionary politics. But the British proletariat was not a revolutionary animal irrespective of its sporting passions. Football mania did not create a reformist Labour Party and a cautious economistic trade union movement; it merely reflected these institutions and their outlook. Thus despite their numerical advantage, the British working classes did not attempt to wrest ultimate control over the nation's sporting or political institutions from the aristocrats and entrepreneurs who ran the state, the FA and football clubs. But by sheer demographic presence and obstinate persistence with football they did leave an indelible impression on the game. In this respect it is the novelist J. B. Priestley, rather than Kautsky the theoretician, who best captures the nature of industrial working-class football. It was an escape, of course, from drudgery, misery and uncertainty. But it was no crude circus handed down from above. It was also created from below. The trademark of the football created by British working men and which is its legacy to the wider world was a spectacle that combined individual and collective excellence; that called upon a balance of grit and inspiration, physical prowess and technical skills; and that offered the opportunity for the public affirmation of an intertwined civic and class-based solidarity.

The working-class colonization of football in the last quarter of the nineteenth century coincided with the maturing of Britain's long process of industrialization and urbanization. However, the connections between football and industrialism were always more than mere coincidences, parallels or reflections. Late nineteenth-century industrialization underpinned the emergence of British working-class football in a number of direct and material ways. (Early-twentieth-century industrialization would spawn the same connections in much of Europe and Latin America). First and foremost, real wages finally began to rise. Although there were big differences between occupations and regions, the last quarter of the nineteenth century saw a general increase in family incomes of around 30 per cent. Lifestyles were hardly lavish but the spare cash for a football match was much more widely available. Moreover, there was time to spend it at last. Employers and government had spent the previous hundred years attempting to impose a gruelling six-day week, eradicating old patterns of labour indiscipline, erratic timekeeping and traditional holidays. They had largely succeeded and in response industrial labour in mines and factories in the 1870s forced a massive wave of change in the working week. A mixture of parliamentary legislation and local industrial action gained the Saturday half-day holiday for many working men. The obvious significance of this for the development of professional football and mass crowds is illustrated by the experience of Liverpool and east London where dockworkers in particular and workers in general were late in gaining their Saturday holiday; local football leagues were slower to develop in both areas by comparison to central Lancashire or south Yorkshire where the half-day holiday was instituted a decade or so earlier.

The industrialization of transport technologies and infrastructure underwrote the increasing size of crowds and the enlarged geographical scope of leagues and cup competitions. Between towns and cities, the rail network was now substantially complete and reasonably priced, although the Football League could still exclude Sunderland in 1890 on the grounds that the cost of travel for other clubs to the far north-east was prohibitive. Trains provided the means for the bigger teams to conduct national Christmas and Easter tours to top up their coffers and for international teams to meet in the annual Home Countries championship, but they were not as yet being used by spectators. Aside from very local derbies away fans were almost absent during this whole period (1880–1914). The one exception was the annual day out for northern fans to the FA Cup Final in London, though the cost required fans to join savings clubs at the start of each season to fund the journey should their club be lucky enough to make it to the final. Within cities, the spread of the bicycle down the social scale and the development at the turn of the century of horse-drawn trams and then electric trams massively increased the radius from which football crowds could be gathered together. The presence of railway stations was a factor in determining where new grounds and clubs were based. Tottenham Hotspur settled at White Hart Lane right next to a station that could handle tens of thousands of fans arriving in less than two hours. Stamford Bridge, Chelsea's ground, was consciously built next to the Underground stop Fulham Broadway. Having established a ground and transport links first, Stamford Bridge's owners simply created Chelsea as a club to use them. Arsenal's move in 1913 to Highbury in north London from their home in Woolwich, south of the river, was primarily determined by the availability of land next to a Piccadilly Line station. Some clubs even had special stations built for them. In south Bristol Ashton station was opened in 1906 to service Bristol City's new stadium on match days.

Finally, industrialism was slowly bringing a widespread literacy to the working classes. Britain's ruling classes had awoken to the fact that an increasingly technical, industrial economy required that a significant part of the workforce be able to read and write. Hitherto the working-class self-help literacy movements had shouldered most of the educational burden. This was now combined with compulsory junior schooling funded by local government. This facilitated the growth of football by creating a huge secondary market around the game for newspapers, magazines and advertising which helped economically sustain the game while at the same time creating a cultural depth to the sport. But if industrialism furnished some of the essential preconditions of organized football, that organization had still to be imagined and invented.

By 1885 nearly all of the key elements of a modern industrialized mass sporting infrastructure were in place. The rules and tactics of the game had evolved to the point where the football played would have been recognizable to us today. The FA had been forced to accept a form of managed, but open, legal professionalism and a cadre of professional players had emerged. A network of clubs existed across much of Britain, albeit heavily concentrated in certain regions and almost absent in others. One key problem remained for the clubs at the leading edge of the game. That problem can be revealed by a glance at their erratic and eclectic fixture cards in the mid-1880s. There was no consistency to the games played over a season. One of industrial society's defining features was its ordered use of space and time which arose from the need for planned and regular use of expensive capital investments, the efficient meshing of interlocking transport systems and technical production processes, and the disciplining and control of an otherwise unpredictable and unruly labour force. These feats of social organization were achieved by the use of new technologies – like accurate clocks – and the introduction of common frameworks of timekeeping, the use of transport timetables and the imposition of inflexible work rhythms.

Football, however, was anything but regular. Leading teams would enter themselves in a multiplicity of cup competitions at national, county, city and local levels, though of course the progress of a team through any one of them would not be guaranteed. Thus each team faced the problems of either too few fixtures if they went out of the cups or too many fixtures and cancellations if they progressed in all of the competitions. Then there were friendlies, charity matches, challenges, testimonials, tours and exhibition games of variable value, drawing power and income. Clubs often found themselves ditched by other clubs that had found a more remunerative game to play or ditched others themselves for the same reason. Even when a fixture was played, that was no guarantee that the right team or the best team would turn out or that they would turn up on time or bring the right number of players with them. Mismatches and one-sided victories were therefore often the order of the day; Preston's 26–0 FA Cup victory over Hyde in 1885 must have been fun for their strikers but was not the kind of taut competitive encounter that would, in the long term, guarantee big crowds and financial security.

The free market in fixtures that was in operation was not, contrary to the dominant economic ideology of the era, providing optimal solutions for clubs, fans or players. The hidden hand of the market was creating chaos not order. The same problem had already presented itself to the two other modern team games that had acquired a mass paying public – baseball in the United States and county cricket in England. In both cases the solution was the creation of a league, in which a central authority drew up a regular and balanced competitive schedule among a group of clubs. It must have been obvious to most of the new commercial football hierarchy that this was the solution for their sport as well, but an example is not enough; someone must actually propose its emulation and in football that someone was William McGregor.

McGregor was a draper of Scottish descent who had moved to Birmingham, set up his business and joined the board of Aston Villa. Like the rest of Birmingham's progressive industrialists and small employers, he was acutely aware of the economic problems that a permanent salaried labour force (players), unpredictable demand (the chaotic fixture list) and expensive underused assets (a stadium) create. McGregor wrote to his fellow directors at the leading professional clubs of the era suggesting that 'ten or twelve of the most prominent clubs in England combine to arrange home and away fixtures each season'.[1] A meeting was held at the Royal Hotel, Manchester in April 1888 and representatives of twelve clubs formed the Football League. Six clubs came from Lancashire – Accrington, Blackburn Rovers, Bolton Wanderers, Burnley, Everton and Preston North End – and six from the midlands – Aston Villa, Derby County, Notts County, Stoke City, West Bromwich Albion and Wolverhampton Wanderers.

---

8 September 1888
Bolton Wanderers 2 Derby County 6
Pikes Lane, Bolton

Time: spend it, save it; keep it, give it; make it, kill it. Victorian capitalism had beaten time into a shape like a sheet-metal plate. Moulded it into regulation seconds and minutes, fixed it on a global grid of zones and meridians. It has riveted down its hours. Like the railway companies that insist on standard time to anchor their timetables, like the stockbrokers and shipping companies who deal in global time, simultaneous coordination needs standard time. Three o'clock in Bolton, is three o'clock in Liverpool, is three o'clock in Preston, Stoke and Wolverhampton. The first five games of the Football League kick-off together.

'The first generation of factory workers were taught by their masters the importance of time; the second generation formed their short-time work committees . . .; the third generation struck for overtime or time and a half. They had accepted the categories of their employers and learned to fight back within them.'

Now the fourth generation is making time work for them.

And with that the basic pattern, the rhythm, the form, the competitive nature of most football, in most of the world, for most of the last 120 years, was set. Preston North End on an unbeaten run won the inaugural

League and then the FA Cup as well to make it a double. In a number of ways the 'Invincibles' set the template for the football characteristic of the late Victorian era and beyond. As with all great winning clubs to come, Preston had their charismatic figurehead. The team was led by Major William Sudell, an ex-military man turned mill manager who was the irrepressible organizing energy behind the club – raising money, arranging transport, poaching strikers, cajoling players and supplying kit. His immense energy, attention to detail and, it later transpired, regular siphoning of cash from his mill job to the football club's coffers made Preston unbeatable. The side boasted ten Scottish professionals who had been tempted south by Sudell. Every other team in the League had their Scottish contingent. Sunderland and Aston Villa, who between them would dominate the League in the next decade, were almost as dependent on immigrant labour as Preston. But it was not just the club's officials and players that set the tone for future football, it was the fans and the town – for when Preston returned north from winning the FA Cup, the town erupted into an immense civil celebration, the players and the cup slowly winding their way to the town hall on an open-top bus.

From 1889 until 1914 clubs were falling over themselves to be admitted to the League. Where they couldn't get in, leagues were set up in emulation of the original. The Football Combination and its successor the Football Alliance were the main competitors, drawing on the strongest clubs in the north and the midlands that had not been allowed into the Football League. Most of their strongest sides joined the League in 1892 when a second division was created. Of the twenty-eight teams in the League in 1892 none was from further south than Birmingham. The Southern League was created in 1894 to cater for the leading clubs there, like Southampton, Portsmouth and Millwall. Scottish football also took its cue from the League, adopting professionalism in 1891 and establishing a Scottish League in 1893. Ireland and Wales, although unable to sustain professional football, both quickly adopted the league format for their leading sides. With the introduction of compulsory promotion and relegation on the basis of league position in England in 1898 the essential format of all league competition in global football was set. By 1905 the two English divisions had expanded to encompass twenty teams each and thus a much longer football season. It remained however an overwhelmingly northern combination with just four clubs – Arsenal,

Chelsea, Clapton Orient and Bristol City – from the south. Only Luton Town and the London sides Tottenham and Fulham would be added to the list by the beginning of the First World War. As the *Manchester Guardian* put it in 1896, 'London is the capital of the kingdom certainly, but who in the football world regards London as a centre of any interest?'[2]

This northern bias in English football extended to more than merely the number of teams in the Football League. In the first place the League itself maintained its offices in Preston and its senior administrative staff were predominantly drawn from Lancashire – in both cases this was a rarity for what was a national institution. The League's champions also all came from the north. In the years before the First World War the championship-winning sides were drawn exclusively from the major industrial conurbations of the north: Preston, Blackburn and Manchester United from east and central Lancashire, Everton and Liverpool from Merseyside, Aston Villa from the west midlands; Sheffield provided champions in the shape of both United and Wednesday while the north-east supplied Sunderland and Newcastle. Not only were these cities in the north but they were from medium to large in size. No club from a city of less than 100,000 people could win the League, and no club from a town of less than 40,000 in size could stay in the League, as Glossop and Accrington found out. The FA Cup was little different and while a number of smaller-town clubs could win it (like Barnsley and Bury) and a few southern clubs made the final, only Tottenham kept the trophy down south, winning in 1901.

The FA Cup Final itself had become a northern day out with working-class crowds saving all year and going into debt to follow their side should they make it to the final. Even the usually hardbitten, unforgiving mine owners of Barnsley gave their workers the day off to follow the team to the 1910 Cup Final; few of the crowd that day had ever been to London before and few would return: 'They don't know English i'London an' stare at us like we was polecats . . . and there's not a happy face in the streets.'[3] As early as 1884, the *Pall Mall Gazette* had commented negatively on the Blackburn Rovers fans who travelled to London for that year's final, describing them as a 'northern horde of uncouth garb and strange oaths'. *Athletic News* was more positive if more patronizing, writing 'the northcountry men hit one another in a playful yet vigorous manner and almost hugged one another in their excesses of joy'.[4]

The enduring political, linguistic, economic and cultural differences between the north and the south of England that were played out through the Cup speak to a bigger truth in early industrial football, that at root the phenomenal popularity and success of the game cannot be divorced from the notion of civic pride and civic identity. For the oppositions and solidarities that these kinds of north–south, provincial–metropolitan contrasts generated could be every bit as fierce and pointed between clubs from the same city (Everton vs. Liverpool), the same region (Newcastle vs. Sunderland) or from different regions altogether. Football, alone among the many forms of working-class urban culture in late Victorian Britain, provided an opportunity for a gathering of people whose origins, identity and purpose cut across very local neighbourhoods, industrial occupations, employers, trade union membership – and united them around a bigger but comprehensible geographical location and identity. It also served to insert these nascent forms of working-class localism into a national framework and national institutions, at exactly the same moment that the working class as a whole and its representative economic and political institutions were beginning to assert themselves in national economic and political forums. The working man, and working families, were finally beginning to lift their eyes up from the most parochial and immediate concerns to assume a wider set of horizons and to claim their rightful place in the national culture. Nothing could do this with more accuracy, simplicity and immediacy than supporting your local football team in the national league and the nation's cup.

So who were those supporters? What did they look like? How did they create the first football-fan culture in the world? In his celebrated 1896 essay *The New Football Mania*, Charles Edwardes, with his tongue only just in his cheek, described the football public in the following terms:

Thrice during the last season, the writer witnessed matches in violent snowstorms; and on one of these occasions, with snow and slush ankle deep on the ground, the downfall was so severe that a layer of more than an inch of snow accumulated on the shoulders and hats of the enthusiasts, who were packed so closely together that they could not move to disencumber themselves. You would have thought that they were all possessed of some sovereign preventative of the many diseases that proceed from simple catarrh. Yet, of course, such was not the case. Probably more than one of them was fast asleep in his grave ere the match of the ensuing Saturday.[5]

More than this, they paid for the privilege and in the twenty-six years between the foundation of the Football League and the outbreak of the First World War they did so in ever increasing numbers. In England the FA Cup Final was the best-attended game of the season. The crowd for the 1888 final at the Oval Cricket Ground was 17,000; by 1913 the game had moved to the Crystal Palace where 120,081 saw Aston Villa beat Sunderland. But it was not just the one-off spectacular that pulled in the crowds. In its inaugural season the twelve-team Football League was watched by around 600,000 people; in the 1905–06 season the crowds had increased more than eightfold to 5 million; and by 1914 attendance at Division 1 matches alone was almost 9 million. With FA Cup ties, Division 2 and the burgeoning and well-supported semi-professional leagues in the south-east and north-east the figure climbs to something around 15 million paying punters in a single year.

The borrowed cricket grounds, simply fenced fields, rented parkland and tiny pavilions that hosted most football matches in the late 1880s could not possibly have coped with this great wave of humanity. Fifty league clubs moved to new grounds between 1889 and 1910 and initiated an era of stadium building.[6] The basic principles of the task were simple. Clubs needed to put a fence up around their ground to keep paying customers in and freeloaders out. Turnstiles were the technology for controlling entrances and taking money. A fence might not always have been enough, particularly where grounds – like Blackburn Rovers' – were overlooked by trees, hills and high buildings. Most clubs built small grandstands or pavilions on their halfway lines and most initially opted for separate dressing-room tents for the players. The rest of the pitch would be steadily encircled with a raised embankment of some kind to provide a vantage point for standing spectators. Some clubs went so far as to invite the dumping of waste and spoil to build this up. When Fulham FC were building Craven Cottage they used street sweepings, while many clubs in mining areas used slag and ashes. Those prepared to invest a little more would construct wooden-frame terracing.

Nearly all of these stadiums were built right in the heart of towns and cities, nestled among a working-class community. Opening ceremonies were elaborate civic events. When Sunderland proudly unveiled Roker Park, the event was marked with marching pipe bands and a flotilla of steamboats on the River Wear with Lord Londonderry as master of ceremonies.

Roker Park's architect was the Scottish engineer and draughtsman Archibald Leitch, and it was Leitch more than anyone else who defined the nature of the early industrial football stadium.[7] Leitch made his name in Scotland where his engineering practice specialized in the design and construction of factories and warehouses; utilitarian and cost-effective models of design that appealed to the impecunious directors of football clubs looking to expand their capacities at the lowest possible cost. Leitch was responsible for the first great wave of stadium building in Glasgow, including Celtic Park, Ibrox and Hampden Park. He then moved on to projects in the north of England and the midlands including Roker Park and Middlesbrough's Ayrsome Park in the north-east, Sheffield Wednesday's Hillsborough, Blackburn Rovers' Ewood Park, Bolton's Burnden Park, Aston Villa's Villa Park and Wolverhampton Wanderers' Molyneux. Leitch's work was so popular that he finally reached the south coast, designing Southampton's The Dell and Portsmouth's Fratton Park, while in London Leitch was also responsible for parts of Stamford Bridge (Chelsea), White Hart Lane (Tottenham) and Craven Cottage (Fulham).

Leitch's early work created an enclosed stadium that had a covered, seated grandstand on one long side of the pitch and open terraces on the other three. As the ambitions of both clubs and designer grew, Leitch innovated by producing two-tier grandstands, some with seating above and standing below, others all seated; and, in his later efforts, he created stadiums with cover on all four sides of the ground and seating and standing on each side as well. Though his work was not austere, it had a certain functionality about it, leavened only by a number of trademark details including criss-cross iron work on grandstand balconies, gabled roofs and pediments. Yet for all the functional eloquence of the stadium, Leitch and his contemporaries built a very low-tech, low-cost infrastructure. There was little appetite for experiment or aesthetic innovation among the patrons of the game and the directors of the board. Floodlights were tried in a variety of forms – strung across and along the side of pitches at Bramall Lane, Sheffield in the 1870s, for example – but not followed up. Nor was there the same kind of ideological aesthetic that would shape the stadium-building programmes of fascist and communist Continental Europe in the inter-war era. Like the industrial revolution that gave birth to British football, its fixed capital assets were functional but crude, initially effective but quickly obsolete, a model for others but soon superseded.

So who were the huddled masses, the crowds that filled Leitch's stands and terraces? The architectural division of his and other early English grounds into covered and uncovered, seated and unseated, cheap and expensive areas probably provides the most accurate indicator of the crowd's social make-up. There was always a small tranche of middle-class supporters in the best seats, perhaps 10 per cent of the total. At the centre of the pavilion or grandstand there would be the club's directors and civic dignitaries – often symbolically separated by the creation of some kind of barrier, though the hermetically sealed executive box was yet to be invented. The other 90 per cent of the ground was filled by what contemporaries would have called a mix of the rough and the respectable. It seems likely that the bulk of those on the terraces were drawn from the lower middle classes – especially young single men – and the skilled working classes; if only because most contemporary reports, observational rather than statistical, say precisely this. The only actual record of a crowd's occupations is a somewhat morbid document – the list of the dead in the 1902 Ibrox disaster – and this confirms the observers' reports. The commitment and income of these social groups was such that the Football League was able to raise admission prices to 6d in 1890, which was more expensive than the cheapest seats at the music hall or later the cinema. That said, it did not put a place on the terraces out of reach for anyone but the very poorest and then there were always ways of smuggling oneself in; security remained fairly lax. Boys were usually charged half-price and made up a small but not inconsiderable portion of the crowd, sometimes given their own enclosure or pen, other times carried aloft over adult heads to the front or even down to the side of the pitch. Initially women were usually granted free entrance, but when over 2,000 came to watch Preston North End in 1884 the club abandoned the practice and others followed suit.

By all accounts football grounds were noisy places. The air was rent with violent oaths and swearing though this could be balanced by the spontaneous rendition of hymns from behind the goals. Rattles, drums and other instruments made their way on to the terraces, and tunes, gags and catchphrases from the contemporary music hall repertoire joined them. In much of the photographic record the crowd on the open terraces is dressed in heavy winter coats, mufflers and the ubiquitous flat cap. From around the turn of the twentieth century, and especially for the big games and the Cup ties, rosettes and ribbons in team colours seem to have made their first appearance. Although it is harder to prove from contemporary photographs, there is little doubt that much of the crowd would have had a drink beforehand and during the game too if they were organized enough to have brought a hip flask or a bottle.

The behaviour of the crowd, outside of major events of disturbance and disorder, can only be gleaned from the many chance remarks, reports and jottings of the era. Although clearly there were occasional incidents of violence, the most fundamental point to make is that the crowd was overwhelmingly good humoured, well behaved and self-policing, with an immense tolerance for the low standards of comfort and scant regard from the authorities for their sightlines or well-being. There is some suggestion that working-class life of the time inured many to the low-level scuffling and drunken fisticuffs that might break out. There is also a hint of the presence of more organized ruffians and gangs from the worst streets in the toughest cities. But there is very little direct evidence that they were an enduring feature of the late Victorian and Edwardian football crowd. What seems incontestable is the degree of passionate interest, detailed observation and delirious pleasure that football could evoke in the fans.

The hunger for football beyond the raw ninety minutes was soon recognized by the media entrepreneurs of the era. In the 1880s scores for the big matches were almost immediately being telegraphed around the country and from town to town. Youths would gather by pubs and post offices to get the news; shopkeepers would chalk up the current scores of FA Cup Finals. Inevitably a specialized press took shape to cater for this interest. By the late 1880s England possessed three sporting dailies: *The Sporting Chronicle*, *The Sporting Life* and *The Sportsman*. They all covered a multitude of sports, especially horse racing, but were steadily more and more focused on football. The *Athletic News* was founded in Manchester in 1875 under the irrepressible H. A. H. Catton who turned it into the leading football newspaper of Victorian Britain.

It emerged each Monday with coverage of every League game and a reported circulation of 170,000. The local press all over the country were quick to follow as they recognized the passion for the game. Special Saturday-evening editions were printed on coloured paper – and thus known as Pink 'Uns and Green 'Uns – at such extraordinary speed that you could pick one up on the way back from the game. The whole report from the game would have been dictated move by move down the phone as the game developed, ready to go to press on the final whistle. Clubs began to reciprocate interest as they understood the virtuous circle of football and press coverage for the bottom line; the first press facilities specially constructed at a football ground were at Celtic in 1894. The love affair of the press with football was ratcheted up even further when the technology for taking action photographs was perfected and in 1907 the *Daily Mail* became the first title to make massive use of football photos to report on the game and sell the paper. Dailies and weeklies were soon joined by a variety of other publications, with Charles Alcock's *Football Annual*, published every year between 1868 and 1908, defining the genre.

Where the press and the public lead, the advertisers cannot be far behind, and the early twentieth-century footballer was used to sell consumer items to the working class. Players and teams sponsored, endorsed, supposedly used and often specially preferred everything from Player's cigarettes to Sloan's Liniment and Eliman's Embrocation. Oxo advertised itself by claiming: 'Remember the English Cup was won in 1911 for the fifth time in succession by a team trained on Oxo.' And for those who simply wanted more football rather than football-endorsed beef drinks there was the first flickering of the memorabilia industry in the form of cigarette cards. Although the heyday of football cards was yet to come, after the First World War, the 1890s were notable for the aesthetically pleasing and much sought-after Ogden's Golden Guinea series. From the very beginning Edwardian football tapped into the range of predominantly male obsessions and traits – collecting, listing, mapping, numbering – that fuel the massive ancillary football industries all over the world today.

IV

If football was consumed primarily by the upper echelons of the skilled working class, who produced industrial football? For most consumer products of the era, the private company and the individual entrepreneur were the main agents of economic organization. In football the club was the hub of production and for this reason football, not just in Britain, has defied the conventional assumptions of rational market economics. Whereas the dynamics of most industries saw the steady concentration of power and production in a small number of big corporations and eventually monopolistic arrangements, football's success was accompanied by the steady proliferation of clubs. While many of the clubs that still make up English professional football were created by the 1890s, many others, including some of the most famous names, were being formed and moving towards top-flight status in the years just before the First World War.

The legal structure of football clubs was a grey area at first, but most appeared to fall under the legal rubric of charitable and voluntary organizations. However, as clubs grew and needed to take on considerable debt to fund their expansion and the creation of football stadiums, there was a steady conversion of clubs into private limited companies (that could take on debt) with private shareholders (providing some of the capital). An examination of those shareholders and the directorial class that was drawn from their ranks gives us a good profile of the make-up of the people in charge of producing industrial football. The cost of initial share offerings in football clubs was relatively low: low enough that by 1915 manual workers constituted 37 per cent of all shareholders. However, each shareholder tended to own only a few sentimental shares and they did not organize themselves in a way to make use of their potential voting power. Only 20 per cent of directors came out of the ranks of manual and clerical workers. The other 80 per cent, who were in general larger shareholders, came from substantially wealthier backgrounds.[8]

The motivations of this intriguing group of sporting entrepreneurs and amateur bureaucrats are complex. Unlike almost any other investment financial gain could not have been the primary return they were looking for. With the Football Association signalling its distaste at too overt an intrusion of commercial logic into football, annual dividends that could be paid were fixed at a maximum of 5 per cent (7.5 per cent after 1918). There were innumerable better ways to invest one's capital. In any case, the profitability of clubs was consistently undercut by the relentless dynamic of catch-up with one's competitors in pursuit of glory. When faced with a choice between a bigger dividend and a better centre forward, there was little option. There were probably some indirect benefits for directors who were in the drink or hotel business, supplying clubs and their fans. Brewers on the board of Manchester City voted against a ground move in 1903 fearing that they would lose their local captive drinking audience. This was an exception rather than the rule. There were unquestionably genuine enthusiasts who loved playing, watching and organizing. But the most plausible return on these investments was the immense local kudos and status that would inevitably arise from occupying such a hallowed position in a hallowed institution. This would be enough for many.

If club directors were the capitalist managers of industrial football then the players were its labour force. By 1914 there were fewer than 5,000 professional footballers in England. The leading players in Edwardian Britain tended to be drawn from the same class that dominated the terraces – the skilled working class – although there continued to be exceptions. In many ways their conditions of labour were not entirely dissimilar to that class as well. In the 1890s players were earning around £3 a week and £2 in the close season: not a fortune but well above what the poorest stratum of the urban working class might earn. Moreover, these young men were doing something that they actually liked doing and experienced minimal supervision and control compared to their factory- and workshop-based peers; there were as yet few coaches with any authority in football clubs, nor any attempt to systematize training.

The most significant form of control that clubs exercised over players was through the retain-and-transfer system. Clubs held or retained players' professional playing licences and a player could only play for the club that held that licence. Of course the licence could be bought and sold for a transfer fee and the obsessive pursuit of talent saw the value of a player's licence steadily climb. Middlesbrough were the first to pay £1,000 for a player – Alf Common – in a desperate bid to avoid relegation in 1905. This system prevented player poaching but the club retained absolute control over where a player could play. The possibility of escalating wages in pursuit of the best squads, with all the implications that had for the concentration of talent in a few clubs and generalized wage inflation, was registered early on by football's administrators. The Football League tried to introduce a maximum wage in 1893 but was unable to muster a sufficient majority of clubs. Then in 1900 the FA did the League's dirty work for them by introducing a maximum wage across all football clubs, set at £4 a week. For the very best players there were a variety of open and hidden inducements, bonus payments, and the opportunity to endorse consumer products. But like the rest of the British working class, life in the long term remained precarious. Little if any provision was made to support players after their short careers ended. Pension systems were nonexistent and the problem of injuries was dealt with by an inconsistent paternalism. Many disappeared after their playing days into the very lowest ranks of working-class destitution, alcoholism was a prominent risk, while a few were rescued by sinecures at their old clubs though often in a humiliatingly lowly position. Others who had husbanded their resources carefully made the traditional but limited transition to small-scale entrepreneurship, running a pub, shop or hostelry of some sort. But whatever the risks of embarking on a playing career, few young men who could make the grade appeared to have had any qualms about taking them on. Once again, Victorian and Edwardian football established a pattern that would be repeated all over the world for decades to come.

It was clear by the early 1880s that Scotland's contribution to football (like its contribution to industrial technological innovations, the British imperial civil service and the British Army) was quite disproportionate to the size of its population. Prominent footballing Scots included Lord Kinnaird, the celebrated Old Etonian forward and FA bureaucrat, William McGregor, the Aston Villa director and initiator of the Football League, and the earliest professionals in Sheffield in the 1870s. From its inception the Football League saw Scots present in huge numbers, making up virtually the entire championship-winning teams of Preston North End in 1888–89 and the great Sunderland sides of the 1890s.

They would soon all be playing in grounds designed by or influenced by the Scottish engineer Archibald Leitch. Scotland saw the first international game in 1872, played between England and Scotland, the first organized women's game, in Inverness in 1888, and the first penalty kick in an official match, at Airdrieonians in 1891. While every urban area in the country took to football, it was in the central industrial belt in general and in the city of Glasgow in particular that football mania was most intense. As George MacDonald Fraser put it in *The General Danced at Dawn*: 'The native highlanders, the Englishmen, and the lowlanders played football on Saturday afternoons and talked about it on Saturday evenings, but the Glaswegians, men apart in this as in most things, played, slept, ate, drank and lived it seven days a week.'[9] Just as the artistic avant-garde has concentrated its creative energies in key cities, and technological revolutions have been focused on key urban areas, so the new sport of football acquired its leading edge, its most modern expression, in a single city. In the years before the First World War that city was Glasgow.[10]

The most compelling indicators of Glasgow's football mania were its stadiums and its crowds. For the first Scotland vs. England international held in 1872 the crowd was a very respectable 3,500, almost double the attendance of that year's FA Cup Final in London. The same fixture in 1876 attracted 16,000 and in 1878 when the first Hampden Park was opened the figure had risen to 20,000. The game at Ibrox held in 1892 also attracted 20,000. But after extensive redevelopment and building work in 1902, Ibrox could pack in 75,000, while Celtic Park, the main venue for the big game in the last decade of the nineteenth century, peaked at 63,000. With two stadiums already taking over 60,000 people a time, it was little wonder that a new record would be set by the completely rebuilt Hampden Park, and in 1906 Scotland's game against England was seen by around 102,000 people. In 1907 the crowd rose again to a record 121,452. Thus by the beginning of the First World War, Glasgow alone possessed the three grandest football stadiums in the world. In Hampden, it possessed undoubtedly the largest. Taking all of the city's grounds together, there was enough capacity to hold over 300,000 people at a time – a very significant percentage of the male adult population of greater Strathclyde.

The sales of the sporting and footballing press are equally instructive. The *Athletic Journal*, launched in 1882 and predominantly about football, began with a circulation of 20,000; and all this over a decade before professional football had started up. Its success encouraged others like *Scottish Umpire and Cycling Monthly* while the most popular magazine *Scottish Referee* could in 1909 boast a circulation of half a million in a total population of only 5 million.

What accounts for such precocity? In the sporting realm football had no significant competition in Glasgow. Rugby union, the main competitor at club level particularly in the amateur era, was overwhelmingly played in Edinburgh and the Borders, where the Anglophile Scottish upper middle classes were concentrated. The sons of Glasgow's industrialists who might have formed a corps of elite rugby or football players were overwhelmingly educated in Edinburgh or England. Similarly, both popular and elite golf were concentrated in Edinburgh and on the east coast of Scotland. Middle- and upper-class Glaswegian sportsmen overwhelmingly played football and not merely the professional middle class, but the emergent strata of clerks, tellers and white-collar office workers, who in Queen's Park created a nucleus of talent and commitment to the game that would catalyse the creation of clubs all over the city and the wider Strathclyde region. In contrast to England, where football was initially colonized by the aristocracy and the public schools, in Scotland the game moved much more quickly into the hands of less exclusive social circles.

If the growth of football is in some sense bound to the growth of industrialism then Glasgow's sporting and economic rise can be linked together. Although in the second half of the nineteenth century already a successful port and small-scale shipbuilding city, Glasgow underwent such massive economic growth that it became the self-styled 'second city of the British Empire'. Only the megalopolis of London could exceed it. Shipbuilding, engineering and metalworking, railways, chemicals and glass all took root along the banks of the Clyde, and with this Glasgow's working-class population soared. While every new industrializing region in Britain drew on migrants to staff its factories, railways and docks, Glasgow was perhaps unique in drawing on so many distinct migrant streams – highlanders, lowland Protestant Scots, Irish Catholics and Northern Irish Protestants. This created a whole series of distinct communities which looked to their local football team as a source of identity, succour and entertainment, and by the same token created the possibility of deep and fearsome rivalries and oppositions. Glasgow was by some way the most densely populated city in Britain and possessed a particularly strong transport infrastructure for a late nineteenth-century city with tram and bus networks that connected many parts of the city with the new football grounds. This combination of density and accessibility helped create an immediate and compelling sense of civic pride that connected football clubs to their communities, physically and emotionally.

Whatever the precise alchemy of Glasgow's urban and class structure, the figures do not lie; football was king. The speed of Glasgow's advance brought with it three other firsts that make its footballing culture particularly important. In the Old Firm – Rangers and Celtic – Glasgow created not only one of the most bitter and enduring feuds in world football, but given the clubs' roots in their respective religious communities and the sectarianism of Scottish society at the time and since, Glasgow's football rivalries were the first to be so intimately connected to the warp and weft of real social divisions and conflicts. The vast crowds, crude commercialism, emotional instability and practical difficulties of such intense sectarian dislike expressed through football meant that Glasgow was also the first city to see a major stadium-based catastrophe – the Ibrox disaster in 1902. Similarly, while not alone in possessing a culture of disorder, violence and intimidation around football, Glasgow was the first to experience a full-scale football riot – the Cup Final replay of 1909 at Hampden Park.

Glasgow Rangers began life at the very start of the working-class football craze in Glasgow. A group of local lads, built around the McNeil family, gathered on Glasgow Green, where the playing mania centred in early 1872. They wore light blue, practised like fury and managed to get fixtures with the likes of Clyde, Argyll and Queen's Park second team. Eleven years later after much roaming around central Glasgow they built Ibrox Park and have been there ever since. Rangers rapidly ascended Glasgow's new footballing hierarchy, taking the more established side Vale of Leven to three games in the 1878 Scottish Cup Final and were soon attracting crowds of around 8,000. It seems that early on Rangers were acquiring a reputation for bad sportsmanship, a lack of humour and a fearsome concern with the bottom line. When Rangers played a charity match with Dumbarton to raise money for the families of the victims of the 1883 Linthouse steamer disaster, to the dismay of the footballing fraternity, Rangers insisted on taking their expenses out of the pot. The fans could be equally bad-tempered, invading the pitch in the inaugural game at Ibrox when Preston North End were thrashing the home side 8–1. The club had a significant tranche of the Protestant business classes on the board and the Protestant working classes in the Govan area in the crowd, but at this stage Rangers' relationship to the Orange Order, Freemasonry and sectarian politics had not been established. The club only began its rise to sporting greatness and social conflict with the arrival of a suitably well-supported opponent.

Celtic were founded in 1887 in the East End of Glasgow by an alliance of Catholic churchmen, rising professionals and publicans. On the one hand the team served as a money-raising tool to feed the Catholic poor of the area, on the other it provided an instrument for keeping Catholic football players in a Catholic institution. In the years before the First World War, the side became the sporting icon of Glasgow's Irish migrant community. The club, which boasted the Archbishop of Glasgow as patron and Irish nationalist politicians among its most prominent fans, lent its facilities to the Church and other Catholic organizations for parades, masses and the like. But despite such obvious links with the Catholic Church, Celtic were never explicitly closed to Protestants.

In the 1890s Celtic and Rangers had clearly established themselves as the best-supported clubs in the city and their capacity to generate massive crowds and thus massive takings earned them the moniker of the Old Firm. The sharpening of the opposition between the two clubs and the depth of animosity only emerged close to the First World War. This occurred in part because the Irish Question had become more pressing in British politics, and after the Belfast firm of Harland and Wolff had opened a shipyard in Govan and staffed it exclusively with Northern Irish Protestant workers. The pre-existing differences between the clubs soon hardened into more systematic and emotionally charged opposition. The First World War kept the lid on the political conflict in Ireland and Scotland, but they would both explode after 1918.

While the Old Firm games were huge money-spinners for the clubs, the biggest and certainly the most lucrative fixture of the year was the Scotland vs. England game. Hampden and Celtic Park had monopolized the hosting of the game at the turn of the century, but in 1902 Rangers had managed to bring it to Ibrox. In anticipation of a bumper pay day the club had installed new terracing at the north-west corner of the ground. As the packed crowd swayed in unison to watch a passage of play, the timbers at the far back corner of the rebuilt terrace gave way. A huge gaping hole opened, into which dozens of men fell to their deaths; many were only saved by falling on the bodies of others. The resultant panic and crush saw more deaths and injuries lower down the stand. Mercifully the referee stopped the game and the players retired to their dressing rooms where they witnessed a macabre procession of mutilated and asphyxiated bodies on their way to the hospital or the morgue. The final death toll was 25 killed and there were more than 500 people injured. Amazingly the authorities decided to finish the game, fearing the response of a disgruntled Glaswegian football crowd that hadn't got their money's worth. As the game restarted men were seen clambering back into the damaged area of the stand to take up a new and better vantage point over the match.

As early as the 1880s when large paying crowds first began to attend games in Glasgow there are reports of bottles being thrown at players and referees, though mud and stones were the missiles of choice. In Glasgow among the shipyard workers a well-aimed rivet was not uncommon, though at this stage the fans of Hearts and Aberdeen had the worst reputations. The gentlemen down at Queen's Park seem not to have been immune from this with the *Glasgow Examiner* often berating the behaviour of the 'pavillionites' and 'covered standites':

Rabid and bigoted partisanship is an exceedingly mild term to apply to their ferocious ebullitions. Were any of them working-class there might be a little excuse for them, but the most of them at any rate are dressed like gentlemen. I am afraid the resemblance ends there. A worse exhibition than these gents favoured us with has never been given in Scotland. It was worthy of a band of drunken cannibals.

In this Scotland and Glasgow were not alone. The record of hooliganism in England in the years before the First World War reveals a large number of minor incidents of crowd disorder and a few that were rather more serious. Research focused on Leicester reveals a great deal of bad language, the occasional scuffle and a variety of missiles thrown at players, officials, police and above all at referees. But in general there were few outbursts of large-scale fighting or disorder; the records of the Birmingham police between 1900 and 1940, for example, do not mention football as a separate or distinct policing problem.[11]

Glaswegian football generated disorder and violence on a level that England had yet to reach. In 1898 the New Year's Day game between Celtic and Rangers at Celtic Park stood at 1–1. The enormous attendance had already spilt on to the pitch on a number of occasions and forty police officers were barely enough to control the crowd of over 50,000. With Rangers pressing for a winner spectators invaded the pitch in such numbers that the tie was abandoned altogether. The crowd at Celtic Park did the same again during a 1905 Cup semi-final, only this time Rangers were leading 2–0 with eight minutes to go. To make matters worse the Celtic player Quinn had been sent off for apparently kicking at a Rangers fullback. As he made for the tunnel, Celtic fans tore up the spiked iron railings in their section of the ground and proceeded to assault the referee.

The causes of the 1902 disaster and this series of crowd disturbances and pitch invasions of Edwardian Scottish football are not hard to fathom. Given Glasgow's massive demand for football, commercial reasoning was central to the directors of the big football clubs. The Ibrox disaster was driven by a combination of enormous crowds, and a commercialism that sanctioned under-investment in shoddy infrastructure. The outbreaks of disorder were fuelled by a combination of an already violent and boisterous working-class subculture, revved up by sectarianism, alcohol and being housed on open terraces with primitive security arrangements. But the events around the 1909 Cup Final illuminate something else: the depth of working-class/middle-class divisions in Glaswegian society manifested in football. Some people had gathered to see the final at Hampden Park. They had paid a shilling each, which given the acute depression in the city's economic fortunes over the previous year was a considerable investment. Celtic and Rangers had played out a 2–2 draw. The replay the following week still managed to attract 61,000 who were treated to yet another draw. The arrangements for such an eventuality were not made entirely clear before the match. Certainly the bulk of the crowd believed that extra time would be played while club officials assumed another replay (and pay day) would be in order. At full-time the Rangers players walked off, but the Celtic team remained on the pitch, encouraging the crowd to think that extra time would indeed be played. What finally triggered a pitch invasion by both sets of fans and a headlong charge for the players' and officials' dressing rooms is not clear, though some reports suggest that an official who ostentatiously uprooted a corner flag may have been responsible. In any case the riot soon assumed the form of a pitched battle with bottles and stones flying at the police and, according to some observers, police horses and their riders pulled to the ground. Goalposts and netting were torn apart and wooden railings around the ground broken up as makeshift weapons. Fires were lit in the stands and on the pitch and the fire brigade were soon called out though their progress was hampered by the crowd stoning them. The middle-class horror at this working-class orgy of violence was evident from the tone of the *Scotsman*'s report:

It would be impossible to adequately describe the many cruel incidents which went to make up a riot now proceeding in almost every quarter of the field. Stricken men fell with blood streaming from their wounds and the rage and tumult became more intense. Many of the police were beaten and injured in the most callous fashion, and the force as a whole were the chief sufferers of the day. It was generally remarked that those of the crowd most active in the disturbance were composed of the most degraded section of the community, the self-respecting portion having as far as possible retired when the character of the fray became apparent.[12]

In the pages of the *Glasgow News* an attempt was made to link the riot to the wider spectre of politicized working-class unrest. Under the banner headline 'Seeing Red' the paper suggested that the same spirit of disorder that animated the Hampden riot had also disfigured meetings earlier in the week of the trades council and Glasgow city council. To the ruling order, it appeared that the once pacific and cowed working classes were sensing their power and flexing their muscles. Any crowd, any hint of disorder and volatility in a world beyond the reach of pulpit and police, was beginning to look worrying. In the years before the First World War the ruling classes would have plenty of reasons for fearing the crowd and linking it to football.

VI

In 1900 a Bournemouth minister wrote: 'The professional footballer is a monstrosity. God did not design a life to be spent in kicking a leather ball about. It was a perversion of God's meaning of life.'[13] He had certainly not designed the human skull for regular heading of a soaking-wet leather ball – for it has subsequently been revealed that many football players would have received considerable if low-level brain damage from the practice. Medical matters aside, the minister was not a lone voice. Football in Edwardian Britain continued to attract the opprobrium of a small fringe of cultural observers. Those close to the scouting movement, founded in 1908, and in the business of creating a fit, healthy and disciplined imperial master race, poured their scorn on the hunch-shouldered, fag-smoking masses that merely watched rather than participated. The trade union and Cooperative movements were mainly indifferent to the sport though there was an undercurrent of Marxist thought in the labour movement that equated football mania with a definite lack of cutting-edge class-consciousness. The temperance movement, many of whose members were drawn from the ranks of labour, frowned upon the drinking that inevitably accompanied football matches, before, during and after: 'Football is a fascination of the devil and a twin sister of the drink system.'[14] The same school of thought was equally disapproving of the gambling that the game attracted. This stony-faced radicalism made common cause with a strain of Edwardian conservatism that launched attacks on the whole panoply of emergent popular mass culture, decrying the music hall, the saloon, the penny dreadful and the Football League all in the same breath.

Yet despite this spectrum of censoriousness ranging from militant imperialists and conservative elites to alarmed teetotallers and frustrated socialists, football was the recipient of increasingly public royal patronage. The Prince of Wales had been invited to become the patron of the FA in 1892 and had accepted. In 1901 the FA postponed all Cup replays for one month as a slightly eccentric mark of respect following Queen Victoria's death. The newly crowned Edward VII replied by retaining his position at the FA, and every monarch has followed suit ever since. More than merely a name on the FA's headed notepaper, George V, who was no particular fan of the sport, became the first reigning monarch to attend a game, watching England vs. Scotland in 1912. Football, like the British working classes, had become just too big to ignore. An intelligent monarch in an era of populism and creeping democratization would be well advised to develop a demotic sheen to his rule. Thus on the recommendation of his confidants George V also attended the inaugural Royal Variety Performance in 1912, tying the House of Windsor to the other great wing of working-class culture, the music hall. This strategy of uncontentious populism peaked when the King attended his first Cup Final in 1914, seeing Burnley dispatch Liverpool at the Crystal Palace.

Football in Britain had thus become more than an innocent pastime; it had become a social phenomenon of such size and centrality that it had begun to accurately reflect, perhaps even shape, the dominant economic, political and cultural contours of Edwardian Britain in its late imperial pomp. British football, like the British economy, had become the leading power not because of its technical sophistication but simply by being first. Both survived on a diet of low and restricted wages, small clannish companies and clubs, and low levels of investment yielding low levels of profit. Politically, the relationship of football associations to professional leagues reflected the broader class compromise of the aristocracy with the new commercial classes of the urban north; while culturally and demographically the game reflected the unmistakable imprint of the working classes whose sheer size rather than the radicalism or ingenuity of their politics ensured that they would have to be included in some way in national politics and sport.

However, direct political manipulation or even indirect exploitation of the game was rare. Swindon Town and England player Harold Fleming actively supported the Unionist candidate Colonel Caley in the 1910 election. T. Gibson Poole, the chairman of Middlesbrough FC, also ran as a Unionist candidate in the town in the 1910 general election. He persuaded members of the team to speak on his behalf at campaign meetings. Poole also tried to bribe Sunderland players to throw the local derby. He lost the election, his scam was uncovered and the FA banned him from football for life. In this the FA was reflecting a distaste for politics among the footballing press and public. The *Green 'Un* for that year began an article with the words, 'Faint not dear reader, for I have no intention of talking politics at this time of day', while the *Swindon Evening Advertiser* was relieved to take its readers 'from the heat of the political atmosphere into the more exhilarating and congenial air of a cup tie'.[15]

Football was certainly an accurate barometer of Britain's relationship with the rest of the world. The immensity of Britain's formal and informal empire, its enormous merchant and royal navies, its engineers, bankers, teachers and travellers, had helped spread the game all over the world. In the decade before the First World War British clubs were touring extensively in Europe and North and South America. The superiority and sophistication of English and Scottish professional football was apparent to all. British amateur football was pretty good too and the British national team won gold at both the 1908 and 1912 Olympic football tournaments. Indeed, the home nations considered themselves so advanced and so superior that they looked at the rest of the world with a certain degree of disdain. Thus when in 1904 the first international football organization – The Fédération Internationale de Football Association (FIFA) – was created, it was founded by Continental Europeans in Paris, without any British involvement.

If Britain's tepid relationship with Continental Europe was typified by its cautious dealings with FIFA, so the underlying conflicts and tensions of Edwardian Britain were also illuminated by football. Three forces in particular were shaking the seemingly stable edifice of British politics: Irish nationalism; the new women's movement; and the seemingly unstoppable rise of organized labour. In Ireland football had become closely enmeshed with the nationalist struggle. The formation of the Gaelic Athletic Association (GAA) had politicized the whole realm of sports in the 1880s and to most Irish nationalists association football was clearly part of the British imperial universe. As a consequence football was concentrated in the north of the country and, within the north, among the Protestant community. However, the dividing lines of religion and sport had not yet become hard and fast, and in 1892 Belfast Celtic was formed.[16] The team was clearly modelled on its Glaswegian namesake and thus while it was never officially or unofficially a club for nationalists or Catholics alone it soon acquired that reputation. The team entered the Irish League in 1896–97 and its presence immediately ignited trouble; Celtic player Terry Devlin was attacked by the crowd when they played staunchly Unionist Linfield, while police had to separate fans later in the season in the game against Glentoran.

Outside the stadium, the Irish Question became more vexed and more intractable. The dependence of the Liberal government in Westminster on the votes of Irish nationalists forced them to concede the possibility once again of home rule. This is turn created the most vicious reaction from Protestants in the north who spent the years before the First World War arming themselves, and preparing if necessary to create their own independent state. As the home rule debate reached new heights of intensity in 1912, a game between Linfield and Belfast Celtic had to be abandoned after there was persistent gunfire from the stands.

While the Irish issue challenged the geographic reach of the British state, the emergent struggle for women's rights and women's suffrage challenged the legitimacy of its ridiculously narrow franchise. In England the game was taken up by public-school and university-educated women – the same cross-class alliance that formed the core of the new suffragette movement. On 23 March 1895 Nettie Honeyball, later secretary of the British Ladies Football Association, and Lady Florence Dixie, youngest daughter of the Marquess of Queensbury, organized the first recorded women's game in England at Crouch End Athletic Club in London. The game was played between a team from the south and a team from the north. Further games followed in a small tour of the country culminating in a game at Newcastle attended by 8,000 people. The response of the male establishment, like their political counterparts, was first to ignore the phenomenon, then to try and claim it was in some sense deleterious to health, and, when that failed to convince anyone, to deploy draconian forms of exclusion. For the FA it all ended in 1902 with a sharply toned note to members informing them that they were not to play with women's teams or support them.

Finally the politics of organized labour could not be kept out of football. The first decade of the twentieth century saw successive attempts by the courts and the state to control, weaken and divert the growing power of trade unions and the nascent labour movement that they were in the business of creating. But whatever obstacles that might be thrown down in their way, the working classes of Britain were demographically growing and finally getting politically organized. A similar tale could be told of football's labouring classes – the professional players. The first attempt to create a players' union took place in 1893 but proved short-lived. A second attempt in 1897–98 created the AFU but its weakness within the profession and its isolation from the rest of the labour movement meant that a refusal of recognition by the sport's governing bodies scuppered it. Almost a decade later the landscape had changed. The 1906 Trades Dispute Act had made union organization and strike action easier, while the music-hall performers' strike of 1907 over contractual restrictions suggested that previously unorganized but skilled workers in the entertainment industry could, under the right circumstances, win a labour dispute. The AFPU was formed in December 1907 at the Imperial Hotel in Manchester, chaired by Welsh international winger Billy Meredith and led by Manchester United centre-half Charlie Roberts. It has been suggested that Roberts's England career (only three caps) was sharply curtailed for his temerity in taking on such a role. Although there were many points of disagreement between players and their employers, the most vicious conflicts took place over, first, the right of players to take their cases of complaint to the formal court system rather than having them dealt with in-house; and, second, the right of the union to affiliate to the wider trade-union movement and thereby gain access to the power, status and financial reserves of the rest of the organized working class. The FA and the clubs strenuously opposed this and were prepared to take the union – which threatened strike action – right to the brink. Indeed all the League clubs prepared lists of amateur footballers that they were prepared to use as strike-breakers. But it was the players that capitulated. Like the wider British labour movement, militancy was not its strong suit. With the organiz-ation financially crippled by a number of unsuccessful court cases fought over the retain-and-transfer system and its membership decimated by the First World War, the players' union struggled on, but its weakness condemned British professionals to a small maximum wage and highly restrictive contracts for almost another half century.

VII

The torrent of political protest that was threatening to break the consen-sus and compromises of liberal Edwardian England was stilled if not eradicated by the advent of the First World War. As the Germans crossed into Belgium en route to France, the often understated nationalism that lay at the core of British sport was suddenly revealed. The aristocratic sportsmen of Edwardian Britain appeared to relish the prospect of a 'good game' with the Germans, believing that they would polish them off quickly. But if sport's call to the colours exposed a deep vein of nationalism it was equally instructive in revealing the depths of class division within British society. The Rugby Football Union took its cue from the *Evening Standard*, who ran the headline 'Duty before Sport', and abandoned its playing programme for the duration of the war. The cricket season was almost over but cricket's credentials were assured by actions like that of Yorkshire's captain A. W. White who left the field during a game with Lancashire to join his territorial regiment.[17]

The Football Association and Football League shared the general consensus that the war would be over by Christmas. Given that football provided a perfect distraction and recreation on the home front, they argued, why close it down now? That was not to say that football did not have a duty to perform. In close collaboration with the War Office the footballing authorities agreed to allow the use of their stadiums and other facilities for drill practice and military storage. Many benefit games were played to raise money for war charities of one kind or another. Most importantly of all, the football clubs agreed to act as recruiting sergeants in the creation of Britain's new mass volunteer army. This was no mean project for despite the authority and imperial might of the British state its actual capacity to intervene in or connect with working-class life, aside from strike-breaking and other forms of labour repression, was actually minimal. Football clubs and football games provided the perfect instrument for engaging with the young working-class men that the armed forces were desperate to turn into the necessary cannon fodder of the new industrialized war they had to fight. *The Times* claimed that over 100,000 men, led by professionals who took the King's shilling on the pitch before a game, had signed up by November 1914. This meant that around half of the country's whole recruiting drive had been achieved through football clubs. Two thousand players out of around 5,000 professionals had joined the armed forces and only 600 unmarried professionals had not enlisted.

But it was all to no avail. The most conservative and bellicose forces in British society were determined to close down working-class professional sport and demonstrate the greater power and moral authority of nation over class. F. N. Charrington, scion of the brewing family, was among the most extravagant in his dismay: 'What an appalling contrast it is to the fact that three well-known international Belgian footballers have already given their lives for their country ... The thickest flannel petticoats should now be provided for our footballers.'[18] He was also prepared to do more than merely write letters; on 5 September 1914 he persuaded Fulham to allow him to speak to the crowd prior to the game on the subject of enlistment. Charrington quickly moved on from this topic to a full-blooded attack on football and its malingering players and fans. He had to be escorted from the ground. E. H. D. Sewell unfavourably compared rugby's manly athleticism and gallant patriotism with degenerative soccer, a game now only fit for the basest elements of the lumpenproletariat: 'the sooner the army as a whole takes up "rugger" . . . the better for Tommy. Let "soccer" remain the exercise of the munitions workers who suffer so much from varicose veins, weak knees, cod-eyed toes, fowl's liver and a general dislike for a man's duty.'[19] It is instructive to note that hunting and field sports did not take the opportunity to engage in any wartime restraint, nor would anyone have asked them to consider doing so.

The war of course was not over by Christmas – it had hardly begun. The declining reputation of the game took a further blow in spring 1915 when relegation-threatened Manchester United beat middle-of-the-table Liverpool 2–0 at Old Trafford. The match had been comprehensively fixed by a group of players from both sides. Their concern was not who went up or down a division for it was becoming clear that there would be no division at all the following season; rather it was the expectation of losing their livelihood that led them to organize a small betting coup. To ensure the 2–0 result that they had bet on, one player missed a penalty and a lot of balls flew into the stands. Players on both sides visibly abused one of the Liverpool strikers who was not in on the coup and who had nearly scored when the game already stood at 2–0. By all accounts the ruse was perfectly obvious to most of the crowd and the scam was subsequently exposed, giving the conservative press another powerful tool with which to denounce the continuation of professional football.

If the Football League was struck at from one direction by the moral lash of hyperbolic patriots, it was struck from another by the raw facts of life in a war economy. As more and more men were called up, sent away and killed, so crowds steadily diminished; only Luton and Watford bucked the trend, but then they were both close to some of the major human marshalling yards where recruits were turned into soldiers. By early 1915 attendances were falling sharply, so income to clubs was in steep decline and the wages of the few professional players left had to be cut. The military requisitioning of the railway made journeys to away games increasingly difficult and the munitions industry was taking more and more people away with every week. The League limped on. Everton took the title. Sheffield United and Chelsea played out the last game of the season, the last game of the war: the FA Cup Final.

24 April 1915
Sheffield United 3 Chelsea 0
Old Trafford, Manchester

If Orwell had it right, that 'Serious sport has nothing to do with fair play ... it is war minus the shooting', then this is very serious sport indeed. Not because Sheffield United have won the FA Cup – Chelsea didn't offer much real resistance – but because here we have almost everything you need for a good war. The Minister of War Lord Derby is in attendance, and the crowd is so densely populated with soldiers, snatching leave or soon to depart for France, that we know it as the Khaki Final. All that is needed is the shooting and that's to come.

The cartoon urging football players to sign up for the slaughter reads, 'The Greater Game: No doubt you can make money in this field my friend but there is only one field today where you can get honour.' Mr Punch and the rest of the gang have been so good at persuading footballers and their followers to join the forces that the money game has had to stop. Crystal Palace, the usual venue for the Cup Final, is now in the hands of the Admiralty. There will be no more finals for a while.

In the single photo that survives of the day, taken from the players' tunnel, a peaked cap in the foreground reminds us of the military presence. But beyond the figure is the field of money lost in a white blur, a fog of light and over-exposure. On the field of honour, in Ypres, on that very day, at that very moment, there is also an impenetrable blur as, for the first time, clouds of chlorine gas silently drift across the battlefield.

The Minister of War presents the Cup and speaks to his men: 'You have played with one another and against one another for the Cup ... play with one another for England now.' Attendance was just under 50,000. A year from now, 60,000 just like them will be killed or injured on the first day of the Battle of the Somme. A whole terrace of mangled corpses, a double-decker stand of the seriously injured; the walking wounded fill another, the shell-shocked and the shattered invade the pitch. The Minister of War is still in the directors' box, the brushed black silk of his top hat spattered with blood.

PART TWO

The People's Game:

Football, Empire and Industry, 1870–1934

4
Perfidious Albion:
The Resistible Rise of
Global Football

The ugly and irritating fact [is] that we are daily importing from England, not only her manufactured goods ... but her fashions, her accents, her vicious literature, her music, her dances and her manifold mannerisms, her games also and her pastimes, to the utter discredit of our own grand national sports, and to the sore humiliation, as I believe, of every genuine son and daughter of the old land.

If we continue travelling for the next score years in the same direction that we have taken for some time past, condemning the sports that were practised by our forefathers, effacing our national features, as though we were ashamed of them, and putting on, with England's stuff and broadcloths, her nastier habits and other effeminate follies as she may recommend, we had better at once and publicly abjure our nation, clap our hands for joy at the sight of the Union Jack and place 'England's bloody red' exultantly above the green.

Archbishop Croke

I

Nearly a century and a half after Britons first started taking their boots, balls and goalposts to foreign ports and imperial postings, and during which football has become the world's most played and popular sport, it is tempting to write its history as one of ineluctable triumph; to read football's contemporary domination back into an unproblematically victorious geographical expansion. It is not a perspective that would have been immediately obvious to contemporary observers of, or partici-pants in, the emerging modern sports cultures of the mid-to-late nineteenth century. The paradox of the global game, the emblematic sport of the imperial Pax Britannica, was not its overwhelming triumph in the outposts of the English-speaking world and the strongholds of the empire where it was first exported. What is notable is that it was in these societies that football was most fiercely rejected, resisted, bypassed or replaced.

Archbishop Croke, the most senior member of the Irish Catholic clergy in the last quarter of the nineteenth century and an active Irish nationalist, was not alone in abhorring the pervasiveness and reach of British imperial culture. Nor was he alone in identifying sport as a central if not the pivotal element of this alien, corrosive threat. As far as one German observer was concerned, sport gave the British an edge in the imperial game over their more cerebral and literary continental European counterparts: 'The great task offered by the empire often demanded the strong energetic character rather than the bookworm.'[1] It was not a view from which many in Britain, and certainly those running its public schools, would have dissented. The 1895 obituary of A. F. Munnery – a legendary and pioneering mountaineer – encapsulates this self-perception. Munnery was the kind of man who 'made our race the pioneers of the world, which in naval warfare won for us the command of the sea, which by exploration and colonization has given the wastelands of the earth to Anglo-Saxon enterprise . . . Whilst Englishmen possess this quality they will manifest it in their sports.'[2] Conversely, attitudes to British rule and British power would deeply colour responses to British sport. The two did not just mix, they were inseparable.

In some cases the equation of British sport with British rule and the rejection of both was simple and unqualified. In the south of Ireland football was disdained by many along with the entire panoply of newly codified British games. In a grand statement of cultural independence and nationalism, Gaelic football and hurling were offered as alternatives and challengers; though even here football was not entirely extinguished south of the border and Irish rugby persisted as a rare instance of non-sectarian and depoliticized middle-class sport. The experience of the United States was similar, in the realm of team sports at least. British games were sidelined by North American variations and innovations: American football, baseball, basketball and ice hockey. In time these sports, like American power more generally, would serve as global competitors to the hegemony of the British Empire and British games.

Football did remain however a hidden part of the sporting universe of the US right up till the Second World War. Its ultimate demise, like the eventual success of professional American football, was never pre-ordained but the contingent outcome of economic upheaval and bureaucratic infighting.

Attitudes towards British sports were perhaps at their most complex in Britain's white dominions, where imperial conquests had been accompanied by significant colonial migration. During the nineteenth century Canada, Australia, New Zealand and the English-speaking whites of South Africa understood themselves as essentially British societies. But even the phlegmatic British abroad could not entirely deceive themselves that they had taken occupation of the Home Counties. British dominance was contested by native Indians and a French-speaking minority in Canada. In South Africa English-speakers found themselves among a black African majority and Afrikaans-speaking colonial competitors. Aboriginal peoples in Australia and Maoris in New Zealand stubbornly held their ground. The precariousness of the dominions' English-speaking populations made membership of the empire a source of security and strength, and psychically and culturally connected these far-flung societies to the metropolis and the old world. On the other hand their very distance and increasing difference from Britain left them searching for an alternative and distinct identity. Sport – imperial sport – offered just the right combination of communality and difference, amity and enmity. Yet in none of these societies was football able to achieve more than a marginal status in their modern sporting cultures.

Of the dominions, Canada's sporting culture diverged most sharply from Britain's. Cricket and football flourished in the elite schools and universities of mid-nineteenth-century Canada. However, neither spread much further. French-speaking Canada showed little inclination to play either of these 'British games' and in the case of cricket particularly elite clubs and schools showed no evangelical fire to take the game beyond the exclusive boundaries of their social circle. The summer-game vacuum that this left was quickly filled by baseball from America and among women especially the peculiarly Canadian sport of lacrosse, a Native American Indian game formalized and organized by white Canada. Football in the universities displayed the same cacophony of rules and styles that had existed in Britain and the United States prior to the process of codification. But rather than following the lead of Oxbridge,

Canadian universities found the influence of Ivy League universities in the American north-east pervasive. Harvard, Yale and Princeton set the intellectual and sporting standards for their poorer and smaller Canadian comparators. Thus by 1891 the Canadian Football Union had come into being presiding over a game that was American football but for a few technical variations. Association football (soccer) was relegated to the working-class neighbourhoods populated by the new waves of English and Scottish immigrants. Enthusiasts persevered, spreading football to the west of Canada along the newly built cross-continental railways, creating clubs and leagues in the industrial cities of Ontario. But Canada was enthralled by ice hockey. Here was a game suited to the climate that could be played by children and amateurs in the long frozen winters when grass pitches were unusable. Although the rules of the game were formalized at McGill University, Montreal, they could be shared by upper- and lower-class Canadians and owed no particular allegiance to either French- or English-speaking Canada. Best of all, Canadians alone were good at the game and the game itself was so good that the Americans had to import it. Football didn't have a chance.

The later settlement of New Zealand meant that organized sport was established on the islands after the formal codification of games in the imperial metropolis; there would be no New Zealand rules football. In fact in the last quarter of the nineteenth century New Zealand was exposed to the formalized rules of football, Gaelic football, Australian football, rugby union and rugby league. By the First World War it was clear that rugby union had triumphed. A local football association was founded first in Auckland in 1886 and then a national organization was established in 1891 in the capital city Wellington; a nationwide competition – the Brown Shield – was established in the same year by a Glaswegian whisky merchant. But from such promising beginnings the pace of development was painfully slow. The Brown Shield, although played annually, had to wait until 1925 before it acquired an actual trophy, a gift from the London FA. By this time it had been superseded as a competition by the Chatham Cup, which did have a trophy donated by the crew of the Royal Navy ship of that name after a spell in New Zealand in 1922. Given that it took over thirty years to acquire a shield for the Shield and that the New Zealand FA was reliant on itinerant sailors of a foreign country for a trophy for its leading club competition, it is little wonder that it did not have the resources to make football New Zealand's national game.

Even had it been a more active developmental bureaucracy the New Zealand FA faced formidable opposition. Contrary to New Zealand's perception of itself as an essentially classless society, sport did reflect and reinforce the nation's stratification. In the 1870s rugby clubs formed all across the dominion and quickly came to dominate the sporting curriculum in both elite high schools and the nascent universities and colleges of the country. Football, unable to get a toehold in educational institutions, seemed to survive best in smaller industrial communities, especially the mining towns of South Island, as well as industrial and workplace-based sides in the cities. Leading teams included Seacliff, made up of the staff of a large mental hospital, Harbour Board from Auckland and Tramways and Waterside from Wellington. This was enough to sustain football as a popular recreation but when compared to the sporting infrastructure created by the professionalization of the game in Britain, New Zealand was never going to be able to compete in international competition with the metropolis or attract its attention by way of profitable tours or promising players. Rugby, however, was another matter. With the pool of talent that British rugby union could draw upon diminished by both amateurism and the split with rugby league in the 1890s, the tiny rugby-playing population of the dominions could actually compete. Indeed, they could prosper. The importance of early victories for both the New Zealand All-Blacks and the South African Springboks over the home nations cannot be underestimated in linking rugby union with nascent national identities and securing its preeminence over football. In 1905 the All-Blacks' tour of Britain saw the New Zealanders win thirty-two out of thirty-three games and they only lost the one game against Wales to a controversial try whose legitimacy is still being discussed today. The Springboks announced their place in the world of rugby union with victories the following year over both Wales and Ireland.

The dynamic of sports history in South Africa was structured by class like New Zealand's, but much more so by issues of ethnicity. Football, cricket, hockey and rugby had arrived in South Africa via the British Army and the other agents of colonial conquest and rule. Rugby found its first institutional home in the elite universities of Cape Town and Stellenbosch, while the army played football. The low status of the average British soldier and his games was further diminished by the army's habit of playing with black South Africans who took to the game in the last decade of the nineteenth century. This, when combined with the increasing working-class aura that the professional game in England exuded, was reason enough for status-conscious white South Africa to make rugby union its own. The early victories of the Springboks certainly helped cement the status of rugby as the dominant element of white sporting culture, but it was the game's adoption by Afrikaans speakers – who had initially rejected cricket and showed little interest in football – that was crucial. The popularity of rugby, like the hegemony of the white South African elite, would rest on an uneasy alliance between an urban English bourgeoisie and a rural Afrikaans farmer class. Football was certainly played by working-class whites and non-English-speaking white immigrants, like the Greeks in Cape Town and the Portuguese in the Rand, but together they never amassed sufficient sporting or cultural weight to displace rugby, cricket or the country's ruling classes. Football, like all the challenges to the status quo, would have to await the emergence of an organized urban black working class in the middle decades of the twentieth century.

Before football could become the national sport in South Africa, it would have to be the sport of the liberation movement. In a cultural equation repeated all across the continent, the colonists' game was turned against them. Embraced by the new urban masses of Africa, football was an instrument of social organization, cultural self-expression and a yardstick for demonstrating the limits and fragilities of the colonizing authorities. This was the role of football in India in the nineteenth and early twentieth centuries, but one that it first shared with cricket. A similar pattern of development can be observed in the English-speaking Caribbean where football proved popular, but for much of the twentieth century was always a poor second to cricket.

Australia is an intriguing example which falls between many of these other cases. Cricket became a national passion; the Ashes series has, for over a century, been emblematic of Australia's complex relationship with Britain. Rugby has dominated the sporting culture of the east (New South Wales and Queensland) and has proved so popular that Australia can sustain international prowess in rugby union and rugby league as well as thriving domestic leagues and sporting cultures. Australia has also embraced the beach cultures and beach sports of the Pacific, most notably surfing. Finally, in Victoria and South Australia it generated its own version of football which pre-empted both football and rugby as the winter game. Indeed in its 1863 variant Australian Rules preempted football itself.

The first decade of the twentieth century was a crucial moment of nation-building in Australia. In 1901 the hitherto autonomous states – New South Wales, South Australia, Victoria and Queensland – had handed over much of their power to a central federal Australian government. While the fledgling nation still saw itself in many ways as a loyal outpost of the British Empire and an essentially British society, there was also a rising current of independence and Australian nationalism. This paradoxical closeness and distance, identification and opposition of Australia with Britain had been encapsulated by the now eponymous Ashes series in Test cricket; Australia's amazing success in beating England at the Oval in 1882 had cemented the relationship between the national team and an emergent sense of national identity. One might therefore have expected the same to be true of Australia and football, but it was not. Indeed in the years before the First World War football was very much a minority sport in every state, a distant second or third in popularity and significance during the winter months to either rugby (in New South Wales and Queensland) or Australian Rules football (in Victoria). Moreover it was Australian Rules football which consciously sought to represent itself as the winter sporting soul of the nation: in 1906 the Australasian Football Council chose to promote the code with the slogan 'one flag, one destiny, one football game', and it was a game to be played with balls of only Australian manufacture and beneath an Australian flag at every stadium.[3] The question remains why should this most anglophone of societies invent its own version of football rather than adopt its metropolitan variant?

As with so many things in sport, it is a matter of timing. Football arrived in Australia unformed, before the rules had been settled in Britain. Melbourne, in the early 1850s, was a booming microcosm of urban Britain, transplanted to the other side of the world. Like the continent's unique flora and fauna it evolved in isolation. The ludic genes of football carried by colonists to Australia would mutate to create a distinct sporting species. The recent Australian gold rush, combined with the fortunes to be made in ranching, saw significant cross-class immigration from Britain to Victoria State in general and Melbourne in particular in the mid-nineteenth century. In the absence of much cultural infrastructure, sporting events of all kinds were popular in the city. Unlike in Britain there was plenty of available land on which to play. Labour was in short supply in Victoria's booming economy and so workers were able to obtain much shorter working hours and thus more leisure time than their counterparts at home. A variety of football rules were played, including large-scale games of folk football among the new working-class colonists and games adapted from and based upon the various English public-school rules of old boys among the elite. A number of the most enthusiastic participants in these games also appear to have engaged with the local aboriginal population – a rarity among colonists – who played their own team-based ball games. It has been suggested the idea of the high catch and the mark – characteristic elements of Australian Rules – was learned in these encounters. The semi-formal games of the era proved very popular, but the rules available were diverse and unclear. So, in 1859 the first set of Melbourne Rules was written down, four years in advance of the FA rules drawn up in London in 1863. This early version of Australian Rules continued to allow handling and catching of the ball and created a game of remarkable speed and fluidity. By the mid-1860s large crowds were gathering on Melbourne's cricket pitches and scrubland to watch the game:

Backwards and forwards, on this side and that, now out of bounds – and this, unfortunately, was too often the case – amongst the crowd and again into the ditch by the fence, now into old Dennis's cabbage patch, and again kicked into the branches of those horrible gums; now kept in exciting closeness to the Melbourne goal and then with a fine spurt taken to the suburban headquarters, wavered the much abused ball; and for two hours and half the closest observer could not tell which side had any the best of it.[4]

A number of key decisions and local preferences shaped Australian Rules football to create a sport quite different from association football. In the first place, the topography of gum-tree fields made any accurate or regular implementation of an offside rule impossible. In any case, the English public-school disapproval of sneaking and goal-hanging that the

rule was designed to offset did not offend the sporting or social sensibili-
ties of Australian colonial society where neither the chancer nor the
short cut were objects of moral opprobrium. Second, while the debates
in England over the rules were constantly driven by deep-seated disagree-
ments between different public schools, determined to preserve their
distinct traditions of handling or kicking, these differences and their
social significance were meaningless 12,000 miles away. Rather, the
founders of the code sought the most enjoyable game, consciously looking to draw upon the best of every previous code. Above all, the new
football was to be open, accessible and available to the new colonists
streaming into Melbourne. Thus the columnist 'Free Kick', when comparing the domestic game with its English competitors, awarded the
Melbourne Rules the 'palm of honour'; for they were, he wrote, 'Short,
very simple, easily understood and remembered'.[5]

Once the alchemy of distance and isolation had generated the particular forms of Australian Rules football, its subsequent development was
remarkably similar to the course of association football. If anything, its
transformation was conducted at an accelerated rate. Within a decade
of codification the game was completely entrenched in Melbourne's
thriving sporting culture. Teams were formed around the same set of
institutions that created clubs in England: cricket clubs trying to keep
fit in the winter; pubs run by enterprising landlords seeking to create
occasions for boosting the sales of drink; churches and Sunday schools
seeking to divert the flock from the former; schools and neighbourhoods
in the new suburbs of the rapidly expanding city looking for an urban
identity and focus; as well as the armed forces and the new University
of Melbourne. The size of the crowds and the degree of press coverage
suggest an insatiable level of interest. The craze was intensified by the
creation of a Challenge Cup in 1862, almost a decade in advance of
the FA Cup in England. Money and the dynamic of competition were
already undermining the game's amateur status by the mid-1860s. In
the absence of the kind of social bloc that underpinned the amateur
ethos in England, fences, turnstiles, money and payment to players
became part of the sport with barely a fight. In the 1880s, once again
ahead of developments in England, an openly professional league was
created in Melbourne and the game began to spread to New South
Wales, South Australia and New Zealand.

Football based on the FA rules finally did arrive in Australia in the late 1870s when a new wave of British migrants settled in the industrial suburbs of Sydney and the small towns of New South Wales and Queensland; but even here the game's hold was precarious. The South British Football Soccer Association was created in 1882, a name redolent of the old world rather than the new and unlikely to appeal in an increasingly nationalistic Australia. Some local leagues and interstate matches began to be played, but the game remained fragmented and amateur. Unlike either Latin America or even South Africa, no leading British teams or FA representative sides considered it worth their while to tour the dominion. A properly constituted national football organization was set up only in 1923, and not until 1925 would even an amateur English FA team deign to tour. By then it was too late for football. The success of Australian Rules effectively excluded the game from Victoria and South Australia. By the turn of the century rugby union and rugby league were proving the most popular winter games in New South Wales and Queensland. Football was stuck as the second or third sport in every state of the country. The game's revival would have to await a new influx of migrants from Greece, Italy, Croatia and other parts of Europe in the late inter-war and early post-Second World War years. For these communities, football connected them to their homelands rather than to Britain. They created a football revival which, in the context of the narrow and provincial racism of mid-century Australia, only served to reinforce the minority status of football or, as it was derisively known, 'wogball'. The entry of football into the Australian mainstream would only be possible when these new migrant communities had been allowed admission into 'white Australia' in the last quarter of the twentieth century.

How is it that football, which has come to be the leading game on every continent, should fare so poorly in the USA? It was certainly not for the lack of early football experiences. The Pilgrims of the seventeenth century record the existence of a Native American Indian game, *Pasukk-quakkohowog*, which translates as 'they gather to play football'.[6] The game was played using an inflated bladder between two large teams on a narrow pitch, up to one mile long. It was probably similar to the game of folk football played by the British colonists and their descendants in the growing villages and towns of New England and Virginia – a game big enough and rough enough for the Boston authorities in 1657 to issue an edict banning it from the centre of town. Football had arrived but in a society which for all its superficial similarities to the old world in general and Britain in particular was actually something quite different. As Andre Markowitz succinctly puts it: 'America's sports exceptionalism ... remains inextricably linked to the other exceptionalisms that have rendered American politics, American social relations, and American culture, so similar yet at the same time so different from other comparable phenomena, particularly in Europe . . .'[7]

Of the many features of American society and social structure which have sent it on its own particular course of modernization, some stand out when considering the nation's sporting history. First, America developed without creating a successful or enduring socialist party and the institutions created by its working classes are among the weakest in the Western world. Football, unlike baseball and American football, was an overwhelmingly working-class sport and suffered accordingly. Second, many features of American life – sport and education in particular – have lacked any kind of central national direction or organization and have been shaped by the market and financial forces to a greater extent than their European counterparts. So it has been with football, which has particularly suffered from the fragmentation and market orientation of social life and from its exclusion from the nation's elite educational institutions.

In the early nineteenth century America's popular and indigenous football inheritance was complemented by an elite football culture in those educational institutions. In the leading universities and colleges the sports culture of British public schools was consciously replicated with all its cruelties, inequalities and hierarchies of power. The games of football played had loose and changing rules and combined the use of hands and kicking; but they proved exhilarating enough to inspire a Harvard student in 1827 to compose a humorous epic poem, 'The Battle of the Delta', the first written record of football in American universities. The game was enshrined at Harvard as 'Bloody Monday' as freshmen and sophomores fought it out on the first Monday of the new term. Harvard was not alone, with games of football being recorded at Dartmouth, Yale, Princeton and Columbia before 1840. But in all of these cases football remained intra-collegiate.

Inter-collegiate football began in 1869 with a game between Rutgers and Princeton played to an eclectic set of rules, with twenty-five-a-side, in a game that combined both kicking and handling. The experiment proved popular, not least as a way of establishing the place of colleges in the emerging educational pecking order, so further matches followed with Yale, Columbia and Cornell – all with a marked preference for kicking rather than catching and running. At Harvard in the 1860s the university authorities had banned the game, dismayed by its violence and fearful of its anarchic potential. When football was reintroduced in the early 1870s the rules used were based on the 'Boston game', a form of football played and codified between 1862 and 1865 by the large and popular Boston club for elite secondary-school and Harvard alumni, Oneida FC. These rules were much closer to the catching- and running-based version of football. Harvard were thus forced to turn north for competition and first played an intercollegiate game against McGill University in Canada in 1874. It was on this occasion that Harvard was first introduced to the rules of rugby union and to an oval ball. Both reinforced Harvard and Oneida's already existing preference for catching and throwing over kicking and passing and, perhaps most importantly, marked them out as the most elite and most exclusive college in an already elite and exclusive field. It appears that this level of prestige was sufficient leverage to encourage other colleges to abandon their round ball and kicking game for Harvard's version of football. Tufts were the first to capitulate followed by Yale in 1876 after which there was a flood of conversions. This culminated in the intercollegiate football association refining the rules of Harvard football to the point where most of the key elements of American football or gridiron – downs and yardage, blocking and scrimmaging – were now present.

By the time association football arrived in the United States it encountered a sports culture in which baseball had already occupied the summer schedules and claimed the mantle of national sport or metaphor. The obvious slot for football, if it were to parallel the English model, was as the winter game of the elite in educational institutions and old boys' clubs, but this had been taken by the newly minted gridiron. This left space for football as a lower-middle-class and working-class recreation and entertainment. Basketball, invented by the YMCA in the 1890s as a way of making use of its underused city-centre gymnasia, would provide a fearsome competitor that was as cheap, simple and flexible, but professionalism was a long way off. Ice hockey, which did eventually grab itself a place in the commercial world of US sport, was still largely a Canadian game. Thus a window of opportunity existed for football to establish itself as a popular and commercially successful sport in the first three decades of the twentieth century. Football, although facing substantial organizational problems and perhaps carrying cultural baggage which would make the United States a difficult environment in which to prosper, was by no means doomed to irrelevance, but its development fell into uncooperative hands.

The weakness of football in the marketplace was demonstrated by the first and ill-fated attempt to establish a professional football league in the USA. In 1894 the American League of Professional Football Clubs (ALPFC) was established by the owners of six National Baseball League franchises who were looking to use their otherwise empty stadiums in the off-season. However, the commitment and seriousness of the baseball franchises was questionable. In the first place, games were not scheduled for weekends when the vast majority of the potential working-class audience might have been able to attend. Second, the NBL's doubts about football were such that they suggested to the public that the football teams would be 'coached' by the baseball squads and that some of the public's favourite baseball stars might be taking the field too; this like many of the league's promises proved to be erroneous. The one area where the league appeared to have real promise was Baltimore whose team began to attract crowds of around 8,000, peaking with an infamous 10–1 thrashing of Washington. The capital's press took such umbrage at this pasting that they made it clear to both the public and the US immigration authorities that Baltimore had, on dubious papers, employed a number of foreign professionals in the squad. But by the time the federal authorities began to investigate this the league had collapsed as the rise of a second national baseball league left all the franchises scrambling to get out of football and protect their core business. After only three months the ALPFC had fizzled out.

Excluded from the universities and a failure in the marketplace, football survived in the street and in the neighbourhoods where a new wave of British immigrants (English and Scottish) had settled as well as communities from Ireland, Germany, the Netherlands, Scandinavia, Central and Southern Europe. Football was particularly strong in the small industrial towns of New England and the East Coast. Fall River in

Massachusetts was populated by textile workers of Lancastrian descent whose footballing tradition was so strong that they defeated the visiting Corinthians on a tour in 1906. In the big cities like New York, Boston, Chicago, Philadelphia and Pittsburgh immigrant communities created ethnic and football islands within the mainstream. St Louis was a particular stronghold of football with a vibrant city league whose players represented the US in the unofficial football tournament at the 1904 Olympic Games held in the city. This thriving grassroots football culture could attract reasonably sized crowds but its growth was limited by perpetual organizational problems. For example, prior to the First World War there were two competing bodies that sought to be the football association of the USA. The American Football Association (AFA) and the American Amateur Football Association (AAFA) both made representations to FIFA in 1912 to be accepted as the single footballing authority in the USA. FIFA bluntly told them to merge and get on with promoting the game. The subsequent merger created the USFA, but the development half of the plan did not fare so well. The USFA, to its own immense cost, decided to ignore college football and created a huge, cumbersome Open Challenge Cup as its leading competition. This massively diluted the available talent and potential spectacle in the American game and was a poor substitute for a functioning league.

Despite this, the popularity of the game at local and semi-professional level continued to grow. After a number of abortive efforts to establish a league before the First World War, Thomas Cahill, a long-standing and entrepreneurially minded US football bureaucrat from St Louis, established the well-organized and well-funded American Soccer League (ASL) in 1921. The ASL survived for twelve years, a period that can be considered the golden age of American football, peaking with a semi-final appearance for the USA national team at the 1930 World Cup in Uruguay. The league was initially made up of eight teams and grew in size over the next decade. Its roster was mainly drawn from the north-east of the country and combined factory or enterprise teams like Bethlehem Steel and Indiana Flooring, ethnic outfits like New Jersey Celtics and Hakoah Brooklyn and the self-consciously showy names that American sport revels in: the Boston Wonder Workers and the Providence Gold Bugs and Clam Diggers. There was good press coverage and media interest – including early radio broadcasts – especially in the smaller towns and markets that the league covered. Attendances were high and the money on offer to players was enough to attract a steady stream of mid-career professionals from the British Isles and elsewhere. Tours from Europe were a regular feature of the scene including the first tour by a women's football team – Dick Kerr's Ladies in 1922 – as well as Hakoah Wien in 1925, the Jewish Viennese team who were champions of the new professional Austrian league. Their celebrity was sufficient to attract a record crowd of 46,000 people to see them play an ASL all-New York XI in New York – a figure not exceeded at a football game in the USA for almost half a century. Tellingly, the money on offer in America was sufficient to entice nearly the whole squad to stay and play in the ASL rather than return home.

Yet in less than a decade professional football in the United States had collapsed, driven by its own internal 'soccer wars'. A long-simmering disagreement between the USFA and the ASL broke into open warfare in 1928. The professional clubs had long argued that the USFA's Open Challenge Cup tournament should take place after the close of the regular season to prevent scheduling conflicts or endangering a team's league performance with cup distractions. The USFA refused to yield and had some supporters among the clubs. The ASL ordered its clubs not to participate and threatened to fine and expel those that did, but to no avail. Newark Skeeters, Bethlehem Steel and the New York Giants all left the ASL, played in the cup and helped set up a rival East Coast League. But the quality of play and the attention of the sport's audience was too thinly spread. Two poor leagues could not match the interest created by one good one. Attendance began to plummet and by the time the league had been re-formed as a single entity economic history had caught up with football in America. The depression triggered by the Wall Street Crash of late 1929 scythed its way through the industrial strongholds of East Coast football. By 1931 key teams like Fall River and Bethlehem Steel had collapsed, their fan base unemployed or under-employed and no longer able or willing to pay to come through the turnstiles. By 1933 the league was finished and there was still no college game to fall back on in hard times like these.

IV

The sheer distance of Australia and America from Britain was a central factor, if not the only one, in explaining the emergence and then triumph of an alternative football code. In both countries the indigenous version of football came with a certain amount of nationalistic baggage, helping assert the independence and difference of the new world from the old; but in neither case could the explicit politicization of the game be considered a central component of its success. The same cannot be said of Ireland on either count. Indeed, it was the closeness of British culture to Ireland, the immediacy and sheer weight of British power exerted upon it, that stimulated the codification and popularity of Gaelic football and deeply politicized it. Football's fate was to arrive in Ireland at the very moment that a broad-based opposition to British rule and the Anglo-Irish landlord ascendancy was being mobilized; sport and politics would become inseparable and the tenor of that politics would be a bitter struggle between the forces of imperialism and nationalism. Football would be aligned with the former. Gaelic games, as they came to be known, were aligned with the latter.

In the 1870s regiments of the British Army, predominantly but not exclusively Protestant communities of the north especially in Belfast and some educational institutions in Dublin, were beginning to play football. In Belfast – a typical industrializing working-class port city – its popularity was quickly established and reinforced by the city's close connections with the football hotbeds of the west of Scotland. In the 1880s the Irish Football Association was formed. Tellingly, of all the national sports associations established in this era, the only one based in Belfast rather than Dublin was football. The IFA established the Irish Cup in 1881 and early competitors included teams from the Black Watch and Gordon Highlanders regiments. A league followed in 1890 and while the cup did go south on a number of occasions before partition, the league championship barely migrated beyond the boundaries of Belfast itself.

Archbishop Croke, with whom we began this chapter, was only one of many Irish voices, if perhaps the loudest, denouncing British sport and British rule in the same breath. In an open admission of the intertwining of sport and politics the left-leaning Irish nationalist paper

The Irishmen – hardly a natural ideological ally of the conservative Catholic hierarchy – declared that: 'If any two purposes should go together they ought to be politics and athletics. Our politics being essentially national, so should our athletics.'[8] It was alleged that those authentic national games had been steadily eradicated or suppressed alongside other elements of indigenous Irish life by the long imperial occupation. However, the decline of indigenous games was more the consequence of massive rural depopulation, migration and dislocation following the mid-century famine than any active programme of cultural repression by the British. Nationalists argued that the insidious impact of British culture could only be properly opposed by the rediscovery and modernization of authentic and indigenous Irish culture. Alongside the Catholic Church, which was increasingly taking a nationalist position in Irish politics, support for Croke's line of reasoning came from Charles Parnell who led the nationalist opposition in the Westminster parliament; the Land League, who supported the widespread struggle for tenants' rights in the countryside; and the more radical Fenians led by Michael Davitt in the Irish Republican Brotherhood (IRB). All these wings of the nationalist movement provided vocal and practical support for Michael Cusak and the small band of enthusiasts who established the Gaelic Athletic Association (GAA) in 1884.

Although created in opposition to the cultural hegemony of Victorian Britain, the GAA was, paradoxically, a very Victorian sporting organization. Indeed its actions paralleled those of the Football Association; the codification and bureaucratization of pre-industrial pastimes and contests was in perfect harmony with the rationalizing thrust of Victorian society. The GAA's equation of national self-consciousness and national well-being with the playing of authentically national games displayed the same belief in the connections between ethnicity, race, athleticism and the body that underwrote the games ethic in that most British of institutions – the public school. The GAA's first task was to codify the rules of hurling – a ball and stick game that had parallels with both lacrosse and hockey – the best established and most unproblematically Irish game.

The GAA did more than merely preserve, codify, invent and sponsor Irish games and culture. It also drew up and enforced a series of rules designed to exclude and marginalize British sport and to challenge British rule. Regulations set down between 1884 and 1887 forbade the playing of any British games on GAA property; banned any member of the British Army or the Royal Irish Constabulary from joining the organization; and promised to expel any member of the GAA participating in British sports or indeed watching them. The GAA was fantastically successful in its first decade of existence; membership soared, clubs were formed across the south of the country, and its adopted sports proved robust enough to prevent the emergence of a strong footballing culture in the towns and cities of the south. While the closeness of the GAA to politics was its strength, it was also its Achilles' heel. It certainly ensured that the British authorities and their secret police and spies would make it their business to infiltrate the organization and keep a careful watch on its senior cadres and their activities. When Parnell and his movement were undone in the late 1880s by the Kitty O'Shea scandal – in which Parnell's affair with a married woman rendered him unsuitable for political leadership in late Victorian Britain – the GAA was similarly broken apart. Some officials and clubs sided with Parnell, others took a stand against him, and all were involved in a vicious post-Parnell struggle for power. The predominantly legalistic and gradualist wing of the nationalist movement that Parnell had headed was now displaced by the radicals inside the GAA. The dominance of the IRB within the GAA became so great that the Church hierarchy actively campaigned to diminish its role, forcing the Fenians to share power with more moderate nationalists.

In 1891 Charles Parnell died a broken man. But he would have been amazed and no doubt proud that at his funeral Gaelic games – and their implicit declaration of an independent Irish identity – should take centre stage in the procession that accompanied his coffin in central Dublin: 'The hurley stick became a symbol of Irish freedom, a weapon to drive out the British. Two thousand hurleys draped in national colours were borne aloft at Parnell's funeral.'[9] With the most vicious infighting behind them the GAA concentrated on entrenching its sporting activities, starting leagues and cups and building a national stadium named after the archbishop himself – Croke Park. By the early twentieth century the all-Ireland Gaelic Football finals held in September would attract as many as 80,000 spectators who along with watching the game participated in much kissing of rings and patriotic ritual. The FA Cup Final may have drawn a few thousand more spectators, but then England had a population perhaps ten times the size of Ireland.

Although the hierarchy were concentrating on sporting matters, the wider and increasingly volatile politics of Irish independence in the years before the First World War could not be kept at bay. By 1914 a majority of the GAA's members were joining Sinn Féin or the Irish Volunteer Movement in expectation of some kind of armed conflict or uprising, and in January of that year the GAA's president James Nowlan came out in support of them, calling upon GAA members to 'join the volunteers and learn to shoot straight'.[10] While officially refusing to get involved in the conflict and refusing the use of Croke Park for drill by the Irish Volunteers, the GAA became increasingly associated with the struggle in the popular mind and in the eyes of the British authorities. Certainly many of the most active members of the 1916 Easter Rising were GAA members, and so many prominent Gaelic football players were interned in the aftermath of the uprising that that year's Wolfe Tone Tournament final between Kerry and Louth was played in Frongoch Prison in Wales where the British authorities had interned much of the republican movement.

The Easter Rising may not have caused the immediate defeat of British rule, but the occupier's days were now numbered. The brutality of the British authorities' response to the rising and the subsequent repression that followed galvanized mass support for the cause of independence. With the end of the First World War, hostilities grew to fever pitch in Ireland and both codes of football were directly caught up within it. By 1919 animosity towards Dublin reached such proportions in the north that Shelbourne refused to play an Irish Cup semi-final at Windsor Park in Belfast, fearing for the safety of their players in this cauldron of loyalism. The following year, as the war of independence between Sinn Féin and the British government intensified, the popular association of Gaelic football with Irish nationalism, independence and resistance was fixed. In mid-November the now armed and active IRA had killed a number of key British agents and members of the Royal Irish Constabulary in Dublin. Later the same day Tipperary were due to play Dublin at Croke Park and despite the violent unrest around 10,000 people showed up for the game. They were not alone. The infamous 'Black and Tans' – the key militia units of the British occupation – also decided to put in an appearance. The soldiers scaled the stadium's walls during the game, entered the ground and opened fire. Thirteen people were left dead, including three children and Michael Hogan, captain of the Tipperary side. Clubs south of the border now withdrew from the Belfast-based IFA and its competitions, and rapidly formed their own organizations – the Football Association of Ireland and the League of Ireland. But there was no official enthusiasm and less money available to the game in de Valera's Irish Free State. It would be seventy years before an Irish national team would grace the World Cup and football would find a place in the heart of a new Ireland and a new Irishness.

Football was played sporadically in India's ports and major cities from around the middle of the nineteenth century by British sailors and soldiers, and, prior to its dissolution, the officers and men of the East India Company. Like British power in India football was concentrated in Calcutta, the capital of British India until the early twentieth century. The city was an enormous, bustling merchant entrepôt, the heartland of the colonial state and the epicentre of India's first wave of industrialization. The first recorded game of football in India took place in Calcutta in 1854 between a 'Calcutta Club of Civilians' and 'the Gentlemen of Barrackpore'. There are also reports of a match in 1868 between Old Etonians and the rest, and one in 1870 that saw Eton, Winchester and Harrow combine forces against the other public schools. Calcutta FC was the first football club established, in 1872, though it seems that they initially planned to play rugby; but there was little appetite for the game and they eventually switched to football in 1894. By then Calcutta had acquired a whole league's worth of teams. Dalhousie Club was formed by the Indian civil service in 1878, Trades Club drew their members from the city's jute mills and both were joined by Naval Volunteers, Police, Customs and an Armenian club. An Indian Football Association (IFA), staffed by a colonial miscellany of clerks, church ministers and retired officers, was established in Calcutta in 1893. While the officer class and the upper echelons of the Indian civil service and the British commercial community played their part in the introduction of football, it was the ranks of the British Army in India – serving long and often tedious periods of service in garrison towns – that really spread and popularized the game. Soldiers formed regimental teams and regularly played in Madras, Bangalore, Hyderabad, Ambalka, Delhi, Peshawar and Dacca. Organized competitions soon followed. The Durand Cup, first held in Simla in 1888, is the third-oldest football tournament in the world (after the FA and Scottish FA cups). Britons in Bombay created the Rovers Cup three years later, while Calcutta could boast both a league and the prestigious IFA Shield; and in all of these competitions there was not as yet a single Indian face to be seen.

Football, like so many other aspects of the life of the Raj, was designed to keep the British apart from their colonial subjects, to demonstrate their difference and to maintain their ties to home. But the dynamics of colonial politics made a rigid and permanent exclusion of Indians impossible. The Indian uprising of 1857–8 demonstrated that Britain could not hope to rule the entire subcontinent, certainly not profitably, by force of arms alone; it would have to enlist the support of India's own royal houses and ruling elites. In return for their political submission and loyalty India's princes were to be invited to become honorary English gentlemen. Lord Curzon, Viceroy of India at the end of the nineteenth century, laid out the curriculum appropriate to this act of cultural and political alchemy: 'Learn the English language and become sufficiently familiar with English customs, literature, science, modes of thought, standards of truth and honour, and . . . with manly sports and games.'[11] By the 1870s and 1880s many of the scions of India's ruling houses were doing just this, passing through institutions explicitly modelled on England's public schools and incorporating their obsessive games culture. The lengths to which the British would go in pursuit of this task and the cultural barriers that they encountered are exhibited most starkly by the extraordinary Cecil Earle Tyndale-Briscoe, a pioneering headmaster at a school in Kashmir charged with teaching football to the sons of local Brahmin families. When first presented with a leather ball and the proposition that they should kick it, the boys fiercely protested, arguing that the leather ball was unholy and unclean, while the very idea of charging headlong around a field in pursuit of the object was quite below their priestly dignity. Resistance was so great that Tyndale-Briscoe and his masters were reduced to surrounding the recalcitrant boys on a marked football pitch brandishing sticks. After waiting five minutes for the boys to start the game voluntarily the staff charged:

All was confusion . . . as [pupils] tried to kick the ball but generally missed it, their clogs flew in the air and their pugaris were knocked off while their night-

gowns flapped in one another's faces; a real grand mix-up of clothes and humanity
... suddenly there were squeals of agony and horror and the game came to a
halt. One unfortunate had stopped the ball with his face. He was polluted.[12]

The cult of athleticism and imperial masculinity imparted by such
an education had a very particular resonance in Calcutta and Bengal.
Although the Indian uprising of 1857 was carried by many different
ethnic groups, Bengali officers in the Indian army were key rebels.
Consequently, the Bengalis were excluded from the reorganized security
apparatus of British India. This purge was given a sheen of intellectual
justification by Britain's bizarre official imperial anthropology which
subdivided the continent into martial (i.e. loyal) and non-martial (i.e.
disloyal) races. The educated Bengali, or babu as he was contemptuously
known, was now constructed by both colonizer and colonized as an
overeducated, effeminate physical weakling fit for the mundane clerical
realities of the Raj but not the defence of its borders or honour. Lord
Macaulay was among the harshest of the many who depicted the received
stereotype:

The physical organisation of the Bengali is feeble even to effeminacy. He lives in
a constant vapour bath. His pursuits are sedentary. His limbs delicate, his movements languid. During many ages he has been trampled on by men who are
bolder and hardier breeds. Courage, independence and veracity are qualities to
which his constitution and his situation are equally unfavourable.[13]

Early nationalists in Bengal in the 1860s responded to these stereotypes by arguing for a return to an indigenous Hindu physical culture
and a rejection of Western sports. In the following decades, the Bengali
middle and upper classes tried to acquire the physical culture they were
supposed to lack. The martial route had been closed to them so they did
so by embracing British sports. As one Briton living in Calcutta in 1885
put it, 'Many educated natives, in Bengal specially, have for years past
felt the reproach which attaches to their want of courage and corporeal
activity and have earnestly set themselves to remedy these defects; hence
on all sides we find efforts to follow the example of Europeans among
native students. Football and cricket are becoming popular...'[14] The
Bengali graduates of the new elite Indian schools, just like their English
counterparts in the 1850s and 1860s, left school and founded sports
clubs to maintain their social networks and recreational pleasures.

Initially there were no integrated competitions in which Britons played Indians, but with the establishment of the Trades Cup ethnically mixed football began in Calcutta. Sovabazar demonstrated the strength of Bengali football by beating the East Surrey Regiment 2–1 in the 1892 final. Manmatha Ganguly's National Association then took over as the leading Bengali team at the turn of the century, winning the Trades Cup themselves in 1900. In contrast to the showy aristocrats of Sovabazar, National drew their players and members from the lower middle classes of Bengal and insisted upon strict, even ascetic discipline and training among their members, arguing like the new Congress that the British could only be beaten after rigorous preparation. The rising militancy and assertiveness of Bengali society went a stage further with the creation and success of Calcutta's Mohun Bagan in 1889. The club was founded by an alliance of Bengal's intelligentsia and aristocracy with a conscious nationalist agenda of creating a new and independent Bengali masculinity. Smoking and drinking were banned in the clubhouse, and players that neglected their school work would not be allowed to play. Most unusually, money and employment were made available for the best players who had no income of their own.

The first decade of the twentieth century saw the political temperature in Bengal steadily rise and the forces of nationalism both on and off the pitch gathered strength. The British response to the growing assertiveness of the Bengali nation was to partition the presidency of Bengal in 1905 between predominantly Hindu West Bengal and the Muslim-majority East Bengal and Assam. The claim that this was a mere matter of administrative convenience in an otherwise vast geographical area was perceived as a cynical act of divide and rule, and initiated a further round of protest from Bengalis against British rule. This antagonism began to find popular expression in the contest between Indian and British football teams in the city, and the team that led the way for Indians was Mohun Bagan. The club won its first major title in 1904 when they took the Cochebar Cup, while success in the Trades Cup, the Minto Cup and the Gladstone Cup all followed. But the real test of the club's football required participation in Calcutta's leading tournament, the IFA Shield, previously closed to Indian teams. In 1909 Mohun Bagan got their first chance, but lost out to the Gordon Highlanders; other Indian teams smirked gleefully at their downfall, claiming that the club was like a 'dwarf reaching for the moon'. But they were back in 1911 and scythed their way through the opposition. By the time they had seen off the 1st Middlesex Regiment team in a two-leg semi-final it was clear that they had a real shot at the title. The East Yorkshire Regiment awaited them at the Maidan. Crowds gathered for the final from all across Bengal and as far as Assam. The authorities put on special trains and steamers to cope with demand and telephone lines were laid at Calcutta FC's ground nearby to transmit the result, as it came through, to the rest of Bengal.

---

29 July 1911
Mohun Bagan 2 East Yorkshire Regiment 1
The Maidan, Calcutta

Sixty thousand people came to the Maidan. Special trains had been arranged to bring them from across Bengal to Calcutta. They chanted the nationalists' mantra '*Vande mataram!* – Worshipping the mother!' Mohun Bagan came back from 1–0 down, scoring twice in the last five minutes. 'When the referee blew the long whistle, shirts, hats, handkerchiefs, sticks and umbrellas started flying in the air.' After that it's urban myth, like the pigeons and kites used to pass news of the score to the back of the crowd, and politics where myths and magic are put to use.

Nayak, voice of the city's educated Bengali elite, had despaired in June 1911:

We English-educated babus are like dolls dancing on the palms of the Englishman . . . English education and the superficial imitation of English habits and manners have made us perfectly worthless, a miserable mixture of Anglicanism and Swadeshism.

How different things looked in late July:

Indians can hold their own against Englishmen in every walk of art and science, in every learned profession, and in the higher grades of the public service . . . It only remained for Indians to beat Englishmen in that particularly English sport, the football . . . It fills every Indian with joy and pride to know that rice-eating, malaria-ridden, barefooted Bengalis have got the better of beef-eating, Herculean booted John Bull in the peculiarly English sport. Never before was there witnessed such universal demonstration of joy, men and women alike sharing it and demonstrating it by showering of flowers, shouts, whoops, screams and even dances.

The *Manchester Guardian*, like much of the imperial press, conceded defeat and emphasized their own magnanimity: 'A team of Bengalis won the IFA Shield in India after defeating a crack British regimental team. There is no reason of course to be surprised. Victory in association football goes to the side with the greatest physical fitness, quickest eye and keenest intellect.' Substitute physical fitness for military power and you have the recipe for keeping political control. Later that year the British moved the capital of the Raj from Calcutta to Delhi and left all those troublesome nationalists and football players behind. They remained there for another thirty years.

Mohun Bagan's defence of the IFA Shield in 1912 was curtailed when two goals were given as offside in a game against Calcutta FC. Whatever the reality of play this was understood as a rebuke and revenge by the British, still smarting from their defeat the previous year. Despite the prowess of Indian teams, only two places were allocated to them in the Calcutta League and no Indians were allowed on the committee of the Indian Football Association. Both of these bars would eventually erupt into conflict, with Indian clubs threatening to boycott the Calcutta League in the early 1930s and setting up an alternative football federation in the middle of that decade. In both cases the British eventually capitulated, allowing Indian clubs into all of the nation's tournaments and on the board of the reconstituted IFA.

It was clear that the balance of power and confidence was steadily slipping from colonizer to colonized in the years leading up to the Second World War. A similar shift could be discerned on the pitch. From Calcutta two new forces had emerged: East Bengal, which represented lower-class recent migrants from the east of the presidency in Calcutta; and Mohammedan Sporting, which was the team of Calcutta's Muslims. Mohammedan Sporting brought a new level of professionalism and organization to Indian football in Calcutta, and in the 1930s repeatedly won the Calcutta League before going on to be the first Indian team to win the prestigious Durand Cup in 1940. They beat the Royal Warwickshires 2–1 in a highly charged game attended by a massive gathering of India's Muslim elite who travelled great distances to see their team.

As Mihir Bose, chronicler of Indian cricket, has written:

While the Indians were fighting the British for independence, one of the most popular games in the country was football. Logically after independence, football should have become India's number one sport. It is cheaper, it certainly permeated more layers of Indian society . . . than cricket and, as in other parts of the world, could have been a metaphor for nationalism.[15]

But it didn't. In a nation that remained riven by the hierarchies of the caste system, cricket proved more accommodating of distinctions than the universalism of football. In any case football had already become deeply entwined with the communal identities and conflicts of the subcontinent; football was too polarized and too contentious to assume the mantle of the nation's favourite sporting metaphor – an argument borne out by the fierce communal and regional rivalries that dominated Indian football in the 1950s and '60s.[16] While after independence the Indian national football team continued to play well, its opposition – such as South Korea and Indonesia – lacked the post-colonial edge of the Test cricket circuit. For some time to come India preferred to represent itself and test itself against perfidious Albion at cricket rather than the upstarts and minnows which the world of Asian football offered.

5

The Great Game and the Informal Empire: The International Spread of Football, 1870–1914

We also have them in our Dutch dunes, those English, and yet I should not be inclined to rank them amongst the pinnacles of earthly hindrances – on the contrary. They would descend as winter set in, migrants by nature, identifiable from a great distance without any difficulty by . . . something that is indisputably English. Just fix your gaze upon those robust, overgrown fellows who have been formed by sport.   Simon Gorter

When everyone is dead the Great Game is finished, not before.
                                                  Rudyard Kipling

I

Simon Gorter's description of Lancastrian textile workers not only records the earliest sighting of football in the Netherlands but also marks the first recorded use of the word 'sport' in Dutch. It remains, like so many words in the English sporting lexicon, embedded in another language. As early as 1866, for Gorter and others like him in Continental Europe, sport and the British were considered synonymous. Sport was no mere reflection of Britishness but an essential element in Britain's rise to global dominance. J. E. C. Weldon, headmaster of Harrow school, would later condense the essence of this belief: 'Englishmen are not superior to Frenchmen or Germans in brains or industry or in the science or apparatus of war'; rather the hegemony of the British rested upon 'the health and temper which games impart . . . the pluck, the energy, the perseverance, the good temper, the self-control, the discipline, the co-operation, the esprit de corps, which merit success in cricket and football . . . [these] are the very qualities which win the day in peace and war.'[1]

Gorter, however, did not come across gentlemen but itinerant proletarian players. This early sighting of football has its parallels elsewhere. Working-class Britons in the lower ranks of the armed forces and the merchant navy, as well as those employed on foreign railway projects, are remembered, if rarely documented, playing the first kickabouts on docksides as far flung as Rotterdam, Copenhagen, Odessa, Rio, Lima and Buenos Aires and in locations as varied as military parade grounds, cricket pitches, public squares, wasteland and railway sidings. Yet the working-class contribution to the initial spread of football was minimal, its status either mythical or marginal – an invented or dim echo of football's later adoption as the people's game.[2] Before the First World War, football spread as the game of the *fin-de-siècle* urban elites of Europe and Latin America. The game also made its first tentative appearance in those parts of Africa and Asia most closely linked to Europe; the first indigenous football clubs had been formed in elite circles in Egypt, Algeria, South Africa and the Ghanaian Cape Coast before 1914. Working-class players never stayed long enough in any of these places to give the locals more than a glimpse of their unusual ball game. More importantly this kind of company lent no social cachet to football; quite the opposite. That required the participation of the eclectic elites and technicians of Britain's informal empire.

In the half century before the cataclysm of the First World War the British were everywhere. Obviously enough Britons staffed the military and bureaucratic machines of the empire, but the pink that coloured over one-quarter of the earth's surface on the conventional maps of the day had been quietly seeping out into almost every region of the world. British merchant seamen criss-crossed every ocean and in every port that they stopped in a British community of merchants, entrepreneurs, middlemen and speculators was gathered. These circuits of trade created a de facto British economic empire that reached to China, South America, Mexico and right the way across Europe, from Lisbon to Moscow, from Oslo to Constantinople. More than just trade, the British exported capital to these unofficial economic outposts, establishing banks, investing in railways, infrastructure and factories. Where local skills and technologies were insufficient, Britain exported technicians, techniques and machines too, most notably for the funding and constructing of Latin America's entire railway network.

While economic relationships were at the core of British influence, the informal empire was always more than just pounds, shillings and pence. British teachers, schools and educational philosophies were in vogue and in demand among many of the elites of Europe and the Rio de la Plata, for Britain was not just the most powerful player in world affairs, it was the most modern. While for much of the twentieth century Britain saw itself as imperturbably tranquil and able successfully to preserve the archaic and traditional, that is not how it looked to others in the late nineteenth century. On the contrary, the whirlwind of its industrial revolution, the modernist might of its iron-hulled navy, its development of new technologies of communication like the telegraph, suggested a society in a process of tumultuous change, riding the very edge of a revolutionary wave of social and economic transformation. Britain meant wealth, power and modernity and who did not wish to be rich, powerful and modern?

In the realms of politics, high culture and football, the terms British and English became synonymous. Despite the obvious contribution of Scotland to the creation of both empire and football, and the existence of separate Home Countries football associations, the nuances were too complex and of little interest to most of Continental Europe. British, English, it made no difference; either way the island empire's place in the great power politics of the era evoked reactions. On the one hand it created significant and powerful pockets of jealousy, suspicion and Anglophobia among the most nationalist political forces in Europe, the Far East and Latin America. An Italian gymnastics magazine of 1906 could write: 'they dress, eat, drink and abuse in English . . . people only play football to look like an Englishman and to be able to use an exotic vocabulary. For some time this was considered fashionable and a sign of good taste. Fortunately, everyone recognizes now the grotesqueness of this attitude.'[3] Perhaps not everyone, for almost everywhere these voices were drowned out by a great wave of Anglophilia; and to embrace England and Englishness was to embrace sport.

The key agents of this sporting diaspora were the peculiar expatriate elites that staffed the economic and educational outposts of the informal empire, or mingled as travellers, gadflies and adventurers in its ambience. Long-standing British colonies in São Paulo, Rio, Lima, Buenos Aires, Oporto and Lisbon sent their sons to be educated at home where they acquired a taste for games that was sufficiently unquenchable that they set up sports clubs on their return. They were joined in the later part of the century by fresh waves of migrant Britons engaged in trade, business and banking in Scandinavia, Italy, Switzerland, France, Russia and the cities of the Austro-Hungarian Empire. The social mix included the sons of both aristocratic and bourgeois families but was heavily weighted towards public-school old boys and in its upper echelons Oxbridge graduates. Alongside them a new class of highly educated technical specialists, particularly engineers, factory managers, railway technicians and teachers were recruited to Belgium, Russia, Spain, Germany and Mexico. All took the fashion and the passion for sport with them.

Consequently, from the 1860s to the 1880s football was just one of a whole panoply of English sports that were played and watched for the first time across the informal empire. While cricket won the affections of some local elites, most notably in the Netherlands, and rugby was immensely successful in south-west France, it was football that seemed most to engage the imagination.

But whose imagination? Who were the first generation of pioneering football players? They were almost exclusively male; there is scant recorded evidence of women's football in England, France, the Netherlands, Russia and Sweden, describing isolated and sporadic events. Above all they were urban, sometimes titled, always moneyed and usually highly educated. One of the few systematic surveys of the social origins of the leading footballers of the era looked at the Dutch national team. Using a three-class – upper, middle and lower – model, Cees Miermans found that between 1894 and 1905 96 per cent of the team came from upper-class backgrounds and only 1 per cent from the lower classes. In the period 1906 to 1918 workers had only taken 4 per cent of the places, middle-class representation had risen to 15 per cent, still leaving 81 per cent of the players coming from upper-class families.[4]

Not everyone from the youthful elites of Europe and Latin America was interested in football. As one Basque observer of football in the region in the early twentieth century wrote: 'Football is a modern and open-minded tendency directed at upper- and middle-class people with "advanced" cultivated ideas.'[5] Those people constituted the Anglophile and often liberal wing of the aristocratic and middle-class urban elites. Students at English high schools or, most prized of all, those who had studied in England, were among the earliest enthusiasts. Business people whose work took them to England or brought them into regular contact with British business supplemented their numbers. Doctors, lawyers, teachers, engineers, all of whom looked to England as a source of liberal thought and advanced professional standards, joined them. The English language itself was considered the mark of modernity and an essential device for excluding any would-be players from the lower classes. In its inaugural statutes the early Parisian club White Rovers stated, 'Football being an essentially English game, all players must use the English language exclusively when playing together.'[6] This homage to the power of English remains in the Anglicized club names of the Netherlands, like Go Ahead Eagles and Be Quick Denver, and of Italy, where it is AC Milan not Milano, and Genoa not Genova. In Switzerland Grasshoppers and Young Boys remain among the leading clubs, while in Latin America Liverpool, Everton, Arsenal, Lawn Tennis, Corinthians and The Strongest still play in Uruguay, Chile, Argentina, Peru, Brazil and Bolivia respectively.

Football also attracted many of the more intellectually inclined, and university students were at the core of the new football clubs in Rio, Copenhagen and Prague. Dr James Spensley, the leading force and player at Genoa Cricket, was the kind of multi-talented, cosmopolitan Englishman who inspired these scholar-players. Spensley was described in his obituary as having 'widespread interest[s] in philosophical studies, Greek language, Egyptian Papyrus, football, boxing and popular university. He even initiated an evening school in Genoa.'[7] Reflecting on the dense network of formal and informal connections among this emergent transnational class the Frenchman Paul Adam wrote in his 1907 book *La morale des sports*:

Over the last fifty years, a general type of elite has emerged. They share a number of common ideas about philosophy, science, arts and morality. They reign and prosper in spa towns, winter resorts and where international conferences take place. This elite is composed of doctors, bankers, professors, rentiers, authors, diplomats, dandies, artists, princes and dilettantes of various kinds ... they consider themselves brothers of the same intellectual family and have faith in universality and rationalism ... through sport they may unite and soon dominate the world.[8]

But football was not the only game competing for the attention of this transnational class. Cricket, rugby, tennis, hockey, athletics and gymnastics were all in circulation at the same time. Cricket, rugby and hockey were certainly English enough in their origins and social trappings to serve many of the cultural and status functions that the uptake of football satisfied. What was it about football, above all about playing football, that captured the imaginations of so many youthful European and Latino elites? On the one hand, the game was successful in this milieu for the same reasons that the British working classes took to the game with such speed and enthusiasm: the simplicity of its rules and scoring system; its flexibility in terms of numbers that can play, how long they can play for and the space required to play in; its lack of equipment; and the lower likelihood of serious injury, compared to rugby especially. But these are the traditional explanations for football's success among the world's urban poor. The *fin-de-siècle* gentleman player could have played whatever he wanted – football was not the only option left after financial and social costs had been discounted. People played because they just loved to play. Once seen, the prospect of trying it out for yourself was irresistible. A match report of a game between Athletic Bilbao and FC Bilbao in 1902 describes a scene that must have been repeated all over the world:

While the aces drank their lemonade in the changing rooms, many of the spectators, numbed by the cold afternoon, played the game in imitation of those who had finished their noble exhibition. Who knows? Maybe one day everyone here will play the game. It seems to be bringing folks together. It seems to arouse extraordinary curiosity.[9]

There are few published reflections by these early players that illuminate their choice of sport. We can reasonably argue that many of the reasons that make football a particularly good game to watch applied to playing it too: its continuous flow, its unpredictability, its combination of teamwork and individual bravado, its respect for both mental and physical labour. But it requires a considerable act of imagination to conceive of a universe without football, to understand just how bizarre and intriguing the game must have appeared. The Russian writer Yuri Olesha, born in Odessa in 1899, recalled first explaining football to his father: 'They play with their feet. The old man replied incredulously, "With their feet? How can that be?" '[10] There is something fantastically cussed and obstinately non-utilitarian about football. It was precisely this oddity that the promoters of the first football game in Seville in the 1880s sought to highlight and explain to the locals on their advertising posters and bills:

Football is a very enjoyable and healthy game since it demands a lot of physical effort. The peculiarity of this game resides in the fact that instead of striking the ball with the hands or with bats it is instead struck by the feet and, in extreme cases, using the shoulders or the head.[11]

Once the game had been established as an amateur pastime of the young and rich in the informal empire, a second wave of Britons helped shape its growth. In the two decades before the First World War, both professional and amateur British teams toured extensively in Europe and Latin America, providing inspiration, reflection and paying crowds wherever they went. A handful of more adventurous figures from within the otherwise rather conservative world of British professional football took the plunge and stayed overseas. Jimmy Hogan, an itinerant Lancastrian professional, had played for Rochdale, Burnley, Fulham, Swindon Town and Bolton Wanderers before moving to Holland and Vienna to coach before the war. The Glaswegian John Madden ran Slavia Prague for over thirty years starting in 1905.

The Great Game was coming to a close. Kipling, no friend or lover of team sports, recognized that for much of his generation that world of imperial rivalry and great power politics was cast in the frame of sport. As tensions rose in the last years of peace, there was, even among the Anglophile footballers, resentment over the exclusivity and haughty air of superiority of expatriate British clubs which saw the formation of breakaway and alternative sporting organizations to challenge their hegemony. Nacional in Montevideo, Stade Français in Paris, and Independiente in Buenos Aires were all created in opposition to English-dominated clubs in their cities and inevitably came to carry a nationalist flag onto the pitch. Simultaneously in Central Europe, Latin America and Sweden the game was spreading beyond the circle of the privileged and on to the toes and heels of the urban working class – who knew nothing of England and cared even less for its modernity or sophistication. But for them to take possession of football, as their English and Scottish equivalents had done thirty years before, the old order would have to be broken, the great game would have to stop, and if not everyone, then around 10 million young men would have to die first.

Football's initial beachheads on the European mainland were the ports and capitals of Scandinavia and the Low Countries. The university students and young urban bourgeoisie of Denmark, Sweden, the Netherlands and Belgium were all early and enthusiastic footballers; a precocity indicated not merely by the date of football's arrival but the rapid and early establishment of clubs, city-based competitions, national football bureaucracies and international teams. All four nations, with their rapidly industrializing societies, possessed many of the key factors required for the growth of popular organized sport: urbanization; the emergence of a large pool of young city-dwelling middle-class men with time on their hands; the development of a geographically concentrated and literate working class; new modes of communication and transport within and between cities. What they did not possess was the ball or the idea that one might profitably kick it around a rectangle of grass. For that leap of sporting faith they needed the British.

The British were certainly around, for Scandinavia and the Low Countries formed an essential element of Britain's informal empire. The economic and trading links across the North Sea were numerous and well-established, thus the earliest reports of football in Denmark describe British sailors playing on the docksides of Copenhagen, Lancashire textile workers were seen with the ball in the Netherlands, while Scottish riveters in Gothenburg and the staff of the British Embassy in Stockholm were among the earliest players in Sweden. But unlike much of Western and Central Europe, the development of football in these societies did not rely on such expatriates and their sports and social clubs. Coming from cultures unencumbered by great power pretensions, the elites of Scandinavia and the Low Countries could comfortably exhibit an Anglophilia that bordered on Anglomania. They did not wait for the British to arrive, they went to Britain or brought the British to them. Thus the leading schools of Brussels, Antwerp and Bruges and their English teaching staff were a hotbed of football, while the Dutch, the Danes and the Swedes who crossed the North Sea in search of social refinement and technical teaching got a sporting education into the bargain.

It was these travelling scholars who established Continental Europe's first football club, København Boldklub, in 1876 and created the first European football association, in 1889. Given a head start of almost a decade over most of the Continent, the Danes were second only to the British in their embrace of football in the years leading up to the First World War. Certainly they were good enough to win the silver medal at both the 1908 and 1912 Olympics. In 1908 they opened their campaign with a 17–1 victory over France, before losing to England in the final. They lost the gold medal to the English again in 1912. The social caste of Danish football can be gauged from the presence of Nils Bohr's brother in the national team. Nils (the Danish Nobel Prize-winning physicist and chemist) himself played for Akademisk, a team that had traditionally drawn its players and support from Copenhagen University, as a reserve goalkeeper. But exclusivity and elitism were not hallmarks of the Danish bourgeoisie who were already conceding political and social power to a democratizing bloc of organized workers and independent farmers. Football was therefore quickly taken up by working-class Danes, often with the active support of progressive trade unions and the Danish Social Democrats; the southern Copenhagen team of BK Frem, founded in 1886, were the standard bearers of workers' football. Both social blocs had their place in the country's (indeed mainland Europe's) first purpose-built football ground: the Idraetsparken. It was opened in 1911, built on open ground at the edge of Copenhagen city centre. On three sides cinder banking provided a cheap vantage point for working-class spectators, while on the fourth side stood what was colloquially known as the 'expensive stand'. For a price, the upper echelons of Danish society could take their place in a mock-classical pavilion with covered seating flanked by porticoes with Doric columns. It was and remains a perfect Hellenic folly, the architectural reflection of the unbending Olympian amateurism of Denmark's bourgeois football elite which could accept working-class participation but only on condition that any trace of commercialism and payment was eradicated from the game – a course of action strongly supported by the puritanical and Lutheran elements of the labour movement. Idraetsparken was opened with a game between the cream of the city's amateur footballers and the professionals of Sheffield Wednesday. In 1911 these Nordic Corinthians could hold their own. However, Danish football, locked into the micro-economics of a small country and technically restricted by the FA's hard line on amateurism, would henceforth disappear from the wider football stage for almost seventy years.

Danish Anglophilia, while strong, was dwarfed by the cultural magnetism of Britain for the Dutch in the late nineteenth century. When the former Mayor of Rotterdam, Drooglever Fortuyn, recalled Pim Mullier, it was with a tone of awed reverence: 'He was a little older than we were, and had the aura of one who had been to England.'[12] Mullier had studied in England in the 1870s and returned a zealous athlete and arch-organizer. He was one of the founder members of the influential multi-sports club Haarlemse FC in 1879 and was directly responsible for switching the club from rugby to football in 1883, the first Dutch club to make the change. He went on to found and edit the first Dutch sports journal *Nederlandsche Sport*. But Mullier was just part of a much bigger educational exodus that saw English-educated Dutchmen set up sports clubs all across the Netherlands in the 1870s; nearly all of these began life as cricket clubs. One participant captured the *raison d'être* of these early sports clubs, when he wrote that the purpose of sport was to play 'on English grounds, with all their English customs and English strategies . . . amid the beautiful Dutch landscape'.[13] The Englishness of early Dutch sports culture went even deeper. In the posed team photos of the era, the settings, postures and uniforms of the Dutch are an exact replica of their English counterparts. They conjure an air of calculated nonchalance, sporting the extravagant droopy moustaches of high Victorian England and 'radiat[e] studied indifference and arrogance'.[14]

By the turn of the century the cricket boom was over and the game was in a state of terminal decline. As the first wave of Dutch sportsmen aged and moved on, they were not replaced in anything like the same numbers. Cricket, which had always been accompanied by an air of exclusivity and elitism, consciously closed its ranks to the new urban masses, both white and blue collar. Cricket-club membership was only available on recommendation and all prospective members were subject to the social tyranny of a membership ballot and the high economic hurdles of substantial membership fees. Most clubs ran systems of fines for poor performance that dissuaded both poor and incompetent alike, while the rigorous sartorial requirements for spotless white flannels reinforced this. With the arrival of the Boer War and the general Dutch distaste for the British Army's treatment of Dutch Afrikaaners in South Africa, much of the remaining appeal of cricket was nullified.

But cricket clubs had provided the seed bed for the development of football. Haarlemse FC was just the first of many hundreds of existing cricket clubs that took on football in the 1880s and 1890s, though they did not take it very seriously at first. Indeed early Dutch soccer had a pleasingly anarchic quality to it, partly because the first generation of players were very young. While their older brothers played cricket, the next generation, still in their teens, played football. At Haarlemse FC the pitch was dotted with trees which were treated as an integral part of the playing field and the players were notorious in their use of them for eluding the opposition. Games were played with an enormous variety of rules and players; some observers believed that no one really knew the rules at all. Olympia FC were known to play regularly with forty or fifty a side.

Most importantly, football was not made exclusive. Indeed many clubs would put on games and invite non-club members to join in for a tiny one-off fee. This exposure would bear fruit in the early years of the twentieth century when the Dutch labour movement secured considerable advances in working hours and wages which in turn made working-class participation in football considerably easier. There was a veritable explosion of wild clubs, unregistered players, spontaneous competitions and chaotic fixture lists. Some sides sprung from pre-existing workers' cycling and shooting and pigeon-racing clubs; others seemed to coalesce suddenly from amongst floating groups of lower-middle-class and working-class youth. While the established elite clubs continued to take a somewhat patronizing attitude to the new clubs, they did not refuse to play them or actively seek to exclude them. Indeed there were many instances in which the older elite clubs supported them by lending their pitches to new clubs or providing officials and equipment. With the arrival of a comprehensive national rail network as well, organized competitive football boomed. Indeed so central was the development of the railways to Dutch football that in 1919 there was an exact correspondence between the remaining towns without a railway station and those without a football team.

Geographically further to the east, Sweden was a decade behind the Danes and the Dutch in their embrace of football. In part this was because football faced more sporting competition: a section of the Swedish middle classes had already taken to their own suitably austere version of nationalist gymnastics – the Ling method. For those that did not fancy the soulless discipline of Ling, the harsher climate both made football harder to play through the year and offered the alternative pleasures of winter sports for the new class of athletes. Nonetheless a combination of British kickabouts and English-educated Swedes was enough to initiate organized football in Gothenburg in the late 1880s where the city's military drill ground hosted Lyckans Soldater (the Soldiers of Happiness) in one of the first matches played in Sweden by Swedes. Örgryte IS, a bourgeois multi-sports club, was founded in 1887 and the craze it helped promote was deep enough to sustain a Gothenburg city championship by 1896. Stockholm was slower to start, but by the end of the 1890s it had acquired three major football clubs: AIK, Djurgården and Hammerby, the clubs of the bourgeosie, aristocracy and working class respectively – though both AIK and Djurgården had working-class origins before being taken over by their social superiors.

In the early twentieth century Swedish football saw an influx of working-class players, clubs and spectators. The same was true of Denmark and the Netherlands, but in Sweden alone this acquired a political dimension. The Swedish bourgeoisie, who up till this point had controlled every aspect of football, had adopted a particularly rigorous form of English amateurism in which the gentlemanly virtues of fair play were married with a marked distaste for commerce and combined with a vision of football as an adjunct to a low-key martial and nationalist masculinity. Working-class players and supporters, however, took to the game without learning or accepting this value system. The Swedish authorities began the century furiously worried about declining standards of play and persistent on-field fighting. Indeed it seems from very early on that football matches provided an opportunity for both spontaneous protest and displays of fearsome neighbourhood rivalry. The two were fused in the responses of the crowd at a game between IFK Norrköping and Västerås in 1906 in which IFK fielded a number of players who the Västerås crowd believed to be strike-breakers in a local labour dispute. The match report recorded that: 'The Koping players were during the game subjected to stone throwing and insulting shouts. The uproar when the match ended cannot be described. The crowd charged onto the pitch shouting "hurra", howling and calling out, "Down with the blackleg, scab", and so on.'[15] The ferocity and volatility of the Gothenburg crowd were certainly enough to worry and disturb Manchester City in their visit to the city in 1910. *Nordiskt Idrottslif* reported that: 'The crowd roared and whistled during the entire match, and the police had to intervene after it. Unfortunately enough, a couple of people from the seated section were guilty of indiscretions, of the kind one would have thought impossible amongst educated people.'[16]

Two years later the simmering class conflicts of Swedish society, symbolically represented by IFK Göteborg (working class) and Örgryte IS (bourgeoisie), exploded at the end of their derby game. The match had been studded with incidents of fighting among players on the pitch and the crowd boiled over when at 1–1 IFK were not given time to take the last-minute penalty that might have decided the game. At the same fixture the following year the crowd rushed on to the pitch, surrounded and jostled Örgryte players and then trapped them in their dressing room as window panes were smashed and stones thrown.[17]

The response of Sweden's ruling classes to this great wave of working-class football was twofold. The threat of commercialism and professionalism that large crowds and working players presented was countered by the implementation of an even stricter formal amateurism – so strict that visits by English professional clubs were banned until 1910 – but with enough flexibility and blind-eye turning to allow the best working-class players some form of payment in kind, particularly for those selected for the national team. The major clashes over professionalism were yet to come. In the meantime Sweden's football bureaucrats sought to counter the divisiveness of class-based domestic football with a focus on the international game and the national team as an instrument of unity. Sweden's sports administrators were among the most conservative and nationalist groups in the country. When the King of Sweden attempted to prevent the breakaway of Norway in 1905, the country's sports pavilions were among the loudest exponents of imperial hubris and punch-drunk patriotism, while the 1909 general strike saw many clubs offer up armed vigilante groups to the government.

The regular game between Sweden and Denmark, beginning in 1908, became the centrepiece of this strategy in which the unruly working-class energies of the terrace could be flared off like a flammable gas in an outward-facing nationalism rather than consumed by domestic class conflict. In the 1913 game against Denmark, the Swedish FA president Anton Johansen could be seen handing out paper megaphones to the crowd and leading the chanting. In later years musicians and music-hall stars were called in, sing-songs were conducted before kick-off and, alongside the standard and official repertoires, the terraces, fuelled by vast amounts of drinking on the train and boat to Denmark, rang with spontaneous and humorous banter. Sweden's working class liked to drink and beat the Danes, but in football as in politics they were far from being silenced; in fact, as the inter-war period would reveal, they had only just begun.

Like everything else from the Old World – invasions and epidemics included – football came to Latin America through its ports. The first sightings of *los ingleses locos* – the crazy Englishmen – playing their crazy game with a stitched leather ball are the stuff of myth. Yet from the 1860s to the 1880s there are enough stories of British sailors playing kickabout on docksides and wastelands all around the coast of the continent to suggest they are more than pure fancy. When the locals gathered to watch them tear up and down the hard scrubby earth in the searing heat, what did they make of it? A Brazilian journalist, who saw one of the very first organized games in Rio de Janeiro, was genuinely bemused.

In Bom Retiro, a group of Englishmen, a bunch of maniacs as they all are, get together, from time to time, to kick around something that looks like a bull's bladder. It gives them great satisfaction or fills them with sorrow when this kind of yellowish bladder enters a rectangle formed by wooden posts.[18]

Our correspondent may not have got the point, but pretty much everyone else did and they started joining in with the maniacs. Across South America a new local slang for the kickabout was coined: *pinchagas* on the Pacific coast, *peladas* in Brazil and *picados* on the River Plate. The British were more than occasional visitors, however. In the last half of the nineteenth century Latin America's immense mineral and agricultural wealth was ripe for development. The industrial revolutions of Europe and the USA provided a growing market for these resources, but Latin America's nations lacked capital, technical expertise and labour. The massive waves of immigration from Europe and Asia that took place over the next fifty years supplied the labour. Capital and expertise came from Britain. By the late nineteenth century the British were making money out of copper in Chile, guano in Peru and government debt everywhere. They ran the banks in Argentina, the meat, hide and wool export industries across the Río de la Plata and took a big chunk of the Brazilian and Colombian coffee markets. From 1863, when the Argentine central railway was first started, the British designed, funded, built and ran the many railway networks that were snaking out from the ports to tap the wealth of the continent's hinterlands. The US consul in Buenos Aires reported back to Washington: 'It almost seems that the English have the preference in everything pertaining to the business and business interests of the country . . . They are "in" everything, except politics, as intimately as though it were a British colony.'[19]

By 1880 there were 40,000 Britons in Buenos Aires, as well as smaller but powerful communities of expatriates in São Paulo, Rio, Montevideo,

Lima and Santiago. Alongside their business, these communities opened newspapers, built schools, ran hospitals, consecrated the occasional church and, with perhaps more gusto than anything else, established sporting clubs. From 1860 the British social clubs of Buenos Aires were organizing athletic competitions and games of cricket, tennis and polo. In 1867 the editor of the English-language daily *The Standard* received and published a copy of the FA's 1863 rules. Thomas Hogg of the Buenos Aires Cricket Club took it upon himself to organize the first game played under those rules in Latin America. In June 1867 a motley collection of the young men that made up the lower echelons of the city's British business community assembled in the Palermo district of Buenos Aires as the Colorados (with red caps) and Blancos (without). They played two fifty-minute halves, held up for some time while a discussion over the propriety and etiquette of wearing shorts in front of the ladies was resolved. The Blancos won 4–0.

Football was certainly played in Buenos Aires through the late 1860s and 1870s but it was just one of many sports played at the Anglo social clubs of the city, and many games were an erratic mixture of the FA rules and the newly developing rugby rules. Two decades later, outside the highest echelons of the city's elite, football was the only game. Its growth was driven by the fearsome games ethic that held sway at the many schools established by the British community in Argentina, the increasing number of expatriate railway workers, and as with many other societies, the arrival of a football evangelist. In Argentina that evangelist was a Scottish schoolteacher, Alexander Watson Hutton. Hutton disembarked in Buenos Aires in 1882 and took up his teaching post at St Andrew's High School. He left to create his own English High School in 1884 having fallen out with St Andrew's management who were not prepared to enlarge the school's playing fields and gymnasiums. For Hutton, as for many late Victorian educationalists, those facilities were the sine qua non of a decent schooling. Football was central to the curriculum at the English High School and it set the tone for elite schools both British and Argentine across the city. Simultaneously the influx of British railway workers and managers to the country created concentrated nuclei of football players who also began to form teams. Rosario, the first provincial city to host football teams, boasted two in the late 1890s – Rosario Athletic for the management and Rosario Central for the workers. Under Hutton's relentless organizational auspices the first competitive mini-league was played in Buenos Aires in 1891. After a short pause, a second and longer competition was played in 1893, the Argentine Association Football League (AAFL). The competition has been played as the Argentine national championship without a break ever since.

A similar pattern of development can be discerned across the Río de la Plata in Uruguay. In 1874 an English High School had been founded to serve the growing community of Britons in Montevideo. There are reports of football being played at the school and across the city through-out the 1880s but again a single charismatic individual provided the impetus for turning kickabouts into regular competition. William Leslie Poole, a Scots physical education teacher at the English High School, was that man in Uruguay. After getting school sports organized, Poole founded Albion Cricket Club in 1891 and created a football section in 1893. Albion, who had little domestic competition as yet, were soon playing teams from Buenos Aires like Belgrano and Lomas. The railways supplied football with an extra infusion of players and competition. However, Montevideo's fledgling clubs only contested their first organized league in 1901, a decade behind Buenos Aires; Uruguayan football was disrupted by the country's seemingly interminable civil wars that continued to rage until early in the twentieth century.

Brazilian football began with the return of Charles Miller in 1894. Son of an English father and Brazilian mother and part of the coffee and commerce elite of São Paulo, Miller was sent to England for his education. He ended up playing football for his school, Bannister Court, his county, Hampshire, and even a few games for the newly professional club Southampton. He returned to São Paulo in 1894 with two leather footballs, some playing kit and the bug. Initially a cricketer at the exclusive São Paulo Athletic Club, he persuaded a few other members to try football. Their first excursions in spring 1895 were played on scrubland to the east of the city centre where the mules that pulled the trams were left to graze. The beasts were chased away and the hastily assembled and named São Paulo Railways faced The Gas Team made up of staff at the municipal gas-supply company. It was agreed after-wards that it was rather a good game and well worth another crack, but opposition was required. In 1897 Hans Nobiling, a German immigrant, arrived in São Paulo with the rules of football in German and a few seasons playing in Hamburg under his belt. His attempts to get a game with São Paulo AC were rebuffed and together with other excluded non-Anglo immigrants they responded by forming their own sports association, SC Internacional. To these two clubs were quickly added three more: a breakaway from Internacional of exclusively Teutonic members called SC Germania; a team formed by American students at Mackenzie College; and CA Paulistino, a sports club and football team for the city's Brazilian elites. By 1902, football was so well established that an extensive league programme and city championship could be staged.

---

26 October 1902
São Paulo AC 2 CA Paulistino 1
Velodromo Paulistino, São Paulo

> CHAMPAGNE: Football gets no kick from *champagne*: 'Carrick
> is trying too many *champagne* balls instead of keeping it simple';
> 'Berkovic is a *champagne* player and doesn't like it up him'.
> **Leigh and Woodhouse**, Football Lexicon

It wasn't always so. On the contrary, in turn-of-the-century São Paulo it was all champagne football. Take the play-off for the first Paulista championship; anyone who was anyone in the city was there. *O Estado de São Paulo* virtually swooned over the game: 'The attendance was extraordinary, about four thousand people, continuously applauding the formidable players . . . The elegant young ladies, who lent the utmost charm to this festive occasion, were visibly agitated whenever the ball went near either goal, agitation that transformed itself into loud cheers when the ball was cleared.'

São Paulo are the Charles Miller gang, young British and Germans staffing the European banks and utilities. Paulistino are the team of the local oligarchs, the scions of hard-nosed coffee dynasties and hard-arsed cattle ranchers, the alliance of *café com leite*. Paulistino's president is Bento Pereira Bueno who just happens to be the state government's Minister of Justice; its squad is littered with the famous names of Paulista society. Together with the Europeans they are making themselves very rich.

São Paulo ran out the winners and Charles Miller accepted the trophy. Amid the backslapping, cavorting, exchanging of laurels and posies, drinking to winners and losers, the assembled gathering offered a toast to the ball and then bathed it in champagne.

Bathed in champagne, the football was irresistible to the Anglophile elites of turn-of-the-century Latin America. In 1895, two years after Alexander Watson Hutton's first AAFL competition, Buenos Aires had acquired an expanded first division and a newly created second division. By 1899 the city could sustain three divisions of competitive league football. In 1902 it was four. The leading teams continued to be British, and Lomas Athletic won the competition eight years on the trot. However, even Buenos Aires' sizeable British community could not on its own supply four divisions of football players. Within a decade of its emergence football was going native. The first truly Argentine institution to field a football team was the elite sports club in La Plata – *Gymnasia y Esgrima* (Gymnastics and Fencing). Gymnasia was founded in 1887 and first played football in 1901. In the first years of the new century the majority of the country's leading football clubs were created. River Plate (1901) and Boca Juniors (1905) were founded by immigrants in and around the docks of Buenos Aires. In the industrial suburb of Avellaneda, Racing Club was started by French migrants in 1903 while neighbours Independiente were a breakaway of Spanish-speakers from the British-owned and run City of London Stores sports club (1905). Crowds were beginning to touch four figures for the biggest games and *La Nación* began regular and comprehensive reporting as early as 1903.

Uruguayan football had trailed the development of the game in Argentina, for the country had been convulsed by two failed uprisings orchestrated by the predominantly conservative and rural Blanco party in 1897 and 1904. The rebels were comprehensively defeated by the Colorado government of the era. Finally freed from the dictates of war, the victorious and liberal Colorado President Batlle y Ordóñez set in motion a raft of progressive policies: the entrenchment of electoral democracy, the creation of a secular state, a massive expansion in public education and pensions and major public investments in economic infrastructure. Uruguay began to boom. Montevideo began to grow, acquiring a new middle class and a new working class in the process. A judicious mixture of economic surpluses and state redistribution kept politics peaceful; exclusion from power was no longer a matter of life or death for electoral losers. The permanent but peaceful conflict between the Colorados and Blancos, the social division of Montevideo into middle and working classes, Hispanics and Italians, *criollo* and immigrant, found its footballing expression through the transformation of an old club and the creation of a new one. Nacional was founded by Hispanic students at the University of Montevideo in 1899. It was always a self-consciously nationalist project, challenging the hegemony of the British at their own game. Nacional took the colours of the nation's *libertador*, Jose Artigas, and sited their ground on the same land as Artigas's own house. In 1903 the Uruguayan FA asked the team to represent the nation in a game in Buenos Aires against Argentina. The Uruguayans won 3–2. Nacional are still celebrating. They acquired their eternal enemy when CURCC (Central Uruguayan Railway's Cricket Club) was transformed into Peñarol, a process completed in 1913 with an official name change and the abandonment of English for official business.

The hold of the British in São Paulo was beginning to dwindle in the first decade of the twentieth century, but in Rio it was all but swept away by the creation of a wave of truly Brazilian elite clubs. In 1897 Oscar Cox, a Swiss-Brazilian, son of one of Rio's richest families, who had studied and played football in Lausanne, returned to the city. Initially Cox persuaded the Rio Cricket and Athletic Association to play football but, dissatisfied by their lack of zeal, created the leading social and sports club of the super rich in Rio: Fluminense. Mário Filho, the leading Brazilian football writer of the 1930s and '40s, described the club:

In order to join Fluminense, the player had to live the same life as Oscar Cox, Félix Frias or Horácio da Costa Santos … all established men, chiefs of firms, first-rate employees of big companies, sons of rich fathers, educated in Europe, used to spending money. It was a hard life. Those who did not have access to a constant supply of ready money couldn't stand the strain.[20]

Sports clubs were pivotal locations for elite socializing; pre-match teas and post-match dinners were added to the social round of weddings, receptions, soirées and dances held in Brazil's splendid new club houses. Fluminense became the benchmark of sophistication and connectedness. The wooden stands and pavilions at its Laranjeiras ground were filled by the wealthiest Rio families, in their smartest clothes. Gentlemen sported a discreet striped band in club colours on their straw hats, a direct echo of English public schools. The team would offer a solemn bow to a crowd that responded with 'Hip Hip Hurrah'. In emulation of and in competition with Fluminense, Botafogo and América were both founded in 1904 and both put out a football team. Flamengo Rowing Club had at the time remained staunchly anti-football, routinely deriding the game as unmanly prancing, but football had become so central to the social life of Rio's elites that when a breakaway group of players from Fluminense were looking for a home in 1911, Flamengo Football Club was created. The Fluminense that Filho described did not last long; the intensity of competition and the demands of the game were too much for the ageing playboys of the Carioca aristocracy. Rio's clubs increasingly recruited from the faculties of medicine, law and engineering at the city's university whose students offered an appropriate mix of rural aristocrats, urban bourgeoisie, eligible bachelors and reasonable strikers. São Paulo's leading footballers before the First World War included building contractors, merchants, engineers, army officers, doctors, bankers, accountants and professors.

The First World War destroyed Britain's economic hold on Latin America. The cost of the war and the debts accumulated saw most of the country's overseas investments liquidated. Britain's cultural and sporting capital were absorbed and appropriated even sooner. In Argentina the AFA, which had first published the rules of football in Spanish in 1903, adopted it as the official language of the organization in 1905. In 1912 it finally Hispanicized its name becoming the Asociación del Football Argentina, but it was not until 1934 that football finally became *fútbol*. The Uruguayan FA moved in step with its bigger neighbour, changing over to Spanish in 1905. Many of the remaining British clubs in Buenos Aires abandoned football whose exclusivity and social status appeared to be declining by the season; polo, cricket and rugby offered a reassuring differentiation between themselves and *porteños* of all classes. *Criollo* football had arrived and the Englishness of football on the Río de la Plata began to dwindle to what it is now: a linguistic and lexical residue. Offside is still *offside*, a throw-in is a *lateral* and English can still be heard when Liverpool in Montevideo, Everton in Viña del Mar, or Newell's Old Boys in Rosario take the field.

The British also initiated international football in the region. As early as 1888 the British were organizing games between Buenos Aires and Montevideo XIs to celebrate Queen Victoria's birthday. The Scottish tea magnate Sir Thomas Lipton was so taken by the game between Argentina and Uruguay played in the first years of the century that he donated a trophy to be awarded to the winner of the now annual games between the two countries. Argentina first sent a team to Brazil in 1907 and, before the First World War, teams travelled to play selections from the leagues in Rio and São Paulo. In 1910 the Argentinian FA organized a tournament to celebrate one hundred years of autonomous government in the country which is considered to be the first, if unofficial, South American Championship. Over 10,000 people came to watch Argentina beat Uruguay 4–1. But the biggest crowds of all were for the visits of English teams. Despite the immense distances and potentially hazardous economics of a Latin American tour, Southampton (1904), Nottingham Forest (1905), a South African XI (1906), Everton and Tottenham (1909), Corinthians (1910 and 1913), Swindon Town (1912) and Exeter City (1914) all made the transatlantic crossing. The English teams flattered the emergent football cultures of the region with their presence. The matches offered local players their sternest tests and a benchmark by which to measure their rapid progress – in particular they seem to have been a lesson in the virtues of teamwork and fearless heading. The games were deemed sufficiently important for the very elite of political, economic and social life to attend. Southampton and South Africa played before the President of the Argentine Republic General Julio Roca and the Minister of War. The cream of Rosario society and the surrounding pampas aristocracy turned out for Nottingham Forest, making the game the centrepiece of a high society soirée.

The proximity of Chile, Paraguay and Bolivia to the football fever of the southern cone created a second wave of football in Latin America just behind the leading edge of the Río de la Plata. Chile, which had the biggest British presence of the three, was the quickest to develop. In the early 1890s Anglo and mixed sports clubs were playing the game in the port of Valparaíso and soon after in the capital city Santiago and in Viña del Mar as well. A Chilean federation was in place by 1895. In Paraguay William Paats, a Dutch PE instructor at the teachers' college in Asunción, arrived with the nation's first ball in the late 1890s. In

1902 he and other enthusiasts founded the club Olimpia and then Guarani (founded in 1903 and named after the indigenous peoples of the country) provided some opposition. The first known competitive game, played intriguingly on a country estate outside of the city, took place in 1903. A national federation and an Asunción-based league followed in 1906 by which time all of the key teams in contemporary Paraguayan football had been established: Nacional, Libertad and Cerro Porteño (named after the site of a Paraguayan victory over the Argentinians in the nineteenth-century War of the Triple Alliance). Bolivia, which in almost every other respect would have been described as behind or underdeveloped relative to the others, was equally prompt in its embrace of football. In 1896 the Oruro Royal Club was founded by a mixture of British and local elites; a year later Northern Sport and Nimbles were formed by workers on the La Paz to Antofagasta railway. Despite the desperately thin air of Bolivia's high mountain cities, clubs multiplied and competitive football was a regular feature of the La Paz social scene.

In the Andean nations, whose British connections were weaker than those in the south of the continent, football arrived later, was slower to develop, and remained in its coastal enclaves for longer. In Venezuela and Colombia, where American economic and political influence was greatest, baseball proved a plausible competitor to football, further slowing its popularization. In 1899 in the Ecuadorian port of Guayaquil, European-educated students at Olmedo School formed Guayaquil Sports Club. Two months later Juan Alfredo and Roberto Wright, returning from their English education, brought the first stitched leather ball back to the country and by 1908 the city could boast a small organized league. But the capital Quito remained oblivious to the charms of the sport until well into the 1930s. The story in Colombia is not dissimilar. There the first set of football rules in Spanish was published in the Caribbean port of Barranquilla in 1906. This created a stir of interest sufficient to support regular competitive football in the city, but the impossible geography of the country and the contempt of the elites of Bogotá, Cali and Medellín for coastal society and its fashions restricted football to Caribbean Colombia; the country would only acquire a national football federation let alone a national league in 1924. Peru, where the port of entry for football was also the capital city and where unlike the other Andean nations there was a significant British expatriate community, acquired the strongest football culture in the region. The British were playing football at their sporting clubs like Lawn Tennis and Lima Cricket and Tennis at the start of the 1890s. The local elites of the city had adopted the game by the end of the decade. Uniquely in the Andean nations, the urban poor were almost as quick to join in, their efforts coalescing in the La Victoria *barrio* where they formed Alianza Lima in 1901. Consequently Lima's football league was a vibrant and active sporting institution before the First World War – but the complete absence of internal communications with the Amazonian basin and highlands of the country left it as an isolated island of sporting modernization.

In all of these societies football changed from being the game of the British to the game of the *criollo* elite. But what distinguished the Latin American experience from the rest of the world is that the game changed from being the mere pastime of the select few to the obsession of the urban masses more quickly and comprehensively than anywhere else. This compressed timetable of football's social diffusion was driven by a combination of very rapid urbanization and immigration experienced by Latin America's key metropolises in the decade before the First World War. In 1869 Buenos Aires had a population of just 178,000; it tripled by 1895 and on the eve of the war it was a city of over 1.5 million people. Rio touched a million and São Paulo's population increased twenty-fold over the same period. In Argentina the bulk of the new urban populace were immigrants, especially Italians and East European Jews. Italians went to Brazil too, joining a stream of Germans, Portuguese and Japanese. These urban demographic cauldrons were superheated by the arrival of the new technologies of urban living in Latin America: mechanized factories, subway systems, trams, municipal gas and electricity supplies, parks and recreational grounds. Sam Allen, the manager of the 1912 touring side Swindon Town, registered the social spread of the game in Argentina and Uruguay:

I have never seen such enthusiasm for the game as shown by the two republics and everywhere one sees the hold it has taken on the people. Boys on the street, on the seashore, down alleys, soldiers on barrack grounds – all have the fever and when I say that one firm alone in Buenos Aires has just given an order in England for 5,000 of one particular make of football the immense attraction the game has out there will be realised.[21]

In this era in Buenos Aires over 300 clubs were playing in numerous unofficial and ad hoc proletarian leagues outside the mainstream AFA organization. Moreover, the newspaper reports of the era indicate that the gentlemanly amateurism and the ethos of fair play that British and Argentine elites had found a useful social lubricant were being swiftly abandoned by the new working-class and immigrant football of the *barrios*. At the bottom end of the social scale football served as an instrument of power and revenge. Teams that arrived late at matches would be forced to forfeit the game, however plausible their excuses. The neutrality of referees was often questioned, the safety of visiting players rarely assured. As for the ever increasing numbers coming just to watch, one observer wrote, 'the behaviour of the Argentinian crowd was not an example of an educated public; they were booing and whistling constantly and a number of the crowd descended to even lower depths.'[22] Charles Miller, reporting back to his old school magazine on the São Paulo football scene in 1904, captured the instantaneous gusto with which football had been taken up by Rio's poor:

You will be surprised to hear that football is the game here. We have no less than sixty or seventy clubs. A week ago I was asked to referee a match of small boys, twenty a side. I told them that it was absurd them playing twenty a side; but no, they wanted it. I thought of course, the whole thing would be a muddle, but I found I was very much mistaken. They played two and a half hours and I only had to give two hands [warnings for foul play] ... even for this match 1,500 people turned up. No less than 2,000 footballs have been sold here within the last twelve months; nearly every village has a club now.[23]

This downward social diffusion was accelerated in Brazil by the widespread emergence of factory teams. Managers and technicians at British-owned companies on the edge of the greater Rio de Janeiro area were isolated from the main concentrations of upper-class footballers in the city centre. Often unable to muster two full elevens they were playing informal games with their Brazilian workers by the turn of the century. In 1904 the textile firm Companhia Progresso Industrial based in the northern Rio suburb of Bangu formalized the practice, establishing its own team of Englishmen, Brazilians and Italians and entering the Carioca Championships. Although paternalistically managed there was no separation of classes and races at their social club or in the ground. Bangu's football team proved reasonably successful on the pitch and a powerful instrument of labour management off it. In 1908 the América Fabril factory in Pau Grande followed suit and more followed. At all of these clubs the team was made up of worker-players. While they were formally employees of the company with regular factory jobs, they were actually semi-professionals combining light work duties with training and playing. Bangu, Pau Grande and the others opened up the hitherto exclusively white world of organized football to the first wave of black and mulatto players. But – factory teams or not – footballers of colour were coming. You just had to look. Members of the 1914 Exeter City touring party, who watched street football in Rio, were 'astonished to discover that the match was between junior teams of about 18 to 20 years old. They were all niggers, as black as your hat, and most of them playing in bare feet.'[24]

Exeter City soon departed and returned to a Europe now engulfed in the first round of its long and bloody civil war. The third Corinthians tour party bound for Brazil, bristling with army officer reservists, was forced to turn round, head home and fight. While Europe was riven and divided, South America, untouched by the carnage, was thinking about unification. Football unification at any rate. The Uruguayan Héctor Rivadavia Gómez, a long-standing MP for the Colorado party, president of Montevideo Wanderers and head of the Uruguayan league, had been making the case and building support for such an idea since 1910. In 1916 the clumsily named CONMEBOL (Confederacíon Sudamericana de Fútbol), the first continental football association – almost forty years in advance of its European equivalent UEFA – was founded during an international tournament organized by the Argentinian Football Association in Buenos Aires. As with its predecessor tournament in 1910, the final pitted Argentina against Uruguay.

The match was never played as the small Gimnasia ground was over-whelmed by people – more tickets had been sold than it could possibly hold. When it became apparent that there would be no football spectators are reported to have taken the naphtha oil from the lamps of carriages waiting behind the main stand. They set the place ablaze leaving only the central pavilion unscathed. And still 10,000 people came on a working day to see the rematch.

IV

Unruly games of football were first reported in Switzerland as early as the 1850s in games between Swiss and English students. Attracted by the country's Alpine scenery, burgeoning wealth and influential banking and engineering industries, many young Englishmen attended elite private schools and technical colleges in Switzerland and stayed to work in the new financial, trading and industrial centres of Lausanne, Geneva and Zurich. In francophone Switzerland the Lausanne Football and Cricket Club, established in 1860, appears to be the earliest sports club in Switzerland. It was followed in 1869 by football teams based on the exclusive École de la Châtelaine in Geneva and private schools in Lausanne. In German-speaking Switzerland, St Gallen were the first football club, founded in 1879. Tom Griffiths, an English biology student and Blackburn Rovers fan, helped establish Grasshopper-Club in 1886. They played, and still do, in Blackburn's blue and white. By the turn of the century nearly all of Switzerland's significant clubs had been created. The Swiss Football Association was founded in 1895, a national championship based on regional leagues began in 1898, and in 1904 they were a founder member of the world governing body FIFA.

Switzerland's place in global football has, since this era, depended upon its traditional virtues of neutrality and secrecy. Both FIFA and UEFA have made their headquarters there. Switzerland's war-time neutrality meant that it was the only European country that could feasibly take on hosting the first post-war World Cup, in 1954. But in the years before the First World War the Swiss were, alongside the British, the great educators, travellers and proselytes of European football. Barcelona were founded by the Zurich-born Hans Kamper. Henry Monnier, the son of a French Protestant banking family, received his commercial and football education in Geneva and Liverpool before returning to France where he founded Sporting Club de Nîmes. Walther Bennsemann, the son of a German Jewish doctor, attended a Swiss private school and then returned home to found Karlsruher SC at the tender age of fifteen. In the course of a trans-European career of travelling and working he founded clubs in other parts of Germany and in Strasbourg before finally settling down to create and publish Germany's first, and still its leading, football journal, *Kicker*.

The Swiss were also instrumental in establishing and sustaining early football in Italy. Franz Cali, who captained the first Italian international team, was educated in Lausanne, and Vitorio Pozzo, who founded Torino and coached the Italian national side to two World Cup victories, spent two years in Switzerland in 1908 and 1909 studying business and languages and playing regularly for Grasshopper's reserve side. Swiss expatriates staffed the teams of northern Italy's leading clubs, especially at Torino, Internazionale and Genoa.

While the Swiss helped diffuse football in the West, it was the contribution of Central Europe and the core lands of the Austro-Hungarian Empire that spread the game to the otherwise inaccessible Balkans. The Central Europeans also did what neither the Swiss nor the Low Countries could manage before the First World War: they created an entrenched popular football culture in which the game was played by a broad spread of the social scale and which could draw on growing and passionate crowds. It was from this base that Central Europe would go on to become the most innovative force in inter-war European football. This success rested on the massive concentration of football in just three cities – Vienna, Budapest and Prague. Vienna was the centre of the British presence in Central Europe where a large diplomatic staff, British banks, and trading and engineering companies created a significant British community. The first game of football took place on 15 November 1894 between the already established Vienna Cricket Club and a team recruited from among the Scottish gardeners of the Rothschilds' estate who were kitted out in the family's racing colours. Vienna Cricket soon lost its English majority, if not their ethos, and played football as Wiener Amateure from 1911. The gardeners called themselves First Vienna and the club continues to play.

The impact of the British presence was magnified by Vienna's footballing contacts with the rest of the Austro-Hungarian Empire. The bizarrely Anglicized *Der Challenge Cup* was established by members of Vienna Cricket in 1897, who immediately threw the tournament open to clubs from across the empire, although in practice this meant just Prague, Budapest and Vienna. The competition attracted considerable interest and social standing. The internal imperial rivalries at this time were being made more acute by the growing politics of nationalism and secessionism in the Habsburg lands, giving an edge and a dynamism to the early development of Central European football. To these powerful ingredients of football development Vienna added two more. First, the Viennese working class acquired its own standard bearer when in 1898 the employees of a hat factory created Wiener Arbeiter FK, and though forced the following year to change their name to the less obviously proletarian Rapid Wien, they provided a solid working-class component to the mix. Second, British teams and British trainers, like Jimmy Hogan, came to Vienna with great regularity. As in Latin America they provided benchmarks, incentives and role models. Oxford University toured in 1899, Southampton in 1900, the Corinthians in 1904. In 1905 both Everton and Spurs made the trip, their game against each other attracting a record crowd of 10,000. The England team came in 1908 and, most exceptional of all, the visit of Sunderland in 1909 saw Wiener AC beat the English professionals for the first time – 2–1. Two years later Vienna had acquired its own football league.

Hungarian football had started as an adjunct to gymnastics in the city's gymnasiums in the late 1880s. In 1885 Újpest Sport TE was the first organized football team to spring from one of those gyms. Liberal nationalist defectors from a hard-core conservative Habsburg gym created the Athletic Club of Budapest in 1888 which would become better known as MTK and acquired members, players and fans dispro-portionately drawn from among the city's intellectuals and Jews. MTK's eternal class and sporting enemy, Ferencváros, was established in a working-class suburb of the city in 1899. Two years later the city could field thirteen clubs in the first Hungarian championship. Like Vienna, Budapest's football was open to the urban poor. Thus despite the country's relative economic backwardness crowds and quality were high enough for Ferencváros to take the plunge and build a new football stadium in 1911. They were closely followed by MTK, who built an even bigger stadium the following year for up to 20,000 spectators.

In Prague the Czechs had taken to their own version of nationalist gymnastics – *Sokol* – very early. Invented by a Dr Tyrs in 1862, Sokol freed the Slavs from German dominance by providing an alternative to their Teutonic *Turnen* gymnastics. Sokol clubs created a sense of soli-darity among Czechs and as with their German counterparts formed a key component of a nascent Czech civil society. Football, which appeared insufficiently Slavic at first glance, therefore began outside of the gymnasiums. One of the first sightings was a team put out by the

Rudderklub Regatta Sailing Club against the visiting Viktoria Berlin in December 1893. For all its nationalist cant Sokol had its roots in Turnen and bore its regimented and authoritarian imprint. For the Czech intellectuals and educated young men who trained in the city's Sokol gyms the winds of modernity were blowing from London and Vienna, where football was the sporting route to the modern world and independence. Slavia Prague were the leading football side of the era and functioned as a sports club, a Czech-language society, a literary club and a gathering place for liberals, nationalists, students and intellectuals. Formed in 1892, they adopted a red and white kit with a red star – the colours of the flag of Czech independence – and could boast the presence of a young Edvard Beneš on their team sheet. Beneš would go on to be the most significant politician in inter-war Czechoslovakia. The city's other main club, Sparta, was established the following year and immediately attracted significant working-class support. Together the two teams provided the mainstay of a Prague league, up and running in the late 1890s, and they also provided the squad that faced a visiting English FA XI in 1899 – an occasion that signified the rapidity of football's development in Prague and to the delight of the nationalist intelligentsia placed the Czechs on a par with the other free nations of Europe. Czech national aspirations were sufficiently developed for the Bohemian FA to apply for membership of FIFA and for it to seek to take an independent team to the 1908 Olympics, but the power of Austria and its fear of real secession were sufficient to keep the Czechs out of both. Hungary, whose status *vis-à-vis* Vienna was considerably higher, fielded an independent Hungarian national team and in 1902 the Hungarians played increasingly well-attended matches with the Austrians.

The relationship between patterns of urbanization and industrialization and the arrival of football is not linear, but the cases of Eastern Europe and the Balkans certainly suggest a strong relationship between the two. By 1900 Northern and Central Europe had established the game as a popular recreation among expatriate and local elites in the biggest cities and the game was even beginning to spread beyond these confined social enclaves. Prague, Vienna and Budapest had taken to the game with alacrity, but the small towns and rural hinterlands of these core Habsburg lands were bereft of football, and east of the Oder and south of Vienna it had hardly begun at all. When the game did arrive in the

Balkans and the East it was truly tiny bands of young and wealthy enthusiasts that sustained it.

It was in Greece, the country in the region with the strongest economic ties to Britain, where football arrived first in the region. In the early 1890s, in central Athens, British bankers, Anglican priests and Belgian military attachés started playing football with upper-class Greeks, many of whom had studied in England. Rules were available in Greek in 1895 and through the Hellenic Athletic Federation football acquired a national bureaucracy of sorts in 1899. Together they seem to have concocted some of the characteristic features of Greek football – petulance, indiscipline and trouble. At the 1906 'intermediate' Olympics held in Athens, the football semi-final pitted an Athenian XI against a Salonika XI. The game never made it beyond half-time as it dissolved into fighting among players and crowd. The Athenians then played the Danes in the final and after taking a 9–0 pasting in the first half refused to show up for the second. However, the passion the game aroused was sufficient to support the formation of a small Athenian league in 1905. Panhellenic – the club of expatriates and Anglophile rich Greeks – was joined by teams from the university, the army and the naval cadet school.

In the Yugoslav provinces of the Habsburg Empire, football was first reported in the 1870s, in the Croatian port of Zadar among British sailors and in the city of Rijeka where British workers were employed building a factory. But with no significant expatriate community of Britons to sustain interest, the first organized games in the Balkans did not begin until almost twenty years later. In 1896 Hugo Bale, the son of a Jewish tailor in Belgrade, returned home from Vienna with a football and a taste for the game acquired while away. Kickabouts under uncertain and possibly ill-remembered rules were played at the city's hippodrome. When a set of rules did arrive the first game was played on a field in the centre of the city, in the shadow of the tower that the Ottoman occupiers had used for internment and torture. The juxtaposition was unintentional perhaps, but it offered an unmistakable contrast that defined Belgrade's shifting horizons: from Istanbul to Vienna, from feudal satrapy to an emergent modern metropolis. Implanted, as Bale's origins suggest, among the artisans and middle classes of Belgrade, they were soon joined by university students who flocked to football. It was not the minority game of the upper middle class or aristocracy, but spread rapidly among the dynamic, nationalist classes below, quickly yielding clubs like Greater Serbia, Serbian Sword and Hawks. A similar process of late but rapid development saw the Croatian cities of Zagreb and Split take to the game with equal relish. In Zagreb the Sokol gymnastic clubs created a football section called HASK in 1903; by 1911 the best players of Belgrade, Zagreb and Split were pitted against each other. In clear parallel with the rising tide of nationalism and separatism in the region, Croatia, still a Habsburg province, created its own national football federation in 1912 and its first national championship in 1913.

Despite its apparent backwardness and extreme eastern location, Romania was just as quick to take up football. It first arrived in the city of Arad in 1888 where a local paper considered it newsworthy enough to report seeing '... a couple of youths running with a ball on the empty ground outside of the town'. Two years later the English-educated dentist Iuliu Weiner returned to the town with the enthusiast's usual kitbag: a ball, a set of rules and the zeal of the convert. With many other young men retuning to Arad and Timisoara from educational sojourns in Switzerland, Vienna and Budapest, where they had been exposed to the game, football clubs began to form; the first club in Arad was established in 1899, although the grasp of the game's rules was perhaps still uncertain as the club's inaugural match was played with four referees. In addition to this Central European zone of influence, Romania began to acquire a footballing infrastructure further east, in the capital city Bucharest and in the oil fields of Ploieşti where substantial British, American and German communities had arrived. With active support from King Carol I the Romanian FA was established in 1909 and a national competition followed. The limits of the nation's game were illuminated in 1911 when nine-man Olimpia Bucharest lost the title to United Ploieşti. Olimpia could not field two schoolboys whose parents would not give them permission to miss college. Football, in the end, was still the ludicrous hobby of a bizarre band of foreigners, students and teenage boys.

The last areas of Eastern Europe in which football developed were Poland and Bulgaria. Poland was almost totally bereft of British sporting influences before the turn of the nineteenth century; it was only in the textile-manufacturing city of Łódź that English managers and workers appear to have introduced football. The limited British presence was a function of Poland's political situation, for there was no Polish nation-state. The Poles were divided up among the German, Russian and Austro-Hungarian empires. All forms of independent Polish organization were treated with political suspicion and some cultural derision by the Germans and Russians. The more open and tolerant rule of the Habsburgs in the south of what is now Poland provided both the route and the context for the emergence of football, centring on Kraków where the first Polish football teams were formed: Cracovia and Wisła Kraków in 1906. Both were composed of students and youths from among the city's middle classes, and Wisla particularly were associated with the struggle for Polish independence – the club's kit sported the emblematic White Star on their strip. However, like the formation of a Polish nation-state, the creation of a Polish national league and football association would have to await the acid solvent of the First World War to weaken and then dissolve the hold of the three Eastern European empires on the nation.

Bulgaria remained under the sway of Istanbul and the Ottoman sultanate until the final decisive battles of the War of Independence in 1908. The country was subject to a Turkish ruling class that treated football with political and theological distaste, officially discouraging it like their superiors in Istanbul. But the antiquated and reactionary state machine of Ottoman Bulgaria could not resist the tide of modernity sweeping across Europe. Desperate for trained educational staff in its new schools, the Bulgarians imported Swiss teachers in the late 1890s and one of them, George de Regibus, first brought a football to the country in 1896. Despite his and other expatriates' enthusiasm, the capital Sofia only acquired its first football club in 1912; but too late. The Balkan war (1912–13) and then the First World War effectively terminated Bulgarian football development until the early 1920s.

The dynamism of football in Latin America and Central Europe at the end of the century had many sources, but two elements were common to both football cultures: the early leakage of the game from the feet of the urban elites to those of the urban poor – and, as a consequence of this, the emergence of powerful local collective identities around football clubs. In both regions, football was overwhelmingly concentrated in single cities and football rivalries coalesced around the axes of ethnicity, class and neighbourhood. In Italy and Spain (and to some extent Portugal whose rates of urbanization and industrialization were slower), the working classes did not gain access to football as either players or mass crowds until after the First World War. Instead of mimicking the class divisions of society, the emotional and cultural mainsprings of early football in the Western Mediterranean were based on regional and urban identities. In Portugal footballing rivalries were at their strongest between north and south, Oporto and Lisbon. In Italy they arose from conflicts between the expatriate and Italian urban bourgeoisie within cities or between regions and cities; in Spain politics and football began to crystallize as a conflict between the forces of Castilian centralism and the ethnic, linguistic and occasionally secessionist nationalists of Catalonia and the Basque country.

That football, indeed any sport, should mobilize such social energies in the Western Mediterranean would from the vantage point of the late nineteenth century appear unlikely. The region was a sporting desert. The Italian and Spanish rural aristocracies were significantly less urbanized than their northern counterparts. As such they did not provide a pool of potential athletes in the cities for modern sport. Rather in the countryside residences, the landowning classes were preoccupied with hunting, shooting and fencing. In the cities of Spain commercial bullfighting had become an entrenched feature of urban life, but it was always closer in ethos to the fiestas and games of small towns and villages and did not offer the possibility of mass participation. Indeed physical exercise of any kind did not seem to preoccupy the Spanish elites. King Alphonse XIII did set up a school at the University of Madrid in 1883 to train physical instructors, but it was closed owing to lack of funds in 1892. The army's engineering corps, headquartered in Guadalajara, managed to sustain their own institute there for only two years. It was as late as 1911 that Captains Salazar and Delkeito were dispatched to Sweden to investigate Ling gymnastics and its use in military training. Even so, it took until 1919 for the army to acquire a school of physical education and provide some training for its desperately unhealthy conscripts. The royal house aside, football would be nurtured in Spain without the help of the state.

In Italy, matters were little better, although a less rural aristocracy offered more support and patronage of sport in general and football in particular. The Italian state made physical education a compulsory element of schooling only in 1909, over forty years after the idea was first proposed in parliament. In any case the government failed to fund, monitor or enforce the decree. When football did arrive it faced no competition from other sports and amid the small elite of upper-class youth disconsolately hanging around the few small gymnasiums of the era it found a pool of players with time and energy to burn.

By a quirk of geology the first football played in Spain was in the heat and dust of Andalusia. One of the poorest, most rural, most backward regions of nineteenth-century Spain, Andalusia was also home to the country's richest copper deposits. The Spanish government, as ever desperate for cash, sold the mining rights to the British company Rio Tinto for a song in the 1860s. The company made the small port city of Huelva its base and with imported technicians and local labourers constructed Spain's first railway line, 60 kilometres into the interior to where the mines were located. More British managers and adventurers arrived to work and run the mines and the railways and to provide other services in Huelva, and from the early 1870s a small but thriving community of Britons made this corner of Spain their home. A British garrison was posted to the town in the 1870s to protect British investments after the violence and chaos of the Carlist wars. In the visitors' book of an inn in Gaucín near Huelva, used by the garrison's officers, Captain W. F. Adams wrote in September 1874, 'Marched out of Huelva on Wednesday. Played foot-ball with some railmen for about an hour out. The only diversion we truly had.'[25] However it was not until 1889 that the British progressed beyond informal sporting practice with the creation of Spain's first sports club and first organized football team – Recreativo de Huelva. The club played its first game in Seville in 1890 against employees of the British-owned and -operated Seville Water Works at the Tabalda hippodrome. Such an early head start for Huelva did not translate into longer-term success. The laws of football economics are not infinitely elastic. The side made a couple of undistinguished appearances in the King's Cup competition in 1906 and 1907 and passed into Spanish hands. Without a significant local population to draw upon and off the transport map of Spain, Huelva disappeared from top-flight football for almost a century.

A better guide to the emergent footballing geography of Spain was the 1902 Coronation Cup. The tournament was held to coincide with and honour the coronation of King Alphonse XIII who was popularly known as a sports enthusiast, relishing hunting, riding and polo in equal measure. The five clubs that contested the tournament, held in the clipped and exclusive surroundings of Madrid's racecourse, were drawn from the three regions that have shaped modern Spanish political and football history: Athletic Bilbao from the Basque country; Barcelona and Espanyol from Catalonia; and from the capital New Madrid FC and Madrid FC, who would in a decade or so become Real Madrid. Add Valencia and the outpost of migrant Basques that became Atlético Madrid, and one has the teams that have won all but five of Spain's league titles. The kind of person who had the ear of Alphonse XIII and was privy to his party arrangements was the kind of person playing football in turn-of-the-century Madrid. The game had been informally played among the staff and pupils of the Institución Libre de Enseñanza, an elite college, many of whom would have received an education in England. From this milieu sprung the delightfully named Sky Football Club which included on its board the Count de La Quinta de la Enrajada, an Oxford graduate, horse breeder and owner of the Madrid hippodrome which hosted the tournament. Sky split in 1900, one wing forming New Foot-ball Club, the other forming Madrid FC. Both teams lost their opening and only games in the Coronation Cup, won by Athletic Bilbao. Madrid's time was yet to come. For the moment, it remained locked away on the cold landlocked sierras of Castille, overwhelmingly inward-looking, traditional and conservative. The leading zones of Spain's changing society were outward-looking and on the coast; that is where football not only emerged but prospered.

The Basque country in general and the port of Bilbao in particular was the initial pole of Spanish industrial development. The rich iron-ore mines of the region and the entrepreneurial instincts of the local merchant class provided the catalyst for the creation of an iron, steel and shipbuilding economy. With the Atlantic rather than the Mediterranean as its obvious point of reference, Bilbao had the country's most extensive contacts with Britain. Specialist miners from Sunderland in the north-east of England and shipbuilders from Southampton in the south worked in the Basque country from the early 1890s and commonly played football among themselves on the banks of the River Nevron. Many young *Bilbaínos* had studied in England and together they challenged the English migrants to a game in May 1894. Short press reports inform us that the locals lost by five goals in the first leg and in the rematch, attended by significant numbers, they went down 5–0. But that was enough; in 1898 the core of those pioneers formed Bilbao FC, while Athletic Bilbao was formed at the fashionable Café García in 1901. Both teams were now mixed British and Basque and two games were played in late 1901 and early 1902. The teams then combined to play a game in Bordeaux, which they won 2–0, and pulled in an extraordinary 3,000 spectators to the rematch at home where they scored seven goals without reply.

Bilbao FC disappeared but Athletic Bilbao went from strength to strength, winning four King's Cups in their first decade. English lessons aside, what imparted social and sporting energy to the club was its ethnicity and political awareness, practically and symbolically. Athletic's growth ran alongside the rise of modern Basque nationalism and its representative political party the PNV. The party drew upon the small businessmen and entrepreneurs that controlled the new Basque industrial economy. It was precisely this class that made up Athletic's hundred or so *socios* (paying club members) who between them were able to raise the astronomical sum of 98,000 pesetas to commission the country's first purpose-built football stadium. Opened in 1913, San Mamés or *La Catedral* was tangible proof of Basque sporting prowess, business acumen and precocious modernity. By now, Athletic had shed its British players, and the notion of *La Cantera* – the restriction of players to those of Basque stock – had already been informally announced.

While Athletic and the PNV, even at this early stage, had come to think of themselves as the authentic standard bearers for a unified Basque nation, their claims to hegemony were challenged politically and sportingly. In this context, regional and inter-city rivalries in the Basque country, when combined with the inflammable passions of a football game, began to turn nasty. Reports of Athletic's game with Club Ciclista de San Sebastián, the predecessor of Real Sociedad, said that the crowd had begun to taunt their visitors with 'demonstrations of hatred'. In 1916 the two teams met in a play-off for the final of the Basque championship. Two weeks before, Athletic had beaten Sociedad in Bilbao in a cauldron of noise, abuse and contested decisions. Negotiations over a neutral venue faltered, the Governor of Guipúzcoa refusing to host the match for fear of wider public disorder. Eventually the game was arranged for Vizcaya, a suburb of Bilbao, but Real refused to attend and forfeited the title. These rivalries reached a football peak in 1918 on the final day of the season. Real Sociedad played Athletic Bilbao in Atocha to which many Athletic fans travelled hoping to see their team secure the title. The game was abandoned on 83 minutes at 2–2 after a crunching collision between an Athletic forward and a Real Sociedad defender sparked a pitch invasion and attacks on the Bilbao players.

Like the Basque country, Catalonia possessed its own language, retained a clear sense of its distance from Spain and Spanish identity, was in conflict with Madrid and in the late nineteenth century underwent something of an economic and industrial boom. However, most of the Catalan bourgeoisie were considerably more conservative than their Basque counterparts and were initially appalled by any sporting activity that involved the display of even a hint of flesh. Consequently it was a mixture of foreigners and migrants from the rest of Spain that initiated football in the region. Most famously Hans Kamper, who had had a hand in creating FC Zürich in his Swiss home town, arrived in Barcelona in 1899. Initially intending to travel on, he remained and took a job as an accountant with a tram company through a contact of his uncle's. His initial attempt to rustle up a game with the members of the Sole Gym he frequented were rebuffed. Undaunted he published a short letter in the newspaper *Deportes*. The response was not overwhelming but it was enough to get started and Kamper and his band of Britons and Swiss created FC Barcelona.

In 1900 Barcelona acquired some tough sporting and ideological opposition in the shape of Espanyol. The club were formed by an engineering student, Àngel Rodríguez, in conscious opposition to Kamper's cosmopolitans, Espanyol's founding statutes declaring: 'We create this club to compete with the foreigners of FC Barcelona.' Like the Basque country, the declining standing of the Spanish state in Catalonia was shaped by its loss of the last of its overseas empire (the Philippines and Cuba to the USA in 1898) and the accurate perception that it was a hindrance rather than a help in the process of economic development. Catalan nationalism acquired political form through the right-wing Lliga Regionalista which began to win seats in the Cortés in the early part of the twentieth century. Catalonia's separateness and superiority were endorsed by the creation of a Catalan league in 1901 and a distinct Catalonian football association in 1904, both long in advance of any national equivalents. Over the next decade FC

Barcelona's crest acquired the cross of St Jordi – Catalonia's patron saint – and the red-and-yellow stripes of the Catalan national flag. Socially, it attracted the same kind of constituency that the Lliga had tapped into. Meanwhile, Espanyol, now Real Espanyol, had asked for and received royal patronage from Madrid.

The potency of regional identities in Spanish life was made apparent by football in the years before the First World War as the game spread further and more cities and regions acquired a focus of civic identity around their clubs: in Galicia, Deportivo La Coruña were founded in 1906, Sporting Gijón in 1905; in 1905 the city of Seville acquired a club of the same name, followed in 1907 by Betis. Similarly, Spanish football was already exposing the rivalry between the centre and the regions and the weakness of national institutions and identities. Although Spain was among the founder members of FIFA, its representative was not the Spanish FA, for no such organization existed. Rather Spain's representative was merely a member of Madrid FC with no national mandate from anyone. Indeed it took until 1913 for a single national Spanish football association to be created and another seven years before a Spanish national team took to the field. The sporting and political consequences of the struggle between nation and region would be with Spain for some time to come.

The Italian nation-state was created in 1861. However, the unification of the country as a constitutional monarchy under liberal Prime Minister Garibaldi was not matched by the creation of an effective nationwide state machine, nor could the ramshackle structure of Italian national government acquire widespread legitimacy or affection. The complete failure of Italian governments to introduce physical education into public schools or the armed forces was but one instance of this. Italy possessed only two institutions and cultural currents that had a national presence: catholicism and socialism. While both were eventually centrally engaged in national politics, neither took much interest in the development of sport. Indeed, in their most extreme forms, they were intensely suspicious of sport's social consequences. In that vacuum, the intense and enduring local identities, inter-city and intra-city rivalries of Italian politics and Italian football would hold sway.

The Catholic Church certainly had the organizational apparatus to shape sport in late nineteenth-century Italy. The need to find and tend

young souls and to establish a carapace of moral orthodoxy around
them before the temptations and heresies of the modern world descended
made youth work a central priority for the Catholic authorities. Sport
of all kinds was initially considered a baleful distraction from the rigours
of prayer and study, as was politics. However, it was clear that Italian
youth did want to play sport and thus in the hands of Father Giovanni
Semeria a restricted Catholic sports theology was fashioned. But there
were limits to the Vatican's enthusiasm. The discipline of repetitive
gymnastics – the callisthenic equivalent of saying the rosary – was
acceptable but cycling smacked of the future and the idea of mobile
peasants worries all theocracies. Football was Anglo-Saxon, unquestionably Protestant and beyond the pale.

Pope Leo XIII's *nonexpedit* decree of 1868 had instructed Catholics
to abstain from political activity in the new secular Italian state. The
decree was lifted in 1904 and sport provided an immediate flashpoint in
the new battlefields of church–state relations. Catholic gymnastic clubs
had applied to join the national federation of gymnastics. The secular
middle-class nationalists who ran the federation refused to accept their
application on the grounds that confessional organizations of any kind
could not be members. The row was sufficiently important that Prime
Minster Giolitti personally intervened in an effort to find some accommodation between the two sides. But the federation would not relent.
The now excluded Church responded by establishing its own national
network of sports clubs.

To its eternal cost, Italy's socialist movement was always intellectually
in advance of its working-class constituency. Indeed until the first decade
of the twentieth century there wasn't much of a working class to organize. In the absence of serious issues of industrial organization and economic struggle, the Socialists took a keen and early interest in questions
of culture, ideology and leisure. Among activists, the majority position
on sport was not merely negative but hostile. As late as 1909, *Avanti!* –
the closest thing to a Marxist tabloid that European socialism has created
– was calling on supporters to throw nails on the road to sabotage bike
races in an act of petulant class revenge and contempt for the ludicrous
and illusory circus of organized sport. The earnest cadres of the Socialist
Party's youth wing spent their 1910 congress decrying modern competitive sport as a degrading and exploitative spectacle that was con-
tributing to the degeneration of the people. More pragmatic socialist

commentators like Zibordi thought the movement should bow to the inevitable and accept the sports craze, but seek to make it more ideologically wholesome:

The generation under 20, entering a world of relatively good conditions, finding the way paved by the older citizens, neglects our organizations, associations and papers, giving itself excessively, uniquely and madly to sport . . . the bourgeoisie undoubtedly intends to spread through its newspapers the contagious microbe of feverish sporting infatuation, an illness far from the healthy sport practised as one of the aspects of human existence and vigorous youth.[26]

In the absence of state, church and socialism, Italian football was created in the most cosmopolitan, industrial cities of the country by a tiny band of British and Swiss businessmen, their Italian counterparts, enthusiastic aristocrats and bored students and upper-class schoolboys. Though the foreign contingent has long departed, the same class, in its post-industrial guise, has remained in control a century later. In 1893 the British Consul in Genoa initiated the creation of Genoa Cricket Club for the city's English and Scottish commercial communities. The arrival of the more cosmopolitan and evangelical all-rounder Dr James Spensley in 1897 led to rich Italians, Swiss and Austrians being admitted to the club. A football section was created and the multinational squad went on to win the first Italian national championship in 1898, though even by Italian standards the claim that it was a national event was threadbare: the three other teams all came from Turin. This Alpine city, on the country's northern edge, was at the heart of both its asymmetrical industrial revolution and football geography. The first game in the city was played in 1887, organized by the travelling businessman Eduardo do Bosio whose trade in optical products and lenses had taken him to England. He returned with a football and among his circle, both Italian and foreign, there was enough enthusiasm to create Ginnastica Torino, Internazionale Torino and FC Torino. In 1897 the privileged but bored youth of the D'Azeglio College emulated their elders by creating Juventus (from the Latin for youth) who played their first national championship game in 1900. By now they were joined by the other pole of Italian development, Milan. In 1899 Alfred Edwards and a group of wealthy British and Swiss businessmen established Milan Cricket and Football Club – now AC Milan – and broke Genoa's control of the national championship by winning their first in 1901.

Among the urban upper class, football began to grow in popularity. Club formation was marked by two key features. First, the relatively fast and dense growth of clubs in the north and their slow and sporadic formation in the south. Second, the creation of breakaway clubs in the big cities as a result of intra-bourgeois rivalries, which in turn spawned the nation's intense inter-city derbies and rivalries. Small English trading colonies provided the impetus for the formation of southern Italy's earliest clubs, Palermo in 1899 and Naples in 1904, while in the capital Rome army officers were instrumental in establishing Lazio in 1900. But beyond this advanced guard there was little depth to football in the *mezzogiorno* with some cities not establishing clubs until after the First World War (like Salerno founded in 1919 and Cagliari in 1920). More tellingly, no club south of Perugia played in the national championship until 1913. When clubs from the south did join in that year their inaccessibility and the absence of reliable transport links required both north and south to play in self-contained competitions each of which produced a finalist. Lazio, who won the southern half of the draw, were then summarily dispatched 6–0 by Pro Vercelli, a team from a small town in Piedmont.

In the absence of a serious threat from the south the early leaders of northern football were challenged by breakaways and rebels in their own backyard. In Turin the first wave of foreign gentlemen's clubs like Torinese and Ginnastica were challenged by the upstart youths of Juventus. The two older clubs were fused to create a solid expatriate bloc; of the twenty-five founder members of the club fifteen were Swiss, its first president was called Schonfeld, and its social cachet was sufficient to attract the Marquis of Ventimiglia and the Duke of Abruzzi, nephew of the King, to its ranks. The role of the Swiss in this era of Italian football cannot be underestimated. They provided the bulk of the Pro Vercelli squad, nine out of eleven in the case of the 1909 championship-winning team. In the same year there were seven Swiss players at Torino, five at Genoa, four at Milan and three at Juventus. The often inhospitable and stifling Anglophilia of AC Milan led to the formation of the breakaway club Internazionale, created in 1908 round a hub of Swiss members and players like Hermann Abei. In Genoa the success of Genoa Cricket and its overwhelmingly foreign membership saw two exclusively Italian clubs established to contest the field – Sampierdarense and Andre Doria – which would fuse after the Second World War to create Sampdoria.

This flicker of Italian nationalism in football was inflamed even further when in 1908 representatives of the gymnastic movement acquired a majority on the Italian Football Federation's governing council. The cabal immediately began to agitate over the power and role of foreigners in Italian football, and Milan, Genoa and Torino – all of whom insisted on fielding foreigners – were excluded from that year's national competition. In a strained compromise, indicative of the fundamental weakness of Italian ultra-nationalism, the ban on foreigners was rescinded in return for the official adoption of *calcio* as the name of the game rather than football: a symbolic victory based on an invented history.

VI

If the concatenation of industrialization, urbanization and commercial contacts with Britain were the sole determinants of the pace of a nation's football development, then France and Germany should surely have been among the leading football cultures on the eve of the First World War. Yet in both of the great Western European powers, while football was an established element of the sports scene it was by no means as widespread, organized or popular as it was in the smaller nations of Western Europe or in Latin America. In France cycling was the most popular and the most commercialized sport. Of the winter sports played, rugby was not merely the equal of football but in terms of participation and spectator-appeal marginally its superior. In Germany Turnen gymnastics remained the unofficial national sport; football operated in its ideological shadow. Perhaps most tellingly, despite the growth of the vast new industrial suburbs of Paris, the intense industrialization of the Ruhr and the geographical spread of manufacturing industry in both economies, football had barely touched the hearts or feet of the French and German working classes.

Modern sport in France was born of the nation's crushing defeat in the Franco-Prussian War in 1870. It was not simply the loss of Alsace-Lorraine that so bore down upon the French, it was the recognition, unambiguously, that in terms of military prowess, social organization and industrial strength, Prussia and the newly unified Germany of 1871 were more than France's match. One of the many confused and conflicting reactions to the war was the idea that France was beaten because it was weak – not in terms of infrastructure or equipment, but because French minds and bodies were weak, decadent and unsuited to the rigour of industrial war. The Germans by contrast were fortified by their disciplined nationalist gymnastics. In fear and emulation a French gymnastics movement came into being, overwhelmingly among middle-class nationalists who gave their clubs names like *La Revanche*, *La Patriote*, *Le Régénératrice* or simply *La France*. Events often began with public declarations of loathing for the Germans before proceeding to activities and routines that were strikingly similar to those performed in gyms across the Rhine.

Gymnastics, however, was never more than a minority pursuit; the marriage of German callisthenics and French nationalism was unconvincing to any but the most militaristic. In fact, the first popular sport in France was cycling. The Penny Farthing was a French invention. Despite its ludicrous appearance, crude mechanics and the sheer difficulty of riding the thing, young and wealthy Frenchmen were buying and racing them in the 1860s. The first organized race took place between Rouen and Paris in 1869 and by the late 1870s a small semi-professional circuit of races and riders had developed, epitomized by bourgeois young men like H. O. Duncan, the leading sprinter of the era, and Frédéric Charon, heir to an enormous grocery business. This bizarre subculture quickly adapted to the development of the modern bicycle, whose ease of use and mechanical efficiency were transformed by the introduction of chain-driven machines, with two wheels the same size and inflatable tyres. Thus transformed, the bike ceased to be a mere curio for the fanatic but a fantastically simple and efficient mode of transport. France took to two wheels faster and more enthusiastically then anywhere else. France's unique history of early but incomplete industrialization in the context of a largely rural society meant that the country possessed enough of an engineering industry to make the bikes, sufficient wealth to purchase the new machines, with a rural, dispersed population – very poorly served by railways – who couldn't get enough of them. In 1893 there were 130,000 bikes in France; by 1914 there were 3.5 million. As the market for bikes grew, the price steadily fell and thus the market expanded even further. Competition in the country's first modern mass-consumer industry was intense, and made even more so by the arrival of American manufacturers. In terms of either price or quality there was actually very little to distinguish different companies' bikes. The industry was therefore among the first to register the potential of sport sponsorship and advertising in pursuit of increased market share and from the 1890s onwards money was pouring into competitive cycling. Initially it was sprinting that the public flocked to, and banked velodromes sprang up in Paris and the other major cities of the country. The first in the capital was known as the Buffalo, built on the site of Buffalo Bill's circus. Appropriately there was never any question that cycling would be anything other than an unashamedly commercial and professionalized sport. The owners of the velodromes were in the business of delivering entertainment to their public. However, while the connoisseur might remain endlessly fascinated by the adrenalin and intricacy of cycle sprinting, most of the public did not. The velodromes experimented with circus-style racing, introducing the curiosities of black cyclists, women, acrobats and animals. Then they switched to ludicrously long endurance tests, races that would last for days on end only to be decided in the final straight. But the future of cycling was not in the velodromes, it was on the roads. While the urban working class watched cycling, the provincial middle classes, farmers and peasants did the cycling themselves; membership of the Touring Club of France topped 125,000 in 1910. In a country with such a dispersed population, road racing offered a uniquely suitable spectator sport. Beginning with the Bordeaux–Paris race of 1891 and culminating in the creation of the Tour de France in 1903, French cyclists, the French sporting press and the cycling industry created modern cycle road racing as a sport and a spectacle. By 1919 around one-third of the entire population would watch part of the Tour. Cycling was now unquestionably the national summer sport of France; its winter equivalent had not yet been established.

If one had picked up a copy of the leading sports periodical of the era *L'Auto* any time between October and March in the years before the First World War, one would have been reading about rugby on the front page a great deal more often than football. While middle-class nationalists had looked to Germany, and the peasantry and urban lower classes had taken to cycling, it was the young Anglophile, metropolitan elite that embraced English sports. Baron de Coubertin, founder of the Olympic movement, was one of many French aristocrats who believed that the survival of French nobility in the Third Republic required them to adopt some of the strategies of the more successful British aristocracy. Sport offered a domain in which the martial heritage of the nobility and its evident moral superiority could both flourish and be transmitted to the new bourgeois component of the French ruling classes. English sports would also toughen up the effete and over-intellectual products of the *lycée* system. The Parisian elite were the first to heed the call when students of the prestigious *lycées* Carnot, Rollin and Condorcet set up Racing Club in 1882 and their compatriots at the *lycée* St Louis created Stade Français in 1883. Racing based themselves in the Bois de Boulogne and possessed the clout and the bare-faced arrogance to fence in their grounds from the rest of the park. When they opened a sumptuous clubhouse in 1886, no lesser figure than the Minister of War General Boulanger was the guest of honour. Stade Français was no less gilt-edged, using the terrace of the Orangerie as their grounds before moving on to the exclusivity of Saint-Cloud. Sunday mornings offered a panorama of the young Parisian elite at play. As one society reporter wrote, 'What struck me was the real distinction of these young men, all of whom came from excellent families.'[27]

However, they were not playing football. Racing Club and Stade Français preferred rugby, rowing and track and field events and were instrumental in spreading rugby to the provincial *lycées* and universities. Despite these lofty origins, French rugby union, unlike in England, was democratized and popularized before the First World War, a development concentrated in south-west France where the English had a long-standing and significant presence in the wine industry and shipping. The small size of many towns in south-west France, and the relative openness of the class structure, saw clubs take on players from the lower middle classes and even skilled workers. Simultaneously clubs like Toulouse, Bayonne, Carcassonne and Béziers acquired substantial local followings. In Aquitaine and Languedoc the peculiar civic patriotism to which English team sports lent themselves was acquired by rugby before football. When Avitoan Bayonasi won the national championship in 1913 crowds were large, socially encompassing and festive.

On Sunday evening after a match large crowds would assemble in the Place du Théâtre, where the latest results would be chalked up on a large board as they came in and jeered or applauded as local prejudice or interest required. The large café on the square was owned by former player, Louis Saubion, who would give public demonstrations of how to heel a ball with the aid of a couple of chairs, and massaged the injured whilst feeding them a special cocktail of cinzano and cassis which was famous throughout the region.[28]

With the added attraction of a serious Paris vs. Bordeaux rivalry at the top of the game, rugby's national championship final became, the Tour de France aside, the country's most significant sporting event. The 1911 final between Bordeaux and Paris attracted an enormous crowd of 28,000, considerably larger than any football match had managed. Yet rugby also retained sufficient social cachet for many cabinet ministers to attend the final and the touts in the bars of Bordeaux could find punters willing and able to pay up to five times the face value for a ticket.

Football, or rather something approximating to it, was first played in France in Le Havre in 1872 by a collection of English Oxbridge graduates who retained the connection by playing in light and dark blue quarters, but without opposition it was hard for the game to flourish. The breakthrough came in 1891 with the creation of White Rovers by Paris-based Scots, and of Standard Athletic Club, founded by Paris-based Englishmen. Le Club Français, inspired by two *lycée* students who had played football at St Joseph's College in Dumfries, offered indigenous opposition the same year. With the gauntlet now thrown down, Racing Club and Stade had little option but to pick it up and begin to field football teams against them. In 1894, a laughably named national championship was played between six Parisian clubs.

Once started, the round ball kept rolling. Football clubs emerged in those parts of France that were most industrialized or had the most significant British and Swiss connections – for by now the Swiss were as enthusiastic proselytes as the British. Over a hundred football clubs had been formed by 1900, concentrated in Paris, the Channel ports, the northern industrial regions around Lille and Lens and in the south-east in Marseilles, Nîmes and Sète. In the north-east particularly, so much football was being played that an athletic administrator lamented that 'the public are becoming obsessed with the round ball at the expense of other forms of sport'.[29] But the north-east was not France; in the Massif Central no one was playing any kind of sport beyond antiquated folk games of skittles, and Bordeaux and Toulouse had no football clubs to speak of before the 1920s. The continuing division of French sports administration among rival secular and confessional, liberal and conservative wings, meant that, despite the foundation of FIFA on French soil and at French behest in 1904, there was no central French football association and no national league or cup. It would take the centralizing and modernizing imperatives of the First World War to drag rural and peripheral France into the twentieth century. Only then would French football acquire national coverage and a significant place in the national culture.

English ball games arrived in Germany among expatriate Britons and a smattering of educationalists and upper-class Germans in the early 1870s. The first record of football in Germany dates from 1874 when two teachers in Braunschweig, Konrad Koch and August Hermann, ordered a round ball from England out of curiosity. The ball duly arrived and they threw it among their grammar-school pupils, though it seems they continued to carry as well as kick the ball. Outside of this kind of informal schoolboy play the first formal clubs established to play football were founded in 1880 in Hanover (which shared a royal house with Britain until 1837) and Bremen, which had extensive trading links with the country. Neither survived for long and thus football was only properly and enduringly established, albeit as a minority pursuit, in Hamburg and Berlin in the late 1880s and early 1890s when FC Germania Berlin (1888), Viktoria Berlin (1889) and Hertha Berlin (1892) were created. The laws of the game were translated into German only in 1891 and by 1900 there were around 200 clubs, with Leipzig, Nuremberg and Stuttgart added to the key footballing cities of the country. The British were of course present as players and administrators including F. W. Moorman, former captain of the University of Wales, who went on to captain Strasbourg University AFC, and Archibald S. White, an English clergyman who served as the first president of the South German FA. But they were a small component of the 10,000 regular football players in the country by about 1900. These pioneering German footballers were predominantly from the upper-class elite and lower-middle-class white-collar occupations. The upper-class component were the usual Anglophile liberals from the big cities. After 1891 they were joined by a huge influx of the lower-middle-class young men – clerks, technicians, shop assistants and unskilled mechanics. The reform of the nation's trading and labour laws in that year opened the way for this class to play football as they were finally relieved of the burdens of Sunday working. The same could not be said for the German working class who despite some easing of the *Kulturkampf* being waged against them by the state remained bound to a six-day week. The German Social Democats and their trade union allies were like their Italian counterparts among the most suspicious of bourgeois sports. Their own brand of super-orthodox Marxism and class war made any engagement with the burgeoning football culture unthinkable. The social location and employment of white-collar Germany brought them into much closer contact with the elites already playing the game. The prospect of not merely exercise but joining or establishing sporting clubs that would enhance their lowly social status was irresistible. The new football clubs of late nineteenth-century Germany aped the mores and fashions of their aristocratic betters, adopted the linguistic etiquette of polite society and craved the recognition and status that victory and medals offered.

The spread and the significance of football were limited in Wilhelmian Germany by the objection of the Catholic and Protestant churches to games-playing of any kind on the Sabbath – by then the norm – and the almost complete absence of the working class from football as either spectators or players, but most powerfully by the systematic and vocal opposition to the game mounted by advocates of the nationalist gymnastics movement. If modern French sport was born of the defeat of 1870, then Pan-German sporting culture grew from Prussian military defeats suffered two generations earlier when in 1806 Napoleon's armies decimated the Prussians at Jena and Auerstädt. The response of the Prussian state was a wholesale reform of the army, which threw open the ranks of commissioned officers to the best candidates from the middle classes and insisted upon a massive improvement in the physical condition and coordination of its conscripts, including the introduction of physical education in schools. But what kind of physical education would be appropriate? The answer to this was developed by the liberal nationalist Friedrich Ludwig Jahn who invented a form of distinctly Germanic nationalist gymnastics. Indeed so nationalist was his fervour that the Latin-rooted *gymnastik* was replaced by the more wholesome Germanic term *Turnen*. For Jahn, Turnen was not a sport but an alternative to sport. It was a system of physical exercises that was not oriented towards competition, efficiency or individual achievement but served as the grounding for a collective national enterprise of physical, spiritual and moral rebirth. Turnen captured the imagination of the German middle classes, who in the mid-nineteenth century were the mainstay of the movement for German political unification and reform. Across the German-speaking world *Turnvereine* multiplied, forming an essential set of nodes in the emerging network of organizations that constituted middle-class civil society. *Turnvereine* provided a meeting place, a source of identification and solidarity, and in their grand festivals they created a public arena in which the invented traditions of a new German nationalism could be displayed.

Initially the Turnen devotees referred to English sports in disdainful and Germanic qualifying terms: *Fussball ohne Aufnahme* and *Fussball mit Aufnahme* were 'football without picking-up' and 'football with picking-up'. But as the game became more popular in the country, more sophisticated arguments and criticism were required, none more caustic or extensive than those offered by one of Turnen's key ideologists, Otto Heinrich Jager, who published a polemic against football in 1898 subtitled 'The English disease'.[30] Jager considered the game to be without moral, physical or spiritual discipline, bereft of serious purpose and an incendiary tinderbox of grotesque individualism. These debates became all the more charged as Germany steadily began to shift to a more bellicose foreign policy, engaged in a naval arms race with the British and pursued African and other overseas imperial adventures. The Englishness of football and its apparent disregard for order made the game deeply subversive and suspect in some circles.

To counter this the Deutscher Fussball-Bund (DFB), which was founded in 1900 in Leipzig, began its programme of work with the Germanization of football language: captain became *Führer*, free-kick became *Frei-Tritt*, and goal turned to *Tor*. The DFB's founding document stressed both the patriotism and imperial utility of football and drew upon and offered descriptions of the game that emphasized this: 'Two parties of usually eleven fighters are in a state of war. The main task is to move a large leather ball into enemy territory . . . the majority of the army will follow behind.'[31] The DFB also attempted, like the Italians, to demonstrate a direct, if completely mythical, path from folk football games in medieval Germany to the present day.

The first national football championships were held in 1903 and won by Leipzig. They were a chaotic affair. The favourites Karlsruhe were thrown out at the semi-final stage after a fake telegram had told them that their game with Bohemians of Prague had been abandoned. On the day of the final itself no ball in a suitable condition for play could be found for half an hour and a meagre 500 people turned up to watch. In 1904 there was no tournament at all and 1905 did not look any more promising. However, that year's champions Germania Berlin received a telegram in April 1905 prior to a game with an English Amateur XI: 'His Imperial Highness the Crown Prince will arrive at 5.30 for the football competition.' And so he did, watching Germania win 3–2.[32] Such an expression of interest and approval from the Hohenzollerns helped lift the ideological opprobrium in which football had hitherto been held.

In the decade before the First World War, football steadily grew in importance, won favour and increasing popularity, although the 3,500 that saw Germania win the championship in 1905 would not be equalled until after the war. In 1910 the imperial army and the navy introduced football into their training programmes and established inter- and intra-service competitions. The seal of imperial goodwill towards football was the invitation, actively taken up, for the DFB to join the paramilitary nationalist youth organization the Jungdeutschlandbund in 1912. Around the edges of the game, the first organized workers' clubs were beginning to emerge – like Rot-Weiss Essen in 1907 – alongside wild clubs of working-class kids in the Ruhr, but until these zones were incorporated into the formal world of German football, the game remained a minority sport and amateur curiosity.

VII

On the eastern edge of Europe where the continent dissolves geographically and culturally into Asia, football finally arrived in the big cities of the two sick men of Europe, Tsarist Russia and Ottoman Turkey. Paranoid about their relative economic and military backwardness, the rulers of these vast empires approached Western European culture with fear, loathing and suspicion, but also fascination and a practical recognition that emulation was a precondition of political survival. Their relationship with football would parallel this.

Football first appeared in Russia in the mid-nineteenth century. British sailors were seen playing in the docks of Odessa in the 1860s. As early as 1868 the Russian journal *Samokat* was reporting a game among British expatriates in St Petersburg. To the bemused Russian elite the game looked bizarre and uncouth. The magazine *The Hunter* described it this way: 'Football is an English game with a big ball. Usually it is played by people with solid muscles and strong legs – a weak one would only be an onlooker in such a mess.'[33] Despite this early exposure to football and the continuing and expanding presence of British multi-sports clubs in the major cities, there was no take-up of the game comparable to Western or Central Europe. Indeed the creation of a Russian football association and a national competition happened later than in Romania, where the game was first played twenty years after it had appeared in Russia.

One cannot account for Russian tardiness in terms of any national distaste for sport. On the contrary, the half century before the First World War saw the Russian aristocracy take with some enthusiasm and talent to yachting, rowing, fencing and riding. The latter, in particular, offered sport as extension of the typical rural and martial pastimes of that class, while the equipment and access required of yachting and rowing were reassuringly exclusive. That was one of the great virtues of lawn tennis – with its exacting requirements for courts, nets, racquets and unblemished whites. The perceived gentility of the game was entrenched and endorsed by the active participation of the Romanov dynasty. The rigorous separation of the Russian aristocracy from the new urban classes was mapped along social, political and sporting lines. The Tsar, the court and the Russian upper classes were unwilling to share social space, political power or their sporting activities with anyone. Into this vacuum the Czech Sokol gymnastics movement, given a definite Russian twist, became popular among the nationalist middle classes while competitive cycling provided the first professionalized and com-mercialized mass spectator sport in the growing cities. In the 1890s, as in France, cheap velodromes were thrown up in St Petersburg and Moscow, attracting vast crowds from among the urban poor. Football by contrast was relegated to the status of a freak sideshow.

Unattached as yet to any Russian social class, football was played and nurtured by the growing community of expatriate Britons and other Europeans. Not surprisingly, St Petersburg, Russia's 'window on the West', was home to most of the foreign community and the first city to take up football in an organized fashion. Among the earliest regular football clubs were Viktoria, formed in 1894 by British and German enthusiasts, as well as teams like the Scottish Circle of Amateurs, English Football Club, Germania FC and Gloria, all of whom drew on the diplomatic and industrial wings of the expatriate community. In 1896 the Russian-born Frenchman Georges Duperont published the first set of rules in Russian and organized an experimental game among his compatriots on Krestovsky Island. It was a good enough game to encourage the formation of the city's first consciously Russian sports and football club, the St Petersburg Circle of Amateur Sportsmen known more often as just Sport. But the gap between Sport and the British was vast. What is generally considered to be the first organized game between club sides is thought to have been played on 24 October 1897 when Sport lost 6–0 to the predominantly English side Vasilevsky – around thirty years after the game was first seen on Russian soil.

In 1901 the St Petersburg football scene was strong enough to support a formal competition between three teams: Nevsky, a club of Englishmen from the Neva spinning mill; Nevka, a group of Scots workers from the Sampson Weaving factory; and Viktoria, who retained their Anglo-German majority but like many clubs were beginning to admit affluent Russians. As if to emphasize the Englishness of the whole affair, local businessman T. M. A. Aspeden donated a trophy and the Aspeden Cup was played for every year until 1917.

By 1904 the league had grown to six teams, the three foreign sides now joined by three Russian teams – Sport, Petrovsky and Nationsaly. The league was a microcosm of Russia's tortured and contradictory relationship with the wave of modernity sweeping in from the West. On the one hand, foreign ideas and practices were perceived to be a necessary condition of national survival, a strain of thinking made even more compelling after the Japanese Navy (consciously modelled on the British) delivered a strategically and emotionally crushing defeat in the Russo-Japanese war of 1904–05. Thus not only did the progressive elite play football, but they actively adopted many of the social mores that accompanied it. Sipping tea at half-time was an essential feature of Russian football matches in the pre-war era. Similarly, the English language was instantly preferred and incorporated into Russian for describing sports in general and football in particular, while the growing crowds of urban Russians praised and gravitated towards the best English players. When a Czech team – the Corinthians – played a tour of Russia in 1910, in striped shirts and shorts, the fashion immediately became the rage across the nation's football pitches. On the other hand the seething resentment and suspicion of the Russians towards foreign interlopers boiled over into the conduct of matches and the organization of football.

In 1903 *Sport* vigorously protested that none of their players, and indeed no Russian, had been picked to play in a St Petersburg XI. Then in a game against Nevsky, one of their players Christov was sent off and banned for a year for his reaction to a vicious tackle by the Englishman Sharples. The outraged Russian sports press argued that Sharples, exonerated by the English-dominated league, had tried to throttle Christov.

This year we have Sharples the throttler! In future we shall probably have Jim the Stabber and Jack the Ripper! Match reports will be crime reports . . . The English in their typical high-handed way, with their large voting majority, are banning a Russian who is completely guiltless and leaving a man who is obviously dangerous . . . Let Russian clubs band together and form their own league.[34]

But they would get their revenge, for in 1908 *Sport* were the first Russian team to win the Aspeden Cup. In that season's game against Nevsky, the English player Monroe was sent off, giving the crowd ample opportunity to display their feelings. The paper *Novoye Vremya* reported the next day: 'Despite the blatant infringement of football rules by Monroe and even of the rules of normal civility adhered to by educated people, the English section of the crowd made a terrible din and began to clamour for the return of Monroe, whose departure the Russian section of the crowd accompanied with loud hissing.'[35] In an act of calculated petulance, the English teams left the St Petersburg league the following year to form their own exclusive competition and organization, the Russian Society of Amateur Footballers, a move followed by their compatriots in Moscow. Russian clubs boycotted both leagues. It was over for the British. Their hosts, now more numerous and organized, accepted the return of the expatriates to a united fold in 1911, but no foreign team would ever win a Russian title again.

Without access to the sea, Moscow was somewhat slower to take up football than St Petersburg. There are reports of expatriates playing kickabouts in the late 1880s on wasteland near the city centre, but organized club football probably began in 1894 with Harry Charnock, a Blackburn Rovers-supporting factory manager at the Orozov textile mills in Orekhovo, a growing Moscow industrial suburb. After playing with other British workers and managers, he created a team open to the Russian factory workers. Initially known as Morozovtsi Orekhovo Suevo Moskva, the team was, in part, an effort to divert the workforce from focusing their rest days exclusively on vodka drinking. The team played in Blackburn's blue and white and as OKS Moskva were a mainstay of Moscow football for the next two decades. While football in St Petersburg had been divided between foreigners and Russians, in Moscow the divisions were more closely aligned to the indigenous class structure. The elite, both foreign and Russian, played in and among their highly circumscribed clubs whose entrance fees and dress codes excluded all but the very apex of the social pyramid. But alongside them football was taken up in the suburbs, or *dachas* as they were known, and for the first time by autonomously organized workers.

The *dachas* were the new towns built alongside the railways that now radiated out from central Moscow like the spokes of a wheel. They provided, for the first time, inter-communal transport for the poor and middle classes – an essential precondition of lower-class organized football. Each of the first five lines built out of Moscow generated its own distinctive *dacha* league, as a contemporary report described:

In recent days soccer has spilled over into the dacha towns. Young people are enthralled by the game, and they are turning their backs on the unhealthy activities of the dance hall. Often these dacha teams are so strong that they travel to play other teams, sometimes even against the organized soccer sport clubs.[36]

While the rich played in the city centre in spring and autumn, the *dacha* leagues played in the summer. It would appear that the game was introduced by holidaying aristocrats prepared to slum it with the locals in improvised kickabouts. Vast waves of seasonally migrating peasants came to Moscow for the summer but departed for the harvests, taking *dacha* football with them. Workers, however, were not included in these teams. Russia's working class faced the same barriers to participation faced by their equivalents all over Europe and Latin America: their systematic exclusion from polite society; the length of their working day; their physical and financial poverty; their lack of transport and of places to play. However, in almost every case, Russian workers faced greater opposition and higher hurdles. The working day was among the longest in Europe, their poverty the most acute. As one observer dolefully wrote: 'sport is primarily an expensive pastime and therefore is not for the workers. Their path is the kabak [vodka bar]. And, in the morning, hunched and scraggy, off they go again to work.'[37] After the failed uprisings of 1905, the paranoia of the tsarist state machine had reached such heights that independent workers' organizations of any kind, including sports clubs, were deemed seditious and revolutionary dangers. Russian historians of the Stalinist era, whose commitment to documented fact is admittedly a little threadbare, went as far as to suggest that some militant workers' groups – the *Druzhinniki* – used football and football training as a cover for military and weapons drill in secret. Referees from the official football organizations were forbidden from taking control of games among this class. When railway workers attempted to play in the cities' railway yards, management stamped out the practice. Workers in south-east Moscow were reduced to playing at the Klaitnikovskoe cemetery until the clergy drove them away. It was precisely these levels of inequality, injustice and oppression that fuelled the nascent and increasingly radical Russian workers' movement of the pre-war era and forced it politically and in the realm of sport into either sporadic wildcat protests or underground and alternative organizations.

The *Dikei* (wild cat) football phenomenon sprang up all over the wastelands and vacant plots of Moscow and St Petersburg. By the second decade of the twentieth century it had become obvious that strategies of oppression and exclusion were not going to keep the lid on the bubbling pot of urban discontent, and the authorities finally relented. Workers were allowed to form their own teams, to join the existing football organizations and form their own leagues.

In the twilight years of the Romanov dynasty the pressing need for faster development and more comprehensive modernization of economy, polity and society was apparent, and football was now perceived to be in the vanguard of Russia's belated efforts to catch up with the West. According to the press it was the only sphere in which the country was making proper progress. *Sport Life* wrote in 1912, 'The only thing that is approaching progress with monstrous steps is football.' By then the game had spread to provincial cities like Odessa, Kiev and Kharkov, and challenge matches were being played between the cities. Women had played a public game of football in Moscow in 1911, astonishing given their generally appalling status in Russia. Robert Bruce Lockhart, the British diplomat and forward for Morozovtsi, wrote in his diary that, 'At a league match the average attendance was about twelve thousand people, and the women must have contributed 30 per cent of the total.'[38] Indeed crowds had become so obsessive and enthusiastic that they would mass around players before and after the game, while the city's hidden gossip telegraph systems buzzed with the latest scores.

Even the vexed question of the creation of a single Russian football federation, affiliated to FIFA and capable of supporting an international team, was finally resolved under the leadership of Georges Duperont, who outmanoeuvred the residual foreign and English bureaucrats and brought peace to the warring Moscow and St Petersburg factions by creating in 1912 the All-Russia Football Union. An international team was duly dispatched to the 1912 Stockholm Olympics, wearing yellow jerseys with the Romanov emblem – a double-headed eagle – emblazoned on their chests. The limits of Russian modernization were, however, sharply illuminated. In their opening game Tsarist Russia, as they were known, were beaten by their recently relinquished colony Finland. Then they faced their most serious geopolitical enemy, the Germans, and were beaten 16–0. It was not quite the humiliation of Brest-Litovsk, but it was an augury of what was to come.

The antipathy of elements of Russia's ruling elite to Western modernity, of which football was just one component, was replicated at a much higher level in the Ottoman Empire. With the accession of Sultan Abdulhamid II to the Ottoman throne in 1876 Turkey entered a brief period of constitutional government which might have unleashed an era of reform and controlled modernization. However, this experiment in liberalism lasted only two years as the pressure of war with Russia destroyed the new government and saw absolute power returned to the sultanate in 1878 where it would remain for the next forty years. In an increasingly desperate attempt to counter the corrosive consequences of foreign ideologies the regime established an immense network of surveillance, spies and censorship. Dangerous Western ideas and their purveyors were ruthlessly hunted down, while indigenous and Islamic elements in Ottoman culture were lauded.

It was in this context that football was first played in Turkey, probably around 1890 among the British commercial community in Izmir. In 1897 mixed British and Greek teams played as Izmir vs. Istanbul. Izmir won 3–1 and the game was quickly adopted by the sizeable Greek community in Istanbul. Istanbul's Jews also took up the game as did other minority communities including the French, Italians and Armenians. While the sultanate was prepared to allow these groups to play football it was not prepared to see the sporting virus spread to the Muslim population of the empire. Football was condemned from a variety of theological standpoints. First it was claimed that football would keep students away from their studies and their Koran. More worryingly, the wearing of shorts and the display of naked flesh was deemed too salacious. Most powerfully of all, the clergy invoked the Karbala Event as the definitive religious case against the game. In 680 CE the would-be Caliph Muaviye murdered the incumbent, Hossein, the grandson of the Prophet Muhammad. It was claimed that after his murder Hossein's head was severed and then kicked around by his killers. It was just a short step from here to arguing that football, symbolically at any rate, was ninety minutes of blasphemy.

Yet there was something irresistible about the game to the emerging stratum of young highly educated urban Turks who watched the Greeks and the British play the game. The first recorded Turk to take to football was Fuad Husnu Bey, a student at the Naval Academy. The archives of the Ottoman Prime Minister's office of the era make it clear that the apparatus of surveillance and the network of informers was used to keep tabs on these scions of the elite and their predilection for the round ball. Bey's team used an English name, 'Black Stockings', to try and throw the sultanate off the scent but to no avail. After playing a game against a Greek team in the late 1890s, which they lost 5–1, the Turks were reported to the palace and forced to stop. Bey himself went on to join one of the first British clubs in the capital, Kadikoy FC. They were joined by the British Embassy's yacht team, Imogene, as well as the British Moda club and a Greek team, Elpis. These sides combined in 1905 to form the Istanbul League. As the sultanate's power began to ebb, Turkish clubs joined them. First to emerge was Besiktas, founded in 1903 as a gymnastics club and protected from the government by Osman Pasha, the pro-Western confidant of the Sultan. Then Galatasaray were formed by the schoolboys of the premier elite school in the city in 1905, and Fenerbahçe were created from Turkish students at the prestigious French college St Joseph's in 1907.

In 1908 the Sultan died and though the sultanate remained, executive power passed to the reform-minded politicians of the Committee for Union and Progress. Under their rule the social and religious strictures on football were relaxed alongside a more open approach to Western influences, itself driven by the desperate need of the empire to acquire the new technologies of industrial production, transport and military force. The pent-up demand for football in Istanbul was clear. The moment the old laws restricting the formation of independent organizations were lifted, new clubs and leagues sprang up. The city's Muslims started playing on Fridays in the Friday league and non-Muslims played in the Sunday league, and by 1913 an Istanbul FA had been formed; estimates suggest there were over 5,000 regular players in the city on the eve of the First World War and substantial crowds for the biggest games. Indeed so great was the demand that in this still predominantly illiterate society Burhan Felek was able successfully to publish the country's first sports periodical, *Futbol,* in 1910. Alongside scores, fixtures and match reports the magazine attempted to ingratiate itself with the hyper-nationalism of the new government by searching for Turkish alternatives to the standard English vocabularies of football.

It was all too little too late. The failures of the last-gasp attempts of both the Russian and Ottoman empires to emulate the West and coerce their own populations were revealed by the iron hand of war. Neither empire nor dynasty would survive its course. Football and the technologies of rule, power and production developed in the West would only be mobilized in Russia by authoritarian communism and in Turkey by a radical secular nationalism.

6

Pay Up, Pay Up and Play the Game: The Commercialization of Global Football, 1914–1934

A gigolo who exploits a prostitute. The club gives him all the material necessity to play football and to enjoy himself with the game and he wants to earn money as well? I will not allow this in Flamengo. Professionalism degrades the man.

Rivadavia Meyer, president of Flamengo

I'm off to Italy. I am tired of being an amateur in football when such a condition has stopped existing a long time ago, masked by a hypocritical system of tips which clubs give to their players while keeping most of the income for themselves. For twenty years I have offered my modest services to Brazilian football. What has happened? The clubs got rich and I have nothing. I am going to the country that knows how to pay players for their skills.

Amílcar Barbuy, Brazilian footballer

I

The words of a Brazilian club president typify the cant and hypocrisy of an old elite pricked by stating the simple economic realities of sport in an industrializing society. From Rio to Paris, from Madrid to Berlin, the same pieties were crushed by the remorseless logic of economic and political change.

British professional football, like its industrial revolution, had over thirty years' head start on the rest of the world. In the whirlwind of social and cultural upheaval that marked the 1920s in the industrial world, football in Europe and Latin America was catapulted through the same processes of commercialization and mass popularization that had made British football, but at an accelerated rate. In an action replay of the erosion of British industrial hegemony by faster, more innovative late industrializers, British football's unassailable superiority and uniqueness were challenged by the first wave of newly professionalized mass football cultures. However, the geography of football did not precisely map that of industrialization. While British capital was most seriously tested by the Americans and the Germans, British football was challenged by Central Europe, Latin America and the Western Mediterranean. What transformed the amateur football of these regions and made them mass football cultures was the defeat, or retreat, of the game's old elites and the rapid colonization of the game by their respective working classes. This required a profound shift in the structure of power and politics; the kind of shift that cataclysmic war can deliver.

At first glance the First World War does not appear a promising environment for football. With the conclusion of the FA Cup Final in 1915, professional football in Britain, and thus in the world, ceased for the duration of the war; a hierarchy of priority given concrete form when the War Office commandeered the FA's office space at 42 Russell Square. In Germany football pitches along with other sports grounds were converted to rough-and-ready vegetable patches in an effort to mitigate the impact of the naval blockade and general food shortages. Football players across the Continent were by age, gender and inclination among the first to volunteer and then increasingly to be conscripted. Hugo Meisl left his seat at the Austrian FA to fight in Galicia; Sepp Herberger, a star player at Waldorf and later Germany's national team coach for a generation, was sent to the Western Front. Players and officials were also among the first to die. The football battalions raised around West Bromwich Albion in England and Heart of Midlothian in Scotland were mown down; Dr Canfari, the president of the Italian refereeing association, and the captain of the national team Virgilio Fossatti were killed in action. Every combatant nation lost a huge segment of the male generation that played football most enthusiastically, not to mention those who returned mutilated, disabled or insane.

In England in particular football began as a key element of the metaphorical experience of war. Boys at Marlborough College thought the war 'was like a glorified football match in which, if peace did not come they might take their places in the England team'.[1] As late as the first day of the Battle of the Somme sport provided a journalistic frame of reference that could transmute the insane slaughter on the Western Front into a kickabout; that could transpose the insouciant, blasé, effortless play of English aristocratic sporting culture to the killing fields. In an account of the experiences of the East Surrey Regiment the *Illustrated London News* published this:

> On through the hail of slaughter
> Where gallant comrades fall,
> Where blood is poured like water,
> They drive the trickling ball.
> The fear of death before them
> Is but an empty name;
> True to the land that bore them
> The Surreys play the game.[2]

Two years and ten million corpses later it would be impossible to write such a poem again. Thus the enduring memory of football imagery from the war is of the game as a peacemaker. Christmas 1914 was the last collective pause in the killing; the last moment, it appeared at the time, at which the machinery of war might be disengaged. The Americans, the Pope and other neutrals had been urging a Christmas truce upon the combatants in the last months of the year. Christmas 1914, for the Germans in particular but the British and French as well, provided a moment of distance and reflection on the process of mechanized annihilation that resolved itself in a tidal wave of sentimentality, nostalgia, homesickness, grief and schmaltz. Christmas presents, Christmas cards, Christmas food and drink descended on the front lines by the sackload. Munitions supplies were disrupted by the delivery of Christmas trees to the German front line. It was in this context that spontaneous encounters and truces between British and German units all along the front line in France were reported. Lance Corporal Hines reported meeting a German in no-man's land who introduced himself by saying, 'Good morning, sir, I live at Alexander-road Hornsey. And I would see Woolwich Arsenal play Tottenham tomorrow.'[3] *The Times* reported a game between the Royal Army Medical Corps and the 133rd Saxons who sang 'God Save The King', drank the monarch's health and then beat the English 3–2. The German regimental records confirm that a Scot provided the ball and 'This developed into a regulation football match with caps casually laid out as goals. The frozen ground was no great matter.'[4]

Christmas 1914 was the last truce. It was impossible to believe that industrial war was a game. Football disappeared from the front line. Yet for all the mud and slaughter a huge amount of time was spent by a huge number of young men sitting around without much to do. The poet-officer Siegfried Sassoon recalled reading the football news to his troops to calm them before an attack was due to be mounted. If you couldn't play, you could talk. If you couldn't leave, you could find a memory of normality and home.

Football reappeared in the embarkation centres, drill squares, training grounds and prisoner-of-war camps, where the simplicity and elasticity of the game were its greatest virtues. As one British officer testily observed, 'However tired the rascals may be for parades, they always have enough energy for football.'[5] The records of the Russian army include extensive orders for footballs in the early part of the war. Only recently introduced into the German army training programme, the game became widespread through the imperial armed forces. These were armies like no others seen in Europe. For the first time the full bureaucratic and coercive might of industrialized states was deployed in the mobilization of entire populations. The constant and horrific haemorrhage of life from the armies of the European powers forced them to draw on their last reservoirs of labour. Young and increasingly not so young men from every region and class were taken into the maw of the conflict. But before they reached the front line they would pass through the embarkation centres, drill squares and training grounds. French peasant boys from the Massif Central, for example, who had never seen a football, let alone kicked one, learned the game from *lycée*-educated officers from Lyons, rough-house street footballers from Paris and factory workers from Lille. The last social and geographical barriers that had kept football a game of the elite were irreversibly breached. The enormous enthusiasm and energy for football, pleasures that the war had stoked up among its participating armies, would be released in the inter-war era, creating a demand so great for the game that it would, in its leading centres, make the fundamental transition that Britain had made thirty years before: from amateur pastime and neighbourhood festival to professional sport and national cultural institution. But first the old order that had sustained amateur football would have to be dismantled. The war did that too.

When the guns went silent in November 1918, four years of war had cracked the social and political landscape of old Europe. At its apex four European empires had been broken. Tsarist Russia had been decapitated by defeat and revolution and then embroiled in civil war. The Ottoman and Habsburg empires held at the centre but were irretrievably fragmented into a host of new nations and League of Nations mandates. The Kaiser abdicated, Germany was shrunk and denuded of its overseas territories. When these imperial dynasties were deposed the aristocratic land-owning classes that had been their mainstay were also economically, politically and socially diminished. In the Russian case they were eradicated altogether. Even in Britain, France and Italy, the notional European victors, the old aristocracies were decimated. Old forms of rule, allegiance and authority were terminally damaged. In Latin America, where the rural land-owning class was socially and economically overwhelmed by the extraordinary growth of the main industrializing cities, the constituency for amateurism in football was always very small. Now in Europe, where it had been strong, its main representatives were overwhelmed too. By contrast the most powerful and energized new social actors in post-war Europe were the new nation-states created by imperial fragmentation and the working class. The new nations would have their say in international football but domestically it was the working class that transformed the game.

The immense and widespread sacrifices demanded by the war made the exclusion of the working class from politics impossible in most of Europe. The creation of universal male suffrage, and increasingly female suffrage as well, transformed the political balance of forces of every society. The Romanovs, who had always held out against the social and political inclusion of the Russian working class and always preferred a judicious dose of repression rather than reform, were now all dead, ignominiously executed. Their fate during the October Revolution and the subsequent emergence across the world of genuinely revolutionary, if often ineffective, Communist parties, made basic labour and social reforms a precondition of survival for governments and elites everywhere. One of the first reforms was to fix in law the length of the working day and introduce half-day working on Saturday or abolish it altogether. Like the British working class thirty years before them, the young men of European and Latin American cities were released at the end of a shorter working day and had weekend and leisure time to themselves. Of the many things that they chose to do with their new-found freedom, a great many chose to play and watch football.

Attendance records of the era are not everything they might be but the growth of football crowds was of such an order of magnitude that there can be little doubt as to what was happening. For example, before the war fewer than 10,000 people would go to the most popular game of the year in Central Europe, Austria vs. Hungary. In the post-war era attendance at games between the now independent nation-states grew almost exponentially: 15,000 went in late 1918 and around 25,000 the following year; then 45,000 in 1921 and in 1922 the crowd had swollen to 65,000.[6] A similar curve could be drawn for international and domestic football across the most advanced zones of Europe and Latin America. Of course, not everyone was actually paying to get in. The size and design of most football stadiums in Europe were not able to cope with these numbers; reports abound of boys lifted over turnstiles, crowds breaking down fences and climbing over walls. But enough people were paying that the economics of football were transformed. Without really seeking out an audience, without advertising campaigns or conscious attempts at branding, the leading football clubs and football associations of Western and Central Europe and Latin America had acquired a mass playing and paying public.

When in the early 1920s the dust had temporarily settled on the cataclysms of war, revolution, hyper-inflation and austerity, there was in all of these societies a profound need and desire for hedonism and escape, for pleasure and play, from the fabulously rich to the appallingly poor. Football was one of those pleasures, its meaning amplified and transformed by the new culture industries. Britain pioneered the popular, gossipy personalized football press, Argentina added epic and historical saga-making, the Viennese coffee house offered poetry of praise. Song writers and band leaders wrote the first football walks, foxtrots and sambas. The first radio broadcasts played them and experimented with live commentaries. Footballers began to acquire a celebrity, if not always an income, approaching the deifications of Hollywood. Some even made it to the movies themselves as a football face or a flimsy football plot became a common trope in British and European cinema. Above all, football sold. Players and teams increasingly endorsed products of every kind from soap, sugar and stock cubes to cigarettes and alcohol.

In Britain the game was being broadcast by the new technology of radio as far as the drawing rooms of suburbia and the *haute-bourgeoisie*. It was acclaimed across the social scale from the man on the Clapham omnibus to feminist novelists on the fringe of the Bloomsbury group. The question remains, why did so many go to watch the football? Why did so many find it so irresistible to watch or listen to? The novelist Winifred Holtby's ecstatic piece in the *Radio Times* on hearing her first football commentary captures something of football's potency as a spectacle and narrative even to the uninitiated.

I was excited. I had not, I have not to this day, the remotest notion of what they were all doing. But I know that I was excited. No one could listen with cold blood or sluggish pulses to the quickening crescendo of the roar preceeding the final shout of 'goal'. I wanted more goals. I didn't care who shot them. I didn't know who was playing or what they were playing, or where or why. But I wanted to feel my spine tickle and my pulses beat, and my hair stir gently at the roots with suspense as that voice cried out from somewhere near our drawing-room curtains.[7]

Whatever sport the industrial world was going to embrace it was surely going to be a team game. In a society becoming dizzyingly complex in every sphere of existence, in which the threats of anonymity, alienation and atomization were the reality of urban life, a sport that offered spectators an enduring collective identity had a psychic edge on individual sports whatever their other allures. That said, rugby, hockey, cricket and American team sports offered an alternative focus for these needs and Wales, south-west France, America, Australasia and the Republic of Ireland embraced them. Everywhere else football trounced the competition. It did so, in part, for reasons of social structure and meaning, and prevalent attitudes towards Britain.

But it seems inconceivable that the game's success can only be accounted for in strict sociological terms. There is something about the game that for more people in more places brought more pleasures. Holtby's account of the radio commentary suggests at least one reason why football had proved a more successful spectacle than many of its competitors: goals. Scoring, as Holtby recognized, is at the heart of the game's appeal. Everyone wants goals, and their meaning is all the more amplified for their simplicity and their rarity. Football has just one way of scoring. Two of its main competitors – basketball which has one-, two- and three-point shots and rugby with its innumerable different scoring systems – make the numerical flow of the game complex and awkward. Better still, goals come rarely; most games in competitive football see between one and three goals. Not only does this create more intensity and anticipation around their arrival but it offers simpler, more compelling and instantly comprehensible narratives of play.

Holtby also seems alert to the pleasures of flow and rhythm in football narratives. Unlike many sports football has no turn-taking, no fixed breaks, timeouts or other official interruptions. It is – as the cliché goes – a game of two halves. But within this simple framework established by its austere systems of scoring and time-keeping it offers a multitude of pleasures and possibilities. The flow of the game was and is its greatest asset. The ball can, after all, move quickly, unpredictably, in every conceivable direction, with great variation in its speed and distance, on the ground, in the air, with and without spin. While football also offers the spectacle of set pieces – penalties, free kicks and so on – they achieve their intensity against a background of predominantly mobile play and free-flowing movement.

Football – and in this case basketball is perhaps its only serious competition – offers a game in which individual brilliance and collective organization are equally featured. Rugby, for all the thrill of its darting attacking wingers, cannot provide the same spectacle of human dexterity and balance that a footballer's dribble evokes. Cricket and baseball highlight individual virtuosity but cannot, even among the most competitive fielding teams, offer a display of collective action that is comparable to football. Football's use of the goalkeeper, a position it shares with hockey and handball but few other games, also reserves a place in a team game for the loner, the idiosyncratic and the odd-one-out. The game's balance of physicality and artistry, of instantaneous reaction and complex considered tactics, is also rare.

Thus football always had the capacity to rouse a crowd but now, in the aftermath of the war, the crowd was overwhelmingly and unmistakably male, working class and increasingly young. Fear of an unruly and unpredictable working class haunted the elites of Europe and the Río de la Plata in the inter-war era and football offers both metaphor and practical example of the social and political challenge of managing this new element in society. Commercialization and professionalization were not the only model for trying to deal with the problem. In Germany and Scandinavia, despite all the obvious preconditions for the emergence of professional football, amateurism was retained. In Sweden's case, this was because the working class was uniquely politically successful; in Germany's case, because they were so comprehensively defeated. But before the forces of conservatism in football accommodated themselves to the working class there was one social group and one social challenge they were not about to accommodate. Women.

Though the evidence is on occasion rather thin, it seems clear that women played some of the many variants of global folk football. Accounts from native North America, the Japanese medieval court and English Shrove Tuesday games all suggest women playing either in mixed games or among themselves. The same cannot be said of the early development of association football. Nurtured as it was in the exclusively male institutions of public school, university, old boys' clubs and the armed forces, women had no immediate access to the sport. From its very inception modern football was tied to a vast ideological raft of Victorian masculinity which presumed that sport like the rest of the public realm was a matter for men alone. In the upper echelons of Victorian society there was among progressives and liberals a more inclusive conception of exercise and recreation that permitted women to play a certain kind of the more gentle sports, tennis and croquet for example. But manly pursuits like cricket, rugby and football were deemed beyond the pale. Even where some kind of access was possible a great ideological wall needed to be scaled – sport was perceived to be a threat to femininity, damaging to the delicate female constitution, and an aberration of the natural order of things. Women of a lower social class, almost universally tied to the domestic sphere in the new and rigid sexual division of labour that industrial societies created, had no access to any formal sport or physical exercise.

In the face of structural and ideological constraints upper-class women in Britain took to the field anyway. Women's cricket clubs became popular in the early 1880s and the first reports of a game of informal football among women come from Inverness in Scotland in 1888 and then a formal game staged by the Scottish FA in Glasgow in 1892. South of the border the first women's football match in England was played in 1895 when the South of England beat North London 7–1 in Crouch End.

But the women's game had hardly begun before the backlash started. The exclusively male members of the Dutch FA banned a women's game between Sparta Rotterdam and an England XI in 1896, following it up with a ban on women's football at all Dutch FA-affiliated stadiums. Similar policies of exclusion were adopted in Germany, while social, medical and sporting commentators across Europe claimed that football was detrimental to women's health. The English FA issued a ruling in 1902 that men's teams were not to play women's teams. In the decade before the First World War there are only the most scattered references to women's football in England. But just as the First World War would finally break the resistance of the establishment to the question of female suffrage, so the economic and social upheavals of the war would open the space for another experiment with women's football.

As the slaughterhouse of the Western Front consumed more and more of the male labour force, there was a correspondingly large increase in female industrial employment during the First World War. In Britain munitions factories were a favourite destination for young working-class women looking for work and it was here that the first wave of women's football was born. In Dick Kerr's factory in Preston the men's team had been performing poorly and subjected to teasing by the women in the factory. Out of this banter came the challenge to play a game and thus two works teams – one male, one female – played a game in a field near Penwortham, Preston. Dick Kerr's Ladies never looked back. The team began to play charity matches in order to raise money for injured servicemen and other war funds and were an instant hit, attracting considerable crowds. Other women's works teams began to form in emulation, particularly in the north of England. There were perhaps 150 teams in existence by 1921 when a Ladies' Football Association was formed in Blackburn from around twenty-five of them. Games were hugely popular with attendances peaking in late 1920 when 53,000 went to Everton's Goodison Park to see Dick Kerr's Ladies beat St Helens Ladies.

Women's football also took off in France towards the end of the war, combining works teams like those in England with footballing sections of more middle-class women's sports clubs. Members of two of these clubs – *En Avant Femina* and the *Fauvettes* – played the first public game of women's football in France in an exhibition that preceded the France–Belgium international in 1918. By 1920 there were around a dozen women's football teams active in the Paris region. A tour of England by a representative French women's XI was arranged, with games played against Dick Kerr's Ladies and other representative XIs in Preston, Manchester and at Stamford Bridge in west London, where the English won the game in front of 20,000 spectators. But just as the wider male elite feared the consequences of women's entry into male employment and ensured that they returned to domestic labour in the post-war years, so the FA feared intrusion by the women's game.

In 1921 Dick Kerr's Ladies and every other women's club were banned from FA-registered stadiums, setting the women's game back seventy years. Women's football was relegated to odd public and private spaces, parks and municipal pitches. Cut off from formal systems of coaching or finances, the game was reduced to a peripheral and rather odd-looking subculture. Having conceded the vote, European male society was in no mood to concede anything else. Women's football, prohibited by regulation, was then diminished by the power of ideology – the widespread belief systems of a medical and scientific culture that could still be claiming in the 1920s, in a journal as august as *The Lancet*, that football was too rough and dangerous a game for the female body. The revival of the women's game would have to await the discrediting of these arguments and an era in which the formal equality of the suffrage was understood as the beginning rather than the end of the matter.

III

28 April 1923
Bolton Wanderers 2 West Ham United 0
The Empire Stadium, Wembley

Are the British more sentimental about their animals or their civility? In the midst of a stupendous, unprecedented, social event in which half a million people converged on the newly opened Empire Stadium in Wembley, north-west London and just under half of them got inside, the British remember the horse. It's not as if it was the only horse and it wasn't even white.

And the civility? The crowd, shot from high in the air, is slowly shuffling backwards before PC George Scorey who felt that they 'respected his horse'. King George V makes his entrance, the Guards Band strike up the national anthem and all and sundry break into song. There's a bit of a squeeze round the touchlines and in the stands, but buckets of good humour, self-discipline and calm in the face of adversity.

Rummaging through the stuff left on the cutting-room floor of the era we find the edits. The moments that suggest that in a two- or three-mile radius around the ground, traffic congestion and sheer numbers have overwhelmed the police. Something closer to a mob than a merry band is descending:

I made my way across a grass field, crossed a railway, scaled a high wall and then found my way into the enclosure obstructed by corrugated iron hoardings with three rows of barbed wire above them. Some of the more daring spirits surmounted this formidable obstacle, whilst others less venturesome burrowed under the hoardings.

All around the walls of the ground are builders' ladders, planks of wood and scaffolding; like a medieval siege left abandoned. The new arrivals scale the castle walls. Inside, the signage is all wrong, the seating plan has gone to hell and the stewards have panicked and run. Punters are clambering into any space, reserved or not, and the continuous pressure of new entrants gradually forces them out of the stands and on to the pitch. There are fifty casualties taken to Willesden Hospital with broken ribs and shock; a seemingly inconsequential detail – if anything a mark of success not failure. The mounted police's intervention looks less than polite from the stands. 'When they started charging at the crowd, there was a stampede for safety.' The game can only start when the vast lines of chain-linked police officers heave the crowd back.

So self-discipline and the strong arm of the law, lightly applied, are enough to quell the mob in all of us. But crowds can become carnivals and we have edited that out too. On the way to the ground there was

. . . a brewer's lorry. It carried a gigantic hammer made out of a very large beer barrel serving as the head, with a large tree trunk serving as the handle inserted into the barrel . . . It was brilliantly decorated with the claret and blue and there were two smaller hammers made in the same fashion placed either side of the long one . . . [it] carried supporters, singing 'Bubbles' and 1–2–3–4–5.

I imagine them marooned in the traffic jams on the North Circular Road.

The sheer size of the crowd at the 1923 FA Cup Final reflects an era in which professional football, already the biggest spectator sport in the country, grew even bigger. In 1919 Divisions One and Two expanded from twenty to twenty-two clubs each. Then in 1920 and 1921 the semi-professionals of the Southern League and a number of northern leagues were upgraded to become Division 3 South and North respectively. No other footballing culture, then or now, could sustain four national professional divisions. The eventual total of ninety-two clubs

reached into every corner of England but for the extreme rural peripheries of Cornwall and Cumberland. Attendances at each level grew
steadily through the 1920s and 1930s, apart from some locally concentrated collapses of support in small towns hit hardest by the depression
of the early 1930s. However, it was not the scale of the Wembley crowd
that was celebrated but its demeanour. This was a mass but not a mob,
collectively displaying humour in adversity, restraint under pressure and
respect for authority. Football was the people's game, but there was
nothing to fear from the people.

This was certainly the way in which the FA and the Football League
wished to present football to the world. The FA had made its peace,
albeit with regret, with the forces of commercialism and professionalism
but no further shift in that direction would be tolerated. All forms of
technological and practical invention were viewed through a sepia tint
that considered the chaotic gentility of late Victorian football to be the
gold standard of football's athletic and aesthetic values. The Football
League and the directors of the leading clubs were also content with the
status quo. They had effortlessly acquired a paying public whom it
would seem required no further servicing, investment or enticement than
the cinder banks and crush-barrier terracing being offered to them. The
maximum wage and the transfer system gave clubs immense power
over their playing staff and put an effective cap on the commercial
exploitation of the game, a cap made all the tighter by FA restrictions
on the amount of dividends that clubs' shareholders could obtain. Football was a business but a very conservative and unusual business. Clubs
did not compete with each other for customers, nor pay their own
supporters any great heed or give their owners much of a profit. It was,
in strictly economic terms, a low-risk, low-investment, low-return game
that distrusted innovation and ignored the competition; that is how
British football's ruling elites preferred it. Like much of Britain's industrial capital, they would eventually be displaced by the methods and
people they so disdained.

The attitude of the FA to the rise of women's football after the war
was indicative of its wider politics, as was its response to the Irish crisis.
When the Irish Free State had the temerity to create its own football
association and join FIFA in 1923, the Home Countries systematically
shunned its clubs and national team. In the late 1920s the FA turned its
fire on creeping professionalism in the upper reaches of the amateur

game. This culminated in a virtual witch-hunt at the leading amateur teams in the north of England and the suspension of 341 players and over 1,000 officials. As if it didn't have enough to do, playing on Sundays was systematically opposed by the FA, floodlights were deemed unnecessary and the press and public were kept at arm's length from decision-making of all kinds.

Football's entanglement with gambling was fiercely resisted. The use of football grounds for dog racing was prohibited; the holding of lotteries by supporters' clubs as a means of raising money for their team was not permitted. The FA, in a rare act of proactive politics, had persuaded the government to pass the Ready Money Football Betting Act in 1920. A cumbersome name for a cumbersome law, the act sought to prohibit all forms of gambling on football save those involving credit facilities. This was clearly an attempt to exclude or protect the working classes, depending on your view. However, the pools industry, which only collected monies after the fixtures that people gambled on had been played, found a loophole in this law. Brilliantly marketed and efficiently run, 'doing the pools' became a national institution, over 6 million people a week participating by the mid-1930s. The Football League's tetchiness with the pools industry eventually broke into open conflict in 1936 when they attempted to destroy it by announcing fixtures only two days before they were due to be played, making the printing of coupons impossible. The pools companies, the press and the clubs – who were losing money from the ensuing chaos – forced the League to back down. Henceforth, fixtures were made available in advance and the League got its cut of the money.

The Football League was equally twitchy about the idea of broadcasting games on the radio. After much discussion with the BBC the first live commentary broadcast in England took place on 22 January 1927 between Arsenal and Sheffield United. More followed that year culminating in the broadcast of the 1927 Cup Final. Over the next four years around a hundred games were broadcast. Commentator George 'By Jove' Allison brought a modicum of populist gush to the proceedings. The spirit of experimentation extended to commentaries that announced players' positions on the pitch according to a numbered grid printed in the *Radio Times*. However, there was mounting opposition to the medium inside the Football League, especially from clubs in the lower divisions who feared that they were losing crowds to the radio coverage of more glamorous teams. In 1931 the League announced a complete ban on live broadcasts.

Intriguingly, and by contrast, the one area in which the FA was prepared to innovate was in broadcasting, especially the FA Cup which remained on air from 1930 to this day. The FA consciously used the tournament as an opportunity to display football as the 'nation at play'. The kudos of live BBC coverage, which put the event on a par with Empire Day, the Boat Race and the King's Christmas broadcast, was a key element in securing this status. But the boisterous crowds of the immediate post-war era, especially those from the north of England let loose in the metropolis for a day, were deemed an unsuitable chorus for the occasion. The FA dealt with the problem by changing the ticketing arrangements for the final, allocating significantly fewer to the fans of the teams taking part and a great deal more to other clubs, affiliated institutions and friends of friends. In 1927 the FA embellished the final by introducing the singing of the hymn 'Abide With Me' before the kick-off. The following year the *Yorkshire Observer* wrote of the Huddersfield Town fans who made the trip to see their team lose 3–1 to Blackburn Rovers: 'The spectacle of the typical sport-loving, merry English crowd lifting their hats as one man, transformed by a single thought into one huge congregation, is a lasting tribute to the depth of religion in the national character.'[8]

This kind of mock arcadianism was replicated in the anachronistic internal structures of professional football clubs. The actual playing of the game was left almost entirely to the informal internal decisions of the players. They were a caste apart from the middle-class and professional directorate of clubs who held complete sway over every other detail of the business including picking the team. Players received little more direction that being told, 'You know what to do when you get out there.' Hierarchies of age and experience predominated among squads and an unstructured learning by doing and watching was the pedagogic core of this essentially artisanal apprenticeship. Training was confined to low-key, unstructured fitness work, a bit of running and a bit of weights. Ball work and practice games were highly restricted on the bizarre assumption that this would keep the team hungry for the ball when Saturday came – though whether they would know what to do with it when it eventually arrived was a moot point. Prior to the change in the offside rule in 1925, this fundamentally conservative culture generated little tactical or skill-based innovation in the playing of the game, Arthur Grimsdell's pioneering use of the long throw for Tottenham in the early 1920s and Bill McCracken's perfection of the offside trap for Newcastle United being two of the very few. By contrast English professional football continued to produce the top-quality tough, colloquially and affectionately referred to as a team's 'killer'. Frank Barson of Aston Villa was one archetype whose ferocity was enough to get him sent off at his own testimonial.

If the price of such conservatism was a lack of innovation, the reward was stability. The dynamic of competition and money was controlled. The leading clubs did try and poach, attract and retain the leading players by finding ingenious ways to break the maximum-wage policy; but the extras seem meagre in retrospect. Arsenal, for example, sought to lure Alex James from Preston in 1929 by getting him a job as a sports-equipment demonstrator in a London department store. But the system held and the players' union was docile, only beginning to contemplate strike action by the late 1930s. Crowds could get out of hand. Carlisle United, Millwall and Queens Park Rangers all suffered ground closures in the 1930s after incidents of crowd disorder, stone throwing and pitch invasions. However, these were genuinely rare incidents. The only outbreaks of sustained public disorder and violence occurred in Scotland where the sectarian division of Glasgow refused to go away.

Scottish football in general, but Glaswegian football in particular, saw regular low-level and occasional large-scale outbreaks of crowd disorder in the first decade after the First World War. Glasgow itself appeared a city constantly on the brink of trouble. The city's economy was in recession for most of the inter-war era, social conditions were exceptionally harsh in the poorest districts of the city and the legacy of early industrialization came to haunt its declining companies and lamentable housing stock. Added to this, the social divisions between Protestant and Catholic created by large-scale Irish migrations of the previous half century were inflamed by the bitterness following the Easter Rising and the widespread and vindictive sectarianism that characterized the birth of the Irish Free State in 1921.

In this context it is hardly surprising that football became an arena in which sectarian differences were expressed, deepened and occasionally turned to violence. In Glasgow there was the additional factor that the long-standing razor gangs who inhabited the grey area between

organized crime, local toughs and proto-football hooligans were powerful players in the street culture of the era. Matters were made worse by
the development of brake clubs. First established in the 1880s, the brake
clubs were the first organized away fans in football history. Initially,
groups of fans would hire, even occasionally own, their own horse-
drawn transport which turned into a mobile drinking parlour on the
journeys to and from away games. By the late 1890s Celtic could boast
an entire federation of brake clubs. In the inter-war era they grew in
popularity and became motorized, massively increasing their radius of
action. Rangers and other clubs soon followed suit and so large numbers
of away fans were regular features of Scotland's most combustible sporting encounters.

The challenges that came from outside the game's inner circles – be
they from women or unruly fans – were in the end seen off. The most
powerful assault on the status quo came from within in the person of
Herbert Chapman, the central figure in the invention of the modern
football manager. Chapman had begun his coaching career embroiled
in a financial scandal at Leeds City. He moved to Huddersfield Town in
1920, winning three League titles before joining Arsenal in 1925. It
was here that he began to invent modern football management. One
footballer's biography recounts his arrival:

Herbert Chapman sat down to organize football much as a business magnate sits
down to organize profits. In his view every device used by the industrialist to
speed up the production of goods could be used equally well to speed up the
production of goals.[9]

In contrast to the hidebound traditionalism, unreflective complacency
and fixed and inefficient division of labour characteristic of British
football and British industry, Chapman was a force of Fordist rationalization. To this end the most profound innovation that Chapman introduced was to carve out a space of autonomous action for himself from
the pre-existing structures of power in football clubs. Previously directors had signed players and selected teams, the players themselves in
their own informal hierarchies had organized the actual playing and
trainers had provided minimalist training, medical and laundry services.
The core of Chapman's new autonomy was his absolute control over
team selection, team play and tactics. Everyone, apart from players and
officials, was banned from the dressing room half an hour before kick-

off. Players that would not or could not take and execute orders were out. Chapman was able to create this power base by not only the force of his personality but the internal disarray at Arsenal. The previous chairman of the board, Sir Henry Norris, had left in disgrace after the disclosure of financial irregularities. Once established, Chapman also had the financial means and playing staff to deploy a range of innovative and much-copied tactical ploys.

Chapman's tactical invention was a response to the transformation of the offside rule in 1925. The post-war era had seen a steady decline in the number of goals scored in English professional football. With three players required between an attacking player and the goal line to put them onside, it was increasingly easy for skilled and alert defenders to step up and put forwards offside. Pressure from the clubs saw the International Association Football Board (the game's ultimate law-making body) reduce the number of players needed to be onside to just two; a flood of goals, nearly a 50 per cent increase, followed over the next few seasons and this in turn led to a new premium on defence in the Football League. Chapman was not the only coach or player experimenting with new formations and ideas for dealing with these problems, but he was the first to devise a systematic response with a team that was able to realize his vision – a vision which has become known as WM. The most obvious shift was to change the role of the centre-half. Under the 2–3–5 formation that had evolved in the 1880s the centre-half was not a defensive role at all; if anything the position served as a kind of primitive playmaker taking the ball out of defence and initiating attacks. Now the centre-half was withdrawn into the defence between the two fullbacks and served as an exclusively defensive player often referred to as the 'stopper'. The other two midfield players in the old system – the wing-halves – could no longer just shadow the opposition's wingers but were withdrawn into the genuine midfield and allocated both defensive duties and the task of shuttling the ball out of defence and up to the forward line.

Under 2–3–5 the forward line tended to advance together and did not take up specialized positions or face additional midfield or defensive duties. Under Chapman, roles, physiques, skills and training for forwards became more highly differentiated. Wingers were glued to their lines and drilled in crossing the ball. Centre-forwards needed to be bigger and burlier. The inside-forwards that played between them were the two points at the top of the M. They were required to link with the defence and be the brains of the team in attack. Chapman's Arsenal thus displayed many of the key characteristics of modern Fordist production processes: a high degree of specialization of tasks; systematic, repeatable sequences of tasks; task design; close observation and control of players by management.

However, once the ball was in play Chapman's sides were expected to show a degree of spontaneity, reactivity and invention that no production line asked of its workers. In particular Arsenal were the masters of the counterattack. They would and could concede space to the opposition, falling back on a highly organized defence, consciously stretching out the other team as they overcommitted players to the front. When Arsenal regained possession, long balls exploited the space vacated by the opposition and with players like Cliff Bastin they had the kind of speed to make the most of it. Arsenal's capacity to soak up the pressure, score on the break and then hold their lead gave rise to the sobriquet 'Lucky Arsenal', but it wasn't luck – they were calculating and playing for it. The response of crowds around the country was testament to their tough, clear-minded modernism, to their success and metropolitan identity: they were seen in Teesside as a club from the 'soft south, from London, from the city of government, where it was imagined, all social evils were plotted and directed'.[10]

If Chapman had merely spearheaded tactical innovation and the development of managerial autonomy, his contribution to the creation of modern football would be substantial, but his energy and invention were also seemingly inexhaustible. He wrote a regular and highly opinionated column for the *Sunday Express*. From this pulpit Chapman argued cogently for the introduction of innumerable technological and practical innovations: floodlit football, the use of white balls, the development of artificial pitches, numbered jerseys, and public stadium clocks counting down the time of the half. All were calculated to spread the appeal of football and improve the quality of the spectacle on offer. The FA, disinclined to further either of these ends, opposed nearly every idea at one point or another. Chapman also understood the potential of publicity and the press. The tube station that served Highbury was named Gillespie Road until Chapman persuaded London Transport to rename it Arsenal. Highbury even got a sprinkle of stardust as Chapman arranged for two stars of 1930s British cinema, actress Anna Neagle and director Herbert Wilcox, to attend a game and for the press to know all about it.

Chapman's successor at Highbury, George Wilson, inherited the mantle of celebrity manager and proved adept at showmanship and publicity, but neither he nor any other leading figure in English professional football before the Second World War was able to replicate Chapman's political mastery of a club, his tactical control of his squad or the modernity of his training and coaching methods. It took until 1938 for Stanley Rous, by some way the most modernizing figure in the football hierarchy, to publish the FA's first book on coaching, nearly eighty years after the organization's foundation. At Newcastle United directors were still picking the team into the mid-1950s and the England team would not acquire a manager in the mould set by Chapman until Alf Ramsey in the early 1960s. The spark of innovation that English football was still able to generate was doused by the suffocating conservatism, inertia and complacency of its rulers. European football, not hidebound by hallowed convention and the self-assurance of past dominance, was eager for ideas and Chapman was part of an emerging cosmopolitan network of football coaching enthusiasts that adopted and absorbed his ideas as well as generating new models of tactics and training. Among the leading figures of the network were Jimmy Hogan in Budapest, Vittorio Pozzo in Turin and Hugo Meisl in Vienna.

Yet there was no simple convergence of playing styles among them. Indeed, under conditions of professionalism and heightened competition there was greater diversification in styles of play as teams and players sought to innovate and differentiate themselves from their more staid and predictable opponents. A few notes of caution should be sounded when considering the early history of playing styles. First, though plenty of footage of football in the 1920s and 1930s exists, there is remarkably little that shows the full pitch or a full game. Reduced to newsreel strips and cuts of the key moments, using primitive camera techniques filming from fixed positions on the touchline, it is remarkably hard to get an accurate picture of the real flow, spacing and positioning of the era's football. Second, what was written by eyewitnesses on football styles was increasingly bound up in wider political debates about national identity. Football was being viewed through nationalist lenses that could shape what they saw to unspoken political and cultural needs.

English football, albeit often caricatured as more monochrome than it actually was, proved a stable reference point for the rest of the world. The English style was perceived to be supremely physical, bordering on the rough. It drew upon unquenchable reserves of running and work-rate, and made ample use of crossing, heading and long balls. In Central Europe the dense network of personnel and sporting interconnections between Vienna, Budapest and Prague appeared to produce a distinct way of playing that self-consciously drew upon the 'Scottish passing game'. Coaching clearly emphasized technique and ball control more than in England and players were called on, in Jimmy Hogan's words, 'to keep it on the carpet'. It was certainly distinctive enough for contemporaries to refer to it as the Viennese system or the Danubian School.

In Latin America the same Scottish inheritance formed one key element in an emerging *fútbol rioplatense*: short passing, good ball control and multi-player build-up play were all the subject of praise in contemporary accounts of the game. But to this Latin America added a greater emphasis on individual trickery and dexterity, the continent's footballers claiming the invention of the bicycle-kick and bending free kicks, and allotting pride of place to the individual dribble.

Both of these models had a significant impact on the game in Italy where a fourth model of play evolved. Through the 1920s Italian football drew heavily on Central Europe, employing up to sixty players from the region a season and importing coaches too. Simultaneously, Italy was also able to draw upon the Latin American experience, importing Argentinians, Uruguayans and Brazilians until the mid-1930s. Out of this unique concurrence of football cultures, and under the aegis of the influential Vittorio Pozzo, there emerged the notion of a distinct Italian method – *il Methodo* – later referred to as *la Sistema* – the system. The Italian contribution was twofold. First, Italian football possessed a nomenclature of playing positions of a complexity and precision that would have appeared quite alien in England. For example, Italian football did and continues to distinguish between various types of fullback: the *terzino marcatore* – a marking fullback – and *terzino fluidificante* – a fullback with licence to roam alongside his less prescribed defensive duties. Second, given the precision and technicality of its language Italian football was much more systematic in its analysis of micro-level tactics than other football cultures: close marking was prized, the denial of space to playmakers pursued.

Alongside these early schools of football we find innovation, emulation and development elsewhere in Europe. In Switzerland Karl Rappan was one of the first coaches to experiment with the use of the sweeper or *libero* – an ultra-defensive player positioned behind a conventional back line of defence. In Germany Sepp Herberger was international football's Herbert Chapman. Not only did his German national teams play a muscular version of Chapman's WM, but Herberger eventually carved out the kind of tactical autonomy and squad control that Chapman created at Arsenal. In his public pronouncements Herberger was also an innovator captivating and infuriating the press. He was perhaps the first coach to perfect the art of the gnomic, tautological non sequitur. Along with the innumerable others playing, watching, following and coaching, he ensured that for the first time since its codification the future of football was made outside Britain. And nowhere more than in Vienna.

IV

Vienna is the football capital of the European continent . . . where else can you see at least 40–50,000 spectators gathering Sunday after Sunday, rain or shine? Where else is the majority of the population so interested in the results of the games that you can hear almost every other person talking about the results of the league matches and the clubs' prospects for the coming games?[11]

The answer was nowhere. Budapest and Prague came close, but they could be considered as part of the same phenomenon as football in Vienna which in 1924 became the first place outside Britain to stage a professional league. The Hungarians and the Czechs followed almost immediately, emboldened by their neighbour and fearful of losing players to the Austrian capital. But why here? Why should Danubian Central Europe, where football had been merely popular before the First World War, experience vertiginous rates of growth afterwards? In part it was a product of fission, of the energies released by the disintegration of the old political and social frameworks of the region. As the war came to its grim conclusion in November 1918 it had became apparent that the game was up for the Habsburgs and their multinational empire. The last Emperor, Karl I, abdicated and within a year was gone to Switzerland. At the peripheries, the Hungarians, the Czechs, the Poles and the Yugoslavs were all asserting their national independence, leaving a diminished micro-Austria at the centre of the now-dissolved monarchy. From the steps of Vienna's Rathaus on 12 November 1918, this new Austrian Republic was brought into being, though it was far from clear who actually wanted it. The pan-Germans wanted *Anschluss* with their larger neighbour, the Socialists and newly formed Communists wanted a workers' republic and the Christian Democrats were calling for a constitutional monarchy. In a series of plebiscites that only just confirmed the state's precarious existence, the Vorarlberg region voted to join Switzerland; the Tyrol and Salzburg to join Germany.

Vienna itself had been transformed from a city of 2.1 million from which a multinational empire of 52 million people was ruled to a city of 1.8 million ruling a nation of predominantly German-speakers numbering just 6.4 million. The singularity of Vienna, which had been in part obscured by the multifaceted character of the Habsburg Empire, was brought into stark relief in the sharply divided cultural and political landscape of the rump Austria. In the national elections of 1919 the Christian Democrat Karl Renner was elected to power and under his auspices the last flames of revolutionary politics were extinguished as soldiers' and workers' councils created in emulation of the Soviets were sidelined or closed down and two attempts at armed putsches by the Communists were quelled. By contrast, the vote in Vienna's municipal elections of the same year gave an overwhelming 54 per cent of the vote to the Social Democrats and their mayoral candidate Jakob Reumann, a hold on power that the party did not relinquish until its liquidation in 1934. Vienna was the laboratory, the showcase and the pride of Austrian social democracy. The party's social reforms, mass housing programmes and cultural policies made *Rotes Wien* – *Red Vienna* – a scarlet island in the sea of black, the colour of the countryside, the cassock and Austrian Christian Democracy. The two were distinguished by more than colour as their conflict pitted the urban against the rural, the modern against the traditional, the secular against the confessional, and cosmopolitans against nationalists. In these polarized conditions, Vienna's overweening control of Austrian football – still barely played outside of a few provincial towns in the rest of Austria – made the game emblematic of the city.

The peculiar social and geographical ecology of Vienna had created a generation of boys and young men for whom street football was the linchpin of their social lives. The massive industrial development of Vienna in the late nineteenth and early twentieth centuries occurred in the *Vorstadt*, conventionally translated as suburb. But the *Vorstädte* were not zones of individualized domestic bliss or utopian garden cities. They were vast, predominantly unplanned and unregulated zones of large-scale commercial properties and factories with high-density housing for the new proletariat thrown up with them. Within and between the new *Vorstädte* there were large areas of unregulated, unclaimed common land – from half-finished building sites, to open fields, to semi-agricultural commons; it was here that Viennese football boomed in innumerable kickabouts and neighbourhood contests made all the more important by the use of the same spaces for carousing, drinking and socializing away from the authority of the state and one's parents.

In December 1918, one of the first acts of the new Republican government was to enshrine the eight-hour working day in law. Once the Viennese working class had been released from the tyranny of long hours, they took to playing and watching more organized forms of football with a vengeance. The Austrian FA, which had 14,000 registered players on its books in 1914, saw the numbers almost triple to 37,000 in 1921. Alongside the wild clubs, the *Vorstädte* could now sustain more organized clubs playing in the leading league – among them Hertha in Favoriten, Wacker in Meidling, and teams in Rudolfshügel, Simmering and Hütteldorf. If Vienna had now become more working class, it had also become a less diverse city. The demise of empire saw the substantial contingents of Croats, Hungarians and Poles depart. As far as football was concerned, only the Slovaks and the Jews remained, represented by their teams SK Slovan and Hakoah. Attendance at international matches quadrupled before 1925. Crowds at league games grew and the ever-increasing presence of the proletariat among them was beginning to worry the bourgeois press. The *Neues Wiener Journal* noted that:

Crowd trouble has not only become more frequent but has also increased in intensity, the larger the group of football fans has grown, and the wider the sections of the population attracted by this sport have become. They grab stones and wooden posts, and if the front-line troops from Fuschen or Drachenfeld are present, they even fight with knives.[12]

The Social Democrats attempted to create an alternative 'red' football culture in which the sporting energies of the Viennese working class could be steered away from overt forms of politically des-tructive local patriotism and the lure of commercialization and towards a more wholesome socialist amateur ethos. However, the Verband der Arbeiterfussballverein (Workers' Football Association) was never able to mobilize more than a fraction of Vienna's footballing energies. The Social Democrats' ambitious cultural policy in this era sought to catalyse 'a revolution in man's soul', but the Viennese soul required more inspi-rational football than the minor red leagues could muster. The leading 'bourgeois' clubs in the city played the football that everyone wanted to see and offered sporting form to the enduring social and cultural conflicts that wracked the city. Rapid Vienna, whose working-class roots were tangible, remained aligned with that class in both support and style. One observer argued: 'They have yet to let their supporters down, because they never give up and fight to the final whistle. Rapid have their roots in the local population, and never neglect their home territory. The green and whites are a suburban club in the best sense of the term.'[13] Wiener Amateure, who transformed themselves into FK Austria, matched Rapid on the pitch and became associated with the liberal bourgeoisie and the city's extensive Jewish intelligentsia and professional classes. Some, perhaps jealous of the kinds of resources such a supporter base could muster, referred to their game as 'salary football' and de-scribed their play as befuddled by 'dense coffeehouse smog'. Karl Geyer, who joined the squad in 1921, admitted he went for the money, but also from his desire to play with a 'more intelligent social group'.[14]

It was in this intense football milieu that Europe's first professional football league was created by the Continent's first significant football thinker and bureaucrat. The organizing intelligence behind the growth of Viennese football was Hugo Meisl. He was born in 1881 in Moleschau, Bohemia, to an upper-class Jewish family who moved to Vienna in 1893. As a teenager Meisl played inside forward for Wiener Amateure while attending a commercial academy, training for a career in business; but it was family connections that secured him a position as a clerk with the Länderbank. Banking never occupied more than a fraction of his time and considerable energy. He served first as secretary of the Austrian FA and then as coach of the national team from 1912 until his death in 1937, but for his period of war service. Meisl was directly responsible for the creation of the world's first regular international club tourna-ment, the Mitropa Cup, as well as the Continent's first tournament for national teams, the Dr Gero Cup. Alongside the illustrious teams of FK Austria which he also ran, Meisl was the coach and creator of Austria's *Wunderteam* which bestrode the world of international football in the early 1930s.

The decisive act that made all of these developments possible was the legalization of professionalism. Remarking on the transition to openly commercial football, Meisl later remarked that it had been a commercial gamble but in practical terms he was merely formalizing what was already in operation. What was already in operation was not merely the usual panoply of under-the-table payments, inflated expenses and invented jobs that characterized pre-professional football everywhere. In addition, Vienna possessed a broad and sophisticated football culture whose intimate interconnections with the city's intelligentsia and the popular cultures of cinema and music were the preconditions for both a successful commercialization of the game and the creation of a unique style of Danubian football. The crucible of this cultural fusion was where most things in Vienna began: the Viennese coffee house.

According to legend the retreating Ottoman Turkish army left coffee behind when they were finally repelled from the outskirts of Vienna in the seventeenth century. As in England, the new coffee houses that opened to serve the brew became an important nexus in the social world of the emergent bourgeoisie of the eighteenth and nineteenth centuries, where the urban classes could meet, talk, offer and form opinions unhindered by the formality and politics of court and officialdom. By the late nineteenth century, the Viennese public sphere was sufficiently large that particular cafés came to cater for particular clienteles and subsections of the city's intellectual and political elites. The Café Greinsteidel acquired an early reputation providing a crucible for the creation of Viennese literary modernism characterized by Arthur Schnitzler, while Victor Adler, the founder of the Austrian Social Democrats, could be found at the table next to him. In the first three decades of the twentieth century the Viennese coffee house nurtured and refreshed an extraordinary cluster of intellectual and cultural movements from the experimental music of Schoenberg, by way of the revolutionary psychiatry of Freud, to the radical design and architecture of Loos; from the rarefied theorizing of Wittgenstein's logical positivism to the austere but engaged radicalism of Austro-Marxism.

But the coffee house was never a mere substitute for the seminar room or the lecture hall. Its essential democracy and openness, its insistence on combining pleasure-taking with theory-making, its geographical location in the heart of the metropolis – all this made the coffee house a place in which the high culture of the neurotic Viennese elite could rub shoulders with the popular pleasures of semi-public banter, gossip and social intrigue, cinema, theatre and football. The Ring Café – originally the watering hole of the Viennese Cricketers – became the social centre for the city's football scene. It was described by one regular attender as 'A kind of revolutionary parliament of the friends and fanatics of football . . . one-sided club interest could not prevail because just about every Viennese club was present.'[15]

Many of these strands of Viennese football culture entwined in the life of Josep Uridil, the most popular footballer of the early 1920s. Uridil was born in 1895, the son of a master tailor in the working-class *Vorstadt* of Ottakring, where the characteristic open spaces and wastelands of Vienna offered his initial training grounds. Uridil was the star striker at Rapid after the First World War and his fantastically physical presence earned him the nickname 'The Tank'. No film survives of this marauding forward, but in a contemporary description we can sense something of his magnetic presence:

Others scored goals before him, but not one of them had his enormous momentum, the irresistible force with which he powered across the football field. Woe betide the opponent who dared to cross the path of this racing machine. He was knocked over, almost crushed and decomposed into his chemical constituents.[16]

In post-war Vienna Uridil was everywhere. The hit of the moment, played in dance halls and ballrooms across the city through 1922, was the lively foxtrot *Heute spielt der Uridil* – 'Uridil will play today' – written by the popular singer-songwriter Hermann Leopold. The following year fans at Rapid welcomed the players on to the pitch with their own accompanied renditions of Uridil's song. Sponsorship, endorsements and advertising followed as Uridil's face appeared on fruit juices, chocolates, soap, underwear and sportswear.

Yet in 1925, the first year in which a professional Viennese football league was held, it was not Rapid that won the championship or Uridil who was the star. The champions were Hakoah Wien, Vienna's leading Jewish sports club. Hakoah, which means 'strength' in Hebrew, was founded in Vienna in 1909. It was not the only, or even the first, Jewish sporting organization established in Austria, but it was by far the most popular and successful. In the late nineteenth and early twentieth centuries Jewish attitudes to sport in Central Europe closely paralleled the wider debate over the place of European Jewry in an increasingly anti-Semitic world. Among an older generation of upper-class, assimilated Jews and more orthodox, recently urbanized peasants, sport was perceived to be the preserve of the ruffian and to be avoided at all costs.

The strongest challenge to these views came from Max Nordau, the Zionist intellectual who coined the term Muscular Judaism – an obvious reference to the Muscular Christians of nineteenth-century Britain. He acknowledged that the dominant view of Jews in Christian Europe was of a weak, physically debased race unsuited to and uninterested in physical activity of any kind. More than that, they were right. The consequences of the ghetto – 'the narrow Jewish streets' – were that 'our poor limbs forgot how to move joyfully; in the gloom of our sunless houses our eyes became accustomed to nervous blinking; out of fear of constant persecution the timbre of our voices was extinguished to an anxious whisper'. This was a situation that could only be remedied by taking active measures to 'restore to the flabby Jewish body its lost tone, to make it vigorous and strong, nimble and powerful' and that meant playing sport.[17]

The Zionist movement of the late nineteenth century proposed the creation of an independent and exclusively Jewish sports movement but only as an instrument to further the migration of Jews to a nation-state to be established elsewhere. By contrast, the rising professional Jewish classes preferred the assimilationist route, joining a select band of the leading bourgeois sporting clubs and institutions like FK Austria. Others within this class gravitated to the secular universalism of Social Democracy and Communism and certainly Jews were prominent in the Viennese workers' sports organization. But Hakoah alone sought a sporting and cultural experience which would simultaneously declare and celebrate Jewish identity, but be active participants in the mainstream structures of Viennese and Austrian society. Hakoah would play in the league alongside Rudolfshügel and Simmering, but when they did they would wear the Star of David on their shirts. They would play gentile Vienna at its own game and win.

Hakoah was always more than a sports club, not least because of its growing importance as a hub of Jewish social life in Vienna. But it was the men's football team, competing in the city's most high-profile sporting competition, that was the public face of Hakoah. Recalling the club's first games with the wild teams of the *Vorstädte* one of the players, Walter Frankl, wrote:

Every week they dragged the goalposts all the way to the field, often stones were thrown by the fans of the opposing team. Hakoah's goalkeeper not only had to fend off the opponent's strikers, but also had to deflect the attacks of the spectators who were behind him. Yet nothing could shatter the fighting spirit, enthusiasm, and courage of these pioneers.[18]

Hakoah were accepted into the formal Viennese league structure. By 1913 they had made it to the second division and found themselves a playing field near the municipal dump.

In the years immediately after the First World War, Hakoah continued to grow and made the transition from clandestine to open professionalism. They were funded by the conservative Jews who had dismissed the rough house of sport a decade or so earlier, now anxious to secure the social position of the embattled Jewish minority. The team had already proved its worth in 1923 when on a short tour of England they had beaten an admittedly understrength West Ham United 5–1. Off the pitch the club was protecting itself at matches and its wider community by enlisting and organizing a formidable band of Jewish wrestlers and boxers. With two games to go before the end of the 1925 league Hakoah won the title when Alexander Fabian scored an 87th-minute equalizer. Fabian, however, was the goalkeeper and had one arm in a sling. In an era before substitutes, he swapped places with a forward after breaking a bone in a collision. Muscular Judaism had come of age.

The summer of 1925 was a turning point for Hakoah. The club went on tour to the east coast of the United States where they were a huge attraction – indeed their game at Polo Fields in New York attracted a then record football crowd of 45,000. Most of the squad never went home as American professional clubs fell over themselves to sign the Viennese. And with higher wages and considerably less anti-Semitism around, who can blame them for staying? Hakoah survived without them, but they were never as good again. Uridil too was past his peak. He stayed with Rapid until the late 1920s before coaching in Slovakia, Italy and Romania, but his fame, which never really reached further than Vienna itself, was soon eclipsed. Matthias Sindelar, playing for FK

Austria not Uridil's Rapid, was beginning to make his name as Uridil left the country. In Sindelar inter-war Vienna had the footballer and the phenomenon that coffee-house society had been waiting for. *Der Tank* gave way to *Der Papierene* – the wafer. Brute force was swapped for intelligence, the charge for the arabesque. From out of the earthy muscular football of the city, Vienna would create the ethereal and cerebral football of Sindelar and the *Wunderteam*.

Central European professional football was born from the collapse of an empire and the death of an old social order. Professional football in Latin America was born of a tumultuous process of emergent economic development and social change. The leading edge of that change was in Argentina and Brazil. At the end of the First World War Argentina was a society transformed. In the fifty years since 1870 a predominantly rural, agrarian, *criollo* society had become urban and industrial. In the cities nearly half the population were first-generation immigrants to Argentina. Politically, the nation had been transformed by the introduction of universal male suffrage in 1912 which had ended the long rule of Argentina's conservative, landowning elites. Those elites had hoped to bind many of the newly enfranchised voters to their cause, but the electoral weight of urban middle- and working-class Argentines put the populist Unión Cívica Radical (UCR) into power and made its leader Hipólito Yrigoyen President in 1916. However, the exclusion of women and immigrant voters from the franchise and the economic turmoil of the immediate post-war years saw many flock to the colours of Argentine anarchism, syndicalism and radical unionism, a tide of support that backed a nationwide general strike in 1918. The erstwhile populists of the UCR government ordered the army and the police to put the movement down. They showed little quarter in doing so. Thus the surge of working-class power in Argentina was checked, but only temporarily. As Argentina's economic and social structure steadily developed a more industrial and working-class character in the 1920s, successive radical presidents were challenged by the growth of socialism and communism and an increasingly confident and vibrant working-class culture in the big cities.

At the heart of that culture was football. The immense growth in playing, watching and following the game experienced before the First World War was sustained afterwards. Alongside four official divisions and countless local independent and junior competitions Buenos Aires could also boast a merchant sailors' league, a communist league and a separate socialists' league. The leading clubs continued to recruit paying *socios* and built themselves extensive social and sporting facilities. Crowds regularly exceeded 10,000 and the old stadiums and grounds were not up to the task. The combination of fierce competition, a pool of predominantly working-class players and the club's access to both money and power made the use of hidden payments, inflated expenses and fake jobs inevitable. The English-language press, always pious and haughty, wrote in 1926: 'The men who compose our leading local teams are every bit as professional as the hardest-headed big leagues in England. Argentine footballers play the game winter and summer and train every day . . . nominally they are engaged in work for gentlemen financially interested in the big teams.'[19]

The gentlemen in question not only had financial interests but political interests too. Argentine politicians had been attending international matches and basking in the team's international triumphs since the turn of the century. In the 1920s they began to turn their attention to the clubs who were happy to acquire influential presidents and directors, like Aldo Cantoni who was a senator for San Juan and president of both the AFA and Huracán; or Pedro Bidegain, president of San Lorenzo and a leading figure in the UCR. In 1926 the whole issue of domestic club football was deemed important enough for the President of the Republic, Marcelo T. de Alvear, to take responsibility for mediating the conflict between the two warring leagues in Buenos Aires who had split after a series of rancorous administrative and financial conflicts in 1919. That football had captured the popular imagination was beyond question, but how, if at all, could it be harnessed to the populist political project of the time? The central ideological dilemma of the radical movement of the 1920s was how to bind its cross-class electoral base together. Where would it find and how would it shape new collective identities that could outflank the threats from the Left? The obvious solution was a shared sense of national identity. But what was Argentina? What was an Argentine? The cultural legacy bequeathed by late nineteenth-century nationalists located the Argentine soul in the pampas, a landscape tamed and managed by the solitary cowboy-gauchos like Martín Fierro whose bone-dry machismo was the archetype of a heroic rural life; that might still work in the backwoods, but in the densely crowded immigrant *barrios*, in the tango halls of Parque Patricios, in the cinemas of Flores and the factories of Avellaneda it was ludicrous. By the end of the 1920s Argentina had swapped Martín Fierro for Guillermo Stábile as the Argentine football player and the Argentine football style became the central icons of new notions of masculinity and the nation.

Instead of the pastoral idea of the nation and the gaucho myth, the nation built in soccer was able to assume an urban form . . . Instead of an idea of the nation anchored in the heroic pantheon of patrician families and Hispanic tradition, soccer introduced a national identity that was represented by the working class . . . the national heroes proposed by soccer's organic intellectuals were members of the existing, recently urbanized working classes, themselves newly literate and pressing for cultural and political influence through the first wave of Argentinian populism.[20]

Soccer's organic intellectuals, who transformed the raw material of *porteño* football into an entire national mythology, were primarily the staff of the magazine *El Gráfico*. *El Gráfico* was founded in 1919 as an illustrated weekly magazine for men covering politics, sports, news, and photos of dancers and singers. By 1921 everything except the sport had been dropped. By 1930 *El Gráfico* was selling 100,000 copies in Buenos Aires alone and had assumed the mantle of Latin America's sports bible, available and quickly snapped up from the downtown news-stands of Santiago de Chile, Bogotá, Lima, Quito and Mexico City. Its tone was often moralistic, usually educative and self-consciously modern. Above all it developed a model of sports journalism that was historical and comparative. Great teams and great players of every era were characterized and evaluated, lineages and golden ages were constantly being constructed and reconstructed. Each new twist and turn in the national championship was understood in relation to its predecessors, who were then required to reshuffle their place in the narrative canon in relation to the newest coup, comeback or bravado performance. Out of this mode of reporting and under self-conscious reflection *El Gráfico*'s Uruguayan editor Lorenzo Borocotó elaborated an historical theory of the development of *fútbol rioplatense*:

It is logical as the years have gone by that all Anglo-Saxon influence in football has been disappearing, giving way to the less phlegmatic and more restless spirit of the Latin . . . it is different from the British in that it is less monochrome, less disciplined and methodical, because it does not sacrifice individualism for the honour of collective values . . . and for that reason it is a more agile and attractive football.[21]

Thus *criollo* football and masculinity came to be defined in opposition to the English and Englishness. The English were focused and disciplined, combining collective organization and physical force – the prerequisites of an industrial labour force turning out an industrial product. On the Río de la Plata where industrialization had yet to completely stamp its imprint on the economy, landscape or rhythms of life, masculinity was more restless, impetuous and individualistic, spurning crude force in favour of virtuoso agility. It is during this era that musical metaphors – teams as orchestras, playmakers as conductors, wingers as soloists – were first used and the recognition of, indeed the demand for, football as art was loudly proclaimed. Comparing the two styles of play, Borocotó asserted that *fútbol rioplatense* had almost caught up with the English:

We say almost on a par as we are convinced that our own play is technically more proficient, quicker and more precise. It perhaps lacks effectiveness due to the individual actions of our great players, but the football that the Argentinians, and by extension the Uruguayans, play is more beautiful, more artistic, more precise because approach work to the opposition penalty area is done not through long passes up field, which are over in an instant, but through a series of short, precise and collective actions; skilful dribbling and very delicate passes.[22]

Borocotó argued that this style of play sprang from the peculiar urban experience of football in Buenos Aires. The *pibe* – the young boy or scallywag – was the archetypal player. He was drawn from the poorest families and *barrios*, playing with a rag or straw ball. The wastelands and open spaces of the city provided the physical canvas on which the *pibe*'s imagination and energy could be expressed. Often finding himself in cramped spaces among huge numbers in informal games, unprotected by the application of conventional rules and refereeing, the *pibe* was forced to invent new moves and modes of playing. Above all, he had to use the essential guile and craftiness learned in the life of the street.

Thus by the beginning of the 1930s Argentine football had assumed a place in the national culture that was equal to that in England and Scotland. In fact, given the competition from cricket for the mantle of the national sport in England and the popularity of rugby in Scotland, football in Argentina was even more prominent; at the highest level the game was solvent and professional in all but name. What tipped the balance in favour of formalizing this arrangement was the loss of the country's leading players to Italy.

Enrico Maroni, the Italian industrialist, owner of the Cinzano drinks company and Torino football club, went to Buenos Aires on business in the early 1920s. He saw the striker Julio Libonatti from Newell's Old Boys play and decided on the spot to sign him. Libonatti was the first leading Argentine player to leave for Italy, moving to Torino in 1925. In 1928, after the all-South American final in the Amsterdam Olympics had shown off the continent's talent, Raimondo Orsi left Independiente for Juventus, enticed by weekly wages of 8,000 lire, a signing-on fee of 100,000 lire and a Fiat 509. The flamboyant international striker Renato Cesarini followed the next year and after Argentina's appearance in the 1930 World Cup finals, defender Luis Monti was also signed by Juventus. A league without stars soon loses its audience, but how to keep them at home? The case for professionalism was becoming compelling.

In 1931 a players' strike was the trigger for the final transition. A deputation of players demanding freedom of contract marched on the presidential palace. President Uriburu directed them to the Mayor of Buenos Aires, who pointed out to all that if freedom of contract was the issue then the players could no longer be amateurs; what amateur had a contract or could be reasonably compelled to keep to it? It was time to deal with what the president of Boca Juniors called 'all that brooms-and-sawdust nonsense'. Twelve clubs declared themselves professional a month later. River Plate and Independiente, the last bastions of the amateur and patrician ethos, held out but only for a few weeks. The first eighteen-team professional league kicked off in May. Argentine football had reached a point of footballing modernity, unparalleled outside Europe, the match of anything within it. The players got paid openly rather than under the table, but they did not and would not get freedom of contract. Uruguay and Chile, which had experienced the same debates and pressures in a minor key, had little choice but to follow suit or see a mass exodus of their own players across the Río de la Plata or the Andes.

Professionalism was not introduced in any other South America nation – where either money or organization or both were in short supply – but Brazil. The process there was of course, as in Argentina and Uruguay, a form of minor class struggle in which the players, overwhelmingly from poor backgrounds, fought the elites that ran the league and the clubs for better payment and improved conditions. However, in Brazil this struggle was overlaid and in some ways subsumed by a further social cleavage – race. Brazil possessed, by some way, the biggest population of African descent in the Americas and it had made slavery illegal only in 1889. Inequality and racism were endemic. The newly emancipated black peasantry of the countryside were landless and destitute and those that made it to the city found themselves at the very bottom of the social and economic scale. The white aristocracy lived in fear of the revolt of the landless in the countryside and the contamination of their bloodlines in the bedroom. Playing football with them in the city was considered simply demeaning. Writing in the 1930s Mário Filho recalled the story of Carlos Alberto, a mulatto who played in the reserves of the factory team América. In 1916 a series of good performances saw him move to Fluminense. The legend has it that in his first game for Fluminense against América he was seen in the dressing room furiously applying rice powder to his face in an attempt to lighten his skin. When he appeared on the touchline the América fans were merciless in their lampooning, shouting out *Po de Aroz* – rice powder – a cry of abuse still hurled at Fluminense by their opponents. When a few years later América recruited a talented black dockworker called Manteiga, nine of their squad walked out and would not play. Even though black and mulatto players were now regularly appearing in the Paulista and Carioca leagues, the President of the Republic refused to allow black players to represent Brazil at the 1921 Copa América in Buenos Aires.

Everything changed when Vasco da Gama won the Carioca championship in 1923. Prior to this all the teams that had won the Carioca were white. Vasco won with four black players. The club was founded by recent Portuguese immigrants to Rio in 1898 as a rowing club and added football to its repertoire in 1915. In contrast to Fluminense and Flamengo its membership was drawn overwhelmingly from businessmen running small family firms or servicing the new Portuguese community. They and their sons, though eager to play sports, did not have the leisure time of their aristocratic counterparts, encouraging the club from early on to recruit players from outside its usual social circle. Moreover, at work, in the street and at play Vasco lived closer to the poor of Rio. For the club's ambitïous *socios*, there were no social or racial barriers to fielding black players. Vasco won the second division championship in 1922 and went on to win the Carioca the following year.

Shocked, threatened and humiliated, the grand clubs withdrew from the league muttering about the poison of professionalism and created their own league, while Vasco and the smaller teams played separately. Undaunted, Vasco initiated the building of the biggest stadium in Rio; the Estádio de São Januário opened in 1927 with a capacity of over 50,000, the biggest in the country until the building of the Maracanã. The crowds spoke, everyone wanted to see Vasco who had a fantastic team at the time. Flamengo, Fluminense and Botafogo were forced to capitulate and a single league was created in 1926; but the elite would have their pound of flesh. All players were required to fill in and sign a complex bureaucratic registration form before games that included details of their place of birth, their parents' places of birth, employment, education and nationality. It was seen at the time as a blatant attempt to exclude the poor and illiterate from the field, but Vasco simply responded by sending their players on crash courses in basic literacy. The league also instituted a permanent commission of inquiry into players' finances, employment and means designed to flush out hidden professionalism and covert payments; Vasco's directors simply provided their stars with ghost jobs in their family businesses.

São Paulo was much less concerned by the issue of professionalism. The elites in the city were mercantile sports fans as opposed to the flamboyant aristocratic Olympians of Rio; market relationships and wage labour were unlikely to bother them unduly. But São Paulo was much whiter at this point than Rio. Its newly emerging clubs, like Corinthians and Santos, were certainly proletarian in their character. Palestra Itália (later renamed Palmeiras) reflected the large Italian community in the city and Corinthians attracted the Syrians, but black players were almost completely absent. São Paulo's elites could concede the football pitch to the poor without having to face issues of race.

As with Argentina it was the flight of players overseas that tipped the balance in favour of professionalism. Italian agents had been active among São Paulo's Italian community in the late 1920s and the Fantoni brothers were the first of many to set out for Italy in the early 1930s. Lazio, then run by leading Fascist General Vaccaro, had a particular penchant for these returning Italians. White Brazilians also made their way to Argentina where San Lorenzo's championship-winning teams of the era could boast up to five of them. Black players, all originally based in Rio, began to try their luck overseas in the early 1930s. On Vasco's tour of Europe in 1930 Fausto and Jaguare were persuaded to get off the bus in Barcelona. Domingos and Leonadis tried Uruguay for a season in 1932 after playing brilliantly for Brazil against Uruguay in Montevideo.

Oscar da Costa, president of América, broke the silence in 1932 and admitted that he paid players, and that it was time for everyone to come clean and go professional. The following year both the Paulista and the Carioca were professional leagues, quickly followed by the emerging football centres of Minas Gerais, Rio Grande do Sul and Paraná. All across the country an escape route for young black and mulatto men had been opened; they would be through it like a shot. In the first professional game in São Paulo in early 1933, São Paulo beat Santos 5–1, playing Artur Friedenreich at the grand old age of 38. Friedenreich, the son of a German father and black Brazilian mother, had been the leading striker in Brazil through the 1920s. His white skin kept him in the national team when politicians were calling for blacks to be excluded; he scored the winner in the final of the Copa América in 1921 and was the first Brazilian to score a thousand goals. Yet he spent his whole career shamed by his tell-tale African curly hair which he often attempted to straighten and control before playing. He scored one of São Paulo's goals; one likes to think that he was no longer embarrassed.

VI

Football in Central Europe and Latin America, amateur, semi-professional and fully commercialized, was the game of the big cities. Czechoslovak football was centred in Prague, Austrian football was Viennese, Uruguayan football meant Montevideo. In Argentina it got as far as Rosario and no further. What distinguished the Western Mediter-

anean – the third pole of growth for professional football – was that the
game developed as an economic and social phenomenon at the same
time that it became a national institution; but it did so in countries
where national institutions and national identities had been weak
or were in some way contested. In Spain, where regional nationalism
was at its strongest and football closely aligned to it, the national
team and national championships generated the most conflict. On
occasion football could function as an instrument of unity, but as often
as not football served as an arena for conflict and dissent. In Fascist
Italy football was not considered a mere reflection of subterranean social
trends but as an active tool of nation-building. Mussolini may not even
have made the trains run on time but the Fascists did sort out the fixture
list. The administrative chaos of immediate post-war Italian football
was transformed in a decade into one of the strongest football leagues;
good enough to nurture the leading force in world football in the 1930s.
The separation of the impoverished south from national life was at least
partially remedied by the creation of a genuine national championship.
In France football grew in parallel with the slow and diffuse industrialization of the economy in which the vast swathes of deepest rural France
and its small towns were dragged into the twentieth century two or three
decades late.

While football's relationship to the national question varied, all three
countries created a mass football culture and a national and professional
league within a decade of each other. Despite its relative economic
backwardness, Spain was the first of the three to create a national league
in 1928, acknowledging and then legalizing professionalism from 1926.
The absence of any significant aristocratic amateur coterie in Spanish
football removed the most important obstacle to professionalism.
Instead, the provincial business elites and professionals that made up
the bulk of paying *socios* at Spain's leading clubs were the dynamic
force in the commercialization of Spanish football: a class unlikely to
have any great moral problems with the principle of free wage labour.
Indeed, Spain almost alone in Europe had no maximum wage policy for
its players. The Italians followed suit in 1929 when the first national
league season was played. This required the heavy hand of Mussolini's
authoritarian sporting bureaucracy to enforce, though it did so with
some trepidation about the moral and practical consequences of professionalization which it quietly introduced after this. In 1932 France,

despite its more advanced economy and longer and deeper footballing roots, was the last to legitimize professionalism and create a national league. In part this tardiness can be explained by France's pattern of industrialization, which left significant parts of the country untouched; it also possessed a larger and more socially influential band of aristo-cratic amateurs in football than Spain or Italy. Despite appearances, the reality of French football was one of *les amateurs marrons*. The en-during hypocrisy of the French elite, on matters of sexuality for example, made stable by the rigid separation of public and private mores, manners and obligations, was reproduced in football where a late, slow and grudging introduction of professionalism was accompanied by the longest and most blatant period of undercover and hidden systems of payment.

The Janus-faced nature of Spanish football's relationship to the Spanish nation is encapsulated in two incidents: the 1920 Antwerp Olympics tournament and the closure of Les Corts – Barcelona's new stadium – in 1925. War may make football popular but it does not make for good football. Death, injury and malnutrition are the enemies of play. Spain, neutral in both world wars, achieved two of its most important international footballing moments in their immediate aftermath: the 1920 Olympics and the 1950 World Cup. The team that was sent to the Antwerp Olympics was the first Spanish national team to play anywhere, including Spain. Most of the squad had never left the country before and the tournament was considered an opportunity to find out just where Spain sat in the international hierarchy of football. Reasonably high was the initial answer, as they beat the Danes and lost to the hosts in the quarter-final. Then in the final the Belgians were ahead when their Czech opponents walked off complaining about the English referee. Gold to Belgium but the silver was not awarded to the Czechs. A hastily arranged mini-tournament for second place was played and Spain beat Sweden, Italy and then the Netherlands to claim the medal. This feat was all the more amazing for the fact that the first two games of the campaign had been embroiled in internal disputes over whether Basques or other Spaniards should play and in what ratios, but in the game against the Swedes in particular the Spanish proved to be a formidable, cohesive and brave-hearted collective. Describing a game in which only fifteen players were left on the pitch at the final whistle, *ABC* newspaper sketched the first account of the mythic event that encapsulated, for those that liked to think of Spain and the Spanish as a warrior kingdom and an indivisible martial race, *La Furia Española*:

This afternoon witnessed the most barbaric and brutal game ever seen on a football field ... the Swedes scored first and decided to protect their lead by turning to violence. Our boys responded by shouting 'go for the man' which is exactly what they proceeded to do. We went on to win by sheer guts and resilience. The Swedes left the field battered to a pulp, which was no less than they deserved ...

What was the impression of the other nations towards us? Enormously positive. No one had previously believed that in Spain this sport was so advanced. They all thought we were just bullfighters.[23]

The First World War might have been good for Spanish football but it did little to calm the rising political and social tumult in the country. The weak and ineffective governments of the immediate post-war era were deposed by a *coup d'état* orchestrated by General Primo de Rivera with the active support of the royal house, the armed forces and other conservative groups. Primo de Rivera dissolved the *Cortes*, banned the communists and the trade unions, rescinded moves towards regional autonomy and imposed a mode of authoritarian political rule and economic planning not dissimilar to the experiment being conducted by Mussolini in Italy.

Nationalist and centralist in its outlook, the government soon found itself embroiled in the politics of football in Catalonia. In Barcelona the two leading teams, FC Barcelona and Real Espanyol, had already firmly nailed their colours to the masts of Catalan and Spanish nationalism respectively. Barcelona's *socios* and directors were among the many petitioning the Madrid government for Catalan independence in the early 1920s. The supporters of Espanyol helped organize a counter-petition in league with militant nationalists of *Peña Ibérica* – a name now adopted by Espanyol ultras. Barcelona's booming economy generated crowds and capital sufficient for Barcelona to build a new stadium Les Corts in 1922, countered by Espanyol building Sarria with a donation from the La Riva textile magnates in 1923. Competition descended into conflict in the derby game of 1924 when Barça midfielder Pepi Samitier was sent off, followed by a hail of coins on to the pitch. The game was called off and the new military government of the city ordered it to be replayed behind closed doors, an act which merely diverted the fight between the fans to outside the stadium. The intervention of Primo de Rivera's government in Catalan life did not stop with football. With its centralist and Castilian caste the administration had cracked down on other forms of cultural independence and difference, passing laws that banned the use of the Catalan language in public life and the education system.

The identification of Barça and Espanyol with their respective political allies was not complete until 14 June 1925. That evening, Barcelona had arranged for a benefit match to be played in support of a Catalan choral society, Orfeó Català, which since the late nineteenth century had been a linchpin of the Catalan high cultural revival. The government was prepared to allow the game to go ahead but not for any public tribute or statement to be made. In response Catalonia's nationalist political elite made a strong showing at the game accompanied by the iconic cultural nationalist Anselm Clave, founder of the Orfeó Català. Into this volatile mix, the Witty brothers, Barcelona's English co-founders and directors, invited a band of the Royal Marines who were temporarily docked in the city's harbour. Unschooled perhaps in the intricate cultural context into which they had unwittingly stumbled, the marines struck up the Spanish national anthem before the game and were met by a crescendo of whistling and abuse. To everyone's relief they paused and switched to 'God Save the King', which evoked an enthusiastic round of applause from the assembled Catalans. The government in Madrid took a rather different view and considered the entire episode a public act of treason and humiliation. They fined the club and the club's directors; closed the stadium and the club down for six months; and suggested that the club president, Hans Kamper, leave the country, which he did. Barcelona's attachment to the cause of Catalan nationalism was always close; now they were inseparable.

Spanish football's remarkable rise and popularity rested on its capacity to combine fierce national, regional and urban identities and conflicts within a single footballing culture. But success also sprang from an early generation of gifted players who offered a potent brew of showmanship and glamour, married to a small elite of highly commercial and ambitious club directors. Real Madrid, who had acquired royal patronage in 1920, were among the most commercial and ambitious. In 1924 they opened their new stadium Chamartín in what would soon be the most exclusive area of the capital and beat Newcastle United 3–2.

The leading forward of the mid-1920s, the Basque José María Peña, was purchased from Arenas Club de Getcho and to cap it all the two most celebrated players of all, Ricardo Zamora and Pepe Samitier, were enticed away from Barcelona.

Zamora and Samitier typified much that was distinct about this era of Spanish football. Zamora, in particular, was a national institution, a living embodiment of Spanish machismo and style. Perhaps the greatest goalkeeper of the era, he was also a real professional. Zamora's career took him from Barcelona to Espanyol, back to Barcelona and then to Madrid, crossing clubs, cultures and regions in search of a better pay day. *El Divino*, as he was known, was famously described as 'more famous than Garbo and better looking'. On the pitch he often sported polo-neck shirts and rakish flat caps – a style that became much copied by other goalkeepers. Off the pitch he lived a life of bohemian excess and revelry, indulging in cigars, nightlife and fine cognac. He joked, with characteristic swagger, that he made the switch from the racquet game pelota to football because 'The ball was so much bigger, and I thought it would be much easier to play.' Pepe Samitier – whose lifestyle was not dissimilar to Zamora's, though his looks and charisma could hardly compete – captivated Spain with his play. Considered to be one of the first players who genuinely saw the whole pitch and every player on it, he orchestrated his team's play from the back of midfield.

Football was harder hit by the war and its aftermath in Italy than in Spain. Despite Italy's being on the winning side in 1918, the war had exhausted its economic resources, the confidence and room for manoeuvre of its liberal elites and much of the country's patience. The introduction of universal suffrage and the elections held between 1918 and 1922 saw Italian politics descend into bitter, violent conflict between the newly formed Communist Party, the socialists, the Catholic Church and its allies, and the new Fascist Party of the hitherto idiosyncratic socialist Benito Mussolini. The organization of football was equally factional and chaotic. The structure of the national championship, so called, became an enduring and irreconcilable point of conflict between the big clubs and the small clubs, the north and the south. The FIGC – the national football association – almost split in 1921 between competing factions. The following year it did split into two leagues and though they recombined, the standing of the national organization sank to a new low when it revealed a sudden and unexpected surcharge on all clubs to cover its inexplicably large debt, yet had the temerity to draw up new legal statutes without consulting the country's regions.

The fate of football was decided in 1922 when Mussolini and his Fascist Party took power after their march on Rome. Effectively handed power by the old elites, the Fascists quickly set about dissolving, imprisoning, banning or killing their opposition and taking control of every important secular institution in the country. The party's attitude to sport was initially rather mixed and unformed. Like Mussolini himself many of the party's cadres had received their ideological training in the radical socialist movement where sport was frowned upon. On the other hand, the party came to power with the express intention of actively intervening in the cultural and spiritual life of the nation and were armed with the usual panoply of biological, racial, martial and Darwinian theories beloved of ultra-nationalists. The confluence of these two streams of Fascist thought required the regime to develop a position on sport and physical education in general and on football in particular, easily the nation's most popular recreation and spectacle.

The spectacle, as far as many in the regime were concerned, was not particularly edifying. The final of the northern championship in 1925 between Bologna and Genoa was emblematic of the problem. After two drawn games, the third played in Bologna stood at 2–1 to the visitors. Muzioli's shot appeared to many to have crossed the line before Genoa's keeper tipped it around the post. The referee awarded a corner. Leandro Arpinati, leader of the local Fascist Party, led a pitch invasion in protest, supported by his thuggish *squadistri*. The referee reversed his position to persuade Bologna to carry on, but hinted to Genoa that the game would be declared 2–1 and he was only continuing to avoid any further disorder. When the whistle blew for full time Genoa thought it was 2–1, Bologna thought it was 2–2 and the referee sided with them calling for extra time. Genoa walked off. Bologna claimed the championship and celebrated. The FIGC forced both teams to hold a fourth play-off in Turin which ended in a draw and an armed confrontation between supporters at the station where trains were taking both sets home. Fighting broke out across the platform and concourse and gun shots were fired from the Bologna carriages. Bologna won the fifth and final game, held behind closed doors, but for the Bolognese Fascist elite in the stands.

The regime finally decided to act. Having already taken control of all sporting bureaucracies in the country though the umbrella sports agency CONI (the Italian Olympic committeee), Lando Feretti, the Fascist president of the organization, appointed a panel of three experts (a senior Fascist bureaucrat, an engineer and a lawyer-referee) to draw up new statutes for top-flight Italian football. A month later the *Carta di Viareggio* was submitted and the foundations of modern Italian football were laid. The document endorsed CONI's and therefore the Fascist Party's control over football through their power over the FIGC – whose key members would all be appointed from above. A new *Lega Nazione* was formed with the leading clubs from across the country – though still concentrated in the north. Initially *La Lega* was still played in geographical groups but in 1929 a fully fledged national league was established, decisively if unequally incorporating the south into the football nation – a point reinforced by the regime's insistence that the national team start playing in Rome and the FIGC's offices be transferred from the north to the capital. A national cup competition was added to give smaller clubs the opportunity to shine on the national stage and though amateurism was the officially sanctioned ideology of the game, the pragmatic category of non-amateur footballers was allowed. As ever, Italian law created a grey area in which the operations of the already well-established market in players' services could be efficiently transacted behind a smokescreen of Fascist amateur ideology. From the accounts of participants it seems clear that Italian football acquired a degree of organizational cohesion and purpose it had hitherto failed to achieve. Vittorio Pozzo wrote of the old regime:

Who can forget those famous meetings that started at nine in the evening and ended at four in the morning without concluding anything; those discussions that took five, six, seven hours to decide what one person could have done in ten minutes ... this used to happen once. The regime, intervening energetically, introduced swift and practical systems, revitalizing the environment.[24]

La Nazione argued that Fascism and its national league were providing football with 'a new impulse, organizing, encouraging and giving it robustness and meaning'.[25] Questions of nomenclature and style were also issues for the regime. The English names of some clubs were frowned upon and for the duration of Mussolini's rule Genoa and Milan reverted to their Italian forms, while Internazionale was deemed all too cosmopolitan, switching to the name of a Milanese saint – Ambrosia. Italian clubs had certainly been cosmopolitan in their recruitment policies through the 1920s, drawing widely on coaching and playing talent from Austria, Hungary, Czechoslovakia and Yugoslavia. This sat uneasily with the increasingly autocratic economic policy of the regime and the nationalist mission it was placing on football. One was hardly likely to produce the new Italian hero if the league was stuffed full of foreigners. But once again the ideological pretensions of Italian Fascism were immediately undermined: foreigners were banned from the national league in the late 1920s only for clubs to switch their recruitment efforts to South America, where innumerable stars of Italian parentage and thus citizenship were available. The *rimpatriato* as they were known would provide new energy and skills for the successful clubs of the era and the Italian national team itself.

As we have already noted, the First World War was good for French football. The vast national mobilization of manpower saw football spread to every last corner of the country. It also proved to be the most popular mass spectator sport during the war which was indicated by the creation of a whole host of new cup competitions run by the many competing French sporting bureaucracies, including the USFAS's Coupe Nationale, the LFA's Coupe Interfédérale and even cups run by the cycling authorities, the Catholic Church and the British Army. Unofficial international games with the Belgians played in 1916 attracted great crowds and finally, their differences eroded and made petty by the experience of war, the various federations were able to unify behind a single football authority – *Fédération Française du Football* (FFF) – and create a single national French cup and championship in 1919. Gymnastics, fatally tainted by its Germanic connections, collapsed as a sport and rugby proved unable to expand out of its traditional strongholds. By contrast, regions and cities previously without a major football team – like Toulouse and Bordeaux – acquired one. The popularity of football was confirmed in 1924 when the football tournament at the Paris Olympics gave France its national stadium – Stade de Colombes – and provided the most talked-about and best-attended competition of the games.

However, despite these outward displays of modernity and prowess the structure of the French league remained baroque, the payment of players was strictly prohibited and the forces of commercialization were resisted by the football hierarchy, made easier by the poor structural preconditions for investment in France. Apart from a handful of clubs crowds remained small, stadiums were minuscule and success often came to tiny provincial teams like Nîmes, Sète and Cannes. The five-and-a-half-day week, which was crucial to the development of working-class football in Central Europe and Scandinavia, arrived exceptionally late in France – it was not enshrined in law or translated into reality until the arrival of the Popular Front government in the late 1930s. That said, hidden professionalism – or *amateurisme marron* – was public knowledge.

The FFF first investigated the matter of professionalism officially in 1929, but the pressure of small teams and regional leagues, afraid that they would be unable to compete in a free market for players with the biggest clubs in a real national league, forced the FFF to conclude that it should be resisted. What broke the stranglehold of both old-fashioned amateur gentlemen and the small clubs was the rising force in French football and the French economy – the new industrial entrepreneurs. Jean-Pierre Peugeot, founder and owner of the car company, created FC Sochaux in 1929 from two smaller clubs in the region of Peugeot's home town and factory complexes.

Peugeot was not alone in his support for football. Across the country, industrialists had been investing in football: a textile magnate was the president of FC Roubaix; a rich brewer, Henri de Jooris, occupied the same slot at Lille; and the Guichard family, who had created a huge grocery business, backed Saint-Étienne. La Cesne, a grain merchant, helped establish Olympique de Marseille, while the Laurent brothers divided their time between a drapery business and the football club in Sedan. The pressure worked. The FFF, now supported by the French sports press, created a new category of registered footballer who could play for fixed wages on fixed contracts. By 1933 the top flight of French football was professional but its clubs and crowd remained small. Uniquely in Europe, apart perhaps from Sweden's foundry-town sides, the clubs of small and medium-sized towns backed by paternalistic family-owned firms acquired an economic and sporting edge over the middle-class associations of the big cities where the potentially largest crowds existed. The French Cup Final, though honoured by the presence of the President of the Republic, attracted crowds around one-quarter of the size of its English equivalent.

VII

The march of professionalism in the most advanced football nations halted north of the Alps. In the Low Countries, Denmark, Sweden and Germany, despite the existence of the preconditions for professionalization similar to the Western Mediterranean, the game remained amateur. Immediately after the First World War all these societies experienced a massive upsurge in the popularity of domestic and international football. Working-class players and crowds flocked to the game, but the wider balance of social forces conspired to limit the commercialization that these changes made possible.

In Denmark the principal constraints were size and ideology. Given the economic, demographic and social power of the country's independent farmers and the relatively small size of its industrial working class, the urban market for football was smaller than perhaps the country's level of economic development would normally warrant. But more importantly the culture of amateurism ran very deeply in Denmark's football elite. The Danish FA had, after all, been established more than twenty years before its French and Spanish equivalents and had absorbed and emulated British football when amateurism was the norm. Danish football's commitment to corinthian notions of fair play in the 1920s was palpable even to the now cynical British press. The same kind of upper-class moral rigour was directed at professionalism. The Swedish national team were roundly condemned in the Danish press for the luxurious overprovision of facilities and training which, for the Danes, bordered on the professional. Any Danish player with the temerity to get paid was, until long after the Second World War, banned from the national team. Professionalism was not defeated or rejected: it barely surfaced.

In Sweden and Germany the challenge and opportunity offered by much faster and more concentrated industrialization and urbanization and a correspondingly larger and more powerful working class brought both football cultures to the brink of professionalization in the early 1930s. But in both cases the move was stopped in its tracks. In the case of Sweden this was because of the wider political triumph of the working class – represented by the strait-laced, teetotal Lutheranism of the Social Democratic Party and its allied social movements; in the case of Germany because the working class and its allies were so comprehensively defeated by the rise of the Nazis.

Football boomed in Sweden in the 1920s. In 1924 the Swedish FA was able to establish a national league for the first time, though over the next twenty years every title but two went to teams from the more industrialized west coast. While before the First World War the Swedish press had been rather conservative and aloof in its coverage of football, the emergence of a large literate working-class constituency saw new forms of football journalism develop. Newspapers were perhaps the key agents in promoting football. Using the same mix of personalized gossip and local rivalry that had been pioneered in the British press, Swedish papers made football a staple element of the popular culture of the nation's cities and many small industrial towns. The kinds of local patriotism and identification that these conditions encouraged were made even greater by the creation and funding of 'foundry teams' like Sandviken, Degerfors and Åtvidaberg. In these small towns a single large employer, usually in the metallurgy or forestry sectors, would dominate the economic and social life of the community. In the face of a rapidly mobilizing working class a combination of class panic and old-fashioned *noblesse oblige* saw factory owners invest in the local football team. In the bigger towns and cities where the economy was more diverse and this kind of provincial paternalism was ineffective, football, already divided before the war, crystallized along class lines. In Gothenburg GAIS and Örgryte formed the lower and upper poles of football's social scale; in Malmö their equivalents were FF and IFK.

The consequences of this enormous growth in Swedish football were twofold. First, the rational amateurism of the 1910s which had permitted small payments in kind and time-off-work money for players in the national team was systematically undermined. As gate receipts rose, Swedish football became riddled with job-fixing schemes for players, lavish drinking escapades, banquets, dinners and other forms of hidden remuneration. Second, the now massively increased crowds at football became steadily more voluble, drunk and disorderly. The nation's first large-scale pitch invasion occurred at a game between the visiting Scots Airdrieonians and a Stockholm team in 1925. Newspapers report that a Swedish player had been assaulted by the Scots, unnoticed by the referee. The Scots then scored and the crowd, already incensed, poured on to the pitch. The following year, in the same stadium, a similar chain of events during the game between Sweden and Italy saw the invasion repeated.[26] Both occasions point to the root causes of the problem: the changing demographic of the crowd, increasingly young, poor and beyond the immediate control of older family members and work colleagues; the potent brew of intense local and national patriotism; the widespread problem of poor refereeing which even the Swedish FA acknowledged was a legitimate cause for anger; and the essential catalyst of strong and rough alcohol.

In response to these problems some of the bourgeois clubs had tried experimenting with high ticket prices in an attempt to keep the rabble out, but this resulted in a widespread spectator strike which forced the clubs to relent. The Swedish FA responded by wringing its hands and putting up a lot of placards imploring good behaviour from the crowd.

By 1933, the peak year for football disturbances in inter-war Sweden, the FA had finally resorted to closing the grounds of the worst offenders. But what really transformed Swedish football was not the Swedish FA but the great sweep of social and political change that began with the election of the nation's first Social Democratic government in 1932. Over the previous decades practical and ideological opposition to the growing popularity of football had been mounting. The old liberal bourgeoisie continued to run the FA, but were finding it increasingly hard to run the game beyond its own Stockholm offices. The declining political and social authority of this class was made palpable by football. They were joined by the traditional buttresses of the social order – the police force and the free churches – and the new forces of popular politics. The temperance movement, which in Sweden's highly problematic drinking culture had risen to a position of quite exceptional political and social prominence, was a staunch opponent of the alcohol-soaked atmosphere at football matches. The trade-union movement and the Social Democratic Party also had their doubts and mimicked their Germanic and Central European counterparts who had attacked elite sport and sought to create alternative workers' sports and football cultures.

The genius of Sweden's Social Democrats – the most electorally successful left-of-centre political party in the twentieth century – was compromise. Where others, like the German Social Democrats and most European communists, had rejected class alliances, held out for total control and been punished for it, the Social Democrats attained power in Sweden by forging a lasting reformist alliance with the nation's small farmers. Having achieved power, they were able to stay there by striking a series of profound bargains with organized labour and the industrial and financial capital that enabled them to steer the economy out of the global recession and embark upon forty years of unbroken growth and welfare expenditure. In the realm of football, the radical socialist alternative was dropped in favour of reform and control of the existing structures from above. The pools industry, which had become a major illegal operation in the previous decade, was in effect nationalized by the creation of AB Tipstjänst – a state-controlled pools company – in 1934. With control over this significant revenue stream, the government was able to exert considerable influence on football. The Swedish FA finally decided to crack down on the hidden professionalism of the leading clubs in the same year. Malmö's successful working-class club FF were the main targets of this assault. Under sustained government pressure the national sports bureaucracies applied themselves to the control of entertainment and expenses budgets, and the game of hidden employment. In alliance with local police forces and the temperance movement the government and the FA brought crowd disorder under control with a characteristically Swedish mix: the public shaming of miscreants; rational reforms to policing and transportation; rigid control of alcohol consumption; and a real attempt to address the problem of refereeing through intensified training and special appointments for inflammatory games.

Although football continued to be popular amongst the ranks of the German Army during the war, civilian football in the dying days of the Wilhelminian Empire descended into chaos. National-level competition was out of the question and in the *Länder* things were little better. The South German FA's Iron Cross tournament was thrown open to any team who could show up at the right place and the right time. Teams were so depleted by conscription that in Stuttgart deadly local rivals – Offenbach and Kickers – temporarily merged in the hope of fielding a full team. Then, as the blockade began to bite, Germany's urban green spaces were requisitioned for growing potatoes and cabbage. When football did re-emerge it did so in the Weimar Republic. The Hohenzollerns had stepped down and a series of shaky coalitions took power in Germany's first experiment with full parliamentary democracy. As in Austria the newly realized weight of the working-class electorate saw the early introduction of the eight-hour day and weekend holidays. The vast corpus of legislation that had restricted associational life in the Kaiser's Germany was abandoned altogether. At breakneck speed workers' clubs formed all across the country, often with the active support of local government, finally in the hands of the Left. Player registrations with the Deutscher Fussball-Bund (DFB) rose fivefold and crowds spilt out of the still puny grounds and pavilions around the country. Around 6,000 had seen the last national championship in peacetime. In the first national championship to be held after the war, 36,000 saw 1.FC Nürnberg beat SpVgg Fürth 2–0.

These two small-town south German clubs were the leading forces in the game in the 1920s, often providing the entire national team between them – though relations were so bad that they travelled to away matches in separate carriages. Nürnberg had the edge over Fürth, winning five titles in a decade and acquiring the nickname *Der Klub* along the way. This was certainly one of the most cosmopolitan of clubs in Germany employing at times a Swiss coach and a British manager, Fred Spikesley. Before the war they had played a lot of games against touring English professional sides, a learning curve that culminated in a 1–1 draw with Tottenham Hotspur in 1914. In the post-war squad, alongside the first German celebrity players like goalkeeper Heiner Stuhlfauth, Nürnberg recruited Alfred Schaffer, the centre-forward with Budapest's MTK. In official matches between July 1918 and February 1922 Nürnberg went undefeated, winning a second national title along the way. In that year's national championship final they met the rising stars of Hamburger SV and gave German domestic football what it had hitherto lacked – a genuine epic. The stuff of which myths can be made.

---

22 June 1922
1.FC Nürnberg 2 Hamburger SV 2
Berlin

A moment of supreme pleasure for the inveterate numerologists and mathematical seers among football fans. It's the German national championship final, Nuremberg against Hamburg, it's 22 June 1922 and it's 2–2 at 90 minutes. There are no provisions for anything other than extra time. The teams played on, players coming and going from the pitch as exhaustion and injuries mounted. Nuremberg's Anton Kugler lost five teeth and kept going. 'They were staggering across the pitch near a complete breakdown. Nobody had any strength left for a shot on goal, but nobody was willing to give up either.' In near darkness, the referee Dr Paco Bauwens calls time after three hours and ten minutes.

The authorities stage a replay in Leipzig and after 90 minutes it's 1–1. The only imbalance after 400 minutes is that Nuremberg's Boss has been sent off, it's eleven against ten. Extra time begins and Nuremberg are down to nine as Kugler retires. Still 1–1. Then Nuremberg are down to eight as Trag is sent off for a spiteful foul. Still 1–1 at half-time in extra time. Nuremberg's Luitpold Popp collapses and they are down to seven. The referee abandons the match and the lawyers step in. Hamburg claim victory, Nuremberg argue that Popp could have recovered in time to continue. The DFB give the cup to Hamburg on the condition they renounce it; which grudgingly they do.

At the replay in Leipzig over 60,000 crammed themselves into a stadium built for 40,000. Industrial football, mass football, had arrived in Germany and was tumbling out of the terracing and on to the cinder track and the pitch.

HSV won the title for real the following year and along with Fortuna Düsseldorf, Hertha Berlin and Bayern München challenged and then surpassed *Der Klub*, playing faster, more abrasive football. Hertha in particular offered the kind of saga that captured popular attention. They were a technically accomplished and well-funded side that made four finals in a row and lost every one of them, magnetically attracting bad luck and misfortune or suffering a terrible breakdown of nerves and confidence. Better still, for the story-makers, in 1930 they won a wild, open final at the fifth time of asking, 5–4 against Holstein Kiel in front of 45,000 hostile, fruit-throwing Kiel fans.

The organization that was notionally overseeing this exuberant new football culture was the same old DFB. Its senior figures and ruling culture remained deeply conservative, subscribing to an unrepentant version of the 'stab in the back theory' which explained Germany's

military defeat and subsequent humiliation as the consequence of spineless politicians who had hamstrung a still capable military machine; the
same politicians that now staffed the Weimar Republic. The extent of
the DFB's corporate allegiance to the new republic can be gauged from
the flag debate of the early 1920s. On its own emblems the organization
continued to use the red, white and black of the empire rather than the
red, gold and black of the republic. In these new circumstances the DFB
held fast to what it knew. Football was still seen to be a healthy and
wholesome contribution to the physical training and moral improvement
of the nation's youth – though quite how far this ideal spread down the
social scale was another matter. The DFB and the middle-class leadership of German football were decidedly unhappy with the flood of new
working-class applicants to their clubs and the new wave of authentic
proletarian teams that were springing up. The social and ideological
divisions between middle-class and working-class support were sufficiently great that the opening of the new municipal stadium in Dortmund was celebrated twice: first by clubs from the bourgeois sports
movement and the following day by workers' sports clubs.

The rising star of working-class German football was Schalke 04, a
club from the small mining town of Gelsenkirchen in the northern Ruhr.
The first mine shaft was sunk in Gelsenkirchen in 1855. By the early
twentieth century there were three huge coal-mining complexes, many
ancillary shafts and facilities and a sprawl of oven factories, engineering
workshops and chemical works that merged with the vast Essen and
Dortmund conurbations. Few places were more representative of the
speed and scale of German industrialization and the new working-class
communities it seemingly conjured out of thin air, for Gelsenkirchen
like much of the region had no indigenous proletariat. Workers were
sucked in from the east as far as German-speaking Poland. It was among
this class of first- and second-generation miners and factory hands that
Westfalia Schalke was founded in 1904, at the time little more than
a street team of teenagers from Hauergasse Strasse. Conditions were
primitive, the boys reduced to buying up the damaged balls from middle-
class clubs and repairing them or nailing calkins to old pit shoes to make
boots. At first the club played on a gully-ridden, stone-strewn field in
the grounds of a ruined country house on the west side of the town. In
1914 the club was able to rent a plot of land in Gelsenkirchen itself, but
they had to clear, drain and rebuild it themselves. Nonetheless, with

little else to provide distraction and entertainment from the unbending rhythms of working life, Schalke became popular and successful.

In the immediate post-war era the steady rise of Schalke and teams like them through the local league pyramids alarmed the bourgeoisie of the regional football association. Ostensibly seeking to damp down a worrisome competitiveness that was mutating into crowd disorder and on-pitch fighting, the association introduced its 'new-way policy' – actually more a case of maintaining the old way by suspending promotion and relegation for two years and keeping Schalke and their kind out of the top division. As one Schalke player remarked: 'They didn't want to have us in their top division . . . the middle-class clubs . . . only wanted to play among themselves.'[27] But the German working class could not be contained for ever, and in 1926 Schalke were promoted to the top division in the west of Germany. By this time they had helped to create an intense and fervent working-class football culture across the Ruhr. Schalke were able to build their first proper stadium in 1928, which could admit 40,000; the club paid a trifling rent to one of the local collieries for the land.

Once the chaotic inflation of the early 1920s had been quelled and the most fearsome implications of the Versailles Treaty blunted, the German economy experienced a brief boom. Combined with the post-war boom in football attendances and the increasing presence of working-class players without visible means or alternative support, the commercial dynamic of professionalism was reactivated. But it had to be done in the utmost secrecy for the DFB remained staunch defenders of a very orthodox model of amateurism.

The DFB's position was so strict that in 1924, in response to the legalization of professionalism in Austria and Hungary, they declared that the national team would not play opponents who fielded professionals. This was all the more rigorous given that Austria and Hungary were among the handful of teams that would contemplate playing the Germans. The mounting anecdotal evidence of hidden professionalism in German football saw the DFB mount a punitive investigation of Schalke in 1930. The result inevitably concluded: 'First-team players have been receiving expenses greatly in excess of what is acceptable.'[28] The DFB followed this up with draconian punishments. Fourteen players were banned from playing; the club received a large fine and could not compete in DFB competitions for a year. The club treasurer

Wilhelm Nier was so humiliated by the case that he committed suicide; and all for nothing. Schalke were allowed back into the championship in 1931 and 70,000 paid to see them in a friendly with Fortuna Düsseldorf.

The logic of amateurism was so out of kilter with the reality of the game that mere fines and bans would not be enough to prevent the commercialization of football. The gap in quality between professionals and amateurs was cruelly exposed in 1931 when the *Wunderteam* annihilated the Germans 5–0 and 6–0. Now, there was movement. In the regions where crowds were biggest and football most popular – the Ruhr, the south, Berlin – the pressure for legalizing payments was mounting. In 1932 the DFB agreed to hold a decisive meeting to address the issue on 25 May 1933. On 30 January 1933 President Hindenburg appointed Adolf Hitler Chancellor. The meeting would never happen and a power greater than anything the DFB could hitherto have imagined, a power great enough to counter the logic of the mass market and reduce Germany and the rest of Europe to rubble, would take control of German football.

7

The Rules of the Game: International Football and International Politics, 1900–1934

The less we do to put diplomatic pressure on football the better
British Foreign Office memo, 1933

Mes p'tits gars! Mes p'tits gars chéris! Mes p'tits gars français!
Listen to me! For fourteen years *L'Auto* has come out every day
and has never given you bad advice, eh? Well then, just listen!

The Prussians are a bunch of bastards . . . dirty square heads,
mindless sheep without the slightest initiative and ready for the
slaughter. You've got to get them this time, those dirty bastards . . .

This is the big match that you have to play and you must use
every trick that you've learned in sport . . . But beware! When your
bayonet is at their heart and they beg for mercy, don't give in. Run
them through!   **Henri Desgrange, *L'Auto*, 3 August 1914**

It is well to remember that if you play football with a man . . . then
you won't want to kill him, no matter what the politicians think
about it. We want to foster a real brotherhood of man, and the
best way to do it, in my view, is by encouraging the nations to meet
each other in games.   **Lord Decies, Vice President of
the British Olympic Association**

I

The clipped, understated wisdom of British Civil Service advice; the virtually deranged, ultra-nationalist editor of the French sports daily *L'Auto*; and the lofty, hopeless naivety of an Olympian cosmopolitanism. These contrasting words illustrate the main ways that European and American elites thought about international sport and international politics in the first third of the twentieth century – that they were best kept well apart; that sport was war or at least politics by other means; that sport could underpin a utopian politics of peace. In the great arc of world history between the foundation of FIFA in 1904 and the 1934 World Cup, the Olympian vision of football, indeed any sport, as a universalist peacemaker was reduced to tatters. Nationalist politics crushed these hopes, hijacking both the staging of sporting contests and the meaning that they were invested with among domestic publics and in the international political arena. The British position – that politics was simply not appropriate or relevant to the conduct of the game – whatever its actual worth, became impossible to sustain in the face of opponents who increasingly invested football matches and football prowess with cultural and political weight.

The Olympians had their supporters among the elites of the industrialized world, and a major constituency among sports that remained resolutely amateur like athletics. Many of FIFA's founders shared the same vision of universalism and pacifism that animated the International Olympic Committee. However, the charnel house of the First World War took most of the gloss off their early optimism; five Olympic Games (1896–1912) did not seem to have put much of a brake on the inter-imperial rivalries that eventually devastated Europe. By the time that the grotesque propaganda exercise that was the 1936 Berlin Olympics had been held, any residual hope that the Olympian spirit was sufficiently powerful to neutralize the pathological passions of nationalism was looking threadbare.

In Britain, certainly prior to the late 1920s, there was general agreement among the football bureaucracies and the Foreign Office that football and politics did not and should not be mixed. Cricket, closer to the social class and sporting hearts of the diplomatic elite, was seen as a vital cultural cement in fusing Imperium and colonies, but football had no such role. Even a voice as often bellicose and nationalist as the *Daily Express* remarked upon a flurry of concern over playing the Germans in 1929: 'Could anything be sillier or more futile? It does not matter in the least whether we beat the Germans at "Soccer" or are beaten by them. But it does matter a great deal that we should be free and willing to meet them in "friendly strifes and rivalries of peace".'[1] However, it was becoming increasingly obvious to political and sporting observers that not everyone agreed. A leader in *The Times* on the same occasion read, 'No appearance of, say, Frenchmen in Germany or of Czechs in Austria can wholly be devoid of meaning to the onlookers. International politics are very deeply rooted in the minds of the average European.'[2] And that of course was the problem. Britain might hold fast to its vision of friendly, depoliticized sport, but if one's opponents – those others, those Europeans – did not do so, then the game was lost. When the British Consul in Turin reported back to the Foreign Office in 1928 on the social significance of Italian football, he argued that the Continental viewed matters from a 'different mental angle'.[3]

Although Latin America and Continental Europe had their own small bands of Olympians and their own version of the 'keep politics out of football brigade', it was the proponents of 'sport as politics by other means' that came to set the rules of the game. Before the First World War, as we have seen, nationalists and armed forces across Europe looked to mass participation in sport as an instrument of national regeneration, racial-biological survival and military advantage. Sport was often described in the language of warfare to make it appear an appropriate practice for military training. Now, as in the case of Desgrange, when the real war began sport would provide the metaphors for its conduct. The triumph of the 'sport as politics' model in international football was in part the result of post-war politics – ultra-nationalists, most notably European fascists, steadily came to power and influence in the 1920s and 1930s. And Britain's refusal to assume a decisive leadership role in the creation of international football gave them space to play.

The great wave of adventurous, outward-looking Britons who took football all over the world in the late nineteenth century were not complemented at home by an adventurous outward-looking football hierarchy. Indeed the peculiar conditions of Britain's early football development and the nation's relationship with the international politics of Europe produced quite the opposite: an elite that tended towards isolationism and a barely masked but overweening arrogance. The early and comprehensive commercialization of British football gave it such a headstart over other nations that the gap in competitive terms was so vast as to warrant no serious comparison. The already lukewarm relationship between British football and FIFA before 1914 was made colder still by the hurts and suspicions produced by the Great War.

Although British football associations would return to the fold, they were if anything less inclined to get themselves embroiled in European affairs. In some senses this was liberating, for Britain's absence opened up the global stage to the new football powers: both Latin America and Central Europe were key innovators in the development of international football. But there was a price to pay too. In the vacuum left by Britain's absence, and despite the best intentions of FIFA and its sincere, gentlemanly, progressive liberalism, international football became deeply politicized, a process that reached its inter-war apogee in Mussolini's Italy at the 1934 World Cup. In retrospect perhaps this was inevitable, for international football came of age at precisely the moment that mass ultra-nationalist politics was at its height in Europe and Latin America. More finely attuned to the manipulation of popular taste, more ready and able to intervene in mass culture than the bumbling empires of *fin de siècle* Europe, the new dictators and populists of the 1920s and 1930s took a close and active interest in the game and there was no one to stop them.

International football was born in 1872 and its origins are remarkably parochial. It is only in the geography of football (and rugby) that England vs. Scotland constituted an international encounter. For the next four years the only such games were between England and Scotland, then in 1876 the Welsh took on the Scots for the first time and an Irish team first played in 1882. At the end of the nineteenth century Britain alone made the rules on and off the pitch. In 1882 representatives of the four Home Nations' (as they were collectively referred to) football associations met and created the International Association Football Board (IAFB) which was to serve as the ultimate football law-making body. The board promptly insisted on the use of fixed crossbars rather than tape or string, and arranged the world's first international football tournament: the Home Championships. It was first played in 1884 and won by Scotland. The centrepiece of the championship was the England–Scotland game and by 1906 representative teams of predominantly professionals rather than amateurs drew 100,000 to Hampden Park to see Scotland win 2–1. On the eve of the First World War the fixture drew 127,000.

English amateur elevens of various kinds played at both the 1908 and 1912 Olympic Games and went on short tours across Western Europe and Scandinavia before 1914. These sides were treated by their opponents as the official representatives of English football, but the FA did not accord them the status of full internationals. An England side including professionals, and deemed to be an official outing by the FA, did not play their first game until 1908 when they trounced the Austrians in Vienna and the Hungarians in Budapest. They repeated the feat the following year but that was that. England would not play overseas again until 1920. The Scots, Welsh and Irish made the English look gregarious. They played no games outside the British Isles whatsoever. By contrast, English amateur club sides were in demand and grabbed the chance of a foreign jaunt: the Corinthians, various Nomads, diverse Wanderers, Old Boys, University and regimental teams, from the London-based English Civil Service to the mining community side Bishop Auckland from the north, all played across Central and Western Europe and in the case of Wanderers as far east as Moscow. Given the kind of paying crowds that these teams could pull in, professional football clubs were not far behind them; over thirty English and Scottish clubs played abroad in the decade before the First World War, touring across Europe and South America. The north London side Tottenham Hotspur were one of the most industrious, going on eight tours between 1907 and 1914, including one to Argentina and Uruguay. Southend United by contrast limited themselves to a single game against Hertha in Berlin.[4]

Overseas football associations proved less reticent travellers than the British. In Latin America, Argentina and Uruguay began to play each other – officially – in 1901. Austria and Hungary followed suit in 1902. Both pairings created a public spectacle and rivalry that was of equal if not greater social intensity than the England–Scotland clash. With the formation of FIFA in 1904, the French, Dutch, Belgians and Swiss joined the international football circuit, followed by the Scandinavians and, just before the shooting started, Tsarist Russia. Alongside this emergent network of international football, the early twentieth century also saw the development of transnational football. In the cultural and political spaces not yet overrun by centralizing, border-closing nation-states the international football scene was full of pleasing anomalies. For example, Scottish, Welsh and Irish teams were often participants in the notionally English FA Cup. The best teams from Hungary and Bohemia were invited to Vienna to play in *Der Challenge Cup*. Stade Helvétique, the team of Swiss expatriates in Marseilles, won the 1911 French championship, while teams from south-western France and northern Spain played in the cross-border Pyrennean Cup before a national tournament existed in either country. Milan and other leading northern Italian clubs crossed the Alps to play the Chiasso Cup in Switzerland from 1901. Yet Milan would not meet a team from Rome for another ten years.

The development of cross-border postal networks, telegraph lines and railways all in the latter half of the nineteenth century was the key infrastructural precondition for any regularized international sport. These new networks of communication necessitated the creation of international institutions of regulation and technical standardization like the International Telegraph Union created in 1865 and the Universal Postal Union established in 1874. Similar bodies were created in the realms of trade, law, scientific nomenclature and above all time, for no industrialized society can operate and certainly no fixture list can be fulfilled without a singular, agreed time. Greenwich in Britain, despite much French opposition, provided the global standard. Against that background it was obvious to a small group of Western European football administrators that some kind of systematic international regulation of football was required.

As with the creation of standardized world time, it was assumed that Britain would be the reference point for the rest of the world. In 1902 the Dutch Football Association sent a proposal for the formation of such a body to the English FA. The letter was allowed to saunter its way around the offices of the other home nations before the FA eventually replied, suggesting rather vaguely that they would invite everyone to England for a meeting but at a time and place not yet specified. Refusing to take 'sometime' as an answer, Robert Guérin, the president of the French sports body the USFSA, was dispatched to London for interminable and unproductive meetings with Lord Kinnaird, the president of the FA. Guerin reported that their conversations were like 'slicing water with a knife'. Undeterred, Guérin called a meeting of interested parties for 1903, which somehow didn't quite happen, and then tried again in 1904. This time, on 21 May in Rue St-Honoré in Paris, FIFA or in its full Gallic glory Fédération Internationale de Football Association was formed by delegates from seven countries: Belgium, Denmark, France, the Netherlands, Spain, Sweden and Switzerland. It should be said, however, that Robert Guérin represented only one of three French sporting associations who claimed a role in the regulation of football, while Spain did not even possess a national football association – the delegate was a member of Madrid FC whose claim to represent Castile let alone Catalonia was questionable. Initially, the British stayed aloof but Germany, Austria, Italy and Hungary all quickly signed up.

In 1906 the English finally arrived and, recognizing the reality of the new dispensation, the FA began to sever its formal links with the football associations of Argentina, Chile and South Africa, all of whom joined FIFA over the next decade, as did the USA. Czech Bohemia applied for membership as well but the Austrians called for their exclusion on the grounds that Bohemia was really an Austrian territory. But then if Bohemia could not join on the grounds of sovereignty, how could Scotland and Ireland, who had also applied, be allowed in? If the Bohemians were allowed in then the Austrians and Germans threatened to make applications for all of their constituent regional states. The

Bohemians inevitably got squeezed out. Scotland and Ireland were allowed in but no applications arrived from the Holstein or Saarland FAs. Finland and Norway, recently released from Russian and Swedish dominion respectively, marked their entry into the club of independent nation-states by both gaining FIFA membership in 1908.

During this era FIFA remained as much a gentlemen's club as it was an international bureaucracy: its membership was exclusively male and upper class or professional in social origin. International tournaments and European championships had been planned in great detail and endlessly proposed within the federation, but FIFA actually organized nothing. Its work was overwhelmingly concentrated on the necessary paper shuffling of regulating international football, providing referees, deciding who could join and who could play with who and when. Yet this could generate friction, particularly during the final years before the war when the German delegates, no doubt emboldened by domestic Anglophobia and rivalry, began to press for FIFA to take control of the laws of the game and subsume the IAFB. In 1913 the IAFB decided to let 'those Continental people' in by giving FIFA one seat on the board, though nullifying its power by insisting that any proposal required a four-fifths majority. The newly constituted board met for the first time in Paris in spring 1914. The British were of course to spend another four long years encamped in France.

Britain's absence from and then wariness towards FIFA in its early years meant more than just relinquishing the name of the world body to the French language. It also meant that the organization's ideological soul was and remains more Gallic than Anglo-Saxon. The entirely disinterested keep-politics-out-of-sport model of the British, although present in FIFA, has always been accompanied by a stronger and more articulate version of Olympian cosmopolitanism, albeit shorn of the IOC's obsessive hard-line amateurism. Before the war FIFA and its small circle of enthusiasts were committed to a notionally depoliticized football and a friendly communitarianism that might help evoke global peace and understanding. In the tense final days of the summer of 1914, as the Continent seemed to be poised for war, FIFA passed a resolution announcing to anyone who might have been listening that they would 'support any action which tends to bring the nations nearer to each other and to substitute arbitration for violence in the settlement of all the conflicts which might arise between them'.[5] But nobody was listening. Later on the same day Archduke Ferdinand was assassinated in Sarajevo and the fateful sequence of events that led to war was triggered.

While the First World War was instrumental in transforming football from the game of the European and Latin American urban elites into the game of the working classes, its immediate effect on international football was destructive. FIFA effectively went into cold storage between 1914 and 1918. Only four nations outside Latin America played any international fixtures during the war: Norway, Denmark and Sweden, who played among themselves in their cocoon of Scandinavian neutrality, and the USA, who received Denmark and Sweden in 1917 just before the U-boat blockade made safe travel for neutrals impossible.

When the war ended in 1918, the victors set about both punishing the defeated and fundamentally redrawing the borders of Europe and the Middle East. FIFA's membership reflected both processes. At the centre of the post-war diplomatic settlement were the various peace treaties, of which Versailles was the most important, and the creation of the League of Nations. The League, which was based in Geneva, was designed to be the expression and instrument of the international community of nation-states – committed to peace. The defeated Central Powers – Germany and the disintegrating Austro-Hungarian Empire – were not initially allowed to join the League of Nations. Sport followed suit. In late 1919 the IOC effectively excluded them from the Olympics by handing over the power of invitation to the Belgians who were hosting the 1920 games in Antwerp. Whatever the legal and diplomatic niceties of the IOC's charter, nobody could reasonably expect Belgium – occupied by the Germans for four years – to invite the defeated powers.

Opinion within FIFA varied. Certainly there was considerable support from the French and the Dutch for the exclusion of the Central Powers, but by far the harshest line was pursued by the notionally depoliticized world of English football. The FA minutes that record discussion on the question tersely note that 'the Football Association could not entertain any association, official or unofficial, with the Central Empire's associations'; a tone that reflected the widespread belief among most of the British public that the aggressors should be punished.[6] Sweden and Italy resisted the British-inspired FIFA proposal that not only the Central Powers but also any national association who played them, or whose clubs played their clubs, should be excluded. Both FAs asserted their right to play who they liked and although the FIFA executive committee reiterated their commitment to keeping the Germans and Austrians out, it was not good enough for the English. They and the three other Home Countries left the organization in 1920. The ramifications of this policy meant that the following year Aberdeen and Dumbarton could play local clubs in Denmark, but not in Sweden whose international side had played Austria early in the year. The burden of proof fell to British clubs to demonstrate the bona fides of their prospective foreign opposition, creating an almost insurmountable hurdle to Glasgow Rangers' European tour of 1922. Gradually, though, the FA, like British public opinion, began to relent in its anti-German stance. Aberdeen were allowed to play in Vienna; then clubs could play anywhere. There was now no reason to remain outside the FIFA fold and in 1924 the home nations rejoined.

The most immediate political impact of the First World War was to shatter the political legitimacy and reach of its imperial dynasties. They were broken by military defeat, economic and social exhaustion and internal nationalist revolts. When the time came to pick up the pieces, they were arranged in accordance with the principles of nationalist self-determination insisted upon by President Woodrow Wilson and the American government at the peace negotiations. Even the British Empire was forced to yield its oldest colony – Ireland. Or most of it at any rate. The end of the Irish uprising was followed by the partition of Ireland and the establishment of the Free State. As with almost every national, cultural or political organization, football divided. The Football Association of Ireland (FAI) was established in 1921 and with the active support of the new Ministry of Foreign Affairs applied for and received FIFA membership in 1923. The Belfast-based Irish Football Association (IFA) was particularly troubled by this and stoked the already smouldering embers of conflict by continuing to claim the right to pick players from the whole island of Ireland. But as the home nations were not at this point members of FIFA, there was little they could do about the FAI's recognition. What they could do, and what in retrospect appears little more than a calculated act of political spite, was to agree collectively that no home country would play the FAI national team or any FAI-affiliated club; a sure way of starving the nation's Lilliputian football culture of competition, income and support.

Before the war Austria and Hungary were both members of FIFA, but with the collapse of Habsburg rule, Bohemia was finally freed and in its new incarnation as Czechoslovakia joined the League of Nations and FIFA. Yugoslavia – an ersatz monarchy created from the demographic chaos of the Croatian, Slovenian and Bosnian provinces of the empire and the previously independent Serbia – joined FIFA in 1919 with the active support of the royal house for what was perhaps the only other functioning Yugoslav national institution at the time. Poland, at last freed from the triple domination of Habsburgs, Hohenzollerns and Romanovs, re-emerged as an independent entity for the first time in nearly two centuries. FIFA membership and international football followed. The three Baltic states of Estonia, Latvia and Lithuania, which had managed to pull themselves free from the wreckage of the disintegrating Russian empire, were even more fervent international footballers, joining FIFA in the early 1920s and establishing their own regular Baltic Cup. Longer-standing football cultures with tardier bureaucracies – like Greece, Romania and Portugal – drifted in late.

The already established nation-states of the New World overcame the tyranny of distance that separated them from Europe. With the exceptions of Argentina and Chile (pre-First World War) and Colombia and Venezuela (1936 and 1952 respectively), the whole of South America (Paraguay, Brazil, Uruguay, Ecuador, Peru and Bolivia) joined FIFA in the 1920s and through their own regional organization CONMEBOL ran the most systematic programme of international football in the world. The USA, which was the only member of FIFA north of Argentina before the First World War, was joined by Canada, Mexico, the Central American states of Costa Rica, Panama, Guatemala, El Salvador and the independent Caribbean islands of Cuba and Haiti. Football, now in the shadow of more established American sports, remained confined to small metropolitan areas in this vast and underconnected region. It was only in the late 1930s that there was any push to develop a programme of international matches or to create confederations and organizations.

The map of the Middle East was transformed by the collapse of the Ottoman Empire at the end of the First World War. From out of the ruins emerged the modern Turkish nation-state under the rule of President Kemal Atatürk. Football, though popular during the short-lived

Allied occupation of Istanbul by British and Empire troops in 1918, virtually disappeared during the turbulence of the war with Greece and the founding of the republic. But once created, Turkey immediately signed up – FIFA and football representing the 'universal civilization' towards which Atatürk was determinedly reorientating the country. The old provinces of the Ottoman Empire had been carved up by and distributed between the French and British. Egypt, the first to throw off the shackles of this latest phase of imperial rule, were next to join in 1923. Lebanon and Syria, which had formed part of the French sphere of influence in the region, drove off the French in the 1920s and early 1930s. Both countries followed their declarations of new republics with FIFA membership in 1935 and 1937 respectively. The British zone of influence included Iraq, Trans-Jordan and Palestine. While football was certainly being played in the southern oil fields of Iraq and in Amman, the main city of Trans-Jordan, there was no question that either would be acquiring independence or applying to join FIFA in the inter-war era; but in Palestine, where British rule and intentions were under much greater assault, it was another matter.

Before the British arrived in Palestine there was a small informal football culture among the European Jewish immigrants to the area and there are reports of games being played with Turkish soldiers in the first half of the First World War and with the British in the second half. The Turks had been defeated and expelled in the break. After a period of de facto occupation, the British received the League of Nations' mandate to administer Palestine in 1922. The football-playing component of the rapidly growing Jewish communities – the *yeshiva* – was reinforced by a new wave of migrants from Western and Central Europe who had been exposed to football at home and in the Continent's armies. By the mid-1920s both the Left and the Right of Jewish politics had formed their own social movements and corresponding sports clubs (Hapoel and Maccabi) and football was the most popular game among the young men that flocked to them. Competition from British army and police teams was stiff; games often descended into fisticuffs over accusations of anti-Jewish refereeing by British officials, but the trouble remained on the pitch. Mainstream Jewish political opinion had not yet begun to regard the British mandate as an encumbrance or problem. It was in this atmosphere of relative civil peace that football enthusiast Josef Yekutieli led an application to FIFA for the accession of the Palestine Football

Federation. A similar attempt to win recognition from the IAAF in 1924 had floundered on the exclusive Jewishness of the athletics movement. Yekutieli offered FIFA the assurance that the federation and the game would remain open to everyone: Jews, Arabs and Christians. FIFA accepted and Palestine became a member of FIFA in 1929. However, when a national team was sent on a tour of Egypt in 1930 they may have displayed a P on their shirt for Palestine, but in small letters on the pocket one could see LD – the initials of the Hebrew name for Palestine. Finally, the few independent states that remained in East Asia outside the reach of either Asian or European empires – Thailand, the Philippines, Japan and China – joined FIFA too.

From just twenty-four members in 1919 FIFA membership had grown to fifty-six in 1939. But there were again four notable absences. After rejoining FIFA in 1924, the Home Nations stayed for only four years before leaving in 1928; and this time they were leaving good and proper. They would not rejoin FIFA until after the Second World War. Extraordinarily, given the comprehensive commercialization and professionalization of English and Scottish football, it was the issue of amateurism and broken-time payments that led to the second withdrawal. As with the wider cultural and political debates of the 1920s, British football was not uniformly isolationist in its attitudes to Europe. Clubs toured even more extensively than they had before the war. Cordial, even friendly personal relationships and correspondences were established among leading administrators and officials across the Channel. Racing Club de Paris and Arsenal played an annual charity friendly on Armistice Day throughout the 1930s and Belgium were even invited to play in England. But there were limits to all this fraternization: the national team's short summer tours were confined to politically uncontroversial hosts France, Belgium, Sweden, Spain and Luxembourg. Scotland only played their first international against non-British opposition in Norway in 1929. Wales would play only two overseas internationals in the 1930s, both against France, and Northern Ireland played none at all. For many, particularly in the professional game, who had their own reasons for opposing too much international football using the players that they were paying, it just did not seem important. Caustically commenting on the matter, the Football League official Charles Sutcliffe said:

I don't care a brass farthing about the improvement of the game in France, Belgium, Austria or Germany. The FIFA does not appeal to me. An organisation where such football associations as those of Uruguay and Paraguay, Brazil and Egypt, Bohemia and Pan Russia, are co-equal with England, Scotland, Wales and Ireland seems to me to be a case of magnifying the midgets. If Central Europe or any other district want to govern football let them confine their power and authority to themselves and we can look after our own affairs.

Such conceit rested on the unshakeable assumption that however much organizing and regulating foreigners managed to get up to, the gulf in quality and experience on the field was so vast, so unbridgeable that international competition was simply not needed as a calculus of merit. This was a certainty so deeply embedded in British football that it was impervious to empirical challenge. England's surprise defeat by Spain in May 1929, 4–3 in Madrid, was simply brushed aside.

This kind of brusque disdain reached its apogee when the English FA was invited to attend the first World Cup finals in Uruguay in 1930. Official attitudes were no doubt influenced by the account of Chelsea's 1929 Latin American tour given by club director Colonel Charles Crisp to the FA. In one game in Buenos Aires a Chelsea player was punched by the crowd when on the touchline. At Boca Juniors crowd trouble had seen the game come to an early end, followed by attacks on the team bus. But Chelsea scare stories or not, England were never going to the 1930 World Cup. The FA's curt response to the Uruguayans dated 30 November 1929 read:

Dear Sir

The letter of the 10th ultimo from the Asociación Uruguaya de Football inviting a Representative Team of the Football Association to visit Uruguay in July and August next to play in the Worlds Championship [sic] in Montevideo has been considered by our international committee.

I am instructed to express regret at our inability to accept the invitation.

F. J. Wall, sec.[7]

What appeared at the time as an almost inconsequential reflex of a brusque and unreflective superiority appears in retrospect an act of colossal hubris.

IV

If the British would not or could not take the lead in organizing international competition then others would. FIFA, the IOC and the Latin Americans were certainly at the forefront of competition between national teams, but Central Europe, the third pole of advanced football in the inter-war era, was also an innovator. The early arrival of professional football in the old Habsburg Empire did not guarantee financial stability. The sudden rise in expenses and salaries was hard to meet for clubs that were inexperienced in business operations and woefully uncommercialized. However, the profitable tours undertaken by English teams to the region and the crowds these exotic encounters drew convinced Hugo Meisl, the president of FK Austria, that ends could be made to meet from the gate receipts of a tournament between the leading clubs of Central Europe. Meisl called a meeting, held in Venice in 1927, attended by the Austrian, Czech, Hungarian, Yugoslav and Italian FAs, and the Mitropa Cup was born.

The Mitropa Cup (or Copa Europa in Italy) occupies a special, even pivotal place in the history of football. In the twelve years that it was contested before the Second World War it created the defining template for international club football competitions. Its format was a simple knock-out tournament between the leading clubs of Central Europe – which would extend to include teams from Switzerland and Romania too. Each round was played over two legs – home and away – to ensure everyone got a cut of the gate receipts, and to provide a genuine test in which a side had to prove themselves both at home and in the hostile environment of another country. The matches were fantastically popular, the standard of play impressive and, as if to confirm the modernity of the moment, the fixtures were the first to be broadcast live on the radio in Continental Europe. The competition also helped to give rise to the widely circulated notion of a distinctive regional style; as the Italians put it, *Calcio Danubio*. These interconnections were reinforced by the creation of a web of migrating players and coaches between all of these football cultures.

However, interconnectedness is no guarantee of harmony. Neither the Mitropa Cup, nor the customs union between Austria, Hungary and Italy that simultaneously came into effect, could induce it. In the realm of high politics Central Europe was beset by discord and manoeuvring. The wider European conflict of the inter-war years hung over the region as France and Germany sought allies and influence and Italy became an increasingly aggressive presence. In such a charged atmosphere, international football was not merely dragged into politics, it was among its most potent lightning rods. In the immediate wake of Mussolini's assumption of power in Rome, Austrian communists called for mass opposition to the visit of 2,000 Italian fans planning to watch an international in Vienna. As one Austrian diplomat rather ruefully noted, the Mitropa Cup seemed to be resolved more often than not in the embassy than in the stadium. Crowd trouble broke out in the first year of the tournament. In the second leg of the final between Sparta Prague and Rapid, with the aggregate score at 7–4 to the visitors, the Viennese crowd armed with fruit and bottles rained objects down on the Czechs.

The Czechs could dish it out as well. In 1932 Slavia Prague were drawn against Juventus in the semi-finals; after a collision between the Italian Cesarini and a Slavia player, the Czech coach is reported to have thrown a bottle at Cesarini and made some interesting gestures to the rest of the team. The game, which finished 4–0 to Slavia, descended into an extended brawl and culminated in a full-scale pitch invasion.

Both the Czech and Italian governments sought to dampen expectations and passions around the return match, but with Juventus leading 2–0 Slavia's goalkeeper František Plánička fell to the ground apparently struck by a stone from the crowd. Slavia left the field and returned to Prague to a hero's welcome. Both teams were expelled from the tournament. On this occasion international football, like international politics in Central Europe, would prove to be a zero-sum game.

If Central Europe led the way in the development of international club competition, then the pioneers of international tournaments among nations were the South Americans, and the South American championship organized under the auspices of the newly created CONMEBOL was the leading model. The idea of a South American football confederation had first been proposed in 1912 by the Uruguayan parliamentarian and president of Montevideo Wanderers, Héctor Gómez. He mounted a concerted campaign in the press around the tournament staged by the Argentine FA in 1916 to celebrate the centenary of independence from Spain. The following year he was running the new organization from Montevideo and arranging the first official South American championship. The competition was played on virtually an annual basis from 1917 to 1929 in the football strongholds of Buenos Aires and Montevideo (thrice each) and Rio (twice) but also in Viña del Mar, Santiago and Lima. The tournament also drew Bolivia and Paraguay into international competition and attracted close attention from political elites and football publics. But for all the brilliance of the football that was being played by the cream of what were now covertly professional leagues in Argentina, Brazil and Uruguay, the progress of the continent had not been registered by the rest of the world. For that Latin American football would require a global stage. In the first third of the twentieth century the pre-eminent global sporting event was the Olympic Games and the most important international sporting organization the International Olympic Committee. Neither provided much of a platform for football until the sheer weight of public interest in the game over anything else elevated Olympic football to a position of international importance.

The IOC was founded in 1892 by the French aristocrat Baron Pierre de Coubertin, who mobilized sufficient money and support for the first games to be held in Athens in 1896. The sports chosen for the event were heavily influenced by their ancient Hellenic counterparts, with track and field events being the centrepiece of the games. Football at this stage was just a minor exhibition sport. The records of the Athenian XI that played have been lost, though it does seem that an Izmir XI were thrashed 15–0 by a team of Danes. At the next two Olympics, in 1900 in Paris and in 1904 in St Louis, football fared little better. In Paris the matches were a haplessly organized and almost invisible side show to the Universal Exhibition to which they had been attached. Upton Park FC, an amateur team from east London, beat a French team 4–0 and a group of Belgian students somewhere in the Bois de Boulogne. In St Louis hardly any Europeans turned up at all, dissuaded by the prospect of 3,000 miles of ocean and another 1,000 on the railways.

The fourth full Olympic Games held in London in 1908 saw a signal improvement in organization and turn-out. Football was included as a full Olympic sport with leading amateur players chosen from France, England, Denmark, Sweden and Holland. The English beat the Danes in the final, a result repeated in the final of the Stockholm Olympics of 1912. After the war, Antwerp hosted the 1920 Olympics. Football, which even in London and Stockholm had been just one among many events, had clearly become the biggest draw of the games. While the athletics and other events were poorly attended the football matches were full to overflowing, 40,000 coming to see Belgium play Czechoslovakia in the final. The Czechoslovaks, 2–0 down in half an hour, decided that the English referee was too biased for their liking and walked off the field nine minutes later.

Hitherto, Olympic football tournaments had been all-European affairs and their status as the world championship of football, although unchallenged, was rather thin. The 1924 Olympics in Paris remedied both of these weaknesses. The participation of Egypt, Uruguay and the USA gave the tournament a real international feel and although neither the Germans nor the British teams were present, the quality of football was immeasurably improved. The public certainly thought so as nearly 300,000 people attended the matches and 60,000 went to Stade Colombes for the final, with 10,000 left ticketless outside. They had come primarily to see Uruguay, a country so small and distant from Paris that the French had managed to print silk scarves celebrating the games with the flag of every participating nation except one. According to Eduardo Galeano, the team were:

Workers and wanderers who got nothing from football but the pleasure of playing. Pedro Arispe was a meat packer, José Nasazzi cut marble. 'Perucho' Petrone worked for a grocer. Pedro Cea sold ice. José Leandro Andrade was a carnival musician and shoe shiner. They were all twenty years old, more or less, though in the pictures they look like senior citizens. They cured their wounds with saltwater, vinegar plasters and a few glasses of wine. In 1924 they arrived in Europe in third class steerage and then travelled on borrowed money in second class carriages, sleeping on the wooden benches and playing game after game in exchange for room and board.[8]

Once they took to the field France took notice. Uruguay, despite having their flag hung upside down and a Brazilian march played instead of the national anthem, dispatched Yugoslavia 7–0, then the USA 3–0, and comprehensively outplayed their hosts beating them 5–1. Uruguay met Switzerland in the final and beat them comfortably 3–0. But the scoreline gives no sense of just how extraordinary the Latin Americans appeared to the Europeans. The ecstatic Gabriel Hanot, later editor of *L'Équipe*, wrote:

The principal quality of the victors was a marvellous virtuosity in receiving the ball, controlling it and using it. They have such a complete technique that they also have the necessary leisure to note the position of partners and team-mates. They do not stand still waiting for a pass. They are on the move, away from markers, to make it easy for their team-mates ... The Uruguayans are supple disciples of the spirit of fitness rather than geometry. They have pushed towards perfection the art of the feint and swerve and the dodge, but they also know how to play directly and quickly. They are not only ball jugglers. They created a beautiful football, elegant but at the same time varied, rapid, powerful, effective. Before these fine athletes, who are to the English professionals like Arab thoroughbreds next to farm horses, the Swiss were disconcerted.[9]

When the news came down the telegraph cables, Montevideo went wild, the government declared a national holiday, stamps were issued commemorating the events, crowds flooded the city's streets and on their return the players were treated to a dockside celebration and financial rewards from the government. The football community on the other side of the Río de la Plata was not happy. Used to thinking of themselves as the leading edge of Latin American football, the Argentines were incensed that the Uruguayans had stolen a march on them by going to the Olympics and having the temerity to win it. A two-game contest between the nations was hastily arranged. The Argentines were determined to show their neighbours and the rest of the world who really was the best team in Latin America. The first game of the rematch was a closely fought 1–1 draw in Montevideo. The return match was played a week later at the ground of Sportivo Barracas in Buenos Aires. However, the enormous and restless crowd encroached onto the pitch after five minutes and both teams were ordered to leave the field. Police and army conscripts forced the bulging crowds back over the touchline, but only just. The game was abandoned and despite some scuffling and the impromptu demolition of a ticket kiosk the crowd dispersed with the promise of a rerun the following Thursday.

When the crowd reassembled they found a 12-foot-high wire fence between themselves and the pitch. In the final minutes of the game the Argentinian crowd stoned the Uruguayan defender Andrade who, true to form, threw the stones back at the crowd and the rest of the

Uruguayans joined in. As the police approached the Uruguayan forward Scarone he kicked a police officer and was arrested. With the crowd baying and flinging anything to hand through and over the fence the Uruguayans walked off. The Argentinians stayed on the field for the last six minutes and were awarded the game. The fences have still not come down in Latin America.

The Uruguayans left the next day; reports politely describe their departure as accompanied by an 'exchange of coal between ship and shore'. The success of the Uruguayans in Paris encouraged three teams from Latin America to embark on European tours in 1925. Nacional left Montevideo in February 1925 and returned in August having played thirty-eight games in a gruelling tour of nine countries and twenty-three cities, of overnight rail journeys and tough competitive matches. The Uruguayans won twenty-six, drew seven and lost only five games. More than 700,000 came to see them including over 70,000 in Vienna where they beat the national team. Boca Juniors played mainly in Spain but won all five of their games in Germany and France. Extensive coverage in the Argentine press of the team's progress provided a great canvas for reporters to elaborate upon and celebrate a distinctive free-flowing, balletic Argentinian style of football. The Brazilian amateur side CA Paulistino which travelled to France and Switzerland also impressed.

At the same time, teams from Europe, now only three weeks away on the fastest steamers, were coming to Latin America: a Basque selection in 1922, Genoa in 1923 and Espanyol of Barcelona in 1926. Their city rivals FC Barcelona arrived in 1928 and the following year, before the Wall Street Crash destroyed the economics of such ventures, Chelsea, Bologna, Torino and Ferencváros of Budapest made the trip. Thus by the time of the 1928 Amsterdam Olympics, Latin American football was no mere curiosity and the two leading teams – Uruguay and Argentina – were the favourites.

It was as it should have been. In the absence of the British, the two best teams in the world, Uruguay and Argentina, faced each other for what was, in the absence of anything else, football's first world championship. A quarter of a million requests from all over Europe were made for the 40,000 available tickets. On the Río de la Plata papers devoted pages and pages to the finals. Life had become structured around the stream of telegraph messages sent from the Netherlands to the offices of Buenos Aires' newspapers, flashing up every chance, every goal, every substitution. Loudspeakers and public-address systems had been set up in the city's major squares to relay the news. The plazas heaved, the balconies groaned with people straining their ears for the news.

In between the intermittent episodes broadcast, excited comment would burst forth from the crowd but as soon as the voice of the loudspeakers was heard again sss-s-s-s went the crowd, and it would have been something akin to suicide to have spoken another word until the voice had stopped . . . The silence of the grave, broken only by the monotonous drone of the loudspeaker and an occasional distant snort of a motor horn, seemed to hang over just those few squares.[10]

It took two games to settle matters. The first was a cautious 1–1 draw. The replay was an altogether more open affair, end-to-end at times; the Uruguayan defence, led by their captain José Nasazzi, had just the better of the Argentine attack and kept them to a single goal. Uruguay scored two. Atilio Narancio, a wealthy Uruguayan patron of football, exclaimed: 'We are no longer just a tiny spot on the map of the world.' Uruguay were the champions of the world.

VI

In 1926 Henri Delaunay, FIFA's secretary, described the organization's central dilemma: 'Today international football can no longer be held within the confines of the Olympics, and many countries where professionalism is now recognized and organized cannot any longer be represented there by their best players.'[11] In the wake of the 1928 Amsterdam Olympics in which football had proved by far and away the most popular event, FIFA was propelled into action, forming its first World Cup organizing committee and settling the internal conflicts that had been rumbling away at its congresses over the basic format of the competition. The World Cup would be open to the whole world, not just to European teams. Any player, professional or amateur, could represent his country. Money made on the deal would be split between FIFA and the hosts and the whole show would happen every four years.

Up till this point a number of European countries had expressed some interest in hosting the event, but the practicalities, the risks and the costs dissuaded them all. The field was left open for the only country prepared to put its money on the table: Uruguay. And Uruguay had money. Its wool, hide and beef industries had grown throughout the 1920s. The welfare state constructed under President Batlle y Ordóñez siphoned off enough of the super profits from export agriculture to keep the social peace and fund an era of progressive politics, high educational invest- ments and urban growth. Eager to entrench and advertise the country's status as undisputed football world champions, Uruguay's government offered to pay visiting teams' expenses, undertook to build a new and fitting stadium for the occasion and proposed that the tournament begin in July 1930 – one hundred years on from the inauguration of Uruguay's first independent constitution. In 1929 at FIFA's Barcelona congress, Jules Rimet awarded the competition to Uruguay and commissioned a golden trophy – then known as the Goddess of Victory and only later as the Coupe Jules Rimet – from French sculptor Abel Lafleur.

Unencumbered by the immense demands of the electronic media, modern telecommunications and international tourism of later World Cups, Uruguay's preparations could centre on building a new stadium. The organizing committee commissioned architect Juan Scasso to design it. They named it *Estadio Centenario* in honour of the coming consti- tutional centenary and chose Parque Batlle at the centre of the newly expanded city as its location. Work started in February 1930 and the park was turned into a human anthill as two separate building companies raced to build their halves of the stadium. Concrete was imported from Germany, as Latin America did not yet possess its own manufacturing capacity. Quite how many teams would actually play in the new stadium was open to question in early 1930 as national association after national association declined the offer to attend. Stayaways included all the British home nations, the Scandinavians, the Germans, the Swiss and the Central Europeans. King Carol of Romania had pledged his personal support to the World Cup in 1928 and true to his word he helped organize a Romanian team and put them on a chartered liner *Conte Verde*. However, most of the team were oil workers employed by British companies in Ploiesti. It was only on the intervention of the King's mistress that their employers permitted their departure. In Genoa the ship picked up the French who had been bullied into attendance by Rimet though he was unable to persuade the country's leading striker Manuel Anatol or the national coach Gaston Barreau to accompany him. The Belgians joined them having been dragooned into going by

FIFA's Belgian vice-president Rudolf Seedrayers. Only the Yugoslavs, who came in style on a pleasure cruiser called *Florida*, seemed to need no incentive other than the glorious thought of two months without work and the adventure of football in its new stronghold – Latin America. These four and the hosts plus a further eight teams from the Americas – Argentina, Bolivia, Brazil, Chile, Mexico, Paraguay, Peru and the USA – made up the thirteen participants who assembled in Montevideo in July 1930.

The Centenario Stadium was not completed by the time the tournament was due to start and the opening games of the first World Cup were played at the tiny home grounds of Nacional and Peñarol, Parque Central and Pocitos respectively. Argentina provided the early entertainment. Their game with France was a hard-fought duel between two impressive midfields. Argentina broke the deadlock with a goal on 80 minutes. The French counterattacked furiously and Marcel Langiller was released only for the referee to blow for time four minutes early. Argentinian fans invaded the pitch, the French surrounded the referee and mounted police rode out after all of them. The Brazilian referee Almedia Rego threw up his hands in despair and embarrassment at his mistake. The pitch was cleared, the Argentine forward Roberto Cherro fainted and the restarted game spluttered to a conclusion. The predominantly Uruguayan crowd jeered the Argentine players and carried the French off on their shoulders. In a fit of pique the Argentinians threatened to withdraw but showed up to beat Mexico 6–3. In their final group game they defeated Chile 3–1 and qualified for the semi-finals.

Uruguay's World Cup awaited the completion of the Centenario and on 17 July it was ready. It was without doubt the finest football stadium yet built. Its capacity was less than Hampden Park or Wembley, but at 90,000 it was the largest outside the British Isles. Architecturally it was in a different league. Flush with overseas investment, government spending and rich, architecturally cultured patrons, the late 1920s had seen a building boom in Montevideo. Along the central avenues of the city and the rolling seafront *ramblas*, a distinct and breathtaking Latino modernism was emerging whose architectural motifs included soaring flat white surfaces, rigorous geometry, curving concrete balconies and glass brick detailing. Uruguay's architectural elite had been among the first and most enthusiastic students of the emergent minimalism and modernism of inter-war Europe. Le Corbusier himself had visited

Montevideo in 1927 both to study and proselytize. It was in this context that Scasso drew up his plans.

The Centenario was to be Latin America's first reinforced concrete stadium, built as a double-tiered ellipse broken into four stands that fanned out like the multi-layered petals of an art-deco flower. The detailing of walkways, walls and seats stayed faithful to a core aesthetic of flush surfaces and simple patterns. Two stands were to be named in honour of the Olympic victories – Colombes and Amsterdam. Expectations were running high; a third stand was to be called Montevideo. For these structures alone, the Centenario was an exceptional stadium, but on the north side of the ground Scasso added his *Tour d'hommage*: a nine-storey tower rising 100 metres above the sunken pitch. It was and remains an extraordinary statement of modernist optimism. At its base the square walls of the tower sprouted the elegant aerodynamic wings of an aeroplane. At the front the prow of a sleek steel-hulled ship pitched upwards. The eye, following the prow of the ship, turned immediately up along the rectangular concrete fluting that runs all the way to the high flagpole at the very top of the tower. Along the way one could catch the nine windows and geometric architraves that match the nine stripes of the Uruguayan flag. In the shadow of the tower, before crowds that were reaching 100,000 (20 per cent of the adult male population of the country), Uruguay dispensed with Peru and then Romania to make the semi-finals. In the first of these the Argentinians swept the USA aside 6–1 and then the following day Uruguay, after going a goal down to Yugoslavia, scored six themselves – the equalizer supposedly scored after a policeman kept a ball in that should have been a Yugoslav throw. Three days later Uruguay and Argentina played the first World Cup Final.

Those three days disappeared in a whirl of frenzied activity and speculation. The historical record is engulfed more than usual by the swirl of myth and mystery. The fog of war, like that which engulfed some of the liners crossing from Buenos Aires to Montevideo, descended. The unfortunate *porteños* on those boats found themselves lost on the Río de la Plata as the final was being played. No one really knows how many Argentinians actually went to Uruguay (estimates cluster around 10–15,000) nor how many of them actually made it into the Centenario, but the port of Buenos Aires had never seen anything like it. The rich set sail in their own private yachts or chartered planes. The Postmaster

General hired a cargo steamer for himself and his friends while six members of the Chamber of Deputies requisitioned a government barge pulled by a tugboat. The offices of the Atlantic liners that passed by Montevideo and the companies running the regular short-trip steamers were besieged by crowds, running into the tens of thousands.

Things were equally frenetic in Montevideo. The Argentina team holed up in Santa Lucia were feeling the pressure. Cherro had been in a state of nervous collapse since the French game and was in no condition to play. Luis Monti reported receiving death threats to his mother that would be carried out by Argentines if the team lost and threats from Uruguayans to be carried out if they won; Monti only played after the directors of his club, San Lorenzo, begged him to. Uruguayans certainly gathered around the team's hotel to barrack and abuse them.

On the day of the game, the teams were accompanied by a large cavalcade of police and soldiers to the Centenario. In Buenos Aires, normal life had shut down. The Argentine factories of General Motors had stopped the production lines; the Chamber of Deputies suspended its sittings; office workers across the city gathered around their radios and crowds massed outside the newspaper offices. In Montevideo the Centenario was full; tens of thousands were left outside to listen to the cries of the crowd. Referee Jean Langenus from Belgium lifted his whistle to his lips, secure in the knowledge that the Uruguayan government had accepted his request for special protection for himself, his assistants, his family and a boat in the harbour ready to depart within one hour of the final whistle.

---

30 July 1930
Uruguay 4 Argentina 2
Estadio Centenario, Montevideo

The Uruguayan flag is hoisted up the pole that sits atop the Torre de los Homenajes. Barely unfurling at first against the empty sky, a fragile wire-strung biplane buzzes past and sends it rippling. The Centenario rings with cheering and salutes to flag, plane, tower and nation.

Standing at the top of the tower, three-quarters of a century later, there is no flag, though finally they have installed a lift, seventy-five years late. Behind the tower, the open sky is now dominated by the great grey concrete hulk of the university hospital. Built a few years after the stadium and funded by the same munificent boom, its fifteen storeys, multiple wings and wards are looking tired, barnacled by decline: peeling plaster, broken guttering.

Looking down on the pitch you strain to see the Uruguayans and the Argentinians. Down 2–1 at half-time, the hosts score three in the second half. But it's hopeless; the grass is filled with the half-dismantled remnants of a rock concert. Football rarely fills the Centenario now.

Soon it will be gone altogether, its experimental reinforced concrete unable to deal with the salt air of the Atlantic. It has, perhaps, less than a hundred years. Maybe climate change will get there first. The Río de la Plata will flood the city and leave it marooned: a carved grey beacon alerting sailors to submerged treasures.

――――――――――

In Buenos Aires a dismal silence hung over the columns of disappointed fans, their Argentine flags still furled on their poles. Silence gave way to night and alcohol and anger. The Uruguayan Consulate and the elite Oriental Club were attacked from the streets, one woman with a Uruguayan flag was stoned and in certain *barrios* the mob played 'Sacarse el Sombrero' ('Take off your hat'), marching through the street with the national flag, insisting that all and sundry offer respect and acknowledgement – those that would not had better look out. By midnight there was gunfire and shootings, and it was only in the early hours of the morning that the police dispersed the gangs. Next day, some Argentine papers expressed their disgust with the team and their lack of courage, others detected Uruguayan skulduggery; the roots of both national footballing paranoia and self-loathing were born. But it was their lack of teamwork that had really let Argentina down. The Italian journalist Berrara who witnessed the game argued: 'Argentina play football with a lot of imagination and elegance, but technical superiority cannot compensate for the abandonment of tactics. Between the two rioplatense national teams, the ants are the Uruguayans, the cicadas are the Argentinians.'[12] Just sixty years since the first international match in Glasgow, the pinnacle of the game had crossed the Atlantic. Football's central irreconcilable polarities of individualism versus collectivism, of art versus results, of skill versus force, of beauty versus efficiency had not merely been transferred but their exploration elevated to a new level of sophistication.

VII

The Europe that the French, the Yugoslavs and the others returned to in the late summer of 1930 was just beginning to descend into the dark valley of economic depression and political turmoil that would culminate in the Second World War. The collapse of the German economy that year precipitated, if not settled, the rise of the National Socialist Party and once the Nazis were in power the fate of Czechoslovakia and Austria was sealed. Italian Fascism and Salazar's Portugal were joined by German totalitarianism and some variant of military, monarchical or authoritarian dictatorships would take power in Athens, Belgrade, Madrid and Warsaw by 1939. The remaining European democracies were steadily squeezed between the rising power of the Soviet Union and right-wing nationalists bent on undoing the wrongs of Versailles. The very fabric of European societies was politicized as never before: capitalism vs. communism, democracy vs. dictatorship, cosmopolitans vs. nationalists. Nation was set against nation, class against class, and many of those struggles were sustained and nurtured by the widespread acceptance and use of voluble mass political ideologies which aimed at not merely the rule of societies but their transformation and control down to the most minute levels. Mass culture of all kinds – from sport to fashion, from cinema to schooling – became in many of these societies more widely and consciously a matter of politics than ever before.

In this context, no single nation can be considered individually culpable for the drift to politicized international sport. The Berlin Olympics of 1936 are often considered to be the defining moment at which international sport descended to the level of a stage-managed nationalist spectacular – though one that pleasingly continued to provide upsets and unexpected outcomes. However, as in so many matters of policy and style shared by the fascist regimes of Europe in the early 1930s, it was Mussolini's Italy that led the way. In 1932, at its Barcelona congress, FIFA awarded the rights to host the 1934 World Cup to Italy. The preparations for the tournament coincided with a steadily more expansionist and aggressive Italian foreign policy that would culminate after the World Cup in the invasion of Abyssinia, intervention in the Spanish Civil War and relentless pressure on Albania and Central Europe. In this context the 1934 World Cup became an explicitly political as well as a sporting exercise. Mussolini, in one of innumerable speeches on the subject that he made in the mid-1930s, said:

You athletes of all Italy have particular duties. You must be tenacious, chivalrous and daring. Remember that when you take part in contests beyond our borders, there is then entrusted to your muscles, and above all your spirit, the honour and prestige of the national sport. You must hence make use of all your energy and all your willpower in order to obtain primacy in all struggles on the earth, on the sea and in the sky.[13]

Britain (and the Scandinavians) almost alone attempted to hold to a different view of sport and public affairs. The gap between the politics of football in Britain and Italy is neatly illustrated by events surrounding England's first game in Italy, played in 1933. Unbeknown to the British government, the FA had accepted an invitation from the Italian federation FIGC to play the fixture. There was considerable excitement and anticipation in the Italian press around the visit. In fact even the *New York Times* was moved to cover the event, writing, 'No other contest in the history of modern Italian sport has caused so much interest.'[14]

Mussolini entered the stadium to loud cheering and the mass waving of handkerchiefs. The public-address system boomed, 'With the Duce one is never lost; neither will we lose today'; and they did not. The game ended 1–1. The German journalist Walther Bensemann, a rare neutral observer, thought it not a great game, for everyone seemed overcome by the occasion. FA secretary Fredrick Wall had not found matters to his liking, writing, 'I have no desire to again be a guest of the Italian Football Federation.'[15] So when the host nation invited England to the World Cup and offered to pay their expenses, for the second time the English and the other Home Nations refused.

The Uruguayans, hopelessly strapped for cash as the global recession decimated its export economy, declined the chance to defend their title. The Argentines, almost as broke, refused to send a full professional team in protest over the recruitment of their leading players into the ranks of the Italian squad. But the amateur side that travelled made a much publicized visit to Mussolini's birthplace where flags and wreaths of friendship were laid. The Brazilians were the only other South Americans to make the journey and they were so enthusiastic about their hosts that a writer and known fascist sympathizer was made the titular head of the delegation.

Like the Uruguayans in 1930 the Italian government was prepared to throw money at the event – around 3.5 million lire. Everything at the tournament was paid in lire, especially foreign teams' expenses. *La Nazione* considered this significant enough to write that this was 'official recognition that Italian currency offers a greater confidence and guarantee than that of other foreign currencies'.[16] The already extensive building programme of the 1920s and early 1930s furnished an array of exemplary stadiums offering an architectural homage to Fascism's Roman pretensions and Futurist aesthetics. Funds were made available to subsidize 75 per cent of the cost of foreign travel for visiting fans, especially from Holland, Switzerland, Germany and France, and internal transport for visitors was free. Match tickets were printed on the best quality card and embossed with an elegant design. The noted Futurist theoretician Marinetti won the competition to design the tournament poster. A hundred thousand copies were printed and the emblematic juxtaposition of ball and the regime's favoured *fasces* insignia was reproduced a million times over on the cigarette packets of the state tobacco monopoly. Similarly inspired designs of sparkling stadiums and soaring aeroplanes adorned a specially issued set of commemorative stamps. FIFA had hoped to issue the stamps themselves in Switzerland, but the Fascist government was not about to relinquish this kind of publicity or revenue stream. Mussolini's personal imprimatur on the event was to commission a rather tawdry trophy named after himself – *La Coppa del Duce* – which was to be awarded alongside the World Cup itself to the eventual victors.

The draw for the finals was held in the palatial surroundings of the Ambassadors Hotel in Rome in the presence of Starace, secretary of the Fascist Party, and General Vaccaro, president of the sports federation CONI. Two naval cadets, one of them the general's son, made the draw and the whole show was flanked by a great chorus of blackshirts, flags, *fasces*, eagles and assorted insignia.

Italy could certainly stage a World Cup, but could they win one? It was very clear that they were expected to. The team and its coach Vittorio Pozzo had been shaken to the bone by their 4–2 defeat three months earlier to the expressive Austrian *Wunderteam*. It was perhaps a necessary shock as old players and tactics were dropped and Pozzo wrestled with the problem of constructing a new side. The spine of his team were Argentinians – referred to generically as the *Rimpatriato* – who had all come to play in the Italian league in the early 1930s; with various Italian grandparents and great-grandparents they were able to take Italian citizenship and play for the national team. At centre-half and at the core of the defence Pozzo had Luis Monti, who had played for Argentina in the 1930 World Cup. On the wings he had two more Argentines, Raimondo Orsi and Enrico Guaita, and up front he had the closest thing that Mussolini's Italy could get to a sporting superman – Giuseppe Meazza. Mussolini attended Italy's opening game with his sons and great populist play was made of the fact that he had paid for his tickets. They were certainly good value. After much Fascist saluting, the Italians took the USA apart 7–1.

The team that everyone would have paid to see at the 1934 World Cup were the Austrians: *Das Wunderteam*. They were the cream of Red Vienna, the toast of European football and had arrived in Italy as the favourites for the tournament. Austrian international football had been strong through the 1920s but in the early 1930s it stepped up another gear. *Das Wunderteam*, as a team and object of public acclaim, was born of the mesmeric performance they put on against Scotland in Vienna in May 1931. Scotland, the football nation with the second oldest football association cup and professional league, a team that rightly possessed an aura of British invincibility, were beaten by the Austrians 5–0. Even the social democrat newspaper *Arbeiterzeitung*, normally suspicious of both sporting hagiography and unfettered nationalism, was roused by the occasion. 'If there was an elegiac note in watching the decline of the ideal that the Scots represented for us, even yesterday, it was all the more refreshing to witness a triumph that sprang from true artistry. Eleven footballers, eleven professionals – certainly, there are more important sides to life, yet this was ultimately a tribute to Viennese aesthetic sense, imagination and passion.'[17]

The Scotland game was one of a run of eighteen unbeaten games for the Austrians, fifteen wins and three draws. Having beaten the Scots the Austrians thrashed Germany 6–0 away and then 5–0 in their new home, the Praterstadion. The stadium could hold 60,000 people and placed football right at the heart of the parks and pleasure grounds in the centre of Vienna. The Swedes, the French, the Italians, the Hungarians and the Czechs – the leading forces in European football – were all given the same treatment as the Scots and Germans. The run culminated with the first visit of the national side to England in December 1932. When the teams took to the pitch at Stamford Bridge, west London, Vienna was transfixed. Huge crowds had gathered in the city centre and around the Heldenplatz, where loudspeakers had been set up to relay live commentary of the game. The home side quickly ran up a two-goal lead but in the second half the Austrians found their feet and both sides exchanged goals. England ran out 4–3 winners of a classic match.

Das Wunderteam was the pinnacle of Austria's inter-war football development. The coach Hugo Meisl was able to select from the large pool of professional players in the Vienna league. Moreover the players from the leading teams were well schooled in the rigours of international competition; FK Austria and Rapid Vienna were regulars in the Mitropa Cup. The team once selected was able to play regularly together in fearsome battles with Europe's toughest opponents in the Central European competition, the Dr Gero Cup. The *Wunderteam* also had Matthias Sindelar, the leading footballer of his generation. Sindelar was born in 1903 in the Czech region of Moravia. His family, like tens of thousands of Moravians, migrated to Vienna and headed for the grim industrial suburb of Favoriten where there was work in the giant brick factories. Sindelar first played for the youth team at the local club ASV Hertha before Meisl arranged for his transfer to FK Austria in 1924. He made his international debut in 1926 and played well before falling out of favour with the disciplinarian Meisl. Four years in the international wilderness followed until Meisl was cornered by a gathering of the city's leading football commentators as he sat in the Ring Café in 1931. Everyone was arguing for Sindelar's recall and Meisl changed his mind. Sindelar played. Scotland were beaten and the *Wunderteam* – already disciplined, organized, hardworking and professional – acquired their playmaker and inspiration, that vital spark of unpredictability.

Sindelar's nickname was *Der Papierene*, literally the man of paper, but perhaps rendered best as 'the wafer', for his ability to slip unnoticed though the tightest defences. There is no footage of Sindelar playing, but for a brief cameo in a corny romance. Perhaps the lack of film has added undue lustre to his career, but the written reports and oral recollections of the player seem consistent. Sindelar, if not the first, was certainly the leading playmaker in European football. At last here was someone with the time and the confidence to look up, be able to judge the space and time available to every player on the field and select a pass or a move accordingly. Sindelar and the teams that he shaped played football with markedly less physical contact and force than either British or Italian football; it relied on guile, balance and brains. Viennese café society at last had a player and a game in their own image: cultured, intellectual, even cerebral, athletic but balletic at the same time. By the time they were writing his obituaries his football had metamorphosed to the level of epic narrative and poetry.

He would play football as a grandmaster played chess: with a broad mental conception, calculating moves and countermoves in advance, always choosing the most promising of all possibilities. He was an unequalled trapper of the ball and stager of surprise counterattacks, inexhaustibly devising tactical feints . . . Sindelar's shot hit the back of the net like a punch line, the ending that made it possible to understand and appreciate the perfect composition of the story, the crowning of which it represented.[18]

Austria lost just one more game until the semi-finals of the 1934 World Cup, a 2–1 home defeat by Czechoslovakia. Between April 1931 and June 1934, the *Wunderteam* had lost just three out of thirty-one games and scored 101 goals. However, when the team of Red Vienna made their way to Italy in June 1934, Red Vienna was no more. The mounting political conflicts between Vienna and provinces, the Left and the Right turned to outright civil war. Austria was still reeling from the economic hammer blow of the Wall Street Crash. Unemployment had touched 40 per cent in the early 1930s encouraging the growth of radical politics of both extremes. The then Chancellor of Austria Engelbert Dollfuss had responded to the external Nazi threat of a forced *Anschluss* or unification with Germany and the internal communist threat with repression, banning both the Austrian Nazi and Communist Parties. Dollfuss would not countenance an anti-Nazi–Communist alliance with the Social Democrats, preferring to seek a pact with Mussolini and to create his own right-wing populist paramilitary force. In February 1934 the armed truce between the Dollfuss government and the Social Democrats broke down when the latter's own armed paramilitaries – the *Schutzbund* – opened fire on the police in Linz. On cue Vienna descended into three days of open warfare. Dollfuss ordered the army into Vienna, who in an act of decisive symbolic and military advantage levelled the Karl Marx Hof housing estate, the pride of Viennese social planning and the last stronghold of its armed retinue. The Social Democrats were outlawed, the party closed down, its leadership imprisoned or exiled.

It was therefore a tired and troubled *Wunderteam* that arrived in Italy and it showed. In the early games, when one would have expected them to coast, they were only able to sneak past the French and Hungarians. But that was enough and in the semi-final they drew Italy. The match was preceded by a short deluge that left the surface of the San Siro wet and muddy. The Italian defence smothered the Austrians. Monti wrapped himself around Sindelar and the Austrians barely got a shot on goal. The Italians effectively bundled the ball and the Austrian goal-keeper into the net.

Italy were through by a single goal again and in the final in Rome they faced Czechoslovakia who had seen off Romania, Switzerland and Germany, improving with every game and displaying the strength in depth of Central European football. In the final itself the Czechs held on for seventy minutes. Then their forward Puč was knocked out by a crunching tackle from the Italian Ferraris. On the touchline Puč was given a blast of smelling salts and returned to the game; within a minute he had received a pass from the brilliant Nejedlý and put a low shot in the net: 1–0. For ten minutes Italy disintegrated and the Czechs hit the post. Then Orsi rescued the Italians; dummying on the edge of the penalty area to make space, he shifted his weight from one side to the other and in an instant scored with the outside of his right boot. Five minutes into injury time Schiavio scored Italy's winning goal, but not before Meazza had handled the ball. Claims persist that the young Swedish referee Ivan Eklind had been wined and dined by Mussolini himself and invited to consider the consequences of an Italian defeat. Delightful as this conspiracy is, there is not a single shred of documentary evidence to support it. Italy coach Vittorio Pozzo was chaired off the field, the team received the World Cup, *La Coppa del Duce*, a signed photo of the man himself and a gold medal in recognition of their conquest of football in the name of Mussolini and Fascism. The national anthems were played all over again and Mussolini and the Fascist Party had their sporting paradigm of the nation's newfound strength.

Within two months of winning the World Cup Vittorio Pozzo was despatched to London to arrange a fixture between Italy and England, for the question of absolute superiority in world football remained undecided. It certainly looked a propitious moment to mount such a challenge. England, albeit with a weak team, had been beaten by both Hungary and Czechoslovakia in the early summer tour of 1934 and both teams had been beaten by the Italians. Pozzo recorded his concern that the game would be played in the cold and wet of the English winter, putting the Italians at a disadvantage. That is precisely what the FA offered him – a game in November. But the regime was full of confidence and eager for the encounter. Pozzo wrote, 'I objected. I telephoned Rome to express my contrary thoughts. Nothing doing. In Rome, at a high level, concern was that the game should go ahead and it was a political interference – somebody was in high spirits. It was necessary to accept.'[19] So they went, rushed on by a vast gale of nationalist and bellicose rhetoric roaring out of the Italian press and sports newspapers. The game was billed from the beginning as 'The Battle of Highbury' and Bruno Roghi, editor of *La Gazetta dello Sport*, cast the match as a 'Theatre of international war'.[20] It appears from contemporary reports that it was indeed a battle. One Foreign Office diplomat described it as a 'less [than] pleasant affair characterised by a range of unsavoury incidents'.[21] England went 3–0 up but the Italians, down to ten men, turned up the heat and got two goals back. The international footballing status quo was shaken but not disturbed.

The Italian press salvaged a moral and aesthetic victory from defeat, writing of the team that these soldiers of sport, athletes of Fascism, 'emanated the class, the style, the technique and the skill . . . the ten athletes played like a platoon of gladiators. Ten Combatants. One heart.'[22] Mussolini's eyes were moving now from the football field to the fields of Abyssinia, from World Cups to world empires, from soldiers of sport to soldiers of war. Not for the first or last time, the regime would believe its own propaganda and the performance of a national football team would prove a most unreliable guide to the performance of the nation's army.

PART THREE

The Beautiful Game:

Football's Short Twentieth Century, 1934–1974

8
The Road to El Dorado: Latin American Football, 1935–1954

Boca,
Perón,
Un solo corazón.
Boca,
Perón,
Un solo corazón.
The crowd at Boca Juniors, *c.* 1946

Uruguay is a country built by two Varelas.
César Aguiar

I

The two Varelas in question were José Pedro Varela, late nineteenth-century Uruguayan social activist, and Obdulio Varela, the centre-half and captain of the 1950 World Cup team. President Varela's social and educational reforms heralded the creation of the most advanced welfare state in Latin America. From the early twentieth century onwards, under Batlle's Colorado party, Uruguay managed to combine successful economic development, relative social peace and the creation of the continent's most liberal democracy. One consequence of these developments was that Uruguay could afford to host the first World Cup in 1930 and were good enough to win it. It is difficult to underestimate the degree to which national identity and pride became tied to the fate of the national team – *La Celeste*. Uruguay, a country of not even 3 million people whose creation was the bizarre outcome of great power politics, had hitherto made no impact on the wider world. Now, as Eduardo Galeano has written, 'The sky-blue shirt was proof of the existence of the nation: Uruguay was not a mistake. Football pulled this little country out of the shadows of universal anonymity.'[1] While Brazil and Argentina had other historical materials and cultural resources from which to fashion a distinct modern nationalism, in Uruguay the cupboard was bare. The equation of the nation and the national football team, already widespread in Uruguay in the 1930s and 1940s, was permanently sealed in 1950 when, under Obdulio Varela's magnificent, obstinate captaincy, Uruguay beat Brazil in the miracle of the *Maracanazo*. As Ondino Viera, coach of the Uruguayan team at the 1966 World Cup, put it: 'Other countries have their history, Uruguay has its football.'[2] Uruguay is perhaps the extreme case, but it is not alone in finding its history suffused with football.

The Wall Street Crash of 1929 and the long global recession that followed it hit Latin America hard; through the 1930s foreign investment dried up, debts were called in and prices for the continent's agricultural and mineral exports collapsed. Political authoritarianism followed economic meltdown as unemployment and poverty fired the militancy of trade unionists and the urban poor across the continent. The antiquated political systems of the region tottered, ruling elites grew increasingly nervous. In the four short years after the collapse of the New York Stock Exchange, the military and its civilian allies took power in Argentina, Uruguay, Peru, Chile, Brazil, Mexico and Cuba. Colombia, Paraguay and Bolivia acquired their own military dictatorships in the 1940s and 1950s. Although the military withdrew from power in many of these states, this did not, with the exception of Uruguay, prefigure a return to democracy. In the Andean nations what followed was the creation of closed civilian coalitions of the powerful. In the two largest states, Argentina and Brazil, where the level of economic development and urbanization had produced an uncontainable urban mass and a small but militant organized working class, power was consolidated by a new kind of populist authoritarianism. Getúlio Vargas in Brazil and Juan Perón in Argentina created innovative political coalitions, combining the military, industrialists, urban workers and the labour movement. Given their similar constituencies and the place that football had already established in Brazilian and Argentine urban popular culture, the game was an obvious instrument for populist gestures and nationalist cultural politics. In Brazil football was deployed alongside Vargas's control over carnival and the education system in a culture that was strictly controlled and monitored from above. In Argentina by contrast the cultural links between football and politics were forged from below. The chant of the crowd at Boca Juniors – 'Boca, Perón, One Heart' – was not staged but spontaneous. Perón's rock-solid political and electoral support really did come from the terraces of *La Bombonera*.

This linkage between football and national identity was all the more important for the peculiar course of Latin American modernity was such that its state machines and its conceptions of nationalism were not developed in the forcing house of industrial war. Of course there had been wars in Latin America: among others the nineteenth century saw Chile, Bolivia and Peru struggle over the Pacific copper lands from 1879–83 and Paraguay dismembered at the hands of the Triple Alliance in the 1860s. All these wars had left an enduring mark on their participants, but in the twentieth century the impact of war was slighter. Latin America's peripheral or neutral status in the two world wars spared the rickety regimes of the continent the forced march of development that total war demands. Paraguay and Bolivia's confrontation in the Chaco War of 1935–9 merely ground their already miserable peasantry further into the dust rather than forcing state and society to undergo a painful and rapid modernization. Thus the military was domestically powerful but could not rewrite national identities in its own martial image for there were no tales of heroic state-building and conquest to draw upon.

In Latin America the nation primarily confronted the world as its football team, and in this sphere the continent could compete and excel like in no other. The Second World War thoroughly, if temporarily, destroyed European football. It would not really recover in international terms until the mid-1950s. In this hiatus, Latin American football was unquestionably the best in the world. But it was no copy, no mere facsimile of Europe. Its victories were not the outcome of a stereotypical industrialized football of simple-minded efficiency, sweat-drenched work horses or the application of sheer force. Latin America aimed higher.

Football in Latin America had become something more than an exercise in sporting rationality. There was among players, coaches, fans and journalists a stubborn objection to the idea that modern football had to be played like a modern business was run; like the patrimonialism, nepotism and clientelism that ran through Latin America's economies and polities, no amount of modernization or development was about to eradicate it. This tenacious resistance to crude utilitarianism pitted playing for love against playing to win, the cult of the dribble against the cult of efficiency. Art and science, bohemianism and professionalism, the modern and the traditional, did not merely rub shoulders in Latin America, they sparked off each other. There were social and sporting fireworks to come.

The rapidity of Argentina's football development was such that when the first professional league was played in 1931 many of the key elements of the nation's football culture were already in place. Argentina had been playing international football for thirty years. They had been champions of South America, and twice runners-up to Uruguay in the 1928 Olympic Final and the first World Cup Final in 1930. In the hands of the new popular press, like *El Gráfico* magazine and the newspaper *Clarín*, a working mythology of a unique national playing style had been articulated. Buenos Aires was blessed with socially and geographically distinct neighbourhoods that flocked to see their neighbourhood clubs, and a public-transport network that could take them to away games too. Thus despite being launched in the depths of the global economic depression of the early 1930s Argentine professional football survived and thrived. It did so, in part, like the wider Argentine economy, by disengaging from the global economy and from global football. The AFA sent only an amateur team to the 1934 World Cup in Italy, which was quickly despatched by the Swedes in a single game. No team at all was sent to the 1938 World Cup, where the Italians won again with a considerable phalanx of Argentine players who had taken Italian citizenship. No Argentine side would appear in a World Cup finals for another twenty years. The migration of high-profile players to Spain and Italy that had spurred the creation of a professional game was soon over. Buenos Aires looked a lot more attractive as the next war in Europe loomed. In South America Argentina were supreme. While Europe and the Pacific burned, Argentina was winning the Copa América: as hosts in 1937; then in Chile in 1941; followed by a trio of bravura victories in 1945, 1946 and 1947.

Having made the breakthrough to professionalism the commercialization of domestic football that sustained these international triumphs was broadened and deepened in the 1930s. The radio finally arrived in the furthest reaches of the country and the music and football of Buenos

Aires came with it. From chilly Patagonian villages 2,000 kilometres to the south, to Tucumán in the far north on the subtropical Brazilian border, people heard the swing and the strut of Héctor Varela's and Osvaldo Pugliese's tango big bands and the new ecstatic, staccato, radio football commentaries of Fioravanti. This created a nationwide fan base for the leading metropolitan teams that persists to this day. Buenos Aires sounded so good that people were leaving Patagonia and Tucumán and heading for the city. Just as the transatlantic migrations came to an end rural migration filled the gap in Argentina's relentless process of urbanization. Buenos Aires was not the only pole of demographic growth. Rural migrants moved to Santa Fe, Córdoba and Rosario too. This demographic and economic shift helped propel the first provincial clubs, Newell's Old Boys and Rosario Central, into the professional league in 1937.

Through the 1930s average ticket sales in the league were recorded at around 7,000, but these figures exclude seats taken by club members or *socios*. The biggest clubs had over 10,000 apiece and the smaller clubs 2–4,000. Crowds of over 40,000 were not uncommon for the very biggest games and they were richly rewarded by a decade of free-scoring football: between September 1936 and April 1938 there were no goalless draws in the Argentinian first division. As Argentina's economy began to boom in the early years of the Second World War, average crowds doubled and continued to increase in the late 1940s and early 1950s. At their peak, River Plate had 72,000 *socios* and could get crowds approaching 100,000; even their third and fourth teams were watched by crowds of 15,000. *El Gráfico* was selling 200,000 copies a week and amateur and recreational football occupied every park, square and vacant lot in the metropolitan areas. The media industries continued to innovate through the 1930s and 1940s. *La Crítica*, for example, redoubled interest in games by offering cash prizes for goalkeepers who could keep a clean sheet against in-form strikers, or who managed to save penalties. The cinema, now a staple of everyday life in Buenos Aires, began to show sport too. Perón's government sponsored *Sucesos Argentinos*: short movie newsreels that combined reports of children's sporting competitions, public works on sports projects and international successes. But football barely needed sponsorship, as around 30 per cent of all commercial films made between 1944 and 1954 in Argentina took sport as their subject – usually football.

What was almost immediately recognized as a golden era in football was known in politics as *la década infame*. Military rule gave way to twelve years of government by a dysfunctional and closed coalition of conservatives, socialists and the dominant Unión Cívica Radical, which by 1940 was resorting to stuffing ballot boxes to survive. For the most part football remained outside of politics. The directors of smaller and medium-sized clubs remained motivated by civic pride as much as political ambition. But the irresistible lure of the game and the essentially clientelistic system of political patronage of the era saw the growth of a tenticular network of interconnections between football and politics. General Juan Justo, president of the Argentine Republic between 1932 and 1938, made it known that he was a fan of Boca Juniors. His daughter married Eduardo Sánchez Terrero who went on to become president of Boca between 1939 and 1946; a term of office that coincided with a massive soft government loan that built their new stadium, colloquially known as *La Bombonera* – The Chocolate Box – in 1940. A subsequent president – of the nation rather than Boca – Ramón Castillo was not himself interested in football, but his son was. Lo and behold, Ramón Junior became president of the Argentine FA between 1941 and 1943.

Four teams dominated the first decade and a half of professional football in Argentina. Boca Juniors, River Plate, Independiente and San Lorenzo occupied the top two spots in the league for sixteen years. The identities and allegiances of the clubs, first established in the 1920s, hardened into self-perpetuating mythologies. Boca Juniors, the team always most explicitly linked to an immigrant, Italian, working-class identity, were the only side to remain in the very heart of old Buenos Aires. By the early 1930s transatlantic migration had come to an end but the impact it had wrought on Argentina's demography was such that Boca could now claim to be the team of the masses, the team of the people; 50 per cent plus one, as they described their support. River, whose crowds remained mixed, had like all social aspirants moved out of the docks and headed north to the more exclusive *barrios* of Palermo and Belgrano. Along the way they acquired a reputation as the aristocrats of the league, with a preference for style over sweat; for good manners over gamesmanship. Independiente retained the grit and grime of Avellaneda – Buenos Aires' industrial sinkhole – while San Lorenzo occupied the space, west of the city centre, in Flores and Almagro where the middle class and working class, the workshops and tango halls rubbed shoulders with one other. While each member of this quartet can claim its own distinctive contribution to the era it is perhaps River Plate's that was most emblematic.

River earned the sobriquet *Millonarios* in 1931 when they began the professional era with a wild spending spree on players like right wing Carlos Peucelle and striker Bernabé Ferreyra. As the best-connected club of the era River were the first to benefit from the government's low-key largesse, investing in the development of new football stadiums in return for both symbolic kudos and the practical use of the property for housing schools and clinics. Argentina's application of this obvious solution to the eternal problem of how to fund a piece of infrastructure that is only really used for ninety minutes a week was considerably in advance of anywhere else. The Estadio Antonio Vespuccio Liberti, always known as *El Monumental*, was opened on 25 May 1938, a national holiday, in the presence of President Ortiz. A two-tiered horse-shoe, El Monumental was Argentina's first industrial, steel and concrete football stadium, with a capacity of around 70,000. It contained a school and a medical practice and was built alongside a whole range of sporting and social facilities for the club's *socios*. It hosted its first game that day in which River thrashed Montevideo's Peñarol. The team that would truly grace El Monumental, matching sporting achievement to architectural ambition, was just evolving. It would mature three years later in 1941, as the champions. *El Gráfico's* editor Borocotó watched them demolish Chacarita Juniors 6–2 that season and wrote that they played like a machine. They were, henceforth, *La Máquina*.

La Máquina won their first title as the Japanese bombed Pearl Harbor. They went on to win another three titles. In 1942 they won the championship by a point from Boca on the final day of the season, while Stalingrad was reduced to dust and ice and corpses. In 1945 they took the title while the rubble of Japan's cities still throbbed with radiation. They claimed the 1947 championship while a winter so fierce gripped Europe that it seemed the war had never ended. But in December, in Latin America, the sun shone. It was another world. In the six years between their first and last title, in this otherworldly haven, *La Máquina* came to define, to embody, everything that was *La Nuestra* – our style, the best football in the world. Cut off from the carnage, freed from the imperatives of war and survival, Argentinian football could create a distinct blend of instrumentalism, art and entertainment. In the 1920s the cults of dribbling and flamboyant individualism had been central to the distinct *criollo* football of the Río de la Plata. Now, under the sterner conditions and imperatives of professionalization, the Scottish legacy of the passing game was added to the repertoire.

The style of play that evolved was an unreservedly attacking game exemplified by River Plate's forward quintet – Muñoz, Moreno, Pedenera, Labruna and Lousteau – then as now, an Argentinian football litany. Even the young Alfredo di Stéfano was a mere addendum to these five. *La Máquina* played for time and searched for space, passing, always passing. They kept possession and could slow the tempo of their game until a chink of light, a hint of a chance, offered up the opportunity of some remarkable feint, shot or dash. Muñoz, in particular, was adored for his trickery. ' "The tango", he'd say, "is the best way to train, you maintain a rhythm then change it when you stride forward, you learn the profiles, you work on your waist and your legs".'[3]

But then there was room to tango on the pitch in Argentina. Defensive play and tactics were woefully underdeveloped. Man-to-man marking had barely been explored. Midfields and strikers did nothing as inelegant or pointedly utilitarian as close down their opponents or press them in packs. Regaining the ball, if it were lost, was not treated as a priority. The man on the ball had time. And there was time for wine, women and song, for *La Nuestra* was not a puritan regime. In the magical air of Buenos Aires, professionalism and bohemianism could coexist. A team that played with artistry could be a machine. Eduardo Galeano retells Muñoz's story in suitably mythic terms:

On Sundays at midday, before each match he would devour a big bowl of chicken stew and drain several bottles of red wine. Those in charge at River ordered him to give up his rowdy ways . . . he did his best. For an entire week he slept at night and drank nothing but milk. Then he played the worst game of his life. When he went back to carousing the team suspended him. His team-mates went on strike in solidarity with this incorrigible bohemian.[4]

An unexpected but telling overview of Argentinian football at the peak of its powers comes in the clipped tones of the British Diplomatic Service. In 1945 the president of the Rio club Botafogo was proposing a post-war South American tour by British clubs, and the Foreign Office had asked their South American embassies to comment on the likely course of events. The British Embassy in Buenos Aires was cautious:

Local interest in football has to be seen to be believed; games between the leaders in the championship draw crowds of 80,000 ... Under their own rules and on their own grounds the Argentine football players are first class and even the best First Division teams from England would have their work cut out to hold their own. Any football team below tip-top standard would do our football reputation more harm than good.

Even then we should have some hesitation in recommending. The local rules differ considerably from the English, particularly in regard to charging; an Argentinian goalkeeper is a sort of untouchable ... Argentine players and spectators are very excitable and the sight of a twelve-stone Arsenal forward charging an Argentine goalkeeper with the ball into the net might easily start a battle.[5]

Argentina's crowds were big, voluble and volatile. There are scattered reports of fighting between fans but for the most part they were crude and rude rather than threatening.

What, it seems, was most likely to ignite trouble were refereeing decisions. In 1932 Sr De Angelis was in charge of a game between Estudiantes and River Plate. River were top of the league and 1–0 up when De Angelis disallowed an Estudiantes goal. He was surrounded by players and fans on the pitch and was forced to retreat to his dressing room. He emerged fifteen minutes later announcing that in fact the goal would stand, inaugurating the now common phrase '*el gol de la casilla*' – scored in the changing rooms. Rumour abounded that the president of Estudiantes had held a gun to De Angelis's head. But what distinguished the crowds of Buenos Aires was that they sang a repertoire of taunts and support, slogans of love and hate that at the time had no equal for their intimacy, intensity, diversity or wit.

After twelve years in their barracks the Argentine army returned to politics. Alarmed by Argentina's fragile and inconsistent foreign policy in the midst of the Second World War and appalled by the pettiness and corruption of the old cabal of civilian politicians, a group of dissident officers staged a successful coup in 1943. They dissolved Congress, pushed the politicians out of the ministries and banned all political parties. A hitherto unknown Colonel, Juan Domingo Perón, was made Minister of Labour and in two short years he unleashed a torrent of social and industrial reform. Perón's immense popularity and personal political magnetism so worried the senior officer corps and the military government that they arrested and imprisoned him in October 1945. In the single greatest gathering of Argentina's working class hundreds of thousands filled the Plaza de Mayo and stood before La Casa Rosada – the presidential residence – demanding his release. Peronism – the cult, the programme, the movement – was born. Perón, now released, began to articulate an intoxicating blend of nationalism, independence and modernization. The working class were captivated by his delivery and the promise of more social reform, economic advance and inclusion in the political process. The new class of industrialists backed his plans for national economic independence and domestically controlled industrialization. This fusion of the two most dynamic sectors of Argentinian society in Perónism attracted the progressive wing of the military and a swathe of middle-class intellectuals. In 1946 Perón ran for the presidency and won.

Once in power Perón made good his promises to his working-class constituency. Real wages leapt as the government aided the trade unions and settled strikes in their favour; at the same time prices for key consumables like football matches were kept low. Foreign influence in the economy was diminished as the government nationalized the British-owned railways, the French-owned docks and the American-owned telephone system. As the economy boomed on exports to a Western Europe beginning the process of reconstruction, Perón paid off the national debt and declared a state of economic independence. Such flourishes hid the regime's awareness of the fragility of Argentina's industrial companies. Tariffs for foreign goods rose, throwing a protective wall around the domestic industrialists that had rallied to Perón's cause. Correspondingly, the nation's self-esteem in its football was protected by limiting the national team's participation in world football. No team was sent to the 1949 Copa América or to the 1950 World Cup. Although bureaucratic differences were publicly cited as the reason for Argentina's absence, it was well known that the regime was acutely aware of the damage that could be done if notions of national superiority were punctured by the realities of open international competition.

The role of sport in domestic politics was considerable. Perón's government merged the Argentine Olympic Committee and the Confederation of Argentine Sport and brought them under direct state control. Perón made himself president of the new body which was launched with a spate of posters and sloganeering that declared 'Perón Sponsors Sports' and 'Perón: the First Sportsman'. Perón, like Mussolini, preferred hunting to sport and was an expert fencer, but he also recognized football's potential role in nation-building and social policy. Strong nations required strong bodies and intense collective experiences. Even so, San Lorenzo's 1946–7 tour of Europe, during which they soundly beat both the Spanish national team 6–1 and the Portuguese 10–4, did not embolden the football authorities. They preferred to draw the conclusions of Brazil's shattering home defeat in the 1950 World Cup; no Argentine team went to the 1954 World Cup either. International athletics, which excited fewer passions and lower expectations than football, was seen as a safer bet. Thus the government made money available for a large and successful Argentine team to travel to the 1948 London Olympics, and Argentina's medallists were presented with special commemorative Perónista medals by the General himself in 1949 at El Monumental. Argentina then hosted the first Pan-American Games in 1951 and the government was happy to bask in the international success of a gifted generation of Argentine boxers and racing drivers.

By contrast, domestic football was politics of a higher order, confirmed by the government's direct interest in and control over senior appointments at the Argentinian FA. AFA presidents Oscar Nicolini and Valentin Suárez were direct Perónista appointments. In return for control the government began to dispense money, with cash for new stadiums at Huracán in 1947 and Vélez Sarsfield in 1951. Every club acquired among its inner circles and boards of directors a *padrino* (godfather), who linked them to the tightly wired new circuits of power in Perón's Argentina. The nation's charismatic and omnipresent first lady Evita Perón possessed an instinctive political populism which led her to football too. The first Evita Perón football championships were played right across the nation in 1950. The competition was open to any team of kids from anywhere that presented itself to the now proliferating offices of the Evita Perón Foundation – a para-statal welfare operation run by Evita herself. Every team was then supplied with kit – for many poor children their first proper playing kit ever – and the players submitted to a compulsory medical, immunization and x-rays. Hundreds of thousands of Argentina's children made their first contact with the country's fledgling health service in this way. After innumerable rounds the finals were held in Buenos Aires. They played the national anthem and a specially commissioned march for Evita who of course took the kick-off. Yet even Evita was aware of her limits. During a four-day rally to back her unsuccessful run for the vice-presidency all football was rescheduled; she knew she could not compete.

The rise of organized labour under Perón did not leave football untouched. Labour relations mirrored the wider urban economy: working conditions were poor, security of employment low. Conflict had been brewing for some time and the labour force had slowly but surely been organizing itself. Players had struck in Uruguay for four weeks in 1939, led by the star of their 1930 World Cup victory, José Nasazzi. In 1944 Mexico had started up its first professional football league and attracted Argentinian and Uruguayan players who had had enough of feudal labour contracts and poor wages. In the wider Argentinian economy of the late 1940s trade unions were growing fast, received government support in the labour market and were winning wage increases, concessions and improvements across the board. The first players' union in Argentina was formed in 1944 and named the *Futbolistas Argentinos Agremiados*. By 1948 the union was demanding recognition from the football authorities, the creation of a minimum wage and the establishment of freedom of contract. The clubs and the football authorities attempted to ignore the union and a strike was set for April. The AFA and the clubs agreed to recognize the union but would not relent on the other issues. The strike was delayed but only until July. Buenos Aires' stadiums went silent. There really was no football through the long winter months. The government then intervened in the dispute, creating a tribunal to adjudge the case. The league restarted, but the tribunal's recommendations were not enough for the players and the strike was back on in November. The clubs were forced to finish the season with amateur teams and rapidly declining crowds. New contracts and wages were agreed for 1949 but by then it was too late as the very elite of the Argentine league had left for the new pirate league in Colombia. Except, of course, for one club: Racing.

Although every club had its *padrino* (godfather), not all *padrinos* were equal. *El Padrino* of Racing Club was Ramón Cereijo, Perón's Minister of Finance. Although he held no formal post at the club his relationship was so close that Racing became known as *Sportivo Cereijo*. When the rest of Argentina's leading clubs were losing the core of their squads to the new leagues of Mexico, Colombia and even Guatemala, Racing lost no one. In 1949, while the other teams were depleted, Racing finally broke the stranglehold of the big four and won the championship.

Such triumphs demanded an appropriate stage and Cereijo arranged for a loan deal of extraordinary generosity to be struck between the club and the government – 3 million pesos to be paid back in sixty-five years. As the new stadium was being built 3 million became 11 million. President Perón, who had once announced his affection for Boca Juniors, attended the opening ceremony of the stadium named in his honour, while Bramuglia, Minister of Foreign Affairs, and Miranda, president of the Central Bank, were made honorary members of the club. The team won the title again in 1950 and 1951, a victory rewarded in the third year by the presentation of a brand new Chevrolet to every player. Perón went on to win his second term in office in 1951; the power of Peronism and its place in history seemed secure. Untouched, as yet, by the harsh realities of the global economy and global sporting competition, Argentina was on the top of its world.

For perhaps a century the Conquistadores had scoured the mountains and forests of what became Colombia, searching for El Dorado, the land of gold. They never found it. At Lake Guatavita outside Bogotá the Indians, it was said, had ritually thrown golden artefacts into the water. Repeated trawling of the lake yielded nothing. It was the wrong time, the wrong game and the wrong place. For foreign adventurers, El Dorado would be found for a few short years on the football pitches of Colombia's major cities. Football in that country had made slow progress in the first half of the twentieth century. From its initial stronghold in Barranquilla on the Caribbean coast where it had been introduced by British sailors and engineers, football's spread was as slow as the still predominantly riverine transport system of the country. Crossed by huge mountain ranges and river valleys, Colombia's geography demanded a level of investment in railways, tunnels and bridges that no one had yet managed to accumulate. But in the 1930s and 1940s Colombia began to change; the engine of change was coffee. Making up nearly 80 per cent of the country's export earnings by the end of the Second World War, coffee fuelled an economic boom and social transformation of the country. Railway construction finally began to link the nation's less accessible parts together. The major cities, Bogotá, Medellín, Barranquilla and Cali, began to industrialize. The merest hint of new work and new wealth saw them rapidly fill and then overflow with rural migrants. The essential urban and economic conditions for the professionalization of football had arrived. In 1947, alongside the Barranquilla-based amateur football federation Adefútbol, a Bogotá-based professional league had been formed: DiMayor. The idea sprang from the massive commercial success of the Argentine team San Lorenzo's tour of Colombia in 1947. But before it could begin, politics intervened.

Over the previous four decades political power in Colombia had been shared between the Conservative and Liberal parties. Elections had been relatively free and fair, power passed between the parties peacefully and moderate levels of state-sponsored industrialization had proved successful. But this tranquillity masked a degree of caffeine-fuelled vertiginous social change. In the cities trade unionists, syndicalists, socialists and communists were becoming active and organized. In the countryside peasant organizations and rural workers' unions were pressing hard for better conditions and access to land. In the person of Jorge Eliécer Gaitán they found their voice and their figurehead. Gaitán began his career in the Liberal Party, rising from a provincial representative to Minister of Education. His mestizo looks and outsider status in the stuffy world of Colombian politics made him a natural lightning rod for the country's tumultuous desire for change. His rhetoric was electric, his favourite slogan incendiary: '*El Pueblo es superior a sus dirigentes*' – 'The people are superior to their leaders'. Gaitán was assembling a coalition of the many, binding the rural poor and dispossessed, the aspirant skilled working class and the marginalized middle classes of the cities. By 1948 he was Mayor of Bogotá and the Liberal presidential candidate in the up-and-coming election – an election he looked certain to win. Colombia's traditional ruling class were in no doubt as to the torrent of social reform that would be unleashed by such an event. On 9 April 1948 Gaitán was assassinated in what remain mysterious circumstances. Bogotá went up in flames. By the time the police had stopped shooting there were 20,000 corpses on the city's streets.

The opening games of DiMayor which had been scheduled for May were delayed until August 1948 by which time the league was not only late but an international outcast. An extensive set of disputes between DiMayor and Adefútbol had reached such proportions in the fetid political atmosphere of the time that Adefútbol asked FIFA to suspend

DiMayor and its clubs from international competition and friendlies with foreign clubs. FIFA obliged. While this initially appeared a formidable sanction, Alfonso Senior Quevedo, a leading Bogotá lawyer, the founder of DiMayor and president of Millonarios, saw a silver lining: leagues and clubs that were no longer members of FIFA were no longer bound by FIFA regulations concerning player transfers. Senior sent Millonarios' Argentine manager Carlos Aldabe to Buenos Aires to sign a leading player. There would of course be no transfer fee and this would fund an alluring level of wages. A week or so later Aldabe sent a telegram saying that he was returning with one of *La Máquina* – Adolfo Pedernera. Unbelievable! When Millonarios presented Pedernera in their stadium the take at the turnstile was $18,000 – five times the average gate-money for a match, let alone a presentation.

There were plenty more ready recruits in Buenos Aires and not just for the wages, but for the relative freedom and dignity that Colombia offered. Pedernera was quoted in the Bogotá daily *El Tiempo* saying, 'I want to express a perfectly logical human aspiration: to enjoy the same freedoms as all men. You understand that it is perfectly impossible that the fact of exercising a profession – that of football – should put us in an exceptional situation in relation to the other professions, in that we are obliged to give up the freedom of labour.'[6] The same arguments held up in Rio, Lima, Asunción and Montevideo. More than that, the same arguments that held for Millonarios held for Independiente Santa Fe, and every other club in the country. In 1949 the Millonarios squad boasted nine Argentinians, a Brazilian, a Colombian, a Chilean and a Peruvian. Then Deportivo Cali got their own Argentinians, Deportivo Pereira signed Paraguayans, Cúcuta Deportivo had Uruguayans, including eight of the team that won the 1950 World Cup, and Independiente Medellín settled on Peruvians; by 1950 there were 109 foreign players of the very highest calibre in Colombian football, fifty-seven of whom were Argentinians. The lure of El Dorado was so strong that in a singular reversal of the normal geographical patterns of the global football transfer market Colombia could attract players from all over Europe, including England, Scotland, Ireland, Hungary and France.

Luis Robledo, the Cambridge-educated Colombian diplomat and president of the other Bogotá team Independiente Santa Fe, sought out Stoke City's Neil Franklin and George Mountford and the Manchester United winger Charlie Mitten. Not to be outdone Millonarios signed

Everton's Billy Higgins and the Scot Bobby Flavell from Heart of Midlothian. Franklin, who had recently been humiliated by Stoke's autocratic directors – kept waiting for three hours before they would condescend to see him to discuss his transfer request – was easy prey. Robledo offered him a signing-on fee of £1,500 – the equivalent fee in England in 1949 was £10. Mitten, who was on £10 a week at Manchester United, was offered wages almost ten times that as well as bonuses, expenses and flights. Despite the money, Franklin, in particular, found the transition too much to handle. The football seemed recklessly individualistic, though he recognized the immense technique of the South Americans. The wider culture appeared too alien and too impenetrable. Franklin lasted just six games; Mitten and his wife managed a whole season.

Yet there was more to this furious global recruitment than the competitive dynamic of the clubs. Alfonso Senior Quevedo of Millonarios put it very bluntly: 'People were desperate because of the political situation . . . So the government, President Perez, supported our bringing in foreign players and gave us the dollars . . . because they knew we would fill stadiums. And they gave us a good rate: 1.75 [pesos] to the dollar!'[7] The Colombian Senate was equally supportive, offering a 10,000 peso prize for the champions. The political situation was indeed desperate. Even Neil Franklin, whose diaries do not suggest a man attuned to the culture and politics of Colombia, could not remain oblivious: 'Never a day passed without some form of demonstration . . . and when the Colombians demonstrate they really demonstrate . . . so electric was the political atmosphere that during the time we were there a curfew was in force.'[8]

The *Bogotazo*, as the outbreak of social unrest had come to be called, had uncoiled into a bloody civil war. The Liberals boycotted the 1949 presidential election won by Conservative Laureano Gómez. Gómez hailed from the furthest reaches of the authoritarian clerical right of Colombian conservatism. He was an open admirer of Franco and Salazar and viewed the threat to property and propriety with such alarm that his regime suspended civil liberties of all kinds. Conservative-backed mobs sacked and burnt the offices of the nation's leading newspapers, Congress was closed down, the High Court was packed with placemen and electoral manipulation became commonplace. The Liberals abandoned electoral politics and formed a guerrilla army in the countryside participating in the land and labour conflicts that followed the uprising. They were met by a government-backed war of terror and repression so furious that 50,000 died in the fighting in 1950 and around 200,000 over the next three years. The cities were made secure by high-intensity policing and repression of the Communist Party and the trade unions. DiMayor football provided the distraction and dreamland of the circus.

But what a circus! In 1950 the league was so open and attacking that there were only six goalless draws in a whole year. Top of the bill were Millonarios, who in addition to Pedernera attracted the young Alfredo Di Stéfano from River Plate and Uruguayan star José Jacuzzi. They won the national championship four times out of five between 1949 and 1953, and were unbeaten throughout 1951, playing mesmerizing football of swirling movement. 'Alfredo Di Stéfano . . . later claimed that their sole method was to attack and beat the opposition without humiliating them. Once they had scored enough goals to win, the ballet would commence. The ball would pass from one player to another with such precision and speed that sometimes the other side stood and watched in sheer admiration.'[9] The crowds flocked in their tens of thousands to what had become known as *Ballet Azul* – the ballet in blue (the colour of the Millonarios strip). Di Stéfano recalled the opulence of the moment and the freedom it offered to play football as art.

The Millonarios players really were living the life of . . . millionaires. Every day they went training at the end of the morning, then everyone was invited for lunch at the club's headquarters. The Colombian cuisine, based on rice, manioc, and pork meat and fried bananas, was a discovery for us. They drank a special kind of beer, the Bavaria, which was fantastic. And after that, we had a Colombian coffee, rightly considered the best in the world. Later a siesta, and sometimes the cinema and a quick visit to the dancing. When you come from the country of the tango, you aren't ashamed to show that you possess the art of dancing.[10]

FIFA and CONMEBOL, strangely oblivious to the sea of blood in Colombia, shuttled officials back and forth between Bogotá and their offices, negotiating an end to El Dorado. At a special congress in Lima in 1951 a deal was struck: the Colombians could see the economic crisis coming at home would make their glorious isolation more and more difficult to maintain; FIFA were prepared to let the fiesta continue just a little longer. DiMayor could keep its stars until the end of 1953 and then they would have to go. Colombia could rejoin FIFA but they would have to play by the rules. Colombia signed. Released from the ban on playing foreign clubs, Millonarios set out on a global tour in 1952. The team astonished and delighted the crowds of Chile, Uruguay, Peru, Argentina and Bolivia. Then they went to Spain, winning in Madrid, Valencia and Seville. They returned home in 1953 to win a final championship and then the foreign players went home or, like Di Stéfano, exposed to the world on Millonarios' tour, moved to Europe.

Halfway through the season President Gómez attempted to remove the army Commander-in-Chief, General Gustavo Rojas Pinilla, from his post. The army responded with a *coup d'état*, widely supported across the now bloodied and shattered elites. Rojas offered an amnesty to the rural guerrilla forces who accepted. The first round of *La Violencia* came to a close and Rojas's dictatorship gave way to a systematic carve-up of power among conservative and liberal elites that excluded the rest of the country for another thirty years. Colombian football shrank back to the level that the country's real level of economic and political development warranted. Marijuana appeared in Bogotá for the first time. Drugs, football and violence would reconvene three decades later when the political and economic settlement that followed El Dorado was exhausted.

IV

For most of the 1920s and 1930s Brazilian football had lived in the shadow of *fútbol rioplatense*. While Argentina and Uruguay were con-testing Olympic and World Cup finals, Brazil were being turned over by Yugoslavia in the 1930 World Cup and by Spain in 1934. The flood of football migrants to Spain and Italy in the early 1930s saw just a handful of Brazilians make the journey, most of whom were unsuccessful. But at the 1938 World Cup in France, Brazil were South America's only representatives. They stepped into the limelight with aplomb. A wildly attacking game against Poland gave free rein to their forwards and exposed their defence. Brazil were 3–1 up at half-time, but the score stood at 4–4 after 90 minutes. Leônidas completed his hat-trick in extra time to finish the game 6–5. Then against the Czechs, Brazil showed they could rough it with the Europeans. A spiteful draw saw three sent off (two of whom were Brazilians) and two Czechs depart with broken bones: Plánička and Nejedlý, arm and leg respectively. In the replay there were fourteen changes in the two sides and a strange shift in atmosphere. In a bizarre, semi-catatonic state Brazil won 2–1 and left for Marseilles to play the Italians in the semi-finals.

Legend claims that confidence in the Brazilian camp was so high that tickets had been booked for the rail trip to the final in Paris and that Leônidas was rested in anticipation of a semi-final win. The tedious reality was that Leônidas was injured and the Italians were good. Piola and Colaussi in particular danced rings around Domingos in the Brazilian defence, Italy winning 2–1. Brazil regrouped and went back to Bordeaux where they thrashed the Swedes to win third place, a result greeted with great acclaim at home. What distinguished this Brazilian team was not only their success, but that their two undisputed stars, striker Leônidas da Silva and central defender Domingos da Guia, were black.

Interviewed in the newspapers on the team's return no less a figure than Gilberto Freyre – one of Brazil's leading social commentators and writers – said:

Our style of playing football seems to contrast to the European style because of a set of characteristics such as surprise, craftiness, shrewdness, readiness, and I shall even say individual brilliance and spontaneity, all of which express our 'mulattoism' . . . Our passes . . . our tricks . . . that something which is related to dance, to capoeira, mark the Brazilian style of football, which rounds and sweetens the game the British invented, the game which they and other Europeans play in such an acute and angular way – all this seems to express . . . the flamboyant and at the same time shrewd mulattoism, which can today be detected in every true affirmation of Brazil.[11]

Freyre had made his name in 1933 when he published *Casa-Grande e Senzala* (the former being the big house of the white slave masters of his native north-east Brazil and the latter the quarters of the African slaves who worked their sugar plantations). The title was translated into English as *Masters and Slaves*. It is an extraordinary book, describing in immense detail every aspect of social life on the plantations, and every aspect led back to sex. While the sexual relationships between slave masters and slaves in Protestant North America were nasty, brutish, short and shameful, in Catholic Brazil – where the demographics of colonialism were so much more heavily weighted against Europeans – miscegenation was a necessity and a virtue. The same could also be said for relationships with the new immigrants to Brazil in the late nineteenth and early twentieth centuries: Italians, Japanese and Germans. This way of thinking gave the Brazilian elite who had always felt queasy about their bastard nation a narrative and an ideology that turned the nation's diversity to their advantage. As Peter Robb has eloquently put it: 'It was immensely seductive, Freyre's tropical pastoral of the vanished world of the sugar estates, conjured in sensuous and loving detail. Most seductive of all was the idea that out of Brazil's sensual and promiscuous past a new society had grown where all races flourished and racism was extinguished.'[12]

Freyre's ideas were adopted and developed by many Brazilian intellectuals and politicians including Mário Filho, the leading football journalist of the era, who had endlessly campaigned in the 1920s and 1930s for the professionalization of Brazilian football and above all the equal inclusion of black players in the game. Both Filho and Freyre argued that not only was this a moral imperative but it was clear that Brazil's essential 'mulattoism' – its mix, its diversity, its African qualities – helped create a body culture, a state of mind and a mode of cooperation that raised football to a new level – an argument invented, illustrated and mythologized in Filho's landmark book of football writing *O Negro no futebol brasileiro*.[13]

Whatever the precise sociological or biological truth of Freyre and Filho's arguments, the sporting impact of black footballers was unambiguous. In Rio the two leading teams that most systematically signed and played black players – Flamengo and Vasco – came to win both the Carioca championship and the hearts of the Rio masses. By contrast, Fluminense, who diligently kept to their whites-only policy by recruiting more and more players from regions further and further from Rio, and Botafogo, who were also initially elitist in their approach, languished. Similarly, in Porto Alegre to the south it was the mixed-race sides of Internacional that dominated the era, while Grêmio with its explicitly German roots and white teams were always a miserable second. São

Paulo, which had hitherto been a much whiter city and had a white footballing culture, received a massive influx of black and mestizo immigrants through the 1930s and 1940s including both Leônidas and Domingos who transferred to São Paulo FC in 1944 bringing Afro-Brazilian football style and glamour to the city.

A similar cross-fertilization of Brazilian culture came through the mingling of Catholicism and African cultic magic. It was widely believed that Vasco da Gama's decade-long wait for a championship victory was caused by the curse of Arubinha, a player from a small team called Andrari which had been humiliated by Vasco 12–0 in 1937. In 1943 and 1944 exceptionally strong Vasco teams were pipped for the Carioca title, and the club actually resorted to ploughing up the playing field in search of buried frogs that held the curse. No frog was found and Vasco begged Arubinha to tell them where the frogs were. He assured them there were none and that the curse was now lifted. Vasco won the 1945 championship.

This cultural effervescence of the new urban Brazil emerged under what at first sight appears an unlikely political regime. Getúlio Vargas, a short avuncular *caudillo* from the tough countryside of Rio Grande do Sul, was the defeated presidential candidate in the 1930 elections, beaten by Júlio Prestes, the representative of the incumbent São Paulo coffee oligarchy. But in the immediate weeks after the election, which was seen by many as a fix, opposition continued to coalesce around Vargas. The consequences of the Wall Street Crash were now beginning to bite very hard on the Brazilian economy; commodity prices were collapsing and the financial orthodoxy of the government which was maintaining a hard currency was sinking the country's export trade and balance of payments. The Brazilian military intervened, and installed Vargas and his cabinet in power in a brief coup in October 1930.

Vargas, however, was never a mere puppet of the military; rather the army was but one wing of a political coalition that he created and that would sustain him in power for the next fifteen years. Vargas's rule was characterized by three interlocking policies: the centralization of power in Brazil in the federal government rather than the states; the creation of a powerful sense of Brazilian national identity; and the marginalization and repression of enduring immigrant identities. This combination of centralization and nationalism was used to create a state and a nation that could embark upon a programme of industrialization and development. Vargas immediately replaced all but one of the country's state governors who were transformed at a stroke from independent power brokers to mere satrapies. In 1932 he ordered the army to crush an armed and organized uprising in São Paulo. His own personal power was consolidated in 1934 by drafting a new constitution that made provision for elections but installed Vargas as the first president of the new regime unelected. A rising tide of dissent and unrest by both Brazilian communists and Brazilian fascists – though neither were serious contenders for power – provided the opportunity for Vargas to cling on to power by declaring an internal coup and creating yet another constitution, the *Estado Novo*. From 1937 to 1945, civil rights were curtailed and political parties were banned. Centralized executive power was fused with a semi-corporatist model of society that owed much to Mussolini's early attempts to control and incorporate working-class power through police repression and state-sponsored trade unions.

In this context football, like carnival which Vargas effectively nationalized, was an obvious tool of populist politics. Vargas bought off some of his opprobrium and opposition in São Paulo by funding the construction of the municipal Pacaembu stadium in the early 1940s. By the same token Rio's Flamengo benefited from a low-cost loan arranged by the President that allowed them to speculate on prime Rio real estate; a favour again extended to the club by Vargas's eventual successor President Dutra. When Vargas had a big announcement to make – like the enactment of Brazil's first worker-friendly labour legislation, or the setting of the vital minimum wage – it was Vasco da Gama's São Januário stadium that often provided the venue. The military's active interest in physical education was fused with strains of the now commonplace developmental and biological nationalism in Brazil. The country and the bodies of its people had to be made fit and strong enough for industrialization, so Vargas created a national council for sport in 1941. The Confederação Brasileira de Desportes (CBD) centralized power and control over every aspect of the nation's sporting development. Located in the Ministry of Education and with military and civilian directors directly appointed by the President, the CBD gave the state a powerful instrument for shaping football.

When in 1943 Brazil finally entered the Second World War on the side of the Allies, the substantial German, Italian and Japanese communities in Brazil came under suspicion. Public displays of these ethnic identities, including those associated with football teams, were abruptly terminated. Thus Palestra Itália, the team of São Paulo's Italians, became Palmeiras, while their equivalents and namesakes in Curitiba and Belo Horizonte reappeared in their new Brazilian incarnations as Coritiba and Cruzeiro.

However, Vargas's nationalist project was always more than one of mere repression. The inclusion, indeed celebration, of Afro-Brazilians within the nation pointed to something both inclusive and infinitely richer in its content. The intellectual and political framework established by the Freyrian celebration of miscegenation, diversity and mulattoism and Vargas's populist nationalism was brought to mass cultural fruition by a gifted generation of Brazilian football intellectuals. For an earlier generation of Brazilian intellectuals football was a pastime, even a passion, but not a subject fit for literature. Coelho Neto, the leading Rio novelist of the early twentieth century, was a fanatical Fluminense fan. He is credited with leading the country's first pitch invasion, running down from the elegant Edwardian stands of the club's Laranjeiras stadium to contest a doubtful penalty decision. He was also the father of the multi-talented Preguinho who scored three goals for Brazil at the 1930 World Cup. But Neto never wrote a word on the subject. His successors were less reticent.

Mário Filho continued to edit, publish and write on sport throughout the era. He acted as a personal counsellor to Vargas on these matters and used his sports journalism as a cover for political and social thinking. He was also, despite the apparent seriousness and sobriety of his style, the first great mythmaker of Brazilian football. His account of the 1941 Carioca derby between Flamengo and Fluminense – christened the *O Fla-Flu da Lagoa* – is a perfect example of the genre. And the best was yet to come: in the late 1950s Filho's younger brother, the scandalous playwright Nelson Rodriguez, would pick up the tradition of football writing established in the Vargas years and take it to new heights of comic intensity and acid social commentary.

A little behind Argentina, radio began to spread across Brazil in the 1930s and football commentaries were a staple element of early broadcasting. In 1942 the horse-racing commentator Rebelo Junior gave Brazilian football its signature exclamation, uttering the first super extended 'Goooooooooooooooooooooooooooooooooooooool!' But the defining voice of the era was the incomparable Ary Barrosa. Barrosa was an easily distracted law student from the provinces who on arrival in Rio spent more time on music, football and dancing than studying. He rose to fame in the newly fashionable Copacabana as primarily a composer but also as a pianist, writer, local councillor and fanatical Flamengo fan. At the height of Hollywood's 1940s infatuation with Copacabana and Carmen Miranda he was offered a very well-remunerated job as musical director with Walt Disney in Los Angeles; in his broken English he delivered a blunt response: 'No have Flamengo.' Flamengo were on the radio and so was Barrosa, who was now the country's favourite commentator. Unlike anyone before or since, Barrosa treated the game as both a blank canvas for fantastical invention and a deeply partisan affair. When Flamengo scored he signalled the goal with a wondrous sprightly trill on his harmonica. When the opposition scored he emitted a rasping screech or a doleful drooping note. He started the practice of interviewing players and referees as they came on and off the pitch and provided a brilliant comic comment on an evident truth of Brazilian civil society: that pretty much everything was viewed through partisan lenses and motivated by the pursuit of individual interests.

On the back of their performance at the 1938 World Cup, FIFA awarded Brazil the 1942 competition. The Second World War intervened but the FIFA congress of 1946 reconfirmed Brazil as hosts of the fourth World Cup, to be held in 1950. Brazil's participation in the grand anti-fascist alliance of the Second World War made Vargas's continuing authoritarian hold on power unsustainable. He stepped down in October 1945 only to take up a senatorial post and build a new network of power through his Brazilian Labour Party. His command over the Brazilian elite remained significant and he was able effectively to anoint the successful candidate for the presidency of the Second Brazilian Republic, General Eurico Dutra. The preparations for the World Cup under Dutra served as both a practical problem for and a proxy debate about Brazil's economic development. Despite the advances of the Vargas era Brazil suffered from a chronic lack of industrial, energy and transport infrastructure. Mário Filho led the charge of the football developmentalists by arguing for the construction of a new stadium in Rio that would provide a proper stage for the World Cup. In its size and styling the stadium would provide concrete testament of Brazil's footballing prowess and its new urban modernity. 'The stadium will be a gift from this generation to the next, strengthening the human wealth of Brazil. This stadium will be a gift from all of us.'[14] Critics argued that scarce capital should be spent on schools and hospitals, to which Vargas Neto responded in Mário Filho's *Jornal dos Sports* that football could also heal the nation: 'I'm not against your request! I'm in favour! But I want you to be in favour of stadiums. It could well be that hospitals will become less necessary.'[15]

In Brazil the case was unanswerable. Money was raised by the government, the project was controlled by the prefect of Rio, Mendes de Morais, the architects Galvão, Azevedo, Bastos and Carneiro were appointed and construction of the stadium began in 1948. By the time of the tournament it was barely finished, but it was magnificent. Brazil had built the largest and most elegantly modern stadium in the world. The Maracanã was an immense double-tiered white concrete ellipse with an official capacity of over 160,000. Its 360-degree flat concrete roof, when viewed from the south on the summit of the Corcovado, gave it the irresistible appearance of an alien spaceship that had chosen to park in a wasteland of vacant lots and exposed steel on the poor fringes of Rio's Zona Norte and Centro. The stadium from Planet Modernity was built with some of the first concrete to be actually produced in Brazil. The main entrance was a long space-age ramp with a roof supported by two lines of simple cylindrical columns with no nod, not the slightest gesture, to any classical colonnade; like the hidden steel cantilevers in the roof they were a bold statement of advanced engineering and minimalist design. The Maracanã's high internal arches and buttresses beneath the stands flanked great circular concourses that swept round the stadium beneath the seating; a people's sporting boulevard. *A Noite* wrote, 'Today Brazil has the biggest and most perfect stadium in the world, dignifying the competence of its people and its evolution in all branches of human activity.'[16] Mário Filho wrote that the Maracanã gave Brazil a new soul, that it prefigured the awakening of the slumbering giant of Brazilian potential.

The Brazilian team's preparations were meticulous, cloistered in a special training camp for a couple of months before the tournament, serviced by an army of cooks, clerics and medical staff. Rio prepared itself. The samba parade on the Shrove Tuesday of Rio's carnival took the World Cup as its theme. The radio was permanently tuned to the hits that implored Brazil to win. The Jules Rimet trophy was put on display in the windows of a shoe shop downtown on Avenida Rio Branco where thousands made a pilgrimage of awe. On the day of the first game the Korean War broke out, but nobody noticed. Everyone was going to the Maracanã.

Five thousand pigeons were let loose and the new stadium thundered to a 21-gun salute. Arthur Ellis, the English referee in the stands that day, reports being showered with a powdery white rain of plaster from the Maracanã's just-completed roof. Brazil sailed past Mexico, scoring four and hitting the woodwork six times. For obvious political reasons Brazil played one game, the next, in São Paulo. They faced Switzerland with five changes to the side. Brazil stuttered, just scraping a 2–2 draw against an organized but unexceptional opponent. The final game of the group stage against Yugoslavia was now critical, for the Yugoslavs had won both their games and could go through at the expense of Brazil. On a day of extraordinary heat 160,000 Cariocas went to the game. The beer ran out. The first-aid posts were overwhelmed; the jittery nervous crowd succumbed in their hundreds to a rash of sun stroke. Yugoslavia began with only ten men as Mitić had gashed his head on an exposed girder in the underground passageways of the unfinished stadium. By the time he had been patched up Ademir had made it 1–0 to Brazil. With eleven the Yugoslavs appeared a match for the hosts and held them until late in the second half when a goal from Zizinho made it 2–0 and Brazil were through.

There was a wait of just two days before the final rounds of the tournament which, unusually, were organized as a four-team mini-league rather than a knock-out competition. Rio's local elections held that week brought Brazil's political class out in force, associating with the national team in the grubby search for votes. Indeed the further Brazil progressed, the more politicians and the powerful sought to have themselves seen or photographed with the squad, the more they showed up at the training camp even though the players' families were excluded, the more they came into the dressing room before and after the game. Yet despite the pressure of expectation, Brazil were a team unleashed as they scythed down Sweden 7–1 and dispatched Spain 6–1. The game

289

against the Spanish was euphoric. By the third goal the entire crowd was whirling their knotted white handkerchiefs above their heads and singing *adios* to the Spaniards. The official supporters' band struck up the insufferably jaunty Carmen Miranda carnival favourite 'Bullfight in Madrid'. It was a moment recorded in both the history of Brazilian football and song: 'The spectacle transformed into one of the largest demonstrations of collective singing ever known; it was like the chorus of the fans was a counterpoint to the Brazilians' game.'[17] Uruguay, the fourth member of the mini-league, had by contrast made heavy weather of their games against Spain (a 2–2 draw in São Paulo) and Sweden (who they only managed to beat with two late goals). Pleasingly, the final game of the tournament between Uruguay and Brazil was in effect a conventional final, but while Uruguay had to win to take the trophy, Brazil only needed to draw.

The twenty years since Uruguay had won their first World Cup Final had been mixed. Uruguay's triumph had been achieved at the pinnacle of the country's economic prosperity. But, just as governments were swept from office in Brazil and Argentina by the shockwaves of the Wall Street Crash, so too was Uruguay's long-standing civilian administration. As commodity prices plunged and the Uruguayan economy took a sharp fall, the army struck in 1932. A brief coup was followed by a decade of militarily supported conservative dictatorship in which political competition was restricted.

Like the beef and wool industries, Uruguayan football disappeared from the world market. No Uruguayan team was sent to the 1934 and 1938 World Cups and the triumphant European tours of the 1920s were not repeated. The best talents continued to cross the Atlantic for Spain and Italy until the mid-1930s; others went to Buenos Aires. When the chance came to go to join the gold rush to Colombia, there was a virtual stampede of players who had been living on the pitiful income that Uruguay's football economy offered. At home, with professional football still restricted to the city of Montevideo alone, competition contracted and the title was shared exclusively between Peñarol and Nacional who had become a self-perpetuating duopoly.

Uruguay's football officials didn't think that the 1950 World Cup Final was going to be much of a competition. Dr Jacobo, president of the Uruguayan FA, is reported as saying to the squad, 'What's important is that these people don't make six goals. If they score only four goals our mission will be successful.'[18] Such defeatism provided the side with precisely the irritant needed to psych them up for the game.

Neither form, nor omen, nor caution restrained Brazil's belief. Over 200,000 are said to have flooded the Maracanã – over 20 per cent of Rio's adult population. It remains the biggest crowd that has ever attended a football match. On a day of superlatives there followed the single greatest act of footballing hubris: seconds before the game was due to kick-off, the Mayor of Rio announced over the public-address system, 'You Brazilians, whom I consider victors of the tournament . . . you players who in less than a few hours will be acclaimed champions by millions of your compatriots . . . you who are superior to every other competitor . . . you whom I already salute as conquerors . . .'[19] You couldn't have scripted it.

———————

16 July 1950
Brazil 1 Uruguay 2
Maracanã, Rio de Janeiro

EXTERIOR; DAY. The small gates of a tiny crumbling football stadium in suburban Montevideo. Half obscured by vines there is a plaque: Estadio Obdulio Varela. We hear Obdulio Varela, Uruguayan captain, in voiceover.

OBDULIO VARELA v/o
Get it in your head: we won, because we won, no more . . . If we had played a hundred times, we would have won only that one.

ARCHIVE: The Brazil squad nervously eat their lunch at canteen tables while a phalanx of suits and fedoras walk between them. We hear Flavio Costa, Brazil coach, in voiceover.

FLAVIO COSTA v/o
The Uruguayan team has always disturbed the slumbers of Brazilian footballers. I am afraid that my players will take the field on Sunday as though they already had the championship shield sewn on their jerseys.

EXTERIOR; DAY. We are inside a rotting goal in the Estadio Varela, moving slowly towards the centre circle.

OBDULIO VARELA v/o
The stands were on fire, there were sparks everywhere, and I had to do what I did. I had to delay putting the ball back into play as much as possible because, if we started up again immediately they would have scored five . . . they went from being happy to booing; they got nervous. We calmed down and that's when I gave up the ball. I was close to being kicked out of the game, so I was lucky even then. Afterwards came Schiaffino and Ghiggia's goals. That was it.

ARCHIVE: Ghiggia advancing on the Brazilian goal. As he scores we hear the voice of Radio Globo commentator Luiz Mendes announce the goal with the usual roar. He repeats his words six times, stunned, quizzical, enraged and bewildered. The camera lingers on the ball in the corner of the net. In the middle distance Ghiggia, in slow motion, turns to embrace his team-mates. A woman in the crowd, in slow motion, turns to the camera, her face breaking.

LUIZ MENDES v/o
GOOOOOOOOL DO UUURUGUAY!!!!!! . . .
gol do uruguay??? . . .
Gol do Uruguay.
Gol do Uruguay?
GOL DO URUGUAY??
GOL DO URUGUAY???? . . .
Gol . . . do . . . Uruguay!
Goool . . . dooo . . . U . . . ru . . . guay!
Gol . . .
Do . . .
Uruguay!

ARCHIVE: FIFA President Jules Rimet stands confused amidst a small clutch of officials and weeping Uruguayan players. He furtively opens a hinged wooden box and offers the trophy inside it to Varela.

JULES RIMET v/o
I find myself alone in the crowd [on the field] jostled by my neighbours, the cup in my arms, not knowing what to do. In the end I saw the Uruguayan captain and gave him the cup, at the same time discreetly shaking his hand.

ARCHIVE: The Maracanã, almost empty, a low wind is audible.

PELÉ v/o
There was sadness so great, so profound that it seemed like the end of a war with Brazil the loser and many people dead.

Uruguay slipped away from the now empty Maracanã and returned to their hotel. The post-match party ended early with the officials of the Uruguayan FA heading off into the night for a whirl through the clubs and the cabarets while warning the players to stay in the hotel in case the locals got hostile. A similar logic had been applied to the official medals awarded by the Brazilian FA: gold for the directors, silver for the players. Varela and the team's masseur Matucho drank the hotel's wine cache dry and then headed off themselves on a drunken odyssey through the city, fuelled by beer and whiskey. They were hailed at every turn by foreign journalists and lamenting Brazilians. In the immediate aftermath of the *Maracanazo* Brazil had neither energy nor inclination for post-mortems or recriminations. Brazil's players ran for cover and consoled their guilt and anguish as far away and for as long as possible. They never wore white shirts again.

In this sombre mood that threw such a heavy shadow of doubt over Brazil's self-acclaim, the electorate were in the mood for safety and nostalgia. Four months later they actually elected Getúlio Vargas as President. Brazil did not play another international match until April 1952, and they only played at the Maracanã again in March 1954. When the time for recriminations did come, the scapegoats were the left-half Bigode, defender Juvenal and goalkeeper Barbosa. All were condemned in the press as cowards, lacking fibre and discipline – and all three were black. Barbosa was singled out for special levels of opprobrium which endured until his miserable poverty-stricken death fifty years later. He recalled walking into a baker's shop where a woman recognized him and told her son, 'Look, there is the man who made all Brazil cry.'[20] Legend tells us that he burnt the posts that he had stood between at the Maracanã and ate a barbecue of revenge from their embers, but to no avail: in 1993 he was shunned by the Brazilian World Cup squad at their Teresopolis training camp and Brazil did not field another black goalkeeper until Dida's debut in 1995. The multiracial, confident, progressive Brazil that Freyre and Filho had conjured from football was dissolved in an acid bath of racism, self-doubt and self-loathing.

Brazil went to the 1954 World Cup under coach Zezé Moreira. Moreira took a team to Switzerland whose strength was at the back, though the attacking line included talents like the young Didi and Julinho. Together they took the team easily past Mexico, coasted to a draw against Yugoslavia, and moved through to the quarter-finals. Since the *Maracanazo* a persistent criticism of Brazilian players and by implication of the African influence on Brazilian football was the psychological dysfunctionality of the stars – their inability to keep their heads, to play in a disciplined fashion. Moreira had absorbed much of these arguments and shaped his team accordingly.

It didn't quite work. In the quarter-finals they met the favourites, Hungary. The Magyars won 4–2 but the game is remembered more for a rising tide of violence. Brazil's captain Bauer brought Bozsik down so hard he had to leave the field for extended treatment. Then Bozsik and Brazilian defender Nílton Santos were sent off for fighting, followed eight minutes later by Humberto. Djalma Santos exacted revenge on Czibor and Hidegkuti pushed Indio to the ground and stamped on his calves. Didi was restrained by the police on the touchline. As the teams left the pitch the free-for-all began which continued into the tunnel and the dressing rooms.[21]

Brazil had imploded and with the political cycle of presidential elections now clearly hitched to the World Cup, defeat was followed once again by a change in regime. In the four years since his election, Vargas had ridden a wave of massive social discontent, ever-mounting demands from the labour movement and a restless military. In a vainglorious sacrifice, he staved off a military coup by committing suicide in the presidential palace.

The 1954 World Cup was also a watershed for the Uruguayans. The defending champions were in imperious form in the early rounds sweeping aside the Czechs, the Scots and England. In the semi-finals they too met the Hungarians and played out one of the World Cup's greatest games. But late equalizers do not win matches and the Hungarians were stronger and better. Uruguay went home and would not return to a World Cup for twelve years. The country's leading players Ghiggia and Schiaffino moved to Italy, took Italian citizenship and played for the Italian national team. Uruguay, now returned to democratic politics, saw national government oscillate between the Colorados and the Blancos and the national championship move between Peñarol and Nacional. But what had once been sources of creative tension, good enough to make Uruguay the sixth-richest country in the world and world football champions four times over, was now a source of sclerosis and decline. Uruguay had a long way to fall, but starting in 1954 it went all the way.

---

30 June 1954
Hungary 4 Uruguay 2 (aet)
Stade d'Olympique, Lausanne

For over three-quarters of this match there's only one team in it. The Hungarians are imperious, in charge and in the lead. The defending champions are 2–0 down and going out. The speed and power of the Hungarians make the Uruguayans look ponderous yet lightweight. Then in the final quarter of an hour two goals from Hohberg, out of nothing, take the game to extra time. In the opening moments of extra time he fires the ball from five yards against the post. The rebound is hustled over the touchline.

That was Uruguay's final flourish: they will never come so close to a World Cup Final again. As the second period of extra time begins the Uruguayans are clearly exhausted, the Hungarians are full of running and Kocsis puts two headers away. Uruguay's economy is heading into a depression that will last for all of the 1950s and most of the 1960s. It too has run out of steam, made to look ponderous and lightweight by Europe and the Far East.

9

Games of Life, Games of Death: European Football in War and Peace, 1934–1954

On 22 June 1941, the day the Germans invaded the Soviet Union, the decisive act of the entire conflict, ninety thousand spectators watched the German league final in Berlin. What were they thinking of?   **Simon Kuper**

People find the war at present completely unsatisfactory as a compensation for sport.   **Mass Observation, 1939**

I

What were they thinking? Mass Observation – the inaugural and innovative British social survey of the everyday, conducted before and during the war – was asking the same question. If the mood in Britain was the same as in Germany, then they were thinking about football. Rapid Vienna, now a team of the 17th Gau of the Greater German Reich, and FC Schalke 04 to be precise, in a game that saw Rapid come back from 3–0 down to win 4–3 in an extraordinary six minutes of chaos. The Germans were not alone. The Italian public had flocked to Serie A through 1940 and 1941 as Bologna raced to the title. At the same time the Italian army attempted to invade Albania and Greece and disintegrated in a fog of its own incompetence; its logistical and technological backwardness cruelly exposed by Italy's smaller neighbours. This concurrence of football and warfare stood in sharp contrast to the experience of the game twenty-five years earlier. Outside of the armed forces and the prisoner-of-war camps, the First World War had extinguished football in all combatant nations. The Second World War, at its points of maximum barbarism and destructiveness, could also extinguish the game: Poland, alone of any major European nation, played no national football championship for the entire duration of the conflict. But beyond the most concentrated firestorms, football continued, formally and informally, nationally and locally. Indeed football was considered important enough that the German Foreign Minister Von Ribbentrop wrote in his early war diaries that he 'placed the highest value on German teams appearing abroad and foreign teams coming to Germany'.[1] In the quarter of a century since the first industrialized war both the social significance of football and the nature of warfare had changed.

In the 1920s and 1930s, in its leading zones, European football industrialized, either in the form of commercialization and professionalization, or it had been taken over by an authoritarian state. In both the surviving democracies and new dictatorships that emerged from the tumult of the 1920s and the global economic recession of the early 1930s, football had become by some way the leading spectator sport, a central national cultural institution and a potent index of national prowess in the world. In the shadow of the real war, football's use as proxy conflict was redundant, but its role on the home front was amplified. Although the First World War had required a level of domestic mobilization, hardship and exposure to violence that no war had hitherto required, it was a mere prelude to the experience of the Second World War. In the Soviet Union alone 20 million were killed. To endure a war that included the terror and destruction of the Blitz, of Barbarossa, the Soviet scorched-earth retreat and the firebombing of Dresden, and still to produce munitions and machines in unprecedented quantities, European states were forced to mobilize, brutalize, cajole and persuade their societies like never before. Football was one element of the strategies that governments pursued to do this.

For the most part football functioned as a cipher for normality. Ribbentrop's support for the maintenance of a circuit of international football through the axis of iron was intended to evoke the sporting rhythms of peace. As Fritz Walter, the enlisted German international, said after being mobbed by German troops on a boat bound for Italy, 'For them I am the embodiment of concepts that seem to be lost for ever: peace, home, sport.'[2] When peace finally came and those who still had a home to speak of could return, European men went to the football. The immediate post-war era saw record levels of attendance at domestic and international games across the entire Continent. The Norwegian Cup Final played in the summer of 1945 saw 158,000 applications for just 35,000 seats to see Fredrikstad play Lyn. In Britain, Germany and France, attendances at the biggest domestic games and biggest internationals were regularly in six figures. For much of the next decade it was a rough-and-ready affair, the game of austerity, rationing and hunger. Only in the mid-1950s had Europe's people and their economies recovered sufficiently that they could field teams which could compete with the Latin Americans who had led the footballing world since the early 1940s; a process consecrated by the 1954 World Cup in Switzerland, the first European World Cup for sixteen years.

But it was not the same continent that had converged on the 1938 World Cup in France. In 1945 the Red Army were stationed in Berlin and Vienna, and were the de facto occupiers of Poland, Bulgaria and Romania. Soon, they were to take up residence in Hungary and Czechoslovakia too. Europe was divided into communist and capitalist, East and West, Warsaw Pact and NATO, American and Soviet zones of influence; the process was complete by 1955, centring on Germany and Berlin, which were both split between the two camps. The course of European football provides an accurate marker of the twin processes of economic reconstruction and political division.

In the West football remained in private and voluntary hands. In the East it was the property of state and parastatal organizations. The Germans had both versions. All across Europe, as the tectonic shifts of the war settled down allowing the formation of new states, new borders and a new pecking order of power, football continued to offer a narrative palette of unity and disunity, triumph and disaster, collapse and recovery. For the English the game served most acutely as an index of relative decline. In Hungary, their main competitor for footballing hegemony, the game spoke to both the nation's hidden pre-war bourgeois past and the exaggerated hopes of its new communist technocracy. In West Germany, most potently of all, it offered the opportunity for a profound reimagining of the nation as a winner of games rather than wars. Football, for so long not merely metaphor or proxy for war, but an actual instrument of the violent struggle between Europe's nations, was for a rare and fleeting moment the sporting and symbolic embodiment of the foundations of peace.

The prelude to the conflagration was Spain. The Wall Street Crash finished off the tottering military authoritarianism of Primo de Rivera's regime in 1930. The general's resignation was followed by elections in which Spain decisively voted for the establishment of a republic. King Alfonso XIII went into exile and a republican coalition government under Niceto Alcalá Zamora and Manuel Azaña took power initiating a programme of reform including agrarian land redistribution and regional, linguistic and political autonomy. The already established and entrenched oppositions between nationalists and regionalists, Left and Right, the secular and the religious, was super-heated by the attempts of the successive governments of the Second Republic to swing Spain violently in their direction. The first Azaña government's assault on the landed aristocracy and the Church was sufficient to evoke a failed military coup in 1932 and then a victory for the Right in the general election of 1933. While the new government attempted to unpick the reforms of the previous three years, the Left went into semi-armed opposition leading a general strike in 1934 and a full-blown insurrection in Asturias later in the year. The political significance of football, already established in the Basque country and Catalonia, reached nationwide proportions in the last King's Cup Final before the looming civil war. The game was held in Valencia, a republican stronghold. Madrid FC – who had dropped their royal prefix as soon as Alfonso had left the capital – faced Barcelona. The crowd of Valencians relentlessly booed and whistled Madrid who had taken a 2–1 lead in the first half. They vented their fury when Ricardo Zamora, Madrid's goalkeeper, saved a last-minute Barça shot.

The general election of 1936 saw the united forces of the Popular Front (socialists, communists, republicans and regionalists) just defeat the right-wing National Front (composed of armed Christian Democrats, Carlists and an indigenous fascist party, the Falangists). The Popular Front re-embarked on a programme of political change, releasing left-wing political prisoners, transferring suspect military officers away from their high commands and granting Catalonia autonomy. The army began to plot a coup in earnest, made all the more urgent by massive capital flight, raging inflation, a rash of strikes and the surreptitious arming of the Left by the new government. The army struck in July 1936 and for almost three years the Spanish Civil War would rage. The national football league, like every other national institution, was split asunder by the violence.

In the initial stages of the war the fiercest fighting was in Madrid where the coup was led by an ex-player and official of Real Madrid, General Adolfo Meléndez. The army was defeated by massive local resistance organized by the city's communists, which culminated in the storming of the Montana barracks. General Meléndez was smuggled out of the city. The prominent Madrid FC board member Santiago Bernabéu was arrested by the city's republican militias. He was only released after the intervention of another Madrid FC supporter: Spain's socialist ambassador to France, Álvaro de Albornoz. Bending to the prevailing balance of power, Madrid had appointed a moderate republican as their president in the immediate pre-war era – Rafael Sánchez Guerra. But in the febrile political atmosphere of Madrid under siege, where the rich lay low and the republican militias ruled the street, Sánchez Guerra was deposed. He was replaced by two political commissars and then by a communist officer in the republican army, Lieutenant Colonel Antonio Ortega. The club's previously exclusive facilities, like its swimming pool, were thrown open to the public, membership fees were cut, and Soviet-style displays of proletarian sporting endeavour and mass gymnastics began to replace the increasingly sporadic and disorganized attempts to play football at the Chamartín stadium.

Madrid, although held by the republic in the first two years of the war, was as far as competitive football was concerned effectively cut off from the rest of the republic's strongholds by a patchwork of shifting front lines and semi-occupied zones However, in Catalonia and the Basque country, which were held much more securely by the republic and retained their coastal escape routes, both regional leagues and overseas tours continued through 1937 and 1938. Foreign tours were a significant source of additional income and an opportunity to advertise the republic's predicament. The already established connection between FC Barcelona and the cause of Catalan independence reached new highs when Josep Sunyol was elected club president. Sunyol came from an impeccably connected and enormously rich Catalan bourgeois family. He had become a parliamentary deputy for the left-wing Catalan nationalists Esquerra Republicana in 1931 and, like any aspiring populist, secured a seat on Barça's board of directors and wrote a football column in his family's newspaper *La Rambla*. He became club president in 1935. Sunyol's contribution to the club is primarily as martyr. In 1936 he drove to Madrid through the mountain ranges of the Sierra de Guadarrama, a contested zone of land in which the republicans attempted to keep open the line of communication between the coasts and Madrid while Franco's forces sought to close in on the capital from their strongholds in Burgos, Valladolid and Salamanca. Quite why Sunyol took the trip is unclear. Some suggest politics, others a bit of ill-advised war tourism; some have even offered a football rationale involving the signing of players. Either way he was detained on the road by Falangist militia and summarily executed. In a coda to the war, the enduring bitterness that the conflict generated saw long and ugly conflicts over the return of Sunyol's remains and the marking of his passing.

Spain, as everybody knew, was the dry run for the war to come. Franco and the Right were strongly supported by the regimes of European fascism: the Italians in Spain were 50,000 strong, mixing army units and a volunteer Fascist militia; the German Condor Brigade brought a level of aerial firepower and destructive technology to the war that the republicans were never able to match. The French and British governments, too preoccupied with their own politics of appeasement and time-buying, chose to condemn the republic with fine words and inaction. The Soviet Union sent what little supplies it could but the European Left's support was primarily confined to the rag-tag enthusiasts of the International Brigades.

By 1937 it was becoming clear which way the conflict would resolve itself. FIFA accepted the Francoist RFEF rather than the republican-nominated institution as the official delegate to the organization even though the war was not over. In early 1938, confident enough that they would soon be attempting to rule a united if decimated Spanish state, Falangist allies of Franco founded Spain's first and still largest sports daily newspaper *Marca*. It first appeared before Christmas 1938. On its cover a blonde girl made the fascist salute, headlined 'To all the Spanish sportsmen and women'. Among its earliest articles was a feature on that man again, Santiago Bernabéu, the ex-Madrid player and director who having fled republican Madrid for France in 1936 returned to Spain in 1937 and joined Franco's army in Irún. Bernabéu, it seems, was already preparing for a different kind of future. In the New Spain, he said, 'The spectacle of a few sweaty youths must disappear and give way to a youth that is healthy in body and spirit under the direction of specialist trainers.'[3]

The end finally came in March 1939. Franco's army entered Madrid. For those who went there, Real Madrid's Chamartín stadium was a sorry sight. Like much of the urban landscape it was a skeletal ruin, its wooden bleachers long since stripped for precious firewood in a city under siege. The club's president Colonel Ortega was one of 100,000 republicans arrested and executed in the immediate blood-letting; another

35,000 died in camps. Sánchez Guerra, his moderate predecessor, was imprisoned and then exiled; the club's vice-president and treasurer Valero Rivera was arrested and murdered. Spain was a country under military occupation and football was subjected to Franco's martial rule. The Copa del Rey was renamed the Copa del Generalísimo. In 1941 the regime took organizational control of all forms of sport in the country creating the centralized overarching bureaucracy DND (mercifully short for *Delegación Nacional de Deportes de Falange Española Tradicion- alista y de la JONS*), which in turn controlled the Spanish football federa- tion REFE. The Falangist hero of the siege of Alcántara, General José Moscardó, was put in charge. Crowds and players were encouraged to begin every game with the standard battle cries of the war. '*Arriba España!*' and '*Viva Franco!*' Singing the Falangist anthem '*Cara del Sol*', although not compulsory, was actively supported. The national team's red shirts were initially replaced with a more politically appropriate blue. The regime's newspaper *Arriba* argued that football had a special place in the new Spain. Reaching back to the international football triumphs of the 1920s, the newspaper linked the rediscovery of the authentic Spanish playing style to the triumph of the Right in the civil war.

The *furia española* is present in all aspects of Spanish life, to a greater extent than ever since the 'war of liberation'. In a sport, the *furia* best manifests itself in football, a game in which the virility of the Spanish race can find full expression, usually imposing itself in international contests over the more technical but less aggressive foreign teams.[4]

In such an atmosphere the lingering linguistic residues of the British had to go. Athletic Bilbao were renamed Atlético de Bilbao, FC Bar- celona was changed to the formal Castilian of Barcelona Club de Fútbol. More substantially the board and presidents of nearly all clubs were replaced by Madrid, with politically safe placemen installed at the most recalcitrant homes of regionalist sentiment, such as the Falangist Basque Eduardo Lastaragay imposed on Atlético Bilbao. Atlético Madrid finished the war with barely any squad to speak of and were merged with the crack air-force team of Colonel Francisco Salamanca as Atlético Aviación. Under coach Ricardo Zamora they were perhaps the only team positively to benefit from the regime's limited largesse and took two titles in 1941 and 1942 before reverting to their Hispanicized Atlético Madrid.

Barcelona's treatment was perhaps the harshest and most humiliating. In late 1939, on the orders of General Moscardó, the club's stadium Les Corts was subjected to a form of fascist exorcism in an attempt to quell and then expel the spirits of Catalan autonomy and identity that lingered there. Ernest Giménez Caballero, a right-wing intellectual who had helped draft the regime's anti-autonomy decree, its key instrument of political and linguistic hegemony, spoke to a huge crowd corralled in the stadium to celebrate the liberation of Catalonia from republicanism. In 1942 Franco came to put his personal stamp on the subjugation of both the club and the nation it represented. His triumphal parade at Les Corts began with the release of 1,000 doves followed by a march-past of 24,000 Falangists. Yet, despite the imposition of the Marquis de la Mesa de Asta as club president, operating in a city under siege from its own government, its normal chosen language of business banned, Barça rose to the challenge, winning the Copa del Generalísimo in 1942. It was as Franco would have wanted it, for at this stage the regime was happy to encourage football in its enemy's heartlands as part of a calculated policy of depoliticization and evasion.

However, there were limits to the regime's generosity. Barça could win the cup but it could not express its triumph politically. One of the semi-finals of the 1943 Copa del Generalísimo pitted Barcelona against Real Madrid. In the first leg, played at Les Corts, Barça won 3–0 while their delirious crowd hooted, booed and whistled at Madrid. In his match report the ex-Real goalkeeper Eduardo Teus, then a journalist for the conservative Catholic daily *Ya!*, claimed that the crowd had shown dishonour and disrespect to the nation. In Madrid they were handing out free whistles to the crowds before the return game. Angel Mur, the Barcelona masseur, remembered it this way: 'The night before the game we had to change our hotel, and even then we didn't leave it all evening because we were convinced we would be lynched. During the game our goalkeeper was so petrified of being hit by missiles that he spent most of the game as far forward from the goal as possible allowing Madrid players to strike at the net from all directions.'[5] Barça players also received a visit in their dressing room from no lesser creature than the notoriously sinister Director of State Security, José Escrivá de Romani. Escrivá is said to have made his preferences for the direction of the game very clear. Barcelona lost 11–1.

The crude injustice of the game was clear to all in Spain, despite the blandishments of a neutered press and the crowing of the Madrid sports papers. It was too much for the upper echelons of the regime. A polity so bent on forging national unity could not allow such open and uncontrollable levels of public disorder or regional conflict to go public. The presidents of both clubs were effectively sacked, both clubs were fined and a series of farcically good-natured peace matches were played in the winter. Barcelona acquired another placeman as president but Real Madrid acquired Santiago Bernabéu. With that, Real Madrid's rise to the very pinnacle of global football began.

Bernabéu's first task was to build a stadium in which the team could play as the old Chamartín remained unusable. In the desperate economic conditions of 1944, in which much of the country was malnourished, there was no chance of any significant investment from the government. The new Chamartín was financed by a series of bond issues, taken up by Real's 45,000 *socios*. The money was invested with care. True to his politics, Bernabéu's evangelical leadership mobilized the capital's middle classes and applied technical competence and financial rectitude to the task. His extensive connections helped him to put together a design committee for the new stadium, which included the architect of Franco's monumental civil war memorial *The Valley of the Fallen*, Pedro Muguruza. It is rumoured that the concrete used to lay its terraces – a commodity in desperately short supply – was part of the same consignment used in the construction of *The Valley of the Fallen*. As the new Chamartín was built the area in which it was located, once the scruffy northern periphery of the city, began to be transformed into the main zone of high-end development in Madrid. Locale, club and class were on the rise. But before the footballing histories of Madrid and Spain could reconnect with the rest of Europe, the Continent would have to undergo its own civil war.

The political organization and ideological mobilization of football by the Spanish state under Franco was a pale imitation of the level of control achieved in the most powerful authoritarian states in inter-war Europe: Italy, Germany and the Soviet Union. While ideologically ambitious, Falangist Spain remained financially penurious. Fascist Italy had pioneered the model in which the state-party took complete control of sporting bureaucracies. Independent religious and workers' sports organizations were dissolved and placemen put in charge of the more recalcitrant or significant clubs. Professionalization was hidden and state-subsidized, and the actual playing of sport was wrapped in a discourse of super-nationalism. Sport in general and football in particular served to unite the nation internally in a single project; prepare, train and harden the nation's bodies for war; and express the prowess and strength of the regime abroad. By 1935 Mussolini and his allies had seemingly perfected authoritarian football having created one of Europe's strongest leagues and having staged and won the 1934 World Cup.

In the early 1930s the unquestioned masters of that league were Juventus. The club had had some success before this, attracting the liberal elite and the old aristocrats of Piedmont to their colours, archetypally their long-standing president and Italian man of letters Corradino Corradini. But the fortunes and social standing of the club were transformed when Eduardo Agnelli, son of the founder of FIAT, became club president in 1923. Founded in 1899, FIAT was the leading industrial and engineering firm in the Italian economy; the Agnellis were the leading family in the complex of business elites in the north of the country. Their team Juventus was the most commercial, carefully organized club in the new hidden professionalism of Serie A. Despite the limited size of the Italian market FIAT grew, diversified and innovated. In the 1930s its Mirofiori factory was the most advanced industrial plant in Italy. FIAT were among the first manufacturers to bring micro-cars and aerodynamic design to production-line vehicles. The wealth and confidence generated by these enterprises saw the Agnellis significantly invest in Juventus, building a new stadium in 1932 initially known as Stadio Mussolini, signing the leading players of Italian descent from South American football like Orsi, Monti and Cesarini, and paying considerable fees and enticements to bring the best Italians too: Giovanni and Mario Varglien, Bertolini, Ferrari and Borel. Under coach Carlo Carcano they monopolized the championship from 1931–5.

Nineteen thirty-five was a decisive year for Italy. Finally all the bluster was turned into real action, though the action when it came – the invasion of Abyssinia – highlighted the large and dangerous gap between the regime's imperial pretensions and the quality of its armed forces. The imposition of sanctions against Italy by the League of Nations following the invasion extended to sporting equipment, but not to sporting encounters. Italian football, more than ever, was an instrument of a foreign policy that was getting more aggressive with every passing month; in 1937 Italy joined the Germans in their anti-Comintern pact as the main lines of Europe's war were drawn. The national team triumphed again at the 1936 Berlin Olympics and in the teeth of sporting and political opposition brought the 1938 World Cup home from France. In domestic football Bologna were the team of the moment; playing in the amazing neo-medieval brick stadium of the Littoriale, backed to the hilt by the ambitious local Fascist Party they won four national championships in the late 1930s and early 1940s and the Mitropa Cup twice.

As the war approached the regime tightened its control over sport. The Italian Olympic Committee (CONI), now an arm of the Fascist Party, tried to take more systematic control of physical education, sports clubs and sports bureaucracies. There was an attempt, more on paper than in reality, to increase the level of physical education in schools, and to shift sporting clubs and recreation towards drill. But in the final days of peace CONI and its leading officials were primarily concerned with organizing a spectacular sporting and athletic celebration of twenty years of Fascism scheduled for the Olimpico complex in Rome in 1942. By the time the date came around no one in the upper echelons of the Fascist movement would be celebrating anything.

German fascism's arrival in power a decade after its Italian counterpart necessitated a faster pace of change in the transformation of the nation. In the short interlude between the Nazi takeover and the beginning of the Second World War German football was forcibly reorganized from above at lightning speed. Having garnered a third of the vote in the 1932 general election, Hitler and the Nazi Party demanded the chancellorship from President Hindenburg and received it early in 1933. In a matter of months they had passed enabling legislation which gave them complete legal authority over almost every sphere of German economic, political and cultural life. A national sports bureaucracy was established, the *Deutscher Reichsbund für Leibesübungen* – the German Reich's Committee for Physical Exercise. Party hack Hans von Tschammer und Osten was put in charge. The DFB was not dissolved but retained as the football and English sports section of the new Reichsbund. The senior members of the DFB joined the Nazi Party immediately. The coaching staff of the German national team followed in the late 1930s. German football, after all, had shown its political acumen and loyalty to the new order.

In June 1933 Minister of Education Bernhard Rust ordered the expulsion of Jews from the nation's welfare, youth and sporting organizations. However, football had pre-empted this, starting the expulsions and exclusions beforehand. In April, in *Kicker* magazine (founded by the Jewish journalist and football evangelist Walther Bensemann), the DFB made its position clear to members: 'Members of the Jewish race and individuals who are members of the Marxist movement are unacceptable in leading positions in regional organizations and clubs, who are urged to initiate appropriate measures, if they have not yet been taken.'[6]

Hugo Reiss, the treasurer at Eintracht Frankfurt, was expelled from the club he had helped build. Former international player Julius Hirsch left Karlsruher FV, ironically one of the clubs founded by Walther Bensemann. 1.FC Nürnberg expelled all its Jewish members immediately; tens of thousands would follow. Almost alone in attempting to moderate or defy the law was Bayern München, the upstart team from the Bavarian capital who had just won their first national championship. Bayern was a secular institution, but counted many of Munich's Jewish community among its board, players and supporters, including its president Kurt Landauer. Landauer was forced to step down by the authorities rather than the club in March 1933. The bonds of club over *volk* were sufficiently strong for Bayern to risk a visit to see Landauer in exile on their 1940 tour of Switzerland.

Then the authorities came for the Left and the Church. The Deutscher Reichsbund and the DFB closed down many independent Church-based football clubs, and explicitly socialist and communist clubs. The older Länder FAs of the Weimar period were dissolved and reconstituted as sixteen Gaue or districts – a Germanic term whose tone was more in keeping with the artificial medievalism of the Nazis. Youth football was completely wrested from the control of clubs and the mainstream football administrators and put under the aegis of the ever-expanding Hitler Youth. Club boards were vetted and occasionally staffed with placemen; British-sounding names like Viktoria and Britannia disappeared and a few mergers, like the one that created VfL Bochum in 1938, were organized by local enthusiasts. However, the regime stopped short of the wholesale dissolution and reconstitution of all football clubs that it had been planning. They were running out of time. There was, after all, a war on the way.

The limits of the Nazi engagement with football were not imposed by time alone. Hitler himself is reputed to have had almost no interest in the game at all. He recognized both the political utility of international sport, the emotional potency of the spectacular, and the economic and military virtues of the sporting, healthy nation, but he played no sport himself and only showed any enthusiasm for boxing and motor racing. The politics of international football was left to others. In the first three years of the Third Reich, the national team functioned as ambassadors for a Germany still feeling its way back into the European balance of power. The 1934 World Cup, where Germany had beaten Austria to take third place, had gone better than anyone had expected. The game against England in London in 1935 was considered a propaganda success, when 10,000 German fans were subsidized to attend and show the new Germany off in a good light. But the key test of football's political utility was at the 1936 Olympic Games and it failed. In their opening game Germany comfortably beat Luxembourg 9–0 and were drawn in the next round against the rank outsider Norway. Hitler, who had never attended a football match before, and the rest of his cabinet were encouraged by Albert Foster, *Gauleiter* of Danzig, to go and watch Germany's triumphal procession to the quarter-finals. Alongside 100,000 in Berlin's Poststadion Hitler, Goebbels, Hess, Göring, Rust and Frick watched Norway win 2–0. The first goal came after just six minutes. Germany spent the rest of the match encamped in Norway's half. Goebbels recalled in his diary the excruciation of the moment: '. . . the Führer is very agitated. I am almost unable to control myself. A real bath of nerves. The crowd rages. A battle like never before. The game as mass suggestion.'[7] The Norwegians stole a second goal with five minutes to go. Hitler got up and left, never to return.

In March 1938 the Austrian *Anschluss* was effected. The Austrian football association was dissolved and reformed as the 17th Gau of the Deutscher Reichsbund. There was a whirlwind purge and reordering of football in Vienna. Hakoah, the explicitly Jewish sports club, was the first target. The club was closed down, its entire resources taken over by the government and its records in the football league expunged. All the teams that had already played Hakoah that season were awarded a 3–0 victory. Secular clubs with significant Jewish membership like FK

Austria and First Vienna were next. FK Austria not only saw its board sacked but had a member of the Austrian Nazi Party imposed as president who attempted to have the club renamed Ostmark, in accordance with Nazi geography. A club official, Egon Ulrich, was fired merely for his Jewish-sounding name. The incorporation of Austrian football into the greater Reich was completed in formal terms, but emotionally and practically an already existing enmity was redoubled. While the vast majority of Austrian society welcomed or accepted the *Anschluss*, including many in the football establishment, there was a strain of thought in Viennese society in general and football in particular that remained contemptuous of German football and the Nazis. The opinions of Hans Presser of Rapid Vienna were widespread: 'They play strictly according to army regulations ... it's their strength-through-kicking football.'[8] The visit of German teams to Vienna, reported on by the secret police, elicited 'anti-German chants, fights, stone-throwing and fanatical support for the home side'.[9] Thus the influx of Austrian talent into the German national team on the eve of the 1938 World Cup, which should have been a great boon, proved disastrous.

The DFB were very clear about what was required when it came to selecting the national team. 'In our sphere as well as in others a visible expression of our solidarity with the Austrians who have come back to the Reich has to be presented. The Führer demands a 6:5 or 5:6 ratio. History expects this of us.'[10] The coach Sepp Herberger complied but the dressing room was rent with resentment and tension. Germany went to the 1938 World Cup, were assailed with rotten fruit by the French crowd, and after grinding out a draw against the Swiss were demolished in the replay 4–2. Football, it seems, would not yield entirely to the Nazi Party. The game retained its insufferable tendency to upset the smooth acclimation of power. It also offered a swansong for the great Viennese football culture and the fragile metropolitan social ecology that had sustained it. Both would be irreparably damaged by the *Anschluss* and the war. Matthias Sindelar, the emblematic player of *Das Wunderteam*, refused Herberger's entreaties to play for the new united German side. He played his last match for the old Austria against Germany in Vienna. Dubbed the alliance game, it was billed as a celebration of the *Anschluss* that had happened three weeks earlier.

3 April 1938
Austria 2 Germany 0
Stadion Prater, Vienna

The film record of Matthias Sindelar is slim: a distant figure, almost unrecognizable, playing England at Stamford Bridge; a cameo in a romantic comedy that intercuts a few shots of a real game with staged shots of implausible headers and crunching tackles. It is just as well, for if we saw more perhaps the memories carried in poetry and prose would be less fantastical. They've been working on both since his final game for the Old Austria. The story goes like this.

Recalled from retirement and plagued by a knee injury, Sindelar is persuaded to play this last game for Austria against the Germans who are about to devour them. Sindelar insists that they play in the old imperial colours of red and white but any chance of a final hurrah is, it seems, prevented by the authorities' quiet insistence that the game finish a well-mannered draw. In the first half Sindelar misses a hatful of chances, some say with such exquisite touch that they could only be read as gestures of defiance. After half-time his patience snaps and he scores. A second goal, an audacious lob from Sesta, seals the game and Sindelar wheels away to dance before the Nazi functionaries and their Austrian satraps in the VIP box. The crowd roar '*Österreich! Österreich!*'

So much for myth, so much for defiance. Three weeks later, 99 per cent of those who voted, vote for the *Anschluss* and the liquidation of *Österreich*. Sindelar, now completely retired from football, buys a Jewish café: the Nazis are forcing Jews out of every business and official position in the country. Sindelar pays a fair price to the owner and quietly serves coffee and beer on the Laxenburgstrasser back in Favoriten. We know from the police files he didn't take kindly to displaying Nazi posters or taking collections for the Nazi Party. We know that he refused Herberger's entreaties to come and play for Greater Germany.

In a photo from the time, we see him, shoulders slouched, hands in pockets, eyes cast down. He looks like a man getting ready to pack it all in.

Sindelar died the following year in mysterious circumstances. He was found with girlfriend Camilla Castagnolla dead in his flat, both apparently asphyxiated by gas from the oven. An accident, suicide, murder? All have been offered as more or less plausible explanations. It makes no difference, Red Vienna and its football had their martyr.

In the immediate aftermath of the October revolution, football, like most organized social activities, ceased to exist in the Soviet Union. It was only with the end of the civil war and the relative social and economic tranquillity of the mid-1920s and the New Economic Policy (NEP) that football, indeed sport of any kind, could resurface. As befits an era of high ideological heterodoxy, in which collectivization and state control sat alongside private initiatives and micro-markets, the regime and its ideologues were divided over the place of sport in the new Soviet society. Marxism-Leninism did not offer a line on football beyond the usual claims that sport was a circus, an instrument of class rule and political obfuscation. But capitalism had been defeated and there was, according to the Communist Party (CPSU), no Soviet ruling class that could use sport for its own oppressive ends. Thus the Soviets were left with the two other Western European models of sport in an industrialized society – Olympianism and professionalism. Both coexisted under the NEP. On the one hand the military, educational and social bureaucracies of the new state saw amateur sport and wholesome recreation as essential instruments in the creation of a new Soviet humanity: fit, disciplined and cooperative. This was the world of amateur Olympianism coalescing around the first multi-sport clubs, like Dinamo Moscow founded in 1923 and TsDKA Moscow created in 1928. Dinamo was formed on the orders of NKVD chief Felix Dzerzhinsky and supported by both the NKVD and the Ministry of the Interior. TsDKA Moscow were the 'Central House of the Red Army'. Closely aligned to the core institutions of the Soviet state, these clubs were initially suspicious of foreign, bourgeois football and preferred mass gymnastics and athletics. Yet, while the new regime proved capable of transforming most aspects of the nation, the established sporting preference for football was immovable. Despite every privation and hardship young men in the cities continued to play and watch football and were prepared to pay, even in those straitened times, to do so. It was this unwavering interest in the game that sustained football in an era of impromptu arrangements and forced even Dinamo and TsDKA to create football sections.

After Lenin's death in 1924 and Stalin's rise to power, the Soviet Union saw a series of considerable departures in economic and sporting politics. The NEP was abandoned and in 1928 the first five-year plan for the Soviet economy was initiated, followed by another in 1933 and a third in 1938. Under the iron hand of the CPSU Soviet economy and society were launched on a course of breakneck forced collectivization and industrialization. Measured by increases in productivity and rates of urbanization, the Soviet Union experienced an industrial revolution which had taken forty years in Western Europe and America compressed into a single decade. Moscow's population almost doubled between 1928 and 1940; new industrial cities sprang up across eastern Russia and Siberia. The necessary corollary of forced industrialization was political repression of the highest order. The purges and terrors conducted by the state security apparatus in this period not only ensured that all forms of opposition were silenced or destroyed but that a steady stream of slave labour was supplied to the harshest projects and environments – and Soviet industrialization offered both of those in abundance. Among the millions of victims were five Ministers of Sport, the heads of the major physical education colleges, leading sports doctors and thousands of sportsmen and women.

But even under these conditions it was still possible, in the cracks and crevices between state and society, to find independent action and semi-autonomous institutions, like Krasnaia Presnia, a Moscow football club founded by the fanatical Starostin brothers around 1919. If Dinamo were the prime example of a top-down model of club formation, Krasnaia Presnia were their mirror image – a club created from the bottom up. Under the charismatic and relentless leadership of Nikolai Starostin, Presnia climbed out of the rubble of post-revolutionary Moscow and started organizing football in the working-class suburbs of the city. Under the NEP, the club was able to survive and even prosper on the basis of its ticket sales and regular wild tours of central Asia and Siberian Russia.

In the early 1930s sports clubs and city-based football leagues were reorganized from the top, the party decreeing that all clubs must be allocated to and ultimately run by public institutions. Starostin, who had proved himself both an exceptional footballer and ice-hockey player, was also a wheeler-dealer par excellence. He persuaded Promkooperas-tiia, the state organization that controlled the small services sector of the Soviet economy (like barbers, tailors and waiters), to fund his side. Better still, he had established a close relationship with Alexander Koso-rov, the head of the party's youth movement Komsomol and a member of the Politburo who furnished essential political support and protection. The new club was called Spartak – the Russian for Spartacus – after the leader of the major Roman slave revolt in the first century BCE. Starostin had played a German workers' team of this name in the 1920s, the club no doubt named after the free-wheeling German communist Spartacus League founded by Rosa Luxemburg and Karl Liebknecht. Alongside Dinamo – which now had branches in many of the provincial cities of the USSR – TsDKA and Spartak, a host of new clubs were created: the railway industry got Lokomotiv; the vehicle manufacturers of southern Moscow had Torpedo. The Soviet Union now had football clubs, a cadre of full-time if unevenly professionalized elite football players, increasingly large working-class industrial cities with precious little entertainment of any kind, and a functioning inter-city transport system: the preconditions of a national football league.

In keeping with the autarchic socialism-in-one-country vision of the revolution, the Soviet Union had, but for a pair of games with the Turkish republic in the early 1920s, played no international matches at all. However on New Year's Day 1936 a combined Spartak–Dinamo team had been allowed to play an exhibition game in Paris against Racing Club. The Soviets were beaten and Starostin took the opportunity of the defeat to argue for the formation of a real national league in an effort to raise standards. Six months later the first league and national cup competitions started and the early industrialization of Soviet football was complete. Initially just seven teams competed from three cities, but attendances were phenomenal – the crowds, suddenly released from the everyday oppression of work and surveillance, were large, boisterous and unpredictable.

What made the competitions so intensely popular was not really the quality of the football but the depth and the meaning of the social conflicts, silently and sometimes not so silently, played out on the field. At the heart of those conflicts was the rivalry between Dinamo and Spartak. Of course, almost nothing at the time was written down, officially or informally. It is only in the post-communist era that the depth and character of football support in the pre-war Soviet Union has been recorded. One Spartak fan of the 1930s remembered it like this:

The relationship of Spartak's fans to Dinamo . . . was highly antagonistic. Dinamo represented the authorities: the police, the organs of state security, the hated privileged elites. They ate better. They dressed better, and they certainly didn't live in communal apartments . . . We lived in a large communal apartment. We were all working class . . .[11]

Thus the Spartak–Dinamo rivalry pitted the elite against the masses, the party-state against society. But Spartak was never a force or symbol of outright opposition. Rather its social meaning hovered between offering an alternative way of being Soviet and providing the opportunity for what has been described as 'a small way of saying no'. The difference between the cultures of the clubs is well illustrated by their attitudes to the first official Physical Culture Day spectacular in 1936. The two sides were due to play an exhibition match in Red Square in front of Stalin himself. Dinamo pulled out at the last minute, deeming the unpredictable nature of football and Stalin's apparent uninterest in the game as sufficient reasons to avoid what could become an unpleasantly political encounter. Spartak, by contrast, were ready to field two teams and volunteers at the club had sewn together an extraordinary green felt rug, 9,000 square metres in area, to cover the cobblestones of Red Square. The game was scheduled for just thirty minutes, acknowledging that the Great Friend of all Athletes was known to have a very low boredom threshold. In the end it was allowed to continue for over forty.

If, at one level, Spartak could play as patriotic celebrants of the Soviet people, there was something else about them:

Spartak was not a team that belonged to any single group. Maybe it was the Starostin brothers, maybe their friendship with the intelligentsia, but there was a kind of mark of democracy on the team. Giving your heart to Spartak, you hung on to some hope that they were somehow apart from their surroundings.[12]

In an era of totalitarianism Spartak offered an enclave of autonomy, made all the more attractive by their evident sporting talents and the spontaneity and fluidity of their play; a style, part real, part imagined, that contrasted to the dour, mechanical manoeuvring of Dinamo.

In the midst of the terror, success could breed resentment, flamboyance was inherently suspicious. In November 1937 Georgii Znamenskii, a leading Soviet athlete, secretly denounced Starostin to the Minister of Sport: 'Nikolai Starostin devotes his time, attention and funds only to football. He ignores other sports. He allows only a few designated people to work with the soccer team, he acts personally for himself rather than being guided by the situation of the organization . . . The method is similar to that of the entrepreneur of a private sports club.'[13] For good measure he was also accused of currency speculation and using his contacts in the army to obtain players. All of this, as Starostin made clear in his biography, was broadly true and standard practice in the new world of Soviet professional football. But in the context of Stalin's reign of terror those practices could, at any moment, be criminalized. Starostin survived, for alongside all of the above, he was also a supremely accomplished political networker. Before Spartak's big games over 1,000 tickets would be distributed among the party-state elite in Moscow and Nikolai Yezhov, a central organizer of the terror, was a personal contact.

With this kind of practical and political support, alongside the most accomplished training and tactical programme in the country, Spartak were unstoppable in 1938, winning both league and cup. But the political tide was turning against them. Lavrenti Beria was made head of the NKVD in 1938 with a remit from Stalin to slow the whirlwind devastation of the purges. Yezhov and his allies were executed. As Robert Edelman put it, 'good for the nation but terrible for Spartak'.[14] Worse, Beria was an ex-player and a very serious Dinamo fan. He began to attend every Dinamo home game. In 1939 Spartak won the league again and looked to have won the double when they beat Stalinets Leningrad in the final of the cup. Then, to the astonishment of even the Sports Ministry, Beria insisted on a replay of the semi-final between Dinamo Tbilisi and Spartak. Spartak had won the game 1–0 despite it being refereed by an ex-Dinamo player. Needless to say he was arrested and disappeared which made getting a new referee for the rematch so difficult that Sports Minister Colonel Snegov was forced to intervene and directly appoint one. Spartak won the match and kept the cup. In his memoirs Starostin describes looking up at the end of the game: 'When I glanced up at the dignitaries' box, I saw Beria get up, furiously kick over his chair and storm out of the stadium.'[15] He was furious enough to try and persuade Prime Minister Vyacheslav Molotov to sign an arrest warrant for Starostin on the same charges made in 1937. Molotov refused, but come the war Beria would have his revenge.

IV

The intense politicization of football in Europe's new authoritarian states did not leave the remaining European democracies untouched. Indeed, the French Minister of Sport saw the social mobilization of sport under fascism and communism as an explicit challenge to liberal democracies: 'We have heard all too often that a democratic country is by its very nature incapable of creating a vast sports and leisure organization. Our ambition is to show the fundamental error of that view.'[16] It was one of many ambitions held by France's new Popular Front government elected to power in May 1936. The global economic recession was now eating away at France's social fabric. The endless succession of right-wing governments had not mobilized the political or economic resources to deal with recession, unemployment and the looming threat of war from across the Rhine; nor had they seemed able to contain a rising tide of French fascist agitation. The Popular Front, named in conscious emulation of their Spanish counterparts, was united by the same twinned threats of national and international fascism. After almost two decades of division on the Left, the socialists, communists and trade unions agreed a combined electoral list and policy programme and won a majority at the polls. Léon Blum was made Prime Minister in June 1936.

France erupted. In the streets and public spaces of its cities mass celebrations were held that verged on an occupation. This mood of working-class confidence released the pent-up political and economic demands of a society sorely tried by the economic hardships of the previous decade; a rash of strikes and factory occupations followed. Extensive workplace reforms and wage increases were conceded by France's employers to the trade-union movement and committed to paper in the Matignon Accords. The government itself was emboldened by these displays of popular power, none more so than Leo Lagrange, the new Socialist Minister of Sport. The creation of the Ministry was itself a measure of the Popular Front's commitment to a politics of leisure; matters of sporting infrastructure and popular sport had hitherto been the responsibility of unaccountable, invisible, elitist bureaucracies. More than that, no consideration had ever been given to the provision of public facilities. France may have hosted two Olympic Games, but its record of building municipal sports grounds and swimming pools was very poor.

The Popular Front lasted less than two years; but in the realm of football it left some indelible traces. The Front itself was a measure of France's belated and incomplete industrialization and its fragmented and disorganized working class. The election of a left-wing government – committed to basic reforms in the labour market and welfare provision – arrived more than a decade after it had in Britain and later even than in Spain. French football, as we have seen, had followed this arc. It was the last of the major nations to accept professional football, only really complete in 1935, and it was predominantly populated by teams from small rather than large cities. This too finally changed as the late 1930s saw the emergence of powerful and successful football clubs from France's largest urban areas: Racing Club de Paris and Olympique Marseille. At the level of amateur and recreational sport the Popular Front's bureaucratic and political innovations initiated the tradition of French state intervention in sport which continues to this day. It also managed to build an impressive array of public sports facilities despite the immense budgetary constraints of the era.

These kinds of domestic developments and innovations were complemented by an attitude which refused to let the spectacular remain the property of authoritarian societies alone. In 1937 Paris hosted the International Exposition; Blum believed it to be an arena in which 'democracy would deal fascism in all its forms a death-blow', though in the football tournament played to accompany the exhibition, Bologna, the team of Emilia Romagna's Fascists, saw off Chelsea. The Italian press exclaimed the strengths of football under Fascism. A year later France would be hosting the 1938 World Cup and the politics of the Continent would be no less charged, its sporting spectaculars no less infused with the coming menace of war. Although the French did not apply the same level of concentrated government action to the event that Mussolini had mustered in 1934, there were considerable funds for the tournament's stadiums. Parc des Princes and Stade Colombes in Paris were extended and the former given an art deco façade. Two stadiums in small and geographically peripheral towns were rebuilt – Stade du Fort Carré in Antibes and the Stade de la Cavée Verte in Le Havre – and two completely new stadiums were constructed: the Stade Vélodrome in Marseilles and the Parc Lescure in Bordeaux. The latter is, without question, the most considered architectural response in stadium design to the grandiose pomposity of fascist arenas and their alliance of concrete modernism with historical duplicity and brutal futurism. Designed by Jacques D'Welles and Raoul Jourde, Parc Lescure was a simple straight-sided oval in shape built entirely from reinforced concrete. Its 360-degree roof, uniquely at the time, required no pillars or supports, thereby offering unimpeded views around the ground. It was built from ribbed concrete sections whose rhythmic undulations echoed the ring of concrete arches that encircled the upper tiers of the stadium. Rather than a single domineering tower or other centralizing architectural device, Parc Lescure offered more democratic features, most particularly the four viewing platforms built on the ends of the main stands. Like the bridge of an art deco cruise liner, these semi-circular structures were embellished with curved glass and porthole windows, while behind them metal gantries passed for mast and rigging, on which the floodlights were hoisted and lowered. This kind of quirky architectural pluralism was replicated on the outside of the stadium. The site itself was tightly packed among residential streets rather than laid out in the opulent emptiness of Albert Speer's Nürnberg or Roma's Olimpico Complex. Instead of a single monumental or triumphal entrance Parc Lescure could be accessed from a number of points: through a simple if monumentally large concrete arch inserted into a terraced street; or via a cluster of small houses around the base of an art deco tower, encrusted with scarlet mosaics. Technologically advanced, architecturally bold, engaging, diverse and playful in design and decoration, open and unthreatening, Parc Lescure rebuked the crudity and delusions of fascism but 'delivering a death-blow' was beyond it.

Once again the democracies would have to deal with fascism without the British who would not only not be attending the 1938 World Cup but whose notionally apolitical football culture had been colonized by the politics of appeasement. English football, in the guise of peacemaker, had reopened relations with Germany in 1930 when England had played their first post-war match there (3–3). Much had changed in the five short years between then and the FA's decision to return the favour and invite the Germans to play in London in December 1935. As usual the British government was not informed of the decision by the FA. Indeed it was only made aware of the fixture and its possible implications by a rash of articles against the match from the left-wing and Jewish press and protests organized by Jewish groups, the trade unions and the umbrella organization the Anti-Nazi Society.

Passions, especially in London, ran higher when it became clear the Germans were intending to bring around 10,000 supporters with them by steamer and train. With a clumsiness that betokened either extreme political naivety or ignorance, possibly both, the FA decided to play the game at White Hart Lane, home to Tottenham Hotspur, who had acquired a significant north London Jewish following in the strongholds of Haringey and Stamford Hill. The *Daily Worker*, among others, reported at the time that a Polish Jewish football player had been murdered. The story was denied by the German Embassy, but became common currency on the streets of north London where activists distributed handbills decrying the murder, the game and the Germans. There was talk that 5,000, maybe more, would march on the stadium on the day of the match. Writing in the *News Chronicle*, Barnett Janner, the Liberal MP for Whitechapel, argued that, 'The great mass of English football followers regard the Nazi persecution of Roman Catholics, church people and Jews as violations of the rules of sportsmanship.'[17] As so often, the belief among British anti-fascists in the 1930s that there was not only a clear and unmistakable groundswell of popular distaste against fascism but a will actively to take it on, was misconceived. Five days before the match the TUC led a protest march to Hyde Park which attracted at most 20,000 people. On the day of the game itself there was a full house but no march. The only person arrested was the plucky youth who scaled the roof of White Hart Lane's main stand and ran the Nazi flag down.

The response of both the government and the majority of the press was encapsulated by the Home Secretary Sir John Simon who said, 'We have to keep up in our country a tradition that the sporting fixture is carried through without any regard to politics at all.'[18] In actual fact the German visit had generated more political discussion about sport in the Foreign Office and Home Office than any event hitherto. Maintaining a pretence of political indifference to the occasion had become just one more political trope. Indeed the government took the view that a simulacrum of normality, amity and political disinterest would be the most effective politics, making clear the differences between Germany and England, authoritarianism and democracy. Thus over 10,000 German fans were welcomed off the train at London Victoria, shepherded around London, in and out of Lyons Tea Houses and feeding stations in Leicester Square, and given German-speaking guides, many of whom inevitably were émigré Jews.

The Germans invited England back to Berlin for May 1938. Once again the Foreign Office found out a week beforehand by which time the gloomiest political prognoses that had surfaced in their discussions three years before had come to pass. Germany had just swallowed up Austria in the *Anschluss*. Czech Germans were mobilizing in Moravia, demanding to be returned to the Reich. The Continent seemed closer to war than it had been for twenty years. British foreign policy under Chamberlain maintained the notion that Hitler's territorial ambitions could be sated, while at the same time believing that this kind of appeasement bought time for rearmament. Given this context, the Foreign Office was now hypersensitive to questions of etiquette and diplomacy around the game and made it clear to the FA that they should accede to German requests that the England team give a Nazi salute to the crowd. The memoirs of players and officials smack, more than most, of hindsight and ghost-writers' sleight of hand. England won the game 6–3 but they had already lost; 110,000 Germans, much of the German Cabinet included, roared their Heil Hitlers and their approval as the England team raised their hands.

One could not read a list of participants and absentees at the 1938 World Cup and not see the shape of the conflict that was to come, and that for Spain, China and Japan had already begun. The British, though still absent, treated the competition with a kind of benign indulgence rather then the indifferent contempt that had met the two previous tournaments. Whereas the British had refused to allow a meeting of the IAFB to be scheduled for Rome before the 1934 World Cup, they were happy to allow such a meeting in Paris in 1938, a measure of the new political and sporting *entente cordiale* across the Channel. More extraordinary, this was the first World Cup at which there was actually an official delegation from the English and Scottish FAs. Had they really not wanted to go and watch it in 1930 and 1934? The Spanish were embroiled in their civil war; the Soviet Union was embroiled in its revolution. The Japanese pulled out to concentrate on the war in Manchuria. The Americans, who had played at both previous World Cups, were keeping out of the European civil war. The Austrians, who had qualified, were now reduced to an administrative district of the Greater German Reich, their FIFA membership extinguished. Other absentees included the Uruguayans who were broke, and the Argentinians who were broke and still smarting from FIFA's refusal to stage the tournament there. This made 1938 the most Eurocentric World Cup of all, with just three sides from elsewhere: the Brazilians, who surprised Europe with their progress to the last four; the Cubans, who came for the first and last time when the Mexicans pulled out; and the replacements for the Japanese, a team from the Dutch East Indies. Cuba amazed with a first-round replay victory over Romania, only to be humiliated by Sweden 8–0 in the quarter-finals. The Dutch East Indies met a similar fate against Hungary.

The Italian squad took the train to Marseilles and were met at the station by a welcoming committee of around 3,000 anti-fascist activists. The crowd were sufficiently intent on reaching the Italians that baton-wielding mounted police were called into action cracking heads among the Italian exile and French communist demonstrators. The atmosphere had been stoked by Mussolini's recent inflammatory speeches on European politics that were reflected in the battle cry of *La Nazione* before the tournament: 'The Fascist revolution . . . has stirred the vigour of the race in sport, it has created the sporting spirit amongst the masses, of which a warlike spirit is known to be a direct descendant.'[19] Italy's opening game against Norway was played in a highly charged political atmosphere. Coach Vittorio Pozzo claimed in his memoirs that '. . . our players did not even dream of making it something political. They represented their country and naturally and worthily wore the colours and insignia.'[20] However, 10,000 anti-fascist demonstrators made it to the Stade Vélodrome and dreamed of little else. When the Italian team raised their hands in the fascist salute during the national anthem, the abuse and heckling reached a climax.

In the quarter-finals the political temperature peaked when the draw pitted the French against the Italians in Paris. Both played in blue, so they had to draw lots for first-choice kits. The Italians lost and had in this situation in the past played in white. A very clear and direct message came to the squad from Rome – play in black, the first and only occasion on which Italy has done so. For all the political connotations of the encounter the Italians were just too good for the French. Two more goals came from Piola after the French goalkeeper Di Lorto had pitifully palmed the ball into his own net from a soft looping Colaussi cross. In the semi-final Italy beat Brazil in Marseilles in an atmosphere that *La Nazione* described as 'manifestly hostile' and which was repeated at the 4–2 victory over Hungary in the final at the Stade Colombes. The team, little fêted in Paris, returned to Rome and a personal audience with Il Duce. Later on that year the Italian cyclist Gino Bartali won the Tour de France and the Italian colt Nearco won the Grand Prix de Paris ahead of the winners of both the French and English Derbies. Mussolini and the Italian press celebrated the nation's might.

Late 1938 was a moment of delusion. Chamberlain returned from Munich with his piece of paper and his assurances. On the occasion of the FA's seventy-fifth anniversary England played the Rest of Europe, with two Germans and seven Italians in the side, and beat them convincingly 3–0. When Chamberlain made his trip to Rome in January 1939, courting the Italians, hoping to delay the war a little longer, the FA was busy still setting up Italian and other European fixtures for both the national and club sides. However, the reprieve of Munich was to be only brief. With the German occupation of Prague, British football started cancelling fixtures with German sides. But a planned Italy–England game still went ahead in May 1939; 300,000 applied for tickets, and the Italian authorities planned to broadcast the match to the new European empire they were carving out in Albania and to the Italian-speakers in Yugoslavia they intended to incorporate. The government even brought a shipload of sympathizers from Malta to 'watch a real football team lick the English'. The English team made their fascist salute once again, this time to all four corners of the San Siro and drew 2–2. The Italian team's reception in Yugoslavia later that month was a better indicator of what was to come as locals barracked the players and stoned their bus. Similar restiveness stirred among Czechs playing the Germans in Prague and among the old Viennese crowd who watched FK Austria Wien play Schalke 04 at the tail end of the 1939 season. Then on 27 August 1939 Hungary beat Poland 4–2 in Warsaw. On 27 September the German army occupied the city. There would be no more organized football in Poland until 1947.

The Germans and the Soviets had devoured Poland by October 1939 after which there was a short pause. The French, Belgians and British, braced for the coming invasion, abandoned their football seasons and improvised with friendlies and mini-tournaments. The Dutch and the Danes, bizarrely oblivious to the fate awaiting them, concluded their seasons. Then in April 1940 the Germans attacked. Denmark fell almost instantaneously, Norway with some British support survived for another two months. Then came the invasions of Belgium, Holland and France and by late June all had surrendered, the remnants of the British Expeditionary Force had been evacuated from Dunkirk and the battle between the RAF and Luftwaffe for air supremacy over the Channel and North Sea was in full swing. Simultaneously the Soviets helped themselves to Finland, Latvia, Lithuania and Estonia, extinguishing international and independent football in the Baltic States for half a century.

Unable to achieve victory in the air the Germans turned their attentions east and south where their Italian allies were being trounced by the British in North Africa and the Greeks on the Albanian–Greek border. To secure their southern flank, before the invasion of the Soviet Union, the Germans invaded Yugoslavia and Greece while the Afrika Korps threw the British and their allies back across the Libyan desert and deep into Egypt. Then in June 1941 in the final decisive act of German aggression, the invasion of the Soviet Union began. By December the Germans had occupied the Ukraine, encircled Leningrad and were at the gates of Moscow. The fate of football in the new European order was for many nations a measure of the harshness or leniency of their occupation; for the remaining combatants it remained a tool of public policy.

The neutral nations of Europe – Sweden, Switzerland, Spain, Portugal, Ireland and Turkey – all continued to play football throughout the war. The only occupied or combatant nation to match this was Denmark whose occupation by the Germans was perhaps the least vicious. The Danes not only managed to keep their league going and avoid starvation but retained control of much of their own government and security forces and spirited their Jews across the Baltic to Sweden. At the other

end of the scale, Greece and Yugoslavia, who offered some of the most
substantial partisan resistance to the German occupiers, held no football
championship at all after the invasion and saw their major football
stadiums reduced to marshalling yards or ashes. Between these two
extremes come the experiences of the Netherlands, France and Norway.

Dutch football, like the Danish, appeared to weather the war rather
well; only the 1945 season was disrupted during the German retreat
and the subsequent Allied liberation. Indeed football boomed in the
Netherlands during the war. Club membership rose, participation in
football increased, the numbers of tickets sold to sporting events of all
kinds soared. The half million or so Dutchmen working in German
labour camps and factories played their own competitions and hungry
urban football fans swapped their tickets for the big games with farmers
for cheese and vegetables. It was certainly the way the Germans and
their Dutch allies liked it: 'He who plays sport does not sin,' said Artur
von Seyss-Inquart, the Government Commissioner.[21] Enthusiasts, like
the editor of Feyenoord's club journal, found the game less a diversion
from sin and more a diversion from boredom.[22]

Under conditions of enforced rectitude not only did football boom,
but the use of libraries, the reading of books and attendance at the
theatre reached record levels. German intervention in culture and sport
was limited. The various separate Catholic, Protestant and labour-
movement football associations were forced to merge in a single, controllable national organization. Residues of English in football terminology
and club names were changed as was any reference to members of the
royal house now in exile in Britain. And then there was the fate of the
Netherlands' Jewish population. From mid-1941 onwards the Germans
began to pressurize the Dutch football authorities to exclude Jews from
club membership, from playing and from officiating in football matches.
Amsterdam's five openly Jewish clubs were closed down. Jewish referees
were banned in 1941, precipitating a crisis in the game as so many Jews
had taken on the referee's role in the pre-war Netherlands. Then the
deportations and the executions began; among the deportees was Han
Hollander, the voice of football on Dutch radio and the man more than
any other responsible for popularizing the game in the 1930s with his
semi-fictitious but always compelling accounts of the national team. In
this as in the wider society, the Dutch were quietly but systematically
complicit with the Final Solution on their own soil. There was, at the

level of officialdom, in football, the police and Jewish organizations themselves, no systematic attempt to obfuscate, delay or mitigate the German demands. The few Dutch Jews that survived did so because of the bravery and humanity of a few key individuals and a few institutions; one of those was Ajax of Amsterdam where the pre-war bonds of intra-club solidarity proved strong enough for gentile members to hide and help some of the club's Jewish supporters, directors and players.[23]

After the surrender, French territory and football was divided into two zones. The north and Atlantic coasts and as far inland as Paris were directly occupied by the Germans. The rump of Mediterranean and Alpine France was controlled by the collaborationist Vichy regime of Marshal Pétain. Shorn of its liberal, urban and socialist elements, Vichy lay bare the depths of French authoritarianism, pathetically reimagining the truncated nation as some unadulterated pre-industrial arcadia. Building on the interventions of the Popular Front but reorientating them to new ideological ends, Vichy took sport seriously. Under the ultra-conservative Commissioner for Sport, Jean Borotra, Vichy declared war on professionalism, arguing that commercialism and competition had poisoned sport and society in the decadent Third Republic. The FFF was sidelined; Jules Rimet quietly resigned and disappeared from football administration for the duration of the war. Professionalism was permitted, but from 1942 every team had to field at least four copper-bottomed amateurs in their side – a degree of commercialism that was still deemed unacceptable by the government. The following season, the category of professional footballer was terminated and all players became civil servants and clubs public institutions. In France, like the Netherlands, in the long grey days of the early 1940s, football was a rare entertainment. The zonal cup winners met in a single national cup final and in 1942 a record 45,000 filled Stade Colombes to see Red Star Olympique Audonien beat FC Sète.

If football in the Netherlands and France trod close to and even crossed the line between normality and collaboration, in Norway it unambiguously took the path of opposition and resistance. Unlike Denmark which had capitulated and then retained a significant degree of independent political authority, Norway had resisted the Germans and was rewarded by the imposition of a local dictatorship fronted by the Norwegian Nazi Party and its leader Vidkun Quisling, backed up by two German divisions. In an attempt to mirror the total control strategies of its German counterparts, Norway's Nazis appointed a *Sportsführer* to run every club in the country. The response was unambiguous. The country went on a nationwide sports strike. Fans stayed away, players did not play, coaches did not coach and administrators would not organize. The response of the nation's great skiing champion Ruud Birger to suggestions that he should continue to compete during the occupation was this: 'When the day comes that it is my duty to partici-pate in a skiing context, on that day I will burn my skis.'[24] Some 800 members of the football club Lyn simultaneously resigned. Oslo's Ullevaal stadium, which had a capacity of 40,000, hosted games with less than a hundred people. In Bergen a semi-final match in the Nor-wegian Cup in 1942 attracted a crowd of 27. By this point teams and crowds alike were reduced to a handful of the regime's toughs and hangers-on. By contrast illegal sporting events sprang up deep in the countryside and these occasions became crucial nodes in the networks of the Norwegian resistance. Himmler was sufficiently concerned by the security situation in Norway to visit in 1943, an event accompanied by the round-up and imprisonment of many officials in the country's remaining independent clubs and sports associations.

While Norwegian football resisted by not playing, British football acquired the same cachet by carrying on regardless. The military invariably fight each war with the lessons learned from the last; so too with the British football authorities. Having been so roundly criticized for maintaining the official fixture list after the outbreak of war in 1914, they responded to the declaration of war on 3 September 1939 by suspending the Football League. However, both the government and public opinion turned out to be against it. The football authorities backtracked. During the long time-killing days of the phoney war in late 1939 and early 1940 Britain played phoney football, replacing the league with regional competitions. The War Office set an attendance limit of 8,000 and in the face of collapsing incomes and dispersed squads professional clubs tore up the players' contracts, abandoned bonuses and cut wages. What money was made went to war charities. Players were henceforth allowed to turn out for any team anywhere. This chaos is fondly remembered, like the historical memory of the Home Front in Britain, for its cheery insouciance in the face of privation and its capacity for improvisation, for its storylines which were part music-hall farce, part ripping yarn. Teams would regularly turn up for a game without the full complement of players or kit and were reduced to asking for volunteers from the crowd, like Sergeant Major Bryson who scored the winning goal for Blackburn Rovers against Burnley in 1941.

In the course of the Second World War Britain suffered 270,000 military and 65,000 civilian deaths. Its territory, although bombed heavily during 1940 and 1941 and never entirely secure till 1945, was never invaded or occupied. The Soviet Union fought a different kind of war. Military casualties were in excess of 15 million, and the civilian dead numbered over 7 million. The agricultural and industrial heartlands of the country were occupied and devastated by the Germans. The entire remaining industrial plant was relocated beyond the Urals. Kiev, Stalingrad, Leningrad were shattered. Those that survived did so because they worked at unbelievable rates and fought with unbelievable stoicism. Neither left much time or energy for football, formal or informal. Indeed the Soviet league completely closed down for the duration of the war. Football was confined to the occasional act of symbolic bravado – like the game played at the half-built Kirov stadium during the siege of Leningrad in May 1942. There was a crowd of 10,000 and the game was broadcast to the city. A match of pyrrhic celebration was played out in the desolation of Stalingrad after the German surrender, between the army and a hurriedly reconstructed Dinamo Tbilisi. Behind the lines the remnants of Dynamo Kiev and the Luftwaffe played in Kiev in 1942. Back in Moscow politics continued as usual. In 1942 Beria persuaded Politburo member Georgi Malenkov to sign the arrest warrant for Nikolai Starostin and his brothers. All four were found guilty by the courts and made their way to Siberia.

Between 1939 and late 1942 the German national team played over thirty international matches on a circuit of allies, satellite states and neutrals. Italy, Hungary, Romania and Bulgaria fell into the first category, while the Croatian state torn out of the old Yugoslavia and the rump Slovakia left after the absorption of the Czech lands into the greater Reich fell into the second category. Spain, Sweden and Switzerland fell into the third. Bulgaria and Hungary, insulated from the worst of the fighting, maintained a full programme of football until the very last days of the German retreat. The Slovakian and Croatian leagues, which were always more fragile constructs, lasted only a couple of years before partisan activity and public opposition made continuing impossible. The Italians played on through 1942 and despite the invasion of the country in 1943 continued to play football afterwards. In Germany itself, football went on much as before for the first four years of the war. Indeed, the authorities were determined to use football's continuation as an indicator to the German people that the war, while a painful sacrifice, would not completely annihilate normal life. In the official programme of the German Cup Final in 1940, the writer crowed that while they were watching the game,

At the same hour the men and women of the British Isles fearfully await the German general attack, where the pitches of English football clubs have been ploughed and torn up, in the hope that this panic measure might be of some use at the decisive hour.[25]

Nineteen forty-two was the pivotal year in the course of the war. The Afrika Korps had been broken by the British at El Alamein; the Sixth Army was about to be annihilated in the wastes of Stalingrad. The German national football team, exhausted by the impossibility of travel and training in a war economy, were exposed. After they lost 3–2 to Sweden in Berlin, Secretary of Foreign Affairs Martin Luther wrote, '100,000 have left the stadium depressed; and because victory in this football match is closer to these people's hearts than the capture of a city in the East, such an event must be prohibited for the sake of the national mood.'[26] The denouement came in Bratislava in November 1942 where the Germans soundly beat Slovakia 5–2. The German player Fritz Walter recalled that the usual minute's silence held for the war dead was accompanied by a bitter, poisonous seething and murmuring from the crowd.

Early in 1943, in response to the reality of Germany's diminishing military and economic capacities, Goebbels asked the people whether they were ready for total war. They were getting it, ready or not. The newspapers announced the vast range of measures, privations, sacrifices and regulations that total war would entail. Among other things, 'International sporting competitions are to be cancelled until further notice ... because soldiers are no longer available and people doing labour service will not be granted leave of absence.' However, some space would be allowed for football at home: 'Sporting competitions of a local character are to be carried through in order to sustain the work ethic.'[27] Indeed so vociferous were the demands from the public for football that a form of national championship was allowed to continue as well.

This last-gasp militarization of German society saw the competition populated by a rash of new teams like Air Force Sports Club Putnitz and Sports Union SS Strassburg. As late as spring 1944 the national championship was played to a conclusion. Dresdner FC took the title a few short months before the city's incineration. By August 1944, with the Russians in the suburbs of Warsaw and the Americans and British in Paris, all men between the ages of sixteen and sixty were called up to fight: game over. The Third Reich was disintegrating, its football structures had collapsed, and as the corpses mounted all around it could no longer even bury its dead. In early 1945, 'a coffin carrying the mortal remains of Fritz Unkel, the revered long-time president of Schalke 04, stood in a cemetery in almost completely destroyed Gelsenkirchen for eight days and nights, until members of the family buried it themselves'.[28]

In the decade after the Second World War Europe divided between East and West. The balance of power and the centre of international politics pivoted on a divided Germany. There is an obvious parallel with the course of football's history. Football in Eastern and Western Europe was reconstructed on profoundly different economic and political lines, no more starkly demonstrated than in the emergent command-economy model of East German Stalinism and the hedged commercialism and provincial power bases of West Germany's social market under Konrad Adenauer. More than that, each of these zones contested the claim to European, even world football hegemony. England, now returned to the global football fold, remained convinced that its pre-war status was undiminished and unassailable. From the East, Hungary's Golden Squad emerged to challenge and ultimately destroy those illusions. But confirmation of their claim to global supremacy required victory in the 1954 World Cup and in this they were thwarted by the new West German national side; like the nation it represented, it was only recently released from international quarantine and returned to the polite society of the new international order.

Italian football offered some competition in this stuggle, in the shape of *Il Grande Torino*, the great northern side which won five championships between 1943 and 1949 and provided the backbone of the Italian national team. The entire squad was killed in an air crash in 1949. On the eve of their sixth title Torino returned home from a friendly game with Benfica in Lisbon. In dense fog the plane crashed into the side of the mountain that lies beneath the Superga monastery that looks down on Turin. A quarter of a million people lined the streets and gathered around the city's cathedral to bury the dead. Italian football would certainly recover, but Torino were destroyed at this crucial juncture of post-war reconstruction. They have never been able to regain their place in the football hierarchy. Similarly, Spanish football, recovering from the civil war, appeared to be producing top players and internationally competitive teams like Barcelona and Espanyol. Barça not only won three Spanish league titles in five seasons but also the new Copa Latina, an international club competition among the French, Italians and Iberians. But their peak came too early. By the time the European Cup had been created and Spain was allowed to re-enter the European mainstream, Barcelona had given way to the new Real Madrid.

British supremacy in the immediate post-war era appeared undiminished. On 10 May Great Britain played the Rest of Europe at Hampden Park and won 6–1. The match was organized to mark the return of the Home Nations to FIFA, signalling both the closure of past conflicts and the reincarnation of international peacetime football. It also raised a few quid for FIFA who were broke. Great Britain, with at least one player from each nation, were almost uniformly a team of pre-war vintage, including Frank Swift, Stanley Matthews, Tommy Lawton and Wilf Mannion. The Europeans had no players from the former Axis powers, the Iberian dictatorships or the emerging communist states of the East, all of whom were out of political favour in Britain. There was one Czech but then Czechoslovakia still possessed a coalition government of which the communists were not in control. The best of the team came from Denmark, Holland and Sweden, whose neutrality or relatively mild occupations left their players better fed and their football in more robust shape than most.

The press and public cast the game in a variety of guises. The main axis of contrast in the British press was Britain's reliance on inborn character and instinct over Europe's reliance on training and coaching. Like the wider culture British football was suspicious of intellectuals, distrustful of theory, disdainful of certified expertise. Great Britain's victory was comprehensive, its scale and ease entrenching the footballing consensus: 'A match which seemed, when it was played, to confirm the power of British football in fact marked its brilliant sunset.'[29] The sun was already setting on the British Empire. Egypt had gone, India too, and Britain was leaving Palestine just as fast as it could. Attlee had abandoned Greece to its fate, recognizing that only the Americans had the resources to play politics in Southern Europe.

It was all the harder to grasp the real position of British football in the world, for at home it was experiencing its own post-war boom. If Nicholas Fishwick is right in saying that English football had become 'the Labour Party at prayer', then football in the immediate aftermath of the war was more revivalist celebration than Church of England mumbling.[30] In August 1945 the British electorate and overwhelmingly its working classes voted in the first majority Labour government in the country's history and one with a mandate to transform profoundly the economic and social structures of the country. Almost a hundred years since the collapse of Chartism the British working classes had got organized and into power. Simultaneously, football, already indelibly stamped as their game, achieved a level of hitherto unparalleled popularity. Already by far the biggest spectator event in the country before the war, attracting over 20 million to matches during the 1938–39 season, attendances effectively doubled, peaking in 1949 at over 41 million and staying above 30 million until the early 1960s. A measure of the nation's enthusiasm for live football was the FA Amateur Cup, now almost invisible, but first played in 1949 when it attracted 95,000 people to Wembley for the final. Football was the pre-eminent game of the age of austerity. Relieved of some of the burden of the government's wartime entertainment taxes, entrance to the game was as cheap as a shilling a shot and unlike almost every other pleasure it was neither rationed nor only available on the black market.

'We are the masters now.' No one ever really said it within the Attlee government, though it was commonly quoted of them. It would, after all, have been too crude, too self-satisfied a proclamation for an administration characterized by economic and emotional austerity. Maybe, as Anthony Howard has suggested, they should have said it. Then their ambition might have matched the tangible sense of working-class power their election represented. For all the successes of the Attlee government – principally the creation of the enduring institutions of the British welfare state – it left the British economy in the same state of under-education and under-investment in which it found it, and occupied by the same conservative cartel of woeful managers and skilled but defensive workers. Nonetheless, the changing balance of industrial power was tangible enough to extend even to the most placid and disorganized sector of the economy – football players. The threat of strike action in November 1945 saw the maximum wage rise to £9 a week and a return to pre-war bonus schemes. Continual agitation by the growing players' union, the Professional Footballers' Association (PFA), saw them score a victory at one of the government's new labour tribunals in 1947. The tribunal raised the maximum wage to £12 and put a decent floor under the wages of juniors, which were notoriously low. That said, no profound rupture with the past was possible. The PFA certainly did not have the power to challenge either the maximum wage itself or the enduring feudal system of contracts and transfer law. Like the trade-union movement in the wider economy, they registered material gains without fundamentally altering the rules of industrial organization and conflict. In such circumstances, the best and the bravest took their chances as a small exodus of British players tried their luck in Italy, France and Colombia in the 1950s.

The football culture and industry that they left behind was thriving. Professional football had been re-established all over the country and the record crowds watched an unusually open and competitive sport. In the decade after the war eight different teams won the league, including four that had never won it before – Portsmouth, Chelsea, Spurs and Wolverhampton Wanderers. Radio broadcasting of league matches carried on from the immensely popular wartime radio commentaries. However, the Football League remained suspicious enough of the impact of broadcasting to insist that the details of which actual game was to be covered were kept secret. Radio was now joined by television which, although in its technological infancy and prohibitively expensive for most, managed to attract an audience of over a million for the 1950 FA Cup Final. By 1953, with televisions more widely available, over 10 million tuned in to see Stanley Matthews finally win an honour.

Beyond the sepia-tinted recollections, the happy, orderly crowds and the sense of normality returning, there were other signs and messages if you chose to read them. In March 1946 an FA Cup tie at Bolton Wanderers' Burnden Park attracted at least 80,000. According to one eye witness, the stadium, especially the cinder banks behind the goals, was not designed for such an influx. 'The bank was pretty crude, just dirt really, with bits of old flagstones they could get for steps. When it rained the gaps filled with water and the mud spilled out.'[31] Some of the crowd, already inside, opened one gate to let friends in. Then the other closed gates were forced open. As the crowd recognized a free-for-all, many hundreds more started climbing over the walls. The immense pressure of this charge on those in the middle of the stand eventually broke the flimsy antiquated barrier and walls. The crowd flooded on to the pitch, released like a cork from a bottle. Thirty-three people died and over 400 were injured. In the aftermath the official judicial report suggested that local government should be given the power to license and inspect football grounds to prevent a recurrence of the disaster. The football industry was not happy. Overwhelmingly conservative in its boardrooms it feared the intrusion of the local state, especially in the hands of the Labour Party, and convinced itself that safety standards would be so high and the cost of compliance so expensive that they would be forced out of business. In the context of post-war politics and the scale of the war dead it seemed to most a minor matter.

But the surest signs were coming from the England team itself. The team's unbeaten run after the war, the pyrrhic glories of the Rest of Europe game and the popularity of domestic football all conspired to hide the decline. The FA even appointed a full-time coach to the England team, Walter Winterbottom, though the power of selection remained with the cumbersome, arcane, secretive and often incompetent selection board. Winterbottom alongside Stanley Rous formed the modernizing axis of the FA. Both made considerable efforts to improve the parlous state of football education and coaching, arguing that the conventional artisanal wisdom of British football needed to be replaced with a more systematic approach to training, fitness and tactics. But they remained minority voices.

The extent to which the opposition was catching up was made obvious by the performance of Dinamo Moscow on their tour of Britain in late 1945, drawing with Chelsea and Rangers, beating Arsenal and embarrassing Cardiff City. If it wasn't obvious by now it surely should have been after England's first disastrous World Cup in 1950. The team that went to Brazil managed to beat Chile but lost first to the USA – a team of lower-league drop-outs and amateurs – and then to Spain, both 1–0. England were humiliated and out. Yet still the illusion was maintained. These defeats could be accounted for in terms of the problems of travel, unfamiliarity of circumstance, unforeseen injuries and sheer flukes. Brain Glanville has condensed this web of self-deceit like this:

The myth of supremacy rested on the fact that neither England nor Scotland had been beaten on home ground by a foreign team. They had failed time and again, away; in the great amorphous never-never land known vaguely as abroad, where defeats, obscurely, somehow didn't count, because one get-them-in-our-British-mud and we would kill them.[32]

This myth too would finally be dissolved and its dissolution would come from the east.

VII

In Warsaw, in the early 1950s, tens of thousands of young Poles laboured for nothing to build the Stadion Dziesięciolecia, named to celebrate the ten years in power of the Polish Communist Party. It opened in July 1955, a year late, but in its unbending industrial asceticism and unadorned architecture it offered real testament to the gruelling process of reconstruction in football and just about every aspect of society, under the blunt and gloomy aegis of East European Stalinism. Simon Inglis captures the essence of this aesthetic: 'The mould of all great Socialist stadiums of the post-war period ... is a vast, serious, open bowl, formed by earth banking and lined with benched seats divided into forty blocks. At both ends are tunnels, faced in severe grey sandstone blocks, through which one might expect a train to emerge.'[33] All across Eastern Europe these great bowls were sunk into the ground or built up with the broken rubble of the still war-destroyed cities. In southern Poland Chorzów's Stadion Śląski was cut into the lunar landscape of half a century's mining wastes. In Leningrad the Kirov stadium was started in 1938; half finished it was used for occasional football and regular anti-aircraft gunfire in the war and was only opened in 1950. In Bucharest the Stadion 23 August, marking the minor Romanian uprising against the occupying German forces in 1944, opened in 1953. The Zentralstadion in Leipzig and the Népstadion in Budapest followed. All were intended as focal points for nationalist sporting spectaculars and a celebration of communist authority.

That authority rested primarily on the Red Army, who in May 1945 occupied most of the region outside of Yugoslavia and Albania whose own partisans – both communist and royalist – had cleared the Germans and Italians out. In Poland, Bulgaria and Romania, where the Red Army's occupation was most emphatic and where either no government existed or had been fatally tainted by alliance with the Germans, national Communist Parties were installed in government. The Bulgarians and Romanians dispensed with their monarchies in referendums held the following year, while clearly rigged elections dispensed with the agrarian and right-wing opposition in Poland in 1947. In Czechoslovakia and Hungary the greater depth and organization of non-communist political forces required the communists to share power with them in national coalitions until 1948. Their full integration into the Soviet sphere of influence was accelerated by the conflict between the Soviets and the US over the Greek Civil War in 1947, and then the Berlin Crisis of 1948–9. By the end of the latter Germany had been irrevocably divided into East and West. In Eastern Europe Communist Parties had taken complete executive power, promulgated new constitutions that made them people's republics and one-party states, began the liquidation and imprisonment of both suspect communists and political opponents, and had taken control of key sectors of the economy and media.

The Soviet model that was instituted at the level of economics and high politics was also reproduced in the realm of sport. The Stalinist template began with the eradication of opponents and alternatives. Across Eastern Europe scouting organizations were incorporated into communist youth movements; YMCAs were closed down and their facilities reallocated; any remaining independent nationalist organization – particularly Sokol gymnasiums in Czechoslovakia and Poland – were put out of business. National Olympic Committees were liquidated and reconstituted as the bureaucratic arm of communist-dominated ministries of education or sport. Above all, sport was unambiguously politicized. East Germany's main youth magazine told it like it was: 'The athletes in the GDR have to understand that they must learn to win competitions for the cause of our workers' and peasants' state.'[34] As with the Soviet Union, there was among the ideological cognoscenti some disdain for football and recognition that its pre-existing popularity and loyalties, large crowds and unpredictability offered an enclave of autonomy that was potentially threatening. Where possible, resources were directed towards gymnastics and athletics. But like their Soviet masters before them they were forced to bend to the seemingly unshiftable popular preference for football. If you can't beat them, join them; football teams were soon allocated to state institutions. Everywhere the armed forces and the Ministry of the Interior – responsible for surveillance and policing – got first choice of the pre-existing clubs or created their own from scratch. Some clubs of suspect social origins and political orientation were either taken over or marginalized, but Eastern European football still had space for independent people's teams on the model of Spartak Moscow and standard bearers for repressed minorities and nationalists.

In Czechoslovak football the regime encountered an already established order of clubs, as in politics the communists encountered already established politicians and parties. Slavia Prague were the team of the city's liberal intelligentsia. In the short interregnum between German occupation and communist domination, they won a league title in 1947. The following year Edvard Beneš, a player for the club in his youth and the grand old man of Czech democracy, resigned the presidency of the republic and died, heralding the complete takeover of Czechoslovak politics by the Communist Party. Under the new dispensation, when Slavia's championship-winning coach, the Glaswegian John Madden, died in post, the party insisted on a name change to Sokol Slavia Praha VII, and players were lost to sides with better party connections. Slavia would not win another title until 1996. Sparta Prague, who despite their suspect pre-war existence could at least claim to have been the team of Prague's working class, were largely left alone by the party, if hardly encouraged. Rather the party's efforts were directed through the army who acquired the minor club ATK in 1947. The club would come to dominate Czech football in the 1950s as Dukla Prague. The other force that Czechoslovak communism was never able to quell entirely was the separatist nationalism of Slovakia. In the immediate post-war era the Slovak Communist Party took control of Slovan Bratislava, the capital's leading team, provided them with the resources to win three league titles, and did not relinquish control until 1989.

In Poland the first post-war championship was won by Polonia of Warsaw, who like Slavia Prague were the pre-war team of the capital's intelligentsia. Those who had survived the war and the fierce fighting of the Warsaw uprising flocked to its colours. But their independent nationalism was deeply suspect to Gomułka's Communist Party and Polonia were consigned to the margins by the new regime. The two arms of party power took over clubs themselves. The army turned Legia Warsaw into CWKS while the interior ministry acquired Gwardia. Like their masters, neither club was able to decisively win the affections of the Polish people or entirely control Polish football. In Bulgaria the sparsity of pre-war football required the army, easily the most powerful institution in the country, to create its own club – CSKA Sofia. The Ministry of the Interior opted to take over Levski, the most popular club of the inter-war era. They also attempted to rename the side Dinamo but found it persistently unpopular with the crowd who considered the club to be theirs not the ministry's. The fans prevailed and the name reverted to Levski. Similarly, in Romania the army created their own club Armata, later known as CSKA and then finally Steaua Bucharest. The secret police merged a number of pre-war clubs to create Dinamo Bucharest and claimed an area of prime city-centre parkland to build a new stadium. Rapid Bucharest, farmed out to the railway industry, remained a hidden repository of dissent.

As with so much in East Germany, any residue of the old order was dissolved as soon as possible. In the case of bourgeois FKs and SCs – football and sports clubs – they were reconstituted as proletarian SGs – sporting groups. These were distributed not merely to the security forces (Dynamo Dresden) and the army (Vorwärts Berlin), but also among the heavy industries that had not been carted off by the Soviets. East German football boasted Lokomotive Stendal, Chemie Leipzig and Turbine Erfurt.

One of the few clubs not to come wholly under the control of a parastatal institution was the leading pre-war team SC Dresden, now known as SG Friedrichstadt. In a key game in the 1950 championship they played Horch Zwickau, a club created by the fusion of three small teams. The game was understood by many participants as a contest between the old and the new, the authentic and the artificial, bourgeois and communist. Eyewitnesses report that after Friedrichstadt had taken a one-goal lead, Zwickau resorted to systematic violence unnoticed by the referee for 85 minutes. Zwickau won 5–1 only for the angry crowd to pour on to the field and assault the Zwickau team who had to be saved by a mounted police cordon. The regime chose to bare its teeth on this occasion, dissolving SG Friedrichstadt and transferring most of the players to BSG Tabak Dresden, a cigar-factory team in the lower divisions.

In compensation, Dresden got a new club, Volkspolizei Dresden, soon to be Dynamo Dresden. Unfortunately it was the property of the Stasi. The club immediately acquired seventeen of the country's leading players from eleven different teams. Not surprisingly Dynamo Dresden began to do well and were East German champions in 1953; that year the Stasi, the party and the entire regime demonstrated their fear and contempt for their own population when the strikes and protests by workers in Berlin were brutally repressed. It was a similar disregard for the public that saw the head of the Stasi, Erich Mielke, insist that his now championship-winning team be relocated nearer the office. Dynamo Dresden therefore became Dynamo Berlin. Similarly, in 1954 Empor Lauter, a civil servants' club from a tiny mountain mining village near the Czech border, went on a run of victories that took them to the top of the table. On the orders of Rostock trade unionist and politician Harry Tisch, who had decided that the city needed a winning team, they were moved wholesale to the Baltic port.

In Yugoslavia organized football began to re-emerge before the war had even ended. Having cleared the Germans from national soil in late 1944, there was time and energy it seems to found new football clubs in Belgrade as early as February 1945. The facilities of old bourgeois club BSK were appropriated by the newly created Metelac with Tito himself as honorary president. The club was later acquired by the federal secret police and renamed OFK. Red Star Belgrade were created by the city's communists in March 1945 out of the remains of the old SK Yugoslavia and began to attract support from the university, the Belgrade police and the Serb political elite. In October, a stone's throw from Red Star, Partizan Belgrade were created by the Yugoslav National Army (JNA). In Croatia the local Communist Party establishment founded Dinamo Zagreb from the fusion of HASK and Gradjanski and though Yugoslavia's communists tried to keep the lid on any display of nationalism, Dinamo Zagreb quickly became the symbol of an underground Croatian nationalism.

The accumulated heritage and experience of the inter-war era was not entirely lost in post-war Yugoslavia. The national team, which was considered unambiguously important by the Yugoslav Communist Party, received considerable talents and practical support. The already essential function of the national team as an expression of federal Yugoslavia rather than Serbia, Croatia or Slovenia was given a further level of significance in 1952 as part of the ongoing conflict between the country and the Soviet Union. In 1948 Tito had broken with Stalin, declaring that Yugoslavia would pursue an independent national road to socialism and maintain a position of equidistance between the emerging power blocs in Europe. Such autonomy of mind earned him the undying hatred of Stalin and the CPSU.

Yugoslavia were drawn to play the Soviet Union in the first round of the 1952 Helsinki Olympic football tournament, a match billed by the press in both countries as a proxy for the deeper ideological and strategic conflict between them. With twenty minutes to go the Soviets were 5–1 down to a rampant Yugoslavia and facing a trip to Siberia. Yugoslavian reports describe the Soviet players foaming at the mouth in their frenzy to get back in the game. The scoreline does not lie, the Soviets scored four goals, all from corners, and earned themselves a replay. Yugoslavia won 3–1 and the Soviet press that had hailed the comeback against Tito's fascist clique went silent. CSKA, the army team who provided the core of the Olympic squad, were quietly disbanded, reprieved only by Stalin's death the following year.

The Yugoslavs went on to the final where they met Hungary who beat them 2–0. Throughout the Olympic tournament the Hungarians had been in brilliant form. They roughed it with the Romanians and came out on top in the preliminary round. The Italians were beaten 3–0 and Turkey humiliated 7–1 in the second round. Against Sweden, who were considered one of the strongest teams in the tournament, they added another six goals. With the two against Yugoslavia, that was 20 goals in five games. But it was not just the goals that brought the entire Finnish crowd behind the Hungarians, it was the way they were made. Although not quite the finished article it was evident, even to the casual observer, that Hungary were playing a different kind of football. As Ferenc Puskás, the team's captain, described it: 'It was during that Olympics that our football first started to flow with real power. It was a prototype of total football; when we attacked everyone attacked; in defence, it was just the same.'[35] One spectator at the semi-final against Sweden was Stanley Rous, secretary to the FA. At the end of the game he turned to Sándor

Barcs, secretary of the Hungarian FA, suggested Hungary come to Wembley and they shook on it. The game was set, after much debate and at as high a level as the Hungarian Politburo, for November 1953.

Why should this extraordinary new football, this unstoppable, unbeatable team come from Hungary? Why should it have prospered under one of the most restrictive Stalinist regimes in Eastern Europe? It was, of course, a matter of chance and luck. A generation of exceptional players came together, with their talents spread around the pitch: Grosics in goal, central defenders Bozsik and Zakariás, the midfield spine of Borski and Hidegkuti, the forwards Kocsis and Czibor – all players of the highest calibre. In Puskás they had the player of truly rare and exceptional qualities. But there is more than luck involved in the creation of a team that did not simply play to win, but changed the nature of the game we play. First, the Hungary of the early 1950s were the inheritors of the great Hungarian football culture of the inter-war era. Hungary had, after all, lost the 1938 World Cup Final, provided the coaching staff for much of Serie A in the early 1930s, and in Ferencváros and MTK possessed two of the best club sides in Europe. Though the war had taken its toll on Hungary's football infrastructure, and its players, the final months of the conflict aside it had escaped the worst of the Allied bombing and the wrath of the Red Army.

Football and politics restarted in 1946. A coalition government comprising the conservative Smallholder's Party, the Communist Party and Social Democrats ruled in the shadow of the Soviet armed forces. In this period of relative calm and openness, the Hungarian football league restarted and a wealth of talented coaches – like Béla Guttmann and Martin Bukovi, both of whom had spent the war elsewhere – came home. In international football, the Hungarians started winning and Puskás proved so good in a game played against Italy in Turin that Juventus openly offered $100,000 for his services. In 1948, as the division of Europe was being finalized, the Communist Party edged their opponents out of power in a highly controversial election. Then in a second election in 1949 they offered the public just communist candidates. Hungary was declared a people's republic, a secret police force, the ÁVH, was created and opponents inside and outside the Communist Party were executed or put on highly public show trials.

Now the inheritance of Hungarian football would be held by the Communists. The usual state reforms put football and the football association firmly under the control of the Ministry of Sport and the party. Clubs were allocated to state institutions. Ferencváros, the traditional team of working-class Budapest, fell out of favour for its wartime association, among crowd and directors, with the Hungarian fascist movement and was humiliated by an enforced change of name and colours. MTK, the team of Jewish, liberal Budapest, had lost much of its natural support to the Final Solution. The empty shell was taken over by the newly founded secret police. Thus the state's patronage fell mainly on the small club Kispest, which was taken over by the army and renamed Honvéd. The majority of the country's leading players were concentrated at Kispest and MTK in the early 1950s in an effort to ensure that the national team would benefit from their familiarity.

The man entrusted by the regime with the task of turning these materials into victory was Gusztáv Sebes, a man of impeccable political credentials. Sebes was a long-standing communist, an industrial organizer at Renault in Paris in the 1930s, and a leading figure in the Hungarian trade-union movement. He was appointed the sole coach of the national side in 1949 in addition to his existing role as Deputy Minister of Sport. Grosics remembered him like this: 'Sebes was deeply committed to socialist ideology and you could feel it in everything he said. He made a political issue of every important match or competition; he often said that the fierce struggle between capitalism and socialism took place as much on the football field as anywhere else.'[36] The regime certainly expected to make political capital from football, and had allocated precious resources to the building of a vast new national stadium – the Népstadion – as the centrepiece of the construction programme of Hungary's first five-year industrial plan. Sebes made use of the considerable power vested in him. He established a national scouting network, co-opted the entire coaching fraternity of the Hungarian league in his plans, arranged special midweek friendlies and training sessions for the national squad and, above all, experimented with players, tactics and ideas.

Paradoxically, at a time when the expression of individuality, the exploration of heterodox ideas and the entrusting of initiative to the public were capital offences in Stalinist Hungary, Sebes created a protected enclave of trust, dialogue and spontaneity. Innovation began at the back where Grosics increasingly played as a goalkeeper-sweeper: more reliant on his feet than his contemporaries, able to anticipate and intercept long balls outside his area, and ready to initiate quickfire counterattack by rolling the ball into space rather than kicking it. At the other end of the pitch Hungary retained two wingers, but expected them to do more than merely run the line, but overlap and interchange with what appeared at the time as two inside-forwards. The fifth forward of conventional football formations – the number 9 or centre-forward – was withdrawn into midfield which had already been depleted by one player progressively playing deeper and deeper. Thus Hungary evolved a formation with four defenders. This left two midfield players whose role was primarily organizational and attacking, breaking from the centre of the pitch into gaps, taking shooting opportunities around the penalty area, supporting slick interplay and passing among the forwards and confusing the dullard defences of the day with unusual runs and shapes. When Brazil played this way at the 1958 World Cup it was called 4-2-4, but Hungary were there first.

In March 1953 Stalin died. The flames of protest flickered on the streets and building sites of Berlin. They spread to Hungary where workers at the Rákosi steelworks downed tools and demanded improvements. The Hungarian countryside and the small towns began to smoulder. The Communist Party leadership was summoned to Moscow and berated by Khrushchev for their failings and obsessive fidelity to the worst excesses of doctrinaire Stalinism. Prime Minister Rákosi, Stalinist-in-chief, was demoted and the more reformist Imre Nagy put in charge. With this tiny thaw in the authoritarian permafrost a mood of change, of optimism and possibility began to seep out in Hungary. In 1952 the Hungarian national team had won ten out of ten matches and remained unbeaten through 1953. Against Italy in Rome, the possibility that the Hungarians really were the best team in the world seemed tangible. Hungary won 3–0 in a superb display of innovative passing and tactical sophistication matched to an emotional intensity epitomized by Puskás, screaming for a quick throw from the keeper when Hungary were already two up with just a few minutes to go. It was England next. Sebes was nothing if not meticulous. After watching England vs. the Rest of Europe at Wembley a few weeks before the Hungarians were due, he thought the ball bounced differently and the turf had unusual properties. He arranged for the Hungarians to train with British balls on a pitch the size of Wembley. On the way to London his team played a friendly with a factory team at Renault in front of 15,000 production-line workers, and took a little international proletarian solidarity into the heart of the old kingdom. Like the Austrians in 1932 and the Italians in 1934, the Hungarians came to England with regicide on their minds.

---

23 November 1953
England 3 Hungary 6
Wembley Stadium, London

In Brazil and Africa, fans bury magic totems, charms and curses beneath their opponents' pitches; but not in England. England is common sense and hard work. England is in black and white. The dense dirty London fog is already circling the pitch. The distant camera picks out the crowd as thousands of serried anonymous dots, the primitive microphones make them sound like slow heavy waves landing on a distant shore. The photographers in heavy coats and hats nearly all scurry off behind the Hungarian goal. They are expecting England to do the scoring.

To a man, the England players look like they have just rolled up their sleeves for another hard shift at the factory. Their kit is baggy; the Hungarians' is fitted. On their feet are heavy, high-cut leather clod-hoppers; the Hungarians wear lighter, low-cut modern boots. Their frames are like oxen; the Hungarians look sinewy. Billy Wright, the England captain, jokes with Stanley Matthews, 'We shall be all right here, Stan, they haven't got the proper kit.' Just before the kick-off, Puskás flips the ball up on the toe of his left foot, twice more, then on to his thighs, back to his foot, spins and flicks the ball behind him off his heel to Hidegkuti. Nervous pre-match juggling, or a calculated display of insouciance in the decrepit palace of English football?

How long does it take for an empire to die? How long does it take to lose a match? Forty-five seconds. Hungary kick-off, a thrust down the right wing is clumsily cleared by the English defence. In a high-speed slalom of one-touch passes, from the halfway line to the edge of the English penalty area, the Hungarians carve up the opposition. Totally unmarked, Hidegkuti rifles the heavy, sodden English ball into the net. England get one back, but then in the next fifty-five minutes the Hungarians score another five. They could have had ten. They did as they

345

pleased. At times England barely touched the ball; when they did, they needed two, three touches to control it. When they had control, they hardly seemed to know what to do with it. The Hungarians plucked the ball out of the air, controlled it on their chests, and barely looked up before passing it into their team-mates' path. The forward line was everywhere, crossing from left to right, running from deep, tracking back into defence, counterattacking at speed. They looked like a modern football team.

The Empire Stadium was thrown up in a matter of months. They say that a locomotive that the builders could not be bothered to move was buried under the pitch. A ramshackle imperial circus built on a long-forgotten industrial revolution.

The spell was finally broken. England, beaten in Europe, humiliated in Brazil, were now beaten at home. Budapest took to the streets. The Hungarians were cheered off from Victoria station, hailed as the heroes of Continental football at the Gare de l'Est and celebrated as the descendants of the *Wunderteam* at Westbahnhof in Vienna. In Hungary every station, every stop, saw them showered with gifts and flowers. In Budapest itself the entire Communist Party hierarchy assembled alongside hundreds of thousands of people in and around Keleti station. The players were publicly honoured with the People's Order of Merit and secretly rewarded with cash. Six months later England came to Budapest for the rematch. There was no mistake; Hungary were that good, England were that bad, and worse had learned absolutely nothing from the Wembley game. Hungary won 7–1 and made England look even more ponderous and out of their depth than before.

VIII

Every football culture has provided a practical and emotional refuge for certain strains of obsessive masculinity that delights in order, control and completeness. Modern bureaucratic sports offer innumerable cabalistic pleasures for record keepers and statisticians. For collectors and completists, the commercial world has added cigarette cards, stamps, coins and sticker books. For the sentimental there has been an ever-mounting range of memorabilia and insignia. On the coaching side, this kind of mania for comprehensiveness has spawned relentless note-takers, dossier compilers, detail-zealots and impossible perfectionists. What place was there for such essential triviality, such total disconnection from the real world at Zero Hour, 8 May 1945, the day of the German surrender? Paradoxically, the desolation, the unutterable ruin of it all, the profound emptiness, was also the moment at which those with a sufficiently narrow vision and an almost autistic relationship with the social and ethical catastrophe around them could survive and even flourish. Sepp Herberger, still officially coach of the German national football team, possessed such emotional autism and narrowness of vision. He was, after all, a man who spent the second half of the war compulsively tracking the fate of his conscripted and dispersed squad, urging them to keep safe and fit and work on the weaker aspects of their games. Throughout the entire war, indeed throughout his entire coaching life, he kept 361 tightly written notebooks in which there is not a single word, not the merest inkling that anything other than football was going on in mid-century Europe. Zero Hour was not a moment for moral reflection or personal introspection; it was simply time to get the team back together. Herberger was not alone in his mania. In southern Germany in the summer of 1945, the ex-official of VfB Stuttgart Gustav Sackmann personally combed the region in an effort to assemble a squad of pre-war players.

The part of the Reich not returned or given to Austria, France, Czechoslovakia, Poland and the Soviet Union was divided between and occupied by the Soviet Union, France, Britain and the United States. In the Soviet Zone, as we have seen, the creation of a communist government and a state-controlled sports system was underway by 1946. In the French and British Zones there appears to have been little sympathy for German football, both administrations refusing to let clubs reform or games be played; there are even reports of posts and nets being confiscated and football kits too close to Nazi colours being burned. By contrast, in the American Zone, where football appeared an oddity of insignificant cultural weight, football was not only permitted but encouraged. A South German FA was established in late 1945 and within a month a small regional *Oberliga* was in action. In 1946 there were four such leagues in the US Zone. Germany's capacity for self-organization was seemingly undiminished. As the emotional tenor of the occupation dissipated, the French and British began to permit the formal organization of football. The heightening East–West conflict drew the Allied Zones closer together in anticipation of the division of Germany to come; monetary union between the US, UK and French Zones was quickly followed by the first West German national championship final played in Cologne in 1948. That said, the apparatus of national championships and regional associations is deceptive. Football in Germany, like its people and its cities, was a ruined, emaciated affair. With over half the entire country's building stock destroyed, the state of pitches, clubhouses and other facilities is not hard to imagine. Through the 1946 and 1947 seasons the squads of leading clubs found themselves playing for soup and bread. In the cities the rag-ball and street football made an unprecedented return, for there really was nothing else. In this interlude of extreme privation a whole generation of urban German children rediscovered their love affair with the simplicity of the game.

Even if there were a national championship there was of course no national team and no international football. FIFA had suspended Germany's membership of the organization and banned its own members from playing German teams at any level. In 1949 the Federal Republic of Germany was created from the fusion of the three Allied Zones and a provisional constitution, sparsely described as the basic law, was agreed. The final questions of Germany's military and legal status were bracketed. The Deutscher Fussball-Bund was reconstituted in the winter of 1949, while in the East its Stalinist mirror image arose. The Saarland in south-west Germany, still occupied by France, attained independent status with FIFA and would play international matches over the next four years until its reabsorption into West Germany. FIFA now lifted its ban and in 1950 Germany played their first home international since 1942 against Switzerland in front of 115,000 people. Like most pre-war German institutions that were reborn in some new guise in the Federal Republic, the DFB had barely been touched by the process of denazification. The president Peco Bauwens, a pre-war football referee and bureaucrat, had joined the Nazi Party in 1933 after which his Jewish wife committed suicide, but this did not debar him from office. Bauwens then recruited a cadre of press officers and organizers who had either been active members of the Nazi Party or personally involved in the implementation of the regime's race laws in sport. On the coaching side, Otto Nerz and Fritz Linneman, who with Herberger had been responsible for the team before the war, were both interned after the surrender as members of the Nazi Party. Neither survived the rigours of imprisonment. Herberger, who had on Nerz's advice joined the party too, was tried and fined as a young fellow traveller and dismissed. After a short spell working in education he was back in charge of his team.

It was Herberger's team that was to provide the defining moment of post-war West German football: victory in the 1954 World Cup, known as *Das Wunder von Bern* – the Miracle of Berne. Immediately recognized as a myth in the making, West Germany's progress from rank outsiders to world champions, from unwelcome guests to honourable champions, tracked the concurrent transition of West Germany from occupied enemy to sovereign nation-state. The epic narrative of nation-building has been constructed primarily around the characters of Herberger and his captain Fritz Walter, with cameos for the radio commentator Herbert Zimmermann, the winning goalscorer Helmut Rahn, and the bootman to end all bootmen – Adi Dassler, the founder of the Adidas sports goods company.

The quotidian qualities of Herberger and Walter began with their consistent lack of interest in the merest hint of politics. Like many of the Germans who made the journey from Zero Hour to the prosperity of the Federal Republic they did so by avoiding politics and history rather than engaging with them. Herberger himself captured something of the patrician authority of the nation's leading Christian Democrat and first post-war chancellor Konrad Adenauer. Both men acquired a definite aura of power in their respective spheres by a combination of apparent all-knowingness and an understated avuncular charm. Both men were given to the utterance of epigrams and clichés whose folksy warmth and self-conscious common sense contrasted sharply with the pomposity and rhetoric of the Nazis. Walter, a midfielder with 1.FC Kaiserslautern, was a man of some footballing sophistication but personal simplicity and an obvious cipher for the characteristics of the German workforce that were hauling the country out of its economic abyss: focused, modest, loyal, unyielding and undying in his dedication to the collective cause. His enigmatic reticence made his life magnetic to myth and legend. At the end of the war Walter was attached to the football team of an air-force unit on the Eastern Front. He was captured by the Americans but handed over to the Soviets who put him on a train for Siberia. At the final stop in the Ukraine he joined a kickabout with the guards. He was recognized by the camp officers and miraculously sent back to Germany. During the war he was said to have contracted malaria, a condition he never entirely shook off, and was ever after strangely energized by dank wet weather – known colloquially as Fritz Walter weather. This was a man who miraculously survived the Armageddon of defeat and occupation, who carried the feverish sickness of the whole experience in his veins, who came back to the same club and the same life that he had left in 1939 and just tried to get on with it.

In keeping with this prevailing mood of national self-abnegation, the German build-up to the 1954 World Cup was very low-key. Publicly expressed bellicose nationalism of any kind remained politically and psychologically unacceptable. The team's performances, while competent, gave no plausible reason to think about victory. Indeed, the very idea of Germany abroad, winning anything, was an emotional and cultural tinderbox best left alone. The exclusion of the Germans from the 1950 World Cup and both the 1948 and 1952 Olympics had put off this eventuality, but with the division of Germany almost complete it could be put off no longer, though the German press did its best. On the eve of the tournament, the team poised to play their opening game against Turkey, the newspapers were overwhelmingly focused on the stormy negotiations between France and Germany over rearmament and the final stage of the Federal Republic's reconstitution as a sovereign independent state. West Germany was a nation-state in waiting. What kind of nation its citizens imagined themselves to be remained in question; the 1954 World Cup Finals offered them the opportunity to find out.

The finals revealed what was already known about Switzerland; neutrality paid. It was the only European state whose economy was in good enough shape to consider hosting the tournament. The finals also revealed the end of Latin America's supremacy over Europe – for the time being anyway – as both Uruguay and Brazil were beaten. England's place in the second rank of global football was confirmed by their own dismal showing, while a taste of the multi-continent cosmopolitanism of the World Cup in the post-war world could be seen in the participation of newcomers Turkey and South Korea.

By contrast to the Germans, the Hungarian build-up had taken on the feel of preparations for a coronation. The team continued to play exceptionally well, were treated to winter training in Egypt and permitted levels of overseas shopping and smuggling that few below the Politburo could access. Hungary had been hung with bunting. Billboard posters of the team were displayed around the country. Invitations to victory parties addressed to every embassy in Budapest had been printed. After arriving in Switzerland the Hungarians swatted Luxembourg aside 10–0 in a warm-up game. In the opening stages they humiliated Korea 9–0 and Germany 8–3. After such a decisive victory, against admittedly a second-string German team, the idea that the Hungarians might meet the Germans again seemed implausible. They barely noticed the Germans' steady progress – beating Turkey, Yugoslavia and then Austria to make the final. Puskás had been injured by a fierce tackle from the German defender Liebrich and was out of the side, but even without him Hungary played two quite exceptional games, both of which illuminated different facets of the game and confirmed their authority and their ranking in global football. Against Brazil, in the 'Battle of Berne', the Hungarians scored four, and held their ground in a series of violent encounters that culminated in a free-for-all in the players' tunnel after the match. Then in the semi-final they played the defending champions Uruguay, scored twice and controlled the game. The Uruguayans were still good enough to score twice themselves and take the game to extra time, but Hungary added self-belief, resilience and another two goals to their tally. Hungary, already Olympic champions, had beaten both finalists from the 1950 World Cup, humiliated England home and away, remained unbeaten in four years and were the possessors of both technical virtuosity and tactical originality. Now they were in the final of the World Cup.

The mists of myth and misinformation have long settled on the mood in the Hungarian camp. But enough seems clear to suggest that they arrived in Berne less than the sum of their parts. Puskás's inclusion, despite not being fully fit, was a source of rancour and just one of a number of selection decisions that provoked jealousy and conflict. The sour mood could hardly have been helped when the Hungarian team coach was stopped some distance from the stadium, locked into impassable crowds. The party were forced to squeeze their way through to the Wankdorf stadium on foot. In the crush Gusztáv Sebes found himself on the end of a Swiss police rifle butt. It was raining and it didn't stop all afternoon.

---

4 July 1954
West Germany 3 Hungary 2
Wankdorf, Berne

Stage Left: Heaven. Angel Gusztáv Sebes sits on his rain cloud, declaiming to no one in particular. Stage Right: Ferenc Puskás, still very much alive, sits in his front room, steadily working his way through a plate of fatty sausages.

Sebes: The night before the match was dreadful. It was the evening of the Swiss brass-band competition, with parades until two in the morning, right outside our hotel. They started playing again just after lunch on the day of the final.

Puskás: (*Without looking up from his sausage*) The world's press had been all over us and everyone knew us and wanted to beat us.

Sebes: And then the rain. It rained all day before the final, and very heavily during the second half as well. The ground was soft, very muddy and tiring for the players.

Puskás: (*Still eating sausage*) It wasn't long before we were two goals up and we had at least half a dozen other clear chances to score which we missed. Then we sat back and tried to keep the ball in midfield.

Sebes: At half-time everyone was complaining about the ref . . . Isn't it odd we always seem to get British referees?

Puskás pushes his plate away and directly addresses Sebes.

Puskás: We gave two silly goals away. We should have pressed on then looking for the third to kill the game off. I got an equalizer right at the death but that Welsh linesman Griffiths . . . disallowed it for offside. Even the English ref Billy Ling had given it.

Sebes: If Hungary had won there would have been no counter-revolution but a powerful thrust in the building of socialism in the country . . .

Puskás snorts and slurps down a small beer.

High above the stage, the gaunt figure of Gyula Grosics appears. He looks down on the image of Helmut Rahn on the edge of the Hungarian penalty area, two Hungarian defenders look at each other and the ball, arguing who is to deal with it. The ball is cleared but only as far as Rahn whose shot crosses the line. The roar of the German crowd, six minutes from time, rises and dies away.

Grosics: I felt – and still feel – an enormous, personal sense of loss; that day something went out of my life that has never been restored . . . On the day they beat us, and in doing so revealed a deep self-conceit in the team that had never showed itself before. After we got the second goal in the eighth minute, we thought it was all over.

In Germany the initial air of uninterest in the team's progress had been blown away. It had now become the centre of popular attention as most of the nation gathered around radios and the first wave of televisions in homes and cafes. On the final whistle the Berlin correspondent of the *Manchester Guardian* reported:

There was wild cheering and people started dancing on the pavements. Crowds had gathered in and outside cafes all over the city to listen to the radio commentary. Knots of excited people danced beside taxi cabs which had their radios on full blast.[37]

Estimates suggest two million people met the team's train on its short journey from the Swiss border to Munich. With uncharacteristic exuberance the press reported a man cheerfully having his head shaved at the barber's after losing a bet in which he was certain Hungary would win. At one of the many impromptu stops the players and officials were showered with gifts:

People hung from the trees like grapes, from the railway lights like flies. The whole town was on its feet; the bands of the auxiliary fire service were in their special uniforms, the local officials in their best suits. Just like how they once would have welcomed Kaiser Wilhelm.[38]

This hot plasma of emotion and public carnival are the moments at which myth and meaning are forged. What gave shape to those meanings was, first and foremost, a materiality rather than spirituality in West Germany's response to winning the World Cup. On the very cusp of their *Wirtschaftswunder* (economic miracle), West Germany's industrial output in 1954 grew at 11 per cent per annum and exports at 20 per cent. Germany might not have been able to build arms but it supplied the rest of the world with all the machine tools to make arms. When the team finally got to Munich a fleet of twelve imperious Mercedes open-top cabriolets awaited them. In the following week, at innumerable civic ceremonies and impromptu gatherings, the squad were given the tangible fruits of the economic miracle – fridges, televisions, sewing machines, carpets, chandeliers – and manufacturers got their endorsements. None more than Adi Dassler whose innovative screw-in studs had allowed Herberger's team to deal with all the weather thrown at the side and whose company Adidas was an exemplar of German manufacturing's export prowess.

From the official victory celebrations held in an underground Munich bierkeller, DFB President Bauwens' speech was broadcast live on Bavarian radio. In an atmosphere heavy with alcohol, emotion and unreconstructed nationalist politics, the speech began with an acceptable level of platitudes about Germans' heart and spirits, moved on to suggest that the team had been inspired by the spirit of the Nordic god Wotan, and reached a climax when he suggested that the team had reaped the benefits of unflinching obedience – *Der Führerprinzip*. Mercifully, Bavarian radio cut the speech short and then lost the tapes, but the spectre of Aryan mysticism allied to authoritarian ultra-nationalism was out. The impact of the speech was multiplied by reports surfacing in the foreign press that the crowd in Berne had sung the first verse of the German national anthem – *'Deutschland, Deutschland, über alles'* – rather than the Federal Republic's officially sanctioned third verse – *'Einigkeit und Recht und Freiheit'*, 'unity, justice and freedom'. The same was often true of public celebrations in Germany itself.

This simplified matters for the East German press which had been allowed a dash of pan-Germanic congratulations but had predominantly taken the path of excruciating forced politeness. Relieved of these obligations it could denounce West Germany's victory as a catalyst for every kind of revanchist, fascist, raging aggressive nationalism it could come up with. A slightly more tempered but no less accusatory tone could be registered in parts of both the French press and public opinion. In

Britain the victory was seen in a wider context of other German sporting triumphs, like Mercedes' recent victories in Grand Prix racing, and the obvious economic success of the Federal Republic. Nine years after winning the war, rationing remained more widespread and severe in Britain than in the defeated Germany. Moreover, it was clear that Chancellor Adenauer's conduct in the rearmament negotiations, although understated, indicated the definite emergence of a rearmed and sovereign West Germany.

Understatement was the characteristic tenor of the high political response to the victory. The team were publicly celebrated in Berlin in front of 95,000 people. The President of the Republic Theodor Heuss took the opportunity to tick off 'the good Bauwens' and his ilk with the patronizing homily, 'good kicking does not make good politics'. Heuss not only asked the crowd to sing the third verse of the national anthem, but read out the words to the verse just in case they did not know them. The headline of the *Süddeutsche Zeitung* captures this mode of conscious depoliticization: 'Great victory. Great day. But only a game.' Such official and establishment nonchalance proved an effective strategy in marginalizing hyper-nationalist interpretations of the World Cup, but that should not obscure the real and widespread political and social meanings that have been and were grafted on to it. The Berlin correspondent of the *Manchester Guardian* reported moments after the victory: 'To understand this joy one must remember both the giant load of bewilderment beneath which this nation has been staggering since one type of German pride came to its catastrophic fall nine years ago, and also, especially in Berlin, the zeal for an emotional release to lift minds out of the ever-present spectacle of surrounding ruin.'[39]

In such a context it is hard not to read the words of the German radio commentator Herbert Zimmermann on the final whistle – 'It's over! Over! Over! Germany is the World Champion!' – as the moment of closure on the humiliation and hardship of post-war occupation and reconstruction. *Der Spiegel* was unabashed in consecrating the victory as the cultural founding moment of the Federal Republic: 'After 2,000 years of taking the wrong path Germans have now discovered the true destiny of their national existence.'[40] And the meaning of that destiny? That it's good to win, but it's better to win a game than a war. That it's good to be the best, but that it's better to be the best at playing than ruling. That the national characteristics of hard work, loyalty, discipline and order could be mobilized to make cars and washing machines rather than tanks; that solidarity and hierarchy could be best expressed on the football field rather than the battlefield.

In Hungary there were low-key riots in the working-class suburbs of Budapest and by nightfall the most angry and the most drunk had set fire to the offices of the state football lottery in the city centre. Then, en masse, the crowd went to the headquarters of the national radio station where they called for the head of commentator Gyorgy Szepesi. The billboards came down, the parties were cancelled and the team were virtually smuggled back into Budapest, under armed guard. Once home they encountered a considerable degree of personal threat and plenty of public animosity. The regime had a re-edited version of the final shown in cinemas in which Hungary had possession for over 90 per cent of the game but they could not change the result. Hungarian socialism would not be invigorated by the success of the brilliant football that it had nurtured. It would be crippled by this sporting defeat and then both party and squad would be finished off by the destruction of the uprising to come.

10
Demons and Angels:
Latin American Football,
1955–1974

Brazil's victory with the ball compares with the conquest of the
moon by the Americans.   *Jornal do Brasil,* 22 June 1970

In fútbol there is art, dignity, genius, bad luck, Gods and Demons,
freedom and fate, flags, hymns and tears, and above all the discovery that although Brazil is bad at a lot of things, it is good with
the ball. It is a football champion which is very important. After
all, it is better to be champion in samba, carnival and football than
in war and the sale of rockets.   *Roberto DaMatta*

I

The normally august, even austere *Jornal do Brasil* was not joking when it made the comparison between the United States' Apollo missions and Brazil's third victory in the World Cup. In 1962 President Kennedy announced: 'The world now looks into space, to the moon and to the planets beyond, and we have vowed that we shall not see it governed by a hostile flag of conquest, but by a banner of freedom and peace.'[1] In so doing, he articulated the irresistible symbolic function of the moon landings as the perfect expression of American modernity. Of course, the case for the Apollo missions would be made in terms of hidden subsidy to the military-industrial complex and a mix of cold war posturing and strategic paranoia but that was always to miss the point. The point was that going to the moon was impossibly hard and gloriously useless. At what appeared the high point of America's rise to global economic and technological dominance its own borders were long conquered and those of the rest of the earth frozen by the military balances of the East–West conflict. The moon offered a new and open frontier for the relentless mental imperialism of the United States; a manifest destiny for an era of technocracy. The Apollo programme was a high-tech pyrotechnic display of what could be accomplished by the massive concentration of scientific, technical and financial resources guided by a diamond-hard instrumental rationality. And all for what? So they could stick their flag in a ball of rock first.

Brazil went one better, for one could not concoct any great power manoeuvres or industrial rationale to explain their conquest of the leather ball. What in the end could be more gloriously useless, transient and utterly unhelpful than a game of football? Like the Americans,

358

though inevitably less lavishly, the Brazilians devoted scientific, psychological and economic resources to the development of domestic and international football and to winning, especially the World Cup. But unlike the dust-dry rational calculations of America's space programme, Brazilian football was guided by other parameters: football as art, as spectacle, as dance and as drama. The impossible hardness of the task that Brazilian football had set was to resolve these two competing rationalities: the instrumental and the aesthetic; the efficient and the beautiful; to play to win but to play for pleasure, and in so doing to reconcile, if only for a moment, a central dilemma of not merely Latin American football but of all modern societies. For Brazil, and by association the rest of Latin America, the football played by the 1970 World Cup winners was one of the clearest and highest cultural expressions of their turbulent arc of social development. And how did that football appear to those who were there? It is hard to improve on the words of Hugh McIlvanney who, under the most primitive technological conditions, instantaneously wrote and telegraphed this account of the 1970 World Cup Final from the bowels of the Azteca in Mexico City:

Those last minutes contained a distillation of their football, its beauty and élan and undiluted joy. Other teams thrill us and make us respect them. The Brazilians at their finest gave us pleasure so natural and deep as to be a vivid physical experience . . . the qualities that make football the most graceful and electric and moving of team sports were being laid before us. Brazil are proud of their own unique abilities but it was not hard to believe that they were anxious to say something about the game as well as themselves. You cannot be the best in the world at a game without loving it and all of us who sat, flushed with excitement, in the stands of the Azteca sensed that we were seeing some kind of tribute.[2]

Football as art, football as drama, football as ballet or orchestral music – Latin America had been casting the game in these terms for over fifty years and insisting on not merely their importance but on their equivalence to the raw pursuit of victory. The great River Plate side of the 1940s – *La Máquina* – staffed by incorrigible bohemians and tango artistes; the *Ballet Azul* danced by Millonarios of Bogotá in the 1950s, and indeed the Brazilian World Cup-winning sides of 1958 and 1962 – all these were among the precursors of Brazil 1970. In this respect Brazil 1970 were no sudden and miraculous one-off but part of a longer tradition. But if football of this type had long been played in Latin

America it raises the question as to why its ultimate expression should happen precisely then, with precisely this team. One answer of course is the concatenation of talents and abilities that the team could draw upon. But viewed with a little distance, Gérson, Tostão, Carlos Alberto, Rivelino and Jairzinho – even Pelé himself – were products of their time; a unique moment in the intersecting economic, political and sporting histories of the continent.

The essential precondition of these emblematic modernist projects – be it a moon landing or *futebol arte* – was two decades of historically unprecedented economic growth. The global economic boom that began with the Korean War and only ended in the mid-1970s was appreciably stronger and deeper in the United States. That was just as well: no one said going to the moon would be cheap. But Latin America too was buoyed by the boom. It furnished a growing market for the continent's raw materials and a breathing space for the domestic industries and companies created by the surge of import industrialization initiated in the 1940s. In Argentina and Brazil employment and wages rose in the 1950s allowing a signficant increase in consumption for the working class and created a new urban middle class as well. However, Latin America was never able even to approximate the high productivity, high employ-ment, and high welfare economies of OECD countries. Poverty remained widespread and the growing gap between city and country was reflected in the continued and new growth of *favellas* and shanty towns in Rio, São Paulo and Buenos Aires. This more sharply divided form of economic growth at the Latino periphery meant that there were sufficient resources available to national governments and football elites to run organized, competitive, professional football. Simultaneously the mean poverty of the cities ensured a steady flow of hungry talent to staff it. Too little wealth and the football infrastructure cannot be maintained. Too much wealth and too many working-class jobs and the social production line of *maldranos* and *pibes* (street toughs, wide boys) will slow down.

The political context of these changes varied across Latin America. The leeway that the economic surpluses of the era generated was suf-ficient to support limited but reasonably stable democracies in Chile and Uruguay and to entrench established elite carve-ups in the Andean nations and Mexico. But in the two key footballing countries, Brazil and Argentina, politics took a more complex course which, at least in part, accounts for the intensity of their football cultures. Both were capable of producing sublime football, both were also capable of playing mean spirited, calculating football marked by cruelty and violence on the pitch. But the balance of these two forces differed. In Brazil it is still *futebol arte* that defines the era. The emblematic modernist football of Argentina was *anti-fútbol*.

The era began with the fall of the old populists and the fragmentation of their ruling coalitions. In Brazil President Vargas had committed suicide in 1954 theatrically preempting a military coup, while in Argentina in 1955 Perón was exiled by the short-lived military regimes of Generals Lonardi and Aramburu. In both countries there followed a decade of increasingly chaotic if predominantly civilian democracy. In Brazil President Juscelino Kubitschek re-energized, indeed super-heated Brazilian economic development by building Brasília and pursuing unsustainable expansionist macro-economic policies. As Brazil's economy soared, the nation's headlong drive for industrial development and global recognition was finally crowned by victory in two World Cups, in Sweden in 1958 and four years later in Chile. Brazil were always going to be good at football in this era – the legacy of the 1930s and 1940s was immense and domestic football was hugely popular – but the buoyant economics and irresistible optimism of the Kubitschek presidency helped create a climate in which it could truly flourish.

By contrast, in Argentina, a series of elected governments attempted to grapple with a wildly gyrating economy that plunged from peaks of growth to troughs of recession and a society so polarized and divided that the social compromises necessary to the process of economic development and social peace could not be sustained. Successive governments proved institutionally and politically unequipped for the task. Finally exposed to the harsh competition of both the global economy and global football after the era of Peronista dictatorship, Argentina was hit very hard. It found itself in chronic balance of payments problems and a decade out of date in international football. The dominant response of Argentine football to the chaos and instability was to play ultra-defensive, ultra-muscular football or, in the case of Estudiantes La Plata, to do the very opposite of Brazil – to abandon every norm and value but winning, to play what became known as *anti-fútbol*.

The political consequences of the dash for growth pursued by the two countries was a long period of military and authoritarian government. But a further factor is required to explain the peculiarly repressive and vicious response to these problems taken in Latin America. In 1959 Fidel Castro and the small core of guerrillas that made up his 26th of July Movement entered Havana. Two years of rural insurgency had been enough to destroy the Batista dictatorship whose flailing repressive measures had served only to alienate US public and political opinion and provide a steady stream of recruits to Castro's small army. By 1960 the shape of the Cuban revolution had become clear. Non-communists were expelled from government, a massive agrarian land reform was implemented, all US-owned and other foreign assets were nationalized and the regime moved closer to a classic socialist authoritarianism at home and towards the Soviet Union abroad. Under the influence of the Argentine cadre and then government minister Ernesto 'Che' Guevara, Cuba also began to seek out and support radical and guerrilla movements across Latin America. The limits of Cuba's capacity to directly export the revolution were sharply demonstrated when Guevara led a short-lived insurgency in the high plateaus of Bolivia in 1967. He was shot in 1968 by US-trained Bolivian soldiers. But the indirect route was infinitely more powerful. In the mid-to-late 1960s, in emulation of the Cuban model of armed struggle, radicals took up the gun in Brazil, Argentina, Uruguay and Colombia, while in Chile the power and ambition of the parliamentary Left, communists included, rapidly grew.

It would take the collapse of the global economy in the early 1970s to propel the already panicky military elites and the upper and middle classes of Chile and Uruguay to go down the route of armed authoritarianism, but in Brazil and Argentina, where the military had a longer history of political involvement, the decision to do so came earlier. In Brazil the military took power in 1964 and remained there for two decades. In Argentina, General Onganía struck in 1966. The disastrous Peronista interlude of 1973–6 aside, the military regime effectively lasted until 1983. Both regimes would reap the last glory and the late triumphs of the *futebol arte* and *anti-fútbol* they inherited. General Médici publicly revelled in Brazil's 1970 World Cup victory. General Onganía saluted the virile masculinity and gamesmanship of Racing and Estudiantes. But in both football cultures violence on and off the pitch rose in parallel with the increasingly repressive measures required to sustain these regimes in power. The message from Cuba, a predominantly baseball-playing culture, was that playing the best or the meanest football in the world feeds no one.

Demonic and angelic, beautiful and ugly, both sides of Latin American football found their place in the tournament which defined the club football of the era: the Copa Libertadores de América. While Latin America had led Europe in creating international competitions between national teams by some four decades, it was slower to develop international competitions for clubs. Of course, teams across the Río de la Plata had played each other since the turn of the century, but there was nothing to compare to the inter-war Mitropa Cup, let alone the European Cup established by UEFA in 1955 as a trans-continental knock-out competition between national champions. One attempt to play a genuinely pan-South American club tournament had been held in Santiago in 1948. The Copa de Campeones had teams from seven countries and was won by Rio's Vasco da Gama, but the basic logistical and economic problems of staging this kind of competition in a continent of immense distances, underdeveloped air-transport infrastructure and restricted budgets could not be overcome. The impetus for change came from Europe; in 1958 UEFA proposed that the winners of the European Cup should, each year, play the champions of South America for an Intercontinental Cup. But who were the champions of South America? Who indeed were the Peruvian or Uruguayan champions in football cultures still restricted to a single dominant city? As ever, it was only the pre-eminent cities of Latin America that were linked to the wider world; the continent's rural hinterlands and provincial cities remained off the map. The patriarchs of CONMEBOL and the national football associations chewed the issue over for almost two years. There was money to be made and glory to be won but then there was also much grumbling that clubs' demands on their players would become so great that the Copa América would suffer (which it did, disappearing from the calendar between 1967 and 1975) and that the costs of staging the competition could not be met (often true as well). But the continent's air links were improving and the prospect of an Intercontinental or World Club Cup was enticing. The first South American Championship kicked-off in 1960 in Buenos Aires where San Lorenzo played Bahia from Brazil's Caribbean coast, 3,000 kilometres to the north.

In the mid-1960s the now firmly established competition was renamed the Copa Libertadores in honour of the soldier-presidents who had defeated the Spanish Empire in the early nineteenth century and defined the politics of the now independent continent. The Copa Libertadores invoked two aspects of that heritage. On the one hand it spoke to the pan-Americanism of the Libertadores era, reincarnating Bolivar's vision of a Latin America without borders. On the other hand, in practice the tournament also retained the same narrow, fissile, partisan localism of the fractious generals that irretrievably split Bolivar's Grand Colombia apart. As with any pan-American enterprise the Copa Libertadores struggled to deal with four interrelated problems: the enduring poverty of the continental economy; the vast and complex geography of the region and its correspondingly weak transport networks; the immense difference in size and levels of economic and footballing development between the nations of South America; and the enduring suspicions and jealousies that existed between many cultures over issues of race, ethnicity and enduring border conflicts. These factors were certainly obstacles enough to prevent any kind of regional economic cooperation and development in the 1960s. Organizing regional football, which was after all a much lesser task, proved almost as hard.

In its first decade of existence the tournament was never played under identical formats two years running. The Copa Libertadores explored the outer reaches of knock-outs, byes, preliminaries, mini-leagues, meso-leagues and round-robins. Numbers of participants fluctuated wildly. To begin with the Peruvians and Ecuadorians stayed away, then they joined. The Venezuelans were in and then out and then in, and in any case were just too weak to compete. Big clubs from small nations – like Peñarol and Nacional of Montevideo – wanted lots of matches to make up for a small home market. Big clubs with tougher domestic commitments, especially in Brazil, wanted fewer games. National associations sometimes wanted no games at all. World Cup preparations kept the Brazilians and Argentinians away on a number of occasions, internal politics and another split between the FA and the league in Colombia did likewise. The economic logic of the competition underlay the decision not to use the away-goals rule to decide two-leg fixtures, or even to use the aggregate-score rule, but to go on games and points won and thus generate plenty of money-spinning play-offs. Even so, it was hard to make ends meet. In the late 1960s the Brazilians, after one of their periodic absences, rejoined the competition only on the condition that their teams got 40 per cent of the away gate when everybody else was getting 20 per cent. The Uruguayans threatened a walkout when they found themselves paired with the Bolivians who really had no money. Racing Club of Buenos Aires, the winners of the 1967 Copa Libertadores, date their long economic decline through the 1970s and 1980s to the debt initially incurred playing the competition in 1967 and 1968.

Yet this rickety economic and organizational infrastructure created the stage on which the Latin American club game could excel. The inaugural champions Peñarol were the quickest to see that there might be money to be made. After a sell-out crowd saw them play a semi-final with San Lorenzo they were falling over themselves to offer their ground for a third game play-off. Peñarol gave the competition something to aim at by winning again in 1961 against São Paulo's Palmeiras, attracting immense crowds in the process. If, so far, the Libertadores had offered the exoticism of foreign competition, the grandeur of a continental crown and in Peñarol an incipient dynasty, it had yet to generate an epic narrative. The 1962 final offered this.

In the first leg Santos won 2–1 in Montevideo. In the second leg, deep in the second half Peñarol were leading 3–2. The Chilean referee Carlos Robles was then knocked unconscious by a stone thrown from the stand. Still on the pitch, when he woke up forty minutes later he decided to abandon the game only to be persuaded by the Brazilians to let play continue. Santos equalized in the final moments of the restarted game, but simultaneously one of the linesmen was knocked out by another projectile. Robles disallowed the goal and abandoned the match – which had by now lasted over three hours – and declared the result 3–2 to Peñarol. Santos won the play-off.

The global recognition and financial rewards that came with Santos's spectacular victory encouraged the president of Boca Juniors Albert J. Armando to take the competition more seriously than any Argentine side had done hitherto. Indeed, in 1963 Boca initiated the strategy of fielding weaker teams in domestic competitions in order to concentrate on the Libertadores. It proved enough to get them to the final against Santos, but not good enough to match the Brazilians at their peak. Goals from Pelé and Coutinho settled the matter. But the Argentinians had arrived and were to win ten of the next twelve competitions, losing only in 1966 and 1971. Over the next decade the Libertadores offered the full range of sporting drama to complement the farce of 1962. In 1965 Santos and Peñarol played out an epic three-leg semi-final goalfest: 5–4 to Santos and 3–2 to Peñarol, then 2–1 to the Uruguayans in the play-off. In 1966 Peñarol staged one of the great comebacks in footballing history in the final against River Plate. A third match was necessary to separate the teams and at half-time in Santiago River Plate were 2–0 up and cruising. Peñarol came alive, equalizing in the 72nd minute and winning 4–2 in extra time. In 1967 Racing offered Libertadores football as a war of attrition, playing a marathon twenty games to win the tournament. The following year Racing abdicated their crown to Estudiantes La Plata in a three-game semi-final of rare unpleasantness and vitriol. Estudiantes La Plata, an unfashionable team from a small beach town to the south of the greater Buenos Aires metropolis, were a key ingredient in expanding the narrative possibilities of the Libertadores, for they were the first real outsiders to claim the title, winning it three times in succession. Their style progressively tended towards the gamesmanship and brutality of their encounter with Racing rather than the free-minded open football with which they won their first title in 1968 against Palmeiras. Estudiantes cut a path from plucky outsiders to pantomime villains.

The South American spectacular, always fissile and combustible throughout the 1960s, was turning nastier. Estudiantes' signature victory in the Libertadores was their gruesome, bitter 1970 triumph over Peñarol, concluded by a stand-up fight among the players in the centre circle of the pitch. Despite having a grandstand view of the whole affair the assembled sages of the CONMEBOL executive decided to do nothing about the matter. The following year, even their tolerance levels were broken when the Copa Libertadores staged the Battle of the Bombonera. In the opening rounds of the tournament Boca Juniors were playing the Peruvians Sporting Cristal in Buenos Aires. With the score at 2–2 and just a few minutes from time a mass brawl broke out which resulted in nineteen players being sent off; only the goalkeepers and a Peruvian playing for Boca managed to keep out of it. The city police decided to jail both the Peruvians and the Argentinians for thirty days only for them to be set free by a hastily assembled special judicial commission. CONMEBOL's Peruvian President Teofilio Salinas, relying exclusively on reports in the Peruvian press, issued an edict banning Boca from international matches and expelled them from the tournament.

CONMEBOL's exchange of impermissible neglect for indefensible partiality was just another facet of an often erratic, highly partisan mode of governance in Latin America.

Outside of Brazil, already under military rule, the failure of that mode of governance had, alongside the enduring inequality of the region, helped stoke the fires of political conflict, armed rebellion and insurrection. Peru came under the rule of a populist military regime in 1968, Bolivia and Mexico were in ferment and the Left were making gains in Uruguay, Chile and Argentina. Military cabals and terrorist cells multiplied. Disorder and disrespect for authority was tangible, violence was in the air, on the streets and heading for the Copa Libertadores. In Buenos Aires in 1972 Independiente were entertaining Barcelona of Guayaquil. When the visitors failed to get a handball decision in the Independiente penalty area, they refused to restart the game and simply walked off. The match was awarded 1–0 to the Argentines. In the 1973 semi-final between Millonarios of Bogotá and San Lorenzo of Buenos Aires, Colombian fans ran on the pitch and attacked the referee after a goal for the home side was disallowed. The Argentinians, lucky to make it off the pitch, had to leave the stadium in a small convoy of armoured cars.

The Brazilian squad returned from their bruising encounters at the 1954 World Cup to a nation whose rancour was every bit as bad as the fist fight in the players' tunnel at the conclusion of the Battle of Berne. President Getúlio Vargas had since 1950 pursued an increasingly populist economic course and in so doing had sufficiently unnerved or alienated enough of Brazil's generals and key industrialists and bankers that there was talk of mutiny in the air. By late August 1954 the plotters were ready to strike. Faced with demands for his resignation, Vargas shot himself through the heart in the presidential palace in Rio. In the outpouring of national grief, mourning and confusion that followed this most political act of suicide, the threat of a coup receded and Brazil limped along with a series of makeshift governments until late 1955. Vargas's legacy was a nation sufficiently developed that it now stood poised between tropical agrarian lassitude and urban industrial dynamism. With the election of Juscelino Kubitschek as president in 1955

Brazil decisively opted for the latter course and thereafter the many pieces of Brazil's football fell into place.

Kubitschek was a centralist politician from the hard school of pragmatic pork-barrel politics in Minas Gerais, but to this he brought an aura of dynamism animated by both his own personal charisma and his unwavering commitment to super-heated economic development. He offered Brazil 'Fifty years of progress in five.' Riding the wave of global economic growth that followed the Korean War, and making the most of Brazil's reasonable credit rating, Kubitschek went on a spending spree. The military were temporarily neutralized by a significant pay rise and given plenty of new equipment to play with. Foreign multinationals were invited in and came in numbers. Public expenditure on significant infrastructure began to grow and in the defining act of his presidency, Kubitschek decreed that the federal capital would finally be moved from Rio and relocated to an undeveloped plateau 600 kilometres north-west of Rio – Brasília. The money and concrete began to flow around the clock. For five years Brazil's economy boomed, growing at over 6 per cent a year. Money was pouring into football as attendance boomed in the big cities where this explosive economic change was concentrated. In the final game of the 1963 Rio state championship between Flamengo and Fluminense, a world record total for a club match of 177,000 attended the Maracanã and saw a goalless draw. Football's hold on Brazil's popular imagination had never been tighter. The legacy of the Vargas years, during which black and mulatto players had been integrated economically and stylistically into a professional game, was strengthened by the influx of resources and new urban migrants and the booming popular cultures they helped create.

Brazilian football in the 1950s was but one strand, albeit an essential strand, of the cultural life of Brazil's emerging industrial cities. As migrants from the countryside flooded into towns, football support offered an immediate urban identity to the lost and confused. For those with a job and income who could join one, clubs offered not only sports facilities but status and communality too. The established connections between Brazilian music and football drew closer as fans perfected their repertoire of flags, fireworks and singing first learned in carnival and the samba schools. The beaches of Rio, where the city gathered to play, were an important laboratory of footballing innovation. It was here that beach football was developed into a more organized sport and foot-volley was perfected on the volleyball courts that lined the sand. Rich and poor, black and white, though still overwhelmingly men, played football as the centre of an organized social life of drinking parties and barbecues.

Brazilian football's muse in this era was Nelson Rodriguez, the younger brother of Mário Filho. Filho's work had both recorded and invented the founding myths of Brazilian football. His prose had something of the twinkled-eyed uncle spinning you a yarn, but with Gilberto Freyre's interpretation of Brazil as a bountiful, Africanized, multi-ethnic melting-pot the essential undertone of its account of football. Rodriguez was cut of very different cloth: playwright, critic, polemicist and columnist, his prose was by turns witty, barbed and scandalous. Alongside football, Rodriguez's writing roamed the Rio ether in search of perversion and infidelity, hysteria and ecstasy; fuelled on a cocktail of caffeine, nicotine and alcohol, he cut a frenetic arc across the cityscape. Writing against a background of accelerating urbanization and economic boom, Rodriguez offered a partiality yet more extreme than even Ary Barrosa had managed. 'I'm Fluminense. I always was Fluminense. I'd say I was Fluminense in my past lives.' His penchant for the mysterious and the conspiratorial led him to personify the role of chance in football as the *Supernatural de Almeida* – a medieval madman living in a northern suburb of Rio whose life was devoted to creating flukes and upsets.

Beyond the ball, beyond the stadium, the rise of Brazilian football was propelled by four interacting factors. First, the nation's economic dynamism produced concentrated centres of wealth and organization alongside a production line of football talent from poor areas. Second, the partial settlement of issues of nation, class and race achieved under Vargas meant that a huge pool of poverty-stricken talent including Afro-Brazilians, mestizos and Indians came streaming into the professional game. To this was added the third ingredient: the creation of an urban civil society that really knew how to play. Nelson Rodriguez, social football and the creative leisure of the Rio beaches are three indicators of a much wider phenomenon that in this era embraced an explosion of popular dance music – most notably bossa nova – and the first experimentation on radio and then TV with the hysterical dynastic sagas and revenger's tragedies that would become the telenovella. However, serious play requires serious money and serious organization. In 1958, Brazil at last had all of these.

The bulk of the money that underwrote the 1958 World Cup campaign came directly from President Kubitschek and was supplemented by a training and earning tour of Italy en route to Sweden. The organization was provided by João Havelange, one of Brazil's growing band of indigenous tycoons, who had just won the presidency of the Confederacão Brasileira de Futebol (CBF). As an indicator of his political prowess to come Havelange won the election by 185 votes to 19. His opponent was Carlito Rocha, president of Botafogo and a man at the far extreme of the football-management-as-voodoo school of thought. Havelange, by contrast, was a supreme rationalist, a sharp politician and a legendary networker. Alongside him, representing São Paulo's interests, was a man of similar caste: Paulo Machado de Carvalho, patron of São Paulo FC and owner of much of the city's electronic media including TV Record and Radio Panamericana. The two assembled a technical commission of experts. The notional head and the man in charge of the team itself was the corpulent Vincente Feola. Feola, who had won the Paulista in 1957 with São Paulo, imbibed the ideas of Hungarian coach Béla Guttmann who worked in the city at the time and was the vital connection in the transfer of Hungary's tactical and positional innovations to Latin America. Alongside Feola, relieving him of all other responsibilities, was a doctor, a trainer, a psychologist, a dentist, a treasurer, and an all-purpose organizer, Carlos Nascimento. Finally, Ernesto Santos was engaged as a full-time spy lurking around their opponents' training camps.

Only a few players from the 1954 squad were called up including Djalma Santos, Nílton Santos and Didi. For the most part the players were the youthful elite of the new generation of football players who came of age in the boom like Joel, Zito, Pepe and Vavá; and included, on the fringes, the mercurial Botafogo winger Garrincha and the teenage sensation at Santos, Pelé. The squad underwent intensive medical checks in Rio's leading hospitals which revealed an extraordinary catalogue of disease, neglect and long-term malnutrition. Almost the entire squad had intestinal parasites, some had syphilis, others were anaemic. Over 300 teeth were extracted from the mouths of players who had never been to a dentist, and but for this episode might never have gone. Epidemiologically, Brazil '58 were a team of the people.

In Brazil the players were cloistered in carefully prepared and remote *concentrações* in the Minas Gerais countryside. The technical commission visited over twenty-five locations in Sweden before settling on an itinerary that was planned to the hour for every single day between the assembly of the squad on 7 April and 29 June, the day after the final. Unlike any team that had been assembled in Brazil before, the management established a microscopic level of surveillance and control over each player's diet, movements, family life and sexual activity. Players were issued with and required to remember a fabulous list of dos and don'ts including what could be worn and when, and who could be spoken to and about what. Nascimento went so far as to insist that the Swedish hotel housing the squad replace its twenty-five female staff with men. However, the technical commission were unable to close the nudist camp nearby.

Once in Sweden the Brazilians opened slightly stiffly in their easy win against Austria and a goalless draw with England. The decisive game of the first round was against the Soviet Union. In keeping with the Cold War paranoia of the time and stoked by the contemporary successes of the USSR's Sputnik space missions, the Brazilians cast the Soviets as exemplars of rational scientific football hardened by the disciplines of industrial gigantism and planning. The rationalists in the Brazilian camp were still arguing against playing Pelé and Garrincha. Psychologist Carvalhaes had deemed Pelé 'obviously infantile. He lacks the necessary fighting spirit . . . he does not possess the sense of responsibility necessary for a team game'.[3] Garrincha's IQ scores were off the low-end of the scale and, according to Carvalhaes, he should not be playing in high-pressure games. But then this was a man whose main experience as a psychologist was testing the suitability of applicants to be drivers with the São Paulo municipal bus company and whose psychological models were deeply enmeshed in the still-present racist assumptions of white Brazil. Reports vary as to whether the technical commission or the players insisted upon their inclusion but both Pelé and Garrincha played. Brazil, still orchestrated by the loping, majestic Didi, found their team. In the first few minutes of the game the Brazilians opened up and played exquisitely. Pelé hit the bar, Garrincha offered a mesmerizing dribble and Vavá scored. The same confidence and verve was brought to the quarter-final against Wales and a wild, high-scoring semi-final against France that ended 5–2 to Brazil, including Pelé's second-half hat-trick.

29 June 1958
Brazil 5 Sweden 2
Råsunda Stadion, Stockholm

They showed football as a different conception; they killed the white skidding ball as if it were a lump of cotton wool . . . Didi, floating about mysteriously in midfield, was always the master link, the dynamo setting his attack in motion; and besides Didi with Vavá and Pelé a piercing double central thrust, they had one man above all the others, to turn pumpkins into coaches and mice into men – Garrincha.

From 1–0 down after four minutes, Brazil are now 4–1 up, and inscribing the field with intricate patterns of interplay, so vivid and clear that every contrast, every difference appears sharp and vivid. Surely the gap between these teams, these peoples, is unbridgeable?

The Swedes are tall, angular, pale, homogenous and blond. The Brazilians are just mixed up – but on the whole shorter, rounder, darker, blacker. Physiognomy is the least of it. The cold boreal north meets the warm lush tropics; Protestants, and strict Lutherans at that, facing fallen Latino Catholics. The new world and the old world, advanced and late industrializers, consensual democracy and febrile populism. Sweden in yellow, Brazil in blue and football in another register.

In Brazil, around the radio, they are cheering anything and everything, even Sweden's second goal is met with delight. In the final minutes of the game, it is no longer clear who the Swedish crowd are supporting. They chant for the home team when they win occasional possession. But, when Garrincha dances over and around the ball, without touching it, leaving two Swedish defenders transfixed on the spot, they cheer. When a Brazilian is down injured and the Swedes play on, they begin to hiss; when a Swedish winger takes the ball to the goal line and slips over as he attempts to cross, they laugh.

A long ball from inside the Brazil half sails through the air towards Pelé. He catches it on his chest and as the ball is dropping to the ground steps over it, effortlessly executing a backheel pass. The cries of joy are palpable and still rising in a crescendo as the return ball comes back into the penalty area and Pelé, diving away from its trajectory, flicks the ball with the side of his head and inside the post. As the celebrations begin he lies still on the ground and his team rush to revive him; his body appears heavy, inert, unconscious. The whistle goes and they haul the boy to his feet: tears, rapture, dizziness, and stumbling embraces.

The Brazilians take their lap of honour carrying a large Swedish flag. The straight-backed Swedish king abandons protocol and descends to the pitch, lost in the mêlée of bodies and hugging and weeping.

By brilliant planning or miraculous coincidence the inauguration of Brasília took place the next day. The team were fêted at ever greater levels on each stage of their journey home. In London, Paris, Lisbon and Recife there were cocktails, receptions, plaudits and crowds. Finally they landed in Rio and were piled on to a municipal fire engine that slowly wound its way from the airport to the vast multi-laned Avenida Brasil heading for the presidential palace.

The bulk of this side went to Chile four years later for the next World Cup. The Chilean football federation's president Carlos Dittborn had plaintively pulled at FIFA's heartstrings when the bid was made: 'You must give us the World Cup, for we have nothing else.' Not quite nothing, but compared to Sweden or even Switzerland it was a small show. Half the matches were played in the truly minuscule provincial cities of Arica and Rancagua, while only 5,000 people in Viña del Mar could bring themselves to watch a World Cup semi-final between the Czechs and the Yugoslavs. Brazil approached the tournament with no less rigour than in 1958. Despite being drawn to play at sea level at Viña del Mar, the squad were still packed off to the mountains for high-altitude training. The local government-licensed brothels received a medical inspection from the Brazilian technical commission. Once again Brazil's opening performances were solid without being spectacular, the team perhaps labouring under the pressure of being favourites, then Pelé's injury in their game against Czechoslovakia put him out of the tournament. In the quarter-final against England Brazil stepped up a gear with a bravura display from Garrincha who was allowed to play a free role across the Brazilian attack. Drifting from the wing to the centre of the field he scored two goals and gifted a third to Vavá who drove home the rebound from his shot.

In the semi-final Garrincha was again the chief architect of Brazil's 4–2 victory over the host nation despite the endless attentions of Chilean defender Eladio Rojas. After kicking the Brazilian for 85 minutes, even poking him in the eye, Rojas eventually got him to snap. Garrincha kneed his tormentor from behind and Rojas threw himself to the ground. Garrincha was sent off and with that was out of the final. The Brazilian political and diplomatic machine went into overdrive. A Brazilian member of the FIFA board persuaded the linesman, crucial to any hearing of the case, to leave for Montevideo. The Peruvian President got his ambassador in Chile to speak to the Peruvian referee on the matter and Brazil's own Prime Minister Tancredo Neves was implored to intervene at the highest level. The referee revoked his decision and Garrincha played in the final against Czechoslovakia. Despite going 1–0 down to the skilful Czechs Brazil never looked concerned and three goals later they were champions again. In the final minutes of the game Garrincha was seen repeatedly standing with his foot poised atop the ball daring the Czechs to take it off him. Brazil's control of this game, of the ball, of football, was unhurried and unassailable.

While in the late 1950s and 1960s Brazilian football was graced with abundant and diverse talents, two players rise above the rest: Pelé and Garrincha. Their parallel biographies and careers stand as testament to both the brilliance and the brutality of the game in Brazil. Both arrived in the world poor, black, provincial and with their given name. Garrincha was born Manuel Francisco dos Santos of mestizo Indian-European family in the small industrial town of Pau Grande beyond the edge of the Rio periphery. As a baby it was clear that his left leg curved outwards and his right leg curved inwards, a condition that never altered but seemed to make no difference to his movements – indeed, it may have made his dribbling even more unpredictable and elusive. From an early age his footballing talents were obvious. Like the entire town Garrincha began his working life at the Pau Grande textile factory, but was quickly placed in the company football team and allowed to slack off. He may well have remained there, had not some of his friends forcibly dragged the teenager to trials with Rio's professional clubs – even then he turned up to some trials late, some without boots, others he abandoned, seemingly unconcerned about the outcome. In a trial at Botafogo Garrincha was put up against the commanding left-back Nílton Santos. Garrincha destroyed him and was immediately signed. He stayed at Botafogo for the vast majority of his career and all of his best years.

Garrincha was carefree, socially unambitious, ignorant and sheltered to the point of other-worldliness in the company of his social superiors. His approach to playing football was equally uninformed and unstructured. He played primarily as a winger and could both beat his man and cross the ball with some alacrity. But such a rigid division of labour and narrow range of tasks were impossible to impose on Garrincha. He drifted inside, played in midfield at will and scored goals in the box. He never knew who was marking him or even who the opposition were, before or after the game. He found it impossible to listen to, let alone absorb, tactical talks at Botafogo. He was allowed to play table tennis while the rest of the side sat around the chalkboard. Yet it was for Garrincha that the olé chant of the bullring and the toreador was transferred to football, the Rio crowd crying out with every feint and swerve that Garrincha inflicted on a hapless Argentine defender, Vairo. If he had a trademark it was this – the capacity to find every way to pass his opponent with the ball. Sometimes he enjoyed it so much he would, on beating his man, turn back and do it all over again.

Pelé, then Edson Arantes do Nascimento, was born in 1940 in the tiny town of Três Corações deep in the back country of Minas Gerais. His father had played semi-professionally in his youth and offered Edson a basic level of coaching and encouragement. The family moved with work to the city of Bauru where the young Edson played in his first team – 7 September – without boots in innumerable slum *peladas*. His precocity was noted by the local side AC Bauru and their coach Waldemar de Brito, a veteran of the 1938 Brazil World Cup team. Edson, now called Pelé, though the origins and meaning of the nickname have been lost, was in the adult team at fifteen. Brito took Pelé to São Paulo to show him off to the big clubs. Pelé signed for Santos at sixteen, scored a goal in his opening match as a substitute and embarked on an unbelievable run of over 1,200 games for the club in the next seventeen years. Santos was a club on the rise, based in the run-down port city of São Paulo state; it hadn't won the city championship since 1935. Now, serving as the gateway between São Paulo's growing industrial might and the oceans, the city began to boom and its team began to win, taking their first Paulista in twenty years in 1955. The following year Pelé was added to a squad that included Gilmar, Mauro, Pepe, Zito and Pagão.

But it was Pelé that stood out. Lula, Pelé's coach at Santos, argued for his uniqueness in this way:

Pelé can no longer be compared to anyone else because he possesses all the qualities of the ideal football player. He is fast on the ground and in the air, he has the physique, the kick, the ball control, the ability to dictate play, a feeling for the manoeuvre, he is unselfish, good-natured and modest. I think he is the only forward in the world who always aims the ball at the precise point in the opposition's net at the moment of shooting a goal.[4]

To their domestic triumphs Santos added international victories, winning the Copa Libertadores in 1962 after their epic three-match marathon against Peñarol and then seeing off Boca Juniors in 1963. After their triumph against Peñarol in 1962, Santos went on to measure themselves against European champions Benfica in the Intercontinental Club Cup. Having won the first leg 3–2 with two goals from Pelé, Santos pulled off a stunning 5–2 victory in Lisbon. Pelé scored an astounding hat-trick and the government declared a national holiday.

Although football offers specialist tasks and positions to many body sizes and types of players and calls on a great diversity of skills and abilities – fitness, suppleness, balance, visual acuity, tactile sensitivity and tactical awareness – Pelé's rarity and brilliance rested on possessing so many of them so abundantly. His touch with his thighs and chest was particularly amazing. Pelé seemed able to stun and drop a ball of any height or angle down on to his toes and the close-hit toe punts that often followed were immaculate. His capacity to stop and turn and shield the ball, all at once, sent him past defences though his sheer pace and physical presence could do the same. Statistically, his longevity and endurance were incredible. Often playing more than 100 games a year on three or four continents, and increasingly harshly marked, Pelé managed to play over 1,300 games between 1956 and 1977. He scored at a rate that was no less incredible, over 1,200 goals – a rate of almost one goal a game. This of course tells us nothing about all the goals he made.

The different arcs of Pelé and Garrincha's lives were illuminated by the manner of their return from Sweden. Pelé was met by a civic gathering and given a small three-wheeled car then manufactured in São Paulo. Unable to drive the car, and unwilling to break the law by taking the wheel, Pelé barely touched it and went training. Garrincha silently slipped away from Rio and returned unnoticed to Pau Grande where he spent the days running up and settling a town-sized bar bill and playing kickabout with his old friends. Over the next decade Pelé lived a model professional life; Garrincha drank and ate like the most dissolute factory worker. While Pelé, even through his teenage shyness, was a talker there is barely an interview of any substance with Garrincha. Pelé, ambitious, knew the value of his talent and though he lost what he had on a number of occasions to unscrupulous business partners, he managed to extract and keep some of the value. Garrincha had a pathological lack of ambition, he neither knew nor cared how much he had made or where it might be going. Pelé planned for the future. Garrincha lived for the moment. Pelé trained. Garrincha slept. In their later years both players acquired another nickname – an essential suffix. Pelé was *O Rei* – 'the King', honoured, but ultimately distant, of another world. Garrincha was *O alegria de povo* – 'the joy of the people', of this imperfect world, disabled, drunk, fragile and ultimately broken. The King was and is revered but Garrincha was loved.

The Brazil of the late Vargas and the Kubitschek regimes which had nurtured these talents was coming to a close. In 1960 the unpredictable, maverick but electorally electric Jânio Quadros, Governor of São Paulo, was elected President on a right-wing anti-corruption, anti-inflation platform. After just seven months his nerve appeared to buckle or a wild bluff was called for he suddenly offered his resignation to the Brazilian Congress which accepted it. His replacement was the vice-president João Goulart, previously the ultra-populist Minister of Labour in the last Vargas cabinet. The army and industrialists, already feeling uneasy as government policy at home and abroad was moving dangerously to the left, looked on askance. Without the balm of economic growth in 1962 and 1963 Goulart attempted to rule with a coalition of unions, Catholic radicals and urban bohemians all of whom disturbed the forces of conservatism but did not panic them. But when the government began to encourage rural unionization, they panicked. The military, with the tacit support of the US government, finally struck in early 1964 and Goulart fled to Uruguay. The new government under General Castelo Branco set about purging the state and society of communist influences, suppressed trade unions, and eventually banned political parties, dissolved Congress and enacted major controls over the press and the economy. Football was not on their agenda other than as a source of unpaid taxes. Through 1964 and 1965 a newly empowered internal revenue service pursued Didi, Mário Zagallo and Nílton Santos for a mass of unpaid dues. Garrincha, whose finances were as chaotic as the rest of his life, had absolutely nothing with which to pay a decade of accumulated tax demands and only escaped the courts when João Havelange, worried that he would not be able to go to the 1966 World Cup, picked up the tab.

It made no difference: Brazil went to the 1966 World Cup looking for their third consecutive title but were cut down to size. Most of the leading players from 1958 – Gilmar, Djalma Santos, Bellini, Orlando, Zito, Garrincha and Pelé – were still there, and if they could stand they got a game. In the opening match it looked like the old formula would be enough; free kicks from Pelé and Garrincha made it 2–0 against Bulgaria. Then the Hungarians beat them 3–1 and Portugal did so too. In all these games Pelé had been repeatedly and harshly fouled especially by Bulgaria's Zhechev and Portugal's Morais. Brazil went home. Santos too were on the slide: there were no more Libertadores triumphs. The Paulistas kept coming but less frequently, and in 1973 only with the aid of a dim-witted referee who declared them champions in a penalty shoot-out with Portuguesa, despite there being two penalties per side still left to take. (The ruling body later declared both clubs joint champions.) Santos were also saddled with Pelé's fabulously expensive contract, not to mention the wage inflation raging through the rest of the squad. The club's directors increasingly relied on foreign tours to make the sums add up. In 1967 alone Santos played in Argentina, Chile, Colombia, Uruguay, Peru, Brazil, Gabon, Zaire, Côte d'Ivoire, Germany and Italy. The following year they took in Europe, the United States and Mexico as well as their usual South American jaunt. When in late 1970 the board realized that Pelé's contract was up at the end of 1972 and that he did not wish to stay they upped the pace of touring to grab a final pay day; 1971 took Santos to Hong Kong, Bolivia, El Salvador, Martinique, Guadeloupe, Jamaica, Colombia and Haiti. The sums were all the harder to compute after board members and their friends had taken their expenses; then the club indulged in property development and speculation, building a fantastic new clubhouse, the Parque Balenario, while the whitewashed Vila Belmiro stadium began its long and still unfinished decline. A fantastical casino development ate up cash but never materialized.

Brazilian football, always a volatile affair, appeared to be spiralling out of control. From the mid-1960s throughout the early 1970s the Rio championship saw more and more players sent off for violent conduct every year. In the decisive game of the 1964 Rio–São Paulo tournament Botafogo played Santos. A fight started that quickly spread. Three players, including the normally mild mannered and unflappable Pelé, were sent off simultaneously. Nine Flamengo players walked together when, at 3–0 down to tiny Bangu in the final of the 1966 Rio state championship, they exploded around the referee in a frenzy of anger and pushing. The following year saw twenty-one dismissed simultaneously in a game between Vasco and Fluminense. Finally in 1968 the full twenty-two were sent from the field in a vicious Olaria versus América game.

Brazil had become an increasingly violent country. Small guerrilla movements, some no more than a few dedicated cells, continued to harass the regime from their hidden urban enclaves and secret rural bases. Students at the country's universities had been a particular target of repression for the military regime. In 1964 they had inaugurated their rule by cracking down on the campuses, arresting, torturing and killing key activists and attempting to close student politics down altogether. Initially driven underground, militant students regrouped and in 1968, acting on accumulated local grievances and the widespread disgust with General Castelo Branco's authoritarian rule, they triggered the country's biggest student protests. On the one hand they attracted support from workers and unions who began a massive wave of strikes, on the other they invited another wave of violence from the state. The remaining guerrilla movements also sprang into action, conducting a series of audacious kidnappings and executions of prominent supporters of the regime. Through 1969 and early 1970 the Brazilian military was thrown on the defensive, forced to use the most extreme measures – such as huge dragnet operations pulling in thousands of suspects at a time and barbaric forms of torture – to defend its authority. That year Brazil were 2–1 down to Peru in the Maracanã with minutes to go when Brazil's midfielder Tostão brutally kicked the Peruvian De la Torre. The ensuing fight lasted forty minutes and required a huge police presence on the pitch; finally João Havelange was forced to plead with the Peruvians to finish the game.

As the 1960s came to a close and the 1970 World Cup loomed, the paths of Garrincha and Pelé, already a long way apart, decisively

separated. The 1966 World Cup had been the last international outing
for Garrincha. He had already played his last game for Botafogo though
neither he nor his public knew it at the time. Sold on to Corinthians for
a few games late in the year, his passing went unmarked. Garrincha's
body and emotional balance had been shattered beyond repair by his
personal and professional life. His knees, which had sustained unbelievable levels of torsion and twist, were the first to go. As early as 1963 he
was spending time in splints, getting high on painkillers and having fluid
drained from his knee joints after every match. An operation was an
immediate necessity but both Garrincha and Botafogo preferred to keep
putting off the inevitable. When he finally did have surgery it was too
late: his knees and his game were never really the same again. Worse,
after experiencing a car crash in which his mother-in-law died, Garrincha
descended into deep depression, exacerbating his already hardcore cach-
aca (sugarcane liquor) drinking. What little energy, form, time-keeping
and appetite for training that remained disintegrated altogether. Brazil
moved on and Garrincha, without any savings and almost entirely
dependent on his wife, drank himself into a decade-long stupor, relieved
only by his death in 1983.

Pelé, by contrast, was going into orbit. Almost alone among his
generation of Brazilian players he had an agent and a manager. Although
he would lose a great deal of money on some of the deals struck, he was
making enough to move in an entirely different social stratum from any
Brazilian player hitherto. He had been declared a national treasure,
trademarked his own nickname, signed up with Pepsi Cola, been incorporated into a popular telenovella and acquired his own radio shows.

In the final weeks and games of 1969 Pele approached his one thousandth goal. The press had seen the milestone coming at about goal 990
in late October. Expectation built as the goals slowly came. At goal 998
in Bahia unmanageable numbers of foreign and domestic journalists and
photographers clustered behind the goalmouth in a writhing mass of
flashlights and lenses, but they only glimpsed his shot ricocheting off the
bar. Back in Rio, Vasco's goalkeeper Andrada was hysterically booed
for saving a shot from Pelé before finally, from the penalty spot, the one
thousandth goal was scored. In a schmaltzfest of tears and declarations,
Pelé dedicated the goal to the children of Brazil. A Brazilian senator
composed a poem in his honour and read it from the floor of Congress.
The following day's newspapers, which in every other country on the

planet covered nothing but the second Apollo moon landing, were split down the middle in Brazil. Apollo 12 on one side, Pelé on the other.

IV

So spoke Alberto J. Armado, president of Boca Juniors, dedicating the team's 1954 championship victory to President Perón. It was the year in which Argentine football recorded its highest attendances. The working classes that packed the stands of Buenos Aires and Rosario in such numbers were at the peak of their collective powers. Perón's government was drifting closer and closer to the trade unions, wages were rising at unfeasible rates and the streets were becoming more bold and raucous. The previous year a Peronista mob had burnt the Buenos Aires Jockey Club – the centre of the Argentine aristocracy's social scene – to the ground. In the year that Boca won the title, Perón and his most radical acolytes had taken on the power of the Catholic Church. Divorce had been legalized, church schools taken into state control and in the ensuing conflicts, cathedrals had been set alight. The Pope excommunicated the whole cabinet, but no one blinked an eye. The sense of power and invulnerability of the moment was sufficient to tempt the cautious Peronista football establishment into risking a series of international matches. They were rewarded as Argentina went to Ireland, Spain and Portugal and won. They were beaten, but only just, on a trip to England in 1951 where they played a game as part of the Festival of Britain; the return game in Buenos Aires in 1953 was eagerly anticipated. In fact there were two games. In the first the English fielded their reserves and recorded the game as an English FA XI playing, but Argentina played their full-strength side and treated the game as the real thing. Argentina won 3–1 and in the delirious atmosphere of triumph and celebration that followed, Perón declared that 14 May, the day of the game, would henceforth be an annual holiday – 'Footballers' day'. England's first team turned out a few days later for the second game only for it to be abandoned as the pitch was flooded. Such sleights of hand can generate a false sense of security. By late 1954 Perón's attack on the Church and the soaring rate of inflation had sufficiently alienated the conservative core of the officer class and leading industrialists that a coup was planned. The generals sent their ultimatum to Perón in mid-1955: resign or face a bloodbath. Perón had no stomach for the fight; unlike Evita he had never been able to contemplate arming the unions in such a situation. He fled to Paraguay and a long exile.

Under General Lonardi and then the more conservative General Aramburu Argentina entered a period of transitional military dictatorship. The Peronista Party was banned and a de-Peronization of sporting institutions and sports policy was initiated. Along with a certain amount of musical chairs at the top of the game's bureaucracy, one clear sign of the demise of Peronism was Argentina's unambiguous return to international football competitions beginning with a victory in the 1955 Copa América in Santiago. In 1957 Argentina went to the Copa América in Lima and dazzled. They put eight goals past Colombia and beat Chile, Uruguay and Brazil by six, four and three respectively. The team's young forward line of Maschio, Angelillo, Sívori – known as *Los ángeles con cara sucia* – 'The angels with dirty faces' – suggested that Argentina's capacity to nurture talent was undimmed. The Italian scouts who made the journey to Peru were convinced. Within a year all three had gone, to Bologna, Internazionale and Juventus respectively, and all three would play for the Italian national team. Argentina's subordinate and exposed position in the international football economy was, despite the autarchic pretensions of Peronism, unaltered. Consequently Argentina went to the 1958 World Cup – its first since 1934 – without its leading players. Indeed so desperate was the search for forwards that Angelo Labruna, the last of *La Máquina*, still playing at nearly forty, was drafted in.

It was a national calamity. In the opening game against the defending champions West Germany, Argentina scored after two minutes, but the stamina and organization of the Germans systematically ground down the Argentinians. It finished 3–1. Though they got an early goal, the Northern Irish offered less stern opposition and left enough space on the pitch for Argentina to assert their superiority and run out 3–1 winners. Argentina could still go through to the quarter-finals if they beat the Czechs. They met in Hälsingborg. Slow and clearly unable to keep pace with the Europeans, Argentina were not ground down, they were overwhelmed and conceded six goals. The team were pelted with rubbish on their return to Buenos Aires and the guts of the disastrous defeat by Czechoslovakia were laid out, dissected and divined for their meaning. The almost universal conclusion of the political press and the football world was that Hälsingborg was a failure of Peronista modernization. The Aramburu military government prepared to hand power back to the civilian political parties in late 1958 hoping that the short interlude of authoritarian rule had broken the back of Peronism, working-class power, trade-union militancy and inflation.

The Argentina that emerged from this brief interlude of de-Peronization was divided. In the 1958 general election the Peronista vote abstained or spoilt its ballot papers, the Socialists split in two, the Conservatives into three and the centre-ground Radicals in half. Arturo Frondizi of the Unión Cívica Radical became President with the most precarious of mandates. But there was a vast deception at the heart of the Argentine polity. Perón, supposedly exorcized by the Aramburu interlude and the subsequent defenestration of Peronista power in state and parastatal organizations, retained a spectral presence. The trade-union movement became a surrogate Peronista party, contesting elections openly as *Organizaciones 62*. The military, supposedly withdrawn from politics, increasingly acted as an armed and politicized police force, implacably opposed to the return of Perón himself and the reformation of the popular coalition that had sustained him. Frondizi, deemed ineffective and too close to the trade unions, was deposed by the army in 1962 and replaced the following year by Arturo Illia. Like his predecessor, Illia attempted to tread a narrow path between the simulacrum of Peronism on the Left and the increasingly disgruntled coalition of industrialists and generals on the Right. The path would shrink to nothing in 1966, but in the decade after Perón just enough middle ground was made available by continued economic growth. Argentinian football of the era was shaped by both the social consequences of this short-lived boom and its high politics of mirrors and duplicity.

Economic growth, which had always been unevenly distributed in Argentina, was once again focused on Buenos Aires. Under Perón it had become a more openly working-class city. The material legacy of his era were the giant multi-tower public hospitals and housing complexes that sprang up in the city's backyard and the vast subsidized stadiums of the inner *barrios*. The intangible legacy of Peronism in the city's memory was made from the tumultuous occupations of the main city squares and avenues by his supporters in innumerable rallies, and by the ingrained cultural significance and popularity of football. With the fall and then exile of Perón the economic good fortunes and cultural presence of the working class in Buenos Aires diminished. In its place a new urban middle class arose – many working in the emerging service and cultural sectors of the economy – whose newfound buying power and changing patterns of consumption set the cultural tone for the city in the early 1960s. The most discernible shift in the habits of *porteños* was the relocation of free time from the streets to the living room, as middle-class Argentina, like everywhere else, began to choose the TV over the cinema; and from the mid-1960s when football was first broadcast live, the armchair over the bleachers.

In the early 1960s the average crowd in the Argentine first division had dropped by 40 per cent from its Peronista peak in 1954 and state aid was decidedly thin on the ground. In the aftermath of Hälsingborg and Aramburu, Argentine football and Argentine business lost their state subsidies and were more fully exposed to global competition. Boca Juniors and River Plate in particular decided to respond to the new competition for people's time and money by upping the ante and offering football more explicitly as a spectacular, supported by a chorus of hype from the popular press. Presidents Alberto J. Armando at Boca and Antonio Vespucci at River started buying foreign exotica to draw the crowds – Uruguayans, Peruvians and Brazilians. But for all the promise of flamboyance their teams and coaches learned zonal marking and flat back fours.

This was the dominant key in which Argentine football modernized: a new emphasis on defence and organization and a new language of professionalism and discipline. It was a mood that found its highest expression in Helenio Herrera, the itinerant Argentine coach who perfected *catenaccio* defence (that is, four man-markers and a sweeper) and spring-loaded counterattack at Internazionale in Milan. In Argentina Manuel Giúdice, coach at Independiente in the early 1960s, had his teams play much the same and with considerable success. Independiente won the league twice in 1960 and 1963 before going on to win two Copa Libertadores, but they were more than a Latino Inter. They took to the field in formation, signalling a V to the crowd with their arms, they played on the mystique of the alcohol massages evaporating through their shirts and their confidence was unshakeable; they won their first

Libertadores by deposing the champions Santos, coming back from 2–0 down in the Maracanã to win 3–2. Argentina's new defensive football was given a muscular twist by Juan Carlos Lorenzo who coached the national team at the World Cup finals in Chile and England. In 1962 the new Argentina were certainly a fitter and more coordinated unit than in 1958 but they still played with an old-style centre-half and were beaten soundly by England before being knocked out of the first stage. The team that went to England in 1966 were better, tough and organized, increasingly adapted to modern tactics, but with plenty of traditional short passing too. Argentina drew with the fancied West Germans and beat the Swiss and the Spanish. Then in the defining game of the era for Argentina's national team they met England in the quarter-finals.

At home the progress of the team was briefly interrupted by the last gasp of Argentina's puny democracy. President Arturo Illia was deposed in a neat coup by General Juan Carlos Onganía. Congress was shut down, the universities were suppressed and the regime planned the further restriction of the trade-union movement The nation, unruffled, sat back to watch the quarter-finals. Across Latin America the tournament had already attracted some suspicion. The harsh and unpunished fouling of Pelé, the early exit of the Brazilians and a perception of refereeing bias by Europeans against Latin Americans all suggested an unspoken plot to defeat Argentina. The game was predictably bad-tempered and foul-ridden, made worse, as Brian Glanville described it, by the German referee Herr Kreitlein, who '. . . ran hither and thither, an exacerbating rather than calming influence, inscribing names in his notebook with the zeal of a schoolboy collecting engine numbers'.[6] Argentina's captain, Antonio Rattín, who had already been booked for what in the scheme of things was an innocuous foul on Bobby Charlton, was also making his considerable lanky presence felt every time Herr Kreitlein made a decision. When he objected to another booking Kreitlein snapped and sent him off.

In the immediate aftermath of the game England manager Alf Ramsey said, 'Our best football will come against the right type of opposition – a team who come to play football, and not act as animals.'[7] This comment stoked the already mile-high pyre of righteous indignation and wounded pride burning on the Río de la Plata. The team returned home to Buenos Aires to a presidential reception and the glow of moral victors. In a political system where no government, civil or military, could be sure of its tenure in office, where plot and counter-plot were increasingly becoming the normal instruments of political life, paranoia was the new common sense and foreign conspiracies were to be expected. The normally more restrained *Crónica* responded with the headline, 'First they steal the Malvinas from us, now they steal the World Cup'.[8] The newspaper would even dispatch a small plane to land on an outlying rock of the island group and plant an Argentine flag.

Onganía appointed his own man, Valentín Suárez, as head of the Argentine FA. Suárez began his term of office by announcing, 'The government never closed its doors on football clubs and never will close its doors on football clubs.' What this meant in practice was that a certain amount of money was made available to cancel historical debts, especially unpaid taxes, in return for instituting a reformed national championship. The single league, dominated by Buenos Aires teams for thirty years, was to be opened up. In the new dispensation two shorter leagues would be played – the Nacional and the Metropolitano – with more access for the small city teams from Córdoba, Santa Fe and Tucumán. If breaking the old monopoly was the intention, it certainly worked; over the next decade titles went outside of Buenos Aires to Rosario Central and Newell's Old Boys, and to small teams in the capital like Huracán, Vélez Sarsfield and Chacarita Juniors. The small team that rose highest was Estudiantes de La Plata who won the 1967 Metropolitano before going on to contest four and win three Copa Libertadores finals in a row. Estudiantes rose that high because they were the evolutionary end-point of the defensive, muscular hyper-professionalism that had been developing in Argentine football. Estudiantes played *anti-fútbol*.

Estudiantes were not a chance mutation. In fact they were the leading edge of the main lines of football development in Argentina, an interpretation confirmed by the prelude to their rise, the 1967 Intercontinental Club Cup played between Racing Club and Glasgow Celtic. The first leg had been played in Scotland and, true to form, Celtic had attacked and won 1–0, Racing wasted time and there was a lot of rough play. The return match was, despite the Irish republican affiliations of the opposition, treated as a rerun of the 1966 World Cup quarter-final – Irish, Scottish, English were considered synonymous. A crowd of over 80,000 emitted a wall of shrill whistles and explosions as Celtic walked out in Avellaneda. The Scots were not allowed a ball to warm up with and the Celtic goalkeeper Simpson was struck by a stone from the crowd and replaced by a substitute. The assailant went unidentified. Celtic played it straight, flooded forward and could have had three early penalties but for the hesitations of the clearly cowed Uruguayan referee. Finally a penalty did come their way and Celtic went 1–0 up only for Raffo to equalize for Racing from what was, according to most of the Argentine press, a clearly offside position. Racing lost no opportunity to garner an advantage: at half-time there was no water in the Celtic dressing room. Then a few minutes into the second half they snatched a lead and closed the game down with a repertoire of trickery and rule-bending. Many minutes ticked away when the crowd took the ball and refused to return it. The ends more than justified the means.

At one game all, a decider was scheduled for the Centenario in Montevideo. Celtic, despite some doubts within the camp, accepted the fixture asking only for security guarantees and a new referee. Twenty thousand Argentines crossed the Río de la Plata to see another game in which the referee completely lost control. This time Celtic were fighting back and trading elbows, but Racing were more subtle in their brutality, more artful with their spite. Celtic lost three players; Racing lost two and then, in the midst of the mêlée, filched a single goal. When it was over the Argentines ran a lap of honour and were showered by objects thrown from the Uruguayan sections of the crowd. The Racing players and officials hid in their dressing rooms as angry Montevideans massed outside, only dispersed by repeated police baton charges. Celtic fined their players. Racing, it is reputed, bought theirs new cars.

While Racing were engaged in intercontinental warfare, Estudiantes, a small team from the polite beach resort of La Plata, were grinding out results. As the press reported they played:

A football that is elaborated over a hard week of laboratory work, and explodes on the seventh day with an effectiveness that consecrates the table of positions. Because Estudiantes continue to manufacture points just as it manufactures its football: with more work than talent . . . Estudiantes keep winning.[9]

Under coach Osvaldo Zubeldía, the team without stars and with the most spartan of training facilities won the Metropolitano in 1967. There was, even at this stage, a hint of something darker to their game, but it was surfacing only as a rumour to be suppressed. Critics rejected the label of *anti-fútbol*, preferring to think of Estudiantes as 'more solid than beautiful'. *El Gráfico*'s leading columnist, Juvenal, went as far as to suggest that they were 'young, strong, disciplined, vigorous, spiritual and physically upright people'.[10] Just the kind of role models that General Onganía and his colleagues wished Argentine youth to look up to.

Estudiantes won their first Copa Libertadores in 1968 after a bruising and plainly violent semi-final marathon against Racing, and a mixture of pugnaciousness and skill against Palmeiras in the final. Zubeldía's team were capable of playing it any number of ways but the core of their game was personified on the field and subsequently captured by the ferric Carlos Bilardo. Bilardo recalls Zubeldía's football as first and foremost one of technical and instrumental rationality: 'All the possibilities afforded by the game were foreseen and practised. The corners, the free-kicks, throw-ins were used to the best of advantage and we also had secret signs and language which we used to make our rivals fall into the trap.'[11] Such attention to detail reaped rewards as Estudiantes scored half of their goals in the Libertadores from set pieces and consistently broke up the attacks of more open and skilful teams. When they had to defend they played a tough man-marking system and kept their shape across the width of the pitch: a contemporary commonplace but a rare instance of discipline in Argentina.

Where tactical acumen was insufficient, Estudiantes had other methods. Midfielder Juan Ramón Verón described it: 'We tried to find out everything possible about our rivals individually, their habits, their characters, their weaknesses, and even about their private lives, so that we could goad them on the field, get them to react and risk being sent off.'[12] Nacional's Cococho Álvarez was watched before the 1969 Libertadores final and his penchant for contesting refereeing decisions by marching on the official was spotted. Estudiantes players would get between him and the referee, goading him into striking them. Álvarez was one of many Estudiantes victims who was out-thought and sent off. When play restarted Estudiantes were the masters of destruction. They knew how to play a foul rough enough to stop the game in its tracks, but just short of a booking. With a single back pass or shift of direction they would change the pace of a game, invariably slowing it down, drawing its sting. When the pace was still not slow enough they would just waste time.

As South American champions, Estudiantes travelled to England to play Manchester United in the second leg of the 1968 Intercontinental

Cup. They had already beaten United 1–0 in Argentina, in the presence of President Onganía. Estudiantes edged a match marked by endless tactical fouling and no little spitting. The return match was the first encounter between the two nations in England since the 1966 World Cup quarter-final and ended a 1–1 draw making Estudiantes world champions. In Argentina it was seen as ugly but necessary; sweet revenge on England and Sir Alf.

If national honour required Argentina to embrace both violence and the cynicism of *anti-fútbol* there were limits. The unspoken tolerance of much of middle-class Argentina for crudely instrumental projects was diminishing. Estudiantes' cynicism was becoming hard to justify, like Onganía's military regime which offered bureaucratic authoritarianism without stability or prosperity. When Estudiantes squeezed out a desperately narrow victory over Peñarol in the 1970 Libertadores final, mustering all their meanness and mischief, the press admitted that they could do no better than to grin and bear it.

The economic and political failures of the Onganía presidency were exposed and deepened at the end of 1969 when the intersecting and mutually supporting student and workers' groups of the rapidly industrializing city of Córdoba began a series of protests that within weeks were tantamount to an insurrection – *El Cordobazo*. The occupations, strikes and sit-downs were violently suppressed and when a similar but smaller uprising in Rosario followed it was given the same treatment. The army were still in power but at the cost of greater violence and greater resentment. Their minimalist defensive programme of economic retrenchment and trade-union suppression was being swamped by social forces and movements beyond their control. When in August 1969 Argentina were beaten by Peru, fatally undermining their chances of qualifying for the 1970 World Cup, Estudiantes and the style of play that they epitomized were made the scapegoats for this national disaster. Under a cloud of opprobrium they went to Milan to play the first leg of the Intercontinental Club Cup and lost 3–0.

----

22 October 1969
Estudiantes de La Plata 2 AC Milan 1
La Bombonera, Buenos Aires

Late May 1969, the provincial industrial city of Córdoba. A spontaneous popular protest erupts against the harsh economic austerity and political repressiveness of President Onganía's regime. Trade unions, students, the whole city, pour on to the streets, occupying the centre. The President orders in the army, including an armoured column. Left-wing radicals take to the rooftops and snipe at the soldiers. The army replies in kind and with more. By the time Córdoba has been occupied over sixty civilians are dead.

Late October, the federal capital, Buenos Aires. A night of increasingly desperate and wilful violence by Estudiantes. Aguirre Suárez elbows Milan's Combin in the face and breaks his cheekbone. Goalkeeper Poletti strikes Milan's Rivera. Manera kicks him to the ground. By the time Estudiantes have lost the tie, they are down to nine men.

President Onganía was horrified: 'Such shameful behaviour has compromised and sullied Argentina's international reputation and provoked the revulsion of a nation.' Poletti, Suárez and Manera are sent to prison for thirty days. Suárez and Manera are banned from football for a year, Poletti for life. The soldiers who killed civilians in the *Cordobazo* are getting medals.

El Gráfico, shocked by the match, cast Estudiantes as the enemy rather than a representative of the nation. 'Television took the deformed image of a match and transformed it into urban guerrilla warfare all over the world.'[13] The once physically upright, serious role models of the mid-1960s had degenerated into the most insidious youths of all – left-wing armed activists. Hidden in the texts of *El Gráfico* and the mainstream press is a metaphorical record of the deep social changes transforming Argentine youth. Old generational hierarchies, conservative forms of etiquette and cultural tastes had begun to dissolve the moment they encountered the egalitarian hedonism of the new pop cultures. But Argentina's youth, once psychically liberated, did not all follow a path of individualist bacchanalia and sartorial statement. Rallying to the cries of the Cuban revolution and the *Cordobazo*, implacably opposed to the authoritarianism of Argentina's government and military, they had formed the Montoneros guerrilla movement in 1970. Estudiantes won their last Copa Libertadores, the Montoneros kidnapped and executed General Aramburu and Argentina was heading for political meltdown.

With the protests and dissent of 1969 and early 1970 now quelled, the Brazilian military regime under a new President, General Médici, turned with renewed vigour to the problem of securing popular legitimacy. Football, but for issues of tax evasion, had not been a concern of the Castelo Branco presidency but Médici was an enthusiast, a rabid Flamengo supporter, and more alert to the kind of PR that might work in contemporary Brazil than his more culturally conservative predecessors. He certainly took an active interest in Brazil's progress towards the 1970 World Cup finals, quietly and not so quietly lobbying for the inclusion of Dario, a striker that he had effectively ordered to leave Atlético Mineiro for Flamengo. The object of his lobbying was João Saldanha, coach of the national team. Saldanha had coached Botafogo back in 1957 and won the Carioca that year, but he had spent the intervening years working as a football commentator and columnist. He was also a known communist in his youth from a wealthy but radical family. He remained a blunt and outspoken character, immensely popular with the public, but deeply suspect to the regime. Saldanha's football strategy was the very antithesis of the kind of regimentation and gruelling fitness regimes preferred by the military. Saldanha appeared to pick the players then let them get on with it. It was certainly a good enough plan for Brazil to get through the qualifying rounds with ease.

Yet for all that, it appears that Saldanha's refusal to play Dario and his curt dismissal of Médici – 'I don't choose the president's ministry and he can't choose my front line' – put him on probation. Saldanha had wintered in Europe and was dismayed at the physicality and brawn of the Continent's football; on his return he began to change his team to respond to these more defensive and physical challenges. When in this mode Brazil lost to Argentina at home and then drew away early in 1970, there were calls for Saldanha's removal. Matters were made worse by his public criticism of Pelé and his walking into a Rio hotel lobby with a loaded pistol looking for his arch critic Yustrich, the manager of Flamengo. The CBD removed him on grounds of emotional instability.

His replacement was Mário Zagallo, a veteran of the victorious 1958 World Cup side and as safe and as calm a pair of hands as could be found in Brazil. The military's presence was bolstered by the employment of Captain Cláudio Coutinho as fitness trainer and the addition of Admiral Jerônimo Bastos to the travelling party. Money was no object and Coutinho had been sent to NASA to learn the fitness regimes and techniques deployed by astronauts. The already legendary levels of preparation for World Cups reached a new high as handmade boots were made for every player from special casts; the team went on a Central American sleeping-and-eating schedule two weeks in advance of their departure; and the kit had been completely redesigned to deal better with the sweltering heat and humidity of Mexico.

The 1970 World Cup was the first to be broadcast in colour and that gives it, for those who saw it, a kind of chromatic magic. Brazil's yellow shirts shimmered and sparkled in the blistering white sunlight of the Mexican noon – the appointed time for kick-offs to suit European TV schedules. Yet those that saw them in black and white, the vast majority, were no less dazzled. At Mexico 1970 Brazil played six games and scored nineteen goals, an unambiguous record of adventure, attack and positive play. They had the decency to keep only one clean sheet, to go a goal behind against the Czechs and to concede two to the Romanians, showing us their mettle and giving their opposition just enough will to entertainingly resist. To this they added moments of sublime invention. In their opening game against Czechoslovakia, with the score at 1–1, Pelé stood just inside his own half, behind the centre circle, and realized that the Czech goalkeeper Viktor was 15 metres off his line. Without pausing for thought he struck a now much-imitated long, high curving ball. Even before it reaches the peak of its sinuous parabola it is clear that it is going somewhere very close to the top corner of the goal. Viktor is now doubling back; gripped by panic he knows it too. The ball just shaves the outside of the post. Brazil put seven past Czechoslovakia and Romania anyway.

If the Eastern Europeans allowed Brazil the space to show off, England offered a more compelling challenge. The defending champions playing at about their very best conceded but a single goal to the Brazilians. Better still it was a defence so tightly marshalled that it required a goal of extreme invention to break them: Tostão's dribble through the packed defence followed by Pelé's immaculate lay-off from the penalty spot to Jairzinho in the only empty space available.

Against Peru in the quarter-final, Brazil played a team that were a less developed version of themselves. As in Brazil, although twenty years later in the 1950s, professionalization had provided one of the few economic escape routes available to young black Peruvian men. Consequently, Peru were now looking demographically Brazilian with a significant group of Afro-Peruvian and mestizo players. They were coached by a Brazilian too, Didi, who like Zagalo was a star of the 1958 and 1962 World Cup-winning squads. Inevitably it was a feast of open play and goals, Brazil winning 4–2. Uruguay in the semi-finals offered the opportunity to exorcize any lingering ghosts from 1950.

---

17 June 1970
Brazil 3 Uruguay 1
Estadio Jalisco, Guadalajara

The eye is immediately drawn to and transfixed by a spot about two metres outside Uruguay's penalty area, empty but for shimmering grass. Three objects are precisely converging on it. Tostão's through ball which rolls at a steady middling pace; Uruguay's black-shirted goalkeeper Mazurkiewicz who after bursting off his line is decelerating in anticipation of a shot or a swerve or a save; and Pelé in glimmering yellow whose long steps and flashing white socks are actually lengthening and accelerating.

Ball, keeper and striker converge. Pelé must surely brake his charge or stop the ball. Your eye remains fixed on that same spot, the point of collision. All that is left is Mazurkiewicz stranded on one knee. It is only in your peripheral vision that you can see that the ball has rolled to his right and Pelé, who had given it the merest, almost feather-like touch, ploughs into his opponent, who is braced for impact. Without breaking stride Pelé cuts past him on his left. With a sharp turn behind the stricken keeper Pelé gathers the ball and shoots just past the left post, the flight of the ball crossing paths with the despairing Uruguayan defender haplessly tumbling across the goal line.

In the final Brazil faced Italy who held it to 1–1 for two-thirds of the game, their circuits hardwired it seemed for deep defence. Then in five minutes Gérson and Jairzinho scored, reflecting the real balance of play in the game. The final twenty minutes were Brazil's, their fourth goal a celebration, now an icon.

Clodoaldo ... began the attack with a dribble that was as brilliant as it was untypical ... he mesmerized five challengers and from the left-half position passed the ball to Jairzinho. Moving inside from the left wing Jairzinho sent it on to Pelé who was twenty yards out in front of goal. Yet again Jairzinho had drawn Facchetti far out of position and Carlos Alberto was coming through on an angled run with the intimidating directness of a torpedo. Pelé, seeing him come, turned unhurriedly and rolled the ball into his path with the relaxed precision of a lawn bowler. Without having to check, deviate or adjust his stride, Carlos Alberto smashed the ball with his right foot low into the side [of the] net ... It was an unforgettable goal and its seeming inevitability increased rather than diminished its excitement.[14]

The team made its well-worn return to Brasília; a national holiday was declared. The streets turned to carnival and the presidential palace, for the very first time since the coup of 1964, was opened to the public for the day. It remained closed for the rest of the military occupation. President Médici spoke to the nation: 'I feel profound happiness at seeing the joy of our people in this highest form of patriotism. I identify this victory won in the brotherhood of good sportsmanship with the rise of faith in our fight for national development.'[15] The government's public-relations machine recycled the tune *Pa Fente Brasil* – 'Forward Brazil', originally written for the World Cup team as the government's song, and recorded it for use in a multitude of adverts, radio jingles and public events.

Pelé's image, leaping to head a goal, was accompanied by the government's slogan *'ninguem segura mais este pais'* – 'nobody can stop this country now' – on innumerable giant posters. Having bound the military presidency, its vision of economic development and national unity and Brazilian football success together, Brazil's generals would spend much of the 1970s trying to bend football more explicitly to their purposes, funding a gigantic stadium-building programme and attempting to colonize football's institutions and ethos. But they would do so without Pelé and without another World Cup victory. He played his last game for Brazil against Yugoslavia in 1971 and though in 1974 President Médici and João Havelange begged him to play in the World Cup, and mobilized a TV-led campaign 40 million strong to persuade him, Pelé refused. After his official retirement from football in 1974, he reappeared in the United States as the star and saviour of the New York Cosmos and America's professional league, the NASL. The year that he left for the US, 1975, was the first in which the Brazilian economic miracle appeared to be truly faltering; the global economic slowdown reducing Brazil's growth to a crawl.

As three-time winners of the World Cup, Brazil were allowed to keep the Jules Rimet trophy. At some unspecified point in the mid-to-late 1970s, as Brazil began to groan under the impact of recession and austerity, the cup was stolen. It has never been recovered and was almost certainly melted down for its value as gold. When there is not enough food, who needs trophies? As Tony Mason has so lucidly summarized of Latin America in this era, the significance of football, even *futebol arte*, has its limits.

Football may indeed be a passion rather than a pleasure and may be better than nothing, but it is certainly not enough.[16]

11
The Glamour and the Glory: High Industrial Football in Europe, 1955–1974

There arose a vision of the future. In 20, even 10 years' time, will all football be played under the stars and the moon? There is much to recommend it. There is a dramatic, theatrical quality about it. The pace of the game seems accentuated, flowing patterns of approach play take on sharper, more colourful outlines. In the background of the night the dark, surrounding crowd, half shadow yet flesh and blood, can produce the effect of a thousand fire-flies as cigarette lights spurt forth.   *The Times*, reporting on England's first floodlit league game, February 1956

The great fallacy is that the game is first and last about winning. It's nothing of the kind. The game is about glory. It is about doing things in style, with a flourish, about going out to beat the other lot, not waiting for them to die of boredom. **Danny Blanchflower**

/

Our man from *The Times* had indeed seen the future, though only a glimpse. Even now not all football is played under artificial lights but its appeal is still undeniable. In the grey evening fogs of austere England in the 1950s, midweek floodlit football offered an exhilarating break from the drudgery of the working week; a taste of theatrical glamour, of limelight and shadows, of the darkened chorus and the spotlit stars. Hitherto football in Europe had been a daytime affair, and though it offered passion and intensity it was hardly glamorous. In the late 1950s and 1960s it acquired a sprinkle of stardust and that rested on more than illumination. First, the game was transformed by the process of

European integration that yielded both UEFA and the European Cup – the competition that provided European football with a new and compelling dramatic form. Second, football was widely televised. This initiated a change in the game's economics and its relationship with the swirling currents of pop culture, youth movements and celebrity but most profoundly it transformed the collective experience and memory of the game, for prior to the advent of the televisual record our historical vision is at best partially sighted; for the most part it is blind. Third, this was the football of affluence, the football of high industrial Europe; buoyed by new money, new methods and new styles of play, the game acquired glamour because the game being played was the best yet seen.

The foundation of UEFA (Union des associations européennes de football) in 1954, and the creation the following year of its first competition, the European Cup (more formally known as the European Champion Clubs' Cup), marks a decisive break in the organization of European football. It is a measure of both Europe's original domination of FIFA and the depth and bitterness of its long civil war that no pan-European football organization had been established before this. The South Americans, despite the fissiparous politics of the continent, had achieved footballing union in 1916.[1] By 1952 it was becoming apparent that Europe's numerical majority within FIFA had evaporated and its de facto command of the organization would eventually be lost. Europe's football administrators, already nervous about the changing geography of post-colonial football politics, were further panicked by a considered demonstration of bloc power and organization among the South American delegates to the 1952 FIFA Helsinki congress. The lead in creating a European football fiefdom was taken by the general secretary of the FFF Henri Delaunay and his Italian and Belgian counterparts. With support from the British and German members of the FIFA executive committee, a meeting of Europe's football administrators – East and West – was held in Berne in June 1954. The Greeks arrived late, but by the end of the day UEFA had been founded. It was football's parallel to the Schumann Declaration of 1950 in which the French Foreign Minister Robert Schumann had announced the initiative to pool the coal and steel production of France and Germany: a plan of dubious economic value but of vital political importance, for it would make war between the two states inconceivable. The idea of European co-operation and integration rather than the substance of policy was all-important to UEFA too. Only after the founding meeting did Henri Delaunay sketch a practical and sporting riposte to the political moment in his key essay, 'Is it possible to build a footballing Europe?' It would take the politicians another six years to negotiate and sign the Treaty of Rome establishing the European Economic Community. UEFA's lesser task – to create a pan-European football competition – was accomplished in a year.

Once again it was the French that were the driving intellectual and organizational force behind European integration; in this case, the senior editors and writers at *L'Équipe* – Gabriel Hanot and Jacques Ferran. Hanot and his colleagues, familiar with the Mitropa Cup and the Copa Latina, had already mulled over the idea of a competition for the Continent's leading clubs. When Wolverhampton Wanderers beat Honvéd in 1954, on a pitch deliberately saturated with water on the orders of Wolves manager Stan Cullis, and then had the temerity to claim that they were the champions of Europe, the French were spurred into action. Hanot laid out his plans in an open letter. The tournament was to be played over a whole season among the leading clubs of the Continent, on a knock-out basis, each tie made up of home and away legs. Games would be played mid-week and under floodlights to fit into the domestic schedules that clubs were already committed to, and to attract the crowds after work. Impeccably connected as he was, Hanot's missive received a warm welcome from the leading clubs and football associations of Europe – apart, that is, from the English whose attitude to European integration at the time veered between uninterest and disdain. Europe moved ahead anyway and in cooperation with UEFA the first game of the new competition was staged in September 1955 between Sporting Lisbon and Partizan Belgrade. From the moment of its birth, the European Cup set a standard of excellence and achievement in club football which remains unmatched.

Over the next twenty years UEFA would organize a European Championship for national teams and two additional knock-out competitions – the European Cup Winners' Cup and the Inter-City Fairs Cup, later the UEFA Cup – and they all offered their highlights, pleasures and wonders; but nothing compares to the European Cup. The history of European football in this era cannot be written without the fate of the tournament and the succession of teams that won it serving as its narrative backbone. For while high industrial football brought forth two generations of gifted players, its pinnacles were reserved for great teams and great clubs. It is a spine with a most particular and illuminating geography. From 1956, with the exception of Eintracht Frankfurt, all the finalists came from the Western Mediterranean until Partizan Belgrade lost the 1966 final. Iberia was the first power in the land. The Spanish, in the shape of Real Madrid, won five cups in a row (1956–60) and a sixth in 1966. Then Benfica, Portuguese pretenders, took their crown and held it before it passed to the Milanese barons: AC Milan and Internazionale. There was a turning point in 1967 as Internazionale fell to the first Northern European champions, Glasgow Celtic. Then in 1968 the shift in power seemed confirmed when Benfica lost to Manchester United. But Northern rule did not mean British rule and they in their turn were superseded by the Dutch and the Germans, the last two major European countries to introduce professionalism and complete the industrialization of their national game. Feyenoord in 1970, Ajax from 1971 to 1973 and Bayern München for three years after that kept the European Cup in the North.

European integration and competition and electric floodlights were important in shaping the development of European football, but it was television that would eventually have the most profound impact of all. Football, in the end, is a visual art and television allowed the audience for that art to swell from tens of thousands to tens of millions. This is not to suggest that football does not enliven all the senses. Metaphorically it allows us to savour sweet victory and bitter defeat. For the players there is the taste of sweat and mud. The game's smells are as various as its crowds and locales; in Middlesbrough and Leverkusen the acrid acetates of chemical plants waft through the game. Marseilles offers thick black tobacco smoke, Soweto the blue and purple plumes of hot bush weed, Sheffield has dodgy meat pies, Belgrade its roasted sunflower seeds. Touch is everything, from the spine-tingling, hair-raising reflex that football brings to the back of the neck, to the soft precision pressure that brings a high swirling ball to a stop. Sound is surely a forte of the game. Johan Cruyff would judge the quality of a shot or a pass by its timbre. His team mate Gerrie Muhren hated high winds because 'You have to hear the ball during a game. You can hear from the sound it makes on the boot where the ball is going, how hard, how fast. If there is a big wind you are angry with the ball. You kick the ball but it doesn't listen to you.'[2] It is amazing that they could hear so much, high winds or not, for football's crowds have not merely cheered and booed but sung, chanted and roared. As Arthur Hopcraft put it: 'The sound of a big football crowd baying its delight and its outrage had no counterpart. It is the continuous flow of football that excites this sustained crescendo.'[3] That flow is based on motion, on the continuous making and breaking of patterns and spaces that so dazzled the man from *The Times* under floodlights; no still photograph, no graphic, no painting can do justice to this.

Thus the introduction of television and the widespread broadcasting and recording of entire games transforms the historical record. Although small archives of football on film exist from before this, their value is limited. Much of the footage, shot for cinema newsreel, is disjointed and episodic without any sense of the overall dynamic of play or the flow, movement and patterns of the players. The dictates of the market and the limited number of cameras at matches have left us with just fragments: play moves out of shot, we see only scraps of goals and from the oddest of angles. Consequently our collective memory of football before this is essentially blind, dependent on the vagaries of radio, still photography and reportage – which for all their strengths simply cannot capture the game like motion pictures. It is no coincidence that the standard canon of great players barely extends before this era. Pichichi, Friedenreich, Sindelar, Bloomer, Andrade, Scarone, Mazzola and Piola – the greatest players of their cultures and eras are barely known beyond the smallest circles of bookish devotees. By contrast, the period between 1954 and 1974 offers a whole slew of candidates for every list of greats. Yet even here it is visual familiarity rather then quality that appears to determine the pecking order. The lesser known players are those whose careers were peaking or had peaked in the very earliest days of TV broadcasts: Alfredo Di Stéfano, Ferenc Puskás, Lev Yashin, Josef Masopust, Stanley Matthews, Didi, Vavá and Garrincha all played their best football before 1964. The players most seared on the collective memory are those that came to prominence after this as TV became a truly mass phenomenon: Eusébio, Gianni Rivera, Bobby Charlton, Denis Law, George Best, Franz Beckenbauer, Johan Cruyff. Only Pelé truly straddles both eras.

The basic technologies of television broadcast and reception had been developed in the early 1930s and the pre-war era saw a number of limited experiments with the live televising of sport. In England the BBC had transmitted pictures of the 1938 FA Cup Final, while in Germany the 1936 Olympics were filmed for transmission to a limited audience. The lead in sports broadcasting after the war came from the United States which not only pioneered the core technologies of live broadcast, but the formal commercialization of sports TV rights. In Europe the pre-war pioneers were the first to return to football. West German television showed live games from the Hamburg region in late 1952 and the BBC broadcast the London Olympics and the FA Cup Final in 1948. In France the first live broadcast of a game – Stade Reims against Metz – came as late as 1956 and television arrived in Spain and Portugal even later. In 1954 the European Broadcast Union (EBU) showed nine live games from the 1954 World Cup; the EBU paid nothing for the privilege, but the sale of TV sets was given a massive boost and the existence of a market for international football was demonstrated. The 1960 European Cup Final, between Real Madrid and Eintracht Frankfurt, was the first to be broadcast across the entire Continent live. It sold for just £8,000, but over the next decade and a half the audience for and value of televised football would sharply rise. With the arrival of colour television in 1970 and the complete diffusion of TV across European society, key matches were attracting audiences in their tens of millions.

The key innovators in football coverage in the 1960s were the British, the Germans and the Italians. The British through the BBC had the most robust institutional framework for developing sports coverage, but faced the most conservative and suspicious football authorities who restricted access to league games until well into the 1960s; the West Germans accessed the leading technology fastest and were the first to organize the actual sale of TV rights, but it was the Italians who were the most alert to the potential of the medium for covering sport and the fastest to invent the new codes and modes of presentation that it demanded. *La Domenica Sportiva*, first broadcast on RAI 1 in 1954, was the earliest and remains the longest-running sports show on European television. With the invention of the VTR machine, which allowed high-speed editing, the possibility of the football highlights show emerged. The Germans were there first with *Sportschau* in 1961, then the BBC's *Match of the Day* began in 1964 and the Italians launched 90° *Minuto* in 1970.

The slow-motion replay was first perfected in the United States in the mid-1960s. It made its first appearance in Italy in 1967 as the *moviola*, and it proved an immediate and compelling element of football on TV. In the hands of the first *moviolisti* Heron Vitelli and Carlo Sassi, the post-match analysis began its ascent from an afterthought to an integral feature of the TV package, from technological curiosity to the central journalistic tool for the creation and investigation of conspiracies, controversies and uncertainties. In their coverage of the 1969 Milan derby the *moviolisti* were the first to report the conclusive sighting of a 'ghost goal' (awarded but not valid) in a European stadium. A similar elevation of the pundit and technocrat was first given conversational and combative dramatic form by the use of a panel of commentators and football personalities on Britain's ITV network during the 1970 World Cup, and again in 1974.

The impact of television on football's finances, though welcome, remained marginal throughout the period. In the absence of commercial television outside Britain and competition for TV rights between broadcasters anywhere, the value of televised football could not be inflated. Match-day ticket sales remained far and away the most important component of clubs' incomes. Attendances, though they continued to decline from their post-war highs, did not collapse; indeed at the leading clubs of the era they actually rose. Television was gradually eating into football's audience but not because of live football broadcasts, but because it was the cornerstone of a new social milieu in which television was just one of the many alternative uses of the leisure time opened up by a society of relative affluence. Football was also competing with trips in one of the new cars on the road, with the new suburban domestic masculinities of DIY and gardening, and with the increasingly powerful role of women in determining how families spent their time and money.

However, television also created moments of collective experience that outstripped anything achieved in earlier eras. England's victory in the 1966 World Cup Final was watched by over 15 million. When Italy played in the 1970 final 17 million Italians were watching. In the whole history of the Republic that number of Italians had never done anything together before. These moments of virtually blanket participation in the high points of the international football calendar offered some of the most powerful and poignant moments of imagined community in post-war Europe, opportunities for the nation, albeit physically dispersed, to gather and fathom the meaning of its own identity.

Like the long wave of economic growth that sustained it, high industrial football was, to a great extent, based on a complex of methods, technologies and social relations first created in an earlier era but only generally diffused under conditions of international stability and domestic class peace. Television and floodlight technologies were first developed before the Second World War but only came into general use a decade after its conclusion. The boots, balls, kits, pitches, stadiums and methods of transport used by the European football industry were technologically virtually identical to the leading examples of each item in the immediate pre- or post-war decades. No football made completely from artificial materials was used in international competition until 1974. The screw-in studs supplied by Horst Dassler and Adidas to the 1954 West German World Cup winners were as advanced as anything to appear in the next two decades. The key innovations in stadium technology – reinforced concrete and steel cantilevers – were both first tried out in the 1930s; and the first artificial turfs were only used in American professional sport. Even the various muscle-building steroids, stimulants, amphetamines and other performance-enhancing drugs that were increasingly used in the 1960s and 1970s were based on pharmaceutical technologies over twenty years old.

What distinguished the football of affluence was that all these innovations were brought together and made accessible to the leading clubs under conditions of heightened internal organization and professionalism. It is remarkable quite how rickety the bureaucratic and organizational capacities of football clubs and national associations were prior to the 1950s. UEFA itself did not have a full-time professional press officer until the 1970s. Few clubs understood the meaning of public relations let alone saw the need to employ anyone in the field. Management at board level was for the most part haphazard, amateurish and risk-averse. Those clubs that prospered did so, in part, by getting organized, though their precise methods and structures of power varied. The Italians in particular were innovators in constructing a new managerial division of labour between a wealthy patron/president, a technical director who dealt with wider sports politics, transfers and organization, and a coach who focused wholly on the team itself. The introduction of full-time, professional coaches was in itself a revelation in many footballing cultures and it was on the basis of this new class of football technocrats and prophets that many of the key playing and tactical advances of the era were made.

Affluence brought more than a rationalization of football's internal bureaucracies and chains of command. For one thing it created a generation of players who were fitter, healthier and with greater longevity than their predecessors. Their levels of training showed on the pitch where pace, speed and stamina were tangibly rising. But affluence also bred discontents. Across Europe in the late 1960s labour movements and trade unions flexed their muscles while wild-cat protests were breaking out in every industry as workers, freed from the fear of unemployment and penury, began to contest not merely the contents of their pay packet, but their conditions of work and the authority of the system that employed them. Football players were not immune to the forward march of labour; indeed given the virtually feudal conditions under which they were generally contracted they were some of the workers most in need of change. In Italy, for example, players received neither insurance or pensions before the early 1970s. In England the decisive encounter between football labour and capital occurred over the abolition of the maximum wage in 1961, while in France, the Netherlands and Italy the belated formation of player unions occurred in the late 1960s, followed by the threat of strike action. But footballers were never going to be in the vanguard of the industrial struggle – indeed the English PFA was expelled from the Trades Union Congress in 1973.

Instead players were cast as a new kind of cultural icon. In the inter-war era Italian Fascism tried to elevate its World Cup winners to the status of fascist supermen. Austrian coffee-house intellectuals cast Matthias Sindelar in their own image of a frail intelligence and doomed beauty. In the post-war era players were unrelentingly loaded with worthy and low-key patriotic laurels: Lev Yashin, the taciturn, loyal hero and stopper of the Soviet Proletariat; Fritz Walter, hardworking, modest emblem of the German economic miracle; Raymond Kopa, the good and dutiful assimilated French immigrant; Billy Wright, England's unflappable, imperturbable finest, a man who knew how to roll up his sleeves and get on with the job. In the 1960s the manufacture of cultural meaning from the raw materials of football clubs and players eluded the direct grasp of politicians and, although the media continued to serve a crucial role in the process, the field of meaning was thrown open by the extensive changes in youth and popular cultures and among the players themselves.

In the 1960s, like the rest of their generation football players grew their hair. The significance of such a trivial act can only be grasped by looking at photographs of the European crowd of the late 1950s and early 1960s. They are overwhelmingly male. Their dress barely varies across the generations: dark suits and jackets, white shirts, dark unpatterned ties. In the rain they wear thick coats and long mackintoshes. Scarves and hats in the winter, short back and sides in the summer. By the mid-1970s the shirt and ties were all but gone, denim was more prevalent than tweed and the hat, but for the woolly bobbler in club colours, was a museum piece. Above all there was hair, a lot more hair; the single clearest defining mark of this generation's distance from and disdain for their parents. On the pitch they had had no shortage of role models. George Best's dark mop and beard made him El Beatle in Spain. Gigi Meroni and Gianni Rivera broke all the sartorial rules in style-conscious Italy when they let their locks touch their collar. Cruyff's straggly mane and Netzer's luxuriant curls announced new types of masculinity in European football – by turns individualist, hedonistic, conspicuous consumers, but also independent and anti-authoritarian and, finally, surely the essence of glamour – with some spark of sexual fire, some embers of a smouldering athletic eroticism.

Europe's high industrial football had acquired glamour. Could it also furnish glory? The forces of money and power, though never far from football, and in Eastern Europe pathologically overbearing, remained at some distance in the West. Football was more rationalized and professionalized than commercialized. The innovations of the era were in coaching, training, tactics and internal organization rather than the invention of new revenue streams. The advent of television had its biggest impact on how we remember the era rather than any more fundamental economic shift. Although there was more money in the game than before the war, it remained for the most part a cottage industry, with all but the stars paid wages comparable to the skilled working classes. Advertising and branding were being invented, but as late as 1973 Tottenham Hotspur would see no need for the ugly intrusion of commercial hoardings at White Hart Lane. Similarly, politics stood at one remove from football. The defeat of fascism had saved the game from its most insistent interferers – though here again East European communism did its best to maintain the tradition of political dalliance. Yet, in an era of deep and abiding division in Europe, UEFA remained one of the only truly pan-European functioning institutions on the Continent, and football was one of very few forms of regular cultural interaction between the two halves of the Continent. In the liberated institutional and psychological space created by a thin commercialism and relative depoliticization, football could pursue a more autonomous course. Football, as Danny Blanchflower argued, is hardwired for glory – for winning, but winning with style. Of course the era also abounds with cruelty, corruption, mean-mindedness, treachery, dishonour and plain simple cheating, but the television record is hard to argue with: European football had glamour and glory in abundance.

Gusztáv Sebes, coach of the Hungarian Golden Team, claimed in retrospect that, 'If Hungary had won the football World Cup there would have been no counter revolution but a powerful thrust in the building of socialism in the country.'[4] But as the Argentinian Junta found out in 1978, no victory on the football field has yet elicited emotions sufficient to negate the weight of a truly discontented and brutalized nation nor offer a plausible defence for a ruling elite whose legitimacy has expired. In any case Hungarian communism would have to face its nemesis without even this delusion. In the aftermath of defeat, the discontent and disappointment of Hungary's football crowds was turned most fearsomely on Puskás, who was dropped for his own safety from the national team for some time. The regime vented its anger on goalkeeper Grosics and coach Sebes. Gyula Grosics, long noted by the security services as a man of dubious political opinions, was arrested in the autumn of 1954 while warming up for a league game. He was imprisoned, interrogated and abused for fifteen months. When finally released he was sent into internal exile, forced to play with a tiny provincial miners' club called Tatabánya.

Sebes was the victim of the fast-changing political landscape. In March 1955 the reformist Prime Minister Imre Nagy was deposed and eventually expelled from the Communist Party by the old Stalinist faction led by party secretary Mátyás Rákosi. The swift return of hardcore Stalinists to power ran counter to the direction of political change in the rest of Eastern Europe which was undergoing a gradual post-Stalin thaw in internal politics. Without the protection of sporting victory or political patrons, Sebes was exposed and came under sustained bureaucratic and ideological attack. In mid-1956 he was publicly condemned for his bourgeois leanings by the Ministry of Sport; many of the most supportive coaches in the national network established by Sebes were sent out of the country on diplomatic coaching missions to Nigeria, Egypt and Brazil. Perks and smuggling opportunities for the whole squad were radically curtailed.

The Golden Team had struggled on through 1955, beating Scotland home and away, but both team and regime were beginning to disintegrate in early 1956. Following a winter tour of Egypt, the national team were beaten in Turkey 3–1 then returned home to be beaten by Czechoslovakia, 4–2 in the Népstadion on a wet day in May. It was Hungary's first defeat in the rebuilt stadium and the crowd were appalled. Then in the summer they threw away a 3–1 half-time lead against Belgium to lose 5–4. The Rákosi regime was then fatally destabilized by its closest ally, the Soviet Union. First, Khrushchev had made his peace with Yugoslavia and called on all of Eastern Europe to rehabilitate the victims of Stalinist purges as well as those that had supported Tito and been punished for it. In Hungary that inevitably meant László Rajk, a leading Hungarian communist executed by Rákosi in the late 1940s, whose rehabilitation was increasingly understood by the Hungarian public as the most important and urgent act of de-Stalinization. The pressure for such a move was redoubled by the impact of Khrushchev's secret but widely circulated speech given in February 1956 to the Soviet Communist Party's Central Committee in which he denounced Stalin and his crimes. Under pressure, Rákosi announced that László Rajk was innocent but tried to shift the blame to the secret services (AVH) and away from himself.

What seems in retrospect the merest admission of guilt and error was, in the context of Stalinist Hungary, like opening a great crack in the legitimacy and credibility of the Rákosi regime. The release of many of the country's intellectuals and writers from prison the following month only added to the growing talk of change. Rajk's widow now called publicly for her husband's rehabilitation, a call increasingly linked with demands for the return of Nagy as Prime Minister. The Soviets removed Rákosi in June, concerned that he could not hold the line domestically and internationally embarrassed by his ultra-Stalinism and his anti-Tito outbursts at a moment of Moscow–Belgrade rapprochement. But his successors were unable to intervene in the gathering wave of protest across the region. In Poland, workers' protests, strikes and riots had been gathering strength throughout the autumn, encouraging thoughts of sedition and culminating in the reformist Gomułka taking power in Warsaw in October. The Hungarian national team had recovered enough from the disasters of early 1956 to score their first victory against the Soviet Union in Moscow, winning 1–0 to tremendous popular approval. Two weeks later, on 6 October, László Rajk, now officially declared an innocent victim of the nation's purges, was reburied in Budapest. An unbelievable 200,000 people attended.

Across the country newly formed and independent student unions, trade unions, writers' groups and intellectual networks were a hive of meetings and conversations assessing the possibilities of the moment, and drawing up a series of new political demands that coalesced around calls for free speech, a free press and free elections. On 23 October around 10,000 protesters gathered in the early afternoon in Petőfi Square, Budapest. They were predominantly students and high-school kids marching in support of the workers' movement in Poland. As the day wore on, more and more people joined them. They began to cross town and make towards Parliament Square, joined by workers coming off their shifts. What had begun as an act of solidarity with the Poles, peppered by Leninist slogans and communist insignia, rapidly mutated into a vast expression of nationalist discontent. One of the city's many vast statues of Stalin was cut down by metal workers, the old dictator's metallic skull filled with petrol and set ablaze. At 6.00 p.m. over a quarter of a million had gathered to call for Nagy's return and the disbanding of the AVH. They were joined by army cadets and more workers; the city was adorned with the national flag, the Soviet emblem cut from its centre. At around 8.00 p.m. that evening the first shots were fired, and the demonstration turned into a city-wide street battle between the protesters, joined by units of the Hungarian army and police, against scattered and confused army units and loyal remnants of the AVH who were hounded all over town. By the 25th the initial battle was over. The AVH were gone, the Soviets had retreated, Nagy had been made Prime Minister and a moment of calm had returned to the streets.

Recognizing the limits of any attempt to resuscitate Communist Party power in its old form, Nagy immediately took his lead from the street, announcing the end of one-party rule, the dissolution of the Communist

Party and its reformation as a socialist party; and most radical of all, the immediate withdrawal of Hungary from the Warsaw Pact. The country's leading footballers, cocooned in their bubble of fame and privilege, were spirited out of the country. Honvéd, who had been told by UEFA that, revolution or not, they were still expected to fulfil both legs of their impending European Cup clash with Athletic Bilbao, headed for Vienna. The squad of MTK joined them there. On 4 November 1956 the Soviet Army invaded Hungary, immediately announcing the formation of a new government under Hungarian communist János Kádár. The result was never in doubt, as the Soviet armoured columns crushed the armed but disorganized resistance of Hungarian urban youth and the unions. Nagy and his allies made their final broadcasts to the West to support Hungary before seeking asylum in the Yugoslav Embassy. They would later be tricked into leaving, and were executed. In the streets the battle raged hardest and longest in the working-class districts of Budapest, most notably in the suburb of Ferencváros where the club of the same name had long fallen out of favour with the communists. Ferencváros fans – the broke, dissolute and alienated young – formed the core of the resistance and were among the heaviest casualties of the fighting. Two weeks after the fighting had stopped the remaining student and workers' councils in Budapest attempted to hold a mass rally of resistance at the Népstadion, but were barred from entering by a ring of Soviet tanks parked around the stadium.

The severance of the Hungarian people from their football team was made complete by the dispersal of its leading talents. MTK had toured Austria, Germany, Belgium and England in late 1956 but eventually returned home. The Honvéd squad, who played in Spain and then Brazil, were more divided. As Tichy said of their game in Bilbao, 'We hadn't even had time to unpack our suitcases before we were surrounded by agents. There wasn't a single player who didn't get some kind of offer.'[5] Sebes was sent to bring them all home, with a mixture of persuasion, threat and incentive, but he returned without three of the squad. Kocsis had gone to Barcelona, and Czibor would join him there after the Italian FA refused to allow him to join Roma. Puskás, like the others, served a short ban that the Hungarian FA had insisted UEFA impose, but there was no going back. In 1957 he took the field for Real Madrid and later for Spain. Hungarian football began its long and still unfinished decline. Without Sebes, who was soon removed from his all coaching posts, and these key players the national team was still good enough to make three World Cup finals in a row (1958–66) and lose quarter-finals at two of them, but it never for a moment looked anything other than a pale imitation of the Golden Team. By the late 1960s the human and spiritual capital of the squad had dissipated altogether.

Timing, in comedy and football, is everything. As Spain finally crawled out of the wreckage of its civil war and began to re-engage tentatively with the world, it was Barcelona that had momentum. The city was at the heart of the country's slowly gathering industrial revival, its population swelled by hundreds of thousands of migrants from the poverty-stricken south; when they arrived they invariably chose to support Barcelona over Espanyol, a quiet integration with the Catalan nationalist majority. They were also the form team. Between 1948 and 1953 Barcelona had won four league titles, three Copas del Generalísimos and two Copas Latinas – a tournament played among the leading teams of France, Spain, Italy and Portugal – their victory over OGC Nice in Paris in 1952 igniting a huge outburst of exiled Catalan nationalist celebrations. But the Copa Latina never had the cachet or the standing of the European Cup and when the latter began in the autumn of 1955, Barça were on the slide and Real Madrid, the new champions of Spain, were poised to replace them not merely as the leading team in Spain but in all Europe.

Spain in 1955, if not hungry, remained desperately poor. Real Madrid were not a team of affluence but the final moment in a long cycle of professionalization and modernization in Spanish football that had begun in the late 1920s, was interrupted and set back by the Civil War and post-war isolation, and only began to recover in the 1950s. The club was ruled by Santiago Bernabéu, a patron of the old order. Real did not, like the Italians or the British that would succeed them as the dominant forces in Europe, implement the new division of labour with a professional and high-profile manager or explore a distinctive and experimental playing style. They were as Bernabéu liked it – an old-fashioned team. Over the previous decade, Bernabéu had laid the architectural, economic and political foundations of Real's success. The new

Chamartín stadium – later to be renamed and better known as Estadio Santiago Bernabéu – had been opened, and the combination of arrow-straight accounting, a large group of middle-class *socios* and the big crowds that Real could now accommodate made the club wealthy by the standards of the day. Although Bernabéu and Real were comfortably associated with Franco and his regime, the club benefited only from the small change of influence: special permits to import foreign cars for star players, access to restricted foreign-currency stashes, favourable planning permissions. Despite the rich vein of conspiracy theory in Spanish football, there is no firm evidence to suggest that at home or in Europe they received help from referees or officials. What decisively changed the fortunes of the club was, after a fierce and acrimonious tussle with Barcelona for his services, the arrival in 1953 of Alfredo Di Stéfano.

The Argentinian midfielder came to Spain from his Colombian adventure with Millonarios.[6] Nicknamed *La Saeta Rubia* – 'the blond arrow' – Di Stéfano was the brains, the lungs, the inspiration and often the sword of Real Madrid for over a decade. Although formally a midfield player he worked the entire length of the field, displaying a work rate and fitness that were unmatched at that time. His expectations of team-mates were equally demanding – apocryphally when Amancio played his first game for Real and found no shield on his shirt, he mentioned it to Di Stéfano who snapped back, 'You've got to sweat in it first, sonny.' He did not merely track back but defended deep, organizing and mar-shalling the team at set pieces. He didn't just instruct but cajoled and ordered and in so doing he visibly raised the game of others around him. He was fast enough to launch stinging counterattacks, perceptive enough to be on the end of other people's passes and inventive enough to constantly create space and danger in midfield and on the edge of his opponents' penalty area. For a player who was not formally a striker, over 800 goals in a career is an unparalleled achievement. And his posture at rest and in flight was remarkably straight and poised; his head was always up, his neck long, eyes always scanning and looking. Herrera, when asked to compare him to Pelé, suggested that if the Brazilian was the violins, then Di Stéfano was the whole orchestra.

Between 1956 and 1960 Real Madrid won five consecutive European Cups and in so doing set a standard of excellence and achievement, a peak of sporting glamour and class, against which all European teams and triumphs were henceforth calibrated. Unlike the Italian and Northern European teams that would come to dominate European competition in the 1960s and 1970s, Real Madrid were not tactical innovators – indeed for much of the era they played with an old-fashioned five-man forward line. Nor were they associated with the rule of a charismatic coach. The run of five titles were achieved under four different coaches: Villalonga, Carniglia, Fleitas and Muñoz, none of whom could stamp their imprimatur on the club. There was no space for such a character. Behind the scenes, Bernabéu could have no peer, while on the pitch Di Stéfano was the motivating intelligence of the team. It was here that Real's strength truly lay – in an exceptional squad nurtured and constantly replenished by Bernabéu. Alongside Di Stéfano he gathered a core of home-grown talents including Gento, Muñoz and Molowny, and added South Americans like Uruguayan José Santamaría and Argentinian Héctor Rial. In 1957 Real acquired Raymond Kopa from the Stade de Reims team they defeated in the 1956 European Cup Final. The following year, Bernabéu picked up the otherwise unemployed and overweight Ferenc Puskás, now in exile from Hungary. Those that did not make the grade or could not accept the systems of authority within the team and the club were weeded out. The great Brazilian forward Didi lasted only a season.

Above all Real had fight. As Di Stéfano said of the home crowd, 'It wants the team to fight . . . It wants it to win . . . but it wants it to win first and then to play.' In the new world of two-leg European ties, unreliable transport and impossibly hard away matches in alien lands, Real showed that they could deal with anything. In the quarter-finals of the first ever European Cup they played Partizan Belgrade at home on Christmas Day 1955 and beat them 4–0. It was Bernabéu's idea to show those atheist Yugoslavs that they were playing in a Christian country. But the victory was truly ground out in Belgrade where they played in temperatures touching minus 10 degrees and with hard packed snow across the pitch. When Partizan's opening volley ricocheted against the bar, 10 kilos of snow fell on Real's goalkeeper. Partizan knew what they were doing in these conditions, and scored three. Real, defending for ninety minutes, hung on. Then in the semi-finals against Milan they showed that they could keep a lead, as twice Milan came back to equalize against them, before Madrid made it 4–2 in the cauldron of the Bernabéu. Real also knew how to stage a comeback and in that year's final against Reims they found themselves two-down in twenty minutes, before a bravado attacking display made it 4–3. The same formula of open attack and unflinching belief could open up the tightest and meanest of Italian defences (against Fiorentina and Milan in the 1957 and 1958 finals) and where and when necessary they could mix it physically and verbally with the roughest of opponents. The 1960 European Cup Final was their peak.

The match was held at Hampden Park in Glasgow and a crowd of 130,000 came to see Real play the West German champions Eintracht Frankfurt. The Germans took an early lead only to find themselves 6–1 down after 70 minutes. Di Stéfano completed his hat-trick shortly after, but couldn't emulate Puskás' tally of four goals. For the generation that watched the game, including the many that saw Real on television for the first time, this was the football that they had only heard and read about but now, finally, they could see. 'Last night Real flaunted all that has made them incomparable. The unflagging generalship of Di Stéfano, the technical perfection and breathtaking ingenuity of Puskás, the industry of Del Sol, the deadly pace of Gento, the striking directness of Canario . . . to list the Real team is to chronicle greatness . . .'[7] The Germans pulled two consolation goals back but they are invisible from the record. Madrid, quicker than any saint, were canonized on the spot.

In the inaugural Intercontinental Cup Real underlined their brilliance. Smart enough to grind out a 0–0 draw against South American champions Peñarol in Montevideo, they took them to pieces at home, winning 5–1. Although Franco's Spain had begun to end its self-imposed diplomatic and cultural isolation in the late 1950s, it remained a relatively closed world. Real Madrid functioned as both its ambassador and as a window on the world. Franco was known to interview club officials and players after their travels, particularly to Eastern Europe, revelling in the details of food shortages and misery. More significantly, on the eve of the 1956 final the Spanish Embassy in Paris found itself more popular and more fêted than it had been for twenty years. As Foreign Minister Fernando María Castiella put it, 'Real Madrid is a style of sportsmanship. It is the best embassy we have ever had.' Governments began to treat the team as de facto diplomats. Forward Ignacio Zoco recalled: 'We would usually be met by government dignitaries. They'd bring flowers for Di Stéfano, Puskás, Gento. As for the rest of us – well, we carried the suitcases . . .'[8] Among the crowds that gathered to watch the team on their European tours, Real attracted both sides of the Spanish diaspora in Europe. Substantial numbers of political exiles, replenished by the continuing oppression and violence of the regime, took the opportunity to protest against Franco, most notably at the 1962 quarter-final against Juventus in Turin, just days after the execution of the leading Spanish communist Julián Grimau García.

Real's reign as European champions was terminated by Barcelona, who had been revived under the mercurial leadership of Argentine Helenio Herrera, and an influx of exiled Hungarians in attack and big Catalans in defence. In the first round of the 1961 tournament, Barça beat Real in the Nou Camp, though Madrid continue to claim that four goals were disallowed by English referee Reg Leafe. Barcelona then went on to lose the final to Benfica and would have to wait over thirty years for a European Cup title. Real's stars were leaving (Kopa returned to Reims in 1960) or ageing (Puskás and Di Stéfano were pushing forty) but they remained good enough to win the Spanish league and lose two more European Cup Finals – both epics of their kind. The first was an extraordinarily open and high-scoring game against Benfica at their peak, and then in 1964 they fell to their nemesis Herrera, now coaching the ultra-defensive Internazionale.

There was an abundance of talent in Spanish football, not only at Real, but at Barcelona and Valencia and Zaragoza who between them won six Fairs Cups between 1958 and 1966. Not only were there indigenous Spaniards but the naturalized Puskás and Di Stéfano too. Yet the national team was never able to reproduce the form of its club sides. Spain failed to qualify for the 1958 World Cup and Franco pulled the team out of the inaugural European Championship in 1960, unwilling to let them travel to Moscow for a quarter-final with the Soviet Union. At the 1962 World Cup, Helenio Herrera was appointed coach. He clashed with the injured Di Stéfano who did not get to play. The team showed little commitment or bite and went out in the first round. The sporting press unleashed a tirade of nationalist anger against the cosmopolitan nature of coach, squad and method. The sports paper *Marca* wrote, 'The national team is so full of foreigners and so conditioned by foreign tactics that it no longer plays like a team of real Spaniards, with passion, with aggression, with virility, and, above all, fury.'[9] The ultra-nationalists now had their moment. In 1963 foreign players were banned from Spanish football, a position maintained for a decade.

Yet in 1960 Franco had decided to open the Spanish economy to foreign tourism and investment, and launch a programme of state-sponsored growth under the guidance of his *Opus Dei* technocrats. In keeping with this cautious opening Spain now hosted the second European Championships in 1964. The team was coached by Civil War Falangist José Villalonga, who promised 'a young, impassioned, aggressive, virile team'. The draw offered a Cold War narrative and Spain duly beat Hungary and then the Soviet Union as the crowd acknowledged team – nation – and Franco himself in the Bernabéu. The supine Spanish press had a field day: 'In this quarter of a century there has never been displayed a greater popular enthusiasm for the state born out of the victory over communism and its fellow travellers.'[10]

The feat was not to be repeated. Spain were desperately poor at the 1966 World Cup, and failed to qualify for the 1970 and 1974 tournaments at all. Real had only one major triumph left in them, when they won the 1966 European Cup against Partizan Belgrade with an all-Spanish team that have come to be known as the *ye-ye's*: a transliteration in strict Spanish phonetics of the Beatles' chorus 'She loves you, yeah-yeah-yeah'. In 1965 the Beatles had played their first and only Spanish concert at the Madrid bullring. The music, the audience response and the haircuts were considered incomprehensible and destabilizing by the political and cultural old guard of the city.

However, no new dynasty was founded, no unbroken run of success initiated. Indeed, 1966 is the beginning of what became known as *los años del desiertos* – the wilderness years. In retrospect the *ye-ye's* are truly the last of the old order, as uncomfortable in the garb of the new Northern pop culture as Bernabéu himself. Bernabéu liked his players to have short hair and no beards. Shirts should be tucked in, socks pulled up, and private lives kept exemplary. Commitment and sacrifice to a higher ideal – in this case Real Madrid – was taken as a prerequisite of the club's representatives. But these were rules and attitudes that were dissolving in the New Spain. The shock of the Beatles was repeated a million times over as Northern Europeans came in their droves to Spain's beaches and émigrés returned with European money and attitudes. Authority of every kind was coming under attack and in the late 1960s erupted into open political confrontation with the regime as Basque nationalists, students and trade unions took to the streets. Bernabéu, speaking in 1969, distraught and confused by changing times, vainly thought that football could still provide a measure and a vision of the old normality.

We are doing the nation a service. What we want is to keep people happy. People like football a lot and with football Spaniards can deal better with their everyday problems. We are living a moment of such misunderstanding and such horrible confusion that what people want is real calm. They don't want problems. Football is the source with which people can periodically forget about their problems.[11]

But they did not forget about their problems and Real Madrid would deliver no triumph or success to soothe the old regime in its dotage. In 1971, for the first time, the team did not participate in the European Cup; instead they underwent, in their own terms, the humiliation of losing a Cup Winners' Cup Final – a tournament they had hitherto disdained. In 1974 as their fortunes plummeted they entered the lowly UEFA Cup, losing in the first round to Ipswich Town.

When the ban on foreigners in Spanish football was lifted later that year, Bernabéu went shopping, but his capacity to determine the sartorial and political make-up of his squad was finished. The arrival of the Germans Gunter Netzer and Paul Breitner brought big hair and Maoist chic to the Bernabéu, and to underline the changing of the old guard, coach Miguel Muñoz, fourteen years in the job, was sidelined and replaced by one of those atheist Yugoslavs, Miljan Miljanić. It was to no avail. European glory remained beyond the reach of the club. In the home leg of Real's 1976 European Cup semi-final against Bayern München they had a penalty appeal turned down. A man leapt from the crowd on to the pitch and punched the referee in the face. Real Madrid had lost not merely the match, they had lost their dignity. General Franco lay on his deathbed. The spectres of revived Catalan nationalism and a revived Barcelona under Rinus Michels and Johan Cruyff rose up, waiting for their moment.

IV

The 1956 European Cup Final is inevitably the point of narrative lift-off in the rise of Real Madrid, but it was also a moment of satisfaction for the losers; for Stade de Reims had been worthy opponents and appeared to represent the ascent of French football to the highest level. The intersecting elites of the French Football Federation and the sports press had been instrumental in the creation of the Inter-City Fairs' Cup (UEFA Cup from 1972) and the European Cup. France was one of the first European nations to embrace floodlight technology. In the immediate post-war era attendances at league football rose to a record average of over 11,000 a game. Stade de Reims possessed the leading strikers in French football, Raymond Kopa and Just Fontaine. They also possessed the leading young coach of the era, Albert Batteaux, whose conscious decision to build the tactics of his teams around the skills of key players made Reims an open, stylish, goalscoring outfit. These three would form the core of France's 1958 World Cup side, the best the nation had ever fielded. And though Raymond Kopa was sold to Real Madrid, Stade de Reims were still good enough to meet him and Real again in the European Cup Final of 1959. Yet ten years later French football would record its lowest-ever attendances, its lowly disregard in the nation's affections only matched by the poverty of performance from the national team and club sides.

Even at the peak in the late 1950s, France was never comfortable in its footballing skin. But then France was not comfortable with itself as a nation. Something of the neurotic and divided debate over the meaning of French identity in the 1950s is captured in the dispute over Raymond Kopa and the French national team. Kopa, born Kopaszewski, was the son of Polish immigrants, tens of thousands of whom came to work in the mines of north-east France. As a player Kopa was small but very quick. He was both an exceptional dribbler and a passer of decisive final balls, either as crosses from the wing or on the end of an inside-forward's rapier runs. In a remarkable reversal of the usual attitudes, the French Left applauded him for his individualism and flair while the Right criticized his wastefulness and neglect of the collective. The correspondents of *Miroir-Sprint* and *Miroir du Football*, journals aligned with the Communist Party, cast football as primarily a people's festival and entertainment. Kopa's open and often highly individualistic play was preferred to the mean-spirited prioritization of collective discipline and winning. But the directorate of *L'Équipe* and *France Football* criticized him on precisely these grounds.

Kopa's standing and the meaning of his immense public stardom were inflected by more than class, but also with questions of ethnicity. His Polish origins were certainly a source of racist taunts: after his and the national team's poor performance at the 1954 World Cup, crowds called out '*Kopa retourne à la mine*'. The problem, however, was bigger than just Kopa; Jacques Ferran argued that French football was a 'Russian salad, a jumble ... a hotchpotch of doctrines'.[12] He was not referring merely to tactical visions but by proxy to the ethnic stock of the team going to the 1958 World Cup. Its leading players alongside Kopa were Roger Piatoni, son of an Italian immigrant family, and Just Fontaine, born to a Spanish mother in Marrakech. Gabriel Hanot had been particularly critical of the national side's instability and individuality, and lack of the tireless runners and rescuers of lost causes that characterized the English game. He was not, it should be made clear, against immigration or immigrants, and he loudly denounced the various bans imposed on foreign players in the French league. The issue was not migration but integration; Kopa, for example, was forgiven his idiosyncratic play in exchange for his exemplary demeanour and work rate and his unflinching commitment to the French cause. How, from this increasingly complex mix of ethnic groups, could an authentic but distinctive and successful French football style be created? It was a microcosm of a wider debate that grew more intense and volatile as the 1958 World Cup drew nearer.

French nationalism had still not quite recovered its poise after the humiliations of defeat, occupation and Vichy collaboration during the Second World War. Despite coming out on the winning side and maintaining the nation's sense of global significance with the acquisition of nuclear weapons and a permanent seat on the UN Security Council, the grandeur of France was still under assault. Its Indo-Chinese empire had been lost in a series of costly, bitter and humiliating military defeats. France had been forced to cede Tunisia and Morocco to the forces of independence, and its African and Caribbean empires could clearly not last much longer. Above all there was the independence movement in Algeria which had erupted into open and armed confrontation with both metropolitan France and the European settlers. Two years of brutal fighting had quelled the initial uprising in Algiers, but it cost three governments, thousands of lives and merely displaced the struggle to the borderlands and backwaters of the vast desert colony. The increasingly desperate and politically restive European settler population were clamouring for strong leadership from Paris. Then in the weeks before the 1958 finals the roar for the return to power of General Charles de Gaulle grew louder. Two of the French squad, Rachid Mekloufi and Mustapha Zitouni, left France and the team to join the FLN football team in opposition in Tunis.[13]

Thus the French squad that left for Sweden in May 1958 went with unanswered questions of nationhood and identity hanging over their heads. The French camp was remarkably low-key with just a few journalists and fans travelling with them. They were cosseted away in a tiny rural town in Sweden, playing cards, petanque and a few friendlies while the country was in a state of extreme political turbulence. When the tournament began they were scintillating, announcing their style and intention in a 7–3 win over Paraguay. They scored two against Yugoslavia but let in three and qualified for the knock-out stage by putting two past Scotland. The Northern Irish were swept aside 4–0 in a swirling game of unbroken attack. Against Brazil in the semi-final, they met their match, scoring two but conceding five. But such was the exuberance of this team that even in the usually anodyne third-place game they raised themselves to win a flamboyant 6–3 victory over the West Germans. Fontaine's four goals brought his tournament total to thirteen, still a record. Yet what would have been in other circumstances an opportunity for an outbreak of national self-confidence and pleasure was received with curious indifference by the nation for the real politics of nation-building and state-making was happening right there right now, at home. Through May and June, France was in a state of flux. With the government poised to negotiate with Algerian nationalists, the army in Algiers seized the city and threatened mutiny unless De Gaulle was returned to power. The general rose to the challenge, and set about dissolving the French Fourth Republic and creating a Fifth Republic in his own image – centralized and presidential. Armed with immense executive powers, he set about detaching France from Algeria rather than maintaining colonial rule.

Kopa and Mekloufi both returned to French club football in the early 1960s, but the course of decline was set: crowds collapsed, bottoming out in 1968 at less than 7,000 a game in the top division, let alone the empty stands of the second and third. Clubs that had once been among the best in the country folded, merged with other stragglers (Toulouse and Bastia) or disappeared into the lower leagues never to return (Roubaix and Sète). No French side would see a European final or semi-final, and the national team qualified for just one of the next four

World Cups. Paris became a football desert as Red Star and Racing first disintegrated before disappearing altogether.

The brilliance of the 1958 World Cup team was neither celebrated nor recognized. But even had it been the basic dilemmas of the sport would have remained unresolved. Football continued to compete for audiences and wider cultural significance with rugby in the south of the country and cycling across all of the nation. Television never developed a symbiotic relationship with the game, indeed its derisory levels of coverage in the 1960s publicly demonstrated football's marginal importance. French sides could not count on the injection of political connections or finance that the leading clubs in Italy, Portugal and Spain were to draw upon, and remained small-town and small-change operations. At the lower end of professional football, players were still part-time and teams were locked into a vicious cycle of low pay, low performance and low crowds. The urban geography and pattern of suburban modernization that they operated within in the 1960s made the clubs' task even harder. No French city, other than Paris, experienced the kind of growth rates or assumed the critical size and density required to support a major football club of the era. While in Britain the new youth and music cultures of the 1960s interacted with football, in France they stood as an alternative and an opponent. The counter-cultures of the late 1960s explicitly rejected football and its antiquated provincial hierarchies.

'Fado, Fatima and Football' – according to exiles and opponents, this was the ideological troika that sustained the authoritarian rule of António Salazar, Prime Minister of Portugal from 1932 until his death in 1968. The frail Portuguese republic had already fallen to a military coup in 1930, after which the generals, unable to fathom any kind of policy response to the nation's economic and social predicaments, handed over power to the reclusive and austere Minister of Finance, António Salazar. Under his premiership all forms of open opposition and dissent were banned, and power rested with a tiny band of politicians, police officers and technocrats. The army withdrew from politics, effectively pensioned off. Unlike the grandiose ambitions and rhetoric of the expansionist fascism of Germany and Italy, Portugal's *Estado Novo*, as Salazar attempted to dignify his dictatorship, pursued a rigidly autarchic form of social and economic conservatism. In an act of educational cruelty, Salazar deliberately cut the budgets of rural schools, arguing that illiteracy was a structural guarantor of social stability and deference. To this criminal imposition of ignorance Salazarian ideology added a strong dose of the most reactionary and deferential Catholicism – the regime actively promoting the Fatima Cult which began in 1917 when three rural Portuguese schoolchildren claimed to have encountered the Virgin Mary.

In the absence of any new urban popular culture, Portugal's isolation from musical and artistic trends abroad, and the very late introduction of new media technologies, Fado reigned supreme – its hypnotic mix of resignation, sadness and nostalgia matched the mood of uncontested repression. When there wasn't Fado there was football. Before Salazar took over, the game had proved popular enough to sustain a national league and draw crowds in their tens of thousands in the bigger cities. Salazar, who was by training an accountant, displayed a personal asceticism matched by a parsimonious attitude to public expenditure and debt that prioritized domestic order over imperial adventure. He therefore recognized football as primarily a potent domestic social sedative rather than an inspirational beacon of national strength. Unlike other authoritarian nationalists he was not prepared to bankroll the national football team. It did not look too good a bet in any case. The national team lost their first international match 2–1 to Spain in 1921, and it took the Portuguese until 1928 even to get a draw against their most regular and important sporting enemy and four years to achieve a win of any kind, finally achieved in a scrappy game against Italy in 1925. Unsupported and isolated from the mainstream of European football, the national team continued to perform very poorly throughout the 1930s and 1940s. The only intervention the regime was prepared to make in developing the game came in the wake of a particularly humiliating 9–0 defeat by Spain in 1934 which provided the occasion for quietly legalizing the prevailing shamateurism of the top league.

Even so professionalization and commercialization made few inroads, for Portuguese society remained overwhelmingly rural, poor and isolated. Like the rest of the economy football was only able to industrialize haltingly and incompletely: it was overwhelmingly concentrated in Lisbon and Oporto. After the Second World War, in an almost unique display of infrastructural investment, the government celebrated the inauguration of a new national stadium just outside Lisbon. They invited England to play and the entire cabinet, Salazar included, were in attendance to see Portugal thrashed 10–0. The country then failed to qualify for the next four World Cups and were again humiliated in the 1954 World Cup qualifying rounds, losing 9–1 to Austria in Vienna.

In the late 1950s change began at a glacial pace, and much against the wishes and intentions of Salazar. Portugal was allowed into the United Nations, despite its poor democratic record, as it was white, anti-communist and expected to vote with Washington. It duly obliged. The desperate and enduring poverty of the Portuguese peasantry, which had no domestic urban escape route, began to push people both to the African remnants of the Portuguese Empire (Angola and Mozambique) and into the booming factories of Northern Europe. Under pressure, internationally and domestically, the regime held rigged elections, hounded opponents, and expanded a quiet but nasty secret police force. But as in Spain, the changing attitudes and new horizons of returning migrants and visiting tourists began to have an impact. In this spirit of cautious growth and optimism, Benfica, Sporting Lisbon and FC Porto built the country's first concrete bowl stadiums and filled them with crowds over 50,000 strong. There was even room in the new dispensation for the championship actually to pass out of Lisbon to FC Porto for a season or two. By 1960 this interlinking of Portugal's economy and society with the rest of Europe and with the African colonies provided the dynamism that would take Portuguese football to the very pinnacle of European achievement and initiate the disintegration of the Salazarian state.

The rise of Portuguese football inevitably centred on Benfica, by some way the most popular, well resourced and well connected of the nation's clubs. At its apex sat the president Maurício Vieira de Brito, scion of a rich and powerful coffee-planter family. De Brito used the rising income of the club to attract the great Hungarian coach Béla Guttmann to Benfica in 1959, enticing him away from rivals Porto with whom he had just won the championship. Guttmann brought new levels of sophistication and attention to detail in the club's preparation and organization. He transformed the training regime of the squad and introduced them to the tactical and positional innovations of Hungarian football. Where only WM or even more antiquated systems had been the norm, Benfica began to look like a modern football team with a flat back four and attacking midfielders. De Brito was also able to fund the acquisition of some considerable talent and to allow them to operate as full-time professionals. Most notable among the recruits were the Africans. The importation of African talent had begun almost a decade earlier in 1951 when the black Angolan Miguel Arcanjo signed for FC Porto and the black Mozambican Lucas Sebastião da Fonseca, 'Matateu', began his professional career at Belenenses – a career that would culminate in regular appearances for the national side. In 1958 Sporting Lisbon had signed Hilário, a mulatto from Mozambique, but it was at Benfica that African talent arrived most regularly. The Angolan José Águas had joined Benfica as early as 1951, followed in 1955 by Costa Pereira and five years later by Joaquim Santana. The side's heartbeat, captain Mário Coluna, left Mozambique for the club in 1955.

Benfica had been stretched and developed by its earlier encounters with the elite of European football in the 1950s, but in 1961 the team came of age, storming through four rounds of the European Cup, scoring almost three goals a game. In a furious and open final against Barcelona in Berne, Benfica rode their luck. An equalizer from Águas after 30 minutes made it 1–1 and changed the feel of the game. Two minutes later the Catalans' goalkeeper fumbled the ball into his own net, and Coluna made it 3–1 just into the second half. Benfica then saw off a storm of Barcelona chances, shots rebounding off the post and the crossbar, and were champions.

Then in 1960 Benfica discovered a prodigious teenage talent through their scouting networks in the slums of Mozambique: Eusébio da Silva Ferreira. After the predictable tussle between Benfica and Sporting over his signature, Eusébio signed for Benfica. In autumn 1961 Benfica faced South American champions Peñarol in the Intercontinental Club Cup. Both sides had won their home leg and in the play-off the Uruguayans were 1–0 up. Guttmann had picked Eusébio for his first major game for the club and was rewarded with a 30-yard strike of such exceptional quality that its memory has long outlived the final scoreline of 2–1 to Peñarol. The following year, with Eusébio now at the heart of the Benfica attack, the club won the Portuguese league and faced Real Madrid in Amsterdam, in their second consecutive European Cup Final. It was a

game that demonstrated their worth, for Real put on a bravura performance. Di Stéfano and Puskás combined in the first half-hour to produce
a hat-trick for the Hungarian, but the Portuguese held on to the pace
and replied twice. Then in the second half Benfica broke Real's defence
and scored three more goals. Eusébio asked Di Stéfano for his shirt and
the Argentine agreed, appearing to pass on his mantle.

Eusébio, who carried not only Benfica but the Portuguese national
team to unheard-of heights, was perhaps the archetype of the modern
football player. He was tall, heavily built, sensationally fit and strong
enough to keep defenders at bay and hold his own in a tackle or a
challenge. His acceleration and top speed on the ball were faster than
almost anyone else at the time and he rode tackles and barges with
considerable aplomb. He had a remarkably powerful shot, from distance
and at free-kicks, as well as a striker's usual poaching instincts. He was
also an uncommonly gentlemanly player who despite receiving a lot of
brutal treatment, often unprotected by referees, never responded and
never displayed unwarranted aggression on the ball. Indeed, when Alex
Stepney kept out a certain goal from him in their 1968 European Cup
Final he stood back and applauded.

The rising standards of the Portuguese game were underlined when
Sporting won the Cup Winners' Cup in 1964. Together with Benfica the
two sides furnished the bulk of the national squad that qualified for the
nation's first World Cup, in England in 1966. The Portuguese were
drawn in a difficult group but to great acclaim saw off the Brazilians
and the Hungarians. They gave the tournament its most helter-skelter
match when the unknown North Koreans took a 3–0 lead in their
quarter-final. Eusébio scored four goals (including two penalties) and
Portugal made it 5–3 before losing in the semi-finals to the hosts. In
retrospect the 1966 World Cup was Portugal's high point. Benfica had
already lost their European crown to Milan in 1963 and failed to regain
it against Internazionale in the 1965 final. On both occasions, this
last representative of Iberia's open attacking industrial football were
outthought by the defensive nous of the new Italian *catenaccio*. Benfica
made it to another final in 1968, but, tiring in extra time, were comprehensively beaten by Manchester United. But then how could Portuguese
football progress and develop to meet the new challenges of ultra-tactical
Italian football or robust and athletic Northern European football if no
player could travel abroad and no foreigner could come to Portugal?

Eusébio, the most obvious target for foreign clubs, was, in the cheap parlance of authoritarianism, declared a national treasure by Salazar – though this rhetorical flourish hides the reality of a crude injustice. Recalling the matter, Eusébio argues with righteous anger:

Juventus came for me when I was 19. After the World Cup, Inter made a big offer, one which would have made me the highest paid player in the world. And yet I was not allowed to move. Why? Salazar was not my father and he was certainly not my mother. What gave him the right? The truth was that he was my slave master, just as he was the slave master of the entire country.[14]

Salazar died in 1968 and handed the reins of power to his successor Marcello Caetano. There were no more finals and no more triumphs to be had. Portugal failed to qualify for either the 1970 or 1974 World Cups, the country's European prowess declined and crowds were thinning by 1974, when over a quarter of the male population was under arms fighting the unwinnable poisonous colonial wars in Angola and Mozambique.

VI

The rule of Iberian football was terminated by a single city: Milan. AC Milan beat Benfica in the final of the 1963 European Cup and returned to win a further title in 1969. Internazionale sealed the city's pre-eminence with two further European Cups, beating Real Madrid in 1964 and then Benfica in 1965. Along the way the Milanese were champions of the world three times, Inter lost another two European Cup finals (in 1967 and 1972) and Milan won the Cup Winners' Cup in 1968. The decade-long reign of Iberian club football was in many ways the completion of an older cycle of sporting industrialization, which had seen the leading edge of Continental European football pass from Scandinavia to Central Europe to Italy and then Iberia. Now under a new economic and political dispensation it would return to Italy.

Milanese football in particular, and Italian football in general, was the first European football born of the new wave of post-war industrialization, of economic miracles and popular affluence. It was high industrial football marrying a new level of detailed professionalism, with rational, systematic, technical and tactical knowledge and a highly organized division of labour on and off the field. In Milan this football was housed in a factory fit for such a modern approach. The newly rebuilt San Siro stadium with its capacity of 80,000 was perhaps the most unusual and original stadium on the Continent. In reponse to the booming crowds, it was decided that four cantilevered tiers would be built above the old stadium terraces. This was accomplished by wrapping the entire structure in a series of concentric striated concrete walkways that took the crowd from street level to their seats without entering the stadium proper. Functionality was married with the boldest of aesthetic statements.

Italy's football might have peaked sooner but for the legacy of the Superga disaster of 1949. The impact of Superga was both material and psychological. Most cruelly, the heart of the Italian national side that would have gone to the 1950 World Cup was dead. Under the management of Ferruccio Novo, president of Torino, the squad that was selected was understandably required to take a two-week boat trip rather than a plane to Brazil. Not surprisingly, the Italians lacked fitness and edge when they got there. In reaction to the highly dictatorial managerial methods of the Pozzo–Mussolini era, the Italian Football Federation now opted for a more pluralist and collegiate committee system of management. Like the emergent politics of multi-party horse-trading that it mimicked, the system served as a persistent source of disunity and infighting that marred every Italian World Cup campaign for sixteen years. In 1954 the team were knocked out in a first-round play-off by their Swiss hosts. They failed to qualify at all for the 1958 finals after losing to lowly Portugal and Northern Ireland. Italy did make it to the 1962 finals, but the tournament is only remembered for the infamous Battle of Santiago in which the Azzurri traded punches and kicks with the Chileans. There was a different kind of disaster in 1966 as a team of considerable talent were decimated by the unfancied but flying North Koreans and then assaulted by their own fans at Genoa airport with rotten tomatoes.

The legacy of Superga hung heaviest over Torino whose financial, spiritual and sporting decline was palpable and desperate. Having won four consecutive championships from 1946–9, the team failed to win a single title of any kind throughout the 1950s and 1960s (save the less-prestigious Coppa Italia in 1968). With every contemporary defeat the memory and the glory of *Il Grande Torino* grew. Superga and its consequences were the centre of a collective act of melancholy myth-making made all the more poignant by Torino's sporting failure and the simultaneous and astronomical rise of Juventus from mere city rivals to the biggest, most successful club in the country. Like the rest of the club the concrete of the Stadio Filadelfia crumbled, to the point in the early 1960s when Torino were forced to ground-share with bitter rivals Juventus at their Stadio Comunale. The mounting sense that Torino were a cursed club, forever condemned to fall short of past achievements and to be locked in an unbroken cycle of seductive but disempowering nostalgia, was clinched by the death of their 1960s star Gigi Meroni. Meroni was so popular at Torino that when the club decided to sell him to Juventus in 1967, demonstrations were held in the streets at the homes of both clubs' presidents. Meroni stayed with Torino only to be killed the following season in a road accident, struck by a car driven by one of the club's and Meroni's most fanatical fans. Something of the past continued to linger around both the Italian national team and Torino – their triumphs were the products of an era that if not entirely forgotten was not being discussed and celebrated in polite political and cultural circles. The new Italy and the new football were being forged elsewhere.

By the mid-1950s Italian football had assumed its recognizable form as the nation's civic religion. The football calendar, its opening rounds, its mid-winter break and late-spring climax, had assumed the status of the Liturgy. Matches were played almost without fail on Sunday at 3 p.m. in a nationally coordinated mass of sporting reverence. Players habitually crossed themselves on entering or leaving the pitch, managers and coaches were seen to sprinkle holy water on the touchline. The language of the game became increasingly inflected with religious vocabulary. An extraordinary save or a last-minute comeback was a *miracolo* (miracle); the enduring and unbreakable support of the fans was *la fede* (faith) which of course was accompanied by suffering; and escape from relegation, regularly cast in the language of a trip to purgatory or hell, was *la salvezza* (salvation). The great Inter team of the 1960s was known as one 'touched by the hand of God'.

Football crowds, already substantial in the immediate post-war era, began to climb, in stark contrast to participation in the Mass on Sunday morning. The steady increase in real wages for urban workers put regular attendance within the reach of all but the newest and poorest urban arrivals. In this, Italian football was exceptional. While all football cultures and crowds of the era were socially mixed, none could claim the breadth of support from every social class and occupational type that Italian football could. The regional and urban identities and rivalries of the inter-war era remained easily more significant than economic markers of social status. Surveys of Milanese fans, in particular, reveal that there has never been any static attachment of any particular economic group or even neighbourhood to AC Milan or Inter. That is not to suggest that Italian football had no hierarchies; rather it demonstrates the extent to which all forms of social life in post-war Italy were organized around vertical hierarchies between patrons and clients rather than horizontal alliances among members of an economic class or occupational group. The depth of engagement with football can easily be measured by the extraordinary scale of Italy's sporting press in this era. The long-established grandee of the Italian media, the Milan-based *La Gazzetta dello Sport*, and its junior, the Rome-based *Corriere dello Sport*, were joined by *Tuttosport* in Turin. Copies of these papers could be found everywhere in Italy from the cabinet office to the smallest bar or barbers in Catania, their daily readership numbering many millions.

Totocalcio, the state-regulated football pools system established after the war, became an inextricable element of family life in every social class and region. Football on the radio continued to be immensely popular for those who could not go to the match, while the new transistor radios were equally popular with those at the match who tuned into *Tutto il Calcio Minuto per Minuto* – the first live and multi-feed football-reporting show that cut from game-to-game around the country as stories developed and goals were scored or missed.

The team that most successfully rode the boom of the 1950s was Juventus. In some ways, Juventus picked up where they had left off in the mid-1930s as the FIAT works team owned and run by the Agnelli family. But FIAT and Turin were transformed in the years after the Second World War. The city itself almost doubled in size, sucking in a huge quantity of cheap labour from the impoverished regions of southern Italy and the even more desperate islands of Sicily and Sardinia. It was these immigrants that staffed the new and expanding production lines of FIAT and similar Turinese industrial companies, and it was Juventus that was their team. In part this can be understood as a form of obvious clientalism as workers aligned with their boss/patron rather than organizing among themselves against their boss. But Juventus offered something more than an expression of subordination. For this generation of migrants Juventus stood for modernity, for the new opportunities and the new life of the city.

In the mid-1950s Juventus underwent the second great phase of the club's history. At the top Giovanni Agnelli remained president of both FIAT and the club, building a team in his own image – 'Simplicity, seriousness and sobriety' – while his brother Umberto became the club's accomplished political fixer and technical director. The squad was strengthened with the purchase of Welsh striker John Charles and Argentinian Omar Sivori, and a run of considerable success in the national championship began. This, together with widespread media coverage, made Juventus increasingly a national institution rather than just a Turinese team. Indeed the new southern migrants to Turin sent home not merely their wages but their love of Juve too. The team's popularity became so great and widespread that in the 1960s its following could include within its ranks figures as disparate as Palmiro Togliatti, the general secretary of the Italian Communist Party, and Giorgio Almirante, the leader of the neo-fascist MSI party.

But success in Europe required something more than sheer financial clout, seriousness and sobriety. Just as FIAT was dominant in the Italian home market, but struggled to break into export markets, so Juventus, so strong at home, struggled to make any impression on the major European competitions. That something more came from Milan, which by the early 1960s understood itself to be the moral capital of Italy; the leading edge of the new niche industrial economy of the north. Milan may not have had FIAT but it had Pirelli, Zanussi, Alfa Romeo and Innocenti. The city exemplified the fruits of hard work combined with sharp style and design. What Milan added to the mix was the refinement of the art of technical, defensive football, known colloquially as *catenaccio* (meaning 'door-bolt'). The great theorist and advocate of defensive football was the editorial director of *La Gazzetta dello Sport*, Gianni Brera. In this era, in which television and other visual imagery were still only part of the media mix rather than the overwhelmingly dominant financial and cultural force, and newspaper readership was high, European football offered an unequalled audience and platform for the written word. In France, *L'Équipe* and *France Football* offered the considered seriousness and brilliant, vaulting organizational ambition of Gabriel Hanot. England, particularly in the 1960s, began to generate sports journalism of the highest, if understated calibre, exemplified by Geoffrey Green and Arthur Hopcraft, while in Brian Glanville England finally found a football writer whose gaze extended beyond the Channel. The Glaswegian Hugh McIlvanney matured into the finest match reporter of the era, capable under the most extraordinary pressures of time and resource to evoke the emotional fibre and sporting dynamics of the moment with precision, wit and well-chosen flourish. In this context Brera is perhaps the first amongst equals.

Born in the Po Valley in 1919, Brera studied for a degree in political science and completed his education by writing a thesis on Thomas More's *Utopia* in 1942. In 1944 he joined the Italian Partisans and saw out the war on active duty, as he put it 'more shot at than shooting'. He was a man of diverse talents, tastes and energies. Eating and drinking were of course a continual backdrop to all the others, which included writing four novels, translating three plays of Molière into Italian and watching and writing about sport. In 1950 at the age of thirty he was made editorial director of *La Gazzetta* and from here he remade the language and reality of Italian football. He was capable of the usual range of journalistic polemic, hagiography, myth-making, gossip-mongering and conflict-stirring, and combined all of them to write a hysterical if anecdotal history of Italian football. His knack for nicknaming players and creating neologisms was immense. What did one say to describe the meandering passing of the ball between the defensive line and the midfield in their own half in an effort to waste time or frustrate their opponents, until Brera coined the term *melina*? And that fragile-looking midfield player who didn't seem to turn and tackle but could play a decisive ball – what was he called in Italian before he was an *abatino* – a young priest? But for all of this, Brera's distinctive contribution was his discussion of tactics. The question of tactics had never been addressed in any football press with the seriousness and persistence of Brera's *Gazzetta*. Two further innovations aided and sharpened those discussions: the evolution of the world's most complex vocabulary for positions on the pitch and for types of players; and the systematic marking or scoring of players after games. Italy, long before most, recognized a complex division of labour that included stoppers, man-markers, liberos, stable and fluid fullbacks, holding and attacking midfielders, water-carriers, destroyers, on-field directors, wingers and *fantasisti*. Out of this engagement with the tactics of the game Brera offered not merely description but a philosophy in which every move had a counter-move, every attacking strategy its defensive nemesis, and under which 0–0 was the perfect score of the perfect game.

Catenaccio as an actual system of play with recognized and distinct on-field positions was first developed by the Austrian-born coach Karl Rappan at Servette in the Swiss league in the 1930s. In the conventional formations of the time three forwards would bear down on three defenders. If anyone managed to beat his man, there was no cover behind him. Rappan withdrew one player from his forward line and played him directly behind his three centre-backs as a sweeper; for perhaps the first time in professional football a player was deputed to mark a space not an opponent. While Rappan never attended to the implications of this ploy for scoring at the other end, it was good enough for the Swiss national team to beat the Germans and the Austrians at the 1938 World Cup. But it was under Nereo Rocco at AC Milan and Helenio Herrera at Internazionale in the 1960s that the system was perfected.

Catenaccio, then and now, also refers to a state of mind, a broad disposition among coaches, players and teams that is characterized by Italy's leading football cliché, 'our first priority is a clean sheet'. But it also alludes to an essential caution and closely honed risk analysis in which the possession of the ball is always valued and squandering it in quixotic attacks or moves is treasonable. Increasingly, *catenaccio* came also to serve as a synonym for gamesmanship, which in Italy was increasingly considered an art in its own right. Italian football may not have invented the tactical or 'professional' foul, but it was among the first to name and refine it. An Italian crowd would applaud the kind of challenge that saves a goal even at the cost of a yellow card, even a red card and dismissal if necessary. With these tactics and this mindset, Milan would conquer Europe.

Both Milanese teams found domestic success in the 1950s, Milan fielding their Swedish forward line of Gunnar Gren, Gunnar Nordahl and Nils Liedholm, and Inter winning a title with a characteristically defensive manager, Alfredo Foni. The leap to European and global success was based on the same core of resources and relationships that Juventus had pioneered in the 1950s, bringing together wealthy and connected presidents and politically and sportingly astute technical directors. Milan and Inter then added charismatic managers. Nereo Rocco, schooled in the art of *catenaccio* with smaller teams, was reunited at Milan with technical director Gipo Viani, who had himself pioneered the technique in Italy over a decade earlier. Together they built a defensive system around Cesare Maldini, created a midfield that worked hard around their single creative passer Gianni Rivera, and possessed a front line that included during the 1960s Jimmy Greaves and José Altafini. *El Paròn* (the Boss), as Rocco was known in the Trieste dialect, was by turns avuncular and an irascible bully. Under his management Milan won the championship in 1962 and the European Cup the following year, courtesy of two brilliant passes from Rivera. After a short sabbatical at Torino, Rocco returned to Milan and won the championship again, the Cup Winners' Cup and the European Cup, thrashing a rising but unworldly Ajax 4–1 in the 1969 final. This team also had a spine of steel, demonstrated when they outfought the combative Estudiantes La Plata in the 1969 Intercontinental Club Cup. As Rocco said to his sides, 'Kick everything that moves; if it is the ball, even better.'

Internazionale's fortunes were transformed by the arrival of Angelo Moratti, a self-made petroleum billionaire, as president in 1955. After getting through almost a manager a year, he settled in 1961 on Helenio Herrera who had just taken Barcelona to two Spanish titles. At Inter he was united with Moratti's money and a fixer and technical director of impeccable connectedness and dubious practices, Italo Allodi. Over the next seven years they created *Il Grande Inter*. Herrera, known in Italy as *Il Mago* (the Magician), was the first manager-as-star in global football. His origins and age were deliberately shrouded in mystery. He was born on an island somewhere on the Río de la Plata around the turn of the century. The son of a Spanish anarchist, he grew up in poverty in Casablanca, escaped through French professional football and then coached there before making his international mark by leading Atlético Madrid and Barcelona. Though not alone, he is one of the key creators of Italian football's hyper-professionalism and attention to detail. His rule, though uneven and combustible, was characteristically dictatorial. The minutiae of the players' personal lives, diet and conduct were under constant scrutiny. Herrera introduced the practice of pre-match retreats, completely cocooning a squad away from the press, family and friends in an act of collective meditation and focus that owed something to Herrera's own Buddhist and yogic practices. Training regimes and expectations of levels of fitness were truly demanding.

Herrera's grasp of the psychological dynamics of professional football led him to place particular stress on the role of the crowd. He encouraged Angelo Moratti to form and fund travelling clubs of Interisti to support the team at away games in Italy and on their European adventures – an action that anticipated the creation of independent *ultra* groups by some way. To this mix Herrera added a meticulous if occasionally incomprehensible body of note-taking, theorizing, speaking and writing. Herrera's mantra was *Taca La Bal* – attack the ball – don't just possess it, use it, make it work for you. In a remarkable anticipation of the spatial thinking of Dutch football later in the decade, Herrera instructed, 'Create empty spaces. In football as in life, in painting, in music, empty spaces and silences are as important as those that are filled.'[15] But if Herrera aspired to a game of open spaces, the reality of his team's play was a game of closed spaces, locked doors and impassable barriers. *Il Grande Inter* created a defence of incomparable effectiveness.

With such a successful domestic football scene in Italy in the late 1960s, the national team finally came good. Italy hosted the final rounds of the 1968 European Championship and though they required the toss of a coin to get past the Soviet Union, and a replay to beat the brilliant Yugoslavs in the final, they claimed their first major trophy for thirty years. The 1970 World Cup marks the high point of this generation of Italian football. Italy made the final, and lost to Brazil, though the event has been so totally monopolized in its global retelling by the performance of the Brazilians that the Italian experience of Mexico 1970 is lost in most accounts of the tournament. For the Italians, the game that really mattered was the 4–3 semi-final win against West Germany, and of that game it was extra time that defined the moment. Uncharacteristically, the last thirty minutes saw an explosion of open attacking football and wanton risk-taking, by an otherwise *catenaccio*-minded Italian team. Not only that, but in a society in which truly national symbols and experiences were rare, the match had an audience of 17 million viewers, easily the biggest in Italian broadcasting history. They were watching a team that for once drew on players from both the northern and southern clubs – especially Cagliari, the tiny Sardinian club led by striker Gigi Riva which had unexpectedly won the Scudetto the previous season. Nando Dalla Chiesa described the experience like this:

In place of traditional defensive tactics, which had so nearly worked, Italy went for broke, on the attack, scoring three goals in an uncontrollable explosion of sentiments, passions, instincts . . . there were no more tactics, no more order, no more cynicism . . . the past was over.[16]

That spirit of youth rebellion, of a challenge to the established order and the denunciation of the rotten compromises, shallow consumerism and antiquated social and political mores erupted first in France in 1968. Then in Italy it took hold in the long hot autumn of 1969 in which workers' strikes and factory occupations joined with the students and utopians of a thousand left-wing micro-groups in the country's biggest open challenge to public and economic authority in seventy years. Beneath the veneer of modernization and democratization, Italian political and public life left much to be desired. For those who chose to look closely at Italian football, it was not the spirit of 1968 that predominated but the creeping pathologies of a closed, clientalistic and cynical world.

The early 1960s saw the first doping scandals in Italian football. Minor players at Internazionale were found to be positive in 1962, throwing continued doubt on the rest of the squad. Five Genoa players were banned for a few games for taking amphetamines in 1963 and Gigi Meroni was banned for refusing to take the dope test. Most seriously of all Bologna players who had beaten Inter in the 1964 Scudetto play-off were accused of taking performance-enhancing drugs. In every case, the notion that the problem might be endemic was raised but no investigation of any seriousness was pursued. The same kind of response was mounted by the authorities to accusations of corruption and bribery which constantly circulated as low-level topics of conversation and rumour. Occasionally, when the evidence was overwhelming, the story would burst into the press – such as the 1955 Catanian refereeing crisis – but for the most part the clubs, the press and the Italian Football Federation denied that any such practices went on. When the British journalist Brian Glanville published accusations that Italian clubs had been engaging in the systematic courting and bribery of match officials in European tournaments, he was ostracized by the Italian press and football establishment who, in an act of self-preservation, denied everything; acts that now appear to be both mendacious and dishonest.[17]

The politics of refereeing was perhaps the clearest and most worrying sign of the problems of Italian football and Italian society in general. The attitude to the authority of the referee offers no better and clearer example of Italian civil society's view of legality, law and authority. By the 1980s this would boil down to an unshiftable cynicism bordering on the paranoid. At this stage it was merely contempt for the obvious structural inequalities in the Italian polity. Giorgio Bertotto, one of the leading referees and football administrators, coined the term 'psychological slavery' to describe the unconscious but systematic bias of referees to the big clubs after a particularly skewed set of decisions in a game between Venezia and Inter in 1967. Inter, after all, went over 100 games at one point without conceding a penalty and that was playing a system with the last man invariably tackling inside the box.

If the Italian establishment had circled the wagons in an attempt to keep out the forces of change in football and society alike, society was not content to just sit back and let them recover. The late 1960s and early 1970s saw wave after wave of collective protests and innovatory micro-groups in Italian politics. So too in football, where football fans began to form the first autonomous fans' organizations – soon to be know as *ultras*. The earliest recorded *ultra* group emerged among AC Milan fans in 1968: the *Fossa dei Leoni*. They were soon followed by the *Inter Boys SAN* and by Sampdoria's *ultras* named in honour of their old star Tito Cucchiari. By 1973, when both Turin teams acquired their first *ultra* groups, the ideological tilt of this unexpected social movement was apparent: Torino's gave themselves the militaristic name of *Granata Corps* while Juve's *Drughi* acknowledged the influence of Anthony Burgess's *Clockwork Orange* gangs.

Football players, despite their relative wealth and status, took the long hot autumn as an opportunity to flex their muscles as skilled labourers, for the contractual systems and welfare support available to players remained absent or primitive: in 1970 there was still no provision for player insurance or pensions. In this they were no different from most of the skilled workers in the Italian economy whose rising pay had not been accompanied by any systematic welfare provisions or any change in the authoritarian hierarchies and daily inequities of the shop floor. Both trade unions and footballers achieved this in the early 1970s by the threat of strike action. Italy was now embroiled in a nationwide series of industrial disputes, runaway inflation and an emergent politics of left- and right-wing extremism, state and private terrorism. The sheen had come off the Italian economic miracle, while Italian football, though still good enough to produce teams that could make the final of the

European Cup – Inter in 1972 and Juventus in 1973 – was no longer good enough to win it.

In 1935 Stalin proclaimed, 'Life has become better: life has become more joyous.' He was admittedly starting from a low base, but by the mid-1930s the pace of purging, working and dying in the Soviet Union had finally dropped and there was time and head space for the re-emergence of a little private leisure and public spectacle. Twenty years later, after the tumult of the Second World War and the initial phase of communist reconstruction, the same could be said once again of Eastern Europe and the Soviet Union. The death of Stalin in 1953 and the rule of Khrushchev in Moscow till 1964 led to the abandonment of the worst excesses of forced industrialization and rule by terror. Though the Hungarian uprising showed there were limits to this newfound tolerance, it became possible to live a relatively normal if drab life again. Although never able to match the long-term growth rates and technological sophistication of Western Europe, Eastern Europe experienced reasonable rates of economic development following the global boom and the continuing industrialization and urbanization of the region. In this context football, although never commercialized, was able to become increasingly professionalized, drawing on large urban crowds, but relying on whatever resources that state and parastatal institutions which ran the game could extract from the central economy.

A combination of a certain amount of luck and a crop of talented coaches and players was enough to give Czechoslovakia and Poland their short-lived place in the footballing sun, but the real powerhouses of football in the Eastern Bloc world were Yugoslavia and the Soviet Union. Yugoslavia's record is quite remarkable. In the inter-war period they had played in the semi-final of the first World Cup – and to this day many believe that only the illegal intervention of Uruguayan policemen prevented them from beating their hosts. In the 1930s Yugoslav players were also making their way to France and Italy to play in the new professional leagues. Despite the sledgehammer blows that the war applied to Yugoslavia's economy and society, the national team made four Olympic Finals in a row between 1948 and 1960. They also

437

played in three World Cups (1954–62) and two European Champion-ship Finals (1960 and 1968). But when the decisive moment came, these teams were nearly always found wanting. Their only victory was the 1960 Olympics, by then a pale imitation of the World Cup.

Yugoslavia were, from their inception, enthusiastic participants in European club competitions: Yugoslavia was the only country east of the Elbe to contest or win a European final in the 1960s, Partizan Belgrade losing to Real Madrid in the 1966 European Cup Final and Dinamo Zagreb winning the Fairs Cup in 1967. The Partizan game, in particular, is the subject of extended and unresolved myth-making and gossip-mongering that are the hallmarks of a paranoid football culture. One version of the match is that the team were offered cash by an intermediary to throw the game at half-time. In another version the referee offered the game to the Partizan Belgrade board beforehand for a mere $15,000 hard currency. However, the army generals decided they couldn't afford it.

Soviet football in the 1950s entered a period of relative stability; in the jargon of the day, 'normalcy'. The break-up of teams on ideological or political grounds, like CSKA in 1952, on the whim of the Kremlin, no longer pertained. As the worst of the war damage was repaired and the Soviet steel and cement industries continued their ludicrous overexpansion, sufficient spare capacity existed to underwrite a massive stadium-building programme. In the 1960s and early 1970s over 2,000 sports stadiums were constructed in the country, and the now bur-geoning provincial cities of the Soviet Union had their football grounds rebuilt or radically reconstructed. Kiev's Republic stadium acquired a second cantilevered tier, and Tbilisi, Minsk, Baku and Yerevan all acquired large, ugly, concrete bowls. Membership of the football league, previously restricted to Moscow, Kiev and Leningrad, grew alongside this urbanization which now saw over 70 per cent of the country living in cities. Total attendance at league games in 1953 was 3.9 million watching an eleven-team league. By the mid-1960s the top division had increased to nineteen teams and attendances had tripled to a peak of over 10 million. When television arrived in the Soviet Union in the mid-1950s football was from the beginning a staple element of program-ming. Initially both coverage and reception were restricted to Moscow, but like the wave of stadium-building it reached the entire country by the end of the 1960s. This pattern of diffusion was haltingly reflected in performances on the pitch as the Moscow monopoly on the title was finally broken by Dinamo Kiev, who won the title in 1961; and then in the early 1970s the championship passed to the truly provincial Zarya Voroshilovgrad and Ararat Yerevan.

In the international sphere, Soviet teams had only started to play non-communist opposition in the early 1950s, appearing at the 1952 Olympics, touring in Eastern Europe and playing friendlies – the defeat of world champions West Germany in Moscow was hailed as a decisive breakthrough. The team that won the 1956 Olympics in Melbourne then qualified for their first World Cup in 1958, where they played out their usual tournament destiny: good in the opening rounds, then a defeat in the knock-out stage. This time they were beaten 2–0 by the Swedes. At the inaugural European Championship in 1960 the squad was consciously drawn from beyond the usual Moscow-based talent pool and tellingly it was players from the provinces and lower leagues that made the winning goal for the Soviet Union in the final against Yugoslavia. However, they were never to repeat this triumph. In 1962 they lost a World Cup quarter-final to Chile, having exhausted themselves in furious and ill-disciplined games against Uruguay and Colombia. In 1964 they were runners-up to Spain in the European Championship – a defeat by Franco's Spain was a sleight of sufficient importance that Khrushchev himself made his displeasure known. Some pride appeared to have been regained when the team made it to the semi-finals of the 1966 World Cup, losing a dreary, foul-ridden game with West Germany; and then in 1968 they were beaten by the Italians in the European Championship on the toss of a coin.

After each of these defeats there was, in private and increasingly in public, a long and agonized debate about team tactics and the strengths and weaknesses of Soviet football. It was clearly recognized that the summer season played in the Soviet Union left its players underprepared for summer tournaments when other nations' players were peaking. Similarly, it was known, but not publicly stated, that the leadership's ideological preference for Olympic sports was a constant drag on football's development. The technical and tactical weaknesses of the Soviet squads were also raised and it was clear that fitness levels did not match the one-gear running game that they seemed to always play – particularly in the heat of Latin America. And despite the taboos of socialist thought, there was also a recognition that Soviet teams lacked individual flair and

initiative. The most explosive outburst of protest came at the end of this
cycle of tournaments. At the 1970 World Cup the Soviet Union once
again made the quarter-finals but were sunk by Uruguay, who stole a
goal near the end of extra time as the Soviets melted in the heat. Encouraged no doubt by greater TV coverage, the degree of public anger and
disappointment was immense: *Izvestia* alone received 300,000 letters of
complaint. The next six months saw both sports press and mainstream
publications littered with critical and tactical discussions. The team
would not qualify for a World Cup for another twelve years and in the
following four years football attendances plummeted to less than half
the peak levels of the mid-1960s. In the fields of both sporting success
and popular entertainment it appeared that football organized under
the Soviet mode of production had reached its limits. The limitations of
the centrally planned economy were countered by operating in the grey
areas of society:

Enterprises were forced by circumstances to adopt the use of a variety of middlemen pushers or *tolkachi*, to obtain the raw materials and other favours required
to fulfil centrally mandated plans. These people had no formal title, but industry
could not have operated without them. The economy was highly controlled, but
in fact, it could not function without a wide variety of supposedly informal
mechanisms.[18]

Making the system work required systematically undermining, cir-
cumventing or dismantling the system; so too with top league football.
Although the club was a supposedly open organization, it was actually
a fiefdom of powerful and connected individuals, though they were not
necessarily members of the club's board or on its pay roll in any way.
Collectively known as the *metsenaty*, these patrons responded to the real
economic signals and pressures of competitive football – that victory, not
fraternal relations, was the purpose of the exercise and if that meant
spending money then money would be found and spent. Although
players were notionally amateurs they were receiving goods, phantom
jobs and perks at a level that exceeded even the leading shamateur
Western leagues of the pre-professional era. Similarly, although no transfer market existed, there was considerable player movement, facilitated
by cash payments, payments-in-kind and a range of proto-agents.

If football demonstrated the hollowness of the command economy, it
made an equal mockery of the official ideological stance in which sport

was cast as an instrument of peace, understanding and proletarian harmony. Violence, although underreported, was tangible. Pitch invasions resurfaced as acts of collective protest, usually in response to refereeing decisions. The term *zaznaistvo* – star syndrome – was coined to describe not merely the bad behaviour (violent, rude, and drunken) of leading players but the whole system of official silences and cover-ups on which they relied.

The peccadilloes and hypocrisy of the Soviet nomenklatura were reasonably well known and well documented. Football was no different in this respect from the broader social order. Where it differed was in the opportunities it offered for the public to misbehave. By the early 1970s *Sovetskii Sporti* would complain:

Why has it become impossible to imagine any soccer game without some drunk, disturbed people, who push you on the shoulders at the entrances and who, in the stands, harass their neighbours for an hour and a half . . . ?[19]

Football was exposing the degenerate state of Soviet civil society, which was responding to the gloomy narrowness and double standards of state socialism with ever-rising levels of vodka consumption and anti-social behaviour. In the 1970s and 1980s, what was left of the illusion of Soviet economic parity was destroyed by its militarism and inflexibility, and Soviet football would expose the pathologies of this fragmenting society ever more starkly.

VIII

Withdrawal from India in 1947; defeat to the USA in 1950; 6–3 to the Hungarians in 1953; Suez, 1956; the relentless litany of defeat. For a decade Britain's declining power in the worlds of politics and football marched in step. Although in reality Britain remained rich, powerful and influential, its conversation with itself and its estimation of its footballing prowess were conducted in the context of decline. In retrospect the twenty years after 1954 appear a period of immense economic growth which transformed the lives of the entire country; yet there was a nagging feeling, occasionally visceral and public, that Britain was falling behind its political, economic and sporting competitors.

The national teams of England, Scotland, Wales and Northern Ireland may have finally thrown off their insularity – indeed, all four qualified for the 1958 World Cup in Sweden – but they were evidently in the second or third rank of global football. England, in particular, were disappointing. Quarter-finalists at the 1954 World Cup, a team that boasted Matthews, Lofthouse and Finney were made to look ordinary by the Uruguayans who beat them 4–2. In 1958 England could only manage three draws in the first-round group and were squeezed out by a mediocre Soviet team in a play-off for the quarter-final. In Chile in 1962, Garrincha's bravura display of trickery put England out of the quarter-finals. As with the products of Britain's manufacturing industry, Britain's football teams did not travel well.

Finding the source of decline became the holy grail of political economy and football politics. There was a whole variety of candidates: the amateurism and conservatism of the ruling elites; the perennially low level of investment; the absence of a serious and competent technocracy in positions of authority; restrictive practices among an inadequately trained and under-educated labour force. All had their football corollaries. The rate of capital formation in the British economy was one of the lowest of any advanced capitalist country – less than 15 per cent of GDP through the 1950s and 1960s. British football was equally parsimonious. Once the worst of the war damage had been repaired – at Old Trafford, for example – the basic infrastructure of British football was left untouched and unmodernized. When England hosted the 1966 World Cup, not a single new stadium was built and those that were used merely received a lick of paint and not much more. Wembley Stadium got a roof, but the toilets and catering remained of an inter-war vintage. Sheffield Wednesday's celebrated steel cantilever stand was the only significant architectural advance of the era. The owners of British firms and British clubs were not only reluctant to invest in plant, they remained slow to appreciate the use of new technology and unwilling to fund the kind of training and apprenticeship schemes that the low-skill economy of the country required.

The general tenor of the governance of English football in the 1950s and early 1960s bore a remarkable resemblance to the antiquated, complacent self-importance of the Macmillan and Home administrations that governed the country. Both the Football League and the FA remained suspicious of many of the key innovations of the era. The pools industry was resisted until the late 1950s; floodlit league football was opposed until 1956; television coverage was sharply restricted – even the advent of the highlights programme *Match of the Day* in 1964 left the game woefully undercovered. Most amazing of all, the Football League champions of 1955, Chelsea, took the decision not to enter the newly created European Cup – an expression of predictable cultural insularity. Even where innovation was tentatively explored, it remained shackled. Walter Winterbottom was appointed as the first coach to the England team in 1946 with a remit to develop the national team and the general standard of coaching and coaching education in the country. That a single post could be responsible for such a massive workload suggests either naivety or lack of interest on the part of the FA. Even then, Winterbottom did not obtain proper control over the squad whose composition remained with the same unaccountable and unfathomable selection committee. Winterbottom, who was an ex-professional and who had trained in physical education, was perhaps the first technocrat in English management. He introduced a measure of tactical thinking and discussion to the England squad, though his inability to anticipate or learn significantly from the Hungarian debacle suggests that his grasp of tactics and communication with the players was limited.

The other modernizing force in English football was Matt Busby's Manchester United. Busby rescued the club when he took over after the Second World War, won the FA Cup in 1948 and created a fabulous team of young players, the Busby Babes, who in various incarnations won the Championship three times in the 1950s and were England's first entrants in the European Cup. Where Chelsea feared to tread, Busby's United stooped to conquer. Busby's innovations were manifold. Above all, in his own words, 'I wanted method' and method is what Manchester United got. Busby took real control of the club by force of charisma and personal authority. He created a youth system, a professional training and support structure and applied his own version of Scottish working-class solidarities to the business of football. In their opening game in the European Cup in 1957 they beat the Belgian champions Anderlecht 10–0 and went on to lose a fiercely competitive semi-final with the defending champions Real Madrid. The following year they flew to Yugoslavia for the second leg of their quarter-final with Red Star Belgrade, where a 3–3 draw was enough to put them through. A semi-final with AC Milan awaited them. And then there was Munich. On the way back from Belgrade, the team's plane crashed on take-off from Munich airport in the driving winter snows; twenty-three people were dead and many others seriously injured. Manchester United had lost the core of its management and its squad. In the semi-finals a makeshift side held their own at home before being despatched 4–0 at the San Siro. The most exciting playing force in English football, backed by the most modern and adventurous management, was finished before it had even started.

The fate of most English professional footballers, like the class they hailed from, was less dramatic. There was a steady growth in real wages to the point where patterns of consumption, expectation and aspiration were being transformed. The legacy of the Attlee Labour government to professional footballers was the industrial tribunal system which pushed the maximum wage up from £12 a week in 1947 to £20 in 1958. Although those on the maximum wage and bonuses earned around 50 per cent more than skilled workers, only 30 per cent of the sporting workforce was getting anywhere near this level of pay. Even those at the top of the scale saw the differentials eroded: in 1948 they had been earning double the wages of a skilled male worker – and that indisputably was the economic and cultural reference point of the British footballer who overwhelmingly continued to emerge from working-class families (well over half of those came from the north of England alone). Despite their public status, they continued to be treated with the same authoritarian contempt that their social equivalents in the engineering and construction industries endured. When Barnsley's Harry Hough put in a transfer request to his chairman Joe Richards, he was told, 'You go where I tell you.'

One possible option for players was to move abroad. But as the Colombian adventures of Neil Franklin and Charlie Mitten demonstrated, the cultural capital and personal confidence of the average British footballer were just not up to the complex and difficult transition to professional football in other cultures.[20] John Charles, the Welsh centre-forward who left for Juventus in 1955, is perhaps the only British player of the era who made that transition successfully. Jimmy Greaves and Denis Law, who were recruited by AC Milan and Torino in the early 1960s, were home within a season.

If the exit option was blocked for players, speaking out did not seem much of an option either. The quaintly named Association Football Players and Coaches Union, despite possessing a loud and abrasive

Scottish half-back Jimmy Guthrie as its general secretary, remained a poorly organized and supported trade union. Players' loyalties to their clubs generally exceeded their loyalty to their class. Nonetheless, discontent was widespread and with the arrival of ex-Coventry player Jimmy Hill as the union's secretary it was at last effectively mobilized. Hill, in contrast to Guthrie, did not see riveters as the reference point for himself or professional footballers. The new, often working-class stars and entrepreneurs of the TV, film and music industries were his models, as his subsequent careers as club manager and director, Middle Eastern football entrepreneur and TV football pundit bore out. Hill was also articulate, sharp, convivial and confident: a mixture of talents and traits that were not associated with footballers of any kind. He changed the union's name to the Professional Footballers' Association (PFA) – a name redolent of the modern white-collar world to which he thought professional football should belong – and he got organized.

In mid-1960 a clear and agreed agenda of change was put to the footballing authorities: the abolition of the maximum wage, a share of transfer fees for players, a new retention system that would give players considerably more freedom when moving clubs, and a new contract. After six months of wrangling the Football League conceded the abolition of the maximum wage but nothing else. Hill and the PFA ran rings around them in the press, got public opinion on their side and in the single most effective display of industrial solidarity in the English game, agreed to strike in early 1961 for the full package. The day before the strike the League relented on everything but the retention system. Hill was ready for this too, and he took up the case of Newcastle United forward George Eastham who had been barred from leaving the club. When the case came to court, the judge stated the obvious: that the entire contractual system of English football was a blatant and indefensible restraint of trade. It would take another decade-and-a-half for the implications of the ruling to be implemented. But wages at the very top of the game exploded overnight with Johnny Haynes of Fulham making the news as the first £100-a-week player, and throughout the decade there was a steady rise in income putting leading players – for the duration of their career – into the salary bracket of the comfortable middle classes.

The struggle over the maximum wage made one thing clear: advances against the establishment would only be won by planning and organization, and they would be resisted if possible and only grudgingly

accepted. Such a situation required advocates of change and modernization to combine a thick skin with a realistic level of internal paranoia
– for they really were out to get you. These were precisely the traits of
both Harold Wilson, leader of the opposition Labour Party, and the
emerging football technocracy of managers and coaches. Wilson became
Labour leader in 1963 and electrified the nation with his promise of
economic and social modernization, correctly identifying the enduring
problems of antiquated systems of management, hapless amateurism
amongst the business and state elites, and the restrictive impact of old
hierarchies and inequalities on the nation's youth and talent. In its place
he offered a vision of Britain in which science, knowledge and those that
possessed them would remake the nation.

In all our plans for the future, we are re-defining and we are restating our
Socialism in terms of the scientific revolution. But that revolution cannot become
a reality unless we are prepared to make far-reaching changes in economic and
social attitudes which permeate our whole system of society. The Britain that is
going to be forged in the white heat of this revolution will be no place for
restrictive practices or for outdated methods on either side of industry.[21]

A similar spirit can be detected among the leading football managers
of the era who, despite their many differences, represented the new class
of football coaches. They were all ex-professionals; they all carved out
a high level of autonomy and authority from their employers and boards
of directors; they were innovative in their training methods and familiar
if not obsessed with questions of tactics. They were also fanatically
detailed in their preparations. The key English managers were Bill
Nicholson at Spurs, Ron Greenwood at West Ham United and Alf
Ramsey, first at Ipswich Town and then as coach of the England team.
The leading Scots were Matt Busby and his post-Munich Manchester
United, Jock Stein at Celtic and Bill Shankly at Liverpool. Between them
this cohort of coaches remade British football and in the mid-1960s
returned it, albeit briefly, to the very pinnacle of the world game.

After Munich the club and coach that proclaimed again the modernization of English football were Tottenham Hotspur and Bill Nicholson.
Nicholson inherited a strong team and passing culture from his predecessor Arthur Rowe, exemplified by Danny Blanchflower. To this he
added the immense attacking and creative talents of Dave Mackay, Cliff
Jones and Jimmy Greaves, and insisted on a game built on possession

and position, thinking spatially, and short accurate fast passing. At their peak, Nicholson's Spurs won the League and FA Cup double in 1961, the first time it had been achieved in the twentieth century. Moreover, this was a team that could really compete in Europe. In the 1962 European Cup they made it as far as the semi-finals, only losing to Benfica. The following year they were the first English club to win a European title – the Cup Winners' Cup – thrashing Atlético Madrid 5–1 in the final.

Ron Greenwood, manager of West Ham United, also brought a more explicitly tactical approach to the game and a more open and even dialogue with his players. He also organized and invested in the country's leading youth programme which nurtured three of the key talents in England's 1966 World Cup squad: captain Bobby Moore, Geoff Hurst and Martin Peters. The club itself went on to win the 1964 FA Cup and 1965 European Cup Winners' Cup.

In 1962 the league title went to Ipswich Town under Alf Ramsey. It was a feat of considerable technocratic and social engineering. The championship had never been won by an East Anglian club and Ipswich was as small, provincial and unfashionable a place from which to fashion a league-winning team as one could imagine. Ramsey took them out of the second division in 1961 and took the major title the following season. He did it with almost no money, deploying his obsessive command of detail, preparation and training, and matching the mode of play to the limitations of his squad. He combined both a relentless focus on his job with an active distate for non-professionals and those outside the magic circle of football knowledge. When the chairman of Ipswich came to congratulate him on the title at a reserve game, Ramsey is said to have stared coldly ahead, snapping, 'D'you mind? I'm working.' When Walter Winterbottom stepped down from the England post, Ramsey was the obvious choice.

Of the Scots, Bill Shankly was the first to make his mark in the 1960s. Shankly arrived in 1959 with Liverpool stuck in the second division. The team were promoted in 1962, won the league in 1964 and 1966, the FA Cup in 1965 and made it to the semi-finals of the European Cup. His achievements were based on an alluring and eclectic mix. Practically, his immediate achievements were to establish absolute authority within the club over football matters, and to create a support team of diverse talents – nicknamed the boot-room – including Bob Paisley, future

Liverpool manager and one of the most tactically informed coaches in English football. At every level of organization, from transport (Liverpool were one of the first teams to travel by air to away games), to investment in training facilities, to the organization of training itself (the famed sweatboxes and small-space five-a-sides), Shankly was an obsessive. But alongside these innovations he established a model of football and team-building rooted in his early years in a small mining community in the west of Scotland. First, he pursued a vision of simple football. Pass the ball to someone else in red and then take up another position in which you can receive it. The local press soon recognized his Continental inclination for possession, short passing, simple movements. But it was also a vision of football that prioritized the team over individual performance. Second, he brought a profound sense of solidarity to the dressing room, denoted by his own preference for tracksuits over lounge suits, for the training ground rather than his office. It was a solidarity materially enforced by a wage policy that refused to allow major differentials to emerge within the squad.

Yet to focus exclusively on Shankly's practical work and his rootedness in the working-class communities of his native Scotland is to miss perhaps the most essential element of his rule: 'With his drill-sergeant's hair-style, his boxer's stance, his staccato hard-man delivery, he did not fit everyone's idea of a romantic. But that is what he was, an out-and-out, 22-carat example of the species.'[22] It was an era of technocracy and order, of method and plan, and Shankly – despite his loathing for the theoreticians and clipboard merchants of the FA's official training courses – was part of that moment too. But unlike so many others he also understood and possessed the powers of love, wit, charisma and solidarity, and it is in these traits that his romanticism resides. Significantly, Shankly was the most avid player of any of the new wave of managers: his inability to resist a five-a-side in the car park was without parallel. And his wit? On addressing the massed ranks of Liverpool fans outside the town hall celebrating a trophy, he told them, 'Chairman Mao has never seen such a show of red strength as this.'

However, Shankly's Liverpool was always more than Shankly, the boot-room, the squad or the club. The phenomenon was also made by the fans and indeed by the whole city of Liverpool. Shankly sat at the very centre of Britain's emergent youth culture, and his instinctive charismatic populism and human openness made him the manager best placed to draw on its energies. Peter Thompson, the Liverpool winger, recalls: 'It was a quarter to three on match day at Anfield and there was no sign of Shanks. Suddenly he came in. His shirt's torn, tie undone, jacket hanging all over the place. "What's happened, boss?" "I've just been in the Kop with the boys." ' High on their shoulders and arms he had been tossed across the stand.

The Kop, like most English stands, was pretty much unaltered from its original form built in 1928. Arthur Hopcraft described the Kop in the 1950s as:

Hideously uncomfortable. The steps are as greasy as a school playground lava-tory. The air is rancid with beer and onions and belching and worse. The language is a gross purple of obscenity. When the crowd surges a man . . . can be lifted off the ground in the crush as if by some soft-sided crane, grabbed and dangled about for minutes on end, perhaps never getting back to . . . the spot from which the monster made its bite.[23]

The monster could still bite. In 1966 over 200 people were injured in a crush at a European Cup game. The same traits could be found elsewhere in England, but the Kop stands as both the clearest example and the greatest innovator in fan culture in Britain in the 1960s. The city that filled it was on a high. The docks and the new light industry of the city were booming. As Liverpool rose, so too did Everton; then known as the School of Science, they had won the league in 1963. As the port of empire, Liverpool was more open to and more connected to the transatlantic currents of Caribbean migration and American music than anywhere outside London. When the market for working-class enter-tainers in television, music and comedy inched open, Liverpool's heritage of spoken wit and word play gave it a head start. Of course there were the Beatles, soon to leave, but there was more to come: Cilla Black, Ken Dodd, Jimmy Tarbuck, Gerry and the Pacemakers and the Merseybeat poets. Given that the centre of popular cultural gravity had for a moment descended upon Liverpool, it was at Anfield that the contact between the new pop music and football was first made.

Prior to the 1960s there were few instances of either spontaneous or organized singing at British football grounds. What there was came from the two principal sources of urban working-class song – the church and the music hall. 'Abide With Me' had become the institutionalized sing-song before the FA Cup Final in 1927, while the post-war success of Portsmouth was accompanied by the Pompey chimes, mimicking the tone and rhythm of church bells – 'Play-up Pompey, Pompey play-up'. Crowds at Newcastle United had adopted 'Blaydon Races' in the 1930s and sung it with particular vigour during the club's run of FA Cup wins in the 1950s. West Ham sang 'I'm Forever Blowing Bubbles', Birmingham City fans took to Harry Lauder's hit 'Keep Right On' and Norwich City supporters revived a very old favourite, 'On the Ball City'. However, the sound of the British football crowd remained a collage of collective roars and one-liners.

Change came in the early 1960s. First, television exposure to the Brazilian fans at the 1962 World Cup and their hypnotic 'Brazil, cha-cha-cha! Bra-zil, cha-cha-cha!' saw the rhythm mimicked in England with a club's name inserted. In the case of the Kop it was used as a commentary on an injured Everton player going off the field: 'Dead Fred, ha-ha-ha!' From here it was a simple step to the adaptation of nursery rhymes and skipping songs learnt in urban Britain's play-grounds: '2–4–6–8, who do we appreciate?'

From late 1963 onwards the Kop began to sing verse and chorus from the Beatles' 'She Loves You', Freddie and the Dreamers' 'You Were Made For Me' and Cilla Black's 'Anyone Who Had a Heart', and adopted Gerry and the Pacemakers' 'You'll Never Walk Alone' as their anthem. The degree to which the Top 40 had become the everyday language of the Kop was illustrated by the Gary Sprake incident in 1967. Sprake, Leeds United's goalkeeper, checked himself as he was poised to throw the ball out. He managed not to give the ball to the Liverpool player bearing down on him, but he did let it slip into his own net. Ten thousand voices broke into Des O'Connor's corny ballad 'Careless Hands'.

The defining moment for Shankly's first Liverpool team came in 1965 when they faced Internazionale in the semi-final of the European Cup. In the home leg Liverpool were the aggressive, moving, passing, scoring machine that Shankly had envisaged. Against a wall of noise and taunts, they ripped Inter's fearsome defence to shreds and won 3–1. But away from home they had yet to find the resilience, the luck and the mendacity required to win in Europe at the time. Inter and the referee beat them 3–0, and British football for all its advances had yet to prove that it had returned to the first rank of the game.

IX

The rising arc of British football was not yet complete. In the next three years England would host and win the World Cup, and Celtic would win the European Cup in 1967 followed by Manchester United in 1968. After that it was downhill. There were international victories after 1968 – Chelsea and Rangers won the Cup Winners' Cup, while there was something of an English monopoly of the Fairs/UEFA Cup, winning every year between 1968 and 1973 – but neither national team nor clubs would scale the same heights again during the period. By 1975 all of the leading teams of the era, but for Liverpool, had entered a period of desperate decline. Simultaneously, the sporadic outbreaks of football-related violence, disorder and vandalism that had been peppering the newspapers in the early 1960s had by the mid-1970s turned into the defining feature of British football culture.

It is hard not to see the same arc in British politics. In the brief interlude between Labour's 1964 election victory and the 1967 devaluation of the pound, the pent-up social energies and demands of the nation were briefly unleashed in a wave of pop-cultural ferment, and in social and sexual liberalization such as the legal reforms of divorce and abortion. The British student revolts of 1968 were, by comparison to their European peers, a trifling affair. What increasingly shook the nation was the conflict in Northern Ireland and the rising tide of trade-union militancy in industry. Indeed, so central had the issue of industrial relations become that the last two years of Wilson's government were consumed with the doomed attempt to regulate them and the wildcat strikes that were paralysing British industry. Wilson went to the polls in autumn 1970 expecting to win but was defeated by Edward Heath's Conservative Party, which in an effort to break the logjam of decline and conflict promised the most rightward shift in economic and social policy for a generation. Wilson blamed his defeat on, among other factors, the national mood that followed England's elimination from the 1970 World Cup. Heath's attempt to impose a wages and prices policy and reform the trade unions ended in the infamous U-turn of 1972 and descended into a series of pitched battles with the miners. By 1974, when two general elections were required to produce a knife-edge Labour majority, both British polity and the British football stadium were beginning to look ungovernable.

There is something of the Ealing Comedy and the *Carry On* movie to the 1966 World Cup. First, in March 1966, the Jules Rimet trophy, which had been put on display at Westminster Central Hall as the centrepiece of a sports and stamps exhibition, was stolen to the complete bemusement of Inspector Knacker of the Yard. A week later a mongrel dog called Pickles sniffed it out, wrapped in newspaper beneath a bush in south London. Then, without a trace of irony, in those formative days of branding and event management, the FA created the World Cup's first official mascot 'World Cup Willie': a cartoon lion who played in a Union Jack shirt. The complete elision of England and the United Kingdom, by both the FA and the English crowds who exclusively flew Union Jacks at games, speaks of a Britain before Irish, Scottish and Welsh nationalism began to challenge the unspoken English hegemony.

Television coverage took a great leap forward at this tournament. For Chile 1962 broadcasters were still flying film back to Europe; now the whole Continent could watch live, and journalists attended from a greater diversity of countries than ever before. Thus the central English narratives of 1966 are entwined with a firmer grasp of the other stories of the tournament – the disconsolate Germans still fuming over the Russian linesman in the final, the South Americans still convinced a conspiracy was afoot to thwart them, the North Koreans' moment of glory and their short summer fling with the people of Teesside. Reporting from Sweden in 1958, Geoffrey Green could still write of the Brazilians as 'dark exotic strangers'. Now they were playing at Goodison Park. England won, which of course makes everyone more generous and open, but it was also a moment of genuinely greater interconnection. If for a month every four years the World Cup has now become the world's playground, it began here.

Alf Ramsey had of course predicted it. He played the percentages and he played them well, though it is a tragedy that this tight-wired, emotionally constipated man could not publicly share his triumph and his glee with players or nation. There was no room in his team for the flamboyance and individuality of Jimmy Greaves, no darting wingers. England, like their captain Bobby Moore, were solid, reliable, positionally astute and professional in defence; through the middle, players like Nobby Stiles and Alan Ball – furiously competitive, hardworking and fit – were emblematic of the ethos of the side; and in attack they had a range of movement and goalscorers to choose from – Bobby

Charlton, Hurst, Hunt, Peters. England were, however, more than hustle and bustle. The coaching and tactical transformations of the previous decade closely informed England's play, indeed they gave them a real edge. The use of a near- rather than far-post cross, an innovation that Ron Greenwood took from the Hungarians to West Ham, was a distinctive ploy for England. More broadly, England were the first team to win a major tournament playing what is now the conventional 4–4–2 formation. Ramsey's use of attacking fullbacks, at which the Brazilians had excelled, made wingers redundant.

The semi-final with Portugal showed, against the tournament's top scorers, how good they were and the final, 4–2 in extra time, against the West Germans was stupendous drama. No wonder when Harold Wilson joined the celebrations later he was keen to get his own hands on the Cup: 'We only win the World Cup under Labour,' he quipped. But the feelgood factor he so desperately sought was never enough to arrest the slide in the nation's stock market and currency, and the inevitable devaluation of the pound that was to come. The World Cup win has, however, had a longer-term resonance. England has not stopped talking about 1966 since and, for all the dismay at the ever-lengthening gap since England won the World Cup, it allowed the nation to live more comfortably with its post-imperial decline. The empire, the right to the number one spot, had gone, but England was still good enough occasionally to occupy it – and that it seems is the destiny of a minor power in the modern world.

If 1966 now has an air of *Carry On Alf* about it, 1967 was *Summer Holiday*. After decades of poor performance, Glasgow Celtic under manager Jock Stein had become the dominant club in Scotland and stood poised to win the European Cup. They won the first of their nine consecutive league titles in 1966 playing very attacking football. Always exuberant and exciting, they played with width and speed and a great deal of heart. The championship squad that Stein, himself a Protestant, assembled was drawn from the same class and locale as the club's fans – overwhelmingly Glaswegian working-class Catholics. Their players' rise mirrored and burnished the social ascent of their supporters, for the prosperity of the 1960s offered a tiny window of individual and collective liberation for the Catholic communities of the west of Scotland from the straitjacket of Scottish sectarianism. When, in 1967, Celtic beat Dukla Prague in the semi-finals of the European Cup they stood poised to conquer Europe. They would not do so alone. The nineteenth-century brake-club tradition of away-game travel was reinvented for an era of Europeanization and mass tourism. An extraordinary cavalcade of transport was put together in Glasgow to take around 20,000 supporters to Lisbon. For many it was the first time they had left Scotland, let alone travelled to Europe. They went two to a scooter, six to a Mini, and seventy to a coach. Laced with crates of brew and armed with their first passports, they crossed France, broke down, hitched lifts and took wrong turns, crossed Spain, slept by the side of the road, and arrived at the last minute, just in time, late or very late. But they got there and assembled at the Estádio Nacional.

---

25 May 1967
Celtic 2 Internazionale 1
Estádio Nacional, Lisbon

From the moment Mazzola scores his seventh-minute penalty you know Inter will just sit on their lead and somehow Celtic have got to score. For the next eighty-three minutes Celtic attack and Inter defend. They have forty-nine shots to Inter's one. The Italians have no corners at all. Celtic take it down the wing, play long and short balls into the penalty area, pass it in triangles on the flanks, control the centre and explore and probe and strike. But every move is covered, every shot blocked or deflected, attacks are broken up, passes intercepted and space denied. Inter are like a crenellated wall, ramparts and watchtowers.

Having been played exclusively in Inter's half, the game now compresses and tightens into the final third in front of their goal, retreating to their last line of defence. Having had occasional possession and control, making runs that relieve the pressure, Inter are now blasting the ball away from their goal only to face its immediate return.

But hope is being flattened into doubt. Breath and time are short. Then Gemmell pivots, shoots and the net roars. Inter are broken, they no longer know where the halfway line is, let alone the territory beyond it. Celtic's winner is an inevitable but delicious pleasure.

In the final minutes the moat around the pitch is suddenly alive with people, clambering out of the stands and on to the concrete wall by the athletics track. Behind Inter's goal they are standing two or three deep with a thicket of heads, hats and banners massing behind them. The flags are homemade sheet-and-pole jobs or cannibalized Irish tricolours, all adorned by hand: *Celts 7–1 Easy, Celts Champions OK* – blocked out in the crude angular letters of black masking tape; the green-and-white striped banner with *Celtic* spelt out in gold-braid curlicues. Cardboard top hats in green and white hoops, home-knitted scarves, tourist sombreros and a green bobble hat with *John Clarke* in white cotton stitch. The blond kid with *Jock Stein* scratched out in green felt tip across his white T-shirt. The weatherbeaten man in his white Arran cardigan, the whole squad, in formation, stitched on the back in green wool.

When the game ends they come tumbling off the wall, bound over the moat, stream down the terraces and surge across the pitch, a cavalcade of delirium. Some immediately peel off to grab their divot and grasp the turf. Others, suddenly realizing that the players, dazed and perplexed, are all around, embrace them in expanding, mutating knots of scarves and bodies, hands grabbing at their shirt and boots. Among those still running, some collide, link with others, embrace, break away, tumble to the floor in heaps, join arms and dance. The perplexed Portuguese stewards in their white caps, astonished, beaming local boys, white-gloved police and besuited photographers – all are caught up in the mix and swirled among them. One man has planted his flag in the centre circle and is genuflecting before it. The girl in the green dress whirls on the touchline. The advance guard run out of pitch and regroup around the corner flag, breaking into song.

When finally Billy McNeil makes it up to the fascist mausoleum where the politicians are sitting and lifts the huge cup, the mayhem barely seems to pause.

And then came the triumph of Matt Busby and Manchester United a year later. Ten years on from the Munich air disaster Busby had created another exceptional team. With a forward line of George Best, Bobby Charlton and Denis Law weaving a fantastical display of attacking football, United re-established their credentials as a European force with an epic semi-final against Real Madrid, holding out for a 3–3 draw in the Bernabéu. In the final they played Benfica at Wembley. A tense 1–1 draw after 90 minutes was recast in extra time as a 4–1 rout.

Best was unquestionably the most talented British football player of the generation. He was rare among his contemporaries as a sublime dribbler of the ball and was possessed of the most exquisite and delicate balance that allowed him to ride or avoid the legions of clod-hopping and scything tackles dealt out to him in the English league. Best's mop of hair, taste in clothes and failed boutique ventures saw him dubbed the Fifth Beatle at home and *El Beatle* in Spain. Best cut an arc of hyper-social mobility and global successes followed by personal crisis and addiction, similar to that which John Lennon would follow. Best's brilliant play for United was counterpointed by an increasingly bohemian lifestyle, a seemingly insatiable desire for women and alcohol, and eventually obsessive and destructive coverage in the popular press. A combination of physical abuse and psychological pressure eventually ate into his fitness, poise and desire. His double hat-trick against North-ampton Town in an FA Cup fifth-round tie in 1970 may be considered his parting shot before leaving Manchester United for good. Like the Beatles, though with many more comeback attempts, he would live through the 1970s but he would not prosper.

Prior to Britain's long summer of football love there had been almost a decade of incidents and reports of trouble of one kind or another. Certainly from the late 1950s serious drinking by young men, teenagers and those in their twenties, followed by horse play descending into vandalism and fisticuffs, was occurring on the cross-country football trains. However, the main focus of the more general moral panic around youth, unhinged from traditional social mores and hierarchies, was on Teddy boys and then mods and rockers. All of these subcultures were released from the constraints of the past by the exploding levels of youth employment and youth wages and furnished with the ready-made signifiers of generational difference and rebellion by American pop and cinema. Teddy boys in particular steered clear of football, preferring to flaunt their rough working-class dandyism on the dance floor, in the milk bar and on the street. Mods and rockers, who acquired the mobility and independence of the scooter and the motorbike, took their joust to the seaside. But in the early 1960s these events provided plenty of material for thought on the terraces, demonstrating the adrenalin buzzes, the politics of territoriality and the short-lived but saturation media coverage that were available from a public ruck. High on a heady mix of disposable income and the disintegration of deference, this crowd who went and stood separately from the older generation were changing the tone.

The press coverage of disorder was finely poised between nonchalance and panic. In 1963 when Everton installed fences at Goodison Park to segregate fans, there was genuine shock and surprise. The *News of the World* sent a reporter who rather tweely wrote, 'Hooligans. They're so friendly?' Yet Everton were not responding to a phantom or invented phenomenon. Something had been happening on the terraces in the late 1950s and early 1960s. Things tipped towards panic in late 1965 when a dead hand grenade was thrown from the Millwall end on to the pitch at Brentford. The *Sun* was working itself up into what would become a permanent state of hysteria: 'The World Cup is less than nine months away. This is all the time we have left to try and restore the once good name of this country. Soccer is sick at the moment!'[24] A similar dismay accompanied the Liverpool–Celtic Cup Winners' Cup semi-final in spring 1966 which saw widespread fighting in and around both Anfield and Parkhead and showers of bottles on the pitch.

The World Cup was entirely peaceful but proved a mere hiatus. The following season (1966–67) was the first in which recognizable gangs definitively established 'ends' in their home grounds and took to taking those of their opponents when away from home. The scale of the ensuing fights are indicated by the clash between Everton and Manchester City followers when over forty people were arrested. The increasing numbers of away fans travelling on the national train network over the previous decade had seen a fair amount of drunken fisticuffs but the football special trains were now serving as the mobile if informal headquarters for whole mobs who were saving their trouble for when they got off the train.

The immediate response of the authorities and police was to attempt the segregation of fans inside the stadium by means of thick police lines or fences, and make them take the laces out of their ubiquitous bovver boots. The immediate impact of this was to sharpen and sanctify the territorialization of the stadium – precisely the goal of the 'ends' in the first place. However, the naivety of the authorities at the time was such that they failed to monitor or control who actually went to the designated ends. Even where these strategies managed to keep people apart for ninety minutes they were not matched by any systematic policing of the railway stations and public areas that fans were using. Saturday afternoon pitched battles at the main London termini of Euston, King's Cross and St Pancras became commonplace.

What truly ignited the already inflammable and chaotic situation was the emergence of skinheads and their rapidly developing relationship with football violence. The skinhead style, having paid its debts to the Caribbean rude-boy cultures it grew up alongside, burst out of the tougher zones of white working-class decline in London. Television, violence, and the simple reproducibility of the style saw the look go nationwide by the end of the decade. It asserted an unambiguous masculinity in a deliberate riposte to the androgyny and femininity of the hippies. Skinheads rejected the inspirational dandyism and fake cool cosmopolitanism of hard mods and their Italian suits and scooters. Shaven heads, working jeans and big boots were the proclamation of their über-proletarian status and the practical instruments of a subculture imbued with the use of force. Skinhead gangs at football, as part of the broader mix of groups in the ends, brought a higher level of solidarity, toughness and spontaneous organization to the fight, which the police and clubs appeared unable to counter. In 1969 a large group of Spurs fans returning from a game had caused so much mayhem on the train the authorities decide to just ditch them 40 miles outside London on the village of Flitwick where they went on a rampage through the high street. The following year, the nation was able to view from the comfort of its armchairs the first televised pitched battle between Leeds and Stoke followers.

Yet just a few years earlier football, in London at any rate, had acquired a degree of social cachet it had never before possessed. Chelsea striker Peter Osgood recalled the atmosphere at Stamford Bridge:

You'd see Raquel Welch, you'd see Honor Blackman, you'd see Richard O'Sullivan, and you'd see Ronnie Corbett and Michael Crawford, Jane Seymour. All these sort of people and Michael Caine used to come along . . . I always remember scoring my hundredth league goal . . . I did a lap of honour and the crowd were chanting my name Osgood . . . I went into the dressing room and who's sitting there but Steve McQueen.[25]

Worlds collided on the King's Road, old and new money, louche aristocrats, luvvie film directors, working-class wide boys and hard mods;

football, music, fashion and the movies. The Beatles had left Liverpool
and the swinging sixties – for the tiny minority that actually lived them
– came to London, and their football team was Chelsea. The decade
yielded a single trophy – the League Cup in 1965 – but location is
everything. The club's Stamford Bridge ground stood between the swish
mansion flats, salons and boutiques of Chelsea and Sloane Square and
the inter-war housing estates and cheap street markets of the North End
Road; its geography, supporters and players reflected this rare but real
moment of class cross-over.

If Chelsea were, in part, a model of the get-rich-quick school of
instantaneous social mobility, Don Revie's Leeds United offered an
entirely different morality tale. Revie had been an accomplished player
who led Manchester City to victory in the 1956 FA Cup using a version
of the Hungarians' deep-lying centre-forward ploy. For this kind of
intelligent innovation and guile he had been depicted as a schemer.
The press never dropped the notion and added layer upon layer of
opprobrium and character assassination to him over his entire career.
Like Harold Wilson, another smart northern boy, his tough hide masked
a paranoid insecurity. Revie was made coach of Leeds United in 1961
with the club close to relegation from the second division. Revie turned
them around, took them up to the first division in 1964 and they were
runners-up that year. Over the next ten years Leeds were never out
of the top four. The year after winning the 1968 Fairs Cup against
Ferencváros they fulfilled Revie's dream by landing the league title, and
later lost a European Cup Final. Their performance in domestic cup
competition was equally strong, winning the 1968 League Cup, and
reaching the FA Cup Final four times, at last lifting the trophy in 1972.

Revie had the same obsession with fanatical preparation as his technocratic peers and established a similar level of maniacal control over every
level of the club's operations, but he was the first to seriously commit
the process to paper. Revie's accumulation of dossiers and files on clubs
and players, temperaments, styles and weaknesses, was the bureaucratic
backbone of his squad. From this grew a form of football that, although
capable of great style, concentrated on negating their opponent's
strength, drawing the sting from the attack and above all, not conceding
goals. There was a touch of the showman about him too: he changed the
club strip to emulate Real Madrid's all-white and encouraged formation
warm-ups to stir up the crowd. But the enduring folk memory of the

team is of a peculiarly northern, gritty masculinity: the use of controlled and premeditated aggression, and a level of sophisticated gamesmanship that the English game had not yet encountered.

Leeds and Chelsea had been shadow-boxing all through the 1960s, their games increasingly cast as north vs. south, province vs. metropolis, grafters vs. chancers. The 1970 FA Cup Final offered a stage on which to play out the end of the sixties. Great drama but poor football, it was full of charge and menace: 2–2 at Wembley, Chelsea just sneaked it in the replay 2–1 and took the chance of a European jaunt the next year, beating Real Madrid to win the Cup Winners' Cup. The party had been incredible and so was the hangover. There was nothing but debt and trouble and relegation for the next two decades

If Chelsea's demise was a signal of the termination of the short-lived alliance of the metropolitan glamour industries with football and the steady descent of the game from prized national asset to embarrassing rust-belt ruin, the sharpest rebuke on the pitch was delivered to the England side. A month after the epic 1970 FA Cup Final England went to Mexico as defending world champions. At their best, in the game with Brazil in the first round, they had shown intelligent defending, tactical sophistication, awareness and timing, only to lose by a single goal. They came home after the quarter-finals, throwing away a two-goal lead to the West Germans and then conceding a third in extra time. What could have been put down to the difficulties of playing in the heat of Mexico, illness and injuries, the vagaries of chance, was confirmed as a more structural set of problems. In 1972 the West Germans came to Wembley to play the quarter-finals of the European Championship. The Germans won 3–1, but the scoreline does not measure the extent to which their movement and rotation baffled and humiliated the home side. Ramsey was becoming more paranoid, more irascible and bitter, more impossible to deal with. Then, in 1973, Poland came to Wembley. Universally underrated, even mocked, they played the game of their lives and England would not be going to the World Cup in 1974. Ramsey stepped down.

A sense of endings in British football was now palpable. Improbably, unbelievably, Shankly retired. He had no pressing need, no cabal against him. The second Liverpool team that he had built had just won the UEFA Cup and the league, but enigmatically he had decided his time had come. In Scotland Rangers' victory in the 1972 Cup Winners'

Cup in Barcelona was overshadowed by the city-wide fighting between Spanish police and the Rangers fans. Celtic, still dominant in the league, lost the 1970 European Cup Final to Feyenoord. Most telling of all, Ibrox was the scene of yet another footballing disaster. In January 1971 at the Old Firm game, a massive crush occurred on a staircase as departing fans returned in response to a late goal. Sixty-six people died in the crush and the subsequent investigation revealed the extent of the decline in Britain's football infrastructure, and belatedly introduced a safety licensing system. It was, as the 1980s were to prove, painfully inadequate. In 1974 Celtic won their last league title in the run of nine achieved under Jock Stein. The big man would be kicked upstairs a few years later and the team he had assembled retired or departed.

But it was perhaps the fall of Manchester United that had been most vertiginous. Busby, now Sir Matt, had moved from the bench to the board in 1971. Bobby Charlton retired, Denis Law was sold to Manchester City and George Best declined, locked into a downward spiral of erratic form and alcoholism. Busby's successor Wilf McGuinness laboured under an impossible weight of expectation and went bald in the process; Frank O'Farrell fared little better and then in 1974, under Tommy Docherty, United were heading for relegation. In the Stretford End, the Red Army had acquired probably the most fearsome reputation for trouble of any of the now established crews. In the strange social and political limbo that existed in Britain between the two general elections of 1974 – the country seemingly divided and irreconcilable on the right response to the industrial, financial and energy crises mounting around them – Manchester United, already doomed to relegation, played their final game of the season against their rivals Manchester City. The depth of their demise was truly registered when, with five minutes to play, Denis Law backheeled the ball into the United net. Law, his arms frozen by his side, rigid and unemotive, was mobbed by his new team-mates. It was all too much for the United fans, who stormed the pitch and the game was abandoned – the first English Football League match to be stopped after crowd disorder. The power of the mob was as illusory as ever. The result stood and the Kings of Europe were no longer even the best team in Manchester.

During the German occupation, football in the Netherlands had boomed and like many other Dutch institutions it emerged from the war without any radical ruptures in its leadership or organization, despite both tacit and explicit collaboration with the Nazis, particularly in the treatment of Dutch Jews.[26] Psychologically and emotionally immobilized by its unspoken complicity, Dutch society lived in a state of suspended amnesia, and in the case of sport it was ruled by an unbendingly stuffy and pedantic conservatism, epitomized by the president of the football federation (KNVB), the known Nazi collaborator Karel Lotsy. To the sports establishment, professionalization was an impermissible act of vulgar commercialism and a threat to their authority. Like the other amateur football cultures of Northern Europe, Denmark, Sweden and Germany, high levels of participation and a competitive although amateur league created a generation of players good enough to make a professional career overseas. For example, Faas Wilkes left to play for Internazionale in 1949 and then Valencia, Abe Lenstra went to Fiorentina, and Kees Rijvers to Saint-Étienne; all were banned from the national team. In 1953 the depth of this professional diaspora was demonstrated when it gathered to play as a Dutch XI in a charity match against France, raising funds after a major flood in Zeeland. Subsequently, the KNVB, under public pressure, was forced to relax its ban on professionalism in domestic and international football. Even so, the Dutch national side performed poorly, losing 5–1 to Spain, and 2–1 to Turkey in Amsterdam, and they did so with the most antiquated of tactics; the WM system was still unfamiliar in the Netherlands, let alone the innovations of the Hungarians. There was perhaps a deeper cultural force at work; as Hans Kraay, an international of the era, argued, 'We had the talent and the football possibilities, but the personality wasn't strong enough – and the way of life. We were too timid; we were not people of the world yet.'[27] The insularity and conservatism of the Netherlands would be swept aside in the early 1960s.

Post-war Dutch society was bound not just by the conspiracy of silence over the course of the occupation, but by the rigid social scaffolding of polarization. The four key religious-political groupings in the Netherlands – Liberals, Socialists, Protestants and Catholics – did not merely organize politically and vote en bloc, but were educated separately, read different newspapers, possessed their own radio stations and, below the thin level of semi-professional clubs, played their football separately too. Such all-encompassing stratification combined with a stifling low-key conformity reigned over Dutch culture. But as the Dutch economy boomed through the 1950s and 1960s and a new generation acquired security, independence, free time and disposable income, all inconceivable twenty years earlier, the attachment of the young to the old identities and social micro-worlds of their parents was gradually dissolved. As one Amsterdammer put it, 'Before young people had to give their money to the household, now we could keep it and we used it to buy records and tickets to football matches and mopeds.'[28] The first stirrings of a distinct youth culture came in Amsterdam with the Pleiners, bikers who hung out around the Leidseplein, and Dijkers, working-class moped riders who favoured leather jackets and the Nieuwendijk neighbourhood. They were joined in the new urban mix by Amsterdam's university students, who had rebelled against the humiliations and hierarchies of the established student societies – more duelling clubs than trade unions – and in 1963 established new progressive organizations in the city. All began to tune into the new sounds of British pop, black American soul and the subversive wavelengths of pirate radio. These groups formed the core audience and participants for the hysterical series of happenings that erupted on the urban landscape between 1962 and 1967.

The surrealist poet Simon Vinkenoog held an 'Open the grave' happening in late 1962 prophesying the downfall of the old ways in newly magical Amsterdam. On Liberation Day in 1965 – the holy day of collaborationist denials – tens of thousands gathered in the city to bizarrely chant '*Wij Willen Bolletjes*' ('We want Bolletjes') – a breakfast-cereal advertising slogan: the transparent historical cover-up of the Netherlands' past was punctured by a brilliant act of collective ludicrousness. Robert Jasper Grootveld – part vandal, part showman, part shaman – deployed similar tactics in a series of magical happenings and events that mixed a deranged assault on the tobacco industry and addictive enslavement to consumerism. The state, in the shape of the city police, found these occasions incomprehensible but threatening, and increasingly acted with a heavy hand, breaking up gatherings and attacking participants. This, of course, doubled and tripled the size of the crowds, the social meaning and cachet of the event and the determination to persist and resist. It was only when the national elites decided that tolerance was a more effective sedative than violence that the events and the crowds began to peter out. By the time Paris was ready to erupt in 1968, Amsterdam had passed through its collective adolescence.

In this heady atmosphere of surreal experimentation and self-conscious flamboyance, Amsterdam underwent a transition in its body cultures. The city exhibited a permissiveness and tolerance of the sex industry's commercialization of the body and the drug subcultures' experimentation with the mind and destruction of the brain. The same impulse to seek personal liberation awakened a cultural renaissance of dance, physical theatre and ballet, and with it an explosion of colour and energy in the fashions and on the dance floors of Amsterdam. This turbulent and disorganized wave of cultural change generated its own distinct and inevitably short-lived political forms, like the white-clad Provos of the mid-1960s whose antics crossed the border between agit-prop political theatre and urban anarchist social interventions. They threatened to fill the city's reservoirs with LSD, covered it in white smoke bombs while Princess Beatrix was getting married, and in an act of optimistic idealism tried to break the hold of both private property and the car on the city by distributing free white bicycles. In 1967 they won a seat on Amsterdam city council and promptly disbanded.

Thus the Dutch counter-culture was potent enough to destroy the old rigidities, hierarchies and systems of deference that had defined the Netherlands, counterposed the play principle to the Protestant ethic and offered a new aesthetic of bodily liberation and adornment. But it was neither strong enough nor was its economic or political vision comprehensive enough to offer anything more than quixotic and symbolic ripostes to the conventional logics of the market. This triple inheritance of social liberation, heightened aesthetic sensibility for the body in motion and hard-headed economic individualism that characterized the modern Netherlands was encapsulated in the iconic figure of its greatest football player, Johan Cruyff.

Cruyff was born in 1947 in Bettendorp, a working-class district of Amsterdam close to Ajax's De Meer stadium. He trained with Ajax from the age of ten. His father, a grocer, died when he was twelve, and his mother subsequently worked as a cleaner in the club's training complex. He was a rakishly thin, angular teenager, seemingly too fragile for the professional game, but in 1964 at seventeen he made his first-team debut. Cruyff was without question the leading Dutch player of all time, exhibiting a superb, ethereal balance and exquisite ball control. He was capable of stunning acceleration and mesmerizing runs, turns and shifts, and appeared to possess an innate and precise sense of geometry and a spatial awareness that allowed him to score goals from impossible angles and see passes through gaps that did not immediately appear visible. He was, as David Miller named him, 'Pythagoras in boots'. But it was as a team player that he truly excelled, for Cruyff was an on-field director, who when not running was talking and when not on the ball was pointing to it, calling for it, ushering others into space, alerting everyone around him to the dangers and possibilities of the moment.

Hubert Smeets has said of Cruyff that, 'You can see both sides of the sixties and both sides of the baby boom; on one side he was against the backwardness of the establishment, and on the other he was rather aware of personal interests.'[29] On the financial side, Cruyff was quick to recognize his own worth, but quicker still to note and challenge the hypocrisy of authority. When he realized that KNVB officials were insured when travelling at the federation's expense but the players were not, he led a successful revolt. He was remarkably open and available to the press, but charged for his time to publications that made millions by featuring him. Having already established a lucrative contract with Puma he painted out the Adidas stripes on his boots at the 1974 World Cup finals. But he was no mere mercenary. Smeets argues: 'Cruyff got into all kinds of conflicts because he started asking the question the whole generation was asking: "Why are things organized like this?"'[30]

If Cruyff was the iconic individual at the summit of Dutch football, he was also part of a remarkable club team. Ajax had a long-established tradition of youth coaching and open attacking play, developed under émigré English managers Jack Reynolds and Vic Buckingham, but in the mid-1960s they were unable to turn this inheritance into victories. Indeed when in 1964 Buckingham was sacked and replaced by Dutch coach Rinus Michels they were threatened by relegation. Seven years later they would be champions of Europe playing the most exceptional and fluid style of football yet seen – what came to be known as *Totalvoetbal* – total football. What made this possible was the combination of Ajax's patrons, Rinus Michels' coaching, the ideas and talent of Cruyff and the cohort of players that emerged with him, and the peculiarities of the Dutch conception of space.

In the early 1960s Ajax had attracted an eclectic but rich set of backers including the Van der Meijden brothers, who had made their fortune building coastal defences and bunkers for the Germans, and some of the leading Amsterdam Jews to have survived the war and stayed in the city. These included the multi-millionaire Maup Caransa, in whose honour the club was occasionally called Caransajax; club president Jaap van Praag; and the textile baron and ex-international referee Leo Horn. Together they nursed the club through the era of semi-professionalism, underwriting transfer fees, providing part-time or phantom jobs for players, sometimes setting them up in business. In the mid-1960s all of the Ajax squad had second jobs. Although there were few Jewish players at the club in this era and the city's Jewish population had dwindled so dramatically that they could only have made up a tiny fraction of the crowd, there was an unmistakably Jewish air about the club and the team, a fact that was embraced by the team – so much so that many believed Cruyff to be Jewish, which he was not.

Rinus Michels' initial contribution was to use these resources to fashion a real professional club culture. Players were now able to train full time and Michels made them do so with a relentless determination: up to four training sessions a day. He introduced new equipment and facilities, for the club did not even possess a proper massage table on his arrival. He also created a high level of internal discipline and insisted upon a relentless attacking style from his teams. Playing something akin to a 4–2–4 formation, Ajax stayed up and started winning, starting with the Dutch championship in 1966. Michels swept out some of the older players and introduced a tough Yugoslav defender and former captain of Partizan Belgrade, Velibor Vasovic, who brought a level of gritty professionalism and an unyielding intent to win to the team; a steeliness then uncharacteristic of Dutch football. Then in the gaps created in the squad Michels promoted and nurtured the club's own indigenous youthful talents, including Gerrie Mühren, Barry Hulshoff, Wim Suurbier, Ruud Krol and Johan Neeskens.

The team came of age in the 1967 European Cup second round when they beat Bill Shankly's first great Liverpool team 5–1 in Amsterdam. Shankly assured the dismayed home support that Ajax would be turned over at Anfield, but they held out for a 2–2 draw. They were beaten in the following round by Dukla Prague, but the centrality of European competition to the new Ajax was set. National championships followed in three of the following four seasons and in 1969 Ajax lost a European Cup Final to a vastly more experienced AC Milan. The richness of Dutch football culture at the time is illustrated by the following year's competition in which Feyenoord went one better, as rank outsiders beating Celtic in the final in Milan. Under their Austrian coach Ernst Happel they showed a similar level of technique to that enjoyed by Ajax and were blessed with the soaring curving crosses of Wim van Hanegem. However, it is for Ajax's three consecutive victories in the European Cup between 1971 and 1973 that Dutch club football of the era is best remembered, for not only did they win but they played the game in a way no one had quite done before.

In the late 1960s Ajax switched from playing a 4-2-4 formation to 4-3-3. This has remained the core of the Ajax system ever since. While this provides a framework for the team's play, and players had their designated numbers, positions and tasks, the single most important innovation was to conceive of these positions as nodes in a fluid network of players. One's position on the field at any moment determined which role one took up, rather than the squad number on one's back. If the Italians had invented marking space rather than players, the Dutch invented playing according to one's space rather than one's pre-allotted place in the division of labour.

As with any elegant system, this not only produced good results, it diminished the amount of energy required to produce them. Ruud Krol emphasized this dimension of the game:

Our system was also a solution to a physical problem. How can you play for 90 minutes and remain strong? If I as left back run 70 metres up the wing it's not good if I immediately have to run back 70 to my starting place. So if the left midfielder takes my place and the left winger takes the midfield position, then it shortens the distances. That was the philosophy.[31]

Alongside this display of positional flexibility and position switching, Ajax attempted to change the space in which the game was being played. When attacking they sought to make the playing space as large as possible, using touchline-hugging wingers and attacking fullbacks. When defending they sought to compress the playing space, crowding the opposition by closely pressing the ball carrier, defining a high defensive line, including the goalkeeper, and playing the offside trap. When they attacked they attacked with eleven, when they defended they defended with eleven. Above all they sought to place the ball with either the player who had the most space or the player whose position on the pitch would allow him to create the most space with the next pass; for in space you can move and score. Positional and functional flexibility, the expansion and compression of playing space, and the tactical pursuit of space required a greater degree of all-round skills from every player as well as tactical and spatial awareness, high levels of concentration and quickness of thought. Such a cohort of players and such a collective working culture could not be managed and organized by the conventional methods of command and control, simple and brutal managerial hierarchies, and deference to age, bullying and experience. Michels, while imposing a level of personal discipline necessary to get the players fit enough to play football at such tremendous speed, also encouraged an atmosphere of honesty, directness and mutual criticism which was, hitherto, alien to the dressing rooms of professional football. He combined a stern professional relationship with players at work with a relaxed and respectful friendship away from it. While the sporting and administrative division of labour in most football cultures was finally approximating to the rational, hierarchical, and inflexible specialisms of classic Fordism, the Dutch had anticipated the key structural elements of the post-Fordist and post-industrial economies that would emerge in Western Europe over the next three decades. It is a measure of Ajax's modernity that, for once, football appeared to be the leading edge of innovatory social organization rather than a mere follower in the wake of others.

The invention of total football was clearly a collective endeavour and a developing project, orchestrated by Michels and Cruyff, but indisputably the product of the whole squad. But why should this admittedly potent institutional and personal chemistry have generated such a distinctive way of playing football; and why in the Netherlands? As David Winner has succinctly put it: 'The Dutch think innovatively, creatively and abstractly about space in their football because for centuries they have had to think innovatively about space in every other area of their lives.'[32] Total football has a number of linguistic predecessors in Dutch cultural life. Total architecture was first proposed by Michel de Klerk as a model in which many separate elements in a building or a large project must be functionally and stylistically integrated into a whole vision – a notion taken up Dan Roodenburgh, a member of the Ajax

1. Ibrox Park, Glasgow, 5 April 1902. At the leading edge of industrial football, Glasgow suffered the first stadium disaster.

2. The informal empire spreads. The German team for the English game,
Stockholm Olympics, 1912.

3. Factory, colliery, dressing room: Ipswich Town take a bath after an
FA Cup replay, January 1938.

4. An altogether more splendid life. The self-regulating crowd in action, Upton Park, 1930.

5. The Glamour and the Glory: Alfredo Di Stéfano scores with the back of his heel as Manchester United lose to Real Madrid, April 1957.

6. High Industrial Football is born. San Siro, Milan, 1955.

7. Grace and power, a dancer in flight: Eusébio scores against Milan in the European Cup Final, Wembley, 1963.

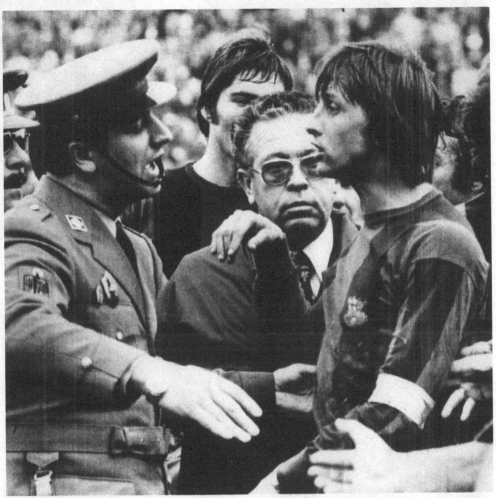

8. The migrant as hero, the club as nation. Johan Cruyff and Franco's police dispute his sending-off, Barcelona vs. Málaga, February 1975.

9. 'Above all, I would like to be remembered as a man who was selfless, who strove and worried so that others could share the glory, and who built up a family of people who could hold their heads up high and say, "We're Liverpool".'

Bill Shankly's final competitive match as Liverpool manager,
August 1974, Wembley.

10. El Pibe d'Oro confronts the rabble. Diego Maradona, Argentina vs. Belgium, Spain 1982.

11. The Descent to the Pitch. Argentina vs. England, La Bombonera, Buenos Aires, June 1977.

12. 'There is in hell a place stone-built throughout,
  Called Malebolge, of an iron hue,
  Like to the wall that circles it about.'

Dante, *The Divine Comedy*: 'Inferno' (canto XVIII, 1–3)

29 May 1985, Heysel Stadium, Brussels

Shrines and memorials

13 and 14.
Paying respect to the dead
of Hillsborough and the
Zambian Air disaster:
Anfield, Liverpool, 1989;
Zambian captain Kalusha
Bwalya, National Stadium,
Lusaka, 1993.

15. Homecoming I. Andrés Escobar *(centre)* after his own goal for Colombia against the USA, World Cup 1994. Escobar would be murdered on his return home.

16. Homecoming II: Wracked by civil war, the nation pauses to welcome the Côte d'Ivoire team home after losing the final of the African Cup of Nations, Abidjan, 2006.

17. The Information Age.
Press stand, Germany, *circa* 2000.

18. We shall not be moved: women celebrate Iran's qualification for the 1998 World Cup. Despite attempts by the authorities to keep them out, they have just forced their way inside. The stadium remains out of bounds to them.

19. The Game at the End of the World. Cambodian monks
watch the league final, 1999.

board and architect of the De Meer stadium. But perhaps the clearest parallels between total football and wider Dutch conceptions of space can be found in the realms of fine art. The way in which the Dutch see space is evident in the extraordinary precision of perspective and composition in the work of artists like Vermeer, while in its stripped-down modern form the same sensibility can be seen in the abstract paintings of Mondrian who progressively reduced landscape and the natural world to the simplest elements of the visual arts – lines and blocks, horizontals and verticals, primary colours, black and white. But the Dutch do more than perceive space with accuracy, even veneration – they have always been in the business of using it.

The Netherlands has long been the most densely populated country in Europe. As a consequence it is perhaps the most systematically planned and humanely constructed landscape on the planet. The Dutch have created space by reclaiming land from the sea, defending space through the vast systems of polders, dikes and flood control, and constantly dividing and redividing space according to the ebb and flow of political powers through the region. Within this precariously constructed parcel of land there are of course no mountains and barely any hills. It is a horizontal landscape of vast unbroken vistas and horizons, whose one-dimensional gloominess appears to have encouraged the Dutch to put great value on the aesthetic of the vertical – expressed in their bizarre love of narrow staircases – and to become expert in the ordering and use of the tiny spaces each had available to them in this cluttered land.

No one since Real Madrid had won three European Cups in a row. Ajax dispatched Panathinaikos in 1971 and opened the mean-spirited defences of Internazionale and Juventus in 1972 and 1973. In an act of audacious showmanship, Ajax demonstrated their mastery of Europe when at 1–0 up in the 1973 semi-final against Real Madrid, Gerrie Mühren received a long cross-field pass on his left foot on the edge of the penalty area. Without breaking step, he juggled it two, three times on his foot and the crowd rose in appreciation of his presumption and skill. A short pass to Ruud Krol went thundering towards the goal and just over the bar.

However, the conditions that underwrote the successes of Ajax were also its undoing. Rinus Michels left the club for Barcelona in 1971. This potentially destabilizing move was remedied by his replacement, the Romanian Stefan Kovacs, who, recognizing the degree of autonomy acquired by the squad under Michels, operated in a low-key manner, essentially allowing them to get on with it. But when he left in 1973 and was replaced by the more conventional George Knobel, the political dynamics of the squad became unstable and volatile. The Ajax compromise between individualism and collectivism had reached its limits, with the squad particularly divided over issues surrounding Cruyff's privileged status but also expressing a certain Dutch cussedness with their leaders, however good they might be. At the start of the 1973–74 season there was an election for the captaincy – it had changed hands three times in three years from Vasovic to Keizer to Cruyff. This year the squad chose Keizer over Cruyff. A few weeks later he had left for Barcelona for a then record fee of just under $1 million. Neeskens followed Cruyff a year later, Johnny Rep went to Valencia, Gerrie Mühren to Seville, others left for Belgium, Germany or retirement. Such dispersals were to be the fate of every great Ajax team – rich enough to produce champions, too poor to keep them at home. But this crop of players had one more great performance in them, one scintillating exhibition of total football left to give – and they would give it on the biggest stage of all: at the 1974 World Cup in West Germany.

XI

After the miracle of Berne, West German football was bathed in a long warm glow of self-satisfaction and complacency. In keeping with the dominant cultural mood of the Adenauer years and its unbroken pattern of economic growth and rising consumption, it was assumed by the football authorities that all was well and there was no need for any further modernization or professionalization – thus by the early 1960s Germany was the only major Western nation not to have open professional football. Players continued to survive on a meagre diet of hidden payments, fiddled expenses, phantom and part-time jobs, tips and perks. Fourth place at the 1958 World Cup did not seem a disaster and certainly not a poor enough performance to initiate change. But it was becoming apparent that West German football was falling behind the rest of Europe. Clubs south of the Alps began regularly to court leading German players and the 1962 World Cup showed just how far the national team had fallen when they were dispatched by Yugoslavia in the quarter-finals. When the rising star of this generation, Uwe Seeler, was almost enticed to Internazionale by Helenio Herrera and three-quarters of a million deutschmarks, it became clear to even the diehard amateurs at the DFB that some kind of change was necessary.

In 1963 the DFB created a sixteen-team national professional league: the Bundesliga. Like all commercial operations in the West German social-market economy, its practices were hedged and limited by a great variety of restrictions and regulations. The newly licensed players of the league could earn a maximum salary of 500 Deutschmarks; they could double that with bonuses, and players in the national team who were targets for foreign clubs could earn double that again. Transfer fees were given a maximum ceiling of DM 50,000. The first championship was won by 1.FC Köln who benefited not only from the booming economy of the Rhineland but from being, by some way, the most organized and consciously professional outfit in the league. There had been some concern that professionalizing the game would produce a concentration of wealth, playing power and titles among a handful of rich clubs – as had happened elsewhere – and which ran counter to the Republic's intense federalism. However, over the first seven years, the Bundesliga was won by seven clubs, competition was fearsome and the general level of West German football seemed to be on the rise as clubs made their mark in European tournaments: TSV 1860 München lost the Cup Winners' Cup Final to West Ham United in 1965, Borussia Dortmund beat Liverpool to win the competition the following year and then Bayern München made it a double in 1967 by beating Glasgow Rangers. West Germany were runners-up in the 1966 World Cup, beaten, as far as the nation was concerned, by some very questionable decision-making by the linesman.

West German football was certainly on the up; attendances rose, and one of the most generous of the early TV deals in Europe filled the clubs' coffers, but in the grey areas and loopholes created by the game's complex system of regulation seethed an entire subculture of hidden payments, hot money, tax havens and corruption. A new kind of football agent or deal-broker emerged, such as the ex-circus artiste Raymond Schwab and Hungarian lawyer Otto Ratz. Teams consistently broke the transfer limit, covering their tracks by adding the excess payments on to their floodlight bills or returfing costs. Players were given ever larger cuts of the transfer deals; at Hertha Berlin they did all of this as well as attempting to bribe opposing players to go easy against them. The DFB could have gone to any club to expose these practices, but in 1965 it went to Hertha and found a hole in the accounts almost DM200,000 deep. Hertha were punished by relegation.

In response to the widespread allegations of corruption made by the protesting Hertha board against the rest of the Bundesliga (much of it clearly documented), the DFB merely raised salary and transfer maxima in an attempt to keep matters above board. They failed miserably. On the final day of the 1971 season three teams were in danger of relegation: Offenbach Kickers, Arminia Bielefeld and Rot-Weiss Oberhausen. Bielefeld managed to beat Hertha in Berlin, Oberhausen drew at Braunschweig, and Offenbach lost to Köln and were relegated. A few days later the club's president, a Spanish-German banana importer named Horst-Gregorio Canellas, invited a select group of officials and journalists to his fiftieth birthday party at which he played a tape of conversations between himself and a variety of Bundesliga players. Köln players were asking for money to lose; Hertha players were asking for money to win, especially as Bielefeld had already offered them money to lose. The DFB's initial response was to impose bans on the players involved and Canellas himself, and leave the relegation standings as they were. Canellas then went off on a maniacal solo investigation into Bundesliga match-fixing and bribery which generated so much irrefutable documentation that at least two-thirds of the entire league were implicated and over fifty players, coaches and presidents ultimately received life bans. There was no alternative but a full-blown open market in wages and transfers.

West German football had, however, already been prospering on the basis of a rigged market and hidden payments which had created the conditions for de facto (if not de jure) professionalism. Like the parallel rise of Dutch football, its development was spurred and shaped by the broader political and cultural transformations of the era. The Bundesliga was born at the end of the long rule of Germany's Christian Democrats (CDU), first under Konrad Adenauer and then his successor Ludwig Erhard. Between 1965 and 1968 the country was governed by a grand coalition of Christian Democrats and the Social Democrats (SDP) led by Willy Brandt. In 1968 Brandt trounced the CDU and became Chancellor, a post he held until his surprise resignation after a spy scandal in 1974. Both German football and German society were transformed in these six years. The Bundesliga title, which hitherto had moved around the country, came to rest with just two clubs for the eight years between 1969 and 1977: Bayern München and Borussia Mönchengladbach. And the national team achieved a new pitch of performance, contesting the best match at the 1970 World Cup with Italy in the semi-finals, and winning the 1972 European Championship with a degree of openness, flair and creativity that no previous German side could match.

In the late 1960s Bayern and Mönchengladbach were seen as two of a kind – the rising stars of West German football, favouring youth and adventure, artistry over efficiency. Like Ajax and Feyenoord in the Netherlands, these were the clubs who most effectively rode the wave of professionalism and new money in football. Both employed coaches that favoured experiment and attack: at Bayern, the Yugoslavs Zlatko Čajkovski, better known as Czik, and Branco Zebec; at Gladbach, Hennes Weisweiler; and Udo Lattek at both of them. Bayern could boast an extraordinary roster of new home-grown players: goalkeeper Sepp Maier, the then midfield playmaker Franz Beckenbauer, and the taciturn goal-poaching striker Gerd Müller. At Gladbach they had Günter Netzer and Jupp Heynckes. Both teams brought in a few foreigners, but they were more cautious in the transfer market than many of their competitors, Bayern favouring Swedes and Gladbach acquiring the mercurial Dane Allan Simonsen. Both teams liked to play and pass, favoured artists over artisans in midfield, and both scored a lot of goals. Bayern won the Bundesliga in 1969. Gladbach came back to win two in a row and then Bayern went one better, winning three in a row between 1972 and 1974. Gladbach, unbowed, responded by winning another three themselves.

The era 1969–77 also saw the peak years of youth revolt and urban terrorism in Germany. The counter-cultural movements and student protests of the late 1960s had politicized the public culture of the Federal Republic out of all recognition. When West Germany went to the World Cup in 1954 it was effectively forbidden to mix politics, the national question and sport; by the early 1970s everything in West Germany was politicized. The new social movements and intellectual currents insisted that the Germans collectively examine their Nazi past with a clarity and honesty hitherto unapproached. The comfortable consumerism of the economic miracle came under assault for its shallowness and psychic pathologies, and the consensus politics of grand coalitions, social markets and the Bundestag were treated with derision by extreme Left and Right as well. In this context, Helmut Bottiger could write:

Gladbach and Bayern: radicalism or rationality, reform or pragmatism. If need be Bayern won 1–0. Bayern never played themselves into rapture, they won in a calculating manner [while] the young foals [of Gladbach] played free of all restraints, irresistibly coming forward.[33]

The contrast between clubs and playing styles was focused even more sharply by comparisons drawn between their stars: Franz Beckenbauer and Günter Netzer. Beckenbauer had acquired an aura of conservatism around him (a disposition borne out by his current politics) reinforced by his nickname 'The Kaiser' – though he had initially been called this because his youthful altar-boy looks resembled the insane King of Bavaria, Ludwig II. He also had an air of ease, aloofness and arrogance, none of which seemed to sit well with the mainstream German football public. Netzer by contrast was cast as a romantic football rebel, long-haired, extravagantly gifted, somehow closer to the fans. Yet none of these contrasts stands up to critical scrutiny. Beckenbauer's private life was certainly more unconventional than Netzer's; he also came from a working-class home, while Netzer, though by no means a scion of the establishment, was the son of a comfortable provincial seed merchant. Bayern may have had Beckenbauer but then they also had Paul Breitner whose giant Afro, self-avowed Maoism and refusal to sing the national anthem at games placed him well to the left of Netzer, let alone Berti Vogts, the mainstay of the Gladbach defence and as conventional a person as one could hope to meet. Netzer also displayed the same kind of steely cynicism about money and power that Beckenbauer possessed: 'There are eleven businessmen on a pitch, each looking after his own interests.'

The same could be said of the team's styles of play, which when dissected actually look rather similar, despite Bottiger's contrasting of them. Gladbach may have taken part in the ritual humiliations of Dortmund and Schalke (12–0 and 11–0 respectively) but Bayern were equally capable of big scorelines, in rousing see-saw matches played with abandon – most famously their 4–1 lead at Kaiserslautern in 1973 which turned in the last half-hour into a 7–4 defeat. Similarly after 1969 Bayern were more likely to build a rolling series of attacks through the middle of the pitch, using Beckenbauer as a free-roaming libero capable of turning a game with his long runs from defence. Gladbach were noted for their counterattacks, based on Netzer's uncanny ability to spot a 50-metre cross-field pass. Over their joint period of rule, Bayern actually scored more Bundesliga goals than Gladbach and conceded more as well. Yet there is little doubt that from the end of the 1960s Bayern München became the team everyone else loved to hate.

In retrospect the debates of the era are a clear projection of political and cultural battles on to football, and the footballing claims cannot be entirely substantiated, though there is a grain of truth there too. In this era Bayern not only began winning, they began to transform the way in which German football business was done – like the rest of Bavaria. Once a sleepy and deeply conservative Catholic agricultural backwater, Bavaria had become the leading edge of the West German economy, long displacing the Ruhr as the industrial heart of the nation. Where the Ruhr had crude steel, chemicals and coal industries, Bavaria had the very latest and most sophisticated toolmakers, engineers, car plants and aircraft-builders. It was this booming economy and increasing political prominence that brought the Olympics to Munich in 1972 and furnished Bayern with the largest and most modern stadium in the country. Crowds became huge and Bayern had the skill to turn crowds into money, appointing the Bundesliga's very first business manager as early as 1966. Bayern was a standard-bearer for Bavarian regional identity rather than a wider reactionary conservatism, but this was and is equally loathed in the rest of the country.

Bayern were also lucky. Their triumphant European Cup campaigns of the mid-1970s owed something to the team's knack for the last-minute reversal and acquiring the rub of the green. Against Atlético Madrid in 1974, Bayern looked outclassed and beaten until they found an equalizer in the dying seconds of extra time and forced a replay which they won. In 1975 their victory over Leeds United, who outplayed them for long periods of the game, turned on a disallowed Leeds goal and the penalty they were never given. Finally, against Saint-Étienne, having put three past Real Madrid on the way to the final, only a single Bayern goal made the difference after the French had hit the woodwork twice. By contrast, Mönchengladbach remained a small club with a tiny if boisterous stadium; in Europe in particular they had a tendency to implode, miss their chances, as if operating under a jinx. Twice, in 1973 and 1977, they made a European final only to be beaten by Liverpool on each occasion.

*

If club football offered West Germany a prism through which to explore its profound internal divisions, then the national team appeared to offer the balm of unity – combining the leading players from Bayern and Gladbach. In the quarter-finals of the 1972 European Championship West Germany played England at Wembley; it was the defining moment of this generation of German football. They won 3–1 against what was an excellent England side and they did so with flourish, movement and intelligence. They repeated the feat in the closing stages of the tournament, beating Belgium and then the Soviet Union in the final in a performance that even the Italian *Corriere dello Sport* saw as full of 'imagination and genius', and the World Cup on home soil now beckoned.

The 1974 World Cup was a tipping point in the history of the tournament, perhaps of all global sport. Behind the scenes at the Frankfurt FIFA congress Sir Stanley Rous had been deposed as FIFA president by the Brazilian João Havelange – a shift in the political geography of global football of tectonic proportions and the herald of an era of hyper-commercialization.[34] Horst Dassler's sports goods conglomerate Adidas, which was the spearhead of global sports commercialization, was also present in the wings, providing the tournament's match balls and making a gigantic marketing coup from the tournament as a whole. The qualifying rounds had easily been the biggest and most global yet and they produced a pleasingly eclectic final sixteen, including novices Haiti and Australia and the first sub-Saharan African entrant in Zaire. In an era when West German foreign policy was consumed by Brandt's *Ostpolitik* – détente with the Soviet Union and normalization of relations with the GDR – Eastern Europe was well represented, including Yugoslavia, Poland and for the first and only time East Germany, who were scheduled to meet the West Germans in the first round. The scale of the operation was also larger than any other World Cup. Attendances were slightly up on 1966 and 1970, but ticket sales provided only a small fraction of the tournament's overall income which like all sports mega-events to come would be predominantly made up of sponsorship deals and TV rights. As a consequence the numbers of accredited journalists at West Germany 74 was more than double the number at Mexico 70 with a massively increased cohort of television technicians. Overall, the tournament was remarkably well organized, and even turned a small profit, most of which was passed to the participating nations. For all that, the feel of the event remained somehow antiquated and provincial, evidenced by the kitschfest that served as the tournament's closing ceremony: two youth bands were followed by the Alberta girls from Canada and then the Fischer choir, 1,500 strong.

The tournament favourites were the hosts and the Dutch, both of whom promised their own versions of attacking open football and dressing-room crises. The West Germans were held in their rural training camp under conditions of extraordinary security, deemed necessary in response to the 1972 Munich Olympics kidnappings and the rising tide of Red Army Faction violence. As the helicopters whirred overhead, the team and coach Helmut Schön were at loggerheads over money; it was a microcosm of the generational conflict being fought out all across Germany over money, status and power. The DFB, still unable to grasp the consequences of their own decision to completely professionalize the game, had offered the squad derisory win bonuses of less than a fifth of the value of those offered to the Italians and a quarter of the Dutch squad's offer. Helmut Schön, on a different wavelength from these new professionals, had packed his bag and wanted to send the entire squad home. Beckenbauer took charge, negotiated a tripling of the bonuses and persuaded everyone to stay – a moment at which, perhaps for the first time in German football, power passed from the DFB and the national team coach to the squad. Peace of a sort reigned and the team did enough to qualify for the second round by beating Chile and Australia but against East Germany, in a strangely artificial atmosphere, they were beaten by a single goal. Schön began to disintegrate emotionally and the squad got drunk until dawn. At the press conference, where the defeat was dissected, Schön remained silent and Beckenbauer took centre stage, offering a calm appraisal of the team's chances. Under this new informal leadership the West Germans were transformed, qualifying for the final by successively beating Yugoslavia, Sweden and Poland. There they would meet the Dutch who had set the competition alight. Rinus Michels and Johan Cruyff had been recalled from Barcelona to coach and captain the team and they forged a formidable unit from the best of the Ajax and Feyenoord squads. They cruised through the first round, beating ultra-defensive Uruguay, drawing with Sweden and thrashing Bulgaria in Dortmund, where for the first time the massed ranks of orange-clad fans had gathered. Then in the second round they humiliated Argentina, despatched the East Germans and fought tooth and nail with the Brazilians, beating them in the tackle and in the air.

The opening minute of the 1974 World Cup Final was entirely Holland's; from the kick-off, to Cruyff picking the ball up from deep in his own half, to the rapid-fire pinball passing down the left, culminating in Cruyff's piercing run into the German penalty area, to Uli Hoeness' loose challenge. Johan Neeskens took the penalty and for the next 23 minutes the Dutch controlled the game, intricately but effortlessly exchanging the ball; a discernible arrogant snap to their movements, a curt edge to their touch. There was more going on here than merely winning the game, there was a palpable sense of intent about the Dutch disdain for their opponents. Johnny Rep recalled: 'We wanted to make fun of the Germans. We didn't think about it but we did, passing the ball around and around. We forgot to score the second goal.' Wim van Hanegem was blunter. 'I didn't mind if we beat them 1–0, as long as we humiliated them.' Which they did, until the West Germans were awarded and scored a penalty themselves. In the second half they took a lead they never relinquished. The Dutch remember the moment in the words of the commentator Herman Kuiphof: '*Zijn we er toch nog integuind* – they've tricked us again' – a turn of phrase that condensed the trauma of the occupation and evoked the unresolved guilt and anger of the war years in the Netherlands. The Dutch dealt with the lost final, as it came to be known, in the same way: silence and rumour.[35]

The celebration that evening was a disaster. The DFB refused to allow players' wives to attend and the squad, to a man, abandoned the official party for a drinking session down town. The Dutch had lost, but they had surely learned how to play and how to celebrate and how to treat professional footballers like adults. As Sepp Maier put it with disgust: 'Germans can organise a World Cup perfectly and crush even the strongest opponent through unflagging discipline. But we don't have the faintest idea about holding a party.'[36]

12

We Can Show Them Who is Really Superior: Football in Africa, 1900–1974

When Dr David Livingstone came to Zambia he brought three things with him in his bag. His medical kit, the Bible and a football.

Dennis Liwewe

They rule us with guns and machines. On a man to man basis, on the field of football, we can show them who is really superior.

Ferhat Abbas

I

Unfortunately there is no evidence that Livingstone did take a football to Zambia, but Dennis Liwewe, Africa's most venerated football commentator, captures a deeper truth. If anything can be salvaged from the harsh and unequal encounter between Western and African cultures, then the list must include the arrival of football. Western medical care, though dismissive of local healing traditions, is a universal demand in Africa. Christianity's legacy is more complex, its relationship with indigenous practice more hybrid, but it has become the faith of just under half the continent. Football's contribution is more unambiguous; it is without competitor Africa's game. Moreover, unlike science or religion this colonial sport has been turned by Africans into an emblem of pride and independence and thus inevitably an instrument of political and social struggle. Ferhat Abbas, the leader of the provisional Algerian government during the bitter war of independence from France (1958–62), recognized that in every area of life where colonizer met the colonized – economic, political and cultural – the playing field was weighted against the latter. The case for traditional healing and religious and political independence could be made, only to be sidestepped and ignored. But on the football pitch, where there is nowhere to hide and no rhetorical sleight of hand that can mask the reality of a goal, then one could see who really was superior. Yet the same dynamic is true of much of Asia, the Pacific Islands and the Caribbean. Why should Africa adopt football so much more quickly and with such greater intensity than the other colonized regions of the world?

Africa's course is all the more surprising when one considers the fact that in the Bantu-speaking cultures that cover most of the continent south of the Sahel, there is no indigenous word for ball. Is it possible that ancient Africa did not play with the ball? There was certainly no shortage of playing. The record of games in Ancient Egypt is particularly rich. The hieroglyphic record shows chariot racing, spear throwing and combat sports. Wrestling can be found all over Africa, from the highly ritualized and disciplined contests of the Igbo in south-east Nigeria to the wild unstructured mêlées of the Bambara in Mali. The peoples of the Great Lakes raced their canoes and rafts and everywhere the lines between war, hunting and sport were crossed as Africans played stick-fighting games and organized archery competitions.

However, it is only on the peripheries of Bantu cultures that we find African ball games. The Ancient Egyptians certainly had them, though their games seem to be closer to volleyball and catch. Among the Berbers – the pre-Arabic inhabitants of the mountains of North Africa – a kind of softball with stones can be found. On the high central plains of Ethiopia Amharic Christians have been playing Genera for over a millennium. On the extreme southern tip of the continent around the Cape of Good Hope the San people also developed ball games.

Balls were thrown and caught and struck, but nowhere in the record was the ball kicked. Feet and legs, perhaps, were for dancing, for Africa's traditions of dancing are richer than in any other region. In African society dance is ubiquitous but diverse, performed in formal and informal settings, by men and women, collectives and individuals. It is irresistible, if unprovable, not to imagine that the precocity of football's growth in Africa was triggered by the simple magic of adding a ball to the dance and watching the universe of playful possibilities that opens up.

The ball, however, did not arrive unaccompanied. It was just a small and almost unintentionally transported component of the long European colonial conquest of Africa, from the end of the fifteenth century onwards. The Portuguese first explored the west coast of Africa founding small trading missions and forts. At the same time the Iberian colonies of South and Central America and the British and French colonies of North America and the Caribbean came into being; with them came an insatiable demand for slave labour to work the recently established mines and plantations of the New World. Arab traders and soldiers had been taking slaves from East Africa for some time before this and now they were joined in the human plunder by the Portuguese and then the Dutch, the French and the English. It is hard to underestimate the impact of this act of destruction and inhumanity on Africa and Africa's relationship with the West. Between the mid-seventeenth and early nineteenth centuries somewhere in the region of 20 million people were forcibly removed from the continent, many enslaved by inland African kingdoms and sold on to the Europeans.

The European slave trade came to an end in the mid-nineteenth century and Europeans began to explore the interior of the continent now in search of booty that was not immediately accessible from their tiny coastal redoubts. The violent and disorganized grab for land and influence that followed was given a spurious dignity by the Congress of Berlin in which the European powers settled their differences and carved Africa up into their respective domains of power. In the last quarter of the nineteenth century this process was accompanied by the late arrival of Italian colonialism, successful in Libya and Somalia but defeated in Abyssinia; the direct military occupation of Egypt and Sudan by the British; and the creation of settler populations by the French in North Africa and the British in East Africa and South Africa. All were accompanied by the destruction or cooption of existing elites and the subjection of African societies to economic, political and cultural domination.

No one knows exactly who or when or even how the cocoa bush first arrived on the Gold Coast, but in retrospect it is clear that it was an epoch-making event; so too the arrival of football. If we cannot date the moment or name the strip of land where the first kickabout in Africa took place, we do know who was there: the agents of the British Empire. First, there were the sailors from merchant adventurers and naval warships putting briefly into port and disembarking with the ball for a game on the quayside. Seafarers took their ball home. Then there were the first waves of soldiers and colonial administrators who brought not just football but the entire sporting, moral and social ethos of competitive games with them, and stayed. Colonial armies and police forces proved to be key agents in the diffusion of football. In the east the King's African Rifles drew heavily on African manpower and, alongside conventional drill and military training, Africans first learned the rules of football and Western styles of boxing. In South Africa the British Army played

African scratch teams at the siege of Mafeking, while in Cape Town military regiments were setting up their own football association and playing a regular football competition as early as 1891.

The civilian wing of colonial power was even more games-orientated. It was not just that many of the recruits to the British colonial tropical service were drawn from the sport-obsessed public schools and Oxbridge universities, but the service itself actively looked for athletic types in their selection procedures. In Sudan between 1899 and 1952, 90 per cent of the British administration had been to a leading public school. One Governor General was known to circulate a leather-bound book among his staff in which sporting activities, records and achievements were punctiliously recorded. The proliferation of successful Oxbridge sportsmen in the ranks of the service prompted a Foreign Office wag to describe Sudan as 'the land of blacks ruled by blues'.[1]

Beyond these central pillars of colonial control Britons arrived in Africa on educational, medical, trading, engineering, mining, construction and religious missions, and duly began to establish their own sports clubs. South Africa saw the largest migration of British settlers to an African colony. Their first recorded game was played as early as 1866 in Pietermaritzburg and the first club, Pietermaritzburg County, was founded in 1879. By 1882 the Natal FA was formed by three exclusively white clubs, Durban Alphas, Umegi Stars and Natal Wasps. Paternalistic European employers backed the formation of white working-class teams in Durban and by the turn of the century in Johannesburg and the Cape. The unusual proximity of a white working class to the new African urban populations meant that football immediately spilt over into the townships where the game was adapted to the terrain of tiny streets and the flat tops of mine dumps in the Rand. In an early indication of the consciously separate development of European and African societies in the country, football never became the national game of white South Africa; the massively successful international tours of the national rugby union team the Springboks in 1906 and 1912 ensured that the game of South Africa's Boers would take that spot. Although football would continue to be watched and played by the British, Portuguese and other white settlers, football would become the game of Africans, Coloureds, Indians and the national liberation movement.

In the early British colonial enclaves of West Africa the key role of the army and the colonial service in diffusing football was replaced by mission and government schools. The colonial educationalist A. G. Fraser took football to his school in Kampala, Uganda in 1900 and then to Achimoto College on the Gold Coast. In 1903 boys from the Cape Coast government school were entranced by the kickabouts and games they had watched and played with visiting sailors. Excited by the match reports of football they read in the scraps of the British press that crossed their classroom desks, they made their own plans; they secretly trained by moonlight on the ceremonial parade ground of Victoria Park Gardens, the only grassed, open space available. After three months' practice they were ready although they possessed neither posts nor pitch markings, or even a full set of rules. They were joined by a voluble crowd awed and amazed by black Africa's first football club, Cape Coast Excelsior. In a political culture in which African nationalism had not yet made its appearance, the British Governor Sir Frederic Hodgson celebrated and indulged the initiative of his imperial subjects arranging their first game against Europeans. They lost 2–1 to a team of sailors but won their second match with British civil servants 3–1. By 1905 they possessed their first book of rules and the first African referees had taken charge of the game. African clubs sprang up in emulation: Everton, Energetics, Sports Swallows and Bolton Wanderers. In 1910 the Invincibles formed in Accra, followed in 1911 by Hearts of Oak – the oldest sub-Saharan club still in existence. Across the colony Europeans organized African leagues and tournaments.

To the east the British were completing the improbable construction of Nigeria. The British colonial presence began in Lagos in 1861 followed by the Oil River Protectorate with its headquarters in Calabar. From this base, the rest of Southern Nigeria was conquered and then Northern Nigeria was notionally purchased from the Royal Niger Company. All three were amalgamated in 1914. Football was introduced to the colony by the Hope Waddell Training Institute in Calabar, founded in 1894 by a group of Jamaican Presbyterians who had been evangelizing in the city for decades. In 1902 the Reverend James Luke arrived to take up the post of headmaster and brought a football with him. The first recorded game played by the boys and teachers of the school occurred on 15 June 1904 when the precocious barefoot Nigerians beat a team from HMS *Thistle* 3–2.

The British encounter with Egypt was quite different from the rest of its African empire. Britain assumed control of Egypt and its ramshackle

Sudanese empire in 1882 to ensure the security of the Suez Canal and the maintenance of interest payments to the country's numerous European creditors. The British encountered a society already incompletely modernized by the voluminous loans taken out by the last Pashas of the Ottoman era. The royal house and urban elites retained a political and cultural influence that could be contained but not eradicated. It is hardly surprising then that the course of football's development should differ too. However, rather than using its accumulated cultural and political capital to reject or resist the emergence of football – as Ottomans had in Istanbul – the Egyptian ruling class embraced and excelled at the game. These elites and their scions, having watched and played the game with the early occupation forces of the British Army in Cairo, founded Al-Ahly – the National Sporting Club – in 1907. The prowess and organizational resources of upper-class Egyptian football were such that as early as 1911 Hassan Hegazi was able to play professionally for Fulham before embarking on the full-time study of Arabic and history at Cambridge University.

Football made slower inroads in French colonial Africa prior to the First World War, reflecting the stricter separation of Europeans and Africans in most French colonies, and the weaker cultural weight of sports in general and football in particular in French colonial institutions. Indeed in French Central and West Africa the only football among Africans was played in Brazzaville where monks of the local Catholic mission introduced the game as they despaired at the impact of urban life on the moral well-being of their putative African charges:

Not having enough to do and receiving high wages, . . . [they] very quickly show in Brazzaville an innate laziness, and acquire intemperate habits and a dissipated lifestyle, which is at odds with the civilizing work that France undertakes in the colonies . . . It is for this reason that we have all kinds of games, and by this means that we will remove them from the influence of immoral dancing and dangerous companions.[2]

In French North Africa settlers had been arriving since 1830 and in Algeria had created the football-playing Club de Joyeuses d'Oran in 1897. Despite incurring the disapproval of much of the French educational establishment in Algeria, schoolboys, students and young bank clerks marked out pitches in lines of plaster powder, shared their boots and took their chances on the bumpy military parade grounds and empty spaces of Algiers, Oran and Constantine. They were playing leagues in the main cities within the decade and people were coming to watch. In 1906 Sport Club d'El Biar attracted over 2,000 spectators to their game with a team from the visiting British ship HMS *Dreadnought*. As in South Africa the physical proximity of a football-playing white colonial working class to the colonized population saw an informal diffusion of the game to the Arab streets of the big cities. In 1910 the first Arab team had donned their green shirts and took to the field as L'Étoile Sportive de Dupere. The colonization of Africa remained incomplete, the diffusion of football had barely begun, but already this strange compelling European game was providing a platform for the assertion of identity and a quiet declaration of independence.

The First World War transformed the political landscape of Europe. Dynasties ended and empires fell, but in Africa the tremors of change only appeared to reach as far as Egypt. In Cairo the local elite regained both their political and sporting independence. The former came in 1922 but Egypt had already made its mark through international football, sending Africa's first football team to the Olympic Games in 1920. In 1928 they were good enough to make the semi-finals, losing to Argentina in Amsterdam. In 1934 they were the first African team at a World Cup finals, having thrashed a Jewish Palestinian team 11–2 over two legs in qualifying games. At the finals in Naples they lost 4–2 to the mighty Hungarians, but the gap between them and the more experienced Europeans did not look unbridgeable. However, the Egyptian upper classes that had staffed the independent Egyptian state and its national team began to lose control of Egyptian society and football. Almost unnoticed, the street had taken to football and was beginning to supply a new generation of players recruited from the urban poor. Dangerously revolutionary ideas circulated in the same neighbourhoods among secular socialists and the Muslim brotherhoods presenting a series of challenges to the central axis of Egyptian politics. That axis lay parallel to the rivalry of Cairo's two leading clubs, Al-Ahly and Farouk. By membership and outlook the clubs stood opposed: liberal republicans vs. royalist conservatives; the Wafd nationalist movement and its parliamentary representatives vs. the King and his coterie. The intensity of their rivalry produced an unstable, increasingly authoritarian and ultimately unsuccessful politics that neither countered the turmoil from below, nor maintained the early status of Egyptian football.

But for the rest of the continent, like colonial authority in general, football had only carved out a small place in the coastal cities and among the new African urban elites that attended government and mission schools. Both empire and football had yet to really impose themselves on the rural areas which were ruled in the most tenuous way imaginable by the ramshackle provincial outposts of the colonial state, or remained under the control of co-opted traditional chieftaincies. The precocity of football's development in Accra and Calabar had yet to reach the northern Muslim territories of the Asante in Upper Ghana or the Hausas of Northern Nigeria. But football and nationalism would prosper from a series of changes that would encompass much of Africa in the three decades after the First World War. First, the German influence on Africa was terminated as defeat in Europe saw their colonies transferred to France, Belgium and Britain, and in the process football began to develop in the Cameroons, Togoland, Tanganyika and South West Africa. Second, football as one of the few activities that colonial authorities would allow Africans to organize openly provided one of the main recruiting grounds and training centres of the new nationalist elites that would spearhead the struggle for independence. The leading Nigerian nationalist Nnamdi Azikiwe recalled his childhood in Lagos in 1916:

When I arrived in Lagos at the age of eleven I found the open spaces in front of King's College, to our neighbourhood boys known as 'Toronto', a mecca for juvenile sports. We played football there with mango seeds, limes or oranges or old tennis balls. Any collection of boys would be divided into two sides and a spirited game would ensue. We made and altered our rules to suit each game and so we emerged to become self-made soccerists.[3]

And self-made soccerists like Azikiwe would arise all over the continent. They were equipped with new organizational skills (often gained in the administration of football), institutional bases of support (attached to football clubs) and the unquenchable self-confidence that accumulated sporting and political victories can bring. In South Africa football clubs and African and Indian football organizations became closely linked to the emerging nationalist movement. An African football association was set up in Durban as early as 1916 under prominent nationalists Charles and William Dube. Albert Luthuli, later president of the ANC, was its vice-president, while the Johannesburg FA was controlled by Dan Twala, nephew of one of the co-founders of the ANC. The game was phenomenally popular: by the 1940s the Johannesburg Bantu FA were getting 10,000 people to their Sunday afternoon games.

Third, colonial power although always incomplete, began to reach out from the coastal cities and the elite summit of African societies to encompass small towns, rural areas and the lower classes. Although economic investment and infrastructural development was limited and deliberately skewed to the interests of colonial companies, African economies and cities began to grow, centring on the tiny hot spots of micro-industrialization in the mining and manufacturing zones. Football, supported by mining firms, colonial railway and port authorities and commercial enterprises, spread among the nascent African working classes. In Rhodesia this parallel development of economy and football became intensely politicized. White settlers had first brought the game there in the 1890s, but the exclusivity of their Salisbury sports clubs meant that Africans first learned the game via South Africa. The poor migrated to the mines of the Rand and the sons of traditional tribal elites went to the leading African schools in South Africa. In both they learnt to play football. Lobengula, the grandson of the Ndebele King, played for his school side Zonnebloem and two teams of Rhodesian migrants played in the Alexander township of Johannesburg. The returning migrants found Bulawayo to be the most receptive city to the new game. Here, nearly all of Rhodesia's industrial and transport infrastructure concentrated and in the years before the Second World War there was large-scale migration and urbanization. Riots, following the economic downturn after the Wall Street Crash, sent colonial officials scurrying south to see what could be learned in South Africa about pacifying an unruly African working class; one of the answers was football. The African Welfare Society (AWS) was allowed to promote the game in Bulawayo in the 1930s. By 1941 this African-run organization had a sixteen-team league playing a nine-month season in the city. The British panicked as Africans showed an alarming capacity for self-organization. The trade-union movement was even more worrying and it grew alongside football. Men like Benjamin Burombo and Sipambaniso Manyoba doubled as union officials and as the captains of Matabele Highlanders and Red Army respectively. When in 1947 the colonial government attempted to wrest control of football from the AWS, Africans responded with a boycott of all official football. The following year they were joined by the rest of the city and then the entire colony in a massive wave of boycotts, strikes and demonstrations. The government backed down on both economic and sporting issues.

In the inter-war years, French North Africa was perhaps the most advanced footballing zone on the continent. South Africa aside, it was here that the highest levels of white colonial settlement and urban industrial development took place. Alongside considerable numbers of French immigrants to Morocco, Tunisia and Algeria, the French also invited Italians to Tunisia. Spanish migrants went to Morocco and a mosaic of trading and ethnic groups could be found in the string of growing port cities on the Mediterranean coastline. The football associations of the region were, in conformity with imperial policy, deemed subsections of the mother country and were thus affiliated to the French Football Federation. Organized competitions were established after the First World War between the colonists' leading clubs; this was a level of international competition that actually exceeded most of Europe and Latin America. In all of these societies, football thus began in the enclosed world of the colonists' sports clubs. The local population first watched, then played. Where possible they joined the more open European clubs, before finding the organizational and political resources to found their own. Given the ambivalence and often hostility of Europeans to mixing with the colonized, it is little wonder that such acts took on the colouring of resistance and opposition to colonial rule. In Tunisia a football league was, in the years either side of the First World War, contested by teams drawn explicitly from the French, Italian, Jewish and Maltese communities in and around Tunis. They finally had to face their Tunisian Arabic subjects on the field in 1919 when key elements in the modernizing elites of Arab Tunis founded the sports club Espérance. There was significant opposition to this from the French colonial authorities and both Espérance and Club Africain were forced to accept French board members. It made no difference; the rising tide of Tunisian nationalism propelled the clubs into the football league in the 1920s and to the championship title in the 1930s.

Morocco's first Arabic club, Wydad Casablanca, was founded in 1937 after a protracted struggle over the use of the beachside swimming pools that had been built by Europeans on Casablanca's coastline. A certain amount of ethnic mixing had been permitted but as Europeans became more fearful of their restive subjects, Arabs were banned from the swimming clubs and their facilities. In response, and with the active support of King Hassan, Wydad Casablanca (WAC) was set up as an alternative sports club for wealthy Moroccans. While in Tunisia and Algeria new clubs were linked personally and ideologically to an increasingly radical republicanism, in Morocco King Hassan tied them to his own more conservative brand of royalist nationalism. He persuaded the French to install a personal telephone line between his palace and the club, calling the team before, during and after matches and rewarding them with lavish receptions and presents. His main political opponent, the socialist and republican leader Abderrahman Youssoufi, spent his time trying to organize the poor. After the Second World War (during which regular football was suspended) he helped found Raja Casablanca, the team of the city's working class. In the febrile atmosphere of the post-war era, the steadily shifting balance of political power from the French to indigenous forces was reflected in the steady improvement of Raja and Wydad, with the latter winning three national championships in the late 1940s. The colonists' monopoly of the North African Club Championship was at last broken, as Wydad won the tournament three times between 1947 and 1949.

In French West and Central Africa the colonial populations enforced a stricter degree of racial separation between themselves and their African subjects. While French sports clubs sprouted in Abidjan and Dakar the process of diffusion and emulation by Africans was impeded. The French authorities' suspicion of the political and organizational potential of independent sports clubs made it slower still. Football does not seem to have arrived in the Ivory Coast until as late as the 1920s and then via migrant Ghanaians rather than French colonists. Nonetheless, in the 1930s in the commercial heartland of Abidjan the growing African population and its early cultural and nationalist leaders, like playwright Germain Coffi Gadeau and politician Robert Champroux, began to create the sports clubs that still control Ivorian football: Bete SC, which later became Africa Sports, and ASEC Abidjan, founded by employees of French commercial operations in the city. In the French Cameroons, meanwhile, Africans set up their own clubs in Douala and Yaoundé. The authorities were sufficiently paranoid not only to segregate spectators but to prevent African teams from adopting French club names like Olympique Marseille. French Army officers were called in to run the fledgling sports bureaucracy.

Congo-Brazzaville underwent its own micro-industrialization as the Congo-Ocean railway opened and new port facilities were built. Brazzaville swelled and the colonial authorities could no longer completely ignore the needs or the disposition of the tens of thousands of Africans in the city. The mission schools redoubled their efforts to provide wholesome sporting recreation. Primary schools for Africans with football on the curriculum were opened and an informal network of boys' clubs began to play in the African districts of Brazzaville: Poto-Poto, Dahomey, Brussels and Aviation. As the boys grew they allied with local traders and skilled Gabonese immigrants to create their own clubs and in 1929 to build their own ground. Bicycle repairman Flavin Bongo approached the Mayor with the idea and, as Emmanuel Daet, a teacher in Brazzaville, recalled: 'Every Sunday and vacation for six months, sometimes in the rain, office workers and labourers armed with hoes, spades and shovels, rakes and machetes, worked to clear the bush, dig out roots and stumps, level the ground and mark out the playing field.' The initiative and enthusiasm of the Congolese impressed and frightened the French. Coinciding with the first stirrings of nationalist agitation in the colony, the imperial authorities pursued a strategy of control by incorporation. A native sports federation, run by Europeans, took control of African football in return for access to playing fields and other resources. Black teams were allowed to play in the main stadium as a warm-up game before the Stanley Pool Championships between white teams from Brazzaville and Kinshasa in the Belgian Congo. They were good. The great players of the era acquired hero status and nicknames to match: D'Artagnan, Bakki – the Train, Sombo – the Butterfly. It was all too much for the French who, in 1936, in an extraordinary display of crassness, ordered African players not to wear shoes or boots when playing. The ban was ostensibly to limit on-field violence but in reality it was designed to demean their subjects the way the Belgians did in the Congo where Africans were already forbidden from wearing shoes when they played. In Brazzaville they refused. The native sports federation was abandoned and organized African football was set back a generation.

Though outright racism and physical segregation were the order of the day among the French in Africa, attitudes were different in France where a certain class of African was encouraged to participate in French elite life as part of the grand if deluded civilizing process that was the French Empire. Raoul Diagne was the son of a Senegalese parliamentarian and a middle-class Frenchwoman, and was educated at a grand *lycée* in Paris before embarking on a long professional playing career through the 1930s and 1940s. Among the Algerian players, Koudier Daho came to study medicine and play; Ben Bouali came from a wealthy family before joining Montpellier. But French football was also open enough to talent to take in great players from the poorest of backgrounds. In 1938 Labri Ben Barek – perhaps the first player to earn the sobriquet 'The Black Pearl' – left his cleaning job in Casablanca and signed up with Marseille where he was a goalscoring revelation with a searing volley. More Moroccans followed as Barek became a key figure in the French national team and at Atlético Madrid in their post-war heyday.

Africans had learned Europe's game and Europe's politics. Could they now overthrow its ideological hegemony, its assumptions of innate superiority and the right to rule? The Second World War forced colonial powers to mobilize their African possessions more systematically than ever before, calling up thousands of troops, marshalling strategic resources at a time of desperate need. The war exposed the material and military weakness of the old colonial powers and forced them to adopt a political universalism in the fight against fascism. But if racism and ethnic inequality was unacceptable in Europe why should it be any more acceptable in Africa? Colonialism had been ideologically unmasked. Now the lessons learned on and off the pitch could be turned against it.

In Nigeria, Nnamdi Azikiwe (known informally as Zik) created Zik's Athletic Club in the 1930s as a conscious attempt to foster non-racial football. He also used the club's tours across Nigeria in 1942 and 1943 as a campaigning tool. The British were forced to allow the tour to proceed for Azikiwe was selling desperately needed war bonds at the events. But every time he had 10,000 or 20,000 Nigerians assembled together to hear his call for self-rule and independence.

The always shaky edifice of colonial power was tottering and football allied to African nationalism was helping to shake it.

Despite the growth of nationalism in Africa and the ideological and economic shocks of the Second World War, the immediate post-war political geography of Africa was starkly revealed when delegates from only four independent African nations attended the 1953 FIFA congress: Egypt, Ethiopia, Sudan and South Africa. They had gathered to press Africa's claim for separate representation on FIFA's executive committee. Initially their efforts had been brusquely rebuffed by FIFA's European majority on the grounds of a barely disguised and contemptuous racism. However, the Africans found anti-imperialist allies among the Soviet satellite states of Eastern Europe and anti-European allies in South America. FIFA were forced to concede. Africa could set up its own continental organization and it would be allocated places in FIFA's corridors of power. It did so, in 1956, in Khartoum, and the first African tournament to be played amongst the founders of Confédération Africaine de Football (CAF) was planned for Egypt in 1957. The first Cup of Nations did take place in 1957, but in Sudan and without South Africa. The Suez crisis and the war of 1956 made Egypt an unfeasible location. Football stopped when the war started and both Al-Ahly and Zamalek offered their stadiums to the authorities as impromptu field hospitals and marshalling yards. The South Africans, in accord with the racial laws of the newly constructed apartheid regime, declared that they could send a white team or a black team but not a mixed team. CAF, which had already come to represent to its members and activists the first pan-African organization in an era of continental liberation, could not contemplate endorsing this. The South Africans were excluded, then thrown out of CAF in 1961, and would eventually be expelled, after intense pressure from the Africans, from FIFA.

10 February 1957
Sudan 1 Egypt 2
Khartoum, Sudan

The beginning. Africa's first continental tournament, the first game, the first goal, the first penalty, for Egypt on 21 minutes. Sudan equalize but Egypt's Ad-Diba finds a winner in the second half. A scrap of film; a general bedecked in braid inspects a military band on the touchline. There, you have the record. Africa's football history sometimes leads to dead ends and silence. The documents of CAF's inaugural meetings have been lost, possibly in a fire, possibly not. The Nigerian FA persistently misquotes its own date of origin. The old men that were there are dead or dying.

Egypt met Ethiopia in the final and Ad-Diba put four past Gila, the Ethiopian keeper. The low grey bowl of Khartoum stadium is, even on the grainy celluloid, white with the cloaks and headdresses of 30,000 Sudanese. Neatly arrayed, closely ranked, cross-legged up to the touchline, they stand in straight lines and tidy curves on the terracing. The scratchy black lines of deteriorating film stock dance erratically across the screen.

Cut to a camera angle low behind the Ethiopian goal.

The origin of the ball's trajectory is hidden but we see it come spinning up from the edge of the penalty area in a high slow loop. It suddenly falls, perfectly, untouchably and fractionally inside the angle of the cross bar and the post. We cannot see Ad-Diba, but it must be him scoring. The film cuts back to the crowd. Some are pressing against barbed wire fences. Kids curiously kneel beside them. The uncannily still ranks of men strain to see to their left; like every crowd, hoping to glimpse the moment of brilliance.

The subsequent fate of football in CAF's four founder members paralleled the course of their political history. In particular, Egypt's early independence and advanced commercial and urban development gave it a decisive edge in the first years of African football. After the 1952 revolution, which had deposed King Farouk and installed first a military council and then Colonel Gamal Abdel Nasser as head of state, the radicalized officer class that ran the country did not ignore football. Nasser was made honorary president of Al-Ahly. Farouk, the team of the now defeated and exiled King, took the name of their neighbourhood Zamalek. The leading Cairo teams possessed better facilities and greater resources than any other African clubs and the national team, the Pharaohs, fed on their strength. The military made sure that they could take advantage of this crucial national resource. Field Marshal Abdel-hakim Amer took personal control of the Egyptian FA. Leading foot-ballers were drafted into the army where they were carefully nurtured and General Abdelaziz Salem, a leading figure in the regime, was elected president of CAF, which was based in Cairo.

As the regime's domestic popularity peaked, Egypt hosted and won the 1959 African Cup of Nations as the UAR (the United Arab Republic) which was a short-lived experiment in pan-Arabism in which Egypt and Syria were joined. But Egypt's advantage was swiftly eroded as other nations caught up, and its own economy and polity began to stagnate. In 1962 they were losing finalists in the Cup of Nations. In Ghana in 1963 they failed to qualify from the group stage and withdrew altogether from the 1965 competition in Tunisia in protest at President Bourguiba's peace overtures to Israel. The seething tension of Egyptian society, its poverty and divisions, remained unresolved by the increasingly clumsy military elite and boiled over in a massive riot at the Al-Ahly–Zamalek derby in 1966; over 300 people were injured when the military opened fire. It was a premonition of disaster to come.

The war with Israel in 1967 devastated Egyptian society and football; indeed, so great were the upheavals caused by such total military defeat and chaos that league football was abandoned altogether for five years. The Egyptian team's performances were a shadow of their former selves. Yet the elite never lost faith in the capacity of football to soothe their masses. Despite the massive costs of the Yom Kippur War in late 1973, and the precarious peace that followed, President Anwar Sadat insisted that Egypt host the 1974 Cup of Nations. But the inherent limitations of Egypt's war-racked infrastructure were cruelly revealed in a match played shortly before the tournament began. Fifty people were killed as the walls of Zamalek's stadium crumbled under the weight of a crowd watching them play Czechoslovak army side Dukla Prague. The panic in the ranks of the Egyptian government saw them, for the first time, arrange live television coverage of the Cup of Nations in an effort to keep crowds down. The Egyptian team limped through to the semi-finals where they were beaten by Zaire 3–2.

The political logic of South African apartheid was laid bare in 1960. The pursuit of industrialization in a racially divided society required a massive apparatus of urban control to contain a huge black working-class labour force in designated townships. But in creating an African working class, the apartheid regime brought its own nemesis into being. Deeply felt opposition to restrictions on movement, the imposition of pass laws and the assault on African political institutions erupted in the Sharpeville riots. Apartheid would henceforth be implemented through teargas and the gun. The same processes of urbanization provided black South African football with a huge new pool of players and fans. Black football entrepreneurs organized tournaments, leagues and clubs. There were cash prizes in township championships. Sometimes, instead of cash, an ox would go to the winning side, often slaughtered and eaten on the touchline. In the upper echelons of the sport African teams like Orlando Pirates and Moroka Swallows were sufficiently big draws that they verged on the professional. But money was always short and the first black South Africans made their way overseas to play professional football in Europe: Stephen 'Kalamazoo' Mokone went to Cardiff City as early as 1956; Albert 'Hurry Hurry' Johansen went to Leeds United in 1961. Despite African football attracting the biggest crowds, sponsorship money from South Africa's companies flowed only to white football. In 1959 *Drum* magazine, a leading voice in the African press, addressed itself to the problem:

Remember that soccer is just another game to the whites. Rugby gets the crowds. Soccer gets what is left. Now, for non-white South Africans, soccer is the national game ... Why shouldn't WE start our own professional inter-racial Soccer League? ... We've asked these questions the past few weeks, and, from clubmen and sports officials, the answer every time has been 'Yes. Let's try'.[4]

And so they did. In early 1961 a group of administrators and club owners broke away from the non-racial but strictly amateur South African Soccer Federation to create the South African Soccer League (SASL). The clubs were underwritten by an odd cross section of the excluded and marginal entrepreneurs of the time: Bernie Katz, a Jewish nightclub owner, backed the Cape Town Ramblers; Daddy Naiddo, an infamous crime boss and boxing promoter, supported Durban Aces United; and the league took its sponsorship money from the United Tobacco Company. Clubs did not own their own stadiums so delicate negotiations with the municipal apartheid governments were required to access playing fields.

Despite such shaky beginnings the league was a massive success. The pent-up desire for top-class non-racial organized football in urban South Africa was immense. Crowds flocked to see Transvaal United from the coloured Soweto township of Noordgesig win the first title. The original six clubs were soon joined by every major non-white club in the country. The quality of football under a professional regime rapidly improved. The social closeness of players and fans made for an intimate and expressive bond. Eric 'Scara' Sono at Orlando Pirates and Difference 'City Council' Mbanya of the Moroka Swallows were the embodiment of physically tough but cunning and mentally determined township football. Supporters' clubs became a rare permitted source of self-organization and football became closely tied to the rhythms of township music, parties, festivals and dances. In this vibrant mix South Africans created new friendships, alliances and communities that cut across divisions of gender, ethnicity, age and class. In the dark shadow of the repressive apartheid state, the solidarity, the exuberance, the resilience and independence of the SASL spoke to and nourished the desire for liberation.

Such a potent cocktail of social and political forces did not go unnoticed. The white authorities had sought to prosecute the Durban team Lincoln City for violating the Group Areas Act by playing mixed soccer, but the Natal Supreme Court concluded that South African law did not actually forbid mixed soccer; however, socializing and taking refreshments together in the same building were a real problem. The government and FASA were spurred into action by this legal loophole and their desire to reassert economic and political control over black football. All municipalities were contacted and ordered to prohibit the use of playing fields by the SASL. On 6 April 1963 thousands of fans arrived at the Natalspruit Indian Sports ground in Johannesburg to find a handwritten note from the city council announcing the cancellation of the game. The fans and the teams climbed over the fence anyway and

15,000 people watched Moroka Swallows take Blackpool United apart, winning 6–1. It was a pyrrhic victory. The league was systematically denied access to playing fields all over the country. The SASL as a spectacle was dead by 1966, and was disbanded the following year.

While its founding members stumbled in the first decades of independence, CAF itself rode the now howling winds of political change across Africa. From just four members in 1957 it had nine members in 1960, twenty-six members in 1965 and by 1970, as the process of decolonization was completed outside of lusophone (Portuguese-speaking) Africa and the white settler colonies of the south, membership had reached thirty-four states. The British, the French and the Belgians scrambled their way out of Africa even quicker than they had arrived, harried by nationalist movements that almost everywhere had become in some way connected to football. Thus nowhere in Africa could football escape the clutches of politics and social conflict. The story of this unstable relationship is exemplified by two states, Ghana and Algeria. In Ghana, football became totally enmeshed in the new state's domestic conflicts and radical foreign policy. The game would initially benefit from the association, but the country's sporting triumph would not outlive its key patron President Nkrumah. In Algeria, football would become a central component of an anti-colonial revolution. That fight would bring independence but leave a bitter legacy of violence in Algerian society and sport.

In 1951 Kwame Nkrumah became the Prime Minister of the Gold Coast. Though he had been initially imprisoned by the British after widespread social disorder in the late 1940s, the colonial authorities turned to the only politician who could halt it. Nkrumah was more than the first African politician to run his country. He was the most inspirational and visionary voice of the first wave of post-colonial African leaders. There were to be no half measures, no lingering colonial suzerainty. Africa must regain its political independence, and Nkrumah rallied his listeners with the cry, 'Seek ye the political kingdom.' In foreign policy he was the most outspoken and articulate advocate of a radical pan-Africanism that sought to create a continent that could transcend the arbitrarily imposed boundaries of European-constructed nation-states. Domestically, he led the way in experiments with African socialism and the creation of an interventionist state. He was also the first leader to go down the authoritarian path of the one-party state, a path that the rest of the continent would soon follow. At each stage of this political odyssey, football was a central element of Nkrumah's repertoire. After six years of African government, the British finally left in 1957. Yet at the very moment that the colonial yoke was broken, Nkrumah organized the celebrations around Ghanaian independence to include a tour by Stanley Matthews. Crowds across the country flocked to see his mesmeric dribbling.

The leading clubs of the pre-independence era were Hearts of Oak from the capital city Accra on the coast and Asante Kotoko from Kumasi in the north. Kotoko's ethnic and geographical affiliation was without question. The club was founded by a taxi driver from Kumasi who was impressed by the football scene in Accra. On his return home he founded the Rainbow football club and provided their kits. The team then became Titanics and then Asante. In 1931 a dreadful run of form saw the club's board consult a local oracle who recommended that they change their name to Kotoko, the Asante word for porcupine and the symbol of an emerging ethnic nationalism. The club had by now become enmeshed with the traditional chieftaincy structure of the Asante people who provided its leading officers for generations. Hearts of Oak's affiliation was urban rather than ethnic. As representatives of Accra they were connected to a multi-ethnic urban population in which the traditional forms of African authority that operated in the Asante lands had broken down, to be replaced by the new order of the independent Ghanaian state. The fearsome rivalry between the two clubs was paralleled by the emergence of two competing football associations – one based in Kumasi, the other in Accra – which made the organization of national competitions increasingly fraught. Similarly, Nkrumah's Accra-based CCP government and the Asante chiefs were locked into a conflict which centred on control over the cocoa-marketing boards. The boards monopolized the sale of Ghana's most precious and taxable commodity. Nkrumah's government needed the revenues to fund their urban constituency and their development programmes, while the Asante leadership looked to divert funds to both themselves and the Asante peasant farmers who grew much of the crop. The battle over the FA went to Nkrumah as the old officials were levered out and his key appointee

Ohene Djan took control of Ghanaian football in a single Accra-based FA. On the field Hearts and Kotoko both won championships in the now national league. But division of the spoils was less easy to accommodate in the world of Ghanaian cocoa politics. By the early 1960s Nkrumah had banned ethnically based political parties, cowed the trade-union movement and was ruling by decree.

As Nkrumah struggled to face down a tide of internal dissent he continued to prosper internationally. His radical pan-Africanism became the commonplace rhetoric of almost every new independent African state. It took on a concrete institutional form when the Organization of African Unity was founded in Addis Ababa in 1963. Ghana had joined its footballing counterpart CAF after independence in 1957 and secured the right to host the 1963 Cup of Nations. With a characteristic rhetorical flourish, Nkrumah named the Ghanaian national football team the Black Stars, in memory of the ship *The Black Star* chartered by Caribbean pan-African leader Marcus Garvey in 1922 to take black Americans and Caribbeans back to Africa. Nkrumah's Black Stars were equipped with foreign coaches and generous government resources. The leading players had immediate access to Nkrumah himself and a steady supply of gifts, inducements and rewards. The already established Jalco Cup with Nigeria was soon supplemented by a Nkrumah Cup between all of the newly independent West African states and the team was sent on diplomatic missions to play exhibition games at Kenya's independence celebrations and the accession of Mobutu to the Congolese presidency. But the serious business of winning competitive matches was not ignored. The Black Stars of the era were tested against the most fearsome opposition. In 1962 they toured Europe playing Fortuna Düsseldorf, Dinamo Moscow, Austria Vienna and Blackpool. In early 1963 they achieved a 3–3 draw with Real Madrid and beat Italy 5–2. The final element in the mix was Nkrumah's determination to rid the Black Stars of the last traces of colonial dependence and domination – a European coach would not be acceptable. Nkrumah turned to Ghana's only overseas professional – CK Gyamfi, who played in Germany – to lead the team at the Cup of Nations. The planning paid off and although Nkrumah was too worried by the threat of assassination to attend Ghana's opening game or indeed the final, he was delighted to reap the rewards of Ghana's flowing play and a decisive 3–0 victory over Sudan to lift the trophy.

The Black Stars were unquestionably the best team on the continent and proved it again under the complete control of CK when they went to Tunisia in 1965 and retained the Cup of Nations, beating their hosts with an extra-time goal in the final. The international prestige and domestic political capital garnered from these victories were not enough to shore up Nkrumah's increasingly contested rule, and in both football and politics international success was complemented by a new push for domestic control. Just as Ghana had led the way in the creation of independent African states, so it was first in the drift to authoritarianism. In 1964 Ghana became a one-party state under Nkrumah's CPP and the new order had its own club in the national league. Sports minister Ohene Djan created the Real Republikans in 1962 by taking the two best players from the leading teams of the Ghanaian league and appointed an Englishman, George Ainsley, as their coach. Protests from the clubs were muted for the most part, but Asante Kotoko complained vociferously. The regime was sufficiently tough minded to threaten to expel them from the league and to create a surrogate club on their patch – Kumasi United – to replace them if need be. In the end, Kotoko like the rest of the Asante elite temporarily acceded to Nkrumah's demands. In their first season in the league, the Republikans played on a non-competitive basis. Like their President they were supposed to be above the interest-ridden conduct of winning points and controlling power. Teams could take points off of them in a game, but they would take none themselves. This of course was not enough and in their second season as one-party rule became more deeply entrenched and more bitterly resented, they played for real and won the league. Domestic football though was always too small an arena for Nkrumah's ambitions. For this team were to be, in his own words, 'ambassadors of the new spirit of African man'. The Real Republikans had been named in emulation of Real Madrid and only the creation and domination of a pan-African tournament would allow them to measure themselves adequately against the European domination that Madrid had exercised in the late 1950s. Thus in 1964 the first edition of the African Cup of Champion Clubs was played out in a four-team tournament in Accra. But the Real Republikans were beaten and the Kwame Nkrumah Trophy headed south with Oryx Douala of Cameroon.

The Real Republikans never did win the African Champions Cup. In June 1966 Nkrumah was deposed by a military coup. Before the end of

the season the Real Republikans were disbanded and Sekondi Independence – a team run by a key Nkrumah political ally – followed them
into oblivion. Other allies, like Djan and CK Gyamfi, lost their protec-
tors, their authority and their jobs. The support that the Black Stars had
received evaporated. Ghanaian international football would be in retreat
for a decade, while at home the only beneficiaries of the decline that
followed Nkrumah's departure were his old adversaries in Kumasi.
Asante Kotoko regained their best players and became the leading team
in Ghana. In 1967 they had drawn their two-leg African Champions'
Cup Final with Zaire's Tout Puissant Englebert. With no provision
for penalties, a third game was required. However, when CAF finally
organized the fixture and phoned the details through to Accra the message got stuck. No one in Kumasi was told and by the time they did
know, the day had gone. The Zairians showed up and claimed their
prize. The two teams met in the final again in 1970 and this time under
thunderous pressure from the Zairian crowd Kotoko's Robert Mensah
stepped up to score from the spot. Ghana had won back the Nkrumah
Trophy but the man was no longer there to receive it. He was dying in
Conakry.

Football and nationalism had become irretrievably bound together in
Algeria in the mid-1930s for the game was no longer restricted to the
French and other colonial communities in Algeria; it had been adopted
by Muslim Algerians, both Arabs and Berbers, as their game. Crowds
had swelled, an independent sports press had been established and games
across the ethnic and political divide were commonplace. Before the
Second World War these encounters seethed with violence. The crowds
were segregated by ethnicity and by class, with the poorest of the poor
reduced to the pirate stands of rooftops and electricity poles around the
ground. Reports from the French colonial authorities single out the
Djidjelli Sports Club in Constantine as a regular location of inter-ethnic
clashes around football games. After the war, as the Fourth Republic's
hold on its Algerian colony became ideologically unsustainable and
practically harder to maintain, the level of agitation at games increased.
General Henri Martins, a French army commander in the colony, listed

the plethora of problems that the game appeared to be attracting: seditious cries, nationalist slogans chanted, the active disruption of games, fist fights between players that crossed over into the crowd.

In 1954 the leadership of the Swiss-based Algerian nationalist movement met as the World Cup finals were played out in Switzerland. They took the decision to pursue an armed struggle for independence and Algeria exploded. As the nationalist FLN fought the French army, the police and their local collaborators, the conflict was reflected at football matches. Algeria's papers report knife fights, attacks on police officers and even the death of a player on the pitch after a protracted riot. The already existing antipathy between colonist and colonized on and off the pitch reached a new intensity. France responded to the conflict with force but also tried to bind Algeria even more closely into mainstream French life. They made Algerians French subjects and allowed Algerian representatives into French parliamentary institutions. Similarly, the Algerian FA at this time was not an independent member of FIFA but was merely affiliated to the French FA. Algerian and Tunisian clubs were encouraged to take part in the French Cup and many Algerian footballers had moved to France to pursue a professional career unavailable to them at home. France also had its Arab supporters, like the former president of the Algerian assembly Ali Chekkal who consistently opposed full independence for Algeria. It was no surprise then to find Chekkal in the VIP box at the 1957 French Cup Final where he was assassinated by FLN activist Mohammed Ben Sadok.

The already close connection between football and nationalist politics was sealed in 1958 when Rachid Mekloufi and eight other Algerian professionals playing in France secretly made their way to Tunis to join the FLN government-in-exile and form the FLN's own national football team. Mekloufi was the leading Algerian-French footballer of his day. He had won the World Military Games title the previous year with the French army team. He was loved and respected at his club Saint-Étienne and in taking the trip to Tunis he abandoned the opportunity to attend the 1958 World Cup with the French team. France was stunned, amazed and appalled. At a time when Algerian politicians were going underground, organizing a war of liberation, *Le Monde* was haughtily surprised that 'The French public is more sensitive to the disappearance of Algerian footballers than Algerian politicians.'[5] The FLN team came to embody the inescapable momentum of the nationalist movement as it ground down the French colonial authorities. The team played in four-teen countries over the next four years (communist states in Eastern Europe and Asia as well as Arab nations in North Africa and the Middle East), playing with élan, bravado and style; they scored an average of around four goals a game. As Frantz Fanon wrote, 'The colonial peoples should win, but they should do so without barbarity.' They did win, and in 1962 the French left. The FLN team was disbanded and Mekloufi headed back to France and Saint-Étienne. In Algeria he was revered for his national service but treated with suspicion and some distaste by the socialist elite for his professionalism. In France Mekloufi's status was equally ambiguous: loathed by the diehards who still bitterly resented their enforced departure from Algeria, but adored and embraced by the majority for his return. As he stepped up to receive the French Cup in 1968 as captain of Saint-Étienne, it was De Gaulle who was waiting for him with the trophy and the phrase, 'La France, c'est vous.'

Mekloufi was not alone. The intensity of football's politicization and the quotidian violence of Algerian society made Algerian football an uncomfortable place for anyone in the years immediately after indepen-dence. The conflict and bloodshed of the previous decade lived on, despite the departure of the French. Indeed, the situation was so bad that, in an effort to calm things down, the authorities banned anyone from attending the final matches of the 1964 championship. The cham-pionship was completed but the wild disorder of the country's stadiums would only be contained for so long.

VII

The legacies of violence and disorder that the Algerian revolution bequeathed to football and Ghana's turn to one-party authoritarianism were just two straws in the wind of African football's development. Almost as soon as the processes of decolonization and independence were complete, the weakness and fractures of African political life began to show. The paucity of the continent's post-colonial infrastructure was crudely revealed at a game between Gabon and Congo-Brazzaville when nine people were killed and thirty injured after a landslide engulfed a fragile stand in the capital Libreville. Kenyan football, like Kenyan politics, quickly descended into a vicious zero-sum battle between ethnic groups struggling for power in the new patrimonial state. Politicians of the Luo people – like Tom Mboya and Oginga Odinga – orchestrated the merger of Luo United and Luo Stars in 1968 to form a single and powerful standard bearer, Gor Mahia. The main body of Luhya support responded to the Luo threat by merging their own sides to create an ethnic super-club Abaluhya FC who became AFC Leopards. These teams and their fans have been fighting each other on and off the pitch for four decades.

In Nigeria football reflected the over-inflated expectations of the country's politicians and the immense difficulties of building lasting national institutions in a society so divided by ethnicity, language and religion. The prospects for Nigerian football seemed strong in 1960. The huge popularity of the game in the Yoruba west and Igbo east had finally spread to the north. The Muslim Hausa elite had initially been suspicious and dismissive of the game, preferring the elitist sports of polo and cricket. But by the 1950s, leading aristocratic politicians from the region like the Sardauna of Sokoto, Ahmadu Bello, had learned to love the game at school. The Emir of Kano – a traditional ruler in the main Islamic city of the north – had actually sponsored football tournaments. The Prime Minister in waiting was the northern Muslim Tafawa Balewa. The man charged with holding the balance of power in Nigeria's hotly contested and unstable political game had become patron of the Nigerian Referees' Association. Independence celebrations were held at the new 30,000-seat national stadium, Surelere in Lagos. The previous month, a World Cup qualifying game against Ghana in Accra announced Nigeria's entry into the world of independent nations. The Ghanaians won 4–1, however, and the front of Nigerian national unity was immediately broken by an official announcement from Nnamdi Azikiwe's NCNC party deploring the loss as a national disgrace. Nigeria's subsequent outings in international football were no better and despite a nationwide spread of clubs and an insatiable demand for football, the Nigerian FA could not even begin to organize a national league before the Biafran civil war of 1967–70 rendered the project meaningless.

But Nigeria, perhaps, was the worst-case scenario. Elsewhere there was a flowering of African football talent. In 1970 Morocco became the first African team to play at the World Cup finals since Egypt in 1934 and in front of a few thousand curious Mexicans in León they took Africa's first World Cup point with a draw against Bulgaria. Morocco's footballing pedigree was well known, but there were surprises to come from the most unexpected quarters. The greatest African player of the post-independence era came from the vast and thinly populated Sahelian state of Mali, where football had been a minor urban pastime under French colonial rule. That player was Salif Keita. He made his debut as a tall wiry sixteen-year-old for Real Bamako in 1963. Within a year he was playing for the national team, and cross-town rivals Stade Malien borrowed him for the 1964 African Champions' Cup campaign. In 1966 he took Real Bamako all the way to the final with an incredible fourteen goals in eight games. Keita accumulated clubs, goals and nicknames: 'Domingo', 'The artist of the ball' and the 'The Bamako gazelle'. His fame spread from Africa to Europe and the call came in 1967 from French club Saint-Étienne. A professional contract awaited. Keita flew to Orly airport in Paris only to find no one there to meet him. He took a cab over 500 kilometres south. The club paid his fare and were richly rewarded by five years of dynamic attacking football. After Saint-Étienne, Keita played with Olympique Marseille, Valencia and Sporting Lisbon and earned himself a pension with the New England Tea Men in the final days of the NASL in Boston. In an era when most of Africa's leading footballers were forced to play at home by authoritarian regimes jealously guarding their talents, or languished in obscurity outside of their homelands, Keita was the pioneer. As he put it, 'When my sun started to shine in Europe, all Africans were happy.'[6]

In the Congo another kind of pioneer was at work, General Joseph Désiré Mobutu – a pioneer in the dark arts of political manipulation and ruthless statecraft. The vast territories of the Congo had been subject to the harshest of colonial regimes – first, under King Léopold of the Belgians and then under the Belgian state itself. They were then subject to the most irresponsible and hasty process of decolonization in Africa. Within a year the Belgians turned a complete volte-face from refusing to acknowledge or support any instance of African political activity to instant independence. Patrice Lumumba became President in 1960 with only the barest trappings of statehood. Within months he was facing an army mutiny and a secessionist movement in mineral-rich Katanga province. Lumumba was arrested and then murdered with the knowledge and connivance of Western intelligence agencies. The Katanga rebellion was controlled by the UN and Congo was made safe for the

Western mining and security interests that Lumumba had threatened to disrupt. From out of this chaos Mobutu, now head of the armed forces, stepped forward and in 1965 became President. He took over a nation in which football and the Church, married to social control and violence, were the central embedded legacies of the European presence.

In the Belgian Congo football had attracted the usual colonial alliance of church missionaries and worried bureaucrats, with the addition of the vast mining corporations desperate for a docile labour force. Together, they supported the development of football in Léopoldville (later Kinshasa) and Elizabethville (later Lubumbashi). When that was not enough there were other forms of pacification: during a labour dispute in 1941 troops shot a hundred striking workers of the copper giant UMHK on the company's football pitch. Mobutu's populist instincts were sharply attuned and a football tournament was held to celebrate his accession to power. In the short hiatus between his arrival and the later descent of the country into economic meltdown and political tyranny, the Congolese economy boomed. Atop it rode an effervescence of Congolese urban popular culture; the music, the dancing, the football were the best. From the irresistible and melodious riffs of Franco and his TPOK Jazz Orchestra to the stylish play of TP Englebert, and AS Vita Club, Congo was in the groove. In 1966 Mobutu invited the Ghanaian Black Stars to Kinshasa where they beat their hosts 3–0. Mobutu liked what he saw and decided to invest. The football authorities were brought within his direct circle of control, Pelé's Santos were invited on tour, a Hungarian coach was imported for the national team and Mobutu bought out the contracts of Congolese players in Belgium. Congolese football talent took its chances. TP Englebert won the 1967 and 1968 African Champions' Cup and were beaten finalists in the next two tournaments. Better still, at the 1968 Cup of Nations in Addis Ababa, Congo became African champions when the towering, lanky frame of Pierre Kalala spun in the Ghanaian penalty area and put the ball under the crossbar. He, like the rest of the team, was flown back to Kinshasa and paraded in one of football's most bizarre homecomings; bedecked with flowers they were presented as strange public chattels descending the aircraft steps with their names printed on large white boards hung around their necks.

Mobutu consolidated his rule in 1970 when an implausible 100 per cent of the country confirmed him as President-for-life. He then began his programme of 'authenticity'. This was essentially a takeover of foreign- and migrant-owned economic assets that he needed to redistribute among his networks of power, but it was dignified and popularized as Africanization. He renamed himself Mobutu Sese Seko, the country was renamed Zaire, Western dress was banned and African dress, especially bearing his image, was the rage. Tout Puissant Englebert, named after a colonial tyre manufacturer renowned for its strength, became TP Mazembe. The national team, formerly the Lions, was rebaptized the Leopards to match Mobutu's own trademark leopard-skin hat. The Leopards continued to progress and, under their chain-smoking Yugoslav trainer Blagoje Vidinic, they won their second African Cup of Nations in Egypt in early 1974 and then qualified for the World Cup in West Germany later that year. A vast entourage of administrators, factotums and witchdoctors of all kinds accompanied the Leopards to Europe. In their opening game they played well but lost to Scotland 2–0; but as the Scottish manager had dismissively claimed that the Scots couldn't fail to beat them by more than two goals it was a moral victory. It was their last and soon forgotten.

---

18 June 1974
Zaire 0 Yugoslavia 9
Gelsenkirchen, West Germany

On the most expensive advertising board in the stadium, now reserved for the very biggest multinational sponsors, it reads 'Zaire – Peace'. One wonders quite what Mobutu had intended; that after nearly a decade of brutal repression Zaire was now entering a period of political tranquillity? Or perhaps subliminally, that a piece of the action was available in Zaire for anyone who wanted to talk to him about it.

At first, it is not possible to watch the Yugoslavs shred Zaire and not read between the lines. Some of the players claim that they were not trying from the start, as the squad saw its FIFA bonus payments disappear into the maw of Zairian football administration. 'Just watch. Just look at us – we weren't running, we were doing nothing.' But in the opening quarter, before the score had got out of hand, Zaire are trying. They are running off the ball, getting in their tackles and although they barely press the Yugoslav midfield and their marking in the penalty area is poor, they are in the game. Do you throw a World Cup game just because the boss has made off with the cash? Like that had never happened in Zaire before.

After three goals have gone in Zaire's Yugoslav coach Vidinic pulls off goalkeeper Kadazi and throws on the untested Tunilandu Dimbi. His first task is to pick the ball out of the net after Katalinksi has scored Yugoslavia's fourth. In Kinshasa they are already concocting the stories that he has taken a bribe to field a substandard team, that he has sold the team's secrets, perhaps its soul, to his home nation. Others suggest that over-attentive even spiteful healers and witches share their part in their disaster.

It's 6–0 at half time. The thin crowd of Yugoslav gastarbeiters, probably straight off the car production lines of the Ruhr, are on their feet. In the second half the Yugoslavs just keep at it and although the Zairians are wilting – I'd wager sickeningly worried by the fate that awaits them afterwards – it's better not to read between the lines. Just watch. Just look at them. The Yugoslavs are bigger, fitter, faster and tougher. Their technical skills are impeccable. The organization is precise but effortless. There isn't much mystery here, nothing between the lines, just the cruel and relentless contrast of poverty and wealth.

The team recovered a measure of dignity in a 3–0 defeat to Brazil but Mobutu washed his hands of the Leopards and of football. No one was at Kinshasa airport to meet the team on their return. Players were left to thumb a lift with friendly taxi drivers. All became personae non gratae in public life in Zaire, and many of the squad disappeared into the impoverished slums of Zaire's cities where, like the rest of the country, they scratched a living. Key forward N'daye Mulamba, who had been awarded the National Order of the Leopard, survived on scraps of coaching for nearly two decades before CAF honoured him and his memory at the 1994 Cup of Nations in Tunisia. On his return to Zaire he was attacked by street thieves looking for the cash they assumed he must have been given. There was none. He still limps from the brutal assault. CAF announced his death at the 1998 Cup of Nations only for him to be found, drunk, sick and penniless in a Cape Town slum. Asked to recall the 1974 World Cup campaign he said, 'It's not just the football that went downhill. The whole country was hurtling towards an abyss.'[7] And so it was. Zaire's national team never looked like serious challengers for honours again, and Mobutu's regime descended into the worst kleptocracy in Africa. The promise of African independence and African football, although undermined and subverted in a thousand places, was most surely abused in Zaire and rudely exposed that night in Gelsenkirchen.

PART FOUR

Things Fall Apart:
Football after the Long Boom, 1974–1990

13

The World Turned Upside Down: João Havelange, FIFA and the Transformation of Global Football

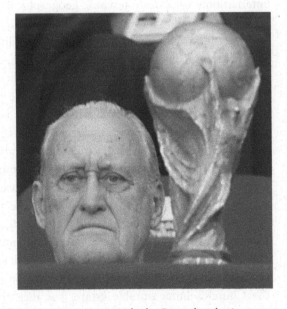

I don't want to make any comparisons with the Pope, but he is criticized from time to time, and his reply is silence. I too am sometimes criticized, so explanations about such matters are superfluous.

João Havelange

I

One should not be fooled by João Havelange's false modesty. The comparison between his office and the Pontiff of Rome was not meant as mere fancy, nor does one have to subscribe to the model of football as secular religion to see the parallels between FIFA and the Papacy. As President of FIFA between 1974 and 1998 Havelange presided over an international organization whose geographical spread was far in excess of the reach of global Catholicism and whose devotees, measured by the viewing figures for the 1998 World Cup Final, were far greater in number than Rome's flock. Michel D'Hooghe, a member of FIFA's executive committee, made the comparison explicit when he described the extraordinary omnipresence of Havelange: 'He is everywhere . . . heaven and hell, like the Pope.'[1] As regards issues of irrefutable authority and doctrinal correctness, Havelange clearly believed in his own version of papal infallibility. In one particularly memorable encyclical Havelange stated that under his control, 'the FIFA administration may be considered perfect.'[2] An audience with the man was as hard to come by as one at the Vatican, if not harder. When Rupert Murdoch gate-crashed the VIP box at the 1994 World Cup trying to get a meeting with Havelange, he was treated with glacial contempt and sent packing. Of course, even the $4 billion cash in FIFA's bank accounts that Havelange bequeathed to his successors is but a drop in the ocean compared to the Church's immeasurable estate; but then they have had almost a two-millennia headstart in the accumulation game. That such comparisons could be touted, even in jest, would have seemed inconceivable to FIFA and the rest of the football world on Havelange's accession to the throne in 1974. That they no longer seem entirely risible is testament to two things. First, the vast transformation in the global geography of football in the half-century after the Second World War which shifted the balance of power sufficiently to the south that for the first time a non-European like Havelange could win control of the organization. Second, the role of Havelange's FIFA in turning the World Cup into, unquestionably, the premier global sporting spectacular, underwritten by its alliance with the global television industry and multinational corporate sponsors.

When FIFA reconstituted itself at the end of the Second World War it had just fifty-four members, over half of them European and around another fifth from South America. By 1974 membership had grown to 140 with Europeans and South Americans making up less than a third of the total. Europe, whose borders seemed permanently frozen by the Cold War, had added an extra Germany and the ex-British micro-colonies of Cyprus and Malta. In South America, Colombia was expelled and then let back in, and Venezuela, always the continent's most backward football nation, finally joined. The other ninety or so new members came from three regions: Africa, Asia and the Caribbean. This in turn was the result of a deluge of state formation that followed the almost total dismantling of every remaining European empire but for the Portuguese, whose final ignominious collapse came in 1975.

The process began in Asia. The British departed the Indian subcontinent in 1947 and after partition the three new states – India, Sri Lanka and Pakistan – became members of FIFA. Over the next decade the British steadily abandoned everywhere east of Suez: Burma, Malaysia and Singapore signed up. Once the Dutch were driven from Indonesia in 1949 the new government applied to and joined FIFA. The division of the Korean peninsula yielded two new members while the ongoing wars of Indo-China generated new states and FIFA members (Laos, Cambodia and two Vietnams) while simultaneously making organized football impossible. European imperial power, more tenuous in Western Asia, crumbled quicker than in the east. Iran had joined FIFA in 1945, Afghanistan in 1948 and Iraq in 1950. In the Gulf the antipathy of the clerical and political elites towards football saw a more substantial gap between independence and FIFA membership than in other regions. Even so, Saudi Arabia had joined by 1959, Kuwait followed in 1962, Bahrain in 1966. The micro-fiefdoms of Qatar, UAE and Oman joined in the 1970s. The process of decolonization was slower to start and quicker to conclude in Africa. Before 1955 only Ethiopia, Egypt, South Africa and Sudan were independent nation-states with national football associations. Beginning with Ghana in 1958 and Morocco in 1960 and finishing with Malawi in 1967, thirty-one African states joined FIFA in a decade. The desperately slow and painful process of economic and social development in Central America saw Nicaragua and Honduras, over a hundred years after independence, join FIFA in 1950 and 1951 respectively; though the weight of America's economic and cultural presence and the popularity of baseball are partially responsible for their lateness. By contrast decolonization and independence in the Caribbean islands was always accompanied by accession to the world of football nations. From just two FIFA members in 1958 – Cuba and Haiti – the Caribbean added another seven: Puerto Rico, Jamaica, Trinidad, the Bahamas, Barbados, Guyana and Antigua. Even in the distant oceanic island chains of the Pacific football and nationalism stirred, Papua New Guinea and Fiji joining FIFA in 1963.

Yet despite this remarkable global expansion FIFA remained what it had always been: a minuscule, cash-strapped, understaffed micro-bureaucracy, institutionally dominated by Europeans, consistently challenged by South Americans. During the post-war presidencies of Jules Rimet (who retired in 1954) and Arthur Drewry (1955–61), the organization did little more than process the paperwork of accession and re-establish the World Cup as a functioning competition. FIFA's fastest growth occurred under the subsequent presidency of Sir Stanley Rous. We have already encountered Rous in his guise as the secretary to the FA, a post he held from the mid-1930s until his election as FIFA President in 1961. Born into a middle-class English home at the close of the nineteenth century, Rous was a grocer's son from Suffolk, a grammar-school boy, Oxbridge candidate and a feverishly enthusiastic, if not enormously gifted, amateur goalkeeper. After imperial military service in Africa during the First World War he trained as a teacher and found his true vocations as an educator and arbiter: the first as a schoolmaster at Watford Grammar School, the second as the leading referee of the era, taking charge of thirty-six international games and the 1934 FA Cup Final. Dedicated to the technical refinement and improvement of the game, Rous introduced the diagonal system of refereeing that became the global standard. He was the architect of the re-editing of the laws of the game; published in 1938, they remain substantially unaltered in content or prose style. He would later champion the introduction of red and yellow cards, first used at the 1968 Olympic football tournament.

In hindsight, as FIFA President Rous was an anachronism in his own lifetime, exemplified by his unflagging commitment to the notion of public service, his enduring affection for Olympian amateurism, his antipathy to both the commercialism and politicization of football and his missionary zeal for spreading football that replicated the racial prejudices of his clerical counterparts. But as secretary to the FA, in contrast to the insular conservatism of his curmudgeonly predecessor Sir Fredrick Wall, he was the leading force of bureaucratic modernity, technical innovation and cosmopolitan openness. In insisting on such simple developments as regular and standardized teaching for coaches, players and referees he was twenty years in advance of the rest of the country. Through Britain's isolation from FIFA in the 1930s, Rous remained on friendly terms and in regular contact with European football. During the Second World War he began to pave the way for the Home Countries' return to FIFA by casting British football as a powerful instrument for maintaining British influence and spreading British values to a world from which the country was about to conduct a vast imperial retreat. He was, in his own way, sophisticated, connected and astute.

When Rous took office as FIFA President in 1961 he was already sixty-five. Securely ensconced as a member of the British establishment for over a decade, the world that had formed him was in the process of disintegrating. In Britain the social transformations of the 1960s, which in time would yield widespread disorder and rock-bottom football attendances, caught his successors at the FA by surprise. Rous escaped that fate only to be caught out by the post-colonial politics of world football – an arena in which he was particularly unlikely to prosper. Unpaid but unwavering, Rous pursued a modest policy agenda of technocratic modernization on a shoestring budget with a skeleton staff. The increasingly politicized and vicious fighting over hosting rights for the World Cup, exemplified for Rous by the spat between Mexico and Argentina over the 1970 tournament, was countered by introducing what he called 'the long look ahead': World Cups were to be allotted many years in advance, technical specification for tournaments becoming more demanding, precise and media-orientated. Rous's zeal was primarily directed to a programme of training for referees and coaches, under which Europeans would tutor what he patronizingly referred to as 'younger associations'. However, there was no move of any kind significantly to improve FIFA's income, or take commercial control of the World Cup itself, despite the massively growing television audience for the tournament.

South Africa was the key issue on which Rous's presidency turned and over which the new faultlines in international football politics were first drawn. In 1948 the National Party government of D. F. Malan began the process of imposing apartheid on South Africa, and sport was ruthlessly segregated according to official racial categories.[3] As early as 1957, when the first African Cup of Nations was played, the rest of the continent had made it clear that racial discrimination in football was not permissible. South Africa was excluded from the tournament and then from CAF. Its membership of FIFA, subsequently under constant attack, was suspended in 1961 pending an investigation into the representativeness of the official white governing body, the Football Association of South Africa (FASA). Rous and Jim Maguire (president of the US Soccer Federation) visited the country in 1963 and produced a report of breathtaking complacency. Rous argued that only FASA could represent South Africa on FIFA.

The members of the dissident federations whom we interviewed would, in our opinion, be quite unsuitable to represent Association Football in South Africa. Their attitude was one of destruction and not construction in any way. We found that they desired to hinder and act contrary to government policy.[4]

Beneath a veneer of apolitical universalism lurked an unreflective racism so deep that collaboration with apartheid was deemed a firmer moral and practical basis for the development of football than resistance to it.

African discontent was further fuelled by the continent's pathetic representation at the World Cup. For the 1966 tournament, Africa's leading team was offered the chance of a play-off with the Asian champions for a single berth at the World Cup. Led by Nkrumah's Ghana, Africa boycotted the qualifications and the tournament. In 1968 Rous attended the CAF conference held in Addis Ababa on the eve of the African Cup of Nations. The CAF delegates had received an open letter from the South African Non-Racial Olympic Committee (SANROC) imploring them to work for the expulsion of South Africa from FIFA and the implementation of a ban on global sporting contacts – matters that the delegates were keen to discuss. Rous responded with a mix of excruciating self-importance and moral complacency.

I have noted that you have attached undue importance to the SANROC. In fact you should take no notice of their letter . . . I know these people. I have been in South Africa to meet them . . . In fact this group in more interested in communist politics than in football.[5]

Central America was treated to a similar ticking-off when Rous spoke at CONCACAF's conference in the early 1970s, expressing his concern at the manifest and multiple forms of malpractice and maladministration in the region: corruption, bribery, low refereeing standards and poor crowd control. All of these accusations were true, but his speech made no difference and fewer allies. Rous's weakened political position was exposed in 1973 when he attempted to arrange a postal ballot of FIFA members in support of a South African government initiative to stage an ersatz multiracial sports festival. Protests rained down on FIFA from the entire Soviet bloc and most of the developing world. This coalition of angry incomprehension was reassembled when Rous insisted that the Soviet Union play their World Cup play-off against Chile in the Estadio Nacional – then in use as a concentration camp and torture chamber by the new military dictatorship of General Pinochet.[6] (The Soviets forfeited the match and their place in the finals in West Germany.)

However, for discontent with Rous's presidency to crystallize into a real opposition there needed to be an alternative to him. The alternative was João Havelange. Born in Brazil to middle-class Belgian immigrants, Havelange played junior football for the team of the Rio elite – Fluminense – before concentrating his energy on swimming. He represented Brazil at the 1936 Olympics and then again in 1952, but this time as a member of the water polo team. While an accomplished sportsman, Havelange's real strength was as a networker, weaving together a tapestry of sporting, banking, political and industrial contacts which allowed him, as part of a small group, to launch Viação Cometa – Brazil's first major private bus company – a move perfectly timed to take advantage of the huge expansion of inter-city highways in the country. The company boomed and by the late 1960s Havelange had amassed an extraordinary portfolio of businesses, offices, sinecures and positions: chemicals and insurance companies were added to the bus business, he was put on the Brazilian Olympic Committee in 1955 and the IOC itself in 1963. But what transformed his prospects in the world of football was his election as president of the Brazilian football confederation (CBF) and his close involvement with the technical commission that supported the national team at the World Cup from 1958 to 1970 – three of which, of course, they won.[7]

Havelange's bid for the FIFA presidency arose from a mixture of vaulting ambition and the simmering discontent in Latin America over the conduct of world football – specifically its control by Europeans – which was entrenched by perceptions of systematic bias against Latin America at the 1966 World Cup and the vitriolic and increasingly violent encounters between European and South American clubs in the Intercontinental Cup.[8] Havelange appears to have committed to running for the presidency in 1971 when he publicly received the backing of the South American football associations. He then mobilized support in Central America and the non-Anglo Caribbean, spontaneously and fortuitously appearing at CONCACAF and national football-association congresses, reaping the support of a region still smarting from the dressing down delivered to them by the headmasterly Rous. Havelange was schooled in the political geography of Brazil's federal football structure, in which states of massively different sizes, populations and levels of development had equal numbers of votes. Thus electoral success was predicated on devising programmes that channelled resources to small needy states in exchange for votes. Applied globally, his strategic master stroke was to concentrate on Africa and Asia, where the majority of FIFA's post-colonial membership now lay.

Havelange began to campaign and to travel. In 1974 alone he visited eighty-six countries with an air ticket that weighed over a kilo.[9] As one close observer and participant in the football politics of the era, Patrick Nally, describes it:

There had never been an election campaign like it for a sports presidency ... Sir Stanley Rous hadn't travelled to all the countries throughout Asia and Africa and certainly not all the little islands. It was such a radical change to suddenly have this dynamic glamorous South American character, brimming with bonhomie, travelling the world with his wife, meeting people, pressing the flesh, bringing over the Brazilian team, travelling with the likes of Pelé.[10]

Havelange explicitly courted the African vote on the issue of apartheid, making it clear, everywhere from the Sheraton Hotel cocktail bar, Cairo, to Government House in Accra, that under his presidency South Africa would never enter FIFA. In Jean-Claude Ganga, the Congolese sports administrator and First Secretary of the ill-fated Supreme Council for African Sport, he had a henchman forged in the murky and manipulative politics of Zaire. By contrast, Sir Stanley's man in Africa, the secretary of the Nigerian FA Oroc Oyo, proved as politically naive and ineffective as his boss. Having promised the support of Nigeria and the rest of the African Commonwealth, Oyo was deposed by his own FA executive in the lead-up to the crucial vote and replaced by Havelange loyalists. But for switching their vote there was more than mere revenge on offer. Havelange proposed a series of key reforms, all of which would dispro-portionately benefit the developing world in general and Africa in par-ticular: an expansion of places at the World Cup to twenty-four with more places for Africa; the creation of a new under-20s World Cup which could be held in countries unable to make a realistic bid for a full World Cup; and the channelling of more funds south for technical support, training and stadium development. For good measure he was also proposing a new headquarters for FIFA, anticipating the organiza-tion's bureaucratic explosion and the need to present a new kind of face to the world, transforming itself from a sleepy sports federation into an international organization of rising cultural significance.

Presidential campaigns cost money and this one cost a lot of money. Havelange had arranged an international tournament in 1972 in Brazil – the Mini-Copa – which served as a sporting front for a gargantuan schmoozefest. The CBF and the government covered the cost of transport-ing and accommodating nineteen teams to the tune of $21 million, and key delegates from around the world were courted. Brazil's embassies often provided suitably imposing stops on Havelange's global tour.

The vote took place at FIFA's Frankfurt congress that preceded the World Cup in June 1974. There was, until the very final moments, an air of fatalism and complacency around the Rous campaign. Almost conceding the contest in a tactical retreat to the moral high ground, Rous's flimsy manifesto stated: 'I can offer no special inducements to obtain support . . . nor have I canvassed for votes except through this publication. I prefer the record to speak for itself.'[11] Unfortunately for Rous, that is precisely what his record on South Africa and other issues did. Yet faced with the obvious, he and his allies could not quite believe that their world could be turned upside down. Havelange's most public intervention at the congress was to raise and support the case for China's readmission to FIFA, a position that won wide support in the developing world. Havelange won by 68 votes to 52. Some years later, and still in a state of shock and denial, Rous recalled the surface tremors but could not fathom the tectonic shifts in global culture and politics that underlay his comprehensive defeat. 'Yes, I think an Indian spoke against and I was surprised at that. People like Indonesia voted against me but I don't think they ... their officers have changed so much in these countries, you know. There were quite a few then who didn't really know me and they were persuaded to vote for Havelange.'[12] Rous departed with his dignity intact but privately he was shattered. The congress hurriedly made him Honorary President of FIFA, a post he accepted, but he refused a pension, on the grounds that the post had always been unpaid, and he also rejected the suggestion that the new World Cup trophy be named after him: an impermissible act of egotism, he thought, for a public servant.

The subterranean geographical shifts in power that paved the way for Havelange's election were made explicit at the first FIFA executive committee he chaired. The meeting was held in Dakar, Senegal, the first to be held in Africa. It was, no doubt, a businesslike meeting, its conduct a signal for the style of governance that the Brazilian would henceforth deploy. Guido Tognoni, a member of the FIFA executive, described Havelange as: 'A master of managing meetings. He was also a master of giving people the feeling that they are important without actually giving power away. He was just a master of power.'[13] If that didn't work he could play hard ball too. When at the 1982 World Cup he realized that the 400 tickets for the Brazil–Russia game that had been allocated to him and his entire Brazilian network were located behind the goals rather than in the VIP stand, he personally paid a visit to the offices of Raimondo Saporta, the man in charge of all ticketing at the tournament and possessor of both a sizeable girth and a heart condition. When Saporta told him that there were no tickets left for the VIP section, Havelange is reported to have closed the windows, drawn the blinds, locked the door and spoken:

I can stay here for seventy-two hours without having a piss, a shit, food or sleep. You on the other hand might well die, because I am not going to let you leave until I have got my tickets in my hands.[14]

The President left with his tickets. After experiencing Havelange's mode of operation during the bidding competition for the 1986 World Cup, Henry Kissinger remarked, 'It makes me feel nostalgic for the Middle East.'[15] What he had perhaps forgotten was the slight he had inflicted on the Brazilian's dignity when Havelange's own party was removed from a VIP box at the 1974 World Cup finals to make way for Kissinger and almost forty security guards. Havelange's capacity to remember names, dates, faces and places, as well as hurts and favours, was as legendary as his capacity to edit the past selectively and fall prey to temporary amnesia, particularly when it came to financial matters.

By contrast Helmut Käser, the German FIFA general secretary he inherited from Rous, was unrelentingly actuarial in his monitoring of FIFA's money. Although the two men disagreed on a whole variety of matters, it was on this issue that they most repeatedly clashed. In a marked shift from the austerity of the Rous regime, Havelange celebrated FIFA's seventy-fifth anniversary at a banquet in Zürich in 1979 – each of the 100 guests was given a Longines Swiss watch. The bill for over 100,000 Swiss francs dropped on to Käser's desk. Many more such bills followed. But this was relatively small change; it was said that he had instructed the main insurers of the 1982 World Cup to place a significant chunk of business with his Brazilian company Atlantica Boavista. Käser may have known where all the bodies lay, but apparently he didn't have the stomach for the fight. With a mixture of malicious wit, bureaucratic evasion and institutional humiliation, Havelange made Käser's position intolerable and the offer of a very generous pension was one he couldn't refuse. Käser left in 1981 to be replaced by Sepp Blatter, a Swiss lawyer who had worked for Longines and who had been groomed for the post after a stint at Adidas and in FIFA's technical department.

Havelange had initially planned to continue his presidency of the Brazilian football confederation, but was forced to trade it for a much-needed amnesty. Just as Havelange was departing for Zürich, it was becoming apparent to key members of the Brazilian Junta that he was leaving a gigantic hole in the budget of the CBF. The Treasury investigation into the organization revealed that over $6 million had completely disappeared since 1958. While some, like Admiral Adalberto Nunes, wanted to put him on trial, the embarrassing international ramifications of pursuing the case made Havelange unassailable if unemployable. The following year the government closed the case by offering technical support to the CBF which amounted to taking $5 million from Brazil's social-assistance fund and putting it into the organization's bank account.

The decisive moment in Havelange's reign came at the first dinner he attended as president of FIFA. Amongst the guests was Horst Dassler, the son of Adi Dassler, founder of the sports goods conglomerate Adidas, and then chief executive of Adidas France. Dassler had encountered Havelange before, attempting to persuade the Brazilian to sign up the entirety of Brazilian national sport to Adidas sponsorship and sports goods. The deal was never done and Dassler was one of Rous's supporters in 1974. Havelange was, no doubt, impressed by the swiftness and directness of Dassler's turnaround. By the end of the evening he had asked Havelange to dinner and the invitation was accepted. Havelange and Dassler were joined by the third member of their troika, Patrick Nally, who had cut his teeth in the world of sports marketing and sports sponsorship in Britain in the 1960s and had begun to amass a global client base of potential corporate sponsors.

The participants' own accounts of the dinner and subsequent conversations are, on many points of detail, at odds with each other, but the core concern of the discussion was clear. How could they catalyse the intersection of the World Cup, the growing global television market and corporate sponsorship to generate a vast revenue stream for all of them? The answer that they came up with and the model of global sporting commercialization that evolved from it over the next decade has provided the template for every major exercise in global sports sponsorship. It had four components. First, only the very largest multinational companies, whose advertising budgets could bear the load and whose global reach matched the TV audience on offer, should be approached as sponsors. Second, sponsorship and advertising would be segmented by product type: there could be only one soft drink, one brand of beer, one micro-electronics firm or one financial services company that could be the official World Cup product or supplier. The exchange developed from merely providing cash in return for advertising hoardings, to the direct provision of services to the tournament in return for around one-third of the tournament tickets at the greatest global corporate-hospitality bonanza ever. Third, FIFA would have total control over all forms of TV rights, advertising, stadium space, etc. Any and all existing deals in a host country would have to go. Fourth, FIFA itself would not handle the details of the sponsorship or TV deals. Marketing and TV rights would be handed over for a guaranteed sum of money to an intermediary who would sell them on. Initially this meant Dassler and Nally, and later Dassler's specially created sports-marketing company ISL, which held the rights until its ignominious bankruptcy in 2001.

In late 1974 Havelange arrived in a private jet at Atlanta international airport. He had recently made a pitch in New York to Warner Brothers – owners of PepsiCo – who had said they would think about it. One suspects they are still thinking rather ruefully about it. Havelange was driven to a meeting with Al Killane, the president of the Coca-Cola Corporation. Nally had not only set up the meeting but done the vast majority of the political groundwork at the company, who after a very stormy board meeting decided to align their precious global brand with football. The final deal was done in London in 1975 and the money began to flow. Quite how much money is almost impossible to determine. Havelange himself claims not to be able to put a figure on it. FIFA's own accounts are impenetrable in this area. Commercial secrecy clauses in sponsorship contracts forbid companies from revealing any real details of the deals. Tracking the flow of money has been made all the more complex by the way in which much of it flowed first to Dassler and then to FIFA, or direct from Coca-Cola to the new facilities and tournaments in the developing world. This system of financing allowed Havelange to deliver on some of his manifesto. Or rather, Dassler delivered, for he and Adidas were central in devising and implementing the new wave of technical assistance to football's developing world. Dassler was also the chief orchestrator of the World Youth Cup, first held in Tunisia in 1977 and then on a biennial basis; the next three tournaments were in Japan, Australia and Mexico. The returns to the company in terms of contacts, deals, sponsorship and ultimately sales and profits were considerable.

However, the key issue was the World Cup. Argentina '78 was not Havelange's show, it was the Junta's. Not that FIFA had any intention of taking the hosts on. Indeed, on the eve of the tournament the organization pointedly refused to accept a copy of an Amnesty International report on human-rights abuses in Argentina; nor did they show any inclination to investigate any of the murkier aspects of the tournament itself.[16] But Spain '82 was Havelange's show. He now needed to deliver on his campaign promises and expand the World Cup from sixteen to twenty-four teams, and that was going to be expensive. He curtly informed Dassler and Nally that FIFA and the Spanish would require significantly more money than they had ever considered raising before. Dassler and Nally went to work. Dassler took control of all marketing rights for the tournament and was able to sell on the North American TV rights as well. Nally found the sponsors, lots of them, with deep enough pockets for over 42 million Swiss francs to make their way to Zürich. Two minor side deals which exemplified the political cunning and commercial toughness of the new global football imperium wrapped things up. Spanish cooperation was assured when Havelange agreed to use his considerable influence in Latin America, Africa and Asia to mobilize support for Juan Antonio Samaranch, Spain's candidate for the presidency of the IOC; a post he duly won. And Coca-Cola's interests were looked after too. When it became clear that Real Madrid had signed what appeared a cast-iron contract that plastered its Estadio Santiago Bernabéu with Pepsi, every last hoarding was removed.

Spain '82 was also notable for the arrival of the FIFA gravy train. According to David Yallop, 'The personal amount of expenses Havelange was being paid exceeded $1 million a year . . . The bill for bringing FIFA officials to Spain . . . was over $3 million more than it cost to transport and accommodate the twenty-four teams.'[17] This kind of largesse was sustained by the ever-increasing television audience and thus evermore-expensive sponsorship packages sold by ISL for the 1986 and 1990 World Cups. Mexico '86 attracted a total global audience over the tournament in excess of 10 billion. Italia '90 more than doubled this and on that basis ISL signed up nine top-tier sponsors – including three Japanese multinationals, four American and two European – for over 100 million Swiss francs and an additional seven Italian official suppliers (including Fiat, Olivetti and Alitalia); not to mention the official-product status which was flogged to, among others, Barilla pasta and Sagit ice-cream.

Havelange ensured that South Africa was expelled and China was levered back into the organization while Taiwan was sidelined. Persistent problems with Israel's place in the Asian Football Confederation were

temporarily solved by relocating them in Oceania for World Cup qualifying purposes. FIFA's membership continued to rise, now easily
exceeding the UN's membership, as the organization mopped up the
new states emerging from the now defunct Portuguese Empire. In keeping with Havelange's political fondness for small associations (whose
votes were equal in power to those of the largest nations, but whose
poverty made them much more coaxable), FIFA added the micro-states
and Lilliputian islands of the world. Between 1976 and 1990 FIFA
accepted the membership of Grenada, Belize, St Lucia and St Vincent
from the Caribbean; San Marino and the Faeroe Islands in Europe; the
Solomon Islands, Vanuatu, Samoa and Tahiti in the Pacific; and just for
good measure Macao, Rwanda, Oman, the Seychelles and the Maldives.

An empire of such global proportions required a new capital and
Havelange supplied it when he replaced the sleepy Swiss villa-office of
the Rous era with the gleaming, angular white concrete and glass of the
new FIFA house, which now held over a hundred full-time staff. The
emperor himself was acquiring a new level of significance and power
too. In the fearsome battle between the Swiss and the French for the
rights to host the 1998 World Cup the Swiss football federation nomi-
nated Havelange for the Nobel Peace Prize. The standing ovation which
followed the announcement would have shamed Khrushchev.

From what was such power born? Within FIFA itself, Havelange's
power was created and sustained by mobilizing the football elites of the
global peripheries. In the wider world, that power was multiplied a
thousand times by the global explosion of access to television. In the
early 1970s there were barely a million TV sets in Africa. By 1990 that
figure had multiplied twenty-times over. In Asia the number of televisions increased tenfold over the same period and fourfold in Latin
America. In 1954, when the World Cup was first televised, there were
fewer than 50 million TV sets in the whole world; the vast majority of
those were in North America, but they were not tuned to football. By
1990 there were almost a billion all over the world and they were tuned
in.[18] Every four years, in early July, television provided the conduit for
the single greatest simultaneous human collective experience: the World

Cup Final. Even global eclipses must travel slowly across the earth's surface. Television transmission was effectively instantaneous.

Now expanded to twenty-four and later thirty-two teams, the World Cup began to provide exposure for peripheral football nations that amounted to the greatest single instance of global recognition that many of them would achieve. We have already touched on the potency of World Cup performance in the politics of Africa, but the tournaments since 1970 have also offered berths for the first time to Honduras, El Salvador and Costa Rica in Central America and to Haiti, Jamaica and Trinidad and Tobago in the Caribbean. In Western Asia, Israel, Iran, Iraq and three Gulf States (Saudi Arabia, Kuwait and UAE) have been to the World Cup. In East Asia, South Korea, Japan and China have participated. However, there are limits to the parallel geographies of global economic dependency and footballing prowess. Two regions, which on any conventional account of wealth and power are at the centre of the world, were, in football terms, at best newly industrializing states, at worst virtually off the map: North America, and the USA in particular; and Oceania, especially Australia. Similarly the demographic weight and advanced urbanization of Asia – over six times the size of Africa – did not translate into stronger footballing cultures.

Since the demise of the professional American Soccer League (ASL) in the 1930s, football in the United States had been confined primarily to ethnically aligned football clubs, playing in small local leagues, under the excruciatingly conservative and amateurish aegis of the United States Soccer Federation (USSF). The national team's remarkable win over England at the 1950 World Cup in Brazil barely registered at home; had it done so, the Haitian roots of the goalscorer, Joe Gaetjens, would have merely reconfirmed the profoundly alien and unassimilated quality of the game to Anglo-America. However, by the early 1960s there was, among a coterie of significant investors and existing mainstream sports-franchise holders (like Lamar Hunt, Jack Kent Cooke and Judge Roy Hofheinz), the growing notion that professional football could be made popular and profitable. In the late 1950s and early 1960s American elite sport had experienced a period of major expansion. The baby-boomer generation, flush with phenomenal prosperity, rising disposable incomes, increasing leisure time and big televisions, was soaking up more sport and more adverts than ever before. American football fully commercialized itself, establishing the Superbowl as the premier television event of the American sporting calendar. Baseball, already fully professional for nearly a century, underwent a further round of expansion. Basketball, overwhelmingly a college and local sport until the late 1950s, began its vertiginous ascent in wealth and status as the newly created NBA. In such a rapidly growing marketplace a space for football appeared to be emerging, a conjecture seemingly confirmed when ABC televised the 1966 World Cup Final from England and the viewing figures and subsequent buzz were, by historical standards, remarkable.[19]

History repeats itself the first time as tragedy, the second as farce. The demise of professional football in the US in the 1930s had been as much a consequence of internal bureaucratic infighting and excessive competition between organizations as it was a problem with the tastes of the US public.[20] Precisely the same mistake was made in 1967 when two new professional leagues were launched in direct economic and legal opposition to each other. The National Professional Soccer League (NPSL) was faster off the mark and had secured a proper TV deal. But the NPSL was a rogue league, unaffiliated to either FIFA or the USSF. The official league was the crudely monikered USA (United Soccer Association) which had no TV deal and was forced to import minor European and Latin American clubs wholesale in the off-season and implausibly rename them. Thus Shamrock Rovers became Boston Rovers, Cagliari the Chicago Mustangs and Stoke City were transmuted into the Cleveland Stokers. Cerro of Montevideo were upgraded to the New York Skyliners, and in the move from the rainy Black Country of the English west midlands to sunny California, Wolverhampton Wanderers turned into champions as the Los Angeles Wolves. The result was a complete disaster as attendances were small and TV viewing figures even worse. The NPSL was reliant on the limited talents of American players and a few freewheeling foreigners. The USA found it had, at best, teams' second-string squads playing in off-season low gears. Faced with economic meltdown, the two leagues agreed to fuse in 1968 and launched the North American Soccer League (NASL) as a seventeen-team nationwide competition. The late 1960s and early 1970s were a period of consolidation at best, mere survival at worst. What transformed the NASL, for a brief but scintillating moment, was the arrival of Pelé.

Until 1975 the New York Cosmos, like every other team in the NASL, were a ragbag of minor-league foreigners and home-grown players, playing a pretty basic game to minuscule audiences in dilapidated stadiums. Cosmos, despite being bankrolled by the enormously wealthy Warner Brothers, put on the show at the decrepit Downing Stadium on Long Island – geographically and culturally at the low-grade periphery of Metropolitan New York. Their games were only covered in the local press by junior reporters; often, it is said, as a punishment detail. Pelé's standing was considerably higher. His global fame was sufficiently large that even the overwhelmingly insular United States acknowledged his celebrity, and the football he had played on tour in the USA with Santos in the 1960s was remembered fondly. With Warner Brothers' money available, he was persuaded to come out of retirement and sign for the New York Cosmos on a three-year contract worth over $4 million. In an instant the club, and by association the league and the game itself, acquired a sprinkling of stardust and celebrity it had never had before. Where once the club had been reduced to handing out Burger King vouchers in an attempt to half-fill their games, on Pelé's debut they were forced to lock the doors; 25,000 made it inside and over 50,000 were left outside.

Over the next five years the New York Cosmos were the glamour team of the NASL. After Pelé came players who, although also at the end of their careers, were of an unimpeachable calibre, like Carlos Alberto, Franz Beckenbauer, Giorgio Chinaglia and Johan Neeskens. Other franchises followed suit and signed among others George Best, Johan Cruyff, Gerd Müller, Eusébio and Gordon Banks. The Cosmos became so popular at home that in 1977 they moved to the Giants stadium in New Jersey. In that year's play-offs they won a fabulously attacking 8–3 victory over Fort Lauderdale and recorded the biggest crowd hitherto for a football match in the USA, over 77,000. Cosmos went on to win the title and did so again in three of the next five seasons. The high cultural status of football and football players in New York, in the dying days of the 1970s, can be registered by their regular presence at the most exclusive node of the Manhattan social circuit – Studio 54. Located on West 54th Street, Studio 54 was a self-conscious haven of debauchery and decadence. As New York City plunged into seemingly unending bankruptcy and financial crisis and the country as a whole recoiled from the poison and failures of Vietnam and Watergate, Studio

54 partied like there was no past and no tomorrow, serving up disco, sexual deviancy and experimentation, cocaine and fame. Henry Kissinger, Mick Jagger and Elton John were as likely to be mixing it with the Cosmos here as they were at the games they regularly attended. In this context, football's otherness was a source of exotic attraction rather than a threatening alien. However, what worked in New York, the most open and cosmopolitan of American cities, did not necessarily work on Main Street.

Pelé played his final game for the Cosmos in late 1977, in a friendly against Santos. He played one half for both sides on a day that poured with rain. With characteristic melodrama the Brazilian press reported that 'even the sky cried', and so did the banks. Although the quality of football in the league had clearly risen with the arrival of Pelé and his cohort, the economics of the league remained out of kilter. Warner Brothers never made a cent on their Cosmos investment though the kudos it brought was immense. Other franchise holders, paying ever bigger salaries for squads that could not fill their stadiums, started piling up the red ink. Worse, for the medium-term prospects of football, few if any home-grown stars emerged and the national team's presence in global football became if anything more invisible. By the early 1980s ABC could no longer tolerate the poor ratings data and pulled the TV plug. When it became clear that Mexico not the USA would get the 1986 World Cup finals, Warner Brothers did the same. Half the league's franchises declared they were bankrupt in 1981 and 1982. By 1984 only five were left to contest the final NASL season. By the spring of 1985 New York Cosmos were reduced to playing ad hoc friendlies and exhibitions.

The failure of professional football in North America had knock-on consequences for the rest of the region, which Mexico aside consisted of the impoverished states of Central America and the Caribbean islands. In international footballing terms, the United States was as peripheral as these countries were in the wider global economy. The Mexicans, in a rare reversal of geographical priorities, consistently looked south for football contacts and ideas, leaving the region and its clumsily named confederation CONCACAF the weakest in global football, but for Oceania. Even had American football been a stronger influence in the region it would still have been dwarfed by the strength of cricket in the English-speaking Caribbean and baseball across the region. In Cuba,

Guatemala, Honduras, Panama and Nicaragua baseball was by some way the most popular sport and ran football close in Costa Rica and El Salvador. In the 1980s and 1990s the phenomenal success of the NBA and the increasing presence of Central American and Caribbean migrant communities in the USA saw basketball become immensely popular in the *barrios* and downtowns of their homelands.

If baseball preceded and excluded football on the isthmus, cricket had the same role in the English Caribbean. In the late nineteenth century, in Jamaica, Trinidad and Tobago, Barbados and the Antilles, the British colonial elite, as well as selected English creoles, had first formed exclusive cricket clubs.[21] Although the game remained stratified by race and class, enough social space existed for teams of mixed ethnicity to play for the West Indies in international contests and for the leading black players of the era to make a small living in the professional leagues in England. Played with fierce dedication in the streets and wastelands of Kingston and Port of Spain, cricket had as much claim on popular as elite affections, and offered the same tiny channel of social advancement to the black and Indian populations of Britain's colonies that baseball or football did elsewhere. Consequently, football was, until the 1980s and even later, an overwhelmingly amateur, at best semi-professional game. Jamaica and Trinidad's remarkable achievements in qualifying for World Cup finals in 1998 and 2006 respectively were not primarily a consequence of the strength of their domestic football. Rather, both squads were staffed by children of the Caribbean diasporas, many of them born in Britain and playing in the lower leagues of English professional football, but taking Caribbean football citizenship. Across the whole of CONCACAF regional competitions between clubs and national teams were of low status, irregularly played, poorly attended and often ignored altogether by the Mexicans. This was a weakness which was reflected in the region's poor performance on the global stage. Of the six nations from the region (Mexico and the US aside) to attend World Cup finals between 1970 and the present, only Costa Rica have made the second round of the competition, and Jamaica's win against Japan in France '98 is the sole other victory.

That said, playing at the World Cup has proved as powerful a lubricant of nationalist politics and as attractive to the local oligarchs and dictators as it has been in the rest of the world. Haiti's remarkable progress to the 1974 World Cup finals was bankrolled by the island's maniacal President, Jean Claude Duvalier. When qualification was secured, as one of the team put it, 'Well, the country was upside down. It was crazy.'[22] The squad then made the mistake of demanding a $5,000 bonus and were rewarded with death threats from the presidential palace. Haiti's opening game of the tournament was against Italy and with considerable aplomb, the Haitians held them 0–0 at half-time. In the second half they actually took the lead when Manno Sanon dribbled the ball around a flailing Dino Zoff. But the Italians clawed their way back into the game and won 3–1. Worse, one Haitian tested positive for drugs after the game. Back at the team's hotel fighting broke out among the squad and the Duvalierists who had accompanied them as junket-junkies and political minders. Demoralized and broken, Haiti were beaten by Argentina and Poland and went home.

El Salvador and Honduras, who have both attended the World Cup (El Salvador in 1970 and 1982; Honduras in 1982), also fought the now eponymous 'Soccer War' in 1969. For over thirty years the two states had been locked into a complex economic and environmental conflict along their border. El Salvador was the most densely populated country in the region and combined this with the most grotesquely unequal distribution of land in a grotesquely unequal part of the world. Consequently there were enormous numbers of landless and destitute Salvadorean peasants. Honduras was a much larger and less populated country and by 1969 around 300,000 Salvadoreans had crossed the border in search of land and work. The two countries met in the first of a three-match series that would decide who went to the 1970 World Cup. At the first game in Tegucigalpa in Honduras, the crowd and authorities made things uncomfortable for the Salvadoreans and their dispirited side lost 1–0. Before the return match in San Salvador:

It was the Honduran team that spent a sleepless night. The screaming crowd of fans broke all the windows in the hotel and threw rotten eggs, dead rats and stinking rags inside. The players were taken to the match in armoured cars . . . the mob lined the route holding up portraits of the national heroine Amelia Bolanios.

The army surrounded the ground. On the pitch stood a cordon of soldiers from a crack regiment of the Guardia Nacional with sub-machine guns. During the playing of the Honduran national anthem the crowd roared and whistled. Next, instead of the Honduran flag – which had been burnt before the eyes of the spectators, driving them mad with joy – the host ran a dirty, tattered dish rag up the flag pole.[23]

El Salvador won 3–0. Honduran fans were attacked on the street as were the country's consulates. In retaliation, attacks against Salvadoreans broke out in Honduras, leading to a massive exodus back across the border. In an atmosphere of press and political hysteria diplomatic relations were severed. Two weeks later, in mid-July, the real war began as El Salvador invaded Honduras. Six days later a ceasefire enforced by the Organization of American States came into effect. The decider was played in Mexico City and won by El Salvador who returned to the city for the finals the following year, and were comprehensively beaten in every game. Some 6,000 people were killed or injured during the conflict. The rickety economies and regimes of both countries were exposed.

IV

Oceania was the land that football forgot. Despite arriving in Australia and New Zealand in the nineteenth century, football remained a poor relation to cricket, rugby and Australian rules.[24] Until 1974 both nations had attempted to reach the World Cup through the Asian qualifying rounds and neither had succeeded. It was only with the establishment of the Oceanic Football Confederation (OFC) in 1966 which conjoined Australasia to the Pacific islands, like Papua New Guinea and Fiji, that a play-off spot for the World Cup was reserved for the region – duly won by Australia in 1974. New Zealand would repeat the trick in 1982. Intriguingly the All-Whites, as the national team was known, achieved this singular moment of global prominence at precisely the time that New Zealand rugby union was at its lowest ebb, embroiled in almost a decade of vicious and sometimes violent conflicts over the sporting ban on South Africa. While this arrangement gave the two anglophone nations of the region a reasonable crack at a play-off place it was ultimately counter-productive. With only the likes of the Solomon Islands and Tahiti to test themselves against, Australia in particular found itself a long way behind the South Americans and Asians that they were playing-off against for a place in the World Cup. In the early twenty-first century, in parallel with the shifting nature of Australia's foreign policy, economic linkages and its sense of political and geographical location, Australia campaigned successfully to join the Asian Football Confederation.

Australia's relative football backwardness was not derived from the geography of isolation alone. At home, in the post-war era, football remained a minority, amateur sport. It was a distant fourth or fifth in the nation's sporting affections behind Aussie rules, both rugby codes and cricket. It also remained, like everything else at the time in Australia, a British concern. The Victoria State League, perhaps the strongest in the country in 1948, boasted neighbourhood teams whose names evoked the old country: Brighton and Box Hill for the English; Moreland for the Scots; and for some an evocation of their suburban fantasy land, Sunshine United. Only Hakoah, the Jewish team in Melbourne, hinted at a more cosmopolitan demographic. This situation was transformed in less than a decade by a great wave of migration from Southern Europe, mixing political migrants, refugees and job seekers, that swept into the booming industrial suburbs and mining towns of the country. In total Australia received nearly 300,000 migrants from Italy, 150,000 each from Yugoslavia and Greece, as well as many other Eastern Europeans. Chain migration, mutual housing support networks and a preference for the major centres of employment saw them concentrated in specific urban neighbourhoods.

The reception of Southern and Eastern Europeans into Australian society was not a smooth one. Although welcomed by labour-short employers their lack of English and their perceptibly darker skins evoked tiresomely predictable patterns of racism, exclusion and discrimination. Unlike the earlier generations of Italians and Greeks that went to the United States, who assimilated in part by adopting baseball, this generation came to Australia with their sporting preference already formed – and that was for football. To many, Aussie Rules appeared ludicrous, while rugby and cricket were so obviously and self-consciously English games that they didn't even bother. Football was another matter, and by 1950 ethnic communities were creating their own social and football clubs. Australia's leading sports newspaper *The Sporting Globe* was worried.

The whole question of these New Australians being allowed to form national clubs should be the subject of special investigation and although one does not advocate a boycott of these recent arrivals from the playing fields it certainly would be much better if they were assimilated into the ranks of teams of mainly British stock and thus became better mixers instead of keeping to themselves and in some cases endeavouring to settle political differences on the football field.[25]

The conflict was intensified by an obvious contrast of playing styles and expectations. The Anglo-Australians were shaped by a wider sports culture in which high levels of on-field violence were tolerated; they played an exceptionally rough and physical version of the already characteristically muscular English game. The Europeans, by contrast, were schooled in an entirely different playing culture which was rather more cerebral. There was, among the first generation of footballers and their clubs, almost no assimilation at all, although no ethnic club systematically excluded outsiders. But then why would they have wanted to join Anglo-clubs anyway? The New Australians were proving themselves adept footballers. By the late 1950s the Victoria State League only retained Box Hill and Moreland from an earlier Anglo-era. Now, alongside them were: Polonia (Polish), Juventus (Italian), JUST (Serbian), Wilhelmina (Dutch), South Melbourne Hellas (Greek), Slavia (Czechs) and George Cross (Maltese). It was the same in New South Wales where the leading teams of the era included Prague, Budapest, Hakoah Eastern Suburbs, Polonia North, Side Sydney Croatia and Pan-Hellenic. Their possession of football in Australia was so comprehensive that the derogatory Anglo-slang for the game was *wogball*. This kind of playing prowess was not reflected in the administration and personnel of the Anglo-dominated Australian Football Association. By 1961 the division between Anglo-football and ethnic football, and between those who wanted to stay strictly amateur and strictly local and those who wanted to move towards a more semi-professional and national form of football, saw the formation of a breakaway Australian Soccer Federation which in time became the official football federation.[26]

White Australia's antipathy towards football was swirled into a minor moral panic by the expression of political differences on the football field and the sporadic violence that accompanied this, particularly when teams from the Serbian and Croatian communities were playing. A small number of Croats had migrated to Australia earlier in the century, but after the war they came in their tens of thousands. Croatia Adelaide was founded in 1952 and teams followed in Melbourne and Sydney. Their members and supporters tended to come from the most conservative and nationalistic elements of Croatian political culture, many fleeing the new communism of Tito's Yugoslavia, and they included in their ranks many supporters and officers of the brutal Ustashi regime that ruled Croatia as a puppet state of the Germans during the Second World War. While they remained a minority among Croatian Australians, the clubs were fiercely nationalist in their display of Croatian colours and insignia. Serbs also came to Australia, including within their ranks some Chetnik supporters – the royalist resistance groups who were allied with and then defeated by Tito's partisans. This community gravitated to teams like JUST and Yugal – though their Chetnik connections were sufficiently small that both retained friendly relations with the Yugoslav embassy in Australia and were treated to flights home by Yugoslav Airlines. The bitter conflicts between Serbs and Croats during the Second World War were certainly not left behind in Europe. In the early 1960s a game between Croatia Melbourne and Yugal descended into a full-scale riot, and in 1972, after a particularly nasty incident in the game between Croatia Melbourne and Hakoah, the Croatian team were expelled from the Victoria league and effectively dissolved, although they were back in it five years later.

Australian football provided an instrument of solidarity and partial integration into mainstream society for Southern Europeans in the 1960s and early 1970s. In turn their contribution was to raise the quality of organization and performance to the point where Australia finally qualified for the 1974 World Cup with a squad that included Anglo- and Slavic Australians. Australia's performance was predictably poor at the finals in Germany, failing to score a single goal, and though the excitement generated around the campaign was enough to convince the football federation that the time had come to create a national league, football remained a peripheral sport in Australia. Its failure to win over the mainstream was in part a failure of its initial policy of de-ethnicization. After the national league was launched in 1977, teams were meant to abandon their ethnic tags and act against overt displays of aggressive nationalism among their crowds. But the clubs were not prepared to take on their hardcore support and the authorities lacked the clout to enforce it. Indeed matters got worse in some ways. A newly created club like Canberra City, which was intended as a model of wholesome non-ethnic family entertainment, became a bitter redoubt of an explicitly Anglo-Australian identity.

Worse, as the temperature of ethnic politics in Yugoslavia heated up, the relations between Balkan teams deteriorated, and this state of affairs endured through the 1990s. The ethnic identities and solidarities that had revived and reinvigorated Australian football would also prove the limiting factor in the successful commercialization of the game.

Before 1970 only three teams from Asia had attended the World Cup finals. With half the world's population, Asia had claimed less than 3 per cent of the tournament's places. Even then the Dutch East Indies team that made it to the 1938 tournament were overwhelmingly Europeans. The South Korean and North Korean sides that played at the 1954 and 1966 World Cups respectively were the only truly indigenous Asian sides to appear. No Asian team qualified for the 1958, 1962 or 1974 World Cups. Japan's miraculous bronze medal at the 1968 Mexico City Olympics remained the continent's best performance in a global tournament until South Korea's semi-final place at the 2002 World Cup.[27] Although the Asian Football Confederation (AFC) was established as early as 1954, it was markedly less successful at creating and sustaining international tournaments than its African counterpart CAF. While the African Cup of Nations has long been an event of considerable political, cultural and sporting significance, the Asian championship languished in scale and status until the 1990s. Similarly, the African Champions League and Cup Winners' Cup, although often haphazard affairs, established themselves as prestigious competitions, while the Asian Champions Cup, six years in the organizing, was abandoned in 1971 after just four tournaments and was revived only in 1986.

Why should Asia exhibit such footballing backwardness? Perhaps the most obvious explanation is that for the entire twentieth century Asia was a continent of peasants, subsistence farming and vast rural hinterlands. Although it could boast of urban enclaves, industrial zones, port cities and majestic capitals, Asia was and remains an overwhelmingly agrarian set of societies. Football, if it is nothing else, is a game of the city. But then Africa was hardly short of peasants. Differences in the geography of the continents and perceptions of ethnicity provide part of the answer to their differential rates of development. While intracontinental transport in Africa has been underdeveloped at best, the continent is considerably more compact than Asia whose sheer scale from east to west, encompassing multitudinous time zones, made international competition of any kind prohibitively complex and expensive for even the very richest football associations and clubs. Moreover, from its very inception CAF acquired a practical and moral authority, albeit a fragile one, as a genuinely pan-African institution. Post-colonial Asia had no comparable rallying cry or notion of shared identity. The AFC, a micro-bureaucracy in Kuala Lumpur, had neither status, nor money, nor clout. Even if it had possessed them, Asia presented a peculiarly unfertile territory in which to nurture professional and international football. Three further contrasts with Africa suggest why.

First, Asia's encounter with European colonialism was profoundly different from Africa's. Although European power was often blunted, eluded or subverted in Africa, no African society was able effectively to resist the force of European arms. Africa paid for the military weakness of its states with a hundred years of servitude. Asia, by contrast, had generated imperial powers and state machines of sufficient resilience, agility and military strength that they could resist. China, although partitioned and corralled, was never fully subdued. Even though the Japanese were shaken from their developmental torpor and geographic isolation by the West, they were not conquered. Siam-Thailand remained independent and India, even under British rule, barely deviated from its own internal ruling beliefs and ideas. In this context, modern sports which appeared an inevitable fact of modern life and progress in Africa were still viewed by many Asian elites as dangerous and distasteful alien practices.

A second contrast with Africa concerns the presence of the Americans who, Liberia aside, played no part in the scramble for Africa, but who from the mid-nineteenth century onwards had a major stake and presence in East Asia combining missionaries, economic investors and occasionally – in Japan, China, the Philippines and Korea – the armed forces. As a consequence baseball was a significant competitor to football in these societies and the most popular sport for most of the twentieth century in all of them but China. The importance of cricket in South Asia is analogous in accounting for the limited development of football.[28]

A third difference concerns the continent's experience of warfare. In Africa war has been a major factor in inhibiting, even terminating, the development of football. The potential of nations like Ethiopia, Angola and Mozambique had been persistently undermined by incessant fighting. Asia has certainly been no stranger to war. But in Asia the key wars and processes of social change have been more tumultuous and all-encompassing, more destabilizing and intense than those in Africa; they have also tended to be inter-state cross-border wars rather than the civil conflicts and wars of secession that have plagued Africa. The scale of death and destruction endured during the Second World War in Asia was obviously far greater than in Africa, but this cataclysm was then followed by: the partition of India, and three subsequent Indo-Pakistan wars; the struggle for Indonesian independence and the ensuing civil wars; the Korean War and the enduring military stand-off that followed; the Malay Insurgency; the long and complex wars in Indo-China; the Chinese civil war and revolution; the Russian invasion of Afghanistan and the Iran–Iraq War. These events dwarf the equivalent struggles and conflicts in Africa. The experience of China, in particular, exemplifies the devastating impact of social upheaval on organized sport in Asia as a whole.

On 1 October 1949 the creation of the People's Republic of China was declared and, as part of the celebrations, the Shengyan football club was invited to Beijing to play a demonstration game in front of senior politicians and Communist Party officials. Enthusiasm did not immediately translate into organization though, as China attempted to recover from almost four decades of continuous upheaval and warfare. In 1951 the first Chinese national football championship was held, although it was contested by just eight sides representing various industries and regions and an army team. Over the next few years the scale of the national football tournament expanded in line with the nation's first five-year plan, which centralized, bureaucratized and politicized the nation's economic and civic institutions, including football clubs attached to trade unions, power plants, navy garrisons and the railway industry. The doctrinaire Marxism of this model of football development was complemented by a close relationship with the football associations of Eastern Europe and communist Africa through the 1950s and early 1960s. Even after withdrawing from FIFA in 1959, in protest at Taiwan's continuing membership, the Chinese national team continued to play an enormous number of games with friendly regimes.

In 1958 Mao Zedong initiated the 'Great Leap Forward', in which he attempted, by force of rhetoric, charisma and coercion, to catalyse a decentralized rural-based industrial revolution. The results were chaotic and ultimately disastrous: agricultural production collapsed, famines were reported across the country and the fragile transport and sporting infrastructure that had been established collapsed. Mao was persuaded by the saner and more cautious elements in the Politburo to abandon this programme in the early 1960s and both the country's economic fortunes and its footballing organization began to recover. Then, once again, football, like every other form of organized leisure and sport, was cut dead by tumult.

In 1966 Mao, fearing his more conservative enemies within the party, initiated the Cultural Revolution; he actively encouraged a youth uprising that claimed to challenge the revolution itself from the Left. In the end it was little more than a grotesque personality cult of Mao, misguided by the vacuous epigrams of the Little Red Book. What began as a purge of the party spiralled out of control and into a self-perpetuating reign of terror and fear that spread to every type of institution in the country. China descended into chaos and virtual civil war for six years, and no competitive football was apparently played. If it was, there are no records. Sports institutions were colonized, broken up, taken over and closed down by the Red Guards. Leading administrators, coaches, players and athletes were condemned for their attachment to capitalist ideologies of competition and elitism, and publicly humiliated; many endured long periods of 're-education' in the rice-bowl gulag of the remote Chinese countryside. In 1972 Mao and the army finally brought a halt to the madness and the following year a national football competition was held for the first time since 1966. With Mao's death in 1976 the new leadership in China began to re-engage with the diplomatic and sporting world. Early discussions with FIFA saw China begin to play international football again. In 1974 the country joined the Asian Football Confederation and FIFA and in the following year foreign clubs began to tour, starting with Pelé's New York Cosmos and Ron Atkinson's West Bromwich Albion. In 1980 China re-entered formal international competitions, though its footballing prowess was pitiful. Mao's successor Deng Xiaoping had now set the country on a course of authoritarian, market-friendly industrialization. Both the economy and football, having lost thirty years to war and revolution, would not look back.

14

If This is Football, Let It Die: The European Crisis, 1974–1990

A slum game played in slum stadiums watched by slum people.

Sunday Times, 19 May 1985

I

European football reached its moral ground zero at the Heysel Stadium, Brussels on 29 May 1985. Thirty-nine people were killed and three hundred people injured, in a tragedy played out in front of a pan-European television audience of over 100 million. Everyone had been expecting the European Cup Final between Liverpool and Juventus, and at the insistence of UEFA and the Belgian authorities the game was duly played as the corpses were ferried to the city's morgues. Juventus won 1–0. *L'Équipe*, midwife of the European Cup, proclaimed its dismay at what its charge had become when it reported on the game the following day: 'If this is football, let it die.'[1]

Heysel was not the only European stadium to descend into a charnel house in the 1980s. The Bradford fire that preceded Heysel by just two weeks claimed fifty-six lives; the Hillsborough disaster of 1989 killed ninety-six. In the Soviet Union, although shamefully covered up and underplayed at the time, a crush on the icy steps of the Luzhniki Stadium in Moscow in 1982 saw over three hundred fatalities while a stampede at the indoor Soloniki Sports Palace, three years later, claimed over twenty victims. However, Bradford and Hillsborough were, in the end, English tragedies, the Luzhniki and Soloniki were Soviet tragedies, while Heysel was Europe's. Unlike the four other disasters, which were all explicable primarily in terms of decaying infrastructure and inadequate policing and crowd control, Heysel alone could count the irresponsible misbehaviour of supporters as one of its causes.

Heysel began with a scuffle.

It was the type of skirmish that you'd seen 100 times before, on grounds all round the country, over a fifteen-year period and you thought to yourself, 'Well, that's a skirmish and within a couple of minutes there'll be a police line there and they'll force both sets of fans back . . .' That didn't happen . . . there was no one taking control.[2]

The culpability of these Liverpool fans at Heysel is not in question, nor can their behaviour be viewed with anything other than disapproval. However, the genesis of their actions had a wider context and their actions could only have mutated into a grotesque killing field with the help of others' disastrous decisions and unforgivable neglect.

Heysel Stadium itself was little short of a disgrace. Its concrete terraces were cracked by grass; its rotten hulking crush barriers were more decorative than effective. The decision of UEFA and the Belgian authorities to allow the final to be played there was reprehensible. This was the least of the Belgians' mistakes, given that they appointed a police officer in charge that night who had no experience of football crowds let alone a European Cup final. Bereft of any serious operational strategy or system of stewarding, the police were so hapless that the key officers inside the stadium had no batteries in their walkie-talkies.

Ticketing and segregation arrangements were alarmingly lax. Although the majority of Liverpool and Juventus fans were to be located in separate areas of the ground, ticketing was sufficiently loose that a large number of Liverpool supporters gained access to a supposedly neutral area where they mixed with the predominantly middle-aged Juve fans who had bought their tickets on spec from the touts. The hard-core *ultras* were elsewhere. First-hand reports suggest that tickets for this section were used and reused by Liverpool fans, that many gained entrance with beer crates over the wall, and that policing at this end was alarmingly thin. The disaster itself happened remarkably quickly as a small group of Liverpool fans began to throw missiles and abuse into the neutral section, which was situated next to theirs; they then tore down the flimsy netting fence and conducted a series of drunken charges which in turn initiated a panic retreat among the Juve fans. A massive crush developed against a dilapidated free-standing wall at the end of the stand. It collapsed and in the crush thirty-nine people were killed.

The aftermath brought no dignity or grace. UEFA, the Belgian authorities and it seems the club managements decided to play the game.

The pitch was surrounded by a belated show of force from the police. Fights and scuffles continued to break out around the ground, while the players moved in a strange, lethargic torpor. The trophy was presented in the Juventus dressing room in a funereal wooden box. Inexplicably, the team did a lap of honour afterwards, justified by President Boniperti, who argued that 'we have earned this cup with the blood of our fans'.[3] Across Italy, in a collective act of disrespect and bad taste, Juve fans celebrated while the supporters of other teams sprayed '*Grazi* Liverpool' on the walls.

In the aftermath of Heysel, English clubs were banned from European competition for five years and Liverpool were banned indefinitely. Thus, in retrospect Heysel was a moment poised between two eras in European football. The high industrial football created in the 1950s and 1960s reached its terminal point in the late 1970s and early 1980s. A measure of its exhaustion was the decline in innovation, for after the development of Dutch total football in the early 1970s European football saw no significant tactical developments until Arrigo Sacchi's Milan sides of the late 1980s. Off the field, the increasing ungovernability of minority but visible fan cultures in Northern and Southern Europe – of which the Liverpool casuals and Juve *ultras* were emblematic – had brought the organizational capacity of the game and its commercial viability to breaking point. In the end, however, football was rescued from its predicament by the forces of the market and the application of an unalloyed commercialism that had been germinating through the 1980s. After Heysel, that whirlwind of technological, social and economic change would provide the instruments for the sanitization and selling of football. The slum game, shorn of its most belligerent and chaotic supporters, excluded by surveillance and cost, would be transmuted from social outcast to one of the central collective cultural experiences of the new millennium. What price football would subsequently pay with its soul was yet to be determined.

The ban on English clubs brought a decade of Northern European (predominantly English and German) dominance to an end. In the space created by their absence there was now room for others to prosper. The leading clubs in the Continent's smaller nations came to the fore. The mid-to-late 1980s saw European triumphs for Aberdeen and Mechelen (Cup Winners' Cup 1983 and 1988), IFK Göteborg (UEFA Cup 1982 and 1987), Porto and PSV Eindhoven (European Cups in 1987 and

1988). At an international level the Dutch finally won a major tournament – the European Championship in 1988. In Italy and France new footballing dynasties were created by the confluence of new money and new media in Bordeaux, Marseilles and Milan. Although after Heysel security and safety arrangements were hastily examined across the Continent, precious little change actually came about. Most European football associations, comforted by the thought that the problem was essentially one of English thuggery and Belgian incompetence, attended to neither their own hooligans nor their stadiums. The Italians, in particular, would reap the consequences of their myopia later. Eastern Europe, in the shape of Steaua Bucharest and Red Star Belgrade, had its final moment of sporting glory before the fall of the Berlin Wall swept its football cultures to the Continent's impoverished periphery.

In the dog days of the decade, football offered two denouements. In 1989 the Hillsborough disaster set the seal on English decline, marking the game's low point before its phoenix-like rebirth around the re-branded Premiership. Italia '90 condensed the new social forces remaking European football: saturation media coverage, high commercial stakes and the repackaged spectacular. It was perhaps the most gruelling, defensive and mean-minded tournament yet staged.

Championships won, wages paid, profits turned; there are many ways of calibrating the successes and strengths of a football culture. One measure stands above them all though: attendances. For without the crowd football is nothing. In its absence it is neither spectacle nor economically sustainable. Even in an era where the game is overwhelmingly mediated by television cameras and sustained by immense TV rights payments, a game behind closed doors remains a financial disaster and an eerie sterile simulacrum. The state of European football culture in the late 1970s and 1980s is sharply illuminated by this one measure.

In Northern Europe attendances fell, at some clubs precipitously. In just ten years attendances at all English professional league games collapsed from 25 million in 1975 to a post-war low of less than 17 million in 1986. In West Germany after peaking at 26 million in the late 1970s crowds shrank to just 18 million in 1990. Over the same period

Dutch annual league attendances virtually halved from 12 to just 7 million. In Sweden the drop was so sharp that by the late 1980s ice hockey was on the verge of becoming, in terms of attendance, affection and income, the national sport. The most vertiginous fall was reserved for the zone of greatest social turbulence. In the dying days of the USSR, the Soviet first division saw average crowds halve over the three years between 1987 and 1990. By contrast, attendances in Southern Europe from Portugal to Romania remained high or even increased. French crowds, which had reached rock bottom in 1968, soared. In Italy, where the large crowds of the 1960s and '70s had not dissipated, they were enlarged by the football fever that swept the country after their victory in the 1982 World Cup.

Whether they shrank or grew, they were not the same crowds that had flocked to European football in the 1950s and 1960s. Emerging on the far side of the Continent's generational ruptures and conflicts, young people, overwhelmingly young men, liberated by work, income and the decline of deference to age and status, began to gather separately from their elders on Europe's football terraces. In their intensity and isolation they began to define themselves in opposition both to other clubs' fans and their own club's traditional, passive supporters. The timing of the emergence of new fan cultures in Europe almost precisely parallels the timing of each nation's youth revolt. Britain was ten years ahead of the Continent and had acquired mobs and ends in the mid-1960s. Italy, France, West Germany and the Netherlands followed a decade later. In Spain the late survival and enduring legacy of Franco's regime froze the relaxation of social norms and discouraged the emergence of any form of public exhibitionism until the early 1980s. East Germany and the Soviet Union, where the old guard and the old culture stayed on so long that they expired in power, were the last to admit the gulf that had opened up between young and old, the powerful and the powerless; autonomous fan cultures, although germinating through the early 1980s, only finally exploded on the football scene in the dying days of both regimes. However, while all of the fan cultures emerged from the debris of national generational conflict and popular cultural revolutions, the particular form they took was not uniform. Three archetypes can be identified: the English gangs and firms; the Italian *ultras*; and the Scots and Danish carnival armies.

The correlation is not perfect, but broadly speaking those countries that saw a significant decline in attendances were also the countries where the most visible of the new fan cultures was a variant on the English hooligan gang. In a vicious cycle of decline, the rise of violence and disorder in football drove many supporters away from the grounds, creating more space for the entrenchment of the cultures of disorder and confrontation. A similar pattern could be found after the emergence of East and West German skinhead gangs, the Dutch *sides* and the Soviet *fanaty*: violence rose, attendances fell and then neo-Nazi and extreme right-wing nationalists began to recruit and organize amongst them. Fan cultures in Northern Europe were never homogenous, and the firms and gangs, even the massed ranks of English and Scottish casuals, were never more than a minority of football's audience. Partly in reaction to the firms, whose significance had been amplified many times over by the hysterical press, there emerged in England and Scotland two alternative fan cultures, both explicitly non-violent. The first, unique to Britain at the time, was primarily a literate response centred on an effervescent fanzine scene which acted as a voice for the pleasures, obsessions and interests of the then invisible phalanx of obsessive but reflective supporters. The second was the emergence in Scotland of a new form of support around the national team. The Tartan Army changed from being predominantly a teenage/casual affair to one dominated by older supporters whose presence transformed the Scots from an invading mob into a carnivalesque parade of alternative national identities; a similar fan culture would develop around the Danish, Dutch, Irish and Norwegian national teams in the 1980s.

In Southern Europe an entirely different form of fan culture took root – *ultra*. Where the gangs and firms of the North were minimally organized, largely concerned with conflict outside the stadium and high on the adrenalin of violence, bravado and confrontation, *ultras* in their original incarnation were highly organized, primarily concerned with support inside the stadium and high on the adrenalin of invented solidarities, formalized emotional melodrama and high-intensity visual display and pyrotechnics. Beginning in the early 1970s in Italy, the *ultra* style was taken up in Mediterranean France, Yugoslavia and Iberia. Swept by a wave of organized, committed and very visible fanatics, countries where the *ultra* model was adopted saw crowds swell. However, by the late 1980s the *ultra* movement had acquired a sinister momentum as the logics of clientalism, fanaticism, hedonism and hysteria combined to produce violent encounters and political extremism.

The invading armies of teenage skinhead gangs who largely dominated the chaotic ends of English football grounds in the mid-1970s were gradually brought under some kind of control by ever heavier levels of police surveillance and by rigid segregation. Over the next decade, those commited to the search for trouble sought to subvert these policing tactics. At some clubs a distinct caste of 'top boys' emerged whose authority over their peers was established by acts of violence and courage in the face of the enemy. These were the people who did not just push and shove, taunt and provoke. When it all went off, they were the people who were there, in the thick of it, able to cope, manage, respond and win. No account of football violence, particularly in England, can begin to comprehend this phenomenon unless it is accepted that for this small subculture, such exploits were not merely a source of kudos and authority but an intensely exciting, pleasurable experience.

When you've run a firm and your adrenalin's gone, know what I mean, and you, and you start. I mean, it's the best. I mean, sixty quid's worth up yer nose won't, like, top that. Truth, no it's the truth. I mean sod the coke and the smack, you know. Because the feeling, the feeling of doing something like that.[4]

Crews, firms and gangs developed around the country, including West Ham's Inter-City Firm, the Chelsea Headhunters, the Leeds Service Crew and other notorious mobs at Sheffield, Millwall, Newcastle and Arsenal. All of them abandoned overt displays of club colours or regalia on security and sartorial grounds. Fans with scarves were easy targets for both police and opposing firms, and although the skinhead aesthetic remained, there was also a turn to the more anonymous hard-mod looks of the 1960s. For similar reasons these groups avoided football specials and public transport, keeping one step ahead of the police's herding strategies. They presented an odd mix of the calculatedly rational and the psychotic as levels of violence and forms of weaponry began to escalate – peaking with Chelsea's use of Molotov cocktails at Brighton in 1983. From the late 1970s onwards, these groups established connections with political organizers in the far-right National Front and British National Party.

Although Liverpool fans had seen and caused their fair share of trouble in domestic football in the 1970s, the fans that travelled across Europe to see them in their European Cup campaigns were by and large peaceable. In preference to violence, the main thrill was shoplifting clothes, especially Continental menswear and exclusive sports gear. By the late 1970s the coolest clobber on the terraces was foreign anoraks, training tops, cycling gear and, above all, the right trainers. The subculture as a whole acquired a name – Casuals. Through the early 1980s, they made up the bulk of the young men looking for trouble at football.

If Celtic's carnivalesque celebrations in Lisbon in 1967 were the *Summer Holiday* of British football abroad, their successors took their cue from *The Italian Job*, the Michael Caine crime caper in which lovable, roguish British villains steal Chinese gold from under the noses of the Mafia and the Italian state against the backdrop of an Italy–England football match in Turin. Thus an act of armed robbery was fictionally transmuted into a victory for Britannia. The real European tour that saw these fantasies made flesh was inaugurated in Barcelona by those perennial innovators Glasgow Rangers. Having hosted the nation's first great football disaster and taken part in its first major football riot, Rangers now celebrated their first European victory in the 1972 Cup Winners' Cup by conducting the first full-scale British football riot abroad. The ferocity of the clash owed something to the collision of Rangers' Orangeism with the clerical conservatism of Franco's police. The following year, Britain's Conservative Prime Minister Edward Heath signed the treaty of accession and the country joined the European Economic Community. Europe had good reason to feel ambiguous about it. In 1974 Manchester United fans rioted in Ostend and Tottenham fans went on the rampage through the streets of Rotterdam before their UEFA Cup tie with Feyenoord, then rioted in the stadium itself. Leeds United fans fought in the streets of Paris following their defeat by Bayern München in the 1975 European Cup Final. The violence was of sufficient scale for the usually insipid UEFA to ban Leeds from European competition for four seasons. In 1977 Manchester United were expelled from the European Cup Winners' Cup after crowd disturbances in Saint-Étienne.

Trouble had, so far, been confined to club games. Now a second football front was opened as violence began to break out at England games abroad. In 1980 there were riots in Turin during England's

European Championship game against Belgium. The following year England fans caused £60,000 worth of damage in Basle after defeat by Switzerland in a World Cup qualifier and at the 1982 World Cup finals in Spain cheap beer and hot sun saw innumerable small-scale bar fights and drunken brawls. Luxembourg was treated to the usual rampage and riot routine in 1983, and Spurs fans returned to Rotterdam for a re-enactment of their previous performance. In 1984 a Tottenham supporter was shot dead in a Belgian grocery store during an act of collective robbery before the club's UEFA Cup Final against Anderlecht in Brussels.

American journalist Bill Buford attached himself to English fans abroad in the 1980s and in *Among the Thugs* wrote one of the most compelling accounts of the phenomenon. He grasped with particular accuracy the collective dynamics at work – simply put, the English fans abroad had established that if a very large number of people simultaneously break the law and act out of order, no one is likely to challenge them or stop them. Buford's account of the locust-like clearance of Italian groceries and the mob's extraordinary capacity to avoid all the normal security checks at an international airport to secure free flights home by lying under the seats of a charter plane are testament to the hysterical highs of collective disorder. He was also suitably amazed at the level of intentionally self-destructive drinking that accompanied this behaviour. Finally, he correctly identified the essential xenophobia of these crowds, a rabid insular nationalism that was just a few notches more extreme than the foreign policy of the most Europhobic government since the Second World War. Through the early 1980s in innumerable incidents in countless cities the conditions for disaster were there. Uncontrollable crowds, befuddled police forces, ancient and crumbling stadiums. The time for Heysel had almost arrived.

In the aftermath of Heysel one response was literary. Over the next two years a dozen football fanzines made their debut. Using the same low-tech technologies of the punk and new-wave music fanzines of the late 1970s, they were written by fans, photocopied, stapled and sold outside grounds. Most were club-based, like the pioneering *Terrace Talk* at York City, *The Pie* from Notts County and Bradford City's *City Gent*, and though uneven, they were often funny, sharp and pointed. Alongside these club magazines three fanzines covered football in general: London-based *When Saturday Comes, Off the Ball* from Birmingham and from Scotland, *The Absolute Game*. All three rapidly grew and by the early 1990s had gone on general distribution in the nation's newsagents, by which time they were carrying the listings and details for perhaps 250 smaller fanzines across the country.

While Latin America, Italy and Central Europe could boast a tradition of serious writing on football, it was the preserve of intellectuals, novelists and senior journalists; Britain was unique in global football in nurturing such a literate grassroots response to the ruling football order. The cultural ground had, in some senses, been prepared a decade earlier by the satirical football rag *Foul*, published between 1972 and 1976. Its editors and contributors were a floating mix of Oxbridge graduates, junior sports journalists and fanatics. In its samizdat look, its mixture of gossip, send-up, parody and pastiche of the football world, and its often biting satirical tone, it was akin to *Private Eye*, though the magazine was never sufficiently read by football insiders to establish the kudos that the *Eye* had earned. In fact the few members of the football establishment who did read it, loathed it, which proved *Foul* was on to something good. The magazine unleashed a torrent of articulate anger and fuming humour at the incompetence, selfishness, stupidity and duplicity of English football.

The crusade to strip the professional game of its public veneer of cliché, evasion and formula was helped by two path-finding books in the mid-seventies: *The Glory Game* by Hunter Davies and Eamon Dunphy's *Only a Game?: Diary of a Professional Footballer*. Davies's fly-on-the-wall season with Spurs was decried at the time for washing dirty linen in public, for its exposure of the real emotional and financial insecurities of the Spurs players and the lamentable amateurish organization of the club. In retrospect it appears a quietly intelligent anthropological study of the previously closed world of the professional football club. Dunphy's short diary of half a season at Millwall towards the end of his career is a masterpiece of staccato compression and brevity, its stark vernacular prose the perfect medium for his lacerating honesty about the mean, bitter micro-politics of squad life.

A decade later, the moment was right for a reprise for such indiscretion. The fanzines tapped into a segment of football supporters whose interests were not strictly parochial, who had hung around on the edges of the goal ends trying to keep out of the aggro and actually watch the game for the previous ten years, and were poorly served by the popular press in either their supine or hysterical mode. It was precisely this audience that were the prime movers in the establishment of independent supporters' associations and the umbrella group the Football Supporters' Association, which served as the voice of the grassroots in the torrid political debates over ID cards and reform in the late 1980s.

In a final coda to a decade of turbulent change, incidences of trouble declined after Heysel. The arrival of acid house, warehouse parties and ecstasy in the late Thatcherite summer of love saw the firms and the casuals mutate into baggy-trousered, loved-up fools – a crossover with the more pacific culture of dance music reinforced by New Order, masters of the thoughtful electronic chill-out, performing the official England song for Italia '90 with John Barnes. Only the police and the travelling England support seemed immune from the new drift of the times, as they would demonstrate at Hillsborough and Italia '90 respectively.

The extensive European tours conducted by English and Scottish fans in the 1970s and 1980s gave the whole of Europe the opportunity to examine closely their style and mode of operation. Most rejected it, but in France, Germany and the Netherlands it retained considerable appeal. In northern France, the kind of intense support and commentary pioneered at the Anfield Kop inspired a new generation of supporters in the industrial cities like Lille, Le Havre and Lens. In Paris, PSG's Boulogne Kop began when the club introduced a policy of cheap tickets for the young in 1979. The crew that began to gather at this end of the Parc de Princes quickly imbibed the punk scene in the early 1980s before dropping it in favour of the skinhead–hooligan nexus. Drawing on predominantly white, working-class youth from the declining *banlieus*, where France's incipient racial conflicts were brewing, the Boulogne Kop was the centre of racism and violence in French football. Kop skinheads were active members of Le Pen's Front National and organized attacks on visiting England fans in 1984. In West Germany a similar brew of urban youth, skinhead gangs and neo-Nazi agitators stalked the Bundesliga through the 1980s.

Dutch fans, who had more opportunity than most to examine the English at work, absorbed the lessons of particularly violent trips by Spurs and Manchester United to the Netherlands. In the late 1970s, *sides* – named after the section of the stadium they habitually occupied – were formed in emulation of the English; among the largest were

Den Haag's Midden-Noord, Ajax's F-Side, Feyenoord's Vak-S and FC Utrecht's Bunnikzijde. Reflecting their roots in older working-class gangs and biker cultures, they combined a love of heavy drinking, heavy metal and heavy weapons. Their gruesome armoury included knives, knuckledusters, bike chains, leather belts and screwdrivers. Fighting inside and outside the stadiums, among themselves and with the police, rose sharply through the 1980s and spilt over into the international arena.

In an interesting contrast to the British experience, the Dutch responded with something more than just segregation and repression, though they tried and failed with that too. Domestically, successive governments leavened the brute imposition of public order with an equal emphasis on issues of public safety and the first fan-oriented initiatives to come out of social-work departments. Internationally, beginning at the 1988 European Championship in Germany, the expected and much-touted hooligan element were completely swamped by the first major outing of the *oranje* supporters – up to 30,000 fans dressed in national colours.

English firms, Dutch *sides* and Scots casuals distinguished themselves from the mainstream by their use and acceptance of violence. Although Italian football would increasingly witness incidences of fighting, the dividing line between the new and old fan cultures was drawn along a line of emotional intensity. *Ultras*, a term borrowed from the vocabulary of political militancy and activism, came to define a fandom in which the highs and lows of a deliberately inflated solidarity and obsession with the club were the core of an entire lifestyle. The established official supporters' clubs were derided for their passivity.

The key reference groups for these fans were the many small political organizations that first sprang up among young workers and university students in the hot autumn of 1969. Occupying every niche of the confused ideological spectrum, Italy's schools and factories sprouted Spartacists, Maoists, Leninists, situationists and anarchists, collectives, co-ops, cells and splinters. Alongside the occasional strike and demonstration there was also the routine occupation of public spaces, parks, squares and street corners, where flags and banners announced their solidarity and the cadres could flaunt the new street style of the militant urban revolutionary. Shorn of nearly all of their political content, these independently established and self-organized groups provided the institutional template, sartorial codes and public postures of the new *ultra*, now busy colonizing the nation's *curva*, or football terraces. The look of the moment was 'green parkas, camouflage combat jackets bearing team badges, blue jeans and balaclava caps or neckerchief on the face, all of which made the *ultra* look like a metropolitan guerrillero'.[5] La Fossa dei Leoni was formed at AC Milan in 1968, but adapted the songs and sloganeering styles of the politicos. Red and Blue Commandos, Bologna's *ultras*, from the political heartland of Italian municipal communism, displayed clear left-wing leanings when first organized. Tupamaros Fedayan, the Sampdoria *ultras* founded in 1971, took their name but little else from the Uruguayan urban guerrilla movement.

Through the late 1970s and early 1980s the essential work of the *ultra* was to take control, practically and morally, of the *curvas*. Territory was marked out by early arrivals – up to three or four hours before a game began. Banners, flags and slogans were draped across the hoardings and fences. Once enough *ultras* had assembled, two or three *capocurva* would face the crowd rather than the pitch and with electric megaphones direct, lead and exhort the fans in the songs, chants and insults that had been broadly agreed among the leadership beforehand. To all of this they added visual *coreografia*. Vast banners and flags were unfurled across the entire *curva* as a prelude to games. In 1976 Lazio's *Irriducibili* set the standard by manufacturing a 56-metre-wide banner of an eagle.

The scale and complexity of these displays demanded both money and organization. Over the first decade of their existence the *ultras* evolved an informal system of internal promotion and hierarchy, with a collective leadership of older and more experienced fans that emerged rather than being appointed – the *direttori*. Initially they were responsible for maintaining premises, organizing materials, commissioning artworks, raising money and organizing transport to away games. As their control of the *curva* became more entrenched and their impact on the atmosphere in the stadium as a whole more pronounced, informal, even covert, relationships were established with the club's management. By the early 1980s an uneasy and unspoken peace reigned between them in which the fanatical support of the *ultras* was exchanged for cheap tickets and lax security, and a blind eye turned to extensive pirate merchandising operations that kept most *ultra* groups afloat.

There was also a rising tide of violence and confrontation. *Ultra* groups sought to steal their opponents' banners and then humiliate them by displaying them. Systems of mutual alliance and antagonism created networks of conflict, attack and counterattack. Bologna *ultras* made their presence felt in knife fights with the Inter Boys during the Milan derby as early as 1977. Vicenza against Verona the following year was accompanied by fusillades of rockets from end to end, and clashes outside the stadiums now erupted in Ascoli, Milan and Brescia. In this vortex of nihilism and aggression the neo-fascist MSI found a rich recruiting ground, especially amongst the *ultras* at Inter, Lazio and Verona. Someone, somewhere was going to get very hurt and at the Rome derby in 1979 that someone happened to be Lazio fan Vincenzo Paparelli. He was struck by a nautical rocket. It had been launched over 150 metres away on the other side of the stadium and entered his brain through his left eye. He was the first person to die in an Italian stadium since a Salerno fan had a heart attack after taking part in a pitch invasion in 1963. The usual short-term panic among the authorities saw the introduction of metal detectors in some stadiums, but the increasingly corrupt relationship between directors and the *ultra direttori*, and the complete failure of clubs or the police to take responsibility for controlling what got taken into the stadium, remained completely unaddressed. This complacency was vividly illustrated and entrenched by the authorities' interpretation of Heysel as someone else's problem.

By the mid-1980s *ultra* groups had been established at every professional and nearly all semi-professional clubs right across the country. The last remnants of the class affiliations and radical political posturing of the 1970s had, like the Socialist party that led the country, been abandoned for either experiment in far-right nationalism, intense regional and municipal parochialism or undiluted hedonism. The enmity between teams from the far north and the deep south – like Verona and Napoli – became particularly charged. But the most chaotic scenes and terrace fights resulted from the internal fragmentation of older *ultra* groups and the struggles that developed between them and new groups in the *curva*. Some *ultras* gradually abandoned military and fascist iconography in favour of the vocabulary of heavy metal and teenage narcotic oblivion – Wild Chaos and Verona Alcohol emerged as a reaction to the now ossified hierarchies of the first *ultra* groups whose original informality and spontaneity had been lost. These younger fans were also tuned into different music, different drugs and different values.

Like its English equivalents, the *ultra* style travelled. In Marseilles, just across the Alps from Turin and Milan, supporters of Italian descent were amongst the earliest to bring *ultra* organizations and choreography to the Stade Vélodrome. The new generation of fans in Belgrade at both Red Star and Partizan had begun to coalesce into independent groups and gangs in the late 1970s and by the early 1980s had imported the organized pyrotechnics, flag-waving and banner-draping of the Italians. Recognized as a potential pool of nationalist heavies by both Croatian and Serbian politicians, the *Delije* (Tough Guys) at Red Star and the Bad Blue Boys at Dinamo Zagreb grew in size and power under their secret patronage.

While France was subject to both English (the Boulogne Kop) and Italian (the Marseilles *ultras*) influences, they were geographically separated. In Spain they were more closely merged, a coincidence that made for a particularly virulent and unpleasant micro-culture of violence and racism in Spanish stadiums – a legacy that the nation has yet to fully address. Franco died in 1975 but, despite the swift introduction of democratic elections, it would take nearly a decade for his regime to die. In 1982 the election of the Spanish Socialists (PSOE) under Felipe González set the seal on Spain's democratization, unleashing wild celebrations among the young and a sense that the country could finally shake off the authoritarian restrictions of the old order.

Like most of Spanish youth, the young men gathered in Spain's football stadiums were increasingly dissatisfied by and alienated from traditional organizations with their narrow horizons and old hierarchies, in this case the supporters' clubs known as *peña*. Now open to foreign influences, these Spanish supporters looked to both Italy and England for alternative forms of fan culture and support. At Real Madrid, a European Cup game with Internazionale in 1981 provided a powerful introduction to *ultra* culture, and extensive contact between the clubs' fans initiated the Spanish into the methods of the *interisti*. The potency of Italian support was reinforced during the 1982 World Cup. The game between Italy and Brazil at Espanyol's Sarriá stadium appears to have been decisive in the creation of the club's first *ultra* group:

Thousands of Italians, with their shouting and their flags – red, white and green – answered the thousands of Brazilians ... with their yellow shirts and green flags with the globe in the middle, dancing a samba ... It was a hallucinating spectacle. Many Espanyol *socios* who were present cried with emotion observing their beloved Sarrià transformed into the centre of a global fiesta.[6]

There was another style on offer at España '82: the English, who spread low-level scuffling and disorder around the tournament. One Real Madrid *ultra* recalls the arrival of the English style rather earlier, at a Cup Winners' Cup game against West Ham in 1980.

We had the opportunity to watch one of the most violent fan groups in the world. Can you imagine what the future *ultras* thought when observing these masses enter our stadium? There were no confrontations between both fan groups because the truth is we wouldn't have had the slightest chance. Once inside the stadium, the hooligans destroyed everything they could ... The young Real Madrid fans decided to end the shame of being attacked in our own stadium. Never again![7]

Over the next three or four years the most radical of the youth support in the old *peña* of the major clubs broke away to create their own *ultra* organizations. Real Madrid's Las Banderas gave birth to Ultras Sur; Atlético Madrid's Peña Fondo spawned Frente Atlético Ultras; Barcelona acquired the Boixios Nois and Espanyol the Brigadas Blanquiazules. In this early phase, the emphasis was on the Italian model, as grounds in Spain were festooned with fireworks and flag displays. However, as early as 1984, elements of English skinhead culture – dress, racism and general behaviour – began to appear. When combined with the already existing enmities between city rivals and regional standard bearers, fighting inside and outside the stadium mushroomed. Uniquely the fighting spilt over into other sports, and there were fatalities at the basketball game between Real Madrid and Estudiantes in 1987 and at the Espanyol–Barça football derby too. But as with the Italian experience the short-lived moral panic that followed failed to yield significant reform, constrained by the covert relationships of mutual interest established between club directors and their *ultras*.

The Tartan Army, Ireland's travelling support, the Dutch *Oranje*, the Norwegian *Drillo* and the Danish *Roligans* – the colours and the language might change but they share this: tens of thousands of predominantly young and middle-aged men gathered in a ludicrous array of mock-national dress and emblematic kitsch, coloured wigs, face paint and other novelty headgear. They are in every imaginable stage of drunkenness and inebriation – tipsy, merry, roaring and blotto. They are singing and laughing, chanting and carousing, falling over, throwing up, and when they remember where they are and why, they are watching their national team play a football match somewhere away from home.

These are the carnival fans of Northern Europe, fanatical only in pursuit of their own collective intoxication. These events and their rituals, which began in the 1980s, did not take their cue either from youth subcultures, as in Britain, or political radicals, as in Italy. Instead, they drew on common Celtic and Nordic drinking cultures of riotous bonhomie, organized dancing and communal singing. Previously the preserve of the private sphere – home, kin and extended family – this kind of collective Bacchanalia could now emerge in a public form. In societies where a peculiarly dour and po-faced conservatism – be it the grim sobriety of Danish Lutheranism or the hypocrisy of reactionary Irish Catholicism – had provided their dominant moral compass for most of the century, the post-liberation party was all the more intense and hedonistic. The emergence of carnival fans had material roots too: rising incomes for those in work, and familiarity with and ease of foreign travel, made these exercises in mass sporting tourism possible.

Denmark's *roligans* – a pun on hooligan in Danish, weakly translated as funsters – were first sighted at the 1984 European Championship in France where the Danes were fielding their best and most successful team for three generations. The mass exodus of fans to France that year was a spontaneous agglomeration, but once in France the travelling Danish support acquired a collective identity constructed both by them-selves and the popular press who were as excited about Denmark's fans as they were about the team. In an orgy of red-and-white face paint and strong lager, the *roligans* not only brought a great repertoire of song to the terraces but surreal caricatures of the nation – blond-plaited wigs, foam Viking helmets and hats with hands that clap. More closely studied than any of the similar groups, the social profile of the *roligans* can stand proxy for the others. The majority were men, but there were more women than one would have found in domestic football. Many of the fans did not go to see live football at home. Socially mixed, the profile of the *roligans* was slightly more wealthy, skilled and educated than the domestic crowd.

However, the rise of carnival fans was not only a matter of the gentrification of football. It was a product of changing nationalisms too. In societies where national identities and meanings were a matter of turbulent, confrontational politics, support for the national team had been blighted by indifference (Italy) or trouble (England, Germany). The emergence of the Irish support at Italia '90 could hardly be separated from Ireland's late but phenomenal economic development and newly found self-confidence in the world. The Dutch, finally coming to terms with their war guilt, found expressions of nationalism less distasteful than in the past.

For the Scots the transformation of the Tartan Army was partly a matter of changing demographics, but it was also a matter of a diffuse but changing popular nationalism. Having rejected devolution in the late 1970s, the Scots now found themselves a social democratic minority hitched to the mad runaway train of neo-liberalism centred in southern and central England. Subject to a coruscating process of deindustrialization, and abandoned by London, one strand of Scottish football support continued on the path of English football: Scottish casuals remained a significant and disorderly element of the crowd at England–Scotland games until the end of the 1980s. But away from home, the Scots discovered the pleasures and the pride in not being English – which meant not being aggressive, boorish or violent. The first hint of this shift in the early 1980s came after the positive reports on the Tartan Army's friendliness in a game against Israel. In a rare virtuous circle, positive press coverage of a hysterically good *craic* swelled the numbers of supporters and encouraged them to repeat the performance at ever higher levels of drunken goodwill.

Helping to burst the ludicrous bubble of pumped-up self-important nationalism that can engorge international football crowds is perhaps the Tartan Army's decisive and lasting contribution to European football.

It was, as they say, an era of two halves. Between 1977 and 1985, there was an English team in every European Cup Final but one and they won seven of them: Liverpool's four in 1977, 1978, 1981 and 1984; Nottingham Forest under Brian Clough won in 1979 and 1980; and

Aston Villa were the champions in 1982. There were also UEFA Cups for Liverpool, Ipswich Town and Tottenham Hotspur and a Cup Winners' Cup for Everton. In the second half of the decade there was nothing; English clubs had been banned from Europe. Such comprehensive strength in international club football was paralleled by the disastrous performance of the England national team who failed to qualify for two successive World Cups in 1974 and 1978, played without distinction (although remained unbeaten) at the 1982 tournament and failed to make the final rounds of the European Championship in either 1976 or 1984. When they did qualify for the latter in 1980 they were dispatched. Only in the second half of the 1980s did the team's reputation begin to recover as they made the quarter-finals of Mexico '86 and the semi-finals at Italia '90; even then the persistent violence and xenophobia that surrounded England away games undercut their value. The collective hysteria and venom of the English tabloid press towards both England managers – Ron Greenwood and Bobby Robson – expressed the furious impatience and perpetual disappointments of the consumer boom that swept parts of the country in the late 1980s.

The political chronology of the era was equally divided. Between 1974 and 1979 the country played out the last act in the long death of social democratic Britain. The intellectual assumptions, institutional mechanisms and class alliances of the post-war consensus fragmented. The Labour government of Harold Wilson and then James Callaghan attempted to steer the UK economy out of its post-oil-shock recession and back to full employment by conventional means: wages and prices policies negotiated with organized labour and capital, and reflationary public spending. The first project foundered on the mounting militancy and organization of the trade union movement, while the latter hit the buffers of the international financial markets, which drove the currency into the ground, and the IMF, who provided the threat and the pretext for self-administered deflation. Against this background of economic decline and social disorder, the crowds at English football entered their steepest point of decline, while the leading clubs embarked upon their era of maximum achievement.

In 1979 the Labour government was toppled from office by the Conservatives under Margaret Thatcher. In a break with post-war Conservatism, Thatcher and her allies pursued a radical strategy of change. The economy was to be liberalized, capital markets deregulated, state industries privatized and the power of trade unions broken. Monetarist economics, a prolonged recession, unprecedented levels of unemployment and authoritarian labour legislation delivered the latter; the social costs of this extended economic restructuring were borne by the old manufacturing cities and regions of the midlands, the north of England, Wales and Scotland. Alongside the free market came the strong state. Resistance, opposition and complaint, at home and overseas, were to be confronted and beaten – not least the increasingly irksome influence of the European Community.

The footballing renaissance of England's old industrial heartlands was always more than one club and one city, but it is with Liverpool that any exploration must begin. The scale of their achievement is unparalleled in English football; perhaps only Real Madrid and AC Milan can boast an era of similar grandeur. Between 1975 and 1990 Liverpool won the English League ten times and were runners-up five times. They won the FA Cup twice, four League Cups, the UEFA Cup and four European Cups. The usual rule, that footballing success and economic development and growth move in step, was turned over. While Bill Shankly's first side had flourished in an age of working-class confidence, full employment and social mobility, the Liverpool FC he bequeathed to the city blossomed under conditions of urban decay, deindustrialization, mass unemployment and widespread disorder, most notably the Toxteth riots of 1981. Liverpool was also the stronghold of Militant, the entryist Trotskyites devoted to penetrating and radicalizing the lumbering wreck of the Labour Party. Their control over Liverpool City Council and their protracted head-on conflicts with the government in Westminster saw the city demonized on the political Right as the last redoubt of a lumpenproletariat that prospered on social security fraud and voted for a lunatic municipal socialism. In a city cast as an outsider in its own land, battered by the deliberately engineered economic downturns and clearouts of the early 1980s, Liverpool Football Club was an enduring source of pride, a magnet for the energies and emotions of a public hungry for success.

After Shankly the managerial seat passed to his boot-room colleague Bob Paisley, a man whose public persona was deceptively avuncular; it hid an acute tactical brain, extensive medical training and an iron will. 'The Liverpool Way' was retained: a tradition of simple football, pass and move, defending and attacking collectively, continuity of staff and players, respecting player autonomy but insisting on solidarity. To this

Paisley added the lessons learned from their European experience of the 1960s and early 1970s and then made them the common-sense culture of the club. Possession was made the first priority, the virtue of patience extolled.

Paisley had the right players and when he lost one, he found another and better. Alongside leading English internationals like Ray Clemence, Phil Neal, Phil Thompson, John Barnes and Kevin Keegan, Liverpool drew on Britain's Celtic fringes, from Welshman Ian Rush to Irish players like Mark Lawrenson and above all the Scots: Graeme Souness, Alan Hansen and Kenny Dalglish.

In this context the achievements of England's other European champions Nottingham Forest and Aston Villa were all the more remarkable. At Aston Villa, who won the league in 1981 and the European Cup the following year, first Ron Saunders and then Tony Barton coaxed two years of unflinching effort and doggedness from a tiny fourteen-man squad devoid of stars. At least Villa had some heritage, albeit based on a victorious era in the nineteenth century. They could claim to be the first team from the second city. When Brian Clough took over at Nottingham Forest in 1975 the club had never won anything. Clough dragged them out of the second division, took them to a league title in 1978 and then two consecutive European Cups. In the two and a half decades since, no club of similar provincial stature has won the tournament, or ever looks like doing so again. PSV Eindhoven managed to win in 1988, but they had the economic and technological might of the Philips corporation behind them. Porto have won the European Cup twice, but then they are the club of the leading industrial city in Portugal, not the side of a declining Victorian manufacturing and mining centre that did not even rank among the eight biggest cities in the UK. Clough, whose media appearances and unconventional methods made him a legend in his own lifetime, kept it simple on the training ground. His teams played the ball to each other's feet, they never argued with referees and they never argued with him. Those that did were shown the door or given a clip round the ear, a fate suffered by both a costumed clown and Forest fans who invaded the pitch within reach of his jab. In this respect Clough was closer to the foreman than the boss, a working-class patriarch whose rule rested on a mixture of charisma and coercion.

If the culture and the support of the nation's leading clubs still bore the stamp of Britain's working classes, the same remained true of its players, who throughout this era continued to be drawn from working-class families. Liverpool's Steve Heighway and Manchester United's Steve Coppell, both university graduates, remained objects of surprise and suspicion in the defiantly anti-intellectual culture of English football. A greater test facing the English game, however, was the incorporation of the new black working class. Where just a generation before Britain was almost exclusively white, now it was becoming mixed. The post-war migration from the Caribbean to Britain and the newly settled communities of black Britons in the nation's big cities supplied a small percentage of the country's working classes and a much bigger slice of its professional football players.

There had been a black presence in English professional football since its inception. West African Arthur Wharton played in goal for Preston North End in 1887 and later for Rotherham. Later pioneers included Walter Tull at Tottenham in the pre-war era, Jack Leslie at Plymouth Argyle in the 1930s and after the war Roy Brown, Charlie Williams and Lindy Delaphena. Perceiving them as a form of imperial exotica, the press rendered these players in the bright tones of an unreflective stereotypical racism. Delaphena, who is recalled in club histories at Middlesbrough as a stocky, gruff stopper, was described in the papers as 'lithe as a snake . . . the coffee-coloured king of the wing', who played with the 'spirit of calypso'.[8] There was, however, an altogether nastier undertone expressed on the terraces. Indicative of this, William 'Dixie' Dean, the star striker at inter-war Tranmere and Everton, got his nickname because the crowd read his dark complexion and thick dark hair as the pejorative signs of a 'half-caste'. The leading black players of the 1960s, South African Albert Johansen at Leeds and Bermudian Clyde Best at West Ham, had to endure, from both the press and the crowd, an assumption of inconsistency, lack of fibre and fighting spirit.

In the early 1970s the first generation of British-born black players, drawn almost entirely from the African-Caribbean community, broke into professional football. Their path was hard but the ascent was explosive. As late as 1977 the England team were all white. In 1978 Viv Anderson became the first black player to be capped and at the 1990 World Cup Paul Parker, Des Walker and John Barnes were leading members of the team. By the early 1990s almost 15 per cent of English professional football players were black, more than quadruple their proportion of the population as a whole. Their ascent is all the more remarkable when one considers the degree of open and institutional racism that they met. Many crowds, and not just those segments where the skinheads and National Front organizers were present, demonstrated the depth of racist attitudes in England. The wave of abuse that could be heard in the nation's stadiums sprang effortlessly from a ready-made vocabulary of invective and a deep historical reservoir of ignorance and prejudice.

Even where clubs and managers chose to flaunt their black charges, players' identities were still yoked to mainstream clichés. Thus the rising stars at West Bromwich Albion, Cyrille Regis, Laurie Cunningham and Brendon Batson, were sold to the world by manager Ron Atkinson as football's equivalent of the female Philly soul group the Three Degrees. Entry into the world of professional footballers was equally problematic; the same strategies of exclusion and closure prevalent in other areas of skilled white working-class employment were practised in football too. John Barnes, the cool, composed but sensational midfielder at Liverpool, only cracked the code by self-mockery. When he was initially ignored and snubbed at the club, he jokingly asked, 'Is it because I'm black?' Barnes endured worse from his own fans who in his early days at the club were not above showering the pitch with bananas – one of the cruder and more cowardly weapons in the armoury of racist abuse.[9] Meantime, the FA saw nothing and the TV coverage and commentary teams miraculously rendered it all invisible.

While the course of English football in the 1970s and 1980s suggested the cultural politics of a nation still ill at ease with itself, forced to reassess its diminished capacities in the world, its ethnic make-up and its relationship with a renascent Europe, the course of Scottish football offers a different narrative of nation-making. Just as the England national team fell consistently below expectations, the Scots seemed to rise above it. The national team qualified for the 1974 World Cup and then for every subsequent tournament until 1998 but for one. Each time the footballing nation underwent a great wave of optimism and over-expectation, peaking in 1978 when manager Ally McLeod headed for Argentina promising to bring the trophy home. What followed, then as always, was a departure from the tournament after the first group round. There was usually a hopeless performance against weak opposition, such as the 1978 draw with Iran and 1990 defeat by Costa

Rica, or a brilliant rearguard action against strong teams that brought qualification tantalizingly close, only for it to be snatched away, like the draws with the Soviet Union in 1982 and Uruguay in 1986. The same kinds of hysterical mood swings, failures of nerve and confidence, near misses and miraculous recoveries, were the stock-in-trade of Scottish national identity – the mixture of public defiance and inner doubt that is the curse of most hidden and submerged nations.

Scottish hostility to England continued to be the guiding light of its international football culture, sharply demonstrated by the pitch invasion of teen tartanery that followed Scotland's 2–1 victory over England at Wembley in 1977. Ironically, the strength of Scottish football rested on English economics, for the majority of the key players in Scotland's international sides over the next fifteen years would play their football with England's leading clubs – Kenny Dalglish, Alan Hansen, Graeme Souness and John Wark at Liverpool, Gordon Strachan at Manchester United, Steve Archibald at Spurs, Joe Jordan at Leeds, Archie Gemmill at Nottingham Forest. It was the kind of unspoken economic umbilical cord between Scotland and England that gave many Scots pause for thought when contemplating devolution or independence. Thus in 1978 when Scottish nationalist pressure finally forced a referendum on whether to establish a Scottish parliament, the Scots voted in insufficient numbers. This cautious regionalism perished with the Labour government in 1979 to be replaced by the explicit and virulent unionism of the new Conservative government in London.

The most notable feature of domestic Scottish football in the 1980s was the short but sharp decline of the Old Firm. After the departure of Jock Stein Celtic seemed to live off an ever-declining stock of sporting capital. A couple of league titles could not mask the fact that crowds had shrunk and finances were in terminal decline. While the incompetent management of the club was bad for results, it provided the perfect foil for *Not the View*, one of the funniest and sharpest of the new generation of independent fanzines. Rangers fell even further. After winning the league in 1978 they were forced to endure nine seasons without, while the Glasgow club's wider standing declined even further. The well-earned reputation for violence among Rangers fans established in the early 1970s endured and became increasingly entwined with private and public criticism of the sectarianism that still animated the club. It remained the case that Rangers had yet to sign a Catholic player; that there were extensive personal links between senior members of the Rangers administration, much of the crowd and the Scots Orange Order. Criticism became louder and longer as the 1980s progressed.

In the space left vacant by the decline of Rangers and Celtic there appeared the short-lived Small Firm of Aberdeen, Dundee United and Hearts, all of whom were challenging for Scottish honours through the 1980s on equal terms with the old duopoly. Aberdeen was Scotland's richest city per capita, the administrative centre of the booming North Sea oil industry, and under manager Alex Ferguson it had the best team in Scotland: winning three league titles in 1980, 1984 and 1985, the Scottish Cup three times in a row (1982–4) and at their peak the European Cup Winners' Cup in 1983. Dundee United won the league in 1983 and were runners-up in the UEFA Cup in 1987. Even St Mirren, the team of Paisley, a western industrial suburb of Glasgow, won the Scottish Cup in 1987.

This era of diversity was brought to a close in 1986 by the arrival of David Murray at Rangers. Murray was a self-made steel millionaire who bought the club, entirely rebuilt Ibrox, and installed Graeme Souness as manager. Murray viewed Rangers with sharper business eyes than any director hitherto. Recognizing the prevailing drift in football towards commercialization, concentration and eventually Europeanization, Murray reasoned that the old Rangers would not be able to survive and prosper in the new world unless there were radical changes, both organizational and ideological. Money was made available to Souness to bring in English internationals and Scandinavian imports. Then in 1989 the sectarian barrier was finally breached by the signing of the Catholic ex-Celtic striker Mo Johnston. The public fury among Rangers supporters was predictable if still unpleasant. Murray and Souness rode out the storm. Rangers fans kept coming to Ibrox and whoever was on the pitch they would keep bringing a visceral anti-Catholicism with them into the 1990s.

The climactic year for Thatcherism was 1985. The voodoo monetarist economics of the previous six years had effectively downsized the nation's industry, working class and inner cities. The enemy without, from the Argentine Junta to the IRA, and the enemy within, from the inner-city rioters and their phantom leftist agitators to the National Union of Mineworkers, the last bastion of serious working-class industrial muscle, had all been seen off by force. In the garden of middle England, now blooming on easy credit and rising house prices, the only demon that remained was football, one of the few cultural zones in which the people and the disorder of rust-belt Britain clung on. In the spring of 1985 these beliefs were confirmed by a series of violent and catastrophic incidents. In March the nation had a ringside seat for the televised battle at Luton Town, between the massed ranks of police and visiting Millwall fans. In May a lit cigarette end, dropped beneath the wooden terracing of a stand at Bradford City, ignited a pile of combustible rubbish. In less than a minute the entire structure was engulfed in flames, drawn fiercely upwards by the design of the roof: fifty-six people lost their lives. On the final day of the domestic season a fan was stabbed and killed at a game in Birmingham, and then came Heysel.

The most immediate response to the year's events was at Luton Town, led by chairman David Evans, a local businessman and Conservative MP. Luton simply banned away fans from their ground, took the losses, and enjoyed an arrest-free season in 1986–87. The Football League didn't like it, banning Luton from the League Cup, but Mrs Thatcher did like it and used it as a way of reviving one of the recommendations of Lord Justice Popplewell's 1985 post-Bradford fire report, that all football supporters who wished to enter a ground must carry an ID card. By early 1989 the Football Supporters Bill that would legislate for this had reached the House of Lords. It would have reached the statute books but for the Hillsborough disaster which demonstrated that the nation's decrepit football infrastructure could not cope with fans with tickets, let alone fans with tickets and ID cards.

For all the bluster of the strong state what really transformed English football was the logic of the market. It was becoming apparent in the late 1970s that the already precarious economics of football clubs were becoming impossible. As attendances and income continued their precipitous decline, the wage-price inflationary spiral of the decade continued to push up costs. Sponsorship first appeared at the very sharpest end of the economic crisis – semi-professional football – when Kettering Town put the first logos on their shirts. The west London club Queens Park Rangers were quick to follow, although they were refused permission to wear logos during televised games. Then in 1981 Arsenal struck gold when they signed a half-million-pound deal with the consumer electronics multinational JVC. The deluge of corporate design and imagery into the visual landscape of football had begun. Not just shirts were for sale, but competitions too as the League Cup became the Milk Cup and the Football League was sponsored by Canon.

Football clubs themselves remained remarkably unchanged in their systems of management and financial operation. The only attempt to introduce the practices of the private sector into the game at club level came at Tottenham Hotspur, whose chairman Irvin Scholar experimented with stock market flotation. Although the initial share sale was successful, being a public limited company brought neither profits nor triumphs to Spurs, and Scholar, perhaps a decade ahead of his time, sold up in the early 1990s. For the rest of the football world, the impact of the market came from outside. Despite the opprobrium that still hung around the game after Heysel, the Football League was able to entice Barclays – a brand of impeccable conservatism – to sponsor the league in 1987. Football might not be Glyndebourne, but the demographic it attracted was big enough to keep major corporations interested.

A similar line of argument motivated TV executives in search of eyeballs for advertisers. The BBC and ITV had been fighting it out over TV rights since 1978 when London Weekend Television had attempted to massively outbid the BBC and acquire a monopoly of TV football highlights. The next decade saw the dynamic of competition, although muted by an effective cartel of price control and rights-sharing between the two broadcasters, ratchet up the value of football. The biggest clubs in England increasingly chafed at what they perceived to be the gap between their pulling power and their share of TV income, and announced a new kind of footballing economy when they withdrew from the practice of sharing gate receipts. The concentration of income this implied – the big clubs with large grounds kept the home receipts – would get ever greater. In 1988 a new consortium made up of BSB (the first UK satellite channel), the FA and the Football League seemed set to take control of TV coverage, only for a desperate ITV to outbid them in a deal worth £52 million over four years – piffling today but astronomical at the time. ITV believed that the key to raising the ratings and selling football was concentrating coverage on a few core clubs; by 1990 the five leading clubs of the era – Liverpool, Everton, Arsenal, Tottenham and Manchester United – were receiving over one-third of the TV coverage. The Premiership of the 1990s was being created in embryo. However, the final piece of the jigsaw remained unaddressed.

The product had to be sanitized, the terraces removed and replaced by seats. Indeed the nation's stadiums as a whole needed to be rebuilt and that is precisely what the Taylor Report of 1990 insisted upon. It would require the Hillsborough disaster to make it happen.

IV

The divergent sporting fortunes of Northern and Southern Europe had an obvious political parallel. While Northern Europe responded to the economic and social malaise of the 1970s by voting its socialist and social democratic parties out of office – even in Sweden the longest-serving social democratic government in the world was finally forced to yield to a right-of-centre coalition – Southern Europe swung sharply to the left. The process began with the election of François Mitterrand as President of France in 1981 and a Left majority in parliament. Greece followed, electing a PASOK government under Andreas Papandreou for the first time in the country's history. The following year Felipe González's Spanish Socialist Party took office and the process was completed in 1983 when the Portuguese Socialists returned to power and the PSI of Bettino Craxi grasped the Italian premiership.

For a brief moment it appeared that Mediterranean social democracy might successfully modernize the region's economies and expand their welfare states as technocratic socialist parties made common cause with dynamic state industries and the entrepreneurs of the new information technologies. The era was framed by two World Cups: in Spain in 1982 and in Italy in 1990. Both flaunted the new and raw commercialism of the moment and bookended nearly a decade of high and growing attendances at football matches, a major change in the relationship between football and the new television technologies of pay per view and cable, and an exponential growth in the amount of money in the game. In retrospect, both Mediterranean World Cups betray the grotesque inefficiency and corruption of the host nations' public sectors and the hidden networks of patronage and influence between public and private capital and the new political class. The matrix of power in domestic football was little different.

The fortunes of French football had reached their nadir in the late 1960s – the lowest annual attendances were recorded in 1968. As both the counter-culture and worker militancy ebbed, French football appeared to revive. Attendances rose through the 1970s and the game began to reap the benefits of changes initiated in the 1960s. Appalled at France's meagre haul of medals from the Rome Olympics, De Gaulle turned his and the French state's attention to the nation's international sporting profile. Although money and energy were initially devoted to Olympic sports, a nationwide framework of state support, financial subvention and technocratic guidance of elite and grassroots sports was established and would provide the infrastructural and ideological backbone of France's formidable youth football training programmes of the 1970s and 1980s. The late 1950s and early 1960s also established the key dynasties of coaching that would staff that apparatus and nurture the players of the next generation. Albert Batteux, coach of Stade de Reims and the 1958 World Cup squad, worked directly with future managers of the calibre of World Cup winner Aimé Jacquet and European Championship winner Michel Hidalgo. José Arribas was the founding spirit of the Nantes academy, where Breton pride and grassroots scouting yielded a rich tradition of one-touch football and a rounded inclusive model of youth development; and the incomparable and idiosyncratic Guy Roux almost single-handedly turned Auxerre into a central force in France. Perhaps most crucial of all, Salif Keita, the brilliant Malian striker, came to play for Saint-Étienne, and France, which had risen on the skills of its European and Arabic immigrants, finally began to harvest the considerable talents of its African colonies.

These intersecting trends found their first expression in the Saint-Étienne teams of the late 1970s. The club won seven French championships between 1967 and 1976, four French Cups and took part in European competition for all but three years from 1967–83. Above all they were the first French club to do it all on TV and their European adventures were the central French footballing experiences of the decade, peaking in 1976 when they made a miraculous recovery in the European Cup quarter-final against the much-vaunted Dinamo Kiev, squeezed past PSV and then narrowly lost the final to Bayern München. They raised the standing of the game in the country and gave it a glamour and collective intensity not achieved before. The club was run by an old-style French patron, Roger Rocher, who gathered the leading talents of the era at the club: the Revelli brothers, Jean-Michel Larqué, Dominique Rocheteau – *L'ange vert* – and the young Michel Platini. Most unusually for France, the club created a ferocious home support that, taking its cue from Liverpool and Anfield, saved its best for European nights when the Stade Geoffroy-Guichard became *Le chaudron vert* and the crowd *Le 12e homme*. Then, in a series of events that would acquire a depressing familiarity in French football, a season's exclusion from lucrative European competition in 1977 precipitated a financial crisis at the club. This in turn exposed a series of corrupt financial practices, slush funds and illegal payments. Rocher was force to resign in 1982 and the club entered almost two decades of relegation, debt and decline.

By the early 1980s French football had expanded its fan base, acquired a new cohort of players drawn from across the country's ethnic spectrum, developed one of Europe's most advanced national training programmes and was led by a generation of talented managers born of a serious and cohesive coaching culture. All that remained were questions of money and glory. Money meant sponsorship and television. Glory meant winning something. There had been considerable resistance to sponsorship among France's leading clubs in the 1960s and 1970s, reflecting both a general suspicion of commercialization and the defence of direct economic interests. In the late 1960s a deal was struck with the mineral water company Vittel to sponsor the top division, but it foundered on the resistance of Bordeaux whose board included many wine growers irked at the thought of displaying the brand of a competitor.

The same kind of arm's-length relationship existed between the clubs and the state monopoly TV broadcaster which paid virtually nothing for the rights to the very few games it did show. In 1980 less than 1 per cent of clubs' incomes came from television. Bordeaux's president Claude Bez extracted a certain amount of additional money out of French state television, but it was the arrival of a competitor and the eventual privatization of the public Channel TF1 that really transformed the economics of French football. Canal Plus, Europe's first subscription channel, was launched in 1984 initially as a film and entertainment channel, but soon realized that football was the single most effective tool in gaining subscriptions. By the end of the decade everything had changed. The total income of Le Championnat had risen from FF37 million in 1970 to FF1.2 billion in 1990; TV and sponsorship income over the same period soared from nothing to over FF500 million. Most tellingly of all, the leading twenty clubs had acquired a collective debt of FF800 million.

Glory and eventually victory came from *Les Bleus*, the French national team. In the early 1980s coach Michel Hidalgo was able to field the most talented midfield in European international football.

Giresse, compact and balanced, a master of clever and penetrative distribution . . . Tigana, lithe and quick, supplying width . . . Luis Fernandez, who had become the first choice enforcer, the versatile Genghini to fill in behind . . . And leading from the front was Platini who had the freedom to do what he did, which could only be described as everything.[10]

Their specialities were seen as pleasingly diverse as their ethnic origins (French, Spanish, Italian and African); their team play as disciplined as the centralized training structures of the French republic that had nurtured them. France had possessed skilful teams before but this one had spine. They lost 3–1 to England in their opening game of the 1982 World Cup finals, but came back with a string of victories that took them to Seville and a semi-final with West Germany. The largest television audience for a football match in the country's history – at least 30 million – gathered to watch a game of compelling narrative twist, that pitted the stylish and buccaneering French against the rough, hard Teutons – a clash immortalized worldwide by the heinous and malicious barge of German goalkeeper Schumacher on the Frenchman Battiston. One-all at full-time the French were 3–1 up ten minutes into extra time, only to concede twice and finally buckle in the penalty shoot-out. The team had lost, but the nation was enthralled.

Then in 1984 France hosted the European Championship. The event proved enormously popular as crowds flooded to games of the national team and visitors alike. The Stade de la Beaujoire in Nantes was a glimpse of the new socialist municipalism. Considerable local and national funding had underwritten the adventurous modernism of its rolling concrete roof and vertiginous stands. Its out-of-town location and vast car parks were a measure of French socialism's drift from the inner city to the suburbs. But the main attraction was *Les Bleus* who in five winning games scored fourteen goals and gave just four away. They offered imperious domination in their 5–0 rout of Belgium, and nail-biting suspense in the seesaw fortunes of their 3–2 victories over Yugoslavia and Portugal. In the final they beat Spain 2–0 to win the nation's first major footballing honour. This generation's last grand outing was the 1986 World Cup where in the quarter-final they played the best game of the tournament, giving a display of style and excellence that lived up to the nation's own billing. One observer described it as a match of extraordinary fluidity with hardly a foul, a 'symphony of wonderful passes, of perfect through balls'.[11] In an act of redemption for the shoot-out defeat in Seville France beat the Brazilians on penalties, only to go out to the West Germans once again in the semi-finals. Mitterrand's France would get the better of Kohl's Germany in Maastricht not Guadalajara.

The new entwinement of business and football in France was first announced by the formation of Paris Saint-Germain in the early 1970s by a consortium of local firms, led by the flamboyant head of a Paris fashion house, Daniel Hechter. He resigned in 1977 after a ticketing scandal to be replaced by another tranche of the capital's business elite, this time led by Francisco Borelli. Riding the new wave of money in football, Borelli built up the team and his audience, constructing the country's first executive boxes and offering cheap tickets to the young – a move that would help create the notorious skinhead mobs in the Boulogne Kop. Borelli brought two French Cups to PSG and in 1986 a league title too, but he also brought an ever-mounting pile of hidden debts; so large that he was forced to resign in 1991 and was later found guilty of serious financial irregularities in court. The same cycle of over-optimistic commercial expansion and debt-laden decline was repeated in a minor key at the once great Racing Club. In the early 1980s the team was bought up by the arms and press conglomerate Matra-Hachette and shamelessly turned into an explicit promotional device – Racing Matra – who climbed out of the lower divisions and into the top flight only to ignominiously descend again, having burned hundreds of millions of francs.

Of course, not all of France's clubs succumbed to the new business elites. Nantes remained true to a presidential tradition of salaried middle managers in local companies, men such as Jean Clerfeuille and Louis Fonteneau who still considered the post a form of civic duty and the club a collective property; but they and their values were in decline. Where once France's clubs were led by doctors, minor provincial civil servants, forestry workers and small-time small-town industrialists, now they were run by the managerial technocrats at the summit of the new banks, media and high-technology industries. Borelli at PSG was the CEO of a major publisher, Aulas at Olympique Lyonnais ran computing firms, Soucaret at Stade Rennais ran the pharmaceutical giant Pfizer-France. But most emblematic of the new televisual football order were the presidents of the two leading clubs of the 1980s, Claude Bez at Bordeaux and Bernard Tapie at Marseille.

Claude Bez may have made his money running the Aquitaine region's biggest accounting firm but he did not strike the observer as a typical provincial bean counter. Sporting an outrageous walrus moustache, transported in a gigantic and luxurious Bentley, he was remarkably cavalier about the getting and spending of money. But then money was not his main concern. 'The basis of my personal philosophy is power. And money for me is just the instrument of power.'[12] So too with football. Girondins de Bordeaux, the club where he was made president in 1977, was another instrument of power. Bez turned Bordeaux from a small club in a rugby-loving region to the leading force in French football, winning three French championships, two Coupes de France (including the double in 1987), and competing in European competition every year between 1981 and 1988. He did it by conjoining the mainstays of Mitterrand's new elite – local government barons and the new television and advertising industries. Bez's first innovation was to approach the Gaullist Mayor of Bordeaux, Jacques Chaban-Delmas, and sell him the club as a standard-bearer of Aquitanian identity, whose success and glamour could act as an instrument of economic development attracting capital to the city. Chaban was convinced and low-interest loans, favourable planning permissions and subsidies of all kinds headed for Parc Lescure. It was deemed so successful that the Grimaldi family, the micro-royal house of the Lilliputian tax haven of Monaco, poured money into the team which so dominated French football in the mid-1980s.

Bez insisted on a 'policy of stars' and each year for almost a decade a cavalcade of pan-European and African talent passed through the squad. Jean Tigana was signed for a then record transfer fee, and with his characteristic delight in conspicuous consumption Bez broke the protocol that kept the ugly details of fees and contracts secret, by splashing the figures all over the press. Tigana was followed by Germans, Yugoslavs, Algerians and Portuguese. Bez introduced professional marketing, revolutionized the level of sponsorship contracts, made a ground-breaking deal with Opel and installed executive boxes. Above all, he realized the true value of football TV rights, especially for the most glamorous

European encounters, and wrung it out of the newly competitive broadcasting companies. His power was so widespread in French football that he was instrumental in the removal of Henri Michel, the national team coach, in 1988 and his replacement with Michel Platini. And then there was more; as Bez himself said, 'Clubs will always find ways to break the rules. Me, I have three million ways.'[13]

While the club was winning and income was buoyant those ways remained hidden – apart from a much publicized and televised slagging match between Bez and Tapie at Marseille, which ratcheted up the ratings but failed to initiate a judicial investigation. However, when defeats and then exclusion from European competition came, in part driven by the incessant, disruptive and costly turnover of players, the club had to admit to debts of FF10 million owed in unpaid tax. It was a grotesque understatement. When Bez was finally forced to step down in 1991 and a true picture of the club's books emerged it revealed a debt of over FF240 million. In 1995 Bez was sentenced to three years in prison for fraud.

The same morality play of vaulting political and sporting ambition, finally laid low by the exposure of corruption and theft, was played out in Marseilles where the influential socialist Mayor Gaston Defferre invited celebrity entrepreneur Bernard Tapie to assume the presidency of Olympique Marseille in 1986. After dabbling in politics and pop in the 1970s, Tapie made his mark in the 1980s as a corporate raider and turnaround specialist whose holding company bought, re-engineered and sold on firms as large as Toshiba, Wrangler France, Kickers and Mazda. Defferre secured a business-minded president and promises of substantial investment from Tapie himself, and the promise of a Mediterranean socialist riposte to the Atlantic Gaullists of Bordeaux. Tapie, a rootless tycoon, acquired a home base and faux regional identity, as well as an entrée into the very highest levels of the Socialist Party regime. The OM *ultras* acquired a team that looked like it might finally win something.

Tapie was a whirlwind of change and public bluster. Olympique Marseille's coffers bulged with monies from his own empire, the city government, new TV deals and hyper-commercial sponsorships and advertising practice, as well as a variety of increasingly desperate and complex accounting practices. Although Tapie declared that he would treat the club strictly as a business it soon became an instrument of his own personal aggrandizement. Again, a huge influx of foreign stars came to the Stade Vélodrome, and coaches too, flying through an ever faster revolving door of transfers, loans, fees and wages which grotesquely inflated the entire wages and transfer market of French football. OM's fortunes rose as they first won the French league in 1989 and then did so again every year in a run of four consecutive titles. They contested and lost a European Cup Final in 1991 – the first French side to do so since Stade de Reims in the 1950s – and finally in 1993 won the European Cup, beating Berlusconi's Milan. Tapie's political career followed a similar arc. He first grabbed the TV limelight in his rumbustious encounters with Jean-Marie Le Pen, leader of the Front National and *bête noire* of the Left. He was elected to parliament as a Socialist deputy in 1989 and served as Minister for Cities in 1992 and 1993. In a deliberate contrast to Agnelli and Juve's three 'S's' – seriousness, sobriety and simplicity – Tapie offered the three 'R's' as the guiding light of the new OM: *Le Rêve, Le Rire, Le Risque* – the dream, laughter and risk.

The fall came in the aftermath of the European Cup triumph. Jacques Glassman, a player with the small league side Valenciennes-Anzin, made public a series of accusations against Tapie; most damagingly that he had offered Glassman and colleagues money to throw a game against Marseille in the run-up to the European Cup Final of 1993. It was so crude and so obvious a fix that Tapie was banned from football and eventually imprisoned on charges of fraud. In the final days of the Mitterrand presidency, as successive socialist administrations were being dragged through the mud in a great wave of corruption scandals, OM were bankrupted and relegated. They were stripped of the European Cup and the 1993 French league title for match-fixing and a range of other improprieties. Yet in the late 1990s Tapie would re-emerge and even return to public life and Olympique Marseille. Something had profoundly changed in French politics and football. 'Both he and his team were corrupt, but his corruption was somehow seen as thumbing his nose at the establishment . . . Tapie was politics as soap, now up, now down, but always fighting back and always in the public limelight.'[14]

V

In parallel with France, Italian football rose as the North declined. The national team won the World Cup in 1982, attendances were large and rising, Juventus won all three European competitions in the late 1970s and mid-1980s and when they faltered their mantle was taken up by Berlusconi's AC Milan, who not only won the European Cup twice but set the template for the kind of high-tempo passing and pressing football that would characterize the next two decades. It was an arc of success that seemed to parallel the course of the Italian economy. In 1987 it was official: the OECD declared that Italy had overtaken Britain to become the fifth largest economy in the world, which appeared as confirmation and embellishment of the self-image of the country's smug political elite. The political and social emergency of the late 1970s had petered out into sporadic acts of random violence from the remnants of the far Left and far Right; kidnappings and shootings persisted but the challenge to the ruling order was over. The Italian Communist Party had been effectively domesticated as a loyal opposition and in 1981 the stitch-up was made complete with the creation of the *pentapartito* – a coalition of five parties dominated by the Christian Democrats of Ciriaco De Mita and the Socialist Party of Bettino Craxi. In one form or another such a government would rule Italy until the explosive effects of *Tagentopoli* – 'kickback city', the mother of all corruption scandals and investigations in 1992 – laid waste to all its members. In its final decade the rotten party system of the Italian republic presided over an era of high economic growth and even higher public expenditure in which hi-tech, conspicuous consumerism became the definitive feature of Italian private life.

Italy's newly elevated status in the world's economic league table, never based on the firmest statistical evidence, proved to be an illusion when the Italian economy entered a period of prolonged stagnation in the 1990s, while the *pentapartito* was revealed to be little more than a bargaining system for appropriating and dividing the spoils of public office and the public purse. Its tentacular systems of power and patronage bypassed the machinery of democratic politics and wired the Italian state into networks of organized crime, sedition and corruption. These same pathologies would also infect the fibres of Italian football culture, but as with the political system there was plenty of reason to suspect their emergence and growth in the 1980s. As we have seen, the decade saw the drift towards organized violence and neo-fascism among some *ultra* groups, the unspoken complicity of many football club directors with their *ultras*, and the abdication of responsibility for redefining public order and public space by the country's many police forces. The era began with the *totocalcio* scandal in 1980.

Totocalcio, the state monopoly for gambling on football, possessed qualities rare for an Italian public institution. It was genuinely national in its coverage and use, and although it could deliver jackpots, it could also, like the British pools system, hand out smaller democratic shares. It was liked, respected and very difficult to rig, in part because there was no betting on the outcome of individual games. To meet that need a vast illegal network of football betting emerged – *totonero* – that reached back to the Camorra of Naples. By the late 1970s, with the same brazen insouciance of the rest of the black economy, *totonero* employees would openly take bets and quote odds at tables set up in *totocalcio* booths and shops. In late 1979 and early 1980 two Rome-based businessmen, Alvaro Trinca and Massimo Cruciani, attempted to rig the outcome of twelve matches. Their instruments were bribes and a network of players they were introduced to via the Lazio players who frequented Trinca's restaurant. Trinca and Cruciani were amateurs of the first order. They failed to achieve most of their desired fixes and were astoundingly lax in their preparations and discretion, talking with increasing frequency and openness as their schemes got out of hand. The papers began to print rumours and Lazio midfielder Massimo Montesi gave an interview to the press that really blew the whistle.

As their losses mounted, Trinca and Cruciani compounded their problems by borrowing wildly from dubious sources of credit. In an atmosphere of mounting rumour in the press and threats from the creditors, they went first to their lawyer, then the police and then the newspaper *Corriere dello Sport*. Two weeks later, at half-time on Sunday, 2 March 1980 the police swooped on the nation's football grounds and dressing rooms and eleven players were arrested. Everyone talked, at length and in detail. Sporting justice was swift and decisive: Lazio and Milan were relegated, many other clubs lost points, and fifty years' worth of bans from football were applied to players and club presidents including international stars like Paulo Rossi and Bruno Giordano. State justice was another matter. The public case against the accused was based on a legal code that did not even recognize the concept of sporting fraud. No one was convicted of anything, not even Trinca and Cruciani. But then this was the same judicial system that despite uncovering unambiguous documentary evidence of a vast secret Masonic lodge, P2 – linking every level of the state security apparatus with organized crime, political parties and business – was unable to successfully prosecute anyone.

If the *totonero* scandal exposed the underbelly of the Italian football economy, Juventus remained its hard-headed public success – the nation's footballing FIAT. Continuity of ownership and management persisted with Gianni Agnelli as the charismatic public face of the club, his brother Umberto the arch organizer and Giampiero Boniperti making an effortless succession from iconic player in the 1970s to triumphal president in the 1980s. The Agnellis installed Giovanni Trapattoni – *Il Trap* – as coach, a tough-minded no-nonsense defensive strategist blessed with his generation's leading goalkeeper, the imperturbable Dino Zoff, and a defence of iron welded from Gentile, Scirea and Cabrini. When in 1983 the ban on foreign players was lifted Juventus went out and bought style, bringing in Irishman Liam Brady, the Pole Zibi Boniek and the incomparable Michel Platini. Between 1977 and 1986 they won six *scudetti* and all three of the major European tournaments – the UEFA Cup in 1977, the Cup Winners' Cup in 1984 and the European Cup in 1985.

The controversy, bad faith and bad taste which surrounded their victory at Heysel also soured their *scudetti* in 1981 and 1982. In the key game of the 1981 season, Roma, who had chased them all year, came to play Juventus in Turin. Juve scraped a draw when a goal from Roma's Turone was ruled offside although he was, to the entire country, clearly onside. In 1982 the challengers were Fiorentina, who had managed to draw level with Juve on the penultimate weekend of the season. Fiorentina played their last game away at Cagliari, who still needed points to avoid relegation. Juve, by contrast, travelled to Catanzaro who were already safe. The day turned on penalties given and refused. Catanzaro were denied a first-half penalty and Juventus were given and scored a penalty with just fifteen minutes to go. Fiorentina appeared to have pulled the situation around with a last-minute goal only to see it disallowed. Repeated viewing suggests that only the Catanzaro decision was incorrect, but the fury and incomprehension of Fiorentina's fans and the rest of the country was so great that the theft of the 1982 championship came to embody the entire system of psychological slavery and structural disadvantage that privileged the already powerful and wealthy in Italian football and society.

Juventus, now more than ever, were a national team with a national following rather than a Turinese team and they formed the backbone of the 1978 and 1982 World Cup squads, supplying seven of the players that began the '82 final against West Germany. A television audience of over 32 million people, the entire adult population of the country, joined them and watched Italy score three times and win their third World Cup.

In the latter half of the 1980s the national team aged and faded: they only made fourth place in the 1986 World Cup. Juventus too went into a short-lived decline, leaving the field open for three clubs to make their mark in domestic football, each of whom pointed to the social forces in Italian life that would survive and emerge from the wreckage of *Tagentopoli*. Hellas Verona, a club from the heartlands of the secessionist Lega Nord (Northern League), won the championship in 1985; Napoli, sunk deep into the social fabric of Western Europe's biggest slum and the Italian mainland's crucible of organized crime, became the standard bearer of the south, matching and surpassing Verona, winning the title twice (1987 and 1990). Above them all was the renascent AC Milan, champions of Italy, Europe and the world, the team of the new money and new TV politics of Silvio Berlusconi.

The extreme north-east of Italy was until the 1960s desperately poor, an economic reality reflected in the underperformance of its leading city teams like Venezia and Verona. Then, the economic miracle brought a dense network of small, interconnected, highly specialized firms into being – especially the niche fashion houses of Diesel, Benetton and Police – and by the 1980s it was among the richest regions of the country. It was in an atmosphere of growing regional renaissance and self-assertiveness that Hellas Verona pulled off the miracle of 1985 – the last team from outside the charmed circle of Milan, Rome and Turin to win the *scudetto*. They achieved this astonishing feat under Osvaldo Bagnoli, a coach of the old school, temperamentally and ideologically imbued with a Milanese working-class communist sensibility and a predilection for philosophical musings; Gianni Brera nicknamed him Schopenhauer. His team without stars, whose most noteworthy individual was an unsung Danish striker, Preben Elkjaer, performed as an unbreakable and immovable unit, supported with a rare fervour home and away by the swelling ranks of the *Brigate Gialloblu*. Alongside their repertoire of song and choreography they also acquired a reputation for the most public and explicit statements of anti-southern sentiment among football fans. In the late 1980s Napoli provided the main outlet for this fury. When Napoli came north, Verona *ultras* displayed the infamous banners 'Welcome to Italy', and '*Vesuvio facci sognare!* – Help us dream, Vesuvius!' Simultaneously the Veneto and surrounding regions began to provide political support to Umberto Bossi, the founder of the separatist Lombard League and first elected to parliament in 1987. Bossi fused his organization with the Liga Veneta to create the Northern League in 1989 and give full political vent to the simmering hostility and resentment of small business and petit bourgeoisie of the north against Rome and its taxes, the south and its subsidies. By the early 1990s, Verona's *curva* was a recruiting ground for the most extreme elements in the new northern separatism.

The anger of Verona and indeed the whole of the north was inflamed by and directed against Napoli. Despite the club's immense support, vast stadium and endless succession of well-connected and wealthy patrons, by the mid-1980s Napoli had won nothing. It confirmed northern stereotypes of the south as a bottomless pit of inefficiency and torpor which devoured any amount of subsidy and transfers but failed to deliver the goods; a reality embodied by the vast but totally unproductive industrial plants that had been artificially located in the region over the previous two decades. Under club president Corrado Ferlaino, Napoli finally bucked the trend by throwing their money at and investing their faith in a single player: Diego Maradona. Ferlaino brought Maradona to Napoli's Stadio San Paolo by helicopter in the summer of 1985. Over 80,000 Neapolitans queued and paid for the privilege of seeing him step out on the pitch and juggle a few balls. It was enough; they were convinced that the saviour had arrived. Napoli sold over 60,000 season tickets a year while Maradona remained with them. Coaches Ottavo Bianchi and Alberto Bigon kept the runaway train of Napoli's combustible squad on the rails over the next five years, marshalling a tough Italian defence around Ciro Ferrara and adding Brazilian Careca to Maradona at the front.

In May 1987, after a season embellished and defined by Maradona's goals, assists and energy, Napoli secured a draw with Fiorentina at home and the city's first *scudetto* had arrived. The celebrations were tumultuous. A rolling series of impromptu street parties and festivities broke out contagiously across the city in a round-the-clock carnival which ran for over a week. The world was turned upside down. The Neapolitans held mock funerals for Juventus and Milan, burning their coffins, their death notices announcing 'May 1987, the other Italy has been defeated. A new empire is born.' Derided by northerners as donkeys, they now dressed as one, dragging Lombard and Tuscan devils by their tails through the gutters of the city. Urban myths flourished and circulated in ascending spirals of ever more ludicrous connectivities: the victory had been preceded by the number 43, Maradona's number, coming up in the city lottery; and it came up again the following week alongside 61, the number of years Napoli had been waiting to win Serie A. Murals were painted of the divine one on the city's ancient tenements in the guise and even the arms of the city's patron saint San Gennaro. Children born or conceived in the moment were named in his honour.

The mutual antagonism between Napoli and their northern rivals was intensified over the next three seasons. In 1988 Napoli collapsed in the final run-in and Milan swiped the title. In 1989 they slugged it out with Inter all the way to the end. Then in 1990 they crawled back to the top with the help of two points won at a tribunal after their goalkeeper had been hit by a coin and injured in a game against Atalanta. All across the north, but especially in Milan, they claimed a theft, and the chief thief for the football public north of Rome was Maradona. They would have their final and bitterest encounter at the 1990 World Cup that summer.

AC Milan, disgraced by the *totocalcio* scandal and relegated to Serie B in 1982, were a shadow of their former selves in the early 1980s. Although they had returned to Serie A, they appeared a spent force. Then in 1986 they were taken over by the Milanese TV and property magnate Silvio Berlusconi. Things were about to change in Italian football. When, at the start of the season, the new team assembled by Berlusconi were displayed before the fans, they arrived at the San Siro in helicopters, accompanied by the hugely amplified sounds of Wagner's 'Ride of the Valkyries'; their descent and emergence endlessly repeated on Berlusconi's cable television network Mediaset. He himself acknowledged that people would laugh, but Milan sold 65,000 season tickets.

Berlusconi was born in Milan in 1936, the son of a bank clerk. As a teenager he was already looking beyond the narrow cultural horizons of white-collar Milan and his conventional Catholic boarding school.

His heroes were French and American, like the smooth crooners and entertainers Frank Sinatra, Nat King Cole and Yves Montand. His first job out of school was working as a chanteur on tourist cruise ships in the Mediterranean. After studying law at Milan University, Berlusconi grabbed his first break when his silver tongue and family connections got him a decent bank loan from his father's boss. Property deal after property deal followed, culminating in Milano 2, the city's first suburban gated community which consciously imported the architectural vernacular and social segregation of suburban southern California; it was a gigantic financial success. No property developer in Italy, however accomplished, could achieve this without friends and it appears that Berlusconi was well connected. His name, for example, appeared on the P2 list of Masonic conspirators.

One feature of Milano 2, and Milano 3 that followed, was the early installation of cable television services. The cables carried space for six channels, most of which were for Italian state television and some foreign stations, but Berlusconi inherited one. Once he had grasped its potential, he moved quickly to plan the launch of a national network: 'In the building trade you plan something today and see it realized in ten years' time. In television you think of it in the morning and in the evening it's already on the screen.'[15]

Berlusconi's TV strategy was content-driven, a televisual replay of the aesthetics of Milano 2. He gave the trash-starved Italian public what they wanted. He showed as much football as he could get his hands on and invented tournaments and tours when nothing else was available. He also imported an enormous volume of low-grade Hollywood movies, American television comedy and drama and, for the kids, eyeball-bursting quantities of cartoons. All came heavily laced with mid-programme commercial breaks, much of it made and conceived by Berlusconi's own giant advertising agency Publitalia. His channels increasingly offered the kind of tacky game show, celebrity fluff and inane gossip that the staid and conservative state channels had never been able to lower themselves to. He even put TV on after 11 p.m. at night – a revelation in Italy. Indeed it was understood as an act of intensely popular cultural transgression. The three RAI channels, carved up among the Christian Democrats, Socialists and Communists, were being outflanked by Berlusconi and the other new cable channels Rete 4 and Canale 1. The only obstacle left was the 1976 Constitutional

Court ruling, which declared that the new commercial stations could only possess a local broadcasting remit.

Berlusconi was prepared to sail closer to the wind than his early cable competitors, pushing to create what was in effect a national channel by stealth, in part because it was his natural inclination and in part because he had really good friends. In the decade's marriage of convenience, Berlusconi had become personally and politically close to the Socialist leader and then Prime Minister, Bettino Craxi. The two families holidayed together at the shrines of the super-elites, Portofino and Saint Moritz, and Craxi was both godfather to Berlusconi's children and witness of his second marriage. In 1984 Berlusconi bought out his cable competitors and established a virtual national monopoly of commercial broadcasting. Milan magistrates invoked the 1976 ruling, declared the channel unconstitutional and ordered transmission to cease. Berlusconi's wider publicity machine went into overdrive, mobilizing the real irritation of the public who found the judicial regulation of their viewing habits to be a step too far. It was a war for *Libertà di telecomando* – the freedom of the remote control – and Berlusconi won. Craxi ensured that his cabinet issued an immediate six-month decree annulling the ruling and when the Italian parliament initially refused to renew it or change the law, Craxi merely issued another decree. By the time that ran out, everyone had moved on and Berlusconi's empire was left untouched.

He then enlarged his domain by buying AC Milan, claiming that he did not see it as a business, but something located in the 'sphere of affections'; for he understood Italian football in the TV age to be neither simply sport nor corporation, but showbusiness, spectacular and circus. Beyond the opening histrionics Berlusconi proved to be a shrewd and active club president. He invested in the country's leading training facilities, attended almost every game and has insisted from all of his coaches that Milan be an attacking and entertaining team.

Berlusconi's first coach was the little known Arrigo Sacchi, then with Parma in Serie B. Sacchi was a man of well-cut suits, unfeasibly large glasses, and even bigger sunglasses usually worn at night. He possessed a squad of considerable ability, including the young Paolo Maldini and Franco Baresi in defence, and hard-working destroyers like Alessandro Costacurta and Carlo Ancelotti. Berlusconi had also obtained the cream of Dutch football: midfielders Ruud Gullit and Frank Rijkaard and striker Marco van Basten. Sacchi's Milan played a game that broke with some of the core principles of Italian football. First they abandoned man-marking altogether: defence like attack became about the use of space. This was not an updated version of *catenaccio*; it was in many ways its definitive rejection. Milan never played with a sweeper or libero, but always with a flat back four, pressing high up the field, drilled in offside traps and mutual cover. Defence continued all the way up the field with systematic pressing and crowding of the opposition when they were in possession. Everyone in Sacchi's teams, from Van Basten at the front to goalkeeper Sebastiano Rossi at the back, had specific pressing duties. In midfield especially the team hunted in packs, closing down space around the player on the ball, but also looking to cut them off from their team-mates, forcing an error that could be intercepted. Set up like this, Milan were constantly poised to attack: as the ball was regained quick passing and lightning movement took over. Milan were brilliant. Gullit, in particular, played with a razor-sharp intelligence and technique. They won the *scudetto* in 1988 and in the following season's European Cup they were at their best, announcing their return to the highest levels of football by shattering Real Madrid 5–0 in the home leg of their semi-final before travelling to Barcelona where they faced Steaua Bucharest in the final.

---

24 May 1989
AC Milan 4 Steaua Bucharest 0
Nou Camp, Barcelona

After the match, once Milan were champions of Europe, their stock enhanced, a journalist asked Berlusconi whether he would be selling the club on: 'Let us be sincere, in the whole of my life I have never bought anything, however small, with the slightest intention of it being sold again.' Who would sell a team that plays like this?

Steaua kick-off, the flare and smoke bombs still drifting across the pitch. In the first ten minutes they only get the ball out of their half three times, and two of those are long hopeless lobs instantly returned with interest by Rijkaard and Ancelotti. Bucharest's Lăcătuş holds the ball under his control just beyond the centre-circle in Milan's half for less than a second before he is ruthlessly dispossessed.

Wherever the Romanians try to pass the ball, Milan are there. Gullit and Van Basten are pressing the ball back into the Steaua's penalty area, harassing and unnerving their centre-backs. When the midfield tries to take it forward, Milan descend in a white snarling pack around them. When they pump the ball forward it is intercepted by the tight back line with ease.

The moment the Milanese regain the ball the patterns on the pitch are suddenly transformed. The defence rolls forward, white shirts break for the wings and through the centre, options and possibilities open up everywhere. The four goals – Gullit's poached shot, a flying Van Basten header, Gullit's miraculous pull-down and volley on the edge of the area, and Van Basten's sinuous run and flick – are almost mere embellishment.

Football, like business, is first and foremost about ownership, be it capital or the ball. The plan, the shape, the possession, the first ten minutes tell us everything we need to know about how football is going to be played. We are still, for the most part, playing 4-4-2, trying to hold on to the ball, pressing our opponents, breaking and interpassing at speed. Berlusconi still owns Milan; he has parted with nothing.

Later that year Milan went to Tokyo and beat Atlético Nacional, the Colombian team of the Medellín drugs cartel, to become Intercontinental Club champions. The following year they would do it all again, beating Benfica in Europe and Olimpia of Paraguay in Japan. Mediaset offered wall-to-wall coverage of a triumphant Milan and its president. Few teams and few impresarios were better poised and better equipped to survive and prosper in the new football and the new politics of the next decade.

In the 1980s there were marked differences in the course of Eastern European football. After the relative successes of the early and mid-1970s, including a Czechoslovak victory in the 1976 European Championship with a team staffed overwhelmingly by Slovaks, football went flat in the most advanced economic zones of the East. The embattled and utterly discredited regimes of Czechoslovakia, Hungary and Poland had no stomach for sporting adventure of any kind; their citizens, it appeared, had little taste for the ersatz clubs and cultures of a tiring bureaucratic socialism. The two states in which football appeared to prosper were those most distant, diplomatically at any rate, from the Soviet Union. In Romania, in particular, the increasingly independent policy of the Ceauşescu regime provided the context for the very late industrialization of Romanian society and sport. Boosted by the competition among segments of the state apparatus and the close links to the ruling family, Romanian football briefly blossomed, most especially at the army's club, Steaua Bucharest. Yugoslavia, which had long broken from the most formal communist orthodoxies, continued on its own distinct path. Its economic openness to the West resulted in a vast exodus of the most talented players and a domestic transfer-fee bonanza for the big exporting clubs. Organized youth groups of fans began to emerge who adapted the Italian *ultra* model of support. By the end of the decade these groups would provide the recruiting grounds and shock troops of the most barbarous forms of ethnic nationalism in the country's bitter civil war.

In the Soviet Union, which still officially preferred athletics and Olympic sports, football retained a glimmer of its outsider status, though in reality it had long settled down into a quiet accommodation with the stagnant ruling polity. Only after Gorbachev's arrival in the Kremlin in 1985, and the dual initiatives of *perestroika* and *glasnost*, did change arrive. Then, as with the wider society, it arrived at such a pace and scale that the old football order was not reformed but swept away altogether. In East Germany, which had cleaved to the Soviet model most assiduously, the final years of communism witnessed a comprehensive colonization of football by the forces of the state. The game endured a maniacal level of micro-control and distortion that in turn evoked an uncontrollable response from violent fan groups who could cast their vandalism as an anti-systemic gesture.

The mid-1970s were the last moment at which the Soviet Union could claim, with any plausibility, military, technological or footballing parity with the West. Its own mode of highly centralized, vertically integrated, state-subsidized, high-tech, military and infrastructural engineering – the supposed commanding heights of the economy – had their sporting parallel in the Dinamo Kiev teams coached by Valeri Lobanovski which dominated Soviet football in the 1970s and early 1980s. Lobanovski, an ex-professional player with training as both a plumber and engineer, began his managerial career at Dnipro Dnipropetrovsk where he teamed up with the sports scientist Anatoly Zelentsov, then based at the local Institute of Physical Education. The two moved to Dinamo Kiev together where they were backed by the Kiev Institute of Physical Culture, the Ukrainian Communist Party and the Ministry of the Interior. This level of support allowed them to develop a philosophy of football rooted in scientific and statistical thinking, generously supplied with computer equipment and the most sophisticated training and medical monitoring equipment in the country.

The core principles were the precise calculation and measurement of player performance with a particular focus on measuring and reducing a player's error rate. Lobanovski argued that a team that makes a mistake in less than 18 per cent of a game's key situations was virtually unbeatable. He knew because Zelentsov had been counting. The pair also reasoned that the speed of modern football was so great that there was insufficient time for any player to react, so predetermined patterns of play, burned deep into the player's spatial circuitry, were at the core of the team's training and tactical thinking. To this was added a phenomenal work rate, with just a touch of the total football of the Dutch, positional switching in particular. On the pitch this mode of operation was primarily expressed by taking control of the ball in midfield and the sending of long diagonal passes to the speedy goalscorer Oleg Blokhin, who would run in predetermined sequences and moves behind the opposition's defence. In the domestic league Lobanovski also favoured a season-long strategy of only playing for a draw away and winning at home. Neither model was particularly pretty, but it was often effective as Kiev won six Soviet championships in a decade and in both 1975 and 1986 they won the European Cup Winners' Cup.

Although Kiev and the Ukraine were tightly bound to the Russian core of the Soviet Union, and Stalin's famine and repression had crushed Ukrainian nationalism for almost two generations, Dinamo were inevitably a quiet reminder of a distant Ukrainian national identity. It was not the only club whose sporting triumphs would warm the embers of a hidden nationalism. In 1973 the Armenian side Yerevan won the Soviet Cup Final, beating Dinamo Moscow with a late equalizer and extra-time winner. In the Luzhniki Stadium 15,000 Armenians chanted out the nation's name and in Yerevan the air rang with car horns and forbidden nationalist songs were sung. The city's sacred Lenin monument was hung with a number *8* in honour of the player who had scored the winning goal. In Georgia Dinamo Tbilisi was a similar lightning rod for incipient nationalism. Strongly supported by Eduard Shevardnadze, then head of the Georgian Communist Party and later President of the independent Republic of Georgia, they won the Soviet Cup (twice), the Soviet League and the European Cup Winners' Cup in a five-year streak of success between 1976 and 1981.

While the peripheries prospered, the core began to degenerate. In 1979 the invasion of Afghanistan by Soviet troops formally ended the period of détente with the West and set the USSR on course for a gruelling guerrilla mountain war on its borders and a draining hi-tech arms race with a newly bellicose America. It would lose both contests and over the course of the early 1980s its decrepitude would be confirmed by the demise of its senior cadres. President Brezhnev died in 1982 and was replaced by KGB chief Yuri Andropov. In 1984 Andropov died and was replaced by Konstantin Chernenko. Chernenko died less than a year later. The Moscow football scene was no less depressing. As the peripheries took control and the economy was squeezed clubs suffered falling attendances and a scattering of violence. As early as 1973 young fans had been separately gathering behind the goal ends, distinguishing themselves by the then frowned-upon display of club colours – often home-knitted scarves and hats – and identifying themselves by their self-ascription as *fanaty* – fanatics. By the late 1970s and early 1980s all the Moscow clubs could boast such groups and the walls of the capital city were increasingly daubed and sprayed with their icons and markers. Scuffles, fights and punch-ups began to dot the Moscow metro and the streets around the stadiums.

This of course was as nothing to the casual violence and structural irresponsibility that the Soviet state inflicted on its citizens. Soviet football's Chernobyl was the disaster at the Luzhniki stadium in Moscow in 1982. A massive crush on the icy winter terraces during a UEFA Cup match saw over three hundred people killed. The authorities predictably stayed silent, denied the problem and then refused to investigate, release information or seek anything but marginal scapegoats for the tragedy. Three years later a crush killing twenty people at the Soloniki Sports Palace, where an international indoor football tournament was being played, was also covered up. It was against this backdrop of systematic neglect, decay, underinvestment and incipient disorder that Mikhail Gorbachev was made general secretary of the Soviet Communist Party in 1985 with a programme, it appeared, of real reform. Its twin pillars were a move to a more open and plural politics, known as *glasnost*; and a gradual liberalization of the Soviet economy and state, *perestroika*.

In the world of elite football this had three key consequences. First, the football authorities and the clubs were expected, like every other parastatal organization, to move towards self-financing, real cost-accounting and to detach themselves economically and politically from state institutions. Second, the sham amateurism and black transfer market in players developed over the previous forty years would have to be formalized. Third, clubs would have to find new sources of income. There were, however, no new magic sources of income to tap into. Sponsorship made little sense in an economy in which consumers did precious little consuming, of brands or anything else. Soviet TV, which continued to show a great deal of football, also continued to refuse to pay anything significant for the rights to games. As the economy began to head into a tailspin in the late 1980s, attendances crumbled, literally halving in the final years of the decade. The only option was to sell players to the West and Spartak Mocow and Dynamo Kiev began what would soon turn into a flood with the 1988 sales of Khidiatulin to Toulouse and Zavarov to Juventus respectively.

Perestroika, rather than initiating a process of smooth transition towards a modern and moderate commercialized football, acclerated its decline. Although a number of clubs took the plunge and became fully independent professional outfits – a trend began by Dnipro Dnipropetrovsk – none could break even let alone financially prosper. At a moment of profound political transformation, oppositional and youthful energies were congregating around Western rock music; football was increasingly the domain of old men and dissolute and marginal youth. The violence that had been brewing throughout the early 1980s exploded into the open. In September 1987 Spartak Moscow travelled to Dinamo Kiev for what was the deciding match of the season. Travelling Spartak fans were attacked in the streets of Kiev, assaulted on their way out of the stadium and the railway station in the city centre turned into a pitched battle involving many hundreds of supporters. This was not an isolated incident and Spartak's 500-strong regular travelling fans met similar if less intense situations across the whole Soviet Union.

The Soviet success in finishing runners-up at Euro '88 was a swansong, not a new beginning. Football was not a source of late imperial unity but a site of simmering conflict and nationalist fragmentation. Across the country Moscow clubs faced a barrage of nationalist and secessionist passions, especially when they played in Tbilisi, Riga or Kiev. Glen Hoddle, the England midfielder, remembers Tbilisi fans cheering England in a match in Georgia against the USSR. In Armenia in games against Zalgiris or Skonto Riga the Yerevan fans would chant 'Lithuania!' or 'Latvia!' to show solidarity with their opponents' national aspiration. And in a portent of the inter-republic fighting to come, games between Azerbaijani and Armenian teams were particularly volatile. On the eve of the 1990 season the newly constituted Georgian and Lithuanian football associations declined to involve themselves or their teams in the new Soviet league. A year later there would be no Soviet league, no Soviet Union and after the 1990 World Cup no Soviet national team. The break-up of the Soviet Union had begun and as it began to disintegrate it would take all of its fraternal socialist brothers with it.

Even as late as the mid-1960s, Romania remained a predominantly rural and agrarian society. Twenty years of Communist rule had created an authoritarian bureaucratic state and a centrally planned economy but precious little infrastructure, industrialization or growth. In 1965 the Communist Party acquired a new general secretary, General Nicolae Ceauşescu, who pursued a path of political independence from Moscow (denouncing the Soviet invasion of Czechoslovakia) and acquiring aid and trade deals with the West which helped stimulate the late industrialization and coercive urbanization of the country. Football, the national sport for many years, prospered on the back of the demographic changes this brought about. Moreover, the very low price of match tickets and the almost complete absence of alternative entertainment kept the stadiums full throughout the 1970s and 1980s. Football was so popular that it was one of the few areas in which opposition to the regime could be expressed. When in 1985 a live transmission of a double-header – Rapid vs. Steaua and Dinamo vs. Sportul – was cancelled, tens of thousands of disgruntled fans descended upon the stadium, broke through police lines and entered the stands. After the second game, there was a pitched battle outside between fans and police with a number of fatalities.

Ceauşescu, although hardly interested himself in football, understood its significance enough to make sure his home town of Scorniceşti had a football team fit for a president's birthplace. In the late 1970s FC Olt Scorniceşti won three successive promotions until it found itself in the top division. The abuse was flagrant. One promotion hinged on their game with Energia Slatina whom they needed to beat by a bigger score than that achieved by their promotion rivals Flacăra Moreni in their game. Olt led Slatina 1–0 at half-time. Reports then came in that Flacăra were 9–0 up, though in fact it was only 3–0; Olt went on to win 18–0. This kind of crass overkill was a *leitmotif* of Romanian public policy under Ceauşescu. Scorniceşti may have got itself a first-division team and a 20,000-seat stadium, but it was also subject to the forced collectivization of the 1980s. The local peasantry was forcibly relocated into concrete blocks that were dilapidated on their completion, turning a small market town into a sprawling slum.

The rest of the Romanian state apparatus were even more persistent in their involvement with football, particularly the leading Bucharest clubs. The army ran Steaua, the Securitate (the Ministry of the Interior's secret police force) ran Dinamo. Rapid was the fiefdom of the Ministry of Transport. Progresul, now FC Nacional, was linked, but only loosely, to one of the trade union federations, its partial autonomy attracting the disgruntled and the dismayed. Like Spartak Moscow under Stalin, support for Progresul was a way of saying 'a small no'. However, unlike Spartak, they had no Starostin and no powerful patrons. When Ceauşescu decided to build his grandiose folly, the Victory of Socialism Boulevard – a huge stretch of urban motorway, flanked by serried concrete towers and culminating in the gargantuan House of the Republic, then the third largest building in the world – 10,000 houses, ancient churches and Progresul's Republic Stadium were flattened in the process. Like many of the occupants of the demolished houses, Progresul were reduced to a life of temporary accommodation, displacement and decline.

The pre-eminent position of the Securitate in maintaining Ceauşescu's rule of terror was reflected in the football hierarchy where Dinamo Bucharest were clearly the dominant team of the 1970s and early 1980s. They were in receipt of the best players, favours and decisions. Steaua and its military masters were second best. Matters were reversed when in 1983 General Constantin Olteanu, Head of the Army Ministry, appointed Valentin Ceauşescu as Steaua's general manager. Valentin was a true fan, a nuclear physicist by training and the son of the President. It proved an inspired signing. Valentin devoted himself to the club, proving a competent, even workaholic manager as well as a powerfully connected patron. He effectively created the first Eastern European club to be run on real commercial lines, agreeing a sponsorship deal with Ford that his father vetoed, and planning the sale of their star Gheorghe Hagi to Juventus in return for the funding for a FIAT car plant in Bucharest. Dinamo and the Securitate did not yield their crown easily. They continued to bug Steaua's offices throughout the 1980s and tried to unsettle the Steaua club captain Tudor Stoica by having the local police arrest his father, a notorious drunk, in his home town of Galati. But for all this the balance of power in football, if not in politics, decisively shifted. Steaua won five successive championships from 1985 to 1989 and at one point went a ludicrous 104 games unbeaten in the domestic league.

The 1988 Romanian Cup Final underlined both this power shift and the now pathological consequences of persistent political interference. With injury-time approaching the score stood at Dinamo 1 Steaua 1. A goal from Steaua's Balint made it 2–1, but he was flagged offside. Most witnesses then report that Valentin Ceauşescu signalled from the stands for his players to leave the field, which they did, never to return. Officials, Dinamo players and the crowd stood around not knowing how to proceed. Perhaps the most effective if crude commentary on the matter came from Dinamo defender Ioan Andone, who dropped his shorts and waved his genitals at the VIP box. The referee abandoned the match and in the dressing rooms the trophy was presented to Dinamo. Matters were reversed the following day when the government ruled that the goal should have stood, the real score was 2–1 and Steaua were the winners. Steaua have, with uncommon good grace, since returned the cup and no winner is now recorded for that year's final.

That Steaua received considerable support from referees and government agencies is not in question. This should not, however, overshadow the extraordinary fact that in 1986 they became the first Eastern European side to win the European Cup – a competition where all their usual advantages were nullified. Steaua crept unnoticed past Kuusysi Lahti in the quarter-finals and Anderlecht in the semis and arrived in the final where they faced not just Barcelona, but Barcelona effectively playing at home in Seville. There were 70,000 for Barça and only 1,000 Romanians, and not all of them were there for the football. Alongside 200 Steaua officials there were 800 Securitate-vetted Communist Party members, 40 of whom defected. Steaua held out for a draw, took the game to penalties and watched Barcelona's confidence and shooting disintegrate. Bucharest erupted in the single greatest spontaneous outpouring of emotion since the Second World War. The army and Securitate, despite their nervousness, could not intervene, even when 30,000 marched to the airport to greet the team.

The win in 1986 was no fluke: Steaua made the semi-finals of the European Cup in 1988 and the final in 1989 where they were defeated by Arrigo Sacchi's AC Milan. They have not returned to such heights since, for within six months of the 1989 final Romania was in flames. Ceauşescu and his wife had been executed and the Securitate were running for their life. Valentin was saved by one of his own players, Marius Lăcătuş, who hid him in his apartment. Steaua Bucharest were perhaps the only real success of Ceauşescu's brutal mode of economic development, but the regime reaped no reward or favour from their victories which were competing with rationing, food shortages and the armed suppression of strikes for the public's attention. When the apparatus of fear was banished, it brought Romanian top-flight football tumbling down with it.

In 1974 the East German regime could be pleased with its new standing in European politics and European football. The *Ostpolitik* of Willy Brandt and his SPD successors in West Germany had brought about the official international recognition of the GDR, its sovereignty and borders confirmed and guaranteed. In May of that year 1.FC Magdeburg, a small provincial club with a team of virtual semi-professionals, won the European Cup Winners' Cup. That summer the national team, which had qualified for its first World Cup finals, had against all expectations beaten the West Germans 1–0 in the opening round of the tournament. Football was by some way the country's most popular spectator sport, and now it appeared to offer a glimpse of normality, a glimmer of national pride and celebration. Although the teams of the Stasi and the armed forces were deeply resented, there was space for clubs who were thought of as local standard bearers at one remove from the tentacles of the police state. In preference to BFC Dynamo from Berlin one could support 1.FC Union, instead of 1.FC Lokomotive Leipzig there was Chemie Leipzig. With the mass acquisition of television in the 1970s, and unrestricted access to West German signals, one could acquire allegiance to a Bundesliga team too – an act that was considered, if not treasonable, then certainly worrisome and decadent.

But East Germany's communists never quite got it with football. When Magdeburg won and the city celebrated through the night, the next day's papers displaced the triumph from the front page with photos of party functionaries celebrating the twenty-ninth anniversary of the Soviet liberation of the country. When Carl Zeiss Jena had the temerity to lose the Cup Winners' Cup Final in 1981 against Dinamo Tbilisi, they were treated as leprous class enemies. The national team, despite playing a marathon round of friendlies in the communist and non-aligned world, never played in an international tournament again. In part this was a consequence of the regime's relentless focus on Olympic sports. Under the auspices of DTSB (the German Athletic and Gymnastics Federation) and its boss Manfred Ewald the GDR turned itself into a global sporting superpower in swimming, athletics and gymnastics. In his memoirs, Ewald reflected on the irreconcilable differences between the GDR's socialist sports project and football: 'Football has its own special value: individualism and fanaticism are often stronger than discipline and rationalism.'[16] The game itself was not amenable to the kinds of super-disciplined programming that brought excellence in endurance and individual events. Teamwork and solidarity can be imposed but are the weaker for it. Spontaneity and individual initiative are vital resources in a game which changes its geometry and form so instantaneously, but these attributes were viewed with deep political suspicion. Football, one suspects, also proved less amenable to enhancement by pharmaceuticals, for it demands so many different and balanced qualities of its players that the super enhancement of one faculty or organ brings only fractional overall improvements.

What, in the end, destroyed the credibility and pleasures of East German football was the elevation of Dynamo Berlin, from being merely the best connected and resourced club, to being the only club to win anything. In the same way all remnants of the regime's legitimacy were shredded by the web of surveillance, control and manipulation that spread out from the Stasi, through every organ of the state and into the personal lives, loves and homes of around one-third of the entire population. The descent into this monopoly of poisonous power began in 1978. Dynamo Dresden had clinched the league title and were celebrating in their dressing room. Enter Erich Mielke, the Minister of State Security, head of the Stasi and president of Dynamo Berlin. He was reported to have told the Dresden squad that it was now Berlin's turn. Dynamo Berlin won the next ten East German championships. The cheating and bias was so crass and obvious that even the usually ultra-supine press were complaining, and other leading members of the *nomenklatura* with a stake in football went public with their dismay. It made no difference, Dynamo Berlin kept winning. But if the Stasi could block any political or sporting countermove to their rule from above, they proved unable to comprehend or quell a small, ugly but vociferous protest from below.

In the late 1970s the Stasi were perplexed by the emergence of East German variants of Western European youth subcultures. On the streets of Berlin, in the parks of Leipzig, Honecker's children took up the sartorial styles, smuggled music and public postures of skinheads, punks, rockers and heavy metal kids. Skinheads, again taking their cue from the West, gravitated towards football where low-level disorder had been stirring for some time. Unofficial supporters' clubs had begun to develop in the mid-1970s especially around trips to away games. In a society in which foreign travel was difficult and most journeys trailed, the trip to Erfurt or Frankfurt an der Oder with your crew looked like a freedom ride. All of these groups were monitored, many had informers placed inside or drafted into their midst, but as quickly as the Stasi neutralized their independence other groups would emerge.

Although the 1970s saw minor forms of vandalism among these groups, an occasional pitch invasion, fighting in stadiums and anti-regime chanting, the arrival of the skinheads in the early 1980s upped the ante. The numbers involved in violent acts increased, their militancy and organization rose and they introduced a previously hidden but deeply rooted and disturbing far-right politics to football grounds, combining neo-Nazism, anti-Semitism and racism in equal measure. At Dynamo Berlin's ground away fans were heard singing, 'Zyklon B for BFC' and 'My father was an SS soldier'; while midweek the same gangs would engage in attacks on the Angolan, Mozambican and Vietnamese communities in the big cities.

The Stasi, for all their vaunted powers, were perplexed. These people could not actually be connected with external fascist powers or imperialist Western plots. They could not be coerced and frightened in the same way that the rest of the population had been corralled. Few would turn informer, and authentic entry by outsiders into the subculture was difficult. They had so little real organization that there was nothing to smash and yet when they massed together inside and outside the stadium club stewards and the police seemed reluctant or powerless to effectively stop them. With arrests running at over 1,000 a year in the late 1980s and recorded violent incidents many times that, football hooliganism appeared the most immediate threat to public order – a threat that peaked in 1988 at the cup final between Dynamo Berlin and Carl Zeiss Jena when over 150 skinheads marched through the city before fighting their way through the fixture chanting fascist slogans. It is testament to the regime's self-hypnosis, duplicity and double-think that for all this, it never once managed to identify its own role in undermining competitive football's legitimacy and alienating its own citizens.

VII

Two months after the Bradford fire and the Heysel disaster, the British Home Secretary Leon Brittan announced the Conservative government's White Paper on public order and policing like this:

People have the right to protection against being bullied, hurt, intimidated or obstructed, whatever the motive of those responsible may be, whether they are violent demonstrators, rioters, intimidatory mass pickets or soccer hooligans.[17]

The Thatcher government and its allies perceived football through the same bullish authoritarian lens that they viewed all opposition: hooligans, miners, unions, peace activists, terrorists were all of a piece. Although the main weapon in this authoritarian response to the crisis of football violence, the planned football ID card scheme, collapsed under its own administrative impossibility, there was a less tangible legacy: a widespread culture and expectation among all ranks of the police that football matches were not primarily a matter of public-safety management but a coercive exercise in imposing order on anarchy. Although few football clubs had gone as far as Chelsea's chairman

Ken Bates, who had considered installing electrified perimeter fences at Stamford Bridge, they were effectively complicit in the culture of neglect, disrespect and disdain. Stewarding arrangements were unsophisticated, even primitive, while first aid and medical services remained sparse and ludicrously overreliant on the voluntary St John Ambulance Brigade. Above all the decrepit stadium infrastructure, from perilously narrow approach roads to sticky turnstiles, from rusting crush barriers to cracked terracing, remained unaltered. The only significant change came in the architecture of segregation, control and surveillance. CCTV cameras arrived, perimeter fences got spikes and the terraces were increasingly divided into smaller high-fenced cages, which suggested a mode of crowd control that took the livestock market and the slaughterhouse as its model.

The language of police operations was even more explicit. Fans were to be fenced in, crowds herded. The mob was to be rounded up at key points – railway stations, approach roads, motorway services – and escorted to and from the ground. As with any herd, stragglers and misbehaviour would need dealing with; the prevailing culture accepted the need to 'go in hard' where and when necessary. Fans were assumed to have a predisposition towards violence, and a predilection for excessive alcohol consumption, until proved otherwise. It was in this context that Liverpool were drawn to meet Nottingham Forest in the semi-final of the FA Cup at Hillsborough on 15 April 1989.

The South Yorkshire police appointed as the commanding officer for the day Superintendent Duckenfield, a man who had no experience of command at a football match let alone a sell-out FA Cup semi-final. It is also clear that he had no more than a passing knowledge of the operational plan, or the range of warning signs and problems identified by the South Yorkshire police during the FA Cup semi-finals played at Hillsborough in the previous two years. A cursory examination of the ground plan would have revealed the core of the problem: 25,000 fans would be entering the Leppings Lane end of the ground and given previous experience most of them would do so in the forty-five minutes before kick-off. They would come in through a series of small iron gates and find themselves in one of two irregular walled courtyards served by twenty-three turnstiles. The rest of the ground, which held 29,000 people, was served by almost triple the number of turnstiles.

Half an hour before the game the larger of the two courtyards became extraordinarily full, the police having made no effort to control or filter the flow of fans into Leppings Lane or the courtyards. A sudden change of atmosphere came over the yards as fans and police struggled for space and breath. Some had already taken to climbing over the turnstiles, and the police continued to treat the situation as an exercise in riot control using mounted officers in the midst of the crowd. After much vacillation, the order was given to open a number of side gates and allow the crowd to flood into the stadium. Inside the ground, at the Leppings Lane end, there had already been a substantial build-up of fans in the small cages behind the goal; indeed before the courtyard crush had developed it was getting very full. Neither police nor stewards had taken any action to divert the crowd who were coming from the turnstiles through the main tunnel into the emptier side pens. The courtyard crowd came piling down the tunnel and headed straight for the light and the central over-loaded pens. The crush, like a relentless vice, tightened and pressed those closest to the front.

Many officers at the ground panicked or froze, others seemed to persist in the engrained belief that the problem was fighting or alcohol. The few who did respond to the gravity of the situation were, in the absence of orders from above, unable to open the locked perimeter gates that would have allowed fans out of the pens to relieve the pressure behind them. Supporters were the first to act, desperately trying to pull people up and into the tier above or over the fence. Incredibly, the game had kicked-off but was abandoned after six minutes, the players left the pitch to jeers from the Nottingham Forest end who still appeared to assume that a fight had broken out. By the time the gates in the perimeter fence were opened the vast majority of the ninety-six who would perish had already died. There were over 400 other injuries.

As people tumbled out of the pens and on to the pitch the immediate response to the needs of the dead and injured was totally chaotic and devoid of serious leadership. It comprised the desperate efforts of an ad hoc crew of police, supporters and medical professionals who had come to the game. Advertising hoardings were ripped down as impromptu stretchers; survivors wept, wandered, screamed, lay down and passed out. Now, live on TV, the country watched the dead bodies lined up on the ground before being moved to the morgue established in Sheffield Wednesday's gymnasium. It took a long political and judicial struggle to establish what was common knowledge on the day: that what had killed ninety-six people was not the responsibility of the violent and

drunken dregs of the working classes but directly stemmed from the
grotesque assumptions and beliefs of the police, and from the neglect
and disdain of the football and political elites who had come to view
football supporters as pack animals and rabid dogs.

If Hillsborough set the seal on a decade of English decline and despair,
the next fourteen months saw Italian clubs win five out of the six
European club tournaments: Napoli and Juventus in the UEFA Cup,
Sampdoria the Cup Winners' Cup in 1990, and Milan two consecutive
European Cups. This set the seal on the nation's comprehensive domination of European football, a process that would be crowned by hosting
the World Cup in June 1990. Yet at the same time this was a moment
of closure: the shape of a new Europe and the new football of the 1990s
and the twenty-first century were emerging. In the limbo between the
death of the old order and the emergence of the new, the Astra TV
satellite was launched, the first link in the digital television networks of
the following decade that would once again revolutionize the economics
of football. Then in December 1989 the Berlin Wall fell and initiated
the landslide of political and social change that would terminate communist rule in Eastern and Central Europe, end the Cold War, unify Germany and transform the map of Europe: Yugoslavia, the USSR and
Czechoslovakia would all make their last appearance in these guises at
the 1990 World Cup.

Our hosts for the World Cup at this historical turning point were the
Italian local organizing committee known as COL, its public face and
internal machinations a perfect example of the deceptively sleek Italian
corporation whose surface modernity thinly masked its subterranean
chaos and corruption. The man in charge was Luca Cordero di Montez-
emolo, who had cut his teeth as manager of Ferrari's Formula One team
and Italy's entry in the America's Cup yacht race; the man, the sports and
the events sat at the intersection of television, show business, politics,
conspicuous consumption and hi-tech fantasy. Beyond the glitz the
essential dynamic of Italia '90's management was a shameless commercialism whose neo-liberal business-school argot did not prevent the
uptake of vast quantities of public subsidy. The Italian state spent
billions of lire on the World Cup, COL raised another 60 billion lire in
sponsorship from Italian companies – and they still lost money.

The tournament was always conceived as an opportunity to flaunt the quality and design skills of Italian industry. At their best the major stadium programmes undertaken did precisely that; at their worst they revealed rather more about Italy's political economy than the COL had perhaps intended. Costs of all the stadiums spiralled uncontrollably upwards: in Turin the Stadio delle Alpi came in at three times its original budget. Despite such generosity, projects were delayed, endlessy revised and completion schedules were perilously tight. During a FIFA inspection before the tournament, one of the cantilevers for the new roof in Palermo collapsed, killing four workers and injuring a number of others. The following day seven of the cantilevers collapsed. Although there were no fatalities this time, overall the stadium-construction programme claimed over twenty fatalities.

In Bari COL created a classic 'cathedral in the desert'. Renzo Piano, a high priest of modernist architecture, was commissioned to build a 60,000-capacity stadium for a city of just 365,000 people and a home team that was only on passing acquaintance with top-division football. Stadio San Nicola fulfilled its brief as a political totem for the local Christian Democrats who orchestrated its creátion, and its car-parking, access roads and hidden tunnels for emergency services and team coaches were exemplary. To accommodate an undulating roof around the pitch, the key concrete components of each segment of the stadium were individually cast to the highest levels of precision and given, unusually for any stadium, a highly finished surface. Since hosting the 1991 European Cup Final, however, the stadium has remained embarrassingly underused, and Bari has been promoted and relegated from Serie A five times. In Turin they managed to build a stadium that nobody liked and subsequently no one would go to. Torino preferred to rebuild the Stadio Filadelfia. Juventus preferred an expanded Stadio Comunale. What they got was the soulless Stadio delle Alpi, stuck on the northern fringes of the city, virtually inaccessible by public transport.

Milan's San Siro had barely been touched since its reopening in 1955. FIFA's insistence that the major stadiums be fully seated and predominantly roofed presented an immensely complex and difficult design challenge to the Milanese if they were to retain the core of the old stadium and its emblematic candy-stripe walkways. The solution was spectacular, grandiose and expensive. Eleven concrete towers were erected around the edge of the old San Siro to support a new third tier of seats. Each tower was wrapped in its own helical spiral of white concrete walkways providing a kaleidoscopic mixture of diagonal lines and ascending and descending curves. The four largest towers actually poked their way up through the second tier and then the third tier. Atop the four corners a vast grid of steel girders was put in place and a Plexiglas roof slung across it leaving a central open rectangle precisely above the pitch. The stage was remarkable but ever since the grass on the pitch would not grow, so they have had to relay the turf up to three times a year.

In the final days before the tournament began, the sleek surface of the country's preparations was beginning to crack; the immense expansion in media and TV coverage of the tournament was creating what one participant described as 'an unreality zone of media and marketing mayhem, a land of hysterical fantasy' – a combustible brew that was laced with a touch of apocalypse. The Italian authorities and press appeared to be preparing for the worst, detecting both the enemy without and the enemy within. The enemy without was the foreign football hooligan, principally the English. The collective memory of Heysel and the enduring crowd trouble around England games since made the Italians acutely sensitive to the dangers of violence and disorder around England games. Indeed, in parallel with the British press they steadily transformed a sense of foreboding into fully fledged panic. Worse, the Dutch, whose reputation abroad veered between thuggery and carnival, were drawn in the same group. Together with the Irish and the Egyptians they were banished to the badlands of the south in Sicily and Sardinia. The English did not disappoint. The stadiums remained relatively trouble-free, but as the long hot days passed in free-flowing drinking, England's drunken, combustible support was perfect tinder for the few firms, both impromptu and organized, who were up for a ruck, and the Carabinieri too appeared enthusiastic about the prospect.

The England fans rose above the scuffles and drunken fighting in Sardinia; coach Bobby Robson finally rose above the incessant and insidious carping of the English press corps and the team rose above their earlier frailties to play open attacking football. Back home, they captured the public imagination like no team since the 1970 World Cup. When the teenage Paul Gascoigne received a yellow card putting him out of the final should England qualify, and shed tears, the English melted. Pearce and Waddle blasted their penalties wide and over and West Germany were through to the final.

*

Napoli's much disputed championship victory in 1990 served as a lightning rod for wider political discontent in the north of the country, and was emblematic of the political and fiscal chicanery and cheating of the south. In the municipal elections which immediately preceded the tournament, Umberto Bossi's Northern League made another leap forward in votes and prominence. Antipathy towards the republic was sufficiently high that some Milan *ultras* declared their support for the Dutch whose key players – Gullit, Rijkaard and Van Basten – all played for Milan, while some *interisti* backed the West Germans who fielded their three stars – Klinsmann, Brehme and Matthäus. Fiorentina supporters found it hard to support an Italian side which fielded Juve's Roberto Baggio, who had, against all promise and expectation, been transferred between the clubs at the end of the season. The move prompted widespread rioting in central Florence. Into this cauldron of anger and disenchantment Maradona made it known that he thought Neapolitans would be better off backing him and the Argentines rather than the Azzurri.

Expectations of the Italian national team under Azeglio Vicini were high; its results preceding the tournament were excellent. The squad seemed to offer the regional variety of specialisms characteristic of Italy: a parsimonious Milanese defence from Inter and Milan, hard-working midfielders like Ancelotti and incisive passers like Roberto Baggio and the aristocratic Vialli from Sampdoria. But in the opening game against Austria the Italians were nervous, cramped and above all, goalless. Late in the second half Vicini introduced the little-known Salvatore Schillaci – known by his diminutive, Toto. A Sicilian of exceptionally humble origins, he had steadily worked his way up through amateur football, Serie C, Serie B, before his transfer to Juventus the previous year. In the 79th minute he scored the game's only goal. Against the USA the original line-up struggled to another unconvincing 1–0 win. Given their chance, the new front line of Toto and Roberto Baggio took Italy to a 2–0 win over Czechoslovakia and then overcame Uruguay and Ireland to reach the semi-finals. In an era of instant hype, over-expectation and national division, Toto became the touchstone of a short-lived but intense Italian national experience. The good immigrant, the hard-working southerner made good, the modest working-class boy who had prospered, he evoked the unequal but mutually beneficial relationship of southern labour and northern capital in the golden era.

Beyond the progress of the Italian team the reality of the spectacle was underwhelming. The progress of Cameroon and Ireland to the quarter-finals was good for the underdogs but the football was meagre fare. Cameroon were tough and uncompromising, the Irish invariably negative and one-dimensional. The Brazilians were among the crabbiest and most defensive to represent the nation, both England and West Germany periodically reverted to five-man defences and sweepers, and the Argentinians, having recovered from their opening and humiliating defeat by Cameroon, scratched and clawed their way back into the competition. The semi-finals were the peak. In Turin the English and the West Germans relived all of their military and sporting history in the tournament's epic, a 1–1 draw that went to penalties. Argentina were drawn to meet Italy in Naples, and the smouldering national question was reignited. Antonio Matarrese, a Christian Democrat parliamentarian, publicly called for the city to reject Maradona and embrace the national team. In a moment of singular lucidity and eloquence, Maradona retorted:

For 364 days out of the year you are considered to be foreigners in your own country; today you must do what they want by supporting the Italian team. Instead, I am a Neapolitan for 365 days out of the year.[18]

It made for a compelling encounter, in which the reactions of the Neapolitans were watched as closely as the game on the field. The Neapolitans sang the national anthem, but they could not bring themselves to boo Diego. It was rough and often ugly. The Italians had most of the game, but Argentina as ever took the tiny scraps offered to them, scraping an equalizer, surviving extra time with ten men and putting their penalties away.

The world gathered to watch the worst final ever. A single German penalty deflated the bubble of theatrical rancour that passed for Argentinian football that evening.

15

Military Manoeuvres: Football under the Latin American Generals, 1974–1990

Well known that as result fascist upheaval overthrown legal government national unity now in chili reveals atmosphere bloody terrorism and repressions COMMA

National stadium supposed be venue hold football match turned by military junta into concentration camp place of tortures and executions of Chilean patriots STOP

Soviet sportsmen cannot at present play at stadium stained with the blood of Chilean patriots STOP

Telegram from Soviet Football Federation
to FIFA President Sir Stanley Rous, 27 October 1973

I

After making the semi-finals of the 1962 World Cup on home soil, Chile performed indifferently four years later and failed to qualify for the 1970 finals, while its leading clubs made no impact beyond the country's borders. But in 1973 things appeared to be turning. Colo Colo, the most popular team in Santiago, had made it to the final of the Copa Libertadores and had only lost to the seasoned Argentine side Independiente in a tie-breaking game in Montevideo. The national team too had beaten off Peru to win a place in a play-off against the USSR for the last berth at the 1974 World Cup. The upsurge in Chilean football had its political corollary, if not its cause, in the Unidad Popular government of Salvador Allende, which had unleashed a programme of radical reform in Chile.

In 1970 Allende, the candidate of the Unidad Popular, had won a close-fought election for the presidency. Latin America's first elected self-proclaimed Marxist government took power and despite opposition from within the army and Congress set about pursuing a strategy of radical but legal change. The country's copper industry, coal mines, steel plants, railways and many of the banks were nationalized. Encouraged by their own government, striking workers and radical trade unions called for further takeovers, and the nationalization of Ford and ITT Chile followed. Wages were increased, prices were frozen and a massive programme of land reform was initiated. By early 1973 the economy had succumbed to roaring inflation, lines of international credit were closing and the massed ranks of industrialists, landowners and conservative bureaucrats were sabotaging and contesting every move of the government. Protest in Santiago by supporters and opponents of the regime was becoming a daily and bitterly fought occurrence. Shut-downs in the copper mines and land occupations by the peasantry were matched by strikes and marches from middle-class associations such as the architects and the dentists, truck owners and shopkeepers. Inside the army the old constitutionalist chief-of-staff General Carlos Prats was deposed and replaced by General Augusto Pinochet, a man of decidedly different political opinions. With the support of the US administration, the armed forces acted. On 11 September 1973 the air force set the presidential palace in Santiago ablaze and Allende, after scorning the opportunity of safe passage to exile, shot himself in the head.

Resistance from the Left was unarmed, uncoordinated and ineffective. The military began a nationwide trawl for subversives. Communists, trade unionists and political activists of almost every hue were swept into a network of large and small detention centres, the most important of which was the Estadio Nacional. Opened in 1938, the Estadio Nacional had established itself as a central part of life in Santiago. After the Second World War it had been used as a clearing house for refugees from Europe. It had hosted concerts and performances of every kind. It was home to the national team, the club side Universidad de Chile, the team of Santiago's intelligentsia, and had hosted the 1962 World Cup Final. Over the next eight weeks more than 12,000 (perhaps as many as 20,000) people passed through the stadium complex; at its peak up to 7,000 were squeezed into its labyrinthine rooms. It served as a detention centre and a torture house. Men and women were herded into the underground maze of dressing rooms and offices, left to starve, subjected to brutal tortures and interrogation and underwent mock firing squads; others were simply executed. Guitarists had their fingers broken and were then asked to perform. The military played the Beatles at full volume from their mobile megaphones to drown out the screams; friends and families gathered outside the newly erected rolls of barbed wire to hear the news of their loved ones. In the 1990s Chile's own human rights commission conservatively put the death toll at forty-one. Others have suggested it was more likely to have been in the hundreds, with many bodies dumped in the Mapocho River or in the gutters of the city's alleyways. Amazingly the regime allowed a visit to the stadium by human rights organizations and the international press on 22 September. Despite the stage management of the event they were not fooled. The air of blood and brutality was tangible.

Four days later the Chilean national team played the USSR in the first leg of their World Cup qualifying play-off and ground out a 0–0 draw in Moscow. The return match was planned for 21 November. Within days the Soviets and their allies in East Germany, Africa and Asia began to petition FIFA, arguing that at the very least the game had to be moved to a neutral venue. FIFA responded by sending a fact-finding mission in early October 1973. It is hard to determine the exact proportions of the duplicity, complicity and sheer naivety that informed the glib and sanitized response of FIFA's inquisitors. Stewarded by the factotums of the new regime, they wrote:

As mentioned before, the stadium is at present being used as a clearing station and the people in there are not prisoners but only detainees whose identity has to be established ... the stadium is under military guard and entry is only with a special pass. Inside the outer fencing everything appears to be normal and gardeners are working on the gardens. Inside the stadium itself the seats and pitches were empty and the remaining detainees were in the dressing room and other rooms. The grass on the pitch is in perfect condition as were the seating arrangements ... Outside the stadium approximately 50–100 people were waiting for news of the relatives who were still detained.[1]

The Soviet telegram that opened this chapter was the last word from Moscow. The East Germans wrote to Sir Stanley Rous asking whether he would contemplate holding a game in Dachau. But FIFA merely responded by pointing out the contents of Article 22 of their statutes: 'If a team does not report for a match – except in the case of *force majeure*, accepted by the organizing committee ... the team shall be considered as having lost.'[2] The game went ahead. The Soviets stayed at home.

---

21 November 1973
Chile 1 USSR 0
Estadio Nacional, Santiago

This is a game beyond metaphor. Its evil is real. Beneath the pitch in the impromptu holding pens and torture chambers are the remnants of Santiago's radicals. Pinochet and his kind are not content merely to handicap their opponents, or subject them to systematic bias; they do not intend to play that game any more. They are going to eradicate the opposition altogether.

The Chilean team and the match officials take to the pitch but the Soviets are not there. A smattering of people are on the terraces, but they make no noise. Many, heads in hands, do not seem to be watching at all. The touchline is ringed by impassive soldiers. The Chileans pass the ball among themselves before rolling the ball over the line. The game ends.

———

So Chile made it to the World Cup. In Germany the local riot police kept the protests of exiles and supporters away from the television cameras, Chile lost to the hosts and managed just two uninspiring draws against the East Germans and the Australians. The squad went home to a country in which all normal forms of democratic politics and civic association had been banned or crushed. Pinochet erected a regime of systematic terror and unusual brutality. Political authoritarianism was then complemented by a bone-dry economic liberalism. All of the Allende reforms, industrial and agricultural, were reversed. Trade unions and peasants' organizations were eviscerated; nationalized industries and redistributed land were returned to their previous owners.

The blood was washed off the walls of the Estadio Nacional and although the national team would make an undistinguished appearance at the 1982 World Cup, football became moribund. The incredible austerity programme imposed upon the population by Pinochet's American-trained economic technocrats saw clubs struggle to survive and attendances at football matches collapse. Colo Colo's board took out the insurance policy of making Pinochet the club's honorary president and in turn arrangements were made between the club and the regime's favourite financial institution, the bank HBC, to keep it afloat. Similar arrangements were made in other countries between military rulers and the so-called people's team in the capital city: Paraguay's General Stroessner was honorary president of Olimpia; Ecuador's military actually had their own team, El Nacional; Uruguay's Junta kept out of the boardroom but bailed out Peñarol from two of their many episodes of penury. However, for those outside the charmed circle life could be more difficult. Universidad de Chile, Colo Colo's eternal Santiago opponents, failed to win a single title under the dictatorship. In Chile the only new source of funding in football came from the privatized copper industries of the north that backed the tiny Cobreloa club from the mining town of Calama; they alone in Chilean football made an international impact, losing two Copa Libertadores finals in the early 1980s. Elsewhere crowds were sporadically violent or depressingly muted.

Perhaps their silence had emboldened Pinochet. He held a referendum in 1988 asking the Chilean public to confirm him in power – and they said no. For once outmanoeuvred, the general was forced to step down in 1989, though not without securing his own position as commander-in-chief of the army and the legal immunity of himself and the killers in his entourage. The return of democracy was not matched by a return to footballing success. In September 1989 Chile faced Brazil in the Maracanã in a decisive World Cup qualifier. The Chileans were 1–0 down and looking like they would take a hammering in the final twenty minutes of the game when goalkeeper Roberto Rojas appeared to be struck by a smoking firecracker thrown on to the pitch. With blood streaming from his head, a brawl among the players rapidly escalated into a free-for-all, followed by a dramatic walkout of the Chileans and their officials helping Rojas from the field. In fact Rojas had pulled a razor blade from his glove as he hit the floor and sliced himself in the hope of getting a replay; the firework never touched him. Brazil were awarded the game, Chile were out of one World Cup and excluded from the next, Rojas was banned for life and the woman who threw the firecracker was signed up by *Playboy* Brazil. FIFA lifted the ban in 2001. 'At 43, I'm unlikely to play again,' said Rojas, then coach at São Paulo, 'but at least this pardon will cleanse my soul.'[3] A few months after the national team's disgrace, Patricio Aylwyn was inaugurated in the Estadio Nacional as Chile's first democratically elected president for twenty years. But neither Catholic prelates nor football matches could begin to exorcize the demons and the ghosts that still lingered.

With the fall of the Allende government in 1973 Chile joined Bolivia, Brazil, Paraguay and Peru in the military camp of Latin American dictatorships. As the 1974 oil-price hike and global economic recession dragged down the already fragile economies of the region, Uruguay and Argentina – beset by social conflict and small guerrilla armies – would join them. Latin American football received its own sharp shock from

Europe at the 1974 World Cup. Chile, unable to score against the Australians, were dismal. Uruguay, Argentina and Brazil all disappointed and all were beaten by the amazing Holland. In the opening round the Uruguayans tried to kick the Dutch off the field, but Cruyff ran rings around them. With an almost careless touch, a casual and cruel arrogance, Rep scored twice. The best the Uruguayans could manage was violence: Montero-Castillo punched Rensenbrink in the stomach and walked. Forlán should have done so for a brutal kick on Neeskens. The Swedes took the battering, scored three goals and then sent the Uruguayans home. They would not return to the World Cup for twelve years.

Argentina scrambled through the early matches, losing to Poland, drawing with Italy and surviving by beating Haiti. But the pretensions of the side were destroyed by the Dutch who beat them 4–0. Hard tackling and swift pressing brusquely pushed the Argentinians aside. In possession the Dutch attack appeared unstoppable, Cruyff's versatility and range highlighted by his dribbling around the keeper for his first goal and finding an impossible angle for his shot to score the fourth goal. After that Argentina failed to beat East Germany. Finally Brazil met Holland in what was in effect the semi-final. They were outplayed, outfought and out-toughed by the Dutch who gave a display of skilled but very forceful football.

The responses of Latin America's footballing elite to this debacle differed. In Brazil, forced to yield their title, the impact was sharpest, the blow to their collective confidence greatest; the philosophical debate between *futebol arte* and *futebol força*, already drifting in the direction of the latter, shifted even further. Aided by the military's own obsession with physicality, muscle and scientifically rigorous training, many Brazilian players ran further and faster, bulked up and played tough. In Uruguay the same debate was conducted in a minor key but the national team under Omar Borrás in the 1980s suggested that the triumph of force over art was even greater here. In both countries the dull hand of militarism and the brutalization of social relations hung over the football field.

Argentina's response was different. The already significant physicality in the Argentine game, exemplified by Juan Carlos Lorenzo's Boca Juniors, twice winners of the Copa Libertadores in the late 1970s, was deemed sufficient. What the Dutch and the Germans had shown in 1974 was the importance of pace and tempo. The man who now injected a greater pace and tempo into the Argentinian game was César Luis Menotti. *El Flaco* – the skinny one – had been a cultured and bohemian midfielder at Rosario Central but had also played in Spain and the USA. Menotti came to prominence as a coach when he took the small Buenos Aires side Huracán to a completely unexpected national championship in 1973 and was then made national team coach in anticipation of the 1978 World Cup. Like a philosopher-prince, Menotti expounded a vision of Argentinian football that was true to its *portero* roots (kick-abouts on waste ground), unwavering in its commitment to the game as a popular spectacle but updated and adapted to the fitness levels and more furious pace of the advanced industrial football of Northern Europe.

However, the liberties and luxuries of Menotti's personal and practical bohemianism always had their critics in Argentinian football, and after his failure in the 1982 World Cup campaign the post passed to his nemesis, Carlos Bilardo. Bilardo was schooled in the *anti-fútbol* of Zubeldia's Estudiantes and though he did not field teams of such unrestrained malice his commitment to winning over art, of the collective over the individual, was forcibly and starkly stated: 'I like being first . . . Because second is no good, being second is a failure . . . for me it's good that if you lose you should feel bad.'[4] In the increasingly bitter conflict between the two men and between these two polar opposites in Argentina's football culture, the sporting and rhetorical record was inconclusive. Like Menotti, Bilardo's record was one World Cup won and one lost. Menotti, the lover of the spectacle and the flamboyant, could not find a place in his squad for Maradona and when he did could not get the best from him. Bilardo, the cynical collectivist, built teams around Maradona's individual brilliance. Bilardo's team at the 1990 World Cup may have sunk to the level of street fighting but Menotti's 1978 side were also capable of calculated spite and gamesmanship. And ironically, Menotti, a man of noted left-wing sympathies and the coded standard bearer for an older, freer Argentina, won the World Cup for the Junta; Bilardo, the ultra-authoritarian manager, won it under Argentina's new democracy. Menotti has argued subsequently that:

Many people could say that I have coached teams during the time of dictatorships, in an epoch when Argentina had governments with which I had nothing in common, and even more, they contradicted my way of life. And I ask what should I have done? Coach teams to play badly, to base everything on tricks, to betray the feelings of the people? No, of course not.[5]

It became abundantly clear in the 1980s that the Latin American military regimes were actually incapable of resolving the political and economic problems that beset their nations. During this brutal interlude they had crushed armed left-wing and rural insurgencies, but the creation of a sustainable authoritarian politics in the face of Latin America's gyrating economies and exploding cities was impossible. What began with the triumph of the military, confident that the application of force was a substitute for the art of politics, ended with them running back to the simplicities and certitudes of life in the barracks.

In 1973 Perón returned from exile in Spain to Eziza airport in Buenos Aires, where cadres of the leftist Peronist Youth movement and gangs of right-wing ultra-nationalist Peronistas had gathered. Before his plane touched down the two wings of Peronism were locked in armed combat. His plane landed elsewhere. It made little difference wherever Perón had chosen to place himself; Argentina was a vortex of industrial and political conflict. His predecessor Campora had negotiated a fragile social pact between industrialists and labour. Soaring inflation and the oil-price hike unravelled it within a few months. Strikes proliferated and turned into mass factory occupations. The nation's oil fields fell to worker councils, syndicalist unions emerged and armed guerrilla groups in both town and country grew in support and boldness. The response of the army and police force was brutal but uncoordinated, and into the vacuum stepped an array of right-wing death squads protecting property and looking for students and radicals.

Perón's health deteriorated rapidly. He died in July 1974 and was succeeded by his widow and third wife Isabelita Perón, originally a nightclub dancer who had met Perón in Panama soon after he began his exile. Government descended into an unholy scramble for power and influence over the frightened and inexperienced *La Presidenta* who was utterly unequipped to negotiate the treacherous waters of Argentina's declining economy, incipient civil war and fracturing Peronista party. In the early months of the new government there was a desperate lurch to the Right, increasingly violent crackdowns on unions and dissidents and an inflation rate of over 300 per cent.

Argentina's football and its World Cup preparations were swept into this chaotic and ungovernable maw. The impossibility of exercising any authority in Argentina was painfully illustrated by the experience of referees and their assistants. In 1973 there had been a protracted officials' strike after a linesman had been heavily beaten on the touchline by fans at Huracán. In a game in Rosario in 1974 between Rosario Central and Newell's Old Boys the score stood at 2–2. Referee Álvarez gave the visitors a disputed penalty in the final minute of the match. A riot ensued almost immediately, five police officers were hurt, and the referee was hit in the eye by a stone and needed an operation that afternoon. Worse was to come. Under an old and ambiguous 'Sports Fraud law' charges were brought against Álvarez by the police in Rosario for fraudulent refereeing of the game. We can assume that the police had plenty of support and advice from Newell's officials. Álvarez was subsequently held in jail until another referees' strike and the widespread threat of a players' strike saw him released. A Mendozan lawyer, Alfredo Goméz Chair, also brought charges of sports fraud against a referee after Gimnasia y Esgrima Mendoza had lost to Estudiantes. Goméz was not even in the stadium in Buenos Aires but at home in Mendoza listening to the commentary on the radio. Violence at football games began to rise. When Boca Juniors played Central Norte in Salta the game was abandoned after tear-gas canisters were fired all round the stadium. The players and referees were corralled by a hail of stones into the centre circle where they remained for three hours as the riot took its course.

And all the time the books of every club were getting redder and redder. The belated attempt to create a national championship incorporating Buenos Aires and the teams of the small cities of the coast and the interior made matters worse, as crowds were often small and air tickets expensive. Successive governments initiated a series of price freezes to try and control inflation, and football tickets were included. Income and outgoings were just not matching up. And yet in this unstable climate Boca Juniors launched the most economically and architecturally quixotic plan in Argentine football in a long time. Trapped in the narrow confines of La Boca in central Buenos Aires, the club proposed building not merely a new stadium but a vast entertainment and multi-sport complex. More than that, they wanted to build it on an artificial island made of reclaimed land in the Río de la Plata. Documents were issued, designs presented and a massive bond issue was made to finance the development. But the stadium was never built. Less than a decade later, like most Argentine investments, the bonds were virtually worthless. Architects argued that the complex would have sunk through the soft reclaimed earth and back into the river.

It was not as if Argentina had not had a long time to prepare for hosting the World Cup. They had been awarded the hosting rights to the 1978 event in 1964 at FIFA's Tokyo congress. But by the time of Perón's death little had been achieved beyond deciding that the country would somehow find the money for three completely new stadiums in cities with minuscule football teams – Mendoza, Mar del Plata and Córdoba; facelifts for other stadiums in Rosario and Buenos Aires; and a major upgrade of air, road and telecommunications links throughout the country. Money was meant to be coming in from the recently established football pools, but somehow it never quite managed to arrive. Organizing committees and executive officers came and went, at a speed that made mainstream politics look placid. By 1975 the fifth World Cup organizing committee had been formed, headed by the football authorities, but its precise remit and lines of authority were crossed by a parallel committee formed by the Ministry of Tourism. Almost nothing had been definitely decided, let alone done, apart from the award and receipt of some very exceptional committee expenses. FIFA's visits to review the preparations verged on the farcical; one trip to a park in Mendoza that would be cleared for a stadium that was not yet designed and no visit at all to Mar del Plata owing to transport problems. Then the generals, in a widely predicted and for some deeply appreciated move, took control.

Civilian government crumbled at the merest push from the military and in March 1976 General Jorge Videla convened the first meeting of the new executive power in the land, colloquially known as *La Junta*. Items for discussion included the prosecution of an all-out war against terrorists, subversives, guerrillas and radicals of all kinds. Plans for a more systematic and aggressive liberal economic policy were set out; then there was the small matter of the World Cup. The political implications of the event and the disastrous state of preparations were of such importance to the generals that they immediately announced the formation of Ente Autárquico Mundial (EAM) under General Omar Actis, charged with the preparations for the Mundial. On his way to his first press conference Actis was assassinated with a bullet from a rifle. The Junta blamed the Montoneros guerrilla groups, but Actis was succeeded by the man most likely to have ordered the execution, Admiral Carlos Alberto Lacoste. Lacoste, together with sidekick Admiral Emilio Eduardo Massera, ran the show and skimmed many millions of dollars off the top of every contract and deal the World Cup required.

The generals set about their tasks that they loftily entitled *Proceso de Reorganización Nacional* – the Process of National Reorganization – but widely known by its more sinister diminutive *El Proceso*. Without regard to domestic or international opinion the Junta launched a systematic dirty war against what was left of the EPZ rural revolt in the north and the Montoneros urban guerrilla movement in the cities. The military then extended the war to include the eradication of all political opposition: radicals, students and workers. Suspects were identified, rounded up, often tortured and many were killed. The precise count will never be known but somewhere between 20 and 30,000 people disappeared. Simultaneously, a harsh economic programme was introduced, slashing public spending and restraining inflation at the cost of widespread industrial recession and unemployment. Nonetheless, money was found to execute the preparations for the World Cup. The roads, airports and stadiums were built or rebuilt, and Argentina acquired colour television though the World Cup itself would only be seen in colour outside the country. The total cost of the spectacular remains uncertain but it was at least $700 million – considerably more than was spent in Spain four years later and far more than was prudently available from the Argentinian national budget.

Opposition to the Mundial at home and abroad was brushed aside. Exiles, human-rights organizations and leftist sympathizers in Europe tried to discredit the tournament and urge a boycott. The Junta responded by employing US public relations firm Buston-Marsteller to manage their public profile. FIFA were adamant: they would not take away the World Cup from Argentina. But could they win it? The military found themselves with a known left-wing sympathizer as coach of the national team. César Luis Menotti showed his independence of mind and distaste for the brutal side of Argentinian football by resisting the clamour to include in the squad the new hero of Argentina – the seventeen-year-old Diego Maradona – and refusing to pick players from the triumphant Boca Juniors team. Boca, who had won the Copa Libertadores in 1977 and 1978, were coached by Juan Carlos Lorenzo, the infamously tough-talking coach of the Argentinian national team at the 1962 and 1966 World Cup. His Boca team were a true rough house and, it had been persistently claimed, they were pumped up on a lot of drugs. Menotti by contrast picked and coached an Argentinian team of swift and direct passing who played at a tempo significantly faster than their predecessors – though rumours of excessive drug use hung over the team's medical preparations, too.

General Videla, in full military regalia, held a reception for the national team on the eve of the World Cup at the presidential palace. His expectations were made clear: 'Like the commander says to his troops before battle, you will be winners.' The next day at the opening ceremony Videla addressed the crowd and the nation to stony, but attentive, silence. In the ESMA military school the desperate routines of torture and intimidation were broken for a moment. The World Cup, Videla said, would be 'played under the sign of peace'. El Monumental was filled with the swirling showers of blue and white tickertape and the aching roars of the crowd. In the Plaza de Mayo the mothers and grandmothers of the disappeared made their last plaintive protests and appeals to the eyes and ears of the international media. But the football had begun.

In the final Argentina faced the Dutch, their own people and the Junta. Menotti remembered it this way:

Each of us had an order when we entered the field the day of the final: to look at the stands. We are not going to look at the stage-box of the authorities people ... I said to the players, we are going to look at the terraces, to all the people, where perhaps sits the father of each of us, because there we will find the metalworkers, the butchers, the bakers and the taxi drivers.[6]

Whatever Menotti's protestations that Argentina would play in the old way, the right way, the Dutch were still taken to the stadium by a long tedious route. Once there they were kept waiting on the pitch by Argentina for nearly ten minutes as the crowd howled them down. When they did arrive, the Argentinians made a massive protest over the protective arm cast worn by Dutch player Rene van de Kerkhof. Given that he had played in it for the last five games it was clear that the protest was designed to throw their opponents off balance. Playing on a carpet of shredded toilet rolls and newspaper, Argentina took the lead in the first half when Kempes burst through the Dutch defence to stab the ball home. Holland squandered chances until substitute Nanninga equalized with eight minutes to go. With a minute left to play Rensenbrink had the winner in his sights only to hit the post. In extra time Argentina had the edge and their attacks took on the aura of a cavalry charge. Kempes' long-legged stepover and dummy put him through for a second goal and then a third from Bertoni made sure of Argentina's victory.

People flooded on to the streets of Buenos Aires, of Rosario, Córdoba, of every tiny town and dusty *barrio. Ar-gen-tina, Ar-gen-tina, Campeón Mundial! Ar-gen-tina, Ar-gen-tina, Campeón Mundial!* On Avenida Corrientes a car with darkened windows moved slowly, gingerly through the pressing, uncontrollable crowds. Inside military officers sat quietly with one of their few remaining living prisoners, a leading figure in the Montoneros: 'You see we have won.' They let her soak up the reality of the situation through the sun roof and treated her to a meal at a restaurant brimming with patriotic reverie. *Asado* never tasted so much of ash.

In 1928 Borocotó, the great editor of *El Gráfico*, proposed the erection of a monument to the inventor of dribbling:

A *pibe* with a dirty face, a mane of hair rebelling against the comb; with intelligent, roving, trickster and persuasive eyes and a sparkling gaze that seem to hint at a picaresque laugh that does not quite manage to form on his mouth, full of small teeth that might be worn down through eating 'yesterday's bread'. His trousers are a few roughly sewn patches, his vest with Argentinian stripes, with a very low neck and with many holes eaten out by the invisible mice of use ... His stance must be characteristic; it must seem as if he is dribbling with a rag ball. That is important: the ball cannot be any other. A rag ball and preferably bound by an old sock. If this monument is raised one day, there will be many of us who will take off our hat to it, as we do in church.[7]

In October 1960 in a hospital built under Perón, but already showing a lot of wear, in the grim Buenos Aires *barrio* of Avellaneda, Diego Armando Maradona was born. Apocryphally his mother Tota announced his birth by exclaiming 'Goooooooooooooool!' The doctor lifted up the child and said, 'Congratulations, you have a healthy son and he is pure ass'.[8] Thus at the very moment of his arrival Maradona was myth made flesh. For while Argentinian football had bred and nurtured real *pibes* who had learnt their art on real *porteros*, Maradona was and still is *el pibe de oro* – the golden boy – whose sporting brilliance, social origins, childhood experiences, glorious but self-destructive eternal adolescence and thus chaotic adulthood matched and indeed extended every element of Borocotó's brilliant mythology.

Maradona's family came from the tiny provincial town of Esquina in the far north of Argentina near the Paraguay border. His mestizo father Chitoro scratched a living from the river traffic and hunting, and played football on a Sunday afternoon. His mother, who came from Italian immigrant stock, struck out for Buenos Aires in the mid-1950s as part of the great wave of Perón-inspired internal migration. Even on the minimum wage the drudgery of domestic labour constituted a massive economic leap for Tota. Reluctantly the rest of the family followed, setting up home in a self-built three-room shack in Villa Florito. His mother continued to work as a domestic, his father took a job in the bonemeal-crushing factories. Maradona, born five years after their arrival in the city, was the fourth child but first son of a family of eight. If he had lived, Borocotó would have wanted his monument here in Villa Florito's dusty wastelands, unpaved alleyways and sewage-strewn flats. Here Maradona played with a ball given him by his uncle Cirollo. Later he recalled, 'That first football was the most beautiful present of my life . . . The day I was given it I slept all night, hugging it.'[9] By the time he was six the neighbourhood was buzzing with talk of the tiny boy with ringlets who could hold the ball on his toe, his head, his shoulder and dribble rings round anyone. Maradona's break came when he was brought to a training session of the youth team of Argentinos Juniors known as *Las Cebollitas* – the spring onions. At the age of nine he was entertaining the crowds at Argentinos Juniors home games in spectacular half-time performances of ball skills and tricks. When he was ten he featured on television shows juggling bottles, oranges, anything, flipping them from toe to toe. By eleven he was playing in international youth tournaments and the Argentinos Juniors main youth team. The first team came for Maradona at just fifteen, making him the youngest player ever to play in the Argentine first division.

At seventeen Maradona just missed inclusion in the 1978 World Cup squad, but in 1979 at the age of eighteen Menotti picked him to captain the Argentine *selección* at the World Youth Cup in Tokyo. Maradona stole the show and Argentina won the tournament. The saturation television coverage was heavily doctored by the Junta, who blacked out protestors and opposition slogans in the crowd. At the same time as the tournament was being played, Argentina was receiving an Organization of American States (OAS) delegation investigating human rights abuses under the Junta. As post-victory hysteria mounted, the venerable commentator José María Muñoz on Radio Rivadavia asked his listeners to head for the Plaza de Mayo where the human rights commission was based and 'show these men from the commission on human rights what is the real Argentina'. And they did, in their thousands, carrying Muñoz on their shoulders around the square. The mothers and grandmothers of the disappeared who had been queuing all day to give evidence to the commission were obstructed and then overwhelmed by the sea of celebrations that flooded over their heads. On his return Maradona was fêted by the military government who conscripted him, cut his hair and then let him out again as soon as he had arrived, exhorting him to continue to be a role model for the nation's patriotic youth.

Maradona's time at Argentinos Juniors was almost up: his wages were clearly going to be intolerable, his value as a transfer too tempting to ignore, and in a series of backroom deals he moved on loan to Boca Juniors in early 1981. Boca, Maradona's team as a kid, were then struggling but Maradona's arrival transformed them. He lifted the whole Boca side, and they took the title with a draw against Racing Club: Maradona can be seen running half-naked, arms outstretched, a hint of crucifixion to his posture, saluting the Boca fans. In the aftermath of this triumph the psychic demons and external pressures that would doggedly follow him at every stage of his career made their first cameo appearances. Maradona's fame and appeal had already achieved global proportions. He was the centre of attention on Boca's European tours; at invited games in the United States and in Japan his reception reached hysterical proportions as fans endlessly photographed him and begged for locks of hair. Maradona's legs, relentlessly subjected to punishment on the pitch, were treated to a fearsome cocktail of injections and treatments. The money now beginning to flow into the Maradona clan's coffers at an ever-increasing rate appeared to be emptying out the other end even faster as commitments and promises were met, retainers and courtiers acquired and properties bought and filled. The crowd may have sung '*Maradona, no se vende. Maradona no se va, Maradona es Patrimonio Nacional*' – 'Maradona is not for sale, Maradona is going nowhere, Maradona is the nation's heritage.' But he was for sale, and he would be going. European money was calling.

As Maradona's star rose, so that of Argentina's economy fell. The military's stringency had failed to quell inflation which was climbing towards astronomical levels again. Output and employment had collapsed and living standards were now lower than ten years before. The opposition, in the form of clandestine trade unions, old political parties and social movements like the mothers of the disappeared were putting steadily rising pressure on the regime. Argentinian football offered evidence of both economic disaster and an incipient resistance to the dictatorship. Although the clubs' books were hardly open, it was clear that they were all in trouble. In 1981 River Plate, despite being given a lot of free land, were over $30 million in debt. Boca's bond issue of the 1970s now had less than junk status. Racing were not only in debt, but running up further debts at ruinous interest rates. San Lorenzo now had no stadium, having sold their old one to the Carrefour supermarket chain to try and eradicate the last mountain of debt that they had accumulated. There was at the time no prospect of getting another one; they seemed to be condemned to a nomadic existence shuffling around the crumbling small grounds of the backyard of Buenos Aires. Their debts were so high and their credit rating so low that the staff were reduced to organizing whip-rounds for towels and soap. Outright opposition to the dictatorship had not previously emerged in the stadiums but there were now the first hints of it. *Rock Nacional* was now the essential musical soundtrack of young football fans in Argentina and artists began to produce clandestine English music in a deliberately provocative linguistic battle with the authorities. At Chacarita Juniors one could occasionally catch the old and presumed lost Peronista chants of the 1950s. Montoneros flags were seen and hidden at Huracán.

General Videla stepped down as President in 1981, giving way to

General Roberto Viola, though his appointment was opposed by the ultra-nationalist cabal in the military administration. Their suspicions were confirmed when Viola, under the pressure of the deteriorating economy, opened extensive talks with the still illegal opposition about a return to civilian rule. The most conservative forces in the military rallied around General Leopoldo Galtieri and together they deposed Viola in December 1981. Two months later Galtieri put in an appearance at the national team's World Cup training camp and in front of the cameras publicly embraced Maradona. But while a World Cup victory later that year in Spain would, like in 1978, provide a major boost to the flagging popularity of the Junta, Galtieri had even bigger plans for rallying the nation. Having rejected war with Chile over their long-disputed Andean border in the south, the general had decided there would be more to gain and less to lose from taking the Falkland Islands/ Las Malvinas from the British, who had occupied the islands since 1833 despite the claims of Argentine sovereignty.

In early April the Argentine military invaded Las Malvinas. In El Monumental, where four years before they had shouted, 'He who does not jump is a Dutchman,' they called, 'He who does not jump is an Englishman.' But much to the astonishment of the Junta the British did not accept the invasion as a fait accompli and launched a substantial task force to retake the islands. Even worse, the Americans, who the Junta had calculated would stay out of it, backed the British. At home the coverage of the conflict was interspersed with football, especially reruns of the 1978 campaign. Buenos Aires, even at war, was strangely oblivious to reality. As the Royal Navy sank the cruiser *Belgrano* and over 300 Argentine sailors, Maradona and his agent Jorge Cyterszpiler were negotiating the finishing touches to Maradona's massive transfer to FC Barcelona with Josep Lluis Nuñez, president of the Catalan club. And as the World Cup squad gathered and flew to Spain to defend the title, the team paraded in front of a banner proclaiming '*Las Malvinas Son Argentinas*'; in the meantime the miserable conscripts and their hapless officers took the bombs and shells in their icy trenches. Argentinian news coverage still treated the British assault in cod football commentary terms.

Fantasy could not keep reality at bay for much longer. Menotti's second World Cup campaign began with none of the brio or hope of 1978. Maradona described the devastating impact of arriving in Spain and encountering that reality in their own language in the uncensored Spanish press. 'We were convinced we were winning the war, and like any patriot my allegiance was to the national flag. But then we got to Spain and we discovered the truth. It was a huge blow to everyone on the team.'[10] Argentina were beaten by Belgium. Humiliating. The next day the British accepted the Argentine surrender at Port Stanley. Maradona seemed to revive a little and the team limped through to the second phase beating Hungary and El Salvador. But no one was convinced. The Italians ground them out of the game with adamantine marking and needle. Then Brazil delivered the *coup de grâce*, Zico and Socrates tripping round Argentina's increasingly wild tackling. Maradona was reduced to stamping on Batista in the 85th minute and walked. Galtieri had walked too and in less than a year so would the rest of the military.

IV

In the dying days of Uruguayan democracy the country's football experienced a late flourish: a semi-final place at the 1970 World Cup and a Copa Libertadores trophy for Nacional of Montevideo in 1971. But the storm clouds were gathering. For over a decade the country had been racked by an ideologically polarizing politics and an active urban guerrilla movement, the Tupamaros, who among their most audacious attacks kidnapped the British ambassador and held him hostage for eight months in 1972. The endless swings in government between the ineffective and macroeconomically incompetent Colorados and Blancos had brought what was once one of the richest countries in the world to the point of penury. The Frente Amplio, a radical leftist coalition, was steadily gathering electoral support and ran the traditional parties close in the 1971 general election.

Football politics was, like much government business, reduced to petty-minded and emotional bickering. In 1971 the president of the Uruguayan FA, Dr Lecarte Moro, had voted to re-elect the incumbent Peruvian bureaucrat Teófilo Salinas Fuller as president of CONMEBOL – a man that Nacional had never forgiven for a refereeing decision that went against them in the 1969 Copa Libertadores. Nacional, in a fit of pique, refused to take part in the national championships. Moro, who had had a long-running feud with the president of Nacional, Miguel

Restuccia, dramatically resigned and then publicly challenged Restuccia to a duel to settle the matter. The chaos and disarray of the country was paralleled by the football league which was often interrupted by player strikes, referee strikes or both. When the 1972 season began three teams were not even in the country: Nacional arrived back a day late from their overseas tour; Peñarol, who never had any intention of getting back on time, followed later on in the week; but Bella Vista, a small team from a working-class suburb of Montevideo, were over a month late. They remained stranded in Guatemala where they had finished a Central American tour. The organizer of the trip absconded at the last moment leaving them ticketless and penniless. An army plane would finally be despatched north to pick them up.

Perhaps this helped shape the thinking of the generals who decided later that year, as the economic and political situation deteriorated, that only they could sort matters out. In late 1972 the army seized power in a short coup. While Argentina's Junta had the active backing of significant sections of the economic and bureaucratic elites, the Uruguayan generals took over with barely any significant support in civil society, nor did they possess the calibre of administrator and strategist that the much larger and more educated Argentine military could call upon. With such meagre cultural and political resources, the military relied on brute force to kill or imprison the Tupamaros, to corral the political parties and to quieten the people. Uruguay, a country of 3 million people, acquired the biggest population of political prisoners in the world.

In this context politicians swiftly migrated to the only important public institutions that were not attracting the generals' attention – football clubs. One of the key figures in the Frente Amplio, Tabaré Vásquez, became president of Progreso. The leader of the Colorado Party and future state president, Julio María Sanguinetti, moved into the presidential seat at Peñarol and Hugo Batalla, a future vice-president, became a senior official at the Uruguayan FA. This safe space for politicians existed because the Junta failed to mobilize football or indeed any other cultural form. The declining performance of the Uruguayan national team, which after its dismal 1974 World Cup performance failed to qualify again for twelve years, did not offer itself as an obvious vehicle for hyper-nationalist politics. Domestically things initially continued much as ever as Peñarol and Nacional racked up yet more national championships in a duopoly that was now unbroken for over forty years. Then a single crack appeared. In 1976 Defensor, another of Montevideo's small teams, finally broke the deadlock, winning the national championship, coached by José Ricardo de León, a known communist sympathizer. When the team made a triumphal circuit of their Estadio Luis Franzini, they chose to do it anticlockwise, a choice immediately and instinctively interpreted as a protest and condemnation of the ruling order. In the stadium and in the streets of Punta Carretas the first sounds of chants and songs critical of the regime and calling for change could be heard.

By 1978 it was clear to all that the military had run out of economic and political ideas; its pitiful efforts at attracting foreign investment and initiating a process of economic development had proved fruitless. But then the generals must have heard the roaring crowds from across the Río de la Plata, the deafening reverberations of 'Ar-gen-tina, Ar-gen-tina, Campeón Mundial', and they remembered just how useful football can be. Conveniently 1980 was the fiftieth anniversary of the first World Cup and Uruguay's first victory: the perfect opportunity to host a tournament commemorating the event. El Mundialito (the little World Cup), or to give it its full title Copa de Oro de Campeónes Mundiales, was planned as a short tournament between all the past winners of the World Cup providing a small showcase for the Junta abroad and an instrument of diversion and pacification at home. The English refused to go, so the Dutch went instead and Uruguay, with a little help from their friends, beat Brazil in the final.

It was a victory that was even more illusory and threadbare than Argentina's in 1978. The Uruguayan Junta lost a key constitutional plebiscite right after El Mundialito that might have initiated a smooth transition to civilian government; then the currency and business confidence collapsed. By 1984 the military were absolutely desperate for a way out and after violent civilian protests a deal was struck and constitutional government returned in 1985 with Sanguinetti moving from the president's office at Peñarol to the presidential palace in Montevideo. In this era of social and political change Uruguayan football experienced its last hurrah. With Uruguayan players still playing in the domestic league and Brazil and Argentina in economic and political disarray, Nacional and Peñarol won four Copa Libertadores, Nacional in 1980 and 1988 and Peñarol in 1982 and 1987. But this was not the Uruguay of the Varelas. Both teams, though good, did not raise themselves to the epic level of past Uruguayan sides. Moreover, the indissoluble link between clubs and fans, players and people, football and national identity was fraying. Richard Giulianotti captured just one manifestation of this in his account of the Uruguayan band Rumbo and their song 'Orsei' (Offside): 'The lyrics tell the story of a garage worker who stops himself acclaiming a goal by his football hero after reflecting on the huge salary differences between them.'[11] It was this generation of players that got Uruguay back to the World Cup in 1986 under coach Omar Borrás. But after a decade of brutalization it was not a pretty sight. Uruguay went down to ten men in two of their three games after ugly challenges by Bossio against Denmark and Batista after 55 seconds in their game with Scotland. Only Enzo Francescoli, desperately trying to hold the ball up front on his own, gave any inkling of their past glory and gentlemanly style.

The euphoria that surrounded Brazil's victory in the 1970 World Cup crystallized the already intimate relationship between football and the military-political complex in the country. In the early 1970s the military government continued to use football as a rather crude element of its 'bread and circuses' cultural politics. In 1973 the national minimum wage was slated to rise by around 15 per cent – a mere fraction of the real inflation rate in the country. The Rio office of the Ministry of Labour attempted to sweeten the medicine by giving away 15,000 tickets to the Flamengo–Fluminense game that coincided with the day of the announcement. Similarly, although the government was unable to make economy-wide price freezes and anti-inflation policies stick, it did manage to keep the cost of going to football at an affordable level by closely and fiercely policing the clubs' ticket sales. When in 1974 another general was installed as President the papers introduced the little known military bureaucrat as a 'Gaucho from Bento Gonçalves, 64 years old, fan of Internacional in Porto Alegre and Botafogo in Rio, brother of two generals, married with one daughter, Ernesto Geisel will be the 23rd President of the Republic', though it was general knowledge that the bookish and introverted old man had not the slightest interest in football at all.[12]

In the 1970s and 1980s these kinds of populist gestures were superseded by an altogether more extensive and ambitious engagement with the very fabric of the game. With the accession of João Havelange from president of the CBF to the FIFA presidency, no less a power than Admiral Heleno Nunes replaced him. Nunes was a football innocent; his key qualifications for the job were that he had previously been head of the government's ersatz political party ARENA and governor of Rio di Janeiro. Brazil's qualifying games for the 1978 World Cup were turned into rallies for ARENA, with military bands, electoral candidates introduced to the punters, and party banners and paraphernalia freely distributed. In an attempt to garner support in Rio itself Nunes regularly pressed for the inclusion of Rio-based players in the national team, most especially Vasco centre-forward Roberto.

In 1969 the Ministry of Finance had created Brazil's first national sports lottery, based on guessing the outcome of football games from all over the country. It was envisaged as both a revenue-raising instrument and an exercise in mass education; there was still no national football championship through which Brazil's poor could become acquainted with the far-flung geography of the country. The government stipulated that the games chosen by the lottery each week had to reflect the geographical diversity of the nation rather than focus on the most famous and popular teams of Rio and São Paulo states. The lottery was a huge success, garnering significant sums for the nation's treasury, some of which were used to fund popular sporting facilities. Encouraged by the nation-building efforts of the lottery, and hungry for more games in the season and therefore more income, the government pressured the football authorities to establish a fully fledged national championship. Brazil's air-transport infrastructure was at last just up to the job of moving teams around the country and in 1971 the first Campeonato Brasileiro kicked-off with teams from seven of the country's biggest states.

The Campeonato served as a perfect metaphor for the pathologies of gigantism and forced development that the government was imposing on the nation. As the global economic downturn of the mid-1970s deepened, Brazil's economic miracle faltered. Industrial investment and growth dropped. The immense government expenditure on tearing down parts of the Amazon, draining river basins and building enormous road systems, dams and industrial plants, were failing to maintain Brazil's rapid pace of economic development and their negative social and environmental consequences were becoming apparent.

The Campeonato Brasileiro began in 1971 with just twenty teams. By 1973 it had risen to forty. In 1975 the government passed a new sports law which gave equal power to representatives of all of Brazil's states within the national sports federation; the vote of Mato Grosso state (population less than 1 million) was the same as Rio state (population over 12 million). This opened the floodgates to vote buying, politicking and demands for more places for peripheral teams in the national championship. Teams were chosen to participate on the basis of political criteria, and insider dealing. There were 54 teams in 1976, 74 in 1978, peaking at an unbelievable 94 in 1979. Formats changed every year, the systems of promotion and relegation were a virtual lottery. Experiments with additional points for winning by two clear goals were tried. Neither sporting, economic or transport infrastructures could cope. Match schedules became impossibly full. Santos completed one national championship campaign on a Wednesday only to start the next season's São Paulo state championship with a game on the following Sunday. Players were required to endure enormously long and physically debilitating seasons, while attendances at many games fell to minuscule levels and the quality of football declined. Financial difficulties at clubs began to mount and accelerated a brusque, instant commercialism with advertising at stadiums beginning in 1977, shirt sponsorship in 1983 and live TV coverage in 1987. However, revenues remained so poor that when changes in transfer laws came into effect in the early 1980s, there was an exodus of players sold overseas. In a last, late burst a rash of stadium-building projects were commissioned in the smaller towns and cities of Brazil to complement those vast edifices built in the biggest conurbations; lapping up the output of Brazil's oversized and uncompetitive concrete industry, stadium capacity would often exceed the population of the city itself.

The military government did not confine themselves to matters of infrastructure. As might be expected of the army in particular, physical fitness and training regimes occupied a significant fraction of their time, energy and money. The raw industrial modernism of the armed forces was not expressed only through organizational and technological projects, but on human bodies too. The Brazilian army took its fitness regimes and training programmes very seriously and, as with the economy, sought to apply modern scientific methods and technological innovation to the creation of disciplined, efficient soldiers. It was a small leap from there to the application of such a vision to football and footballers. In the aftermath of the 1974 World Cup defeat this strain of physical-education ideology in Brazilian football was in the ascendant.

Brazil went to the 1978 World Cup coached by Captain Cláudio Coutinho, who in his prime had been an exceptional volleyball player, was a serving military officer and a fitness and endurance fanatic. Indeed he had been responsible for the physical preparation of the 1970 and 1974 World Cup squads and 1976 Olympic Games team. His response to Brazil's 1974 World Cup defeat was to try and emulate something of the spirit of Holland's total football. Often using the term 'scientific football' he sought to field a team that really did play as a team, in which roles were less circumscribed and individualism restrained, and tactical nous in an ever-changing fluid formation was at a premium. Such a team would need to be remarkably fit and well organized. Coutinho was able to deliver the former but, in the context of Brazilian football at the time, the latter was inconceivable. With such a footballing prospectus Coutinho tended to avoid individualists, dribblers and the flamboyant players like Paulo César Caju, Marinho, Falcão and Serginho. One Brazilian commentator argued that Coutinho defined 'the dribble, our speciality, as a waste of time and proof of our weakness'.[13] In the run-up to the World Cup, his smartest players Zico and Rivelino were out of sorts, the former forced to stay with the team while his baby son was born, the latter overweight and rather past his best.

Brazil went to Argentina and played defensively and uninspiringly, scraping their way through the opening group matches. So dismal was their game against Austria that Coutinho's effigy was burned by travelling Brazilians in Mar del Plata. Before the second-phase match against Poland Admiral Nunes protected himself in the increasingly outraged press by describing Coutinho as a man of 'scant technical ability'. Coutinho retreated into his shell, refusing to give press conferences for the rest of the tournament. Under this cloud of opprobrium Brazil beat Peru and drew in a tight game with Argentina but went home when the hosts pulled a 6–0 win over Peru out of the hat. Coutinho was relieved of his post.

The military had tried to model Brazilian football in its own image, but they could not mould its soul and they could not win its heart. The same could be said of Brazilian civil society, which despite having been stripped of any autonomous political leadership and subject to censorship and harassment, continued to elude, provoke, subvert and challenge the narrow cultural horizons and drab political vision of the dictatorship. Where the state sought to impose order, science, reason, duty and progress, carnival insisted on disorder, African religions offered magic, popular music spoke of love and longing and fantasy and codedly of freedom. When offered the merest opportunity to express their preference in local elections, the public consistently rejected the military and their political puppets. Through the late seventies and early eighties successive president-generals tried to find a way out, an opening in which popular political demands could be acceded to without the military losing total control. The military regime, now almost two decades old, was running aground. The economic miracle was not merely long gone, but had been put into reverse. The excessive borrowing of the late 1970s finally halted when in 1982 Brazil suspended payments on its ballooning foreign debt – then the biggest in the world. The inflation rate was climbing into four figures and with a rescheduled debt regime came an excruciatingly painful IMF structural adjustment programme that bore down on the jobs and the incomes of Brazil's urban poor. Having cancelled elections in 1980 that they knew they would lose, the generals were forced to allow elections in 1982, for every level of government in the country except the presidency. They duly lost everything but for a slender hold on the electoral college for the indirect presidential elections of 1985. The Brazil that the military had failed to corral or transform was emerging again.

In domestic football the Flamengo teams of the early 1980s offered Zico in his prime and *futebol arte* that won championships and trophies; a mode typified by their effortless domination of Liverpool in the 1981 Intercontinental Club Cup. At an international level, the 1982 and 1986 World Cup squads coached by Telê Santana played an exuberantly gifted and open style of football, quite the reverse of the 1974 and 1978 sides. In Spain, Santana was able to play a midfield brimming with talent. Indeed so big was the pool of talent available to him that coverage of both tournaments in Brazil was overshadowed by bitter argument over the squad and the team's selection. In the opening group games the Brazilians scored at will, mesmerizing the USSR, Scotland and New Zealand. In the second phase, as the final surrender of the Argentine

631

army in the Falkland Islands was being arranged, Brazil finished off a dispirited Argentine team; no blows were sharper or more perfectly executed than two killer passes from Zico that made it easy for Serginho and Junior to score. In the final game of the round, needing only a draw to qualify for the final, Brazil met the resilient Italians in Barcelona. It finished 3–2 and the Brazilians were out.

The core of the 1982 team went to Mexico in 1986 again under Santana and again were determined to play attacking football, though it took them a couple of games to warm up; having only crept past Spain and Algeria, they swatted Northern Ireland and Poland aside. However, the passage of time and accumulating injuries were taking their toll. In the quarter-finals they met their match in Platini's France at their peak. In the 75th minute at 1–1 Zico, who had been on for only two minutes, put a sliced pass into the area, where the French goalkeeper Bats brought Branco down. Zico stepped up and made it easy for Bats to save his shot. In the shoot-out after extra time Socrates and Júlio César missed spot kicks. Brazil went home and the administrators panicked so much about the failure of the country to score penalties when it mattered that it was decreed that all tied national championship games would be decided by penalties to furnish extra practice. A number of clubs resisted and refused to play the shoot-outs. They were forced to back down, treating spectators to the ludicrous spectacle of Fluminense and Botafogo returning to the Maracanã just for a shoot-out.

Corinthians of São Paulo offered the politics of democratization with their art. The art was provided by players of the calibre of Socrates, Juninho, Wladimir and Casagrande. The politics of their brief rise in the early 1980s was centred on a fiercely fought election for the presidency of the club. Simultaneously the debate over the re-democratization of Brazilian politics was gathering pace; a national campaign for a directly elected president was in full swing. The two movements converged. As the most popular team in São Paulo, with some cross-class appeal, Corinthians had the kind of support which offered a reasonable approximation to the mood of the Brazilian public. This gave the contest the aura of a plebiscite, but the choice being offered in the election made the connections irresistible. On the one hand there was the ludicrously and inappropriately named 'Order and Truth' slate, representing the old guard of Corinthians directors who were wedded to a model of club politics that was highly personalized, opportunistically populist, authoritarian, secretive and paternalistic. On the other hand there was 'Corinthian Democracy', the liberal ticket committed to a democratization of the relations between club and fans, players and coaches. *Placar*, the football magazine, described the choice as between 'liberalization and heavy handedness, efficiency or paternalism, new times or old methods'.

The election cost around $500,000, both sides used paid-for TV and radio adverts, and showered the streets of São Paulo with campaign paraphernalia. In an unheard-of act, the players publicly and collectively gave their support to the liberal wing. Socrates went as far as to say that he would leave the club and go abroad if Order and Truth won. It was a defining moment. Corinthian Democracy won the election and in the last year before shirts were taken over by corporate sponsors' logos, they carried slogans imploring fans to vote in the first open elections for the governor of São Paulo. Then with just Corinthian Democracy emblazoned on their shirts they won the 1982 São Paulo state championship; and they won it in style. Speaking at the time, Socrates remarked, 'I'm struggling for freedom, for respect for human beings, for equality, for ample and unrestricted discussions, for a professional democratization of unforeseen limits, and all of this as a soccer player, preserving the ludic, and the joyous and pleasurable nature of this activity.'[14] In the stands the *torcidas* hung the banner 'Win or lose but always with democracy'. A dressing-room culture was created which permitted smoking and drinking, and limited the authority of the coach. This heady brew of charismatic leadership and personal liberation took Corinthians to another Paulista title in 1983, but a national title was beyond them. The following year Socrates stood before 1.5 million people in central São Paulo, gathered to press the Brazilian Congress to vote for a constitutional amendment that would allow for free presidential elections. He was poised to move to Italy but said that if the amendment were to pass he would remain at home. The amendment did not pass, Socrates went to Fiorentina, and Corinthians relinquished their Paulista crown to Santos. Casagrande, who had been lent out to São Paulo, was picked out by the television cameras crying in the stands.

Socrates and Corinthians had reached the limits of football's democratic revolution; departure from military rule would be orchestrated by the generals. In 1985 Tancredo Neves was elected as the first civilian president in twenty-one years but under the electoral college system set up by the military. Almost immediately he fell ill, dying before he could be inaugurated. His vice-president and successor José Sarney, an old-time politician closely linked to the military, did little more than preside over the hyper-inflation that was impoverishing the country. In 1989 Fernando Collor de Mello, an unknown governor from the small and little-known state of Alagoas in the north, was elected president. In the early 1970s Collor had cut his populist political teeth as the president of Alagoas's leading football club. But unlike all his predecessors Collor had registered a shift in the nation's tastes. On the television at any rate football was being displaced by telenovellas – Brazil's indigenous soap operas, subtropical, trashy revenger's tragedies that held much of the country entranced with their heady brew of lust, greed, paternity suits and conspicuous consumption. Collor, rather than pursuing the people through football, lived the life (on kickbacks and credit) and presented an image closer to the alpha-male, libidinous patriarchs of the small screen. He remained unknown until Brazil's media and industrial elites were sufficiently frightened by the rise of the trade-union movement, the Workers' Party (PT), and their charismatic presidential candidate Lula, to throw their lot in with this telegenic Alagoan populist. The combination of these forces crushed Lula and the PT and demonstrated that in the new Brazil, the old elite would continue to fight dirty. The price of such an incomplete democratization was a presidency of the calibre of Fernando Collor: macro-economically incompetent, unremittingly chaotic, venal, patrimonial, corrupt and self-serving, an instrument for the enrichment of an extraordinarily narrow circle of Brazilians and the inflation of Collor's ego. An already deeply unequal society was further polarized by the bungled application of stringent neo-liberal policies of privatization and deregulation, while the withdrawal of the security forces from power was followed by a steady breakdown in law and order, a surge in the crime rate, the rise of an indigenous narcotics industry and with it armed and organized urban gangs.

Brazilian football seemed to follow suit. There were the first hints that the *torcida* organizations were putting on more than choreographed firework displays as guns and knives began to make an appearance in and around Brazil's football stadiums. On the pitch a new wave of coaches and players returned to *futebol força* with a vengeance. Teams from the smaller industrial cities of Paraná and Rio Grande do Sul were among the leading exponents of this approach; Grêmio and Coritiba won the national championships on this basis. Telê Santana warned, 'In

Brazil the way you win does not matter. A very violent form of football is being practised.'[15] Twenty years on from their last World Cup victory, the Brazilians travelled to Italia '90 under Sebastião Lazaroni, a coach of the military school of obsessive physical preparation and muscle building, combined with a rigid commitment to the European sweeper system. Indeed Lazaroni was so convinced that the sweeper system was the cure for Brazilian football maladies that he had written an entire doctoral thesis on the subject. From the outset the mood in the Brazilian camp seemed sour as rumours swirled around the squad: that Dunga and Careca were at each other's throats; that the team were not paying the enormous drinks bills they were running up; that they were failing to meet the expectations and contractual obligations of their corporate sponsors. On the field it was worse. Brazil played four games and scored only four goals. So cautious and negative was their mood that Lazaroni continued to play with a sweeper and a defensive midfield against Costa Rica. Brazil squeezed through by a single goal. A single goal against Costa Rica? Argentina put them out of their misery. After 81 goalless minutes Maradona made space and time for the charging Claudio Caniggia and Brazil were going home without the World Cup again.

#

In 1973 Dr Borrero, President of the Colombian Republic, welcomed a FIFA delegation to the country which was then bidding to host the 1986 World Cup.

It is in everyone's mutual interest to demonstrate to the world that a country such as ours is perfectly competent to put this challenge to our sports administrators, thus conveying to all other nations just how capable it is of organizing an event of this magnitude in 1986.[16]

They were optimistic words; but that was in 1973, before coca. A decade later the country, tragically, did not prove competent. As the curtain went down on the 1982 World Cup in Madrid the steadily escalating numbers of killings and kidnappings, as well as recent football stadium disasters, were making FIFA very nervous. While the Colombians tried to maintain their position, FIFA prepared a special investigative delegation whose sole purpose would be to declare Colombia unable to host the tournament. Bogotá maintained some face by returning the hosting rights to FIFA in late 1982 rather than having them stripped away.

With the prize now up in the air hurried bids came in from Canada, the USA, Brazil and Mexico. The Canadian bid never looked serious. The Brazilian bid, given the chaotic state of the national football bureaucracy, was a very risky venture. More tellingly, FIFA's João Havelange was insisting that the president of the CBF step down before any business could be done. In the end the incumbent resigned and was replaced by Havelange's hapless son-in-law, Ricardo Teixera. Brazil then withdrew its bid. Havelange had other plans. The real fight it seemed was between Mexico and the USA. The Americans put together an impressive bid, backed by the vast Time-Warner conglomerate, who were the central sponsors of the struggling American professional league, the NASL. Time-Warner certainly had enough leverage to make Henry Kissinger, Secretary of State for Presidents Nixon and Ford, the front man for the bid. Kissinger put in six months of global schmoozing, culminating in a comprehensive and detailed presentation to the FIFA executive committee in Stockholm. However, the deal had already been done over breakfast, when Havelange persuaded the committee to accept the recommendation of his own parallel special commission: Mexico. The Mexican delegation made an eight-minute presentation and headed off to celebrate. Henry Kissinger considered suing FIFA. Time-Warner pulled the plug on the NASL. Both had met their match in the shape of Televisa, the gigantic Mexican media conglomerate.

Mexico was a place where Havelange could do business: a rock-solid Latin American political stitch-up without recent resort to unpleasant military interference or unsightly televised violence and an advanced communications infrastructure. The origins of both, in different ways, led back to Televisa. The foundation of Mexico's political stability was the monopoly on power held by the Partido Revolucionario Institucional (PRI), which had ruled Mexico since the dust settled on the Mexican revolution of the 1920s. Regular elections, legal opposition parties and a modicum of press freedom made no difference to the highly organized and institutionalized systems of patronage and power, doc-tored elections and bought votes that kept the PRI in power. Televisa possessed a similarly hegemonic control over Mexican television, barely challenged by the small state-funded system. The fortunes of the

PRI and Televisa became increasingly intertwined as the government ensured that Televisa's dominant position was not challenged on the airwaves, while Televisa's political reporting – and non-reporting – reciprocated the arrangement. Regular donations to presidential election funds passed from the company's founder and president, Emilio Azcárraga, to the PRI.

In the early 1960s Azcárraga had recruited Guillermo Cañedo, the president of the club Zacatepec, to run the television side of his company. He managed the development of Club América as the company's in-house team and his assiduous lobbying and charm combined with Televisa's impressive technical infrastructure allowed Mexico to win the hosting rights for the 1970 World Cup ahead of Argentina. Cañedo went on to run the World Cup and fell in with Havelange during his challenge to Stanley Rous for the FIFA presidency in 1974. Cañedo's reward was a vice-presidency of FIFA, though it is said he never forgot that he was a Televisa employee first and foremost. Cañedo also acted as an intermediary in a whole series of media deals involving FIFA, Televisa, Azcárraga and Havelange. Things had become so cosy that Havelange returned home to Brazil from the World Cup in Spain in Azcárraga's private jet. Televisa was now an enormous conglomerate, owning networks and companies across the USA and Latin America, producing more Spanish-language programming than any other corporation and with investments across the range of Mexican industries. With the World Cup in Mexico again, Cañedo was put in charge of the organization. Televisa picked up the TV rights for a song and made a fortune leasing and selling studio space and other media facilities to the foreign press.

The Mexico City earthquake of 1985 was the country's worst recorded natural disaster; at least 12,000 people died and huge sections of the city's infrastructure became inoperable. Neither Televisa nor Havelange let it faze them. Noting that the disaster had not affected the football stadiums of Mexico City, Havelange sent Cañedo a telegram: 'the earthquake respected football'. Televisa made sure that the news focused on rebuilding and normality with not too much unnecessary lingering on people crushed by buildings. But even Televisa's practised sleight of hand could not entirely conceal the real Mexico behind the World Cup show. A comparison of Mexico '70 and Mexico '86 is instructive. Whereas the 1970 World Cup had used marketing and advertising practices so amateurish that a single menswear shop on Carnaby Street – John Stephens – could afford to take up a quarter of Guadalajara stadium for the Brazil–England clash, this time things were different, with the whole show being reserved for the multinational corporate sponsors that FIFA had now signed up. More tellingly, the crowds were well down on 1970 and ticket prices significantly higher. When criticized for the high cost of tickets, Cañedo tartly replied, 'People have TV.' He was equally unrepentant when challenged over tobacco sponsorship.

On the field Latin America had a mixed World Cup. Uruguay were ransacked by the Danes (6–1) only to scrape through to the next round by drawing with Scotland. Argentina then swatted them aside. Paraguay, at their first World Cup since 1958, were pleased to qualify for the knock-out stages before being seen off by England. Hosts Mexico had their moments but lacked goals and went out in the quarter-finals after a goalless draw with the West Germans was followed by penalties. Brazil too went out in the same way and at the same stage to France. But Mexico '86 was all about just one team from Latin America and just one player: Argentina and Diego Maradona. As we have seen, Argentina went to the tournament coached by Carlos Bilardo whose approach to football was diametrically opposed to his predecessor Menotti's: defensive, cautious, disciplined, with a really hard edge in the tackle and plenty of spike off the ball. The majority of the squad was cast in this mould, but Bilardo had talents smarter and bigger than this – Burruchaga, Valdano and Maradona. For all his apparent rigidity Bilardo had the wit to give them enough freedom and space to use that talent. The draw went one better. The draw gave Maradona a stage befitting a performance of canonical status; it offered a quarter-final with England.

---

22 June 1986
Argentina 2 England 1
Estadio Azteca, Mexico City

> Angels and ministers of grace, defend us!
> Be thou a spirit of health or goblin damn'd,
> Bring with thee airs from heaven or blasts from hell,

> Be thy intents wicked or charitable,
>
> Thou comest in such a questionable shape
>
> *Hamlet*, Act I Scene IV

The high hot Mexican sun is almost directly above the Azteca. The public-address system strung above the pitch casts the shadow of a spiked mace on the centre-circle. In the line-up during the anthems, his feet paw the ground like a restless colt. His nostrils flare, sucking in the thin air and snorting it out. His upper body seems absurdly swollen on his slender legs, his ribcage high and wide like a baby bull. He is a Minotaur.

Maradona has drifted into empty space. Now he receives the ball and turns towards the English goal. As if there were some force field, some pentagram around him, the English players close by appear to fall back, the midfield parting to let him through. A flick to the right finds Valdano on the edge of the area. The ball slides off his foot and behind him where Hodge's outstretched leg slices it up into the centre of the penalty area. Shilton comes off his line, Maradona continues his run and both leap towards the ball. Maradona's body is taut and compressed, his head sunk deep on to his chest, his knees bent and his legs behind him; one fist is clenched. The other hand, above his head, punches the ball. Frozen at that moment with mouth agape, his thick arched brows low on his face, he is a gargoyle.

Five metres inside his own half, his back to goal with Reid and Beardsley descending upon him from two directions. Maradona appears to retreat only to trap the ball dead. He turns himself through 180 degrees, without his boots leaving the ball unattended. Scampering from spin to run, he takes the ball past both English players and begins to accelerate, his legs becoming longer and lighter and faster than ever. At the point of maximum acceleration you can see him take winged flight. Framed against the crowd, his front foot is precisely poised above the ball, his toes delicately pointed. Suddenly he decelerates, shortening his steps, preparing for the swerve that will take him past the defenders scrambling towards him. He swerves, dummies, feints, eluding and deluding the sprawling English, slipping past Shilton and the despairing Butcher. His feet do not appear to return to the ground.

Maradona went out and scored a goal of the same calibre against Belgium in the semi-finals, sending a long thin line of red Belgian shirts, hot and bothered in the Mexican afternoon sunshine, skittling across the turf before checking and shooting. In the final against West Germany, unquenchable German efforts and set-piece goals hauled them back from two goals down to 2–2. In the 85th minute Maradona, sensing a chink of light in the now stretched German defence, threaded a ball to just outside the right of the penalty area and Burruchaga made it 3–2. It was the last World Cup where the crowd actually stormed on to the field at the end of the final. Maradona would be the last captain to hold the trophy aloft in not merely a scrum of FIFA bureaucrats and the global media, but with the people who came to see him. When they write his history again in future worlds will writers be tempted to say that this was the moment of his ascent to another realm? For when he came back down to earth again that autumn in the San Paolo stadium of Napoli in southern Italy, he did so as divinity.

VII

If military rule and an uncertain return to democracy provided the framework for the vicissitudes of football in the Southern Cone, football in the Andes was shaped by a different context. Peru and Colombia, both of which had experienced eras of international footballing success or notoriety, and created intense urban football cultures in the 1930s and 1950s respectively, had failed to sustain their momentum. But both experienced a revival, Peru in the 1970s and Colombia in the 1980s, alongside major transformations in their political and economic fortunes. Colombia's professional football fiesta of the early 1950s was an exotic and exceptional import sustained by exclusion from FIFA and its transfer rules, the windfall profits of the coffee-export industry at its peak and politically nurtured by an elite threatened by popular uprisings in both the country and the city. Colombia's return to FIFA in 1953 terminated the experiment. Colombian football survived and maintained a precarious professionalism in the biggest clubs but it made no impact on the outside world. When in the early 1970s Colombia first bid to host the 1986 World Cup not a single stadium of sufficient size or quality existed that could host a match. The question remains: why, despite the political stability and modest urbanization and economic progress of the 1960s and 1970s, did football remain moribund?

In the 1930s Peruvian football had acquired many of the key features that a successful football culture requires. Football had decisively shifted from being the game of the Anglo and *criollo* elites, to being the game of the urban masses. Not only that, but football had crossed the racial divide between white Peru and the mestizo and black populations. In Lima crowds were big enough to allow a move to semi-professionalism in the mid-1930s, a shift confirmed in law in 1951. Clubs in the capital were well established; a central rivalry between Alianza Lima and Universitario de Deportes on sporting and social grounds gave the game edge and dynamism, and the national team attended the first World Cup in 1930. Football had yet to spread to the countryside and internal communications were so poor that no national league between cities could be contemplated, but the concentration of football in a single city had done the game in Uruguay no harm.

The promise of Lima as the Montevideo of the Andes was confirmed at the 1936 Olympics. Peru's multiracial team, the jewel of the country's first Olympic delegation, were good enough to get to the quarter-finals in Berlin where they faced Austria. In the first half they went 2–0 down, they then equalized in the second half and scored another two in extra time to win the game 4–2. A few exultant Peruvians ran on to the pitch as Villanueva put number four away. Later that day FIFA ordered a replay arguing that the 'pitch invasion' had invalidated the result. Rumours circulated that Hitler, robbed of the chance of a German victory (they had lost to the Norwegians in their opening game), insisted on an Austrian presence in the tournament. Either way the incensed Peruvians were recalled to Lima and the Austrians lost the final. The 1936 Olympics were not an aberration as Peru hosted and won the Copa América in 1939, albeit in the absence of Brazil and Argentina. But that was that. Peru would not qualify for a World Cup until 1970, its team would make no impact on the Copa América or the Copa Libertadores, and its players were barely seen outside the country. Despite all the apparent preconditions for footballing growth and success Peruvian football disappeared.

What then distinguishes the experience of the Río de la Plata and Brazil from these Andean footballing cultures? Why should the former have been able to create successful professional leagues and sustain and develop them subsequently? The central difference is the nature of the political regimes that oversaw the industrialization of football in Latin America. In Peronist Argentina and Vargas's Brazil the state took an active interest in the development of football, because both regimes, for all their differences, were attempts to incorporate the new urban working classes into a nationalist political and economic project; and the urban working classes, whatever else they were doing, were watching and playing football. In Peru and Colombia the upsurge of social, sporting and political organization among the urban and rural poor was decisively checked in the 1940s and 1950s. In Peru a short-lived uprising by the radical APRA party was crushed, after which political power was held by a narrow circle of Lima elites and the army. In Colombia *La Violencia* of the mid-1950s terminated the immediate threat from the Left and from peasant uprisings. Sufficiently scared by the threat from below, Colombia's conservative and liberal parties created a political system which systematically distributed patronage, money and power between them. Neither Andean elite sought or desired any further populist mobilization of their publics; football was of no use to them.

The volatility of the Lima masses and the fragile brutality of the Peruvian state were clear to see in August 1964, when Peru played Argentina in an Olympic qualifier at the Estadio Nacional. Argentina were leading 1–0 when Peru equalized only for the referee to disallow the goal. A similar situation had occurred in Peru's game with Brazil at the 1957 Copa América held in the same stadium. With Brazil already ahead from a Didi penalty, the referee had awarded the Brazilians a second spot kick only to find himself attacked by the whole Peruvian squad. The game was abandoned and the referee smuggled out of the country that evening for his own safety. This time a member of the crowd leapt over the wall and on to the pitch to remonstrate with the referee. A second man followed him and as they reached the official a fusillade of objects began to rain down on the pitch from the stands. The police reacted. Volleys of tear gas were fired directly into the crowd, batons were drawn and an extraordinary stampede away from the trouble began. With locked doors, crumbling stairs and a complete absence of stewarding the result was inevitable: the worst disaster in football's history. Over 350 people died, mainly asphyxiated, and over 500 were injured.

Peru's politics were transformed in 1968 by an army coup led by

General Juan Velasco Alvarado. Under the slogan 'a second independence', Velasco initiated a programme of radical industrial nationalization, land reform and land redistribution. The army, which had been
radicalized by its long and fruitless repression of rural misery and ban-
ditry, attempted the incorporation of Peru's popular classes that the
political elites had put off for so long by organizing and mobilizing
peasants and workers. This new Peru revelled in the generation of players
that social upheaval seemed to release. In 1970 at their first appearance
at a World Cup finals since 1930 Peru went through to the quarter-finals,
losing an entertaining and open game 4–2 to Brazil. It was a defining
moment. For the first time people across the entire country watched the
games on Peru's first national television broadcasts and the military
government made great play of the team as an icon of national unity
and independence.

The squad went one better in 1975. After an aggregate draw with the
Brazilians in the semi-finals of the Copa América, Peru progressed to
the final on the toss of a coin and went on to beat Colombia to win the
title. The core of that side went to the 1978 World Cup and was, on
paper, even better. The midfield trio of César Cueto, José Velasquez and
Teófilo Cubillas were, according to *El Gráfico*, 'the best in the world',
though their 6–0 defeat by Argentina questioned both their talents and
their propriety. This cluster of players came to the end of the road in
1982 in Peru's last appearance in a World Cup, terminated by a crushing
defeat to the Poles 5–1. By this time Velasco's redistributive military
populism had long run out of steam and political allies. Conservative
army officers displaced him in 1975 and then for five years racked up a
massive international debt to keep a crumbling economic show on the
road while they dithered about their political future The army slipped
away from government in 1980 handing a ravaged economy and an
unsustainable debt back to President Belaúnde. Moreover, now rural
Peru was either in revolt, as the Latino Maoists of *Sendero Luminoso*
(Shining Path) mounted a destabilizing campaign of terror, or in the
hands of a new generation of narco-traffickers and coca processors.

Football, like every other aspect of Peruvian society, was battered by
the increasing violence of everyday life, the bitter and dirty counter-
terrorism war conducted in both city and countryside. The economic
meltdown that the debts of the 1970s bequeathed to the country
was made worse by the IMF structural adjustment programmes that

followed. In 1986 the recently elected García administration began to implement its policy of decentralizing power and resources from Lima to the rest of the country. The Peruvian Football Federation followed suit by arranging for three regional champions and runners-up to contest a mini-league that would produce the country's first genuinely national championship. However, the country's transport infrastructure did not match up to the geographical ambitions of the government or the football federation. Without a functioning nationwide road or rail system, air travel was the only option and the costs of flying were not being met by the paltry income that Peruvian sponsors and crowds could generate. Even if the clubs could have afforded to fly, half of the country's commercial aircraft were inoperative owing to defects and neglect and a chronic lack of spare parts. Into the breach stepped the military, offering their cargo planes for charter at highly competitive rates in an environment where regulation and inspection were best described as lax if not absent. It was in this context that the young squad of Alianza Lima, lying top of the table with eleven games to go, beat Deportivo Pucallpa 1–0 in the Amazonian jungle. The team left immediately afterwards on a navy transport plane. Taking off at 6.30 p.m., the last contact with the plane was at 8.15 p.m. as it approached Lima over the Pacific Ocean. The plane crashed and sank. The entire complement of forty-three people died. The immediate response was spontaneous and immense. Everywhere in the traditional *barrios* of Alianza Lima support, especially La Victoria, people gathered; club shirts and regalia were laid in instant memorials and shrines with candles and photos. Fans and families combed the beaches searching for the inevitable washed-up bloated bodies; corpses were carried in procession to family homes when they were found. Football matches in Lima at every stadium assumed the form of a wake. Religious ceremonies at all of Lima's churches held masses for the dead. In acts of public mourning President García and the Archbishop of Lima Cardinal Ricketts offered their sense of loss and disbelief. Only the navy remained silent.

Lima was a city getting increasingly used to grief. The military conflict in the Andean highlands and in the Amazon between Shining Path, the narco-traffickers, the army and freelancing vigilantes was approaching its peak. In the twenty years between 1980 and 2000, 69,000 people were killed and by 1987 the war was coming closer to Lima. Shining Path had announced their capacity to reach the capital when in 1986 they assassinated Rear Admiral Carlos Ponce. Then in early 1987 a riot by political prisoners and others in Lima's main jail timed to coincide with the visit of international socialist leaders to the country resulted in a massacre in which 300 inmates were shot by the navy. The guerrillas retaliated by returning to Lima and shooting the naval Commander-in-Chief, Vice-Admiral Cafferate. In an atmosphere of fear, coupled with a widespread distaste for the armed forces in general and the navy in particular, rumours began to circulate – stories that sought a more satisfying explanation for the Alianza tragedy than the thin narrative gruel of a mechanical accident. From the streets to the newspapers to the television, the tale circulated that the players had discovered cocaine on board the plane, confirming the suspicion that the military were deeply implicated in drug trafficking. Found out, the naval officers were forced to shoot the players and crash the plane. Whatever comfort urban myth could provide there would be no succour from the game; Alianza Lima, utterly devastated, lost the title that year to Universitario and then failed to win another title for a decade.

Colombia's footballing record since the 1950s was even more undistinguished than Peru's. Yet by 1990 its teams had contested five Copa Libertadores finals, one won of them and made a brave showing at the 1990 World Cup. This sudden and accelerated development of Colombian football required more than just the removal of the old regime, it needed an injection of funds that the country's old elites were not prepared to make and the country's formal economy did not appear able to generate. Both problems would be solved by the rise of Colombia's narcotics industry; but there would be an increasingly violent price to pay for the cocaine-induced high. The political carve-up of the 1950s between the liberals and the conservatives may have prevented an inter-elite civil war but it did nothing to address the nation's widespread rural poverty and urban discontent. With all political space occupied by the incumbents, dissent found military and violent outlets. Beginning in the mid-1960s, FARC – a loose alliance of Marxist and revolutionary groups – began a long campaign of rural guerrilla warfare and peasant insurgency. An already unstable farming economy was shattered by the global economic downturn of the 1970s and the disintegrating value of coffee. Into the vacuum of state control and profitable crops stepped the cartels and the coca leaf.

Once the insatiable demand for cocaine in the United States and then Western Europe was factored into the equation, no sector of Colombian society was left untouched by the polyhydrous power of the drug industry; politicians, police, the armed forces, judges, journalists and football clubs were all bought. In the late 1970s and the early 1980s the drug cartels took control of the key clubs in Colombian football. By the mid-1980s at least seventeen of the twenty teams in the top division had major connections to the drug cartels. The attractions of football for the new narco-elite were numerous. Some were just fans: Pablo Escobar's attachment to Atlético Nacional was no fakery. Football and its transfer market offered a useful channel for money laundering and the movement of funds across borders. Perhaps most importantly, football offered an instrument of civic patronage and a public measure of power and status where most of the conventional institutions of the state and civil society had dissolved. Escobar in particular spent money on practice pitches, floodlights and kits for kids in the *barrios* of Medellín.

The country's parlous economic state and deteriorating security situation gave politicians second and third thoughts about hosting the World Cup in 1986. Deaths were mounting on the terraces as well as in the streets. In 1981 eighteen fans were killed when a wall collapsed during fighting between fans of Deportes Tolima and Deportivo Cali. In 1982 drunk fans pissing over the edge of the top terrace provoked a stampede at Cali's Estadio Pascual Guerrero; the crush left 22 dead and over 100 injured. Colombia handed back the hosting rights to FIFA. The events of the next few years would prove them right. In 1983 the Minister of Justice, Rodrigo Lara Bonilla, declared, 'The mafia has taken over Colombian football.'[17] Six months later he was shot dead. The degree to which football, politics and the drug cartels were entwined was then sharply demonstrated in mid-season 1984 when a leading member of the Medellín cartel and the president of Atlético Nacional, Hernán Botero Moreno, was extradited to the USA on charges of drug trafficking and money laundering. The Colombian first division shut down for a week in solidarity. The cartels viewed such extradition procedures as so threatening to their position that they unleashed a war of sustained terror and killing on Colombian society and the judicial system. Among the many thousands gunned down, kidnapped or disappeared over the next five years, the dead included 200 judges, 1,200 policemen and over 150 investigative journalists. Football officials were also a target. The presidents of Deportivo Medellín and Deportivo Pereira were shot as was the president of Millonarios, Germán Gómez García. The coach of the national youth team and the president of the professional league were also assassinated. Football journalists who asked searching questions like Jaime Ortiz Alvear and Carlos Arturo Mejia received similar treatment and then players were targets too. Eduardo Pimentel of Millonarios was injured and his teammate Uriel de Jesús was shot by a fan in the crowd as he was about to score. Squeezed between the cartels and the US Drug Enforcement Administration, Bogotá pleaded with Washington to back down and in desperation saved what remained of its judicial personnel by declaring the extradition of Colombians to the USA unconstitutional.

The team that first rose the highest on this narcotic injection of money and patronage was América de Cali. They won their first national title in 1979 and then five consecutive titles from 1982 to 1986. Money was spent on major players from across Latin America. Argentinians came to Colombia for the first time since the era of *El Dorado*, including international strikers Richard Gareca and José Luis Brown. Argentine coach Carlos Bilardo was put in charge and América proved good enough to make it through to three consecutive Libertadores finals (1985–7) and lost all three of them. Something other than money and imports was required. Atlético Nacional under Pablo Escobar's regime had pursued a similar strategy of throwing money at foreign players and coaches but had only one title in 1981 to show for it. Escobar changed this in 1987 when he appointed Francisco Maturana, a black Colombian coach. Maturana, in turn, created an Atlético side that was strictly Colombian.

At first sight Maturana appeared an unorthodox choice. Despite an illustrious playing career with Atlético themselves and a short international career, Maturana was also a university graduate and a practising orthodontist; except for a single year at a tiny provincial team, Once Caldas, he was an unknown quantity as a coach. But as one commentator remarked, 'More than drug money, it was drug imagination . . . Escobar had the instinct that Maturana was a great coach. Nobody knew then.'[18] Under Maturana Atlético played a distinctive variety of 4-4-2, tightly organized zonal marking at the back, with two central defensive midfielders who could create the space and time for some of the extravagantly gifted playmakers and short passers around them. Maturana encouraged his sides to express themselves and to use and to experiment with their skills. Maturana's football consciously drew upon the musical and dancing traditions of Colombian popular culture. In the Copa Libertadores of 1989 Atlético danced past Millonarios of Bogotá in the quarter-finals and sidestepped Danubio of Montevideo in the semi-finals. Then it appeared dancing was not enough. In the first leg of the final Atlético Nacional lost 2–0 to Olimpia of Paraguay away in Asunción. On the day of the return game in Bogotá, Argentine referee Juan Carlos Loustau was offered $100,000 over breakfast to secure the game for Atlético. He refused the money. That evening Atlético reversed the score, taking the game into extra time and then a penalty shoot-out that they won. Loustau was treated to a 45-minute ride through the riotous celebrations in the city streets afterwards and was informed: 'Now you know we can do whatever we want to you. Make sure you remember that for next time.'[19] Then they turfed him out of the car as gunfire and fireworks erupted. By morning the revelry had left twenty people dead.

The stakes in Colombian football were rising as the cartels and their cash-flush members took to wild bouts of gambling on football matches. In November 1988 referee Armando Perez was kidnapped by six armed men in Medellín and driven round the city for almost a whole day, the 'representatives' of the leading clubs reminding him that 'whoever gives the wrong decisions we'll kill'. Alvaro Ortega made the wrong decision in a game between Independiente Medellín and América de Cali early in the 1989 season. After the return match in Medellín in November he was gunned down. An unknown informer called a local newspaper to say that other referees who were also making incorrect decisions would suffer a similar fate: 'I'm not going to give you figures but we and our bosses lost a lot of money because the result of the Deportivo–América game was not right.'[20] The Colombian officials slated to appear at the 1990 World Cup resigned. Jesús Diaz, the country's most senior referee, wrote to João Havelange, 'My wife and children have begged me to give up refereeing. When it's a matter of life and death you have to consider the feeling of others. I can't keep on tormenting my family.'[21] The Colombian Football Federation announced: 'The law of the bullet is killing our sport. We cannot allow a competition to continue that is dominated by psychological coercion and physical threats . . . no more deaths, no more massacres, and no more blood.'[22] The rest of the season was abandoned. There was no champion for Colombia in 1989, but there was much more blood to come.

16

Football and the Belly: Africa, 1974–1990

A political entity that, for an appreciable period, has saluted a common flag, adopted a common anthem, a motto, or a common pledge for ceremonial or instructional occasions, a polity that loses its collective sense of proportion when its football team goes to battle, fights a war or two as one entity, flaunts a common passport, and pools and distributes its economic resources by some form of consensus, even where such a system of distribution is periodically challenged . . . such an entity may indeed be deemed a nation.

Wole Soyinka

It can cause young men to faint, holy men to swear and strong men to become impotent for a day.

Samuel Akpabot, on Nigerian football

I

A military helicopter hovers above the centre-circle, uncertainly nodding and dipping. The side door slides open and out of its round metal belly a few footballs are tossed on to the parched and patchy grass of the Accra stadium. Then a few more. Then another sackful spilling across the halfway line, coming to rest in hastily assembled constellations on the pitch. The 1978 African Cup of Nations is about to begin. Ghana's military government is so broke it seems it cannot offer bread with its circus, so this birdseed will have to do. It is not as if they haven't had time to prepare. In 1972 General Acheampong led the coup that displaced the civilian government of the Second Ghanaian republic led by President Busia. The generals denounced the corruption and flagrant self-interest of the political classes that had seen the relentless decline of both Ghana's economy and national football team. Acheampong made himself chairman of the ruling National Redemption Council and took the post of Minister of Sport as well. Two years later, the general has secured the 1978 African Cup of Nations for Ghana, hoping for a political and sporting success for his regime. But that is perhaps all that had been secured. Despite Acheampong's unilaterally renouncing many of Nkrumah's and Busia's international debts, rescheduling others and nationalizing foreign companies in a bid for economic self-reliance, capital was fleeing the country, the currency was soft as cocoa butter and the economy continued to shrink. Ghanaians took to the streets where they were met by harsh repression epitomized when armed troops stormed and then closed the country's universities. The military shut down independent newspapers and Canute-like passed a law forbidding the spreading of rumours. General Acheampong's way out was to create

650

a government based on a civilian constitution, but with permanent places in the cabinet for the military and a ban on political parties in perpetuity. A referendum on this issue had been scheduled for the week after the final of the Cup of Nations. All that was required was for Ghana to win it for the first time since 1965. Acheampong and the chairman of the tournament's organizing committee, Colonel Simpe-Asante, devoted themselves to the task. The Black Stars were bankrolled properly for the first time since the fall of Nkrumah and a variety of trials and tribulations were prepared for any visiting team with the temerity to actually play Ghana. So, of course, they made the final. Their opponents were Uganda.

In the years immediately before and after independence from Britain in 1962 Ugandan football was a backwater. The national team, the Cranes, failed to qualify for the Cup of Nations in the 1960s and their club sides made no impression beyond their borders. This was to change with the arrival in power of General Idi Amin. The then Prime Minister Milton Obote left Uganda in 1971 for a Commonwealth Conference in Singapore. He left instructions to the effect that Amin and his supporters in the army should be arrested. Amin struck first and, in a short coup, seized control, immediately setting about the slaughter of large numbers of troops whose loyalty was uncertain. Military officers were appointed to senior posts in every institution in the country and military courts placed above the civilian system; the country was ruled from the army's barracks. Amin, who had been a talented boxer in his youth in the British Army, also looked to the national football team to bring glory and prestige to his regime.

The national team were one of the very few institutions outside the army to receive any of Amin's notoriously short span of attention. The talents of strikers like Philip Omondi and Stanley 'Tank' Maribu were combined with small but regular injections of cash and shopping trips to Tripoli in the presidential jet, and suddenly Uganda had made three consecutive Nations Cup tournaments (1974, '76, '78). Now in Ghana they were good enough to beat the Moroccans and the Congolese in the group stages and sweep the Nigerians aside to make their first and only final.

18 March 1978
Ghana 2 Uganda 0
Accra, Ghana

General Ignatius Kutu Acheampong has swapped his fatigues for a white suit and sits sweating in the dignitaries' box, the final of the African Cup of Nations in front of him. His head glistens with perspiration. He sips, then gulps from his glass of cognac. He lights cigarette after cigarette. He is waiting for the goals that will win the game, that will win the cup, that will win his referendum, that will keep him in power. Somewhere near Kampala General Idi Amin is listening to the radio, waiting for the goal that will win the game, that will win the cup, that will keep him in power. It has come to this, ruling elites so flimsy that they cast their lot on a game of football.

The Black Stars lead by a single first-half goal from Opoku Afriye, but that is no guarantee of anything. Then Afriye strikes the ball past the fingertips of the Ugandan keeper. General Acheampong pulls out his big white handkerchief and mops his brow. Ghana are the champions. He hands over the trophy and leaves by helicopter for Government House. He won his referendum in March, but only just. In the end it made no difference. A year later he was deposed in another coup and then executed by firing squad. Colonel Simpe-Asante was sentenced to ten years' hard labour. General Amin sent his army to Tanzania and lost.

It is no coincidence that Wole Soyinka, one of Africa's leading intellectuals of the last half-century, should see nationhood and football as self-evidently intertwined. In the dismal decades after the oil shocks, the political potency of football revealed by Nkrumah's Ghana in the 1960s and Mobutu's Zaire in the early 1970s would be taken up across the continent. In societies that were bereft historically, institutionally or demographically of any meaningful site of national unity, nothing would prove more effective, if shortlived, in creating a symbol, a locus of national pride, than Africa's football teams. But as Acheampong and Amin found, football is a capricious game. There is always more failure than success and its successes are either ephemeral or uncontrollable. In the end the belly requires more than trophies and ecstasy.

Yet football proved utterly irresistible to Africa's elites. International football in particular provided the sole arena in which post-colonial Africa could register a faster rate of advance than the rest of the developing world. The importance of Africa to João Havelange's campaign for the FIFA presidency in 1974 gave CAF a level of institutional leverage that no African alliance had achieved in international political or economic forums. Football also provided a space in which the remnants of a meaningful pan-Africanism could be sustained. CAF itself was in comparison with the Organization of African Unity a model of efficiency and effective collaboration. Despite the economic and infrastructural constraints on travel and administration in Africa, CAF successfully organized and expanded the African Cup of Nations every two years, and at club level added a Cup Winners' Cup to the African Champions Cup. At the same time a new post-colonial migration of African footballers had begun to showcase the continent's talents in Europe. Africa's claim to be the third continent in global football ultimately rested on the vivid qualities of the players it produced and the football they played. Nigerian sports writer Samuel Akpabot's acclamation of the dynamism and excitement they generated can stand proxy for the wave of emotion and energy unleashed by football across Africa.

Beyond its own borders, Africa was judged at the World Cup. Zaire's dismal performance in 1974 had left a question mark hanging over the quality of African football but in Argentina in 1978, Tunisia began to change perceptions. In their opening match in Rosario Tunisia went 1–0 down to Mexico after conceding a very questionable penalty just before half-time. However, after the interval the Tunisians scored three times to win the game, the last two goals coming in the final ten minutes as the North Africans demonstrated greater fitness and tenacity than the Mexicans. It was the first match won by an African side in a World Cup finals. Tunisia's coach Chetali remarked, 'The world has laughed at Africa, but now the mockery is over.'[1]

Four years later in Spain, Africa had two qualifiers in the expanded tournament, Algeria and Cameroon. The West Africans were unbeaten – drawing all three of the games with Peru, Poland and Italy – and earning their sobriquet the 'Indomitable Lions'. Only goal difference prevented them progressing from the group. The Algerians came even closer to the next round. In an extraordinary opening match they beat the eventual finalists West Germany 2–1 with goals from their stars Rabah Madjer and Lakhdar Belloumi. After defeat to Austria 2–0 they looked like they were on their way home but the team rallied to beat Chile 3–2 and give themselves, depending on results in the other game in their group, a chance of progressing to the next round. West Germany were playing Austria, and a 1–0 victory to the Germans would see both teams through. The Germans scored ten minutes into the match and the next eighty minutes were played out as a grotesque and interminable kickabout. Algerian fans furiously waved banknotes through the perimeter fence at the players.

The Algerians were back in 1986 and this time they were joined by Morocco. Algeria's campaign in Mexico was less successful, losing to Spain and Brazil and only managing a 1–1 draw with Northern Ireland. Morocco, however, passed another milestone for African football, making it beyond the group stage. They began with goalless draws against Poland and England – more a consequence of their almost neurotic caution than their lack of talent – but summoned their best in a 3–1 demolition of Portugal to top their group. Once again West Germany was Africa's World Cup nemesis. Morocco held the Germans for almost the entire match; extra time approached, the Germans had a free kick outside the Moroccan box. The North Africans failed to organize their defensive wall and then Lothar Matthäus took his chance, driving a low shot inside the post.

The African teams at the World Cups of the 1970s – Morocco, Tunisia and Zaire – were exclusively made up of domestic players who existed in the grey area between the impoverished amateurism of most of African football and the semi-professionalism of state-sponsored sport. The early trickle of migrants from Africa to European football of the 1950s and 1960s had dried up as post-independence African sports ministries banned migration and brought players home. The economic downturn of the mid-1970s saw many European states impose import controls on consumer goods, economic migrants and professional footballers alike. In any case, before 1982, foreign clubs were not obliged to release their

African professionals for international tournaments. Africa's national sides were denied access to the few pioneers that had made the great trek north. Until the mid-1980s nearly all of these players began their careers in France and Belgium. Belgium had relaxed its player import laws in 1978 and immediately Zairians began to play in considerable numbers in the top league. Other West Africans joined them like Senegalese sensation Jules Bocandé. Anglophone Africans, unable to break into small-minded English football, began their careers in Belgium too, including Nigerians like Stephen Keshi and Daniel Amokachi, and the Zambian Kalusha Bwalya.

African players in Belgium were economic migrants with a foreign passport. In France, the other major destination for African players, the situation was more varied, reflecting the complex relationship between ethnicity, nationality and migration that faced all Africans in Europe. First, French football had never stopped fielding the children of Algerian migrants to France who possessed dual nationality. When the Algerian government allowed them to play in their national team, Algeria acquired a whole crop of seasoned professionals, including Mustapha Dahleb, captain of Paris Saint-Germain. Second, many African-born players took French citizenship, such as Jean Tigana, who was born in Bamako in Mali, and Marcel Desailly, born in Ghana, who both played for the French national team. Third, there was a small but growing band of genuine football migrants, notably the Cameroonians like Jean-Pierre Tokoto, Roger Milla, Thomas N'Kono and Eugene Ekeke. But of all this generation of African migrants the sinuous Ghanaian midfielder Abédi Pelé stands out. He first came to the world's attention as the seventeen-year-old wonder who helped Ghana to victory in the 1982 Cup of Nations. Over the next decade and a half he played top-flight football in Qatar, Switzerland, France, Italy, Germany and the UAE, peaking in the early 1990s when he captained Olympique Marseille (the first African to lead a major European club) as they won four French league titles and the European Cup in 1993.

The wider impact of this generation of football migrants was twofold. First, they paved the way in European football culture for the massive wave of African footballers that would follow them in the 1990s. Their initial presence alongside black Europeans exposed the enduring racism of European football's dressing rooms and terraces; but their professionalism and talent forced open a habitable space for those that would follow. But they also took African football a step further up the down escalator – an almost impossible balancing act of developing the game by engagement with the highest levels of professional football and under-developing the game by draining domestic football of its leading talents and attractions.

The breakthrough of African football on the world stage in the 1970s and 1980s rested on the consolidation of deeply rooted and intensely experienced domestic football cultures, irresistible to the urban masses and the political elites alike. In the rapidly growing cities of the continent, football was not just the most popular sport but one of the central hubs of urban popular culture, cultures that were no mere emulations of Europe and Latin America but constituted Africa's own distinctive con-tribution to global football. By the mid-1970s it was clear that, for the overwhelming majority of Africa, football would not just be the national sport – it was the only sport. Among whites in South Africa and Zim-babwe cricket and rugby continued to exert a considerable hold, but they were embattled and embittered minorities clinging to their pre-eminent political status and their elitist minority sports. In East Africa athletics, especially distance running, provided the only alternative source of inter-national sporting glory, but despite the brilliance of Kenyan, Tanzanian and Ethiopian athletes their exploits were never going to form the basis of a potent national popular sporting culture for spectators or participants.

Beyond the arena of formal, semi-professional sports, football's domi-nance was even more uncontested. Games could be found on almost any half-empty piece of land in any African city from Tunis to Dar-es-Salaam, from Lusaka to Lagos. Neighbourhood football tournaments between informally constituted local sides with micro-backers and spon-sors began to grow up alongside the official leagues run by national football associations. As Simon Kuper put it after visiting Cameroon:

On my first morning in Yaoundé, I discovered why Cameroonians are good at football; they play a lot. Forget all that nonsense about African suppleness . . . all you need to know is that at lunchtime, in the evening and all weekend,

Yaoundé turns into a football pitch. Some kickarounds draw dozens of spectators, and the quality of play is rare.[2]

The strength and depth of youth football in Africa was given an opportunity to shine in the new tournaments established by João Havelange and FIFA in the 1970s. Part of Havelange's agenda, bankrolled by Coca-Cola, was the creation of World Cup tournaments at under-20 and under-17 levels. While this would be good for the development of promising talents everywhere, the access such an event provided to FIFA money and global exposure was of particular value to developing nations. The first World Youth Cup (under-20s) was held in Tunis in 1977, while African teams have done particularly well in the under-17 title championship with both Ghana and Nigeria winning twice. The failure of the senior sides to maintain this kind of competitive record demonstrates the importance of the resources, facilities and experience that are available to football players in the richer countries of Europe and Latin America and the inadvisability of putting over-age players into tournaments designed for youth development. Yet the victories in the youth tournaments also point to the exceptional pool of precocious talent that urban African football has thrown up.

African football also benefited from an influx of foreign coaches. Yugoslavs were particularly prominent in the 1960s and 1970s, reflecting the country's regular diplomatic contacts with developing nations through the non-aligned movement. Nigeria's international team was nurtured in the 1970s by Father Tiko and both Morocco and Zaire went to the World Cup under Blagoje Vidinic. Soviets and other Eastern Europeans, whose anti-imperialist credentials could be assumed, were also employed. For those who could afford the wages Brazilians were the preferred option; for example, Otto Gloria coached Nigeria to their first Cup of Nations victory in 1980. The 1970s and 1980s saw more Northern Europeans take jobs in Africa; the indefatigable German Peter Schnittger managed Cameroon and the intolerant and irascible Dutchman Clemens Westerhof went to Nigeria. In the 1990s they would be succeeded by a deluge of French coaches. Within Africa this has been and continues to be a matter of almost neurotic debate. On the one hand, club and national teams have clearly benefited from access to the specialist knowledge foreign coaches brought from the professional game: tactics and formations, specialization and technique, training and preparation. On the other hand, foreign coaches have been denounced as racists, authoritarians, neocolonials who have kept local coaches from progressing, who take the money and run, and who lack any sensitivity to local cultures. What they often lacked was in fact sensitivity to local politics: they had the misapprehension that their role and powers were the same as they would be in Europe. But football in Africa was just not the same: the uniqueness of African football cultures must be explained by its intersection with two other key elements of popular African urban cultures – music and *muti*.

If football does have a competitor in the heart of Africa's cities then that can only be music, and it has offered the stiffest competition. Whereas Africa's pre-colonial games and pastimes have been all but lost in the colonial deluge, African traditional music has proved more resilient. While football has seen the wholesale importation of the game and its subsequent modification and embellishment in Africa, the continent's musicians have retained the brilliance of their own historical traditions, modifying and modernizing them in more selective and controllable ways; taking new rhythms from Latin America and the Caribbean and new technologies of production and reproduction from the West. While the leading musicians have a domestic public profile often greater and more venerated than footballers, their international impact has been less recognized. The conservatism of mass consumer markets in the West has proved a sturdier defence than the drilled back lines of European football teams. But in reality the two are not opposed but enriched by each other.

African football stadiums did not ring with the dry spontaneous wit of the English or the organized sentimentality of the Italian *tifosi*; they vibrated to a different energy. Percussion is ubiquitous in African football: drums, rattles and shakers of every kind and size provide the essential beat of the stands. Customs vary but unlike European crowds whose music rises and falls with the fortunes of their side, African crowds maintain their rhythm throughout a game – some do not even pause to celebrate a goal or take a dumbfounded break when they go behind.

Muti, ju-ju, m'pungu, blimba are just some of the many words in African languages for the complex of beliefs that are held in the supernatural, in the animist realm of the spirit and in practices of witchcraft, magic and divination. It is also just one of many belief systems in the world of sport; viewed from even the narrowest perspective it is blindingly clear that in games as uncertain as football and in contexts where so much personal and collective emotion is riding on the outcome, systems of superstition and hopes of influencing the outcome of unknowable events will be widespread. In Latin America and the Mediterranean Catholicism, which has always retained elements of the cultic and the magic, fulfils this function as players cross themselves on entering the pitch and offer prayers and sacrifice before and after to whatever motley collection of saints and spirits they choose. In the Protestant and Anglican cultures of Northern Europe, where magic had been so much more successfully driven from religion, these practices merely reappear as secular and traditional superstition: players who must enter the pitch ninth, managers who wear the same lucky suit, fans who touch the same lucky charm in their jacket pocket. Malian team Djoliba all shaved their heads after a spiritual consultation. The Romanian team at the 1998 World Cup all dyed their hair blond. African football possesses the same repertoire of behaviour as other football cultures but it is connected to a much richer living tradition of magic and ritual.

It has not been uncommon to see players walking backwards into a stadium or climbing over its outer walls because a witchdoctor or *sangoma* has told them that they can avoid curses and charms in this way. An excavation of Africa's pitches would reveal a skeletal menagerie. In Kinshasa in 1969 groundsmen unearthed a human skull in the centre-circle of the May 20th stadium where the home team had been unbeatable. A similar examination beneath African football's stands and inside its dressing rooms and kitbags would throw up carved figurines, cryptic messages, bracelets of gut and rings of copper, ointments, potions and herbs. Although leading players and administrators in the game have argued that only professionalism, discipline and work can bring success, though they never tire of repeating the occasions on which these supernatural practices have failed to deliver the expected result, governments, fans, players and club officials have consistently turned to *muti*.

For some, safety comes in numbers. In Côte d'Ivoire before the 1984 Cup of Nations around 150 witchdoctors were assembled in the host team's hotel. Gadji-Celi, then captain of the team, recalls:

Our rooms were loaded with pots of various sizes and filled with all kinds of concoctions. Every player was made to take a bath in the odious liquids at what we jokingly called 'the laboratory' after which he would be invited to say his wishes privately into the ear of a living pigeon.[3]

A similar gathering was held at the behest of the Sports Ministry in 1992 before the Elephants left on their victorious journey to the Cup of Nations in Senegal. However, some of the staff were not paid and they put a curse on the national team which has failed miserably since. In 2002 the new government of the country took the curse seriously enough to try and lift it with a gift of booze and $2,000 in cash to the disgruntled priests.

Nigeria's FA and national team took the potency of Ivorian *ju-ju* seriously enough that before a game in Abidjan in 1993 they refused to shake hands with the country's Prime Minister and Sports Minister under orders from the team's own spiritual advisers. In the end they are in the majority. While the modernizers and rationalists in African football deplore *muti*, and CAF has sought to ban its overt use in its competitions, magic is still alive and well throughout the continent.

IV

African football had arrived. Born of the struggle against colonialism and nourished by the euphoria of independence, its curse was to assume its settled form under the weight of economic decline, political instability, military violence and widespread corruption. Its growth and successes are thus testament to the resilience and invention of its players and fans. The mid-1970s saw two long historical movements come to an end in Africa: the long capitalist boom of the post-war era and the process of decolonization. The wounds of late decolonization and the enduring uncertainty of national boundaries and national identities born of early decolonization left their mark on football and society in lusophone Africa, Morocco, Ethiopia and Mauritius. By late 1975, the Portuguese had left their African colonies. As the last migrants' crates landed in Lisbon, Guinea-Bissau, the Cape Verde Islands, Angola and Mozambique declared independence. The fragility of these states and the extent of their civil wars meant that, unlike for an earlier generation of independent countries, membership of CAF would not be declared immediately. Football would have to wait on the outcome of their civil wars. Mozambique and Angola joined CAF in 1978 and 1980 respectively. The Angolan league did not start until 1979 and in both countries football was overwhelmingly concentrated in their capital cities – the only places where their governments' writs actually ran. Cape Verde, Guinea-Bissau and São Tomé and Príncipe were even later starters, joining CAF in 1986.

In 1975 King Hassan of Morocco marched a motley civilian cavalcade of around 300,000 people, part-volunteer part-drafted, into the disputed territory of Western Sahara which they claimed for the Moroccan state. Despite a long guerrilla war with Polisario – the local Sahrawi nationalist movement – and a long cold war with neighbouring Algeria, Morocco held the territory. One of the central planks of Casablanca's policy of integration and normalization in the region was to build a 30,000-seat football stadium in the capital city Laâyoune. It now houses the only watered turf for hundreds of kilometres and is home to Jeunesse Sportive Al Massira which has become an integral part of the Moroccan first division. Five years later, the long war in Rhodesia would end; Zimbabwe declared independence and joined CAF in 1980. Only South Africa and Namibia remained in European hands and outside of African football's institutions and competitions.

Yet if the borders of African states were being finalized, the meaning of the nations that lived within them was by no means settled. That question was particularly acute in Ethopia. The Italian colony of Eritrea had, despite internal opposition, been federated by the UN to Ethiopia in 1952. Although some degree of autonomy was allowed to the Eritreans, a process of absorption saw the country officially annexed to Ethiopia in 1962. Eritrean football remained strong in this era with the region's leading clubs playing in a now national Ethiopian league, while fearsome rivalries developed among teams in the local league; between Hamassien from the capital Asmara, Seraye from the southern highlands and Akale Guzay in the south-east. These rivalries were strong enough to ignite violence on occasion. Indeed, the now growing and armed Eritrean nationalist movements – the EPLF and EPF – believed that the Ethiopian authorities were deliberately stoking these conflicts in a bid to destabilize Eritrean politics. In 1974 the Eritrean liberation movements sent a joint letter to the clubs asking them to stop playing in an effort to douse the conflict. Then Haile Selassie was overthrown in a military coup in Addis Ababa. The Eritreans took to the battlefield and by 1977 controlled all of the country but for Asmara. Football came to a grinding halt.

Questions of ethnicity and nationality also plagued politics and football in the island state of Mauritius. The island's demographic and footballing mosaic contained Muslims (Muslim Scouts), Chinese (Dragons FC), Hindus (Hindu Cadets), Tamils (Tamil Cadets), Franco-Mauritians (Dodo Club), Creoles (Fire Brigade) and Coloureds (Racing). All of these clubs had exclusive ethnic memberships, coercing their own community to play for them and rejecting those from outside of it. Violence during and after games between the different groups had been commonplace for over two decades and had at times proved so bad that the government had suspended football altogether (in 1956, '64, '69 and '75). In 1982 the ruling MMM party (Mouvement Militant Mauricien) attempted to control the situation as part of a wider policy of Mauritianism. Ethnic affiliations were to be banned; clubs were to be made open to all, name changes were insisted upon, but to no avail. Ethnic identity among the clubs remained as strong as ever and in the 1990s these differences would turn to violence in island-wide rioting at football matches.

For those states that were not primarily occupied with war, there was the fallout from the oil-price rises of 1973 to deal with. The global economic slowdown that followed struck a devastating blow to the already fragile economies and overstretched states of the continent. Non-oil producers were hit by massive import bills, while commodity prices for minerals and agricultural exports plummeted. Much of Africa – including its football clubs and players – would become caught in a downward spiral of escalating debts, political authoritarianism and administrative meltdown. Three broad political responses to the enduring economic and political problems of African societies emerged. First, across the continent many ruling parties and presidents claimed to be pursuing some variant of African socialism. Second, in North Africa relatively authoritarian states were constructed on the basis of Africa's most homogenous religious and ethnic populations, and those states were used as tools of economic development. Third, in West, East and Central Africa politics became characterized by a combination of authoritarianism and patrimonialism, as states became instruments for the division of the spoils rather than social and economic development. In all three cases football became enmeshed with these distinct structures of power.

Almost all the leaders of Africa's post-colonial states declared their adherence to some kind of socialism at some points in their careers – even those that were clearly not socialists of any fashion. European socialism's opposition to imperialism and its vision of a developmentalist and interventionist state had obvious appeal, even if its presuppositions of the existence of an industrialized economy and a society stratified by class rather than geography or ethnicity doomed it to irrelevance in Africa. One of the continent's leading teams in the immediate post-imperial era, Congo-Brazzaville, was run as a self-proclaimed Marxist state. After the national team had performed poorly at the 1968 Cup of Nations in Ethiopia, leaking eight goals and losing all their games, the Minister of Sport announced his displeasure with what was called the 'debacle of Asmara'. He disbanded the squad and began a period of intensive state support. The Red Devils went on a victorious run in the 1972 African Cup of Nations where they beat Mali 3–2 in the final.

However, Afro-communism proved an unstable master. After a series of internal military coups in the 1970s Congo's footballing prowess collapsed. The Marxist regimes in Dahomey and Upper Volta proved unable to stimulate either sporting or economic development. General Mathieu Kérékou came to power in Benin in 1972. The declaration of Marxism-Leninism as official state ideology (and the renaming of the country as Benin) coincided with the disappearance of league football altogether for three years. In Upper Volta (renamed Burkina Faso in 1984) the endless cycle of coup and counter-coup within the army saw the football season lost (in 1981 and 1982) to the chaos of civil war. However, in all of these regimes the impact of socialist ideas on the actual organization of state, economy and society was very limited. To explore a stronger relationship between football, politics and socialist planning we must look at two other African states: Guinea in the west, Tanzania in the east.

Tanzania was created in 1964 by the fusion of two newly independent states Tanganyika and Zanzibar. The former was led by Julius Nyerere and his socialist Tanganyikan African National Union (TANU), the latter by the revolutionary Afro-Shiraz Party (ASP). Both had forged close connections between football and nationalism during the struggle for independence. In Dar-es-Salaam membership of the Young Africans club and TANU were synonymous. In Zanzibar the ASP and Wananichi Sports Club had the same relationship. The clubs had offered a convenient front for political meetings during the colonial era and through their mutual aid and annual cultural festivals provided an early forum for discussing the union of the two colonies. In 1965 the two parties merged and Tanzania became a one-party state. The ideology that would shape that state emerged as the Arusha declaration after TANU's long congress in 1967. Arusha, the single most considered and coherent document to emerge from the African socialist tradition, proposed an indigenous and alternative model of development. Tanzanian socialism would emphasize the rural over the urban, pursue agricultural reforms and self-reliance, and look to indigenous cultural traditions rather than colonial imports. It proved, economically and politically, to be deeply flawed. But in the late 1960s and 1970s Arusha provided a socialist framework for governing every aspect of Tanzanian life, including sport.

Almost uniquely in Africa, sporting glory was not the central concern of the new sporting elite; rather power and control were their aims. TANU created a new centralized sports bureaucracy and gave itself ample powers to interfere in any aspect of sporting business. It decried the indiscipline of players, the incompetence and larceny of administrators, the disrespect and instability of spectators and eventually the entire colonial sporting heritage that had displaced and destroyed indigenous games and pastimes. While other African one-party states pursued victory, TANU harassed and then sacked the board of the Football Association of Tanzania and appointed its own placemen. Tanzania's very poor record in international and club competition bears out these priorities. Then in 1975 the Young Africans crisis saw TANU strictly apply its policy of national self-reliance to football. Young Africans' Zairian coach went on record after a defeat in the Champions Cup: officials at the club were corrupt, money had gone missing, and preparations had been hopeless. In the ensuing row the club was split down the middle and the players refused to take the field at a number of special TANU events. A police investigation was begun, the club was suspended and its officials were charged with conspiracy. TANU claimed that there were foreign and subversive agents at work. Young Africans' coach was forced to leave the country as was the Guinean boss at city rivals Sunderland. Then all foreign coaches were banned and an edict issued to all clubs to Africanize their names and show patriotism and nationalism. Despite these displays of strength TANU's hold on Tanzanian society was always short of the rhetoric. Just as their model village programmes totally failed to control rural life, so its failed attempt to create a model patriotic footballing culture was exemplified by the game held in late 1975 to celebrate the independence of fellow socialist state Mozambique; the match was cancelled as fighting in the crowd became uncontrollable.

Whereas East African socialism saw a decline in sporting fortunes, the tiny West African state of Guinea had its moment of brilliance and oil-rich Algeria rebuilt its football heritage on new socialist lines. Guinea was the first French colony to achieve independence. The nationalists were led by the mercurial Ahmed Sékou Touré who had cut his political teeth in French West Africa as a communist and a trade-union organizer. When the region was offered independence or continued membership of the French Empire in a referendum in 1958, Guinea alone voted overwhelmingly for independence. Sékou Touré became President and announced both his authoritarianism and his canny grasp of popular culture immediately. There was a sharp clampdown on the trade unions that had brought him to power, a programme of collectivized agriculture was begun and Guinea's musicians were marshalled and organized by the state to ensure that the country danced to the right tunes. In the early 1970s Sékou Touré turned his attention to football, taking over the running of the nation's leading club Hafia FC Conakry. He ran it the way the Soviets would have done. The club became state property, its players state employees. Migration of the considerable talent in the team – including Petit Sory, Cherif Souleyman and Papa Camara – was banned. Hafia showed what a little centralized control could do as they won the African Champions Cup in 1972 and 1975. In 1976 they had the temerity to lose the final to Moloudia Algiers on penalties and on their return the team were sent to the infamous Camp Boiro for political re-education; for some, their visit meant an abrupt termination of their careers. It seemed to work as the following year saw Hafia win the cup again, beating Ghana's Hearts of Oak. Sékou Touré was sufficiently appeased that he chose this occasion to release a trickle of the many political prisoners rotting in his jails. But there are limits to the strategy of intimidation and fear. The following year Hafia lost their title to Cameroon's Canon Yaoundé and in his increasingly erratic rage Sékou Touré issued a presidential decree placing seven players in irons. It was Hafia's last final. Sékou Touré's plan to nationalize the entire economy finally hit the rocks in 1977 when he attempted to make the country's markets subject to state regulation. The women who ran the stalls led a riot in Conakry of such fury that the regime retreated from its policy and lost control, which it never regained. The Guinean economy went into free fall and the funds for football dried up.

VI

Algeria may have been a socialist state in the 1980s but it was also a North African Arabic state and in that regard its successes and failures were shared with the other states of the region. Algeria, Egypt, Morocco and Tunisia all made it to the World Cup, and Algeria, Egypt and Morocco all won the African Cup of Nations. But the enormous strength of football in the region was only revealed when, after many years of scepticism regarding African club competitions and deep cultural and political reticence to accept that their sporting fate lay south of the Sahara rather than east of Suez, North African football clubs began to participate in African competitions. When they did, they were un-stoppable. Al-Ahly, still the leading club of Egypt, announced the shift of power when they beat Ghana's Asante Kotoko to win the Champions Cup in 1982, and lost the following year's final to the Ghanaians by a single goal. Not to be outdone, their old Cairo adversaries Zamalek took the title in 1984 and 1986. They were joined by the clubs of the Moroccan army and the Casablanca working class – FAR Rabat and Raja Casablanca – who won the cup in 1985 and 1989. The Algerians Entente Plasticiens Sétif (1988) and JS Kabylie (1981 and 1990) maintained the trend. In the mid-1980s Egyptian teams won the African Cup Winners' Cup five years in a row; two for the nouveau-riche Al-Mokaoulun and three in a row for the old money of Al-Ahly, while Club Athlétique Bizerte's Cup Winners' Cup victory in 1988 announced the arrival of Tunisian teams at the summit of African club football; they were to remain there all the way through the 1990s.

Why should this be? North Africa's international performances were better than sub-Saharan Africa's in the World Cup but poorer in the African Cup of Nations; however, in club football they became unassailable. The heart of this matter is not for romantics. First, the number of players migrating from North Africa was insignificant. Although no North African league was officially or fully professional at this time, the level of wages and other rewards that star players could expect was significantly greater than their equivalents in Nigeria or Ghana. Governments also lent a hand, dissuading the leading players and entreating them to remain at home. North Africa's governments were capable of a level of surveillance and control that could not be matched by the brutal but disorganized security apparatus of a Zaire or a Liberia.

But most importantly football in North Africa reflected a level of institutional stability, organization and wealth that could not be equalled south of the Sahara. Egypt, whose football and society had been shattered by the impact of the continuing wars with Israel, began to rebuild. Nasser's death had seen his vice-president Anwar Sadat take power and sign the region's first and only peace accord with Israel in 1977. Although this elicited very negative responses from the rest of the Arab world and militants in Egypt, it gave the Egyptian economy a breathing space and opened the door to massive American aid. Tunisia continued under the grim but steady authoritarianism of President Bourguiba whose gradual decline into senility was quietly handled by a bloodless coup organized within the upper echelons of the military. Bourguiba was tactfully put out to grass in 1987 and General Ben Ali took the helm where he has remained undisturbed since. Morocco too, apart from its imperial adventures in Western Sahara, remained politically unaltered throughout the era, run by the royal house and its compliant political elite. Even Libya under Colonel Qaddafi, which displayed the most erratic and unlikely foreign policies, was domestically very clearly and firmly under his command. Although none of these states could be described as wealthy, steady economic progress was made. In Algeria and Libya oil and gas were the key to this. Morocco and Tunisia saw tourism, agriculture and light industries prospering, while Egypt was buoyed by peacetime reconstruction and the lifting of the previously suffocating level of inept state control of the economy.

In this context the leading clubs of each state could establish and maintain a level of facilities that were the envy of Africa. Clubs like Al-Ahly, Zamalek, Raja and Wydad Casablanca had their key patrons within the country's ruling elites. Espérance of Tunis were effectively the team of the presidency. Al-Mokaoulun were the team of the fabulously wealthy Osman family who had made their money in construction. These clubs could also draw on large paying crowds. Given this kind of income they could run extensive scouting and youth-training programmes and maintain larger and more stable squads. Transport, accommodation, equipment, support staff and medical experts were all available. The cumulative impact of all of these factors gave the clubs a decisive advantage over the rest of Africa in club competitions.

North Africa's relative economic and sporting prowess also meant that these states had the infrastructure and influence to regularly win the right to host the African Cup of Nations. In a ten-year run they staged four out of five tournaments: Libya in 1982, Egypt in 1986, Morocco in 1988 and Algeria in 1990. Not surprisingly all these states sought to make considerable political capital from the occasion. Qaddafi certainly did not waste the opportunity of a 60,000 crowd and the continent's television cameras to make a big splash. In fact, two and a half hours of it. In an amazingly wide-ranging speech that barely stopped for a moment to discuss football, the crowd, the teams and the sporting press were treated to a long discussion of French foreign policy in Chad, the situation in the Sudan, the evils of American foreign policy and, of course, a good dose of radical pan-Africanism. Qaddafi saved his best bile for the Egyptians and their treacherous peace deal. The Egyptians, however, were not present. President Sadat had done his best to stop the tournament going to Tripoli at all. Egypt had then qualified for the tournament and was due to play in Libya's group. Sadat was assassinated soon afterwards by Islamicists and in the political chaos and repression that followed the Egyptians decided to pull out of the tournament. Backed by intensely partisan crowds, the Libyans made it to the final where they faced a resurgent Ghana under coach CK Gyamfi and a new government under coup leader Flight Lieutenant Jerry Rawlings. The Ghanaians won 7–6 on penalties and the crowd responded to the spirit of pan-Africanism infusing the games by showering their visitors with stones and abuse, invading the pitch and disrupting the presentation ceremony. The Black Stars ran for it, past giant posters in French, English and Arabic proclaiming that 'Blacks will inherit the world'.

The vicissitudes of national politics were at play again in 1986 in Egypt. The tournament opened against a background of political insecurity. President Mubarak's security forces had just finished suppressing a failed revolt by police conscripts; a good Cup of Nations was a political necessity.

---

21 March 1986
Egypt 0 Cameroon 0
(aet; Egypt won 5–4 on penalties)
National Stadium, Cairo

He has sat with all of them. Selassie, Bourguiba, Mengistu, Sadat, King Hassan, Ahmadu Ahidjo, General Acheampong, Colonel Qaddafi, Felix Houphouët-Boigny and the rest. Squat Ethiopian sphinx Mr Tessema has sat at the heart of the African body politic for twenty years, but he has remained untouched by their pathological use of power. Unwavering, gently spoken bull.

Today is Mubarak's turn. Everyone is nervous. The Egyptian authorities are frightened by their radicals and desperate for their team to win. The Cameroonians are frightened by the crowd as they play out an unfamiliar, crab-like, cautious 0–0 draw in front of 100,000 baying Egyptians. It is not clear whether the 5,000 troops that ring the lower stands are here to protect or intimidate. It's a nasty, spiteful, mean game.

Mr Tessema is dying. In Egypt's semi-final their star Tahar Abouzid scored and celebrated wildly with the crowd. The referee booked him for his exuberance. Abouzid would be suspended from the final. The Egyptians pleaded with Mr Tessema; just for once, just this once, could he, could he please just bend the rules a little? Mr Tessema never bent the rules.

Mr Tessema is dying of cancer. It is eating his body. The Tanzanian referee is made to write an excruciating letter of apology in which he rescinds the yellow card. CAF concoct a line that he has misinterpreted FIFA regulations and directives. Abouzid plays. The Egyptians win when Cameroon miss the final penalty. Mr Tessema will not sit in the box again.

VII

If on occasion socialist planning and North African developmentalism could sustain football success, in much of post-colonial Africa the politics of the belly – of the patrimonial state – tended to undermine it. Across West and Central Africa multi-party states were turned into one-party states; ruling parties in which debate was permitted gave way to parties that were solely devices for distributing patronage. Democratic institutions and alternative centres of power were steadily eroded and all-powerful executives and charismatic presidents became the undisputed centres of political power. From that centre networks of clientalism and obligation were established. In all these states the military were an important component of those networks and in Ghana and Nigeria were more often than not the executive as well. Ethnic identities, despite the rhetoric of post-colonial nationalism, were the key to accessing power and resources.

The consequences of these arrangements were exemplified by post-independence Nigeria where the progress of football had been as faltering and hesitant as the progress of the nation itself. In 1966 a coup organized by middle-ranking Igbo officers in the Nigerian army began with the assassination of numerous political leaders, including the Prime Minister Abubakar Tafawa Balewa, and the replacement of Nigeria's civilian government with a military administration headed by Major-General Ironsi. Ironsi espoused a typical military populism in which the armed forces would cleanse society of its incompetence and inefficiency, banish corruption and get things done. In the Muslim north the administration was seen as a grab for power by the Igbo. With the active support of the local elites, the massive Igbo diaspora in the cities of northern Nigeria was subject to riots, burnings and executions. Tens of thousands of Igbo headed home while a coterie of northern officers conducted a second coup, assassinating Ironsi and replacing him with General Gowon. In the Igbo-dominated east, where the fat oil spigots had just been turned on, these events were considered so alarming that it appeared that only secession could protect Igbo interests. The independent state of Biafra was soon declared and Nigeria plunged into a three-year-long civil war only resolved by Biafra's surrender to the federal government in 1970.

It is hardly surprising that a nation at war with itself should fail to produce a national team capable of winning. Despite Nigeria's enormous population, long experience of the game and ferocious interest in the huge cities of north and south, the Green Eagles managed to qualify for only one Cup of Nations before 1976 and one Olympic Games tournament in 1968. More significantly, the Nigerian FA had been unable to create a national league while the FA Challenge Cup competition was dominated by teams from the south-west of the country in Lagos and Ibadan. Yet football was unquestionably at the centre of Nigeria's popular imagination. It remains an enduring myth that when Pelé's Santos visited Nigeria in 1969 during the civil war, hostilities stopped for the duration. They didn't, but in the immediate post-war era the government of General Gowon recognized the potential of football to forge a unified national identity. To his credit, Gowon had decided on a non-retributive peace in which national unity and reconciliation would be paramount. Nigeria was deliberately fragmented into many small states to blur the lines of ethnicity, religion and geography in politics. The economy began to recover from the war and the arrival of oil money gave real hope that Nigeria's infrastructure and society could be renovated. Gowon personally ordered the enlargement and refurbishment of the national stadium in Lagos where Nigeria hosted the 1973 All Africa Games. The Nigerians won the football tournament with a team notable for its ethnically mixed composition. The government also gave its support and blessing to the creation of the first national league in Nigerian football in 1972. In Enugu City, in the heart of what was Biafra, the bitter pill of military defeat was sweetened by the creation of Enugu Rangers. Riding on a wave of local patriotism they came to dominate Nigerian football in the mid-1970s. They were also the first Nigerian team to contest an African club cup final, losing in the Champions Cup in 1975.

The national team showed a corresponding improvement in its fortunes, coming third at the 1976 and 1978 Cup of Nations, while later in 1976 Shooting Stars of Ibadan won the Cup Winners' Cup. Gowon himself was not around to see the footballing triumphs he had planned for. He was deposed by his own officers in 1975. Out of the ensuing conflict General Olusegun Obasanjo became head of state. In his three years of rule, the oil really began to flow, and with it confidence rose. Nigeria prepared for the handover of power to a democratically elected civilian authority and the hosting of the 1980 Cup of Nations. The presidency of the Second Nigerian Republic went to Alhaji Shehu Shagari. The Cup of Nations was the chance not just to cement the new regime's rule but to celebrate the rebirth and reinvention of Nigeria – oil-rich, unified, democratic, a leading force in Africa, in football, in the world. Shagari charged the Green Eagles on the eve of the tournament, 'A victory for Nigeria would further make her stand above other African countries and also justify her claim to be Africa's leader in all aspects of life including sports.'[4] Nigeria, under Brazilian coach Otto Gloria, blew Tanzania away in their opening game, scratched a nervous draw against Côte d'Ivoire and beat Egypt to make the semi-finals. Another single goal took them past Morocco and to the final.

---

22 March 1980
Nigeria 3 Algeria 0
Surelere Stadium, Lagos

Football like politics requires that you take your chances when they come. Nigeria's first democratically elected head of state since the civil war, Alhaji Shehu Shagari, has positioned himself on a makeshift scaffolding dais at the centre of the main stand. Dressed in traditional embroidered white robes, Shagari and his entourage, like the rest of the crowd, are beside themselves with excitement, skipping impatiently from one leg to another. Nigerians have made their chances, can they take them?

Not everyone senses their urgency, but they will. The TV commentators are thirty seconds late going on air as the Nigerian and Algerian midfields are already trading tackles. People are still filtering into the stands. The crowd generates a simmering, skin-pinching aural fuzz. Two minutes gone. A long crossfield ball from Christian Chukwu seems to innocently meander its way to the left-hand side of the Algerian penalty area. There is no obvious danger or opening. Segun Odegbami, back to goal, easily outjumps the defender, flicking the ball with the side of his head. It bobbles above him. Suddenly, he has turned to face the goal, arched his back and taken it on his chest. The ball, stunned, drops plumb-line straight to his feet, but there is no way that he could find room to swing such fantastically long legs and strike it cleanly. Segun leans back and scoops the ball on to his toes, flicking his bent leg like a can-can dancer above his chin. The seething white noise of the crowd is set alight by the sparkling cries of relief, surprise and acclamation.

The Algerians, stung and hurting, go on the attack, but as the half nears its end Nigeria's hard-tackling midfield wears them down. Then, from thirty metres out Atuegbu is running into the penalty area, the ball is passed just into his path. He launches himself into a hurried opportunistic volley, catching the ball but only to shoot sharply down onto the pitch. It could have gone anywhere, but today ... The ball lurches over the Algerian centre-back who turns his head to see the sliding body of Segun Odegbami stealing in behind him, stretching and reaching with his pointed toes to take his chance ...

In the second half the Nigerians are released and relaxed and loving it. It's show time now. Nigeria are trying out all of their tricks. Odiye is dummying and opening space with backheels almost too daring for the riven, rutted turf of Surelere. He takes the ball down the left. Stops on it and runs on. Felix Owolabi picks it up, drives towards the Algerian goal and shoots. Cerbah parries it, but today Nigeria are taking their chances. Muda Lawal is there to turn the ricocheting ball back into the net.

On the dais the President gathers his robes and dances. His aides whirl old-fashioned wooden rattles and flick their horsehair whips, the crowd has descended to the pitch and the running track clamouring around the team, the cup, the 'Cup of Unity'. The stadium gates are opened and the ticketless human tidal wave that has been pressing against the walls and the doors floods in.

The Nigerian renaissance was not to last. It collapsed first in the political realm as Shagari's re-election in 1983 was undermined by widespread allegations of intimidation and ballot-rigging. He and Nigeria's short democratic experiment were swept aside by plotters on New Year's Eve 1983 led by General Muhammadu Buhari. The political shackles were screwed down even tighter when Buhari was replaced in a bloodless coup by General Ibrahim Babangida, who accelerated and extended the already widespread systems of corruption and the elite's access to the country's enormous oil wealth. By the late 1980s the Nigerian economy was broke, bled dry by the rapaciousness of its elite and the incompetence of its institutions; its domestic and international football were fatally undermined. The country's immense wealth of talent and invention came up short every time as Nigerian clubs successively lost African club finals, while the newly renamed Super Eagles lost two African Cup of Nations finals to Cameroon. Exhausted by the military incubus, the country was close to collapse. In a vital World Cup qualifier against Angola held in 1989 at the national stadium, the Nigerian midfielder Sam Okwaraji collapsed with a heart condition and died. Nigeria still won but in the ensuing crush on the overcrowded stands, full of hope and desperation, another five people died, the life squeezed out of them against the stadium's barriers.

VIII

Immediately to the south of Nigeria lies Cameroon. While the politics of the belly proved disabling for Nigerian football, Cameroonian football appeared to thrive on it, as the strands of African football and African politics were woven together to create the leading African football power of the era. Cameroon is a country of extraordinary complexity. It is home to around 200 ethnic groups, and has been the colonial possession of Germany, France and Britain. Its ethnic variety is supplemented by two further divisions. In the north it is predominantly Muslim, in the south Christian; in the west it is anglophone and in the east overwhelmingly francophone. It is this distinction that is the most enduring and powerful in its politics. Finally, the course of colonial and post-colonial economic history has seen major migrations of many ethnic groups from their traditional rural areas to the major cities, especially Douala and Yaoundé. The formation of indigenous football clubs from the 1930s onwards was clearly in step with these various forms of stratification. In the early days of Cameroonian football the players, administrators and fans of African clubs all came from the same ethnic group; though over time the demands of success have seen teams field players from other groups.

The two dominant ethnic groups in francophone Cameroon are the

Bamileke and the Beti. Beti is actually a collective noun for a whole series of southern ethnic groups whose languages are closely connected and whose unity has been forged by the networks of political patronage that they have controlled since independence. Their teams have been Canon and Tonnerre Yaoundé though both have attracted distinct subgroups of the Beti to their colours. The Bamileke (who are also a recent colonial amalgamation of a number of grassland groups) originated in the west of the country and have settled as successful economic migrants all over Cameroon. Perceived as critics and opponents of the Beti-dominated regime, their teams include Racing Bafoussam, Diamant Yaoundé and Union Douala. In the impoverished west of Cameroon the anglophone population did not originally have the resources to create football teams alone, dependent as they were on foreign agricultural companies. Thus the local state stepped in and created Public Works Department Bamenda as the region's sporting standard bearer, as well as clubs linked to the prison department, city councils and power companies. PWD were considered enough of a sporting and political threat that their journey to Yaoundé to play Dynamo Douala in the 1979 cup final saw them arrested and imprisoned en route only to be released and allegedly drugged with a sedative in their pre-match meal.

The potentially fractious nature of the new Cameroonian state was demonstrated when independence in 1960 under President Ahmadu Ahidjo was followed by two years of popular insurrection. Ahidjo ended the insurrection and then created a one-party state in 1966. National unity was to be further enhanced by a decree the following year that all football clubs were to de-ethnicize themselves. Needless to say, the decree was barely implemented and Ahidjo was notable for his lack of direct interest in football at any level. Thus before the late 1970s the best that the national team had managed was third at the 1972 Cup of Nations hosted by Cameroon and best remembered for the phenomenal level of funds siphoned off by the organizers. Oryx Douala had won the inaugural African Champions Cup in 1964 but Cameroonian clubs had lived in the shadow of the Ghanaians, Guineans and Zairians. Perhaps helped by a level of benign presidential neglect and stimulated by an enduring ethnic rivalry, the late 1970s saw Cameroonian clubs nurturing a generation of exceptional players and beginning to win African competitions. In 1977 Canon Yaoundé lost a Cup Winners' Cup Final but went on to win in 1979 and take the Champions Cup twice in 1978 and

1980. Union Douala grabbed their piece of the action when they won the same trophy in 1979. But it was under Ahidjo's anointed presidential successor Paul Biya that the Cameroonian national team reaped the benefits of these victories.

Biya inherited the presidency on Ahidjo's death in 1982 and the immense national pride that accompanied Cameroon's World Cup campaign that year did not escape his attention. Biya would need such a political resource more than his predecessor. For Ahidjo, a northern Muslim, had attempted to keep a lid on ethnic differences while Biya from the Beti of the south actively promoted his own networks within the state on ethnic and linguistic lines; anglophone Cameroon consistently accused the authorities of discriminating against their players when selecting the national team. But it was hard to argue with success. A mix of domestic players in the leading Beti clubs with the first crop of overseas professionals, under Yugoslav coach Rade Ognanovic and then French coach Claude le Roy, took Cameroon to three successive Cup of Nations finals, winning twice against the Nigerians in 1984 and 1988. This was a team that was not intimidated by occasion or reputation, that knew how to keep its shape and its nerve; that had learnt some hard lessons in physical football, sharply taught in Europe. But in Théophile Abega and Roger Milla they had talents of invention and exuberance. Those that saw them beat a determined and accomplished Nigerian team in Abidjan in the Cup of Nations Final of 1984 would not be surprised by their later exploits.

Those exploits were to go to the World Cup in 1990 and irrefutably bury the memories of Zaire '74 and with it every ignorant clichéd characterization of African football. Cameroon had the temerity to beat Maradona's Argentina – the reigning world champions – in the tournament's opening game by a single goal, a simple header from François Omam-Biyik. The Lions fiercely defended their lead even at the cost of two red cards to counter the rampaging threat of Argentinian forward Claudio Caniggia. This was not naivety as many commentators lazily cast it – it was old-fashioned cynicism. They then secured their passage to the second round by beating Romania 2–1. With the score at 0–0 and only a quarter of an hour to go, Roger Milla, a late substitution, stepped up. At 38 he was the oldest man to score in a World Cup final tournament, yet he was strong enough to barge the Romanian defence off the ball, sharp enough to show real acceleration around the box and sure enough to thrash the ball home – twice. With his celebratory gyrations at the corner flag his iconic status was assured. Milla had been placed in the squad at the insistence of President Biya, despite the opposition of the team's captain, the team's Russian coach, Milla's age and his recent departure from French professional football to virtual retirement in the Indian Ocean in the Réunion league.

Biya has been living off the call ever since. But what a call. In the second round, after 106 minutes of stalemate against Colombia, Milla first beat their goalkeeper Higuita at his near post to take the lead. Then, three minutes later, as Higuita and his defensive line pushed upfield, Milla snatched the ball from the Colombian's feet 10 metres outside his area, before humiliatingly sending it into an empty net. Cameroon became the first African team in the quarter-finals of the World Cup and no one wanted to meet them.

July 1990
England 3 Cameroon 2
Stadio San Paolo, Naples

They are looking ragged, out of their depth, overwhelmed by an opposition brimming with confidence and invention. Their star midfielder clumsily and unnecessarily fouls his man on the edge of the box; a needless, naive penalty to give away in a World Cup quarter-final. The spot kick is taken with aplomb. Cameroon have equalized to make it 1–1 and England who have held on to their slender, lucky lead for 36 troubled minutes are properly exposed. There is no doubt who the poorer team is tonight. There is no doubt which side keeps losing its shape. There is no doubt which side is living from moment to moment. England are being shredded.

The outsiders, the unknowns, the naive, the quaint, the untutored, natural, spontaneous, rhythmic, supple, happy-go-lucky Africans are in charge and are delivering a lesson in learned, patterned, organized, tough-minded and sharp-elbowed football. Roger Milla and Mark Wright clash heads and the Cameroonian just walks away. Wright is consigned to the touchline and returns swathed in bandages.

Cameroon can do it all: they take possession, hold it, tease the English midfield, make the English backline look slow, invent and find space, play with precison and control. Milla is orchestrating the Cameroonian charge. He delays his pass on the edge of the box for just a second, just enough to leave Ekeke unmarked in the box, and he imperiously chips the ball beyond Peter Shilton's reach. It's 2–1 and finally the score reflects the balance of play.

Of course, this is cup football, and in cup football the better team does not necessarily win. England, without a penalty for over four years, get two in one game. The first takes it to extra time. The second takes them to the semi-finals. Cameroon are still the better team.

_____

PART FIVE

The Only Game:
Football and the
End of History,
1990–2006

17

Football through
the Looking-Glass:
Europe, 1990–2006

Alice laughed: 'There's no use trying,' she said; 'one can't believe impossible things.'

'I dare say you haven't had much practice,' said the Queen. 'When I was younger, I always did it for half an hour a day. Why, sometimes I've believed as many as six impossible things before breakfast.'
          Lewis Carroll, *Through the Looking-Glass,
          and What Alice Found There*

I

The Queen of Hearts had surely been reading the European sports press at the turn of the millennium. Here she would have found ample material for practising the absorption of the implausible, the contradictory and the bizarre. Had she been steeped in the cultural norms of an earlier generation of European football, the daily digest would have seemed incomprehensible. Could she have swallowed the conundrum of Winston Bogarde, a player who did not play? Bogarde was a Dutch international who moved from Barcelona to Chelsea in 2002. While at Chelsea he played twelve games in four years, and drew a salary of around £40,000 a week. After manager Claudio Ranieri decided he was surplus to requirements no other club would contemplate matching his wage or anything like it. Bogarde decided to stay at Chelsea where he not only failed to make the substitutes' bench but was humiliatingly relegated to training with the juniors, an arrangement that worked out at just under £500,000 a game. Thomas Brolin's nineteen games for Leeds United came in at around £240,000 a shot.

But why play in any case when you could be paid more from advertising and endorsements than from your football? In 2005 David Beckham earned more than two-thirds of his €25 million annual income from something other than playing football. Italian striker Alessandro del Piero took home €4.5 million from Juventus and another 8 million from his sponsors. By the same token, why lose money on football when you could squander it in innumerable other ways? At the turn of the century Chelsea Village lost more money on its property developments than on its football club. Dinamo Kiev traded in nuclear technologies and engineering products. Manchester United planned to build a chain of a hundred Red Devil-themed sports bars across South-east Asia. Would there be any players left at all? As professional footballers became ever leaner and more conditioned, playing more games at a faster pace, the audience was becoming ever fatter and more out of condition as the slow wave of obesity oozed across the already portly terraces of European football. As playing fields, pitches and open spaces were consumed by the voracious property booms of the 1990s, youth football retreated to teenagers' bedrooms and the pixilated images of football played out on a video game console.

While the leading clubs of the Continent were busy with their property portfolios, ancillary activities and creative accounting techniques, they increasingly understood themselves as not just clubs, not just mere businesses, but as brands. What were once the unintended repositories of a local patriotism, collective identity or neighbourhood solidarity became consciously designed icons, signifiers of aspirational values and symbols of identity that could be purchased rather than inherited, learned or felt. This was no mere addendum to the business of winning football matches but increasingly a task of equal, even greater significance. One Real Madrid director, when asked why the club had not purchased the Brazilian Ronaldinho, without question the most exciting and beautiful player of his generation, replied: 'There was no point in buying him, it wasn't worth it. He is so ugly that he'd sink you as a brand.'[1]

And who could afford to sink their brand when there was a whole world of consumers who might want to buy in? In the early twenty-first century, the opening day of the Italian season, the Super Cup, was played in New York and Tripoli. Liverpool and Manchester United consolidated their hold on the pockets and affections of the new rich of Malaysia and Thailand. Real Madrid toured China, Internazionale opened a club shop in Tokyo. Clubs offered not merely the usual ephemera – mugs, keyrings, scarves and shirts – but credit cards, mobile phone services and TV channels. They did not merely offer season tickets for sale, but asked their fans to pay for the right to be at the head of the queue. On the websites, in their club magazines and official celebrations they offered history as heritage, stripped of any meaningful reference to the world beyond the closed circuits of cups and championships.

Inside the stadium the audience was bombarded with visual distractions. Advertising boards became bigger and more prominent. When that was insufficiently obvious advertising boards began to rotate and when even this could not force your eyes away from the ball, animated electronic strips were introduced around the perimeter. Should you have been able to keep your eyes on the game long enough, they would still have had to filter the increasingly ugly and cluttered landscapes of logos, brand names, trademarks and website addresses that were layered on shirts, shorts, hats, socks, dugouts, bags, players' tunnels, tickets and balls. The television viewer would have to cope with digitally generated emblems, scores and straplines superimposed on the pitch. The officials were branded and emblazoned and stadiums renamed for a price: the Reebok in Bolton, the Allianz in Munich, represented the unconscious insertion of corporate capital into the deepest recesses of the game's vocabulary. Arsenal ended almost a century of history at Highbury by moving not to Ashburton Grove but to the Emirates Stadium, £100 million the price for giving your north London address to the airline of an oil-rich Gulf micro-kingdom. Even Barcelona, the only major club on the Continent not to put a sponsor's logo on its shirts, was taking a premium price for keeping the holy raiment of the Catalan nation clear of anything but the kit manufacturer's discreet but unmissable swoosh.

The unparalleled commercialization of European football in the closing decade of the twentieth century signalled the ideological and institutional victory of capitalism that had swept across the societies of the Continent, a tidal wave unleashed by the fall of the Berlin Wall and the eradication of state socialism in the East. Yet what is so extraordinary about the economic transformation of European football is that beyond the telephone-number salaries and transfer fees and the exponential curves of income and turnover, its ranking in the wider economy was never more than as an industry of minor importance in the leisure or entertainment sector. The workforce of an entire top division in Europe would be no more than 500 players, 200 coaches and a few thousand administrators, managers, factotums and shop workers: barely the equivalent of a medium-sized car factory or local-government department. With a turnover of €1.5 billion the English Premier League is not even comparable to a single member of the big four accountancy firms in the UK, let alone a major supermarket or retail bank. The profits made by Europe's major oil companies were bigger than the turnover of entire national football economies.

If football's economic significance lies not in its size, could it perhaps lie in its representativeness, as an exemplar of the dynamic and successful working of the market and private sector? In this case football has not merely failed the test but utterly confounded it. It has become apparent that football flouts many of the core assumptions of rational choice theory and neo-liberal economics. The notion that a football club is the key unit of economic analysis fails to understand the necessity of cooperation alongside competition in football. If the market rewards success and punishes failure too systematically, then the gap between rich and poor, efficient and inefficient will widen. In so doing the competitiveness of games and seasons will necessarily diminish which is bad for everyone. The mainstream notions of consumer choice and competition flounder on the inelasticity of demand from fans, breaking the link between performance and preference. It remains the case that long-term allegiances in football are rarely changed. As for the bottom line, football is better cast as a bottomless pit for absorbing foolhardy investments. It has proved almost impossible, by legal means, to make a football club profitable. The stock market does not lie: of the twenty-two clubs that have been listed in the UK only twelve remain, and those that do have consistently traded at a mere fraction of their initial offer price.

Like the wider economy, the new European football economy was highly uneven. In Eastern Europe the boom never arrived, bypassed by the explosion in the value of TV rights; the relative importance of the region declined, its domestic football stagnated and was blighted by the same kinds of problems – constant loss of skilled labour, susceptibility to corruption, involvement in organized crime – of all post-communist economies. Only in the twenty-first century, in zones of oil-based wealth have football clubs from the East begun to compete with the West.

Two arcs of semi-peripheral football nations were strung along the northern and southern edges of the Continent. Scandinavia, Scotland and the Low Countries although richer than Eastern Europe could never manage to accrue the kind of TV deal that would allow them to compete regularly on even terms – all had to make do with the occasional European triumph and a depleted domestic game. A similar set of problems, made worse by their relative economic underdevelopment, affected football in Greece, Turkey and Portugal, though their most recent bursts of urbanization and industrialization beginning in the 1990s allowed all three nations short moments of sporting significance. The core of European football by any measure – income, quality, prestige – remained in the big five leagues of England, France, Italy, Spain and Germany.

Yet the wider social significance of European football at the turn of the millennium cannot be explained, despite the centrality of economic forces and pressures, by recourse to the dismal science alone. In the realms of pleasure and pain, meaning and vacuity, identity and idolatry, the economist is mute. The reading and meanings of football have ranged from the trivial to the profound. The sheer quantity of football in Europe's public sphere and conversation, in the print media, television and Internet has grown immensely. From almost no live football at all, between one-third and two-thirds of all games in the top divisions are now screened live in some form or another. In Italy a comparison over time of televised football on the first Sunday in February showed that in 1956 there was one late-night programme; twenty years later it had grown to five; by the mid-1990s there were fifteen different football shows on TV, running from mid-morning until late at night.[2] A decade later, armed with the correct set of subscriptions and smart cards and judicious channel surfing, one could watch football in an unbroken twenty-four-hour stretch; indeed a recording device would be required to catch the entire available output.

The scale and range of newspapers and magazine reporting spiralled upwards. Despite the wider decline in newspaper sales the specialist sports press of the Mediterranean continued to expand. In Spain four daily sports papers devoted themselves overwhelmingly to football, in Portugal and Italy there were three each, in Greece at least nine. In Northern Europe both tabloids and broadsheets created football supplements, introduced football to the business pages, ran their rich lists and their personal scandals at the front rather than just the back of the paper. Both the fawning and the scurrilous ends of the celebrity news market flocked to players and their heavily carpeted living rooms, their fairytale weddings and soap-opera divorces.

The cycle of hysteria has also resulted in the most astonishing elevation of minutiae. When David Beckham, the England captain, broke his fifth metatarsal in the run-up to the 2002 World Cup, the country's newspapers, chat shows, and news broadcasts scrambled for every last consultant podiatrist in the country, annotated x-rays appeared on the football pages and the nation became conversant with the strategies and timetables of osteopathic rehabilitation. In Spain, *Marca* published a double-page spread with a graphic of the seating arrangements on a chartered plane carrying the Real Madrid squad and officials on their return from a disappointing European away match. The diagram was annotated by discussion of who was or was not talking to whom and which plots and cabals they might have been in on. *Gazzetta dello Sport* created maps that showed where the leading members of the national team were taking their summer holidays, and in which restaurants in Milan the stars of the victorious 2003 Champions League team toasted their success.

The coverage of football on the radio had expanded well beyond the narrow range of scores, updates and commentary, but has increasingly become the realm of the phone-in and the rant. Combined with the chatrooms and football blogs on the Internet, a vast buzzing cacophony of rancour, rumour and reflection is the everyday background noise of Europe's football obsession. Even Hollywood, unable in the twentieth century to grasp the economic potential or narrative meanings of football, has attempted to bring its mastery of generic blandness to bear on the subject; the results, like *Goal!* (a rags-to-riches player story) or *Green Street* (an American among the thugs), have proved to be embarrassingly poor. If the popular cultural circuits of Europe now hummed with football, its high cultural conversations were not immune. The market for new kinds of personal and political writing on football was tangible. From Martin Amis to Salman Rushdie, from Umberto Eco to Günter Grass, the leading male novelists wrote on football; new fanzines and magazines inspired by the British model took off in Scandinavia, France and Germany

At the level of high politics, football was captured and celebrated. In July 1998 a million people, perhaps two million, gathered in exuberant carnival mood in the Champs-Elysées, Paris, to celebrate the French national team's victory in the World Cup Final. On the sides of the Arc de Triomphe, the marble cynosure of French imperial pride, the face of Zinedine Zidane, the French star of Berber North African roots, was projected. In the greatest gathering since the liberation, France decided to celebrate itself as a multi-ethnic republic and to hold a carnival of the triumph of civic over ethnic nationalism because it won a game of football. When Turkey made it to the semi-finals of the World Cup in 2002, the President declared it worthy of a national holiday. In the aftermath of Italy's agonizing defeat to France in the final of the European Championship in 2000, the then leader of the opposition Silvio Berlusconi broke off from the tiresome details of politics and policy in a televised press conference to say that he had to get something off his chest:

We could and should have won ... There were certain things happening on the pitch that you could not ignore. You cannot leave the source of their game, Zidane, free to run the show and prompt all their actions, especially in a final. Even an amateur coach would have realized what was happening and would have won the final by stopping Zidane ... It was simply unworthy.[3]

Football had been elevated to such giddy heights of cultural significance that the leading contender for the most powerful political office in one of the biggest European economies appeared more concerned with (and more knowledgeable of) the tactics of the national team coach than the multiple intersecting fiscal, legal and political crises dragging the nation down.

The game has simultaneously served as an exemplar of the new economy, an instrument of civic, regional and national identity, a vehicle for personal and political promotion, but in the early twenty-first century it has increasingly begun to show another face. Despite the almost complete failure of the supine European sports press to examine these problems and the inability of Europe's judiciaries, tax offices and police forces to scrutinize football's operations with anything approaching the rigour and attention devoted to less glamorous industrial sectors, the sheer scale of corruption, collusion, deception, incompetence, fraud and forgery in the game has become apparent. Beneath the gloss of its newly acquired desirability, European football may yet force us to face the Continent's underbelly: its unreformed clientalism, its closed and self-serving elites, its deficient democracies, its shallow consumerism, its desperate inequalities and its systemic racism. Whether football can survive this kind of critical scrutiny with the same ease that it accepted easy money and public acclamation remains to be seen.

In the 1990s European football's long economic decline was spectacularly reversed: the ailing rustbelt of Fordist football was transformed into a booming post-industrial service sector awash with money and hubris. The economics of the process were relatively simple. Almost everywhere in Europe, before the 1990s, there was a single monopoly purchaser of football broadcast rights – invariably state-owned, inflexible and conservative. With nowhere else to go and often fearful that greater exposure would lead to lower gates, football clubs and leagues took what little they could get. However, as the British case showed, where there was competition between broadcasters – in this case the BBC and the established independent channels of ITV – then the value of TV rights could be inched upwards. The emergence of Canal Plus in France in the mid-1980s – the Continent's first subscription channel – demonstrated that football, especially if live and exclusive, was the singularly most effective form of TV content for persuading people to pay for subscriptions in a market where hitherto they had always received television free. Both the number of competitors in the TV market and the number of subscription-dependent channels rose sharply in the 1990s as first satellite analogue systems came into use, then cable television networks became more universally available. Finally, in the late 1990s the switch from analogue to digital television multiplied the number of possible outlets again. With the arrival of broadband internet and G3 mobile phone systems, the number of bidders for new media rights and thus their value rose too.

It was in this context of technological change, industrial deregulation and fearsome competition that the value of football's TV rights was sent through the roof. The thousands upon thousands of hours of televised football generated the kind of exposure and hype that saw the value of sponsorship deals, replica kit sales and perimeter advertising rise just as sharply. In 1992 the newly launched English Premier League broke the mould by detaching itself from the lower (and poorer) divisions, and by signing away its entire live football coverage to the satellite broadcaster BSkyB, a division of Rupert Murdoch's News International empire, for the then astonishing sum of £304 million over three years. In 1996, concerned by the potential threat to their business coming from the new telecoms and cable companies and recognizing the centrality of football to their business model, Sky bid £670 million. By 2003 the value of just part of the TV package to BSkyB was £1.1 billion – a fourfold increase in income for the Premiership in a decade. In Germany the Bundesliga grew at a similar rate as the value of annual TV rights rose from €23 million in 1990, to €84 million in 1995 and €168 million in 2000. Under the ill-fated Kirch media deal of 2001, annual TV income for the

Bundesliga was €355 million. In France rights values rose from less than half the value of the leading nations at the beginning of the 1990s to values just short of the Premiership in 2005. In Spain and Italy income rose but more slowly due to Spain's smaller market, and to the difficulty of making pay-per-view football work in Italy where nearly 60 per cent of viewers were using pirated smart cards.

The degree of economic concentration in European football was extra-ordinary. In 2003 the top divisions in the big five made up 54 per cent of the European football market. If one added the lower-level professional leagues in the big five then they accounted for 69 per cent of the market. If one then added the revenue from the Champions League which overwhelmingly flowed to the top clubs of these five nations then their total share of European football revenue was nearly 80 per cent, leaving 20 per cent for the other 46 members of UEFA – a polarized income distribution that would make even Brazil or Saudi Arabia blanch.[4]

A similar pattern of concentration could be discerned within national leagues. The structure of the TV deals in England, for example, ensured a minimum payment for every club from a common pool; the rest was allocated according to the numbers of games televised and the club's final position in the league. The difference between the teams at the top and the bottom of the league could be as much as £20 million a season. In Italy and Spain inequality was built into the system by allowing individual clubs to negotiate TV rights deals rather than the league as a whole. Predictably the lion's share of income went to the top three clubs in Italy (Juventus, Milan and Inter); indeed Inter alone were receiving more than the eight smallest clubs in Serie A put together. When the knock-on effects of stadium capacity, sponsorship and advertising income are added, the gulf between the top and bottom was becoming unbridgeable. In all of these nations a self-replicating aristocracy of clubs dominated competition. It would require the kind of cash injection brought by Roman Abramovich to Chelsea or Sergio Cragnotti to Lazio to force entry into the charmed circle. By the same token the gap between the bottom of the top divisions and the tiers below became ever more difficult to bridge, with clubs locked into a constant cycle of boom and bust, promotion and relegation that would catch the unprepared and the incautious – like Leeds United and Napoli – sending them into calamitous bankruptcies.

In addition to this avalanche of TV and sponsorship cash, there was more. Clubs received considerable capital injections from floating on the stock market, others obtained cash in the form of very soft loans, others ran large debts with obediently negligent bankers. Yet football as a whole was barely profitable. Even in the peak years of the early twenty-first century, only the Bundesliga and the Premiership were running anything approaching a surplus and then only at a handful of clubs. Take Bayern München and Manchester United out of the equation and there was hardly an institution in European football that was in the black, let alone delivering a rate of return on invested capital comparable to even the most risk-free savings bond. It would have made more economic sense to put your money under the bed than into football. The reasons for such appalling economic performance are not hard to fathom. The key indicator is the ratio of wages to turnover. In the big five leagues the era of increasing revenue saw an increasing percentage of that cash head straight into players' wages and agents' pockets. In England between 1995 and 2002, wages rose from half of clubs' income to nearly two-thirds. In Germany and Spain it was touching 80 per cent of income and in Italy, the worst offender of all, the wages bill was 90 per cent of Serie A's turnover. At the most profligate and chaotic clubs wage bills were considerably in excess of annual turnover.[5]

Players and their agents were able to capture a growing share of the massive new income streams because they continued to operate in an unusual labour market, where employers were locked into a fearsome competitive cycle in which the temptation to outbid one's opponents was high. Moreover, while in many businesses investment in new capital, product lines or managerial restructuring are the preferred strategies for success, in football new stadiums, training grounds and even coaching staff were seen as small contributors to success. Victory turned more than anything else on the quality of the labour force – the players. Where the difference between success and failure was small yet the gains to be made from being first rather than second so enormous, there was a structural propensity towards over-optimism and over-expansion. Given that there was neither significant shareholder or customer pressure to deviate from this strategy, nor collective mechanisms of wage restraint like salary caps to slow the process down and that the Bosman ruling had increased the exit options for players, it was inevitable that wage inflation would run riotously ahead of income generation. By 2005, most players in the leading clubs in the leading leagues were earning around £1 million a year.

Like every other aspect of life in Europe, football came increasingly within the regulatory ambit of the European Union (EU) with the ultra-free-market Competition Directorate taking a close interest in the sale of TV rights, the creation of monopolies and exclusivity deals with broadcasters and ticket agents. However, its most significant intervention was in the field of player contracts and labour-market regulations. A long, slow dialogue between the European Commission and UEFA through the 1980s had produced a 'gentleman's agreement' over nationally imposed limits to foreign players in football teams, which as far as players from the rest of the European Union were concerned were an infringement of the free movement of labour enshrined in successive European treaties. By 1991, teams were allowed to field three non-nationals as well as two assimilated players, who had been continuously in the country for five years. The European Court's 1995 Bosman judgement broke this compromise by ruling that both internal payments between clubs for players who were out of contract and nationality limits on squads were in contravention of European law. FIFA and UEFA complained and dragged their feet. While the key points of the ruling were accepted, nearly four years of legal fencing followed before a deal was brokered which has forced the abandonment of all citizenship restrictions on team composition – though migrants must still negotiate national immigration procedures. Players out of contract are now free to move to the club of their choice without recompense to their previous club.

Until the early 1990s UEFA remained a remarkably small and penurious bureaucracy. It faced a political threat from above as the EU appeared to be contemplating striking out many of its most cherished practices, and a challenge from below as the biggest clubs and their media allies pondered new and better ways to keep more of the new money in European football to themselves. Under the presidency of Lennart Johansson, a provincial Swedish businessman, and his inner circle of Scandinavian and Northern European officials, UEFA attempted to respond to these threats and in so doing began to transform itself and European football. Moreover, this was carried out with an unspoken but entrenched ideology of solidarity, egalitarianism and universalism pursued by a strategic compromise between capital and the social regulation of economic activity; the same values and strategies of Swedish social democracy and the German social market.

First, UEFA adeptly absorbed the many new European states, embracing not merely the successor states to Czechoslovakia and Yugoslavia but all of the former Soviet republics west of the Caucasus. UEFA would also provide a home for the transient Israel in 1992 and in 2002 it accepted the ex-Soviet central Asian state of Kazakhstan. If nothing else, UEFA had almost doubled its voting power within FIFA. UEFA was not only faster than NATO or the EU to expand its membership across Europe, but more successful at pooling the potential power of a united continent. The logic of the single European market was that an open competition between firms within the EU would raise standards all round, benefit consumers and create new continental champions who could compete in the global marketplace. UEFA's Champions League operated in a parallel fashion.

The idea of more regular and lucrative Pan-European competition, be it a new form of European Cup or a super-league, had been mooted in the late 1980s by Berlusconi and his associates. The example of the breakaway Premier League in England demonstrated the will and the capacity of leading football clubs to defy the old order. In 1992 UEFA acted by cautiously expanding the European Cup, creating a group stage in the later half of the competition and by rebranding the enterprise as the UEFA Champions League. However, there was more at work than simply a change of name and format. UEFA adopted the FIFA–ISL model of centralized TV deals and segmented exclusive sponsorships. Then in 1996 with the design and marketing agency TEAM they reinvented and standardized the European football spectacular, ready for easily digestible consumption, a wondrously blank canvas for the new-minted logos of global corporations. Without a trace of irony or shame the TEAM brochure for prospective sponsors of the new competition put it this way:

The UEFA Champions League sponsorship concept allows communication in a clutter-free environment and creates a pan-European package that delivers significant impact, acting as a prestigious platform delivering volume audiences in prime-time programming.[6]

Having taken total control over the TV rights for the competition (previously sold by individual clubs on an ad hoc basis), UEFA now annexed the marketing and design. They introduced the ubiquitous star-ball logo that encrusts every football shirt and document associated with the competition. Its design was drawn from the same lexicon of abstract universalism that informed the EU's twelve-star ring, and possessed something of its anodyne slickness too. UEFA also took control of advertising space inside and outside the stadiums, on tickets, programmes, and of course on the all-important sponsors' name boards behind half-time and post-match interviews. UEFA also specified stricter stadium standards, eventually insisting on all-seater arenas.

From the very beginning, the money started rolling in as television rights deals were struck across the entire world. Latin America screened the tournament at a similar level of intensity to their own Copa Libertadores. Asia's own Champions League was a poor second best in terms of local TV coverage. By 2000 the Champions League was being shown live on every continent, in over 200 countries. Within Europe itself the competition was gaining a huge television audience with finals attracting around 70 per cent of the viewing public when a home team was playing and over half when they were not. When Galatasaray played Juventus in 1999, over three-quarters of the Turkish audience was watching. In broadcasting and sponsorship terms, the Champions League was in the same department as the World Cup and the Olympics – but better than either it was annual and delivered the drip-drip-drip of constant exposure over the entire football season. Sponsors fell over themselves to get a piece of the 'clutter-free environment', the immense hospitality packages and licences for one of the over 8,000 branded products associated with the tournament.

Within two years it was becoming apparent that any club that could not get regular access to the tournament would be systematically disadvantaged in national competitions. The big clubs in the rich leagues lobbied UEFA to expand the competition to allow up to four teams a year from the biggest leagues to play and to introduce qualifying rounds to keep the peripheral and the riff-raff out of the most lucrative stages of the competition. Over the next four years the competition expanded to take in three qualifying rounds, thirty-two teams playing in groups, followed by a second group stage of sixteen teams and then two-leg quarter-finals and semi-finals. When Valencia made it to the final in 2000 they had played 19 games to get there – half a season in itself.

The impact of the Champions League has been profound, transforming not only the economics of football, but football itself. To grasp the economic consequences of the competition, as Deep Throat put it, 'Follow the Money'. In 2006 the total budget was around €580 million, €30 million of which went to the national leagues of Europe. UEFA's take was about €150 million, to cover costs and provide a small surplus, but the bulk was returned to the Continent's smaller and poorer national football associations as solidarity payments for youth development, training courses and infrastructure. The pot of gold that remained, at around €400 million, went to the thirty-two clubs that started the group stage. This was split down the middle with the first half handed out at a flat-rate on a game-by-game basis for all clubs with bonuses for winning and progressing from round to round. The other half of the pot was handed out in a similar manner but with the amounts determined by the size of the club's national TV market. Thus clubs from the core were guaranteed a minimum pay day of around €10 million for just showing up. Winning the competition, for a club from one of the big five would reap around €40 million. However, when Porto won the competition in 2004 they received less than half of the money received by Manchester United, whom they had knocked out in the second round.

The effect of this system of payments has been further to entrench the inequalities of European and domestic football. Since Ajax's victory in the 1995 competition, the only team to have won the final from outside the four biggest leagues has been Porto. Indeed along with their opponents Monaco they are the only teams from outside the big four to have made the final at all. In the richest leagues, a small group of clubs has steadily pulled away from those in the second tier, a fact of economic life that has made the last qualifying spot for the Champions League one of the most significant end-of-season races. The gap between qualifiers and non-qualifiers in the smaller and poorer leagues has become even greater: thus Rosenborg, from Trondheim in Norway, who became expert in negotiating the qualifying rounds of the competition and getting into the group stages, won an unprecedented and virtually uncontested run of thirteen Norwegian championships. A similar logic of separation kept the big three in Turkey and Greece in a different realm from the rest of their leagues.

While the Champions League may have entrenched inequality and introduced a new level of homogenization into the presentation of European football, it is almost certainly fairer than any of the ludicrous, self-serving ideas for European leagues that have been proposed by the clubs and various maverick media groups whose only motive is profit. Furthermore the competition has attracted such enormous global audiences because the football played in the first decade of the UEFA Champions League was of a rare and exceptional quality. In all probability it has regularly produced the finest, most technically accomplished high-tempo football ever.

The logic of economic concentration has allowed the leading teams in Europe to assemble the global elite of football talent, drawing on players from every continent. Most teams in the final stages possessed a majority of internationals, the leading players from Africa and Latin America as well as the very best from Europe, the concentrated talent of which has been sharpened by the regularity of European games. Teams that are regularly running away with their own domestic championships are forced to raise and test themselves against their equals, and in contrast to earlier eras, no club has been able to retain the title. The sheer volume of games has allowed the audience to balance the pleasures of exoticism and familiarity. Midweek floodlit games against foreign opposition continue to exert a peculiar fascination over the public but occur often enough that the particular narratives and meanings associated with other football cultures can be learnt. The competition has even begun to acquire its own internal logic and rivalries. The regular encounters between Barcelona and Chelsea pleasingly pitched the most arrogant club cultures together, while Manchester United, Real Madrid and Bayern München are locked in a triangle of rivalry. The regular encounters between the two Milan clubs in the later stages has offered the Continent exemplars of the most gruelling and tightly fought football contests. The goalless 2003 final between Juventus and Milan was surely the apotheosis of Gianni Brera's vision of the perfectly balanced game. By contrast Manchester United's injury-time goals in their 2–1 victory over Bayern München in 1999 and Liverpool's whirlwind comeback from 3–0 down against Milan in the 2005 final were perfect displays of the relentless driven energy of English football. Porto's triumph in 2004 left just enough room for us to believe that the monopoly of wealth and power is not completely watertight.

15 May 2002
Real Madrid 2 Bayer Leverkusen 1
Hampden Park, Glasgow

Real Madrid, in their centenary year, have already blown the Spanish Cup and league. But no matter, La Nueva – their ninth European Cup – is within their grasp. They won their fifth, at this ground, on this pitch; the electrifying 7–3 defeat of Eintracht Frankfurt in 1960. The greatest exhibition of club football ever. A golden age that can never be bettered.

It's 1–1. Solari, on the edge of the centre-circle, scans the field and sends a pass of exquisite weight into the thunderous path of Roberto Carlos. Leverkusen's Placente stays with him as they hurtle together down the left touchline, the ball skimming and surfing in front of them. The gap between them is barely a boot. The ball rises sharply and the Brazilian sees his chance, impudently catching it at the peak of its bounce to send a high loping cross diagonally backwards to the edge of the penalty area. And there is Zidane. He has already run half the length of the pitch. He has already stolen a metre on Michael Ballack, stepping into the space no one else could see. He is already changing the weight and balance of his body, shaping his shoulders, gliding into position to take it on the volley. Ballack seems to know that he cannot stop Zidane. His body deflates as Zidane rises. The goalkeeper tries to make himself large, but he is already shrinking into nothing.

The ball is still coming. Time is slowing down. The world revolves on the axis of Zidane's twisting torso. The ball begins the final and steepest curve of its descent. Zidane, pirouetting, brings his outstretched leg above and impossibly behind the ball's trajectory. There is £20 million riding on this. There's a century of Castilian pride to be defended. There are the grainy white ghosts of 1960, the flamboyant unrepeatable arabesques of Di Stéfano and Puskás circling. As his curving boot cradles the ball, time stops. The ball screams. A white streak. A blink of the eye. No one but Zidane could have scored it. Memory, history, money, ghosts and golden ages are scattered in the night sky, rising on the billowing roars of the crowd.

While European football was being transformed from above by the intersecting forces of private corporations unleashed, new media technologies and European institutions, it was also being shaped from below by the Continent's changing social structures. In particular, Europe's football and society were being reshaped by a transformation in its gender relations and identities and its ethnic demography.

The growth of women's football in Europe had been stopped in its tracks after the First World War. The women who had occupied male jobs in the war industries and taken a small step on to the football field were summarily dismissed in peacetime. A combination of football association bans and the wider disapproval of society (including parts of the medical profession) condemned women's football in Europe to the very margins. It remained a game for rough girls of dubious sexuality and inappropriate deportment, a real fringe activity until well after the Second World War. An attempt to organize women's football in Europe was made with the creation of the International Ladies Football Association in 1957 and the holding of a women's European Championship. FIFA, UEFA and national football associations remained indifferent.

The second wave of feminism that emerged out of the tumult of the 1960s and early 1970s saw the gender politics of work and play challenged once again, and this time women's football was more successful in organizing itself. An Italian-based international women's football federation was formed in 1969 and held informal women's World Cups in Italy in 1970 and in Mexico in 1971. Driven by fear of losing control and by some dim recognition that women's football was a significant sporting force, FIFA and UEFA acted. UEFA called for all member nations' FAs to incorporate women's football into the mainstream.

In terms of participation and sporting success women's football has three strongholds: North America, China and Northern Europe, and it is gaining ground in sub-Saharan Africa. In America and China the relative weakness of men's football created the space in which the game could grow. Indeed the US has been the only country able to set up a fully professional women's football league, though a year after the launch of WUSA in 2003, it was in deep and irrevocable financial trouble. In Northern Europe the egalitarianism and social engineering of social democratic governments has helped promote women's football and a form of semi-professionalism has emerged in Scandinavia, England and Italy. It remains the case that when Italy played Germany in the

1997 women's European Championship, fewer than 2,000 attended a game broadcast to 135 countries.

It remains a favourite cliché in most European football languages that it is 'a man's game'. However, there does appear, at the edges and particularly in Northern Europe, some minor feminization of football. In the lower professional leagues a number of women officials, particularly as assistant referees, have begun to emerge. There are now a few women administrators in the upper reaches of the game, most notably Karen Brady, the chief executive of Birmingham City, while in Italy Carolina Morace was for a short time the coach of the third-tier side Viterbese. Compared with almost any other managerial sector women's representation in football is remarkably low.

Where perhaps there has been the greatest degree of feminization is in the crowd at the stadium and at home. Certainly in England the numbers of women at football matches has inched up, from below 10 per cent to something near 20 per cent and the regular viewing public for live football is probably nearer 25 per cent female. During the big international tournaments, the football nations of Europe are closer to a fifty-fifty split. Similar increases in female attendance have been registered in France and Spain, but in Eastern Europe, the Balkans and the Eastern Mediterranean the overwhelmingly male culture of the terrace remains relatively unscathed.

The post-colonial migrations of the 1960s and 1970s had already begun to create ethnically heterogeneous populations in the United Kingdom, France, Germany and the Low Countries. The issues of race and ethnicity surfaced in English and French football with a vengeance. In England an explicit and vocal racism within stadiums had reared its head when the first generation of black British players broke into the game. In France the 'Russian salad' of ethnicities that seemed to make up the national football team was often a source of uncertainty, challenge and contradiction to the prevailing notions of Frenchness. The emergence of black Dutch players in the late 1980s began to force the issue of race and nation in the Netherlands. South Americans of Italian descent had been incorporated into Italy's national team, and Franco's Spain was catholic enough in its tastes to make Hungarians and Argentines Spaniards for the purposes of football. For most of the Continent, however, the issues had not emerged at all.

In the decade and a half since the end of the Cold War Europe has undergone a demographic revolution. Within Europe there has been a steady and increasing flow of people from the East to the West: Albanians to Italy, Poles to Germany and Britain, Russians to just about everywhere. From beyond Europe's borders the migrations have been coming even faster. North and West Africans have been climbing on to the lowest rungs of the newly wealthy Mediterranean labour markets, from Portugal to Italy to Greece. Turkish, Kurdish and West Asian and Middle Eastern migrations have headed further north. Asylum seekers, displaced persons and refugees from the worst war-torn zones of the developing world have made their way to London and Paris, Stockholm and Vienna, Dublin and Rome. The percentage of the labour force that was born abroad has climbed in the wealthiest and previously homogenous states of Europe – like Germany, Sweden, the Netherlands and Austria – to over 10 per cent. In London it is over one-quarter, in Brussels over one-third. The economic consequences of all this have been by and large positive, as Europe has cherry-picked the most skilled and talented workers from the developing world, drawn to its infinitely more attractive salaries. However, the social and political consequences have proved less benign.

Across the Continent the 1990s saw the rise of various extreme right-wing, anti-immigration and ultra-nationalist political parties and social movements, including the Danish People's Party, the Progress Party in Norway, the Vlaams Blok in Belgium, the Northern League in Italy, the British National Party in the UK and the Front National in France. Winning significant and concentrated support amongst the poorest and most marginalized white working-class communities, these groups have almost invariably forced mainstream parties of both the Right and Left to adopt more authoritarian and exclusionary stances towards migration and minorities. Everywhere the discourse is essentially the same: the white, indigenous nation was being threatened and undermined economically and politically by the influx of new arrivals who took jobs and depressed wages.

To its eternal shame, the world of European football has paralleled many of the worst excesses and crude ignorance of mainstream European politics and society. In terms of migration, European football has experienced its greatest ever influx of foreign players. The steady deregulation of labour markets in the 1990s saw all remaining restrictions on the nationality of players in a team abandoned. At the bottom of the labour market football migration is akin to the people-trafficking networks and indentured labour gangs. Unscrupulous agents and middlemen have brought young players, particularly from Africa, to Europe lured by the promise of contracts and pay packets. The reality for hundreds of them has been a short and unsuccessful trial with a minor club and then abandonment on the streets of an alien city. Others have played, but found their wage packets and the freedoms disappearing. In the middle range, there is now a considerable conveyor belt of young footballers from key football academies in Africa coming through connected smaller clubs before being sold on for profit in the upper reaches of the football market. The connection with the academies of Côte d'Ivoire and the Belgian club Beveren (a feeder club for Arsenal) was perhaps the sharpest example of this: the Belgian first division outfit fielded up to ten Africans in its side. At the upper end of the market, European football has been able to attract the best football players from all round the world. In 2004 there were 500 Latin Americans and nearly 1,000 Africans playing in the top divisions of European football, but there was also a smattering of the best players from Asia, Australasia, the Caribbean and Central America. At the extremes, leading clubs were beginning to field entire teams made up of foreigners, for example Chelsea and Arsenal in England and VfL Wolfsburg in Germany. Even then the laws and regulations have not been lax enough for some, with the repeated emergence of scandals concerning faked passports, forged identity documents, and invented grandparents.

While nearly every European nation had received a considerable influx of migrants in the late twentieth century, the ways in which those migrants were incorporated into the host society varied considerably – a variation illustrated by the makeup of its football teams. In England the first and second generation of black Britons with Caribbean roots broke into football in the 1970s and 1980s and as in the wider society have survived a storm of direct and institutional racism to carve out their own place in professional football – a place that does not as yet extend very far into the administration and management of the game. In Scandinavia, which has seen a systematic attempt at state-subsidized integration and assimilation, the first black Scandinavians have emerged to represent their country, like Martin Dahlin and Henrik Larsson in Sweden and John Carew in Norway. In Germany, where integration proved harder and rules of citizenship remain bound to Germanic bloodlines rather than place of birth or length of residence, the massive Turkish population has yet to make a significant impact on professional football. In some places migrants have founded their own ethnic teams as a form of local solidarity and identity; among the most successful of this kind of team has been the now semi-professional Stockholm side Assyriaka, the team of Sweden's Assyrian community. In Eastern Europe old local racism directed at national minorities, Jews and the Roma has provided a repertoire of ignorance and hatred easily applied to the new African and Asian migrants filtering into the big cities as well as black players from other nations that come to play there with foreign football teams.

▌▌▌

In the immediate aftermath of the fall of the Berlin Wall, the patronage and protection of communist states melted away and Eastern European football appeared in the cold light of day: decrepit stadiums, embarrassing allegiances, allegations of match-fixing, drug-taking and collusion with the secret police. Football, like every other social institution, was subject to a whirlwind of change. Centrally planned socialist economies were transformed into wild, unregulated capitalist economies. There followed a massive decline in economic output, socially destabilizing levels of unemployment and a more or less corrupt transfer of economic assets from the state to the new economic elites. Entire state bureaucracies and legal systems had to be transformed in an effort to create a public sphere and democratic polity that could conform to European Union standards.

In the process football endured a complete collapse of revenues. Clubs underwent a change in ownership as émigré businessmen, new entrepreneurs and the old apparatchiks tussled for control. All three groups shaded into the burgeoning world of organized crime. Anyone with marketable skills, like professional footballers and coaches, got out if they could, even if it meant the second or third tier of the German or Italian leagues. Those that remained faced diminished wages and dilapidated facilities. The crowds, no longer subsidized and often no longer in work, disappeared, in some countries never to return.

Some clubs were so broke that they operated without showers or dressing rooms. Presiding over this calamity, the national football associations were run by the same unsavoury characters who had been there under the communists. In the international game, the Czechs, Croats and Bulgarians had their moments, but for the club sides and the rest of the national teams the 1990s were a catalogue of failure. In the grim and marginal spaces of Eastern European football, in the shadow of national decline, football's cultures of violence and the new right-wing extremists met and the expression of a virulent, bitter racism could be seen and heard.

The Czech Republic, long the most economically advanced and politically plural society in Eastern Europe, was also the most successful in shifting to the market economy. Its domestic football remained a small-scale and increasingly unedifying affair through the 1990s, but it produced an exceptional generation of players who lost the final of Euro '96 to a German penalty. Inevitably, almost the entire team departed for Western European clubs. Sparta Prague, the leading team of the era, passed from state to private hands and through a chain of investors, its appeal increased by regular appearances in the group stages of the Champions League and transfer fees from the West. Sparta won seven of the first eight league titles in the newly independent Czech Republic.

The significance of the Champions League in Eastern European football was more than just economic; it served as lightning rod for the brooding jealousy, paranoia and anger of the region in its relationship to the European Union. In 1995 Ferencváros, in their first Champions League campaign, managed a 1–1 draw at home to Real Madrid. The Hungarian commentator exclaimed, 'One point from Europe. Every point scored by Ferencváros is a national feat, one more step towards European integration.'[7] Earlier in the competition they had played Ajax in Budapest. Ajax won 5–1, demonstrating the real gap between Hungary and Western Europe, while at the post-match press conference the Dutch coach Louis van Gaal angrily rebuked the Hungarians:

The atmosphere in the stands was hostile from the first moment of the warm-up; spectators emitted monkey hoots to show their scorn for our black players who were completely taken aback. What kind of nation is this that greets its guests by emitting jungle sounds?[8]

Van Gaal's comment unleashed a torrent of bruised pride and national dismay, made all the more intense by the publication of an open letter

in the Spanish newspaper *Marca* from leading Dutch sportspeople asking
Real Madrid to eliminate Ferencváros from the competition in the name
of the Netherlands; Real duly beat them 6–1 at the Bernabéu.

Racism, however, is alive and well. The first major injection of cash
into Hungarian football came from Gábor Várszegi, the owner of the
major retail and property group Fotex Holding who bought ailing giants
MTK in the mid-1990s. In 2001 Várszegi bought a majority stake in
the club's main rival Ferencváros which sparked a wave of protests and
racist outbursts among both fans and the country's right-wing parties.
László Bognár, deputy president of the Hungarian Justice and Life Party,
put it candidly:

Those who consider themselves proper, working-class Hungarians oppose the
spirit of business conduct practised by upper-class Hungarians with foreign roots.
The upper class supports MTK, and Fradi [Ferencváros] supporters have always
felt that they are the oppressed, ordinary children of the nation, while the Jews
have secured their place in high society.[9]

The Polish transition to capitalism was perhaps the hardest and most
brutal of all in Eastern Europe. Under the first post-communist governments Poland decided to take its medicine early and virtually overdosed.
The entire panoply of outdated Polish heavy industry, mining and
metallurgy disintegrated, generating an unemployment rate of over 30
per cent. The correlations between catastrophic deindustrialization, high
male youth unemployment and a declining and violent football culture
– first suggested by Britain in the 1970s and reinforced by elements of
the Dutch and German experience of the 1980s – were reconfirmed by
the gruesome realities of Polish football. The complete withdrawal of
state subsidies, ministerial affiliation and government backing for football happened at speed. Poland's stadiums remain among the worst kept
in the region. The decrepitude of the Stadion Dziesięciolecia in Warsaw,
reduced to hosting the region's biggest flea market, left the country
without a functioning national football stadium; not that the Polish
team's performances had anything to recommend them as they failed to
qualify for any international tournament for twelve years after the fall
of communism.

Match fixing blighted the league in 1993 when ŁKS Łódź were found
to have bribed opponents and bugged dressing rooms. Ludicrously

implausible results on the final day of the 1996 season saw both Legia Warsaw and Łódź punished. However, it is the violence and racism of the emergent skinhead gangs in Polish football that is most worrying. From the mid-1990s on, anti-Semitic and racist graffiti has been daubed across the nation's stadiums.

Swastikas and Celtic crosses had become intermingled with club emblems and 'Jew' became the standard term of abuse towards one's opponents. A website and fanzine culture – including titles like *Pyscho-fanatic* and *Football Bandits* – gave voice and organization to the gangs, and leading members became active in the neo-Nazi party NOP. Violence, spontaneous and organized, has been the inevitable corollary of this. During the 2005–06 season there were eight football-related stabbings in Kraków alone. At the Warsaw derby between Polonia and Legia 1,300 police with ample supplies of CS gas and rubber bullets failed to separate or quell 3,000 fighting fans.

While in 1989 Poland and Hungary were long past their peak of industrial development and urbanization, Bulgaria and Romania were approaching theirs. Both had seen a considerable improvement in the strength of their football culture in the closing years of the 1980s and despite the upheavals and chaos of the immediate post-communist transition, both were able to field international sides of considerable quality. In Hristo Stoitchkov, the Bulgarians had a player of the very highest calibre – as his tempestuous but brilliant career at Barcelona was to demonstrate. His six goals made him joint top scorer at the 1994 World Cup; he led the team out of the group stage, and then past Mexico and Germany to the semi-finals where they were beaten by Italy. Romania, led by the immensely talented Gheorghe Hagi, went to all three World Cups in the 1990s and the European Championships of 1996 and 2000, making the second round in all of them. But by the latter part of the decade the ageing squads of both sides declined, with the stars playing out their careers abroad, and no generation of comparable quality could emerge under conditions of domestic penury and chaos.

In both Bulgaria and Romania the political and economic transitions of the post-communist era were at best incomplete. Neither society possessed an opposition intellectual class, free trade unions or alternative networks of civil organization that could plausibly depose and replace the political, bureaucratic and technical elites of the state socialist era.

The nomenklatura stayed in power, not because they had any serious support, but by the sheer inertia and lack of alternatives from civil society that had been starved of light and space for so long. Mircea Sandu remained president of the increasingly discredited Romanian Football Federation while his Bulgarian equivalent Ivan Slavkov lasted a decade until he was finally expelled from both the IOC and the Bulgarian Football Union on grounds of corruption.

Bulgaria's two biggest clubs, the Sofia rivals CSKA and Levski, were taken over by an ex-communist businessman and a rich émigré respectively. The army relinquished CSKA to the vast, amorphous, post-privatization conglomerate Multigroup, while Levski were bought up by Greek-born Bulgarian Thomas Laftchis; the two have continued to share most of the country's titles since. The only exception, and a good example of the new indigenous business class, was the emergence of Litex Lovech. Lovech was a tiny provincial club whose stadium was located on an industrial estate. Local entrepreneur Grisha Ganchev, an ex-wrestling promoter who is now the country's key petroleum distributor, snapped up the club in 1996, got it promoted to the first division in 1997 and then saw it win both the 1998 and 1999 titles.

Romania's disengagement from state socialism was even slower, and Bucharest's leading clubs Steaua and Dinamo remained the sporting wings of the army and the interior ministries a decade after the fall of Ceauşescu. Both were rumoured to be hotbeds of financial irregularity and embezzlement – a suspicion confirmed in 1999 when Dinamo president Colonel Vasile Ianul and his sidekick Petre Buduru were sentenced to prison for their involvement in forgery, corruption and the disappearance of €2.5 million. But while this kind of self-serving corruption was bad, the systematic distortion of Romanian football made a mockery of the sport and every law enforcement agency in the country. For a decade results were determined by the *Cooperativa*, a loose cartel of around a dozen clubs who exchanged home wins to ensure that none was ever relegated. It became so pointless for teams from outside the *Cooperativa* to try and compete that in 2001 Baia Mare (not a member of the *Cooperativa*), who had won promotion to the top division, sold their place to Bacau (who were members), who had been relegated. It was only with the national team's shock failure to qualify for the 2002 World Cup that politicians and officials were panicked into admissions of guilt and the need for reform – the issue becoming incontrovertible when the president of Bacau admitted on a live football talk show that he had been involved in fixed matches.

If Poland is the heartland of a wider racism in Eastern European football, Romania is the centre of a wider anti-Roma racism. Football's connection with ultra-nationalism and racist politics is systemic. The chairman of the Romanian football league, Dumitru Dragomir, was also a member of parliament for the extreme right-wing Romania Mare party. Steaua Bucharest were bought up by Gigi Becali, one of the country's richest men and an open supporter of Noua Dreaptă (New Right), the spiritual and political descendants of the Iron Guard, Romania's wartime Nazi party. Games with Rapid, who have considerable Roma support, offered the biggest stage for flaunting their bile. The popular canon of racist songs was not merely sung by the crowd but played at high volume over Steaua's public-address system. At Dinamo Bucharest fans have unveiled giant banners that mix club emblems and colours with drawings of Ion Antonescu, the Romanian politician primarily responsible for the killing of hundreds of thousands of Jews and Roma during the Second World War. Needless to say, the Romanian Football Federation's official reports on these matches tell that 'all was normal'.

Normality is relative. Next to football in Yugoslavia it was positively serene. Outside the Maksimirska stadium in Zagreb, the capital of Croatia, a monument stands to fans of the club who died during the war with Serbia. Indeed, it is claimed by the club's *ultras* – the Bad Blue Boys – that their role was more than mere cannon fodder but as catalysts: the inscription reads, 'To the fans of this club who started the war with Serbia at this ground.' In this reading of history the war began in spring 1990 during a Yugoslav league game at the Maksimirska between Dinamo Zagreb and Red Star Belgrade. Games between the two teams had seen mounting levels of violence and animosity since the death of Tito. This drift towards open conflict was accelerated by the rising torrent of nationalist politics in both of the constituent republics of the Federal Yugoslavia. As the old Communist Party structures and powers began to wane, the leading force in Croatian politics was the ultra-nationalist Franjo Tudjman. Tudjman had been a general in the Yugoslav army and a director of Partizan Belgrade before transferring his allegiances to Croatian nationalism and Dinamo Zagreb, where he had actively nurtured the *ultras* and the role of the club as a vehicle for aspiring Croatian independence. Red Star had increasingly come to represent Serbian national aspirations, as against the Yugoslav federalism of Partizan; Serbian President Slobodan Milošević had come to power on a wave of deliberately manufactured fear and extreme nationalism.

The immediate context of the game was the upcoming Croatian elections and a referendum on independence. All sides came to the match well prepared. The Croats had stockpiled rocks; Red Star *ultras* had brought acid to cut though stadium fences. Dinamo fans stoned the Red Star fans, billboards and fences were ripped down, and a stadium-wide mêlée ensued in which the federal police appeared to be favouring the Serbs. Croatian defender Zvonomir Boban made the most symbolic intervention of the game when he aimed a flying kick at a Yugoslav police officer attempting to arrest a Croat. Helicopters were required to get the Red Star players out of the stadium.

The Red Star club of this era was the last great functioning institution in Yugoslavia. Despite the Serbian affiliations of fans the team was resolutely multiethnic, reflecting the diversity of the country. Robert Prosinečki was a Croat, Refik Šabanadžović a Bosnian Muslim, Marović and Savićević were Montenegrins, and Ilija Najdoski and Darko Pančev were Macedonians. In early 1991, as the country definitively fragmented and headed for war, Red Star were making their way through the final rounds of the European Cup. In April 1991 the Serbs in the Kraijina region of Croatia declared that they were seceding and Croatian armed forces and the Yugoslav army clashed in eastern Croatia around the town of Vukovar. Among the earliest and most advanced units in the new Croatian militias were detachments recruited from Dinamo Zagreb's Bad Blue Boys, who wore their football insignia alongside their military emblems.

In a sensational European Cup semi-final against Bayern München, a second-half goal in the away leg gave Red Star a 2–1 lead. In a seething cauldron of football nationalism in Belgrade a late own goal from the German defender Klaus Augenthaler sent them into the final against Olympique Marseille in Bari. A desperately anxious game produced 120 minutes of stalemate broken only by the penalty shoot-out. Red Star were champions of Europe and late in the year in Tokyo they beat Chile's Colo Colo to become world champions. At the party to celebrate the victory in Belgrade a known *ultra* – Arkan – brandished to great acclaim the street signs from incinerated Croat villages.

Born Željko Ražnatović, the son of a Yugoslav air force colonel, Arkan embarked upon a career of foreign bank robbery, audacious prison escapes, and most likely murky dealings with the Yugoslav secret service. In 1986 he returned to Belgrade and opened a patisserie near Red Star's stadium. Arkan was directly approached by President Milošević and his Interior Minister who asked him to discipline and mobilize the huge band of ultra-nationalist but chaotic Red Star *ultras*. Under Arkan's leadership over the next four years, the Gypsies, as the mass ranks of the Red Star fans had been known, were converted into a violent paramilitary force that was used extensively in the early part of the war with Croatia and in Bosnia too as the shock troops of ethnic cleansing. In such an environment a Yugoslav institution like the Red Star squad could not last. With war raging across the region, UEFA announced in April 1992 that no more games could be held in Belgrade. Red Star had to defend their European title from Sofia in Bulgaria where they were beaten by Sampdoria. The squad was sold off, and the rump Yugoslavia was expelled from that summer's European Championship.

Arkan's political power and personal worth were considerably enhanced as the paramilitaries ran amok in Croatia and Bosnia. Suitably emboldened he attempted to take over Red Star in the mid-1990s, but was thwarted by the board. Instead, he alighted on the small Belgrade side FK Obilić. Obilić was a Serbian knight present at the Battle of Kosovo in 1349 where medieval Serbian independence was lost to the Ottoman Empire. Obilić vowed to kill the Ottoman Sultan in revenge, which he did only for his own head to be cut off. Arkan's arrival coincided with a remarkable turnaround in the club's fortunes. The introduction of the same kind of militaristic discipline imposed on the Red Star *ultras* was now imposed on Obilić, and they were promoted to the first division. They won the championship the following season, deploying the full panoply of threat and terror learned in eastern Croatia.

By 1998 the beginning of the end for ultra-nationalism in Serbia was perhaps in sight. The continuing conflict over Kosovo, the economic embargo and NATO bombings all served to undermine the Milošević regime. Serbia was divided within itself, exemplified by the spiralling decline of the already testy relations between Red Star and Partizan. By 1998 things had deteriorated to the point that Partizan fans, probably with the connivance of club officials, smuggled a rocket-propelled grenade into the stadium and launched it across the length of the pitch at the Red Star terraces; a twelve-year-old boy was killed among the carnage and the chaos. His seat remains empty at the stadium.

In the summer of 2000 with presidential elections on the horizon Milošević's hold on power was looking ever shakier. In a qualifying round of the Champions League between between Red Star Belgrade and Torpedo Kutasi, the fans sang, 'Do Serbia a favour Slobodan and kill yourself.' In the ensuing fight with the police Red Star's *ultras* decisively switched their allegiance away from the ultra-nationalist regime and towards the opposition. In late September that year Milošević lost the presidential election to Vojislav Koštunica. Milošević refused to concede defeat and appeared to be manoeuvring in an attempt to declare the results null and void and so remain in power. Velja Ilić, the mayor of Čačak, an agrarian town south of Belgrade, thought otherwise and arrived in the city at the head of a vast motorcade of cars and agricultural machinery intent on deposing Milošević. Once in Belgrade, they made common cause with a significant phalanx of Red Star *ultras* who joined them in storming the national TV station and then confronted the police at the Serbian parliament. As the police prevaricated it was the *ultras*, used to rushing their lines, that stormed the building and Milošević's hold on power was clearly over. At the following week's game against Partizan, whose President Mirko was a close Milošević collaborator, Red Star unveiled vast banners: 'Mirko to jail, Partizan to the second division' and 'The sun of freedom rises on our victory'.

The Soviet Union lasted slightly longer than Yugoslavia, but the end came in late 1991. A botched and half-hearted military coup initiated by the kidnap of Mikhail Gorbachev was halted on the streets of Moscow and at the parliament building in a spontaneous movement headed by the ex-communist mayor of the city, Boris Yeltsin. When Muscovites refused to yield to the tanks and soldiers refused to fire, the conspirators ran for cover. Yeltsin took charge and, in his single-most important action, dissolved the Communist Party of the Soviet Union. With a stroke of the pen the organization was eradicated. Over the next nine years of Yeltsin's successive presidencies, the Soviet Union broke up into fifteen separate states. In Russia the economic shock therapy was so fearsome and the social dislocation so great that Russian life expectancy declined by five years for both men and women. Under Yeltsin the largest sell-off of state assets ever undertaken turned into a grotesque swindle, concentrating the nation's vast natural resources and functioning industry into the hands of a small group of interconnected businessmen and politicians known as 'the family' or the oligarchs.

Russian football's transition was equally skewed. The vast majority of clubs simply collapsed. The Moscow clubs Dinamo, CSKA, Torpedo and Lokomotiv, despite their state connections, were virtually bankrupt for most of the 1990s. The only team with money was Spartak Moscow. Like Boris Yeltsin, Spartak had a Soviet heritage of privilege but were sufficiently detached from the ruling order that they could reinvent themselves as the heralds of the new Russia. Spartak won every single league title but one between 1992 and 2001. In a nation surviving on vodka, and killing itself at the same time, the only other champions were provincial side Alania Vladikavkaz whose wealth was based on home-brewed illegal alcohol. Spartak's edge was partly political, their main sponsors being Gazprom, the gigantic state oil and gas company and one of the few truly solvent Russian institutions. Spartak also had access to hard currency – Champions League currency. Regular appearances in the group stage put them head and shoulders above their competitors. However, the endemic short-termism and asset-stripping mentality of the decade saw them win all the group games in 1995 only for them to sell their four best players before the quarter-finals, from which they were ejected.

Since Yeltsin's resignation in 1999 and the election of Vladimir Putin as President in 2000, Spartak's monopoly has been broken, the oligarchs have been reined in by an aggressive judicial and political campaign from the Kremlin, and the power of the state has been partially reasserted. In this environment Lokomotiv and CSKA Moscow have won the league and CSKA in 2005 won the UEFA Cup. CSKA was finally sold off by the army in 1997 and is now owned by the mysterious AVO Capital and Blue Castle but it is clear that its main backers have been the oil conglomerate Sibneft. The game, now suddenly awash with money, remains a focus of violence as Spartak and CSKA gangs in particular fight it out.

Football in the Ukraine went through a similar pattern of change. In the years immediately after 1991 the game was dominated by Dinamo Kiev whose long-standing nationalist connotations were redoubled in an era of independence. Like Spartak, they were the sole beneficiary of

Champions League money, big transfer fees from Western Europe and ancillary economic activities. Ukraine's own internal divisions became clear after the break from the Soviet Union. In the west the population is primarily Ukrainian; in the east there are more Russians. The economy of the west is more oriented towards the European Union; the heavy industries of the east are more tied to Russia. By the early twenty-first century Ukrainian football was caught in the conflict between the two halves of the country. Dinamo Kiev is linked to Kiev's business elite, especially the club president Grigory Surkis who doubled up as head of the Ukrainian FA and a member of the clan around outgoing President Leonid Kuchma. Shakhtar Donetsk, their new challengers, were linked to the Donetsk clan centred on club president Rinat Akhmetov. Akhmetov, the Ukraine's richest man, inherited his fortune and his football club from his oligarch mentor Aleksander Bragin, who was blown up by a bomb in 1995. Akhmetov drew on the coffers of his vast natural-resources and manufacturing empire to turn Shakhtar into real contenders, winning the title in 2002 and, through access to the Champions League after this, matching Dinamo in successive close contests.

However, the limits of football's pluralism were revealed in the Ukraine during the election for president in late 2004. Viktor Yanukovich was the candidate from the east, pro-Moscow in his outlook, endorsed by outgoing President Kuchma and supported by both the Kiev and the Donetsk clans. His opponent was the pro-European reformer Victor Yushchenko. Yanukovich campaigned in blue (Dinamo's colours), Yushchenko in orange (Shakhtar's colours). The political atmosphere had become so supercharged in what turned out to be a deeply corrupt electoral process, that when Shakhtar landed in Milan to play a Champions League game in their usual orange scarves, they were accused of being pro-Yushchenko by the Yanukovich press. When they took to the field in their change strip of blue, they were accused of being pro-Yanukovich by the Yushchenko press. In reality neither team or clan had the stomach for a politician who was for neither clan but against the oligarchs' hold on power. Kiev's president persuaded Andriy Shevchenko, the country's star striker, to appear on his TV channel endorsing Yanukovich. Like much of Eastern Europe, a decade and a half after the fall, Ukraine's footballing oligarchs are prepared to share power with each other but not with anyone else.

IV

In the early 1990s it was still possible to argue that there would be an enduring place for Europe's small northern nations in the new football geography. The 1992 European Championship was held in Sweden, where almost four decades of declining football attendance was finally reversed – an upward trend as yet unbroken. Both Sweden and Denmark had created small, efficient, sustainable professional leagues. At an international level there were two spectacular successes: Denmark at Euro '92 and Sweden at the 1994 World Cup. As war raged in the Balkans, Yugoslavia's team were withdrawn from Euro '92 and UEFA called up the Danes, then on holiday, to replace them. Denmark scraped through the first round, but showed both tenacity and adventure when they beat the Dutch in the semi-finals and then the reigning world champions Germany in the final. Sweden made it all the way to the semi-finals of the 1994 World Cup on the back of immaculate teamwork and goals from Kennet Andersson and Martin Dahlin, before a single goal from Brazil's Romário knocked them out.

However, no Scandinavian club or national team has managed to repeat the successes of the early 1990s. Regular qualification for international tournaments and an early undistinguished departure has been the predominant lot of Scandinavian national teams in the last decade. No club side has contested a European club final since IFK Göteborg won the UEFA Cup in 1987. The looming threat of marginalization from the core of the emerging new Europe was a Scandinavian preoccupation. On the eve of the 1992 European Championship, the Danish electorate had by a narrow margin rejected the European Union's Maastricht Treaty. Among the many arguments mobilized by the No campaign was the fear that small countries like Denmark would be overwhelmed in the new institutions of the European Union, their interests sidelined by the big powers – above all the now unified and gigantic Germany. After the Danes beat the Germans in Stockholm the celebrations in central Copenhagen were the biggest public gathering since the liberation in 1945. Indeed, the Danish press could not resist alluding to parallels between the events: Denmark had said no to its marginalization in a Europe dominated by the Franco-German axis, on the pitch and off it. Yet for all this, eleven months later when the crunch came, a second referendum was held on the treaty and the Danes said yes. The Swedes and the Finns, when their chance came, would say yes to the EU too. Only the Norwegians, the richest society in the world, flush with North Sea oil, could seriously consider staying out.

No moment of sporting nationalism could halt the inexorable logic of the European project towards centralization and concentration. In a European football economy where the value of TV rights and sponsorship income was primarily determined by market size, smaller nations were at a permanent disadvantage. The Low Countries, Scotland, Sweden and Denmark together constituted just over half the German market alone. The biggest clubs in these countries were penalized further by their lower payouts and seedings in the Champions League. Consequently they were constantly forced to sell on, if they could, their best players to richer leagues, widening the gap between them even further; a process most sharply illustrated by the relative decline of Dutch football.

In 1995 Ajax won the Champions League. A single goal from the teenage Patrick Kluivert was the difference against the holders Milan. This Ajax side was the creation of coach Louis van Gaal who took the club's inheritance of total football from the 1970s and refined it for an era of increasingly fast and muscular football. Van Gaal argued, 'With space so congested, the most important thing is the ball in circulation.'[10] Drilled relentlessly in training through multiple complex triangular passing routines and games, this Ajax side were the master of retaining possession, taking the ball under control and passing at speed and at distance. Van Gaal's assistant Gerard van der Lem claimed that in many of their European games they would have 70 per cent possession.

Ajax reached the final of the Champions League the following year but this time Juventus were too much for them. Having unveiled his new improved product to the world, Van Gaal saw it sold off within two seasons as Seedorf, Davids, Kluivert, Reiziger, Bogarde, Litmanen, Kanu, Overmars, Finidi, the De Boers and Van der Sar all left for foreign clubs. In the end Van Gaal himself went to Barcelona. Since then Ajax have never been further than the quarter-final of the competition. The only club from the northern periphery to make any impression in the Champions League has been PSV Eindhoven who reached the semi-finals in 2005, while Feyenoord won the UEFA Cup in 2002. Anderlecht and Club Brugge, Belgium's leading clubs, have looked consistently outclassed and overwhelmed in the group stages of the Champions League. Celtic, despite some rousing performances, have never qualified from the group stages and Rangers have yet to progress beyond the second round.

That the Dutch have managed to perform better than the Belgians or the Scots is partly a matter of size and partly a matter of strategy. In keeping with the nation's position as a central hub in European transport networks and Rotterdam's status as the Continent's most important container port, Dutch clubs have become expert in the importation and resale of foreign football talent, often adding value to their charges through exposure to the country's rigorous training schemes. PSV have been among the boldest clubs in signing Latin American players – like Ronaldo and Romário – before selling them on at a big profit. The club has also benefited from the substantial resources of the Philips electronics corporation which continues to use the club and its stadium as bearers of its brands and a laboratory for its new technologies.

Ajax and Feyenoord have established feeder clubs in South Africa and Ghana respectively to attract and develop talent. Ajax have scoured the furthest reaches of the Baltic and Scandinavia to bring in players they have nurtured and sold, like the Swede Zlatan Ibrahimović and the Finn Jari Litmanen. However, none of the leading Dutch clubs have relied on imports alone. The youth schemes of these clubs continue to produce players of the highest technical calibre, who are so prized at the leading clubs of Spain, Italy and England. In this sense Dutch football exists as much in its diaspora as in its homeland. Not only are its leading players in demand, but its coaches as well: Guus Hiddink, for example, has been coach to Real Madrid, South Korea, Australia and Russia. Ronald Koeman has run Benfica, Frank Rijkaard is the latest Dutchman to coach Barcelona, and Dutch coaches have taken charge at Chelsea, Newcastle, Tottenham, Rangers and Celtic.

The structural inequalities of European football have squeezed the Dutch out of the running in club competitions, but the Dutch national team remained a side overflowing with talent. Yet on successive occasions in international competition it has fallen short of its promise. The Dutch campaign at Euro '96 was beset by open rumours of racial conflict and cliques within the squad. A stunning series of performances at the 1998 World Cup, culminating in a breathtaking Dennis Bergkamp goal and victory over Argentina in the last minutes of their quarter-final, ended with a loss of nerve in the penalty shoot-out against Brazil, a scenario re-enacted at even higher levels of self-doubt at Euro 2000. In the semi-final against Italy the Dutch managed to miss two penalties during normal time and three of their shots in the shoot-out.

Scottish football has operated under the same kinds of constraint as pertaining in Holland, but not only is the football nation smaller, it suffered even greater levels of financial concentration. No team from outside the Old Firm of Celtic and Rangers has won the Scottish league since 1985. When Rangers won the title nine times in a row (1989–97), it looked as if the duopoly might be reduced still further. Between 1995 and 2005 no team from outside the Old Firm could win second place. Hearts only managed to break the sequence in 2006 with the aid of their own Eastern European oligarch, the Lithuanian oil magnate Vladimir Romanov. Over the same period Celtic and Rangers have won more than half the cup competitions as well, monopolizing income from European competition.

European money aside, the Old Firm towered financially over the rest of the league. Both clubs underwent a period of explosive commercialization and expansion. Rangers were underwritten by the personal wealth of chairman David Murray, a series of share issues and a never-ending stream of businessmen ready to throw some fun or nostalgia money into the Rangers pot. Celtic mobilized the capital of its own supporters too. Under the ownership of Fergus McCann and then Dermot Gallagher, Celtic raised tens of millions of pounds. Both clubs have entirely rebuilt their stadiums with capacities well in excess of all but two or three Premiership sides, and both boasted full houses and long waiting lists for season tickets.

As a consequence Celtic and Rangers were operating on budgets that are the equivalent to the middle rank of the English Premiership in a league where the competition was operating on budgets equivalent to the lower end of the Championship. When the decline in the value of TV rights after 2002 began to bite, the Scottish Premier League as a whole found itself £100m in debt, three clubs were declared bankrupt and Inverness Caledonian Thistle were on the verge of turning down their promotion. The club feared it would cost more to upgrade their stadium to comply with SPL rules than they would receive in additional revenue.

In the early twenty-first century, the chief Scottish clubs have seriously considered leaving the SPL and have quietly been lobbying among the powers of English and European football to find an alternative home. Politically and bureaucratically it has, so far, proved impossible. The Old Firm's dash across the border is not the only attempt by the marooned big clubs of Northern Europe to try and rejoin the financial core. The leading clubs from Scandinavia, the Low Countries, Scotland and Portugal seriously considered the formation of an Atlantic League to supersede or run alongside their own national leagues – but neither UEFA nor the marketing people could quite square the concept.

Over the last decade and a half, the Tartan Army has continued to display a carnivalesque caricature of Scottish identity. In the mid-1990s when Scotland had been toiling under seventeen years of increasingly English Tory rule from Westminster, the national team's progress and its following were swept up by the same tide of cultural and increasingly political nationalism. The creation of a generously funded Scottish parliament and executive by the Labour government that swept the Conservatives out of office in 1997, took the sting out of the politics. However, the enduring bitterness of attitudes towards England, clearly on display in the play-offs for Euro 2000, appears undiminished; an ersatz anger quite inappropriate to the real economic and political order. Drunken exuberance, nationalist lampoonery and bacchanalian good-will were also the dominant notes of the travelling support for the Dutch, Danish and even the Swedish national sides. However, like the Scots they are the outward face of football cultures that were more troubled and divided than they appeared at international football tournaments.

In Scotland the enduring sectarian dimension to football has not been eradicated by either commercialization or political challenge. While Dundee and Edinburgh have not been immune to the sectarian virus, its locus remains the conflict between Celtic and Rangers. Indeed, as the two clubs have become institutionally more similar and more closely tied to each other economically, so the degree of rancour between fans has risen. Despite Graeme Souness's signing of the Catholic player Mo Johnston and the official renunciation of any anti-Catholic bias by the club, the relationship between Rangers and the forces of Unionism and Orangism were clear when player Andy Gorham turned on the Christmas lights in the heart of militant unionism, Belfast's Shankhill Road. In 1999 Rangers director Donald Findlay was forced to resign for leading fellow directors and fans in the singing of sectarian songs.

The skinhead gang finally made its appearance in Sweden in the early 1990s where the Black Army, associated with AIK Stockholm, dabbled in public disorder, extreme right-wing politics and a cocktail of hard alcohol and nihilism. The economic downturn and uncertainties of the early 1990s in Sweden spawned the country's first right-wing populism and open racism for a generation, but also served to crack the dour carapace of seriousness that had traditionally enveloped Swedish crowds. Spontaneous singing, jokes at the enemy's expense and hurled abuse made their first appearance in Swedish stadiums. In the Netherlands the now established repertoire of fighting and vandalism among the four or five key sides in the country continued. Intensified policing and new stadium architecture seemed to push most of it out of the grounds, and the turn of the century saw a whole series of prearranged fights on wasteland, motorway intersections and industrial estates. The relationship between Feyenoord and Ajax fans was the most regularly violent. What had always been an inter-urban rivalry now acquired a strange ethno-religious twist. Although Ajax had long had a reputation as a Jewish club, by virtue of its location, support and backers, it was never exclusively or even predominantly so. Since the liquidation of most of Amsterdam's Jews during the Second World War, the link though still real was of declining significance. Yet through the 1990s, Ajax's sides increasingly took to the emblems and language of Judaism to express their club identity. Ajax's terraces were bedecked in Star of David flags, the symbol cut into innumerable skinhead crops, the crowd singing, 'Jews, Jews, We are Super Jews.' Inevitably, Feyenoord responded in the language of both European and Middle Eastern anti-Semitism, 'Hamas Hamas, Jews to the Gas.' Thus at the end of the twentieth century, in one of the world's richest and most ordered societies, people chose to take on the identities and politics of an ethnic rivalry on another Continent at a game of football. Surely even the Queen of Hearts would have had trouble with this one?

The early 1990s in Italian football belonged to AC Milan. Under coach Fabio Capello, they were champions three times in a row from 1992 to 1994, playing exhilarating, expansive football and going on the longest unbeaten run in Serie A history – fifty-eight games. The spectacular was alive and well and Milan's boss Silvio Berlusconi busied himself with the explosive growth of Fininvest, now in command of majority stakes in Italian television, advertising and publishing. And yet there was a show in town that was, for a moment, even more compelling: *Tagentopoli*. In the early 1990s a growing wave of judicial activism, led by Francesco Borelli and other magistrates in Milan, put a huge swathe of the post-war political elite, particularly the ruling Christian Democrats and Socialists, on trial for a range of corruption and embezzlement charges. Socialist leader Bettino Craxi fled the country, the electorate abandoned them all, and a significant fraction of the entire political and business executive class were retired or imprisoned. Into this political vacuum stepped new forces from the right – the Lega Nord and the Allianza Nazionale, formed from the old neo-fascist party of the south, the MSI. On the Left the Communist Party transmuted into the avowedly social democratic Party of the Democratic Left, while its hard core splintered off to form Rifondazione Comunista. Berlusconi himself was initially barely touched by the *Tagentopoli* revelations, but he had plenty of reasons to worry: the liquidation of his closest political allies left him exposed; Fininvest's mountain of debt was looking unmanageable; and a polity where a party of the Left could now realistically hope to form the government, alongside over-inquisitive reforming judges, was an unpalatable prospect.

I heard that things were getting dangerous, and that it was all being played in the penalty area, with the midfield being left desolately empty.[11]

Thus Berlusconi described his motivation for making the move from mere football club impresario and media mogul to politician and aspiring Prime Minister of Italy, what came to be known emblematically as *la discesa in campo* – the descent to the pitch. With this declaration, the total elision of Italian football and society was made complete. What in most cultures remain connected but parallel universes became fused into one. Nowhere has the *Society of the Spectacle*, first described by French situationist Guy Debord, been so fully realized. Debord had written that 'The spectacle is not a collection of images; rather it is a social relationship between people that is mediated by images.'[12] The amalgam of football, television and politics as show business and spectacle perfected by Berlusconi in the 1990s would indeed create and reshape the social relationships of Italian society. In time the spectacular would lay bare the country's hierarchical and profoundly corrupt clientalism, the tenuous hold of any meaningful rule of law, the supine unreflective consumerism of mainstream civil society and its entwinement and symbiotic interdependence with networks of organized crime. But in the mid-to-late 1990s Italian domestic football underwent a short era of spectacular achievement and confidence.

In late 1993 Berlusconi launched Forza Italia. Never has a political party been so self-consciously and professionally researched, designed and marketed as a form of predominantly televisual consumption. The name, then the favourite cry in support of the Italian national team, captured the now indissoluble intersection of the sporting spectacular with the syntax of politics, advertising and television. The party's initial infrastructure was provided by the network of AC Milan supporters clubs up and down the country, while Berlusconi's own commercial empire provided media support and many of the party's candidates. A whirlwind campaign for the legislature in spring 1994 saw Forza Italia win 21 per cent of the vote and in an alliance of the Right, with the Lega Nord and the Allianza Nazionale, he was asked by the President to form a government. As Berlusconi attempted to stitch together a majority in the legislature, AC Milan wound their way, once again, to the European Cup Final, where they faced Barcelona. On the same evening a crucial vote in parliament would allow a Berlusconi-led government to be formed. As *Corriere della Sera* put it the next day, '4–0 and 159–153, both Cruyff's Barcelona and Occhetto's centre-left were wiped out.'[13]

Berlusconi's stay in power was short but illuminating. One of the new government's very first actions was to issue a decree law that would in effect put a stop to the *Tagentopoli* investigations and trials. It was released on the eve of the World Cup semi-final between Italy and Bulgaria. The Italian press and public did not fall for this one, the law was withdrawn and Berlusconi was out of office by the end of the year. He was not however out of politics. In or out of power, Milan and Italian football prospered in the 1990s. Invigorated by the new stadiums and panache of the 1990 World Cup and by a steady influx of foreign talent, attendances, TV money and sponsorship all grew. More than that, the cachet of club ownership was now so great that a phalanx of the wealthiest entrepreneurs and companies in the Italian economy wanted to invest. Fiorentina were bought by the film producer and would-be TV baron Mario Cecchi Gori in the early 1990s. After his death both club and business were run by the man with the worst fake tan in *calcio*, his supremely incompetent son Vittorio. Parma became an appendage of the burgeoning Parmalat corporation, both owned by the Tanzi family whose patriarch Calisto had made a fortune from selling UHT milk, juice, yoghurt and biscuits. Parmalat's money took the club from Serie B to Serie A and from relegation candidates to winners of the Italian Cup, the European Cup Winners' Cup and the UEFA Cup; a team able to attract an abundance of expensive talent.

Lazio were purchased in 1991 by Sergio Cragnotti, owner of the Cirio agribusiness empire, whose impenetrably complex structure seemed able to pump money into the club at will. An acknowledged master of the dark arts of corporate finance, Cragnotti was the first president to take an Italian club to the stock market and offered stock options and board membership to the squad. Under coach Sven-Göran Eriksson and armed with a transfer budget of almost £100 million, Lazio were the first side to break the Milan–Juve duopoly, claiming the championship in 2000.

In 1995 Internazionale were bought by Massimo Moratti, the billionaire inheritor of the oil refining giant Saras and, as the son of popular 1960s Inter President Angelo Moratti, a life-long fan. Massimo, like all *Interisti*, was desperate to win the league – they last won the *scudetto* in 1989 – and he put his money where his heart was. Between 1995 and 2001 Moratti spent around €260 million and recouped less than half of this on the sale of an incredible seventy-five players. He has spent about another €200 million since, including breaking two world transfer records to bring Ronaldo to Inter from Barcelona for £18 million in 1997 and Christian Vieri from Lazio for £32 million in 1999. He has also been through twelve coaches. For all this Inter had just the 1998 UEFA Cup to show for the blizzard of money. Moratti was closely involved in the purchase and management of players and he proved himself to be generous-hearted and fatally compromised by his passion for Inter. When Nigerian Nwankwo Kanu was purchased from Ajax he was found to have a hole in his heart. Moratti neither dispensed with him, nor sued Ajax, but took the Nigerian under his wing, underwriting his medical expenses.

Inter have tended to hoard players. When the defence was looking particularly thin, Moratti went to market and created a squad with three alternative back fours. When the team already possessed attacking midfielders who liked to play behind the strikers of the calibre of Youri Djorkaeff and Roberto Baggio, Moratti went out and bought two more – Andrea Pirlo and Recoba. Under the relentless pressure and increasing paranoia that the club seemed to generate, genuine stars have seen their career falter at Inter only to miraculously recover when they moved on. Clarence Seedorf and Dennis Bergkamp, who resurrected themselves at Real Madrid and Arsenal respectively, are cases in point.

Inconsistency, turmoil and a mounting sense of frustration created a feeling of *nervosismo* at the club made ever worse by Inter's consistent failure to win their decisive games; they are now the country's longest-running and most compelling public psycho-drama, matching the excruciating sense of frustration and failure of any Italian who has to steer a course through the country's public services and legal authorities. The club, fans, players and directors tend towards bursts of anger, a deep cynicism, and glorious but melancholy black humour.

The mid-1990s was another era of dominance for Juventus. Under the stern technocratic coaching of Marcello Lippi, Juventus fielded teams of unyielding character and increasingly unyielding muscularity, armed with some of the era's finest attacking players: Vialli, Del Piero, Zidane and Nedved. The trophy cabinet began to swell. League champions in 1995, 1997 and 1998, they won the UEFA Cup in 1993 and lost it in 1995. They won the Champions League and the Intercontinental Club Cup in 1996 and lost the finals of the former in 1997 and 1998. Juventus also had the most connected and astute power broker in the Italian game as their director of football: Luciano Moggi, a reptilian football politician of the highest order. The club had long been suspected of exercising undue influence in the corridors of football power over referee selection and the hidden working of the transfer market. In the late 1990s and early twenty-first century these claims grew more insistent.

Three incidents in particular stoked the widespread belief that Juventus were stealing victories. In 1998 the key game of the season was Juve vs. Inter. Juve were 1–0 up after seventy minutes when Ronaldo was clearly checked in the Juventus penalty area. No penalty was given and then another one was given to Juventus a few minutes later. Juve missed their penalty but the damage was done as the Inter squad went wild, the normally mild coach Gigi Simoni sent off for berating the referee. The scale of the referee's bias was so great that it became the subject of parliamentary debate and was christened *la grande ruberia* – the great theft. In May 2000 Parma had a perfectly good goal disallowed against Juve which kept the Turinese in the title race just behind leaders Lazio. Five hundred Lazio fans were so incensed that they attacked the football federation's offices in Rome and fought a three-hour running battle with police. They would later unfurl the gigantic banner: 'Juventus. History repeats itself. Lots of thefts, lots of victories.' Finally the ex-Roma and Napoli coach Zdeněk Zeman was interviewed in *L'Espresso* in 1998 where he said, 'Football must get out of the pharmacy.'[14] He went on at some length to suggest that Juventus had been systematically involved in doping their squad and pointed to the explosive muscular growth of some of its hitherto more callow players. At the time his allegations were denied by Juventus and he was cold-shouldered by the Italian football establishment.

The unravelling of these claims against Juventus was still to come. There were so many examples elsewhere of blatant match-fixing and points trading. For example, in 1999 Venezia and Bari were drawing 1–1 in a mid-table game when Venezia's new Brazilian Tuta came on and scored in the last minute. The reaction of colleagues and opponents, caught by lip synch on television, made the extent of their displeasure clear. Most brazen of all, it was revealed in 2000 that Roma's president Franco Sensi had made a present of a brand new Rolex watch, worth around £10,000, to every referee on the Serie A roster.

At the same time, although not endemic, violence and disorder in Italian football was certainly growing: the Roma vs. Brescia game in 1994 had seen city-wide fighting between police and over 500 Roma fans. In 1995 the Genoa fan Claudio Spagnolo was stabbed by Simone Barbaglia in a fight outside Genoa's stadium before their game with Milan. Barbaglia was a peripheral associate of the Barbour Gang, a small faction of violent Milan *ultras*. The game kicked-off but as news of the death seeped out and the Genoa crowd began to riot the game was called off – the first time this had occurred in Italian football. The fighting between Genoa fans and the police inside and outside the stadium was so intense that the Milanese were kept behind under police guard for seven hours before being secretly bussed out of the city. Barbaglia was arrested, tried and sentenced, and Spagnolo turned into a martyr by the *ultra* movement. Nationwide contacts and meetings between *ultra* groups resulted in a variety of melodramatic declarations and proclamations calling for an end to knives and violence while protesting for the right of the *ultra*-lifestyle to be protected and honoured; a lifestyle in the late 1990s which, despite these protestations, increasingly involved intimidation, extortion, illegal but permitted control over club's merchandising and close ideological and practical links with right-wing extremists and neo-fascists.

In Germany the end of the Cold War unravelled faster than anyone could initially have imagined. While the French, the British and the Soviets were all initially opposed to anything but a slow and managed transition to a united Germany, events on the ground outran them. Italia '90 was the last World Cup that West Germany would appear in; victory over Argentina appeared to confirm the nation's rising status as the future hegemon of the European continent. Less than six months later East Germany had effectively been dissolved and a unified Germany had emerged. However, the reunification party would not be represented by football. In the new Germany the game suddenly appeared to belong to a working-class industrial past and the distressed and declining rust-belt regions of the country where the SPD or the old Communist Party still held sway. Under the long rule of the conservative CDU and Chancellor Helmut Kohl, the individualistic middle-class sports of tennis and golf were in the ascendant. Indeed football was almost eclipsed as the national sport by the successive achievements of Boris Becker, Michael Stich and Steffi Graf in tennis and Bernhard Langer in golf.

By contrast the national football team performed poorly. Defeat by Denmark in the finals of the 1992 European Championship was considered humiliating, the team's exit from the 1994 World Cup at the hands of Bulgaria even worse. The squad and its mode of play appeared to be tired and antiquated; its overreliance on the use of sweepers an anachronism. Victory in the 1996 European Championships – the sole success of the decade – was deemed to be the consequence of a few key battling players, like Jürgen Klinsmann and Matthias Sammer. Germany's performance at France '98 was truly woeful and the Germans were dispatched by Croatia in a display of petulance and rancour made all the worse by an outbreak of fighting among German supporters and the French police which left one officer in a long coma. The decline in German football's standing was confirmed by a first-round exit in the

European Championship of 2000 where they scored a single goal and won a single point before going home.

The situation was even worse for football in the East. The deal at unification was that the two best teams in the East German league would be allowed to join the Bundesliga and the next six would go into the second division. The two teams to make the Bundesliga in 1991 were Hansa Rostock and Dynamo Dresden. While Hansa have proved to be the great survivors of East German football, holding their own in the Bundesliga for most of the decade, Dresden's story is more representative. Within four years they had been entirely stripped of their leading players, who were snapped up by clubs in the West. Unfamiliar with a truly commercial football environment, Dresden were embezzled by their new president, a carpet-bagger from the West. By 1994 they were DM18 million in debt and had their playing licence revoked. Both Dynamo and Union Berlin fared so poorly that they were reduced to playing in the regional amateur leagues, pulling crowds of less than 2,000. Like the state industries of the former GDR they were either asset-stripped or left to dwindle into virtual oblivion.

Yet despite these challenges and calamities, German football demonstrated a remarkable resilience. The Bundesliga, long considered a poor and lacklustre cousin of the Latin leagues, steadily grew in quality, income and status over the 1990s. It was a question of money. New money, old money, TV and sponsorship money, from what remained the largest and richest economy on the Continent, came flooding into the Bundesliga. The DFB was forced by the leading teams to allow private investment in clubs and even their stock-market flotation.

With the avalanche of money came saturation TV and tabloid coverage, foreign stars, high-intensity competition, rising attendances and eventually European success. By 1997, Germany could boast three of that year's Champions League quarter-finalists, and the eventual winner and Intercontinental Club champions Borussia Dortmund. German industry was a major investor. The pharmaceutical giant Bayer upped their investment in Bayer of Leverkusen, Hertha BSC Berlin were transformed by finance from the media group Bertelsmann from a team forced to train on rented British army polo fields into serious contenders, while VfL Wolfsburg were dragged from sporting obscurity by Volkswagen. Dortmund, who were attracting among the biggest crowds in the whole of Europe, received a huge boost from their stock-market debut, their shares snapped up by the blue-chip industrial banks. The entertainment value of the league was further enhanced by the initial failure of Bayern München, the undisputed power in the land before reunification, to prosper in the new environment. Interminable managerial chaos and vicious squabbling among the players and directors produced acres of gossip and earned the club the sobriquet FC Hollywood. With the arrival of the nation's leading coach Ottmar Hitzfeld, the club turned its huge national fan base and commercial potential into an imperious team that began to dominate domestic football, lost the Champions League final in 1999 and finally won it again in 2001.

While Bayern monopolized much of the glory and the gossip, the great hinterland of German football produced fan cultures who took their pleasures in other ways. In the eastern *Länder*, the football of the former GDR was a locus for a wider nostalgia for lives and times lost. German groundhoppers, maniacal visitors to football stadiums across Europe and beyond, sustained their obsessions with fanzines and websites. Borussia Dortmund maintained a commitment to terracing in the age of the all-seater stadium, only adding seats for European games. As German deindustrialization continued apace, football in the Ruhr and other provincial manufacturing zones remained an enclave of mythic solidarities, beer and sausages, denim, leather and heavy-metal anthems. On the margins, where the appetite for carnival was dimmed by serious marginalization and decline, the neo-Nazi and fascist movements of the new Germany found voice and support.

Spanish football began the 1990s with a transfer of power. After five consecutive titles, the Real Madrid of the late 1980s – *la Quinta del Buitre* or the Vulture Squad as they were colloquially known – were finally toppled by a renascent Barcelona under the idolized Johan Cruyff. Cruyff completely rebuilt the side, nicknamed the Dream Team, with a mix like that of Herrera's great Barcelona teams of the early 1960s. First, a Catalan core that pleased the nationalist obsessions of the crowd, exemplified by the young playmaker Pep Guardiola, who made a point of conducting his interviews in Catalan and wrapping himself in the national flag. Second, a sprinkling of talented foreigners who prospered in the cosmopolitan environment of Catalonia, like the Bulgarian Hristo Stoitchkov, the Dutchman Ronald Koeman and the mercurial Dane Brian Laudrup.

Simultaneously the city of Barcelona underwent its own transformation, hosting the 1992 Olympics, reinventing itself as Spain's premier post-industrial city. Barcelona were certainly entertaining, free-scoring and attacking, but they were also lucky. Three times, they took the title on the final day as their nearest challengers collapsed. Real Madrid, the title within their grasp, were twice beaten by lowly Tenerife and forced into second. The newly revived Galician club Deportivo La Coruña threw the championship away in 1994 when Miroslav Djukic missed a penalty in their decisive final-day match against Valencia. Even the 1992 victory in the European Cup over Sampdoria at Wembley was only won with a singular moment of brilliance from Ronald Koeman's explosive free kick. After Cruyff's departure Barcelona's love affair with Dutch football was extended by the appointment as coach of Louis van Gaal who brought a slew of his compatriots to the Nou Camp. Van Gaal's Barcelona, twice La Liga champions, played with the intricate graft of an Ajax side, but failure to progress in the Champions League and a vast and mounting debt led to his dismissal. At the end of the 1990s the club's descent into chaos was made all the uglier by the increasingly violent actions of the *Boixos Nois*, the neo-fascist *ultra* group that took to intimidating presidential candidates, like Joan Laporta. When Luís Figo returned to the Nou Camp as a Real Madrid player in 2002, they threw a severed pig's head at his feet.

The writing was on the wall for the Spanish socialists and their allies long before the decisive general election of 1996. Successive scandals over party funding and public contracts and a long-running series of accusations that the government had sanctioned semi-official death squads in the war against the Basque separatist group ETA had reduced the credibility of the Felipe González government to zero. They were buried by a landslide victory for the Partido Popular and their leader José María Aznar, political centralizer, economic liberal and a *socio* and season-ticket holder at Real Madrid.

The Real Madrid of the early 1990s, under president Ramón Mendoza, remained successful. During his presidency (1985–95) Real won six league championships and the UEFA Cup, but were unable to return to the European heights of the 1950s and 1960s, a fact made worse by Barcelona's succcess. As Catalan novelist Manuel Vásquez Montalbán put it, 'For these prisoners of the myth of Real Madrid – the winner of six European Cups – the conquest of the seventh has become an indispensable condition for affirming an identity that has always revolved around domination.'[15] But Mendoza's regime was never going to be able to deliver on this. Where once the club had been at the leading edge of club football it had become an insular and conservative anachronism. As *El País* reported, 'There are computers that have never worked, most of the staff can't speak any other language than Spanish . . . recently, candidates for jobs that have fallen vacant at the club were shortlisted on the basis of emotional attachment and their family ties to the club. Club officials are very resistant to innovation.'[16] Mendoza resigned and was replaced by his vice-president and patron, the property developer Lorenzo Sanz, who slowly began to modernize the club, buying off and removing the old guard of managers and administrators.

Boosted by the rising income of the club, but unrestrained by any concern for financial or personal stability, Real under Sanz went through nine coaches in his five short years in office and managed to accumulate debts that were touching £170 million; but it was all worth it when in 1998 they beat Juventus by a single goal in Amsterdam to win their seventh European Cup, the first since 1966. Over a million people gathered in the centre of Madrid in the Plaza de la Cibeles, to celebrate in a mood that was simultaneously triumphalist and aggressive, as much a Spanish national celebration as a display of civic success. King Juan Carlos resealed the identification of club, city and nation when he spoke at the city parade: 'This is a victory not just for Madrid but for Spain.'[17]

In 2000 Real were imperious on their way to the Champions League final again. In the spring Aznar and the Partido Popular were re-elected with an even bigger majority. In the Champions League Final Real met Valencia, a city which provided part of the bedrock of the PP's support outside the capital. Real won 3–0. The enduring connection between the club and the centralizing nationalism of the Aznar regime was given symbolic form when the striker Raúl Gonzalez, after being handed the trophy by Crown Prince Felipe, picked up a Spanish flag and in imitation of a matador taunting a bull, swirled the flag before the cameras. Yet just as Sanz had fired successful coaches, so he too was fired by the *socios* of Real Madrid after this great triumph. For while the victories were welcome, his flagrant disregard for any kind of economic probity was no longer acceptable. The Partido Popular and Prime Minister Aznar had been re-elected on the basis of their sound economic management and tight control of public spending. Sanz and his 'spend now, ask questions later' style of governance no longer fitted the bill. His failure to persuade the Madrid city government to buy Real's training ground and lift their debt was the final nail in the coffin. His successor was construction magnate Florentino Pérez whose central campaign promise was to bring Luís Figo, the Portuguese star at Barcelona, to Real. The *socios* chose Pérez, Figo came to Real and the Galacticos were born.

The forecasters' advice to the English FA went like this:

In the 1990s and beyond, patterns of affluence and the associated fragmentation of circumstances and interests [mean] hard choices have to be made as to the consumer segment to which the offer is to be targeted, and hence the ingredients of that offer . . . The response of most sectors has been to move upmarket, so as to follow the affluent 'middle class' consumer in his or her pursuits and aspirations. We strongly suggest that there is a message in this for football and particularly for the design of stadia for the future.[18]

English football heard the message and acted upon it. The continual manoeuvring among the biggest clubs to create a breakaway league and keep more of the ever-rising value of TV rights to themselves was consummated in alliance with the Football Association. In its *Blueprint for Football*, the FA chose to jump ship with the newly founded Premiership and leave the rest of the Football League to make do with the crumbs that would be available. In a bidding war the TV deal with the new Premiership went to the subscription satellite channel BSkyB owned by Rupert Murdoch's News International group, for the then-astronomical figure of £304 million over three years. Henceforth live televised football would only be available to subscribers. While this key deal and its successors have provided the main spigot of money for the development of English football over the last decade and a half, the appeal of the spectacle on offer was ultimately secured by the process of gentrification undertaken at the leading clubs.

Gentrification, the emblematic term for social and architectural transformation, had a wider currency in English football. The relentless and explosive property boom in England in the 1990s and early twenty-first century was also the key economic force in changing and polarizing the

English class structure. Those who were able to join the boom saw their assets rise astronomically in value, while those unable to get into the property market found themselves increasingly marooned. The process of change in football was initiated by the Taylor Report of 1990, commissioned in the wake of the 1989 Hillsborough disaster. While Taylor surveyed and diagnosed many of the intersecting ills of football its central concern was with the unacceptable dilapidation of English football stadiums – testament to the chronic underinvestment in infrastructure that afflicted the entire economy. Taylor, under the rubric of health and safety, insisted that all grounds in the upper reaches of football should become all-seater and a variety of other expensive safety measures and forms of crowd regulation be introduced.

The clubs, some receiving considerable subsidies, set about removing terraces and introducing plastic seating and increasingly intrusive stewarding arrangements. This reached its apogee ten years later when Manchester United attempted to regulate and even ban over-boisterous singing, and there were regular reports of fans removed from grounds for swearing or having the temerity to be supporting the away team in the family section. The widespread introduction of CCTV and a renewed stringency on the part of the police and courts saw truly troublesome elements in the crowd removed and then permanently excluded. Meanwhile, English clubs were putting up the prices of their tickets many times faster than the rate of inflation. From an average price of around £8 for a ticket in the Premiership in 1992, the average price in 2005 had risen to nearer £40. The scale of executive boxes and hospitality suites grew in every stadium. The architectural harvest from this immense process of renovation and transformation was remarkably thin. Aston Villa's failure to maintain the irreplaceable brickwork designs of Archibald Leitch's Villa Park and the destruction of Wembley's twin towers were just the most obvious casualties of a building boom whose aesthetic heart was closer to the supermarkets and retail sheds built on the land vacated by football clubs moving out to the ring road.

Nonetheless, the strategy has proved immensely successful. Despite the astronomical increase in prices, attendance at football in every division of the professional game in England rose to heights not seen since the 1960s. By 2004 the Premiership was reporting occupancy rates of over 99 per cent at some clubs and overall a rate above 95 per cent. The social composition of the crowd has shifted, reflecting demographic change across society. Although all social classes continue to be represented there has been a clear shift, most pronounced in London, away from unskilled and manual workers towards skilled and professional workers. By 2002, over one-third of Chelsea season-ticket holders were earning more than £50,000 a year – twice the average income of the country as a whole. The crowd was also travelling further. While over 80 per cent of season-ticket holders at Newcastle and Sunderland were born locally, the figure fell to as low as 40 per cent for Manchester United. The age of the average fan is rising as the cost of tickets deters the young on low wages and many parents from taking their kids. The crowd remains overwhelmingly male and white although the numbers of women have risen and in London, particularly, a black presence can be seen in the stands.

Those that do go have been spending an increasing amount. The massed ranks of replica shirts, although common in much of Western Europe, are denser in England then anywhere else. Indeed in all areas of ancillary commercialization English football clubs have shown themselves to be smarter and faster movers than any of their Continental competitors By 2005 the Premiership had become the richest league in Europe by turnover, attracting the biggest television deal, the highest rate of sponsorship and the biggest match-day incomes. The Championship, the recently renamed second tier of English football, was by itself the sixth largest league in Europe. The seemingly insatiable and price-inelastic demand for football in England cannot be explained by recourse to the processes of gentrification or commercialization alone; two other factors are required. First, English football was reinterpreted and re-experienced through the lens of a wave of new football writing and talking. And second, the football played in the Premiership was immeasurably better.

Fever Pitch by Nick Hornby was the defining football book of the 1990s. A diary of youth and young adulthood told through the author's obsessive emotionally charged relationship with Arsenal, *Fever Pitch* wore its learning and its thinking lightly, its tone quirky, humorous and honest. It opened up a vast emotional, narrative and psychological terrain that genuinely reflected the consumption of football among a large section of the public, but that had never been aired in this form. At different moments of Hornby's life football had offered a source of ritual emotional connection to a distant father, and a source of exotic and experimental proletarian identities. It caught the moment of transition between two footballing cultures, lambasting the old culture of violence and racism, but suspicious of the new commercialism. The book's limit was its strength – a relentless focus on the individual. For a sense of the depth and richness of the collective cultures of football in England, Harry Pearson's *The Far Corner: A Mazy Dribble Through North-East Football* is a powerful and achingly funny anthropological corrective. Simon Kuper's *Football Against the Enemy* offered a popular idiom in which the hitherto unthinkable connections between societies and their football cultures could be explored.

If the new football writing has helped provide a geography of the emotions and a vocabulary in which football's relationship to personal and social narratives could be explored, the bulk of the ensuing conversation happened on the Internet and on the radio where discussion sites, blogs, and radio phone-ins have multiplied many times over. This was a Europe-wide phenomenon but in England, where class distinctions and territories were policed more fiercely than anywhere else, the emergence of football as a subject of concern among the intellectual elite was considered a moment of historic transition, and for many a signifier of inauthenticity and betrayal – the key terms in the popular conversation attempting to wrestle with the economic and cultural transition being wrought upon the game from above.

The spectacle around which this conversation has been built and to which the new audiences have flocked was for its first decade dominated by Manchester United. Under the chairmanship of Martin Edwards and Glaswegian manager Alex Ferguson, United won the Premiership eight times in its first eleven years, including two League and Cup doubles. In 1991 Edwards floated the club on the stock market, initiating a wave of share issues by English clubs. By 1994 United were already employing twice as many people in merchandising and marketing as playing and coaching, giving them a massive head start in the commercial game. Ferguson's harsh Glaswegian charm and authoritarian personal management lent the enterprise an aura of the industrial football that the club's economic progress was eradicating. In the early years of United's predominance its team, indeed the rising cachet of the Premiership as a whole, depended on the unpredictable, haughty Frenchman Eric Cantona, whose combination of open passion, daring football and theatrical sensibility lit up the Premiership. These facets of Cantona's character combined when he aimed a flying kick at a Crystal Palace fan insulting his French roots; a long suspension followed.

Although United had won the European Cup Winners' Cup in 1991 on the return of English teams to European competition, they had been unable to translate their domestic and financial success into progress in the Champions League. In a recapitulation of the Holy Grail narratives of the Matt Busby era, Ferguson's United turned their attention more and more to the European arena, undergoing the same kinds of learning processes that the English teams of the 1970s and '80s had undergone. This team peaked in 1999 when United won a treble of League, Cup and European Champions League, with a core of young players nurtured at United – Ryan Giggs, the Neville brothers, Paul Scholes, Nicky Butt and David Beckham. Their progress to the Champions League Final, a bravura display of comebacks and battles against the odds, was crowned by a final in which they trailed Bayern München for eighty-four minutes before finding two goals in added time.

Arsenal, under French coach Arsène Wenger, provided the stiffest opposition to United, winning the Premiership in 1998 and 2002; in 2004 they won again after a mesmerizing undefeated season. Wenger's Arsenal were perhaps the best example of the much deeper and wider impact of foreign coaches, players and methods on English football. In contrast to Arsenal's traditional defensive style and hard-drinking dressing rooms, Wenger brought a culture of attack and adventure on the field and a cerebral, ascetic professionalism off it. Behaviour, diet and training regimes were completely revolutionized. Salad, chicken and mineral water displaced bacon, eggs and beer. English players were brought up to technical and tactical speed and encouraged to play a more expansive game. Dennis Bergkamp's play under Wenger brought a degree of sophistication and invention in attacking, passing and play-making that was both the side's signature mode and the foundation of their success. Wenger's French imports turned the club into champions. A midfield marshalled by Patrick Vieira had new steel, and Thierry Henry was transformed from an underperforming winger to the most sumptuously talented striker in the country. Elegance, grace and a cool understated charm radiated from the man and his football.

From less than 5 per cent of the Premiership playing force in 1992, foreign players comprised nearly 60 per cent of Premiership squads in 2004, hailing from sixty-one different countries. Foreign coaches had taken over at Chelsea, where Ruud Gullit, Gianluca Vialli and Claudio Ranieri all held the post. Tottenham experimented with Argentine, Swiss and French coaches till they settled on a Dutchman. Gerard Houllier, previously coach of the French national team, was called to Liverpool, where his adventurous multinational squads were good enough to win a treble of cups in 2001 including the UEFA Cup, but lacked the solidity and endurance to win a league title. The significance of the foreign contingent can be gauged from the Football Writers' Association Player of the Year Award, which since Alan Shearer won it in 1994 has been awarded only twice to an Englishman (Teddy Sheringham in 2001 and Frank Lampard in 2005).

However, the influence has not all been one way. While English football has been transformed by the influx of foreign players and coaches, they too have been shaped by the force of the English crowd. It is quite remarkable how many migrant players report that the crowd at English football demands and insists upon a style of play and level of effort unlike any other. The collective cultural insistence on a degree of honesty and transparency in the game, alongside the influence of foreign technique and tactics, is perhaps the alliance on which the Premiership's popularity and success has rested.

If the Premiership has come to signal the renascent successes and costs of England's new commercially minded private sector and the tastes of its comfortable middle classes, the fate of the national team has offered more complex readings. The years after the high point of Italia '90 were immensely disappointing. Under the management of Graham Taylor, who had made his mark at Watford, a small club on London's periphery, England played appallingly at the European Championship in 1992 and failed to qualify for the 1994 World Cup. The team's failure chimed with a wider sense of national gloom that had enveloped the country as it waited for the Conservative government of John Major, now irredeemably tarnished by economic failure and widespread corruption, incompetence and hypocrisy, to expire. Taylor, never the most adept or charming of communicators, was destroyed by the sports press who hunted him down with the same maniacal vigour and cruel humour that was being applied to the Conservative cabinet on the front pages.

The revival of the national team and the elevation of international football to a level comparable to the Premiership began at Euro '96. Thirty years on from winning the World Cup, five years after the UEFA ban on English teams in Europe had been lifted, England hosted an international tournament which passed off entirely peacefully. England's unlikely theme tune was 'Three Lions', penned by Britpop band the Lightning Seeds with lyrics and singing from the blokish TV comedy duo David Baddiel and Frank Skinner. A massive commercial success, the song was taken up on the terraces, re-establishing English football's love affair with pop music and nostalgia. What distinguished the song was that alone among official anthems it addressed past failure, reflected on and enjoyed its own melancholy. It also offered a reassuring confirmation of the elevated social status of football in England: 'Football's coming home'. In a rare display of adventure the FA appointed the roguish Terry Venables coach of the England team. Venables had the luck and the chutzpah to get the last really great display out of the rapidly disintegrating Paul Gascoigne – just the most prominent of the many footballing casualties resulting from undermanagement and overexposure to money and fame. Alan Shearer and Teddy Sheringham showed the country could still produce strikers of power and guile and on a vast wave of support the team qualified for the semi-finals, where a penalty shoot-out with the Germans was once again cast in the epic antiquated imagery of the Second World War.

Euro '96 transformed the status of the England national team. Any lurking antipathy among the mainstream public about supporting their team was dispelled. Although an element looking for trouble and associated with the far Right continued to make their presence felt around England away matches, particularly in Marseilles at the 1998 World Cup and in Charleroi, Belgium during Euro 2000, they were increasingly drowned in a vast flood of new England travelling support. For Japan–Korea 2002 the hard core were either unable to travel because of police intervention or put off by the high cost – England's support in Japan was virtually carnivalesque. In Portugal 2004, the nation's familiarity with Algarve holidays and cheap flights combined to create a gigantic level of sunburnt, drunken England support – easily surpassing any other contingent of away fans. With each passing international tournament, support for the national side at home had become more fervent. Television audiences, replica shirt sales, and the number of St George flags flown on car roofs have all grown. By the time England met Brazil in the 2002 World Cup quarter-final – at breakfast time in Europe – the entire country ground to a halt.

The St George flag had of course been a staple of the crowds at England matches but not for that long. Its ubiquity was quite new. Looking back to the crowd at the 1966 World Cup, barely any St George crosses can be seen as the stands appear to be waving British Union flags. As late as Italia '90 the balance between the two flags is half and half. But from 1997, as the devolution plans of the New Labour government took shape and Wales, Scotland and Northern Ireland all acquired a significant level of political autonomy, the Englishness of the football team rose in importance. For it remains the case that there are precious few English institutions around which the notion of a distinctly English civic nationalism could be created. The royal family, the armed forces and parliament remain British; the legal system is shared with Wales. This leaves the Church of England and English National Opera as potential repositories of an English national identity. The England football team remains the most potent public expression of the imagined English national community available.

The team itself fell short of the heights of 1996. Under Glenn Hoddle's troubled reign as manager England were knocked out of the 1998 World Cup in the second round. After David Beckham was sent off for petulantly flicking his foot after provocation by Argentina's Diego Simeone, England were down to ten men – an epic of defending took the game to penalties but England were out. Hoddle, representing a small but unmistakable strain of middle England's increasing fascination with new-age therapy and alternative healing practices, was eventually dismissed for claiming that disabled people had most likely received their karmic dues for misdemeanours in a previous life. His departure revealed the degree of internal rancour and disbelief caused by the introduction of his personal faith healer Eileen Drewery into the England coaching set-up. His successor was Kevin Keegan who brought the same kind of brittle bonhomie and optimism that marked his time at Newcastle. Keegan's England, though graced with considerable talent from the improving Premiership, looked out of their depth – sent home from Euro 2000's group stage after throwing away their game against Romania. When England lost a World Cup qualifying match 1–0 to Germany in the final international at the old Wembley Stadium, he resigned.

The senior management of the FA had fared little better in the four years since hosting the European Championship. Its senior officers Keith

Wiseman and Graeme Kelly proved to be deeply incompetent and politically naive – failings illustrated most starkly by England's failed bid for
the 2006 World Cup and the commissioning of the new Wembley
Stadium. The ill-fated bid for the World Cup dates back to the early
1990s when Bert Millichip, then chairman of the FA, believed he had
struck a deal with the power brokers of European football to back an
English bid. All the accounts of these conversations from Europeans
suggest that the deal was an entirely plausible 'gentlemen's agreement'
in which UEFA would back the Euro '96 bid in return for Germany
having a free run at 2006. The English World Cup bid was launched by
Wiseman and Kelly in 1997, with the support of the dying Conservative
government.

Over the next few years they demonstrated themselves to be political
bunglers of the highest order, a fact gradually understood by the New
Labour government forced by circumstance into backing the increasingly
forlorn and embarrassing bid. Having completely blown any chance
of support from the Europeans by reneging on their deal, Wiseman's
transparently obvious switch of England's vote to Sepp Blatter during
the bitterly contested 1998 FIFA presidential election yielded nothing
but further damage to the reputation of the English FA abroad. Worse,
Wiseman and Kelly had secretly but clumsily arranged a series of loan
payments from the FA to the Welsh FA in return for their support in
key UEFA and FIFA meetings. When this was disclosed, Kelly resigned
and Wiseman, whose grasp of political realities was never more than
minimal, attempted to hold on, only for the FA board to dismiss him
ignominiously. England's bid was an embarrassment and never had any
chance of success. If politics was not the FA's strong suit, nor was project
management. The World Cup bid centred on the building of a new
Wembley, the rotting carcass of the Empire Stadium deemed finally to
be beyond renovation. The FA established a committee and then a
separate company to monitor the project and award the contract, headed
by none other than Ken Bates – a man whose talent for property speculation and construction management had taken Chelsea FC to the edge
of ruin.

The machinery and personnel of English football governance had
primarily come to power under the Conservative governments of the
1980s and 1990s during which the kind of hands-off regulation and
market mechanism were the norm of public life. Under the New Labour

government of Tony Blair, elected in 1997, the political environment was changing. Devolution was just one political upheaval to shape the English game. The clarion calls of the moment were for modernization and controlled commercialization in public life, a tempering of the very worst excesses of the market and the introduction of small reforms and ameliorative social programmes. The FA caught precisely this moment with their appointment of Adam Crozier as the new chief executive of the organization.

Crozier was the sharp, high-flying head of the Saatchi and Saatchi advertising agency. As head of the Football Association he set in train an immediate programme of change. He negotiated an improved and highly commercial set of TV sponsorship and advertising deals for the FA Cup and the England team. He cleared the organization out of its decrepit rabbit warren of offices in Lancaster Gate, taking it to the centre of London medialand – Soho Square. He also armed the FA for the first time with a serious body of commercial managers and press officers. Most important of all, he removed, at considerable political cost, Ken Bates from the Wembley project. Although the cost of the stadium has risen considerably, necessitating the use of exotic financial arrangements, and the actual building programme has consistently slipped from its timetable, Crozier at least ensured that a national stadium rather than a retail or office development would be built.

Perhaps Crozier's most radical move was his response to the demise of Kevin Keegan. For the first time, England appointed a foreigner as manager of the national team – the then coach of Lazio, the Swede Sven-Göran Eriksson. Read by some as a deep blow to national pride and a sorry reflection of the depleted ranks of English coaches, others saw it as a symptom of a changing England possessed of a confident cosmopolitanism, an openness to learn from others. Initially Crozier basked in the glory brought by his smart appointment. England's 5–1 victory over Germany in Munich ensured their place at the 2002 World Cup finals and suggested that the burgeoning talents of the Premiership could now compose a truly world-class side. Crozier, however, was not able to stay around long enough to enjoy the fruits of England's passage to the quarter-finals.

Alongside the headline-grabbing initiative Crozier's FA had attempted to address the parlous state of the local governance of football, and the complete failure of the professional game to invest in or cross-subsidize the grassroots development of the game. In keeping with the government's priorities they attempted to imagine ways in which the cultural power of football could be deployed through social and educational projects in local communities. Crozier's communitarianism was backed up by a slew of reports from the government itself, the Football Task Force it had set up, and the parliamentary all-party inquiry into football finances. All of these bodies made the same arguments. The distribution of money in football was unhealthily skewed towards the top of the game. The pricing policy of the top leagues was exclusionary; malpractice and financial irregularities were widespread and under-investigated. Football, a national common good, should not be so systematically distorted by the interests of a tiny minority of big clubs and their boards.

By late 2002 Crozier had been hustled out of power, undermined by constant leaks from within the organization to supportive elements in the press and by the determined manoeuvring of the Premiership's representatives inside the FA. His replacement, Mark Palios, was an ex-professional footballer and accountant whose affair with an office junior saw him culled by the tabloids. The England team under Eriksson qualified for Euro 2004 and again made the quarter-finals. Wayne Rooney, the sensational teenage forward, made his international competition debut and carried the side before injuring his foot. England under Eriksson looked, as they often did, bereft of an alternative plan, unable to react to adversity; skilled and committed but without any innovatory capacity.

The power of private capital remains undiminished in English football. Neither the FA nor the New Labour government has been able to devise or impose interventions that would equalize the distribution of football money or rein in the power of the unaccountable. Both have settled for investment in youth training schemes, homework clubs and community activism as the palliative for the exclusion of most of the football world from the transfer markets and ticket prices they will never be able to afford.

VII

In the 1990s English football had found a new respectability and social prominence, primarily as a form of sanitized entertainment and voracious consumption. The Premiership was celebrated as a product of the Anglo-Saxon model of capitalism – free market, deregulated and entrepreneurial. French domestic football continued to be organized in accordance with its own version of social market capitalism, in which the game was seen to be a form of public good, and in which the state was therefore entitled to regulate the most volatile economic forces at work. As with the wider economy it was not a cost-free approach. During the 1990s France's high labour costs, high public debt and high interest rates saw its share of world trade shrink, its rate of growth slow and above all, a structural rate of unemployment established at around 10 per cent of the work force – considerably higher amongst the young and minority ethnic groups.

French football clubs were unable to compete. After Olympique Marseille's tarnished victory in the 1993 European Cup and the subsequent investigations into match-fixing which resulted in the club's demotion and bankruptcy, no French team would make the final of the tournament until Monaco in 2004. Governments of both Left and Right continued to resist moves to allow the conversion of clubs into PLCs, let alone let them float on the stock market; corporate ownership of clubs was limited to just one-third of the share capital. The French Football Federation maintained a steady flow of solidarity payments and cross-subsidies from the elite to the grassroots of the game. Above all, the high tax rates and social costs of the home labour market meant that for a French club to match the take-home salary of a player in more lightly taxed economies like Italy and England, they would have to come up with almost twice as much money. As a consequence there was a relentless movement of French players, increasingly young players as well, from the club academies where they had been nurtured, into the squads of the leading clubs in Serie A and the Premiership. Of the twenty-two players in the French squad at the 1998 World Cup only nine played their club football at home, and most of those spent the tournament on the subs' bench.

With the decline of Marseille, who have yet to recover from the shame, demotion and bankruptcy of 1994–95, the French league became the most open and competitive in Europe with seven different clubs winning the championship between 1994 and 2002. Paris Saint-Germain were the first to take the title in 1994, fuelled by a massive cash injection from their new owners Canal Plus, who sought not merely to relay the spectacular but to directly control and shape it. A wave of foreign signings and a dash of discipline from new coach Luis Fernández saw them win the French Cup and the European Cup Winners' Cup in 1996, before descending into a soap opera of internal fighting and financial chaos so bad that Canal Plus were forced to disinvest. The turmoil in the club was matched by the turmoil in the stands. *Ultra* groups like the white working class Boulogne Boys in the Boulogne Kop contested PSG's identity with the mixed-race supporters from the suburbs gathered around the group Tigris Mystic on the Auteuil terrace. Monaco, the team of the Riviera tax haven and their royal family the Grimaldis, took the title twice with a FF50 million annual subvention from the Principality's governing council. Lens, at the other end of the social scale, were the enduringly proletarian team of the whole Nord-Pas de Calais region, committed more emphatically than any other to low prices, access for children and families, and well-organized official fan clubs. In Marseilles, close in temper to Italy, the feelings of resentment and isolation that the club and city had always cultivated were redoubled by their exclusion. Over the 1990s up to six different *ultra* groups occupied particular spaces in the stadium, drew on distinct classes, neighbourhoods or ethnic groups, and at least two were systematically making a living from the manufacture and sale of club merchandise. At the turn of the century they and the management under Robert Louis-Dreyfus, the new CEO of Adidas, vied for control of the Stade Vélodrome, marketing and ticketing. The Marseille crowd showed itself capable of the most withering contempt towards the team and club officials – declaring on a banner at a game against Lens during one of the team's lowest points: 'You merit only our scorn and our silence' – a level of contempt that bubbled over into the same antics as their Italian counterparts: attacks on police, the players and the training grounds.

Yet all these developments were no more than an addendum to the mainstream concern of French culture in the 1990s. Football, though popular, had not become all-pervasive, its sporting appeal was still limited, its symbolic potential unrecognized. All of this would change in 1998 when France hosted and won the World Cup finals. France approached the staging of the World Cup in the same manner that they tackled *Les Grands Travaux* of the Mitterrand years. The project was always state-led and though the pit was not bottomless, the financial support available for football and transport infrastructure was plentiful. As with many of France's public–private joint ventures, the state shouldered most of the risks and the construction companies took most of the profit. After much internal fighting over its name, location and look, a new national stadium was commissioned to the north-east of Paris, to be named Stade de France. For if the World Cup was to be a celebration of anything it was going to be a celebration of the nation. What kind of nation would fill the rough-hewn concrete and breeze blocks of the stadium in Saint-Denis was yet to be seen.

Certainly the state of the nation was on the minds of the French. Increasingly the politics of the 1990s were understood as a struggle between the force of the global economy and the French nation-state, between undiluted Anglo-American capitalism and the Continental European model of regulation and solidarity; but the capacity of France to survive in this context, let alone win or prosper, seemed more and more quixotic. In the pre-tournament skirmish between the government's health policy and global capital, the French state won, refusing to allow Budweiser – the US brewer and category 1 sponsor of the World Cup – to advertise alcohol on television via stadium boards. But this gesture aside, France '98 saw another ratcheting up of the level of TV and media coverage for a major tournament and the immense presence of commercial sponsors and ambush marketing. The merchandising rights for the tournament were sold by ISL, FIFA's marketing arm, to the newly formed venture Sony World Cup Paris, who in turn sold 230 licences on over 1,500 product lines. The central indicator of the French team's progress and popularity was the phenomenal rise in sales of *Les Bleus* replica shirts, as the bourgeoisie and celebrity class abandoned their distaste for the synthetic and the suburbs abandoned their support for Brazil.

The England fans got into fights in Marseilles, and the Germany–Croatia encounter turned ugly when a French policeman was knocked into a coma by German fans, but England and Germany were sent home early. France '98 was about France, all the more so as the tournament was played out against the background of the biggest and most unforgivable revelations of doping, cheating and drug-taking in professional cycling in the Tour de France. The scandals centred on the Festina team and France's national cycling icon Richard Virenque. What was once the sporting heart of France was looking tarnished. By contrast the French football team was getting better and better, beating the Italians on penalties in the quarter-finals and Croatia in the semi-finals with two goals from defender Lilian Thuram – who had never scored an international goal before. With each passing game the TV audience became vaster, the post-match celebrations bigger, longer and more intense. In the aftermath of the Croatia game there were 300,000 people on the Champs-Elysées and 30,000 in central Lyons. Marseilles was already partying long into the night.

The meaning of the team and its play had begun to take shape in the collective psyche of the French. This was a team of all France, its ethnic roots testament to a hundred years of French empire and retreat, immigration and emigration. Lama was born in Guyana, Vieira in Senegal, Karembeu in New Caledonia and Desailly in Ghana. Thuram and Henry, born in France, came from families from Guadeloupe. Zidane's parents were Algerian Kabyles, Trezeguet's father was Argentine, Barthez had Spanish roots. Lizarazu's were Basque, Djorkaeff's and Boghossian's Armenian. Before the tournament both team and event had been criticized by the Left and Right: the Trotskyites decrying the commercialization of the people's fiesta, while Le Pen continued to suggest that a national team of mixed heritage and what he called 'French citizens by convenience' could never play as a unified force for the nation as a whole. Both views were confounded by the public's response. President Chirac and Prime Minister Jospin were both increasingly public in their attendance at the games and support for the team. In the wake of the semi-final, Chirac made a point of celebrating Lilian Thuram.

From within the team goalkeeper Barthez, captain Deschamps and coach Aimé Jacquet himself all called for less suits and ties, less corporate politeness at France's games and more football fans in jeans and trainers, national football strips, passion and support. By the time of the final they had it all. So prevalent was the national shirt and its Brazilian equivalent, so intense had been the marketing, advertising and exposure of the key brands and logos during the tournament that it was almost impossible not to read the final as not only France against Brazil, but Adidas against Nike. Adidas won, with two goals from Zidane, a third from Petit, Ronaldo in another world and laughable defending from Brazil. The World Cup passed from Chirac's hands to Deschamps'.

The streets of France had not seen such a public expression of emotion since the liberation; dwarfing *les évènements* of 1968, bigger even than the Gaullist counter-demonstration to the riots. The party that ran long into Monday saw over a million people crowd the Champs-Elysées to greet the team bus. The nation, amazed that it could be more than a worthy and stylish loser, now saw itself as '*La France qui gagne*' – the France that wins, built on the provincial virtues of hard work, solidarity and modesty that Aimé Jacquet embodied. Even *L'Équipe* and the French football establishment that had lambasted the coach for his lack of adventure were forced to eat their words. And of course the team that worked together was the team of many colours – the new multiracial France and its football team. Zidane's face was projected on the Arc de Triomphe, his name cheered in every city square.

France were not the only show in town. Leading up to the tournament those with a taste for a revenger's tragedy could have enjoyed the sight of FIFA at war in a bitter fight for the presidency of the organization and the future direction of global football. In 1996 João Havelange finally decided to retire and set the 1998 World Cup for the end of the long goodbye. Two candidates emerged for the throne: UEFA's president, the Swedish truck magnate Lennart Johansson, and Havelange's chosen successor, his pugnacious henchman of nearly two decades, FIFA's general secretary, the Swiss lawyer Sepp Blatter.

Johansson's candidacy grew out of two of UEFA's long-held concerns: that the balance of power within FIFA did not recognize Europe's unquestionable financial pre-eminence in the global game; and that the organization's closed and secretive mode of governance needed to change. Johansson offered solidarity between rich and poor, but under conditions of openness and financial transparency. His candidature was officially supported by UEFA and an open alliance was established with Issa Hayatou, the president of CAF, whose organization continued to chafe at Africa's marginality in decision-making. Blatter and Havelange's strategy was silence. While Johansson began a round of global glad-handing, Havelange and Blatter upped their own rate of travel, visiting innumerable football associations, confederations, tournaments, projects and unveilings in Havelange's old strongholds in Africa, Latin America and the Gulf. This transparently obvious electioneering under the guise of official business was repeatedly challenged by the Europeans in FIFA's executive, but they were only able to force Blatter into the open in spring 1998. With Michel Platini at his side he launched his candidacy at a champagne reception in the French IOC offices in Paris. The details of the election are simple. Blatter began the competition with the entirety of South America, Central America, the Caribbean and the

Middle East in his pocket. He broke Johannson's European and African blocs apart over the next two months with a mixture of bluff and bluster. When it came to the vote Blatter won the first ballot 111–80 and Johansson knew he was finished, conceding without the necessity of a second round of voting.

Many things in the world are badly governed. There are many elites who are incompetent, self-serving, self-important and arrogantly blasé about their evident limitations. None of them can begin to compare with the circus masquerading as the global governance of football. Sepp Blatter's first eight years in power make one nostalgic for the authoritarian certainties, the despicable charm and haughty, patrician discretion of the Havelange years. At the level of everyday management and internal politics, Blatter's regime has been a disgrace. From the very start of his reign he attempted to create new circuits of bureaucratic power among his hand-picked staff and within the presidential office. The conduct of official FIFA business, always an opulent intercontinental affair, has spiralled to the levels of the grotesque. The massively enlarged carbuncle of football bureaucrats on FIFA business, deliberately created by Blatter as a phalanx of kept support, have lived the high life. In addition to the five-star hotels, the business-class flights, the black Mercedes, they have all been allowed a daily expenses rate of $500 for which no receipts or records are required. Members of the executive committee were handed $50,000 honorariums and President Blatter's salary, emoluments, expenses and accounts remain, despite repeated requests from the press and UEFA, a matter of complete secrecy.

Along the way some gigantic debts owed to FIFA by confederations and national associations were written off without any further investigation. FIFA's interest in following up where its development monies have gone would shame even the Greek and Italian agencies monitoring the Common Agricultural Policy. A whole raft of large payments were made without good reason: like the $100,000 given to Viacheslav Koloskov, president of the Russian Football Union; like the $25,000 to a referee in Nigeria for information concerning African football official Farah Addo, who had publicly voiced the accusation that Blatter had bought votes before the Paris election. Blatter still had time to ruminate publicly on the possibility of holding the World Cup every two years; a whim that demonstrated his complete incomprehension of any kind of connection between scarcity and value. In the FIFA universe only more is good with the sole exception of the length of women footballers' shorts. The president had suggested that women's football might flourish if the clothing were a little more revealing.

Blatter's FIFA bathed in the froth atop the gathering economic boom in European football. The first three years of his presidency coincided with the introduction of digital television, another round of inflated TV rights deals and the expansion of the Champions League into its largest and richest format. The transfer market, which had seen a steady inflation in prices, went on a new and steeper curve. In strictly economic terms football's boom was just a minor current in the wider stock-market bubbles of the early twenty-first century, driven by the wild levels of investment and speculation in dotcom companies, information technology, telecoms and media firms. Football's boom appeared to break in 2001 when FIFA's main marketing partner ISL (the Swiss-based sports sponsorship and marketing company International Sports and Leisure) went spectacularly bankrupt. According to the Swiss courts the company had $1.25 billion of debts. Among the many extraordinary financial transactions uncovered in the still incomplete process of dissolving the company it was found that $60 million due to FIFA from the Brazilian TV company Globo for World Cup rights had been diverted into secret accounts. Up to £200 million of sponsorship money was simply missing. FIFA's official line was that they were a mere $32 million out of pocket, but as Michel Zen-Ruffinen, the organization's general secretary, would later argue, it was nearer $116 million down and that was without taking into account the avalanche of largesse that FIFA had been spending over the previous three years.

Blatter resolved his immediate economic and political dilemmas by authorizing, without recourse to his executive committee, a huge, private securitization deal – in short, a large loan at above market interest rates secured for the creditors against the income FIFA would receive for selling the TV rights to the 2002 and 2006 World Cups in the future. Through late 2001 and early 2002 opposition to Blatter and his methods mounted inside FIFA and among the Europeans who sought, without success, to press Blatter into revealing the true state of the organization's finances and practices.

A sense of collapse was redoubled as in quick succession a number of European companies that had gambled massive investments on television rights for subscription channels folded, or were forced to cut back, merge and renegotiate their investments. ONdigital in the United Kingdom collapsed in 2002. The Greek newcomer Alpha Digital disappeared altogether and desperate mergers were required to keep Italian and Spanish pay-per-view television afloat. When ISL collapsed the mighty German conglomerate Kirch Media, who already held the European television rights for the World Cup in 2002 and 2006, took the rest of the tournament rights and set out to sell them across the world. However, in April 2002 it too crumpled under a mountain of debt and unachievable income projections.

Discontent was so rife that the failed UEFA–CAF alliance of 1998 was reactivated with Issa Hayatou now the lead anti-Blatter candidate and the South Koreans among his most enthusiastic backers and supporters. Hayatou campaigned but it was clear that Blatter's support was as strong as ever, nurtured and fed by the massively expanded networks of internal patronage. The depth of that support, its seeming imperviousness to anything other than self-interest, can be gauged by the limited impact of the Zen-Ruffinen affair.

At the FIFA executive committee meeting in May 2002 the general secretary Michel Zen-Ruffinen blew the whistle, making and distributing statements outlining in depth the scale and scope of mismanagement within the organization. So detailed and comprehensive was the account that eleven members of the FIFA executive committee lodged a criminal complaint based on its contents to the Swiss public prosecutor's office in Zürich, including thirteen specific cases of unaccountable financial transactions. The show at the Seoul Hilton before the start of the 2002 World Cup was a masterclass in the miserable politics of FIFA. The day before the vote, an extraordinary congress was held to investigate and air all the grievances and accusations concerning FIFA's finances. Suspicions were aroused when it transpired that the congress had been called at the instigation of CONCACAF, a region whose allegiance to Blatter was unquestioned and whose own finances would not bear a single shaft of auditing sunlight. In an open, amateurish display of micro-political bullying, obfuscation and filibustering the day was filled with long paeans of praise to Blatter and incoherent criticism of his opponents from football association presidents closely bound to the Blatter camp. Critics from within the executive were not given any space to speak, and despite the Norwegian delegate insisting that precisely those that had been excluded should now be allowed to speak, they were not. Adam Crozier, the head of the English FA, described it as 'an absolute disgrace from start to finish. There was no attempt at transparency in two hours of manipulation.'[19] When the votes rolled in the next day Blatter had won by an even bigger margin than in 1998, 139 to 56. When Leo Mugabe, nephew of Robert Mugabe and dictatorial president of the Zimbabwean Football Federation, could comment, 'It is shocking . . . this is a travesty of democracy' then one has reached a moral ground zero.[20]

In the years since the 2002 World Cup FIFA has celebrated its centenary in a global fest of unreflective kitsch, sanitized history and self-congratulation. The now-global pandemic of corruption and match-fixing, the growing power of the biggest clubs and leagues, the threat of intervention from serious international bureaucracies like the European Commission, and the continuing legal cases arising from the ISL collapse forced Blatter to adopt the language of his opponents – now he promised probity and transparency, now he decried the commercialization of domestic and European football from the alchemist's laboratory where the whole process was dreamed up in the 1970s. On the practical side of things FIFA did what it does best and formed a committee of investigation.

To this committee, among others, Sepp Blatter has appointed Ricardo Teixeira, president of the Brazilian Football Confederation, and Jack Warner, president of CONCACAF and the Trinidad and Tobago FA.[21] Of all the many football bureaucrats he could have chosen, Blatter could hardly have alighted on two characters whose public records of financial and administrative probity were worse. When in spring 2006 it was revealed that Jack Warner's family travel agency was selling World Cup ticket packages straight out of the football association's allocation, he was asked by Blatter to explain himself. Warner announced that he had resigned from the board of the travel agency, as had his wife, and therefore a conflict of interest, if there had ever been one, no longer pertained. This conduct of business is so laughable that it would not survive a moment's scrutiny in the most modestly democratic public sphere. That it can continue to happen is testament to the brazen indifference of an elite that faces no opposition, little scrutiny and is bound by no single legal jurisdiction. The sooner it can be challenged, the sooner it can be swept away.

VIII

When the digital TV bubble burst in 2002, it looked for a moment like the entire ramshackle structure of the European football economy might come tumbling down with it. For the first time in a decade clubs were required to deal with a sharp decline in income and a sudden collapse in the value of their most valuable assets – players. The season before Zinedine Zidane had been sold by Juventus to Real Madrid for a record £45.8 million. Juan Sebastián Verón, the Argentine midfielder, had left Lazio for Manchester United for £28 million. Just a year later Ronaldo, fresh from winning the World Cup with Brazil as the tournament's top scorer and in imperious form, was sold by Inter to Real for almost the same amount. In a deflationary cascade that led down from Ronaldo and the leading clubs and leagues to the bargain basements of semi-professional football, the value of players plummeted as expectations of income declined.

Balance sheets were crumbling, and at clubs across Europe, from Lausanne in Switzerland to Lommel in Belgium, from PAOK Thessaloniki in Greece to FC Tirol Innsbruck in Austria, creditors and tax departments came calling, administrators and bankruptcy proceedings were initiated. Numerous smaller clubs in Spain and the Netherlands were only saved by cash injections from their local councils. While the main consequence of this in football's peripheries was to encourage alternative income streams from match-fixing and gambling rackets, in Germany, Spain and England a combination of public and private investments and a new round of vast TV deals steadied the ship for all but the most reckless and overstretched clubs. In Italy, however, the downturn of 2002 accelerated an already perilous process of economic meltdown and moral decay.

In Germany, where football clubs were hit most directly by the collapse of Kirch Media, the entire second division and two-thirds of the first were facing bankruptcy in spring 2002. Displaying an unprecedented degree of economic illiteracy and spineless naivety, Werner Hackmann, chairman of the Bundesliga, argued, 'In the final analysis football is not to blame for the situation it finds itself in.'[22] Kirch might have been responsible for their own collapse and the drop in income to clubs, but the company could hardly be held responsible for the Bundesliga's cumulative collective debt of €600 million. Gerhard Schröder's Social Democratic government intervened to shore up the industry; indeed it did so with greater speed and generosity than was the case for many other failing sectors of the ailing German economy. In effect, the federal government agreed to underwrite the Bundesliga, while some of the holes in club finances left after a new and smaller TV deal was negotiated were filled by across-the-board salary cuts.

In the same tone as the Christian Democratic opposition, Uli Hoeness, general manager of Bayern München, argued, 'We ought to be giving preference to businesslike solutions.'[23] However, as it later transpired, the kind of business solutions he had in mind was the secret deal that Bayern had negotiated with Kirch to secretly receive an extra €20 million in return for the club not going down the path of individual rather than collective TV rights sales. Extraordinarily, when the deal was made public, and Bayern were revealed to be in flagrant breach of the German FA's rules, they were allowed to get away with paying just €2.5 million back and making a small donation to charity. Franz Beckenbauer, Bayern president, scornfully claimed that the club could and should move to Serie A on the other side of the Alps, while fans displayed banners reading, 'Milan, Juve, Lazio'. Even with the German government's guarantee of football's gigantic salaries and bonuses, described as a 'giant scandal'[24] by Willi Lemke, former coach of Werder Bremen and then a local government minister, it was insufficiently generous to halt the decline of Borussia Dortmund, who had gambled most heavily on the promise of regular Champions League football only to regularly fail to qualify. Despite having the largest average attendance in the whole of Europe – over 80,000 – at the Westfalenstadion, Dortmund found themselves over €150 million in debt by 2005, running at a loss and abandoned by their main shareholder Deutschebank.

While German football went down a state-led route of economic restructuring, Spain's biggest clubs relied more heavily on banks, property sales and private investors. The collective debt of Spanish professional football clubs was estimated at around €500 million in 2003, with Real Madrid and Barcelona accounting for nearly €250 million and Valencia another €100 million. Large sums were owed in unpaid taxes to the government. While some smaller clubs have had to face insolvency, the bigger clubs have been saved by a mixture of property deals (Real Madrid and Barcelona have sold their old training grounds located in now fashionable real estate zones) and the kinds of lines of credit that come from the extensive networks of friendship and patronage among Spain's football, financial and construction industry elites.

In England the market was the key instrument of change, operating with a directness unseen elsewhere. As the *Financial Times* bluntly asked: 'Has there ever been a sector where the shares have performed so badly as football clubs?'[25] Of the twenty-two clubs that had floated in Britain during the 1980s and 1990s, ten were taken off the market altogether. The rest remained, but at a fraction of their initial value. Apart from Manchester United shares, all proved to be appallingly poor investments. Bankruptcies fell most heavily among smaller clubs like Leicester City and Watford. Of the bigger clubs the most spectacular casualty of the downturn was Leeds United.

Despite the collapse of some digital TV ventures and teams as seemingly well supported and successful as Leeds United and Borussia Dortmund, football's finances in England, Germany, Spain and France recovered over the next four years. The money just never stopped coming in. In particular the next round of TV deals in the major leagues saw yet another jump upwards. In 2005 Canal Plus briefly made French TV rights the most expensive in the world, bidding €1.8 billion over three years, until the English Premier League sold its TV rights the following year for over €2 billion. Saturation coverage wasn't keeping the crowds away either. Although there were small variations across clubs, the unmistakable trend in the twenty-first century has been for attendances and match income to rise across the core of European football; everywhere that is except Italy, where what were once the biggest crowds on the Continent began a steady and as yet unbroken decline – just one symptom of the many maladies and afflictions in Italian football's body politic. Indeed, in some ways it was the least of its innumerable worries.

In 2000 Lazio finally broke the Juventus–Milan duopoly on the *scudetto*, winning the title under Sven-Göran Eriksson. That summer the Italian team managed their best international football performance since the 1994 World Cup, meeting France in the final of Euro 2000, where they defended a 1–0 lead until deep into added time before a French equalizer and an extra-time golden goal gave the game to the French. The following year Roma matched Lazio's triumph by winning the *scudetto* themselves. Could the axis of Italian football power be shifting south from

Turin and Milan? It was all a mirage. Within a year Milan and Juventus were back at the top of the table, positions that they have yet to yield; the national team was heading for the most humiliating World Cup performance since 1966; and Roma and Lazio, like the rest of Italian football, were in the throes of economic collapse.

Gazzetta dello Sport announced the 'Crisis in Calcio' in spring 2001. The immediate prompt was the failure, once again, of Italian sides to progress in the Champions League beyond the group stage; but this was merely the sporting surface of a deeper and more profound set of problems. Attendances, which had grown and peaked after Italia '90, were now in steady decline. Average crowds in Serie A fell more than a quarter from their mid-1990s peak. Although the value of television rights continued to escalate, the potential value of those rights and the stability of the TV companies buying them were being dragged down by the widespread and flagrant pirating of services. The *ultras* professed to despise the new broadcasting regime, hanging banners that read, '*Questo calcio ci fa sky-fo*' – this football disgusts us. One cannot imagine BSkyB broadcasting similar images in England. The football, though still on occasion remarkable and of a consistently high technical standard, was becoming unmistakably more cautious and mean-minded. The number of goals needed to win a title was in steep decline, the number of 0–0 draws in the ascent.

Scandals were multiplying, even by Italian standards. In 1999 a judicial investigation revealed that Juan Sebastián Verón, Lazio's Argentine midfielder, held faked passport documents. Dozens of players and their clubs were subsequently investigated and numerous cases of invented Italian ancestry were found. A series of leading players, including Fernando Couto at Lazio and Edgar Davids at Juventus, tested positive for nandrolone and received bans, later drastically shortened. The initial response of the Italian doping agencies was to argue for an increase in the permissible levels of nandrolone.

The violence and racism of the *ultras* also appeared to be mounting: Napoli fans threw a homemade bomb in a game against Bologna, and another one into the garden of the club president Corrado Ferliano. Tear gas was used inside the stadium on the rioting crowds at Inter–Juventus and Milan–Roma. Brescia supporters attacked a car carrying the club president's daughter, Inter's team bus was hit by a Molotov cocktail at Parma, and the *ultras* began to haunt the training grounds and players' car parks of Roma and Lazio, looking to vent their spleen.

National elections held in March 2001 saw the defeat of the centre-left Olive Tree alliance that had attempted to rule Italy for the previous five years. Its record was at best limited, confined mainly to massaging Italian public expenditure sufficiently that the country could join the Eurozone. Voters were preoccupied by the declining quality of public services, the chaotic legal and administrative system, the profound north–south divide in the country, the continuing power of organized crime and the rising tide of illegal immigration. Enough put their faith in Berlusconi to deal with these problems for him to take office as Italian Prime Minister. In the five years of Berlusconi's second government, an alliance again of Forza Italia, the Lega Nord and the Allianza Nazionale, the crises in the Italian economy, Italian public life and Italian football were left completely unaddressed. Once again the predominant concern of the government was to fight by legal and political means the outstanding roster of corruption cases against Berlusconi and the companies and executives that made up the empire, and to prop up the most decrepit institutions. The government tried to block the creation of a European arrest warrant lest it should be used against Berlusconi; it attempted to pass a law in 2003 that would have allowed Italian football clubs to write off their tax bills, debts and depreciation over ludicrously long timescales. Both measures were struck down by the European Union. European institutions were the guarantors of a modicum of order in football too where UEFA were significantly more active in tackling and punishing racism and attacks on referees during Champions League games than the Italian football federation had ever been. Even so, neither Berlusconi, UEFA nor anyone else could prevent the economic implosion of *calcio*.

Fiorentina were the first to go down having run up a debt of €100 million by 2002. Cecchi Gori's own media empire was losing money hand over fist and the sudden sale of the squad's stars – Gabriel Batistuta to Roma, Rui Costa to Milan and goalkeeper Toldo to Inter – indicated the depth of the problem. It transpired that Cecchi Gori had already borrowed €25 million from Fiorentina to keep his other businesses afloat and had already borrowed against and spent the income from TV money for the next two years and season tickets for the next four. When the players, unpaid for months, went on strike, it was the end. The club was liquidated and in a new legal incarnation demoted three divisions.

The situation at Lazio first came to light in 2000 when they failed to pay the transfer fee to Manchester United for the newly purchased Dutch defender Jaap Stam. The club's already precarious position was made impossible by the sudden disintegration of Cragnotti's Cirio empire when the endless and increasingly frenzied movement of funds, debts and bonds could no longer hide the gigantic hole in the balance sheet. Parma's collapse two years later was even more spectacular, for Parmalat at the time was the eighth biggest company on the stock market and an apparently successful multinational corporation. Even Italian auditors could no longer account for the €8 billion gap in the company accounts.

On the last day of the 2001–02 season, Inter went to Lazio for their final game. If Inter won, they would take the title that they had been missing so hysterically for the previous thirteen years. Over 50,000 *Interisti* went to the Olimpico in Rome. Inter's Ronaldo and Vieri were fit and the Milanese took the lead twice in the first half only to give it away again. In the second half they just cracked. Lazio won 4–2, Juventus beat Udinese and took the title. The pressures of Italian football could only be resisted by the very hardest hearts. At the 2002 World Cup, Italy were knocked out by South Korea after sitting on a 1–0 lead and then conceding a late equalizer and golden goal. Ecuadorian referee Byron Moreno became a national figure of disgust, berated for his failure to allow Italian goals. The president of Perugia, the lurid Luciano Gaucci, declared that Ahn Jung-hwan, the South Korean who had scored the winning goal and who played for Perugia, would never play in Italy again.

The following season of 2002–03 was almost aborted after a summer-long wrangle over TV rights, the smaller clubs refusing to accept the pathetic crumbs being offered them. The situation was resolved at the last minute when the big three clubs agreed to pass back some of their cash to the bottom of the league. The season opened with the Super Cup held in Tripoli and Juventus announcing that the Libyan state oil company and the Qaddafi family were taking a 7.5 per cent stake in the club and a seat on the board. Saad Qaddafi, son of the country's president, was signed by Perugia. His playing career was minimal and terminated by a positive drugs test. Violence was now widespread across the league as police and fans clashed regularly, particularly at Como and Atalanta. After Como were denied three penalties in one game a pitch invasion ensued and the Como president Enrico Preziosi, a toy manufacturer, demonstrated the wider culture's contempt for authority when he released a 'hit the ref' board game.

Juventus won the league again and the country was able to distance itself from a disgraceful season by celebrating an all-Italian 2003 Champions League final. Getting there had not been an edifying experience. Milan, Juve and Inter all got to the semi-finals playing steel-hard, super-cautious, no-mistakes, no-flair football. Rafa Benítez, coach of Valencia, had called Inter 'the death of football' and their semi-final with Milan went three-quarters of the distance without a goal, before turning on the thinnest of margins. The final, decided on penalties after 120 minutes in which neither side could clearly be accused of making a mistake, had its own peculiar metallic beauty and deadly symmetries. Milan won the shoot-out, because they lost their nerve less. Such were the sources of glory in Italy. Some chose to read the occasion as the turnaround for Italian football. It appears now as the epitaph of a dying culture.

The following summer was consumed by yet another protracted dispute over TV rights, and a great web of interlocking court cases over which division which clubs should be playing in. The Italian Football Federation's initial plan to expand Serie B, readmitting the relegated teams and sneaking Fiorentina back into the second flight, resulted in a flurry of court cases by affected parties and was only stopped by an emergency government cabinet meeting and the expansion of Serie A and Serie B. Attacks on players multiplied, exemplified by the Avellino player injured at Cagliari airport after missing a penalty earlier in the day. At Inter the inconsistency and underperformance had so exasperated even Moratti that he resigned as president. The *ultras* became more bitter and bizarre: in the home game against Atalanta, a scooter was dragged to the top of the third tier of the San Siro and thrown over the edge into the away fans below. Restaurants owned by Inter players Fabio Cannavaro and Christian Vieri were attacked. In 2004 Inter fans left the *curva* early at the end of the season displaying the words, 'We no longer know how to insult you.' The Rome derby was brought to a halt by the Roma *ultras*. Rumours had been circulating around the ground that a child had been killed in an encounter with the police. Leaders of the Roma *ultras* came to the edge of the pitch and spoke to Roma captain Francesco Totti, asking for the game to stop. Although there was and never has been a shred of evidence to substantiate the story, all concerned from both clubs and the Italian federation bowed to the unmistakable and febrile power of the stadium. The evening was spent in riots between both sets of fans and the police.

Italian football just got uglier. In 2005 when Inter were losing their Champions League quarter-final with Milan, a salvo of flares and objects thrown on to the pitch forced the game to be abandoned as well as injuring Milan's keeper. Allegations of match-fixing became increasingly regular and obvious, sending newly promoted Genoa back down to Serie C. Paolo di Canio, Lazio's talismanic midfielder, repeatedly and openly made Fascist salutes to the Lazio crowd and despite a murmur of disapproval was never properly challenged by the club or the law. Messina's African forward Marc Andre Zoro demanded that their game with Inter be called off when he could stand the racist chanting no more – the game was played to a conclusion.

The longest-running saga of duplicity through this era though was the investigation into claims that Juventus had been illegally administering banned substances to their players throughout the 1990s. Investigations had begun as early as 1998, but it was only in early 2002 that the case came to court with Juventus managing director Antonio Giraudo and club doctor Ricardo Agricola on trial. Juventus players called as witnesses all suffered unprecedented lapses in memory about the medical treatment they were given during their time at the club. After two years of wrangling Giraudo was acquitted for lack of evidence and Agricola was found guilty, though Juventus immediately took the case to appeal which they won in late 2005. However, what appeared at the time as a closed case, just another of the interminable legal trials in post-war Italian history where the truth had been ground to dust by the powerful's manipulation of the system, proved to be the mere prelude to a moment of truth.

Berlusconi narrowly lost the general election in the late spring of 2006. A new centre-left government under Romano Prodi was formed promising another clean-up of the Italian public sphere. In May Juventus won their twenty-ninth *scudetto*. No sooner had the celebrations died down than a significant number of transcripts of conversations involving key figures in the Juventus hierarchy, including the general manager Luciano Moggi, were released. The conversations had been taped during the doping affair. Finally, it became clear to anyone, even the Juventus board and the Italian federation, that the thefts, the pressures, the hidden networks of power and influence were not the creation of their febrile imaginations, they were real. Moggi sat at the centre of a network of favours and influence that ran from Juventus to the Italian Football Federation, the committees that chose referees, Italian representatives at UEFA, the sports press, the boards of other clubs, and – through the huge player agency GEA controlled by Moggi's son – the dressing rooms of other clubs. After the head of the Italian federation had talked about more transparent refereeing, Moggi spoke to Innocenzo Mazzini, the vice-president, saying, 'Tell him not to bust our balls. Better yet, I'll talk to him and put him in his place.' Later Mazzini would tell him, 'You're the boss of the Italian game. You own Serie A.'[26]

The entire board of Juventus resigned, as well as the president and vice-president of the Italian FA. Juventus looked as if they might be stripped of their title and demoted. One hopes this will prove to be the *Tagentopoli* of Italian football: a judicial assault that breaks the old order apart and sweeps the worst of the decrepit elite from power. It may do, but it is just as likely that they will be replaced, as the old political parties were, with new elites whose conduct is every bit as despicable as their predecessors'.

In the immediate aftermath of the Cold War, European football's southern periphery – Portugal, Greece and Turkey – appeared consigned to permanent exclusion from the emerging core of the new Europe. In the 1960s Portugal, despite its political and economic marginality, could have considered itself close to the centre of European football; even as late as the 1980s Porto could win and Benfica could lose a European Cup Final. The 1990s, which began with the economic boom that followed accession to the European Union and the emergence of a 'golden generation' of young players (including Figo, Rui Costa and Couto) who won the 1991 World Youth Cup, were ultimately disappointing. Portugal could perhaps have followed a similar course to Austria: a football culture once at the very peak of the global game that became increasingly marginalized. The persistent failure of the national team to qualify for the World Cup and of its leading club teams to make an impact beyond their own borders in the 1990s seemed to confirm this.

Post-war Greek football was a chaotic affair. Hugely popular in the cities, its notional amateurism was flagrantly disregarded by clubs, players and the football federation. Trapped in the twilight zone of marginal illegality, it remained an undercapitalized and urban affair in a still predominantly rural society. The game received a considerable boost from the short-lived military dictatorship between 1967 and 1974. In the absence of almost any other coherent social policy, the regime built stadiums, supported clubs, put live football on television and backed the national team. When Panathinaikos made it to the final of the European Cup in 1971, the government sent Orthodox relics with the squad to Wembley where they were beaten by Ajax. The fall of the Junta came in 1974 after their ill-advised total mobilization against the Turkish occupation of Northern Cyprus turned into a nationwide no-show. Greek football regressed. Tarnished by its association with the military and bereft of financial support, football only turned professional as late as 1979 and then only at the bigger clubs in the bigger cities where a motley collection of ship-owners, industrialists, nightclub impresarios and local politicians held sway. International results were dismal and in the only major tournaments for which they qualified – the 1980 European Championship and the 1994 World Cup – Greece failed to win a single match.

Turkish football was an even weaker force in the world. Their single appearance at a World Cup finals in 1954 saw them steamroller the South Koreans 7–0, but they were in turn thrashed by the West Germans 4–1 and then 7–2 in the group play-off. Domestically, the game boomed as Turkey's long-stalled process of urbanization and industrialization began to get under way. Professionalism arrived in 1959 and by 1967 there were three national professional divisions, sustaining a nationwide fixture list despite a transport infrastructure that was sparse and archaic. Both the popularity and the precariousness of Turkish football were illustrated by the 1967 Kayseri disaster. Kayserispor vs. Sivasspor was a fiercely contested derby game between the two cities struggling for economic and political control of central Anatolia. The football teams were supported by the urban merchants and politicians, and popular support was so great that 5,000 fans came from Sivas in a caravan of minibuses and at least 21,000 attended the game. When the referee rescinded a sending off twenty minutes into the game, rock-throwing and fighting broke out in the stands. A surge away from the rocks in the Sivas end saw hundreds crushed in exit tunnels against locked gates.

Forty-two people were killed and over three hundred were injured. The sole European triumph for the nation in this era was Fenerbahçe's victory over Manchester City in the 1968 European Cup; a victory whose lustre grew with Turkey's lengthening absence from international competition.

All three of these Mediterranean football cultures were transformed in the late 1990s and in the early part of the twenty-first century, but the economic and sporting boom of the moment dragged in its wake widespread cultures of violence, archaic policing, corruption and match-fixing. Turkey was the first of the three to make an impact. After a military coup in 1980 a series of authoritarian civilian administrations in alliance with the army set the country on a course of economic liberalization and fast but uneven industrial growth, oriented increasingly towards the European market and eventually membership of the European Union. These changes helped fund the expansion of Turkish professional football, especially its stadiums. Galatasaray made it as far as the semi-finals of the European Cup in 1989.

The familiar Turkish lament that 'we do not exist beyond Edirne' – the most westerly city in the country – applied to football too. Progress in European competition provided the most cherished measure of success, but the encounter was always shot through with a paranoid insecurity. In 1991 Fenerbahçe played a testimonial game with Atlético Madrid which was abandoned when the electricity supply failed and the floodlights went out. In the following day's papers the headline lamented: 'We fell into disgrace against Germany and Spain . . . Europe laughs at us.'[27] On the other hand, Galatasaray's aggregate victory over Manchester United in 1993, and Fenerbahçe's win at Old Trafford in 1996 (the game which ended Manchester United's unbeaten record at home in Europe), were hysterically celebrated as a testament to the growing power of Turkey.

These kinds of unresolved tensions nurtured a political culture of extreme mood swings between unbounded confidence and optimism and crippling self-doubt and pessimism, accentuated by an economy that flipped back and forth between raging boom and inflationary meltdown. Galatasaray fans, despite their side's 3–0 defeat away to the Swiss side Neuchâtel Xamax in the 1989 UEFA Cup, packed the stands for the home leg in expectation of a turnaround and got it when Galatasaray finished 5–0 ahead. On the other hand when Fenerbahçe had lost 4–0 to Cannes in the 1995 UEFA Cup, fans expecting a similar turnaround were crushed by another heavy defeat and, spitting with the anger of disappointment, lit fires across the stands.

By the late 1990s the Turkish national team were beginning to benefit from the growth and enrichment of the domestic game. For the first time in over forty years, Turkey qualified for an international tournament – Euro '96 – and then qualified again for Euro 2000, where they progressed to the quarter-finals. A month earlier Galatasaray had won the UEFA Cup – the country's first European trophy. Even the imprisoned leader of the fifteen-year-long Kurdish rebellion – Abdullah Öcalan – was demanding a television set in his cell to watch the game. By now, the fate of the national team had been embraced by politicians of all colours; the President regularly attended their games. More darkly, the MHP ultra-nationalist movement were making their presence felt at football grounds, handing out literature, orchestrating chants and displaying provocative anti-Kurdish banners. Celebrations, always boisterous, were becoming wilder, the regular use of pistol shots resulting in a number of injuries, and some car drivers were attacked when they refused to toot their horns in support of post-match nationalist festivities.

The festivities reached fever pitch during the World Cup in 2002 at which Turkey progressed to the semi-finals, where they matched Brazil at every turn until Ronaldo broke the deadlock. Over 90 per cent of the Turkish TV audience watched the game, Prime Minister Bülent Ecevit declared a national holiday and on the squad's return presented them with half a million pounds in republican gold coins. However, in the aftermath of 2002, Turkish football has plunged. The game has become caught up in wider anti-corruption campaigns that the government aimed at banks, city councils and the security forces. The newspaper *Milliyet* revealed how organized crime syndicates had been placing bets on Turkish league matches on the Internet and fixing games with the appropriate referees. Worse, the violence around Turkish football, for example the stabbing of two Leeds United fans during the team's UEFA Cup visit to Istanbul in 2000, refused to go away.

The joint Turkish–Greek bid to stage Euro 2008, made in defiance of the continuing state of military confrontation between the two in Cyprus and the Aegean, was derailed by widespread fighting around the UEFA Cup game between Fenerbahçe and Panathinaikos. The qualifying rounds for both Euro 2004 and the 2006 World Cup proved fraught and unsuccessful. After two Euro 2004 qualifying games against England were played in an atmosphere of spite, Turkey were then knocked out in a play-off against Latvia, and the newspaper headlines were hysterical: 'From third place in the world to third world.' When the Swiss knocked them out of the 2006 World Cup, the squad and officials physically attacked their opponents. Beyond the testosterone and the machismo, these events speak to a deeper national crisis. Turkey, still queuing to join the European Union, still troubled by Kurds and Islamicists without and within, continues to find its footballing encounters with the world a deeply troubling experience.

While football seemed to be languishing in Portugal, its economy was booming. The influx of European Union money and foreign investment generated a virtuous circle of growth that brought Portugal from penury in the mid-1970s to a standard of living close to the European average, and turned the country from a net exporter of labour to a net importer. In the micro-economy of football, the equivalents of these forces were the money coming to the leading clubs from the Champions League, a steady growth in TV and sponsorship income, and an influx of Brazilian and African footballers – by 2002 over 120 Latin Americans, nearly all Brazilians, were playing in Portuguese professional football. When the country was awarded the hosting rights for the 2004 European Championship another round of state-led infrastructural investment began.

The influx of money was sufficient to dislodge the prevailing order. Porto, having won five consecutive championships in the late 1990s, were forced to cede their crown. Boavista, the second club of the city, won their first league title in 2001. Sporting Lisbon were champions in 2000 and 2002, and there were serious challenges and tough games from well-supported provincial teams like the Madeira club Marítimo and Campomaiorense, the creation of the country's leading coffee manufacturer.

Benfica, by contrast, disintegrated. Once the most powerful club in the country, the champions of Europe and the world, they won their last league title in 1994. Through the 1990s, under the leadership of João Vale e Azevedo, Benfica became a byword for administrative chaos and financial profligacy. In 2001 they hit rock bottom finishing sixth in the league and failing to qualify for Europe for the first time since the 1950s, having been through three coaches in a season. One of the dismissed troika, Toni, remarked on his departure, 'The most stable thing about Benfica is the instability.'[28] At this point the club had only enough cash to pay players a single month's salary and were already £25 million in debt with over £25 million of payments due on transfers. Azevedo was later sentenced to three years in prison for embezzling monies notionally involved in the transfer of Russian goalkeeper Ovchinnikov from Alverca to Benfica in the late 1990s. He was also convicted on three counts of forgery in the 'EuroArea' affair, involving land deals on the plot where the old Estádio da Luz had stood. He was found not guilty of embezzlement from the club and money-laundering, though it was clear that these practices were close to endemic in the Portuguese game. The president of Sporting Lisbon António Dias da Cunha told Radio TSF: 'There's a lot of money passed under the table in the Portuguese game, a lot of creative accounting, a lot of dirty money.'[29]

Porto were everything Benfica were not. Under the long-standing presidency of Pinto da Costa, Porto were organized, solvent and discreet. After yielding their title to Sporting and Boavista, the club regrouped and recruited coach José Mourinho. Both rose together. Mourinho, who had worked at Barcelona with Bobby Robson and at the small provincial club União Leiria, demonstrated his outstanding abilities: to move players into new positions and roles to which they were best suited; to create and enforce patterns of play that made the best use of the available talents; and to insist on a high work rate from all. In 2003 they stormed the Portuguese league, won the cup and, after crushing Lazio in the semi-finals, went on to win the UEFA Cup, beating Celtic 3–2 after extra time in the final. Then in 2004, with the country preparing to host the European Championship, Porto won another treble – the league, the Super Cup and the Champions League – in a relentless season of organized hard-willed football. Mourinho barely stayed to celebrate when they won the European Cup in Gelsenkirchen and was soon heading for Chelsea. Much of his squad followed him out the door.

There was a similar transience to the pleasures and prospects of the European Championship. The stage was truly spectacular. The Portuguese had built ten stadiums – easily the most varied, adventurous and colourful selection of grounds to host an international championship. Tomás Taveira's work on the Alvalade in Lisbon and the stadiums in Leiria and Aveiro combined sinuous curvature, perfect functionality and a stunning display of playful shape, colour and detail almost entirely absent from most of the stadium-building of the previous decade in

Europe. In sensational weather Europe came to play. At least 100,000 English fans made the journey, not only filling more than three-quarters of the seats at England games but comprising a significant part of the crowd at many games that England did not play in. Germans, Swedes, Danes and Dutch flocked to the country. In a sign of newfound wealth, the Croatian and Russian crowds were surprisingly large, all mingling in this post-industrial theme park, where most of the time the visitors themselves were the main attraction. Portugal's increasingly confident progress to the final was greeted with ever larger spontaneous motorcades in the big city centres and all-night dancing at the foot of the Lisbon memorial to the Marquis de Pombal.

Portugal, like everyone else, could not find a way past the Greeks and lost the final. The hangover was all the sharper as the sports pages turned their attention from the national team to the nationwide police action codenamed Operation Golden Whistle. Since the end of the season, police had interviewed and arrested over sixty players, referees and club presidents at the highest level over allegations of corruption and match-fixing. In the national elections that followed, the governing right-wing coalition clumsily tried to seize on the football mania of the summer by running under the banner of '*Força Portugal*', a football chant, but went on to suffer the worst electoral result in two decades.

In the last years of the millennium it was hard to overestimate how obsessed with football the average Greek man had become. Not content with newspaper supplements, pull-outs and specials of every conceivable kind there were nine daily sports tabloids, each fiercely partisan with direct links to the owners of the big clubs. Not only did they cover Greek football in microscopic detail but they served as form guides for betting on football. Nearly 5 per cent of Greek GDP was going to the bookies and nearly all of that on football: Greek, English, Spanish, Italian, Danish, Icelandic, anything. Two channels spent the whole of Saturday and Sunday afternoons broadcasting goal updates on the scores in the Scottish Second Division and the third round of the Norwegian Cup.

This insatiable demand for foreign football betting was, at least in part, linked to the monotony and predictability of results in Greek domestic football. Since 1994 only the two biggest Athens clubs – Olympiakos and Panathinaikos – have won the league and Olympiakos won seven of those in a row. Coincidentally Olympiakos were owned by the richest, best-connected businessman in Greece, Socrates Kokkalis. Kokkalis was the son of a Greek communist who fled the country after the Greek civil war (1944–9) and settled in East Berlin. The precise details of his childhood life in the home of Teutonic Marxism are hazy, but he reappeared in Greece in the 1980s as a member of the board of a company called Intercom: a Stasi-related front company which seemed to spend its time purchasing the kinds of telecommunications technologies that were normally off-limits to East German companies. With the fall of the Berlin Wall, the ultimate owners of Intercom went into liquidation and the East German staff and board members melted away. This left Socrates Kokkalis with a corporate vehicle and a very full hard-currency bank account. Over the next decade he turned Intercom into the biggest telecommunications and hi-tech company in Greece. He bought Olympiakos and he also owned most of the Greek football betting industry. In Greece this was not seen as a potential conflict of interest in any way. However, Olympiakos were unable to turn domestic dominance into European success, and the dismal performance in every Champions League campaign of those seven years culminated in a 7–0 drubbing by Juventus in 2003. Panathinaikos, by contrast, were good enough to make the quarter-finals of the Champions League in 2002.

Suspicions that Olympiakos's stranglehold on the title was down to more than money and players were confirmed in 2002 when the journalist Makis Triantafyllopoulos played tapes on his TV show *Zougla* ('The Jungle') – a bizarre half-hour current affairs slot with a rainforest backdrop – exposing the 'Hut'. The 'Hut' was the colloquialism for the presumed but then unexposed cabal of referees, officials and club owners that had predetermined matches for years. Highlights of the tapes included conversations about preferred results with Thomas Mitropoulos, the owner of small Athenian club Egaleo and brother of Victor, the ex-president of the league, and Yannis Spathas, the head of the Piraeus Referees' Union. Spathas coud be heard berating his colleagues, 'Only Olympiakos and Egaleo should win, and screw the rest of them.' To this day no one has been investigated, arrested or questioned.

Of all the football economies struck by the 2002 TV rights crisis, Greece was hit hardest, but then the deal struck by the football clubs with Alpha Digital was the most ludicrous. Alpha had lured the league away from its long-standing relationship with Super Sport by offering triple the value of the previous deal. Whatever the actual breakpoint might have been for the company, its pitiful take-up by paying sub-scribers made the entire adventure unsustainable. However, the clubs had spent the loot and landed themselves with immense and implausible wage bills. A desperate league declared that football was going on strike until someone else paid up. Officials suggested that the money might come from the football pools, or failing that the government, or failing that anyone, anyone but them. The government held surprisingly firm and after a month the strike disintegrated. The truly parlous state of Greek football was now exposed. The government estimated that the top division was €185 million in debt, in an industry whose total gate income was just €6.7 million and shrinking.

The process was too much for AEK, whose debt included a massive backlog of unpaid tax. Ownership of the club had passed between Dutch TV firm Netmed, UK investment vehicle ENIC, and a gang of Greek businessmen whose reputations ran from dubious to unsavoury. The club's financial position completely collapsed under the rule of Makis Psomiadis, a tycoon who escaped twelve years in prison after his convic-tion for forgery, by claiming he was suffering from tuberculosis – a condition that did not seem to affect his consumption of cigars and whiskey in the AEK directors' box. His other important contribution to the club was to physically intimidate striker Demis Nikolaidis, who subsequently went on strike. The fans who idolized Nikolaidis turned their ire on coach Dušan Bajević, who received death threats through the post and on the phone.

The whiff of scandal and chaos hovered over the national team too, UEFA being forced to initiate an official investigation after receiving allegations of match-fixing before Greece's Euro 2004 qualifying game in Yerevan, Armenia. Greece went on to qualify for the tournament under the German coach Otto Rehhagel. They arrived as cannon fodder and were thrown an opening game against the hosts. To everyone's amazement, including their own, they beat the Portuguese, and did enough by drawing with Spain to qualify for the quarter-finals. The game plan had now become clear. Greece were going to stifle, man-mark and break up everything that came their way and then take their chances from the few set pieces that they could garner. It worked. France were completely stymied, the attacking Czech midfield muffled and the Portu-guese sat upon. Each time Greece got a corner or a free kick they scored: 1–0 to Greece, champions of Europe.

Like Portugal and Turkey, Greece's football success was short-lived; within months, triumph had given way to obscurity. Qualification for the 2006 World Cup proved impossible. Most of the Olympic infrastructure is mothballed, costing €100 million a year. Olympiakos are still winning the title. As Greece struggles with its vast public debt and high unemployment, racism and anger towards its expanding Albanian minority are gaining currency. When Greece were beaten in Tirana in 2004 in a World Cup qualifier, rioting at home saw an Albanian immigrant murdered. Before the return match in 2005, a game between the youth teams was interrupted when Greek fans tore down an Albanian flag at the Athens stadium. When it came to the full international, the Greek state seemed to declare its preference for segregation and silence. A spokesperson for the Ministry of Public Order curtly informed the world that, 'We did not sell any tickets to Albanians, only to Greeks.'[30]

Since the fall of the Berlin Wall cracked opened the frozen borders and politics of Europe, the whirlwinds of capitalism and commercial television have howled through the football cultures of the Continent, blowing from boom to bust and back to boom again. The cultural landscape they left in their wake was, if not unrecognizable when compared to 1990, then profoundly reformed. Its singularly most important feature was the profound degree of economic polarization between and within national football cultures. Just as the income-distribution profile of almost every European nation had shifted in the direction of greater inequality, so too in football.

The pathologies of poverty, most virulent in Eastern Europe, left a legacy of crumbling infrastructure, social disorder, corruption and violence. Match-fixing and betting rackets have been a staple feature of European football for at least forty years. In the early twenty-first century the practices were certainly alive and well in their traditional Mediterranean homes, but the global explosion of Internet betting, and the creation of new zones of underdevelopment, created the preconditions for their spread. Between 2004 and 2006 criminal investigations and trials were conducted in Italy, Portugal, Greece, the Czech Republic, Belgium, the Netherlands, Finland, Poland and even in Germany where referee Robert Hoyzer was closely linked to a Croatian betting syndicate.

In the ghettos of wealth at the high end of the major European leagues, the excesses of affluence took hold with a change of leadership or ownership of the biggest clubs. At Real Madrid the 2000 presidential elections saw the incumbent Lorenzo Sanz return to the electorate with two Champions League titles to show for his trouble. His opponent Florentino Pérez was an impeccably connected centrist politician turned construction magnate. In the image of the recently elected Partido Popular, Pérez mobilized a coalition of right-wing and left-wing *socios*, businessmen and trade union leaders. He cast himself as the candidate of financial rectitude and entrepreneurial acumen, claiming that he would wipe out Real's huge historic debt and bring Luís Figo from Barcelona to Real. Sanz was swept aside and Pérez embarked on a six-year odyssey of galactic hubris. His connections ensured that the sale of Real's old training ground for €480 million went through the planning procedure effortlessly. Then, taking Manchester United as his model, Pérez intended to turn Real Madrid into a global brand of equal reach, wealth and glitz. The transfer policy that would achieve this was a consciously designed game of annual brinkmanship as Pérez manoeuvred to bring another Galactico to the Bernabéu. Zidane came in 2001, Ronaldo in 2002, David Beckham and his image rights in 2003, strikers Michael Owen and Robinho followed. As for the rest of the squad, Pérez's regime relied on the youth team and what was left of the old defence.

In 2002, Real's centenary year, Pérez orchestrated a global media cavalcade. The club visited, among others, the United Nations, the Pope and the King of Spain, and embarked on yet another world tour. The Spanish league and the cup were lost, but Zidane's volleyed winner in the Champions League Final allowed the club to crown the year. Pérez's masterstroke was to sack the coach who had won this, Vicente Del Bosque. It was rumoured that Del Bosque was against the arrival of the next Galactico – Beckham. Del Bosque or Beckham? In a Real Madrid where they were building a sales machine first and a football team second, there was no choice. In the next four years Pérez hired and fired five managers, blew over €200 million on the transfer market, allowed the dressing room to take control, nurtured a culture of glamour over graft, reputation over performance, and watched the team's fortunes plummet. In 2004 as the Partido Popular were swept out of government by José Zapateros' Socialist Party, Real had slumped to fourth in the league and were knocked out of the Champions League and the Spanish Cup in the quarter-finals. By 2006, Real had finally achieved Pérez's ambition; they were, by turnover, the richest club in the world. They had also endured their longest period without a trophy in fifty years. The finance director announced that the club's debt still stood at €80 million and Pérez resigned.

While the economics of European football offered a microcosm of the wider transitions and inequalities of twenty-first century capitalism, the politics of European football have their mainstream parallels too. National football associations continued to be powerful, if often cumbersome and ill-equipped actors still at the heart of football politics. There was, however, a steady leakage of power and influence away from national football governing bodies, to European institutions, clubs and media companies. At a European level, the growing power and wealth of UEFA was contested by the European Commission, the European courts and a pan-European group of elite clubs, the G-14. The latter, later expanded to eighteen members, operated as the pan-European trade association.[31] More than a mere talking shop, the group has been central in articulating the economic and political interests of the big clubs, steering UEFA policy on the carve-up of Champions League money and taking UEFA and FIFA to court over the injury of players on international duty. G-14 has argued that national football associations should cover any losses to clubs resulting from this. If successful it will place the conduct of the entire international football calendar in the hands of clubs.

Football associations and club owners have on occasion been challenged from below. The Glazer takeover of Manchester United provoked an intense response among a small core of the club's fans. The arrival of the Glazer brothers at Old Trafford turned into a small-scale riot. A few thousand broke away to set up their own side, FC United, playing in the amateur leagues of the Greater Manchester area. Wimbledon fans, speechless with indignation at the Football League giving permission for the club's owners to transfer the team to Milton Keynes, a new town 80 kilometres to the north, voted with their feet and formed a similar breakaway club, AFC Wimbledon. The economic fragility of many clubs in the lower reaches of English professional football created a window of opportunity in which organized fan groups could take control of their clubs through new forms of social ownership and community mobilization.

While issues of ownership have, at a few clubs, provided the stimulus for collective action among supporters, the most pressing issue around which they have mobilized has been racism. Indeed, Europe's demographic profile is changing more quickly and thoroughly than at any point in the last few centuries. When questions of migration, race, ethnicity and religion became the core issues of national politics across the Continent, the struggle between the forces of racism and anti-racism in football was not just a reflection of a wider conflict but one of the most public and important components of it. The case of France makes depressing reading. The extraordinary imagery and acts of collective celebration that accompanied the 1998 World Cup appeared to herald the emergence of a successful, harmonious and diverse multi-ethnic France. Politics, football and the street proved otherwise.

The French national team continued to play with authority and won the European Championship in 2000, beating the Italians in the final with a last-minute equalizer in normal time and a golden goal from David Trezeguet in extra time. The same multi-ethnic, multi-faith side were champions but the mood of France was moving on. In the immediate wake of 9/11 France played Algeria in a specially arranged friendly at the Stade de France – the first meeting between the sides since Algerian independence. The game was abandoned early when French Arab youths, many openly declaring their support for Osama Bin Laden, invaded the pitch. The forces of French reaction made their reply, voting Jean-Marie Le Pen, for the first time ever, into the final round of the presidential election, forcing the dilapidated French Left to support Jacques Chirac for re-election. If this turn of events had shown the political demise of the New France, the notion of *la France qui gagne* was dealt a terminal blow in 2002. As the French economy continued to labour under the impossibly hard strictures of the Euro Zone it had created, an ageing, injury-prone French side crashed out of the World Cup, defeated in their opening game by their former colony Senegal. Euro 2004 was little better as the side ran out of ideas and energy against Greece. A year later, the suburbs of Paris, and then all urban France, were in flames as protracted race riots and running battles between youths and police racked the country.

While the French experience suggests how transient the impact of football on racism can be, the efforts of anti-racist groups in European football point to a more secure and lasting advance. Beginning in the early 1990s in Britain with Kick It Out and Football against Racism and repeated now in France, the Netherlands, Italy, Germany and Poland, supporter-led initiatives against racism in football have become established agents for change; they have forced national football associations and UEFA to make open racism an unacceptable form of behaviour in European football stadiums. Since 2002 UEFA has begun to raise its engagement with the issue, investigating and fining more clubs and associations for more incidents.

Football clubs have long been bought and sold amongst national elites, but foreign ownership of clubs in Europe was rare. When English clubs were put up for sale the only takers were a few investment houses buying shares, Milan Mandarić – a maverick Serbian-American computer magnate who fancied Portsmouth – and the ultra-Anglophile Egyptian tycoon Mohammed Fayed who having bought Harrods department store added Fulham football club to his portfolio of eccentric English memorabilia. The Qaddafi family's stake in Juventus was the only foreign purchase of Italian football shares. Opinions tilted between delight at the arrival of saviours and investors and a sense that the bond between locality and club, already tested by the creation of cosmopolitan squads, was being taken to breaking point. In England that bond was tested most severely when two of the biggest clubs, Chelsea and Manchester United, were taken over by a Russian oligarch and a family of American venture capitalists respectively.

After the BSkyB takeover of Manchester United was vetoed by the UK competition authorities, rumour swirled around the likely future ownership of the club, with up to five different investors seen to be building positions for a takeover. Among them was Malcolm Glazer, an East Coast venture capitalist who had made his name and a good deal of his fortune from buying and turning around an ailing American football franchise, the Tampa Bay Buccaneers. In May 2005 he tabled an offer for the club that valued it at over £750 million. Everybody took the money and ran, the club was delisted and Glazer's sons took over. The complex transaction required to make it happen involved the Glazer family saddling Manchester United with an additional £250 million in debt secured against its assets as well as recourse to a variety of exotic financial instruments and loans from Wall Street. The business plan was at best opaque. The Glazers could not realistically expect more TV income by breaking away from the Premiership's collective bargaining arrangements, nor do they seem immune to the arms race of wages and transfers in the football labour market or the vagaries of form and chance. Squeezing more money out of Asia for more trinkets stamped with the club brand seems to be the summit of their innovation. It remains to be seen whether these avatars of American capitalism's deracinated imagination will be able to solve the unpredictability of football's economy.

Chelsea and their gigantic debt were bought in the summer of 2003 by Roman Abramovich, the then unknown Russian oligarch. Abramovich had cut his business teeth in the dying days of the Soviet Union, running one of the few permitted private oil trading companies. During the gigantic state sell-off of the Yeltsin years, Abramovich adroitly obtained a majority share in the giant oil and gas conglomerate Sibneft, as well as a significant share of the state airline, Zil motors and the aluminium industry. The methods of the oligarchs, who came to own over £50 billion of ex-state assets, combined being close to Yeltsin's inner circle, receiving preferential treatment in auctions for companies, exchanging loans for shares with the government and orchestrating an underhand buy-back of publicly issued share coupons from an ignorant and desperate population. Chelsea was the first step in Abramovich's exit strategy from Russia. Having acquired his West London address, he divested himself of his Russian holdings, creating a cash pile of over £7 billion.

Abramovich has, for the moment, devoted himself to Chelsea. He cleared the club's debts, covered its losses to give it an annual income in effect twice that of Manchester United, and unleashed a transfer budget of almost £300 million over three years; even Inter's Moratti cannot compete with such profligacy. Although the club claims to be heading for financial self-sufficiency in 2010, it posted the biggest annual loss in English football history in 2005 of £140 million. Coach Claudio Ranieri was allowed one season in charge. Chelsea came second in the league and reached the semi-final of the Champions League, but it was not enough. Ranieri was dismissed and José Mourinho from Porto arrived. It was under Mourinho that the real outline of the Chelsea project became clear. In his first two seasons in charge Chelsea have dominated the English Premiership with a systematic authority that was both alarming and incredible. As Manchester United, Arsenal and Liverpool were all swept aside, Chelsea never looked for a moment anything other than champions. Mourinho disciplined and organized his expensive squad to produce unflinchingly efficient, precisely calibrated football. Defeat in the Champions League to Liverpool in 2005 and Barcelona in 2006 hinted that the cost of such super-efficient domestic domination might be a lack of the sparkle required to win a cup competition in Europe. But the sparkle keeps arriving. The signing of Andriy Shevchenko and Michael Ballack in summer 2006 demonstrated with ruthless clarity that the best players in the world will go to Chelsea and they will keep going until they win the Champions League. Then when they have won it more than anyone else, what then?

---

17 April 2006
Chelsea 3 Everton 0
Stamford Bridge, London

It's come to this. On the big screen they play digital images of the Chelsea fans who took to the pitch at Fulham earlier in the season; confidential hotlines and rewards. At half-time you're running down the stairs to see if you can have a quick smoke out the back of the Shed, where you never had the bottle to go in the 1980s – because you can't smoke inside the stadium any more – only to find that six or seven hooded boys have got there before you and they're already being hassled by the uniformed security.

You bite on the nicotine craving clawing at the back of your throat and drift through the concourse beneath the stands – ugly unfinished breeze blocks, a carpet of grubby betting slips, the flat brown smells of lager and burnt meat fat overpowering without the clouds of fag smoke that used to mask them. You're in old jeans and trainers, just another unironed specimen of the middle-aged male, except you came to watch them not the football.

That was all over before it started. Everton down to ten men, Chelsea four points from the title then, now just one. Time to go home. Some of them do go home, maybe ten minutes before the end, not staying to savour the victory parade that parts of the crowd are trying to drum up.

They're not celebrating where you are. You're not supporting Chelsea. Your man who got you the tickets isn't either. His man, who gave him the tickets, got them from his boy on the pitch and that is who he is supporting. The guy behind you is supporting his cousin who he tells you will surely be man of the match.

At the other end they're singing, 'Come on, Roman, give us a wave', and the diffident boyish-looking figure who skulks around the door to the box behind him makes a sheepish gesture. Yet somehow the roars of triumph are weak, the cry of 'Champions, Champions', just short of the rasping gale it should be. The queue to the tube is so quiet and orderly that some drunken chanting excites a ripple of embarrassment. You went to watch them crow and gloat, but they too sense that the game may soon be over. On the train the silence is oppressive, broken only by the rustle of programmes. West Brompton cemetery is sliding by us. You imagine our epitaph.

> Hedonists without heart.
> Spiritualists without soul.
> This nullity imagines itself
> The apex of civilization.

18

The Crisis Will be Televised: Football in the Americas, 1990–2006

América TV . . . made a giant flag approximately 150 metres wide and costing $40,000 which was 'donated' to an 'Argentine supporter' to be used at the home match against Ecuador. The flag was in Argentine colours, with the logo of the channel printed in its lower half; along with a legend saying 'Argentina is passion', the motto of the television channel is 'América is passion'. It was shown at the beginning of the game and during the intermezzo, filling a whole terrace of the stadium . . . Meanwhile sheltered from view beneath the flag, spectators were threatened by dozens of pickpockets who demanded that they hand over their belongings. Thus, between the sponsorship of patriotism and delinquency, our national story continues.   **Pablo Alabarces**

Magic and dreams are finished in football.

                                        Carlos Alberto Parreira

I

Television transforms football, but not in circumstances of its own choosing. In post-Cold War Europe, the new media corporations, in alliance with UEFA, some national governments and police forces and the oligarchs at the peak of the club game, rationalized, commercialized and sanitized the football product. In Latin America television transformed the game without being part of such a stable and powerful coalition. The product would not be sanitized; reason, commerce and wholesomeness were in short supply. Indeed the impact of television on what, in the late twentieth century, remained developing economies and fragile democracies was to accentuate the emotional and bureaucratic mania of the region's football and to deepen its financial predicament. Pablo Alabarces captures something of these complex interrelationships in his description of the World Cup qualifying game between Argentina and Ecuador in 1997. Where once authoritarian and populist national governments had sought to harness football to their projects, commercial television now holds sway. The creation of national identities and national sporting mythology has become interlaced with commercial branding and exposure. Beneath the veneer of technological modernity and national unity, the economic inequalities and personal insecurities that constitute urban life in the region remain unaddressed.

Yet television is a Latin American success story. Although slightly behind the leading edge of new technology in the USA and Europe, Latin American television companies are appreciably closer to that edge than almost any other industrial sector. From Televisa in Mexico to Globo in Brazil and Torneos y Competencias in Argentina, domestic capital secured an unusual, almost unique position of dominance, though the arrival of Fox Sport and CNN Española, parts of the News International and Time Warner conglomerates respectively, showed that Western corporations had not given up on the Latin American market. All of these networks show football, a lot of football: live, recorded, highlights, extended highlights, round-ups, résumés and newsflashes. Coverage extends to domestic leagues and international competitions, qualifying rounds and finals, higher and lower divisions, European and Latin American, leagues, cups, friendlies and one-offs. People are watching a lot of football. A survey of the late 1990s reports that 71 per cent of Latin Americans watch football regularly on television.[1] During World Cups the audience approaches 100 per cent. When there is no football, there is chat, classic games and analysis. There are shows about fans, shows about the stars, music shows about football and football set to music. Football, a central strand of urban life in Latin America for seventy years, has become utterly pervasive. The television audience, and to some extent the crowd at the stadium, has become more cross-class, and, though still a definite minority, it has became more feminine. The huge increase in wages for the playing and managerial elite and their often flamboyant and erratic behaviour has combined with the aesthetic of Latin America's TV conglomerates to turn footballers and their private lives into an extended telenovela: scandal, rivalry, paternity suits and conspicuous consumption form an essential element of the expanding football mediascape. Brazil slavered over the details of Romário and Edmundo's feud which was only intensified when they both played for Vasco. Ronaldo's grotesquely kitsch Valentine's Day party thrown in a chateau in Chantilly, north of Paris, was front-page news.

Television has done more than shape the reception of football. It has directly changed the staging and the conduct of the game. One unambiguously positive development was the introduction of multi-camera coverage of games, improved close-ups and more air time for post-match analysis, all of which contributed to reducing the most grotesque excesses of violent play and intimidation that were common-place until the late 1980s. More prosaically, although the value of TV rights in Latin America is a fraction of their value in Europe, television continues to channel enough money into the top leagues, albeit unevenly and unequally, to keep the show on the road. The economic situation may be precarious in Latin America but it would be desolate without television money.

The power of the industry in shaping match schedules has been less benign. In the conflict between security concerns and advertising dollars the latter has always had the upper hand; for example, the Buenos Aires police have long argued for schedules that allow for the geographical separation of travelling Boca and River fans in the city. TV executives have been oblivious. Broadcasters resisted the introduction of the away-goal rule and extra time in Copa Libertadores games, because the proliferation of penalty shoots-outs is cheap drama and less disruptive to the precious scheduling of all the other cheap drama they screen. In 1999 the third and decisive game in the final of the Brazilian championship between Corinthians and Atlético Mineiro had been scheduled by Globo and the CBF for the Wednesday afternoon before Christmas; a ludicrous time to play the game. The mayor of São Paulo took the case to court in an effort to change the timing and on the morning of the game fans still did not know where and when the game would be held. The court gave the Mayor an injunction to move the kick-off to 9 p.m. The CBF then went to a different court an hour later to try and overturn the ruling, but the first court's decision was upheld. Fans either missed the rescheduled game or went and were left stranded after midnight in São Paulo. Those that did stay watched Corinthians creep through after a miserable goalless draw and got soaked by a torrential downpour.

Television has reconnected Latin American football to the wider global game and to the global economy in new ways. In Europe television money generated the revenues to allow the leading clubs to buy the very best talent from all over Latin America. Global coverage of football has hastened that process by making Latin American football and its players more accessible to potential buyers. When Garrincha was taking Botafogo to the Rio State championship hardly anyone in São Paulo was taking notice let alone in Madrid or Milan. Now, the global network of showreels, international scouts, agents and go-betweens means that a player like Ronaldo played barely three seasons in Brazil (for the tiny Rio club São Cristóvão and then Cruzeiro) before, at the age of seventeen, departing for PSV Eindhoven. But you didn't need to be Ronaldo to play abroad. The scale of the exodus of Latin American footballers in the last fifteen years has been immense.

In 1978 a single member of the Argentine World Cup squad of twenty-two – Mario Kempes – played in Europe. None of the Brazilians or Peruvians at the tournament played outside of their home countries.

By the time of the 1990 World Cup numbers had crept up as authoritarian nationalist controls on player movement were lifted and the economic gap between Europe and Latin America widened. As early as 1989 when Platense sold striker Vincente to Grasshopper-Club of Zürich, the $400,000 fee was bigger than the Argentine club's gate receipts for the entire season. The majority of the Uruguay and Argentina squads were now playing in Europe as were just under half the Brazilians. A decade later the financial gap between the two continents made the journey to Europe irresistible to players and clubs alike. At the 2002 World Cup only two of the Argentine squad were home-based, the majority of the Brazilians played in Europe or Japan and many more followed on immediately afterwards. The best Paraguayans and Colombians played in Europe and many others filled the spaces left in the new migratory hierarchy in the squads of Argentina's and Brazil's leading teams. The top-class Latin American football players were now contracted to a handful of leading European clubs, especially in Italy and Spain. But unlike earlier eras of transatlantic transfers, this was always more than just an elite migration. Latin Americans came to Europe to play at every level of football and in every corner of the continent. By 2002 there were over 600 Latin Americans playing in the top divisions in Europe. In Portugal alone there were 123, almost all Brazilians. There were 94 in Spain and 70 in Italy. But then there were Brazilians in Finland, the Faeroe Islands and Albania, Chileans in Hungary, Paraguayans in Germany and Argentines in Russia. Japan, also, provided a major source of employment for younger Brazilian players who struggled in the big squads at home as well as older stars who were winding down.

In Uruguay the sale of the country's football talent has created perhaps the only export-oriented corporate success of the 1990s. Tenfield, a company owned by ex-player Paco Casal, holds the contract of almost every significant player in Uruguayan football. The clubs are desperate for money, having signed over significant chunks of their future transfer revenues to Tenfield in exchange for immediate financial relief. Casal has recouped super profits from the hundreds of Uruguayans Tenfield has managed in the last decade, at the same time as Uruguayan football as a whole appears to be disappearing into an ever deeper financial black hole. A sign of the times? Tenfield also owns the TV rights to Uruguayan football and to Montevideo's carnival – the two institutions that the military dictatorship was never able to control. In the new Latin America money speaks louder than the gun.

Why has Latin America continued to produce players of such high calibre? The answer to this question takes us to the heart of Latin America's economic and political pathologies. Jorge Valdano, the Argentinian midfielder, put it crisply: 'Poverty is good for nothing except football.'[2] Despite almost a century of fitful economic development and industrialization in Latin America, its reserves of urban poverty were undiminished. Indeed, its enduring rural poverty and the widespread violence in the countryside (especially in Peru and Colombia) continued to replenish those reserves. By 2000 São Paulo and Mexico City had over 25 million inhabitants, Rio and Buenos Aires more than 12 million; Lima had swollen to 8 million. The process of urbanization that produced these mega-cities was then gruesomely deformed by a decade of economic neo-liberalism, administered by authoritarian populists like Menem in Argentina, Fujimori in Peru, Cardoso in Brazil and Salinas in Mexico. Sharp reductions in state expenditure, especially on the poor, and a collapse of public-sector jobs for unskilled men combined to impoverish the peripheral *barrios* of the continent. Of course, the widespread existence of malnutrition and poor health and the constant loss of open space and playing fields in poor areas took its toll on the social manufacture of football talent. But the dilemma that faced Pelé – football or a safe government job through a family connection – ceased, like those safe government jobs, to exist. Football, unbelievably remunerated at the highest levels, was a way out like never before. The grinding urban poverty that constituted the essential backdrop to Latin America's production line of globally renowned footballers was the same grim context in which social and familial dislocation, drug use and trafficking, gangs, crime and violence were nurtured. They all made their way to the stadium.

Latin American football had been no stranger to violence, spontaneous and organized, but in the 1990s the incidence of both grew and both were given greater exposure than ever before by television. The intersection of gangs, drugs, football and violence centred on the unofficial but organized supporter groups – variously known across the continent as *barra bravas* or *torcidas*. These groups fought among themselves over control of the stands, with other clubs' fans over bragging rights and with the police in the streets. In a new development, they also took on their own players, managers and directors in innumerable incidents of intimidation, protest, complaint and revenge. This unquestionable shift in the power and presence of the hard core in Latin American football was not just the result of economic and social conditions, but a consequence of the byzantine governance of football.

In keeping with the neo-liberal logic of the era, national governments – populist flourishes aside – withdrew from the direct support of football clubs, national teams and football associations; all, as a consequence, have been drawn closer to, and become more dependent upon, television companies and multinational sponsors. However, the opaque organization and legal grey area within which Latin American football operates has meant that none of the putative benefits of such a commercial environment, like long-term planning, rational investment and stable governance, have emerged. Clubs and national football associations have resolutely remained personal political fiefdoms of the rich, connected and powerful and no-go areas for conventional forms of accounting and audit. The money that has not ended up in players' and agents' pockets has certainly not reappeared in the guise of new stadiums, improved facilities or stellar squads. In fact the main consequence of the influx of commercial expertise and money into Latin American football seems to have been to help pile up an ever-increasing mountain of debt made even worse by falling stadium attendances across the region. Poverty and insane scheduling play their part in that decline, but there are two key reasons for the pitiful level of attendance at many games. First, the persistence, even the intensification, of violence, at its worst in Argentina, Brazil, Colombia and Chile. Second, the declining standards, perceived and real, of much of the domestic football on offer. While there are ample social reasons to explain the rising tide of football violence in Latin America, it is also clear that the football authorities have been culpable in its development and its persistence. In the era of the dictatorships and in the transition to democracy, club directors paid, organized and used fan clubs for their own political and sporting purposes. They have invariably refused to cooperate with the police or national governments in addressing the problem, where the police have been prepared to contemplate anything more than brutal riot control. Neglect and repression have proved ineffective responses to violence and crime inside and outside the stadiums.

The perceived decline in standards of domestic football was an inevitable consequence of the global transfer market. With the best talent playing in Europe, Latin American club squads are often a mixture of the very young awaiting a transfer, and the old who have returned to their homeland to see out their career. Those in the middle were not good enough to go or did go and couldn't survive. The same technologies that have facilitated the export of Latin America's best have also exposed the region to European football in greater depth than ever before. By the early twenty-first century the European Champions League, be-jewelled by the best Argentine and Brazilian talent, became as televised and almost as closely followed as the Copa Libertadores. The evident superiority of top-notch club football in Europe was undeniable.

In his words at the head of this chapter, Carlos Alberto Parreira, the coach of the 1994 Brazil World Cup-winning squad, captured the blunt professionalism of a survivor and winner in contemporary Latin America. He is not alone and he was by no means the most cautious or cynical. A whole generation of Brazilian and other Latin American coaches have grown up telling ball boys to disrupt play and their own players to foul opponents who look like getting into space. Alongside *futebol arte*, *futebol força* and *futebol de resultados*, sadly Brazilians could now play *futebol brutal*. In a game in 2003 between Coritiba and Santos, Coritiba striker Jaba displayed some close-quarter trickery on the ball, juggling it elegantly near the touchline. Santos players were incensed and went for him. But referee Leonardo Gaba booked Jaba for deliberately provoking his opponents. If magic and dreams are finished, then what will be the fate of Latin American football? How long can the passion be sustained when it is colonized and appropriated by television conglomerates? How long can a culture, nurtured on the fantastical and the spectacular, prosper on a diet of pragmatism?

Pragmatism was certainly the guiding principle behind FIFA's decision to stage the World Cup in the United States in 1994. As a *New York Times* columnist put it, 'The United States was chosen by the way, because of all the money to be made here, not because of any soccer prowess. Our country has been rented as a giant stadium and hotel and television studio for the next 31 days.'[3] To be fair, FIFA and its commercial and bureaucratic allies in the USA had a bigger vision than this kind of commercial hit and run. They believed that an American World Cup was the perfect launch pad for the recreation of professional football in the United States and the virtual completion of football's expansion as the world's game. But to achieve this they would have to avoid the pitfalls that previous attempts to run professional football in the USA had encountered and work with the very particular sociological and sporting material available to them.

The death knell for the NASL (America's second attempt to make a national professional football) was the decision to give the 1986 World Cup to Mexico. Time Warner, the main corporate sponsors of the NASL, pulled the plug on what had become an unsustainable business.

When the NASL did collapse in 1984 what was left of professional football in America went indoors. Playing a specially tailored five-a-side game, small professional indoor football leagues survived through the late 1980s and early 1990s. Indeed, so popular was the game in small pockets of the USA that on the same day in June 1994 and at the same time that South Korea were playing Spain in Dallas's first World Cup game, 7,000 people chose to go and see the local indoor football team play instead. In Latin America and Europe indoor football, futsal and other variants of the game had been complementary to the development and popularity of conventional professional football; in the USA it appeared to fragment an already limited football audience.

A diehard core of indoor football fanatics is the least of the United States' footballing peculiarities. Three others stand out. First, in contrast to almost everywhere else on the planet, football in the USA became a middle-class rather than a working-class game; by the late 1990s over half of the country's regular football players came from households with an annual income of over $50,000. Second, the relative significance and prowess of women's football is greater in the US than anywhere else. Finally, the American national team – male or female – has been unable, despite successful international performances, to mobilize a significant level of nationalist support and public interest.

Since the mid-1970s, in the predominantly white and upper middle-class suburbs of the USA, playing football flourished among children, teenagers and women. The NASL's development work, its soccer clinics and evangelical promotion of the game certainly helped account for this, but it was working with a powerful current in American culture. For the middle classes, whose emotional and political disposition had been shaped by the parenting techniques of Dr Spock and the enduring psychic ripples of the counter culture, America's dominant professional sports presented a series of problems. American football was too violent, too confrontational and too authoritarian in its internal structures. Baseball's high-pressure solitary performances for pitcher and batter were suspect. Basketball was rapidly becoming the game of the African-American ghetto. Football offered a game to the suburbs that could be moulded and made markedly less confrontational and violent than gridiron. It is worth noting that the paranoia of the American middle classes was so great that heading the ball was actively discouraged (owing to potential brain damage) and a small industry emerged attempting to sell protective gear to the enthusiastic header of the ball. Unlike baseball, football offered a game in which teamwork was at a premium over individual performances and in which the precious and fragile egos of the players could be protected.

Football was also feminized. Soccer mums took the lead in organizing the game at a grass-roots level and the number of girls and women playing the game in organized leagues soared. By 2000 the USA had 7 million registered female footballers, compared to around 300,000 in Germany, one of the stronger European nations in women's football. Pro rata, America had six times the participation rate of Germany. Success followed; the USA won the inaugural Women's World Cup in 1991, gold medals at the Atlanta and Athens Olympics, the silver medal at the Sydney Olympics, and hosted and won the Women's World Cup in 1999. In Mia Hamm America had the most accomplished female football player of the era, while Brandi Chastain gave them the iconic photographic moment with which to launch women's football into the mainstream. After scoring the winning penalty in the 1999 World Cup Final shoot-out with China, Chastain peeled off her top to reveal her sports bra. That finally got women's football on the cover of *Sports Illustrated*. The moment had come to launch the first fully professional women's football league – WUSA. It lasted three seasons and consumed around $100 million of investors' and sponsors' cash. Average attendances were around 8,000 in the opening season and around 6,000 thereafter. Hardly the NFL, but more than enough to keep the lower divisions of Europe afloat and in some cases, the highest divisions. But

WUSA could not get a game on network TV; it could not get a meaning-ful TV deal of any kind. Similarly they could not find big-time corporate sponsors and could not turn the euphoria of 1999 into sustained support for a domestic league. Despite huge pay cuts for the players, the commer-cial limits of women's football were rapidly reached. A few weeks before the 2003 Women's World Cup, hurriedly moved from a SARS-infected China to the USA, WUSA folded and the USA ceded the title to the Germans.

What explains the reticence of the whole nation to follow the men's national team despite a plausible performance at the 1994 World Cup and successful qualification campaigns for the 1998, 2002 and 2006 World Cups? The former threw up the USA–Iran clash, a game which in any other universe would have served as an irresistible proxy for America's neurotic relationship with the Middle East. The latter pro-duced a stunningly gutsy series of performances in which the USA beat Portugal and went on to lose the quarter-final to Germany. What would in almost any other nation have brought life to a complete, if momentary, halt barely flickered on the collective radar. Football continued to be suffocated by the mainstream belief that it was just not American.

US football did however have another constituency on which to draw: the steadily rising number of Latino immigrants to the nation. Of course, many came from predominantly baseball-playing countries like Cuba or Puerto Rico, but there were major concentrations of Mexicans and Central Americans in the country who might have provided a substantial pool of players and fans. But the social exclusivity and geographical separateness of suburban football culture from these Latino communi-ties, the dependence of recreational football on the self-organization and funding of parents and the lack of access to green space in inner-city communities were major factors in limiting the development of US football. As a consequence the Latino communities of the USA over-whelmingly chose not to engage with the football mainstream in America. Latino football remained a small-scale urban and amateur affair. When the USA national team played against Central Americans or the Mexican national team they might as well have been playing away as expats, green-card-holding immigrants and illegals gathered to cheer Honduras, Costa Rica and Guatemala against the alien nation they were living in. When in 1998 the USA took the field in the final of the Gold Cup (CONCACAF's regional championship) they faced Mexico.

A lone American flag fluttered at half mast on the perimeter, surrounded by a whole host of Mexican tricolors. Any remaining doubts about the identity of the home team were dispelled when the two teams took the field. The fans came, saw, booed and threw things – at the United States. Whistles greeted the US national team when it took the field and during its national anthem. Every lost possession was greeted with cheers. Every US throw-in or corner was hailed by flying debris. Cups and bottles containing beer, soda water and the end product of consumption rained onto the field.[4]

The game was played in Los Angeles.

The opening ceremony of the 1994 World Cup took place on 17 June in Chicago in the burning yellow sunshine and intense humidity of the afternoon. Perfect for the television cameras and European audiences; impossible for the players. Chat-show queen Oprah Winfrey was the mistress of ceremonies, presiding over the lip-synched altrock band the B-52s, cavorting representatives of the nation's ethnic communities matched to the tournament's participants, and most memorably Diana Ross. The soul and disco diva sang the national anthem and then tried to score a penalty into a makeshift goal which had been carried on to the pitch. With all the inelegance and ineptitude of a body schooled in a culture where kicking is an alien technique for propelling balls, Ross stumbled, dragged her foot and missed the goal from three metres. Then the goal collapsed. Oprah fell off the temporary stage and Germany struggled to beat Bolivia. But the stadium was packed to capacity and the crowd loved it and that was true of pretty much every game in the 1994 World Cup. Even the third-place match – usually a neglected affair – got a crowd of 85,000. Getting people in was not the problem. Americans love a big event and can pay the entrance fee. Getting the games out of the stadium and into the US media was a problem. Germany–Bolivia had to compete with the OJ Simpson murder case then dominating the sport and news headlines. The NBA play-offs were in full swing and there was plenty of hockey, baseball and golf action if you wanted it. Host cities got interested, TV coverage was available but most of America remained blissfully or wilfully ignorant of the World Cup.

As if to highlight the peculiarity of the United States, 1994 was the most intensely covered and televised World Cup for the rest of the Americas. Colour television was available across the region for the first time, television-ownership levels had risen enormously, even in the country-side and the urban peripheries; satellite-transmission systems had improved and with a small boom going on at home, Globo, Televisa and their smaller equivalents could all afford to send large numbers of journalists and crews. Bolivia, at their first World Cup since 1950, were showing wall-to-wall coverage of the tournament: 'People are demanding to know who's hurt, what the players are saying, every detail, every word. And not just Bolivia, they want to know how the other teams are doing.'[5] It was just as well, for Bolivia did not stay too long. Defeat by the Germans was followed by an excruciating 0–0 draw with South Korea and defeat to Spain 3–1. At least they got a World Cup goal after their previous outings, going down 4–0 to both Brazil and Yugoslavia in 1930 and 8–0 to Uruguay in 1950. In La Paz they wrote, 'Bolivia played like never before but lost as always.'[6]

Argentina arrived in the USA in some disarray. They had been humili-ated during the qualifying rounds by an unprecedented 5–0 defeat to Colombia in Buenos Aires. Argentina had only managed to squeeze into the World Cup after beating Australia 2–1 in a two-leg play-off. Maradona had, despite all his mounting problems with mental and physical fitness, been recalled to the squad. Although he lacked the ferocious pace and acceleration of his prime, Maradona looked fit and had lost a lot of weight. *El Pibe* lifted Argentina to a crushing 4–0 victory over Greece. Maradona scored the third, letting fly from 20 metres, and then ran for the sidelines where his contorted, demonic face burned its outline on to the world's television screens. Against Nigeria, two goals for Claudio Caniggia were enough against a side that dropped two gears below their best. Then Maradona was called for a random drugs test and the following day it was revealed that his blood contained a cocktail of five drugs, some of which were connected with weight loss and appetite control but could also be considered as performance-enhancing. Maradona was immediately banned from the tournament. Argentina went wild, television was deluged with Maradona tribute shows, his greatest goals set to music. The governor of Buenos Aires sent his personal support. Maradona retreated to a very lucrative seat in the commentary box and the squad declared they would win the World Cup for him. They went out and lost to the Bulgarians, but were still through to the second round where they met Romania. At first Argentina seemed revived, energized by Ariel Ortega, who had stepped into Maradona's space if not into his shoes. Argentina attacked in the heat but sudden Romanian counterattacks left them a goal down. A Batistuta penalty made it 1–1 only for Romania's Dumitrescu to catch them out again with another lightning attack. Gheorghe Hagi ended all hope by making it three. At the end of a 40-metre run Hagi was ready for Dumitrescu's pass and struck a clean, crisp first-time shot. Balbo's effort with quarter of an hour left was not enough to save Argentina. In the aftermath one commentator lamented: 'Ours is a country in which it's the speculators who win, a country that violated its own constitution every time it felt like it. Yesterday Argentina paid with Maradona for a way of life of not heeding the law.'[7]

Colombia would pay for their defeat differently. The team arrived in the USA much fancied if not favourites. Their thrashing of Argentina in the qualifiers was just one of a long sequence of wins and superb performances. Francisco Maturana had replicated the model of play he first developed at Atlético Nacional. The national team played a winning blend of organized zonal marking, a pair of hardworking midfield players and creative, defence-splitting passing from the generously coif-fured Carlos Valderrama. The build-up to the World Cup was not perhaps the best managed of the qualifiers. Colombian beer giant Bavaria had the team play an endless string of advertising friendlies, eventually provoking a players' revolt when they were asked to play another Italian second-division side; though when the company awarded $300 for every goal celebration that matched their own advertising logo – a single pointed finger – the squad were more than happy to collaborate. As Chris Taylor has argued. 'The fact that one of the country's biggest business groups . . . was not only sponsoring the team but also owned many of the country's most important media outlets led to a vicious circle of self-congratulation.'[8] Worse still, as pressure and expectation unstoppably and unreasonably mounted, the kiss of death arrived: Pelé was now tipping them as World Cup winners. *El Tiempo*, in Bogotá, reported that astrologers foresaw great things for the national team. What they had not foreseen was Gheorghe Hagi. In their opening game Colombia played fifteen minutes of brilliant, short passing until Hagi found a long pass to release Romania's striker Răducioiu; 1–0. Then Hagi himself sent a long ball over the mis-positioned Colombian goal-keeper, Córdoba; 2–0. The game finished 3–1, but Colombia were never in it. Yet all was not lost; after all Colombia now had only to face the

USA and Switzerland. Two wins should not have been impossible. On the day of the game against the Americans, Maturana, his assistant Hernán Dario Gómez and Gómez's brother and midfield player for Colombia, Gabriel Jaime Gómez, all received threats by fax and telephone. The message was the same: their Medellín homes would be bombed if Gómez played. Gómez gave way to Hernán Gaviria.

Against the Americans Colombia were a shadow of their former selves. A hopeful but hardly dangerous cross from John Harkes was turned into the Colombian net by defender Andrés Escobar. The USA made it two early in the second half and Colombia were beaten and going home. Escobar, who wrote a column for the newspapers, reflected back on his mistake: 'Don't let the defeat affect our respect for the sport and the team. See you later, because life goes on.'

On their return to Colombia all members of the squad were subject to some kind of abuse. Maturana and Gómez got theirs mainly in the press. Valderrama was cross-examined and criticized for his supposed laziness, Asprilla and Rincón for their attitudes, midfielders Lozano and Álvarez were roughed up and hospitalized. But the biggest price was paid by Andrés Escobar who was shot six times in the chest in the car park of a Medellín nightclub, by a minor mobster's heavy – Humberto Muñoz Castro. The details remain unclear. Most likely Muñoz interceded with his gun rather than his brain in an argument between Escobar and his bosses, the Gallón brothers, who had been taunting the player in the nightclub. Some 120,000 people attended his funeral.

Before, during and after the 1994 World Cup, the Brazilian squad and their coach Carlos Alberto Parreira were accused, charged, tried and found guilty of playing dull football, European football, football without soul or joy. It is certainly true that the squad of 1994 did not possess the luxurious skills of the 1982 World Cup squad or even that of 1986. But then they were something different, they were winners. Parreira has consistently argued that his team was not negative, they were organized. They were organized at set pieces. They were tight in defence. Above all, they were organized and focused when the opposition had the ball – focused on getting it back. They swept aside the Russians and then the Cameroonians, who were at war with themselves over money. Then they coasted to a 1–1 draw with Sweden and into the second round. In Palo Alto they met the USA. Parreira's Brazil showed its sharp edges when fullback Leonardo was dismissed after 43 minutes for crashing his elbow into the skull of American playmaker Tab Ramos. The Americans, who had never looked like making a game of it, went into their shell despite facing only ten men. A pass of some finesse from Romário opened them up and Bebeto calmly put it away. In the quarter-finals the Brazilians continued to make heavy weather of their work, allowing the Dutch back into the game after taking a two-goal lead. A singular moment of excellence from a Branco free kick was the difference between the two teams. Brazil made even heavier weather of their semi-final against ten-man Sweden, who absorbed everything that came through the centre of the Brazilian attack until a single sneaked header from Romário put them in the final against Italy. It was, of course, billed as the rematch of the legendary 1970 final and the 1982 second-round classic, an opportunity to re-create the beautiful game. Brazil won it on penalties, the first and only World Cup Final to be decided in this way, after 120 goalless minutes in which neither side appeared to have the energy or the will to break the other.

So the United States could host a World Cup and make money out of it. Could it now do the same with its own professional league? Major League Soccer (MLS) kicked off its first season in 1996 with ten teams. In a conscious effort not to replicate the mistakes of the NASL, MLS was established as a single entity. The league controlled player recruitment and distribution through a draft system. It took charge of commercial and sponsorship issues and created club franchises in which owners had a stake in the league as a whole rather than just their own team. MLS also managed to attract some sponsors with very deep pockets, $250 million deep, including NFL franchise-owner Lamar Hunt, the Kraft family and Phillip Anschutz who eventually came to own six franchises. MLS also attracted some considerable foreign talents. Veterans of the 1994 World Cup who ended up settling in the MLS included Colombia's Carlos Valderrama, Bolivia's Marco Etcheverry and Jaime Moreno, Romania's Gheorghe Hagi and Bulgaria's Hristo Stoitchkov. While MLS did, like the NASL, provide a lucrative retirement destination for leading foreign players, their centrality to the league's profile was always less than Pelé, Beckenbauer et al. had been in the NASL. This was in part because some players, like Mexican star Jorge Campos and German defender Lothar Matthäus, stayed only a few matches before deciding that MLS's restrictive wage structures and minority cultural status were not to their liking. In compensation MLS did manage to nurture the spine of the US national team and launch a few players – like Landon Donovan at Bayer Leverkusen or Jo Max Moore at Everton – into the lower reaches of top-class European football.

Overall, in its first ten seasons, MLS's primary achievement was survival. But financially and culturally it remains no more than survival. Could it have done better? After all, the late 1990s and early twenty-first century offered a precious moment during which to mount something more than a permanent rearguard action. The greed and intransigence of players, owners and networks had tarnished the reputation of America's leading sports. An entire ice-hockey season and chunks of a number of baseball seasons have been lost to strikes and irreconcilable financial conflicts. Drugs, gambling and sexual scandals have continued to mount. However, MLS had its own problems. With just ten or twelve teams and a play-off structure that mirrors the laborious multi-leg play-offs of basketball's NBA and baseball's MLB, MLS played a thirty-two-game regular season that eliminated only two (or four) teams from the running. Worse, there has been no cup competition or relegation struggle to ignite the narrative imagination. Even if one's imagination had been ignited it would have to try and burn in enormous, cavernous stadiums built for mainstream US sports in which even respectable 25–30,000 football crowds were vaporized. The league did begin to acquire its own smaller, purpose-built stadiums, but progress was slow. Thus handicapped, MLS had to compete on cable television with European and Latin American football, which had acquired a considerable following of US global football fans. The marketing departments of Celtic, Manchester United and Milan had certainly identified them, and the American tours conducted by these and other leading European clubs in the early twenty-first century were major media events and complete stadium sell-outs. However, this audience for football has not translated into a regular audience for the MLS.

Most important of all, MLS, like the national team, had little initial success in attracting the now enormous Latino community in the US – fast approaching one-quarter of the population. In 2005 the most radical attempt to redress this situation was pursued. In a singular reversal of the usual pattern of investment, Mexico bought into the USA's own sporting *Maquiladora*, or cross-border assembly plant. Jorge Vergara, owner of Guadalajara football club – known colloquially as Los Chivas and understood as an icon of Mexican nationalism and independence – bought an MLS franchise in Los Angeles and called it Chivas USA. The club's footballing debuts were uneventful but they did coincide with the election of the first Latino Mayor of Los Angeles. If such a shift of power is possible in City Hall why not in MLS, why not in the whole peculiar landscape of American sport?

When the World Cup-winning squad returned to Rio airport in 1994 they had managed to accumulate around 12 tonnes of goods and presents, which of course carried a very substantial level of taxes and import duties. The squad refused to pay, encouraged by CBF president Ricardo Teixeira, and after a five-hour, televised wrangle involving the CBF, the tax authorities and the Ministry of Finance, they were allowed through, the CBF promising to pay the bill and later removing it from the players' bonus payments. Seventy per cent of Brazilians thought they should have paid up like everybody else. The country had of course gone predictably crazy when the World Cup was actually won, but few expected there to be a repetition of the 1970s triumph in which footballing prowess had been converted into a wave of support for the military government. As Lula, the opposition presidential candidate for the left-wing Partido de Los Trabajadores, argued, 'The people know how to distinguish between football and politics. When the festivities are over the people know how to separate fantasy from reality.'[9]

Brazil's new-found sobriety was reflected at the polls in October 1994 when Fernando Henrique Cardoso decisively beat Lula in the presidential elections. Cardoso, once an exile from the military regime, had made the move from left-wing sociologist to neo-liberal finance minister and unlike almost all of his predecessors he had managed to curb Brazil's runaway inflation levels. That kind of sober achievement, virtually a miracle in Latin American economies, made him a certainty. On his election, Cardoso proclaimed that Brazil had reached the 'end of the Vargas era'. The state would withdraw as far as possible from the running of the economy and the deliberate engineering of society. Cardoso's government preferred to conduct massive privatizations, encourage foreign investment, and implement IMF-style spending controls and monetary policies. They also got the constitution changed so he could have a second term in power.

However, the disengagement of the Brazilian state from football was not total. On the contrary, a neo-liberal model of state and society assumes that the rule of law exists, that there is transparency in accounting, and that the state and its agencies are neutral as regards its social actors. The limits of Cardoso's neo-liberal project were clearly illuminated by the failure of successive regimes to reform the legal framework of Brazilian football and create either financial or administrative transparency. The first attempt had been made under President Collor, who had appointed Zico as Sports Minister in 1990. Zico fashioned a limited set of reforms which attempted to bring some order to the chaos of Brazilian football administration and the law duly passed the Brazilian Congress in 1993 – but it passed because the changes merely tinkered with the system. In 1995 Cardoso appointed Pelé as Extraordinary Minister of Sport – though whether the appellation was for footballing or political reasons was not made clear. Pelé appeared a good choice not merely because of his prestige but because he had genuinely fallen out with the dominant powers in Brazilian football – João Havelange, the CBF and its president Ricardo Teixeira. In 1993 Pelé and his sports company had sought to win the TV rights for Brazilian domestic football. It was made very clear during the negotiations that no rights would be going near anyone who did not deposit a significant chunk of cash in the relevant bank accounts. Pelé refused, went public, protested, won the undying love and support of the reformers within the Brazilian sports media and was then cold-shouldered by the establishment. Havelange was so furious that in an act of calculated spite he refused to invite Pelé to the 1994 World Cup draw.

Pelé spent most of his four-year tenure as minister drawing up what became known as the Pelé Law. Taking the Zico Law as its basis, the Pelé Law sought to force clubs to open their books, and convert from charitable or social-club status to private limited companies. The law also attempted to systematize and regulate players' contracts in their favour and force the chaotic organization of Brazilian football to be more rational and open – especially on the question of the control of leagues and competitions. After much argument, the law was passed by Congress in 1998 but the football lobby of club presidents and administrators doing a little politics on the side effectively emasculated the legislation, forcing changes, rewrites and whole sections to be dropped.

One section that was not lost was the regulations allowing foreign companies to invest in Brazilian football clubs. So by the late 1990s the circuits of power in Brazilian football appeared to connect four groups: the *cartolas* or 'top hats', the well-connected businessmen and politicians who filled the administrative positions and presidencies of the nation's leading clubs; the bureaucrats, drawn from the same class who ran the state and national football authorities; the Globo television conglomerate; and a small number of American banks and European companies who had been bold enough or foolish enough to put real money into some of Brazil's best-supported sides. As we shall see, foreign capital was effortlessly outmanoeuvred by their Brazilian counterparts who really did take the money and run. Globo's relentless focus on big and unsuccessful clubs to the detriment of provincial teams and small clubs doing well, resulted in less than the best football actually being shown. Globo's reluctance to take the Copa Libertadores seriously even when Brazilian teams were playing was a marker of wilful insularity and ignorance. Combined with scheduling decisions that fitted football around the pivotal needs of the telenovela and trash shows, Brazilian television was like an absentee landlord that took its cut and left its declining assets in the hands of cheap hoods.

The cheap hoods were the *cartolas*. Almost no club was exempt from their baleful influence. Only among some of the better-supported clubs of the north-east in Bahia and Fortaleza was there anything close to a benign, open, accountable set of football directors. Emblematic of Brazilian football's ruling class was Eurico Miranda, president of Vasco da Gama. Miranda was a scion of an industrious Portuguese immigrant family, working as a child in their bakery business. He made his way up the treacherous lower slopes of Brazil's class structure by taking a law degree and dabbling in car dealerships. With a small war chest and a local network established, he ran for election to Vasco's board in the 1970s and by 1986 he was president of the club – a post he has held ever since. In addition to his presidency, Eurico acquired the two other key elements of the *cartolas'* portfolio: wealth and power. The former is of essentially unknown origin. Miranda's job at Vasco is notionally unpaid, but his property portfolio is legendary, his business operations are far reaching, his yacht is enormous and his lifestyle without being as grotesquely flamboyant as many is nonetheless opulent. As the maestro himself, João Havelange, once said, 'I just take enough expenses to live comfortably.'[10] In Eurico's case, very comfortably, given that he is known to have once left the Maracanã with $30,000 of gate receipts in his own pocket. The money was subsequently lost when Eurico was 'robbed'. Power came in the shape of a seat in the Brazilian Chamber of Deputies, notionally on the ticket of a small right-wing party, the PSBS – but Miranda had been refreshingly honest in his approach: 'I am for Vasco . . .' And so he was, aggressively pursuing their narrow self-interest in the football courts, the high courts, Congress and the football bureaucracies. He has led pitch invasions by Vasco fans protesting refereeing decisions and prevented visiting teams to Vasco from even warming up. The alchemy of money and power has brewed among this whole stratum a grotesque blend of cynicism, disrespect and disregard for the law. Brazil's most outspoken and astute football writer Juca Kfouri puts it like this: 'In Brazil there is still the ideology of "*rouba mas faz*" – it's OK to steal if you get things done. In football this is stretched to the most far-reaching consequences. Everything is forgotten in the light of victory. I have always said that God put the best players here and the worst bosses to compensate.'[11]

The organization responsible for policing and regulating *cartolas* and their clubs alike was the CBF. Although the organization continued to receive modest government subventions and a share of the pools money, it was, under the hapless stewardship of Ricardo Teixeira, substantially in debt. Of course there were costly outgoings involved in running Brazilian football – taking five Rio High Court judges on an all-expenses-paid trip to the USA to see Brazil win the World Cup does not come cheap. But then nor does losing law suits. The five judges were all sitting on at least one of the perhaps forty outstanding legal cases that the CBF and its football allies were embroiled in at the time. In the new spirit of entrepreneurialism that the Cardoso era was meant to inaugurate, the CBF finally cashed in on its central asset – the *Seleção*, the Brazilian national team. In 1996 Ricardo Teixeira signed a secret, long-term commercial sponsorship deal with Nike. It was subsequently revealed to be the largest ever sponsorship deal of a national football team, amounting to $160 million over ten years. Between 1997 and 2000 the income of the CBF quadrupled yet the total percentage of the budget actually allocated to football fell; travel and hotel costs increased four-

or fivefold. The debt remained unpaid. In the meantime Teixeira was selling milk from his ranch to the CBF – quite what they were doing with huge quantities of milk remains unclear – and letting out his nightclubs to the organization for a variety of expensive hospitality events.

The state FAs could be both venal and eccentric. The São Paulo FA became the centre of bizarre innovation and rule changes in a series of leftfield efforts to deal with the inherent pathologies of the domestic game. Ever subservient to television interests, the president of the São Paulo FA introduced a three-minute timeout in each half and sweetened the pill by offering paid-for cheerleaders. In a desperate attempt to deal with the ludicrous level of fouling São Paulo experimented with two referees on the pitch at once and tried to counter the inevitable yard-pinching of defensive walls by giving referees foam spray to mark the line with. Fouling did not diminish and the foam ate the turf. Taking basketball as their model, São Paulo introduced the idea of an extra free kick on the fifteenth foul – resulting in a number of comic games where bodily contact would cease for the last ten minutes. Most sensationally, in 2001 São Paulo declared the end of the 0–0 draw. In the event of a goalless draw neither side was to be awarded any points at all. In the case of score draws matters would be decided by penalties with three points for the winner and one for the loser. More conventional forms of rule-bending saw the once mighty Fluminense, who finished second from bottom in the 1996 national championship, escape the drop. Relegation should have followed but miraculously the CBF decided to expand the league the following season from an overlarge 24 to a ludicrous 26 teams. The following season Fluminense were relegated again.

In December 1997 Juventude from Rio Grande do Sul played Portuguesa of São Paulo in a quarter-final of the national championship; fifty-five people paid on the door. Crowds as laughably small as this were not uncommon in Brazil in the 1990s. In a poll conducted by *Lance!* – a leading football paper – nearly three-quarters of the readers said that violence was keeping them away from the game. The vast concrete bowls built under the military echoed to the tiny cries of shrinking crowds deterred not just by violence, but by the ludicrous scheduling decisions decided by Globo, and by the physical decline of the stadiums themselves. In 1992 before a Flamengo–Botafogo game in the Rio championship a fence on the upper tier of the Maracanã gave way and fifty people plunged to the next concrete level – three Flamengo fans died and fifty more were injured. The rest of Rio is still cruelly reminding them of these deaths in song at the stadiums. The Maracanã was closed and patched up, its ever-diminishing official capacity in the 1990s testament to the fundamental inability of adapting 1950s architecture to the crowd-control issues and safety standards of the 1990s.

The audience for many football matches not only shrank but was reduced to a hard core of organized fans – the *Torcida Organizada*. These fans' clubs and organizations had first emerged in the late 1970s and early 1980s, taking their cue from the student movement and the samba schools as forms of permissible association under military government. Their activities had been devoted to planning displays and other forms of support at the game, and they had developed a considerable repertoire of songs, chants, displays, flags, fireworks and balloon-waving. Some mutated into or acquired samba schools which paraded in the major carnivals of the big cities. But by the mid-1990s the tone of support was becoming more aggressive and confrontational, with local branches of the *torcidas* shading into the informal networks of local gangs in the poor peripheries. Fighting between fans was not, however, the only problem.

In 1997 Santos beat Corinthians 1–0 in a tense and violent game that saw two Corinthians players sent off and three more booked. Many Corinthians fans had already left which was unusual as they usually stayed to boo the team on such an occasion. The Corinthians team coach left Santos an hour or so later with a military police escort as far as the beginning of the winding mountain road that would take them back to São Paulo, 60 kilometres to the north. The coach soon found itself chased and harassed – first, by a couple of cars with blacked-out windows and then a wayward lorry – before it was forced to a halt by another coach strung across the road. This coach was packed with Corinthians *torcidas* known as O *Gaviões da Fiel* – 'the Hawks of the Faithful'. The *Gaviões* proceeded to stone and then storm the team's coach, physically and verbally abusing the players.

The violence finally spilt out from the stadium and a mere internal footballing matter into the very heart of Brazil's biggest cities. In 1999 Palmeiras won the Copa Libertadores beating the Colombian side

Deportivo Cali on penalties in São Paulo. The banned but still functioning *Mancha Verde* had gathered many ticketless fans outside the stadium before the game and together they tried to storm the turnstiles during the match. Endless scuffling and fighting among the police and the *Mancha Verde* turned into a full-scale riot as they were joined by the delirious Palmeiras crowd. Riot police were called in and many volleys of tear gas were fired ahead of massed baton and shield charges down Avenida Paulista – the very heart of the country's banking district – while the Palmeiras *torcidas* tore up the paving stones and erected impromptu barricades.

The paradox of Brazilian football remains: how, given declining crowds, the mass export of players, crumbling infrastructure, precarious finances and a venal elite, did football remain so intensely popular and Brazilian players and some Brazilian teams continue to be so good? In the early 1990s São Paulo under Telê Santana were South American and Intercontinental champions, playing old-school samba football. Phil Scolari's Grêmio won the Copa Libertadores and fulfilled the stereotype of football in Rio Grande do Sul. Closer in temperament and ethnic make-up to Uruguay than Brazil, the industrial cities of the region played tough, uncompromising but successful football. Scolari's equally successful Palmeiras teams of the late 1990s were little different. The national side after twenty-four years without reaching the World Cup Final, made it to three in a row. Success, of course, breeds success; football's grip on the Brazilian popular imagination is nourished by every triumph. But Brazilian football is nourished by more than baubles. It is wired into many of the main circuits of Brazilian culture – music, dance, carnival, beach life, religion. Brazilian Portuguese has nearly forty synonyms for the ball.

Another indicator of the polymorphous quality of the game in Brazil is the sheer variety of types of football that are played. At the eccentric end of the scale, Brazilian stockbrokers and beach boys before the crash of 1974 played autoball with their Volkswagen beetles and a giant leather ball – a cast-off from a forgotten advertising campaign. In the interior games have been played with bulls as a rodeo novelty. Keepy-uppy has been raised to the level of art form and turned into a minor competitive sport. Button football, Brazil's own version of table or flick football, won the hearts of a generation of football fantasists. Less bizarre adaptations include beach football and footvolley. In a few decades, beach football has moved from a sandy kickabout to being a corporate-sponsored and FIFA-regulated branch of the football family. Most tellingly of all, indoor football, which has been played in a multiplicity of formats and rules around the world, was under FIFA's aegis systematized and given a global standard as its Brazilian variant – futsal. It now has its own panoply of global FIFA competitions.

Modern Brazilian football's relationship with religion reflects the religious diversity and change in the rest of the country. What was once, officially, a 100 per cent Catholic society no longer appears so homogenous. On the one hand, evangelical Protestant churches have grown at an extraordinary rate among the lost and hungry souls of the urban peripheries of industrial Brazil. On the other, African religions and belief systems have completed their transition from the country to the city, from a secret slave ritual to an Afro-Catholic religion of cults and gods – *candomblé* – and urban magic – *macumba*. Officials of leading clubs, openly and not so openly, employ *candomblé* priests, medicine men, conjurors and magicians of all kinds to exorcize stadiums, curse opponents, heal injuries and influence games.

In the centre ground the majority of Brazil's fans and players remain Roman Catholics. Every major club has a chapel built as part of the stadium – Vasco's is the size of a church and embellished with blessed earth from the pitches of Benfica, Porto and Sporting in the home country. At the national shrine of Our Lady of Aparecida the room of miracles overflows with sporting memorabilia and football shirts alongside the waxwork organs that plead for health and recovery.

Evangelical Protestantism's main advance has been with players. For many Brazilian players the trajectory of their career sees them and their families catapulted from a grim anonymous poverty to unprecedented wealth and public exposure. The psychic, emotional and practical challenges of the shift have left a trail of family breakdowns, drug addiction, emotional instability and financial calamity in its wake. 'Athletes for Christ' was founded in the early 1980s by 'God's goalkeeper', João Leite. The organization has found the squads of the national championship a rich recruiting field. In the late 1990s it had 7,000 members including six of the 1994 World Cup Squad.

By the same token, Brazilian football continues, along with its monks, to have its hedonists, playboys and bon viveurs of the highest order. Romário, star of the 1994 World Cup, has been perhaps the most visible example of this. Alongside being one of the craftiest goal poachers in Brazilian football, Romário is one of its biggest party boys. A regular in Rio's clubs, he then went one better and bought and ran his own.

Hedonists and monks, Catholics and Protestants, black, white, Indian, mestizo – Brazil continued to produce an amazing roster of talent. In 1998 Mário Zagallo took the Brazilian national team to the World Cup in France as holders and favourites. His squad included old hands like Dunga, Leonardo and Bebeto from 1994 but he also had new stars at his disposal, including Rivaldo, Ronaldo and Roberto Carlos. Their progress to the final was not unexpected, though a first-round defeat by Norway and penalties needed against Holland made them look less than imperious. Brazil went on to lose the final, but it was the manner of the loss that mattered.

Brazil's defence was laughable, conceding two goals in the first half, both scored by Zidane with his head, in both cases completely unmarked. But defence was not Brazil's calling card. The ignominy of defeat was multiplied by the absence of attack. The day had been rife with rumour as news leaked out of the Brazilian camp that Ronaldo was ill. His name was removed from the team sheet only to reappear just before the game began. Utterly anonymous, he played in a catatonic trance, detached from proceedings.

IV

In 1989 Carlos Menem, the candidate of the Peronista Party, was elected Argentina's President. The suavely coiffured and handsomely sideburned Menem charmed and bullied his way to power and transformed himself from a star of the left wing of Peronism into an acolyte of the IMF. His government massively concentrated power within the Argentine executive, emasculating the Supreme Court and corralling a supine Peronista Congress. Menem cleared the historical decks by granting an amnesty to almost everyone involved in *el processo*, practically and symbolically sweeping everything under the carpet while purging the last diehards in the military. He then executed a classic divide-and-rule manoeuvre among the trade unions and broke their power in the labour market, and began a programme of liberalizing the Argentine economy, opening the country to foreign investment and foreign trade. The

Peronist welfare state and labour laws were dismantled and the government's international creditors kept at bay using the proceeds of a deeply corrupt privatization of Argentina's main state industries. In 1991 the perennial problems of hyperinflation seemed cured by pegging the peso to the dollar and Menem's ego and desire for power were sated by constitutional manipulations that allowed him to run for and win a second term in 1995. For five years Argentina boomed and Menem's popularity soared.

Argentinian football boomed too. The dismantling of trade barriers and the surging value of a dollar-linked peso saw a massive rise in personal consumption for those in work or with significant capital assets – and along with the clothes and the cars, Argentina consumed football. The take-up of cable television in Argentina was massively in advance of many richer and more technologically advanced nations and that was driven by football. In 1997 the ten most-watched television programmes in Argentina were football matches. Argentinian football raked in the money from television, but also from sponsorship deals inflated in value by the nation's vast spending spree of the mid-1990s. The relentless whirl of the game was given new impetus when the national championship was split into two: the Apertura and Clausura, two twenty-team, nineteen-game leagues. Twice the relegation battles, twice the championship struggles, for the price of one. Within a game or two of the start of such a short league the new media industries could conjure instant and high-level speculation, dissent and pressure from thin air. With nearly three-quarters of the league based in the greater Buenos Aires area, every weekend brought not one but two, three, perhaps more, derbies or as they were now graded *clásicos* and *superclásicos*. Argentina bubbled to the fizzing torrent of games and gossip and success. The national team won the Copa América held in Ecuador in 1993 and between 1994 and 2001 Argentinian clubs won four Copa Libertadores – Vélez Sarsfield in 1994, River Plate in 1996, and Boca Juniors in 2000 and 2001, as well as a hatful of the miscellany of other Latin American copas, recopas and supercopas. A quarter-final defeat by the Dutch in the 1998 World Cup was progress after the 1994 debacle, the pill sugared by the pleasure of knocking out England on penalties and playing a superb match of precision, control and elegance against Holland.

Argentina had of course experienced football and economic booms before, but this one was different. It is instructive to compare the football boom of Menem's era with that of the late 1940s and early 1950s – the era of Perón. In the 1940s Argentine football, like its economy, grew under the aegis of an engaged developmentalist state. In the 1990s Argentina's football boom grew under the aegis of private television companies and liberalized global and domestic markets. Menem may have liked his box at River Plate and the photos of him playing in the national shirt with the national team, but there were no government subsidies for new stadiums and no control over player migrations. Indeed, as his presidency continued, it was increasingly thought that Menem's presence at a game or a visit to a team was a sign of bad luck. Perón's boom occurred under conditions of industrialization, urbanization and trade-union mobilization. The new Argentine working class, emboldened by these reforms and the football culture it sustained, was thrust into the cultural limelight. The game provided a central strand of an emergent national identity and nationalist project in which immigrant and working-class Argentina was not marginalized but celebrated. By contrast, Menem's boom occurred under conditions of deindustrialization. Indeed, so effective was the combination of open trade policies and currency overvaluation that most of the country's indigenous medium- and small-size industrial concerns were liquidated. The working classes, fragmented by the destruction of the trade unions, and widespread unemployment, now formed a less homogenous component of crowds that were increasingly cross-class and at the margins feminized.

There was a shift at the top as well. The football clubs of Peronism had been run by *Los Padrinos* – senior politicians and state bureaucrats whose position and influence were dependent on political power and access to the state. After the fall of Peronism, power in football clubs most often lay with middle-ranking businessmen. In the 1990s, as the Argentine state was ransacked and dismantled, power in society and football migrated to the increasingly concentrated forces of big business. Thus while Boca Juniors had been controlled by politicians in the 1940s and the glorified car salesman Armando in the 1960s and 1970s, in 1995 the presidency of the club was won and retained by Mauricio Macri, a civil engineer who also happened to be the oldest son of the family that controlled Argentina's biggest construction and infrastructure firms. The Macris were one of the few families to do well out of Menem's economic policies, as the family company swept up cut-price deals from privatization and won among other contracts the newly privatized motorway toll systems. With this kind of economic muscle behind him and using his American business education, Macri has gone further than any other president in turning his club into a local and a global brand – a strategy that has seen Boca concentrate on winning Libertadores and Intercontinental titles rather than the domestic league.

For supporters the meanings of the game and the identities it nurtures have also changed. Explicit political affiliations among Argentinian fans, like those of Racing and Boca Juniors with Peronism in the 1940s, evaporated. The only remnants of such explicit political leanings among fans was the lingering far-right anti-Semitism at Chacarita Juniors and a strain of romantic revolutionary Marxism in Rosario where Ernesto 'Che' Guevara had once been counted among *Las Hinchas* of Rosario Central. While under Perón football had served to integrate urban *barrios* and the wider nation, football in the 1990s deepened local, neighbourhood and tribal affiliations to clubs. It did so at the price of exacerbating the opposition and hostility between cities and neighbour-hoods in an Argentina that was increasingly divided and in which, for most, trust and loyalties accrued to an ever-diminishing circle of people and institutions. Post-industrial Argentina had thus acquired post-modern football. The once homogenous crowd has been fragmented by class, consumption patterns and belief systems. For older, middle-class men football became a refuge of nostalgia and *jouissance* in a world turned upside down. For some new fans football was just one of the innumerable, ephemeral trinkets of status-marking consumption.

What then remains of the working-class component of the crowd, both the organized *barras bravas* of the 1980s and the crowd around them in the cheap seats? They too have been transformed by Argentina's economic boom and bust, but they have not been passive recipients of historical forces. To paraphrase E. P. Thompson, historian of the English working classes, the Argentinian *barras bravas* 'did not, like the sun, arise at an appointed time, they were present at their own making'.[12] Argentina's post-industrial poor have elevated football support to a level of unprecedented intensity and drama.

What distinguishes and sustains the post-modern *barras bravas* is *aguante*. Crudely translated as 'strength' this has a complex of meanings. *Aguante* is the sheer bodily resistance of the fan who, like the very poor, has nothing to offer but his body. *Aguante* is endurance, to maintain one's support through long lean years of defeat and calamity. *Aguante* is the capacity for collective resistance, a strength that is only fully realized in common with others. Such support and such loyalty in Menem's Argentina was at a premium. Players and managers, whose income and lifestyle now placed them in a different world from the fans, came to be seen as fickle mercenaries whose relationship with the club was contractual and transitory. Directors and officials were venal, corrupt or both and clearly inadequate custodians of club identity. Only the fans were faithful to the colours – an association so profoundly powerful that even Coca-Cola's branding department had to bow before it. When Coke were Boca's sponsors, their advertising at the stadium appeared uniquely in blue and yellow rather than their own (and River Plate's) red and white. This self-perception was swirled with the militant obligations of Latin machismo, mixed with the bravado of alcohol and confused by the starry-eyed misconceptions of strong weed. Thus, when Argentina's *barras bravas* understand themselves as *La Doce* – 'the twelfth man' – they are not operating at the level of metaphor alone.

The semi-clandestine structures of the *barras bravas* groups were inherited from the era of military dictatorship. It is these groups that occupy the core space of the terrace and provide the music and the backbone of the singing: for example, *La Guarda Imperial* at Racing, *La Doce* at Boca, *Los Borrachos del Tablón* – 'the drunkards of the terraces' – at River. Nearly all of these groups overlap with criminal organizations. Drug dealing, extortion and smuggling are among their most popular extra-curricular activities, helping to fund the endless round of away-game journeys. When these methods will not suffice, tickets, money, transport, accommodation and legal cover have all been arranged by club boards, individual directors and even players for their fans.

However, the kind of benign disorder and carnivalesque chaos practised by these fans has been consistently overshadowed by the other side of disorder: violence. In 1986 there were 46 officially recorded instances of violence at football matches, which resulted in 81 injuries and 451 arrests. By 1990 those figures had grown around fivefold to 258 incidents, 413 injuries and 2,255 arrests.[13] With a small but shocking death toll of crushes, stabbings and beatings clicking steadily upwards a government commission was appointed in 1991 to propose a serious solution to the problem. The committee recommended the installation

and extensive use of CCTV in football stadiums to identify and prosecute violent offenders. They also insisted upon a regime of regular
stadium inspection and improvements in safety, security and hygiene.
Money for updating facilities and paying for surveillance would come
from a mix of PRODE (the football pools) and the clubs themselves.
The clubs would also be required to take further measures to prevent
pitch invasions and to take control of ticketing; this was a coded reference to the relationship between clubs and their *barras bravas*. The level
of violence reached a peak in 1992 with 502 incidents, 660 injuries,
6,036 arrests and 12 deaths. The following year saw a sharp decline in
incidents and injuries but not because the clubs had invested more in
security, stewarding or cameras, but because the increasingly active
police had arrested a record 10,702 people in a season.

Forms of violence multiplied. Rival fans fought each other in the
streets and in stadiums, spontaneously and at prearranged venues. In
the case of Boca and River, their fans clashed across the entire country,
not merely in Buenos Aires. They fought the police in all these locations
but they also began to target managers and players at press conferences,
training grounds and in their team coaches going to and from games.
Daniel Passarella, when coach at River Plate in the early 1990s, was
involved in a particularly nasty fight with a fan who had been pestering
him for money. San Lorenzo saw an unpleasant internecine fight between
the old and less militant group *La Gloriosa* and the Young Turks of *La
Butellier*. The failure of the clubs to implement their side of the bargain
in dealing with violence was in part, as always, a question of money and
incompetence, but the continuing dependence of key factions of club
boards on the *barras bravas* for political support considerably dimmed
their enthusiasm for reform. They were, in any case, hardly role models
themselves. In November 1993 the directors of Racing taunted the home
fans at Vélez Sarsfield when Racing went a goal ahead. Someone in the
Vélez crowd nearby chucked a chair through the front window of the
executive box whereupon Racing replied with gunfire. The sound of
shots had not been uncommon inside and outside football stadiums for
the previous decade and a half. Police corruption and complicity with
both the gangs and club directors kept the progress of innumerable
anti-violence campaigns to a minimum. Despite the general economic
boom of the early 1990s the state of Argentina's stadiums did not
improve. Under Menem there was neither state nor private investment

in public architecture. With the exception of El Monumental and La Bombonera the stands were crumbling. On the open-plan terracing of the 1950s and 1960s a crude and ugly architecture of control was installed piecemeal.

In the aftermath of a Boca–River game in 1994 two River fans were shot on the street by Boca fans careering through the neighbourhood on a flatbed truck. José Barritta – aka *el abuelo* (the grandfather) – the leader of Boca's *La Doce*, was eventually convicted and imprisoned in 1997 but on charges of extortion and racketeering, having been cleared of the murder charge. *La Doce*'s bank account was found to contain over $3 million. The level of violence reached such a point in 1998 that Buenos Aires judge Victor Perrotta ordered the first ever judicial suspension of Argentinian football in a ban that extended to every level of the game for over a month. The judge insisted that the key conditions for restarting the league would be the installation of CCTV, banning fireworks and flags, the compilation of lists of known violent offenders by the clubs and their exclusion from football stadiums. The clubs refused to bear the cost of the first, accepted the second but left the policing of it to the police, and delivered the lists. This proved what everyone had always known: that the directors were in cahoots with their *barras bravas*. Football started up again. Fans attended stadiums with their lawyers claiming their exclusion to be unconstitutional, people continued to come with their flags and the CCTV issue remained unresolved. Violence continued to flare every week and the league was suspended again, this time for three months into spring 1999 while all the same old arguments were reheated.

While the show went on, its financial underpinning was beginning to disintegrate as early as 1996. Menem had dismissed his Finance Minister Domingo Cavallo – the architect of his pegged-peso policy – as an economic recession began to arrive and the union movement revived, holding a general strike in 1996. When the ripples of the Asian financial crisis of 1997–8 reached South America and the Brazilian currency collapsed, Argentina's position looked increasingly threatened. The dollars needed to pay the country's debts became harder and harder to earn. Menem slipped away before the final reckoning of his decade of economic irresponsibility and graft. In early 1999 new President Fernando de la Rúa inherited an unbelievable $118 billion debt and a crisis in the beef and soya industries that had hitherto kept the country's balance-of-payments problem in check. In a premonition of what was to come Racing Club were finally declared bankrupt in March 1999. Racing fans filled the stadium that day and employed their full repertoire of singing, fireworks and flags to an empty pitch. The club was then held in judicial and financial limbo until the private company Blanquiceleste became the first corporate owner of an Argentine club in a deal whereby it ran the club as a concession for ten years while paying off its debts. Racing fans put their faith elsewhere as 100,000 descended on the ground to conduct an exorcism of the seventh and undiscovered black cat buried by Independiente fans at the ground in 1967. However, the team's disastrous run continued until coach Reinaldo Merlo ordered the digging up of a moat that had been concreted over. There lay the seventh black cat. Racing won their first championship for thirty-six years in 2002.

By 2001 the wider economic situation was so bad that three cabinets were appointed and fell in three weeks as the government attempted to pilot incredibly severe and unpopular austerity measures through Congress. In July 2001 a general strike paralysed the country, followed shortly by a footballers' strike that paralysed the league. Players claimed £35 million in unpaid wages. Although a short-term loan from the Argentine FA got the league restarted it was suspended again in December when the government, so desperate to halt the tsunami of capital flight from the country, froze all the nation's bank accounts. Another general strike followed and then came the countrywide rioting in which twenty-five people died and the football league came to a halt. De la Rúa resigned, his successor Saá lingering for a week before handing over to Eduardo Duhalde. The inevitable devaluation of the peso was announced early in the New Year; at a stroke the value of the nation's savings was cut by two-thirds. The banking system was suspended again in April precipitating another wave of demonstrations, riots and protest.

Argentina went to the 2002 World Cup representing a nation that seemed irretrievably fractured and openly desperate for sporting redemption. They opened with a win over Nigeria which the government used as a convenient opportunity to announce that they would be attempting to convert everyone's remaining savings into government bonds of dubious value. It was buried in the financial press while the football nation celebrated. Then it was England. How perfect – another chance to outwit the plodding Anglo-Saxons.

The game turned on a single moment. Michael Owen received the ball on the edge of the penalty area and slipped the ball past Pochettino. The Argentine defender stuck his leg out and then immediately began to retract and Owen, like every great Argentine forward, headed straight for it. England got the penalty, scored and won the game. The papers in Buenos Aires exclaimed in horror, 'They've learnt!'

Argentina went home, the riots continued, and finally in November the country defaulted on its unmanageable foreign loans. The financial situation of Argentinian football in late 2002 was equally pitiful. Racing were the worst off, over $60 million in the red. San Lorenzo weren't far behind and they had already laid their hands on tens of millions of dollars' worth of advance TV and sponsorship revenue. Vice-president of the club Rafael Savino said, 'There's no money coming in at the moment. We have almost 90 lawsuits against us and 30 requests for bankruptcy.'[14] Boca, River and Independiente's debts stood at around $40 million each. The devaluation of the peso meant that debts in US dollars were even more enormous and the value of sponsorship deals and TV rights plummeted alongside the incredible shrinking purchasing power of the domestic market. Independiente were the first among many clubs to announce that there would be no bonuses and no signing-on fees. Belgrano Córdoba put their entire squad up for sale. Even Mauricio Macri was reduced to suggesting that fans pay $2 a shot on a premium-rate phone line to fund the cost of keeping Juan Román Riquelme at Boca. He went to Barcelona anyway. President Duhalde reduced taxes on tickets and asked clubs to pay only for the police inside the stadiums. Clubs abandoned away games and reserve games, the Argentine FA stopped paying and supplying fourth officials. Yet in the previous twenty-five years nearly 5,500 players had been sold by the top Argentine clubs for around $570 million, and most of that money had arrived in the previous five years.

The closing games of the Apertura 2002 saw an unprecedented wave of chaos and violence. Banfield, a small club on the southern periphery of greater Buenos Aires, played River Plate in October. Banfield had not beaten River for twenty-eight years, but ten minutes into the second half it was 5–0 to Banfield. In an attempt to halt the humiliation, River supporters invaded and occupied the pitch. Worse was to come the following week as River were beaten 2–1 by Boca at home. Normal practice would have been for the Boca followers to leave first and disperse before River fans could catch them. But *La Doce* refused to leave and River fans were forced to endure their celebrations in what was now heavy rain. The bulk of River's *Los Borrachos del Tablón* then started trying to leave the stadium, pushing past police gates and checkpoints. The police response was a particularly heavy use of tear gas, rubber bullets and baton charges. The tear gas, usually reserved for the open terraces, was let loose through all the corridors, offices and rooms of the stadium. The bathrooms overflowed with hundreds of supporters cleaning their eyes and vomiting. Some fans began fighting the police in the streets, and one group stormed the press conference that was underway, physically attacking River coach Manuel Pellegrini. Meanwhile in the dressing rooms River Plate's doctor was removing a rubber bullet from a fan's eye. A thousand miles away in Mendoza the club's provincial fans rioted in the streets.

On the last day of the Apertura Independiente went to San Lorenzo needing a win to take the title and found themselves 3–0 ahead. San Lorenzo fans ripped open a corner of the fencing and attempted to invade the pitch and prevent any championship celebrations. They were only stopped from doing so by the police deploying a battery of high-powered water hoses during the game.

The election of President Néstor Kirchner in May brought some semblance of financial and political stability to the country and the new government appointed the latest commission and commissioner to deal with issues of violence in Argentine football. But perhaps this was an appointment with a difference? In the early 1990s Javier Castrilli, nicknamed *El Sheriff*, was Argentina's most unbending referee, one of the few who had been considered unbuyable and who was prepared to flout the conventional, for example, by sending off players in derby games. But Castrilli had his work cut out as the 2004 and 2005 seasons were peppered with violent encounters. The goalkeeper of Talleres Córdoba revealed in a hastily retracted statement that he and his club were still paying the *barras bravas* protection money. When the 2004 Paralympics team slugged it out in a televised brawl with Brazil, it was clear that the resort to violence was ingrained in Argentine football.

And the old gods? Maradona had returned to Argentine football in 1995, first as a coach with lowly Deportivo Mandiyú where he took just four points from twelve games. Then he moved on to Racing in late 1995, and won the hearts of the Racing crowd by presiding over the team's first away win at Boca in twenty years; but twelve points from twelve games and a sending off for dousing a linesman with water saw his managerial career abruptly ended. As his appetite for training declined, Maradona played out a desultory season or two at Boca after his FIFA ban ended and then failed another dope test in 1997. This time he really did retire. Jorge Valdano remarked: 'Poor old Diego. For so many years we have told him repeatedly, "You're a god", . . . that we forgot to tell him the most important thing: "You're a man".'[15] Now he was reminded, as he succumbed to a heart attack and retreated to a cocaine-addiction clinic in Cuba at the suggestion of his friend Fidel Castro.

He remained in Cuba through 2001 and then returned to Buenos Aires early the following year. Within weeks his neighbours were campaigning for his eviction and were saved the trouble when the house was set alight. The fire engines could not get close enough to the house because of Maradona's giant lorry parked outside with a flat battery. He recuperated in Cuba, hid on the beach in Mexico, turned up for ad shoots and failed to show for TV interviews. He was refused access to Japan for the World Cup because of his drug convictions until President Duhalde intervened. Then when Argentina were knocked out he went to Panama. He had a Chilean wine named after him and a Rosario-based church established in his name. Italian courts chased him for unpaid taxes and Argentine courts for unpaid child support. His long-suffering wife began divorce proceedings. And all the time – you could see it when he appeared in his box at Boca Juniors – Maradona was getting fatter and more unhealthy; Coca-Cola was as much the problem as coca. In early 2004 he was rushed to hospital with lung and heart problems and another cocaine overdose; thousands gathered, laid tributes, erected flags, sang songs and in his own words 'called me back to life'. Argentina would not let the old god die, for there is no one and nothing that can replace him.

The deathly whirlwind of the market was unleashed not just across Argentina and Brazil but across all Latin American societies in the 1990s. As a consequence the continent was locked into its traditional subordinate position in the global economic division of labour, and domestic inequalities were sharpened. The same was true of its football economies, which exported their best talent abroad to the detriment of their domestic leagues. Foreign earnings from player sales and the size of their domestic markets kept Brazilian and Argentinian football afloat. For the smaller states of South America there was no such cushion. The precarious financial condition of the game in Bolivia, Chile, Paraguay, Peru and Uruguay through the 1990s tipped into crisis after the Argentine default of 2001. Colombian football, when severed from its coca-money addiction, was in an equally parlous state and continued to labour under conditions of near civil war. The long-standing minnows of South American football, Ecuador and Venezuela, were hardly awash with money either, but remained healthy enough to register relative improvement as the economies of the states to their south declined. Ecuador made their first World Cup finals in 2002, and qualified again in 2006, and Venezuelan football, although unable to displace the dominant position of baseball, did at least begin to win some games in World Cup qualifiers and the early rounds of the Copa Libertadores.

In Chile the 1990s had begun on a wave of optimism. Pinochet gave way to the elected President Aylwyn, the terror was over and Colo Colo of Santiago won the country's first and only Copa Libertadores in 1991, beating Nacional of Montevideo and Boca Juniors on the way. Chile's economy was the success story of South America, but as the country's great central defender of the 1970s Elias Figueroa put it: 'Our football has not kept up with the development of our society ... Normally football is a reflection of the state of the country but that is not happening in Chile. Our clubs are badly run. There may be some corruption but incompetence is much more important. There's no responsibility.'[16] Responsibility and accountability were indeed in short supply. Chile's economy grew but its transition to democracy was halting and partial; Pinochet remained commander-in-chief, the human-rights commission that catalogued the abuses of the military regime was muted, the nation still spoke to itself in whispers and there would be no more football triumphs. In 1998 Chile appeared at their first World Cup since 1982. Their strike force of Zamorano and Salas was good enough to bear comparison with the rest of Latin America. But in the end the Chileans were only good enough to manage three draws and a capitulation to Brazil in the second round. These are not the materials from which powerful social myths of a nation reborn can be manufactured.

Football remained by far Chile's most popular sport, but its most intense social meanings were strictly local, especially in the *barrios* of Santiago where the economy's growth had yet to arrive. Here Universidad de Chile's *Los de Bajo* and Colo Colo's *Garra Blanca* fused intense football and local territorial allegiances. In a clear and sometimes conscious parallel of football in Buenos Aires, an escalating pattern of organized stadium violence, crude policing and irresponsible club management, the 1990s culminated with the death of Ricardo Pitcon, a Colo Colo fan killed after the city derby with Universidad de Chile. The following season Universidad had already won the league in their penultimate game. Their final game – a victory parade – was against Colo Colo, who had other plans. Universidad lost 3–0 which was taken as the cue for a riot so widespread among the crowd that over 1,000 arrests were made. When Colo Colo reclaimed the national title in 2002, the *Garra Blanca* – on gigantic quantities of red wine and potent marijuana – treated central Santiago to a full-scale city-centre riot. There was more of the same in 2003. In Universidad de Chile's match at home to Huachipato, fans hurled stones on to the field in protest at their team's performance. Eleven police officers were hospitalized, most in the wave of looting that followed the game. The following week Universidad played Colo Colo away. The match started fifteen minutes late after dozens of fans climbed the fencing surrounding the pitch. Late in the first half Universidad de Chile defender Nelson Pinto was about to take a throw-in when he was struck in the face by a missile from the crowd and sustained a cut on his left cheek and upper lip. The referee immediately called off the match. Universidad de Chile's team and coaching staff left the field under a hail of missiles and in the following fights 168 fans were arrested.

Attendances collapsed in Chile. League games in the provinces regularly had less than a thousand paying spectators. Even the Santiago derbies were only half-filling the stands. In January 2002 Colo Colo were declared bankrupt with debts of £21 million, a huge backlog of unpaid wages and a trail of lawsuits from frustrated creditors. Peter Dragicevic, their president, was accused of defrauding the taxman. The start of the season was delayed as players struck for some of their wages and the clubs responded by trying to sack those they couldn't or wouldn't pay. CONMEBOL subbed the Chilean FA £160,000 to pay a few weeks' wages and get the league started. Colo Colo's attempt to sack their own squad was stopped in the courts, but being on the payroll at the club was a metaphorical experience only. Players resorted to organizing friendlies among themselves in an effort to make ends meet and were rewarded by big turnouts.

The same story of rising violence, declining crowds, economic implosion and labour disputes characterized football in Paraguay, Peru and Bolivia. By 2002 and 2003 clubs were declaring unsustainable levels of debt, from Cerro Porteño in Asunción, to Universitario in Lima, to Bolivar and Oriente Petrolero in La Paz. The coffers were bare and the lines of credit were gone. Players' strikes over wages and referees' strikes over personal security delayed and interrupted seasons in Uruguay, Bolivia and Peru.

The murder of Andrés Escobar in 1994 had shocked the football world, but it was a drop in the ocean, a single figure in Colombia's epidemic of homicides. In the 1990s the murder rate was running at ten times US levels. In Medellín alone the body count stood at over eighty a week. Arturo Bustamante, a member of the Colombian FA executive, was shot in Caldas. The president of Deportivo Independiente Medellín, Pablo Correra, and the president of Deportivo Pereira, Javier Alonso, were gunned down. The drug baron Pablo Escobar was himself shot dead in 1993 attempting to evade arrest. Escobar's death appeared to herald a defeat for the power of the narco-traffickers in Colombian politics and football. Juan José Bellini, previously president of América de Cali and the Colombian Football Federation, was jailed on extensive drug and money-laundering charges in 1997. Deportivo Cali's national title in 1996 was hailed as part of the same change, for the second team in Cali had been considered relatively free of drug connections. Given that América de Cali was the first team, this was not a difficult trick. But with a Federal President, Ernesto Samper Pizano, whose 1995 election campaign was partly funded with narco-money, Colombian society, football included, clearly remained closely enmeshed with the drug industry. Anthony de Avila dedicated his winning goal for Colombia against Ecuador in 1997 to the then-jailed Rodríguez Orejula brothers who had been behind both América de Cali and the Cali cartel. More defeats in the finals of the Copa Libertadores followed for Colombian teams: in 1995 Atlético Nacional lost to Brazil's Grêmio, in 1996 América de Cali lost again, this time to River Plate, and in 1999 Deportivo Cali blew it against Palmeiras. The national team, still orchestrated by a now elderly Valderrama, squeaked into the 1998 World Cup, and departed after only just managing to beat Tunisia. As one observer put it, 'Valderrama was a parody of himself and not just for his yellow fright wig. No one made more passes in a career but most of them were so short that they only loaned you the ball.'[17]

The generation of players at the 1994 and 1998 World Cups began to dissipate. Valderrama played out his last, languid days for the financially decrepit Tampa Bay Mutiny and Miami Fusion in the MLS. His home-town club Unión Magdalena celebrated the end of his career by erecting a 7-tonne, 12-metre-high statue of the man, cast in bronze. The club and statue then passed into the hands of the government's anti-narcotic agency as their owner Eduardo Dávila had been convicted finally of drug trafficking and his assets including the club were taken over by the state. The increasingly erratic René Higuita made his final return at Atlético Junior Barranquilla where he was sacked for not turning up for training, before making his final, final return to Colombian football in 2002 by playing two games for the tiny provincial side Deportivo Pereira before he inevitably failed a drugs test for cocaine. Tino Asprilla, whose form and career had been in free fall for some time, returned to Atlético Nacional and celebrated by getting sent off in his first game. Andrés Estrada survived a mistaken kidnapping in 2000. Only Freddy Rincon, ending his days away from Colombia labouring in the midfields of Corinthians and Santos in Brazil, continued to play to his full potential.

Under President Andrés Pastrana Colombia's civil war had become yet more complex. A four-way struggle was now being conducted be-tween drug traffickers, the FARC guerrilla movement, right-wing death squads that merged with property owners' vigilante groups, and the Colombian military bristling with US advisers and hi-tech weaponry. However the traffickers themselves had multiplied; breaking the main Cali and Medellín cartels was like smashing a ball of mercury, since the drug trade reconstituted itself in hundreds of smaller, leaner operations no less deadly but harder than ever to police and decapitate. It was in this context that Colombia was due to host the Copa América in July 2001. The country's fragile peace process was sorely tested by a spate of bombings in Cali, Medellín and Bogotá – all host cities for the tournament – in which twelve people were killed and hundreds were injured. A number of Colombian footballers were hit by a car bomb in Cali. CONMEBOL repeatedly confirmed Colombia as hosts and

President Pastrana orchestrated a massive troop deployment across the country. Then, in late June, two weeks before the tournament was due to start, Hernán Campuzano, vice-president of the Colombian Football Federation, was kidnapped by FARC guerillas. CONMEBOL panicked and announced that the event would be cancelled, that it would be rescheduled, that Colombia would still be the host, that an alternative host would be chosen at a meeting in Buenos Aires four days later. Campuzano was promptly released and headed straight from captivity to Buenos Aires to argue Colombia's case. Pastrana was on television declaring the Copa a vital national interest, the TV companies were getting ready to go to court and CONMEBOL flipped once again, reconfirming Colombia as hosts for 2001. The Argentinians and Canadians decided that they didn't fancy it at any price. Both pulled out and were replaced by Costa Rica and Honduras.

The tournament was a huge success: the ceasefire was kept; crowds were large, even for games without the hosts; the football was open and attacking; Honduras beat Brazil and provided a giant-killing story; and Colombia won their first Copa América, beating Mexico before 47,000 delirious fans. But as with Chile the materials for the construction of national unity were too meagre to provide anything more than a mere suspension of hostilities. Pastrana lost power to the even more militarized and conservative government of Álvaro Uribe, Colombia failed to qualify for the 2002 World Cup and the killing just went on. In 2002 the Atlético Nacional versus Independiente Medellín game saw police and fans shot after a 1–1 draw. Aldemar Sánchez, a retired player from Deportivo Cali, was shot soon afterwards, and very public death threats were made to Héctor Hurtado of Atlético Nacional and Millonarios' Venezuelan keeper Rafael Dudamel. Millonarios, the aristocrats of the league, fell into a terrible decline, severed from the drug money of Gonzalo Rodrigues Gacha. They went bankrupt and lived constantly under the threat of relegation. In the small towns it was even worse: players at Atlético Huila publicly complained of not having enough money for food or even transport to the training ground.

VI

Brazil lost, but Cardoso still won. Ignominious defeat in Paris was followed by the re-election of the President. His second term in the post was characterized by economic stringency and political torpor. What reforming energies the government had possessed were now exhausted by the task of steering the economy through devaluation and the Argentine default. Thus began the long post-mortem on the 1998 World Cup Final. It was generally agreed that Ronaldo had had some kind of fit on the afternoon of the game. He was rushed to a clinic for tests and left off the team sheet by Zagallo. He was passed fit by the medical staff and Zagallo put him back on the team sheet. Within weeks of the game one enterprising Rio lawyer began a legal action in the state courts to explore the events. The team's doctors were cross-examined by the Rio Medical Council's ethics committee and absolved of blame. Suspicion fell on Nike who had perhaps insisted on Ronaldo's involvement; a claim that acquired more bite when the CBF–Nike contract was leaked to the press in early 1999. The contract revealed that Nike did have a measure of control over how many friendlies the team would play, where they would play and who was on the field. In Brasília a communist congressman Aldo Rebelo filed a petition with the Congress calling for an official investigation into the CBF–Nike contract. It joined the queue and for over a year nothing happened.

Nothing happened to the petition, but in surreal contrast to the torpor of the political and judicial process, Brazilian football whirled at an evermore hysterical rate. Flamengo, the country's most popular club, whirled faster than most. The speed of rotation substantially increased when the Swiss sports marketing firm ISL invested $13 million in the club with no discernible improvement in training facilities, stadiums, playing staff or success rate. Indeed Flamengo found themselves perennial relegation candidates rather than champions and in the process chewed every dollar up until ISL itself went bust in early 2002. Despite such a massive injection of cash, in Brazilian terms, Flamengo's Gávea stadium was infested with cockroaches, the pitch was covered in cat shit and the club's debt grew and grew.

Flamengo was not alone in its profligacy with other people's money. The American investment trust Hicks, Muse, Tate and Furst had invested and lost similar sums in Corinthians and Cruzeiro before they walked away. Palmeiras' association with the Italian dairy conglomerate Parmalat collapsed when the latter became insolvent. Vasco da Gama hoovered up cash from the Bank of America who departed with their fingers well and truly burnt. Matters at Flamengo reached a low point in 2004 when the club found itself with two warring boards of directors. President Márcio Braga had set up a new board to run the professional football club as distinct from Flamengo's multi-sports operations. However, the directors of the non-football board were not prepared to leave football matters alone as both sides continued to issue directives to staff and sign players.

Flamengo have not only managed to have two boards of directors; at one point in 2001 they had seven first-team coaches on their payroll, having sacked six in the previous year: Carlos Alberto Torres, Carlinhos, Joel Santana, Mário Zagallo, João Carlos and Lula Pereira. Pereira's replacement was Evaristo de Macedo, who had only just been paid out from his previous stint at the club which had ended with his sacking in 1999. This phenomenon, the most emblematic of the administrative chaos and volatility of Brazilian football, is the 'Dance of the Coaches', the seemingly endless sacking and hiring of a small coterie of insiders and preferred candidates who, irrespective it seems of their performance or track record, whirl through the revolving doors of the elite clubs in the national championship. There are, for a certain privileged class of Brazilians, still no consequences for failure, and no meritocracy of preferment; for example, between 2001 and 2004 Joel Santana coached and failed at Flamengo, Vitória, Fluminense, Guarani and Internacional. When Vasco fired Geninho, in he came, saying, 'This is not the first or the last time that I'm going to work here. Vasco have always taken me in.'[18] In 2004 there were, among the twenty-four teams in the top division, an astounding forty-two coaching changes. Guarani got through five, two of whom did not last more than a week. Atlético Mineiro, Grêmio and Flamengo chewed over four coaches, and only four teams actually kept the same coach for the whole season.

The instability of personnel in Brazilian football was matched by the instability of the rules. Once again a season would culminate with *una virada de measa*; literally, a turning of the tables, a sudden reversal of the rules to the benefit of the powerful and the detriment of the weak. In 1999 two big clubs – Botafogo and Internacional – were relegated from the national championship. In a post-season coup the CBF announced that both teams would be awarded extra points for their games against São Paulo who had fielded the ineligible Sandro Hiroshi. Hiroshi had played twelve games for São Paulo, but curiously only Botafogo and Internacional would receive compensation and São Paulo were spared the usual punishment of losing five points for playing ineligible players. The net result of these mathematical tropes was that Botafogo and Internacional would stay up and Gama – a small provincial team – would be relegated instead. Gama fans and their congressman José Arunda took the CBF to court. The court ruled that Gama should stay up and Botafogo should go down. The response of the CBF was to abolish its own national championship and hand the organization of the league to the Group of 13 – the cartel of twenty big clubs – whose authority would not be affected by the court's ruling. The clubs duly created the most monstrous and complex competition yet devised in Brazil: the João Havelange Cup had four divisions, 116 teams and no Gama. The CBF also mobilized support at FIFA who banned Gama from all FIFA-affiliated competitions until the lawsuits against the CBF were dropped; except of course that CBF had failed to inform FIFA that the club itself had not issued any lawsuits. In any case, Gama went back to the Brazilian courts to argue that their exclusion from the João Havelange Cup was illegal; the court again ruled in their favour, forcing their inclusion in the bloated new tournament. Even by Brazilian standards it was a mockery. The schedule was so chaotic that some teams went without a game for a month while others played four in a week. One-third of games were rescheduled, home and away games were distributed unfairly and, of course, Fluminense were allowed to sneak out of the third division and back into the first. The final of the knock-out stage was perfectly cast with the villainous Vasco da Gama playing the previously unheard of São Caetano, a second-division team that had crept into the play-offs. The opening game was a 1–1 draw; the second leg was at Vasco.

---

30 December 2000
Vasco da Gama 0 São Caetano 0
São Januário, Rio de Janeiro

'Nothing serious happened. But something could if the game doesn't continue. I want these fucking ambulances out of here.'

Those fucking ambulances are here because Vasco, having refused São Caetano any tickets, have sold out the whole stadium and then some. It's 0–0, and Romário is substituted 20 minutes into the game. The story has circulated that an argument among spectators at the top of the stand resulted in a cascading crush all the way to the crumpled iron spiked fence on the touchline.

The pitch is awash with hundreds of injured fans, two helicopters, a dozen ambulances, officials, medical staff and police and in the middle of it is Vasco president Eurico Miranda who has already secured the agreement of his guest, the Rio State Civil Defence Secretary, that the game should go on.

Watching on television, the state governor calls the stadium and puts an end to the nonsense. The game will not be played. Eurico leads his team to the small table where the João Havelange trophy is sitting. They take it and perform a lap of honour.

São Caetano agreed to a replay, which Vasco won 3–1. Eurico got his cup and São Caetano somehow managed to end up in the first division when the national championship was reconstituted the following season. But stadium disasters, financial meltdown, scurrilous accounting practices, blatant abuse of power and privilege, violence and corruption – none of these things could shake Brazilian football. That would have required something altogether more serious: an unspeakable possibility, the failure of the national team to qualify for the World Cup in 2002. After the 1998 tournament Zagallo was replaced as coach of the national team by Wanderly Luxemburgo, the sharp-suited, smooth-talking boss at Corinthians. He appeared an excellent choice. His teams played attacking football, he was prepared to take risks, but was not prepared to take nonsense from club directors. His spells at Palmeiras and Corinthians had been successful. His appointment certainly appeared vindicated by Brazil's victory in the 1999 Copa América, but then things began to take a turn for the worse. In the early rounds of qualification for the 2002 World Cup Brazil lost successive games to Paraguay and Chile – previously unheard-of phenomena. Worse, the side Luxemburgo took to the Sydney Olympics went out in the quarter-finals to nine-man Cameroon. Luxemburgo was making plenty of other news as well. His ex-lover Renata Alves had caught the attention of the tax authorities who found her buying an extraordinary amount of property and cars on Luxemburgo's behalf. As the tax investigators got to work, Alves revealed that Luxemburgo had taken his cut from many player transfers while in club management. A week after the side returned from Sydney Luxemburgo was gone. Finally, at the peak of recriminations and accusations in the press, Brazilian politicians acted. Rebelo's CBF–Nike inquiry became a reality and the Senate created an even more far-reaching and powerful committee of inquiry to look into the whole gamut of problems in the nation's game.

The two commissions sat for over a year and reported late in 2001. The Rebelo Commission failed to prove any connection between Nike and the disastrous World Cup Final of 1998. This, despite extensive, sometimes ludicrous cross-examination of Ronaldo, Zagallo, Edmundo and numerous other members of the cast of the Brazilian football telenovella. But Rebelo had along the way uncovered detailed evidence of corruption, nepotism, incompetence and larceny. The hapless president of the Minas Gerais football federation Elmer Guilherme Ferreira was found to have employed twenty-seven relatives at the federation. Copious evidence of players with fake passports and fake birth certificates was uncovered; tax evasion, bad loans, and misinformation came tumbling out of the closet. Yet when it came to the vote, the football faction – a group of ten congressmen on the Rebelo Commission – scuppered it. Led by Eurico Miranda, this motley collection of football club presidents, ex-presidents and directors ensured that though the report was published none of the thirty-three recommendations for criminal prosecution of all the leading figures in Brazilian football administration could be followed up.

The Senate investigation dug even deeper. Ricardo Teixeira was sufficiently scared of facing their questions that he temporarily handed over the presidency of the CBF to his deputy, claiming exemption on the grounds of poor health. The imperious Edmundo dos Santos Silva, president of Flamengo, was subjected to such a grilling that he was reduced to tears. In his conclusion the committee chairman, Senator Álvaro Dias, described the CBF as 'a den of crime revealing disorganiz-ation, anarchy, incompetence and dishonesty'.[19] Seventeen *cartolas* were recommended for criminal prosecution. The CBF desperately attempted to buy influence with senators, offering campaign expenses and taking out full-page newspaper adverts right to the last minute, but amazingly the report was endorsed. Yet to this day not one of those criminal prosecutions has been followed up, not one of the many serious allega-tions of fraud, corruption or embezzlement has gone to court. Brazil's football elite was saved by the timidity of its judiciary and the brilliance of its national team.

Luxemburgo's first replacement as national team coach was Émerson Leão who presided over humiliating defeats by Ecuador and Australia in the Confederations Cup in 2001. His reign was quickly terminated and his replacement Luiz Filipe Scolari installed. Known colloquially as Big Phil, Scolari had been a successful coach at Grêmio and Palmeiras, winning the Libertadores at both. He had pioneered a particularly abras-ive style of play in his teams and in his dealings with the press. His gamesmanship was legendary – he had allegedly encouraged ball boys to disrupt play in closely fought games, but perhaps his greatest asset was a thick skin. Scolari and his squad suffered an unrelenting tirade of criticism, scorn and despair from the Brazilian media through 2001 and early 2002. There was much to despair over. At the Copa América in 2001, the champions were knocked out by Honduras. In the World Cup qualifiers, Brazil followed their defeat to Ecuador with a draw against Peru and a loss to Uruguay – Brazil failing to reach the World Cup was a real possibility and with further defeats by Argentina and Bolivia to come, it was only a final-round victory over Venezuela that saw them through.

For the first time since 1938 Brazil did not arrive at the World Cup as one of the cast-iron favourites. Bookmakers in the UK were offering ludicrously good odds for a team that included Ronaldo, returned from injury, the angry and ballistic Rivaldo and the rising and precocious talents of attacking midfielder Ronaldinho. Brazil offered the very best and a hint of the worst that the nation's football possessed. Against China and Costa Rica they were imperious and free scoring. Against Turkey they showed they could match a tough technical team with both skill and trickery: Rivaldo's dive after being hit on the leg by a ball rather than in the face by a hand was perhaps the most disgraceful and certainly the most blatant act of cheating in the tournament. Belgium were dispatched in the second round though only with Brazil's full dose of tournament luck, but England who held a short lead were dismembered even with Brazil down to ten men after Ronaldinho had been unfairly dismissed. Turkey in the semi-final was a taut and brilliantly close reprise of the first-round game. It was settled by the smallest of margins: a few seconds of exceptional, coiled acceleration over a few metres by Ronaldo. With three Turkish defenders around him, this minuscule burst of pace was enough to open up a narrow space for a low shot.

By contrast the final was easy. Germany, who had played badly but crawled their way to the final, offered plausible resistance and organization but Ronaldo, now in extraordinary form, was not to be denied his and Brazil's moment of redemption. CBF chairman Ricardo Teixeira and the Brazilian football elite breathed a collective sigh of relief. Congressional investigations were over and World Cup number five was coming home. Teixeira's cheek was undiminished, corralling the team to attend a homecoming ceremony in Fortaleza to support his favoured presidential candidate, Ciro Gomes. Lula, his left-wing opponent, had claimed in 1994 that Brazilians knew the difference between sporting fantasy and political reality. Maybe they did now. The trip did Gomes no good. He came last of three candidates in October and Lula, finally, was President of Brazil.

VII

In the early twenty-first century Latin America's fragile and incomplete transition to democracy reached a defining moment; power was being transferred peacefully by electorally defeated governments to victorious oppositions. Many of those oppositions were made up of left-of-centre parties or coalitions of the Left whose initial rise to power had been curtailed by military rule in the 1970s. The socialists were back in the presidential palace in Santiago de Chile, Lula won in Brazil, the Frente Amplio took over in Uruguay and Hugo Chávez was acquainting Venezuela with his radical military populism. Indeed by 2005 President Uribe in Colombia was the only head of state in South America that came unambiguously from the Right. The political complexion of the continent was transformed by the ideological and practical exhaustion of the Latin American Right, their glaring economic and social failures and a weary moderation of the Left. The consolidation of democracy was a central concern for many of these new governments. In Latin America that required two things: first, the creation of a more even playing field in economy and society, and some reduction in the degree of economic, educational and political inequalities between individuals and classes. At current levels, inequality remained so immense that the formal institutions of liberal democracy were consistently undermined. Second, the systematic and endemic levels of violence, corruption and clientelism in all their many forms, which manipulated and distorted social and sporting life, needed to be reduced. Progress on solving both of these problems in the continent's football was an interesting, if of course partial, barometer of those projects.

In 2002 Olimpia of Asunción won their third Copa Libertadores. The Paraguayan national team qualified for both the 1998 and 2002 World Cups and in both cases put on a bravura, fighting performance that took them past the group stage. At its best Paraguayan football was played with a tough, technical simplicity and an unwavering level of solidarity. José Luis Chilavert, Paraguay's bear-like goalkeeper, brought a peculiar resolve to the side, but livened his intensity with a predilection for taking brilliant free kicks and heavy-pressure penalties and his generous and practical philanthropy. Paraguay is still living with the consequences of the War of the Triple Alliance (1864–70), in which a British-supported coalition of Brazil, Uruguay and Argentina destroyed the fledgling autarchic dictatorship of Francisco Solano López. In the process the Triple Alliance killed or injured most of Paraguay's male population and destroyed its independent economic and political aspirations. Defeat condemned Paraguay to landlocked poverty for over a century. Its pitiful level of economic development and infrastructure was such that though they organized the Copa América in 1953 the Paraguayan FA had to stage the tournament in Lima. The 1999 Copa in Paraguay was almost lost to an outbreak of furious political violence and uncertainty following the assassination of the vice-president. From such a point of marginality the Paraguay national team's heroic resistance against overwhelming odds could, unlike Colombia and Argentina, continue to reinforce and remake that notion of nationhood. Paraguay's organization, collective endurance and capacity to resist in the war – the fulcrum of the nation's conception of itself – was powerfully reproduced on the football pitch.

The social meanings of domestic football were, however, somewhat less savoury. Olimpia won their three Libertadores (in 1979, 1990 and 2002) under the thirty-year presidency of Osvaldo Domínguez Dibb, businessman, politician and oligarch. Dibb's power and influence rested on three pillars: his immense wealth, mainly garnered from the contraband tobacco factories of Paraguay's counterfeit capital, Ciudad de l'Este; his ownership of the newspaper *La Nación* and a host of other media institutions; and his early marriage into the family of General Stroessner, Paraguay's dictator from 1954 to 1989. Dibb's influence has long outlasted the General's. He was and remains a central figure in the Colorado Party that ruled under Stroessner and has, just about, continued to rule since the introduction of democracy in Paraguay. His personal control of Olimpia over three decades illustrates the extent to which football remains an essential element of the political portfolio of any aspiring populist politician in Latin America. Olimpia's success, like that of Atlético Nacional in Colombia, suggests that illegal or black monies remain one way in which the smaller nations of Latin America can compete with Argentina and Brazil. But, most tellingly, Olimpia under Dibb points to the fragility and inconsistency of this kind of semi-feudal personalized politics. Dibb's erratic mode of governance included taking out full-page adverts in his newspapers criticizing refereeing decisions. Challenges from the Paraguayan FA were met with counter-suits and counter-attacks, like the lawsuits he took out against the FA accusing them of corruption in the distribution of expenses during the national team's World Cup campaigns.

Olimpia played the Brazilian team São Caetano in the final of the Copa Libertadores in 2002. São Caetano, themselves a pleasing illustration of a more even playing field in Brazilian football, were founded as recently as 1990 in this booming industrial suburb of São Paulo and funded by the local fridge and washing-machine companies. The team won promotion to the second division in 1995 and jumped through one of the loopholes in the insanity of the João Havelange tournament of 2000 to make the national championship final. São Caetano won the first leg at home 1–0, prompting an extraordinary explosion from Dibb mid-week between the two games. He publicly accused his players of late nights, drinking and womanizing, and he announced his resignation. He was of course back in the presidential seat come the second leg. Dibb finally left Olimpia in 2003 and with that the club disintegrated. The money simply disappeared. Argentine coach Nery Pumpido, who had won the Libertadores, left with a huge salary unpaid. Players were so strapped for cash they refused to attend pre-season training and the club came within a whisker of relegation a year after winning the Libertadores.

Olimpia though is not the only small club to have recently triumphed in Latin America. In Argentina in 2004, the Rosario club Newell's Old Boys broke the stranglehold of Buenos Aires teams over the national championship and San Lorenzo, the most decrepit of the grand old clubs, underwent something of a revival winning the inaugural Copa Sudamericana. In Mexico, América, the team most closely aligned to the ruling but declining PRI and its Televisa allies, consistently failed to win the national title, with smaller teams from the provinces like Pachucha, Monarcas Morelia and Toluca taking most of the prizes. In Uruguay, Nacional and Peñarol succumbed to national champions Danubio, whose home ground Jardines del Hipodromo has little grass, no floodlights, turnstiles or roof. The opportunities for smaller clubs, smaller cities and smaller nations in Latin American football is worryingly more a product of levelling down rather than levelling up.

Once Caldas, an obscure team from Manizales in central Colombia, won the Copa Libertadores in 2004 and Cienciano, from Cuzco, a town high in the Peruvian Andes, won the Copa Sudamericana in 2003. Once's strategy was defensive. Get a 0–0 draw away and steal a goal at home as the opponents tired in a stadium 2,150m above sea level. It was a strategy that got them past Santos and São Paulo before a 1–1 draw with Boca Juniors at home in the second leg of the final took the competition to penalties. The Colombians held their nerve and Boca, defeated, ran for the dressing rooms and did not emerge for the awards. Boca's coach Carlos Bianchi explained their discourtesy: 'We didn't know they awarded medals to second place ... because we always won.'[20] The magnitude of Once Caldas' victory was surely equalled by

Cienciano who beat the aristocrats of River Plate in a high-scoring final. Juvenal Silva, the president of Cienciano, summed up his winning formula: 'the club pays everyone's salary and bonuses on time'.[21] The press made much of the fact that the squad were blessed by a Peruvian shaman and that they were also eating a lot of Maca, an indigenous radish-like root that the Incas had eaten before battle and that was currently being marketed as a wholefood Viagra. Magic has been relegated from the playing field to the training field. Dreams have shrunk to the desire for a small regular salary.

In the case of Cienciano and all the clubs of the Andes, those salaries and bonuses were small. In Argentina and Brazil, players' wages, though nothing compared to those of their Europe-based compatriots, were astronomical compared to pretty much everyone else. This deepening and increasingly visible inequality resulted in a wave of football kidnappings, at least twenty publicly reported cases between 2002 and 2005, which were part of a much wider wave of kidnappings of the wealthy all across the continent.[22] Cristián Riquelme, the younger brother of Boca Juniors star Juan Román Riquelme, was abducted in 2002 and released two days later after a ransom of around $100,000 had been paid. The kidnapping of the father of Independiente captain Gabriel Milito followed, as did that of Florenci Macri, the sister of Mauricio Macri, president of Boca Juniors. Six men staged a car accident in broad daylight in central Buenos Aires as cover for snatching the father of River Plate's captain Leonardo Astrada. In Brazil 2004 saw four high-profile football kidnappings, beginning with the mother of Santos star Robinho. She had driven her brand new Mercedes to a barbecue with old friends in a notoriously troublesome district of the city. She was held for forty days. Campinas, a small and wealthy town north-west of São Paulo, became the centre of the crime wave with the kidnapping of the mothers of São Paulo forward Gratife, and Luís Fabiano and Fidélis Rogério of Porto and Sporting Lisbon respectively. So far, all of these high-profile kidnappings have been resolved by paying up rather than bloodshed. Yet lawlessness, turmoil and the spreading ownership of firearms continue in Colombia and Ecuador. The Once Caldas coach Luís Fernando Montoya was shot twice in a fight with two men who were attempting to rob his wife on the doorstep of their home. His wife's mistake was to withdraw too much cash in too much daylight from a bank machine. The coach of the Ecuadorian national team Hernán Darío Gómez left

Dalo Bucarám out of the squad. Bucarám happened to be the son of the former and then fugitive Ecuadorian president Abdalá Bucaram. Gómez was subsequently shot in the leg in the lobby of a Guayaquil hotel, an incident traced back to Joselo Rodríguez, president of the second division side Santa Rita. Rodríguez was a business partner of Bucarám and had another of his sons on Santa Rita's playing books. Gómez resigned and went back to Colombia only to return when thousands of Ecuadorians took to the streets of Quito begging him to come back. The national side under Gómez went on to qualify for their first World Cup ever in 2002. However, their stylish contribution to the competition was eclipsed by Byron Moreno, the Ecuadorian referee who rose to prominence on the back of some of the worst decisions to grace a World Cup. For the enduring tragi-comedy of the relationship between football and politics in contemporary Latin America we need look no further.

In 2003 Moreno took charge of a game between Liga Deportiva Universitario of Quito and Barcelona from Guayaquil. Barcelona were 3–2 up with only added time to come. Moreno had already failed to award Barcelona a couple of certain penalties, awarded another goal and then disallowed it and invented two sendings-off, but he finally made his allegiance crystal clear when he awarded six minutes of injury time and played thirteen. Liga equalized in the 99th minute and won the game in the 101st minute. Moreno was, at the time, running for election to the city council of Quito. He was subsequently banned from football and has retired from refereeing, but not politics.

Of all the political changes in Latin America the most important was the victory, at the fourth time of asking, for Luíz Inácio da Silva; Lula, the São Paulo metal worker, trade union leader, presidential candidate for the Partido dos Trabalhadores (Workers' Party) that he helped found, and finally in late 2004 President of the Brazilian Republic with an unquestionable mandate to remedy the worst inequalities and most grotesque forms of corruption. In the dying days of the Cardoso presidency a temporary football law had been drawn up and passed. Lula immediately ratified the fantastically named Law for the Moralization of Sport, more popularly known as the 'Fans' Statute'. The law constituted an embryonic bill of rights for fans covering matters such as minimum standards in stadium hygiene, safety and facilities, standardized and open ticketing and the advance publication of fixture lists.

Even this kind of mild reform provoked a predictably furious reaction from the entrenched vested interests in Brazilian football. After fighting the law tooth and nail in Congress, Eurico Miranda of Vasco da Gama led a revolt by the leading clubs and their directors, who announced that they would not be participating in the national championships. The government's nerve held and the revolt collapsed within twenty-four hours – a rare victory for the average football fan in Brazil.

Lula, himself a long-standing Corinthians fan, created a cabinet devoted to both social reform and football. The President's social kick-abouts were notoriously well attended and well contested, evidenced by the Minister of Finance Antonio Palocci entering parliament on crutches after a crunching game between the President's team and the Ministry of Fisheries. Lula's football populism though has been of a very different hue to his military predecessors. In contemporary Brazil there remain considerable levels of under under-nourishment, malnourishment and hunger. Ronaldo and other leading players have been used as figureheads in the government's campaign to ensure three meals a day for everyone. In foreign affairs, Brazil took the lead in the creation of a peacekeeping force for Haiti, embroiled in a messy civil war after the ousting of President Baptiste. In a gesture of solidarity, Lula arranged for the *Seleção* to play a friendly in Port-au-Prince. Hundreds of thousands of Haitians lined the streets to see Rivaldo, Ronaldinho and Roberto Carlos in a convoy of white tanks, while 15,000 at least crammed into the stadium to see Haiti lose 6–0, each goal cheered louder than the last.

Some semblance of reason appears to have cooled the administrative lava of the football timetable as unnecessary tournaments have been dropped, fixture congestion has diminished a little and the national championship abandoned play-offs and modules. Now the team with the most points wins and those with the least go down. Such quotidian simplicity is, in this context, modernization. Most tellingly of all, big clubs – Palmeiras and Botafogo – have gone down and stayed down. In the prevailing spirit of pragmatic but successful caution Carlos Alberto Parreira took Brazil's second team to the Copa América in Peru in 2004 and, without being the best team, worked hard and won. There was even space for *futebol moleque* – the cheeky schoolboy football of Diego and Robinho at a revitalized Santos who won their first ever national championship in 2002.

Yet for all of this Lula and the PT have, so far, only scratched the surface of Brazil. Marco Antonio Eberlin, the vice-president of Ponte Preta, spoke with a bluntness that characterizes an entrenched and complacent elite, not one that is about to be displaced or radically curtailed: 'Unfortunately there are no ethics in football at all. It's really a rotten business and I include myself in that.'[23] Ironically, the rotten stink was at its worst at Lula's club. In 2004 Corinthians announced a partnership with the hitherto unknown London-based Media Sports Investment fronted by a hitherto unheard-of young Iranian, Kia Joorabchian. MSI and Corinthians went on a buying spree that included among others the South American Footballer of the Year Carlos Tévez from Boca Juniors, and a recall to Brazil for Carlos Alberto from Porto. Many puzzled over the football strategy at work in this whirl of transfers; a guiding thread was Corinthians' preference for deals with Brazilians overseas or foreigners, neither of which required the oversight or involvement of the Bank of Brazil. In the absence of concrete information about the ownership of MSI, the origins of its capital, and indeed its purposes, rumours mounted that the entire thing was a money-laundering operation based somewhere in the Caucasus.

Corinthians went on to win the 2005 championship after a season of predominantly rough football that saw a massive match-fixing scandal and a mounting number of deaths and serious violent incidents in and around football matches. Brazilian football, however, still had more to offer than the magic of hot money and at its best still aspires to something more than merely winning. The Brazilian team in the qualifying rounds of the 2006 World Cup possessed bountiful attacking and creative resources. Against all known form, Carlos Alberto Parreira, back in the managerial seat, chose to play with four at the front in a shape and style that recalled the World Cup-winning teams of 1958 and 1962 – and he still could not include all of his best forwards. But above all he had Ronaldinho.

8 March 2005
Chelsea 3 Barcelona 2
Stamford Bridge, London

Ronaldinho stands on the edge of the penalty area, Chelsea defender Carvalho is braced directly in front of him. The Brazilian pivots and twists his bent leg above and over the stationary ball, his hips half-samba, half-Charleston. At each turn he forces his opponent to twist his body shape in parallel in the hope of blocking the shot that must surely come. With each swing of Ronaldinho's knees, Carvalho's posture becomes more ludicrous, his defiance more hapless, as the movement of his hips, abdomen and upper and lower legs progressively fly out of sync. Each gyration sees him ignominiously sink to the ground under the weight of his own bodily confusion. As he does so, Ronaldinho impudently stabs the ball with the tip of his toes, punting it into the net. He could have played the percentages and shot first time. He could have tried to bend or chip the ball round the defence, but he chose to entertain us and amaze us and made it look like the right decision. Latin American football is still capable of magic. Whether anyone but the aristocracy of European elite football can afford to stage it is another matter.

19
Accelerated Development: Football and Asia's New Industrial Revolution

The Japanese worked from Meiji in order to catch up with the Western nations. Then they started the whole thing from zero all over again after the Second World War. But what did they work for? . . . It can't just be in order to stare at the bar chart of growing trade surplus and give a satisfied smile? The J-League gave a clear answer to this: we are living to enjoy sport.   **Masayuki Tamaki**

The twenty-first century belongs to Asia and we are sitting on a gold mine that is waiting to be tapped.

Peter Velappan, AFC General Secretary

I

At the 1990 World Cup, Asia was represented by just two teams, the United Arab Emirates and South Korea. Neither gained a single point. Twelve years later, the continent would host the tournament, boast four entrants, and in South Korea a worthy semi-finalist. The gap between Asian football and the rest of the world, so painfully evident in the 1970s and 1980s, had begun to close. In 1990 Asia did not possess a single professional league of sporting note or serious commercial potential. By 2002, professional football was firmly established in Japan and South Korea, and was threatening the previously dominant sport of baseball. China, India, Vietnam, Thailand, Malaysia and Indonesia – between them over two-fifths of the entire world's peoples – had acquired professional national leagues for the first time. In the western half of the continent oil money continued to flow into the clubs and competitions of the Gulf States and football climbed out of the wreckage of war in Lebanon, Palestine and Iraq or from under the thumb of religious censure in Afghanistan and Iran. Football even organized itself in the most remote corners of Asia as Mongolia, Bhutan and Guam joined FIFA. The disintegration of the Soviet Union saw the emergence of five independent Central Asian Republics, all of whom moved into the Asian Football Confederation (AFC). From Gaza to Guangdong, with the sole exception of south Asia, football had become the national game of Asian societies. When the world sits down to watch the World Cup Final more than half the audience is now in Asia.

The AFC itself both reflected and organized the changes sweeping through Asian football. What was once an impoverished and ineffective bureaucracy whose writ barely ran beyond its isolated Malaysian headquarters, had in the 1990s become something closer to the developmental bureaucracies of the Asian economic miracle. Like Japan's industrial catalyst – MITI, the Ministry of International Trade and Industry – the AFC borrowed where appropriate the best models from around the world. For international competitions, UEFA's commercial vision and success was the obvious choice. The AFC renovated and expanded the Asian Cup and made sure it went to China for 2004. Its international club competitions were rationalized and commercialized. The Asian Champions Cup was relaunched with small countries excluded, regional groups in the early stages followed by mini-tournaments in fixed locations to cut down on exorbitantly expensive air travel, all underwritten by new sponsorship and television marketing. Alongside creating a continent-wide logistical and technical infrastructure for the game, the AFC has invested in training and development at a national level. Its Vision Asia programme that encapsulates these efforts comes from the same ideological stable as South Korea's five-year plans: concentrating resources on the most important but underperforming markets (China, India, Vietnam, Indonesia), funding youth development and youth tournaments, and providing training for coaches and administrators in order to catalyse a process of independent local growth.

Control over television and sponsorship money has given AFC the autonomy to pursue this kind of top-down developmentalism, but like all autonomy it has had its limits. On certain issues the AFC has remained in thrall to the continent's national associations and the regional blocs they have formed. Much of the decade was taken up by squabbles over hosting rights for tournaments between the Middle Eastern bloc and the South-east Asians. The longstanding enmities between Japan, China and Korea prevented the development of a similar East Asian group though each was powerful enough to join the fight alone. AFC also had to tend to the potentially inflammatory implications of games between long-standing enemies and recent combatants: Iran vs. Iraq, Iraq vs. Kuwait, Palestine vs. Jordan, and North Korea vs. South Korea. Like many regional Asian organizations AFC has responded to conflict and division by excelling itself in the art of diplomatic blandishment. It is this combination of commercial sporting acumen and faux political naivety that allows AFC's general secretary Peter Velappan to make the easy elision between the growth of Asian football and the broader rise of benign Asian wealth, power and influence. He is not alone in thinking that the twenty-first century will be Asian on the pitch and across the planet. But the relationships between economic and sporting success, between social change and sporting preference, are more complex than this kind of lazy continental boosterism suggests.

The case of African football shows quite different connections. It grew accompanied by only the most fitful and ramshackle industrialization. The game first acquired its central place in African cultural life at the moment of decolonization and independence. The imprimatur of the politics of resistance and liberation can be clearly seen on its subsequent history. Asia's stories are not the same. East Asian economics has left the greatest imprint on football's development, but not all economies are the same. In Japan and South Korea football has arisen at the moment of transition from industrialism to post-industrialism. As Masayuki Tamaki, a key mover in the creation of the J-League eloquently states, football in the 1990s became emblematic of the shifts and changes in the economic and social structures of Japan and South Korea. Having matched or outstripped their Western competitors in the game of industrial production, the developmental elites of these states sought to create new service industries and new consumers to match; professional football leagues and addicted football fans fitted the bill perfectly. In China and South-east Asia the growth of football has accompanied a decade of hyper-industrialization. The unparalleled speed of economic change in the region, with China recording growth rates in excess of 13 per cent in some years, has created a form of capitalism characterized by massive social dislocation. The country has moved to the city and the rural family structures, traditions and religious beliefs that came with East Asia's peasantry have been shredded in the process. Deeply entrenched and systematic forms of corruption have made a core of families phenomenally wealthy and a thin layer of urban middle-class professionals rich; but poverty, inequality and urban squalor are their shadow. In the space left by the decline of traditional religion and communism, an insatiable and corrosive materialism burns. Fuelled by the stream of Western advertising and imagery, materialism has become the dominant culture of modern urban Asia. All these changes have their footballing corollaries: a preference for glamorous foreign clubs and leagues over domestic football; widespread problems of illegal football gambling and match-fixing; and the emergence of the region as the world's supplier of football boots, balls and strips, assembled at the bottom of the global value-chain in hot, cramped sweatshops.

Between the two poles of East and West Asia, South Asian football has grown, especially in India, but cricket remains king. The allure of the world's game has been limited by the rise of a resurgent inward-looking Hindu nationalism, the region's preoccupations with its own disputed borders and India's cautious engagement with the global economy. The deepest tensions and preoccupations of the subcontinent are still best illuminated by the atmosphere of an India vs. Pakistan Test match rather than a World Cup qualifier. West of Islamabad, football although long established has been decisively shaped in recent years by a context of international wars, civil wars and religious upheaval. In Iran the Islamic revolution ran its course and football was allowed to return to the centre of social life where it has become a rallying point for opponents of the conservative elements in the theocracy. Football in Iraq made the transition from doleful servant of a cruel regime to an icon of post-Saddam rebirth. In the Gulf the immense strains that oil-driven development and regional conflicts placed on the old ruling orders made football an evermore important source of legitimation and distraction. Six thousand miles from Tokyo, on the shores of the Mediterranean the Palestinian nation looked to their national team as an instrument of state-building. If in Japan they are now living to enjoy sport, at the other end of this most diverse of continents, they were playing sport in order to live.

In South Korea football, indeed organized sport of any kind, was effectively halted by war – the Pacific War and the Korean War – and then retarded by the material and psychological burdens of reconstruction. The massive presence of the US Army and Navy in South Korea helped solidify the popularity of baseball. Football was consigned to the realm of corporate-sponsored amateurism, schools, universities and benign neglect. Even so South Korea's footballing culture was deep enough to keep football alive. South Korea qualified for the 1954 World Cup, though they only managed to arrive ten hours before their first game against the favourites Hungary. They were beaten 9–0 and did little better against the Turks three days later, but the team are remembered fondly at home for being there when the country was at its lowest ebb. The national team went on to win the early Asian Cup tournaments in 1956 and 1960. Perhaps South Korea's greatest achievement was to produce two footballers good enough to survive in professional European football in the 1980s: Cha Bum-Keun, who played for many seasons in the Bundesliga (1979–88), and Huh Jung-Moo, who played at PSV Eindhoven in the same era. But there were no more trips to the World Cup, no more trophies of any kind. For South Korea there was work and study and grind.

The recent triumphs of South Korean football, like its surging economic progress, rest on the authoritarian, militaristic and nationalist foundations of the long Park Chung-Hee dictatorship (1961–79). Under Park South Korea was transformed from one of the poorest nations on the earth to one on the verge of affluence. The economic agencies of the Korean state and the multi-headed industrial corporations known as *chaebols* channelled funds into key industries, excelled at exporting and kept unions weak and labour costs low. South Korea worked very, very hard and there was little time and little support for professional or elite sports. Under Park's successor Chun Doo-Hwan, South Korea's elite began to look to sport as a way of demonstrating the nation's newly acquired wealth. The country's first Ministry of Sport was only established in 1982 and then as a subsection of the nation's Central Intelligence Agency. It made up for lost time. The Seoul Olympic bid was its first task, successfully achieved. Then baseball was told to go professional and a small professional football league was encouraged. Initially, the Super League was not very super. It combined amateur teams like the Seoul-based Hallelujah, appropriately run by evangelical Christians; semi-professional teams from the Kookmin and Hamil Bank; and three professional clubs with explicit backing from the *chaebols*, Pusan Daewoo, Pohang Steel and Yukong. It was a motley arrangement, with no systematic home and away games, the teams moving round the country like a travelling football circus. But with little hype and less fuss, the South Koreans started qualifying for World Cups again; indeed they qualified for every finals tournament from 1986 to 2006.

The K-League as it became known in 1996 slowly grew, shed its residual amateurism and its odd formats. Crowds were small to begin with but began to rise steeply at the end of the 1990s. The rest of the *chaebols* joined the fray, backing teams like Suwon Samsung Bluewings and Ulsan Hyundai. With this kind of investment Korea's leading clubs have gone on to enjoy considerable success in Asian club competitions. Local governments too have emerged as founders and sponsors of clubs. Hallelujah have long since returned to the amateur level of the game, unable to keep up with the forces of mammon, but they have been ably replaced by the phenomenally successful Seongnam Ilhwa Chunma – the club owned by the Unification Church of the Reverend Moon, more commonly known as the Moonies. South Korea's football stadiums are the venue not only for World Cup games but some of the biggest mass-marriage services ever seen.

South Korea's progress stands as a brilliant example of authoritarian-accelerated development. The same can be said of South Korea's bid for the 2002 World Cup. FIFA president João Havelange had made it clear in the mid-1980s that the World Cup should go to Asia and if it was to go to Asia then it should go to Japan. With a decision to be made in 1996 on the host nation for the 2002 World Cup, Japan took the hint and got their bid committee up and running a long way in advance. South Korea only formed a bid committee two years later. Japan's bid was conducted by the salaryman technocrats at the Japanese football association and cast entirely in terms of the country's amazing infrastructure and facilities. South Korea, by contrast, deployed the full weight of its economic and political elites, and they were not afraid to play politics. The bid committee was staffed by, among others, Chung Moon-Joon, chairman of Hyundai, Koo Pyong-Hwoi, chairman of Lucky Goldstar, and the Deputy Prime Minister, Lee Hong-Koon. Indeed Lee considered the bid so important that he attended a reception at the 1994 World Cup finals to promote South Korea's case, in preference to attending the funeral of the nation's nemesis, North Korean leader Kim Il-Sung. The Koreans also placed a multilingual bid emissary in their embassies which happened to be in countries that had a seat on the FIFA executive committee that would decide matters. Chung Moon-Joon had a seat on the FIFA executive which not only guaranteed Korea one vote but gave them access to all the inside politicking and bargaining that they needed. South Korea matched Japan's ambitious plans and claimed that a Korean World Cup could be used to bring North Korea back into the fold of nations by promising to stage a game or two in Pyongyang. The Koreans also hinted that to give the tournament to Japan would be to condone its continued silence or half-hearted apologies for its behaviour during the Second World War in Korea, China and other parts of Asia. When it came to the crunch Europe lined up behind Korea, Havelange and his allies behind Japan. The bids were both good, the balance of forces close and the costs of losing for either side in terms of loss of face were huge. When the possibility of co-hosting was raised – UEFA had already sanctioned this for their own European Championship in 2000 – the participants jumped at the chance.

South Korea's model of footballing development could not be pursued in Japan. In a more democratic polity, central government was less directly linked to sport and less capable of forcing change upon the nation. Japanese industry and people would need to be lured rather than led. There was also more competition. Baseball was more deeply entrenched in Japanese popular culture than in Korea. Indeed in the 1970s baseball seemed to provide the perfect model for Japanese corporate management and organization. Omnipotent coaches and managers issued instructions to hyper-focused and disciplined players and workers in a strict hierarchy.

But Japan was changing. In the late 1980s the economy stood at the peak of what would later be called the Japanese bubble economy, overheated by bad debt and grotesquely inflated property and stock markets. Corporations were flush with money but worried. Japan was not creating the new industries and economic sectors to replace cars, electronics and ship manufacturing at which it had excelled. More significantly, Japan's companies and their workforces seemed ill-suited to the tasks that they would face in a service-dominated, post-industrial, open economy. Individual initiative, creativity, flexibility and innovation would be more important than tightly organized hierarchies and disciplined followers.

It was in this context that the transformation of Japanese football was planned inside the football association in the late 1980s. A hundred years of semi-professional football, organized and sponsored by suffocating absent-minded corporatist benevolence, was to be swept aside in a spectacular act of reverse cultural engineering. The J-League would create professional clubs with European-type geographical loyalties. The new league insisted on the old teams dropping their corporate names, building proper modern football stadiums, diversifying their sponsor base, establishing professional contracts with their staff, running youth teams and connecting themselves to their localities. Football as entertainment was precisely the kind of new economic sector Japan needed to move into. While it remained a team game, it allowed much greater room for individual initiative and flamboyance than baseball. Coaches could set frameworks, but players needed to think for themselves. Corporate sponsors and local government fell over each other to support the J-League.

The J-League now had its product, what it needed were consumers. From the US sports industry the Japanese learned how to produce and sell sports merchandise, how to maximize revenue from a franchise and above all how to sell the thing big. The J-League was to be the ultimate *Shinhatsubi*, which translates as 'new improved product, now on sale'. The league's strips were redesigned by Mizuno and exhibited in a high-profile fashion parade. Rejecting the chromatic simplicity of conventional football shirts, Mizuno splashed painterly stripes across shoulders, experimented with the tie-dye look, whirled polygons and other abstract shapes over stripes and matched purple with orange. For mascots and emblems, key elements of the club's new branding, the league turned to Sony Creative Producers who had cut their teeth designing and merchandising the *Sesame Street* and *Thomas the Tank Engine* kids' brands: 'Yokohama Marinos were given a seagull dressed in a uniform . . . Yokohama Flugels . . . got an aeroplane with a hat on . . . and Kashima Antlers got a deer.'[1] Foreign stars were signed up to give cachet and style to the product. Early arrivals included England's Gary Lineker, Argentina's Ramón Diaz, the Brazilian Zico and German Pierre Littbarski. In the countdown to the first season the J-League organized a vast wave of advertising through Japan. The sponsors of the league added their own marketing campaigns. So successful was the enormous round of hype and novelty that the opening game of the J-League could have sold out six times over.

The meeting of European, Latin American and Asian football cultures in Japan and South Korea has been illuminating, not least for the light it sheds on the relationships between the individual and collective in different cultures. Foreign coaches have been among the most astute observers of differences in players' attitudes and behaviour. Leonard Petrov, a Russian who worked with the South Korean national team, put it like this:

The Confucian tradition of fraternal respect often contradicted the basic principles of football. The very idea of a team is understood in Korea as a strictly hierarchical body with a captain at the top and the youngest member at the bottom. Each player knows exactly his role and position in the team and prefers to abstain from taking any extra responsibility. For example, when dribbling with the ball in the rival's penalty area a virtuous Korean player would never use a golden opportunity to score the goal himself but invariably look for an elder 'brother' who could do it.[2]

The same description could be applied to early Japanese and indeed Chinese football. Deference to hierarchy was accompanied by a draining lack of self-confidence in the face of authority. Stuart Baxter, the English coach of Sanfrecce Hiroshima, describes the contrast: 'In other countries if you drop a player they'll come and batter your door down and it's "Why aren't you fucking picking me?" In Japan, they come and say "Mr Baxter, is there anything I can do to improve my game?" '[3] Players would apologize to each other when a mistake was made on the pitch. Osvaldo Ardiles, the Argentinian midfield star, experienced just how deep that deference could go when coaching Shimizu S-Pulse. He told a defender to touch the goalpost he was defending before a corner kick (just to know where it was). During a game, when the ball was kicked from the corner to the outside of the area, the player remained transfixed with his hand on the post. But perhaps the most crucial lesson learned in Japanese football was delivered by players like the Yugoslav Dragan Stojković and Brazil's 1994 World Cup-winning captain, Dunga. Both brought a level of passion and commitment to play that no one in Japan had encountered before. Dunga was notorious and immensely popular for shaking up his team-mates and screaming at their mistakes. It took nearly a decade for its footballers to shed some of Japan's neurotic fear of individual brilliance and public failure. As the then coach of Kashima Antlers, Arsène Wenger, said of his players: 'They wanted specific instructions from me. But football is not American football, where the coach can give instruction for each play ... The player with the ball should be in charge of the game. I had to teach them to think for themselves.'[4]

One player who could think for himself was Hidetoshi Nakata, perhaps the most gifted of the new-generation Japanese players. They were all drawn from a generation that spurned the corporatist work ethic of the post-war years, that preferred individualism to suffocating conformity and that insisted on the priority of talent and ability over age and seniority; this attitude was made public when Nakata was filmed screaming at a more senior player in the Japan national team – Miura – for making a mistake, and not merely shouting but calling him plain Miura rather than *Miura-san* using the deferential suffix. Not surprisingly, Nakata found Japan a hard place to play and made his club career in Italy and England.

The same cultures of hierarchy, deference and conformity shaped the behaviour of Japanese fans. Although the football stadium was always understood as a place where the most restrictive rules governing personal interaction in Japan could be temporarily suspended, it was also clearly thought that deviant behaviour was not appropriate outside. The core supporter groups following the Japanese national team could whip up an intense barrage of drumming and chanting, but, according to one observer at a match, they were completely drowned out by a few hundred Peruvians in the approaches to the ground. At J-League matches opposing fans would clap each other; the idea of abusive chanting was anathema and no one knew how to intimidate away sides or boo their own underperforming players. In fact there was a tendency to try and support and encourage players having a bad day. During the early years of the league Tokyo Verdy could boast the most voluble support and the largest crowds, who were organized as an official fan club called *Camisa Doze* – 'the twelfth shirt'. Their distance from *La Doce*, their namesakes at Boca Juniors, could not have been greater. Of the 16,000 members of *Camisa Doze* at its height, 10,000 were women and most of those were schoolgirls who had adopted the team like an exotic fashion label; they treated the games as if they were in the large-scale crowds they were used to – pop concerts. Where *La Doce* would sing of narcotic intoxication, sexual deviance and malicious insinuation, the Japanese sung a poem of excruciating blandness penned by none other than Pelé.

> Olé, Olé, Olé Olá
> Hey, Verdy, Fantastic Technique!
> Come everyone, and have a good time together,
> Together with Verdy – kick-off time!

The end of a J-League game displayed an etiquette that would have been incomprehensible in Buenos Aires:

They ended with two sides lining up side-by-side in the middle of the pitch and waving towards the main stand. Then the players went over to greet the supporters, standing in a row on the goalline and bowing in unison.[5]

The phenomenon of football as pop concert or friendship ritual dissipated towards the end of the 1990s. As the initial exoticism and novelty of the J-League declined a smaller, more committed fan base emerged. In a few clubs a new kind of fan culture and supporting style began to develop. Urawa Red Diamonds, previously the team of the Mitsubishi corporation based in the undistinguished Tokyo satellite town of Saitama, are perhaps the best example of this. Founded in 1993, a group called Crazy Calls have been innovating and orchestrating support in Uruwa's home stadium. They borrowed Italian *tifosi* forms of collective display and regimented chanting, but also absorbed the mordant wit and knowing pop culture of English crowds; as the team plummeted towards the bottom of the league in 1993 and 1994, the crowd hummed the Elvis tune 'I can't help falling in love with you'. They also introduced the booing of players, referees and opposing fans. The In Fight group at Kashima Antlers deployed their own samba bands and collective singing. The fans of Kashiwa Reysol staged a revolution against their own authoritarian chant leaders, initiating forms of pre-match discussion and democracy in planning how to support the team. All across the country the saturation coverage of European football brought Italian, Spanish and English songs to the J-League. In this at any rate Japan's small band of *ultras* were following a well-worn path – studying and importing advanced foreign technique. But in many other ways they were considered to be and saw themselves as most un-Japanese. In *The Red Book*, a manual for new supporters at Urawa Red Diamonds, they wrote:

Maybe we need to give up being Japanese just a little. It is not easy to change from a mentality that dislikes confrontation to one that insists on its own point of view. Unfortunately, the red blood of the race of football supporters did not flow in our ancestors.[6]

Football, it was thought, would showcase and nurture the psychological, intellectual and emotional skills that the new post-industrial Japan needed – flexibility, initiative, adaptability, judgement by performance rather than hierarchy. This has been evident to a degree on the pitch, but it is among the tiny groups of football *ultras*, with their relative spontaneity, rudeness, unruliness and occasional drunkenness that spring from football's potential for the carnivalesque, that the norms of industrial Japan have been most regularly and publicly transgressed.

'Korea and Japan have a long history of exchanges. But we had few experiences of doing something together,'[7] said Choi Sang-yong, former Korean ambassador to Japan when reflecting on the imminent 2002 World Cup – the first to be co-hosted, the first in Asia, the first of the twenty-first century. However, the degree to which the Koreans and Japanese did stage the World Cup together rather than alongside each other is open to question. The vast choreographed opening ceremony in Seoul managed to make not a single reference to Japan in any of its vast panoramas or displays. The run-up to the tournament had seen conflicts and disputes between co-hosts, most bitterly over the Japanese plans to name the event World Cup 2002 JapanKorea on its tickets rather than the agreed official FIFA title World Cup 2002 KoreaJapan. The two countries also diverged in their expectations about the significance of the coming event.

In South Korea the World Cup was widely understood as an opportunity to showcase the country to the world. The Seoul Olympics of 1988 had, in the end, been the fruit of the nation's authoritarian workaholic capitalism. In the intervening years the steady if incomplete democratization and demilitarization of Korea had created a different, more open and plural society that the Koreans were keen both to advertise and test against the rest of the world. Civic-improvement campaigns exhorted Koreans to smile more (as Westerners were confused by the perceived passiveness of the nation's facial expression), to spit less and stop eating dogs. Traditional street food stalls were cleared from the streets in the weeks before the tournament on spurious health and safety grounds to make more room for the blandishments of microwaved burgers. Most mean-spirited of all, the lively tented and alleyway drinking parlours of the nation's cities – the *pojangmachas* – were temporarily closed down. Particular energy and concern was focused on the state of the nation's antiquated public toilets and the 'Clean Toilet Clean Korea' campaign promised both a complete infrastructural overhaul of the nation's facilities and a higher standard of bathroom cleanliness and etiquette from the people. Koreans were asked to abandon the traditional multiple-queue, multiple-cubicle system for Western-style single-file queuing outside lavatories.

Japan by contrast had already shown the world what it could do at the Tokyo Olympics in 1964. The World Cup was seen much more as a mere sporting event and carnival than an exercise in national boosterism. That said, a mood of introspection – already entrenched by the dismally static Japanese economy – descended further upon the nation. Japan was more interested in what the World Cup would tell it about itself than what the rest of the world might make of it. The arrival of foreigners was viewed as a source of concern rather than a business opportunity, a low-key panic about English hooligans being the leitmotif of Japan's emotional preparations for the tournament. In sporting terms, both press and public had set the expectations very low. Japan after all had lost all three games at the 1998 World Cup, including a really poor performance against Jamaica. The South Koreans felt the same.

When the world started arriving in East Asia in the late spring of 2002 what they found, first and foremost, was the most hi-tech and expensively assembled football infrastructure of any tournament. The World Cup had been getting steadily bigger and more complex to stage for some time, but a number of factors sent World Cup 2002 through the roof. The co-hosting arrangements, which had done so little to cool the burning embers of resentment and mistrust between Korea and Japan, virtually ensured a stadium-building race for architectural pre-eminence between them. Both countries have exceptionally powerful and influential construction industries which both governments believe to be key engines of economic growth. The same could also be said of the consumer electronics and telecommunication industries which took the World Cup to be one vast marketing exercise. World Cup 2002 was staged in twenty stadiums, more than double the number used in Italia '90 let alone the handful that hosted Mexico '70 or Brazil '50.

Alongside these similarities there were two interesting differences between the Koreans and Japanese, which help explain something of the different experiences of the World Cup in the two countries. In Korea the government and audio-visual industries positively encouraged outdoor viewing on big screens – over 2,000 of them across the country – while in Japan it was actively discouraged. Similarly, in Korea the new stadiums were built with football exclusively in mind. In Japan, where large federal funding subsidies were attached to the staging of the annual national athletics championships, stadiums were built with athletics tracks and facilities overwhelmingly in distant and lonely out-of-town sites. As a consequence, the atmosphere in Korea's stadiums, cultural differences between the crowds aside, was far more intense and the collective experience of the tournament vastly more evocative – but then South Korea came within an ace of the final itself. Japan, though doing far better than the doubters expected, went out in the second round.

What if anything did the Japanese discern about themselves through the prism of their football team and their World Cup? Japan were coached by the Frenchman Philippe Troussier who, above all, had promoted youth and encouraged a degree of individualism in the players – expressed most exuberantly in the array of coloured, shaped, gelled and shaved manga-comic hair-dos of the squad. They were also good enough to win their first-ever World Cup points in a draw with Belgium and then two victories against Tunisia and Russia to see them through to the second round. The Turks were too good for them, but it was no shame to lose to the team that was to finish third in the tournament. The crowd held up a banner that could only have been made before the game, saying to the team 'Thank you for giving us a dream'. Muted expectations produced muted celebrations. Although the crowd was noisy enough in the stadiums, outside it was only a few brave souls who leapt into rivers and urban canals after Japan's victories and who were hailed as the face of the new non-conformist Japan. The fact that Junichi Inamoto actually smiled when he scored against Belgium was of considerable public note. Japan perhaps knew in its soul that while it had nurtured individualism and spontaneity, it had also swapped the Samurai for the celebrity and found a less bellicose nationalism. Reflecting on the meaning of the World Cup in Japan, the newspaper *Asahi Shimbun* suggested:

Probably it will be the season of *Hinomaru* [the national flag] and *Kimigayo* [the national anthem]. Especially *Hinomaru*. It could be that it was the first time that the country was filled with *Hinomaru* since World War Two, though the meaning is quite different. Young people deal with *Hinomaru* and *Kimigayo* casually, not reverently. The lightness and casualness were impressive. Next day, they raised the national flag to support the other country.[8]

South Korea's World Cup was transformed, first and foremost, by the extraordinary performance of its team. The football authorities had closed down the K-League for most of the year to allow Dutch coach Guus Hiddink uninhibited access to his squad. The public braced themselves for the possibility that the team might be the first host to fail to get beyond the first round, but began to believe that things might turn out otherwise in the preparations for the tournament when South Korea thrashed Scotland 4–1, earned a draw with England and lost to France by the smallest of margins. Hiddink, like Troussier, had announced his arrival in Korean football by pursuing systematic meritocracy. Age and standing counted for nothing in selection policy. To augment the already considerable levels of fitness and technique of the players, Hiddink encouraged a degree of multi-functionality, allowing players to cover more efficiently for each other, and built a tangible degree of cohesion and confidence. The team's progress can be charted from the estimated crowds that gathered around the big screens – from the giants of the Kwang Hwa Mun intersection in downtown Seoul to hastily rigged-up affairs hung from a municipal dump-truck in a small-town car park. For the opening game against Poland just half a million gathered to see South Korea win 2–0. Against the USA it was three-quarters of a million for a draw, but qualification was now a real possibility. Nearly 3 million were out for the decisive match against Portugal – a single goal from Park Ji-Sung enough to secure victory. The second-round game against Italy, won in extra time, attracted 4.22 million; the quarter-final against Spain 5 million; and for the semi-final against Germany 7 million Koreans, over a million in central Seoul alone, daubed their faces, dressed in red, packed their lunch pails and headed for the squares, the streets, the screens and each other.

It was still 3 million for the profound anti-climax of the third-place game against Turkey and, though 3–1 down for over an hour, the South Koreans did not stop running and trying for a single second. The injury-time goal from Song Jong-Gook was testament to the indefatigable mental and physical stamina that was the hallmark of the team and the nation, which without raw materials and devastated by civil war had transformed itself from among the poorest and most ravaged in the world into one of the richest by dint of social organization, centralization and phenomenal hard work. The crowds that gathered were initially predominantly in their twenties or younger, but as their

845

numbers swelled they became more demographically inclusive: children, teenagers and the elderly all took their places in these impromptu theatres of civic nationalism. The generation that found the journey hardest were the 386ers – born in the 1960s, now in their thirties and at university in the 1980s and thus on the cutting edge of the democracy protest of the mid-1980s when the same public spaces and squares had been the crucible of the conflict, awash with tear gas and riot police. One veteran of the pro-democracy conflicts described the ambiguity of the moment:

I desperately wanted to cheer for the team. However, I was embarrassed, and simply couldn't. The people around us looked down on us as if to say 'Why aren't you cheering?' Their attitude was 'Why won't you cheer together?'[9]

It appears that many did learn to cheer. Kim Jae-Gyan, another veteran of the democracy protests, joined the throng at Seoul City Hall:

In 1987, what united all the people at this place had been a sense of urgency to fight. This time it was different. We could afford to enjoy ourselves while thinking of others. Even when the crowd numbered hundreds of thousands, everything was orderly. I came to think that I played a part in our progress to the present and I feel pride and responsibility.[10]

Chinese football, like the Chinese economy, spent the late 1970s and 1980s repairing the damage done during the Cultural Revolution and incubating new hopes and desires. After Mao's death in 1976, Deng Xiaoping steadily acquired supreme power within the Chinese Communist Party and initiated a programme of economic change. Foreign investors were invited to make use of the world's biggest pool of cheap labour and Chinese farmers were allowed to sell their crops on the open market and make a buck. Organized football, which had disappeared during the Cultural Revolution, was first re-established and then aligned more closely with international norms. The inclusion of the national team and the army side 1st August in the league, both of whom played but not for points, was dropped. The 1973 experiment which gave bonus points for headed goals in the top division was also shed. After thirty years outside the mainstream of international sport, China rejoined both the IOC and FIFA.

The expectations of a now enormous football public grew; press, fans and politicians longed for the national team to qualify for either the Olympic Games or the World Cup. The first attempt to make it to the Olympics in 1980 was pitiful: the men's team lost in the qualifying rounds of the Asian section, losing to tiny Singapore in the process. China fared better in the qualifiers for the 1982 World Cup, and though they didn't reach Spain they did manage a victory over the eventual Asian qualifier Kuwait. The reaction at home to this victory illustrates the degree to which China's obsessions with football and economics had become intertwined. Hundreds of thousands of Chinese took to the streets of the big cities chanting '*zhenxing zhonghua*', which translates best as 'vigorously develop China'.

In 1984, emboldened by the success of his reforms, Deng extended them to industry, services and state companies. Football clubs responded by seeking commercial sponsorship and a team from Guangzhou were the first to carry a corporate logo. Then in the grey areas of the new economic order they began to establish themselves as professional clubs run on a commercial basis. Still China came no closer to the World Cup and in 1985 the country was plunged into introspective gloom after losing a crucial qualifying game to Hong Kong 2–1; 60,000 fans in Beijing watched China take a 1–0 lead and then freeze. The 'May 19th event', as it has become known, saw China's first football riot as thousands of exasperated fans, humiliated by the defeat, smashed shops and windows, overturned and burnt buses, hassled foreigners and set about the city's metro stations. Hundreds were arrested and a handful sent to prison. China's football fans had pitched their hopes too early and too high; so did the student protesters in Tiananmen Square in 1989. In the square the call was not for World Cup qualification, but for something perceived as an equally necessary complement of the new Chinese economy – democracy. The Communist Party could not guarantee the former and was not prepared to concede the latter. The army cleared the square. The dead numbered over 1,000.

Secure now from any challenge, either within or outside of the Communist Party, in 1992 Deng announced the irreversible historic decision that the Chinese Communist Party would oversee the creation of a capitalist industrial economy in China. An epoch of hyper-industrialization began. The Chinese economy grew furiously. Indeed no economy has ever grown so fast, over such a sustained period, nor undertaken so massive a series of interlinked structural changes; agrarian, rural, socialist China has become, for the half a billion or so who live on its Pacific coastline, industrial, urban and capitalist. Football rode the wave of change.

Almost simultaneously with Deng's speech the Chinese football authorities gathered in the country's first national football congress to provide an outline plan for putting domestic football in order and getting China to the World Cup. The leading clubs broke their remaining ties with old state institutions, like the army and the railways, and forged new commercial alliances with local government and local entrepreneurs. Clubs legally reconstituted themselves as businesses and took control over gate money, advertising, sponsorship and television rights. The Chinese FA's income quintupled in a decade, club budgets multiplied faster and players' wages in the top league, once no different from those of a middling civil servant, were by 1998 twenty times greater. Foreign coaches were recruited to every level of the game including the national team. Foreign players from Latin America and West Africa began to appear in the top division – Jia A. Most implausibly of all, Paul Gascoigne, the English midfield star, sought a late career break in China to top up his pension fund. No Jia A club would have him, but he did join Jia B side Gansu Tianma, the Heavenly Horse club, in 2003, before they too dispensed with his now limited services.

In a sporting parallel with the enormous sponsored migration of Chinese students to the world's business schools, teaching hospitals and elite engineering departments, the Jianli Bao soft-drinks group deemed the pursuit of footballing glory important enough to send twenty-two Chinese youth players to Brazil for five years to train and play. The best of China's new footballers also found a place for themselves in leagues overseas: most notably the Chinese who played in the English Premiership. Crystal Palace signed Sun Ji Hai in 1998 who then moved to Manchester City. Everton boasted Li Tei in their defence and Kejian – a Chinese telecoms company – as their sponsor. The clash between the two teams in 2003 gained a Chinese television audience estimated at 150 million people.

In 1997 the Chinese economy momentarily faltered as it absorbed the shock waves of the wider economic crisis in East Asia. South-east Asian stock markets and property values collapsed and the fall-out would take Suharto in Indonesia with them. China failed to qualify for the World Cup. But both football and the economy were unstoppable. As the twenty-first century began it was palpably clear to all that it was only a matter of time before China became the world's largest economy. On 7 October 2001 China beat Oman, watched by a domestic TV audience of 250 million, and finally qualified for the World Cup. A spontaneous celebration erupted, and the crowds in Tiananmen Square chanted 'Milu' in honor of the Serbian coach Bora Milutinović who had guided them to the finals.

In an unscriptable but magnificent coincidence, on the following day the country's biggest corruption and match-fixing scandal exploded – the affair of the Black Whistles. The games played in Jia B the previous weekend had already aroused suspicions. The penultimate round of the league saw Shanghai Zhongyuan Huili promoted after beating Guangzhou Jili Cars 3–2. Shanghai's winner, scored by South African striker Mark Williams, came in the last minute of injury time from what was to all and sundry a very offside position. Chengdu Wuniu Guoteng, who were chasing the second promotion spot, improved their chances greatly by beating Sichuan Minyang Taiji 11–2. The following week left Chengdu, Changchun and Jiangsu in contention for promotion. Chengdu beat Jiangsu 4–2 and went second in the league. In Hangzhow Changchun were leading 2–0 in their game against Zhejiang. They needed four more goals to take second spot on goal difference. In the remaining five minutes of normal time and some rather generous injury time, four goals were duly scored. Changchun were promoted.

Even in China this level of naked corruption was no longer tenable. The Chinese FA fined everyone, cancelled Changchun's promotion, banned the coaches and sent Sichuan down a division for their laughable 11–2 defeat. Then the presidents of Guangzhou and Zhejiang went on national television and explained how they had been bribing referees and fixing games. More revelations followed, more clubs admitted fixing games, more referees were named. Despite this Changchun's promotion was confirmed in the law courts. In the new China the old problems of corruption and collusion among elites and the ineffectiveness of the rule of law remain. Consequently there has been a collapse of trust in public authority, be it government or football associations. This was highlighted the following season in the game between Shaanxi Guoli Haus

Beer and Qingdao Beer. Qingdao were 2–3 down to Shaanxi when they were awarded an injury-time penalty. Qingdao scored, making it 3–3, and the Xian stadium exploded. First, the chant 'black whistles, black whistles' went up, then there was a hail of mobile phones and coins. Qingdao players were struck by plastic trumpets and steel lighters. Then the plastic seats were on the pitch and China's first full stadium riot took off. Fires were started in the stands, the post-match press conference descended into a brawl and only the use of water cannons inside and outside the stadium restored some semblance of order.

The 2002 World Cup proved a salutary experience as China not only failed to get a point, but they failed to score a goal in successive defeats to Brazil, Turkey and Costa Rica. The following year saw the SARS virus strike the region and the Women's World Cup, which had been planned for China, was cancelled and relocated to the USA. Away from home the Chinese women's team failed to live up to their pre-tournament billing as one of the favourites. But these setbacks are surely the inevitable consequences of overextension, of a society and economy in tumultuous change, in which expectations are rising even faster than production and everyone is looking for the shortcut to success. In 2004 China hosted the Asian Cup, now expanded to sixteen teams, and the national team, backed by hysterical support, made it to the final in Beijing. Their opponents were the Japanese, who in every game thus far had been on the end of whistling and booing from a section of the Chinese crowd. This was redoubled during the final and inflamed by Japan's superiority and a clear case of handball for their second goal. The match finished 3–1 to Japan followed by a series of disturbances in and around the stadium: a Japanese diplomat's car had its window smashed, Japanese flags were burned in the street and the small contingent of Japanese fans was kept back in the stadium for hours. Anti-Japanese feeling in China is hardly news; the legacy of the occupation remains unresolved, contemporary conflicts over gas resources and islands simmer. What is more surprising is the fear that the Chinese authorities now appear to feel about their own subjects. The people who brought us Tiananmen Square described what in Latin America or parts of Europe would be considered a minor outbreak of containable antisocial behaviour, as a full-blown riot. More than that, they were not prepared to intervene inside or outside the stadium.

In 2008 China will host the Olympic football tournament in Beijing, and when the World Cup returns to Asia there can be little doubt it will be going to China too. The probity and performance of Chinese football have been and will continue to be more than just metaphors for China's breakneck development; they will be direct measures of the promise and pathologies of hyper-industrialization.

The countries of South-east Asia lie in a great crescent around southern China. They run from Burma in the west, through the Malay Peninsula (Thailand, Malaysia, Singapore and Brunei) and Indo-China (Laos, Cambodia, Vietnam) to the island archipelagoes of Indonesia and the Philippines in the east. To the north lies the island state of Taiwan, excluded from Asian football by China, forced to play its international fixtures in Oceania. Nearby, on the mainland, the colonial palimpsests of Macao and Hong Kong have retained their international football status with FIFA despite their transfer of sovereignty to China. Not one of these thirteen countries has ever qualified for the World Cup (the 1938 showing of the Dutch East Indies aside) nor have any of them really looked as if they might. There were in the 1950s and 1960s some occasional showings for teams from the region in the Asian Cup (though none better than a semi-final spot), but their record at international level is undoubtedly poor.

The domestic football scene is hardly any stronger. Thai Farmers Bank won the Asian Champions Cup twice in the mid-1990s but in international competition the region's clubs have been swept aside and occasionally humiliated by teams from North-east Asia and the Middle East. Attendances at games can on occasion be very large but the averages are depressingly small, barely enough to sustain the leagues economically. Professionalism, legally and practically, has come very late. Hong Kong did sustain a professional cadre of players in the 1970s, but like the American NASL on which it was modelled, the professional league succumbed to consumer indifference and the economic downturn at the end of the 1970s; it has not subsequently recovered. Singapore's S-League was formed in 1995 when economic and political conflict made the city-state's continued participation in Malaysia's M-League untenable. Vietnam and Indonesia have only created professional national leagues in the 1990s, while the Philippines, Cambodia, Laos and Burma are at best semi-professional.

What accounts for the weakness of the region's football and its late development? In the Philippines and Taiwan, both of which have served as direct client states of the USA in the last half-century, baseball continues to be the most popular sport. The long colonial wars of independence and the post-colonial wars of border dispute have occupied the Indo-Chinese peninsula for some time. Cambodia, Vietnam and Laos have experienced levels of physical damage and social dislocation that make the organization of anything, let alone professional nationwide football, a small miracle. Harsh military rule and internal civil wars have had much the same effect in Burma, despite the regime's active interest in football. Worse perhaps, the regime has attempted news blackouts when the national team has lost a match overseas; this level of paranoia and defensiveness is unlikely to encourage Burmese football to develop. Singapore has got too rich too quickly, so that hardly anyone wants to embark on the risky and poorly rewarded career of a professional footballer in the S-League. Even the Singaporean state, notorious for its social engineering and control-freakery, has not been able to shift those perceptions. Indonesia's vast size and poor transport infrastructure does not lend itself to the easy organization of league football with conventional patterns of home and away games.

Yet even allowing for geographical and historical factors like these there remains an unexplained gap between public interest in football (huge, bordering on obsessional) and the quality of club and international football (both low). One needs to ask, what football is South-east Asia obsessed with? And how do they like to consume it? The answers are revealing. South-east Asians prefer European football to domestic football; they like it on the TV and not at the stadium; and they like it best with a bet riding on the outcome. South-east Asia's football cultures are truly distinct in their preference for foreign clubs and leagues over local teams and competitions – and the sheer scale of illegal football gambling and the degree of corruption that it brings.

At the turn of the twenty-first century a 50-metre image of Alessandro Del Piero, the Juventus striker, appeared on the sides of Jakarta skyscrapers. David Beckham was used to sell engine oil, sunglasses and mobile phones from Singapore to Seoul. Manchester United opened Red Devil theme bars with United Megastores attached in Malaysia, China and Indonesia and then announced that they would license one hundred of them across the whole of South-east Asia. Although European football has had its devotees in South-east Asia since the 1970s and clubs have made low-profile visits to the region (for example, West Bromwich Albion's visit to China in 1979), it was only in the mid- to late 1990s that European football clubs realized that their Asian following was more than a quaint, if inexplicable addendum to their domestic support. Manchester United estimated their core fan base in the region to be over 10 million and led the way in conducting promotional tours, putting their web sites and merchandising into Asian languages. Where United have led, others have followed hard on their heels. Liverpool toured Thailand, and Chelsea, Everton and Newcastle went east too. Internazionale and Milan opened stores in Tokyo. Real Madrid went to China and Japan, and Barcelona followed them. But what has really driven this phenomenon has not been the tours, but television. On satellite TV in East and South-east Asia you can watch the European Champions League, La Liga, Serie A, the Bundesliga and the Premiership, live, recorded, full length and highlights. How can domestic football compete with this?

Unlike Latin America, South-east Asia underwent industrialization in an era of global communication networks. Unlike the nouveau riche of inter-war Rio or Buenos Aires, the new urban middle classes could choose between readily available, high-quality foreign football and underdeveloped domestic football. They have unswervingly chosen the former. In part it is a question of quality and convenience, but it is also a matter of brands. The new consumers of South-east Asia have proved ravenously hungry for the global labels that carry status. Manchester United, Juventus and Real Madrid were brands that said class, glamour, success and wealth. Selangor, Thai Farmers Bank and Armed Forces said provincialism and poverty. The apogee of this attempt to buy into European football was the bid mooted in 2003 by Thaskin Shinawatra, the millionaire Prime Minister of Thailand, to buy a large chunk of Liverpool Football Club.

If support for European clubs reflects the aspirational consumerism that has swept the new rich in South-east Asia, the nature of gambling on football reflects the massive presence of the illegal and underground economy in the region's development. Gambling is illegal almost everywhere in South-east Asia and sits alongside the sex industry, the drugs trade, the music-pirating business and the illegal trafficking of hard-woods and gemstones as a shadowy but significant economic sector. Legal gambling exists only in Hong Kong, where betting on the horses is allowed, and in Macao's casinos. Gambling boats continue to ply their trade from both harbours, taking punters into unregulated international waters. Yet the Asian betting industry is turning over $100 billion a year. That is three times the GDP of Vietnam. The vast majority of this is illegal. On an average weekend during the European soccer season $150 million is wagered with the main underground bookmaking net-works of South-east Asia. These are concentrated in Malaysia, Thailand, Singapore and Indonesia. Betting really takes off during the big inter-national tournaments. Since the arrival of live television coverage of the World Cup in 1998, the volume of bets has grown enormously. During Euro 2004, for example, Thais gambled around $800 million in three weeks; that is half a per cent of the country's GDP. In Singapore $294 million was laid out; that's $70 for every man, woman and child. The tournament was preceded by dire warnings of arrest, prosecution and punishment from governments but the reality is a few minor busts, in a few places. The core of the businesses and the vast majority of the punters are left untouched. As one Malaysian put it, 'You got bookies, you got people, it's normal.'[11]

While no one, as yet, has suggested that games at the World Cup or European Championship have been thrown or distorted by the needs of Asian gambling syndicates, there is no shortage of scandal. Malaysian and Indonesian betting syndicates were intimately connected to the incidents of floodlight sabotage in England, where a sudden failure in electricity supply saw an early end to games at Wimbledon, West Ham and Charlton. In Indonesia and Malaysia the score at the time a match is abandoned stands for betting purposes. When these games reached the desired score, the lights went out, just in case anyone should want to do something inconvenient like score another goal. The same syndi-cates were tied to the long-running accusations of match-fixing in English football in the late 1980s and early 1990s, which touched leading players like Liverpool goalkeeper Bruce Grobbelaar and Wimbledon's John Fashanu. In 1996 the Malaysian authorities arrested and questioned over a hundred domestic players linked to systematic bribery and match-fixing. The police found that nearly 90 per cent of the fixtures in the inaugural season of the professional M-League in Malaysia were fixed, one way or the other. Despite the enormity of the problem, very few players, punters or bookies were actually put away. The Hong Kong player Chan Tse Kong was one of the few, sentenced in 1997 to one year in prison and a lifetime ban from football for his role in throwing a game against Thailand. Arrests and bans of referees in Indonesia mounted up so quickly in 1998 that the league was seriously disrupted by the lack of trained officials, but somehow the problem has not gone away. In 1997 seven players at Ho Chi Minh City Customs, Vietnam's national champions, were investigated and charged. The investigation had been triggered by the sight of a goalkeeper in a national league match running to the halfway line as one of his defenders, now 20 metres behind him, scored in his own goal. It transpired that enormous bribes had been handed out. But despite repeated waves of arrests and crackdowns in Hanoi and Ho Chi Minh City the Vietnamese punters and players just keep coming back for more. The 2004 Samsung Cup, in which Song Lam Nghe An lost 2–1 to The Cong club, saw seven of the losing side arrested and prosecuted for what was considered to be the most blatant display of match-fixing Vietnam has seen.

Unlike the experience of Latin America or Europe, football in South-east Asia at its moment of professionalization was a middle-class game. South-east Asia's new urban proletariat is also part of the football world. But whereas the working classes of industrializing Europe steadily colonized the world of football, in South-east Asia their only foothold has been in the factories of the global sports-goods industry. In the late 1980s and early 1990s, the American companies Nike and Reebok began to shift production from the US and Mexico to East Asia where labour costs were a fraction of those in the US and safety and environmental overheads were minimal. Of course, neither company directly employed anyone, they merely subcontracted local firms to do their dirty work. They were soon followed by the major European companies Adidas and Puma. Phenomenal profits followed for all of these corporations, but none more than Nike.

From the mid-1990s onward reports steadily leaked out describing conditions in these plants.[12] One example will suffice. In 1997 the Tae Kwang Vina factory in Bien Hoa City, 20 miles north of Ho Chi Minh City in southern Vietnam, employed 9,200 workers making 400,000 sports shoes a year. According to accountants Ernst and Young, the vast majority of the workforce were women under the age of 25, working twelve-hour days, six days a week, in grotesque levels of noise, heat and foul-smelling air, and all this for around $10 a week. Dust and chemicals caused skin and breathing problems, protective clothing was not available. The same story could be repeated over and over again, especially in China and Indonesia, not just for Nike but for all the others too. Despite repeated public exposure and promises from the companies to change these practices in their subcontractors, reports of dangerous working conditions, abusive labour practices and harrowingly low wages have continued to emerge. Perhaps worst of all has been the manufacture of hand-stitched balls. Pakistan produces around three-quarters of the world's footballs. They are stitched by pitifully paid labourers, many of them children, who do three or four on a good day. At 20 cents a ball that is not even a dollar a day. Without them the often grotesquely wealthy circus of global football grinds to a halt.

The streets are empty. The roads are silent. Everyone is in front of a screen; from antiquated black-and-white sets balanced precariously on old beer crates at the centre of the village to giant flat slabs of chrome hung in the new malls. The nation's attention is so closely focused that even the prolific film industry has been forced to shut down. No new movie has been released since the tournament began. The contest is spellbindingly good, closely fought, unpredictable, with plenty of twists and turns. If it were China or Korea then it must be the football World Cup. But this is India, the game is cricket and the nation is entranced by India's first tour of Pakistan in fourteen years. India's absence from Pakistan and the high dramatic stakes of their cricketing reunion were rooted in real conflict. The 1990s opened in South Asia with a Muslim separatist rising in the long-disputed region of Kashmir between India and Pakistan. The conflict has dominated relations between the two countries ever since; the two have fought sharp border engagements, come close to a wider war and both have gone nuclear. Two years later, the always latent and now organized, angry core of militant Hindu nationalism marched on Ayodhya in northern India which they believed to be the birthplace of the Hindu deity Lord Rama. On arriving they razed the sixteenth-century Brabi mosque in the centre of the city, triggering the worst sectarian conflict in India since partition. They have been demanding that a Hindu temple be raised on the site ever since. Hindu vs. Muslim, India vs. Pakistan – for both nations cricket has assumed the mantle of both surrogate war and an instrument of reconciliation. Football lives culturally and economically in its vast shadow.

The surface of contemporary Indian history appears dominated by religious, ethnic and territorial conflicts, but something else has been stirring in the shadows: economic and administrative change. The Indian state, while capable of achieving nuclear status, was for the most part an institution of byzantine complexity and legendary inefficiency. It was constructed of innumerable jurisdictions and overlapping geographical layers. The Indian civil service that staffed it was characterized by an immense rigidity and a sclerotic disposition. All of this was held together by networks of corruption, patronage and graft. The Indian economy, by comparison to the dynamism of the states to its east, appeared slow, antiquated, inward-looking and over-protected. Indian football was cast from the same mould. Despite its long tradition of national football competitions, the country still had no national league, no significant commercial sponsorship or acumen and no television deal. Over a hundred notionally national tournaments were held every year in the 1980s which served only to confuse and diminish the game rather than promote it. The only companies that were involved in football were the lumbering giants of India's public sector like India Telecoms and Air India. Players were barely semi-professional at even the biggest clubs in Goa and Calcutta, never mind the lesser football states. The football calendar was an incomprehensible multiplicity – literally hundreds of national, sub-national, regional, inter-regional, city-based and inter-city tournaments were played. The only institution capable of giving a national lead – the All India Football Federation (AIFF) – was universally derided for its conservatism, amateurism, inefficiency and slowness. The performance of the national team was consistently poor and not getting any better. Indian players were not good enough to go overseas and no one was coming to India to play or coach football. Barely engaged with the wider structures of global football, India remained an immense convoluted backwater.

Then, in 1991 the government under Prime Minister Narasimha Rao and Minister of Finance P.M. Singh began a slow programme of economic liberalization. Foreign capital was welcomed, trade restrictions were eased, great swathes of the economic bureaucracy were cut and the tax system was simplified. By 1995 India was ready and willing to join the GATT trade agreement and integrate itself with the global economy. The results were uneven but impressive. While much of rural India remained close to destitution, the cities boomed. Growth has run at historically high levels. Indian entrepreneurs have built enormous and successful export-oriented companies in software and computers, television and films, textiles and garments. It is in this context that a revival of Indian football has been mounted.

In 1996 India's first national football league NFL was launched. Philips, the Dutch electronic giant, were the league's inaugural sponsors, followed by Coca-Cola. Indian companies also moved into the game. United Breweries bought into the big three teams in Calcutta (Mohun Bagan, East Bengal and Mohammedan Sporting) and added one of their beverage brands to their names. FC Kochin was the first completely professional club in the country, set up by leading elements in the Keralan commercial sector. In Mumbai the jeep and tractor manufacturers Mahindra and Mahindra, who had previously sponsored cricket and hockey teams, switched to football, creating Mahindra United. Expatriate Bengalis in the city set up Bengal Mumbai FC. Most important of all, Zee TV – the most dynamic of the indigenous television conglomerates – bought the Goan team Churchill Brothers which became Zee-Churchill Brothers.

Returns on these investments have, so far, not been too generous. Certainly there has been a boom in players' earnings, allowing the leading clubs to import foreign players into their squads. The 1980s had seen a few Nigerians and Iranians play in India. The NFL in the 1990s was graced by players from Ghana, Kenya, Zimbabwe, Jordan, Uzbekistan, Nepal, Thailand, Bangladesh and Brazil. Foreign coaches have come in greater numbers, including to the Indian national team (Stephen Constantine was appointed to the post in 2002). None of this appears to have improved the quality of the game. Only one Indian has played in English football. Baichung Bhutia had a spell with Bury in the lowest reaches of the Football League; the national team continues to linger in the basement of the FIFA rankings, unable to qualify for any significant tournaments. Neither Philips nor Coke have stayed with football. Both failed to achieve the kind of public profile that they were looking for from what remained a minority sport in India. Coke had an additional incentive to get out. After opening a new bottling plant in Goa, the company was approached by the state Minister of Industry, Churchill Alamao, owner of Churchill Brothers. Reports circulated that Alamao 'asked' Coke to sponsor the club at exorbitant rates. Coke politely declined, only to find that the Goan government was cutting off the water supply to their new factory. The increasing power and autonomy of Indian private capital was further clarified in 1998 when Mahindra United and Churchill Brothers were spared the drop despite coming bottom of the league. The same reasoning was not applied the following year when the clubs of two public-sector corporations, Air India and India Bank, found themselves occupying the relegation zone.

Most tellingly of all, the leading professional clubs, exasperated by the incompetence and venality of the AIFF, went on strike in 2000. They quickly forced the AIFF to concede significant control over the league to them, but the new arrangements have yet to yield any real growth in the game in India. Whether football will eventually be drawn along in the wake of economic growth in the cities, or whether Indian development will be so unique that it will be the only major nation to modernize with cricket as its national game, remains to be seen.

VI

As Ayatollah Khomeini was eaten by prostate cancer in the early months of 1989 the social limits of Iran's Islamic Revolution were being exposed. Almost ten years since the abdication of the Shah and the collapse of organized football in the country, a semi-professional national league was re-established. Of course, this was still the Islamic Republic and the league was placed under the auspices of the foundation for the war injured and the war martyrs. The league's moniker – Azadegan – referred to the stream of Iranian veterans returning from Iraqi prisoner-of-war camps after the conclusion of their long and bitter war. That the creation of the league could be registered as a defeat for the clerical regime indicates the degree to which they had attempted to suppress the game in the previous decade. But neither fearsome sermons from the theocracy nor the grinding realities of the Iran–Iraq war had been able entirely to extinguish Iranian football. Although many clubs were disbanded and competition discouraged, football moved into the streets where neighbourhood games and spontaneously formed local teams worried the guardians of moral purity and social order. When nearly every other form of public entertainment had been banned, football still pulled in the crowds. Three months after the start of the league Ayatollah Khomeini died. His final act would be fatally to disrupt Iran's unsuccessful campaign to qualify for the 1990 World Cup. The whole nation, including the national squad, went into a long period of mourning; the Asian Football Confederation duly rearranged Iran's qualifiers and on their return they duly failed to qualify.

Now, under the quietly reformist President Rafsanjani Iran began its slow, cautious re-engagement with the rest of the world. At home the government looked to soften the very harshest edges of their puritanical control of public and private life. Khomeini's direct successor as the leading spiritual guide of the nation, Ayatollah Khamenei, extended his approval to the game and to sport more generally. A thin trickle of Iranian athletes, especially wrestlers and Paraolympians (whose prowess reflects the devastating impact of the Iran–Iraq war on the bodies of the Iranian people), began to take part in international competitions. Iran approached the qualifying campaign for the 1994 World Cup with high expectations. The regime had indicated that the World Cup itself would, for the first time since 1978, be broadcast on Iranian television. However, the long years of isolation, the lack of serious foreign competition and the weakness of the domestic league saw Iran knocked out in a mini-qualifying tournament played in Qatar. The coach of the national team, Ali Parvin, was phenomenally popular. He had first made his name as a player before the revolution and was part of the squad that went to the 1978 World Cup. After the Qatar failure he was fired by Iranian football federation boss Mohammed Safizadeh. Safizadeh was then fired by the government and Parvin was forced into a form of internal football exile unable to coach at any level. The authorities were trying to do more than exile Parvin. They were trying to exile the historical legacy of football under the Pahlavi, and the most important legacy was the idea of the secular football nation. Parvin's mere presence as a leading light of the pre-revolutionary football elite alluded to this dangerous concept; the idea was kept alive by the Persepolis crowd in the Azadi stadium who during his exile would chant Parvin's name whatever the game.

Football's reformist credentials were extended in the 1997 presidential election campaign which pitched the conservative Nateq-Nouri against the more moderate Khatami. Nateq-Nouri shared his platform with the leading Iranian wrestlers of the day, Ghadem and Jadidi, while Khatami drew on footballers among his political entourage. Khatami won the election. The opening months of his presidency coincided with the culmination of Iran's long journey to qualify for the 1998 World Cup. The more conservative elements within the religious hierarchy continued to voice their general disapproval of football, and specifically attacked the diversion of religious and social energies into the national team's progress. Yet some of them could not resist using the team's fortunes as an instrument of political struggle. When Iran were defeated by Qatar, losing them an automatic qualification spot and forcing them into a play-off against Japan, the conservative forces in Iran's parliament summoned the team's coach Mayeli Kohan for an interrogation. They also took the opportunity to attack the Minister for Physical Education, Hahsei Tabe, who was a leading moderate. But Khatami and his supporters had by now taken control of Iranian football. Iran lost the game to the Japanese, Kohan was sacked, but for the first time since the Shah's demise a foreigner was called in to lead the team – the Brazilian Valdeir Viera. No clearer statement of the moderation of Islamacist isolationism could have been made. Having lost the play-off to decide the third Asian qualifier, Iran had one last chance – a play-off against the champions of Oceania, Australia. The Australians preferred to stay in the sterilized air conditioning of the UAE and arrived in Tehran only at the last minute. They played out a 1–1 draw in front of over 100,000 Iranians and took their precious away goal home for the second leg.

---

29 November 1997
Australia 2 Iran 2
Melbourne Cricket Ground

A man runs on to the pitch when Australia are 2–0 up. He grabs a net and brings down the crossbar. He is hurried off, the net is repaired and Australia's concentration is shattered.

He is not a well man. He says that for the most part he invades public events that coincide with the predictions of Nostradamus. He is going to be President of Australia too. Although he has disrupted parliaments and commissions, pop stars' funerals and live television shows, he has a thing for sporting events. He has stopped horse races and tennis matches, he has tried to steal the Olympic torch and he has ridden a tricycle with a cage of monkeys into the centre of an Aussie Rules game.

After trailing for nearly the entire game the Iranians have just equalized and now they are going to the World Cup in France, not the Australians. The next six years of football in Australia are a write-off, as the league collapses and the national team disintegrates. The man gets a manager and starts trying to charge for his services.

As the final whistle blew, the streets of Tehran and every provincial city began to fill with people and noise. Estimates vary as to the precise numbers – 3 million in Tehran, perhaps 5 or 6 million nationwide – but the social meaning of the victory was not in doubt. Crowds defied and taunted clerics and the Basiji militias. Women and men openly mixed. Loud music boomed. Some women abandoned the veil, others danced on the roofs of the Toyota trucks used by the moral militias. A vast crowd gathered at the gates of the French embassy where petrified staff feared the worst, but the crowd had brought flowers and threw them into the embassy compound shouting 'See you in Paris'. It was a victory for the secular football nation.

In some places supporters were invited to pass under a huge Iranian flag. This was a symbolic substitute for passing under a copy of the Koran, the ritual whereby travellers (and footballers coming out of changing rooms) are placed under the protection of the holy book.[13]

The regime, both clerical and secular, appeared panicked and bemused. Unable either to corral the festivities or turn events to their own advantage, the government delayed the team's return for two days while they attempted to grasp the meaning of the situation. A celebration at the Azadi stadium was planned, and television, radio and newspapers implored women to stay away and the crowds to remain calm. Neither was listening. Around 100,000 gathered at the Azadi, among them 5,000 women insisting on their place in this, the greatest display of secular nationalism for eighteen years.

When the draw for the 1998 World Cup was made, Iran were put in the same group as the USA; as politically charged a fixture as it is possible to imagine. Both sides went out of their way to defuse its political symbolism. The air was thick with declarations of fair play. The Iranians shaved their beards, handed out bouquets of flowers and won 2–1, although they were not able to make it out of the group stages. On the team's return President Khatami met them at the airport and issued a sermon calling on the nation to emulate the unity and discipline of its football team.

Of these two great events in Iranian football – qualification for the World Cup and beating the USA at the World Cup – there is no contest as to which has lived longer in the hearts of Iranians. Beating the Americans was good, but qualification for the World Cup itself was another matter, for in that moment alone the simmering discontents of young urban Iran, who had known neither the Shah nor Khomeini, crystallized around football. Those discontents have not gone and will not be going away. The following year, Iran was racked by the biggest outbreak of public disorder and protest against the regime since it took power. The riots were triggered by the closure of moderate newspapers but were rooted in the increasing distance between conservative and reformist visions of Iran. The fighting escalated over a five-day period from minor scuffles to full-scale pitched battles between urban youth and students and the state, the same forces that had met on the streets in 1997. Despite this level of protest, change and liberalization in Iran have been painfully slow. The reform of Iranian football was no less tardy. A legally sanctioned professional league was only permitted in 2001, finally severing football's connection with the martyrs' foundation.

In the same year the national team under a Croat coach looked poised for another trip to the World Cup. The final games of the campaign came in late October and early November 2001. Iran beat Iraq 2–1 and over 20,000 people gathered in the streets and public squares of northern Tehran to celebrate. They were met by the police who dispensed tear gas and made hundreds of arrests. President Khatami called for people to keep off the streets in the event of Iran beating Bahrain ten days later. A victory would guarantee qualification; defeat would force the team into a play-off with the UAE. Iran lost 3–1 to the Bahrainis. On the street the rumour spread that the team had been instructed by the theocracy to throw the game in order to prevent another outburst of public celebration and protest. Initially small groups of youths attacked government buildings and banks. They were met by a sharp response from the police as well as the hated religious Basiji militias. Rocks and fireworks went one way, baton charges the other. Both sides returned to the fray the following evening for further pitched battles in the squares, parks and main thoroughfares of Tehran and Esfahan.

As the line between sporting and social issues disintegrated on the streets, the Iranian team recovered its poise and won the play-off with the UAE for the right to play Ireland in a final pair of games that would decide who went to the World Cup. The Irish won, but the legacy of that game was not the score; it was the debate that the game reignited over the presence of women in Iran's football stadiums. Since the revolution not a single Iranian woman had been knowingly allowed into a game. The clerics still considered attendance to be akin to the viewing of naked flesh. Despite this disapproval football appeared amazingly popular with Iranian women. They had formed indoor football and futsal leagues among themselves, playing without men in the audience, and were, at a pinch, allowed to view the game on television; rumours abounded of girls disguised as men sneaking into matches. Twenty Irish women were allowed into the Azadi for the World Cup game, albeit under strictly enforced dress codes and in a separate section of the ground. But their very presence forced the issue out into the open. Reformist papers including women's weekly magazines claimed that Iranian women were being discriminated against in their own country. Six months later, in a rare act of reform, the Iranian cabinet approved women's return to the stadium, though under 'suitable conditions'. Finally, in 2003, women were present at the Iran Khodro stadium in Tehran to watch Peykan FC play live. The suburban Tehrani team had been chosen because, it was said, its fans swore and cursed the least of any crowd in the country. The game passed without any noted descent of the nation into moral turpitude, but the clerical elite and their minions remained deeply suspicious. When David Beckham's face appeared on Tehran billboards in 2003 advertising engine oil these images were draped in black cloth.

Saddam Hussein was not it seems a fan of football, but he and his entourage understood its value. His half-brothers Barzan and Watban

Ibrahim took control of the club in their home town of Tikrit. A tiny club from a tiny town suddenly looked like championship contenders, coming fourth in the league in 1982 and winning it the following year. General Hussein Kemil, Saddam's son-in-law, backed the army team Al-Jaish. On patriotic grounds he ordered the Iraqi FA to hand over the country's best players to his team in an effort to raise the morale of an army being ground to dust on the border with Iran. In 1984 at the height of the war Saddam handed control of Iraq's International Olympic Committee and then its Football Association to his son Uday. In a political system in which fear and violence were the dominant currency of rule, Uday was perhaps the most brutal and psychotic of the regime's inner circle. The Iraqi IOC building became his personal and political headquarters. All the sports federations were summarily ejected. Bullet-proof glass arrived along with his personal offices and PR department. The basement was given over to his sports-car collection and a thirty-cell prison was installed on the first floor. An understanding of his approach to sports management and motivation is best left to Sharar Hayday, a regular member of the Iraqi national football team in the 1980s and 1990s:

I was tortured four times after matches. One time after a friendly against Jordan in Amman that we lost 2–0, Uday had me and three team-mates taken to prison. When we arrived they took off our shirts, tied our feet together and pulled our knees over a bar as we lay on our backs. Then they dragged us over pavement and concrete, pulling the skin off our backs. Then they dragged us through a sandpit to get sand in our backs. Finally, they made us climb a ladder and jump into a vat of raw sewage . . . The next day, and for every day that we were there, they beat our feet. My punishment, because I was a star player, was twenty per day. I asked the guard how he could ever forgive himself. He laughed and told me that if he didn't do this Uday would do it to him.[14]

Uday liked to vary his instruments of terror. The national team and youth teams were often told that he would blow their plane up if they returned defeated from a foreign fixture. He had a direct telephone link from his office to the national team's dressing room. During big international fixtures loudspeakers would relay his half-time instructions – a mixture of curses, threats, abuse and screaming. After games he would sometimes simply have a team held for hours, allowing them to sweat it out as they awaited an uncertain fate. Domestic football and other sports were treated to the same kinds of brutality. The tall national volleyball team was forced to half-stand, half-sit in specially constructed low-ceilinged rooms for days on end. Defeated boxers were treated to a personal going over in Uday's office. After the invasion and occupation of Kuwait, Uday created a special committee drafted from the entire nation's sporting federations with a mission systematically to loot the equipment of Kuwait's IOC and other sporting bodies; those that refused to participate were imprisoned and tortured. In his early years in the job, Uday's passion was the club he created for himself, Al-Rasheed. Uday handpicked the best players from around the country and advised referees on the likely outcome of Al-Rasheed's games. In the three years before the first Gulf War, they duly won the national championships, together with three consecutive Arab Champions Cups from 1985.

The limits of coaching by terror, the desperate impact of defeat in the Gulf War and the subsequent era of sanctions, shortages and isolation took their toll on Iraqi sport in general and football in particular. While the country had sent large teams to the Olympics in the 1970s and early 1980s there were only four Iraqi athletes present at Sydney in 2000. The national football team, which had been good enough to make the 1986 World Cup finals if not able to gain a point, was unable even under sentence of death to repeat the feat. Failure to qualify for the 1994 World Cup left the squad kicking concrete footballs till the bones in their soles and toes were broken. That the national team managed to qualify for the 1996 Asian Cup in the UAE was astonishing. After this Iraq and its national team were subject to an ever tighter policy of containment and sanctions. They found themselves excluded from the Asian Games and unable to fulfil their home fixtures in World Cup qualifying games. Al-Rasheed were not able to win the national championship again nor even the newly created Mother of all Battles Cup. Uday himself was demoted within the ranks of his father's entourage and an assassination attempt in 1996 left him crippled. At least the leading footballers, once forced to play kickabouts with the man in which he predictably needed to star, were now spared this particular humiliation.

What was common knowledge inside Iraq and increasingly voiced by international human-rights organizations took rather longer to penetrate the world of global sporting bodies. Indeed the IOC never did quite get around to investigating the conduct of the president of its Iraqi branch.

FIFA at least sent a delegation in 2001 after rumours of torture following Iraq's 4–1 defeat by Japan in an Asian Cup match in October 2000 could not be ignored. The FIFA mission made one flying visit to see twelve players and the coach, a few months after the event. The heads of the Malaysian and Qatari FAs and a doctor conducted the interviews with the players. Members of the Iraqi security service were also present at all of these: no allegations of torture were made, no reports of punishment substantiated. FIFA's belief that these interviews would yield anything plausibly connected to the truth points not to the organization's naivity but its gutless cynicism.

Two years later Uday was dead. The Olympic Committee building had been reduced to a bombed-out shell. The national team's boots, shirts and training equipment had been looted. Iraq was occupied by the US and UK armies, and the national football stadium served as a parking lot for the US army's biggest trucks and specialist vehicles. The crude bleachers and concrete walls were pockmarked by shot and shell fire. All international fixtures were played outside the country and facilities for training were virtually non-existent. Yet the Iraqi national team, under German manager Bernd Schuster, managed to get themselves to the 2004 Athens Olympics with a 3–1 victory over Saudi Arabia. Schuster would later resign after receiving repeated death threats. The team then progressed all the way to the semi-finals in Greece before Paraguay beat them. Victories over Portugal, Costa Rica and Australia were followed by massive bursts of tracer and gun fire over Iraqi cities; even in the battle-torn city of Najaf the fighting seemed, to some observers, to lull during the games. The Bush presidential re-election campaign had the cheek to run adverts at the time showing pictures of the Afghan and Iraqi flags with the words: 'At this Olympics there will be two more free nations – and two fewer terrorist regimes.' Iraq's national team coach Adnan Hamad replied, 'The American army has killed so many people in Iraq. What is freedom when I go to the stadium and there are shootings on the road?' So the fairy tale ends; the Italians beat them to the bronze medal.[15]

VII

Osama Bin Laden spent the early months of 1994 in London making contact with his supporters and his bankers. While there this scion of the Saudi Arabian ruling elite took the chance to pay a few visits to Highbury. He seems to have had a particular liking for Arsenal's European games; it was after all the season that they won the European Cup Winners' Cup. He also shopped at the Arsenal megastore in Finsbury Park, buying souvenirs for his sons. Subsequently the chant was heard at Highbury, 'He's hiding in Kabul, he loves the Arsenal, Os-a-ma, Os-a-ma.' Whether Bin Laden has continued to follow the Gunners is not known, but he and Al-Qaeda have certainly stayed in touch with football. The Algerian-based Salafist Group for Preaching and Combat linked up with Al-Qaeda in 1998 and planned attacks at matches during the 1998 World Cup in France, thwarted by a series of arrests before the tournament. More recently, Bin Laden has been seen on a videotape recounting one of his followers' dreams in which Al-Qaeda and the Americans played a game of football. Al-Qaeda put eleven pilots on the pitch and won the game. Another of Bin Laden's colleagues recalls seeing an Egyptian family watching the events of 9/11. 'They exploded with joy. Do you know when there is a soccer game and your team wins? It was the same expression of joy.'[16]

Football metaphors form a central element of the vocabulary of Al-Qaeda because in Saudi Arabia (Bin Laden's home and the movement's base) football is immensely popular. This is somewhat surprising as in Saudi Arabia in general, and among fundamentalist Islamic groups like Al-Qaeda in particular, all other forms of Western culture are viewed at best with suspicion and often with downright hostility. The faces of models in adverts for Western consumer goods are still blacked out in the kingdom and in recent years it has not been uncommon to find decapitated Ronald McDonalds outside the air-conditioned malls. Yet Saudi Arabia has not gone down the Iranian route of repression and attitudes to football remain untouched by this anger.

The story of Saudi Arabian football is the story of how to turn oil into football and success at football into political legitimacy. The money from the country's massive oil industry that does not go to the foreign corporations that extract it is overwhelmingly in the hands of the extended royal House of Saud. These people also staff the upper echelons of government, parastatal corporations and the armed forces, and control as personal fiefdoms the Saudi Arabian Football Federation and all of the leading football clubs. As in many areas of social and economic life in the kingdom, these organizations have been developed by employing short-term imported expert labour working under the constant and inconsistent interventions of the Saudi aristocracy. There are well-founded suspicions that match outcomes are often affected by the place of a team and its backers in the royal hierarchy. Coaches and players find themselves subject to the whim of princes: Al-Hilal's Portuguese coach Artur Jorge was fired for refusing to select players favoured by the club's princely backers, and others have had their tactics and training methods questioned.

Oil money, as well as funding a three-decade bout of ludicrous, ostentatious over-consumption for this narrow stratum, has also been applied to the increasingly difficult problem of how to stay in power. Lavish expenditure on very high specification infrastructure is one element in the mix. Saudi Arabia has motorways that would grace any American conurbation and in the King Fahd stadium it has a national arena that is of world-class standard; few stadiums can boast the intricacy of its finishing or the flamboyance of its Bedouin tent canopies.

But try as they might, the political and religious elites cannot keep Saudi society in a feudal and theological straitjacket; oil has changed the nation. Saudi Arabia has acquired growing and restive urban populations. The cities of the coast, some built from scratch, now house a small, newly educated and frustrated middle class, the indigenous poor, recently urbanized Bedouins, and a large imported proletariat from Egypt, Palestine and South Asia. The foreigners are on short-term contracts, obsessively policed and excluded the moment trouble threatens. But the locals cannot be deported. The government has attempted to sate them with free healthcare, accommodation and education as well as stipends and sinecures of various kinds. And then there is football. Women are banned from the stadiums, foreigners are there only as staff, and the poor can't afford to get in. In Saudi Arabia, a society that has been economically modernized without going through industrialization, it is the new middle class that is the threat to the *ancien régime*. Over-educated and underemployed, without access to power and with few routes for upward social mobility, it is this class that goes to football matches and it is this class that has staffed the secular and fundamentalist opposition in Saudi Arabia.

The national team in particular has provided a patriotic circus and diversion in the 1990s, qualifying for four successive World Cups (1994–2006), winning the Asian Cup twice and in 1994 becoming the first Arabic side to make it out of the group stage of the World Cup. But football success is not necessarily sustainable. While the top teams have lavish training facilities, football beyond this tiny charmed circle is penurious. Most local players, at most levels, must contend with sand and tarmac rather than astroturf or grass. As a consequence the flow of talent upwards is restricted. The development of players that do make it into the top league is retarded in two ways. On the one hand, the huge influx of foreigners into the league, only recently brought under control, keeps some domestic players out. But worse, because the kingdom has – despite the wages on offer – relatively low-skilled football labour from Central Asia, its players are not exposed to the best. The performance of both clubs and the national side has dipped, the nadir being a total trouncing 8–0 by the Germans at the 2002 World Cup. Inequality, paranoia and closure stalk Saudi politics and football alike; they have already taken their toll on the game, the House of Saud may be next.

The Saudi Arabian approach to the maintenance of royal patrimonial power and the pursuit of footballing success was not the only strategy pursued in the Gulf. The United Arab Emirates (UAE), a federation of seven minor sheikhdoms, controlled by the Al-Nahyan family in Abu Dhabi and the Al-Maktoums in Dubai, has opted for a more open path. Football players, Western tourists and foreign companies are all actively courted in the UAE and there are fewer restrictions on publishing and broadcasting here than in Saudi. In footballing terms it has paid considerable dividends. The UAE has a population of 3 million of which three-quarters are foreigners, unable to play for the national team since the UAE's liberalism does not extend to awarding citizenship to poor Palestinians and Pakistanis, however good their football skills. Yet the UAE managed to qualify for the 1990 World Cup – the country with the smallest population ever to make it to the finals.

The Al-Nahyans, although based in Abu Dhabi, have maintained connections with their roots in the desert interior of the country where they have sponsored the club Al-Ain since 1968. A glance at the club's board reveals the very highest-ranking officials from the military, government and royal house with Sheikh Zayed himself as honorary president. In 2003 Al-Ain won the Asian Champions Cup. It is as if Malta's Sliema Wanderers had won the European Champions' League. The UAE's cosmopolitanism extends to the national airline. Emirates has been a major sponsor of European football clubs, most notably Arsenal.

Qatar has taken a similar path to the UAE and has also emerged as a force in football in the Gulf. Qatar is one of the more liberal and open Gulf States. It is home to the Arabic TV station Al-Jazeera and remains closely aligned with the West. Its ruler Sheikh Hamad Al-Thani handed control over football and the local Olympic committee to Crown Prince Tamim Al-Thani in the late 1990s. Tamim had big ambitions for football in this tiny country of fewer than half a million Qataris and under 3,000 registered players. In 2003 Qatar got systematic about this as the Olympic committee gave each of the top clubs $10 million to spend on foreign players. At the start of the season the young semi-pros of Al-Sadd, Khor, Al-Arabi and Al-Rayyan were joined by luminaries of the calibre of Argentinian striker Gabriel Batistuta, French defender Frank Leboeuf and the legendary German midfielder Stefan Effenberg. The Qataris argued rightly that only by bringing in this kind of experience could local players hope to raise their game to world standards. But impatient for success Tamim and the Olympic committee devised a perfect shortcut: don't just buy the player's labour, buy his citizenship. Qatar tempted two leading Kenyan athletes to take Qatari citizenship and run under their flag. They then went on to approach three Brazilians playing in Germany, Ailton, Dede and Leandro, offering them millions of dollars to take the plunge. But before Ailton and his friends could decide, FIFA decided for them, declaring that players must either have grandparents of the nation they play for or have lived in the country for two years before taking citizenship.

West of the Gulf the oil dries up and football like every other aspect of society in the Levant has been shaped by the wars and conflicts, international and civil, that have racked the region since the creation of the state of Israel in 1948. The bitterness of those conflicts led to Israel's expulsion from the AFC in 1974. Israel joined UEFA in 1992 and thus its contemporary footballing history is European. Nonetheless its presence remains deeply felt in the football of the region. Palestinians played football during the British Mandate but like the Palestinian nation football was profoundly dislocated by the 1948 war, the formation of Israel and the massive migration of Palestinian refugees to Jordan and Lebanon. Palestinians were scattered across many national borders, often housed in desperate refugee camps and bereft of international representation. Organized football barely existed in Gaza and the West Bank after the 1967 war and their annexation by Israel. What little progress had been made was swept aside in the Intifada of the late 1980s, when even street football was impossible. The Palestinians' only footballing representatives were Al-Wihdat, a team in the Jordanian league that grew out of the refugee camps on the East Bank of the River Jordan. Yasser Arafat described their importance to the diaspora during the team's tour of the West Bank and Gaza: 'One day when we had no voice, Al-Wihdat was our voice.'[17]

The signing of the Oslo peace accords by the Israeli and Palestinian leaderships in 1993, and the abatement of fighting in the occupied territories, opened the way for a revival of football in Palestine. Within a year the Palestinian Football Association had been created and for a few short years, regular competition was possible. Though Israel still refused to concede the existence of either a Palestinian nation or a Palestinian state, referring only to the territories under the control of the Palestinian Authority, FIFA were unambiguous. Palestine was made a member of the organization in 1998 and significant development money was made available. The Palestinian diaspora has been drawn upon and the national team has fielded players who have grown up in Jordan, Syria, Lebanon and Chile, where a considerable Palestinian community was established early in the twentieth century. Domestic football has not prospered in Palestine. The reignition of the Intifada in 2001 and the breakdown of the peace process has created the same impossible conditions for football in Gaza and the West Bank as before. However, the national team, though forced to play its home games in Qatar, has continued and acts as a hugely popular public representative of Palestinian national aspirations.

Lebanese football stuttered through the climactic years of the late 1960s and early 1970s when Palestinian guerrilla forces started to use the Lebanon as a base for attacking Israel. The instability led to civil war in 1973, the expulsion of the PLO, the division and destruction of Beirut and armed intervention by Syria and Israel. The national football championship did not survive. As the war came towards its close in the late 1980s a national competition was revived, but the 1988 season was never completed and most games descended into brawling. Only in 1991 after the formation of a government of national unity and the dissolution of the militias was a full football programme able to go ahead.

The national team which had also been absent from the world of football during the civil war was reformed at the beginning of the 1990s. Its role is a mirror image of the Palestinian team. Lebanon, at the end of the civil war, was a state. Indeed the end of the civil war was recognition that the country could not be divided into mini-states nor its borders changed. The problem for the Lebanese state was the absence of a nation. Domestic football illustrates the problem, for every major team remained closely linked to Lebanon's ethnic and religious groups. Leading club Al-Ansar are the team of the powerful Sunni Muslims. The wealthy businessman Rafiq Hariri was president of the club and Prime Minister of Lebanon through the 1990s and early 2000s when Al-Ansar won eleven consecutive championships. Al-Nejmeh are the team of the Shiites. Hemki are the team of the Christian Maronites. Christian Phalangists with Armenian roots have Homenetmen if they are on the Right and Homenmen if they are on the Left. Even the Islamicist Hezbollah militia maintains a team, Raia FC, though they have yet to climb out of the lower divisions. The degree of trouble on Lebanon's terraces suggested that the war might be over but national unity was a long way off.

But Lebanon has survived these testing times as a single entity and its national team has served a small part in this. The ex-Welsh international Terry Yorath was made coach of the national team in 1994 and showed a refreshingly uninformed attitude to the conflict, picking players according to ability rather than ethnicity. The 2000 Asian Cup was held in Lebanon – itself a measure of the enormous process of material reconstruction that has happened in the last decade – and the Lebanese team received support from all quarters. For the moment Lebanon's search for a nation through its football team looks a more promising enterprise than the contribution of football to the Palestinians' struggle for a state.

20

Small Mercies:
Football in Africa
after the Cold War, 1990–2006

We are now more cognizant of our children prodding us. Their faces are coming into focus. The grumble in our bellies is becoming prominent. We can hear the voices of our wives as they shout, 'You never listen to me.' We have no excuse to buy beer instead of food. Our televisions are off and we must now pay attention to what the kids are doing in school.   **Soneka Kamuhuza, in the wake of the Zambian National Team's air crash**

I

Kenneth Kaunda was a rarity: an African President who not only backed football, but actually liked it. Disengaged from the dynamics of power, Nkrumah never mentions the game in his letters and memoirs from exile. Mobutu was never seen in a stadium after 1974. Amin liked to play, to join in, and to offer a lot of advice, but his attention span was limited. Kaunda liked to watch, often attending minor league games in Lusaka. He was, in addition, one of the very few African leaders to relinquish power peacefully in an election. Zambia had been a one-party state since 1972 and that party was Kaunda's UNIP. Although his rule was relatively benign Zambia remained desperately poor. Its copper-belt cities lived in thrall to the vagaries of the international commodity markets. The countryside remained mired in desperate poverty. Zambia's admirable stand in the struggle against apartheid and colonialism in Southern Africa did little to alleviate its endemic systems of corruption and patronage at home. Food riots in 1990 heralded the end of Kaunda and victory for the opposition Movement for Multiparty Democracy and the new President Frederick Chiluba. It was a moment of heady optimism for Zambia captured by the rising prowess of the national football team – the *Chipolopolo* ('Bullets').

This generation of players had announced their arrival at the 1988 Olympic Games in Seoul where, to the nation's delight, Zambia had beaten Italy 4–0. They went on to take third place in the 1990 Cup of Nations. Power Dynamos, the copper-belt club that provided most of the national team's home-based players, had won the country's one and only African club prize – the Cup Winners' Cup in 1991. In April 1993 the national team had qualified for the following year's Cup of Nations in style, hammering Mauritius 3–0. Now, two days later, they were heading north for Dakar to play a World Cup qualifier against Senegal with a real prospect of making the finals for the first time. The country was entranced. On the morning of 28 April, rumours began to spread along the main streets of Lusaka: the plane has crashed, yes crashed, off the coast of Gabon, over the Atlantic Ocean. The director of the Zambian Broadcasting Corporation himself came on air to read the news: a military aircraft carrying the squad had taken off from Libreville in Gabon, en route to Senegal. It had crashed in the sea soon afterwards. There were thirty people on board; crew, administrators, players. There were no survivors. When the ghastly bloated bodies were returned to Lusaka they arrived in the Zambian Airways plane that had proved too expensive for the Zambian FA to charter a week earlier. The streets were lined all along the 25-kilometre route to the Independence stadium. There the dead lay in state. President Chiluba led the service of mourning. In the new Zambia, he promised, there would be a full investigation into the causes of the crash and a trust fund established for the players' now destitute families. And hope? Hope would rest with the remains of the team. Offers of support from the Danish Football Association were taken up. The nation's Europe-based professionals who had travelled separately for the Senegal game – like Kalusha Bwalya and Kenneth Malitoli – formed the core of the squad. New and untested players were called up. Qualification for the World Cup proved too much for them as they lost their final qualifying game away to Morocco by a single late goal. A draw would have done. A cross had agonizingly drifted across the Moroccan line begging for a tap in. It never came.

Zambia made it as far as the semi-finals of the African Cup of Nations in early 1996. Later that year Chiluba won another presidential term. The still-heady brew of football, nationalism and hope saw an enormous crowd pack the national stadium in June to see Zambia play Sudan in a World Cup qualifying game. The stadium had been hastily erected in 1964 to host Zambia's Independence Day celebrations. There had been plans to complete the works and replace the temporary structures. Thirty years later nothing had been done. A chaotic stampede in the crowd, made immeasurably worse by locked exit gates, left nine dead and seventy-eight injured. Zambian football and politics entered a steep and persistent decline in their fortunes.

The government refused to publish or release its own investigation into the aircraft disaster. There were persistent rumours that they had chosen a cheap military plane, rather than buy expensive tickets with Zambian Airways. Reports emerged that one of the plane's engines was faulty; it had sat on the runway in Lusaka for some years before suddenly being pressed back into service. Chiluba had by this time ridden out an attempted coup, but the persistent charges of corruption and embezzlement would not stop. Hope and trust were running out. The national team failed to qualify for any tournaments, domestic football shrank, and still no money was forthcoming for the families of the players. The families took the government to court and the Zambian High Court ordered the government to pay, which it didn't. But Chiluba's government did find time to ease many families out of their government-sponsored housing. The widows began to die off and Chiluba and his cronies – whose rottenness and venality had now become clear – were thrown out in the 2002 elections. President Mwanawasa has made sure that Chiluba has been charged with the theft of $30 million while in power, but there is no money for the widows and their orphans and no Zambian team that can bring hope.

The fate of Zambian football traces the arc of African politics in the decade after the end of the Cold War. First, a moment of rare optimism as the constraints and alien imperatives of superpower conflict and intrigue appeared to evaporate. The apartheid regime in South Africa and all the ramshackle one-party states to its north would be forced to reckon with the real needs of their people. And then the reality: for Zambia, like many nations, the acquisition of a new but equally rapacious and incompetent elite; for some, like Zaire, Liberia and Côte d'Ivoire, the descent into war, civil war and secession; for most, enduring economic hardship; for all, the iron logic of the global capital and commodity markets. The same constraints shaped the course of African football. Buoyed by the brilliance of Cameroon at the 1990 World Cup, African football was in the ascendant, but its rise was checked. Although Africa's representation at the World Cup climbed to five teams it was not until 2002 that Senegal would repeat Cameroon's quarter-final placing. The economic logic of world football saw a mass migration of talent to Europe and elsewhere that would diminish a domestic game already hobbled by insecurity and underinvestment. The political logic of democratization in Africa saw football clubs and national teams undercut and undermined by bitter local feuding and barefaced embezzlement. The wars of the decade removed many nations from the football map altogether and ushered in an era of simmering violence and disorder into African cities and football stadiums. The combination of all these factors would culminate in 2001 in a series of cataclysmic stadium disasters across the continent. Over 200 people lost their lives and Africa's first serious bid to host the World Cup – South Africa in 2006 – was undermined as the continent's internal divisions and political weakness in world football's corridors of power were cruelly exposed. And yet as Josiah Johnson, a Liberian coach, recognized in his plaintive call to the child-soldiers of West Africa, football continued to offer small mercies, hopes and aspirations where there were precious few alternatives: 'Put down your guns and go to the stadium and enjoy the game; you don't become a millionaire shooting someone, [but] you might if you can play good football.'[1]

In the past two decades Africa has undergone a huge demographic shift that has hugely enlarged football's constituency. Africa's population is getting bigger, younger and more urban. In 1960 the population of Africa was around 200 million people; by 2000 it had tripled to 600 million. While Europe, America and Japan got older, Africa was getting younger. In Algeria, one-third of the population was under 18, half the population was under 30. The severity of the HIV epidemic that swept the continent in the 1980s and 1990s, striking primarily at adults, skewed the demography of much of Africa even further towards its new youthful majority. Historically comparable rates of population growth in the West took place under conditions of rapid urbanization and industrialization. In Africa they were accompanied by the former but not the latter. Neither formal nor informal economies could begin to absorb this tidal wave of humanity, yet such has been the economic and environmental marginality of much of rural Africa that a vast migration to the exploding shanty towns and shack settlements of Cairo, Accra, Lagos, Kinshasa, Nairobi and Johannesburg has occurred. And what did they do in these vast impoverished metropolises? Here, where there was little land and no public services, there was and continues to be football, in the street, on the scrub, on bare earth and on TV.

Television, which arrived in Africa four decades after the US and Britain, and whose diffusion was always restricted by the state's limited investment in broadcasting and by widespread social deprivation, finally took off in the 1990s. In 2000 Tanzania became the last mainland African state to acquire a terrestrial national broadcasting network. Sets of every make and vintage, illegally run off the mains cables in the towns, arduously wired to car batteries in the countryside, began to spread. Above all the new satellite technologies started to beam international football to Africa. The connection wasn't always that good and the TV rights didn't always get paid, but Africa finally got to look at itself on the world stage and it was playing football.

And in between World Cups and Nations Cups, on those long days of passing time and surviving? Africa's young didn't just watch, they played; from the endless rotating kickabouts on the few patches of open land left in the new urban sprawls, to the organized tournaments between neighbourhoods, *quartiers*, villages and regions. In Senegal the Nawetane leagues in the slums of Dakar were better attended than the national league. In Gambia the Nawetane, which are often held around key dates in the agricultural calendar, became so popular that President Yahya Jammeh threatened to ban football during the harvest and jail anyone taking part in or organizing it: 'The time wasted organizing football matches could be better spent in the fields.'[2] At the same time the official league, barely semi-professional and based in the cities rather than the country, virtually collapsed through lack of interest. Attendances had fallen so low in 2003 that the Gambian FA announced that in 2004 all league football would be free.

In the deep mire of poverty that is Mathare – a giant rotting shanty town of Nairobi – Mathare Youth Sports Association (MYSA) has tapped the enormous passion for the game to create a unique programme of football coaching and social and personal development. Founded in 1987, MYSA has become Africa's largest youth organization, running around 100 leagues for 1,000 teams, including 200 girls' teams. Participation and coaching is linked to voluntary public service. The senior team – Mathare United – built on this huge foundation and supported by Norwegian development aid gained national league status and then won two of three Kenyan Cup Finals in the next four years. The message has not been lost on aid agencies elsewhere who have sought to use football as an instrument of post-conflict reconciliation in Liberia and Sierra Leone and where the reintegration of psychologically scarred child-soldiers into mainstream society has used football as a tool of therapy and socialization.

As the work of MYSA and Unicef shows, the last quarter of a century has also seen the emergence of the women's game. Africa has proved no different from any other part of the world where football has been at every level and in every role an overwhelmingly male domain. African football inherited the male culture of European football and reproduced it in the patriarchal institutions of education, state service and the military, which fed the growth of the game. African women's access to education and sport has grown in the main urban centres but faces the entrenched opposition of traditional attitudes to women, physicality and the public realm. This is most extreme in Islamic societies. As recently as 2003 the northern Nigerian state of Niger banned women's football altogether; similar attitudes have restricted the development of the game elsewhere in West and North Africa.

Nonetheless, in Nigeria, Ghana and South Africa the women's game has grown. The Nigerian entrepreneur Christopher Abisuga created a women's exhibition team, the 'Sugar Babes' Ladies FC, in the early 1980s, while Princess Bola Jegede sponsored the first women's national tournament in Lagos in 1990. Sponsors, players and money have all followed. Women's football had surely arrived when in 2000 the match between South Africa and Nigeria at the African Women's Championship had to be abandoned after fighting and rioting in Johannesburg, and in 2004 the Liberian Football Association appointed Izetta Sombo Wesley as the first woman to head an African FA and Ophelia Doeway as their first female referee. With the victory of Ellen Johnson-Sirleaf Liberia acquired Africa's first popularly elected woman head of state when she beat the Liberian football star George Weah in a bitterly contested election in late 2005.

A powerful indicator of the grip in which football holds Africa's popular culture is the number of political leaders that have been prepared not merely to back football through the usual hidden channels of money, power and influence, but actually to take to the field. In a quite extraordinary display Nigerian President Obasanjo played central midfield in a match between the Nigerian Federal Executive and Legislature. The two wings of the Nigerian government had been at loggerheads for months over the shape and size of the federal budget. Played in Abuja in 2000, the Executive won with a single goal from the President – though the game was stopped halfway through the second half when it started raining. The televised event proved sufficiently popular to be replicated by state executives and legislatures that had the same problem. Ugandan President Yoweri Museveni sought to underwrite his inclusive no-party politics by leading a joint cabinet–parliament side in a game against the Ugandan FA. Museveni's side won 2–1. Kenya's parliamentarians have formed their own cross-party team – Bunge FC – and taken to the road playing their opposite numbers in Uganda and Tanzania, promoting public-health messages and themselves. As one eyewitness reports, it is a risky strategy for Africa's legislators: 'You see them . . . with their pregnant stomachs and tiny legs trying to run after the ball but actually walking after it, and kicking just the way kids kick.'

The 1990s were another poor decade for the economies of Africa and its football, with a sharp acceleration in the intensity of economic globalization. Global flows of capital, technology, trade and labour all grew. But with the exception of the oil-based economies, Africa's intersection with the global economy actually shrank. Increasingly draconian immigration policies in Europe attempted to stem the flow of workers and their families from former colonies, though levels of illegal migration continued to rise. Africa's share of world trade declined and despite its desperate need for investment of all kinds, Africa has been a net exporter of capital. Debt repayments and the accumulation of stolen fortunes in foreign bank accounts have starved Africa's economies. The only area of real growth in Africa's economic connectedness has been the persistent and malign impact of IMF structural adjustment programmes on domestic economies, and the migration of Africa's most skilled workers – including its leading football talents. These two processes are not unconnected for while Africa has continued to produce players of exceptional quality its domestic football economy has become less and less able to hold on to them; and as the stars have departed so the interest in and quality of club football appears to decline, locking African football into a familiar downward spiral of underdevelopment. In response the 1990s saw an effort by many of the leading African nations – including Algeria, Morocco, Nigeria, South Africa – to officially professionalize their leagues, but none has managed to match such a formal commitment with the level of funding that could reverse the current migratory flows.

Money and resources were always very tight in most of Africa but the 1990s saw a further decline in income and attendances for most clubs. While European football grew rich on massively inflated sponsorship and TV rights income, African football fed on the crumbs; the African Champions League, for example, received TV rights income of less than 1 per cent of its European equivalent and less than a quarter of the Arab Champions League. Indeed the only regular and reliable source of income for many clubs was from the transfer of players. Not surprisingly, many clubs and individuals have created football schools and develop-ment programmes to tap and nurture the abundant talent of Africa's cities before selling it off to the north. The steady successes of African nations in the World Cup and the impact of key African football migrants of the late 1980s and early 1990s like George Weah, Abédi Pelé and Jules Bocande encouraged European clubs and agents to take a closer look at African players, and in turn African players and clubs sought out European transfer fees, contracts and wages. Weah, in par-ticular, raised the status of all Africa's footballers with his sparkling performances and pitch-long dribbles for AC Milan. In 1995 he was the first African to be made World Player of the Year. So great were the disparities of wages between Europe and Africa, and so deep was the well of talent, that the migration of African footballers, primarily but not exclusively to Europe, constitutes one of the biggest sporting migrations in history – the equal of the movement of South Americans to Europe or of any group within Europe. From fewer than a hundred players in professional European football in 1990, there were nearly 1,000 Africans playing in 2000.[3] Their main destinations were France, Belgium, Portugal and the Netherlands, with significant numbers in the big leagues of Germany, Spain, Italy and England. But unlike previous migrations that had seen foreigners move to the very summit of Euro-pean football, this migration was broader and deeper. Africans found their way to Greece and Turkey, every Scandinavian country and most surprisingly of all to Eastern Europe – particularly Russia and the

Ukraine, but also to smaller leagues in Poland, the Czech Republic, Romania and Bulgaria. The bulk of this labour force came from West Africa, especially Nigeria, Ghana, Côte d'Ivoire, Cameroon and Senegal. Algeria and Morocco were also major suppliers (unlike Egypt and Tunisia whose football talent was primarily retained at home). Angola exported many players but almost entirely to Portugal while the collapse of Zaire and its uncertain rebirth as the Democratic Republic of Congo saw its players spread far and wide in an effort to escape the poverty and chaos at home.

The recruitment and transfer system for African players has been controlled by a shadowy world of agents, football schools and academies. The ex-French international Jean-Marc Guillou helped establish the ASEC Abidjan academy, which was one of the leading schools alongside Nigeria's Pepsi Academy and Ajax Cape Town's programme. Guillou left ASEC to set up his own unregistered outfit and supplied Belgian club Beveren with an entire first team of young Ivorians in 2003. While leading players have been financially rewarded with secure and lucrative contracts there have been many casualties. Young players have signed up with unscrupulous and unregistered agents, taken the trip to Europe only to fail an unexpected trial and find themselves, suddenly, as penniless and homeless illegal immigrants in a strange land. Others have signed contracts of worthless legal and financial value, played for nothing and found themselves on the scrap heap. Above all, many in or out of work have been subjected to the historic racism of Europe inside and outside the stadium.

Parastatal institutions that were the mainstay of many leagues saw their incomes decline and football teams were often the casualty of such cuts. Nkrumah Red Devils were decimated by the decline of the Zambian copper industry. Nzoia Sugar, from the western Kenyan town of Bungoma, won the league only subsequently to go into liquidation. By contrast teams that were backed by oil companies and the army and police did better. Angola's Petro Atlético and Gabon and Rwanda's army teams – FC 105 and APR respectively – all prospered in the early twenty-first century. If government funds were to be tapped by football clubs then they needed to come higher up the food chain than a mere public utility; in Malawi President Muluzi was the redoubtable backer of the Bata Bullets, while in Nigeria nearly half of the first division in 2000 was directly owned and sponsored by state governments. The other half were the creatures of large companies (like the German construction firm Julius Berger) or of powerful and wealthy individual businessmen. Yet in the absence of a public rich enough to pay for tickets and television, all the material and symbolic investment in these leading clubs still leaves professional football a precarious economic and social enterprise in modern Africa.

IV

While most of the continent faltered, the great hope for Africa's economy and for the advance of its football was newly liberated South Africa. Football and the liberation struggle had been closely connected for more than four decades. Before any other international body decided to place pressure on the apartheid regime, South Africa had been expelled from CAF for refusing to field a multi-ethnic team at the first African Cup of Nations. Although mixed teams had increasingly played in the 1960s and 1970s it was not until 1991 that a truly multi-ethnic national football association was formed. When Nelson Mandela was released from prison his first major speech was given at a rally in the FNB soccer stadium in Johannesburg. With constitutional talks under way, the international community began its process of re-engagement and again first in line were CAF and FIFA who allowed the South Africans back into world football in July 1992. In football as in politics and economics, South Africa was going to be a beacon of hope and reform. Football, rather than the white-dominated sports of cricket and rugby, would be able to take its rightful place as the nation's game. Democratic and technologically and economically advanced as the country was, South Africa's football would not be held back by the constraints of underdevelopment, nor warped by the patrimonial authoritarianism of the rest of the continent.

For a few years, everything seemed possible. Despite the protracted violence of the townships and the vicious struggle between the ANC and Inkarta in Kwazulu-Natal, a constitution was agreed by the elites, accepted by the public in referendums and exercised in a free and fair election that saw Mandela elected to the presidency and the ANC to government. In club football, from which South African teams had also hitherto been excluded, Soweto giants Orlando Pirates won their first

African Champions Cup in 1995. The same year the bankrupt Kenyan state and football association were forced to withdraw their offer to host the 1996 Cup of Nations. South Africa stepped in and not only hosted the tournament but went all the way to the final where they beat Tunisia. A multi-ethnic crowd saw a multi-ethnic team receive the trophy from Nelson Mandela, F. W. De Klerk and Zulu King Goodwill Zweli-thini. Two years later they were back in the Cup of Nations Final only to lose to Egypt, but consolation followed when they qualified for their first World Cup in France in 1998.

In retrospect that was the peak. In successive Nations Cups South Africa have displayed a relentless decline. In 2000 they came third, in 2002 they only made the quarter-finals and in 2004 and 2006 they were eliminated in the group stages; when they failed to quality for the 2006 World Cup, the event was sufficiently calamitous that President Mbeki mentioned it in his State of the Union speech and established a presiden-tial commission to reorganize the national team's preparations for the 2010 World Cup. The exuberance of liberation will only get you so far for so long. The enduring legacy of apartheid was a woeful record of under-investment in facilities, talent and organization. Clubs still do not own their own grounds and thus have little control over the management of games and little incentive to invest in the improvement of facilities. Sponsorship has arrived but given the poverty of many black football fans, the game cannot attract a rate similar to smaller but whiter sports like cricket. What sponsorship there is has been concentrated at a few big teams. Some investment from overseas has come into South Africa, with Dutch club Ajax buying and rebranding the Cape Town Spurs who now compete in the top flight as Ajax Cape Town. But for most clubs and players economic reality has been harsher.

The promise of modernized administration also receded. Just as the ANC has found itself, post-liberation, ensnared by economic stagnation, internal feuds and cases of minor corruption, so South African football has been caught out. The Pickard Commission of Inquiry set up by then Sports Minister Steve Tshwete in 1996 to probe corruption led to the resignation of SAFA executive president Solomon Morewa. The com-mission also recommended the resignation of all executive members who served under him. But the problems have endured. In 2001 match officials and the manager of Johannesburg club Classic FC were banned from football after it was revealed they had colluded to ensure the club won vital matches in its premier-league relegation struggle. Irvin Khoza, the 'Iron Duke', owner and president of Orlando Pirates and vice-chairman of both the FA and the league, was arrested in 2002 on charges of tax evasion and diversion of transfer fees received for two Pirates players – Mark Fish and Helman Mkhalele – from the club to his own trust fund. In the run-up to the 2004 Cup of Nations, South Africa managed to first suspend and then sack coach Shakes Mashaba only a fortnight before the tournament. He was not the first, as national coaches Carlos Queiroz and Clive Barker had suffered similar fates. Indeed, the instability and hysteria of South Africa's relationship with Bafana Bafana saw twelve coaches pass through in ten years. The South African team then promptly lost a warm-up game 2–0 to the ultra-minnows of island state Mauritius. Tellingly, more officials went on the trip to the Indian Ocean resort than players. Shakes took SAFA to court, won his case for wrongful dismissal and was quietly bought off while the squad headed for the tournament in Tunisia where they humiliatingly crashed out. The Herculean task of cleaning out the stables of South African football was further demonstrated when the country won the right to host the 2010 World Cup in spring 2004. The announcement was immediately followed by another attempt to cleanse the domestic game in a wave of mass arrests and trials of corrupt match and club officials, but a year later the trial had ignominiously collapsed without a single successful prosecution.

Rather than conflict, the end of the Cold War was meant to herald a process of democratization in Africa. The superpowers were no longer available to support dictatorial regimes. International aid agencies and banks began tying development funding to the process of good govern-ance. More importantly authoritarian government had proved to be a dismal failure everywhere in Africa. What little economic and social development that they had not managed to stifle was now creating restive urban working and middle classes who through the media, trade unions and other organizations were contesting political power. Begin-ning with Benin in 1990 and Zambia in 1991 and culminating in Nigeria's presidential elections in 1999, almost every African state has seen some kind of democratization. Old leaders have been forced to cede power, one-party states have given way to multi-party systems, and elections of various degrees of probity have been held. The record is inevitably mixed. Africa's notoriously corrupt and inefficient football administrations have, along with other parastatals, been exposed to more searching international and domestic scrutiny. FIFA was particularly active in suspending football associations whose autonomy from the government has been compromised. Pursued to its logical limits, not a single member of CAF would survive such an audit of their independence, but FIFA focused on the worst cases of, for example, electoral malpractice, unconstitutional dissolution of football associations by governments and the illegal sale of World Cup tickets allocated by FIFA to African FAs. Since the late 1990s, Cameroon, Guinea, Gambia, Kenya, Sierra Leone and Tanzania have all been suspended from FIFA for such practices; but this barely scratches the surface.

On occasion the administrative weakness of African football descends into farce. In 1996 shortage of funds saw the Cameroonian team arrive in Johannesburg only two days before their first game in the Cup of Nations. That gave the team two days to acclimatize to the thin air of the high veldt. They didn't and one of the pre-tournament favourites was out of the group stages. When Zimbabwe played El Salvador in a warm-up game for the 2004 Cup of Nations, the following day's papers found that not a single member of the Central Americans' squad had ever played for any of the national senior or junior teams before and that the side appeared to have been cobbled together by the kit manufacturers who had promised Zimbabwe the game. They managed a 0–0 draw.

The continent's transport infrastructure remains a massive impediment to regular international football. For example, imagine the surprise of the crowd in Accra who went to see Ghana play Gabon and found them up against Lesotho. The Gabonese were stuck on a broken-down coach in Togo. The air link to South Africa, 3,000 kilometres away, was more reliable than local West African roads. The very low incomes of match officials and most players leaves the game open to match-fixing and bribery. In Zaire, by the end of Mobutu's reign, there were no incomes of any kind being paid to anyone. There was only flagrant predation. The money allocated for the team at the 1996 Cup of Nations completely disappeared only to reappear in the shape of a new villa for the team's senior administrator. The renamed Democratic Republic of Congo just made it to the 2004 Nations Cup with the help of the Egyptian FA. The squad found themselves penniless in Cairo and reduced to dormitory accommodation as the money from Kinshasa never arrived. Again the Egyptian FA stepped in to pay their hotel and flights. Such benevolence was not carried over on to the pitch. In a warm-up game between the two nations the Congolese players were celebrating their equalizer on the touchline with a small band of fans. The Egyptians decided to restart the game and scored as the Congolese goalkeeper helplessly flailed down the pitch. The match officials, needless to say, found no problem with this.

---

31 October 2002
Stade Olympique de l'Emyrne 0 AS Adema 149
Toamasina, Madagascar

Relinquishing your crown is hard to do. General Didier Ratsiraka, Madagascar's President for twenty years, lost the 2001 election. His stuttering AREMA party was no match for millionaire Marc Ravalomanana and his I Love Madagascar outfit. The vote, despite rigging, went against him. Ratsiraka tried to ignore the vote, but he couldn't ignore the general strike and the mass protests Ravalomanana orchestrated. The courts ordered a recount. They did the recount and the result was the same. Ratsiraka said he'd ignore the recount. Then in the summer of 2002 the US recognized Ravalomanana and Ratsiraka was gone, fled into exile with the funds he had embezzled.

Stade Olympique de l'Emyrne were Madagascan champions. They could still retain the title in the final game of the season against challengers AS Adema, but first they needed to beat DS Atsimondrano. It was 2–1, close to the end of the game; penalty. Stade's players and manager Ratismandresy Ratsarazaka protested the decision furiously but to no avail. Atsimondrano equalized and the crown was gone. Later that afternoon Stade had to play out the final game of the tournament already beaten.

Ratsarazaka has positioned himself in the stands rather than the dugout and is gesticulating wildly. The referee blows his whistle. Stade thread the ball back through their half and turn it into their own net. Adema's players and management, puzzled and astonished, remain at their posts. The referee signals for the game to restart. He blows his whistle. Stade thread the ball back through their half and turn it into their own net. Ratsarazaka is yelling to his side to hurry up. The referee signals for the game to restart. The referee blows his whistle. Stade thread the ball back through their half and turn it into their own net.

Reports make no mention of injury time. I think we can assume they didn't play any. That makes it 149 goals in 90 minutes. A goal every forty seconds for ninety excruciating minutes. That requires discipline, efficiency and concentration on the task in hand. Ratsarazaka was exiled from football for six years with most of the squad he had drilled so well.

Ghanaian football has been particularly undermined by financial malpractice; for despite the strength of its domestic football and the quality of its overseas professionals, Ghana had to wait almost four decades to make their World Cup finals debut in Germany 2006, and have not won the Cup of Nations for over twenty years. Here the impact of democratization has been mixed. On the one hand Ghana can boast that genuine rarity in African football, an administrator who was not only caught and lost his job but was convicted in a court of law. In 2001 Sports Minister Mallam Yussif Issah took $46,000 of government money, earmarked for the players, to Khartoum where Ghana were playing Sudan. Issah arrived but the money didn't. He was found guilty at his trial in 2002, imprisoned for a year and ordered to repay the money. But this laudable episode of transparency has been fatally undermined by the conduct of the Ghanaian FA itself. In July 2001 Ghana played Nigeria in Port Harcourt in a key World Cup qualifying match. Ghana were on a seventeen-year unbeaten run against their long-standing anglophone adversaries in West Africa. Liberia were at that time the top of the qualifying group and Nigeria needed to win to make it to Korea and Japan in 2002. Nigeria got their three points but it was later revealed that the governor of River State passed $25,000 to Ben Koufie, president of the Ghanaian FA, before the match. The cash was shared out among administrators and the Ghanaian press corps in the team's hotel. When questioned about the money Koufie managed a level of faux naivety which was breathtaking even by the shameless standards of Ghanaian football administration: 'I initially refused the money because of the rumours and suspicions . . . But I changed my mind after the Nigerian governor said that it is part of their tradition to extend hospitality with such a donation.'[4]

In Libya football was not entangled with the process of internal democratization. Since taking power in a military coup in 1969, Muammar Qaddafi had pursued a domestic agenda of authoritarian Arab socialism underwritten by oil money, force and Qaddafi's unquestionable personal charisma, and there has been little change in this department. In 1996 the Tripoli derby between Al-Ahly and Al-Ittihad erupted into violence around the ground after anti-Qaddafi chants saw a major police response. It left eight dead and thirty-eight injured.

However, Libya did pursue a major shift in foreign policy. For nearly thirty years Qaddafi had followed an eclectic and active engagement with the world. In the early 1970s he looked to a merger with Egypt. When this failed he explored a union with Tunisia and when that failed he tried one more time to combine with Syria in 1980. In the absence of any partner, Qaddafi went on his own idiosyncratic course, sending troops to Uganda in support of Amin and intervening in Chad's civil war. Above all he proclaimed a strident anti-Western position supporting a range of militant Islamic groups, most notably those involved in the Lockerbie aircraft bombing. The 1990s saw Libya internationally isolated and placed under UN sanctions. But in 1999 the regime finally handed over the suspects in the Lockerbie bombing case for trial in the Netherlands and a process of international re-engagement began.

While Qaddafi himself concentrated on the high politics, he did let it be known that he was a big fan of Ronaldo. His son Al-Saadi Qaddafi got the Brazilian's autograph and pursued the low politics of football. Like his father, he was not averse to taking on multiple offices and roles. He played for Tripoli's leading side Al-Ittihad, then became the club president, and subsequently president of the Libyan Football Federation. With this kind of backing, money and power flowed into Libyan football. An extraordinary selection of advisers was brought in to shape Libyan football development, including disgraced athlete Ben Johnson, the ever-available English coach Terry Venables and of course Diego Maradona. The Italian coach Franco Scoglio was brought in to manage the national team though he was soon sacked, so he claimed, for failing to pick Al-Saadi for the team. The Italian connection was further developed as first the Libyan State Investment Corporation took a 7.5 per cent stake in Juventus and a place on the board, then both Qaddafi father and son ostentatiously supported Italy during the 2002 World Cup; rumours abounded all autumn that Al-Saadi would be investing in a major Greek club or a second Italian one. The immediate pay-off was that the Italian Super Cup that opened the 2002 season, between Parma and Juventus, was played in Tripoli. One cannot accuse the Qaddafis of being anything other than adventurous. While the Colonel was busy negotiating his way back into the world and divesting himself of a nuclear weapons programme, Al-Saadi was offered a contract with Serie A side Perugia, opened a campaign to win the presidency of CAF and launched a bid to host the 2010 World Cup. Football, in the end, has proved more fickle than high politics as Al-Saadi's playing career at Perugia barely flickered before being extinguished when he tested positive for banned drugs.

VI

If football in parts of West Africa has paralleled those nations' descent into violence and civil war that has accompanied the process of democratization, in Nigeria football has punctuated the process and commentated upon it. The fortunes of the national team – the Super Eagles – have served as a barometer for the state of the nation. In the early 1990s it seemed that both the Nigerian nation and its football might fulfil some of their immense promise. After almost a decade of military rule, General Babangida was orchestrating a civilian presidential election and a transition to civilian rule. Elections were held in 1993 and the Yoruba Muslim businessman M. K. O. Abiola was elected as president. The generals panicked, abrogated the results of the election, installed a stooge cabinet and started putting down the protests with their customary unpleasantness. Into the vacuum stepped General Sani Abacha whose own coup inaugurated Nigeria's harshest period of authoritarian rule. The already vicious police apparatus was enlarged, dissidents of all kinds were ruthlessly pursued, the media were controlled, and trade unions banned.

Football came under the rule of the ominously named Directive 101, giving the military regime carte blanche to interfere in all aspects of Nigerian football at will. In this context the brilliant victories of the Nigerian team at the 1994 African Cup of Nations, the 1994 World Cup campaign that took them to within a hair's breadth of the quarter-finals, and even the huge prize of winning the gold medal at the 1996 Atlanta Olympics were tarnished; few in Nigeria wanted to hand such accolades, such prestige, to the despotic Abacha and his coterie. The unrepentant viciousness of the regime was highlighted by their execution of the Ogoni leader Ken Saro-Wiwa and his colleagues in November 1995. This elicited condemnation of such clarity and strength from South African President Nelson Mandela that Abacha withdrew the Nigerian team from the African Cup of Nations to be held in South Africa. The process of exclusion worked both ways as FIFA withdrew the country's right to host the 1995 World Youth Cup and moved it to Qatar.

Fate intervened on the eve of the 1998 World Cup. Sani Abacha had a heart attack and Nigeria could breathe more easily. The team performed brilliantly in the group stage to beat Spain and Bulgaria. But in the second round they imploded, losing to Denmark 4–1, crumpling under the massive expectations of a country that was heady on its unexpected deliverance from evil. Nigeria's interim military leader General Abdulsalami Abubakar began a process of democratization and return to civilian rule. In characteristic Nigerian style, the presidential election won by ex-general Obasanjo was followed first by the 1999 World Youth Cup which almost no Nigerians attended, and then by the actual writing of a Constitution that would define the parameters of Obasanjo's rule. The reticence of the Nigerian public to support the 1999 World Youth Cup, held under military auspices, evaporated the following year when Nigeria co-hosted the 2000 Cup of Nations under civilian rule. Originally planned for Zimbabwe, whose political and economic chaos made hosting the tournament impossible, the tournament was switched at the last minute to Ghana and Nigeria. Almost uniquely in the tournament's recent history, the host nation's head of state President Obasanjo did not attend the opening game, wary of throwing his political fate in with the brilliant but unpredictable Super Eagles. But most Nigerians were not so wary. Expectations of Nigerian rebirth were high. Suleyol Mngerem wrote, 'Truth be told, the unity you see in our faces, the hope you feel in the air, the oneness of spirit which is so thick you can cut it with a knife is beautiful. I don't care much for football, but I just have a good feeling when it's football season.'⁵ The Lagos papers reported heart attacks across the city. The crowds roared the team on as they swept Tunisia and Morocco aside. By now Obasanjo was interrupting meetings with President Chirac to watch the game, but between those wins a pitiful goalless draw with Congo saw the NFA offices attacked and the Super Eagles' bus was stoned. Against Senegal in the quarter-final an extra-time winner prompted a massive pitch invasion; the cowed Senegalese were only just coaxed back for the rest of the game. The nation had truly lost its collective sense of proportion.

---

13 February 2000
Nigeria 2 Cameroon 2 (aet; Cameroon won 4–3 on penalties)
Surelere Stadium, Lagos

Nigerians like to talk, a lot. So when they are not talking, it's a matter of concern. When they are silent it should be taken seriously. It is silent at Surelere, 50,000 silent Nigerians. No, you can't hear a pin drop, for there is noise. A low ominous steely buzz in the air. The hollow, uncoordinated snaps and blasts of desultory firecrackers; they have the pattern of drunken, sullen gunshot. But in the space that has been filled with the drums and the horns, the clapping and the singing, the pulsating energy of the Surelere crowd, there is nothing.

It had been an epic befitting the occasion. Thirty minutes of taut stalemate broken by two Cameroonian goals and the first bitter silences of the day. But the horns kept playing, the crowd rallied, the Nigerians maintained their unity and composure and on the stroke of half-time Chukwu scuffs the ball past Cameroon's Boukar. Surelere finds its voice again. The second half opens with Jay-Jay Okocha sending the sweetest, curving volley into the Cameroonian net. But he and Nigeria stay serious, they mute their celebrations, they reform their huddle, they pray, they resolve to press and play. The ninetieth minute passes, Surelere roars. Extra time passes, Surelere roars. Penalties. Surelere drops its voice, the horns play thinly on.

At 2–2 Kanu's casually conceived shot is saved. Surelere gasps. By contrast Njitap's riposte is driven with unwavering determination.

Ikpeba steps up, the ball strikes the crossbar and flies down over the line and out. Surelere doesn't know what to think. In or out? The scoreboard says yes, the referee is not saying, the linesman says no, but for sure it has crossed the line. Foe misses to keep the Nigerians in it and Okocha's shot is true: 3–3. Song is on the spot, the horn's melody has disintegrated, the trumpet is off on its own squawking improvisational trills, and Surelere can't seem to raise itself to shout him down. Goal. Silence. A wall of hard silence.

The Cameroonian bus and the last of the fleeing journalists escape in convoy, the mounted police and soldiers barely able and barely willing to keep the last of the crowds back from the roads they engulf. Obasanjo calls it 'the verdict of God'. Then God has decreed that Nigeria will face its national questions without divine or sporting intervention. A blessing and a curse.

#

The Cameroonians, accompanied by a hastily despatched unit of the presidential guard, made it home to Yaoundé, but not everyone in Africa has made it back from the stadium. The 1990s saw, even allowing for earlier underreporting of disasters, an unprecedented wave of fatalities and injuries in and around football stadiums. These rotting hulks were microcosms of Africa's urban crisis. Their crumbling concrete stands were testament to the disastrous management and maintenance of what precious little infrastructure many African cities possessed. Their policing by trigger-happy gendarmes and brutal army units was no different from the erratic and often violent control exercised in the shanty towns and slums of the continent's cities. And yet for the big games and the big occasions they were full. They were more than full. The brooding sense of unease and violence that could accompany a big game is captured by a Moroccan observer:

Match days are days of huge flux. It's like a controlled explosion from the districts of the south-west. To the stadium and back the walk has the feel of a great diffuse insurrection, without reason or explanation. The smallest incident might set off an explosion. The young take the route to the stadium in small groups or bands. The caretakers are vigilant on match days and everybody who owns something is on the lookout.[6]

In the face of the ticketless masses, security would disintegrate at the gates; alternative methods of entry would be found. The decade began with the worst football disaster since the mid-1970s. In January 1991 at the big Soweto derby game between Kaizer Chiefs and Orlando Pirates forty people were killed and fifty injured in rioting after a controversial penalty was awarded. On such decisions lives can turn. In 1999 referee Stephen Lungu died after a league game in Zambia between Kabwe Warriors and Green Buffaloes. Contesting his rulings Buffalo fans beat him unconscious. But as Buffaloes are the Zambian army's team the club's punishment was simply to play all remaining home games as away fixtures.

Many deaths were attributable to crushes and collapses as the heaving weight of unregulated and enormous crowds was flung against the flimsy infrastructure and nonchalant supervision of the football authorities. A crush in Nairobi during Kenya's Cup of Nations qualifier against Mozambique left one dead and twenty-four injured after a stampede. Three years later Liberia played Togo in Monrovia; in this desperate war-torn society the national team attracted vast crowds that the decrepit Samuel K. Doe stadium could never handle. A barrier collapsed, two people died and twenty-four were hurt. Doe would fall but his stadium got no better and another three Liberians were crushed to death at a World Cup qualifying game against Chad in 2000. Win or lose the result would be the same; an ecstatic Nigerian crowd at Surelere turned to a crush as Nigeria beat Guinea and five people were killed. The death count rose even further when the police, the army or both went into action. The Kinshasa derby in 1996 between DC Motema Pembe and AS Vita Club saw fights break out in the crowd which were met by volleys of tear gas from the police. In the ensuing chaotic exodus and fighting seven died and more than 100 fans were injured. The same fixture in 2000 saw another four deaths when soldiers switched from tear gas to live fire into the crowd. When Zimbabwe went two-down to South Africa in a World Cup qualifier police fired tear gas, provoking a panic that left thirteen dead at Rufaro stadium in Harare.

The worst was to come in spring 2001. A decade of tragedy had begun at the Kaizer Chiefs–Orlando Pirates clash; now its closing chapter would begin there as well. The match was played at Ellis Park, Johannesburg. The stadium was already overflowing as ticket sales exceeded capacity, but large numbers of ticketless fans remained outside. During the first half they broke down the perimeter fences and charged into the stands. The match was abandoned at 1–1 after half an hour, when forty-three people died. A week later the big Congolese clash between TP Mazembe and FC St-Eloi Lupopo descended into rioting in Lubumbashi; seven people were trampled to death and around fifty injured. The chaos appeared to be catching. In Kenya the May Day derby game between Gor Mahia and AFC Leopards saw widespread violence and use of tear gas and there was still another fissile derby to be played. All season the tension between Accra's Hearts of Oak and Kumasi's Asante Kotoko had been rising. A pre-season friendly had descended into a scuffle between club officials. Kotoko fans had been flamboyantly celebrating Hearts' early exit from the African Champions League. Africa's worst-ever stadium disaster awaited.

----

9 May 2001
Hearts of Oak 2 Asante Kotoko 1
Accra Sports Stadium, Ghana

All across Accra, all across Ghana, people are getting the news. He, she, they are dead. Not passed away, gone over or gone to sleep, but struck down, snatched, killed. And then? Pain, shock, grief, hysteria, but there is more and worse to come than all of these. There is also a question. A question that racks the twisted tissues of your head. Why? Why did this happen? Why did this happen to us?

The reports that have disappeared into the netherworld of the Ghanaian state acknowledge that the exits were too small and the gates should not have been locked and the police overreacted and so on. So that's that. The Football Association has acknowledged its failings and told Ghanaians to forget about it all and get back to the stadiums. So that's that. The trial of the senior police officers in charge on the day collapsed for lack of evidence. So that's that. Except it's not. It's not, because no one who has had to ask the question 'why?' trusts them.

This is a problem of trust. The state does not trust the people because their allegiance cannot be counted upon. The people do not trust the state because it has never delivered on a modicum of its promises. Therefore they both fear and assume the worst of the other.

83 minutes. Addo scores for Hearts of Oak, the TV commentator bawls, 'It's a winner. It's a winner.' The Kotoko fans in the Ade Coker stand were already angry. They don't trust the referee. The Hearts equalizer was very questionable. And because they know how much the referee earns, and they all know how they would spend his bribe and because once again Hearts are going to steal the title, and because they're young and they don't give a shit, they start tearing up the plastic seating. It later transpires that no one has got any meaningful paperwork to cover the multi-million-pound refurbishment of the stadium with these new seats.

90 minutes. the fourth official is indicating four minutes of extra time but the referee seems to want to blow his whistle. He doesn't trust Hearts to keep their lead. The seats and bottles are flying on to the running track. But the fans are not fighting among themselves, nor does that look likely. The huge spiked fences that ring the pitch mean that there is little chance of a pitch invasion. Only the most practised and athletic can throw a plastic seat as far as the police lines. But the police don't trust the crowd, not enough to stand back and let this one burn out. They fear them, so they fire volleys of tear gas directly into the stands.

91 minutes. Now it's the crowd's turn to feel the fear and immediately many of them are heading for the tiny concrete exits. The gates are locked. The police and the authorities don't trust the crowd enough to leave them unlocked. The stampede is unstoppable. 126 people are dead. That's why. That's why I am looking at a photo of abandoned children's shoes, bent railings and a blood-spattered staircase, wondering how you live when you have to carry that image with you.

Nima, a poor Accra suburb, is home to the city's Muslim migrants from the north, Kotoko fans and many of the victims and their families. Three days later they marched on the local police headquarters, burning tyres in the street. They didn't trust the police's apologies, they didn't trust the process of inquiry and they wanted to know why? The police answered them with armoured cars, helicopters and volleys of tear gas.

_____

In the aftermath of Accra, the call went up from every quarter for the reform of African football, investment in its stadiums, the control and retraining of the police and army, for clubs to be more responsible in their ticketing policies. But the deaths continued. Two fans were shot in Zimbabwe at the supercharged Highlanders vs. Dynamos game where police claimed that the open-hand sign of the opposition MDC was being made among the Bulawayo Highlanders fans. In the Gambia vs. Senegal Nations Cup qualifying game in Dakar in 2003, fighting broke out between Senegalese soldiers and visiting Gambian fans who saw their team lose 3–1. The fighting was vicious and spread beyond the stadium. Senegalese in Gambia were attacked, Gambians in Senegal were attacked, and the border was sealed. The Champions League final in 2003 between Egypt's Ismaily and Nigeria's Enyimba, which saw the Nigerian team win, ended in a ludicrous pitch invasion that almost prevented the Nigerians receiving their trophy at all. African football continues to value its fans' lives pitifully low and by the same token the fans hold the authorities in contempt. The same can be said of the continent's elites and their publics.

VIII

In 2004 CAF opened its new headquarters in Cairo. Like most of CAF's operations it was paid for by FIFA and the Egyptian government. Most of the organization's members remain so poor that their payment record to CAF makes the US's relationship with the UN look good. The economic dependence of CAF on international bodies is hardly dissimilar to the continent's economic predicament. Its political fate also has parallels. Africa, by virtue of sheer numbers, must occasionally be attended to at the UN and in other global bodies, but its power is limited and its capacity to act as a coherent united force undermined by internal divisions. CAF has been a player in the biggest struggles and decisions made in global football. On the retirement of João Havelange from the presidency of FIFA, CAF and its new Cameroonian president Issa Hayatou backed UEFA president Lennart Johansson for the top job. But CAF was unable to deliver the votes of its member associations who flooded into Sepp Blatter's camp on the eternal promise of more development money and rumours of other inducements. In 2002 South

Africa, long considered favourites to host the 2006 World Cup, lost the slot to a politically astute German bid. Hayatou himself stood for the presidency of FIFA with UEFA backing in an attempt to unseat Blatter after the financially disastrous collapse of FIFA's marketing arm ISL. Once again, Hayatou failed to muster all of CAF's votes let alone UEFA's or elsewhere. African football's claims to global representation remained morally and practically strong enough to force FIFA to allocate the 2010 World Cup to South Africa (as part of a bigger deal in which the World Cup would automatically rotate around the six confederations in a thirty-year cycle), but the limits of its political power were laid bare.

Like the wider African polity, CAF is divided along francophone and anglophone lines – a division that has been illuminated and exacerbated by the failure of many anglophone countries to host the Cup of Nations (Zambia, Kenya and Zimbabwe have all had hosting rights withdrawn from them) and the success of poor francophone nations in holding on to it (Burkina Faso in 1998 and Mali in 2002). Its poorly paid and funded officials and national administrations remain open to the temptations and accusations of corruption in a world where organizational talent can be a positive encumbrance in career development. Most worryingly of all, CAF presides over a footballing tradition that is fast being caught by the Middle East, East Asia and even parts of the Caribbean and Central America. While Senegal's brilliant performance at the 2002 World Cup gave Africa its second World Cup quarter-finalist, South Korea's semi-final place eclipsed them. While Africa struggles to organize and fund its international and club competitions, the money is just rolling into the Asian Cup and the Arab Champions League. And all the while the yawning gap between the talent of the continent and its dismal domestic infrastructure and economy sees its players spread all over the world and its home leagues abandoned. In this regard African football faces harder tasks than any other continent and does so with less administrative and economic resources than its competitors. South Africa has been awarded the 2010 World Cup – though at the price of exposing the sharp north–south divisions in the continent – and thus Africa's third place in the global football hierarchy seems secure for the moment. But only for the moment. As any African head of state would tell you, football in Africa remains the only game but it is a capricious and uncertain game to be in.

Conclusion:
The Game at the End
of the World

The old gods . . . are dying, and others are not yet born . . . it is not a dead past, but life itself which can give rise to a living cult. The only way of renewing the collective representations which relate to sacred things is to retemper them at the very source of religious life, that is to say in assembled groups . . . Men are more confident because they feel themselves stronger: and they really are stronger because forces which are languishing are now reawakened into consciousness.

Emile Durkheim

Football's status as the most popular global sport was not inevitable. It is a consequence of both historical forces beyond the game, and the intrinsic qualities of its own structure, rhythms and appearance. Football emerged and spread in an era when many other sports were also being codified: rugby, hockey, tennis and golf in Britain; baseball, American football and basketball in the United States; martial arts in Japan, and gymnastics in Germany. The political and military fate of these great powers determined much of the initial distribution of sports. Baseball was established as the leading sport where the USA was an occupying or intervening military power—Cuba, Venezuela, the Philippines, Guatemala, post-war Japan and South Korea. The spread and status of Japanese martial arts and German *Turnen* were terminated by their ultimate military defeats and subsequent loss of empire. British sports, by contrast, spread through both the formal empire and the immense informal empire of Britain's global economic and cultural connections.

However, the geographical reach and cultural cachet of Britain and British sports did not guarantee their adoption in general, let alone that it would be football that would catch on. In an age of explosive industrialization, the mass societies of the nineteenth and twentieth centuries were unlikely to embrace individual sports—not only did they betoken a world quite separate from the majority of those publics, but the spaces that they are played in do not offer the possibility of a truly huge spectacle. Tennis and other racquet sports can only physically accommodate a limited number of spectators around their courts. Basketball suffers from the same problem. You just cannot build a stadium of 100,000 around a basketball court. Golf necessarily separates both spectators and players.

The appeal of football among team sports as a game to play, watch and follow is well rehearsed: it is simple, cheap and flexible in terms of numbers and playing spaces; it is easy to learn, accommodating of a great diversity of physiques, and favours no single set of skills, attributes or virtues but requires a command of many. Its insistence on the use of feet and head over hands has proved an infectious and enticing prospect. As a spectacle it offers space for inspired individuals and dogged collectives, creates instantaneously comprehensible narratives, operates in a perpetually changing three-dimensional space and balances the exhilaration of flow with the orgasmic punctuation of the goal.

These lines of reasoning help us explain the scale of football's reach and its victory in the competitive struggle among modern sports for hegemony. What it does not explain is why having taken hold it should exert such an extraordinary level of social fervour. Few have been bold enough to venture such a general theory; to wonder what it is that sustains and animates the spectacular at the heart of modern life. Some have cast football as the circus, a theatre of distraction, an elite conspiracy devoted to the manufacture of consent and the marginalization of dissent. Some see football as the universal religion for an age of disenchantment. Others see its elevation as the triumph of the empty pleasure, the conversion of the ephemeral to the status of the transcendent where, in the ultimate joke at the end of history, ideology is replaced by vacuity.

The notion of football as the bread and circuses of the industrial city is not entirely fanciful. The records of European fascism and communism, Latin American populists and military oligarchies and authoritarian ultra-nationalists all over the developing world, demonstrate the degree to which political power has sought directly to control football and use it as an instrument of legitimacy, distraction or glorification. However, all of these political forms are in decline, if not extinct. They have been replaced by variants, more or less savoury, of representative liberal democracy and bureaucratic authoritarianism that are the dominant polities of the twenty-first century. Everywhere, beyond the tiniest enclaves of actually disintegrating socialism, variants of capitalism and the market constitute the economic order. For the most part, neither liberal democracy nor advanced capitalism requires the degree of active allegiance and collective acclaim that authoritarian and penurious regimes demand of their subjects. They have no need for conscript armies, militias or incendiary mobs. They can sustain their legitimacy without epics and supermen. And if citizens choose not to participate and consumers continue to passively consume, that is enough. Consent is sustained on the Valium of affluence. Only Silvio Berlusconi's experiment in televisual authoritarian demagogy with its umbilical connection to Italian football approximates to the old model. Elsewhere, at worst, modern commercial football could be seen as the mall rather than the circus; insidiously bland, decaffeinated and pre-packed, its relentless formulaic repetition an instrument for disabling consciousness rather than manipulating it.

If the conditions under which football could be used as a form of crude populist propaganda are past, the image of the circus still points us to the intensely dramatic quality of the football spectacle. The theatre has certainly been offered as an alternative model and football could credibly be seen as a parallel but infinitely more popular art form, offering live and improvised performance, narrative twist, character and plot. Yet this captures only a fraction of the practices and pleasures of football cultures, minimizing the non-narrative qualities of a game whose shapes and choreographies are closer to dance than drama. Despite the best attempts of experimental theatre companies, actors and audiences remain rigidly separated in the stage's division of labour. In football the crowd is unquestionably the chorus, not only supplying ambience, commentary and income, but actively shaping the tone and the course of the game. When in full carnival mode, the crowd can even move from out of the wings and take a place on stage. The opportunity that this provides for the collective dramatization of identities and social relationships, both spontaneous and organized, is without parallel in the field of global popular culture.

It is precisely this bounded emotional fervour, this seeming rupture from the everyday, that has led many to interpret football as a form of lay or pagan worship. The homologies and parallels between the two are now thought so obvious, so commonplace, that a satellite television broadcaster could, without irony, advertise its coverage by claiming 'football is our religion'; 'cathedrals of football' is a sporting cliché across Christendom. Football supporters are the congregation, stadiums are holy places, the touchline marks the division between the sacred and the profane. The game itself is the central ritual, its oppositions and outcomes invariably cast in terms of good and evil, its narratives the theological text that yields spiritual insight.

The language of football culture is suffused with this self-understanding: the suffering but still the faith of the fans, the season as liturgy, the player cast as divinity or demon. In a world that seems to be polarizing between the secular hollowness of individualism and disenchantment and a revival of unbending fundamentalism within all the world religions, football appears between them as what Manuel Vásquez Montalbán has called 'a religion in search of a god'.[1] But religion in the end turns on the notion that there really is a supernatural, metaphysical force at work in the universe, an organizing purposeful intelligence and direction that gives moral order to the chaos of creation. Football does not and cannot offer this. Players are not divine, though they come as close as any mortal can do in a world that has made such an elision impossible. Pundits are not priests, though we all pay a tithe for their contorted truisms. Football can be read as a morality tale but it cannot, alone, generate a moral framework or offer a salvation to a species doomed to live in full consciousness of their mortality. The gods of football are just a linguistic sleight of hand for the statistical randomness of risk, chance and uncertainty. Shorn of metaphysics the roar of the football crowd is no song of praise for deities; it announces the birth of Durkheim's living cults, the celebration of the miracle of our own solidarities, innumerable imagined communities of class, ethnicity, nation, region, neighbourhood and community, struggling to be born.

The Peruvian novelist Mario Vargas Llosa, when covering the 1982 World Cup, explained football's popularity more straightforwardly:

Football offers people something that they can scarcely ever have: an opportunity to have fun, to enjoy themselves, to get excited, worked up, to feel certain intense emotions that daily routine rarely offers them . . . a good game of football is enormously intense and absorbing . . . it is ephemeral, non transcendent, innocuous. An experience where the effect disappears at the same time as the cause. Sport . . . is the love of form, a spectacle which does not transcend the physical, the sensory, the instant emotion, which unlike, for example, a book or a play, scarcely leaves a trace in the memory and does not enrich or impoverish knowledge. And that is its appeal; that it is exciting and empty.[2]

On the one hand, Vargas Llosa clearly overreaches himself. The crowd as chorus and carnival demands an account of the spectacle that includes their contribution, participation and creativity. The degree to which football theatricalizes social conflicts and the fulcrum of imagined communities and solidarities, suggests that it leaves real traces that endure beyond a single game, connections that circulate in the world beyond the stadium. Reducing the experience of football to a single match underestimates the degree to which whole seasons, long historical traditions, derbies and grudge matches generate their own accumulated storehouses of memory and knowledge. If the calibre of the argument, the quality of the conversation and the veracity of its histories might be in question, their existence is not.

And yet there is unmistakable accuracy about Vargas Llosa's argument. Beneath the encrusted layers of ritual and meaning, the peaks and troughs of winning and losing, there are just people playing a game—and play is only play when at some level it is done for no other reason than its own sake. Despite the active collusion of the football elite with the institutions of money and power, Eduardo Galeano senses the game's ingrained resistance to their logics.

Professional football does everything to castrate the energy of happiness, but it survives in spite of all the spites . . . The more the technocrats programme it down to the smallest detail, the more the powerful manipulate it, football continues to be the art of the unforeseeable. When you least expect it, the impossible occurs, the dwarf teaches the giant a lesson, and a scraggy, bow-legged black man makes an athlete sculpted in Greece look ridiculous.[3]

Football's cultural ascent and popularity are rooted at the very deepest level in humanity's need and desire to play. What does it mean to place the world under the sign of play? What does it mean when a culture chooses over time to honour a *game* with the status we have accorded football? There is precious little in the canons of social and political theory, economics and psychology to help us. Most of these disciplines do not even recognize play for what it is, the most obvious universal human characteristic in a world that seems irretrievably diverse. When the imaginative resources of the social sciences fail us there is literature. In Hermann Hesse's novel *The Glass Bead Game* we can find one of the few systematic thought experiments into what a civilization might look like if its aspirations, hopes, values and identities were built around a game. In his alternative modernity Hesse sketches a society in which a monkish scholarly elite of Buddhist disposition have been liberated from the mundane realities of power by their poverty, devotion and independence. Alongside the production of their treatises and theses, their central roles in public life are the control of the education system and the playing of the Glass Bead Game. The latter is an exercise in competitive philosophical and personal reflection, in which the participants use a complex mathematical and musical language and notational system to harmoniously reconcile the polarities and contradictions of ethical, aesthetic and spiritual life.

The world beyond the game is barely sketched by Hesse but we must assume that it could not possibly look like our own. The game our modernity plays could never be so meditative, cerebral, controllable or exclusive. While Hesse's world was infused with the inner tranquillity of Buddhism, ours is propelled outwards by its evangelical religions of salvation and its querulous secular ideologies. The Glass Bead Game was played under conditions of stability, order and economic and technological stasis; we are forced to play in the whirlwind of global capitalism and exponential rates of technical change. Like the world we have fashioned our game would surely have to be a runaway, relentless, physical, maniacal, popular affair. Our play was always more likely to favour experiment over consolidation, spontaneity over reflection, the visual over the aural and laughter over awe. It might create its own elites, but it would be inconceivable that they could prosper without including the masses. Football has precisely these qualities. The Glass Bead Game aimed for synthesis, bringing order and harmony to chaos. We have abandoned this project. Final resolutions, the eradication of uncertainty, the removal of risk, absolute knowledge and absolute security have all been scrapped. We cannot seek to eradicate chaos; we must learn to live with it. Football knows this in its heart. No other art form or sport attracts such a wide and diverse range of superstitious practices, personal charms and magical routines.

If football embraces the relentless uncertainty of play, it also holds fast to the generosity, universalism and egalitarianism of play. When we play power games, we are not playing at all, for we have crossed into the realm of instrumentalism, self-interest, manipulation and inequality. Play can encompass none of these. Indeed, play that does not descend into bullying is necessarily democratic. Play rests on consensus, negotiation and turn-taking. It recognizes the virtues and the limits of collaboration and competition. Too much of the former and you have an oligarchy; too much of the latter and you have the war of all against all. Play, like democracy, is open to revision, responsive to change and necessarily open-ended. The future is never closed. How could it be? On the pitch and in the vortex of change that grips contemporary societies, the possibility of shifts and upsets, the emergence of reversals and opportunities hang, tantalizingly, in the air. At any moment the game's flow can be radically disrupted, turned on its head, transformed by a concatenation of the unexpected. No game embraces both the chaos and uncertainty and the spontaneity and reactivity of play like football. At no moment in our history has humanity faced a world so threatened by the former and been so in need of the latter.

After nearly a century and a half of global industrialization, whose geographical course and social organization carved the main channels into which the planet's football cultures have flowed, the world sits on the brink. Six billion of us today have already taken the world's ecosystems to the point of catastrophe. In 2050, when they play the twenty-ninth World Cup finals, there will be ten billion of us. China and India, absent from Germany 2006, will surely be there in 2050 consuming and competing at levels approaching the West. A vast, unintended and unstoppable experiment into the carrying capacity and robustness of the world's climate systems, biodiversity and hydrological cycles has been set in motion. It is not the gods of chaos that have unleashed this cataclysm; it is us. Living with profound risk and uncertainty is now the destiny of humanity. We are lucky then that the game we have chosen as our collective metaphor, the avatar of our social dilemmas, should so closely parallel our predicament. To place the world under the sign of play is to expose ourselves to the caprice of the ball. We must be bold enough to think that we have the guile, the heart and the wit to bring it under control.

Notes

1 Chasing Shadows: The Prehistory of Football

1. 'Football Fever Hits Beijing', FIFA press release, 20 July 2004.
2. On the mythologization of Chinese sports history, see B. J. Peiser (1996), 'Western theories about the origins of sport in China'.
3. On the historical records of *kemari*, see A. Guttmann and L. Thompson (2001), *Japanese Sports: A History*.
4. W. Strachey (1849), *The Historie of Travaile into Virginia Britannica*, London: Hakluyt Society. Quoted in A. T. Cheska (1970), 'Games of the native North Americans'.
5. For a wide-ranging account of both archaeological evidence and interpretation, see E. Michael Wittington (ed.) (2001), *The Sport of Life and Death*; V. Scarborough and D. Wilcox (eds) (1991), *The Mesoamerican Ballgame*.
6. See P. Mártir de Anglería (1964), *Décadas del Nuevo Mondo*, vol. 2, p. 547.
7. For an overview of this, see S. Miller (2004), *Ancient Greek Athletics*; for original sources, see S. Miller (1991), *Arete*.
8. Taken from Athanaeus' *The Gastronomers*, written *c.* 228 CE, in which he quotes the 4th century CE comic poet Antiphanes, reproduced in S. Miller (1991), pp. 115–16.
9. Quoted in M. Marples (1954), *A History of Football*.
10. Quoted in ibid., p. 24, attributed to Nicholas de Farndone, Lord Mayor of London.
11. Quoted in J. Walvin (1994), *The People's Game*, p. 13.
12. Ibid., p. 18.

2 The Simplest Game: Britain and the Invention of Modern Football

The first epigraph is from Joseph Strutt's 1903 edition of *Sports and Pastimes of the People of England*. The Eton notice is quoted in R. Holt (1989), *Sport and the British*, p. 76.
Match Report: Blackburn Olympic (p. 43)
Details of the players' diet and training in J. Walvin (1994), *The People's Game*.

1. Quoted in R. Holt (1989), p. 38.
2. See H. Cunningham (1980), *Leisure in the Industrial Revolution*; A. Delves (1981), 'Popular recreation', p. 90.
3. A. Delves (1981), p. 105.
4. Cited in R. Holt (1989), p. 79.
5. See J. Chandos (1984), *Boys Together*.
6. J. Walvin (1994), *The People's Game*, pp. 33–4.
7. Quoted in R. Holt (1989), p. 75.
8. Quoted in ibid., p. 81.

9. Ibid., pp. 89–90.
10. Ibid., p. 98.
11. Quoted in ibid., p. 93.
12. Quoted in ibid., p. 82.
13. Quoted in J. Walvin (1994), p. 41.
14. These words from FA minutes, first quoted in G. Green (1953), *Soccer*, pp. 31–3.
15. Cited in J. Walvin (1994), p. 48.
16. Quoted in T. Mason (1980), *Association Football and English Society*, p. 121.
17. Ibid., p. 122.
18. C. Alcock (ed.) (1880), *Football Annual 1880*, p. 10; C. Alcock (1906), *Association Football*, pp. 33–7.
19. F. Wall (1935), *Fifty Years in Football*.
20. Quoted in M. Taylor (1997), 'Little Englanders'.
21. K. Farnsworth (1995), *Sheffield Football*, vol. 1. See also G. Curry (2004), 'Playing for money'.
22. Quoted in S. Tischler (1981), *Footballers and Businessmen*, p. 44.
23. See G. Curry (2004).
24. *The Times*, 21 July 1885.
25. Quoted in T. Mason (1980), p. 122.
26. Cited in R. Cox, D. Russell and W. Vamplew (eds) (2002), *Encyclopedia of British Football*, p. 26.

3 An Altogether More Splendid Life: Industrial Football and Working-class Britain, 1888–1914

The J. B. Priestley epigraph is from his 1929 novel *The Good Companions*.
Match Report: First day of the League (p. 56)
The quotation is from E. P. Thompson (1967), 'Time, work, discipline, and industrial capitalism'.
Match Report: The Khaki Final (p. 82)
Lord Derby's words cited in R. Holt (1989), *Sport and the British*.

1. Quoted in S. Inglis (1989), *League Football and the Men who Made It*, p. 6.
2. *Manchester Guardian*, 23 November 1896.
3. Cited in T. Mason (1996), 'Football, sport of the north'.
4. *Pall Mall Gazette*, 31 March 1884; *Athletic News*, 2 April 1884.
5. C. Edwardes (1892), 'The new football mania', pp. 622–32.
6. S. Inglis (1983), *The Football Grounds of England and Wales*, p. 13.
7. See the incomparable survey of the man and his works, S. Inglis (2005), *Engineering Archie*.
8. See T. Mason (1980), *Association Football and English Society*, pp. 35–41; W. Vamplew (2004), *Pay Up and Play the Game*, pp. 154–73.
9. George MacDonald Fraser (1981), *The General Danced at Dawn*, London: HarperCollins.
10. On Glasgow's football history see the incomparable work of Bill Murray, especially Murray (2001), *The Old Firm*.
11. E. Dunning et al. (1984), 'Football hooliganism in Britain before the First World War'.
12. Anonymous, 'Riot in Glasgow', from the *Scotsman*, 1909, repr. in I. Hamilton (ed.) (1992), *The Faber Book of Soccer*.
13. *Southern Daily Echo*, 10 February 1900, quoted in D. Russell (1997), *Football and the English*.
14. Cited in R. Cox, D. Russell and W. Vamplew (eds) (2002), *Encyclopedia of British Football*, p. 10, attributed to an Anglican vicar from Leeds, 1893.
15. *Swindon Evening Advertiser*, 31 January 1910.
16. On Belfast Celtic, see P. Coyle (1999), *Paradise Lost and Found*.
17. Quotations from R. Holt (1989), p. 276.

18. Quoted in N. Fishwick (1989), *English Football and Society.*
19. Ibid., p. 145.

4 Perfidious Albion: The Resistible Rise of Global Football

Archbishop Croke's words are taken from his letter to Michael Cusack – founder of the Gaelic Athletic Association – in which Croke accepts the position of patron and outlines his muscular Catholic nationalism. Cited in J. Sugden and A. Bairner (1993), *Sport, Sectarianism and Society in a Divided Ireland*, p. 28.
Match Report: India (p. 109)
Nayak quoted in P. Dimeo (2001), 'Football and politics in Bengal', p. 68.

1. Quoted in R. Holt (1989), *Sport and the British*, p. 204.
2. Ibid., p. 207.
3. See R. Hess and B. Stewart (eds) (1998), *More than a Game*, pp. 97–9.
4. *Bell's Life*, 29 July 1865, quoted in ibid., p. 15.
5. *Bell's Life*, 14 May 1864, quoted in ibid., p. 12.
6. R. Williams (1643), *A Key into the Language of America.*
7. A. Markowitz and S. Hellerman (2001), *Offside*, p. 39.
8. Quoted in R. Holt (1989), p. 238.
9. Ibid., p. 241.
10. Quoted in E. Corry (1989), *Catch and Kick*, p. 96.
11. Quoted in Sir Thomas Raleigh (1906), *Lord Curzon in India*, p. 245.
12. Quoted in J. A. Mangan (1986), *The Games Ethic and Imperialism*, p. 184.
13. Thomas Macaulay (1961), *Critical and Historical Essays*, London: Dent, vol. 1, p. 562, cited in K. Bandyopadhyay (2001), 'Race, nation and sport'.
14. Originally from Anonymous (1895), *Ought Natives to be Welcomed as Volunteers?*, Calcutta: Thacker, Spink, cited in P. Dimeo and J. Mills (eds) (2001), *Soccer in South Asia*, p. 63.
15. M. Bose (1990), *A History of Indian Cricket*, pp. 16–17.
16. On regional and communal rivalries in post-independence India, see B. Majumdar and K. Bandyopadhyay (2005), 'Regionalism and club domination'.

5 The Great Game and the Informal Empire: The International Spread of Football, 1870–1914

Simon Gorter's comments are taken from M. Van Bottenburg (2001), *Global Games*, p. 101; the Rudyard Kipling line is from *Kim*, London: Macmillan, 1949.
Match Report: Champagne Football (p. 129)
Details of the match, including match reports, in A. Hamilton (1998), *An Entirely Different Game*; J. Leigh and D. Woodhouse (2005), *Football Lexicon.*

1. R. Holt (1989), *Sport and the British*, p. 205; J. A. Mangan (1986), *The Games Ethic and Imperialism*, pp. 35–6.
2. The role of English shipyard workers in Bilbao is one of the few cases where the key agents of football's diffusion were working class.
3. T. Morgagni and V. Brusca (1907) *Annuario Sportivo 1907–1908*, Milan; *Corriere della sera*, quoted in P. Lanfranchi and M. Taylor (2001), *Moving with the Ball*, p. 22.
4. C. Miermans (1955), *Voetbal in Nederland*, quoted in M. Van Bottenburg (2001), p. 113.
5. J. Walton (1999), 'Football and Basque identity', pp. 261–89.
6. A. Wahl (1989), *Les archives du football*, p. 34.
7. Quoted in P. Lanfranchi and M. Taylor (2001), *Moving with the Ball*, p. 27.

8. P. Adam (1907), *La morale des sports*, pp. 189–91.
9. Quoted in ibid., p. 76.
10. Y. Olesha (1979), *No Day Without a Line*, Ann Arbor: Ardis, pp. 124–5.
11. Quoted in P. Ball (2001), *Morbo*, pp. 61–2.
12. Quoted in M. Van Bottenburg (2001), p. 102.
13. Ibid., p. 108.
14. M. Van Bottenburg (2001), p. 104.
15. As reported in *Kopings-Posten* and *Westmanlands Allehanda*, 17 September 1906, quoted in T. Andersson (2001), 'Swedish football hooliganism, 1900–39', p. 4.
16. *Nordiskt Idrottslif* 22, 1910, quoted in ibid., p. 5.
17. *Nordiskt Idrottslif* 58, 1912, quoted in ibid., p. 5.
18. Quoted in A. Hamilton (1998), *An Entirely Different Game*, p. 40.
19. Quoted in J. Smith (1979), *Illusions of Conflict*, p. 191.
20. M. Filho (1964), *O negro no futebol brasileiro*, Rio de Janeiro: MAUAD (reissue 2003), p. 10.
21. *Buenos Aires Herald*, 13 October 1912.
22. *The Standard*, 27 July 1909, p. 3, cited in E. Archetti (1997), *Masculinities*, p. 55.
23. Letter from Charles Miller to *Bannister Court School Magazine*, vol. III, no. 31, March 1904, repr. in A. Hamilton (1998).
24. Quoted in A. Bellos (2002), *Futebol*, p. 31.
25. Quoted in P. Ball (2001), p. 44.
26. *Avanti!*, 11 October 1910, quoted in S. Martin (2004), *Football and Fascism*, p. 21.
27. Quoted in R. Holt (1981), *Sport and Society in Modern France*, p. 66.
28. Ibid., p. 3.
29. Quoted in ibid., p. 75.
30. O. Jager (1898), *Fusslummelei*.
31. F. W. Racquet (1882), *Moderne englische Spiele. Zum Zweck der Einführung in Deutschland*, Göttingen, p. 50, quoted in U. Merkel (2000), 'The history of the German Football Association (DFB), 1900–1950', p. 174.
32. Quoted in U. Hesse-Lichtenberger (2002), *Tor!*, p. 44.
33. Quoted in J. Riordan (1977), *Sport in Soviet Society*.
34. *Sport*, 6 October 1913, quoted in ibid., p. 24.
35. *Novoye Vremya*, 30 September 1908, quoted in ibid., p. 25.
36. *Moskovskie Vedemosti*, 18 July 1910, quoted in P. Frykholm (1997), 'Soccer and social identity in pre-revolutionary Moscow', p. 145.
37. *K Sportu*, 1912, no. 11, p. 16, quoted in J. Riordan (1977), p. 39.
38. R. B. Lockhart (1958), *Giants Cast Long Shadows*, p. 175.

6 Pay Up, Pay Up and Play the Game: The Commercialization of Global Football, 1914–1934

The epigraphs to this chapter are both quoted in T. Mason (1995), *Passion of the People?*, p. 51.
Match Report: White Horse Final (p. 182)
K. Blows and T. Hogg (2002), *The Essential History of West Ham United*.
J. Hill (2004), ' "The Day was an Ugly One" '.
Match Report: Nuremberg (p. 222)
Key details of the match are cited in U. Hesse-Lichtenberger (2002), *Tor!*.

1. Quoted in R. Holt (1989), *Sport and the British*, p. 276.
2. *Illustrated London News*, 29 July 1916.
3. *Chester Chronicle*, 9 January 1915.
4. Quoted in S. Weintraub (2002), *Silent Night*, p. 118.

5. Quoted in ibid. (2002), p. 111.
6. R. Horak (1992), 'Viennese football culture: some remarks on its history and sociology'.
7. W. Holtby, *Radio Times*, 21 February 1930.
8. *Yorkshire Observer*, 24 April 1928.
9. J. Cox (1962), *Don Davies – An Old International*, extracted in I. Hamilton (ed.) (1992), *The Faber Book of Soccer*.
10. Quoted in D. Russell (1997), *Football and the English*, p. 117.
11. Quoted in R. Horak (1992).
12. *Neues Wiener Journal*, 10 December 1922.
13. *Illustriertes Sportblatt*, 8 October 1927. Quoted in R. Horak (1994), 'Austrification as modernization'.
14. Ibid., p. 49.
15. *Welt am Montag*, 22 March 1948.
16. Quoted in R. Horak and W. Maderthaner (1996), 'A culture of urban cosmopolitanism'.
17. W. Frankl (1983), 'Erinnerungen an Hakoah Wien, 1909–1939'.
18. Ibid., p. 82.
19. *Buenos Aires Herald*, 22 May 1929.
20. E. Archetti (1997), *Masculinities*, p. 66.
21. Quoted in ibid., p. 59. Original in *El Gráfico* 470, 1928, p. 15.
22. E. Archetti (1997), p. 62. Original in *El Gráfico* 366, 1926, p. 17.
23. Quoted in P. Ball (2001), *Morbo*, pp. 214–15.
24. Quoted in S. Martin (2004), *Football and Fascism*, p. 68.
25. *La Nazione*, 5 July 1929, quoted in ibid., p. 69.
26. See T. Andersson (2001), 'Swedish football hooliganism, 1900–39', pp. 8–9.
27. Quoted in S. Gehrmann (1997), 'Football in an industrial region', p. 350.
28. Quoted in U. Hesse-Lichtenberger (2002), p. 61.

7 The Rules of the Game: International Football and International Politics, 1900–1934

A selection of delightful annotations and notes to Foreign Office memos on the subjects of football and politics, including this memo, can be found in P. Beck (1999), *Scoring for Britain*, chapter 4. Henri Desgrange's extraordinary editorial in *L'Auto* is quoted in R. Holt (1981), *Sport and Society in Modern France*, p. 195. Lord Decies is quoted in P. Beck (1999), p. 165.

1. *Daily Express*, 1 January 1929.
2. *The Times*, 2 January 1929.
3. Quoted in P. Beck (1999), p. 118.
4. www.rsssf.com
5. FIFA, Minutes of 11th Congress, Christiana, 27–28 June 1914, p. 10.
6. FA, Consultative Committee, Minute 10, 1 September 1919, 1914–20.
7. Quoted in T. Mason (1995), *Passion of the People?*, p. 39.
8. E. Galeano (2004), *Football in Sun and Shadow*, p. 42.
9. *Miroir des Sports*, 12 June 1924.
10. *Buenos Aires Herald*, 14 June 1928.
11. Cited in B. Glanville (2002), *The Story of the World Cup*, p. 15.
12. Quoted in G. Brera (1978), *Storia critica del calcio italiana*, Milan, translation in E. Archetti (1996), 'In search of national identity'.
13. Quoted in A. Teja (1998), 'Italian sport and international relations under Fascism', p. 162.
14. *New York Times*, 14 May 1933.
15. Quoted in P. Beck (1999), p. 151.

16. *La Nazione*, 11 January 1934, quoted in S. Martin (2004), *Football and Fascism*, p. 186.
17. *Arbeiterzeitung*, 17 May 1931, quoted in R. Horak and W. Maderthaner (1996), 'A culture of urban cosmopolitanism', p. 150.
18. Alfred Polgar in *Pariser Tageszeitung*, 25 January 1939, quoted in ibid. pp. 147–8.
19. V. Pozzo (1960), *Campioni del Mondo*, pp. 213–14.
20. Quoted in ibid., p. 205.
21. Quoted in P. Beck (1999), p. 158.
22. Quoted in S. Martin (2004), p. 204.

8 The Road to El Dorado: Latin American Football, 1935–1954

The Boca Juniors chant ('Boca, Perón, One Heart') is recalled in M. Cappros (2005), *Boquita*. César Aguiar is quoted in R. Giulianotti (2000), 'Built by the two Varelas'.
Match Report: Brazil vs. Uruguay (p. 291)
A. Bellos (2002), *Futebol: The Brazilian Way of Life*; C. Freddi (2006), *Complete Book of the World Cup 2006*; B. Glanville (2006), *The Story of the World Cup*; A. Cantor (1996), *Goooal! A Celebration of Soccer*.
Match Report: Hungary vs. Uruguay (p. 295)
C. Freddi (2006), *Complete Book of the World Cup 2006*.

1. E. Galeano (2004), *Football in Sun and Shadow*, p. 42.
2. Quoted in B. Glanville (2002), *The Story of the World Cup*, pp. 15–16.
3. E. Galeano (2004), p. 76.
4. Ibid., p. 76.
5. Quoted in T. Mason (1995), *Passion of the People?*, pp. 102–3. Mason reports that these diplomatic premonitions came to pass when Arsenal toured Brazil in 1949. A shoulder barge on Flamengo's goalkeeper in Rio triggered a fight on the pitch, a small pitch invasion and police intervention. Bryn Jones, the offending Arsenal forward, was struck on the head with a truncheon.
6. *El Tiempo*, 4 November 1950, quoted in C. Taylor (1998), *The Beautiful Game*.
7. Ibid., pp. 168–9.
8. Neil Franklin, quoted in T. Mason (1994), 'The Bogotá Affair'.
9. *Miroir du Football*, 14 June 1961.
10. Quoted in T. Mason (1994), p. 59.
11. *Correio da Manhã*, 15 June 1938.
12. P. Robb (2004), *A Death in Brazil*, pp. 24–5.
13. M. Filho (2004), *O Negro no futebol brasileiro*.
14. Quoted in G. Moura (1998), *O Rio corre para o Maracanã*.
15. *Jornal dos Sports*, 10 June 1947.
16. Quoted in A. Bellos (2002), p. 46.
17. Ibid., p. 48.
18. Quoted in A. Cantor (1996).
19. T. Mason (1995), p. 89.
20. On Barbosa, racism and myth-making, see A. Bellos (2002), pp. 55–7; J. Leite Lopes (1999), 'The Brazilian style of football and its dilemmas'.
21. Some sources say the sidelined Puskás split Pinheiro's head with a bottle; see C. Freddi (2002), *Complete Book of the World Cup 2002*.

9 Games of Life, Games of Death: European Football in War and Peace, 1934–1954

Simon Kuper's question used in the opening quotation is taken from S. Kuper (2003), *Ajax, the Dutch, the War*, p. 13. The Mass Observation quotation is cited in ibid., pp. 147–8.
Match Report: Sindelar's Swansong (p. 312)
R. Horak and W. Maderthaner (1997), 'A culture of urban cosmopolitanism'; S. Kuper (2003), *Ajax, the Dutch, the War*.
Match Report: England vs. Hungary 1953 (p. 345)
G. Green, *The Times*, 26 November 1953.
Match Report: West Germany vs. Hungary 1954 (p. 352)
R. Taylor and K. Jamrich (1997), *Puskas on Puskas*; P. Legg (2003), *The 1954 World Cup*.

1. Cited in S. Kuper (2003), p. 163.
2. Ibid., p. 158.
3. Cited in J. Burns (2005), *When Beckham Went to Spain*, pp. 158–9.
4. Ibid., p. 176.
5. Ibid., p. 145.
6. Cited in U. Merkel (2000), 'The history of the German Football Association', p. 185.
7. Cited in S. Kuper (2003), p. 37.
8. Ibid., p. 89.
9. Ibid., p. 162.
10. Ibid., p. 104.
11. Y. Oleshchuk, *Sportekspress zhurnal*, 1999, R. Edelman (2002), 'A small way of saying "No"'.
12. Cited in R. Edelman (2002).
13. Ibid.
14. R. Edelman (2002).
15. Cited in ibid.
16. Cited in R. Holt (1981), *Sport and Society in Modern France*, pp. 205–6.
17. *News Chronicle*, 16 October 1935.
18. Cited in P. Beck (1999), *Scoring for Britain*, p. 199.
19. *La Nazione*, 2 June 1938, cited in S. Martin (2004), *Football and Fascism*, p. 183.
20. V. Pozzo (1960), *Campioni del Mondo*, p. 265, cited in ibid., p. 182.
21. Cited in S. Kuper (2003), p. 93.
22. Ibid., p. 94.
23. Ibid., chapter 8.
24. Cited in S. Kuper (2003), p. 136.
25. Ibid., p. 159.
26. Ibid., p. 168.
27. Cited in U. Hesse-Lichtenberger (2002), *Tor!*, p. 119.
28. Ibid., p. 121.
29. B. Glanville (1963), 'Britain against the rest'.
30. N. Fishwick (1989), *English Football and Society*, p. 150.
31. The quotation is from Bert Gregory, a member of the groundstaff, in the *Guardian*, 9 March 1996, cited in M. Johnes (2004), ' "Heads in the sand" '.
32. B. Glanville (1963), p. 139.
33. S. Inglis (1990), *The Football Grounds of Europe*, p. 161.
34. U. Hesse-Lichtenberger (2002), p. 280.
35. R. Taylor and K. Jamrich (1997), pp. 82–3.
36. Ibid., p. 40.
37. Cited in P. Legg (2003).
38. Ibid.

39. Ibid.
40. Ibid.

10 *Demons and Angels: Latin American Football, 1955–1974*

The second epigraph is taken from R. DaMatta (1986), *Explorações?*, p. 130.
Match Report: Brazil vs. Sweden (p. 372)
The quotation is from G. Green, *The Times*, 30 June 1958. See also B. Glanville (2006), *The Story of the World Cup 2006*; R. Castro (2004), *Garrincha*.

1. The full text of Kennedy's speech at Rice Stadium, Rice University, can be viewed at http://www1.jsc.nasa.gov/er/seh/ricetalk.htm
2. H. McIlvanney (1994), *McIlvanney on Football*, p. 168.
3. Cited in R. Castro (2004), p. 101.
4. Cited in *The Pelé Albums* (1990).
5. T. Mason (1995), *Passion of the People?*, p. 70.
6. B. Glanville (2002), *The Story of the World Cup 2002*, p. 147.
7. Cited in H. McIlvanney (ed.) (1966), *World Cup '66*, p. 117.
8. Cited in A. Ciria (1984), 'From soccer to war in Argentina'.
9. *El Gráfico*, 3 May 1967. All *El Gráfico* quotations cited in P. Alabarces, R. Coelho and J. Sanguinetti (2001), 'Treacheries and traditions in Argentinean football styles'.
10. *El Gráfico*, 20 July 1967.
11. E. Weil (1983), 'History of the Libertadores Cup', pp. 18–19.
12. Ibid.
13. *El Gráfico*, 17 December 1969.
14. H. McIlvanney (1994), p. 178.
15. Cited in J. Lever (1983), *Soccer Madness*, p. 68.
16. T. Mason (1995), p. 131.

11 *The Glamour and the Glory: High Industrial Football in Europe, 1955–1974*

The Times is quoted in S. Inglis (1983), *The Football Grounds of England and Wales*, p. 41.

1. See Chapter 7, pp. 242–3.
2. Quoted in D. Winner (2000), *Brilliant Orange*, p. 136.
3. A. Hopcraft (1968), *The Football Man*, p. 178.
4. R. Taylor and K. Jamrich (1997), *Puskás on Puskás*, p. 160.
5. Ibid., p. 165.
6. See Chapter 8, pp. 277–81.
7. H. McIlvanney, *The Scotsman*, 19 May 1960.
8. Quoted in J. Burns (2005), *When Beckham Went to Spain*, p. 241.
9. Quoted in ibid., p. 230.
10. Quoted in P. Ball (2001), *Morbo*, p. 235.
11. Quoted in J. Burns (2005), p. 259.
12. J. Ferran (1958), 'Ne pas confondré.
13. See Chapter 12, pp. 503–4.
14. Eusébio (2004), 'The agony of '66'.
15. Quoted in J. Foot (2006), *Calcio*, p. 212.
16. Ibid., pp. 462–3.
17. On the golden-fix, see B. Glanville (1999), *Football Memories*.
18. R. Edelman (1993), *Serious Fun*, p. 181.

19. Ibid., p. 191.
20. See Chapter 8, pp. 278–9.
21. Harold Wilson's speech at the Labour Party conference, 1 October 1963.
22. H. McIlvanney (1994), *McIlvanney on Football*, p. 31.
23. A. Hopcraft (1968), p. 189.
24. Quoted in P. Murphy, J. Williams and E. Dunning (1990), *Football on Trial*, p. 83.
25. R. Taylor and A. Ward (eds) (1993), *Kicking and Screaming*, pp. 179–80.
26. See Chapter 9, pp. 326–7.
27. Quoted in D. Winner (2000), *Brilliant Orange*, pp. 7–8.
28. Ibid., p. 9.
29. Ibid., p. 25.
30. Ibid., pp. 36–7.
31. Ibid., p. 44.
32. Ibid., p. 25.
33. Quoted in U. Hesse-Lichtenberger (2002), *Tor!*, p. 213.
34. See Chapter 13, pp. 521–2.
35. Quotations in this paragraph from D. Winner (2000), pp. 93–9.
36. Quoted in U. Hesse-Lichtenberger (2002), p. 248.

12 We Can Show Them Who Is Really Superior: Football in Africa, 1900–1974

The Denis Liwawe quotation comes from an interview in the documentary *History of Football: The Beautiful Game*, vol. 6: 'Africa', Freemantle Video, 2004. Ferhas Abbat cited in A. Versi (1988), 'Striking power'.

1. Quoted in A. Guttmann (1994), *Games and Empires*.
2. Quoted in P. Martin (1991), 'Colonialism, youth and football in French Equatorial Africa'.
3. N. Azikiwe (1970), *My Odyssey*, p. 402.
4. *Drum*, August 1959, quoted in P. Alegi (2004), 'Football and Apartheid society'.
5. Cited in P. Lanfranchi and A. Wahl (1996), 'The immigrant as hero'.
6. Quoted in BBC Sport (2003), *Keita: Mali's Living Legend*, viewed at http://news.bbc.co.uk/sport1/hi/football/africa/3218333.stm
7. Interview with N'daye Mulamba, *African Soccer*, May/June 1998.

13 The World Turned Upside Down: João Havelange, FIFA and the Transformation of Global Football

The opening quotation is taken from J. Sugden and A. Tomlinson (2003), *Badfellas*, p. 74.

1. J. Sugden and A. Tomlinson (2003), p. 72.
2. Quoted in ibid., p. 68.
3. See Chapter 12, pp. 496–8.
4. J. Sugden and A. Tomlinson (2003), p. 136.
5. Ibid.
6. See Chapter 15, pp. 608–10.
7. On Havelange's early football career, see Chapter 10, p. 370.
8. See Chapter 10, pp. 386–9.
9. See D. Yallop (1999), *How They Stole the Game*, pp. 95–105.
10. Quoted in J. Sugden and A. Tomlinson (2003), p. 37.
11. Ibid., p. 59.

12. S. Rous (1978), *Football Worlds*, p. 203.
13. J. Sugden and A. Tomlinson (2003), p. 54.
14. D. Yallop (1999), p. 164.
15. Quoted in J. Sugden and A. Tomlinson (2003), p. 68.
16. See Chapter 15, pp. 615–19.
17. D. Yallop (1999), p. 155.
18. D. Held et al. (1999), *Global Transformations*, p. 358.
19. See A. Markowitz and S. Hellerman (2001), *Offside*, p. 164.
20. See Chapter 4, p. 100.
21. See M. Manley (2002), *A History of West Indies Cricket*.
22. C. Arthur (1999), 'Up for the Cup'.
23. R. Kapuscinski (1990), *The Soccer War*, pp. 158–9.
24. See Chapter 4, pp. 92–5.
25. *The Sporting Globe*, 12 April 1950, p. 13.
26. See the work of Roy Hay on ethnicity and Australian football: for example R. Hay (2001).
27. Korea's football history is discussed in Chapter 19, pp. 834–7.
28. See Chapter 4, pp. 107–11.

14 If This Is Football, Let It Die: The European Crisis, 1974–1990

Match Report: AC Milan vs. Steaua Bucharest (p. 586)
The Berlusconi quotation is cited in P. Ginsborg (2004), *Silvio Berlusconi*, p. 56.

1. *L'Équipe*, 30 May 1985.
2. Peter Hooten, quoted in R. Taylor and A. Ward (1993), *Kicking and Screaming*, pp. 243–4.
3. Cited in J. Foot (2006) *Calcio: A History of Italian Football*, p. 336.
4. Cited in J. Williams (1991), 'Having an away day', p.166.
5. C. Podaliri and C. Balestri (1998), 'The Ultras, racism and football culture in Italy'.
6. Cited in R. Spaaij and C. Vinas (2005), 'Passion, politics and violence', p. 82.
7. Ibid., p. 83.
8. D. Russell (1997), *Football and the English*, p. 172.
9. Cited in D. Hill (1989), *Out of His Skin*, pp. 129–30.
10. P. Barclay (2000), 'The Fab Four'.
11. J.-P. Leclaire (2000), 'First samba in Guadalajara'.
12. Interview in *France Football*, 27 October 1984, cited in G. Hare (2003), *Football in France*, p. 161.
13. Cited in A. Flynn and L. Guest (1988), *The Secret Life of Football*, p. 90.
14. R. Gildea (1997), *France Since 1945*, p. 200.
15. P. Ginsborg (2004), p. 32.
16. Cited in M. Hesselmann and R. Ide (2006), 'Football and national identity in GDR', p. 40.
17. Cited in P. Scraton (1999), *Hillsborough: The Truth*, p. 30.
18. Cited in P. Lanfranchi (1994), 'Italy and the World Cup', p. 154.

15 Military Manoeuvres: Football under the Latin American Generals, 1974–1990

The opening epigraph is taken from J. Sugden and A. Tomlinson (1998), *FIFA and the Contest for World Football*, p. 191. The original telegram is in the Sir Stanley Rous archives.

1. Cited in J. Sugden and A. Tomlinson (1998), p. 189.
2. Ibid., p. 192.

3. Cited in *Observer Sports Magazine*, 2 November 2003.
4. Cited in C. Taylor (1998), *The Beautiful Game*, p. 71.
5. Cited in E. Archetti (1996), 'In search of national identity', p. 214.
6. Ibid., p. 215.
7. Cited in E. Archetti (1999), *Masculinities*, p. 182.
8. J. Burns (1998), *The Hand of God*, p. 9.
9. Ibid.
10. Ibid., p. 94.
11. R. Giulianotti (2000), 'Built by the two Varelas', p. 93.
12. *Jornal do Brasil*, 19 June 1973, cited in J. Lever (1983), *Soccer Madness*, p. 64.
13. J. Leite Lopes (1999), 'The Brazilian style of football and its dilemmas'.
14. *Folha de São Paulo*, 13 February 1983, cited in M. Shirts (1988), 'Socrates, Corinthians and questions of democracy and citizenship'.
15. Cited in T. Mason (1995), *Passion of the People?*, p. 135.
16. Cited in J. Sugden and A. Tomlinson (1998), p. 106.
17. Cited in C. Taylor (1998), p. 152.
18. *When Saturday Comes* 104, October 1995.
19. Cited in J. King (1996), 'When drugs rule football', p. 292.
20. Cited in C. Taylor (1998), p. 151.
21. J. King (1996), p. 293.
22. Ibid.

16 Football and the Belly: Africa, 1974–1990

Wole Soyinka's words are taken from W. Soyinka (1996), *The Open Sore of a Continent*. Samuel Akpabot's exclamation comes from S. Akpabot (1985), *Football in Nigeria*.

1. Cited in C. Freddi (2002), *Complete Book of the World Cup*, p. 209.
2. S. Kuper (1994), *Football Against the Enemy*, p. 114.
3. Quoted in 'Magic and mayhem', *African Soccer*, August/September 2001.
4. *New Nigerian*, 8 March 1980, quoted in W. Boer (2004), 'A story of heroes, of epics'.

17 Football through the Looking-Glass: Europe, 1990–2006

1. Cited in J. Burns (2004), *When Beckham Went to Spain*, p. 375.
2. *Gazzetta dello Sport*, 1 March 1996.
3. Cited in P. Agnew (2006), *Forza Italia*, p. 11.
4. D. Jones and G. Boon (eds) (2004), *Annual Review of Football Finance*.
5. Ibid., pp. 13–19.
6. J. Sugden and A. Tomlinson (1998), *FIFA and the Contest for World Football* (1998), p. 95.
7. Cited in J. Bal (2001), 'Ferencváros, Hungary and the European Champions League', p. 254.
8. Ibid., pp. 254–5.
9. Cited in D. Brennan, 'Trip down memory lane reveals the ugly rivalry between Hungarian old firm', *Scotland on Sunday*, 10 April 2003.
10. D. Winner (2000), *Brilliant Orange*, p. 139.
11. Cited in P. Ginsborg (2004), *Silvio Berlusconi*, p. 63.
12. G. Debord (1967), *The Society of the Spectacle*, p. 1.
13. Cited in P. Agnew (2006), p. 123.
14. Cited in J. Foot (2006), *Calcio*, p. 267.

15. Cited in J. Burns (2004), p. 303.
16. *El País*, cited in ibid., p. 316.
17. Ibid., p. 306.
18. Football Association (1991), *Blueprint for Football*.
19. Cited in Sugden and Tomlinson (2003), *Badfellas*, p. 17.
20. Cited in A. Jennings (2006), *Foul!*, p. 225.
21. For an account of Ricardo Teixeira's public record see Chapter 18, pp. 794–5.
22. 'German government to bail out Bundesliga', *Guardian*, 5 April 2002.
23. Ibid.
24. Ibid.
25. 'Football clubs a bad investment', *Financial Times*, 29 August 2005.
26. G. Marcotti, 'You are the boss. You own Serie A', *The Times*, 15 May 2006.
27. Cited in C. Kozanoglu (1999), 'Beyond Edirne', p. 120.
28. P. Town, 'Letter from Portugal', *When Saturday Comes*, February 2001.
29. Cited in *Review of the Year 2002*, viewed at www.footballportugal.com.pt
30. 'Albania fans cry foul at Greek ban', viewed at http://news.bbc.co.uk/1/hi/world/europe/4397921.stm
31. The members of the expanded G-14 are Ajax, Arsenal, Barcelona, Bayer Leverkusen, Bayern München, Borussia Dortmund, Internazionale, Juventus, Liverpool, Milan, Manchester United, Olympique Lyonnais, Olympique Marseille, Porto, Paris Saint-Germain, PSV Eindhoven, Real Madrid, Valencia.

18 The Crisis Will be Televised: Football in the Americas, 1990–2006

The Pablo Alabarces quotation is taken from P. Alabarces and M. Rodriguez (2000), 'Football and Fatherland'. Carlos Alberto Parreira was interviewed in the *New York Times*, 1 July 1994.

1. *Los Medios y Mercados de Latinamérica*, 1998.
2. Quoted in J. Valdano (2002), 'Poverty is good for nothing except football', www.fifaworldcup.com, 9 May.
3. G. Vecsey, *New York Times*, 12 June 1994.
4. Source unknown.
5. *Washington Post*, 29 June 1994, quoted in T. Mason (1995), *Passion of the People?*, p. 142.
6. *Time*, 18 July 1994, quoted in ibid.
7. *Guardian*, 2 July 1994, quoted in ibid., p. 146.
8. C. Taylor (1998), *The Beautiful Game*, pp. 176–7.
9. Cited in T. Mason (1995), p. 145.
10. Cited in J. Sugden and A. Tomlinson (1998), *FIFA and the Contest for World Football*, p. 210.
11. Juca Kfouri interview in *History of Football: The Beautiful Game*, vol. 3: 'Brazil', Freemantle Video, 2004.
12. E. P. Thompson (1980), *The Making of the English Working Class*, p. 8.
13. Data from V. Duke and L. Crolley (1994), 'Fútbol, politicians and the people'.
14. Quoted in *World Soccer*, October 2002.
15. Valdano cited in M. Amis, 'In search of Dieguito', *Guardian*, 1 October 2004.
16. T. Vickery (2004), 'Identity crisis', p. 27.
17. C. Freddi (2002), *Complete Book of the World Cup*, p. 374.
18. *World Soccer*, November 2004, p. 25.
19. Cited in 'Crime, anarchy, incompetence: how the blazers betrayed Brazil', www.guardian.co.uk, 6 December 2001.
20. Cited in 'Boca apologise for Libertadores snub', www.reuters.co.uk, 8 July 2004.

21. Cited in 'Cienciano of Cuzco is Peru's Cinderella story', www.si.com, 20 December 2003.
22. The report can be viewed at http://news.bbc.co.uk/1/hi/world/americas/3824331/stm, 20 June 2004.
23. *World Soccer*, October 2004, p. 21

19 Accelerated Development: Football and Asia's New Industrial Revolution

The opening quotation from Masayuki Tamaki is taken from M. Tamaki (1993), *J League Kara no Kaze, Shueisha*, p. 6. Peter Velappan is quoted from 'Asian football in twenty-first century', viewed at http://english.people.com.cn/english/20010/2353353.html.

1. S. Moffett (2002), *Japanese Rules*, p. 26.
2. L. Petrov (2002), 'Korean football at the crossroads'.
3. S. Moffett (2002), p. 110.
4. Ibid., p. 107.
5. Ibid., pp. 57–8.
6. Ibid., p. 88.
7. Cited in H. Morita (2002), 'Nippon's blue heaven', p. 154.
8. Ibid., p. 155.
9. Cited in Whang Soon-Hee (2004), 'Football, fashion and fandom', p. 155.
10. Ibid., p. 163.
11. Cited in 'Illegal bookmaking syndicates cashing in on soccer craze in Malaysia', viewed at www.channelnewsasia.com, 15 June 2004.
12. 'Nike in Vietnam: The Tae Kwang Vina Factory', viewed at http://poverty2.forumone.com/files/14826Nike-web.pdf
13. C. Bromberger (1998), 'A third half for Iranian football'.
14. Cited in D. Yaeger (2003), 'Son of Saddam', *Sports Illustrated*.
15. Quoted in 'Iraqi footballers' fury at Bush', viewed at http://news.bbc.co.uk/1/hi/world/middleeast/3584242/stm
16. See S. Kuper (2002), 'The world's game is not just a game'.
17. D. Tuastad (1997), 'The political role of football for Palestinians in Jordan'.

20 Small Mercies: Football in Africa after the Cold War, 1990–2006

The opening quotation is taken from a longer piece by Soneka Kamuhuza, viewed at http://www.rsssf.com/rssbest/zambia.html.

1. Quoted in G. Armstrong (2004), 'Life, death and the biscuit'.
2. Quoted in BBC Sport (2003), 'Play football and go to jail', viewed at http://news.bbc.co.uk/sport1/hi/football/africa/2725467.stm
3. Data calculated from F. Ricci (2001), *African Football Yearbook*.
4. BBC Sport (2001), 'Bribery scandal or hidden agenda?', viewed at http://news.bbc.co.uk/sport1/hi/football/africa/1646692.stm
5. *Nigerian Guardian*, 5 February 2000, quoted in W. Boer (2004), 'A story of heroes, of epics'.
6. A. Saff (1999), *Carnets de Bus*, p. 28.

Conclusion

The epigraph is taken from E. Durkheim (1912), *The Elementary Forms of the Religious Life*, (1954 edn) trans. J. W. Swain, New York: The Free Press, pp. 475–6.

1. M. Vásquez Montalbán (2005), *Fútbol*.
2. M. Vargas Llosa (1996), *Making Waves*, pp. 167–8.
3. E. Galeano (2004), *Football in Sun and Shadow*, p. 204.

Bibliography

Adam, P. (1907), *La morale des sports*, Paris: Librairie Mondiale.

Agnew, P. (2006), *Forza Italia: A Journey in Search of Italy and its Football*, London: Ebury Press.

Ahlstrom, F. (ed.) (2005), *Fifty Years of European Club Football*, Nyon: UEFA.

Akpabot, S. (1985), *Football in Nigeria*, London: Macmillan.

Alabarces, P., R. Coelho and J. Sanguinetti (2001), 'Treacheries and traditions in Argentinean football styles: the story of Estudiantes La Plata', in G. Armstrong and R. Giulianotti (eds) (2001), *Fear and Loathing in World Football*.

Alabarces, P. and M. Rodriguez (2000), 'Football and Fatherland: the crisis of national representation in Argentinean soccer', in G. Finn and R. Giulianotti (eds), *Football Cultures and Identities*.

Alcock, C. (ed.) (1880), *Football Annual 1880*.

—— (1906), *Association Football*.

Alegi, P. (2004), 'Football and Apartheid society: the South African soccer league, 1960–66', in G. Armstrong and R. Giulianotti (eds), *Football in Africa*.

Andersson, T. (2001), 'Swedish football hooliganism, 1900–39', *Soccer and Society*, vol. 2, no. 1.

Arbena, J. (ed.) (1988), *Sport and Society in Latin America*, New York: Greenwood Press.

Archetti, E. (1992), 'Argentinean football: a ritual of violence?', *The International Journal of the History of Sports*, vol. 9, no. 2.

—— (1996), 'In search of national identity: Argentinian football and Europe', in J. Mangan (ed.), *Tribal Identities*.

—— (1997), *Masculinities: Football, Polo and Tango in Argentina*, Oxford: Berg.

Arlt, R. (1995), 'Soccer and popular joy', in G. Nouzellis and G. Montaldo (eds), *The Argentina Reader*.

Armstrong, G. (2004), 'Life, death and the biscuit: football and the embodiment of society in Liberia, West Africa', in G. Armstrong and R. Giulianotti (eds), *Football in Africa*.

Armstrong, G. and R. Giulianotti (eds) (1997), *Entering the Field: New Perspectives on World Football*, Oxford: Berg.

—— (1999), *Football Cultures and Identities*, London: Macmillan.

—— (2001), *Fear and Loathing in World Football*, Oxford: Berg.

—— (2004), *Football in Africa: Conflict, Conciliation and Community*, London: Palgrave.

Arthur, C. (1999), 'Up for the Cup: the man who beat Dino Zoff', in M. Dash and C. Arthur (eds), *A Haiti Anthology*.

Azikiwe, N. (1970), *My Odyssey*, London: C. Hurst and Company.

Bal, J. (2001), 'Ferencvaros, Hungary and the European Champions League', in G. Armstrong and R. Giulianotti (eds) (2001), *Fear and Loathing in World Football*.

Bale, J. and J. Maguire (eds) (1994), *The Global Sports Arena*, London: Frank Cass.

Ball, P. (2001), *Morbo: The Story of Spanish Football*, London: WSC Books.
—— (2002), *White Storm: 100 Years of Real Madrid*, Edinburgh: Mainstream.
Bandyopadhyay, K. (2001), 'Race, nation and sport: footballing nationalism in colonial Calcutta', *Soccer and Society*, vol. 2, no. 1.
Barclay, P. (2000), 'The Fab Four: France win the European Championship', in C. Ruhn (ed.), *Le Foot*.
Beck, P. (1999), *Scoring for Britain: International Football and International Politics, 1900–1939*, London: Frank Cass.
Bellos, A. (2002), *Futebol: The Brazilian Way of Life*, London: Bloomsbury.
Blei, D. (2003), *Identity Crises: Jews, Sport and Vienna, 1900–1914*, unpublished.
Blows, K. and T. Hogg (2002), *The Essential History of West Ham United*, London: Headline.
Boer, W. (2004), 'A story of heroes, of epics: the rise of football in Nigeria', in G. Armstrong and R. Giulianotti (eds) (2004), *Football in Africa*.
Bose, M. (1990), *A History of Indian Cricket*, London: Andre Deutsch.
Bottenburg, M. Van (2001), *Global Games*, Urbana: University of Illinois Press.
Bredekamp, H. (1993), *Florentiner Fussball: Die Renaissance der Spiele*, Frankfurt-am-Main: Wagenbach.
Brera, G. (1978), *Storia critica del calcio italiana*, Milan, translation in E. Archetti (1996), 'In search of national identity'.
Bromberger, C. (1998), 'A third half for Iranian football', *Le Monde diplomatique*, April.
Brown, A. (ed.) (1998), *Fanatics: Power, Identity and Fandom in Football*, London: Routledge.
Burns, J. (1998), *The Hand of God: The Life of Diego Maradona*, London: Bloomsbury.
—— (2005), *When Beckham Went to Spain: Power, Stardom and Real Madrid*, London: Michael Joseph.

Cantor, A. (1996), *Goooal! A Celebration of Soccer*, New York: Simon and Schuster.
Cappros, M. (2005), *Boquita*, Buenos Aires: Planeta.
Castro, R. (2004), *Garrincha: The Triumph and Tragedy of Brazil's Forgotten Footballing Hero*, London: Yellow Jersey Press.
Chandos, J. (1984), *Boys Together: English Public Schools 1800–1864*, New Haven: Yale University Press.
Cheska, A. T. (1970), 'Games of the native North Americans', in G. Luschen (ed.), *Cross-Cultural Analysis of Sports and Games*.
Ciria, A. (1984), 'From soccer to war in Argentina: preliminary notes on sports-as-politics under a military regime, 1976–1982', in R. Arch and M. Ritter (eds), *Latin America and the Caribbean*.
Corry, E. (1989), *Catch and Kick*, Dublin: Poolbeg.
Cox, J. (1962), *Don Davies – An Old International*, London: Stanley Paul, extracted in I. Hamilton (ed.), *The Faber Book of Soccer*.
Cox, R., D. Russell and W. Vamplew (eds) (2002), *Encyclopedia of British Football*, London: Frank Cass.
Coyle, P. (1999), *Paradise Lost and Found: The Story of Belfast Celtic*, Edinburgh: Mainstream.
Cunningham, H. (1980), *Leisure in the Industrial Revolution*, London: Croom Helm.
Curry, G. (2004), 'Playing for money: James J. Lang and emergent soccer professionalism in Sheffield', *Soccer and Society*, vol. 5, no. 3.

DaMatta, R. (1986), *Explorações: Ensaios de Sociologia Interpretativa*, Rio de Janeiro: Rocca, cited in T. Mason (1995), *Passion of the People?*
—— (1992), 'Notes sur le football brasilien', *Le Debat* 19, pp. 68–76, cited in T. Mason (1995), *Passion of the People?*.
Dash, M. and C. Arthur (eds) (1999), *A Haiti Anthology: Libète*, Princeton: Markus Wiener.

Bibliography

Davies, Hunter (1972), *The Glory Game: A Year in the Life of Tottenham Hotspur*, London: Weidenfeld and Nicolson.

Debord, G. (1967), *The Society of the Spectacle* (1992 edn), London: Rebel Press.

Delves, A. (1981), 'Popular recreation and social conflict in Derby 1800–1850', in S. and Y. Yeo (eds), *Popular Culture and Class Conflict*.

Dimeo, P. (2001), 'Football and politics in Bengal: colonialism, nationalism, communalism', in P. Dimeo and J. Mills (eds), *Soccer in South Asia*.

Dimeo, P. and J. Mills (eds) (2001), *Soccer in South Asia: Empire, Nation, Diaspora*, London: Frank Cass.

Duke, V. and L. Crolley (1994), 'Fútbol, politicians and the people: populism and politics in Argentina', in J. Mangan and L. P. Da Costa (eds), *Sport in Latin American Society*.

Dunning, E. et al. (1984), 'Football hooliganism in Britain before the First World War', *International Journal of the Sociology of Sport* 19.

Dunning, J. (ed.) (1971), *The Society of Sport: A Selection of Readings*, London: Frank Cass.

Dunphy, Eamon (1976), *Only a Game?: Diary of a Professional Footballer*, Harmondsworth: Penguin.

Edelman, R. (1993), *Serious Fun: A History of Spectator Sports in the USSR*, Cambridge: Cambridge University Press.

—— (2002), 'A small way of saying "No": Moscow working men, Spartak soccer and the Communist Party, 1900–1945', *American Historical Review*, vol. 107, no. 5.

Edwardes, C. (1892), 'The new football mania', *Nineteenth Century*, October.

Elias, N. and J. Dunning (1971), 'Folk football in Medieval and Early Modern Britain', in J. Dunning (ed.), *The Society of Sport*.

Eusébio (2004), 'The agony of '66', interview with Gabriel Marcotti, *The Times*, 16 November.

Farnsworth, K. (1995), *Sheffield Football: A History*, Sheffield: Hallamshire Press, vol. 1.

Ferran, J. (1958), 'Ne pas confondré: l'équipe de France et le football français', *France Football* 648, 8 July.

Filho, M. (1964, 2004), *O negro no futebol brasileiro*, 4th edn, Rio de Janeiro: MAUAD.

Finn, G. and R. Giulianotti (eds) (2000), *Football Culture: Local Contests, Global Visions*, London: Frank Cass.

Fishwick, N. (1989), *English Football and Society, 1910–1950*, Manchester: Manchester University Press.

Flynn, A. and L. Guest (1988), *The Secret Life of Football*, London: Queen Anne Press.

Foer, F. (2004), *How Soccer Explains the World*, London: HarperCollins.

Foot, J. (2006), *Calcio: A History of Italian Football*, London: 4th Estate.

Football Association (1991), *Blueprint for Football*, London: The FA, cited in J. Williams (2006), ' "Protect me from what I want" '.

Frankl, W. (1983), 'Erinnerungen an Hakoah Wien, 1909–1939', *The Bulletin of the Leo Baeck Institute of Jews from Germany* 64, pp. 55–84, quoted in D. Blei (2003), *Identity Crises*.

Freddi, C. (2002, 2006), *Complete Book of the World Cup*, London: Collins Willow.

Frykholm, P. (1997), 'Soccer and social identity in pre-revolutionary Moscow', *Journal of Sport History*, 24, 143–54.

Galeano, E. (1997, 2004), *Football in Sun and Shadow*, London: 4th Estate.

Gardner, P. (1994), *The Simplest Game: The Intelligent Fan's Guide to the World of Soccer*, New York: Collier Books.

Gehrmann, S. (ed.) (1997), *Football and Regional Identity in Europe*, Münster: Lit Verlag.

—— (1997), 'Football in an industrial region: the example of Schalke 04 Football Club', *The International Journal of the History of Sport*, vol. X, no. 10.

Gildea, R. (1997), *France Since 1945*, Oxford: Oxford University Press.

Ginsborg, P. (2004), *Silvio Berlusconi: Television, Power and Patrimony*, London: Verso.

Giulianotti, R. (2000), 'Built by the two Varelas: the rise and fall of football culture and national identity in Uruguay', in G. Finn and R. Giulianotti (eds), *Football Culture*.

Giulianotti, R., N. Boney and M. Hepworth (eds) (1994), *Football, Violence and Social Identity*, London: Routledge.

Glanville, B. (1963), 'Britain against the rest', in M. Sissons and P. French (eds), *Age of Austerity*.

—— (1984), 'FIFA knows how to blow its own trumpet!', *World Soccer*, October.

—— (1999), *Football Memories*, London: Virgin.

—— (2002, 2006), *The Story of the World Cup*, London: Faber.

Green, G. (1953), *Soccer: The World Game*, London: Pan.

Guttmann, A. (1994), *Games and Empires: Modern Sports and Cultural Imperialism*, New York: Columbia University Press.

Guttmann, A. and L. Thompson (2001), *Japanese Sports: A History*, Honolulu: University of Hawaii Press.

Hamilton, A. (1998), *An Entirely Different Game: The British Influence on Brazilian Football*, Edinburgh: Mainstream.

Hamilton, I. (ed.) (1992), *The Faber Book of Soccer*, London: Faber.

Hare, G. (2003), *Football in France: A Cultural History*, Oxford: Berg.

Hay, R. (2001), 'Those Bloody Croatians': Croatian Soccer Teams, Ethnicity and Violence in Australia, 1950–99, *Fear and Loathing in World Football*, pp. 77–90, Oxford and New York: Berg [B1].

Held, D., A. McGrew, D. Goldblatt and J. Perration (1999), *Global Transformations*, Cambridge: Polity.

Hess, R. and B. Stewart (eds) (1998), *More than a Game: An Unauthorised History of Australian Rules Football*, Melbourne: Melbourne University Press.

Hesse-Lichtenberger, U. (2002), *Tor! The Story of German Football*, London: WSC Books.

Hesselmann, M. and R. Ide (2006), 'Football and national identity in GDR', in A. Tomlinson and C. Young (eds), *German Football*.

Hill, D. (1989), *Out of His Skin: The John Barnes Phenomenon*, London: Faber.

Hill, J. (2004), ' "The Day was an Ugly One": Wembley, 28th April 1923', *Soccer and Society*, vol. 5, no. 2.

Hill, J. and J. Williams (eds) (1996), *Sport and Identity in the North of England*, Keele: Keele University Press.

Holt, R. (1981), *Sport and Society in Modern France*, London: Macmillan.

—— (1989), *Sport and the British: A Modern History*, Oxford: Oxford University Press.

Holt, R., P. Lanfranchi and J. A. Mangan (eds) (1996), *European Heroes: Myth, Identity, Sport*, London: Frank Cass.

Hooten, P. (1990), 'The Good, the Bad and the Ugly', *The Face*, November, cited in S. Redhead, 'Football and youth culture in Britain'.

Hopcraft, A. (1968), *The Football Man*, London: Collins.

Horak, R. (1992), 'Viennese football culture: some remarks on its history and sociology', *Innovation in Social Sciences Research*, vol. 5, no. 3.

—— (1994), 'Austrification as modernization: changes in Viennese football culture', in J. Williams and R. Giulianotti (eds), *Games Without Frontiers*.

Horak, R. and W. Maderthaner (1996), 'A culture of urban cosmopolitanism: Uridil and Sindelar as Viennese coffee-house heroes', in R. Holt et al. (eds), *European Heroes*.

Hornby, N. (1992), *Fever Pitch*, London: Gollancz.

Horne, J. and W. Manzenreiter (eds) (2002), *Japan, Korea and the 2002 World Cup*, London: Routledge.

—— (eds) (2004), *Football Goes East: Business, Culture and the People's Game in China, Japan and South Korea*, London: Routledge.

Inglis, S. (1983), *The Football Grounds of England and Wales*, London: Collins Willow.
—— (1989), *League Football and the Men who Made It*, London: Willow Books.
—— (1990), *The Football Grounds of Europe*, London: Willow Books.
—— (2005), *Engineering Archie*, London: English Heritage.

Jager, O. (1898), *Fusslummelei: Über Stauchsballspiel und englische Krankheit*, Stuttgart.
Jennings, A. (2006), *Foul! The Secret World of FIFA; Bribes, Vote Rigging and Ticket Scandals*, London: Harpersport.
Johnes, M. (2004), ' "Heads in the sand": football, politics and crowd disasters in twentieth-century Britain', *Soccer and Society*, vol. 5, no. 2.
Jones, D. and G. Boon (eds) (2004), *Annual Review of Football Finance*, Manchester: Deloitte.

Kapuscinski, R. (1990), *The Soccer War*, London: Granta.
Keane, R. (2002), *Keane: The Autobiography*, London: Michael Joseph.
Kelly, S. (ed.) (1996), *The Pick of the Season*, Edinburgh: Mainstream.
King, J. (1996), 'When drugs rule football', in S. Kelly (ed.), *The Pick of the Season*.
Kozanoglu, C. (1999), 'Beyond Erdine: football and the national identity crisis in Turkey', in G. Armstrong and R. Giulianotti (eds), *Football Cultures and Identities*.
Kuper, S. (1994), *Football Against the Enemy*, London: Orion.
—— (2002), 'The world's game is not just a game', *New York Times Magazine*, 26 May.
—— (2003), *Ajax, the Dutch, the War: Football in Europe during the Second World War*, London: Orion.

Dal Lago, A. and R. De Biasi (1994), 'Italian football fans: culture and organization', in R. Giulianotti., N. Boney and M. Hepworth (eds), *Football, Violence and Social Identity*.
Lanfranchi, P. (1994), 'Italy and the World Cup', in J. Sugden and A. Tomlinson (eds), *Hosts and Champions*.
Lanfranchi, P. and M. Taylor (2001), *Moving with the Ball: The Migration of Professional Footballers*, Oxford: Berg.
Lanfranchi, P. and A. Wahl (1996), 'The immigrant as hero: Kopa, Mekloufi and French football', in R. Holt et al. (eds), *European Heroes*.
Leclaire, J.-P. (2000), 'First samba in Guadalajara', in C. Ruhn (ed.) *Le Foot*.
Legg, P. (2003), *The 1954 World Cup*, unpublished.
Leigh, J. and D. Woodhouse (2005), *Football Lexicon*, London: Faber.
Leite Lopes, J. (1999), 'The Brazilian style of football and its dilemmas', in G. Armstrong and R. Giulianotti (1999), *Football Cultures and Identities*.
Lever, J. (1983), *Soccer Madness*, Chicago: University of Chicago Press.
Lockhart, R. B. (1958), *Giants Cast Long Shadows*, London: Putnam.
Luschen, G. (ed.) (1970), *Cross-Cultural Analysis of Sports and Games*, Champaign, IL: Steips Publishing.

Majumdar, B. and K. Bandyopadhyay (2005), 'Regionalism and club domination: growth of rival centres of football excellence', *Soccer and Society*, vol. 6, no. 2.
Mangan, J. (1986), *The Games Ethic and Imperialism: Aspects of the Diffusion of an Ideal*, London: Frank Cass.
Mangan, J. (ed.) (1996), *Tribal Identities. Nationalism, Europe and Sport*, London: Frank Cass.
Mangan, J. and L. P. Da Costa (eds), *Sport in Latin American Society: Past and Present*, London: Frank Cass.
Manley, M. (2002), *A History of West Indies Cricket*, London: Andre Deutsch.
Markowitz, A. and S. Hellerman (2001), *Offside: Soccer and American Exceptionalism*, Princeton: Princeton University Press.

Marples, M. (1954), *A History of Football*, London: Secker and Warburg.

Martin, P. (1991), 'Colonialism, youth and football in French Equatorial Africa', *International Journal of the History of Sport*, vol. 8, no. 1.

Martin, S. (2004), *Football and Fascism: The National Game under Mussolini*, Oxford: Berg.

Mártir de Anglería, P. (1964), *Décadas del Nuevo Mundo*, Buenos Aires: Editoria Bajel.

Mason, T. (1980), *Association Football and English Society*, Brighton: Harvester Press.

—— (1994), 'The Bogotá Affair', in J. Bale and J. Maguire (eds), *The Global Sports Arena*.

—— (1995), *Passion of the People? Football in South America*, London: Verso.

—— (1996), 'Football, sport of the north', in J. Hill and J. Williams (eds), *Sport and Identity in the North of England*.

Mazzoni, T. (1950), *Historia do futebol no Brasil, 1894–1950*, São Paulo: Ed. Leia.

McIlvanney, H. (ed.) (1966), *World Cup '66*, London: Eyre & Spottiswoode.

—— (1994), *McIlvanney on Football*, Edinburgh: Mainstream.

Merkel, U. (2000), 'The history of the German Football Association (DFB), 1900–1950', *Soccer and Society*, vol. 1, no. 2.

Miermans, C. (1955), *Voetbal in Nederland*, Assen: Van Gorcum.

Miller, S. (1991), *Arete: Greek Sports from Ancient Sources*, Berkeley: University of California Press.

—— (2004), *Ancient Greek Athletics*, New Haven: Yale University Press.

Moffett, S. (2002), *Japanese Rules: Why the Japanese Needed Football and How They Got It*, London: Yellow Jersey Press.

Morgagni, T. and V. Brusca (1907) *Annuario Sportivo 1907–1908*, Milan.

Morita, H. (2002), 'Nippon's blue heaven', in M. Perryman (ed.), *Going Oriental*.

Moura, G. (1998), *O Rio corre para o Maracanã*, Rio de Janeiro: Fundação Getúlio Vargas.

Murphy P., J. Williams and E. Dunning (1990), *Football on Trial: Spectator Violence and Development in the Football World*, London: Routledge.

Murray, B. (1994), *The World's Game: A History of Soccer*, University of Illinois Press.

—— (2001), *The Old Firm: Sectarianism, Sport and Society in Scotland*, London: Collins.

Nouzellis, G. and G. Montaldo (eds) (2005), *The Argentina Reader: History, Culture, Politics*, Durham, NC: Duke University Press.

Olesha, Y. (1979), *No Day Without a Line*, Ann Arbor: Ardis.

Pearson, H. (1994), *The Far Corner: A Mazy Dribble Through North-East Football*, London: Little, Brown.

Peiser, B. J. (1996), 'Western theories about the origins of sport in China', *The Sports Historian*, vol. 16, pp. 117–39.

The Pelé Albums (1990), vols 1 and 2, Sydney: Weldon Publishing.

Perryman, M. (ed.) (2002), *Going Oriental: Football after World Cup 2002*, Edinburgh: Mainstream.

Petrov, L. (2002), 'Korean football at the crossroads: a view from inside', in J. Horne and W. Manzenreiter (eds), *Japan, Korea and the 2002 World Cup*.

Podaliri, C. and C. Balestri (1998), 'The Ultras, racism and football culture in Italy', in A. Brown (ed.), *Fanatics*.

Podalsky, L. (2004), *Specular City: Transforming Culture, Consumption, and Space, in Buenos Aires, 1955–1973*, Philadelphia: Temple University Press.

Pozzo, P. (1960), *Campioni del Mondo: Quarant' anni di storia del Calcio Italiano*, Rome: Centro Editoriale Nazionale, cited in S. Martin, *Football and Fascism*.

Raleigh, Sir Thomas (1906), *Lord Curzon in India: Being a Selection from His Speeches as Viceroy and Governor General, 1898–1905*, London: Macmillan.

Bibliography

Redhead, S. (1991), 'Football and youth culture in Britain', in J. Williams and S. Wagg (eds), *British Football and Social Change*.

Ricci, F. (2001), *African Football Yearbook*, Rome: Prosports.

Riordan, J. (1977), *Sport in Soviet Society*, Cambridge: Cambridge University Press.

Riordan, J. and P. Arnaud (eds) (1998), *Sport and International Politics: The Impact of Fascism and Communism on Sport*, London: Routledge.

Ritter, A. (ed) (1984), *Latin America and the Caribbean: Geopolitic Development and Culture*, Ottawa: Canadian Association of Latin American and Caribbean Studies.

Robb, P. (2004), *A Death in Brazil*, London: Bloomsbury.

Rous, S. (1978), *Football Worlds – A Lifetime in Sport*, London: Faber and Faber.

Ruhn, C. (ed.) (2000), *Le Foot: The Legends of French Football*, London: Abacus.

Russell, D. (1997), *Football and the English*, Preston: Carnegie Publishing.

Saff, A. (1999), *Carnets de Bus: essais sur le quotidien des quartiers Sud-Ouest de Rabat*, Casablanca: Eddif, quoted in G. Stanton (2004), 'Chasing the ghosts'.

Scarborough, V. and D. Wilcox (eds) (1991), *The Mesoamerican Ballgame*, Tucson: University of Arizona Press.

Scraton, P. (1999), *Hillsborough: The Truth*, London: Mainstream.

Shirts, M. (1988), 'Socrates, Corinthians and questions of democracy and citizenship', in J. Arbena (ed.), *Sport and Society in Latin America*.

Sissons, M. and P. French (eds) (1963), *Age of Austerity, 1945–51*, London: Hodder and Stoughton.

Smith, J. (1979), *Illusions of Conflict: Anglo-American Diplomacy toward Latin America 1865–1896*, Pittsburgh: University of Pennsylvania Press.

Soyinka, W. (1996), *The Open Sore of a Continent: A Personal Narrative of the Nigerian Crisis*, Oxford: Oxford University Press.

Spaaij, R. and C. Vinas (2005), 'Passion, politics and violence: a socio-historical analysis of Spanish Ultras', *Soccer and Society*, vol. 6, no.1.

Stanton, G. (2004), 'Chasing the ghosts: narratives of football and nation in Morocco', in G. Armstrong and R. Giulianotti (eds) (2004), *Football in Africa*.

Sugden, J. and A. Bairner (1993), *Sport, Sectarianism and Society in a Divided Ireland*, Leicester: Leicester University Press.

Sugden, J. and A. Tomlinson (1998), *FIFA and the Contest for World Football: Who Rules the People's Game?*, Cambridge: Polity.

—— (2003), *Badfellas: FIFA Family at War*, Edinburgh: Mainstream.

Sugden, J. and A. Tomlinson (eds) (1994), *Hosts and Champions: Soccer Cultures, National Identities and the USA World Cup*, Aldershot: Arena.

Tamaki, M. (1993), *J League Kara no Kaze*, Shueisha, cited in S. Moffett (2002), *Japanese Rules*.

Taylor, C. (1998), *The Beautiful Game: A Journey through Latin American Football*, London: Victor Gollancz.

Taylor, M. (1997), 'Little Englanders: tradition, identity and professional football in Lancashire', in S. Gehrmann (ed.) (1997), *Football and Regional Identity in Europe*.

Taylor, R. and K. Jamrich (1997), *Puskás on Puskás: The Life and Times of a Footballing Legend*, London: Robson Books.

Taylor, R. and A. Ward (eds) (1993), *Kicking and Screaming: An Oral History of Football in England*, London: Robson Books.

Teja, A. (1998), 'Italian sport and international relations under Fascism', in J. Riordan and P. Arnaud (eds), *Sport and International Politics*.

Thompson, E. P. (1967), 'Time, work, discipline, and industrial capitalism', *Past and Present* 38.

—— (1980), *The Making of the English Working Class*, 3rd edn, London: Penguin.

Tischler, S. (1981), *Footballers and Businessmen: The Origins of Professional Soccer in England*, New York: Holmes and Meier.

Tomlinson, A. (2006), 'Germany 1974: on the eve of the goldrush', in A. Tomlinson and C. Young (eds), *German Football*.

Tomlinson, A. and C. Young (eds) (2006), *German Football: History, Culture, Society*, London: Routledge.

Tuastad, D. (1997), 'The political role of football for Palestinians in Jordan', in G. Armstrong and R. Giulianotti (eds) (1997), *Entering the Field*.

Valdano, J. (2002), 'Poverty is good for nothing except football', *www.fifaworldcup.com*, 9 May.

Vamplew, W. (2004), *Pay Up and Play the Game: Professional Sport in Britain, 1875–1914*, Cambridge: Cambridge University Press.

Vargas Llosa, M. (1996), *Making Waves*, London: Faber.

Vasili, P. (1995), 'Colonialism and football: the first Nigerian tour to Britain', *Race and Class*, vol. 36, no. 4.

Vásquez Montalbán, M. (2005), *Fútbol: Una religión en busca de un dios*, Madrid: Debolsillo.

Versi, A. (1988), 'Striking power: Arab football kicks off', *The Middle East*, March.

Vickery, T. (2004), 'Identity crisis', *World Soccer*, March.

Wahl, A. (1989), *Les archives du football*, Paris: Gallimard.

Wall, F. (1935), *Fifty years in Football*, London, repr. Cleethorpes: Soccer Books, 2006.

Walton, J. (1999), 'Football and Basque identity: Real Sociedad of San Sebastian, 1909–1932', *Memoria y Civilización 2*.

Walvin, J. (1994), *The People's Game: The History of Football Revisited*, Edinburgh: Mainstream.

Weil, E. (1983), 'History of the Libertadores Cup', *World Soccer*, October.

Weintraub, S. (2002), *Silent Night: The Remarkable Christmas Truce of 1914*, London: Pocket Books.

Whang Soon-Hee (2004), 'Football, fashion and fandom: sociological reflections on the 2002 World Cup and collective memories in Korea', in J. Horne and W. Manzenreiter (eds), *Football Goes East*.

Williams, J. (1991), 'Having an away day', in J. Williams and S. Wagg (eds.), *British Football and Social Change*.

—— (2006), ' "Protect me from what I want": football fandom, celebrity cultures and "new" football in England', *Soccer and Society*, vol. 7, no. 1.

Williams, J. and R. Giulianotti (eds) (1994), *Games Without Frontiers*, Aldershot: Arena.

Williams, J. and S. Wagg (eds) (1991), *British Football and Social Change: Getting into Europe*, Leicester: Leicester University Press.

Williams, R. (1643), *A Key into the Language of America*, London: Gregory Dexter.

Wilson, J. (2006) *Behind the Curtain: Football in Eastern Europe*, London: Orion.

Winner, D. (2000), *Brilliant Orange: The Neurotic Genius of Dutch Football*, London: Bloomsbury.

Wittington, E. Michael (ed.) (2001), *The Sport of Life and Death: The Mesoamerican Ballgame*, London: Thames and Hudson.

Woodward, P. (2004), 'Extra time', in G. Armstrong and R. Giulianotti (eds) (2004), *Football in Africa*.

Yaeger, D. (2003), 'Son of Saddam', *Sports Illustrated*, 24 March.

Yallop, D. (1999), *How They Stole the Game*, London: Poetic Publishing.

Yeo, S. and Y. (eds) (1981), *Popular Culture and Class Conflict, 1590–1914*, Brighton: Harvester Press.

Acknowledgements

Thanks, praise and love are due to: Simon Kuper for being there at the start and the end; Ben Lyttleton for connecting me to his world and believing it was possible; Andre Markowitz for insisting on it in a fanfare of enthusiasm; Tim Vickery for being a generous host, informed guide and astute reader and setting me right in all sorts of places; Simon Inglis for thinking about stadiums when he didn't want to and teaching me the vocabulary of architecture; Paul Moss because one must. For a miscellany of wisdom and direction, thanks also to Johnny Acton, Gary Armstrong, Sammy Cheung, Liz Crolley, Vic Duke, Richard Giulianotti, Gavin Hamilton, David Held, Simon Lawson, Colin Legum, Liz Legum, Javier Lizarazu, Charlotta Lungberg, Huw Mackay, Ben McPherson, Tim Mansel, Bert Mirra, Chris Oakley, Guy Oliver, Nick Regan, Gregory Salter, Mark Salter, Sebastian Secker Walker, Jo Smith and Yo Takatsuki.

I am hugely grateful to Brian Sayers for reminding me to look at art; Gabrielle Marcotti, Simon Martin and John Foot for putting me right on Italy; ditto Christopher Young and Paul Legg on Germany, Vladimir Soldatkin on Russia, Sorin Dumitrescu on Romania, Jonathan Wilson on everything east of the Elbe. Matti Goskar helped me navigate Norway, John Horne offered help on Asia, Mamoud Mahdi on Iran, Colin Jose on the USA and Paul Dimeo on South Asia. Most of all the biggest thanks to the Sancho Panza of Southend, the encyclopaedic and extraordinary Peter Law.

On the road, hospitality, intoxication, enlightenment and entertainment were generously provided by: David Elleray and the boys of Harrow School; Chris Gregory, Emma Cohen and the Leicester City away crowd; in Newcastle, by Tom Shakespeare, Caroline Boditch, Ivy Broadbent and Peter Thompson; in Sheffield, by Kath and Steve Woodward; in Denmark, by John Idorn, Jeppe Olsen, Morten Olsen, Hans Larsen, Maiken Maigaard, Mogens Madsen, Eric and Nora Skovfoged and Brigitta Pettersen; in Sweden, by Marcus Svensson, Marie Grahn, Samuel, Adrian, Louvisa and the IFK Göteborg brothers – boys, that was the best game of football played anywhere; thanks also to Kennet Andersson, Mattias Goransson, Jesper Högström, Tomas Peterson, Christian Svensson and Gellert Tamas; in Austria, by David Dadge, Roman Horak, Wolfgang Maderthaner, John Bunzel, Michael Fanizadeh, Georg Spitaler, Hansjoerg Egerer, Klaus Federmair, Reinhard Krennhuber and Julo Formanek; in Greece, by Daniel Howden, Korrina Patelis, Naya Hadzipani, Rosy Voudouri, Panos Polyzoidis, Yannis Nikolaou, Jonus Pontusson, Alketas Panagoulias, Efthymious Athanasopolous and the Kalithea massive; in Scotland, by Tom, Sophie and Adam Salter, Charlie Johnstone, the one and only Gerry Mooney, Richard Haynes, Richard McBrearty, all the staff at the Scottish Football Museum, and the whole Dumbarton Harp for letting me come on the ride; in Serbia, by Dejan Nikolic, the man with the Fiat who rescued my luggage, Damir Jovanavic and the amazing Mr Kos; in Tunisia and around Africa, by Martin Davis, Durosimi Thomas, Mary Harper, everyone connected with the BBC World Service Africa, James Copnall, Steve Bidmead, Emenike Ikolodo, Hedi Hemel, *mon oncle* Frank Simon, Mark Gleeson, Emmanuel Maradas, Sami who taught me about Libya, and Conrad Leach who taught me about writing match reports; in Portugal, by João Van Dunem, Mary Van

Acknowledgements

Dunem, Francisca Van Dunem, Julian and Kathy Flanders, Dan Levy, Elliot Hool, Silvestre Rosa, Paulo Delgado and Carlos Henriques; in Argentina, by Andres, Lolly, Philipe, Osvaldo and Christina Garavaglia, Ernesto Dufour who taught me a thing or two about Peronism, Fabi Poricin, Eric Weil, Ezequiel Fernandez Moores, Pablo Alabarces, Julio Frydenburg and his lovely *empanadas*; in Brazil, by Alex Bellos, Juliano Xavier, Christian Xavier, Jose Leite Lopes, Antonio Holzmeister and Bernardo Hollanda; in Uruguay, by Roberto, Carmen, Maite and Daniel Elissalde – *Viva el malo!* – Rafael Bayce, Jose Ballardi, Jose Elosegi, Patricia Pujol, Juan Deal, Joselo Gonzalez, Juan Capellan and all the staff at the Museo de Fútbol in Montevideo.

Back home, big thanks to my Bristol posse who endure and hope in the face of failure: Tim Ruck, Alix Hughes and Steve Roser. Geoff Bond, Vanda Skavaas and Anabelle Mbotchwa helped me do the real work through this thing. In the back office and the big bad world thanks are due to Felicity Bryant and Andrew Heritage for taking a punt on me in the first place; Sally Holloway for licking things into shape. At Penguin maximum respect to my editor Tony Lacey for his long-suffering support and unerring eye for the bum note; Zelda Turner for her meticulous work on photos and illustrations, and to my copy-editor John English for his endurance, stamina and picking up my mistakes.

Bringing up the rear, but heading for the future, love and thanks to Sarah, Molly and Luke, who have permitted me the contradiction of writing a book about play, for so long and so hard, that there was never enough time to play with them. OK guys. I'm done. Let's play!

Illustrations

The publishers would like to thank the following photographers and organizations for their kind permission to reproduce the copyright material in this book:

Inset Pictures

1. Hulton Archive/Illustrated London News/Getty Images
2. From FIFA
3. London Express/Getty Images
4. S. R. Gaiger/Topical Press Agency/Getty Images
5. Keystone/Getty Images
6. Keystone/Getty Images
7. Central Press/Hulton Archive/Getty Images
8. Central Press/Hulton Archive/Getty Images
9. Keystone/Getty Images
10. Steve Powell/Allsport/Getty Images
11. Peter Robinson/EMPICS Sports Photo Agency
12. Eamonn McCabe/Hulton Archive/Getty Images
13. Pascal Rondeau/Allsport/Getty Images
14. Gideon Mendel/Corbis
15. Michael Kunkel/Bongarts
16. KAMBOU SIA/AFP/Getty Images
17. German Football Association
18. Abbas/Magnum Photos
19. John Vink/Magnum Photos

Acknowledgements

Chapter Headings

1. Japanese *kemari* player
3. Drawing, *circa* 1850. Hulton Archive/Getty Images
4. Maori team visiting London, 1926. Fox Photos/Getty Images
5. Hugo Meisl. Austria Press Agency
7. German football team, White Hart Lane, 1935. PNA Rota/Getty Images
8. Eva Péron at Argentinian youth tournament, 1951. Keystone/Getty Images
10. Pelé in Paris, 1971. AFP/Getty Images
11. Stanley Rous chooses football for 1966 World Cup tournament. Robert Stiggins/Getty Images
12. Nigerian team on tour in England, 1950. Charles Hewitt/Getty Images
13. João Havelange at World Cup Final, 1998. Gabriel Bouys/AFP/Getty Images
15. DHM, Berlin
17. Getty Images
19. Chinese fan after 3–1 defeat by Japan, Beijing, 2004. Chien-min Chung/Getty Images
20. Nelson Mandela with Jules Rimet Cup 2004. Franck Fife/AFP/Getty Images
Conclusion. Raymond Depardon/Magnum Photos

Every effort has been made to trace the copyright holders. We apologize for any unintentional omission and would be pleased to insert the appropriate acknowledgement in any subsequent edition.

Index